BUSINESS
RESEARCH METHODS

Fifth Edition

Emma Bell
Alan Bryman
Bill Harley

OXFORD
UNIVERSITY PRESS

OXFORD
UNIVERSITY PRESS

Great Clarendon Street, Oxford, OX2 6DP,
United Kingdom

Oxford University Press is a department of the University of Oxford.
It furthers the University's objective of excellence in research, scholarship,
and education by publishing worldwide. Oxford is a registered trade mark of
Oxford University Press in the UK and in certain other countries

Second Edition 2007
Third Edition 2011
Fourth Edition 2015

Impression: 3

Published in the United States of America by Oxford University Press
198 Madison Avenue, New York, NY 10016, United States of America

British Library Cataloguing in Publication Data

Data available

Library of Congress Control Number: 2018949231

ISBN 978–0–19–880987–6

Printed and bound by CPI Group (UK) Ltd, Croydon, CR0 4YY

BRIEF CONTENTS

DETAILED CONTENTS

LEARNING FEATURES

ABBREVIATIONS

AoIR	Association of Internet Researchers
AOM	Academy of Management
ASHE	Annual Survey of Hours and Earnings
BHPS	British Household Panel Study
BRES	Business Register and Employment Survey
BSA	British Social Attitudes; British Sociological Association
CAPI	computer-assisted personal interviewing
CAQDAS	computer-assisted qualitative data analysis software
CATI	computer-assisted telephone interviewing
CEO	chief executive officer
CMD	common mental disorder
CSR	corporate social responsibility
CV	curriculum vitae
CWP	Changing Workforce Programme
ECA	ethnographic content analysis
ESRC	Economic and Social Research Council
EWCS	European Working Conditions Survey
FTSE	Financial Times Stock Exchange (London)
GDPR	General Data Protection Regulations (European Union)
GMID	General Market Information Database
GSS	General Social Survey (USA)
HISS	hospital information support system
HP	Hewlett Packard
HR	human resources
HRM	human resource management
ICI	Imperial Chemical Industries
ISP	internet service provider
ISSP	International Social Survey Programme
IT	information technology
JDS	Job Diagnostic Survey
LFS	Labour Force Survey
LGI	Looking Glass Inc.
LPC	least-preferred co-worker
MBA	Master of Business Administration
MORI	Market & Opinion Research International
MPS	Motivating Potential Score
MRS	Market Research Society
NASA	National Air and Space Administration (USA)
NHS	National Health Service
NOS	National Organizations Survey (USA)
OCS	Organizational Culture Scale
OD	organizational development
OECD	Organization for Economic Cooperation and Development
ONS	Office for National Statistics
R&D	research and development
RTW	return to work
SIC	Standard Industrial Classification
SME	small or medium-sized enterprise
SSCI	Social Sciences Citation Index
SRA	Social Research Association
TDM	total design method
TQM	total quality management
UKDA	UK Data Archive
VDL	vertical dyadic linkage
WERS	Workplace Employment Relations Survey (previously Workplace Employee Relations Survey)
WOMM	word-of-mouth marketing

ABOUT THE AUTHORS

Emma Bell is Professor of Organisation Studies at the Open University, UK. She completed her PhD at Manchester Metropolitan University in 2000 based on an ethnographic study of payment systems and time in the chemical industry. Prior to this, Emma worked as a graduate trainee in the UK National Health Service. Her research is informed by curiosity about the ways in which people in organizations collectively construct meaning in the context of work and organizations. Recently, she has been involved in projects related to visual organizational analysis, understanding craft work, and power and politics in the production of management knowledge.

Emma's research has been published in *British Journal of Management*, *Academy of Management Learning and Education*, and *Organization*. She has an enduring interest in methods and methodological issues and has published articles, chapters, and books related to this including, *A Very Short, Fairly Interesting and Reasonably Cheap Book about Management Research* (Sage, 2013), co-authored with Richard Thorpe, and *Sage Major Works in Qualitative Research in Business and Management* (2015), co-edited with Hugh Willmott. Emma served as a co-chair of the Critical Management Studies Division of the Academy of Management; at the time of writing she is joint vice-chair of research and publications for the British Academy of Management and joint editor-in-chief of *Management Learning*.

Alan Bryman was Professor of Organizational and Social Research at the University of Leicester from 2005 to 2017. Prior to this he was Professor of Social Research at Loughborough University for 31 years.

His main research interests were in leadership, especially in higher education, research methods (particularly mixed methods research), and the 'Disneyization' and 'McDonaldization' of modern society. In 2003–4 he completed a project on the issue of how quantitative and qualitative research are combined in the social sciences, as part of the Research Methods Programme of the Economic and Social Research Council (ESRC).

He contributed articles to a range of academic journals, including *Journal of Management Studies*, *Human Relations*, *International Journal of Social Research Methodology*, *Leadership Quarterly*, and *American Behavioral Scientist*. He was a member of the ESRC's Research Grants Board and conducted research into effective leadership in higher education, a project funded by the Leadership Foundation for Higher Education.

Alan published widely in the field of social research. Among his writings were *Quantitative Data Analysis with SPSS 17, 18 and 19: A Guide for Social Scientists* (Routledge, 2011), with Duncan Cramer; *Social Research Methods* (Oxford University Press, 2008); *The SAGE Encyclopedia of Social Science Research Methods* (Sage, 2004), with Michael Lewis-Beck and Tim Futing Liao; *The Disneyization of Society* (Sage, 2004); *Handbook of Data Analysis* (Sage, 2004), with Melissa Hardy; *Understanding Research for Social Policy and Practice* (Policy Press, 2004), with Saul Becker; and the *SAGE Handbook of Organizational Research Methods*, with David Buchanan (Sage, 2009). He edited the *Understanding Social Research* series for the Open University Press.

Bill Harley is Professor of Management in the Department of Management and Marketing at the University of Melbourne. Bill was awarded a PhD in political science from the University of Queensland in 1995, for a dissertation on the impact of changes in industrial relations legislation on labour flexibility at the workplace level. Prior to undertaking his PhD, Bill was a graduate trainee with the Australian government and subsequently worked for some years in policy roles in Canberra. He has served as a consultant to numerous national and international organizations, including the OECD and the ILO.

Bill's academic research has been motivated by an abiding interest in the centrality of work to human life. Informed by labour process theory, his primary focus has been on issues of power and control in the workplace. Much of his published work has focused on the ways in which managerial policy and practice shape employees' experience of work. Bill has also published a number of papers on research methodology. His work has been published in journals including the *British Journal of Industrial Relations*, *Journal of Management Studies*, *Industrial Relations*, and *Work Employment and Society*. Bill was previously general editor of *Journal of Management Studies* and at the time of writing is on the editorial board of the same journal and that of *Academy of Management Learning and Education* and *Human Relations*.

ABOUT THE STUDENTS AND SUPERVISORS

For this edition of the book we have fully updated the **Student experience** feature, in which undergraduate and postgraduate students share their experiences of doing business research. In addition to the three UK-based undergraduates and one postgraduate student who were interviewed for the second edition of this book, we have interviewed another UK-based student and four business degree students in Australia about their experiences of doing a business research project. For those students who completed their degrees in 2004/5, we provide an update below on their careers to date. As we believe their experience demonstrates, the skills involved in doing business research are highly transferable into a range of business careers and we are delighted to include details of how they have progressed since doing their university degrees. We are extremely grateful to all these individuals for their willingness be interviewed and we hope that sharing what they have learned from this process with the readers of this book will enable others to benefit from their experience. Videos of the student interviews are among the online resources that accompany this book.

Amrit Bains completed a degree in Business Management with a year in industry at the University of Birmingham, UK, in 2017. Amrit's research question focused on understanding the causes and consequences of mental health problems at work. His dissertation project involved reviewing existing research on this topic, in the form of a systematic literature review (as described in Chapter 5). This method did not require him to collect original quantitative or qualitative data himself, but instead relied on his analysis of existing material. Amrit's dissertation project highlights the importance of understanding the methods used by researchers, so that you can evaluate the quality of the claims that are made.

Lucie Banham completed an MA in Organization Studies in 2005 at the University of Warwick, UK, where she had previously studied psychology as an undergraduate. Her dissertation project focused on how governments seek to foster the development of enterprising behaviour among students and young people. Her fieldwork concentrated on the activities of a UK government-funded institute responsible for promoting enterprise. Lucie's qualitative research strategy combined participant observation, unstructured and semi-structured interviews, and documentary data collection. When we spoke to Lucie again in 2017, she had become a Director of Banham Security, the largest supplier of burglary and fire prevention systems in London.

Jordan Brown completed an honours degree in Commerce at Monash University Australia in 2017 after doing a double degree in Arts and Business, also at Monash. Her dissertation focus in her honours year was on authentic self-expression at work. Jordan adopted a quantitative research strategy and her data collection method involved a correlational field study survey. She is planning to begin a PhD focusing on the aesthetics of art in organizing resistance within political conflict.

Tom Easterling first spoke to us in 2005, having just completed an MSc in Occupational Psychology at Birkbeck College, University of London, UK. He had been studying part-time over two years, combining this with a full-time job as an NHS manager in London. Tom's dissertation research project focused on wellbeing in the workplace, focusing on telephone call centre workers. His research involved a qualitative case study of a public-sector call centre, where he interviewed people at different hierarchical levels of the organization. Tom is currently director of the chair and chief executive's office for NHS England and works in London.

Anna Hartman completed a Master's of Commerce in Marketing at the University of Melbourne, Australia, in 2017. Her interest in marketing ethics led her to focus her research project on women who become commercial egg donors and how these services are marketed to prospective consumers. Anna's research strategy was qualitative in nature; she conducted semi-structured interviews via Skype with women who had been commercial egg donors. She is now enrolled at Melbourne as a doctoral student and is focusing on the market system dynamics of commercial egg donation, using discourse analysis and phenomenology.

Ed Hyatt, before studying for a PhD, worked in a variety of industries, both public and private. His most extensive experience was as a public procurement manager and contracts officer for several US government agencies and universities. When we spoke to him in 2017, Ed Hyatt was completing a PhD at the University of Melbourne, Australia, in the field of human resource management, recruitment, and selection. His focus was on organizational policies that promote a more fulfilling work experience for both individuals and organizations, looking specifically at whether structured job interviews can enable better person–organization fit. His quantitative research strategy involved conducting online panel experiments among hiring managers, using scales to measure their behavioural responses.

Karen Moore completed a Bachelor's degree in Business Administration and Management at Lancaster University, UK, in 2005. Her final-year research project came about as the result of her third-year company placement, when she worked in a human resources (HR) department. Karen became interested in the concept of person–organizational culture fit. She carried out an audit of the organizational culture in the company and explored whether the recruitment and selection process operated to ensure person–organization fit. Her mixed methods research design involved a questionnaire and semi-structured interviewing. Following her degree, Karen joined the logistics company Gist as a part of their HR graduate programme. She was promoted to HR manager before taking a career break and travelling to Australia, where she is an HR adviser at Lizard Island Resort.

Chris Phillips did his undergraduate degree in Commerce at the University of Birmingham, UK, in 2004. His third-year dissertation investigated the career progression of women employees in a global bank where he had done an internship in his second year. His research questions focused on understanding how and why women employees progress hierarchically within the bank, including factors and barriers that affect their career progression. His questions were informed by the concept of the 'glass ceiling' which explores why women experience unequal treatment that hinders career progression in organizations. His research strategy was qualitative and involved semi-structured interviews. Chris works in London as a marketing controller in Sky VIP, Sky's customer loyalty programme.

Alex Pucar did a dual Bachelor of Business degree majoring in Marketing, Management, and Economics at Monash University, Australia. As part of this, he completed an honours dissertation in 2017. He is now employed in marketing. Alex's research focused on understanding how and why companies that start online make the decision to open physical stores—which is referred to as the 'clicks to bricks' strategy in retailing. His interest was on the impact of this strategy on the growth and progression of small and medium enterprises. Alex's research strategy was qualitative and involved semi-structured interviewing.

GUIDED TOUR OF TEXTBOOK FEATURES

Chapter outline

Each chapter opens with a guide that provides a route map through the chapter material and summarizes the goals of each chapter, so that you know what you can expect to learn as you move through the text.

CHAPTER OUTLINE

This chapter introduces some fundamental considerations in conducting business res outlining what we mean by business research and the reasons why we conduct it. The three main areas:

- *Business research methods in context.* This introduces issues such as the role of th ethical considerations; debates about relevance versus rigour; and how political co business research.

Key concept boxes

The world of research methods has its own language. To help you build your research vocabulary, key terms and ideas have been defined in Key concept boxes that are designed to advance your understanding of the field and help you to apply your new learning to new research situations.

1.1 KEY CONCEPT
What is evidence-based managemen

Evidence-based management is 'the systematic use of the best available evide practice' (Reay et al. 2009). The approach is proposed as a way of overcomin et al. 2016), which seeks to address the problem whereby, according to some insufficiently relevant to practice. The concept developed during the 1990s to was subsequently applied in other fields such as education (Petticrew and Ro

Research in focus boxes

It is often said that the three most important features to look for when buying a house are location, location, location. A parallel for the teaching of research methods is examples, examples, examples! Research in focus boxes are designed to provide a sense of place for the theories and concepts being discussed in the chapter text, by providing real examples of published research.

1.3 RESEARCH IN FOCUS
A research question about gender bia towards leaders

The research question posed in the title of the article by Elsesser and Lever (2 female leaders persist?' They begin by reviewing the literature, which suggests female leaders still persist. However, they question whether prior research can

Student experience boxes

The student experience boxes provide personal insights from a range of individuals; they are based on interviews with real research students, business school supervisors, and lecturers from business schools around the UK. In this way we hope to represent both sides of the supervision relationship, including the problems faced by students and how they are helped to overcome them and the advice that supervisors can provide. These boxes will help you to anticipate and resolve research challenges as you move through your dissertation or project.

STUDENT EXPERIENCE
The influence of personal values on

Many students are influenced in their choice of research subject by their ow This can be positive, because it helps to ensure that they remain interested the project. Amrit explained that his decision to focus on the topic of mental was

Tips and skills boxes

Tips and skills boxes provide guidance and advice on key aspects of the research process. They will help you to avoid common research mistakes and equip you with the necessary skills to become a successful business researcher in your life beyond your degree.

TIPS AND SKILLS
Making a Gantt chart for your resear

One way to keep track of your research project is by using a Gantt chart. The h
the total time span of the project divided into units such as weeks or months. T
involved in the project. An example is provided in Figure 4.1. Shaded squares
of time you expect to spend on each task. The filled-in squares may overlap, fo

Thinking deeply boxes

Business research methods can sometimes be complex: to raise your awareness of these complexities, thinking deeply boxes feature further explanation of discussions and debates that have taken place between researchers. These boxes are designed to take you beyond the introductory level and encourage you to think in greater depth about current research issues.

4.1 THINKING DEEPLY
Marx's sources of research questions

Marx (1997) suggests the following possible sources of research questions:

- Intellectual puzzles and contradictions.
- The existing literature.
- Replication.

Checklists

Many chapters include checklists of issues to be considered when undertaking specific research activities (such as writing a literature review or conducting a focus group), to remind you of key questions and concerns and to help you progress your research project.

CHECKLIST
Questions to ask yourself when reviewing th

○ Is your list of references up to date? Does it include the most recent

○ What literature searching have you done recently?

○ What have you read recently? Have you found time to read?

Key points

At the end of each chapter there is a short bulleted summary of crucial themes and arguments explored in that chapter. These are intended to alert you to issues that are especially important and to reinforce the areas that you have covered to date.

KEY POINTS

- Quantitative research can be characterized as a linear series of step
  conclusions, but the process described in Figure 8.1 is an ideal typ
  departures.
- The measurement process in quantitative research entails the searc
- Establishing the reliability and validity of measures is important for

Questions for review

Review questions have been included at the end of every chapter to test your grasp of the key concepts and ideas being developed in the text, and help you to reflect on your learning in preparation for coursework and assessment.

QUESTIONS FOR REVIEW

- Why are ethical issues important in the conduct of business resear
- Outline the different stances on ethics in social research.
- How helpful are studies such as those conducted by Milgram, Han
  understanding the operation of ethical principles in business resea

GUIDED TOUR OF THE ONLINE RESOURCES

www.oup.com/uk/brm5e/

For students

Research guide

This interactive research guide takes you step by step through each of the key research phases, ensuring that you do not overlook any research step and providing guidance and advice on every aspect of business research. The guide features checklists, web links, research activities, case studies, examples, and templates and is conveniently cross-referenced back to the book.

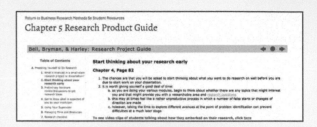

Interviews with research students

Learn from the real research experiences of students who have recently completed their own research projects! Download video-recorded interviews with undergraduate and postgraduate students from business schools in the UK and Australia, and hear them describe the research processes they went through and the problems they resolved as they moved through each research phase.

Multiple-choice questions

The best way to reinforce your understanding of research methods is through frequent and cumulative revision. To support you in this, a bank of self-marking multiple-choice questions is provided for each chapter of the text, and they include instant feedback on your answers to help strengthen your knowledge of key research concepts.

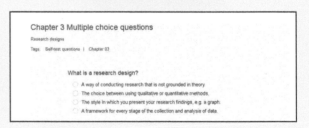

Web links

A series of annotated web links organized by chapter are provided to point you in the direction of important articles, reviews, models, and research guides. These will help keep you informed of the latest issues and developments in business research.

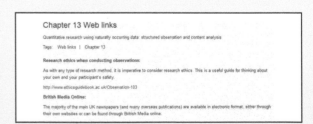

Guide to using Excel in data analysis

This interactive workbook takes you through step-by-step from the very first stages of using Excel to more advanced topics such as charting, regression, and inference, giving guidance and practical examples.

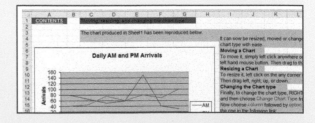

For registered adopters of the text

NEW: test bank

Test banks for every chapter are available with this fifth edition which includes a mixture of multiple-choice, true or false, and multiple-answer questions. There are 10-15 questions per chapter available, providing you with ready-made assessments for your students.

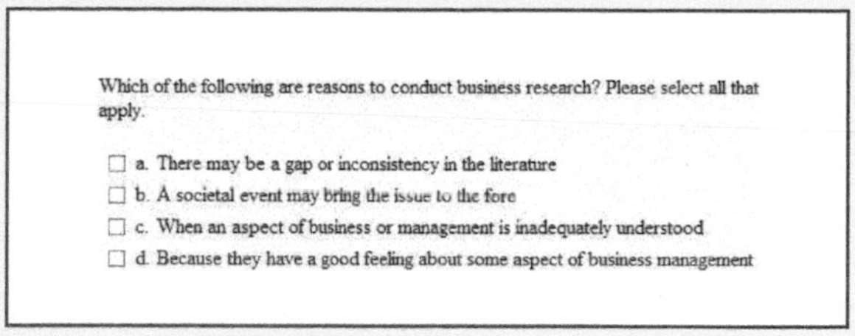

Which of the following are reasons to conduct business research? Please select all that apply.

☐ a. There may be a gap or inconsistency in the literature
☐ b. A societal event may bring the issue to the fore
☐ c. When an aspect of business or management is inadequately understood
☐ d. Because they have a good feeling about some aspect of business management

NEW: discussion questions

Each chapter is now accompanied by two discussion questions with suggested responses and guidance, to help you plan seminars or lectures and generate debate.

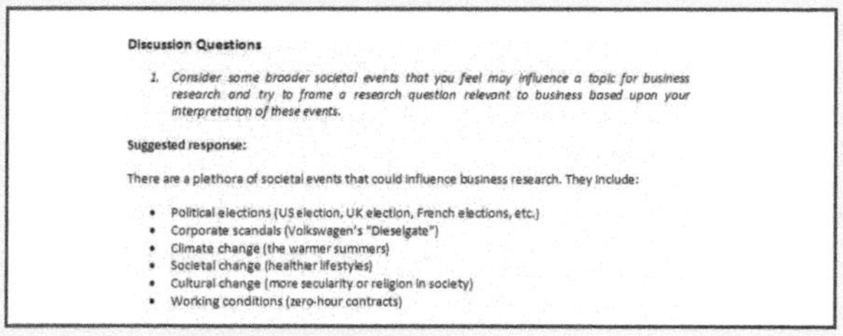

Discussion Questions

1. Consider some broader societal events that you feel may influence a topic for business research and try to frame a research question relevant to business based upon your interpretation of these events.

Suggested response:

There are a plethora of societal events that could influence business research. They include:

- Political elections (US election, UK election, French elections, etc.)
- Corporate scandals (Volkswagen's "Dieselgate")
- Climate change (the warmer summers)
- Societal change (healthier lifestyles)
- Cultural change (more secularity or religion in society)
- Working conditions (zero-hour contracts)

Case studies

Fully refreshed for this edition, varied, real-life case studies illustrate some of the key concepts discussed in the chapters, helping students better understand research in a wider context and saving you time in finding additional examples.

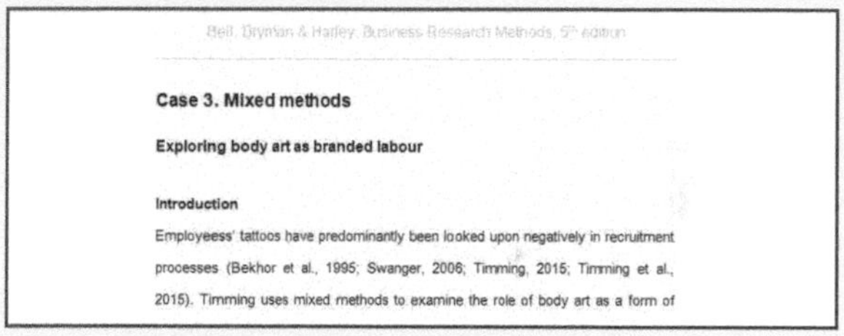

Bell, Bryman & Harley: Business Research Methods, 5th edition

Case 3. Mixed methods

Exploring body art as branded labour

Introduction

Employeess' tattoos have predominantly been looked upon negatively in recruitment processes (Bekhor et al., 1995; Swanger, 2006; Timming, 2015; Timming et al., 2015). Timming uses mixed methods to examine the role of body art as a form of

Lecturer's guide

A comprehensive lecturer's guide is included to assist both new and experienced instructors in their teaching. It includes reading guides, lecture outlines, further coverage of difficult concepts, and teaching activities, and is accompanied by instructions on how the guide may be most effectively implemented in the teaching program.

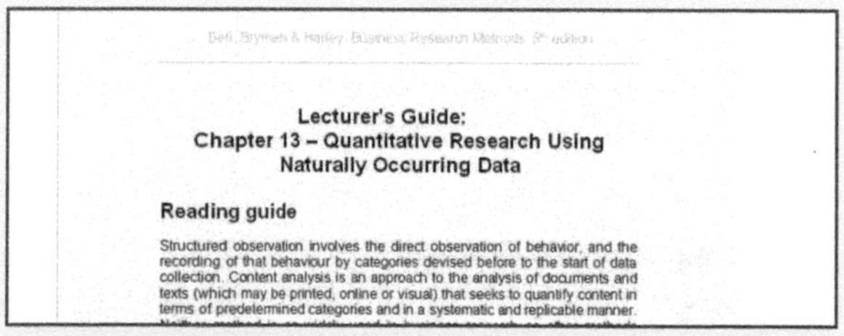

Bell, Bryman & Harley: Business Research Methods, 5th edition

Lecturer's Guide:
Chapter 13 – Quantitative Research Using Naturally Occurring Data

Reading guide

Structured observation involves the direct observation of behavior, and the recording of that behaviour by categories devised before to the start of data collection. Content analysis is an approach to the analysis of documents and texts (which may be printed, online or visual) that seeks to quantify content in terms of predetermined categories and in a systematic and replicable manner.

PowerPoint® slides

A suite of customizable PowerPoint slides is included for use in lecture presentations. Arranged by chapter theme and tied specifically to the lecturer's guide, the slides may also be used as hand-outs in class.

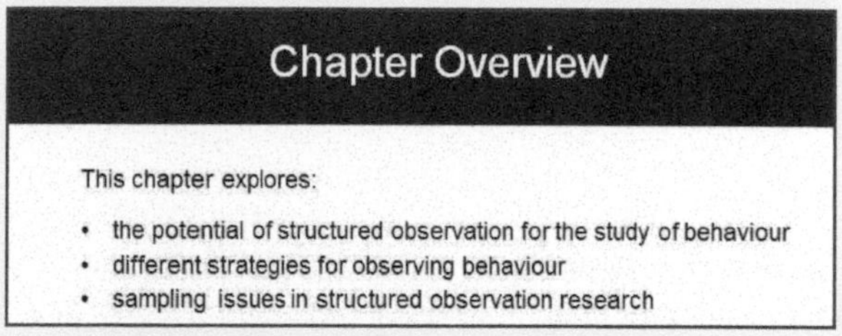

Chapter Overview

This chapter explores:

- the potential of structured observation for the study of behaviour
- different strategies for observing behaviour
- sampling issues in structured observation research

Figures and plates from the text

All figures and plates from the text have been provided in high resolution format for downloading into presentation software or for use in assignments and exams.

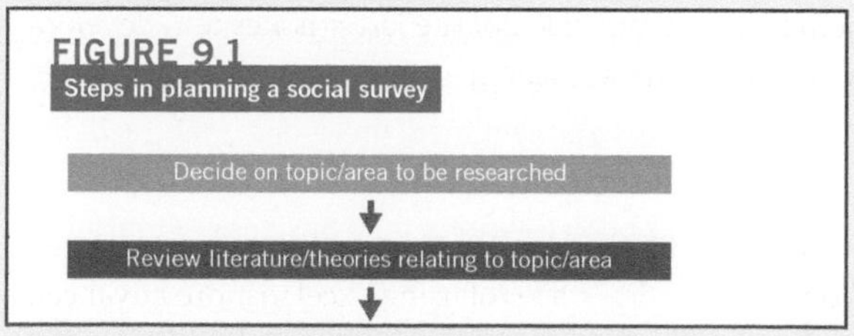

FIGURE 9.1
Steps in planning a social survey

Decide on topic/area to be researched

↓

Review literature/theories relating to topic/area

↓

ABOUT THE BOOK

The focus of the book

This is a book that will be of use to all students in business schools who have an interest in understanding research methods as they are applied in management and organizational contexts. *Business Research Methods* gives students essential guidance on how to carry out their own research projects and introduces readers to the core concepts, methods, and values involved in doing research. The book provides a valuable learning resource through its comprehensive coverage of methods that are used by experienced researchers investigating the world of business, as well as introducing some of the philosophical issues and ethical controversies that these researchers face. So, if you want to learn about business research methods, from how to formulate research questions to the process of writing up your research, *Business Research Methods* will provide a clear, easy-to-follow, and comprehensive introduction.

Business Research Methods is written for students of business and management studies. The book originally grew out of the success of Alan Bryman's book *Social Research Methods*. Writing the fifth edition of *Business Research Methods* has entailed changes enabled in part by bringing in the third author, Bill Harley. A key purpose of the authors has been to further internationalize the book's coverage, based on Bill's expertise in the Australian business and management context. A further aim has been to streamline the text, for example by integrating the coverage of online research throughout the chapters, rather than having a separate chapter on it as in previous editions of the book. We have also sought to be responsive to the needs of today's students and lecturers, who require a guide to business research methods that is comprehensive and informed by the latest developments, but which also remains concise and focused. In so doing our goal has been to ensure that *Business Research Methods* remains a streamlined, up-to-date, and readable textbook.

Because this book is written for a business school audience, it is intended to reflect a diverse range of subject areas, including organizational behaviour, marketing, strategy, organization studies, and human resource management (HRM). In using the term 'business research methods', we have in mind the kinds of research methods that are employed in these fields, and so we have focused primarily on methods that are informed by other disciplines within the social sciences such as sociology, anthropology, and psychology. Certain areas of business and management research, such as economics and financial and accounting research, are not included within our purview. These are self-contained fields with their own traditions and approaches that do not mesh well with the kinds of methods dealt with in this book.

In addition to providing students with practical advice on doing research, the book also explores the nature and purpose of business and management research. For example:

- What is the aim or purpose of business research?

    Is it conducted primarily in order to find ways of improving organizational performance through increasing effectiveness and efficiency?

    Or is it mainly about increasing our understanding of how organizations work, and their impact on individuals and on society?

- Who are the audiences of business research?

    Is business research conducted primarily for managers?

    If not, for whom else in organizations is it conducted?

- Is the purpose of business research to further the academic development of the field?

- What is the politics of management research, and how does this frame the use of different methods and the kinds of research findings that are regarded as legitimate and acceptable?

- To what extent do researchers' personal values impact upon the research process?

- Should we worry about the feelings of people outside the research community concerning what we do to people during our investigations?

These questions are the subject of considerable ongoing debate. Being aware of them is important in understanding how to select a research topic and the methods that can be used to address it. There are four points that can be made in relation to this.

1. **The researcher's role.** In order to evaluate the quality of management and business research it is necessary to know as much as possible about the researchers' *own* role in this process—including how they collected and analysed the data and the theoretical perspective that informed their interpretation of it. This understanding relies on examination of methods used by business researchers, which is why, throughout this book, we have used real examples of published research to illustrate how researchers deal with and justify these methodological choices.

2. **Identifying research methods.** Business research methods tend on the whole to be more eclectic and explained in less detail than in some other social sciences such as sociology. Perhaps this is due to the emergent nature of the field or because it draws from such a diverse range of disciplines. In practice, it means that novice researchers can sometimes find it difficult to identify examples of existing research to inform their own work. One of the reasons we use so many examples in this book is to draw attention to the types of methods that business researchers use, in a way that can be understood by those who are new to this field of study.

3. **The range of methods available.** In some instances, it is hard to identify examples of particular research methods, while in others, such as the case study method, there are numerous studies to choose from. We believe, however, that there are opportunities for new researchers to make use of less popular or less commonly used methods to gain insight into a research problem. In other words, we hope that through reading this book students will possibly be encouraged to use research methods that are less common, as well as those that are well established in the field.

4. **Relevance to business studies.** Finally, where possible we have tried to confine our choice of examples of research in business and management. This is because by getting to know how other business researchers have approached its study you will build up an understanding of how you can apply similar methods.

Why use this book?

This book has been written with two groups of readers in mind. The first comprises undergraduates and postgraduates in business and management schools and departments who take a module or course in the area of research methods. The second group, which overlaps with the first, comprises undergraduates and postgraduates who do a research project as part of the requirement for their degree programmes. This can take many forms, but one of the most common is a research project and a dissertation, thesis, or research report based on the investigation. The chapters in Part One of the book have been written specifically for students doing research projects, especially Chapters 4 and 5, which include a discussion of formulating research questions and reviewing the literature, reinforcing topics that we see as key to the whole process of doing research. In Parts Two and Three the emphasis is on the practice of business research and the methods that may be used. These chapters will help students make informed decisions about doing their research.

There are likely to be two main circumstances in which this book is in your hands at the moment. One is that you have to study one or more modules in research methods for a degree in business and management, or there are methodological components to one of your taught modules (for example, a course in organizational behaviour). The other is that you have to do some research, perhaps for a dissertation or project report, and you need some guidelines about how to approach your study. You may find yourself reading this book for either or both of these reasons during the course of doing your degree. It may be that you are wondering why you need to study research methods and why such people as the authors of this book do business research at all. In the rest of this section, we will try briefly to address these issues and concerns. Before that, what do we mean by the term 'business research'?

What do we mean by 'business research'?

The term 'business research', as it is used in this book, refers to *academic* research on topics relating to questions that are relevant to the field of business and management and have a social science orientation. We include in this category research in areas such as organizational behaviour, marketing, accounting, HRM, and strategy, which draw on the social sciences for conceptual and theoretical inspiration.

In the previous paragraph, the word 'academic' is emphasized, and there is an important reason for this in setting out this book's approach. Academics carry out research to investigate research questions that arise out of the existing literature on topics (such as 'What are the implications of low levels of job satisfaction in a workforce?'), or that may be influenced by developments in business and management generally (such as 'What is the impact of the introduction of total quality management in companies?'). We discuss in some detail in Chapter 4 what research questions are and how they arise in the research process, but for the time being the purpose of this discussion is to make it clear that, when we use the term 'business research', we are referring to research conducted for the illumination of issues that arise in the context of academic thinking in the area of business and management. The term 'business research' in this book does not include research conducted by organizations for the investigation of issues of concern to them. For example, commercial organizations conduct market research to explore how their products or services are received or when they want to launch a new product or service. This is not the kind of research that we focus on in this book. This is not because we view such research as unimportant or irrelevant or because we view it as inferior in some way. Rather, it is because the rationales for doing such research and the ways in which it is done are different from those associated with academic research. Consequently, it would be difficult to incorporate both approaches to business and management research within the covers of a manageable volume. This is the reason why almost all of our examples in this book are based on academic research. To include commercial business research would make the book unmanageable and potentially confusing.

We do not wish to drive a wedge between academic research and that originating from business and management practitioners. Indeed, there is a great deal of soul-searching among academics in the business and management field concerning this issue (see, in particular, the June 2006 special issue of the *Journal of Occupational and Organizational Psychology*), and in Chapter 1 we address further some of these issues in the context of a discussion of what are known as Mode 1 and Mode 2 forms of knowledge (the first is more or less synonymous with traditional academic research in this area; the second is research conducted by academics *and* practitioners to address applied organizational issues and problems). The point of this discussion is to highlight our point of departure and our rationale for emphasizing academic research in this field. It is also worth pointing out that there is often considerable cross-fertilization between academic and practitioner-based research in the

field. Practitioners often draw on methodological developments in academic fields, such as sampling, to refine their techniques, while a research method such as focus groups was largely developed in the applied context of market research before making its way into academic research. Further, the skills from one domain are invariably transferable to the other.

Why do business research?

The rationale for doing business research has been outlined in the previous subsection to a certain extent. Academics conduct such research because, in the course of reading the literature on a topic or when reflecting on what is going on in modern organizations, questions occur to them. They may notice a gap in the literature, or an inconsistency between the findings of different studies, or an unresolved issue in the literature. These circumstances act as springboards for business research in academic circles. Another stimulus is when there is a development in organizations that provides an interesting point of departure for the investigation of a research question. For example, noting the increasing use of social media platforms by organizations, a researcher might be interested in studying whether this is accompanied by changes in the nature and quality of interactions within an organization. In exploring this issue, the researcher is likely to draw upon the literature on technology and organizational change to provide insights into how to approach the issue. As we say in Chapter 1, there is no single reason why people do business research of the kind emphasized in this book, but at its core, it is done because there is an aspect of understanding what goes on in organizations that is to some extent unresolved.

Why is it important to study methods?

Some students do not seem to see a great deal of point to studying research methods. They might take the view that, if they have to conduct an investigation, why not adopt a 'need to know' approach? In other words, why not just look into how to do your research when you are on the verge of carrying out your investigation? Quite aside from the fact that this is an extremely risky approach to take, it neglects the opportunities that training in research methods offers. In particular, you need to bear in mind the following:

- Training in research methods sensitizes you to the *choices* that are available to business and management researchers. In other words, it makes you aware of the range of research methods that can be employed to collect data and the variety of approaches to the analysis of data. Such awareness will help you to make the most appropriate choices for your project, since you need to be aware of when it is appropriate or inappropriate to employ particular techniques of data collection and analysis.

- Training in research methods provides you with an awareness of the dos and don'ts when employing a particular approach to collecting or analysing data. Thus, once you have made your choice of research method (for example, a questionnaire), you need to be aware of the practices you need to follow in order to implement that method properly. You also need to be aware of the many pitfalls to be avoided.

- Training in research methods provides you with insights into the overall research process. It provides a general vantage point for understanding how research is done. As such, it illuminates the various stages of research, so that you can plan your research and think about such issues as how your research methods will connect with your research questions.

- Training in research methods provides you with an awareness of what constitutes good and poor research. It therefore provides a platform for developing a critical awareness of the limits and limitations of research that you read. This can be helpful in enabling you to evaluate critically the research that you read about for modules in fields such as organizational behaviour and HRM.

- The skills that training in research methods imparts are transferable ones. How to sample, how to design a questionnaire, how to conduct semi-structured interviewing or focus groups, and so on, are skills that are relevant to research in other spheres (such as firms, public-sector organizations, etc.).

We feel that training in research methods has much to offer, and we trust that readers of this book will recognize the opportunities and advantages that it provides.

The structure of the book

Business and management research has many different traditions, one of the most fundamental of which is the distinction between quantitative and qualitative research. This distinction lies behind the structure of the book and the way in which issues and methods are approached.

The book is divided into four parts.

- **Part One** deals with basic ideas about the nature of business and management research and with the considerations involved in planning and starting a student research project.

  — Chapter 1 outlines the main stages involved in doing most kinds of business research. It also explores how business research is understood in a wider context, including discussion of the political and wider societal issues that affect its current practice. This provides the basic foundations from which you will be able to explore these issues in more detail and depth.

  — Chapter 2 examines such issues as the nature of the relationship between theory and research and the degree to which a natural science approach is appropriate for the study of business and management. It is here that the distinction between quantitative and qualitative research is first encountered. They are presented as different research strategies with different ways of conceptualizing how business and management should be studied. It is also shown that there is more to the distinction between them than whether or not an investigation includes the collection of quantitative data.

  — In Chapter 3, the idea of a research design is introduced. This chapter provides an introduction to the basic frameworks within which social research is carried out, such as social survey research, case study research, and experimental research. Chapters 2 and 3 provide the basic building blocks for the rest of the book.

  — Chapter 4 takes you through the main steps that are involved in planning and designing a research project and offers advice on how to manage this process. It also includes a discussion of research questions—what they are, why they are important, and how they come to be formulated.

  — Chapter 5 is designed to help you to get started on your research project by introducing the main steps in conducting a critical review of the literature.

  — Chapter 6 considers the ways in which ethical and political issues impinge on researchers and the kinds of principles that are involved in addressing them.

  — Chapter 7 has been included to help with writing up research, an often neglected area of the research process.

- **Part Two** contains nine chapters concerned with quantitative research. After a chapter introducing the subject, there are four chapters dealing mostly with social survey research and two that discuss the use of data that is already available. The final two chapters cover the analysis of quantitative data.

  — Chapter 8 explores the nature of quantitative research and provides a context for the later chapters.

  — Chapter 9 deals with sampling issues: how to select a sample and the considerations that are involved in assessing what can be inferred from different kinds of sample.

  — Chapter 10 is concerned with the kind of interviewing that takes place in survey research—that is, structured interviewing.

  — Chapter 11 covers the design of questionnaires. This involves a discussion of how to devise self-completion questionnaires.

  — Chapter 12 examines the issue of how to formulate questions for questionnaires and structured interviews.

  — Chapter 13 covers two quantitative methods which rely on naturally occurring data. The first is structured observation, which is a method that has been developed for the systematic observation of behaviour. The second is content analysis, a method that provides a rigorous framework for the analysis of a wide range of documents.

  — Chapter 14 deals with the analysis of data collected by other researchers and by official bodies.

  — Chapter 15 presents a range of basic tools for the analysis of quantitative data. The approach taken is non-technical. The emphasis is upon how to choose a method of analysis and how to interpret the findings. No formulae are presented.

  — Chapter 16 shows you how to use computer software—in the form of SPSS, the most widely used software for analysing quantitative data—in order to implement the techniques learned in Chapter 15.

- **Part Three** contains nine chapters on aspects of qualitative research.

  — Chapter 17 provides an overview of the nature of qualitative research and provides the context for the other chapters in this part of the book.

  — Chapter 18 examines the main sampling strategies used in qualitative research. Just like quantitative researchers, qualitative researchers often sample people, documents, or organizations as units of analysis. As this chapter shows, though, the sampling principles used for qualitative research are quite different from those usually employed by quantitative researchers.

  — Chapter 19 is concerned with ethnography and participant observation, which are the source of some of the best-known studies in business and management research. The two terms are often used interchangeably and refer to the immersion of the researcher in a social setting.

  — Chapter 20 deals with the kinds of interview used by qualitative researchers, typically semi-structured interviewing or unstructured interviewing.

  — Chapter 21 explores the focus group method, whereby groups of individuals are interviewed on a specific topic.

  — Chapter 22 examines several ways in which qualitative researchers analyse language: discourse analysis, narrative and rhetorical analysis, and conversation analysis.

  — Chapter 23 deals with the examination and interpretation of documents in qualitative research, including historical documents.

  — Chapter 24 explores some approaches to the analysis of qualitative data.

  — Chapter 25 shows you how to use the computer software NVivo to assist with your analysis of quantitative data.

It is striking that certain issues recur across Parts Two and Three: interviewing, observation, documents, and data analysis. However, as you will see, quantitative and qualitative research constitute contrasting approaches to these activities.

- **Part Four** contains chapters that go beyond the quantitative/qualitative research contrast.

  — Chapter 26 deals with some of the ways in which the distinction between quantitative and qualitative research is less fixed than is sometimes supposed.

  — Chapter 27 presents some ways in which quantitative and qualitative research can be combined to produce what is referred to as mixed methods research.

How to use the book

The book can be read in different ways according to your interests and focus of study. Your lecturer may give you guidance about which chapters to concentrate on. However, we suggest the following as a useful place to start.

- *Setting the scene* Chapter 1 is a scene-setting chapter which will give you an overview of the main stages and processes involved in business research. It introduces the topics that will be covered in greater depth and detail later in the book.

- *Wider philosophical issues* Chapter 2 discusses philosophical issues about the nature of knowledge and how to go about obtaining it, which guide methods choice in business research. While these issues might initially seem esoteric and difficult to understand, they are fundamental to business research. We therefore encourage you to at least try to read this chapter!

- *Developing research questions* As we have already said in this Guide, we see the asking of research questions as fundamental to the research process. Advice on what research questions are, where they come from, and how to develop them is provided in Chapter 4.

- *Doing your own research project* We hope that the whole of this book will be relevant to students doing dissertation research projects, but Chapters 3, 5, and 7 are where much of the specific advice relating to this issue is located. In addition, we would alert you to the 'Tips and skills' and 'Student experience' features and to the Checklists of points to remember.

- *Responsibilities of researchers* As business researchers we have a responsibility to the people and organizations that are the focus of our research. Chapter 6 focuses on these important ethical issues, and it is vital that you are aware of them before embarking on a research project.

Once you have covered these introductory issues, you will be in a strong position to plan your reading of the other chapters in this book. We recommend that you read the chapter outline at the start of each chapter to give you a sense of the issues addressed in each case and to decide how you want to engage with them.

We hope that you enjoy reading this book and find it useful as a basis for thinking about and doing business research—and we hope that you find business research as fascinating as we do!

New to this edition

- Five new students provide first-hand accounts of their experiences of doing business research for the 'student experience' feature, with accompanying video footage available as part of the online resources.

- Extended material on ethical considerations, 'big data', and writing academically is provided.

- E-Research is now woven throughout the text, better reflecting how internet research methodology is taught.

- A new test bank and new discussion questions for lecturers are available with this edition as part of the educator-only online resources.

- Two chapters have been combined and significantly reduced in length for this edition. Chapter 12 on Structured observation and Chapter 13 on Content analysis have now been merged into Chapter 13: Quantitative research using naturally occurring data.

- This edition has been extensively streamlined to focus on all the necessary areas of business research whilst also being concise.

- Jargon has been simplified throughout and clear, full, explanations of methodologies and philosophies are provided.

ACKNOWLEDGEMENTS

The fifth edition of this book is shaped by the loss of our dearly missed colleague Alan Bryman, with whom Emma Bell has collaborated in the writing of this book for over 15 years. Alan's legacy to business research methods and social science methodology more generally is immense, and the field of business research is indebted to him for his significant contribution in this area. It is thus with great sadness that Emma Bell and Bill Harley have written this edition of the book without him, while also seeking to sustain the intellectual curiosity about methods that Alan so effectively cultivated in others.

As in previous editions, this book has benefited from students and colleagues who have shared their ideas about, experiences of, and problems encountered in business research. This includes through Emma Bell's teaching of research methods and organization studies at the Open University and other institutions in the UK, Alan Bryman's teaching of research methods at Loughborough University and the University of Leicester, and Bill Harley's teaching of HRM, organization studies, and research methods at the University of Melbourne, Australia. The number of colleagues who have provided advice, suggestions, and permission to share insights from their research grows longer with each edition. It includes Alan Beardsworth, Michael Billig, Dave Buchanan, Jane Davison, Lauren McCarthy, Albert Mills, Cliff Oswick, Jonathan Schroeder, Samantha Warren, and Tony Yue. We also thank the students who agreed to be interviewed about their experiences of doing business research for this book. In addition, we appreciate the contributions made by Max Theilacker, who revised the coverage of quantitative data analysis in Chapter 15 and the use of IBM SPSS in Chapter 16, and Akash Puranik, who updated Chapter 25, 'Computer-assisted qualitative data analysis: using NVivo' for this edition. For this edition of the book we have substantially updated the accompanying online resources, and have introduced some new features. We thank Charlotte Smith and Aidan Kelly for authoring and updating these – their work on these resources has been exceptional. Finally, our thanks also go to the referees, readers, and book adopters for their detailed, helpful comments, informed by substantial experience of teaching research methods to business students, on this and previous editions of the book.

EDITORIAL ADVISORY PANEL

The authors and Oxford University Press are immensely grateful to the following reviewers, who provided invaluable feedback at multiple stages of the writing of this edition of the book. This feedback informed the book's development and has helped to ensure that it fulfils its aims.

Dr Adolf Acquaye, University of Kent

Professor Robert Ackrill, Nottingham Trent University

Gunilla S. Andersson, Linköping University

Dr Saurabh Bhattacharya, Newcastle University

Dr Shirley Y. Coleman, Newcastle University

Dr Adina Dudau, University of Glasgow, Adam Smith Business School

Dr Katherine Duffy, University of Glasgow

Dr Richard Hewison, Edith Cowan College

Dr Aidan J. Kelly, University of East London

Associate Professor Jennifer (M.I) Loh, University of Canberra

Dr Malliga Marimuthu, La Trobe University

Professor Alan McKinlay, Newcastle University

Professor Wim Naudé, Maastricht University

Professor Stephen Procter, Newcastle University

Dr David A. Savage, The University of Newcastle

Sawsan Al-Shamaa, Senior Lecturer, Auckland Institute of Studies

Dr Charlotte Smith, University of Leicester

Ken Stevenson, University of New South Wales

Dr Nicoleta Tipi, University of Huddersfield

Dr Casey Cross, Lancaster University

Dr Chloe Wu, University of Hull

PART ONE
THE RESEARCH PROCESS

THE NATURE AND PROCESS OF BUSINESS RESEARCH

CHAPTER OUTLINE

This chapter introduces some fundamental considerations in conducting business research. It begins by outlining what we mean by business research and the reasons why we conduct it. The chapter considers three main areas:

- *Business research methods in context*. This introduces issues such as the role of theory; values and ethical considerations; debates about relevance versus rigour; and how political considerations affect business research.

- *The elements of the research process*. The whole book is dedicated to the elements of business research, but here an overview of the essential stages is given. The elements are: a literature review; formulating concepts and theories; devising research questions; sampling; data collection; data analysis; and writing up.

- *The messiness of business research*. This section acknowledges that business research often does not conform to a neat, linear process and that researchers may find themselves facing unexpected contingencies and difficulties. At the same time, it is suggested that a familiarity with the nature of the research process and its principles is crucial to navigating unexpected issues.

All of the issues presented here are addressed in greater detail in later chapters, but they are introduced at this stage to provide you with an early opportunity to think about them.

Introduction

This book is concerned with the ways that business researchers go about their craft. It covers the research process in all its phases—formulating research objectives; choosing research methods; securing research participants; collecting, analysing, and interpreting data; and disseminating findings. Understanding business research methods is important for several reasons, but three stand out. First, such an understanding will help you to avoid the many pitfalls that are common when relatively inexperienced people try to do business research, such as failing to match research questions to appropriate research methods, asking ambiguous questions in questionnaires, or engaging in practices that are ethically dubious. If you are expected to complete a research project, an education in research methods is important, not just to ensure that correct procedures are followed but also to gain an appreciation of the choices that are available to you. Second, an understanding of business research methods is important from the point of view of consuming published research. If you are doing a degree in a business subject, you will probably read a lot of published research in the substantive areas you are studying. A good grounding in the research process and a knowledge of potential pitfalls provides an invaluable critical edge when reading about research done by others. Finally, an understanding of research methods will enable you to satisfy your curiosity about topics that interest you by undertaking your own research project, either for a dissertation or in a work-related context. Such a project may generate insight into important business issues and allow you, in a small, incremental way, to contribute to business knowledge.

What is 'business research'?

The term 'business research' as used here refers to the academic study of topics related to questions relevant to business, including management and organizations. Business research is situated in the context of social science disciplines, such as sociology, psychology, anthropology, and economics. These inform the study of business and its specific fields, which include marketing, human resource management (HRM), strategy, organizational behaviour, accounting and finance, industrial relations, and operational research. Business research may be motivated by developments and changes in organizations and societies, such as concerns about rising levels of executive pay or a desire to improve the environmental sustainability of businesses, but social scientific ideas are key to illuminate and explain those changes. The social sciences also provide ideas about how to formulate research topics and how to interpret and draw implications from research findings. In other words, what distinguishes business research as discussed in this book is that it is deeply rooted in the ideas and intellectual traditions of the social sciences.

Why do business research?

Academics conduct research because in the course of reading the literature on a topic or reflecting on what is going on in organizations, questions occur to them. They may notice a gap in the literature, or an inconsistency between a number of studies, or an unresolved issue in the literature. A societal development may also provide a point of departure for the development of a research question. For example, one of the authors of this book, Emma Bell, was interested in observing the behaviours of consumers who prefer a particular technology brand, Apple. She therefore decided to study how consumer groups develop and express strong loyalty to a particular brand through exploring their relationship to its co-founder and former CEO, Steve Jobs, following his death in 2011 (Bell and Taylor 2016). In exploring this issue, the researchers drew on organizational studies literatures on leadership and culture, and on sociological and philosophical literatures related to cultural practices of mourning and loss, to generate insights. As we note in Chapter 2, there is no single reason why people do business research, but, at its core, it is done when there is an aspect of business and management that is believed to be inadequately understood.

Business research methods in context

Business research and its associated methods do not exist in a vacuum. The following factors form aspects of the context within which business research takes place.

- The *theories* that social scientists develop to understand the social world influence what is researched and how research findings are interpreted. The topics of business research are deeply influenced by the theoretical position adopted. Drawing on our earlier example, Bell and Taylor (2016) were interested in understanding the behaviours of brand-loyal consumers in mourning the death of a leader, so they took into account existing theories concerning the collective cultural processes whereby groups of people develop deep attachments to organizational leaders and brands and use this to construct a shared sense of identity. This illustrates how current research is informed and influenced by existing theory. Research also contributes to theory because new research feeds into the stock of knowledge to which the theory relates.

- Existing knowledge about an area also forms an important part of the background in which business research takes place. This means that someone planning to conduct research must be familiar with the *literature* on the area of interest. You have to be familiar with what is already known so that you can build on it and avoid covering the same ground as others. Reviewing literature is the main focus of Chapter 5 and is also discussed in other chapters, such as Chapter 7.

- The researcher's views about the nature of the *relationship between theory and research* are also important. For some researchers, theory should be addressed at the beginning of a research project. The researcher engages in theoretical reflections from which a hypothesis or hypotheses are formulated and then tested. This was the approach taken in the study by Elsesser and Lever (2011: 1559), discussed in Research in focus 1.3, in which they proposed nine hypotheses based on their review of relevant theory. An alternative position is to view theory as an outcome of the research process—that is, as something that is arrived at after the research has been carried out. The

first approach implies that a set of theoretical ideas drive data collection and analysis, whereas the second suggests a more open-ended strategy in which theoretical ideas emerge out of data. Of course, the choice is rarely as stark as this, but there are contrasting views about the role of theory in research. This issue will be a major focus of Chapter 2.

- Assumptions and views about *how research should be conducted* influence the research process. It is often assumed that a 'scientific' approach should be followed, in which a hypothesis is formulated and then tested using precise measurement techniques. Such research exists, but the view that this is how business research should be done is not universally accepted. These are epistemological considerations. They focus on how the social world should be studied. Some researchers argue that people and organizations are very different from the subject matter of the natural scientist and require an approach that is more sensitive to the special qualities of people and social life. This issue will also be a major focus of Chapter 2.

- Assumptions about the *nature of social phenomena* influence the research process too. It is sometimes suggested that the social world is external to social actors and that they have no control over it. It is simply there, acting upon and influencing their behaviour, beliefs, and values. The culture of an organization, for example, can be seen as a set of values and behavioural expectations that exert a powerful influence over people who work in it, and into which new recruits have to be socialized. But we could also view culture as something that is constantly being reformulated and reassessed, as members of the organization modify it through practices and through small innovations. Considerations of this kind are ontological. They focus on the nature of social phenomena—are they relatively inert and beyond our influence, or are they a product of social interaction? This issue will also be discussed in Chapter 2.

- The *quality criteria* used to evaluate research are a further important influence on the research process. How do you do good research, and how do you know that a piece of research is good when you read it? Assessments of quality relate to all phases of the research process. As we shall see, assessing research quality has become a prominent issue among business researchers and policy-makers. There are several reasons for this, but the key point here is that debates have arisen about whether there are universal quality criteria that apply to all forms of research. As we will discuss in Chapter 17, some methodologists argue that a more sensitive approach is required whereby quality criteria need to take into account the kind of investigation to which they are being applied.

- The *values* of the research community have significant implications for research. *Ethical issues* have always been a point of discussion and controversy in research, but in recent times they have become even more prominent. Universities and funding bodies routinely scrutinize research proposals for ethical integrity to ensure that ethical principles are upheld. Ethical values and the institutional arrangements that are used ensure them have implications for what and who can be researched and for how research can be conducted, to the point that certain research methods are rarely used. Ethical issues are addressed in Chapter 6 and touched on in several other chapters.

- So far, we have stressed the academic nature and purpose of business research. However, much business research has a practical purpose and seeks to make a positive difference to organizations and the people who work in them. This means that studies focus on issues that are likely to have *implications for practice*. Some business research, such as **action research**, discussed in Chapter 17, involves those being researched (such as managers, employees, and consumers, as well as policy-makers) participating in the research process, perhaps by helping to develop research questions. While opinions differ about the need for business research to be directly relevant to practice, this is an issue that researchers are expected to reflect upon.

Relevance to practice

The diverse nature of business research means there is considerable debate about its relationship to practice. Some suggest that management research can be understood as an applied field that is concerned with understanding organizations in order to solve problems of managerial practice. Gummesson (2000) sees academic researchers and management consultants as groups of knowledge workers who place a different emphasis on theory and practice. He writes: 'Backed by bits and pieces of theory, the consultant contributes to practice, whereas the scholar contributes to theory supported by fragments of practice' (2000: 9), but fundamentally their roles are closely related. Gummesson sees researchers and consultants as both involved in addressing problems that concern management, so the value of both groups is determined by their ability to convince the business community that findings are relevant and useful. Other writers, such as Tranfield and Starkey (1998), noted that business researchers have at times lost touch with the concerns and interests of practitioners and that researchers must be responsive to them in order for research to retain its value and purpose. Since the first decade of the twenty-first century there has been some debate around the concept of evidence-based management (Key concept 1.1). Advocates of evidence-based management suggest that managers need to move their 'professional decisions away from personal preference and unsystematic experience toward those based on the best available scientific evidence' (Rousseau 2006: 256). However, others are more cautious, arguing that the changing and context-dependent nature of management and business makes it difficult to identify generally applicable best practices. Reay et al. (2009) carried out a review of articles that used evidence-based analysis and found that none of them demonstrated a link between adoption of evidence-based management and improved organizational performance. Other researchers (Morrell and Learmonth 2015) have expressed concern that evidence-based management privileges certain kinds of research evidence. They argue that evidence-based management restricts our ability to understand the diversity of problems in management and business studies. These writers further suggest that evidence-based management is characterized by a selective, narrow, and exclusionary view of what counts as evidence, a view that devalues narrative forms of knowledge. Specifically, what is considered to be 'trustworthy and relevant' (2015: 522) by those who favour evidence-based

1.1 KEY CONCEPT
What is evidence-based management?

Evidence-based management is 'the systematic use of the best available evidence to improve management practice' (Reay et al. 2009). The approach is proposed as a way of overcoming the 'research–practice gap' (Wright et al. 2016), which seeks to address the problem whereby, according to some commentators, business research is insufficiently relevant to practice. The concept developed during the 1990s to enhance patient care in medicine. It was subsequently applied in other fields such as education (Petticrew and Roberts 2006). There are four sources of information that contribute to evidence-based management:

1. practitioner expertise and judgement;

2. evidence from the local context;

3. critical evaluation of the best available research evidence;

4. perspectives of those who may be affected by a particular decision (Briner et al. 2009: 19).

Point 3 is based on the practice of **systematic review** of the literature (see Chapter 5), a cornerstone of evidence-based management practice. The value of evidence-based management depends on whether it enables research findings to be transferred or translated into practice. What is distinctive about evidence-based management is that managerial decision-making is based on explicit, systematic use of research evidence (Wright et al. 2016). Based on their study of an operations management problem in an Australian hospital emergency department, Wright et al. (2016) describe how an evidence-based approach was enacted by a physician manager. Their analysis highlights the importance of 'fit' between the personal characteristics of the decision-maker and the organizational context in ensuring the success of this approach. They argue that there is a need for a balanced view that takes into account the critiques of evidence-based management, recognizing the situated expertise of managers in addition to relying on scientific evidence.

management is research that privileges a positivist view of knowledge. Morrell and Learmonth conclude that despite claiming to be scientific and impartial, evidence-based management is managerialist, i.e. it privileges and supports management rather than critically analysing it. This builds on earlier arguments by Learmonth (2009), who argues that, because management research operates from within conflicting paradigms (see Key concept 2.14), it is not possible to develop a consensus-based notion of evidence that transcends these fundamental philosophical differences.

A further debate that influences understanding of the role of business research stems from the thesis developed by Gibbons et al. (1994). These writers suggest that the process of knowledge production in society falls into two contrasting categories or types, which they describe as 'mode 1' and 'mode 2'.

- *Mode 1*. Within this traditional, university-based model, knowledge production is driven primarily by an academic agenda. Discoveries tend to build upon existing knowledge in a linear fashion. The model makes a distinction between theoretically pure knowledge and

applied knowledge, the latter being where theoretical insights are translated into practice. Limited emphasis is placed on the dissemination of knowledge, because the academic community is viewed as the most important audience or consumer of knowledge.

- *Mode 2*. This model draws attention to the role of *trans-disciplinarity* in research, which refers to a process that causes the boundaries of single contributing disciplines to be exceeded. Findings are closely related to context and not easily replicated, so knowledge production is less of a linear process. Moreover, the production of knowledge is not confined to academic institutions. Instead, it involves academics, policymakers, and practitioners, who apply a broad set of skills and experiences to tackle a shared problem. Knowledge can be quickly disseminated and findings used to enable practical improvement.

Although mode 2 research is intended to exist alongside mode 1, rather than to replace it, Tranfield and Starkey (1998) argue that business research is more suited to mode 2 knowledge production. Recently, attention has turned towards the challenges of complexity that arise from the relationship of business research to business practice. This includes the study of complex social issues which are referred to as 'wicked problems' (Conklin 2006) or 'grand challenges' (Ferraro et al. 2015). The study of wicked problems involves the acknowledgement of large-scale social changes, such as climate change, poverty, and migration, which transcend national boundaries and involve multiple stakeholders with diverse interests. The complex nature of these issues makes it very difficult to work out exactly what the problem is, or how to study it, and the interlocking nature of variables makes it hard to establish patterns of attribution. Hence it is likely that it will be impossible to accurately trace their cause or identify solutions to the problem (Ferraro et al. 2015). The pervasiveness of business in society means business researchers are increasingly likely to be involved in the study of wicked problems, sometimes as members of interdisciplinary research teams.

The process of business research

In the rest of this chapter, we introduce the main elements of a typical research project. It is common for writers of textbooks on business research methods to compile flow charts of the research process, as you will see from, for example, Figures 2.1, 8.1, and 17.1. However, at this stage we do not present the stages or elements of the research process in a sequence, because the order in which they are carried out will vary according to research strategy and design. We therefore introduce the main elements that are common to most types of business research and which will be addressed in more detail in later chapters.

Literature review

Existing literature represents an important element in all research. When we have a topic or issue that interests us, we must read further to determine

- what is already known about the topic;
- what concepts and theories have been applied to it;
- what research methods have been used to study it;
- what controversies exist about the topic and the ways in which it is studied;
- what clashes of evidence (if any) exist;
- who are the key contributors to research on the topic.

Many topics have a rich tradition of research, so it is unlikely that you will be able to conduct an exhaustive review of the literature. What is crucial is to identify and read key books and articles by some of the main figures who have written in the field. As we suggest in Chapter 5, you must know what is known, so that you cannot be accused of naively going over old ground. Linking your research questions, findings, and discussion to existing literature is an important and useful way of demonstrating the credibility of your research and the contribution to knowledge that you are making. However, as will become clear in Chapter 5, a literature review is not simply a summary: it is expected to be critical. This does not necessarily mean that you must be highly critical of existing work, but it does mean that you should assess its significance and how each published item fits into the overall narrative you construct about the literature.

Concepts and theories

In the social sciences, concepts are how we make sense of the social world. They are the labels we give to aspects of the social world that have significant common features. As will be outlined in Chapter 2, the social sciences have a strong tradition of using concepts, many of which have become part of the language of everyday life. Concepts such as bureaucracy, power, social control, status, charisma, labour process, McDonaldization, and alienation are all part of the body of theory that generations of social scientists have constructed. Concepts are a key ingredient of theories.

Concepts serve several purposes in business research. They are important to how we organize and signal our research interests. They help us to think and be more disciplined about what we want to find out about, and help with the organization of research findings. The relationship between theory and research is often depicted as involving a choice between theories driving the research process in all its phases, or theories as a product of the research process. This is invariably depicted as a choice between deductive and inductive approaches, which will be expanded upon in Chapter 2. Unsurprisingly, this choice has implications for concepts. Concepts may be something we start out with that represent key areas around which we collect data in an investigation. In other words, we might collect data in order to shed light on a concept (or more likely several concepts and how they are connected). This is the approach taken in the investigation reported in Research in focus 1.3. The alternative view is that concepts are outcomes of research. According to this second view, concepts help us to reflect on and organize the data that we collect.

One of the reasons why familiarity with existing literature is so important is that it alerts us to the main concepts already in use in an area of research and enables us to assess how useful or limited those concepts have been in helping to unravel the main issues. Research in focus 1.3 provides an example of this. Even when we are reading the literature solely as consumers of research—for example, when writing an essay—it is crucial that we know what the main concepts are, who is responsible for them, and what controversies (if any) surround them.

Research questions

Research questions are important in the research process because they force you to consider that most basic of issues—what is it that you want to know? Most people begin research with a general idea of what they are interested in. Research questions require you to consider much more precisely what you want to find out about (see Key concept 1.2).

Researchers vary in terms of how specific their research questions are, as discussed in Key concept 1.2. In business research it is commonly expected that you will have a clear research question. However, not all business research starts with a clear question. Some researchers start with a general topic or phenomenon they want to study. They choose not to constrain the process of discovery by imposing a predetermined question. These researchers tend to work inductively and build knowledge and theory after they have collected their data. It is important, though, to be aware of the danger that without a clear research question your research may become unfocused. The value of a research question is that it can

- guide your literature search;
- guide your decisions about the kind of research design to employ;

1.2 KEY CONCEPT
What are research questions?

A research question provides an explicit statement of what it is the researcher wants to know about. A research purpose can be presented as a statement (for example, 'I want to find out whether [or why] … '), but a question forces the researcher to be more explicit about what is to be investigated. A research question is interrogatory, i.e. it has a question mark at the end of it. However, research questions are sometimes worded as an overall aim or objective of study and hence not in question format. Research questions can be quite broad, for example 'How do graduates experience job searching?'; or very specific: 'Does frequency of use of social media influence how quickly or slowly graduates obtain employment?'

Denscombe (2010, first edn 2002) provides a list of types of research question:

1. Predicting an outcome: does *y* happen under circumstances *a* and *b*?
2. Explaining causes and consequences of a phenomenon: is *y* affected by *x* or is *y* a consequence of *x*?
3. Evaluating a phenomenon: does *y* exhibit the benefits that it is claimed to have?
4. Describing a phenomenon: what is *y* like or what forms does *y* assume?
5. Developing good practice: how can we improve *y*?
6. Empowerment: how can we enhance the lives of those we research?

White (2009) is critical of Denscombe's last category, arguing that an emphasis on political motives of this kind can impede the conduct of good quality research. To some extent, this difference of opinion can be attributed to differences in viewpoint about the purposes of research. White proposes an alternative:

7. Comparison: do *a* and *b* differ in respect of *x*?

There are many ways that research questions can be categorized, but these seven types provide a rough indication of the possibilities as well as drawing attention to a controversy about the wider goals of research.

1.3 RESEARCH IN FOCUS

A research question about gender bias in attitudes towards leaders

The research question posed in the title of the article by Elsesser and Lever (2011) is 'Does gender bias against female leaders persist?' They begin by reviewing the literature, which suggests that negative attitudes towards female leaders still persist. However, they question whether prior research can be generalized to 'real world scenarios' because much of it is based on 'student samples surveyed on vignettes of hypothetical leaders, attitudes about ideal leaders, or ratings of task leaders in laboratory settings' (Elsesser and Lever 2011: 1556). The aim of their study was therefore to examine whether biases exist towards actual female leaders and, if so, the conditions and management styles that cause such biases to emerge. At one level, this research addresses a practical issue by identifying factors which prevent or discourage women from assuming leadership positions. As noted earlier, it is generally viewed as a good thing that researchers address relevant problems with a view to improving practice. But the authors also draw on theory, in this case role congruity theory, to help explain the processes whereby gender bias against female leaders persists. This theory states that individuals who behave in ways that are incongruent with stereotypically defined sex roles are likely to be viewed negatively. Based on their literature review, the authors present nine hypotheses which they aim to test through data collection and statistical analysis. Hypotheses are typically based on questions but are very specific questions framed as propositions which can be tested.

Their method of data collection was a US-based national survey, titled 'Rate Your Boss', posted on the popular news website msnbc.com in 2007 for ten days. A total of 60,470 people responded to the survey. The majority (68 per cent) had a male boss, but most (89 per cent of women and 78 per cent of men) had experience of both male and female management. Measures included 'relationship quality', 'competence', 'competitiveness', 'sensitivity and directness', and 'preference for a male or female boss'. Preliminary findings were reported in *Elle* magazine before being written up academically. In addition to statistical analysis, the researchers identified a random stratified subsample from 12,440 responses to an optional open-ended follow-up question which asked participants who had expressed a preference for the gender of their boss to explain why. The researchers identified common themes that emerged from these narratives using a grounded theory approach (see Key concept 24.3), providing quotes that were supportive of the themes.

The researchers found a cross-sex bias in how respondents rated their bosses: men judged female bosses more favourably, and women judged male bosses more favourably. A further finding from the qualitative results of the study was that while respondents who said they preferred female bosses cited such things as their compassion or understanding, those who said they preferred male bosses justified this by referring to the negative attributes of female leaders, describing them as too 'emotional', 'moody', 'gossipy', and 'bitchy'. The authors conclude that the answer to their research question is 'yes' and 'no', as participants were less likely to show gender bias when evaluating their own boss, indicating minimal 'bias against women for violating their sex role by adopting a leadership position', but a high level of descriptive bias—'where women are seen as having less potential for management' (Elsesser and Lever 2011: 1571). We return to this example in Chapter 7, where we use it to illustrate the process of writing up **quantitative research**.

- guide your decisions about what data to collect and from whom;
- guide your analysis of data;
- guide your writing-up of findings;
- stop you going off in unnecessary directions; and
- provide your readers with a clear sense of what your research is about.

It is possible that reading the literature may prompt you to revise your research questions and may even suggest some new ones. Therefore, at an early stage of a research study, research questions and the literature relating to them are likely to be intertwined. At the beginning of a research project your initial reading of the literature may generate one or two research questions; further reading guided by the initial research questions may lead you to revise them and possibly generate new ones. In Chapter 4, there will be more discussion of research questions and how they can be developed.

Sampling

As will be discussed in later chapters, there are a number of principles behind the idea of sampling. Many people associate sampling with surveys and the quest for representative samples. Such sampling is usually based on constructing a sample that can represent (and therefore act as a microcosm of) a wider population. The principles that lie behind the quest for the representative sample will be explained in Chapter 9. These principles often apply to questionnaire survey research of the kind described in Research in focus 1.3. In that research, Elsesser and Lever (2011) point out that their sample was unusually large and broadly representative in terms of gender (51 per cent men and 49 per cent women). Respondents covered a wide range in terms of their educational experience and the sector of employment they worked in. However, the sample 'was not nationally representative, and the survey did not include information on race or ethnicity' (Elsesser and Lever 2011: 1574). This sample may have been affected by the fact that participation relied on internet access, although in the USA where the study was carried out, internet samples are relatively diverse with respect to gender, age, and socio-economic status. A final limitation relates to the self-selecting nature of the sample, which means that it may be skewed in ways that do not reflect overall patterns of employment. For example, 94 per cent of respondents in Elsesser and Lever's study were employed full-time and 36 per cent of female and 51 per cent of male participants described themselves as managers; these proportions are not representative of the overall population.

As this example illustrates, even business research, which is traditionally seen as prioritizing representative samples, involves convenience, i.e. making use of the data collection opportunities that are available. In Part Three we encounter sampling principles based not on the idea of representativeness but on the notion that samples should be selected on the basis of their appropriateness to the purposes of the investigation. This is common in case study research, where there may be just one or two units of analysis. Here, the goal is to understand the selected case or cases in depth. Sampling issues are still relevant to such research because cases have to be chosen according to criteria relevant to the research, and individuals who are members of the case study context have to be sampled according to criteria too. The key

issue is that sampling is an inevitable feature of most kinds of business research and therefore constitutes an important stage of any investigation.

It is also important to remember that business research is not always carried out on people. For example, we may want to examine mass-media content and employ a technique such as content analysis, covered in Chapter 13. In such a situation, we are collecting our data from newspapers or television programmes rather than from people. Because of this, it is common for writers on business research methods to use the term 'case' to cover the wide variety of objects on whom, or from whom, data will be collected. Much if not most of the time, 'cases' will be people. In business research we are rarely in a position in which we can interview, observe, or send questionnaires to all possible individuals who are appropriate to our research; equally, we are unlikely to be able to read and analyse the content of all articles in all newspapers relating to an area of media content that interests us. Time and cost issues will always constrain the number of cases we can include in our research, so we almost always have to sample.

Data collection

Data collection is the key point of any research project, and therefore this book gives more space to this stage of the research process than any other. Some methods of data collection, such as interviewing and questionnaires, are likely to be more familiar to readers than others. Some methods require a structured approach—that is, the researcher establishes in advance the broad contours of what he or she wants to find out about and designs the research accordingly. The questionnaire is an example of a structured method; the researcher designs questions that will allow data to be collected to answer specific research questions. Similarly, a structured interview—the kind of interview used in survey investigations—includes questions designed for exactly the same purpose.

Many methods of data collection are less structured than this. In Part Three we concentrate on research methods that emphasize an open-ended view of the research process, so that there is less restriction on the topics and issues being studied. Research methods such as participant observation and semi-structured interviewing allow the researcher to keep an open mind about what he or she needs to know about, so that concepts and theories can emerge out of the data. This is the inductive approach to theorizing and conceptualization referred to above. Such research is usually still geared to answering research questions, but these are expressed less explicitly than in more structured research. This can be seen by comparing the specificity of the hypotheses developed by Elsesser and Lever (2011, Research in focus 1.3) to address their overarching research question, with the question that guided the study of academics in business schools in UK universities by Clarke et al. (2012):

> Our objective is to understand how the historical, cultural, economic, political and institutional relations in higher education (and in our case specifically UK business schools) shape or reshape the conditions of identity work and how academic subjectivities are sustained or transformed. In particular, we examine how the cultural, institutional and managerial changes of the last decade or so have affected academic identities.
>
> (Clarke et al. 2012: 6)

This research question, which the authors describe as an 'objective', is derived from and illuminated by concepts of managerialism, audit, and performativity. To address the research question, semi-structured interviews were conducted with 48 academics in business schools in UK universities. The interviews were 'conversations with a purpose' (Burman 1994)—that of elucidating the impact of new public management on academic identities (Clarke et al. 2012: 8). This is a noticeably less structured approach to data collection, and it reflects the open-ended nature of the research question. Data collection, then, can entail different approaches in terms of how structured or open-ended the methods are.

Data analysis

Data analysis is a stage that incorporates several elements. At the most obvious level, this might mean the application of statistical techniques to data. However, even when data is amenable to quantitative data analysis, there are other things going on when it is analysed. For a start, the raw data has to be *managed*. This means the researcher has to check the data to establish whether there are any obvious flaws. For example, in the research by Clarke et al. (2012), the interviews were audio-recorded and transcribed. **Transcription** enables the researcher to upload the transcripts into a computer software program of the kind discussed in Chapter 25. In the research by Clarke et al., once the transcripts had been uploaded into the software, the authors began by **coding** each transcript. This is a process whereby the data are broken down into component parts which are then given labels. The analyst searches for recurrences of sequences of coded **text** within and across cases and for links between different codes. Clarke et al. began

by identifying 'descriptive first order' categories such as 'emotion' and 'changes in the higher education system' (2012: 8), which they later expanded or collapsed as the analysis progressed, refining them into more analytic categories such as 'professionalism', eventually arriving at core themes which they concentrated on. This approach is referred to as **thematic analysis**. There is a lot going on here: data are being made more manageable than they would be if the researcher just kept listening and relistening to the recordings; the researcher is making sense of data through coding; and data are being interpreted—that is, the researcher is linking the process of making sense of the data with the research question, as well as with the literature and theoretical concepts.

The data analysis stage is fundamentally about *data reduction*—that is, reducing the large corpus of information gathered to make sense of it. Unless the researcher reduces the data collected—for example, in the case of quantitative data by producing tables or averages, and in the case of qualitative data by grouping textual material into categories such as themes—it is more or less impossible to interpret the material.

Data analysis can also refer to interpretation of secondary data. Primary data analysis means that the researcher who collected the data conducts the analysis, as was the case with Elsesser and Lever (2011) and Clarke et al. (2012). Secondary data analysis occurs when someone else analyses such data. Researchers in universities are encouraged to deposit their data in archives, which allows others to analyse it. Given the time and money involved in business research, this is a sensible thing to do: it increases the value of an investigation, and a researcher conducting **secondary analysis** can explore the research questions in which he or she is interested without having to go through the time-consuming and lengthy process of collecting primary data. Secondary analysis is discussed in Chapters 14 and 24. As Thinking deeply 1.4 illustrates, the possibilities for analysis of secondary data have grown exponentially because of the internet as a context for business activity such as shopping and career networking. Much information about people's internet usage is digitally recorded, creating vast potential sources of data.

Writing up

The finest piece of research is useless if it is not disseminated so that others can benefit from it. We do research so that others can read about what we have done and about our findings. Writing up is often neglected, so Chapter 7 is devoted to this topic.

1.4 THINKING DEEPLY
What is big data?

The term 'big data' refers to the vast quantities of digital information generated, stored, and circulated, including via the internet. While understandings of this term vary, Ruppert et al. (2013: 41) provide the following definition:

'big data' refers to large volumes of digital content that is generated either online or offline in social, commercial, scientific and governmental databases. But the term does not simply signify an increase in the volume but also the velocity of data collection and the increasing variety of data sources and formats.

Hence data can be understood as 'big' in several different ways: in addition to volume, we may consider its *velocity* (it can be produced in real time), its *variety*, and its *scope* (it can cover vast populations) (Hand 2014). Big data research has tended to be commercial, often involving big technology corporations such as Google, Facebook, and Amazon. However, social science researchers are becoming increasingly attuned to the potential of big data. One of the challenges they face is that much algorithmically-produced data generated through people's internet usage, including via social media, is relatively unstructured and unformatted. Big data research therefore additionally involves 'the innovation of data structures, computational capacities, and processing tools and analytics to capture, curate, store, search, trace, link, share, visualize and analyse big datasets' (Ruppert et al. 2013: 41). A final issue raised by big data research concerns ethical questions about who owns the data and how it can be accessed (see Chapter 6).

There are different ways to write up research. More structured research, like that presented in Research in focus 1.3, is sometimes written up differently from more open-ended research of the sort represented by Clarke et al. (2012). However, there are core ingredients that dissertations, theses, research articles, and books usually include.

- *Introduction*. The research area and its significance are outlined. The research questions will also probably be introduced.
- *Literature review*. What is already known about the research area is examined critically. This section often relates to theoretical concepts that are the focus of the research, as shown in Table 1.1.

- *Research methods*. The research methods (sampling, methods of data collection, methods of data analysis) are presented and justified.
- *Results*. The findings are presented.
- *Discussion*. The findings are discussed in relation to the literature and the research questions.
- *Conclusion*. The significance of the research is reinforced.

These elements are discussed in detail in Chapter 7. This is not an exhaustive list, because writing conventions differ, but these are recurring elements of the completed research.

Table 1.1 summarizes the seven elements of the research process.

The messiness of business research

There is one final point we want to make before you read on. Business research is often a lot less smooth than you might assume based on accounts of the process that you read in books such as this. Our purpose is to provide an overview of the research process and to give advice on how it should ideally be done. In reality, research is full of false starts, blind alleys, mistakes, and enforced

changes. We know that research is messy from the confessional accounts that have been written over the years (e.g. Hammond 1964; Bell and Newby 1977; Bryman 1988b; Townsend and Burgess 2009; Streiner and Sidani 2010). It is therefore important for business researchers to remain flexible and to modify and adapt their research plans in response to opportunities and problems

TABLE 1.1
Stages of the research process in two studies

Stage	Description of stage	Example: Elsesser and Lever 2011 *	Example: Clarke et al. 2012
Literature review	Critical examination of existing research relating to the phenomena of interest and relevant theoretical ideas.	Literature concerning gender bias in organizational leadership, focusing on role congruity theory.	Literature concerning identity and new public management (including managerialism, audit, and performativity) related to business school academics.
Concepts and theories	Ideas that drive the research process and shed light on the interpretation of resulting findings.	Stereotypes; role congruity; female managers; female bosses.	Audit and performative culture; new public management; identity; managerialism.
Research question	Question that provides an explicit statement of what the researcher wants to know about.	'Does gender bias against female leaders persist?' (Elsesser and Lever 2011: 1555)—followed by nine hypotheses (see Research in focus 1.3).	'Our objective is to understand how the historical, cultural, economic, political and institutional relations in higher education (and in our case specifically UK business schools) shape or reshape the conditions of identity work and how academic subjectivities are sustained or transformed.' (Clarke et al. 2012: 6).
Sampling	Selection of sample relevant to the research question(s).	60,470 men and women who responded to a US-based national survey, 'Rate Your Boss', posted on the msnbc.com website for 10 days in 2007. Subsample of 1000 narratives from 12,440 responses to an open-ended follow-up question asking respondents to explain their gender preferences for a boss.	Sample of 48 lecturers, senior lecturers, readers, and professors working in 8 different UK business schools in the field of organization studies who were interviewed in 2009/10. The sampling approach was both purposeful (i.e. participants worked in a range of different universities) and self-selecting 'because the onus was on participants to respond to a detailed invitation to take part in this study' (Clarke et al. 2012: 8).
Data collection	Gathering data from sample so that research question(s) can be answered.	Large-scale web survey involving an online questionnaire (as described in Chapter 11).	Semi-structured interviews between 45 and 70 minutes in length.
Data analysis	Management, analysis, and interpretation of data.	Statistical analysis of the questionnaire data.	Thematic analysis of interview transcripts.
Writing up	Dissemination of research and findings.	Initial descriptive findings published in *Elle* magazine and in msnbc.com's financial section in 2007, before being written up as an academic article (see also Chapter 7 on writing up).	Research written up as an article in Clarke et al. (2012) and also in Clarke and Knights (2014) (see also Chapter 7 on writing up).

*Clarke and Knights (2014).

that arise. Of course, research often does go relatively smoothly and, in spite of minor difficulties, may proceed roughly according to plan. However, what we read in reports of research are often quite sanitized accounts of how the research was carried out, without a sense of the difficult problems the researcher faced. This is not to say that business researchers seek to deceive us, but rather that research when written up tends to follow an implicit template that emphasizes some aspects of the research but not others. This tendency is not unique to *business*

research: in Chapter 7 a study of how natural scientists present and discuss their work shows that here too certain core aspects of the production of 'findings' tend to be omitted from the written account (Gilbert and Mulkay 1984). Bell and Thorpe (2013) draw attention to the role of research communities, including the relationship between research student and supervisor, in passing on research skills: for example, by telling stories about their research experience and by doing research in groups. As we explain in Chapter 4, developing a good working relationship with your supervisor is crucial in ensuring the success of your research project because this relationship will support you in dealing with unexpected events.

It is also the case that, regardless of the various ways in which research happens, this book can deal only with generalities. It is quite possible that, when doing your research, you will find that these generalities do not fit perfectly. We therefore urge a degree of caution in the way that you read this book, and we encourage you to adapt the advice we provide to suit your individual circumstances. However, it is also crucial to have an appreciation of businesss research methods as they are explained in the rest of this book because this will provide you with a road map for the journey ahead.

KEY POINTS

- Business research is embedded in a wider context that requires ethical and practical considerations to be taken into account.
- Business research comprises some common elements that are nearly always present. These include: a literature review; concepts and theories; research questions; sampling of cases; data collection; data analysis; and writing-up of research findings.
- Rigorous engagement with these steps is what distinguishes academic business research from practitioner research, such as market research done by private companies.
- Although we can attempt to formulate general principles for doing business research, it is important to recognize that things do not always go entirely to plan.

QUESTIONS FOR REVIEW

What is meant by 'business research'?

- What is distinctive about academic business research?

Why do business research?

- If you were to start a research project now or in the near future, what would you study and why?

Business research methods in context

- What contextual factors affect the practice of business research and researchers' choice of methods?

Relevance to practice

- What are the differences between mode 1 and mode 2 forms of knowledge production and why is this distinction important?
- What are 'wicked problems' and how might business researchers be involved in addressing them?

The process of business research

- Why is a literature review important when conducting business research?
- What role do concepts and theories play in the process of business research?
- Why are researchers encouraged to specify their research questions? What are the different kinds of research question?
- Why do researchers need to sample? Why is it important for them to outline the principles that underpin their sampling choices?

- Outline one or two factors that might affect a researcher's choice of data-collection method.
- What are the main differences between the kinds of data analysed by Elsesser and Lever (2011) and by Clarke et al. (2012)?
- How might you structure a report of the findings of a research project that you conducted?

The messiness of business research

- If research does not always go according to plan, why should we bother to learn business research methods at all?

 ONLINE RESOURCES
www.oup.com/uk/brm5e/

The Interactive Research Guide that accompanies this book contains exercises relevant to each chapter of the book.

BUSINESS RESEARCH STRATEGIES

CHAPTER OUTLINE

In this chapter we introduce the concept of research strategy and discuss the main strategic considerations that you are likely to encounter in your business research project. Research strategy refers to the overall approach you take in your research project. This includes the philosophical assumptions that inform your research design, your choice of research questions, and the methods you decide to use in order to try to answer them. To understand what is involved in developing a research strategy, we address the following key questions:

- *What is the role of theory in business research?* The choice of a particular theory involves making certain assumptions about the nature of the reality that one is researching and how that reality should be studied. The type of theory adopted also has implications for the relationship between theory and research, or the logic of inquiry. Two of the main options here are taking a deductive approach or taking an inductive approach.

- *What philosophical assumptions—about the nature of reality and how to study it—are made in business research?* Philosophical considerations might seem rather abstract in the context of a practical research project. However, philosophy enables us to examine our underlying assumptions about reality. This is important in enabling us to be clear in articulating what we know about business and deciding how we should go about studying it. Thinking philosophically about these assumptions before starting your research project is vital in ensuring that the claims that you make are valid. There are two further questions that follow from this.

- *What is meant by ontology in business research?* 'Ontology' refers to theories about the nature of reality. When we do research, we are trying to understand reality, so it is important to consider what reality is. As mentioned briefly in Chapter 1, different ontological positions provide rather different answers to questions of what reality is. The main distinction is between those that see the social world as something external to social actors—the viewpoint known as objectivism; and those that see reality as something that people are in the process of constructing—constructionism.

- *What is meant by epistemology in business research?* 'Epistemology' refers to theories about what is known, or what we can know. As introduced in Chapter 1, the ontological assumptions that we make about the nature of reality also have implications for how we try to know, and go about studying, that reality. This includes debates about whether the 'natural science' model of research is suitable for studying the social world of business, or whether alternatives are needed that are more sensitive to the distinctive realities of the social world.

- *How do philosophical assumptions inform the choice of business research methods?* A key distinction is commonly drawn in business research between quantitative research and qualitative research. The use of these terms generally reflects the type of research methods that are used in a study: whether these are based on the collection of numerical data—quantitative research—or based on the collection of data that comprises written or spoken words and images—qualitative research. The overall approach that is taken in a particular study is likely to be based *either* on a quantitative *or* a qualitative research strategy. Hence the rest of this book is organized according to this logic. However, while the terms 'quantitative' and 'qualitative' normally represent different kinds of research strategies, we should be wary of driving a wedge between them. Therefore, towards the end of this chapter we introduce the concept of mixed methods research, which is covered in more detail in Chapter 27.

- *Other issues that impact upon business research.* While philosophical issues are important in business research, they can only take us so far in dealing with the practical issues that researchers have to deal with. This chapter ends by reflecting on how your values and prior experience are likely to shape you as a researcher, and also on practical decisions that you will have to consider.

Introduction: the nature of business research

Many people might expect a book such as this one to be exclusively concerned with the different methods that business researchers use. The purpose of the book would therefore be to explain how to choose between them and apply them. But the practice of business research does not exist in a bubble, hermetically sealed off from the social sciences. Two points are relevant here. First, the methods of management and business research are closely tied to different visions of how organizational reality should be studied. Methods are not simply neutral tools: they are linked to how social scientists envisage social reality and how it should be examined. However, while methods are not neutral, they are not entirely dependent on intellectual inclinations either. Second, there is the question of how business research methods and practice connect with the wider social scientific enterprise. Research data are invariably collected in relation to something. The 'something' may be a pressing organizational problem, such as the effect of a merger on corporate culture or the impact of new technology on employee motivation. Research is also carried out when a specific opportunity arises. For example, the NASA space shuttle *Challenger* disaster in 1986 stimulated business and management research into the decision-making processes and group dynamics that had led to the decision to launch the shuttle despite indications that there were significant safety problems (Shrivasta et al. 1988; Vaughan 1990). Yet another stimulus for research comes from personal experiences. Lofland and Lofland (1995) note that many research projects emerge out of the researcher's personal biography. Certainly, one of the authors of this book, Alan Bryman, traced his interest in Disney theme parks back to a visit to Disney

World in Florida in 1991 (Bryman 1995, 1999), while he attributed his interest in the representation of social science research in the mass media (Fenton et al. 1998) to a difficult experience with the press (reported in Haslam and Bryman 1994). Similarly, the experience of being involved in the implementation of a quality management initiative in a UK National Health Service hospital trust prompted another of the book's authors, Emma Bell, to investigate the symbolic meanings that organizational members attach to these initiatives (Bell et al. 2002).

Whatever the stimulus, research data become significant, and make a contribution to knowledge, when they are viewed in relation to theoretical concerns. This means that the nature of the relationship between theory and research is crucial.

Theory and research

When we conduct research, we collect and analyse data in order to generate knowledge. While much knowledge has practical applications, business researchers are fundamentally interested in using data to inform theoretical understandings of the world. This means that regardless of what kind of study business researchers are conducting, theory is absolutely central. Making a contribution to theory, usually a very modest one, is a precondition for publication in many business and management journals and also for being awarded a PhD. But what precisely is theory and what role does it play in research? These are not simple questions to answer, and we do not pretend to be able to do so fully here. However, there are a number of important issues pertaining to the relationship between theory and research. Two stand out, and we will focus on them in the discussion that follows. First, the link between theory and research depends on what form of theory is being referred to. Second, there is the question of whether data are collected and analysed in order to test or to build theories.

What is theory?

The term 'theory' is used in a variety of ways, but its most common meaning is as a way of explaining observed patterns of associations between phenomena: for example, why women and ethnic minorities are under-represented in higher-paid managerial positions, or why alienation associated with the introduction of new technology varies according to methods of production. The sociologist Robert Merton referred to this as *middle-range theory* (Merton 1967) because it consists of theoretical explanations for social phenomena which can be explored using empirical data of various kinds. Merton formulated this idea as a means of bridging a widening gulf between 'grand theory', which refers to abstract, high-level theoretical *perspectives* on the world, and empirical findings.

Middle-range theories, unlike grand ones, operate in a limited domain. Whether research is about strategic decision-making or organizational identity, middle-range theories are characterized by their application to specific phenomena. In other words, they sit between grand theories and empirical findings. They represent attempts to understand and explain a limited aspect of business organization. An example of middle-range theorizing concerns contingency theory. Contingency theory is based on a number of assumptions: first, there is no one best way to organize; second, one way of organizing is not equally effective under all conditions; and, third, to be most effective, organizational structures should be appropriate to the type of work and environmental conditions (Schoonhoven 1981). Some researchers, such as Lawrence and Lorsch (1967), use contingency theory descriptively to show the factors in the environment that should be taken into account. Others apply the theory in a normative sense, recommending its use to inform managerial action based on 'best fit' in a particular situation (e.g. Fiedler 1967).

However, the term 'theory' is also used to refer to the background literature in an area of social enquiry. In many cases, the relevant background literature on a topic defines the focus of research and acts as the equivalent of a theory. That is, while it does not frame theoretically-based propositions, the literature is nonetheless used to define the research agenda. For example, in Ghobadian and Gallear's (1997) article on total quality management (TQM) and the competitive position of small or medium-sized enterprises (SMEs), there are virtually no allusions to theory. Instead, the authors use existing literature to generate research questions about what they argue is a neglected topic, as the majority of TQM research focuses on large companies. Background literature influences the focus of research in other ways, too: a researcher may discover from the literature that a particular aspect of a topic has been neglected; that certain ideas have not been tested; or that existing approaches used to study a topic are deficient.

Social scientists are sometimes dismissive of research that is not framed and conducted with explicit reference to theory. Such research is sometimes dismissed as naive empiricism (see Key concept 2.1). This includes policy or practice-oriented research which starts by gathering and analysing data on specific phenomena. For example, research in industrial relations that focuses on the detail of current employment practices in a variety of sectors or cultural contexts has sometimes been criticized as empiricist and lacking theoretical development (Marsden 1982; Godard 1994). The problem with this type of research, according to Marsden (1982: 234), is that 'empiricists tend to assume that theory will somehow arise from the facts "like steam from a kettle". But facts are never given, they are selected or produced by theory.' However, it would be harsh and inaccurate to brand all studies which use background literature as theory as naive empiricism simply because their authors have not been preoccupied with theory. Such research is conditioned by and directed towards research questions that arise out of critical reading of the literature. Data collection and analysis are geared to illumination or resolution of the research issue or problem identified. The literature can act as a proxy for theory; theory is latent or implicit.

This brings us to our next question: in so far as any piece of empirical research is linked to theory, what was the role of that theory? Specifically, how did the theory and the data relate to one another? Up to now, we have written as though theory guides and influences the collection and analysis of data. In other words, research is done in order to answer questions posed by theoretical puzzles. But an alternative position is to view theory as something that develops after collection and analysis of data. This takes us to a second important issue in the relationship between theory and research—whether theory and data are being used in a deductive or an inductive way.

Deductive and inductive logics of inquiry

The most common view of the relationship between theory and research is associated with a *deductive* approach. The researcher, on the basis of what is known about a domain and the theoretical considerations within it, deduces a hypothesis (or hypotheses) that must be subjected to empirical scrutiny (this approach to research is most commonly associated with a research tradition known as positivism, which we will return to later in the chapter). Embedded within the hypothesis will be concepts that need to be translated into researchable entities. The social scientist must skilfully deduce a hypothesis and then translate it into operational terms. This means there is a need to specify how data can be collected in relation to the concepts that make up the hypothesis.

This view of the role of theory is very much what Merton had in mind with middle-range theory, which 'is principally used in sociology to guide empirical inquiry' (Merton 1967: 39). Theory and the hypotheses deduced come first, and they drive the process of gathering data (see Research in focus 2.2 for an example of this). The sequence can be depicted as a series of steps, as outlined in Figure 2.1. The last step involves a movement that is in the opposite direction from deduction—it involves *induction*, as the researcher infers the implications of his or her findings for the theory that prompted the whole exercise. In other words, the findings are fed back into the stock of theory. This can be seen in Whittington's (1989) case study research on strategic choice in the domestic appliance and office furniture industries. Whittington's approach is primarily deductive, since it is based on the contention that strategic choice enables the recognition of plural and contradictory social structures for human agency. However, as he points out towards the end of his book, 'after the empirical interlude of the last four chapters, it is time now to return to the theoretical fray' (1989: 244) to assess how

2.1 KEY CONCEPT
What is empiricism?

The term 'empiricism' is used in a number of ways, but two stand out. First, it is used to refer to an approach to the study of reality that suggests that only knowledge gained through experience and the senses is acceptable. In other words, ideas must be subjected to the rigours of testing before they can be considered knowledge. The second, and related, meaning of the term refers to a belief that the accumulation of 'facts' is a legitimate goal in its own right. It is this second meaning that is sometimes referred to as 'naive empiricism'.

FIGURE 2.1
The process of deduction

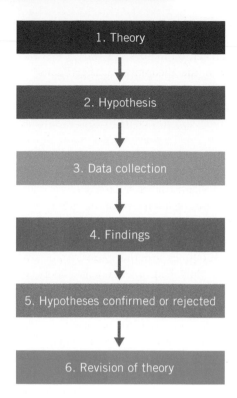

1. Theory

2. Hypothesis

3. Data collection

4. Findings

5. Hypotheses confirmed or rejected

6. Revision of theory

well realist approaches to strategic choice account for the behaviour within the eight case study firms. At this stage he claims that, although dominant actors within the firms 'began from their structural positions within the capitalist enterprise, this starting point was neither unambiguous or exhaustive' (1989: 282). This finding confirms his central proposition that organizational structures could be converted into 'the effective instruments of private agency'.

The deductive process appears very linear—one step follows the other in a clear, logical sequence. However, while it is common to represent it in this way in published research, in practice deduction is often less linear and more 'messy'. A researcher's view of theory or literature may change as a result of analysis of collected data for several reasons:

- new theoretical ideas or findings may be published before the researcher has generated his or her findings;
- the relevance of a dataset for theory may become apparent only *after* data have been collected;
- data may not fit with the original hypotheses.

The Hawthorne studies (see Research in focus 3.7), undertaken at the Western Electric Company's Hawthorne plant between 1927 and 1932, illustrate how deductive research can produce unexpected findings. This research explored the human effects of work and working conditions (Roethlisberger and Dickson 1939); the aim was to examine the relationship between conditions of work and fatigue and monotony among employees. To test this relationship, a series of experiments were undertaken to establish the effects of variables such as lighting, temperature, humidity, and hours of sleep that could be isolated and measured separately. These first experiments involved adjusting the level of artificial illumination at stated intervals to see if this had any effect on efficiency. However, researchers were not able to make sense of changes in productivity, which increased and remained high despite manipulation of a range of variables. This led them to move away from the 'test room method' and adopt a more qualitative strategy based on interview and observation. By moving to a more inductive position, researchers made sense of the data through an alternative explanation that focused on informal social relationships. Eventually, this led to an alternative method for the study of the informal work group. In the Bank Wiring Observation Room investigators spent a total of six months observing informal social relationships within a group of male operators. The Hawthorne research thus made an important methodological contribution to the study of work organizations by showing that research questions and methods could change over the course of an investigation (Schwartzman 1993).

A similar shift occurred during the conduct of the study by Ghobadian and Gallear (1997) that we examined earlier in the chapter, which set out to examine the impact of total quality management (TQM) on the competitive position of small and medium-sized enterprises (SMEs) as compared to large organizations. The researchers developed a large number of research questions through analysis of the TQM literature. Although they describe their research as deductive, they also point out that hypotheses were not easy to formulate because the variables and issues identified were mainly dependent on context and therefore did not translate into simple, general constructs. The researchers therefore shifted towards a more inductive approach in the later stage of the study, using four case studies to explore the research questions and develop a ten-step framework for the implementation of TQM in SMEs.

As a consequence of this kind of realization, business researchers often rewrite their hypotheses after having collected their data because the data does not fit the

2.2 RESEARCH IN FOCUS
A deductive study

Parboteeah et al. (2009) tested the influence of religious values on individuals' work obligation norms. They argue that 'given the prominent role of religion in societies, it is imperative that international management research acknowledges its potential influences on how organizations and people within them operate' (2009: 121). Based on a review of the literature on how major religions around the world describe work, the researchers suggest that 'all major religions prescribe work as an individual's obligation' (2009: 123). This leads them to propose that 'if an individual is raised and educated in a country with a stronger religious environment, that individual is more likely to get exposed to values consistent with stronger work obligation than a similar individual residing in a country with a weaker religious environment. Individuals in stronger religious environments are thus more likely to see work as an obligation' (2009: 124). To assess the countries studied, the researchers use the 'country institutional profile', a theoretical model developed by Kostova (1999) to explain how a country's government policies, shared knowledge, and values affect domestic business activity. This enabled them to specify the contextual determinants of work obligation in different countries and to propose the following five hypotheses.

- *Hypothesis 1*. There is a **positive relationship** between the cognitive aspect of religious institutions and work obligation.

- *Hypothesis 2*. There is a positive relationship between the normative aspect of religious institutions and work obligation.

- *Hypothesis 3*. There is a **negative relationship** between the regulative aspect of religion and work obligation.

- *Hypothesis 4*. Religious pluralism moderates the relationship between the cognitive aspect of religion and work obligations, such that the effect of the cognitive component decreases with more religious pluralism.

- *Hypothesis 5*. Religious pluralism moderates the relationship between the normative aspect of religion and work obligations, such that the effect of the normative component decreases with more religious pluralism.

The researchers used data from the World Values Survey conducted in 2000, in which a consortium of universities from around the world worked together to conduct political and social research. The **sample** comprised 62,218 individuals in 45 different countries. The researchers designed a **questionnaire** that was translated into different languages and that permitted **secondary analysis** of the dataset. The results revealed that hypotheses 1, 2, and 3 were supported. However, the effects of religious pluralism were found to be mixed, and hypothesis 4 was not supported. The researchers conclude that religious institutions do have a significant influence on the work-related attitudes of individuals, regardless of the individual's personal religiosity. They note that this finding is consistent with Max Weber's (1930) thesis on the importance of religious values in shaping the development of modern capitalism.

hypothesis as originally anticipated (Anonymous 2014). As one highly experienced researcher confesses, 'in most of my previous experience, I had used data that in my own mind was guided by propositions or "quasi-hypotheses". Then, post-hoc, I frequently constructed more precise hypotheses to supersede the loose hypotheses' that formed the initial basis for the study (Anonymous 2014: 214–15). The fact that this article was published anonymously gives an indication of the sensitivities involved in acknowledging the existence of these ambiguities and the potential adverse consequences for researchers who admit to them.

This may seem rather surprising and confusing. There is a certain logic to the idea of developing theories and then testing them. In everyday contexts, we think of theories as things that are quite illuminating but that need to be tested before they can be considered valid or useful. However, while the process of deduction in Figure 2.1 does undoubtedly occur in research, it is better considered as a general orientation to the link between theory and research. Its broad contours may frequently be discernible in business research, but it is also the case that we often find departures from it.

However, in some research *no* attempt is made to follow the sequence outlined in Figure 2.1. Some researchers prefer an approach to the relationship between theory and research that is primarily *inductive*. With an inductive stance, theory is the *outcome* of research. In other words, the process of induction involves drawing generalizable inferences out of observations. To put it crudely, whereas deduction entails a process in which:

theory → observations/findings,

with induction the connection is reversed:

observations/findings → theory.

However, just as deduction often entails an element of induction, the inductive process is likely to involve some deduction. Once theoretical reflection on data has been carried out, the researcher may want to collect further data to establish the conditions in which a theory will or will not hold. This strategy is often called iterative: it involves weaving back and forth between data and theory. It is particularly evident in grounded theory, examined in Chapter 24, but in the meantime the basic point is that induction represents an alternative strategy for linking theory and research.

However, as with the deductive approach, we have to be cautious about the use of the term 'theory' in the context of the inductive strategy too. Some researchers undoubtedly develop theories, but it is important

to be aware that many researchers end up with little more than empirical generalizations of the kind Merton (1967) wrote about.

Inductive researchers often use a grounded theory approach to data analysis and theory generation. This approach was first outlined by Glaser and Strauss (1967) and is regarded as useful in generating theories out of data. This contrasts with many supposedly inductive studies, which generate interesting and illuminating findings but whose theoretical significance is not entirely clear. Moreover, in much the same way that the deductive strategy is typically associated with a quantitative research approach (although not exclusively), an inductive strategy of linking data and theory is typically associated with a qualitative research approach. Research in focus 2.3 describes research that is inductive in the sense that it uses a grounded analysis of focus groups, interview data, and participants' drawings to develop a theoretical understanding of the metaphors that workers use to describe their emotional experience of bullying. However, as will be shown below, the inductive strategy is not always associated with qualitative research: not only does much qualitative research *not* generate theory, but also theory is often used as a background to qualitative investigations.

It is useful to think of the relationship between theory and research in terms of deductive and inductive strategies. However, as we have emphasized, the issues are

2.3 RESEARCH IN FOCUS
An inductive study

Tracy et al. (2006) wanted to understand what bullying feels like to those who are the target of it. They suggest that workplace bullying encompasses a range of persistent abusive workplace behaviours including harassment and mobbing (when a group of co-workers gang up on an employee). However, they argue that previous research has overlooked the emotional experience of bullied workers. Using focus groups, in-depth interviews, and creative drawing, they asked participants to tell stories about workplace bullying. As they explain, through early interpretation of the data 'we found that participants often spoke metaphorically' (2006: 157). This led them to focus on the metaphors that bullied workers used to articulate and explore the emotional pain associated with these experiences. This in turn led them to revise their research question to: 'What types of metaphorical language do participants use to describe the emotional experience of bullying?' The authors suggest the complexity and diversity of workplace bullying meant that 'an inductive approach is especially worthwhile for making sense of messy interactive processes, such as bullying, that have no definite "face"' (2006: 174). They identified a series of metaphorical themes in the data that reflected bullied workers' experiences, including the bullying process as noxious substance, the bully as demon, and the target of bullying as a slave or animal. Importantly, the researchers did not commence their study with a view that metaphors were the key to understanding their chosen topic, but came to this conclusion through the collection and analysis of the data. By focusing on metaphorical images of bullying, they shift the focus 'from how researchers label workplace abuse to how those targeted perceive and make sense of abuse and its impacts' (2006: 173).

not as clear-cut as sometimes presented. Deductive and inductive strategies are therefore better thought of as tendencies rather than as a hard-and-fast distinction.

In recent years it has become popular to approach business research as an abductive rather than either a deductive or an inductive process (Key concept 2.4). Mantere and Ketokivi (2013) distinguish between three types of reasoning in organizational research:

- *Theory-testing research:* this involves developing hypotheses from *a priori* theoretical considerations, enabling them to be tested through statistical inference. This is closely associated with the deductive approach described above.

- *Inductive case research:* this involves theory being developed in a 'data-driven manner' using qualitative data, often taking a grounded theory approach. As in theory-testing research, theory is understood as 'a set of propositional statements linking the key concepts in the theory to one another' (Mantere and Ketokivi 2013: 75). The idea is that, once developed, theories can be tested. Both theory-testing and inductive case researchers tend to adopt a realist ontology: see Key concept 2.11 for more on this.

- *Interpretive research:* while this also involves qualitative data, theory is developed in quite a different way, involving a dialogical process between theory and the empirical phenomenon; this results in the production of 'reflexive narratives, not explanatory models or theoretical propositions' (Mantere and Ketokivi 2013: 75). Interpretive research is founded on an interpretive epistemology and is sometimes associated with abductive reasoning (Key concept 2.4). It is also associated with analogical reasoning, which involves interpretation of one entity in terms of its similarity to another, as in metaphorical analysis.

As these distinctions highlight, the way in which business researchers build theory reveals much about the assumptions which researchers make about the nature of the social world and how best to build knowledge about it. Shepherd and Suddaby (2017) argue that there is insufficient clarity about how to build theory in business research. To address this problem, they propose 'pragmatic empirical theorizing' which involves using quantitative empirical findings to build theory through abductive inquiry. This approach to theory building starts with an unexplained puzzle, an anomaly or a tension,

2.4 KEY CONCEPT
What is abductive reasoning?

Abduction is a mode of reasoning which has grown in popularity in business research, as well as in other social scientific research disciplines. Like inductive and deductive approaches, abduction is used to make logical inferences and build theories about the world. However, abduction is proposed as a way of overcoming the limitations associated with deductive and inductive positions. The weakness associated with deductive reasoning is its reliance on a strict logic of theory-testing and falsifying hypotheses, but a problem arises because it is not clear how to select the theory to be tested. The difficulty with inductive reasoning arises from the criticism that no amount of empirical data will necessarily enable theory-building. Abductive logic is proposed as a third way which overcomes these limitations. It is based on the pragmatist perspective (in particular the work of philosopher Charles Pierce). Abduction starts with a puzzle or surprise and then seeks to explain it. Puzzles may arise when researchers encounter empirical phenomena which existing theory cannot account for. Abductive reasoning involves seeking to identify the conditions that would make the phenomenon less puzzling, turning surprising facts into a matter of course (Mantere and Ketokivi 2013). This involves back-and-forth engagement with the social world as an empirical source for theoretical ideas, and with the literature, in a process of 'dialectical shuttling' (Atkinson et al. 2003; Schwartz-Shea and Yanow 2012).

Abduction involves the researcher selecting the 'best' explanation from competing explanations or interpretations of the data (Mantere and Ketokivi 2013). It highlights the limited ability of researchers to think rationally, in terms of computational reasoning, and acknowledges the importance of cognitive reasoning in theory building. This is related to hermeneutics (the study of interpretation) and the philosophical idea of the 'hermeneutic circle', through which understanding is seen as a continuous dialogue between the data and the researcher's preunderstandings. Researchers such as Alvesson and Kärreman (2007) see this as crucial in enabling the researcher to remain open to the possibility of being surprised by the data, rather than using it to confirm their preunderstandings.

which may either be derived from the literature (see Chapter 5) or through engagement with the phenomena of interest. This provides the basis for the inquiry. A further feature of their approach to theory building concerns storytelling—which Shepherd and Suddaby argue is crucial to the success of a theory. Theory building in this way involves choosing a narrative frame to guide the inquiry, which can take one of the following forms:

- *Shifting ontology*—by changing their ontological assumptions about the nature of the phenomena, e.g. from objectivism to constructionism, researchers can 'generate creative insights for the development of mid-range theory' (Shepherd and Suddaby, 2017: 69). For example, by thinking about phenomena as processes (e.g. organizing) rather than entities (e.g. organizations), researchers have created whole new ways of asking questions about, and theorizing, business and management.
- *Moving up or down the ladder of theory complexity*— this involves either reducing or increasing the level of abstraction of a theory, i.e. the extent to which it is middle-range in Merton's terms. This can help to facilitate development of second-order concepts (see Chapter 24 for more on first- and second-order concept development).
- *Moving back and forth between empirical evidence and literature*—Shepherd and Suddaby argue that iterative cycles of engagement with literature and examination of empirical evidence is important in enabling theoretical development in both quantitative and qualitative studies.
- *Crossing levels of analysis*—this entails shifting the level of theorizing from micro (i.e. individual, group) to macro (organization, institution, society).

What Shepherd and Suddaby's account emphasizes is that theorizing is a process that requires disciplined imagination in the development of a convincing story—with characters, a narrative arc, and a resolution to the problem statement articulated at the outset. The next section of this chapter is concerned with questions of philosophy, which are closely related to, but conceptually distinct from, questions of theory.

Philosophical assumptions in business research

As discussed above, how we go about conducting research is shaped in fundamental ways by the way we understand and use theory. Theoretical orientation, however, is not the only factor which influences the practice of business research. To understand research and to conduct it effectively, we need to engage with a body of knowledge that is commonly referred to as the philosophy of social science (see Key concept 2.5). It is common to think of business research as an applied discipline. That is, we tend to think of business researchers as conducting research primarily to help solve practical problems in organizations. In spite of the emphasis on practice in much—but

2.5 KEY CONCEPT
What is the philosophy of social science?

Very often, when we conduct research we do not think about our philosophical assumptions, but simply follow standard and accepted procedures in our specific disciplines. Yet all research is underpinned by a set of implicit or explicit philosophical assumptions, which shape the practice of research and the theoretical conclusions which we draw on the basis of the data we collect and analyse. The philosophy of social science seeks to make explicit, and understand, assumptions in three spheres: ontology—our understanding of what reality is; epistemology— our understanding of how we can know reality; and methodology or research strategy—our understanding of the best way to do research given our ontological and epistemological assumptions. Much of what is regarded as 'common sense' or 'normal' in research can be traced back to the ideas of philosophers who grappled with ontological, epistemological, and methodological questions. For example, the attempt to falsify hypotheses, which is the standard approach in positivist research, reflects to a very significant extent Karl Popper's attempt to develop a philosophically-informed way to develop claims which could be regarded as truly scientific (Popper 2003).

by no means all—business research, a basic understanding of philosophy is essential to business researchers. Specifically, we need to understand a sub-branch of philosophy commonly referred to as the 'philosophy of social science'.

Why should you care about philosophy? You may find philosophy of social science a fascinating topic in its own right—as we do—but even if you don't, there are very important practical reasons to think about your ontological, epistemological, and methodological assumptions as you conduct research. Put simply, if you do not understand these issues, and do not ensure that your assumptions are consistent with each other and with your chosen research methods and design, it is much less likely that you will generate valuable knowledge about reality. Unless you are able to generate such knowledge, practical application of your research findings is unlikely to be effective. To understand why the philosophy of social science matters, it is necessary to understand its components, starting with ontology.

Ontological considerations

Ontology is a term derived from the Greek terms *on*, which means 'being', and *logos*, which means 'theory' (Delanty and Strydom 2003). That is, ontology is concerned with theorizing about the nature of reality. Ontology is about the assumptions we make about what it means for something to exist. Perhaps the most important question addressed by ontology is whether the social phenomena that we study should be understood as existing objectively, external to observers (an objectivist ontology), or whether they are 'made real' by the activities of humans and the meanings which observers attach to them (a constructionist ontology).

These concerns might seem rather far removed from the practical task of business research. Why should we concern ourselves with questions of ontology? As social researchers, our fundamental aim is to understand reality. Differential ontological positions define reality in different ways. The ontological assumptions which we make thus determine *what* it is that we seek to understand through research. Further, our understanding of what reality is should determine *how* we go about researching reality (which will be discussed later in this chapter when we consider the importance of epistemology). By understanding ontology and thus our own ontological assumptions, we can design research studies which are most effective in capturing the reality which we seek to understand. The importance of ontology can be understood by considering the two positions highlighted above: objectivism and constructionism. Their differences can be illustrated by reference to two of the most common terms in social science—'organization' and 'culture'.

Objectivism

Objectivism is an ontological position that implies that social phenomena confront us as external facts beyond our reach or influence and that they exist whether we are aware of them or not (see Key concept 2.6). That is, they have an *objective* reality independent of our role as an observer.

We can discuss *an* organization as an observable object. It has rules and regulations. It adopts standardized procedures for getting things done. People are appointed to different jobs as part of the division of labour. There is a hierarchy. It has a mission statement. And so on. The degree to which these features exist from organization to organization is variable, but in thinking in these terms we take the view that an organization has a reality that is external to the individuals who inhabit it or the researchers who study it. Moreover, the organization represents a social order in that it exerts pressure on

2.6 KEY CONCEPT
What is objectivism?

Objectivism is an ontological position that asserts that social phenomena and their meanings have an existence that is independent of social actors. It implies that social phenomena and the categories that we use in everyday life have an existence that is independent or separate from actors.

individuals to conform to certain requirements. People learn and apply the rules and regulations. They follow the standardized procedures. They do the jobs to which they are appointed. People tell them what to do and they tell others what to do. They learn and apply the values in the mission statement. If they do not do these things, they may be reprimanded or even fired. The organization is therefore a constraining force that acts on and inhibits its members.

The same can be said of culture. Cultures and sub-cultures can be viewed as existing independently of the people who are part of them or researchers who observe them. They exist as repositories of widely shared values and customs into which people are socialized so that they can function as good citizens or full participants. Cultures and subcultures constrain us because we internalize their beliefs and values.

Both organization and culture can be understood as social entities that are external to the actor, with an almost tangible reality of their own. An organization or a culture has the characteristics of an object and hence of having an objective reality.

Constructionism

However, we can consider an alternative ontological position—*constructionism* (see Key concept 2.7), which is related to the postmodernist viewpoint (see Key concept 2.8). This position challenges the suggestion that categories such as organization and culture are objective phenomena which confront social actors as external realities. Rather, it regards them as socially-constructed entities—entities which are made real by the actions and understandings of humans.

Let us take organization first. Strauss et al. (1973), drawing on insights from symbolic interactionism, carried out research in a psychiatric hospital and proposed that the organization was best conceptualized as a 'negotiated order'. Instead of taking the view that order in organizations is a pre-existing characteristic, they argue that it is worked at. Rules were far less extensive and less rigorously imposed than might be supposed from classic accounts of organization. Strauss et al. refer to them as 'much less like commands, and much more like general understandings' (1973: 308). Because relatively little of the spheres of action of doctors, nurses, and other personnel was prescribed, the social order of the hospital was an outcome of agreed-upon patterns of action that were themselves the products of negotiations between the people involved. The social order is in a constant state of change because the hospital is 'a place where numerous agreements are continually being terminated or forgotten, but also as continually being established, renewed, reviewed, revoked, revised …. In any pragmatic sense, this is the hospital at the moment: this is its social order' (Strauss et al. 1973: 316–17). The authors argue that preoccupation with the formal properties of organizations (rules, organizational charts, regulations, roles)

2.7 KEY CONCEPT
What is constructionism?

Constructionism is an ontological position (also referred to as *constructivism*) which asserts that social phenomena and their meanings are continually being accomplished by social actors. It implies that social phenomena and categories are not only produced through social interaction but are also in a constant state of revision.

In recent years, the term 'constructionism' has also been used to refer to the idea that social phenomena are made real by research processes themselves. When we conduct research, we assign meanings to the phenomena that we study and it is this assignment of meaning which constitutes the reality of the objects of study. For example, when business researchers developed the concept of the 'post-bureaucratic' organization, describing it in terms of various characteristics such as flat structures, flexible roles, and so on, this made such organizations real, in the sense that people began to understand 'post-bureacratic' as a legitimate category for organizations, and other researchers began to study phenomena related to this conceptualization (Alvesson and Thompson 2005). This illustrates the point that the researcher always presents a specific version of social reality, rather than one that can be regarded as definitive. Knowledge is viewed as indeterminate and to a degree subjective. This is related to the concept of postmodernism. The first meaning of constructionism might be thought of usefully as constructionism in relation to the social world, the second as constructionism in relation to the nature of knowledge of the social (and indeed the natural) world.

2.8 KEY CONCEPT
What is postmodernism?

Postmodernism is a philosophical approach to thinking about the social sciences and how knowledge claims are constructed through the language of science. Postmodernists are deeply suspicious of the idea that it is possible to arrive at a definitive version of reality. Research findings are viewed as versions of reality that are constructed—the key issue becomes one of plausibility rather than whether they are right or wrong in an absolute sense. Postmodernist writers are more interested in issues of writing and representing social science findings, rather than data collection, although they are often more sympathetic to qualitative than quantitative research (Alvesson 2002).

Postmodernists tend to emphasize the notion of **reflexivity** (see Chapter 7), which highlights the significance of the researcher in the research process and consequently the tentativeness of any findings presented (since the researcher is always implicated in his or her findings). As this account of postmodernism implies, postmodernists are critical of any view of research that implies that there are, or can be, accepted foundations to knowledge, as is suggested by positivists (see Key concept 2.10). In so doing, postmodernism fundamentally problematizes and questions our capacity to know anything.

neglects the degree to which order in organizations is accomplished in everyday interaction. This is not to say that the formal properties have *no* element of constraint on individual action, but they are not the primary reality.

Increasingly, constructionism is being discussed in relation to the nature of knowledge, but in this book we use the term mostly in relation to the first meaning, as an ontological position relating to social objects and categories—that is, one that views them as socially constructed (see Research in focus 2.9 for an example).

The same point can be made about culture. Instead of culture being seen as an external reality that acts on and constrains people, it can be taken to be an emergent reality in a continuous state of construction and

2.9 RESEARCH IN FOCUS
Constructionism in action

Much research has been devoted to considering the impact of delayering and downsizing on middle management. Some studies draw attention to increased job insecurity and rising levels of stress experienced by those who remain in employment. Others suggest delayering as a solution that enables managerial work to become more intrinsically motivating. These pessimistic and optimistic predictions for the future of middle management form the basis for empirical testing and debate.

Adopting a social constructionist framework, Thomas and Linstead (2002) suggest an alternative way of thinking about the 'reality' of middle management based on the assumption that the term itself is a social construct. This leads them to a focus on how middle managers' identity is continually created and contested through prevailing discourses. In other words, they are interested in understanding how managers make sense of the language and practice associated with their changing work roles.

Through the analysis of individual managers' subjective accounts of their work, Thomas and Linstead analyse how they construct identity and deal with feelings of insecurity, ambiguity, and confusion that cause them to 'feel that they are losing the plot in their organizations' (2002: 88). Constant changes in terms of roles and status make it difficult for middle managers to retain a sense of identity. The authors conclude: 'What is apparent … is that these middle managers, for a range of reasons, are searching for stability and sense in their reflections on their lives' (2002: 88).

In sum, the social constructionist perspective enables the question of 'What has become of middle management?' to be recast. Instead it asks: 'How are middle managers becoming?'

reconstruction. Becker (1982: 521) has suggested that 'people create culture continuously .... No set of cultural understandings ... provides a perfectly applicable solution to any problem people have to solve in the course of their day, and they therefore must remake those solutions, adapt their understandings to the new situation in the light of what is different about it.' Like Strauss et al., Becker recognizes that the constructionist position cannot be pushed to the extreme: it is necessary to appreciate that culture has a reality that 'persists and antedates the participation of particular people' and shapes their perspectives, but it is not an inert objective reality that possesses only a sense of constraint: it acts as a point of reference but is always in the process of being formed.

Neither the work of Strauss et al. nor that of Becker pushes the constructionist argument to the extreme. Each accepts the pre-existence of their objects of interest (organization and culture, respectively). However, they both have an intellectual preference for stressing the active role of individuals in the social construction of social reality. Not all writers adopting a constructionist position are similarly prepared to acknowledge the existence or importance of an objective reality. Walsh, for example, has written that 'we cannot take for granted, as the natural scientist does, the availability of a preconstituted world of phenomena for investigation' and that we must instead 'examine the processes by which the social world is constructed' (1972: 19).

Constructionism also suggests that the categories people use to understand the natural and social world are in fact social products. The categories do not have built-in essences; instead, their meaning is constructed in and through interaction. Thus, a category such as 'masculinity' can be treated as a social construction. This notion implies that, rather than being treated as a distinct inert entity, masculinity is construed as something whose meaning is built up during interaction. That meaning is likely to be ephemeral, in that it will vary according to both time and place. This stance displays a concern with the language used to present categories. It suggests that the social world and its categories are not external to us but are built up and constituted in and through interaction. This tendency can be seen in discourse analysis, examined in Chapter 22. As Potter (1996: 98) observes: 'The world ... is *constituted* in one way or another as people talk it, write it and argue it.' This sense of constructionism is antithetical to realism (see Key concept 2.11). Constructionism frequently results in an interest in the representation of social phenomena, as Research in focus 2.13 illustrates.

Clearly ontology shapes how we conduct our research, but to fully understand how this happens, we need to consider the second component of the philosophy of social science—epistemology.

Epistemological considerations

Like ontology, the term epistemology is derived from Greek: *episteme*, meaning 'knowledge', and *logos*, meaning 'theory' (Delanty and Strydom 2003). Epistemology is, therefore, the theory of knowledge. Epistemology follows logically from ontology. A given ontological position—a particular understanding of what reality is—will imply a particular epistemological position—a particular understanding of how we can gain knowledge of that reality. If, for example, we adopt an objectivist ontology, then logically we can gain knowledge of the world only by direct or indirect observation or measurement of aspects of it. If, conversely, we adopt a constructionist ontology, then we would need to gain knowledge in very different ways, for example by observing and interviewing social actors in an attempt to understand how they shape

and understand the world. Epistemology is, therefore, underpinned by ontology.

In a practical sense, epistemology is crucially important in business research. It allows us to answer the question of how we should conduct research. We seek to make sense of business-related phenomena by gathering and analysing data. We need to feel confident that the studies which we design and the techniques which we employ allow us to generate knowledge which provides a sound basis for making claims about the business world and informing policy and practice. Consideration of epistemological issues provides us with a means to ensure that the knowledge we produce is sound.

A particularly important epistemological question for social scientists concerns whether or not the social

2.10 KEY CONCEPT
What is positivism?

Positivism is an epistemological position that advocates the application of the methods of the natural sciences to the study of social reality. Although the term stretches beyond this principle, and constituent elements vary between authors, positivism is widely understood to rely on the following principles:

1. Only phenomena, and hence knowledge confirmed by the senses, can genuinely be warranted as knowledge (the principle of phenomenalism).

2. The purpose of theory is to generate hypotheses that can be tested and that will allow explanations of laws to be assessed (the principle of deductivism).

3. Knowledge is arrived at by gathering facts that provide the basis for laws (the principle of inductivism).

4. Science must (and can) be conducted in a way that is value free (that is, objective).

5. There is a clear distinction between scientific statements and normative statements, and the former are the true domain of the scientist.

This last principle is implied by the first, because the truth of normative statements cannot be confirmed by the senses.

world can and should be studied according to the same principles, procedures, and ethos as the natural sciences. The position that affirms the importance of imitating the natural sciences is associated with an epistemological position known as positivism (see Key concept 2.10).

A natural science epistemology: positivism

Positivism is an epistemological position which is informed by an objectivist ontological position. Positivism holds that, because reality exists objectively and externally, the appropriate way to gather data is to observe phenomena directly or to 'measure' them using surveys or other instruments. In social science, positivism involves the attempt to conduct research which follows the same general rules and procedures which are adopted in the natural sciences. The logic of positivist social science is deductive. It mimics that of experimental research in the physical sciences, following the sequence of framing hypotheses, collecting data to test them, seeking to falsify them, and, if they are not falsified, accepting the hypotheses as representing provisionally true statements about reality.

The five principles in Key concept 2.10 link the points that have already been raised about the relationship between theory and research. For example, positivism contains elements of both a deductive approach (2) and an inductive strategy (3). Also, a sharp distinction is

drawn between theory and research. The role of research is to test theories and to provide material for the development of laws, collecting and analysing data in a way which enables generalizable propositions, in the form of hypotheses, to be tested. An example of a positivist approach is Elsesser and Lever's 2011 study (described in Research in focus 1.3). These researchers were guided by the realist ontological assumption that gender bias exists as a concrete entity about which data can be collected. Their conclusions are drawn in such a way as to enable a degree of generalizability to be claimed about the effects of gender bias on female leaders.

Although positivist epistemology in business research has its roots in the physical sciences, it would be a mistake to treat positivism as synonymous with science and the scientific. Philosophers of the natural and social sciences differ over how best to characterize scientific practice, and, since the early 1960s, there has been a drift away from viewing it in positivist terms. Realism (in particular critical realism) is another philosophical position that provides an account of the nature of scientific practice (see Key concept 2.11).

Interpretivism

Interpretivism is a contrasting epistemology to positivism (see Key concept 2.12). The term interpretivism comes from writers who have been critical of the application of the scientific model, in the form of positivism, to the

2.11 KEY CONCEPT
What is empirical realism?

Empirical realism shares two features with positivism: a belief that the natural and the social sciences can and should apply the same approach to data collection and explanation, and a commitment to the view that there is an external reality to which scientists direct their attention (in other words, there is a reality that is separate from our descriptions of it). Empirical realism simply asserts that, through the use of appropriate methods, reality can be understood. This is perhaps the most common meaning of the term. When writers employ the term 'realism' in a general way, it is almost invariably this meaning they refer to.

study of the social world. They share a view that the subject matter of the social sciences—people and their institutions—is fundamentally different from that of the natural sciences. This approach is underpinned by a social constructionist ontology, which holds that reality is constituted by human action and meaning-making, rather than existing objectively and externally. The study of the social world therefore requires a different logic of research that reflects the distinctiveness of humans as against the natural order.

Whereas the underlying purpose that informs positivist research is the *explanation* of human behaviour, interpretivism is primarily concerned with *understanding* human behaviour. Interpretivism is also concerned with the 'how' and the 'why' of social action, including the processes whereby things happen. This contrast reflects long-standing debates that preceded the emergence of the modern social sciences. They are expressed through notions such as a *Verstehen* approach (meaning 'understand' or 'interpret' in German), advocated by Max Weber (1864–1920). Weber described sociology as a 'science which attempts the interpretive understanding of social action in order to arrive at a causal explanation of its course and effects' (1947: 88). Weber's definition seems to embrace both explanation *and* understanding, but the task of 'causal explanation' must refer to the 'interpretive understanding of social action' rather

than to external forces that have no meaning for those involved in social action.

One of the main intellectual traditions responsible for the anti-positivist position has been phenomenology, a philosophy concerned with how individuals make sense of the world around them and how, in particular, the philosopher should bracket out preconceptions in his or her own engagement with that world. The initial application of phenomenological ideas to the social sciences is attributed to Alfred Schutz (1899–1959), whose work did not come to the notice of English-speaking social scientists until its translation from German in the 1960s. His work was profoundly influenced by Weber's concept of *Verstehen*, as well as by phenomenological philosophers such as Husserl. Schutz's position is well captured in the following often-quoted passage:

> The world of nature as explored by the natural scientist does not 'mean' anything to molecules, atoms, and electrons. But the observational field of the social scientist—social reality—has a specific meaning and relevance structure for the beings living, acting, and thinking within it. By a series of common-sense constructs they have pre-selected and pre-interpreted this world which they experience as the reality of their daily lives. It is these thought objects of theirs which determine their behaviour by motivating it. The thought objects constructed by the social scientist, in order to grasp this so-

2.12 KEY CONCEPT
What is interpretivism?

Interpretivism is an alternative to the positivist orthodoxy that held sway for many years in business research. It is based on the view that a strategy is required that respects the differences between people and the objects of the natural sciences and therefore requires the social scientist to grasp the subjective meaning of social action. Its intellectual heritage includes Weber's notion of *Verstehen*; the hermeneutic–phenomenological tradition; and symbolic interactionism.

cial reality, have to be founded upon the thought objects constructed by the common-sense thinking of men [and women!], living their daily life within the social world.

(Schutz 1962: 59)

Two points are worth noting in this quotation. First, Schutz asserts that there is a fundamental difference between the subject matter of the natural sciences and that of the social sciences and that an epistemology is required to reflect and capitalize upon that difference. The fundamental difference is in the fact that social reality has a meaning for human beings and therefore human action is meaningful—that is, it has meaning for human beings and they act on the basis of the meanings that they attribute to their acts and to the acts of others. This leads to the second point—that it is the job of the social scientist to gain access to people's 'common-sense thinking' and hence to interpret their actions and their social world from their point of view. It is this feature that social scientists claiming allegiance to phenomenology typically emphasize. As stated by Bogdan and Taylor, the authors of a research methods text whose approach is phenomenological: 'The phenomenologist views human behavior . . . as a product of how people interpret the world . . . . In order to grasp the meanings of a person's behavior, *the phenomenologist attempts to see things from that person's point of view*' (Bogdan and Taylor 1975: 13–14, emphasis in original).

This explanation skates over some complex issues. In particular, Weber's examination of *Verstehen* is more complex than the above suggests, because the empathetic understanding that seems to be implied above was not how he applied it (Bauman 1978), while the question of what is and is not a genuinely phenomenological approach to the social sciences is disputed (Heap and Roth 1973). However, the writings of the hermeneutic–phenomenological tradition and the *Verstehen* approach, with their emphasis on social action as meaningful to actors and therefore needing to be interpreted from their point of view, coupled with the rejection of positivism, contributed to a stream of thought often referred to as interpretivism (e.g. Hughes 1990).

Verstehen and the hermeneutic–phenomenological tradition do not exhaust the intellectual influences on interpretivism. The theoretical tradition in sociology known as *symbolic interactionism* is also regarded as an influence. There has been heated debate over the implications of the ideas of the founders of symbolic interactionism, in particular George Herbert Mead (1863–1931), who discusses the way in which our notion of self emerges through an appreciation of how others see us. The school of research known as the Iowa school has drawn heavily on Mead's concepts and ideas but has proceeded in a direction that most people would prefer to depict as largely positivist (Meltzer et al. 1975). Some writers have argued that Mead's approach is far more consistent with a natural science approach than has typically been recognized (McPhail and Rexroat 1979). However, symbolic interactionism is generally viewed as occupying similar intellectual space to the hermeneutic–phenomenological tradition and so broadly interpretative in approach. This is largely the result of the writings of Herbert Blumer, a student of Mead's who acted as his mentor's spokesman and interpreter, and his followers (Hammersley 1989; R. Collins 1994). Not only did Blumer coin the term 'symbolic interaction'; he also provided a gloss on Mead's writings that has interpretative overtones. Symbolic interactionists argue that interaction takes place in such a way that the individual is continually interpreting the symbolic meaning of his or her environment (which includes the actions of others) and acts on the basis of this imputed meaning. According to Blumer (1962: 188), 'the position of symbolic interaction requires the student to catch the process of interpretation through which [actors] construct their actions', a statement that brings out clearly his views of the research implications of symbolic interactionism and of Mead's thought.

Although the connection between symbolic interactionism and the hermeneutic–phenomenological tradition should not be exaggerated, the two are united in their antipathy for positivism and have in common an interpretative stance. However, symbolic interactionism is usually understood as a type of social theory that has distinctive epistemological implications; the hermeneutic–phenomenological tradition, by contrast, is best thought of as a general epistemological approach in its own right. There are other intellectual currents that have affinities with the interpretative stance, such as the working-through of the ramifications of the works of the philosopher Ludwig Wittgenstein (Winch 1958), but the hermeneutic–phenomenological, *Verstehen*, and symbolic interactionist traditions are the major influences.

Taking an interpretative stance can mean that the researcher comes up with surprising findings, or at least findings that appear surprising if a largely external stance is taken—that is, a position from outside the particular social context being studied. The Hawthorne studies, referred to earlier (see also Research in focus 3.7), provide an interesting example of this: it was the failure of the investigation to come up with answers to the original research questions that stimulated the researchers to change their approach and methods and adopt a more interpretative epistemological position. Of course, when the social scientist adopts an interpretative stance, he

2.13 RESEARCH IN FOCUS
Interpretivism in practice

Leitch et al. (2010) discuss research conducted on women business owners that was interpretivist in terms of the approach to both data collection and analysis. They were interested in how women perceived their experiences of obtaining external finance for their businesses at the initial start-up stage and later in nurturing the growth of the businesses. The interpretivist stance was apparent in the researchers' commitment to giving '"voice" to women's experiences in their own right' (Leitch et al. 2010: 77). **Semi-structured interviews** were carried out with a **purposive sample** of ten women business owners (Leitch et al. 2006). One strand of the interview included the use of the critical incident technique (see Research in focus 10.5) when interviewees were asked to reflect on specific experiences in raising venture finance. The researchers elicited the women's 'personal perspectives . . . in their own words' and the analysis was undertaken to reflect 'the issues and topics identified by research participants as being important in understanding the phenomenon of interest' (Leitch et al. 2010: 77, 79). This focus on the perspectives of research participants during data collection and analysis is the motif of the interpretivist approach. For example, the researchers found that their interviewees had predominantly negative perceptions of banks as routes to financial support. One commented: 'The company is not interested in bank finance because the banks are risk averse and don't understand the needs of small businesses' (quoted in Leitch et al. 2006: 171). What we see in an interpretivist stance is a preference for research methods that elicit participants' world views in relation to the topic of interest, and for analyses that ground concepts and connections between them in the words and elicited perspectives of participants.

or she is not simply exposing how members of a social group interpret the world around them. The social scientist will almost certainly be aiming to place the interpretations that have been elicited into a theoretical frame. As Research in focus 2.13 illustrates, there is a double interpretation here, where the researcher is providing an interpretation of others' interpretations of effective leadership. Indeed, there is a third level of interpretation going on, because the researcher's interpretations have to be further interpreted in terms of the concepts, theories, and literature of a discipline.

The preceding discussion has outlined how epistemological considerations—especially the question of whether a natural science, and in particular a positivist approach, can supply legitimate knowledge of the social world—are related to research practice. This links to the earlier discussion in this chapter about the relationship between theory and research, in that a deductive approach is typically associated with a positivist position. Key concept 2.10 does try to suggest that inductivism is also a feature of positivism (third principle), but, in the working-through of its implementation in the practice of research, it is the deductive element (second principle) that is emphasized. Similarly, the third level of interpretation that a researcher engaged in interpretative research must bring into operation is part of the inductive strategy described in the previous section.

Ideally, a researcher's epistemological assumptions ought to lead to particular approaches to conducting

research. Indeed, this is something which researchers should pay attention to when conducting their research, because a mismatch between epistemological assumptions and method are likely to undermine the soundness of the data produced and, by extension, the knowledge generated. However, while such interconnections between epistemological issues and research practice exist, it is important not to overstate them, since they represent tendencies rather than definitive points of correspondence. Epistemological principles and research practices do not necessarily go hand in hand in a neat, unambiguous manner. For example, Hofstede's (1984) study of cultural differences between members of a large multinational business organization, referred to as the HERMES Corporation, shows that inductive researchers do not always rely on qualitative methods. Survey data were collected between 1967 and 1973, from employees in over 40 different countries where HERMES had subsidiaries, producing a total of 116,000 self-completion questionnaires. Statistical analysis based on factor analysis underpinned Hofstede's development of a theoretical framework consisting of four main dimensions on which country cultures differ, labelled 'power distance', 'uncertainty avoidance', 'individualism', and 'masculinity'. The dimensions were not developed deductively as hypotheses prior to data collection; instead they emerged inductively through the process of analysis. We will return to this point on several occasions and will focus on it in Chapter 26.

Research paradigms

A classic source that enables understanding of how philosophical assumptions inform business research is Burrell and Morgan's (1979) 'four paradigms' model, which summarizes and categorizes the assumptions that researchers make about the nature of organizations and how to study them. Their use of the notion of paradigm draws on the work of Kuhn (1970; see Key concept 2.14).

Burrell and Morgan suggest each paradigm contains assumptions that are either:

- *objectivist*—there is an external viewpoint from which it is possible to view the organization, which is comprised of consistently real processes and structures; or
- *subjectivist*—an organization is a socially constructed product, a label used by individuals to make sense of their experience.

Each paradigm makes assumptions about the function and purpose of business research as either:

- *regulatory*—to describe what goes on in organizations, possibly to suggest minor changes to improve them, but not to make any judgement; or
- *radical*—to make judgements about the way that organizations ought to be and suggest how this can be achieved.

Plotting the assumptions of researchers along these two axes provides a framework for four paradigmatic positions in the study of organizations:

- *functionalist*—the dominant framework for the study of organizations, based on a problem-solving orientation which leads to rational explanation;
- *interpretative*—focuses on the conceptions of social actors and implies that understanding must be based on the experience of those who work in organizations;
- *radical humanist*—proposes that organizations are social arrangements from which individuals need to be emancipated and that research should be guided by the need for change;
- *radical structuralist*—views an organization as a product of structural power relationships, which result in conflict.

Each paradigm results in the generation of a quite different type of organizational analysis to address specific organizational 'problems' in different ways. Though time has passed since Burrell and Morgan proposed this model, Shepherd and Challenger (2013) argue that the paradigms debate continues to be influential in business research. However, the ways in which the concept is used varies considerably, encompassing notions such as 'perspective', 'theory', 'discipline', 'school', and 'method'. Burrell and Morgan's model has significantly influenced business researchers by encouraging the exploration of assumptions about the nature of the social world and how to study it. The notion of paradigms also draws attention to the ways in which philosophical assumptions inform the development of either a quantitative or a qualitative research strategy, which we turn to in the following section.

2.14 KEY CONCEPT
What is a paradigm?

Kuhn's (1970) highly influential use of the term 'paradigm' derives from his analysis of revolutions in science. A paradigm is 'a cluster of beliefs and dictates which for scientists in a particular discipline influence what should be studied, how research should be done, [and] how results should be interpreted' (Bryman 1988a: 4). Kuhn depicted the natural sciences as going through periods of revolution, whereby normal science (science carried out in terms of the prevailing paradigm) is increasingly challenged by anomalies that are inconsistent with the assumptions and established findings in the discipline. The growth in anomalies eventually gives way to a crisis in the discipline, which in turn occasions a revolution. The period of revolution is resolved when a new paradigm emerges as ascendant and a new period of normal science sets in. An important feature of paradigms is that they are *incommensurable*—that is, they are inconsistent with each other because of divergent assumptions and methods. Disciplines in which no paradigm has emerged as pre-eminent, such as the social sciences, are deemed pre-paradigmatic, in that they feature competing paradigms. One of the problems with the term 'paradigm' is that it is not very specific: Masterman (1970) was able to discern twenty-one different uses of it by Kuhn. Nonetheless, its use is widespread in the social sciences (e.g. Ritzer 1975; Guba 1985).

Developing a research strategy: quantitative or qualitative?

The discussion above highlights that particular ontological assumptions lead researchers to particular epistemological assumptions. While there is not always a neat correspondence between epistemology and research practice, nonetheless particular epistemological assumptions lead scholars toward particular methodological assumptions. From the Greek (yes, again!) *methodos*, 'procedure', and *logos*, 'theory', the term 'methodology' refers to the theory of how we should do research. It is common for people to use the term methodology to refer to their chosen research method, but strictly speaking methodology is about theory and method is about practice. Having said that, of course one's chosen method(s) ought to reflect one's methodological assumptions, which in turn ought to follow from epistemological and ontological assumptions. We use the term 'research strategy' here to refer to the general approach to research adopted, which will reflect one's methodological assumptions.

Many writers on methodological issues find it helpful to distinguish between quantitative and qualitative research as two general approaches. The status of the distinction is ambiguous, because it is regarded by some writers as a fundamental contrast and by others as not useful or even simply as 'false' (Layder 1993: 110). However, there are no signs that the use of the distinction is decreasing and there is considerable evidence of its continued, even growing, currency. The quantitative/qualitative distinction will be used frequently in this book, because it represents a useful means of classifying different methods of business research and because it is a helpful umbrella for a range of issues concerned with its practice.

On the face of it, there seems little to the quantitative/qualitative distinction other than the fact that quantitative researchers employ measurement and qualitative researchers do not. It is certainly true that there is a predisposition along these lines, but many writers have suggested that the differences are deeper than the superficial issue of the presence or absence of measurement and quantification. We can see quantitative and qualitative research as having different epistemological foundations. If we take the areas that have been the focus of the last three sections—the connection between theory and research, epistemological considerations, and ontological considerations—quantitative and qualitative research can be understood as two distinctive *research strategies*. By a

research strategy, we simply mean a general orientation to the conduct of business research.

Quantitative research is a research strategy that emphasizes quantification in the collection and analysis of data and that:

- entails a deductive approach to the relationship between theory and research, in which the emphasis is on the testing of theories;
- has incorporated the practices and norms of the natural scientific model and of positivism in particular; and
- takes a view of social reality as an external, objective reality.

By contrast, qualitative research is a research strategy that usually emphasizes words and images, rather than quantification, in the collection and analysis of data and that:

- predominantly emphasizes an inductive approach to the relationship between theory and research, in which the emphasis is placed on the generation of theories;
- has rejected the practices and norms of the natural scientific model and of positivism in particular in preference for an emphasis on the ways in which individuals interpret their social world; and
- takes a view of social reality as a constantly shifting and emergent property of individuals' creation.

There is, in fact, considerably more to the quantitative/qualitative distinction than this contrast. In Chapters 8 and 17 the natures of quantitative and then qualitative research are outlined in much greater detail, while in Chapters 26 and 27 the contrasting features will be further explored. In particular, a number of distinguishing features flow from the commitment of the quantitative research strategy to a positivist epistemology and from the rejection of that epistemology by practitioners of the qualitative research strategy.

However, the contrasts and interconnections between different features of quantitative and qualitative research are not as straightforward as this implies. While it is useful to contrast the two research strategies, it is necessary to be careful about hammering a wedge between them too deeply.

For example, although it is common to describe qualitative research as concerned with the generation rather than the testing of theories, there are examples of studies in which qualitative research has been employed to test rather than to generate theories. Hochschild's (1983) theory of emotion work (see Research in focus 17.2) emerged from a questionnaire study of university students. The theory was subsequently tested to establish its broader significance in employment, using two occupational groups and a wider range of qualitative methods, including interviews and participant observation. This enabled development of the theory to incorporate the idea of emotional labour, which is emotion work that forms part of paid employment. This study shows that although qualitative research is typically associated with generating theories, it can also be used to test them. Moreover, it is striking that, although Hochschild's study is broadly interpretivist in epistemological orientation, with its emphasis on how flight attendants view their work role identity, the findings have objectivist, rather than constructionist, overtones. Hochschild describes the

marketing and advertising strategies used by Delta Airlines, explaining how they create a discrepancy between promise and fact. Flight attendants are thus forced to cope with the disappointed expectations of customers through their emotional labour. She relates the demand for emotional labour to the structural conditions of the airline industry market, thus suggesting a social world that is 'out there' and has a formal, objective quality. It is an example of qualitative research in the sense that there is no quantification or very little of it, but it does not have *all* the other features associated with qualitative research. Thus it has interpretivist overtones despite the use of quantitative research methods.

The point is that quantitative and qualitative research represent different research strategies and that each carries with it striking differences in terms of the role of theory, epistemological issues, and ontological concerns. However, the distinction is not a hard-and-fast one: studies that have the broad characteristics of one research strategy may have a characteristic of the other. Many writers argue that the two can be combined within

2.15 RESEARCH IN FOCUS
Mixed methods research—an example

Holmberg et al. (2008) conducted an investigation into the role of leadership in the implementation of evidence-based treatment practices for drug abuse and criminal behaviour in Sweden. The chief method of data collection—a self-completion questionnaire administered by mail to treatment personnel involved in the implementation of treatment programmes—resulted in largely quantitative data that allowed the researchers to examine hypotheses relating to the factors that are likely to enhance or inhibit the implementation of evidence-based programmes. These quantitative data showed that the leadership behaviour of those charged with leading such programmes was related to the job satisfaction, work output, and perceptions of the organization by those members of staff who had to implement the programmes on a day-to-day basis. Qualitative data were drawn from in-depth interviews, which were conducted with 65 individuals who worked for organizations associated with the programmes. Over half were treatment staff and the rest were managers and others. Further qualitative data were obtained from observation of meetings where the programmes were discussed and from participation in training workshops. The interviews revealed the importance of managers taking an active interest in what staff were doing to implement the programmes and being available for support. Where staff had difficulties with implementation, a key factor was that managers were uninterested and failed to provide support and resources that were important to success. The authors write in the discussion of their findings:

Methods that focus on subordinates' perceptions and reports about leader behaviour through questionnaires may be insufficient for capturing the dynamics of managers' impact on processes of implementation and a combination of methods will probably give a more balanced understanding of leadership … In this study we conducted interviews and observations in order to be able to make a more context-sensitive interpretation of the implantation process.

(Holmberg et al. 2008: 168)

The point that the authors are making is that the use of a mixed methods approach that combined quantitative and qualitative research enabled a more rounded and complete picture to be drawn.

an overall mixed methods research project, and in Chapter 27 we will explore the ways in which management researchers combine these two strategies.

Research in focus 2.15 is an example of a mixed methods study. It is presented here partly to provide an early insight into the possibility of doing mixed methods research, but also to show how a wedge need not be driven between quantitative and qualitative research. By contrasting the two approaches, it is easy to see them as incompatible. As the example in Research in focus 2.15 shows, they can be fruitfully combined within a single project. This point will be developed further in Chapter 27.

Other considerations

We are beginning to get a picture now that business research is influenced by a variety of factors (see Figure 2.2). Here we add two more—the impact of *personal values* and *practical considerations*.

Values

Values reflect either the personal beliefs or the feelings of a researcher. On the face of it, we would expect that social scientists should be value free and objective in their research. After all, one might argue that research that simply reflected the personal biases of its practitioners could not be considered valid and scientific because it was bound up with the subjectivities of its practitioners. This view is held with less and less frequency among social scientists nowadays. Émile Durkheim (1858–1917) wrote that one of the corollaries of his injunction to treat social facts as things was that all 'preconceptions must be eradicated' (1938: 31). Since values are a form of preconception, his exhortation was at least implicitly to do with suppressing them when conducting research. His position is unlikely to be regarded as credible nowadays, because there is a growing recognition that it is not feasible to keep the values that a researcher holds totally in check. These can intrude at any or all of a number of points in the process of business research:

- choice of research area;
- formulation of research question;
- choice of method;
- formulation of research design and data collection techniques;
- implementation of data collection;
- analysis of data;
- interpretation of data;
- conclusions.

There are numerous points at which bias and the intrusion of values can occur (see Thinking deeply 2.16 for an example). The researcher may develop an affection or sympathy, which was not necessarily present at the outset of an investigation, for the people being studied. It is quite common, for example, for researchers working within a qualitative research strategy, and in particular when they use participant observation or very intensive interviewing, to develop a close affinity with the people whom they study to the extent that they find it difficult to disentangle their stance as social scientists from their subjects' perspective. This possibility may be

FIGURE 2.2
Influences on business research

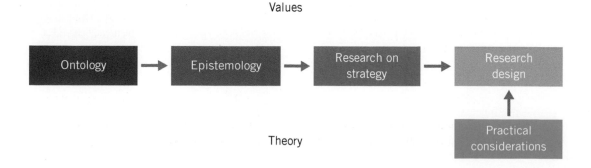

exacerbated by the tendency of some researchers to be very sympathetic to underdog groups. For example, following publication of his classic study of the Ford factory in Dagenham, Beynon (1975) was criticized by the press for having become too emotionally involved in the lives of workers. Equally, researchers may feel unsympathetic towards the people they study. Having sympathy for the people or organizations studied is a particular issue for business researchers, many of whom are part-time students who choose to study issues or problems in their employing organization. Hence they are already immersed in the organization as complete participants and have an understanding of it that is based on this. This is particularly pronounced in an action research project (see Chapter 17), where the aim is to intervene in situations and study them at the same time. According to Coghlan (2001), researchers in such situations face three interrelated sets of issues:

- *their preunderstanding of the setting*—this refers to the knowledge, insight, and experience that researchers have about the lived experience of their own organization; for example, they already know the history, key events, and jargon used within the organization and who to turn to for information;

- *their role duality*—they are doing research on the organization while at the same time being part of it, which sets them apart from other organizational members and can affect the data that are generated, particularly when they are engaged in research that may threaten existing organizational norms;

- *organizational politics*—this relates to the potential role of action research in destabilizing organizational norms and questioning established ways of doing things, requiring a high level of political skill. Although this is particularly salient in action research, the ability to deal with organizational politics is common to much business research (see Thinking deeply 2.16).

Another perspective in relation to values and bias suggests that research cannot be value free. Researchers can

2.16 THINKING DEEPLY
Factors that influence methods choice in organizational research

Buchanan and Bryman (2007) identify six types of factor that influence researchers' choice of methods in organizational research.

- *Organizational:* this includes factors such as organizational size and pace of change. For example, Buchanan describes a situation where the question 'What is your job title?' produced a bemused response from managers whose roles were shifting every few weeks.

- *Historical:* this relates to previous studies of the topic.

- *Political:* this type of influence includes negotiating research objectives, obtaining permission to access respondents, aligning with groups of stakeholders, and the way that different methods are perceived by different journals, which affects researchers' ability to publish their findings.

- *Ethical:* this relates to the increasing ethical scrutiny that is faced by researchers and the role of ethical review in regulating their conduct (see Chapter 6).

- *Evidential:* this relates to the different expectations that academic and managerial audiences have of business research; the former expect knowledge and insight, and the latter want practical recommendations. The rise of evidence-based management, which will be discussed in Chapter 5 (see also Key concept 1.1), has only amplified these tensions and debates.

- *Personal:* researchers are also influenced in their choice of methods by such factors as the extent to which they enjoy face-to-face contact, some researchers opting for methods that rely heavily on interpersonal interaction and others choosing methods that confine them to the computer screen.

Buchanan and Bryman (2007) argue that these unavoidable issues should be treated not as unwelcome distractions but as a central aspect of the research process. They conclude, as a result, that it is difficult to sustain a view of the researcher as a neutral observer. Methods choice is not a single rational process of selecting the most effective tool to address a particular question but rather a highly complex and continually evolving process.

therefore only ever try to exercise reflexivity in relation to their values. This view is based on the assumption that a researcher's prior knowledge, experience, and attitudes will influence not only how they see things but also *what* they see. The example in Research in focus 2.17 considers some of these issues in organizational research.

Another approach is to argue for consciously value-laden research, or what some feminist researchers refer to as '*conscious partiality*', which is achieved through partial identification with the research objects' (Mies 1993: 68, emphasis in original). Many critical, feminist and postcolonial researchers argue that quantitative research is informed by a desire to control the research subject or respondent and the research context. They reject positivist epistemologies which position research as a value-neutral, one-way process, where the task of the researcher is to extract information from the people being studied and give little or nothing in return. Instead they engage with the people being studied as people and not simply respondents, and they aspire to develop equal and emancipatory relationships with research participants. Qualitative research is generally seen as more consistent with these values. These issues will be returned to in Chapters 17, 26, and 27.

There are, then, different positions that can be taken up in relation to values in business research. Far fewer researchers than in the past overtly subscribe to the view that the principle of objectivity can be put into practice. There is a greater awareness today of the limits to objectivity, and there is more criticism of the aura of objectivity that tends to surround quantitative research. A further way in which values are relevant to the conduct of business research is as a consequence of ethical considerations, which are dealt with in Chapter 6.

Practicalities

Finally, we must not neglect the importance and significance of *practical issues* in decisions about how business research should be carried out. There are a number of dimensions to this. Choices of research strategy, design, or method have to be dovetailed with the specific research question being investigated. If we are interested in teasing out the relative importance of a number of causes of a social phenomenon, it is quite likely that a quantitative strategy will fit our needs, because, as will be shown in Chapter 8, the assessment of cause is one

2.17 RESEARCH IN FOCUS
Influence of an author's biography on research values

Brewis (2005) explains that her research on sexual harassment and the sex industry impacts on her being-in-the-world more generally. She considers the reasons why she chose to research sex and organization, even though 'links between my life story and my research, whilst they indubitably exist, are not causal or easily drawn' (2005: 540). For Brewis, readers act as biographers, 'shaping and constructing authors as particular types of individual' (2005: 494). In her own case this has involved them making 'certain assumptions' about her personal life based on her research interests. She explains:

> whether others meet me in settings such as conferences, listen to my presentations, read or hear about my work, their constructions of who I am and what I do derive in no small part from the ways in which they attribute a gender and a sexuality to me … Certain deeply embedded paradigms seem to have constructed me as the kind of author who has intimate relationships with her collaborators. Because I am gendered-as-female, and because I tend to collaborate with others who are gendered-as-male, these signs have apparently been read—through the heterosexual matrix—to imply that my relationships with these individuals go further than straightforward 'professional' contact.

(Brewis 2005: 498)

This biographic construction of professional identity serves to confirm the sexist belief that women can progress in organizations only if they trade on their sexuality. Brewis's analysis suggests a cyclical dynamic to the role of values on the choice of research subject. Not only does biography influence the choice of research subject, but the chosen research subject can also affect how readers construct the researcher's biography.

of its key features. Alternatively, if we are interested in the world views of members of a certain social group, a qualitative research strategy that is sensitive to how participants interpret their social world may be the direction to choose. If a researcher is interested in a topic on which very little research has been done, a quantitative research strategy may be difficult because there is little prior literature on which to base propositions. A more exploratory stance may be preferable in this case. This is likely to involve qualitative research, since it is typically associated with the generation of, rather than the testing of, theory and involves a relatively unstructured approach to the research process (see Chapter 17). Another dimension may have to do with the nature of the topic and of the people being investigated. For example, if the researcher needs to engage with individuals or groups involved in illicit activities, such as industrial sabotage (Sprouse 1992) or theft (Ditton 1977), it is unlikely that a social survey would gain the confidence of the subjects involved or achieve the necessary rapport. It is not surprising, therefore, that researchers in these areas have tended to use a qualitative strategy.

While practical considerations may seem rather mundane and uninteresting compared with the lofty realm of philosophical debates surrounding discussions about epistemology and ontology, they are important. All business research is a coming together of the ideal and the feasible. There will be many circumstances in which the nature of the topic, or of the subjects of an investigation, and the constraints on a researcher loom large in decisions about how best to proceed. Consequently, in certain circumstances, business researchers exercise a degree of opportunism in their choice of research setting and in their focus on a particular subject. Alvesson (2003) draws a distinction within qualitative research between a 'planned-systematic' approach to data collection and an 'emergent-spontaneous' one. The researcher who takes a planned-systematic approach has a reasonably clear idea of his subject of study and plans the process of data collection with the aim of producing a pile of notes and interview transcripts to analyse at the end of it. For example, to study organizational identity, notes made during fieldwork and questions asked in interviews reflect this subject focus. The results of this data collection process then form the basis for writing up findings.

An emergent-spontaneous study, on the other hand, is carried out when something revealing happens. 'In such a study the researcher waits for something interesting/

STUDENT EXPERIENCE
The influence of personal values on student research

Many students are influenced in their choice of research subject by their own personal values and life experiences. This can be positive, because it helps to ensure that they remain interested in their chosen subject throughout the project. Amrit explained that his decision to focus on the topic of mental health at work in his research project was

> quite a personal decision. It was based on experiences of people that were close to me. People I've worked with before, friends, family friends, who I know have experienced feelings of loneliness, anxiety or stress. Work can be quite daunting at times and sometimes you can feel like you're trying to be a person that you're not, just to fit in, or the type of work that you are doing is quite daunting. It starts off as anxiety, maybe stress, but a lot of the time people don't know what that can spiral into. Those are the kind of boundaries I wanted to explore in this project.

Jordan was clear from the outset of her research project that she wanted to give something back to the organization where she had worked as a youth worker.

> I went into the honours program with a very clear idea that I wanted to work with the organization that I have been involved with since I was young. They have a social enterprise model in the not-for-profit sector. They now have business partners in the corporate sector, so they're running the same workshops that I experienced as a young person in the business sector. I just became very interested in that process and wanted to be involved, and saw the honours project as an opportunity to to give back and to work with people that I have gotten a lot out of. I know the central social enterprise manager, so I went to her and said 'I have this opportunity, I would be interested to work with you.' She said, 'Yes, that's great.'

generative to pop up' (Alvesson 2003: 181). Although there are disadvantages associated with this—namely, it might appear somewhat arbitrary and unscientific—Alvesson suggests there are some advantages: 'the most significant one is that it increases the likelihood of coming up with interesting material. The researcher does not find the empirical material, it finds him or her' (2003: 181). By developing sensitivity to rich empirical data and willingness to respond to situations where such data may emerge, the researcher takes a more opportunistic approach to the task. For example, the experience of one of the authors of this book, Emma Bell, led to her study of the closure of a Jaguar car manufacturing plant in Coventry, near to where she lived. In this emergent-spontaneous study, it was the result of existing local contacts she already had with members of the local community that enabled her to trace events relating to the closure as they unfolded (Bell 2012). Alvesson recommends care in presenting studies based on emergent-spontaneous research, as the conventions that guide research may generate a hostile response to this method of research topic selection, even if the research strategy and research design are well informed. It is also potentially a risky strategy, in that it presumes that something important or significant will materialize while the researcher is around. Finally, it requires a high level of vigilance on the part of the researcher—blink and you might miss it!

STUDENT EXPERIENCE
The influence of practical issues on student research

In setting up a research project, it is advisable to make use of whatever practical resources and personal contacts are available to you, providing that you are working within ethical guidelines (see Chapter 6). The idea for Alex's dissertation project arose when he was offered a job with a wholesale distribution business specializing in cosmetics—an organization where he had worked as an intern in the previous year. The company offered Alex the opportunity for further work—on a flexible basis—during his final honours year of undergraduate study. 'Part of what I was working on in this year with the cosmetic company was revamping their online presence and starting a whole new e-commerce side of things.' Alex sought to apply his learning from his undergraduate degree and 'actually try to tie in' with what he was doing at work, 'that way I could sort of put the two together and I wouldn't stretch myself as thin. So that shifted my focus for the thesis.'

Karen gained access to her research site as the result of a placement opportunity as part of her university degree course. She found that gaining the agreement of her line manager to carry out the research was relatively straightforward. 'Once I had decided that this was a topic I was interested in doing, I had a discussion with my manager and discovered that it was something that she was quite interested in as well and other people in the department who did recruitment were all quite interested in it. So access wasn't really a problem. Obviously, it was difficult to get time with people but the management wasn't opposed to me doing it.' However, gaining access through her placement meant that Karen was constrained by the need to combine her full-time employment with a research role.

> Obviously when you're involved in the organization it's quite good because you can get access to people that you know. If I asked them for a favour, they helped me because I'd helped them with something else, so that was quite good. But then, on the other hand, because I was so involved in the organization, I was concerned that I had brought my own opinions into the analysis. I think to some extent I probably did do this, although I tried as much as possible to keep my university head on and remain distanced from it a little bit.

Tom's research access was enabled by a friend who was a manager in a local government call centre. Studying call centre work in a public sector organization was attractive to Tom because 'the majority of call centres are managed in the private sector and almost all the literature that's been published is about call centres in the private sector'. However, Tom was aware that his selection of this particular research setting was driven partly by having a friend as an organizational 'contact'. 'I'm not quite sure how I'd have gone about it if I hadn't had that contact ... I'm sure you could just approach people cold, but it's a lot easier if you've got a link.'

KEY POINTS

- Theory can be used to inform business research according to a deductive logic of inquiry, or can emerge out of a study inductively.

- Philosophical assumptions are important in business research because they enable us to think about the nature of reality (ontology) and how to go about studying it.

- The distinction between objectivism and constructionism is an important dimension of the quantitative/qualitative contrast.

- Epistemological concerns—about how we can know or understand something—loom large in considerations of research strategy. To a large extent, these revolve around the desirability of employing a natural science model (and in particular positivism) versus interpretivism.

- Quantitative and qualitative research constitute different research strategies and are usually associated with different epistemological and ontological considerations.

- Values and practical considerations may also impinge on the research process.

QUESTIONS FOR REVIEW

Theory and research

- If you had to conduct some business research now, what would the topic be and what factors would influence your choice? How important was theory in your consideration?

- Outline, using examples of your own, the difference between grand and middle-range theory.

- What are the differences between inductive and deductive theory, and why is the distinction important?

Philosophical assumptions in business research

- What are the four main paradigms identified by Burrell and Morgan, and how do they shape the type of research that is likely to be conducted?

Ontological considerations

- What are the main differences between epistemological and ontological considerations?

- What is meant by objectivism and constructionism?

- Which theoretical ideas have been particularly instrumental in the growth of interest in qualitative research?

- What are the main arguments for and against paradigm commensurability within management and business research?

Epistemological considerations

- What is meant by each of the following terms: positivism, realism, and interpretivism? Why is it important to understand each of them?

- What are the implications of epistemological considerations for research practice?

Research strategy: quantitative or qualitative?

- Outline the main differences between quantitative and qualitative research in terms of

    the relationship between theory and data;

    epistemological considerations;

    ontological considerations.

- To what extent is quantitative research solely concerned with testing theories and qualitative research with generating theories?

Influences on the conduct of business research

- How might your own personal values influence your choice of research topic?

- If you were undertaking a research project now, list the three most important practical issues that you would need to take into consideration in planning your project.

....

ONLINE RESOURCES
www.oup.com/uk/brm5e/

Visit the Interactive Research Guide that accompanies this book to complete an exercise about business research strategies.

....

RESEARCH DESIGNS

CHAPTER OUTLINE

In focusing on research designs, this chapter introduces the different frameworks that can be used to collect and analyse data. A research design relates to the criteria that are used to evaluate the quality of business research. A research design is, therefore, a framework for generating evidence that is suited both to a certain set of criteria and to the research question that is being addressed. The chapter is structured as follows:

- Reliability, replicability, and validity are presented as criteria for assessing the quality of business research. Validity can be broken down into several other criteria covered in the chapter: measurement validity; internal validity; external validity; and ecological validity.

- The suggestion that such criteria are mainly relevant to quantitative research is examined, along with the proposition that alternative criteria should be employed in relation to qualitative research. These alternative criteria, which are concerned with the issue of trustworthiness, are outlined briefly.

- Five prominent research designs are then outlined:

  — experimental and related designs (such as the quasi-experiment);

  — cross-sectional design, focusing on the most common form, social survey research;

  — longitudinal design, including the panel study and the cohort study;

  — case study design;

  — comparative design.

- Each research design is considered in terms of the criteria for evaluating the quality of research findings.

Introduction

In Chapter 2, the idea of research strategy was introduced as a broad orientation to business research. The specific context for its introduction was the distinction between quantitative and qualitative research as different research strategies. However, the decision to adopt one or the other strategy will not get you far along the road of doing a piece of research. Two other key decisions will have to be made (along with a host of tactical decisions about how the research will be carried out and the data analysed). These decisions involve choices about research design and research method. On the face of it, these two terms would seem to mean the same thing, but it is crucial to draw a distinction between them (see Key concepts 3.1 and 3.2).

Research methods are associated with different kinds of research design. The research design guides the execution of a research method and the analysis of the subsequent data. The two terms are often confused. For example, one research design covered in this chapter—the case study—is often referred to as a method. As we will see, a case study involves detailed exploration of a specific case, which could be an organization or a person. Once a case has been selected, a research method or research methods are needed to collect data. Simply selecting an organization and deciding to study it intensively are not going to provide data. Do you observe? Do you conduct interviews? Do you examine documents? Do you administer questionnaires? You may in fact use any or all of these research methods, but the crucial point is that deciding to choose a case study approach will not provide you with data. This choice is further complicated by the fact that what counts as data is not an entirely straightforward matter. Bartunek et al. (1993) acknowledge the diversity in the way management researchers define the concept of data to include responses to questionnaire items, transcripts of public inquiry hearings, case studies, and advertisements.

In this chapter, five different research designs will be examined: experimental design and its variants, including quasi-experiments; cross-sectional or social survey design; longitudinal design; case study design; and comparative design. However, before discussing the nature of and differences between these designs, it is useful to consider some recurring issues in business research that cut across them.

3.1 KEY CONCEPT
What is a research design?

A research design provides a framework for the collection and analysis of data. Choice of research design reflects decisions about the priority being given to a range of dimensions of the research process. These include the importance attached to

- expressing causal connections between variables;
- generalizing to larger groups of individuals than those actually forming part of the investigation;
- understanding behaviour and the meaning of that behaviour in its specific social context;
- having a temporal (i.e. over time) appreciation of social phenomena and their interconnections.

3.2 KEY CONCEPT
What is a research method?

A research method is simply a technique for collecting data. It can involve a specific instrument, such as a self-completion questionnaire or a structured interview schedule, or participant observation whereby the researcher listens to and watches others.

Quality criteria in business research

Three of the most prominent criteria for the evaluation of business and management research are reliability, replicability, and validity. All of these terms will be treated in much greater detail in later chapters, but in the meantime a basic introduction to them is likely to be helpful.

Reliability

Reliability is concerned with the question of whether the results of a study are repeatable. The term is commonly used to address the question of whether or not the measures that are applied to concepts in business and management (such as teamworking, employee motivation, organizational effectiveness) are consistent. In Chapter 8, we will look at the idea of reliability in greater detail, in particular the different ways in which it can be conceptualized. Reliability is a particular concern in quantitative research. The quantitative researcher is likely to be concerned with whether or not a measure is stable. After all, if scores on IQ tests, which were designed as measures of intelligence, were found to fluctuate, so that the same people's IQ scores were often wildly different when tests were administered on two or more occasions, we would be concerned about the IQ test as a measure. We would consider it an unreliable measure—we could not have faith in its consistency.

Replicability

The idea of reliability is closely related to another criterion of research—replicability. Sometimes researchers choose to replicate the findings of others. There may be a host of different reasons for doing so, such as a suspicion that the original results do not match other evidence that is relevant to understanding the topic. In order for replication to take place, a study must be capable of replication—it must be replicable. This is a very obvious point: if a researcher does not spell out his or her procedures in great detail, replication is impossible. Similarly, in order to assess the reliability of a measure of a concept, the procedures that constitute that measure must be replicable by someone else. Ironically, replication in business research is not common. In fact, it is quite rare. When Burawoy (1979) found that by accident he was conducting case study research in a US factory that had been studied three decades earlier by another researcher, Donald Roy, he thought about treating his own investigation as a replication. However, the low status of replication in academic research persuaded him to resist this option. He writes: 'I knew that to replicate Roy's study would not earn me a dissertation let alone a job … [In] academia the real reward comes not from replication but from originality!' (Burawoy 2003: 650). Nonetheless, an investigation's capacity to be replicated—replicability—is highly valued by many business researchers working within a quantitative research tradition. See Research in focus 8.9 for an example of a replication study.

Validity

A further criterion of research, and in many ways the most important, is validity. Validity is concerned with the integrity of conclusions that are generated from a piece of research. Like reliability, we will examine the idea of validity in greater detail in later chapters, but in the meantime, it is important to be aware of the main types of validity.

- *Measurement validity*. This type of validity applies primarily to quantitative research and the search for measures of social scientific concepts. Measurement validity is also often referred to as *construct validity*. Essentially, this type of validity is concerned with whether a measure captures the phenomenon which it is intended to capture. For example, does the IQ test really measure intelligence? In the study reported in Research in focus 3.4 later in this chapter, the researchers' hypothesis was that in deciding which job applicants to invite for a job interview, managers discriminated on the basis of the obesity of the applicants. To test this hypothesis, the researchers needed to measure two issue-related concepts: 'magnitude of consequences' and 'issue framing'; they also needed to measure two context-related concepts: 'perceived social consensus' and 'competitive context'. The question then is: do these measures really represent the concepts that they are intended to? If they do not, the study's findings will be questionable. It should be appreciated that measurement validity is related to reliability: if a measure of a concept is unstable in that it fluctuates and hence is unreliable, it simply cannot provide a valid measure of the concept in question. In other words, the assessment of measurement validity presupposes that a measure is reliable.

- *Internal validity*. This type of validity relates mainly to the issue of causality, which will be dealt with in greater detail in Chapter 8. When we conduct quantitative research, we are commonly interested in causal relationships between variables, although in most research designs we can only infer causality rather than demonstrating it conclusively. Internal validity is concerned with understanding whether a conclusion that incorporates a causal relationship between two or more variables holds. If we suggest that x causes y, can we be sure that it is x that is responsible for variation in y, and not something else that is producing an apparent causal relationship? In the study examined in Research in focus 3.4, Agerström and Rooth (2011: 797) conclude that there is a 'a strong and consistent relationship' between 'automatic antiobesity bias' and the probability that hiring managers will invite an obese job applicant for interview. Internal validity raises the question of whether we can be confident that this apparent causal relationship is genuine and not produced by something else. In other words, can we be sure that 'automatic antiobesity bias' is responsible for these patterns of behaviour, and not another variable such as the perceived physical attractiveness of the job applicant? In discussing issues of causality, it is common to refer to the factor that has a causal impact as the independent variable and the effect as the dependent variable (see Key concept 3.3). In the case of the research of Parboteeah et al. (2009) in Research in focus 2.2, 'religious belief' was an independent variable and 'work obligation' the dependent variable. Thus, internal validity raises the question: how confident can we be that the independent variable really is at least partly responsible for the variation that has been identified in the dependent variable?

- *External validity*. This issue is concerned with the question of whether the results of a study can be generalized beyond the specific research context. It is in this context that the issue of how people or organiza-

tions are selected to participate in research becomes crucial. This is why Scase and Goffee (1989) went to such great lengths to detail the process whereby their sample of UK managers was generated (see Research in focus 3.14). External validity is one of the main reasons why quantitative researchers are so keen to generate representative samples (see Chapter 9).

- *Ecological validity*. This criterion is concerned with the question of whether or not social scientific findings are applicable in everyday, naturally ocurring social settings. As Cicourel (1982: 15) has put it: 'Do our instruments capture the daily life conditions, opinions, values, attitudes, and knowledge base of those we study as expressed in their natural habitat?' This criterion is concerned with the question of whether business research sometimes produces findings that, while they may be technically valid, correspond in only a limited way with what happens in people's everyday lives. If research findings lack ecological validity, they are of limited value in enabling understanding of how things work in the real world. The more the social scientist intervenes in natural settings or creates unnatural ones, such as a laboratory or even a special room to carry out interviews, the more likely it is that findings will be ecologically invalid. This was an important finding to have emerged from the Hawthorne studies (see Research in focus 3.7). The conclusions deriving from a study using questionnaires may have measurement validity and a reasonable level of internal validity, and they may be externally valid, in the sense that the findings can be generalized to other samples using the same questionnaire, but the unnaturalness of having to answer a questionnaire may mean that the findings have limited ecological validity.

One feature that you may have noticed about most of the discussion so far is that it seems to be geared mainly

3.3 KEY CONCEPT
What is a variable?

A variable is simply an attribute on which cases vary. 'Cases' can obviously be organizations, but they can also be people, offices, shops, production plants, cities, or nations. If an attribute does not vary, it is a **constant**: for example, if all manufacturing organizations had the same ratio of male to female managers, this attribute of such organizations would be a constant and not a variable. Constants are rarely of interest to business researchers. It is common to distinguish between different types of variable. The most basic distinction is between independent variables and dependent variables. An independent variable is understood as potentially having a causal influence on dependent variables.

towards quantitative rather than qualitative research. Both reliability and measurement validity are essentially concerned with the adequacy of measures, which characterize quantitative research. Internal validity is concerned with the soundness of findings that specify a causal connection, an issue that commonly also characterizes quantitative research. External validity may be relevant to qualitative research, but the specific question of representativeness of research subjects with which external validity is concerned has a more obvious application in the realm of quantitative research through the preoccupation with procedures that generate a representative sample. The issue of ecological validity relates to the naturalness of the research approach and seems to have considerable relevance to both qualitative and quantitative research.

Some writers have sought to apply the concepts of reliability and validity in qualitative research (e.g. LeCompte and Goetz 1982; Kirk and Miller 1986; Peräkylä 1997), but others argue that the grounding of these ideas in quantitative research renders them inapplicable to, or inappropriate for, qualitative research. Writers such as Kirk and Miller (1986) have applied concepts of validity and reliability to qualitative research but have changed only slightly the sense in which the terms are used. Qualitative researchers sometimes propose that their studies should be judged or evaluated according to different criteria from those used in quantitative research. Lincoln and Guba (1985) suggest that alternative terms and ways of assessing qualitative research are required. For example, they propose trustworthiness as a criterion of evaluation in qualitative studies. They describe four aspects of trustworthiness, some of which have parallels with the quantitative research criteria we have discussed.

- *Credibility* parallels internal validity—i.e. how believable are the findings?
- *Transferability* parallels external validity—i.e. do the findings apply to other contexts?
- *Dependability* parallels reliability—i.e. are the findings likely to apply at other times?

- *Confirmability* is concerned with objectivity—i.e. has the investigator allowed his or her values to intrude to a high degree?

These criteria will be returned to in Chapter 17.

Hammersley (1992*a*) occupies a kind of middle position here in that, while he proposes validity as an important criterion (in the sense that an empirical account must be plausible and credible and should take into account the amount and kind of evidence used), he also proposes relevance as a criterion. Relevance is taken to be assessed from the vantage point of the importance of a topic within its substantive field or the contribution it makes to the literature on that field. These different views reflect the particular objectives of qualitative research, which many of its practitioners argue are distinctive. The distinctive features of qualitative research will be examined in later chapters.

However, it should also be borne in mind that one of the criteria previously cited—ecological validity—may have been formulated largely in the context of quantitative research, but is in fact a feature in relation to which qualitative research fares rather well. Qualitative research is often based on principles of naturalism. This means that the researcher seeks to collect data in naturally occurring situations and environments, as opposed to fabricated, artificial ones. This characteristic applies particularly to ethnographic research, in which participant observation is a prominent method of data collection, but it applies also to the interview methods typically used by qualitative researchers, which are less directive than the interviewing methods used in quantitative research. We might expect that much qualitative research is stronger than quantitative investigations in terms of ecological validity.

Some of these issues in business research will emerge in the context of the discussion of research designs in the next section, but in a number of ways these criteria also represent background considerations for many of the issues to be examined later in this book.

Research designs

In this discussion of research designs, five different types will be examined: experimental design; cross-sectional or social survey design; longitudinal design; case study design; and comparative design. Variations on these designs will be examined in their relevant subsections.

Experimental design

True field experiments are relatively rare in business and management research, comprising around 2 to 3 per cent of research published in journals such as *Administrative Science Quarterly* (Scandura and Williams 2000). This is mainly because of the problems of achieving the requisite level of control when dealing with organizational behaviour. Why, then, bother to introduce experimental designs at all in the context of a book written for business researchers? The chief reason, quite aside from the fact that they are sometimes employed, is that a true experiment is often used as a yardstick against which non-experimental research is assessed. Experimental research is frequently held up as a touchstone because it engenders considerable confidence in the robustness and trustworthiness of causal findings. In other words, true experiments tend to be very strong in terms of internal validity. It is also suggested that field experiments are of particular value in researching sensitive organizational topics about which participants are likely to be cautious in sharing information or opinions, such as unethical behaviour, bullying and harassment, or illegal drug use (King et al. 2012). The framing of many quantitative studies in terms of hypotheses involving dependent and independent variables reflects the profound influence of experimental design on how we think about quantitative research in general.

Manipulation

If experiments are so strong in this respect, why then do business researchers not make far greater use of them? The reason is simple: in order to conduct a true experiment, it is necessary to manipulate the independent variable in order to determine whether it has an influence on the dependent variable. Experimental subjects are likely to be allocated to one of two or more experimental groups, each of which represents different types or levels of the independent variable. It is then possible to establish how far differences between the groups are responsible for variations in the level of the dependent variable. Manipulation, then, entails intervening in a situation to determine which of two or more things happens to subjects. However, the vast majority of independent variables with which business researchers are concerned cannot be manipulated. If we are interested in the effects of gender on work experiences, we cannot manipulate

gender so that some people are made male and others female. If we are interested in the effects of variations in the economic environment on organizational performance, we cannot alter share prices or interest rates. As with the huge majority of such variables, the levels of social engineering that would be required are beyond serious contemplation. However, where social conditions can be engineered in such a way as to control variables, the research findings can be very powerful. King et al. (2012) take the example of whether gender differences in pay are due to discrimination of decision-makers or differences in behaviour between men and women. An experimental approach to understanding gender differences in pay might involve randomly assigning participants to evaluate either the curriculum vitae (CV) of a man or that of a woman. In this study, the researchers presented fictitious CVs that were identical in every way except the gender of the target. Differences in evaluations (and pay expectations) could only be due to gender. Thus, experimental manipulations in conditions of random assignment can nullify such questions by providing a single causal explanation for effects (King et al. 2012: 505).

Before moving on to a more complete discussion of experimental design, it is important to introduce a basic distinction between the *laboratory experiment* and the *field experiment*. As its name implies, the laboratory experiment takes place in a laboratory or in a contrived setting, whereas field experiments occur in real-life settings, such as in workplaces or retail spaces, as the example in Research in focus 3.4 illustrates. It is experiments of the latter type that are most likely to touch on areas of interest to business researchers. However, in business research it is more common to find field experiments in which a scenario is employed as a substitute for a real-life setting. Furthermore, and somewhat confusingly, researchers will sometimes refer to their research as a field study. This simply means that the research was conducted in a real-life setting; it need not imply that a field experiment was involved.

3.4 RESEARCH IN FOCUS
An example of a field experiment to investigate obesity discrimination in job applicant selection

Agerström and Rooth (2011) conducted a study to investigate the issue of weight discrimination in employment. Specifically, they wanted to understand whether automatic stereotypes were a predictor of hiring discrimination against people who are obese. The study built on research by Rooth, who had earlier conducted field experiments to test hiring managers' willingness to invite to interview job applicants with native Swedish versus Arab-Muslimsounding male names. In the study of obesity discrimination, the researchers sent fictitious job applications to 985 real job vacancies in Sweden. The applications were identical apart from a facial photograph of the applicant, which was of someone who was either obese or normal weight.

The 48 photographs were obtained from an internet photo site of individuals who were approximately 20–30 years old. A group of student volunteers were asked to rank the photos by physical attractiveness and they were then matched into 'approximately equally attractive' pairs. 'The photo was then sent to a photo firm, whose task was to make the person in the photo look obese' (2011: 793). Several months after the decision on who to invite to interview had been made, the researchers contacted the hiring managers and asked them if they were willing to complete an Implicit Association Test (IAT) for measuring automatic stereotypes. The test involved showing the hiring managers a series of photographs of normal-weight and obese people and asking them to quickly select a word to describe them—the words used related to high job performance (e.g. effective, productive, hardworking) and low job performance (e.g. incompetent, slow, lazy). A strength of this test relates to its usefulness in measuring individual spontaneous attitudes and stereotypes, thereby reducing the likelihood of **social desirability bias** (see Research in focus 10.11): that is, the people taking the test are unlikely to modify their responses based on what they may feel is socially acceptable or desirable.

By demonstrating the existence and effects of biases on recruitment decisions, field experiments such as this can potentially demonstrate causal relationships in a way which engenders considerable confidence in the robustness and trustworthiness of the research findings. Agerström and Rooth claim that they found 'a strong and consistent relationship between hiring managers' automatic anti-obesity bias and the probability that they would invite an obese, but not normal-weight, job applicant for an interview' (2011: 797). Because it is often difficult for researchers to assign participants randomly to experimental and control groups, Agerström and Rooth did not use a control group in this study. The absence of a control group limits the extent to which we can be confident that discrimination against job applicants was attributable to manipulation of the independent variable—anti-obesity bias. However, Agerström and Rooth's field experiment did involve random assignment: i.e. the fictitious CVs were sent to a random sample of hiring managers, and the selection of hiring managers for IATs was also done randomly. This helps to ensure that at least some of the principles of experimental research are maintained.

Field experiments such as this are 'quasi-experiments' (see below)—that is, studies that have some of the features of a real experiment but are lacking in one or more ways. This arises in part because organizations are unable to surrender sufficient control to researchers to allow them to fully manipulate the relevant variables, because they are in a workplace and ongoing work has to be attended to. One of the strengths of Agerström and Rooth's study is that it was relatively unobtrusive, thereby reducing the likelihood of **reactive effects**: that is, effects coming from the participants' possible awareness of the study being conducted, which would affect the **generalizability** of the findings. In this case, participants' behaviours in deciding which job applicants to interview were unlikely to have been influenced in this way because they were unaware that they were the focus of investigation (see also Research in focus 3.7). The authors suggest that this type of research can help to enable changes in business practice, such as by encouraging organizations to review personnel selection procedures or by supplying policy-makers with evidence that can be used to justify changes to anti-discrimination laws.

Yet field experiments are not without problems, even when they exhibit some of the features of a true experiment. As Agerström and Rooth note, of the 985 hiring managers who had been sent fictitious job applications, some could not be contacted again due to job and organizational changes. Others were ineligible because they had not handled the entire hiring process of screening and selecting applicants alone, which was a condition for participation in the second stage of the study. Furthermore, the majority of hiring managers did not select either of the two fictitious applicants for interview. And finally, of 384 managers who accepted the invitation to complete the IAT, only 153 actually completed it. As a result, the confidence that can be claimed in the causal relationship between automatic anti-obesity bias and not inviting obese job applicants to interview is somewhat limited.

Classic experimental design

In what is known as the classical experimental design, two groups are established and this forms the basis for experimental manipulation of the independent variable. The *experimental group*, or *treatment group*, receives the treatment (some kind of manipulation of the independent variable), and it is compared against the *control group*, which does not. The dependent variable is measured before and after the treatment, so that a before-and-after analysis can be conducted. Moreover, the subjects are assigned randomly to their respective groups. This enables the researcher(s) to feel confident that any difference between the two groups is attributable to manipulation of the independent variable.

Thus, the classical experimental design comprises the following elements: random assignment to the experimental and control groups; pre-testing (measurement of the dependent variable) of both groups at the start of the time period, T_1; manipulation of the independent variable so that the experimental group receives it but the control group does not; and post-testing (measurement of the dependent variable) of the two groups at T_2. The difference between each group's pre- and post-test scores is then computed to establish whether or not the treatment has made a difference. See Figure 3.1 for an outline of these elements.

Classic experimental design and validity

Internal validity of an experiment

The purpose of the control group in a true experiment is to control (in other words, eliminate) the possible effects of rival explanations of a causal finding. We might then be in a position to take the view that the study is internally valid. The presence of a control group and the random assignment of subjects to the experimental and control groups enable us to eliminate rival explanations and eliminate threats to internal validity. These threats include the following.

- *Testing*. This threat refers to the possibility that subjects may become sensitized to the aims of the experiment (see Research in focus 3.7). The presence of a control group, which presumably also experiences the same 'experimenter effect', allows us to discount this possibility if there is no difference between the experimental and control groups.

- *History*. This threat refers to the possibility that events in the experimental environment that are unrelated to manipulation of the independent variable may have caused the changes. If there is no control group, we would be less sure that changes to the independent variable are producing the change. If there is a control group, differences between the control and experimental groups can be more confidently attributed to manipulation of the independent variable.

- *Maturation*. Quite simply, people change, and the ways in which they change may have implications for the dependent variable. Since maturation should affect the control group subjects as well, the control group allows us to discount the possibility that changes would have occurred anyway, with or without manipulation of the independent variable.

- *Selection*. If there are differences between the two groups, which would arise if they had been selected by a non-random process, variations between the experimental and control groups could be attributed to pre-existing differences in their membership. However, if a random process of assignment to the experimental and control groups is employed, this possibility can be discounted.

FIGURE 3.1
Classical experimental design

T1		T2
Measurement of dependent variable	**Control group** No treatment	Measurement of dependent variable
Measurement of dependent variable	**Experimental group** Treatment	Measurement of dependent variable

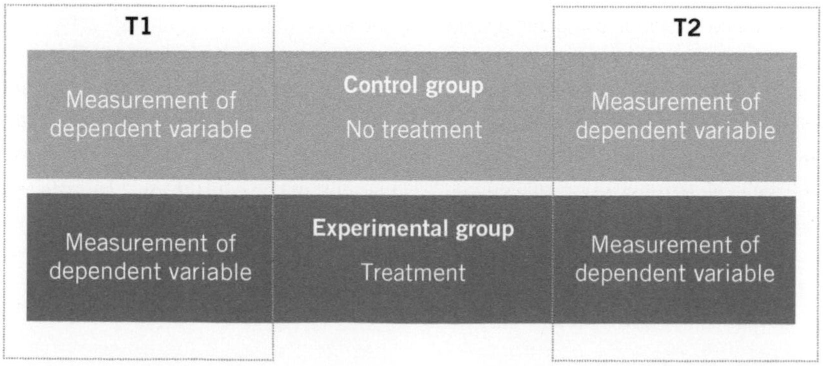

- *Ambiguity about the direction of causal influence.* The very notion of an independent variable and dependent variable presupposes a direction of causality. However, there may be occasions when the temporal sequence is unclear, so that it is not possible to establish which variable affects the other. The existence of a control group can help to make this clear.

These threats are taken from Campbell (1957) and Cook and Campbell (1979), but not all the threats to internal validity they refer to are included here. The presence of a control group coupled with random assignment allows us to eliminate these threats. As a result, our confidence in the causal finding is greatly enhanced.

Simply because research is deemed to be internally valid does not mean that it is beyond reproach or that questions cannot be raised about it. When a quantitative research strategy has been employed, other criteria can be applied to evaluate a study. In the case of the study by Nielsen et al. (2010), for example (see Research in focus 3.8), there is a potential question of measurement validity. Even though measures of intrinsic job motivation and intrinsic job satisfaction may appear to exhibit a correspondence with manager training—that is, to possess face validity—in the sense that they appear to exhibit a correspondence with what they are measuring, we might feel somewhat uneasy about how far increases in job motivation and satisfaction can be regarded as indicative of improvements in training. Does it really measure what it is supposed to measure? The second question relating to measurement validity is whether or not the experimental manipulation really worked. In other words, did the training programme create the conditions for improvements in employee involvement and work satisfaction to be examined?

External validity of an experiment

Campbell (1957) and Cook and Campbell (1979) identify five major threats to the external validity and hence generalizability of an investigation. These can be summarized as follows:

- *Interaction of selection and treatment.* This threat raises the question: to what social and psychological groups can a finding be generalized? Can it be generalized to a wide variety of individuals who might be differentiated by gender, ethnicity, social class, and personality? For instance, many influential studies of leadership, conducted on samples comprising a majority of men, appear not to treat gender as a significant variable (Wilson 1995). It is possible that the findings of these studies simply reflect the characteristics of the predominantly male samples and therefore cannot provide a theory of effective leadership that is generalizable across both men and women.

- *Interaction of setting and treatment.* This threat relates to the issue of how confident we can be that the results of a study can be applied to other settings. For example, in Research in focus 3.4, Agerström and Rooth conducted their study in Sweden, a society which consistently ranks highly in global equality indexes which measure attitudes towards discrimination, and which has directive legislation to protect employees against discriminatory workplace policy and practice on the grounds of gender and race. As a result, the setting may have been unusual by comparison with the wider world and may have had an influence on the experimental participants' behaviours.

- *Interaction of history and treatment.* This raises the question of whether or not the findings can be generalized to the past and to the future. The original Aston studies (Research in focus 3.5), for example, were conducted in the early 1960s. How confident can we be that these findings would apply today?

- *Interaction effects of pre-testing.* As a result of being pre-tested, subjects in an experiment may become sensitized to the experimental treatment. Consequently, the findings may not be generalizable to groups that have *not* been pre-tested and, of course, in the real world, people are rarely tested in this way. The findings may, therefore, be partly determined by the experimental treatment as such and partly by how pre-test sensitization has influenced the way in which subjects respond to the treatment. This may have occurred in Nielsen et al.'s research (Research in focus 3.8).

- *Reactive effects of experimental arrangements.* People are frequently, if not invariably, aware that they are participating in an experiment. Their awareness may influence how they respond to the experimental treatment and therefore affect the generalizability of the findings. This was a major finding of the Hawthorne studies (Research in focus 3.7).

Ecological validity of an experiment

Are the findings ecologically valid? King et al. (2012) argue that an advantage of field experiments is their high ecological validity, which arises from the naturalistic character of the conditions. This, they suggest, provides a welcome alternative to the use of business-school-student subject pools, which are a common research design in psychologically-oriented experimental studies of organizational behaviour.

3.5 RESEARCH IN FOCUS
Establishing the direction of causality

The Aston studies (Pugh et al. 1968) was a highly influential programme of research carried out in 46 organizations in the West Midlands of England during the 1960s. Based on an initial survey study of correlates of organizational structure, the study was guided by the hypothesis that characteristics of an organization's structure would be related to characteristics of its context. However, there was little in the way of detailed hypothesis formulation on exactly how these characteristics were related. The view taken by the researchers was that, although there was a considerable amount of case study research describing the functioning of organizations, very little in the way of systematic comparison had been attempted. Moreover, generalization was made difficult because it was not possible to assess the representativeness of a particular case study. The strategy developed by the Aston researchers was therefore 'to carry out comparative surveys across organizations to establish meaningful stable relationships which would enable the particular idiosyncrasies of case studies to be placed into perspective' (Pugh 1998: xv). A key assumption on which the research was based was that 'the nature, structure and functioning of an organization will be influenced by its objectives, context and environment, all of which must be taken into account' (1998: xv). The researchers concluded that organizational size and production technology were important potential correlates of organization structure, although their findings implied that size, rather than technology, was the more critical factor. This finding contradicted other studies of the time, such as Woodward (1965), which suggested technology was a more important causal factor. However, in later analysis of the same data using a different statistical technique, Aldrich (1972) and Hilton (1972) were able to show other possible patterns of relationships between the three variables—suggesting that technology was an important cause of organizational structure, which in turn affected size. From this we can see some of the difficulties in identifying the causal relationship between variables using survey data.

Replicability of an experiment

A fourth issue that we might want to raise relates to the question of replicability. For example, Pugh et al. (1968) lay out clearly the procedures and measures employed in the Aston studies. This has enabled other researchers to replicate this study in business and non-business organizations, including trade unions, churches, schools, and public bureaucracies. However, analysis of the same data by Aldrich (1972) and Hilton (1972) using a different statistical technique showed other possible relationship patterns between the variables in the Aston studies (see Research in focus 3.5). This failure to replicate casts doubt on the external validity of the original research and suggests that the first three threats referred to above may have played an important part in the differences between these two sets of results.

Laboratory experiments

Many experiments in disciplines such as social psychology are laboratory experiments rather than field experiments. When we use the term 'laboratory' here, we do not mean experiments conducted in a science laboratory, but simply experiments conducted in an artificial

environment where conditions are much easier to control than in field experiments. Some of the most well known of these, such as Milgram's (1963) electric-shock experiments or Zimbardo's prison experiments (see Research in focus 6.3), have informed our understanding of how individuals and groups behave in modern work organizations. One of the main advantages of laboratory experiments is that the researcher has far greater influence over the experimental arrangements. For example, it is easier to randomly assign subjects to different experimental conditions in the laboratory than to do the same in an ongoing, real-life organization. The researcher therefore has a higher level of control, and this is likely to enhance the internal validity of the study. It is also likely that laboratory experiments will be more straightforward to replicate, because they are less bound up with a real-world milieu that is difficult to reproduce.

However, laboratory experiments such as the one described in Research in focus 3.6 suffer from a number of limitations. First, external validity is likely to be difficult to establish. There is the interaction of setting and treatment, since the setting of the laboratory is likely to be unrelated to real-world experiences and contexts. Also, there is likely to be an interaction of selection and

3.6 RESEARCH IN FOCUS
A laboratory experiment on voting on CEO pay

Krause et al. (2014) were interested in the factors that influence the way shareholders vote on the pay of their chief executive officers (CEOs). In particular, they were interested in the relative impacts of two factors—CEOs' current levels of pay and the firm's performance—on shareholders' propensity to vote in favour of a pay increase for the CEO. They formulated hypotheses concerning the impacts of these variables on voting. Students in a Master of Business Administration (MBA) programme were randomly assigned to one of four scenarios which simulated notices to shareholders about the opportunity to vote on CEO pay. The scenarios were identical but varied in terms of information supplied about the two variables of interest—CEOs' current levels of pay, and firm performance. Firm performance was described as either strong or weak. For scenarios in which firm performance was strong, the CEO's pay was either described as currently high or as low. Thus, there were four groups to which students had been randomly assigned. The students were told to imagine that they were shareholders of a Fortune 500 company and were being given the opportunity to vote on pay. CEO pay was found to have no impact on propensity to vote for an increase, whereas poor performance by the firm was found to have an adverse effect on the inclination of the 'shareholders' to vote for an increase. Krause et al. also showed that whether an increase in a CEO's pay is approved is highly affected by firm performance.

treatment. In the case of the experiment by Krause et al. (2014; see Research in focus 3.6), there are a number of difficulties. The subjects were students, who are unlikely to be representative of the general population, so that their responses to the experimental treatment may be distinctive. Also, they were volunteers, and it is known that volunteers differ from non-volunteers (Rosnow and Rosenthal 1997: Chapter 5). There will have been no problem of interaction effects of pre-testing, because, as in many experiments, there was no pre-testing. However, it is quite possible that reactive effects may have been set in motion by the experimental arrangements. As Research in focus 3.7 illustrates, reactive effects associated with an experiment can have a profound effect on the outcomes of the research. Moreover, the ecological validity of the study may be poor because we do not know how well the findings are applicable to the real world and everyday life. However, while the study may lack what is often called mundane realism, it may nonetheless enjoy experimental realism (Aronson and Carlsmith 1968). The latter means that subjects are very involved in the experiment and take it very seriously.

Quasi-experiments

A number of writers have drawn attention to the possibilities offered by quasi-experiments—that is, studies that have certain characteristics of experimental designs but that do not fulfil all the internal validity requirements.

A large number of types of quasi-experiment have been identified (Cook and Campbell 1979), and it is not proposed to cover them here. A particularly interesting form of quasi-experiment occurs in the case of 'natural experiments'. These are 'experiments' in that they entail manipulation of a social setting, but as part of a naturally occurring attempt to alter social arrangements. In such circumstances, random assignment to experimental and control groups is invariably not possible. An example is provided in Research in focus 3.8.

The absence of random assignment in the quasi-experiment described in Research in focus 3.8 casts a certain amount of doubt on the study's internal validity, since the groups may not have been equivalent. However, the results of such studies are still compelling, because they are not artificial interventions in social life and because their ecological validity is therefore very strong. Hofstede's study of cultural differences (discussed in Chapter 2) falls into this category, because the research design enabled some degree of control to be maintained over variables—all employees belonged to the same multinational organization, even though the research took place in a natural setting. This meant that corporate culture constituted the dependent variable and differences in national cultures and mentalities of employees constituted independent variables, where Hofstede anticipated the main differences would be seen. In addition, some requirements of internal validity were fulfilled through replication

3.7 RESEARCH IN FOCUS
The Hawthorne effect

The effect of the experimenter, or the fact of being studied, on the subject is commonly referred to as the Hawthorne effect. This phrase was coined as a result of the series of interlinked investigations carried out during the late 1920s and early 1930s at the Hawthorne works of the Western Electric Company in the USA (Roethlisberger and Dickson 1939).

One phase of the investigations entailed a group of women carrying out manual tasks being taken away from their department and working in a separate room. The aim of the study was to discover how changes in the number and duration of rest pauses, in length of the working day, in heating and lighting, and so on affected productivity, as this quotation from the study illustrates:

> First, the amount of light was increased regularly day by day, and the girls were asked each day how they liked the change. As the light was increased, the girls told the investigator that they liked the brighter lights. Then for a day or two the investigator allowed the girls to see the electrician come and change the light bulbs. In reality, the electrician merely took out bulbs of a given size and inserted bulbs of the same size, without in any way changing the amount of light. The girls, thinking that the light was still being 'stepped up' day by day, commented favourably about the increase of light. After a few days of this, the experimenter started to decrease the intensity of light, keeping the girls informed of the change and soliciting their reaction. After a period of this day-by-day decrease in illumination, he again allowed the girls to see the electrician change the bulbs without really changing the intensity of illumination. Again the girls gave answers that were to be expected, in that they said the 'lesser' light was not so pleasant to work under as the brighter light. Their production did not change at any stage of the experiment.
>
> (Roethlisberger and Dickson 1939: 17)

However, as the study went on, it was found that productivity *did* increase, irrespective of the changes that were being introduced. Eventually it was recognized that the women were responding to the positive attention and special treatment they were receiving. The researchers concluded that increases in worker productivity were due not to any changes in the conditions of the working environment, but instead to the favourable circumstances that the experimental arrangements had produced. While this finding did much to stimulate the 'human-relations' approach to the study of work, by pointing to the potential advantages of providing people with psycho-social support in the workplace, it also neatly demonstrates that experimental arrangements may induce an effect—a 'reactive effect'—over and above the intentions of the investigator. This has been referred to, more generally, as the 'experimenter effect', where the researcher creates a bias in the data through participation in the research situation or by inadvertently communicating his or her preferred research outcome.

The Hawthorne effect also draws attention to the way in which researchers themselves represent 'an audience to the actors being studied', and it is therefore likely that the researcher's activities will have an influence on the research setting. This draws attention to the fact that, 'while the researcher attends to the study of other persons and their other activities, these other persons attend to the study of the researcher and his activities' (Van Maanen and Kolb 1985: 6). The results of fieldwork thus depend in part upon the outcomes of the unofficial study that the observed make of the physical nature and psychological character of the observer, as well as the other way around.

of the questionnaire survey on two separate occasions, once in 1967–9 and again in 1971–3.

Most writers on quasi-experimentation discount experiments in which there is no control group or basis for comparison (Cook and Campbell 1979). However, some experiments do involve manipulation of the independent variable within experimental groups without a control group as the basis for comparison. For example, in an experimental study of electronic brainstorming, Gallupe et al. (1992) wanted to test the effect of group size on performance. The researchers wanted to find out if electronic brainstorming could more effectively support the generation of ideas within large groups (six and twelve persons), as well as in small groups (two,

3.8 RESEARCH IN FOCUS
A quasi-experiment

Nielsen et al. (2010) studied a situation where a team-working intervention was being introduced in a workplace. They were interested in whether providing managers with training during the introduction of the team-working intervention might enhance the impact of the intervention. To test this, the researchers employed a quasi-experiment involving a mixed methods approach, where they collected qualitative as well as quantitative data. The research was driven by hypotheses, such as:

> *Hypothesis 1*: Implementing teams will bring about improvements in employees' perceptions of task design (increased team interdependence and autonomy) and team processes (increased motivation and improved social climate). Because of the change in the role of the manager brought about by the change we predict that employees will also rate their manager as exerting more transformational leadership behaviours. In addition, organizational and individual outcome measures will improve (for example, perceptions of increased team effectiveness, employee involvement and job satisfaction).

(Nielsen et al. 2010: 1721)

The experiment was conducted at two elderly care centres in Denmark. The centres are described by the authors as 'almost identical'. In both centres employees experienced a teamwork intervention, but in one of them managers were trained in the course of the change and were therefore treated as the intervention group; in the other they were not trained, and that group was therefore treated as a comparison or control group. The two groups were compared in terms of how far they changed over time (18 months) for a wide range of dependent variables that would allow the researchers' hypotheses to be tested. Nielsen et al. found that the effects of the introduction of teamwork on most of the dependent variables was limited when it was not accompanied by manager training. Overall, they found that teamwork accompanied by training made a difference for several variables, notably employee involvement and job satisfaction. Contrary to expectations, the control group fared better than the intervention group in respect of one variable (interdependency).

This study uses a quasi-experimental design, in which a control group is compared to a treatment group. It bears some of the hallmarks of a classic experimental design, but there is no random assignment; participants were in groups according to their work location, and subjects could not be randomly assigned to the two groups because of practical constraints. While the two centres are viewed as nearly identical, the memberships of the two groups are of unknown equivalence, so we cannot be certain that the findings associated with comparison of the groups are not due to differences between them. On the other hand, the fact that this is a real-world study makes it of considerable interest, especially in view of the difficulty of conducting experiments with random assignment in the field. Further, the study collected qualitative data which allowed the researchers to gather a wide range of additional information; this allowed them to make inferences about such issues as the mechanisms that lay behind the changes that teamwork and the training intervention engendered.

four, and six persons)—unlike the traditional, verbal brainstorming technique. In this study, both the large and the small groups received the experimental treatment—that is, electronic brainstorming—and both received the control treatment—that is, verbal brainstorming. It was anticipated that large and small groups would show similar levels of productivity in the verbal brainstorming experiment, but that large groups would outperform small groups in the electronic brainstorming experiment. Because there was no control group, i.e. there was no group in which the independent variable was not manipulated, this study cannot be seen as a classic experimental design. However, the internal validity of the findings was reinforced by the fact that both the experiments were also carried out on small groups, where it was found that electronic brainstorming made no difference to group performance. Comparison between large and small experimental groups helped to reduce threats to the internal validity of the findings. The study thus exhibits some of the characteristics of an experimental design, even though no control group was used.

3.9 KEY CONCEPT
What is evaluation research?

Evaluation research, as its name implies, is concerned with the evaluation of such occurrences as organizational programmes or interventions. The essential question that is typically asked by such studies is: has the intervention (for example, a new policy initiative or an organizational change) achieved its anticipated goals? A typical design may have one group that is exposed to the treatment—that is, the new initiative—and a control group that is not. Since it is often not feasible or ethical to randomly assign research participants to the two groups, such studies are usually quasi-experimental. The use of the principles of experimental design is fairly entrenched in evaluation research, but other approaches have emerged in recent years. Approaches to evaluation based on qualitative research have also been developed. While there are differences of opinion about how qualitative evaluation should be carried out, the different views typically coalesce around a recognition of the importance of an in-depth understanding of the context in which an intervention occurs and the diverse viewpoints of the stakeholders (Greene 1994, 2000).

Finally, experimental designs, and more especially quasi-experimental designs, have been particularly prominent in evaluation research (see Key concept 3.9 and Research in focus 3.10).

Possibly because of the various difficulties with quasi-experiments that have been noted in this section, Grant and Wall (2009) have noted that they are used relatively infrequently in organizational research. However, they also note that there may be ways of addressing some of the concerns regarding internal validity that beset quasi-experiments. For example, they suggest it may be possible to strengthen causal inferences when it is not possible to assign experimental and control group participants randomly and the researcher has limited or no control over the experimental manipulation. This might be done by seeking out further information that will help to discount some of the rival interpretations of a causal link that arise from the lack of a true experimental design. However, it is unlikely that such a view will find favour among researchers who adopt a purist view about the need for experimental designs in order to generate robust causal inferences.

3.10 RESEARCH IN FOCUS
An evaluation study of role redesign

The purpose of research conducted by Hyde et al. (2006) was to examine the introduction of role redesign in the NHS (the UK's National Health Service) under the Changing Workforce Programme (CWP), to highlight implications for employment relations and to identify characteristics of successful CWP initiatives. This was a qualitative, rather than an experimental, evaluation that was based on secondary data analysis, **semi-structured interviews**, and observations. The two-phase study was carried out by the research team in 2003 and funded by the Department of Health. The first phase of the evaluation focused on the 13 pilot sites where the CWP had been introduced and 'involved documentary review of reports relating to this initiative. In addition, individual interviews were conducted with participants from each of the pilot sites' (2006: 700). In total, 30 interviews were conducted across the 13 sites. The second phase involved a case study design 'to study the process of role redesign and identify examples of good practice' (2006: 700). Four of the 13 pilot sites were selected as case studies 'to illustrate varying degrees of progress in relation to individual roles; variation in type of redesign attempted; different types of partnership arrangement; differing means of involving those receiving the service; and relevance to the wider NHS and other care sectors' (2006: 700). The fifth case study involved the CWP team itself, to gain an overview of the development of the programme. A further 64 interviews were carried out in the five case study sites. In addition, the research team attended meetings and conducted role observations. This approach to evaluation enabled the researchers to 'take account of the heterogeneity and complexity of CWP interventions' (2006: 703) in different health service contexts.

Significance of experimental design

As was stated at the outset, the chief reason for introducing the experiment as a research design is because it is frequently considered to be a yardstick against which quantitative research is judged. This occurs largely because a true experiment will allow doubts about internal validity to be allayed and reflects the considerable emphasis placed on the determination of causality in quantitative research. As we will see in the next section, cross-sectional designs of the kind associated with social survey research are frequently regarded as limited, because of the problems of unambiguously imputing causality when using them.

Logic of comparison

However, before exploring such issues, it is important to draw attention to an important general lesson that an examination of experiments teaches us. A central feature of any experiment is the fact that it entails a *comparison*: at the very least it entails a comparison of results obtained by an experimental group with those engendered by a control group. In the case of the experiment in Research in focus 3.6, there is no control group: the research entails a comparison of the effects of two variables, CEO pay and firm performance. The advantage of carrying out any kind of comparison like this is that we understand the phenomenon that we are interested in better when we compare it with something else that is similar to it. The case for arguing that charismatic leadership is an effective, performance-enhancing form of leadership is much more persuasive when we view it in relation to other forms of leadership. Thus, while the specific considerations concerning experimental design are typically associated with quantitative research, the potential of comparison in business research represents a more general lesson that transcends matters of both research strategy and research design. In other words, while the experimental design is typically associated with a quantitative research strategy, the logic of comparison provides lessons of broad applicability and relevance. This issue is given more specific attention below in the section on comparative design.

Cross-sectional design

The cross-sectional design is often called a social survey design, but the idea of the social survey is so closely connected in most people's minds with questionnaires and structured interviewing that the more generic-sounding term *cross-sectional design* is preferable. While the research methods associated with social surveys are certainly frequently employed within the context of cross-sectional research, so too are many other research methods, including structured observation, content analysis, official statistics, and diaries. All these research methods will be covered in later chapters, but in the meantime the basic structure of cross-sectional design will be outlined here.

The cross-sectional design is defined in Key concept 3.11. It will be useful to examine the elements of this definition.

- *More than one case*. Researchers employing a cross-sectional design are interested in variation. That variation can be in respect of people, organizations, nation states, or whatever. Variation can be established only when more than one case is being examined. Usually, researchers employing this design will select a lot more than two cases for a variety of reasons: they are more likely to encounter variation in all the variables in which they are interested; they can make finer distinctions between cases; and the requirements of sampling procedure are likely to necessitate larger numbers (see Chapter 9).

- *At a single point in time*. In cross-sectional research design, data on the variables of interest are collected more or less simultaneously. When an individual completes a questionnaire, which may contain 50 or more variables, the answers are supplied at essentially the same time. This contrasts with a classic experiment, in which someone in the experimental group is pre-tested, then exposed to the experimental treatment, and then post-tested; days, weeks, months, or even years may separate the different phases.

- *Quantitative or quantifiable data*. In order to establish variation between cases (and then to examine associations between variables—see next point), it is necessary to have a systematic and standardized method for gauging variation. One of the most important advantages of quantification is that it provides the researcher with a consistent benchmark. The advantages of quantification and of measurement will be addressed in greater detail in Chapter 7.

- *Patterns of association*. With a cross-sectional design it is possible to examine only relationships between variables. There is no time ordering to the variables, because the data on them are collected more or less simultaneously, and the researcher does not (invariably because he or she cannot) manipulate any of the variables. This creates the problem referred to in Research in focus 3.7 in establishing the direction of causal influence. If the researcher discovers a relationship between two variables, he or she cannot be certain whether this denotes a

3.11 KEY CONCEPT
What is a cross-sectional research design?

A cross-sectional design entails the collection of data on more than one case (usually quite a lot more than one) and at a single point in time in order to collect a body of quantitative or quantifiable data in connection with two or more variables (usually many more than two), which are then examined to detect patterns of association.

3.12 KEY CONCEPT
What is survey research?

Survey research comprises a cross-sectional design in relation to which data are collected predominantly by questionnaire or by structured interview on more than one case (usually quite a lot more than one) and at a single point in time in order to collect a body of quantitative or quantifiable data in connection with two or more variables (usually many more than two), which are then examined to detect patterns of association.

causal relationship, because the features of an experimental design are not present. All that can be said is that the variables are related. This is not to say that it is not possible to draw causal inferences from research based on a cross-sectional design. As will be shown in Chapter 15, there are a number of ways in which the researcher is able to draw certain inferences about causality, but these inferences rarely have the credibility of causal findings deriving from an experimental design. As a result, cross-sectional research invariably lacks the internal validity that one finds in most experimental research.

In this book, the term 'survey' will be reserved for research that employs a cross-sectional research design and in which data are collected by questionnaire or by structured interview (see Research in focus 3.13). This will allow us to retain the conventional understanding of what a survey is while recognizing that the cross-sectional research design has a wider relevance—that is, one that is not necessarily associated with the collection of data by questionnaire or by structured interview.

Reliability, replicability, and validity

How does cross-sectional research measure up in terms of the previously outlined criteria for evaluating quantitative research: reliability, replicability, and validity?

- The issues of *reliability* and *measurement validity* are primarily matters relating to the quality of the measures that are employed to tap the concepts in which the researcher is interested, rather than matters to do with a research design. In order to address questions of the quality of measures, some of the issues outlined in Chapter 7 would have to be considered.

- *Replicability* is likely to be present in most cross-sectional research to the degree that the researcher spells out procedures for selecting respondents; designing measures of concepts; the administration of research instruments (such as structured interview or self-completion questionnaire); and the analysis of data. Most quantitative research based on cross-sectional research designs specifies such procedures to a large degree.

- *Internal validity* is typically weak in cross-sectional research. As has just been suggested above, it is difficult to establish causal direction from the resulting data. Cross-sectional research designs produce associations rather than findings from which causal inferences can be unambiguously made. Procedures for making causal inferences from cross-sectional data will be referred to in Chapter 15, though most researchers feel that the resulting causal findings rarely have the internal validity of those deriving from experimental designs.

- *External validity* is strong when, as in the case of the Study of Australian Leadership (see Research in focus 3.13), the sample from which data are collected has been randomly selected. When non-random methods of sampling are employed, external validity becomes questionable. Sampling issues will be specifically addressed in Chapter 9.

- Since much cross-sectional research uses research instruments, such as self-completion questionnaires and structured observation schedules, *ecological validity* may be jeopardized because these very instruments disrupt the 'natural habitat', as Cicourel (1982) put it.

3.13 RESEARCH IN FOCUS

An example of survey research: the Study of Australian Leadership (SAL)

The 2015 Study of Australian Leadership (SAL) was the first nationally representative survey of Australian workplaces—focusing on leadership, work, employment, and organizational performance—since the Australian Workplace Industrial Relations Survey of 1995. The survey population was all workplaces in Australia that have five or more employees (excluding those in agriculture, forestry, and fishing). The main objectives of the survey were to

- map leadership and management practices and capabilities and their associations with organizational performance;
- provide a 'snapshot' of work and employment practices and the experiences of employees;
- inform policy and practice and stimulate debate;
- provide a comprehensive and statistically reliable dataset on Australian workplaces for public use.

The SAL contains data from a representative sample of 2561 Australian workplaces collected from

- senior leaders;
- workplace leaders;
- managerial and non-managerial employees.

The main unit of analysis in SAL is the 'workplace', a single site at which productive activity takes place. Some organizations in the sample were single-site, which means that the organization and the workplace were one and the same, while some workplaces were part of multi-site organizations.

The survey contained the following elements.

- *Senior leader questionnaire*—a questionnaire administered by phone, which was completed by the manager with overall responsibility for the whole organization, e.g. the CEO or the general manager. This questionnaire collected data about 'big picture' issues such as organization strategy, the competitive environment, governance and management systems, and leadership capabilities.

- *Workplace leader questionnaire*—a questionnaire administered by phone, which was completed by the manager with responsibility for the workplace. It collected data about issues including workplace management practices, human resource management systems, workplace management capabilities, union density, and training. In single-site organizations, this questionnaire was administered to the same person as the senior leader questionnaire.

- *Frontline leader and employee questionnaire*—a self-completion questionnaire distributed to a sample of managerial and non-managerial employees within workplaces which were part of the survey. It collected data on perceptions of management practices and competencies, engagement, satisfaction, turnover intentions, and perceptions of senior leadership. In the case of managerial employees, additional questions about their perceptions of their own managerial competence were asked.

- *Workplace performance questionnaire*—an online self-completion questionnaire which collected data on a range of performance measures.

These data enable researchers to build up a picture of workplace practices and outcomes that links the views of employees with those of managers and workers in the same workplace. A key strength of the survey is thus derived from its representation of multiple interests in the workplace, rather than just relying on the account given by a senior manager.

Further details can be found at https://www.workplaceleadership.com.au/sal/.

Non-manipulable variables

As was noted at the beginning of the section on experimental design, in much, if not most, business research it is not possible to manipulate the variables in which we are interested. This is why most quantitative business research employs a cross-sectional research design rather than an experimental one. Moreover, some of the variables in which social scientists are interested, and which are often viewed as potentially significant independent variables, are non-manipulable: they simply cannot be manipulated, other than by extreme measures. At the individual level of analysis, age, ethnicity, gender, and social background are 'givens' that are not really amenable to the kind of manipulation that is necessary for a true experimental design. To a lesser extent this also applies at the organizational level of analysis to variables such as size, structure, technology, and culture. On the other hand, the very fact that we can regard certain variables as givens provides us with a clue as to how we can make causal inferences in cross-sectional research. Many of the variables in which we are interested can be *assumed* to be temporally prior to other variables: they happen first. For example, we can assume that, if we find a relationship between gender and entrepreneurial behaviour, then gender is more likely to be the independent variable, because it is likely to be temporally prior to entrepreneurial behaviour. In other words, while we may not be able to manipulate the gender variable, we can draw some causal inferences from cross-sectional data.

Structure of the cross-sectional design

The cross-sectional research design comprises the collection of data in the form of observations on a series of variables (Obs_1 Obs_2 Obs_3 Obs_4 Obs_5 ... Obs_n) at a single point in time, T_1. The effect is to create what Marsh (1982) referred to as a 'rectangle' of data that comprises variables Obs_1 to Obs_n and cases $Case_1$ to $Case_n$, as in Figure 3.2. For each case (which may be a person, household, city, nation, etc.), data are available for each of the variables, Obs_1 to Obs_n, all of which will have been collected at T_1. Each cell in the matrix will have data in it.

Cross-sectional design and research strategy

This discussion of the cross-sectional design has placed it firmly in the context of quantitative research. Also, the evaluation of the design has drawn on criteria associated with the quantitative research strategy. It should be noted, however, that qualitative research often entails a form of cross-sectional design. A fairly typical form of such research is when the researcher employs

FIGURE 3.2
The data rectangle in cross-sectional research

	Obs_1	Obs_2	Obs_3	Obs_4	. . .	Obs_n
$Case_1$						
$Case_2$						
$Case_3$						
$Case_4$						
$Case_5$						
. . .						
$Case_n$						

unstructured interviewing or semi-structured interviewing with a number of people. Research in focus 3.14 provides an illustration of such a study.

While not typical of the qualitative research tradition, the study described in Research in focus 3.14 bears some research design similarities to cross-sectional studies within a predominantly quantitative research tradition, such as the SAL (see Research in focus 3.13), while retaining some research design features more typical of qualitative studies. The research was not directly preoccupied with such criteria of quantitative research as internal and external validity, replicability, measurement validity, and so on, but it is clear that the researchers took considerable care to ensure the representativeness of their sample of managers in relation to the overall population. In fact, it could be argued that the use of interviews in conjunction with self-completion questionnaires makes the study more ecologically valid than research that uses only more formal instruments of data collection. It is common within business and management research to see such a *triangulated* approach, where attempts are made to cancel out the limitations of one method by the use of another in order to cross-check the findings. Hence, cross-sectional studies in business and management tend not to be so clearly divided into those that use either quantitative or qualitative methods.

Longitudinal design

The longitudinal design represents a distinct form of research design that is typically used to map change in business and management research. Pettigrew (1990) has emphasized the importance of longitudinal study

3.14 RESEARCH IN FOCUS
A representative sample?

Scase and Goffee (1989) conducted a survey of 374 managers employed in six large organizations—four of which were privately owned and two of which were in the public sector. A number of issues were taken into account in order to ensure that the sample was representative of a wider population.

1. The sample of 323 men and 51 women chosen for the questionnaire survey was designed to reflect gender proportions within the wider UK management population.

2. The researchers attempted to achieve a broad spread of ages within their sample, to reflect the relative proportions of male and female managers in each group.

3. They also sought to reflect labour market patterns and functional groupings—for example, by including more women in the sample who were engaged in personnel management, training, and industrial relations.

4. They included more men in senior and middle-level management positions to reflect the fact that women are under-represented in these positions.

5. Finally, the sample was selected to reflect patterns of employment, levels of education, salary levels, and marital status broadly representative of patterns in the wider population.

From the questionnaire survey, a smaller representative group of 80 men and women was selected for in-depth interviews. However, Scase and Goffee make no claim for the statistical representativeness of their sample. Instead they suggest that their findings can be 'regarded as indicative of broader trends . . . affecting the work, careers and personal experiences of men and women managers during the closing decades of the twentieth century' (1989: 197).

in understanding organizations as a way of providing data on the mechanisms and processes through which changes are created. Such a 'contextualist' research design involves drawing on 'phenomena at vertical and horizontal levels of analysis and the interconnections between those levels through time' (1990: 269). However, partly because of the time and cost involved, longitudinal design is relatively little used in business and management research. In the form in which it is typically found, it is usually an extension of social survey research based on self-completion questionnaires or structured interview research within a cross-sectional design. Consequently, in terms of reliability, replicability, and validity, the longitudinal design is little different from cross-sectional research. However, a longitudinal design can allow some insight into the time order of variables and therefore may be more able to allow causal inferences to be made.

With a longitudinal design, a sample is surveyed and is then surveyed again on at least one further occasion. It is common to distinguish two types of longitudinal design: the *panel study* and the *cohort study*. With the former type, a sample, often a randomly selected national one, is the focus of data collection on at least two (and often more) occasions. Data may be collected

from different types of case within a panel study framework: individuals, organizations, and so on. The cohort study selects either an entire cohort of people or a randomly selected sample of them as the focus of data collection. The cohort is made up of people who share a certain characteristic, such as all being born in the same week, or having a certain experience, such as being unemployed or getting married on a certain day or in the same week. However, this design is rarely used in business research.

Panel and cohort studies share similar features. Data are collected in at least two waves on the same variables on the same people or organizations. Both panel and cohort studies are concerned with illuminating social change and improving the understanding of causal influences over time. The latter means that longitudinal designs are somewhat better able to deal with the problem of ambiguity about the direction of causal influence that plagues cross-sectional designs. Because certain potentially independent variables can be identified at T_1, the researcher is in a better position to infer that purported effects that are identified at T_2 or later have occurred *after* the independent variables. This does not deal with the entire problem about the ambiguity of causal influence, but it at least addresses the problem of knowing which variable came first. In all other respects, the points made above about cross-sectional designs also apply to longitudinal designs.

Panel and cohort studies share similar problems. First, there is the problem of sample attrition through employee job changes, companies going out of business, and so on, and through subjects choosing to withdraw at later stages of the research. The problem with attrition is largely that those who leave the study may differ in some important respects from those who remain, so that the latter do not form a representative group. Secondly, there are few guidelines as to when is the best juncture to conduct further waves of data collection. Thirdly, it is often suggested that many longitudinal studies are poorly thought out and that they result in the collection of large amounts of data with little apparent planning. Fourthly, there is evidence that a *panel conditioning* effect can occur whereby continued participation in a longitudinal study affects how respondents behave.

Case study design

The basic case study entails the detailed and intensive analysis of a single case. As Stake (1995) observes, case study research is concerned with the complexity and particular nature of the case in question. The case study approach is a popular and widely used research design in business research (Eisenhardt and Graebner 2007), and some of the best-known studies in business and management research are based on it. A case can be

- *a single organization*, such as Pettigrew's (1985; see Research in focus 3.16) research at Imperial Chemical Industries (ICI), Joanne Martin's (1992) study of organizational culture at 'OzCo', a high-technology industry company based in California, or Born's (2004) study of managerialism in the BBC;

- *a single location*, such as a factory, production site, or office building—for example, Pollert's (1981; see Research in focus 19.8) research in a tobacco factory, Linstead's (1985) study of humour in a bakery, or Milkman's (1997) investigation of an automobile assembly plant (see Chapter 20);

- *a person*, as in Marshall's (1995; see Key concept 17.3) study of women managers, where each woman constitutes a separate case—such studies are characterized as using the life history or biographical approach; or

- *a single event*, such as the NASA space shuttle *Challenger* disaster in 1986 (Vaughan 1990; see Chapter 23).

What is a case?

The most common use of the term associates the case study with a geographical location, such as a workplace or organization. What distinguishes a case study from other research designs is the focus on a bounded situation or system, an entity with a purpose and functioning parts. The emphasis tends to be upon intensive examination of the setting. There is a tendency to associate case studies with qualitative research, but such an identification is not appropriate. It is certainly true that exponents of the case study design often favour qualitative methods, such as participant observation and unstructured interviewing, because these methods are viewed as particularly helpful in the generation of an intensive, detailed examination of a case. Knights and McCabe (1997) suggest that the case study provides a vehicle through which several qualitative methods can be combined, thereby avoiding too great a reliance on a single one. In their study of quality management in a UK retail bank, they combined participant observation with semi-structured interviewing and documentary data collection of company reports, total quality management (TQM) guides, and newsletters. Findings from the case study were used to identify insights into why so many quality management programmes had failed. However, case studies frequently use both quantitative and qualitative, or mixed, research methods, an approach that will receive attention in Chapter 27. In business research the dominance of positivism has meant that the way that case studies are done has been heavily influenced by this epistemological tradition. Lee (1999) reports that qualitative research that is published in American journals tends to cite the work of Yin (1984), who adopts a relatively narrow view of case study research (Lee et al. 2007) (see Thinking deeply 3.15). In some instances, when an investigation is based exclusively upon quantitative research, it can be difficult to determine whether it is better described as a case study or as a cross-sectional research design. The same point can often be made about case studies based upon qualitative research.

With a case study, the case is an object of interest in its own right, and the researcher aims to provide an in-depth elucidation of it. Unless a distinction of this or some other kind is drawn, it becomes impossible to distinguish the case study as a special research design, because almost any kind of research can be construed as a case study. It also needs to be appreciated that when specific research illustrations are examined they can exhibit features of more than one research design. However, in some case study research, cases are selected to represent a population, and in such instances more formal sampling is required. What distinguishes a case study is that the researcher is usually concerned to highlight the unique features of the case. This is known as an *idiographic* approach. In contrast, research designs such as the cross-sectional study are referred to as *nomothetic* because they are concerned with generating statements that apply regardless of time and place.

Stake (1995) suggests the selection of cases should be based first and foremost on the anticipation of the opportunity to learn. Researchers should, therefore, choose cases where they expect learning will be greatest. He distinguishes between three different types of case study. *Intrinsic* case studies are undertaken primarily to gain insight into the particularities of a situation, rather than to gain insight into other cases or generic issues. *Instrumental* case studies are those that focus on using the case as a means of understanding a broader issue or allowing generalizations to be challenged. Finally, there is the category of *multiple* or *collective* case studies that are undertaken jointly to explore a general phenomenon. Stake (2005) notes, however, that the boundaries between these three types are often blurred.

With experimental and cross-sectional designs, the typical relationship between theory and research is a deductive one. This means that the research design and collection of data are guided by specific research questions that derive from theoretical concerns. However, when a qualitative research strategy is employed within a cross-sectional design, the approach tends to be inductive. In other words, whether a cross-sectional design is inductive or deductive tends to be affected by whether a quantitative or a qualitative research strategy is employed. The same point can be made of case study research. When the predominant research strategy is qualitative, a case study tends to take an inductive approach to the relationship between theory and research; if a predominantly quantitative strategy is taken, it tends to be deductive. Thinking deeply 3.15 illustrates how the strategy adopted affects the type of case study approach that is taken.

Reliability, replicability, and validity

The question of how well the case study fares in the context of the quality criteria cited early on in this chapter—measurement validity, internal validity, external validity, ecological validity, reliability, and replicability—depends in large part on how far the researcher feels that these are appropriate for the evaluation of case study research.

3.15 THINKING DEEPLY
The case study in business research

Piekkari et al. (2009) suggest that the way that researchers in the area of international business use case study designs is different from how they are used in other social science disciplines. To find out how the case study research design is used, the authors argue that it is necessary to look at how researchers use it, rather than at how methods textbooks say it can be used. Based on a review of 135 case study articles in international business journals, Piekkari et al. argue that the way that case studies are understood is relatively narrow and is dominated by the positivist tradition as developed by Yin (1984) and Eisenhardt (1989), at the expense of alternative, interpretative approaches. They distinguish between:

- *positivistic approaches*, as propounded by Eisenhardt (1989), where the goal is to extract variables from their context in order to generate generalizable propositions and build theory, often by conducting multiple case studies and using a variety of data collection methods to triangulate and improve the validity of the study;

- *alternative approaches*, where the aim is to produce rich, holistic, and particularized explanations that are located in situational context by using multiple methods of data collection to uncover conflicting meanings and interpretations.

They argue that these conventions 'affect judgments about the proper role of case studies in research, how case studies should be conducted, and the criteria for evaluating the quality of case research' (Piekkari et al. 2009: 570). The authors express the concern that variable-oriented approaches can be constraining for international business researchers by limiting the extent to which they can be flexible in their research. They conclude that researchers need to be more aware of the type of case study approach they are adopting and to justify their choice more explicitly.

Some writers on case study research, such as Yin (1984), consider that they are appropriate criteria and suggest ways in which case study research can be developed to enhance its ability to meet them. Other writers, such as Stake (1995), barely mention these criteria at all. Writers on case study research whose point of orientation lies primarily with a qualitative research strategy tend to play down or ignore these quality criteria, whereas writers who have been strongly influenced by the quantitative research strategy tend to depict them as more significant.

However, one question on which a great deal of discussion has centred concerns the *external validity* or *generalizability* of case study research. How can a single case possibly be representative so that it might yield findings that can be applied more generally to other cases? For example, how could the findings from Pettigrew's (1985) research into ICI (see Research in focus 3.16) be generalizable to all large multinational pharmaceutical corporations?

Although many researchers emphasize that they are interested in the detail of a single case, they do sometimes claim a degree of theoretical generalizability on the basis of it. For example, in her study of Indsco Supply Corporation, Kanter (1977) explains that the case enabled her to generate concepts and give meaning to abstract propositions, which she then sought to test in three other large corporations. It is, therefore, clear that she is seeking to achieve a degree of theoretical generalizability from this case. Lee et al. (2007) suggest that particularization rather than generalization constitutes the main strength of case studies. Flyvbjerg (2006) argues that the idea that one cannot generalize from a single case is a common misconception about case study

research. He suggests that in-depth cases provide the basis for 'concrete, context-dependent knowledge', which is the only thing that social science can reliably produce (2006: 223). Citing the example of Galileo's rejection of Aristotle's law of gravity, Flyvbjerg argues that social and natural scientists have been using techniques of 'intense observation', working with 'critical, i.e. strategically selected, cases, rather than random and large samples, as the basis for development for centuries'. Whether or not one agrees with Flyvbjerg's assertions, most writers agree that the goal of case study analysis is to concentrate on the uniqueness of the case and to develop a deep understanding of its complexity.

Types of case

Following on from the issue of external validity, it is useful to consider a distinction between different types of case. Yin (2003) distinguishes five types.

- *The critical case.* Here the researcher has a clearly specified hypothesis, and a case is chosen on the grounds that it will allow a better understanding of the circumstances in which the hypothesis will and will not hold. Flyvbjerg suggests that selection of critical cases relies on the judgement and experience of the researcher. He states: '[t]he only general advice that can be given is that when looking for critical cases, it is a good idea to look for either "most likely" or "least likely" cases, that is, cases likely to either clearly confirm or irrefutably falsify propositions and hypotheses' (2006: 231). Flyvbjerg cites Robert Michel's (1962) classic study of oligarchy in organizations to illustrate how one might select a critical case by looking where something is

3.16 RESEARCH IN FOCUS
A longitudinal case study of ICI

Pettigrew (1985) conducted research into organizational development (OD) at Imperial Chemical Industries (ICI). The fieldwork was conducted between 1975 and 1983. He carried out 'long semi-structured interviews' in 1975–7 and again in 1980–2. Some individuals were interviewed more than once, and care was taken to ensure that interviews included people from all hierarchical levels in the company and from the different functional and business areas within the firm. A total of 175 interviews were conducted. During the period of the fieldwork Pettigrew had fairly regular contact with members of the organization through his involvement with the company as a consultant. He also had access to archival materials that explained how internal OD consultants were recruited and how external OD consultants were used. He writes: 'The continuous real-time data collection was enriched by retrospective interviewing and archival analysis' (1985: 40). The study thus covered 10 years of 'real-time' analysis, complemented by over 20 years of retrospective data analysis. Consequently, this longitudinal case study spans more than 30 years, although Pettigrew (1990) acknowledges that this is rarely feasible in organizational research.

'least likely' to arise. 'By choosing a horizontally structured grassroots organization with strong democratic ideals—that is, a type of organization with an especially low probability of being oligarchical—Michels could test the universality of the oligarchy thesis; that is, "If this organization is oligarchic, then so are most others"' (Flyvbjerg 2006: 231).

- *The unique case.* The unique or extreme case is, as Yin observes, a common focus in clinical studies. However, this type of case is also related to Flyvbjerg's (2006) category of the 'extreme or deviant case', which may be used to gain information about something that is unusual or puzzling and can enable the researcher to get a point across in a dramatic way.

- *The revelatory case.* The basis for the revelatory case exists 'when an investigator has an opportunity to observe and analyse a phenomenon previously inaccessible to scientific investigation' (Yin 1984: 44). While the idea of the revelatory case is interesting, it seems unnecessary to restrict it solely to situations in which something has not previously been studied. Much qualitative case study research that is carried out with a predominantly inductive approach to theory treats single case studies as broadly 'revelatory'.

- *The representative or typical case.* This type seeks to explore a case that exemplifies an everyday situation or form of organization.

- *The longitudinal case.* This type of case is concerned with how a situation changes over time.

Any particular study can involve a combination of these elements, which can be viewed as rationales for choosing particular cases. However, Lee et al. (2007) argue that Yin's categorization of cases is still rather narrow and defers to the positivist tradition.

Unfortunately, case studies are sometimes perceived as poor relations to positivistic, quantitative research. Some writers argue that exploratory case studies should be conducted as preliminary research, in advance of wide-scale surveys, to map out the themes that subsequent research will explore. Alternatively, descriptive case studies are sometimes recommended to expand on trends and themes already discovered by survey research. Yet Flyvbjerg (2006) argues that case study research also enables theory testing, including through the falsification of existing theory on the basis of a single observation.

Exponents of case study research counter suggestions that the evidence they present is limited, because it has restricted external validity, by arguing that it is not the purpose of this research design to generalize to other cases or to populations beyond the case. It is only the explanatory case that seeks to derive a detailed understanding of a particular phenomenon where the case is not seen as ancillary to more quantitative methods (Lee et al. 2007: 170). This position is very different from that taken by practitioners of survey research. Survey researchers are invariably concerned to be able to generalize their findings to larger populations, frequently using random sampling to enhance the representativeness of the samples on which they conduct their investigations and therefore the external validity of their findings. Case study researchers argue strenuously that this is not the purpose of their craft.

However, the meaning of case study research is not universally agreed on. Tight (2010) has reviewed a range of methodological writings on the case study, including a book written by Bryman (2004a). He notes that the term is used in a wide variety of ways, and many different kinds of study can end up being described as case studies. Indeed, he asserts that 'we simply use case study as a convenient label for our research—when we can't think of anything "better"—in an attempt to give it some added respectability' (2010: 337). He goes on to propose 'why don't we just call this kind of research what it is—small-sample, in-depth study, or something like that?' (2010: 338). While this is one solution to the problem of the term 'case study' being used in different ways, it ought to be possible for researchers who use the term 'case study' to justify why the label is warranted.

Case study as intensive analysis

Case study researchers tend to argue that they aim to generate an intensive examination of a single case, which forms the basis for theoretical analysis. The success of this intensive form of analysis relies on developing a 'good narrative', focusing on the situational details and specific events and writing about them in a way which captures the 'complexities and contradictions of real life' (Flyvbjerg 2006: 237). It is for this reason that case studies are often associated with qualitative methods. A central issue of concern is the quality of the theoretical reasoning in which the case study researcher engages. How well do the data support the theoretical arguments that are generated? Is the theoretical analysis incisive? For example, does it demonstrate connections between different conceptual ideas that are developed out of the data? The crucial question is not whether or not the findings can be generalized to a wider universe, but how well the researcher generates theory out of the findings (Mitchell 1983; Yin 1984). Such a view places case study research firmly in the inductive tradition of the relationship between theory and research. However, a case study design is not necessarily associated with an inductive approach, as can be seen in the research by Whittington (1989) referred to in Chapter 2. Thus, case studies can be associated with both theory generation and theory testing. Moreover, case study researchers vary in their approach to both theory generation and theory testing. Eisenhardt's (1989) article on case studies has been highly influential in promoting a view of case-based theory-building that relies on strategic sampling of cases from which generalizations can be made. She recommends that researchers avoid getting too involved in the particularities of individual cases, because this will lead them to develop overly complex theory. Other researchers see case studies as a means of refining or refuting existing theories, rather than building entirely new explanatory frameworks (Jack and Kholief 2007).

It may be that it is only at a late stage in the research process that the nature and significance of the case becomes apparent. An example of this phenomenon is provided by Buchanan's (2012) account of his work with a team of researchers on the implementation of strategic change in six hospitals and five primary care organizations within the UK's NHS. This was a multiple-case study design (see next section and the discussion of comparative design later in the chapter). Each case focused upon an area of activity which exhibited change. Buchanan was mainly involved in research on one of the hospitals (referred to as Grange) which had significantly improved its prostate cancer services. He found that responsibility for the changes had been widely distributed and varied over the change process itself. When compared to other hospitals that were included in the research, Grange and its cancer care specialty in particular emerged as a case study of 'distributed leadership', as it is referred to in the literature (e.g. Gronn 2011), though they use the term 'distributed change leadership'. However, Buchanan and his co-researchers had not set out to conduct a case study of distributed change leadership at this hospital. That it was a case study of distributed change leadership emerged only after the data had been collected and analysed.

More than one case

Case study research is not confined to the study of a single case. Multiple-case study designs have become increasingly common in business research. They are extensions of the case study design. The multiple-case study design is considered in the section on comparative design because multiple-case studies are largely undertaken for the purpose of comparing the cases that are included. As such, they allow the researcher to compare and contrast the findings deriving from each of the cases. This in turn encourages researchers to consider what is unique and what is common across cases, and frequently promotes theoretical reflection on the findings.

It might be asked what the difference is between a multiple-case study involving several cases and a cross-sectional design. After all, if an investigation involved, say, eight cases, it could be viewed as either a multiple-case study involving several cases or as a cross-sectional design. A simple rule of thumb is to ask: what is the focus? If the focus is on the cases and their unique contexts, it is a multiple-case study and as such is an extension of the case study approach; if the emphasis is on producing general findings, with little regard for the unique contexts of each of the eight cases, it is better viewed as a cross-sectional design. In other words, with a multiple-case study design, the emphasis is on the individual cases; with a cross-sectional design, it is on the sample of cases.

Longitudinal research and the case study

Case study research frequently includes a longitudinal element. The researcher is often a participant of an organization for many months or years. Alternatively, he or she may conduct interviews with individuals over a lengthy period. Moreover, the researcher may be able to inject an additional longitudinal element by analysing archival information and by retrospective interviewing. Research in focus 3.16 provides an illustration of longitudinal case study research. A further example of longitudinal research is given in Research in focus 3.17. This study relies on secondary, large-scale social survey data that researchers are able to access.

Another way in which a longitudinal element occurs is when a case that has been studied is returned to at a later stage. An interesting instance of this is Burawoy's (1979) study of a factory in Chicago, which he claims was the same one as was originally studied by Roy in the 1950s. This is a somewhat loose connection, however, as the theoretical focus adopted by the two researchers was markedly different, although their research methods, based on participant observation, were quite similar. Generally speaking, it is difficult for the researcher to establish how far change over the two time periods is the result of real differences relating to the phenomena that they are trying to observe, or the result of other factors, such as different people in the organization, different ownership of the company between the two time periods, and the possible influence of the initial study itself.

3.17 RESEARCH IN FOCUS
A longitudinal panel study of older workers' pay

Smeaton and White (2017) conducted a longitudinal panel study of the wages and earnings of older workers in Britain (aged 45–60) during the period from 1990 to 2006. The motivation for the study arose from wanting to understand how increased competitive and financial pressures associated with globalization and with organizational and technological changes were having differential effects on older workers, in comparison with younger employees. The researchers' goal was to explore whether the relationship between employees and employers is being altered by changes in distribution of financial rewards over the working life. Specifically, they hypothesized that structural changes were likely to have had a detrimental effect on the pay of older workers, who historically had tended to benefit from more favourable financial treatment relative to younger employees. The researchers also incorporated a gender element into their study of these changes. To test their hypotheses, the researchers used data from the British Household Panel Survey, a large UK official data source (see Chapter 14 for more on secondary data analysis). The researchers analysed structured interview data drawn from a random stratified sample of 9912 individuals aged between 20 and 60 from 5538 UK households. The respondents who formed part of the panel study were interviewed annually over a period of 16 years. The research provided strong confirmation for the hypothesis that wages and earnings for British older workers have declined (by approximately 20 per cent) relative to those of younger workers in this time period. Older male employees have fared worse than older female workers, which is consistent with the researchers' hypothesis and explained by the emphasis among employers on overall cost reduction, since male workers in UK benefited from higher pay relative to women at the start of the 1990s.

Interestingly, the researchers note that they were unable to extend their longitudinal study beyond 2006 because the British Household Panel survey was replaced by the Understanding Society longitudinal survey 'with many changes in questioning, and a decline in response rate' (Smeaton and White 2017: 4). This meant that comparisons over time could no longer be made accurately. This was unfortunate given that the end date of the longitudinal period of study was just prior to a major global recession in 2007/8, which is likely to have had a significant effect on wages and earnings.

Comparative design

It is worth distinguishing one further kind of research design: comparative design. Put simply, this design entails the study using more or less identical methods on two or more contrasting cases. It embodies the logic of comparison, in that it implies that we can understand social phenomena better when they are compared in relation to two or more meaningfully contrasting cases or situations. The comparative design may be realized in the context of either quantitative or qualitative research. Within a comparative research design there are at least two cases (which may be organizations, nations, people, etc.) and data are collected from each, usually within a cross-sectional format.

One of the more obvious forms of such research is in cross-cultural or cross-national research (see Key concept 3.18). In a useful definition, Hantrais (1996) has suggested that such research occurs when individuals or teams set out to examine particular issues or phenomena in two or more countries with the express intention of comparing their manifestations in different socio-cultural settings (institutions, customs, traditions, value systems, lifestyles, language, thought patterns), using the same research instruments either to carry out secondary analysis of national data or to conduct new empirical work. The aim may be to seek explanations for similarities and differences or to gain a greater awareness and a deeper understanding of social reality in different national contexts.

Cross-cultural research in business and management tends to presuppose that culture is a major explanatory variable that exerts profound influence on organizational behaviour. In business research, there have been numerous attempts to assess whether management theories and practices apply to other, particularly non-Western, cultural contexts. There has also been mounting criticism of universalist, colonizing tendencies in business research that are based predominantly on unacknowledged Anglo-Saxon values. These pressures have led to greater interest in cross-cultural and postcolonial research. Within this overall category, however, there are some important distinctions. International management research concerns itself with how and why companies

3.18 KEY CONCEPT
What is cross-cultural and international research?

As its name implies, cross-cultural research entails the collection and/or analysis of data from two or more nations. There are a number of possible models for the conduct of cross-cultural research.

1. A researcher, perhaps in conjunction with a research team, collects data in a number of countries. Hofstede's (1984) research on the cultural differences between IBM workers in different countries (discussed in Chapter 2) is an illustration of this model, in that he took comparable samples of IBM employees from all hierarchical levels, allowing for a similar representation of gender and age, in 66 national subsidiaries of the company. More than 40 countries were eventually compared using this method.

2. A central organization coordinates a portion of the research work of national organizations or groups. An example is the Global Disney Audiences Project (Wasko et al. 2001), whereby a research group in the USA recruited researchers in a variety of countries who were interested in the ways Disney products are viewed, and then coordinated the ways questions were asked in the research. Each nation's research groups were responsible for sampling and other aspects of the interview process.

3. Secondary analysis is carried out using data that are comparable, but where the coordination of their collection is limited or non-existent. This kind of cross-cultural analysis might occur if researchers seek to ask survey questions in their own country that have been asked in another country. The ensuing data may then be analysed cross-culturally. A further form of this model is through the secondary analysis of officially collected data, such as unemployment statistics. However, this kind of cross-cultural research makes it particularly important to be sure about the accuracy of data, which will probably have been produced by several different agencies, in providing a suitable basis for cross-cultural comparison. For example, Roy et al. (2001) suggest that business researchers have tended to avoid relying on secondary data about China because of concerns about the reliability and representativeness of government sources. Research units associated with local authorities may overstate certain factors to give the impression that the economy is doing better than it really is, statistical approaches and classification schemes may differ from one province to another, and data may have been censored at certain points in time or even lost. Business researchers must therefore be cautious in their use of secondary data for the purpose of cross-cultural analysis.

4. Teams of researchers in participating nations are recruited by a person or body that coordinates the programme. Each researcher or group of researchers has the responsibility of conducting the investigation in his, her, or their own country. The work is coordinated in order to ensure comparability of research questions, survey questions, and procedures for administering the research instruments. This model differs from (2) above in that it usually entails a specific focus on certain research questions. An article by Terence Jackson (2001) provides an example of this model: Jackson relied on academic associates to collect data in their respective countries using the questionnaire instrument he had designed for this purpose (see Research in focus 8.3).

internationalize; it may focus on a specific country, or make cross-cultural comparisons between several countries. Usunier (1998) distinguishes between:

- *cross-cultural approaches*—which compare national management systems and local business customs in various countries; and

- *intercultural approaches*—which focus on the study of interaction between people and organizations with different national/cultural backgrounds.

Comparative research should not be treated as solely concerned with comparisons between nations. The logic of comparison can be applied to a variety of situations to inform a number of levels of analysis. For example, Hofstede's (1984) research on cultural differences has informed a generation of studies that have explored cultural differences in organizations other than IBM, and the framework has also been applied to understanding specific organizational behaviours, such as ethical decision-making.

Cross-cultural research is not without problems: for example, gaining and managing the funding for such research (see Key concept 3.18); ensuring, when existing data such as official statistics or survey evidence are submitted to a secondary analysis, that the data are comparable in terms of categories and data collection methods; and ensuring, when new data are being collected, that the need to translate data collection instruments (for example, interview schedules) into another language does not undermine genuine comparability. This raises the further difficulty that even when translation is carried out competently, there is still the potential problem of an insensitivity to specific national and cultural contexts. On the other hand, cross-cultural research helps to reduce the risk of failing to appreciate that social science findings are often, if not invariably, culturally specific. Cross-cultural research also creates particular issues in achieving equivalence—between the samples, variables, and methods that are used (McDonald 2000). For example, in many cases nationality is used as a surrogate for culture; differences may thus be attributed to culture even if they could be more readily attributed to national situation. Equally, people inhabiting a country under the same government may belong to quite different cultures that reflect historical or religious affiliations. Further issues are raised by language differences, which can cause translation problems. Adler (1983) claims that many comparative cross-cultural studies in business and management do not adequately acknowledge these distinctions.

In terms of issues of reliability, validity, replicability, and generalizability, the comparative study is no different from the cross-sectional design. The comparative design is essentially two or more cross-sectional studies carried out at more or less the same point in time.

The comparative design can also be applied in relation to a qualitative research strategy. When this occurs, it takes the form of a multiple-case study (see Research in focus 3.19). Essentially, a multiple-case study occurs whenever the number of cases examined exceeds one. In business research this is a popular research design that usually takes two or more organizations as cases for comparison, but occasionally a number of people are used as cases. For example, Marshall (1984) adopts a multiple-case study approach in her study of women managers; she retains a focus on intensive examination of each case, but there is qualitative comparison of each woman manager's situation with the others. The main argument in favour of the multiple-case study is that it improves theory-building. By comparing two or more cases, the researcher is in a better position to establish the circumstances in which a theory will or will not hold (Yin 1984; Eisenhardt 1989). Moreover, the comparison may itself suggest concepts that are relevant to an emerging theory.

Research in focus 3.19 describes one approach to selecting cases for a multiple-case study that involved researchers in each country selecting two workplaces from retail and financial service sectors. Another example is found in the study of TQM by Edwards et al. (1998), where the researchers selected two case studies from each of the three main sectors of the UK economy: private services, public sector, and manufacturing. Their selection of two cases in each sector, rather than just one, was intended to allow for variation; the limitation to two cases, rather than three, was due to time and resource constraints. To identify their cases the researchers searched press reports and listings of leading quality institutes such as the National Society for Quality through Teamwork. However, they were also keen to avoid companies that had a high profile as 'success stories', instead choosing cases that 'had made significant moves' in quality management but 'were not among the leading edge examples' (1998: 454). From this they identified 25 potential cases, and, on the basis of interviews with quality or human resources managers in each one, narrowed their sample down to just six. With a case selection approach such as this, the findings that are common to the firms can be just as interesting and important as those that differentiate them.

However, not all writers are convinced about the merits of multiple-case study research. Dyer and Wilkins (1991), for example, argue that a multiple-case study approach tends to mean that the researcher pays less attention to the specific context and more to the ways in which the cases can be contrasted. Moreover, the need to forge comparisons tends to mean that the researcher has to develop an explicit focus at the outset, whereas it may be advantageous to adopt a more open-ended approach in many instances. These concerns about retaining contextual insight and a rather more unstructured research approach are very much associated with the goals of the qualitative research strategy (see Chapter 17).

The key to the comparative design is its ability to allow the distinguishing characteristics of two or more cases to act as a springboard for theoretical reflections about contrasting findings. It is something of a hybrid, in that in quantitative research it is frequently an extension of a cross-sectional design and in qualitative research it is frequently an extension of a case study design. It even exhibits certain features that are similar to experiments and quasi-experiments, which also rely on the capacity to forge a comparison.

3.19 RESEARCH IN FOCUS
A comparative analysis panel study of female employment

Collins and Wickham (2004) used data from 'Servemploi', which is a study of women's employment and career prospects in the information society. The project had eight European Union partners, comprising members of universities or research institutes in Ireland, Denmark, Germany, Italy, Spain, Sweden, and Belgium. The main objective of the study was 'to examine the implications for women workers of technical and organizational changes in the retail and financial services sectors' (2004: 36). Each national team studied four workplaces, two in each sector, and each case involved workplace observation and interviews with managers and employees.

As well as being comparative, the study was also longitudinal, as it involved a two-year panel study of women based on semi-structured interviews. As the researchers explain: 'using a variety of sources, in particular, contacts in the trade unions, we located four women working in each sector (but not in the case study companies) who would be prepared to participate in the study' (2004: 36). The reason for keeping the sample for the panel study separate from the comparative cases was because they wanted to follow the women as they moved between workplaces, so it made sense to focus on individuals rather than on workplaces. This generated a total of 500 interviews.

Level of analysis

A further consideration for business researchers that applies to the research designs covered in this chapter relates to the concept of level: in other words, what is the primary unit of measurement and analysis? Hence, research might focus on

- *individuals*, for example studies that focus on specific kinds of individuals such as managers or shopfloor employees;

- *groups*, as in research that considers certain types of groupings—for example, human resources departments or boards of directors;

- *organizations*—in addition to studies that focus on companies, this would include surveys, such as WERS (see Research in focus 3.13), that treat the workplace as the principal unit of analysis;

- *societies*—the main focus of this kind of analysis would be on the national, political, social, environmental, and economic contexts in which business organizations are located.

However, some research designs draw on samples that combine different levels of analysis—for example, organizations and departments within organizations. This begs the question as to whether it is possible to combine data from different levels to produce a meaningful analysis. The complexity of organizational types can make the issue of level particularly difficult to determine.

Rousseau (1985) suggests that in order to avoid misinterpretation, it is important to make explicit the problems of using data derived from one level to represent something at another level. For example, processes of individual and organizational learning may be constructed quite differently at different levels. If researchers make inferences about organizational learning on the basis of data about individuals, they are at risk of making a cross-level misattribution. Since the phenomenon of learning is an essentially human characteristic, as organizations do not behave but people do, this leads to the attribution of human characteristics to a higher-level system. Misattribution can also occur when metaphors are used to interpret organizational behaviour. It is, therefore, good practice to identify and make clear in your research design the level of analysis that is being used and then to switch to another level only after having made this clear (Rousseau 1985).

Another illustration of mixed-level research cited by Rousseau (1985) is found in the area of leadership studies. The 'average leadership style' approach assumes that leaders display the same behavioural style toward all subordinates. Research therefore relies on eliciting subordinate perceptions of the leader, which are averaged and treated as group-level characteristics. In contrast, the 'vertical dyadic linkage' model assumes that a leader's style may be different with each subordinate, thereby treating leadership as an individual-level phenomenon rather than as a group one. Each model thus conceptualizes leadership at a different level.

Bringing research strategy and research design together

Finally, we can bring together the two research strategies covered in Chapter 2 with the research designs outlined in this chapter. Table 3.1 shows the typical form associated with each combination of research strategy and research design and a number of examples that either have been encountered so far or will be covered in later chapters. Table 3.1 refers also to research methods that will be encountered in later chapters but that have not been referred to so far. The Glossary at the end of this book will enable quick reference to terms that are not yet familiar to you.

The distinctions that we make here are not always perfect. In particular, in some qualitative and quantitative

TABLE 3.1
Research strategy and research design

Research design	Research strategy	
	Quantitative	Qualitative
Experimental	*Typical form:* most researchers using an experimental design employ quantitative comparisons between experimental and control groups with regard to the dependent variable. See, for example, the study of CEO pay by Krause et al. (2014) (Research in focus 3.6).	*No typical form;* however, the Hawthorne experiments (Chapter 2 and Research in focus 3.7) provide an example of experimental research design that gradually moved away from the 'test room method' towards use of qualitative methods.
Cross-sectional	*Typical form:* social survey research or structured observation on a sample at a single point in time. See, for example, the Aston studies of organizational size, technology, and structure (Chapter 3 and Research in focus 3.5); Parboteeah et al.'s (2009) study of the influence of religious values on work obligation norms (Research in focus 2.2); and Berg and Frost's (2005) telephone survey of low-skill, low-wage workers (Research in focus 10.3). This can also include content analysis on a sample of documents such as in Harris's (2001) study of courage (see Research in focus 13.6).	*Typical form:* qualitative interviews or **focus groups** at a single point in time. See, for example, Scase and Goffee's (1989) research into managers in large UK organizations (Research in focus 3.14); or Blackburn and Stokes's (2000) study of small business owner-managers (Research in focus 21.3). Can also be based upon **qualitative content analysis** of a set of documents relating to a single event or a specific period in time.
Longitudinal	*Typical form:* social survey research on a sample on more than one occasion, as in the Study of Australian Leadership (SAL) (Research in focus 3.13); or may involve content analysis of documents relating to different time periods.	*Typical form:* ethnographic research over a long period, qualitative interviewing on more than one occasion, or qualitative content analysis of documents relating to different time periods. Such research warrants being dubbed longitudinal when there is an effort to map change, as in Pettigrew's (1985) study of ICI (Research in focus 3.16).
Case study	*Typical form:* social survey research on a single case with a view to revealing important features about its nature. An example is Hofstede's study of cultural differences based on a survey study of a large multinational business organization (discussed in Chapter 2).	*Typical form:* the intensive study, by ethnography or qualitative interviewing, of a single case, which may be an organization—such as Tracy et al.'s (2006) study of organizational bullying (Research in focus 2.3); a group of employees within an organization—as in Perlow's (1997) study of software engineers in a high-tech organization (discussed in Chapter 27); or an individual—as in Marshall's (1995) study of women managers (Key concept 17.3).
Comparative	*Typical form:* social survey research in which there is a direct comparison between two or more cases, including cross-cultural research.	*Typical form:* ethnographic or qualitative interview research on two or more cases where some comparison is sought between them, as in Hyde et al.'s (2006) evaluation study of role redesign in the NHS (Research in focus 3.10); and Collins and Wickham's (2004) panel study of patterns of female employment across Europe (Research in focus 3.19).

research it is not obvious whether a study is an example of a longitudinal design or a case study design. Life history studies, research that concentrates on a specific issue over time, and ethnography, in which the researcher charts change in a single case, are examples of studies that cross the two types. Such studies are perhaps better conceptualized as longitudinal case studies rather than as belonging to one category of research design or another. A further point to note is that Table 3.1 shows no 'typical form' in the cell representing qualitative research strategy with experimental research design. Qualitative research in the context of true experiments is very unusual. However, as noted in the table, the Hawthorne studies (Roethlisberger and Dickson 1939) provide an interesting example of the way that a quasi-experimental research design can change over time. What you will also notice as you encounter many of the examples in this book is that business research designs often use a combination of quantitative and qualitative methods, so the distinction between quantitative and qualitative research strategies that is suggested in Table 3.1 is rarely as clear as this suggests. In Chapters 26 and 27 of the book we will consider the implications of this and discuss research that combines quantitative and qualitative methods, which is referred to as mixed methods research.

KEY POINTS

- A research method is a technique for collecting data, while a research design is a framework for generating research evidence according to certain quality criteria.

- It is important to become familiar with the criteria that are commonly used to evaluate research: reliability; validity and types of validity (measurement, internal, external, ecological); and replicability.

- There are five major research designs covered in this book (experimental, cross-sectional, longitudinal, case study, and comparative).

- True experimental business research is rare but important to understand, as it is the yardstick against which other research designs are often measured.

- Although the case study is often thought to be a single type of research design, it in fact has several forms. It is also important to be aware of the key issues concerned with the nature of case study evidence in relation to issues such as external validity (generalizability).

- Comparative, including cross-cultural, research is an important way of testing the generalizability of organizational theories.

QUESTIONS FOR REVIEW

- What are the main differences between the following: a research method; a research strategy; and a research design?

Quality criteria in business research

- What are the differences between reliability and validity and why are these important criteria for the evaluation of business research?

- Outline the meaning of each of the following: measurement validity; internal validity; external validity; and ecological validity.

- Why have some qualitative researchers sought to devise alternative criteria besides reliability and validity when assessing the quality of investigations?

- What is the 'experimenter effect' and how might it contribute towards bias?

- What is 'social desirability bias' and how might its effects be reduced?

Research designs

- What are the main research designs that have been outlined in this chapter?
- Why is level of analysis a particular consideration in business research?

Experimental design

- 'The main importance of the experimental design for the business researcher is that it represents a model of how to infer causal connections between variables.' Discuss.
- Following on from the last question, if experimental design is so useful and important, why is it not used more in business research?
- What is a quasi-experiment?

Cross-sectional design

- What is meant by a cross-sectional research design?
- In what ways does the social survey exemplify the cross-sectional research design?
- Assess the degree to which the survey researcher can achieve internally valid findings.
- To what extent is the survey design exclusive to quantitative research?

Longitudinal design

- Why might a longitudinal research design be superior to a cross-sectional one?
- What are the main differences between panel and cohort designs in longitudinal research?

Case study design

- What is a case study?
- Is case study research exclusive to qualitative research?
- What are some of the principles by which cases might be selected?

Comparative design

- What are the chief strengths of a comparative research design?
- Why might comparative research yield important insights?

ONLINE RESOURCES
www.oup.com/uk/brm5e/

Visit the Interactive Research Guide that accompanies this book to complete an exercise about research designs.

PLANNING A RESEARCH PROJECT AND DEVELOPING RESEARCH QUESTIONS

CHAPTER OUTLINE

The goal of this chapter is to advise students on the issues that they need to consider when preparing a dissertation based on a research project. Many business students are required to produce a dissertation as part of their degrees. As well as helping students to understand research methods, this book provides specific advice on the process of doing and writing up research for a dissertation. The chapter provides advice on issues including:

- planning and time management;
- how to generate research questions;
- how to write a research proposal;
- expectations and requirements of a good dissertation.

Introduction

This chapter and the remaining chapters in Part One of the book provide advice for readers who might be carrying out a research project of their own. The chapters that follow in Parts Two, Three, and Four of this book then provide more detailed information about the methods available to you and how to implement them. Many business students are expected to write a dissertation as part of their degree programme. Sometimes the terms 'thesis' or 'research report' are used, but for the sake of brevity we will use the term 'dissertation' in this book. The dissertation may be based entirely on what is referred to as 'desk research'—developing a research question and then searching and reviewing existing literature that reports the findings of research that has already been done. This is the focus of Chapter 5, which explains how to conduct a literature review, a necessary component of all dissertations. Even in a dissertation project based in desk research it is important to understand how research methods are used, in order to be able to make an informed evaluation of existing research. However, many, if not most, dissertations are based on an original empirical research project. A student research project is expected to be on a smaller scale than would be expected for a published article. It involves the student collecting and analysing some data that they have collected, or conducting a secondary analysis of existing data. Whether a dissertation involves only desk research or includes a small-scale empirical research project, there are issues of planning and of developing research questions that are common to both.

Getting to know what is expected of you by your university

Your university will have specific requirements about what your dissertation should comprise and how it should be presented.

The advice here is simple: *follow the requirements, instructions, and information you are given*. If anything in this book conflicts with your university's guidelines and requirements, ignore this book! We very much hope this is not something that will occur very much, but if it does, keep to the guidelines your lecturer gives you.

Thinking about your research area

The chances are that you will be asked to start thinking about what you want to do research on well before you are due to start work on your dissertation. It is worth allowing a good deal of time for this. As you are doing various modules, begin to think about whether there are any topics that interest you and that might provide you with a researchable area. This may at times feel like a rather unproductive process in which a number of false starts or changes of direction are made. However, taking the time to explore different avenues early, at the point of problem identification, can prevent difficulties at a much later stage.

STUDENT EXPERIENCE
The importance of starting early

For Lisa, one of the main lessons she learned from her experience of doing a research project was the importance of starting early. 'Time management is definitely a big thing with your dissertation. Starting it early, starting the reading early as well, because the paper trail can take for ages to trace back authors and what they've written in the past. It's really important to start early, I think.' Karen expressed similar views: 'I started my dissertation very early on. A lot of people didn't start it until they got back to University in September/October time, whereas I'd already started mine in January. I actually finished it a bit early because it was due in at the beginning of May and I finished it for the beginning of April.'

These views were also confirmed by the supervisors we surveyed.

STUDENT EXPERIENCE
Why do a research project?

For some students, doing a dissertation based research project is an optional part of their degree programme. In such cases, the decision about whether or not to do research becomes more personal. For Chris, doing a research project was an opportunity 'to find things out from the horse's mouth' by investigating how things worked in the 'real world' after three years of studying theories of business and management.

> I thought it would be interesting to actually find out what people really think about a subject. When you read these textbooks you read theories, you know, papers, and you get told things in lectures or newspapers or whatever and you think 'Right, great. That's interesting and I'm sure that must be right.' I mean sometimes I used to question. 'Well, I don't agree with that.' And I thought 'Well, now I've got this really good opportunity to find out things in an organization.'

For Amrit, choice of research question was

> quite a personal decision based on experiences of people that were close to me. People I've worked with before, friends, family friends, who I know have experienced feelings of sometimes loneliness, or anxiety, or stress and because it's so common and because, you know, after university much of our life is dedicated to work, you know, you can't help but feel for them, they feel trapped, and they kind of need that person to go to. I really wanted to explore why, firstly, why what causes them to feel like this, is it the nature of the work, is it a personal trait? And then secondly, what's being done to deal with it, so does the organization they work in help? Are there ways that they can help themselves, feel more comfortable in themselves, you know? So it was a lot of unanswered questions for me, and I saw a big crossover between mental health and working.

Karen explained that doing her research on something that she was genuinely interested in was crucial in maintaining her enthusiasm for the project.

> My manager said 'Just make sure that it's something you're interested in, because, if it isn't, then you're not going to get through it and you're going to get disheartened.' If it is something you're interested in, you can really enjoy doing the research and it becomes really good for you. You feel like you're really getting something out of it.

These views were confirmed by one of the supervisors we questioned, who said: 'A piece of research can be a talking point for a job interview, as it is something the student has done!' Another commented: 'By the end of the research project, students have an awareness of the need for flexible thinking and the ability to adapt in order to make progress.'

Using your supervisor

Most universities that require a dissertation, or a similar component, allocate each student with a supervisor whose role is to advise and guide the student in their project. It is important for students to understand the role of a supervisor and what can be expected of them. Our advice here is simple: use your supervisor to the fullest extent that you are allowed, and follow the guidance you are given by them. Your supervisor will almost certainly be someone who is experienced in research and they will be able to give you help and feedback at each stages of the process. If your supervisor is critical of your research questions, your interview schedule, drafts of your dissertation, or whatever, try to respond positively. Follow the suggestions that they provide, since critical feedback will invariably be accompanied by suggestions for how to improve. Supervisors regularly have to go through the same process themselves when they submit an article to a peer-refereed journal, apply for a research grant, or give a conference paper. This is your opportunity to address deficiencies in your work before it is formally examined.

Students who get stuck at the start of their dissertations or who get behind with their work sometimes respond to the situation by avoiding their supervisors. They can then get caught up in a vicious circle that results in their work being neglected and perhaps rushed at the end. Try to avoid this by confronting the fact that you are experiencing difficulties and seek out your supervisor for advice.

STUDENT EXPERIENCE
Maintaining a good working relationship with your supervisor

Expectations concerning the frequency and format of meetings between students and supervisors can vary. Of the supervisors we contacted, the majority met students individually, but some hold meetings with groups of students so that common issues could be shared. Face-to-face meetings are often complemented by email communication, Skype and telephone calls, or online discussion groups.

Amrit recalled his first meeting with his supervisor:

> She must've thought 'this guy knows absolutely nothing' because I literally went in and said 'I want to study mental health. It's something that has been bothering me for a while and I want to explore it but I just don't know how.' From that moment onwards, she was kind of like 'you need to give me something to work with here.' To be honest with you, I think I am incredibly, incredibly lucky to have someone of her ability because it's not only the skill that she brought in terms of knowing what I wanted to explore without me being able to say it myself but it was the way she articulated things and the way she spoke to me. After that, she had a very busy schedule so it was quite difficult to have face-to-face meetings with her, so we would do it via Skype a lot of the time. I think we were allowed four or five meetings with our supervisor. In fact, I think I got pretty much everything I need with one interview to spare which just goes to show how independent I became. I began to dictate the project myself. Considering I was so clueless at the start, the fact I managed to develop it into something was great. She gave me that freedom; she gave me a guideline and then she was like, 'you choose what you do with that just make sure it stays relevant.' I don't think I could've asked for a better supervisor in that respect.

Karen said 'my supervisor was really good for me, because he wasn't very prescriptive about what to do and what not to do. He was really good in that sense for me. He never said that that's wrong or that's right. He just used to ask questions and guide me.' Karen enjoyed the independence afforded to her by her supervisor but felt this would not have suited all students equally.

> I think that, if a supervisor thinks you are a bit lost, that's when they come in and they say, 'Right, well let me have a look at it,' or something like that, because they think you need guidance. But the good thing about him was that he recognized I had my own ideas. The reason I feel so good about my dissertation is because it is all my work and my supervisor hasn't put anything into it.

A supervisor whom we spoke to also talked about the importance of good working relationships between supervisors and students. 'Doing research and writing a thesis are things that you learn by doing. Supervision at higher levels therefore becomes much more guiding and discussing ideas (working *with* the student) rather than suggesting how to do something (working *for* the student).' Students can find these expectations disconcerting at first, but in the long run they tend to pay off. When asked what makes a successful supervision meeting, one supervisor replied: 'the moment when you know the student sparks off a new insight for you … or vice versa'. This last comment highlights the reciprocal nature of learning in research supervision relationships.

Managing time and resources

All research is constrained by time and resources. There is no point in working on research questions and plans that cannot be seen through because of time pressure or cost. Two points are relevant here.

1. Work out a timetable—preferably in conjunction with your supervisor—detailing the different stages of your research (including the review of the literature, discussed in Chapter 5, and writing up, covered in Chapter 7). This is particularly important if you are a part-time student combining your studies with other commitments. The timetable should specify the different stages and dates when you plan to start and finish specific tasks. Some stages of the research are likely to be ongoing—for example, searching the literature for new references—but that should not prove an obstacle to developing a timetable.

2. Find out what, if any, resources are available to carry out your research. For example, will you receive help from your university with such things as travel costs, printing or software? Will your university be able to loan you hardware such as digital audio recorders so that you can record interviews to enable transcription? Has it got the software you need, such as SPSS or a qualitative data analysis package such as NVivo? Alternatively, will you be able to contact potential participants by email and either attach the questionnaire to the email or provide a URL link to a web-based questionnaire (see Chapter 11)? This kind of information will help you to establish how far your research design and methods are financially feasible and practical.

STUDENT EXPERIENCE
Finding time to do a research project

For many students, doing a research project is combined with work and family demands. Such students develop ways of managing their time, but this can be difficult. For example, women MBA students interviewed by Bell described how they gave up social activities and family time in order to find time to work on their dissertation at weekends or during holidays. They also highlighted the importance of partners and other family members in helping to providing emotional and practical support in doing their research project. One student who was working full-time and had two young children said:

> My son is growing up really quickly and, yes, people can take him off so I can work on my MBA dissertation, but I'm at work all week and I actually quite like seeing him at the weekend. I'm just conscious that, as the gap between the MBA course and the project gets longer, the project gets harder because you can't remember anything that you've done.

(Bell 2004: 69–70)

Students who don't fully take these time pressures into account can find themselves unable to meet the deadlines for submitting the dissertation. The important thing is to be realistic and proactive in planning your research project and to communicate with your supervisor if you fall behind so that they can help you, for example by supporting you in applying for an extension.

TIPS AND SKILLS
Making a Gantt chart for your research project

One way to keep track of your research project is by using a Gantt chart. The horizontal axis of the chart represents the total time span of the project divided into units such as weeks or months. The vertical axis represents the tasks involved in the project. An example is provided in Figure 4.1. Shaded squares on the graph represent the amount of time you expect to spend on each task. The filled-in squares may overlap, for example to indicate that you intend to continue to review the literature at the same time as collecting data. However, one of the limitations of Gantt charts is that they do not indicate task dependencies, so you cannot tell, for example, how falling behind with one task will affect the timing of others. In a student research project, you will almost certainly be working to a fixed deadline for submitting your dissertation, so falling behind with your literature review will necessarily reduce the amount of time that you have to devote to later stages such as data analysis. Gantt charts also encourage the research process to be seen as linear and sequential. This is less appropriate in **qualitative research** projects, where many tasks are done **iteratively** or repeatedly.

FIGURE 4.1

An example of a Gantt chart for a student research project

	Sept.	Oct.	Nov.	Dec.	Jan.	Feb.	Mar.	Apr.
Identify research area	■							
Formulate research questions		■						
Formulate research strategy and research design, and select methods		■	■					
Write research proposal			15th					
Negotiate access			■					
Literature review			■	■	■			
Data collection				■	■			
Data analysis					■	■		
Write first draft						■	■	
Write second draft							■	
Write final draft								■
Dissertation due								21st

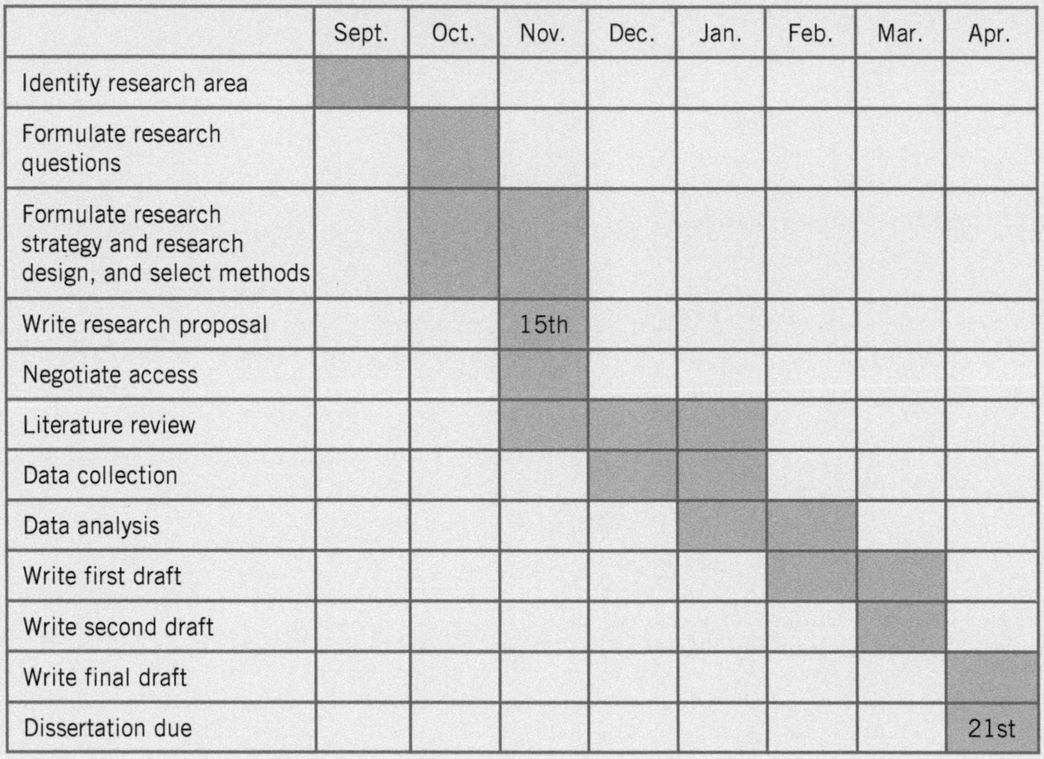

Developing suitable research questions

Research questions enable you to focus on what is it about your area of interest that you want to know. Many students want to do research into current challenges faced by businesses or on business issues that are of personal interest to them. This is not a bad thing at all and, as we noted in Chapter 2, many academic researchers start from this point as well (see also Lofland and Lofland 1995: 11–14). However, most business research involves moving on from this to develop research questions. The specificity of the questions that are used to guide business research varies. The type of research questions asked will also depend on your research strategy (see Chapter 2), i.e. the ontological assumptions you make about the nature of social phenomena as well as your epistemological assumptions about how the social world should be studied. As we will go on to explain in Chapter 17, qualitative research is more open-ended than quantitative research. Chapter 19 includes some notable studies that are driven by interest in a particular topic or type of organization rather than by clearly formulated research questions. However, very open-ended research is risky and can lead to the collection of too much data without a clear sense of what to observe or what to ask your interviewees. This can also lead to confusion about focus when it comes to writing up the research. Some qualitative researchers therefore advocate a more focused approach to their craft (e.g. Hammersley and Atkinson 1995: 24–9).

If you do not specify clear research questions, there is a risk that your research will be unfocused and you may therefore be unsure about what it is about or what you are collecting data for. So, unless your supervisor advises you to the contrary, we advise you to consider developing some research questions, even if they are less specific than the kind often found in quantitative research. Research questions will help to guide various aspects of your work:

- your literature search (see Chapter 5);
- decisions about the kind of research design to use (see Chapter 3);

- decisions about what data to collect and from whom;
- analysis of your data;
- writing-up of your data.

Marx (1997) suggests a wide range of sources of research questions (see Thinking deeply 4.1) and outlines the features that research questions should exhibit. Figure 4.2 summarizes the main steps in developing research questions.

We usually start out with a general research topic or phenomenon that interests us. It may derive from any of several sources.

- *Personal interest/experience.* As we pointed out in Chapter 2, Bryman's interests in theme parks could be traced back to a visit to Disney World in Orlando in 1991, while Bell's interest in 'Investors in People' stems from her involvement in managing the implementation of this quality standard in a UK National Health Service trust hospital. Harley's interest in work organization arose because of his working in routine jobs during his undergraduate studies.

4.1 THINKING DEEPLY
Marx's sources of research questions

Marx (1997) suggests the following possible sources of research questions:

- Intellectual puzzles and contradictions.
- The existing literature.
- Replication.
- Structures and functions. For example, if you point to a structure such as a type of organization, you can ask questions about the reasons why there are different types and the implications of the differences.
- Opposition. Marx identifies the sensation of feeling that a certain theoretical perspective or notable piece of work is misguided and exploring the reasons for your opposition.
- A social problem—but remember that this is just a source of a research question; you still have to identify a suitable empirical context where this problem can be studied in order to explore 'Gaps between official versions of reality and the facts on the ground' (Marx 1997: 113). An example here is Delbridge's (1998) ethnographic analysis of company rhetoric about Japanized work practices which is compared with how they operate in practice.
- The counter-intuitive: for example, when common sense seems to fly in the face of social scientific truths.
- Empirical examples that 'trigger amazement' (Marx 1997: 114). Marx gives, as examples, deviant cases and atypical events.
- New methods and theories. How might they be applied in new settings?
- New social and technical developments and social trends (Marx 1997: 114).
- Personal experience.
- Sponsors and teachers–but do not expect your teachers to provide you with detailed research questions.

FIGURE 4.2
Steps in selecting research questions

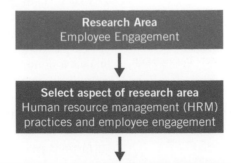

- *Theory*. Someone might be interested in testing an existing theory, such as contingency theories of organization structure (see Chapter 2).

- *Research literature*. Studies relating to a research area such as Japanization in British industry could be an example of a literature that might stimulate interest in the nature of shopfloor work in such a context. Sandberg and Alvesson (2011) note that spotting gaps in the literature is a common way of identifying research questions. This involves looking for overlooked or under-researched topics or identifying phenomena that have not been previously examined using a particular theory or perspective. In another work published in the same year, Alvesson and Sandberg (2011) also recommend development of research questions through what they call 'problematization'. This involves challenging the assumptions that are embedded in the literature. Such assumptions might be located within a root metaphor (Morgan 1997) or a paradigm (Burrell and Morgan 1979). Challenging them can result in the

development of alternative assumptions that can be used as a springboard to generate innovative research questions. However, as Alvesson and Sandberg recognize, 'gap spotting' is itself a creative process because gaps in the literature are often identified by arranging or positioning the literature in certain ways. Yet because such a process rarely involves challenges to assumptions, research questions generated in this way are rarely innovative and rarely likely to engender significant theoretical departures.

- *Puzzles*. For example, how are team and individual empowerment, both of which are topics in research on quality management, compatible?

- *New organizational developments*. Examples might include new developments in social media marketing or the role of corporate social responsibility in responding to climate change.

- *Organizational problems*. An example might be how to manage mental health issues at work or how to develop and manage global supply chains.

As these types of source suggest, in research we often start out with a general research topic that has to be narrowed down so that we can develop a tighter focus out of which research questions can be developed. We can depict the process of generating research questions as a series of steps, as suggested in Figure 4.2. The series of stages is meant to suggest that, when developing research questions, the researcher is involved in a process of progressive focusing down, so that we move from a general research area to specific research questions. In making this movement, it is important to remember several points.

- A research question ends with a question mark. If you are able to articulate what you are interested in as a question, this is generally a positive indication that you are developing a clearer focus in what you are studying.

- We cannot answer all the research questions that occur to us. This is not just because of time and cost constraints. It is also because research questions need to be connected to existing research in a way which builds on, or challenges, what other researchers have already found.

- We therefore have to select from the possible research questions that we arrive at.

- In making our selection, we may end up with two or three research questions that are logically and conceptually related to one another. If these questions are not related, our research will probably lack focus. Thus, in the example in Figure 4.2, the selected research questions relating to employee engagement are closely connected.

The section below on 'Criteria for evaluating research questions' provides suggestions about the considerations that should be taken into account when developing your research questions.

Research in focus 4.2 describes some considerations that went into Watson's (1994*a*, *b*) exploration of management at ZTC Ryland, a UK-based telecommunications firm. Watson (1994*a*, *b*) has also provided a useful account of the process of 'crafting research', as he puts it. Before embarking on the task of research design and choice of research methods, it is a good idea to ask yourself a series of questions about your research and the findings that you hope to produce. Crafting a research design relies on addressing a series of what, why, and how questions (see Figure 4.3), which eventually result in the production of a set of 'findings' or conclusions. Watson (1994*b*) sees management research as an intellectual craft that relies on the acquisition of a set of skills, which, when combined imaginatively, result in the production of findings.

Watson's figure illustrates how central research questions are to the overall research process and the way in which they are embedded in the many decisions that have to be made during it. In his own research, Watson found that his research questions were pushing him in the direction of needing to appreciate 'issues of language and meaning'. He goes on to say:

STUDENT EXPERIENCE
Finding a research area

Lucie's choice of research subject reflected her personal experience of having been exposed to entrepreneurial discourses while she was a student at university.

> As a student I was being exposed to kind of these enterprise courses. I was bombarded with messages like 'Join this course', and I was quite interested in enterprise, so I attended one of these courses as an undergraduate and that's how I became interested in it. Also, a lot of my friends are really interested in enterprise, and a lot of them kind of have started to try and run businesses while at university. So I was interested in what was provoking students to do this.

Lucie's choice of research area illustrates how practical considerations (see Chapter 2) can impact upon choice of research area, since Lucie already had social contact with the kinds of people who might become the focus of her research, in this case university students, and had already had contact with the research setting on which she was intending to base her study. Lucie was thus studying a social group of which she was a member—university students. This is interesting, because it raises particular considerations about the nature of the relationship between the researcher and research subjects, an issue that we will return to in Chapter 17.

4.2 RESEARCH IN FOCUS
Developing research questions

Watson (1994*b*) describes the process by which he developed his research questions for his **participant observation** study of ZTC Ryland, 'a plant of three thousand or so employees engaged in developing, making and selling telecommunications products' (Watson 1994*a*: 4). The company was involved in several change initiatives at the time and this made it very interesting to Watson. His initial aim was to understand how people doing managerial work 'shape' their own lives and identities in organizations (1994*b*). He writes that he 'sharpened' this general area of interest by reflecting on how the culture change management programmes and HRM practices that were being implemented affected managerial identity. In developing his interests into research questions, Watson was influenced by previous research which had been critical of existing knowledge in this area. In particular he notes that they recommended greater attention be paid to the terms managers use to reflect on their work; more emphasis be placed on explaining why managers engage in the forms of behaviour that have been uncovered; and more appreciation of the way in which managerial behaviour is embedded in organizational arrangements. This gave rise to Watson's research questions, which focused on the language that managers use in talking about their work.

This implies investigative techniques which take one close to individuals, which allow close attention to the way people use language and which enable the researcher to relate closely the individual to the context in which they work. The basic research design shaped to meet these criteria was one of participant observation within the management team of a single organization combined with detailed interviews with a cross-section of that group of managers.

(Watson 1994*b*: S82)

In other words, the way Watson's research questions were framed influenced both his research design (a **case study**) and his research methods (participant observation and **semi-structured interviewing**). Decisions about research questions are therefore crucial to how research is designed and to data collection. Some researchers advise that you do not decide on your research methods until you have established what your research questions are. However, other researchers prefer to use particular methods and therefore frame their research questions according to those preferences (Bryman 2007*b*).

FIGURE 4.3
A 'what, why, and how' framework for crafting research questions

What?	**Why?**
What puzzles/intrigues me? What do I want to know more about/understand better? What are my key research questions?	Why will this be of enough interest to others to be published as a thesis, book, paper, guide to practitioners or policy-makers? Can the research be justified as a 'contribution to knowledge'?
How—conceptually?	**How—practically?**
What models, concepts, and theories can I draw on/develop to answer my research questions? How can these be brought together into a basic conceptual framework to guide my investigation?	What investigative styles and techniques shall I use to apply my conceptual framework (both to gather material and analyse it)? How shall I gain and maintain access to information sources?

Source: Watson (1994*b*: S80). Reprinted with permission of Wiley Publishing.

A final point to make is that a research question is not the same as a hypothesis. A hypothesis is a specific type of research question. It is an informed speculation, which is set up to be tested, about the possible relationship between two or more variables. Hypotheses are not as common in quantitative research as is sometimes supposed and in qualitative research they are typically avoided, other than as speculations that arise in the course of fieldwork.

If you are still stuck about how to develop research questions (or indeed unclear about other aspects of your research), it is a good idea to look at research reported by other researchers—in journal articles, books, or past dissertations—to see how they have done this.

Criteria for evaluating research questions

Research questions for a dissertation or project should meet the following criteria.

- *Questions should be clear.* They must be understandable to you and to others.

- *Questions should be researchable.* They should be capable of development into a research design (Chapter 3), so that data may be collected in relation to them. This means that extremely abstract questions are unlikely to be suitable.

- *Questions should connect with established theory and research.* This means that there should be a literature you can draw on to help illuminate how your research questions could be approached. Even if you find a topic that has been scarcely addressed by business researchers, it is unlikely that there will be no relevant literature (for example, on related or parallel topics or in other social science disciplines). Making connections to theory and existing research will also allow you to show how you have made a contribution to knowledge and understanding through your research.

- *Questions should be logically and conceptually linked to each other.* This can involve having an overall research question and two or three related subsidiary research questions. All of the research questions posed need to be connected to a common theoretical perspective or literature.

- *Questions should offer you the potential to contribute to knowledge.* They should at the very least hold out the prospect of being able to make an original, novel contribution—however small—to the topic. However, this is not usually a requirement for a dissertation project.

- *Questions should be neither too broad nor too narrow.* The research questions should be neither too large (so that you would need a massive grant to study them) nor too small (so that you cannot make a reasonably significant contribution to your area of study).

STUDENT EXPERIENCE
Using your supervisor to help you to develop research questions

In the initial stages of a research project students often tend to be overly ambitious in their research questions. Working with your supervisor will help you to overcome this. As Karen explained, her supervisor 'kind of narrowed me down when I was trying to take on too much, when I was saying: 'Well, I think I might do this and I might do that as well.' Then he would just sort of ask me questions and get me to narrow it down.'

This was echoed by a supervisor:

Undergraduate students tend to be unrealistic about what can be achieved and to assume that doing research is easy and not very time consuming. Many choose something which is 'fashionable' or 'current', often without much apparent initial investigation, only to find later that the topic has limited foundations in the existing literature. Apart from the usual problem of students having a broad question, underpinned by multiple more focused research questions, each of which might be the basis for a more effective proposal, it is striking that many students will not narrow the focus, despite numerous signals that it is necessary. I also notice that very few revisit and refine the research question as they proceed. Another substantial minority of students feel that they have to have both a qualitative and a quantitative aspect to the project, irrespective of the context or the specific research question. The outcome is that the project typically falls 'between both stools' and lacks conviction.

Working closely with your supervisor will help you to avoid these pitfalls.

The importance of planning

One of the most important things Karen learned from doing a research project was the importance of planning.

For our dissertation we actually had to do a proposal and submit it and get that approved by our dissertation tutor before we started the actual writing. I think that's really important for them to check that you're on the right lines and just to clarify for you because I think when you first start you think 'Oh, it's such a lot of pages or a lot of words' and you have the desire to do so much, but then once you start writing you realize that it's much better to be a lot more focused and then you can go a lot deeper into things. So I think having that plan right at the beginning is really important.

Writing your research proposal

You may be required as part of your dissertation to write a short proposal or plan outlining what your research project will be about and how you intend to go about it. This is a useful way of planning your research, and it will encourage you to think about many of the issues covered in the next section. In addition to outlining the research design and methods that you intend to use (see Chapter 3), the topic area in which your study is going to be located, and the research questions that you intend to address, the proposal will enable you to demonstrate some knowledge of the literature in your chosen field—for example, by identifying several key authors or important research studies. This information may be used to allocate a supervisor who is knowledgeable in your area of interest. The proposal is also a useful starting point in discussions with your supervisor, and if it includes a timetable for the project this can provide a basis for planning meetings to review progress. Even if you are not required to produce a research proposal, it is worth constructing a timetable for your research and asking your supervisor to look at it, so you can assess how (un)realistic your goals are and whether you are allowing enough time for each stage of the process.

When writing a research proposal, there are a number of issues that you probably need to cover:

- What is your research topic?
- Why is your research topic important?
- What is your research question or questions?
- What does the literature have to say about your research topic and research question(s)?
- How are you going to go about collecting data relevant to your research question(s)? In other words, what research methods are you intending to use?

- Why are the research methods you have selected the appropriate ones for your research question?
- Who will your research participants be and how will they be selected (or if the research will use documents, what kinds of documents will you use and how will they be selected)?
- If your research requires you to negotiate access to organizations, have you done so, and if not, how will you do this?
- What resources will you need to conduct your research (for example, travel costs, recording equipment, printing, software) and how will those resources be obtained?
- What is your timetable for the different stages of the project?
- What are the ethical issues associated with your research (this area will be discussed in Chapter 6) and what steps will you take to address them?
- How will you analyse your data?

Writing a proposal is useful in getting you started on your research project and encouraging you to set realistic objectives. It is important to remember that this is a working document and the proposal can be refined and developed as your research progresses. However, if you keep changing your mind about your area of research interest and research design, you will use up valuable time needed to complete your dissertation within the deadline.

Having planned your research project and developed your research questions, the next step is to conduct a review of the literature, which is the focus of Chapter 5.

STUDENT EXPERIENCE

Listen to the advice of your supervisor, but make your own choices

We asked the supervisors we surveyed to tell us what the most important advice they gave to students at the start of their research project was. This is what they told us.

- Choose a topic that interests *you*.

- Ask yourself whether you can answer the research question.

- Read a lot; read thoroughly and appropriately (this includes articles in refereed journals).

- Identify your strengths, weaknesses, interests, and personal development opportunities and take them into account in designing the project.

- Don't pre-commit to one idea, approach, research design, data source, and so on, to the exclusion of other possibilities.

- Use opportunities to talk to others in your own field and other fields about your proposed research and assess its importance, characteristics, and possible relationship to what others are doing.

- Research something that is likely to be interesting to others: either to business practitioners or to researchers (or both).

- Start writing early. Build in a cushion round the deadline; analysis takes much longer than you think. This is where 'added value' can be gained.

- Remember that this is not your life work or a bid for a Nobel Prize.

- Listen to our advice, but make your own choices.

CHECKLIST
Planning a research project

○ Do you know the requirements for your dissertation, as set out by your university?

○ Have you made contact with your supervisor?

○ Have you left enough time to plan your research, collect and analyse the data, and write up your research project?

○ Do you have a clear timetable for your research project with clearly identifiable milestones for the achievement of specific tasks?

○ Have you got sufficient financial and practical resources (for example, money to enable travel to the research site, audio recorder) to enable you to carry out your research project?

○ Have you developed research questions and discussed these with your supervisor?

○ Are the research questions you have identified capable of being answered through your research project?

○ Do you have the access that you require in order to carry out your research?

○ Do you know which research participants or what sources (e.g. documents) are needed to answer your research questions and how to locate them?

○ Have you established which research method(s) you are planning to use and why?

○ Are you familiar with the data analysis software that you will be using to analyse your data?

KEY POINTS

- Follow the dissertation guidelines provided by your university.
- Thinking about your research subject can be time-consuming, so allow plenty of time for this aspect of the dissertation process.
- Use your supervisor to the fullest extent allowed and follow the advice offered by them.
- Plan your time carefully and be realistic about what you can achieve in the time available.
- Develop some research questions to express what it is about your area of interest that you want to know.
- Writing a research proposal is a good way of getting started on your research project and encouraging you to set realistic objectives.
- Consider access and sampling issues at an early stage and consider testing your research methods by conducting a pilot study (discussed in Part Two of this book).
- Keep good records of what you do in your research as you go along, and don't wait until all of your data have been collected before you start **coding** it (coding will be discussed in Chapters 13 and 24).

QUESTIONS FOR REVIEW

Managing time and resources

- What are the main advantages and disadvantages associated with using a Gantt chart to plan your research?

Developing suitable research questions

- What are the main sources of research questions?
- What are the main steps involved in developing research questions?
- What criteria can be used to evaluate research questions?

Writing your research proposal

- What is the purpose of the research proposal and how should it be used?

ONLINE RESOURCES
www.oup.com/uk/brm5e/

Visit the Interactive Research Guide that accompanies this book to complete an exercise in planning a research project and developing research questions.

GETTING STARTED: REVIEWING THE LITERATURE

CHAPTER OUTLINE

This chapter provides guidance for students on how to get started with their research project. Once you have identified your research questions (see Chapter 4), the next step in any research project is to search the existing literature and write a literature review. In many research projects, the literature review provides the basis for empirical study involving primary or secondary data collection using quantitative or qualitative methods, or a combination of both (see Chapter 27). However, in other projects that are based on desk research, the literature review is the final outcome which forms the basis for the dissertation. The principal task at this early stage involves reviewing the main ideas and debates in a field and the research that is relevant research in your chosen area of interest. This provides the basis for the writing of a literature review, which forms an important part of any dissertation. The chapter explains:

- how to search the literature and engage critically with the ideas of other researchers;
- what is expected in a literature review and the criteria that are used to evaluate it;
- how to assess the quality of existing research in your subject area;
- the role of the bibliography and the importance of referencing the work of others;
- the importance of understanding what constitutes plagiarism and the penalties that are associated with it.

Introduction

This chapter helps you to get started on one of the most important tasks in carrying out a research project—reviewing the literature in your chosen subject area. The literature review is a crucial part of any dissertation. It is usually presented as a separate chapter or substantial section near the beginning of the dissertation. This provides the basis for the justification of research questions and explanation of the research design. The literature review also informs how you collect your data and enables you to analyse your data in an informed way. However, doing a literature review can feel quite daunting, perhaps because so many other researchers have written so many books and articles about your chosen subject, or because your subject area does not seem to have a clearly defined boundary. Consequently, you may feel that there are various bodies of literature that you could review and you may be unsure how to choose between or combine them. Reviewing the literature therefore involves making judgements about what to include and exclude from your literature review, reading what other researchers have written about your subject, and writing about it in a way that demonstrates your understanding. The advice we give in this chapter is designed to assist in this process. A substantial proportion of what you review will be articles that have been published in academic journals (see Key concept 5.1).

5.1 KEY CONCEPT
What is an academic journal?

An academic journal, also referred to as a scholarly, peer-reviewed, or refereed journal, is a place of publication where research papers have gone through a process of 'double blind' peer review (i.e. the authors do not know who reviews, and the reviewers do not know who wrote the initial manuscript submitted for review). Between two and four experts in the specialist subject read the manuscript, and a decision is made by the journal editor based on these reviews. If the reviewers raise serious issues, the editor may reject the submission, judging it unsuitable for publication. Alternatively, the editor will require the authors to revise their research paper on the basis of the reviewers' comments, then decide after revision and resubmission whether to accept it, usually after sending it back out to the referees for further comment. This process may happen up to four or five times. The editor may decide at any stage to reject the research paper. In prestigious academic journals in the business and management field, it is common for more than 90 per cent of submitted papers to be rejected, and it is very unusual for an article to be accepted on its first submission. Consequently, the articles that are eventually published in peer-reviewed journals are not just the culmination of a research process, but are also the outcome of a lengthy feedback and review process than can take in excess of two years. Many of the examples used in the Research in focus boxes in this book have been published in academic journals, which means that they have gone through a review process similar to this. Above all, this enables the reader to have confidence in the quality of the research because it has been reviewed and approved for publication by other experts in the field.

Most academic journals are published by a commercial publisher such as Sage or Wiley, sometimes in association with a professional association, such as the British Academy of Management or the Academy of Management. In recent years, commercial publishers have come under critical scrutiny because of their practices, which are extremely lucrative and generate substantial profits (Lilley et al., 2012). The rapidly rising costs of subscription to academic journals is borne by university libraries, at a time when universities are facing greater budgetary constraints and many students face rising fees. This has led some researchers to set up 'open-access' journal publishing, where research can be read, free of charge, online for an unlimited time. One example in business and management studies is the journal *Ephemera*, founded in 2001 to provide peer-reviewed research free of charge. Several articles published there have become well cited in their fields. Another free route to reading research is via university repositories, where pre-publication versions of accepted journal articles are made available online. This is an entirely reliable way of accessing an academic article if you do not have institutional access to the published version, because it contains exactly the same text as the published version; the only difference is that it is not typeset, so citing specific page numbers for direct quotes can be a problem.

Open-access publishing has the potential to enable the majority of the world's population to access research even if they cannot afford access to academic journals via expensive institutional or individual subscription. On the other hand, the rise in open-access journal publishing has also led to some more unscrupulous practices. The website Scholarly Open Access, commonly referred to as Beall's List, is the work of Jeffrey Beall, a US-based university librarian. Beall is unhappy with the proliferation of open-access journals, especially those with unscrupulous publishers behind them, who use a variety of tricks to fool people into thinking that their journals are legitimate scholarly publications. Examples from Beall's List in the field of business include a Taiwan-based organization which publishes papers in three open-access journals, including the *Journal of Global Business Management*. This journal requires each author to pay a publication fee of between $500 and $700, and there is no peer review. Beall's List may be seen at **https://beallslist.weebly.com/**.

Reviewing the literature and engaging with what others have written

Why do you need to review the existing literature? The most obvious reason is that you want to know what is already known so that you do not simply 'reinvent the wheel'. Your literature review is where you demonstrate that you are able to engage in scholarly debate based on your understanding of the published work of others. Engaging with the existing literature is a means of developing an argument about the significance of your research and where it leads. The simile of a *story* is also sometimes used in this context (see Thinking deeply 5.2). Whatever the approach you choose, the process is always directed

towards achieving the same thing: a competent review of the literature is a means of affirming your credibility as someone who is knowledgeable in your chosen area. This is not simply a matter of reproducing the theories and opinions of others; you must interpret what they have written, often by using their ideas to support a particular viewpoint or argument of your own. Reading the existing literature will help you address the following questions:

- What is already known about this area?
- What concepts and theories are relevant?

TIPS AND SKILLS
Ways of approaching a literature review

Bruce (1994) suggests the task of reviewing the literature for a dissertation can be experienced in any of the following ways:

1. as a *list* of relevant studies in the area;
2. as a *search* for relevant information;
3. as a *survey* of existing research on a subject;
4. as a *vehicle* for learning that leads the researcher to increase their knowledge and test their understanding;
5. as a *facilitating device* to enable identification of a topic, to aid in the development of a methodology, to provide context, or to enable a change in research direction;
6. as a *report* on previously conducted investigations.

The earlier approaches in this list are more indirect—the student works with items that represent the primary literature, such as bibliographic citations—and the latter conceptions are more direct—the student works with source material rather than, for example, a representative abstract. Students may use more than one approach in combination, for example using direct approaches (4–6) as a way of making indirect approaches more meaningful.

- What research methods and research strategies have been used?
- Are there any significant controversies?
- Are there any inconsistencies in findings relating to this area?
- Are there any unanswered research questions?

This last issue points to the possibility that you will be able to revise and refine your research questions in the process of reviewing the literature.

Reading critically

Much of the time during the early stages of your research project will be taken up with reading existing literature in order to write your review. It is important to make sure that the process of reading prepares you well for writing your review. Getting the most from your reading involves developing specific skills that enable you to read actively and critically. When you are reading, try to do the following.

- Take good notes, including the publication details of the material you read. It is infuriating, and very time-consuming, to go back to your notes later and find that you forgot to record where and when something was published—details that you will need when you finalize your bibliography.
- Develop critical reading skills. Reviewing literature must do more than just summarize what you have read; you should be critical in your approach. This doesn't necessarily mean saying that published research has flaws; you have to empathize with the researcher's difficult task, and recognize the challenges of developing new knowledge. Feminist researchers call this practice 'reading with'—it can be critical, but in a constructive way (Plate, 1993). This kind of critical reading involves moving beyond description of published research, to ask questions about the process and significance of the work. A good critical reader attends to issues such as: how does the research relate to what you have already read? Are there strengths and deficiencies—perhaps in methodology or in the credibility of the conclusions drawn? What theoretical ideas have influenced the research? Do you find the research interesting or surprising?
- Your review of the literature should show why your research questions are important. For example, if your research questions are based on the argument that although a lot of research has been done on a topic, such as the psychological contract, female entrepreneurship, or employee absenteeism, but little or no research has been done on a specific aspect of that topic, the literature review enables you to justify your particular focus. Alternatively, perhaps there are two competing positions with regard to a topic, and you want to investigate the one that you think provides a better understanding. The literature review allows you to locate your own research within a tradition of research in an area, or as part of a specific debate. In this situation, reading the literature is an important source of research questions.

- The literature that you examine at the start of your research should also form the basis for discussion of your findings and conclusion.

- It is not necessary to get everything you read into a literature review. Trying to force everything into a review just because of the hard work involved in uncovering and reading the material is not going to help you to do well in your dissertation. The review assists you in developing an argument, and bringing in irrelevant research undermines your ability to get that argument across. All researchers 'read around' topics to decide what is important. This time is not wasted, because as you read, you think.

- Reading literature is not something you stop doing once you begin your data collection. You should continue your search for and reading of relevant literature throughout the process. This means that, if you have written a literature review before beginning your data collection, you regard it as provisional. Indeed, you may want to make quite substantial revisions of your review towards the end of writing up your work, because the data collection process can change how you think about a subject or research question.

- Further suggestions for how to develop your use of the literature are in Thinking deeply 5.2. The different ways of approaching literature presented in this box come from a review of qualitative studies of organizations, but they have a much broader applicability, including to quantitative research.

Systematic review

Recently, considerable thought has been devoted to the notion of systematic review (see Key concept 5.3). This is an approach to reviewing the literature that adopts explicit, often quantitative, procedures.

5.2 THINKING DEEPLY
Composing a literature review in qualitative research articles

Useful insight into writing a literature review can be found by examining how articles based on **qualitative research** are composed. In their review of articles based on the qualitative study of organizations, Golden-Biddle and Locke (1993, 1997) argue that good articles develop a story—that is, a clear and compelling framework around which the writing is structured. This idea is very similar to Wolcott's (1990: 18) recommendation to 'determine the basic story you are going to tell'. Golden-Biddle and Locke suggest that the way the author's position in relation to the literature is presented is an important component of storytelling. They distinguish two main processes—coherence and problematizing—which are used to tell a story about the literature.

1. **Constructing intertextual coherence**—this refers to the way in which existing knowledge is represented and organized; researchers show how contributions to knowledge relate to each other and to the research being reported. The following techniques are often used for this.

   - *Synthesized coherence*—putting together work that is generally considered unrelated: theory and research previously regarded as unconnected are pieced together. There are two prominent forms of this:

     a. the organization of incompatible references;

     b. making connections between established theories or research programmes.

   - *Progressive coherence*—showing the accumulation of knowledge about a topic around which there is considerable consensus.

   - *Non-coherence*—recognition that there have been many contributions to a certain research topic, but that there is considerable disagreement among researchers.

   Each of these strategies is designed to show there is space for a new contribution to be made.

2. **Problematize the situation**—literature is subverted by locating a problem within it that falls into one of the following categories.

   - *Incomplete*—the existing literature is not fully complete: in other words, there is a gap.

   - *Inadequate*—existing literature about a phenomenon of interest overlooks ways of seeing it that can greatly improve our understanding; alternative perspectives or frameworks can then be introduced.

   - *Incommensurate*—making a case for an alternative perspective that is superior to existing literature; differs from 'inadequate' because it portrays the existing literature as 'wrong, misguided, or incorrect' (Golden-Biddle and Locke 1997: 43).

The key point about Golden-Biddle and Locke's account of the way literature can be read is that approaches are used by researchers to achieve a number of things:

- They demonstrate their competence by referring to prominent writings in the field (Gilbert 1977).

- They develop their version of the literature to show and to lead up to the contribution they will be making in their research.

- They show that the gap or problem in the literature that is identified corresponds to their research questions.

The idea of writing up research as storytelling is a useful reminder that reviewing literature is a key part of the story and should link seamlessly with the rest of the article rather than be considered separately.

Systematic review emerged as an approach to engaging with existing research for two main reasons. First, some researchers argue that many literature reviews tend to 'lack thoroughness' and reflect researcher biases (Tranfield et al. 2003). Proponents of systematic review argue that explicit procedures make such biases less likely to arise. Second, as discussed in Chapter 1, in applied fields such as medicine, education and business there has been a growing movement towards evidence-based solutions. Systematic reviews are seen as

5.3 KEY CONCEPT
What is a systematic review?

Systematic review is defined as 'a replicable, scientific and transparent process, in other words a detailed technology, that aims to minimize bias through exhaustive literature searches of published and unpublished studies and by providing an audit trail of the reviewer's decisions, procedures and conclusions' (Tranfield et al. 2003: 209). Such a review is often contrasted with traditional narrative review, the focus of the next section. Enthusiasts for systematic review argue that it is more likely to generate unbiased and comprehensive accounts of literature in a research field, especially where the aim is to understand whether an intervention works. A systematic review that includes only quantitative studies and which summarizes those studies quantitatively is a meta-analysis (see Key concept 14.8). The development of systematic review procedures for qualitative studies has attracted attention. Meta-ethnography (see Key concept 24.8) is one approach to the synthesis of qualitative findings, but there are several other methods, none of which is widely used (Mays et al. 2005).

a cornerstone of evidence-based approaches. Their purpose is to provide advice for practitioners based on all the available peer-reviewed research evidence. Such reviews are valuable for decision-makers, particularly in areas where there is conflicting evidence concerning the best way of doing things, as in the case of business.

However, Tranfield et al. (2003) acknowledge that, unlike medical science, business research is a relatively young field that stems from the social rather than biological sciences and is characterized by low consensus concerning key research questions. Also, medical science is often concerned with research questions related to whether or not particular interventions, such as a medicine or a therapy, are effective. Such questions are well suited to systematic review but are not often encountered in business research. So, can a review process developed in a discipline that is largely based on a quantitative research strategy inform the development of a more systematic literature review process in business research?

STUDENT EXPERIENCE
Reasons for doing a systematic review

Dissertations based exclusively on reviewing existing research are increasingly common. This is a reflection of the tremendous growth of research in certain areas and a need to ascertain its quality. This type of dissertation also has the advantage of removing the need to gain access to a research site and obtain ethical approval (see Chapter 6).

Amrit's dissertation focusing on mental health at work was based on a systematic review of the existing literature. One of the reasons Amrit decided on this was because of the sensitivity of the topic he was interested in and the potential difficulties in gaining research access.

Amrit described this as

> a filtering process. You start with your search terms, the broader idea and then you go through a five-stage process. Stage one was to derive some key search terms which would help me find relevant articles. I had seven key search terms: 'employee mental health', 'employee mental illness', 'employee workplace anxiety', 'employee mental burnout', 'mental health workplace', 'employee workplace stress', and 'workplace depression'. I entered all those combinations into an online database, Web of Science, which was recommended by my supervisor. I found 6886 articles. Obviously, I could not read every one of them. So I applied the Web of Science 'business or management' category filter. This was probably one of the most important parts of the review because my research question was specifically about business and management. That left me with 500 articles. This was

when the reading kicked in. I visually scanned all 495 articles, including the title and abstract. From that I gauged whether or not they were relevant to my research question. That left me with 139 articles. The final stage was a full-text screening. I went through every article and read them. This took around two months, and I ended up with 50 articles.

By systematically following established protocols he was able to generate a manageable number of academic journal papers which he could analyse. The analysis involved looking for themes and developing an analytical framework to reflect the theoretical perspectives represented in the research. Amrit was thereby able to summarize how researchers have analysed mental health at work and identify gaps in the study of this subject. As he explained: 'I went into this thinking "I want to find out why this happens, I want to find out what's spoken about, I want to find out what's not spoken about", and that's precisely what I did.'

The main steps of the systematic review process are as follows.

- *Specifying the question and planning the review*. The research question must be clearly answerable. Denyer and Tranfield (2009) suggest that this involves looking at the relationship between variables and examining why, and in what circumstances, the relationship occurs. There are four elements to this:

  - *context* (what individuals/relationships/institutional settings/systems are being studied);
  - *intervention* (what effects, relating to events, actions, or activities, are being studied);
  - *mechanisms* (what mechanisms explain the relationship between interventions and outcomes);
  - *outcomes* (the intended and unintended effects of the intervention and how they will be measured).

  Denyer and Tranfield (2009: 682) give an example of a suitable question to illustrate: 'Under what conditions (C) does leadership style (I) influence the performance of project teams (O), and what mechanisms operate in the influence of leadership style (I) on project team performance?' Next, a group of stakeholders, including practitioners and researchers, meets at regular intervals, first to define and clarify the boundaries of the review and later to monitor its progress. This includes setting the criteria for inclusion and exclusion of studies from the review. 'This helps ensure that reviews are impartial and balanced, preventing reviewers from including only those studies supporting their particular argument' (Briner et al. 2009: 26).

- *Conducting the review*. This involves carrying out 'a comprehensive, unbiased search' (Tranfield et al. 2003: 215) based on keywords and search terms.

  - The search strategy must be described in terms that allow it to be replicated, and searches should include unpublished (for example, working or conference papers) as well as published articles.

  - The information search leads to the production of a list of all the articles and books on which the review will be based. These articles and books are examined and sifted on the basis of two types of consideration. First, all studies that fail to relate to the review's research question have to be excluded. Second, those studies that are relevant are examined for study quality. Sometimes, systematic reviewers will exclude studies that fail to meet minimum criteria, although that can sometimes mean that the review is then conducted on an extremely small sample of remaining studies. More often, reviewers will categorize studies in terms of the extent to which they meet the quality criteria that are specified. Checklists for assessing quality are available, but it is necessary to use those that are appropriate for the kinds of research being examined; the issue of quality criteria in relation to quantitative and qualitative research is covered in Chapters 7 and 17.

  - Once the items to be included in the review have been identified, the analysis begins. The aim of this is to achieve a cumulative understanding of what is known about the subject through applying techniques of research synthesis. Often, systematic reviewers seek to arrive at a 'narrative synthesis' of the research: this uses text to summarize key findings relating to the research question, often accompanied by simple statistical summaries such as the percentage of studies that examined a certain issue or that adopted a particular perspective. One advantage of a narrative synthesis is that it can be used as a platform for reviewing and summarizing both quantitative and qualitative studies.

- *Reporting and dissemination*. This involves reporting in a way that provides a descriptive map of the research on the subject, including who the contributors are, where they are based, and when the main temporal periods of research activity on the subject occurred. A further criterion for reporting is accessibility and readability. The review process should make it easier for the practitioner to understand the research, so that it is more likely that it will be translated into practice.

Tranfield et al. (2003) suggest that the systematic review process provides a more reliable foundation on which to design research, because it is based on a more comprehensive understanding of what we know about a subject. Research that involves systematic literature review is argued to be more strongly evidence-based because it is concerned with seeking to understand the effects of a particular variable or intervention that has been found in previous studies. This is useful in subjecting widely held assumptions about a subject to empirical scrutiny. For example, it is widely assumed that workplace stress produces ill-health effects in employees. Systematic review provides a way for the researcher who is interested in this subject to find out whether or not previous studies have found this to be the case. This can be helpful in encouraging researchers to think critically about their subject. Proponents of systematic review also commend the approach for its transparency: in other words, the grounds on which studies were selected and how they were analysed are clearly articulated and are potentially replicable.

It is important to be aware that systematic review has limitations. A key issue stems from research questions not always being capable of definition in terms of the effect of a particular variable, or when subject boundaries are fluid and open or subject to change. Since, as we discussed in Chapter 1, business is an applied field of study that borrows theory from a range of social science and other disciplines, this is relatively common. Another criticism of systematic reviews is the argument that it can lead to a bureaucratization of reviewing, because it is more concerned with the technical aspects of how research is done than with the analytical interpretations and understandings it offers. A third potential limitation of the systematic approach relates to its application to qualitative research studies, and in particular the methodological judgements that inform decisions about quality that determine the inclusion or exclusion of an article from a literature review. These stem from differences between qualitative and quantitative research in relation to the criteria used to assess their methodological quality (see Chapters 7 and 17). The systematic review approach assumes that an objective judgement about the quality of an article can be made. Such judgements have the potential to be controversial for all research, but are likely to be especially so for articles based on qualitative research. Among quantitative researchers there is more agreement about the criteria that might be applied than among qualitative researchers, who are not even close to consensus (see Chapter 17).

In contrast to systematic review, some researchers say that they measure the quality of published research in terms of what they find interesting. This is clearly incompatible with the systematic approach, which requires articles to be evaluated in terms of methodological criteria or according to place of publication. Researchers

TIPS AND SKILLS
Important considerations in using systematic review in a student research project

A systematic literature review requires a transparent way of searching and examining the literature as well as keeping records of what you have done. These practices are entirely feasible for a student research project. If you are undertaking a systematic literature review for your dissertation project it is important to meet regularly with your supervisor during the planning stage to define the boundaries of the subject and develop search terms. Your supervisor's knowledge of the subject, databases, and journals is invaluable.

However, as Amrit's experience shows, students undertaking a systematic review can risk being overwhelmed by the sheer volume of literature that has to be screened and analysed (see Daigneault et al. 2012 on this). The decision to conduct a systematic review should therefore not be taken lightly. It is easy to underestimate the time required to screen articles for relevance, and the difficulty of doing so when faced with article titles and abstracts that are not as informative as they could be.

in the medical sciences have found the process of identifying relevant qualitative studies time-consuming, and almost impossible to do on the basis of title and abstract (M. L. Jones 2004). Finally, whether or not the systematic review approach makes sense to you depends somewhat on your epistemological position (see Chapter 2). As Noblit and Hare (1988: 15) state: 'Positivists have had more interest in knowledge synthesis than interpretivists. For them, knowledge accumulates. The problem has been how best to accomplish that accumulation.' For these reasons, researchers who adopt an interpretative approach to understanding the social sciences and who use qualitative methods may find the systematic review approach problematic. Fortunately, they have an alternative approach.

Narrative review

Rather than reviewing the literature to find out what their research project can add to existing knowledge about a subject, interpretative researchers (see Chapter 2 for an explanation of interpretivism) can have quite different reasons for reviewing literature, since their purpose is to enrich human discourse (Geertz 1973) by generating understanding. A literature review is for them a means of gaining an initial impression of the topic area that they intend to understand better through their research. They

often use narrative review. This type of review tends to be less focused and more wide-ranging in scope than a systematic review. It is also less explicit about the criteria for exclusion or inclusion of studies. An example of this type of review is given in Research in focus 5.4.

If your approach to the relationship between theory and research is inductive rather than deductive (see Chapter 2), setting out all the main theoretical and conceptual terms that define your area of study prior to data collection is extremely problematic, because theory is to be the outcome of the study, rather than the basis for it. This means that during the process of researching a topic, researchers may discover issues that they did not previously anticipate as important. As a result, researchers can become aware of the limitations of the field as currently understood, leading them towards an unanticipated way of understanding it (Noblit and Hare 1988). Interpretative researchers are more likely than deductive researchers to change their view of theory or literature as a result of the analysis of collected data, and so require greater flexibility to modify the boundaries of their subject as they go along. This means that narrative review may be more suitable for qualitative or inductive researchers, whose research strategies are based on an interpretative epistemology.

Despite the increasing popularity of systematic review, most reviews are still narrative, regardless of whether

5.4 RESEARCH IN FOCUS
A narrative review of narrative research

Rhodes and Brown (2005) conducted a review of the management literature on **narrative analysis** (see Chapter 22 for an explanation of narrative analysis). Their use of narrative review is consistent with an interpretive epistemology which informs narrative research and tends to use qualitative research methods. Examining literature from the 1970s to 2004, they identify five principal research areas that narrative analysis explores, assessing the theoretical value of each in understanding organizations.

1. *Sensemaking*—focuses on the role of stories as a device through which people make sense of organizational events.

2. *Communication*—explores how narratives are used to create and maintain organizational culture and power structure.

3. *Learning/change*—analyses how stories help people to learn and subjectively to make sense of change.

4. *Politics and power*—considers the role of shared narratives in the control of organizational meaning.

5. *Identity and identification*—focuses on the role of stories in creating and maintaining organizational identity.

While they do not make explicit their criteria for inclusion or exclusion of certain studies, the authors assess the main contributions, implications, and limitations of narrative analysis. They also cite a number of their own publications in this subject area. This helps to convince the reader of the credibility of the authors' evaluations of other people's research on the subject.

Reasons for writing a literature review

Here is a list of good reasons for writing a literature review.

1. You need to know what is already known in connection with your research area because you do not want to be accused of reinventing the wheel.
2. You can learn from other researchers' mistakes and avoid making them.
3. You can learn about different theoretical and methodological approaches to your research area.
4. It may lead you to consider the inclusion of variables in your research that you might not have thought about.
5. It may suggest further research questions for you.
6. It will help with the interpretation of your findings.
7. It is expected!

they are meant to be springboards for the reviewer's own investigation (when the literature is reviewed to specify what is already known, so that research questions can be developed) or are ends in their own right (as a means of summarizing what is known or not known). When we examine examples of writing up research in Chapter 7, we will see that literature relevant to the researcher's area of interest is always reviewed as a means of establishing why those researchers conducted their research and what its contribution is likely to be.

However, the gap between systematic and narrative review approaches is beginning to narrow, as some of the procedures associated with systematic review are incorporated into narrative review protocols. As a result, there is a growing tendency for researchers to spell out in some detail the procedures they used for conducting a literature search, and the quality criteria that guided inclusion and exclusion (e.g. Bryman 2007a). For example, Purkayastha et al. (2012) conducted a narrative review of research on the relationship between firm diversification and performance in developed and emerging markets. They were very explicit about the two questions they employed in selecting articles for inclusion. For the research on diversification in emerging economies, the researchers searched two online databases—ABI-Inform and EBSCO—using keywords such as 'diversification', 'firm performance', and 'emerging economy/ies' (see the next section for more on using databases). Each of the articles found in this way was examined to establish how well it dovetailed with the review's research questions. In the end, 37 relevant articles concerned with diversification and firm performance in emerging economies were employed.

Searching databases

Usually, students will have in mind a few references to start with when they begin work on a project, probably from recommended reading in course modules, or from textbooks. The bibliographies provided at the end of textbook chapters or articles provide you with a lot of relevant references that can be followed up. A literature search relies on careful reading of books, academic journals, and perhaps management consultancy of government reports. Once you have identified keywords that help to define the boundaries of your area (see below), it's time to go to online databases that bring together published literature from journals that can be searched.

Online databases

Online databases are the most valuable source of academic journal references. They also often provide access to the full text of an article in digital format, usually pdf. You will need to check what online resources are available through your university. A good place to start is on your university library's homepage, or you can ask your supervisor or a member of library staff to talk you through the databases available. Here are three that we recommend:

1. ABI/INFORM provides business research and more general information from a wide range of periodicals and reports, coverage is international, and it is possible to search by keyword or to browse by topic to search for relevant articles by subject. The database can be accessed at proquest.com.

2. EBSCO Business Source Premier/Complete is an increasingly widely used business periodical database that now rivals ABI/INFORM in scope and coverage. Its popularity is in part due to the provision of comprehensive full text access to key business and management journals, including titles such as *Harvard Business Review* and *Academy of Management Review,* although older issues of journals are not all included. In addition, it provides indexing and abstracts for over 3000 business journals as well as access to some company and market reports. It can be accessed via EBSCO Publishing at ebscohost.com.

3. We also strongly recommend use of the Social Sciences Citation Index (SSCI), which fully indexes over 1700 major social science journals covering all social science disciplines dating back to 1970. The citation indexes collectively are also known as Web of Science. The SSCI can be accessed through your library website, or through the ISI Web of Knowledge at wokinfo.com.

The SSCI/Web of Knowledge database is a little less intuitive and easy to use than the others, but it provides the best coverage and many useful features for refining searches. Some libraries add full-text links for articles from some of the most important business journals published worldwide. The database also covers related fields such as accountancy and finance, economics, and public administration. It is, therefore, very useful as an initial source in your literature search because, if you search the database effectively, you can be confident that you have found the majority of published articles on your topic. Here are some introductory guidelines for searching it.

- Use the 'Basic Search' box. Note that the default is to search 1900 to date. You can change this by using the pull-down menus.

- You can then search by a number of fields including TOPIC or AUTHOR.

- Refine your search. There are many ways to do this: by language, by article type, by year. Your supervisor's or a librarian's guidance is essential here.

- One other key way of searching is known as CITED REF SEARCH. This helps you find research related to your key article, to see what other authors thought of it and how they used it.

A number of academic publishers also make full text of their journals available through their own websites: Cambridge University Press (Cambridge Core) and Sage (Sage Journals) are the two most prominent examples. Again, you will need to check with your librarian to find out which of these resources you can use and how to access them. The INGENTA website offers full text from various publishers, but you will only be able to access full text for titles to which your library subscribes.

In addition to scholarly books and journals, newspaper archive databases provide a valuable supplementary resource to review the emergence of new topics in business and management. Most newspapers require subscriptions to be able to search their online databases (e.g. *Financial Times*, *Daily* and *Sunday Telegraph*, *Wall Street Journal*, *The Economist*). However, most academic libraries will have a subscription to these newspapers or to a service such as Proquest or Nexis, which allow you to search several newspapers at once. The level of analysis can be high. However, for an academic dissertation, newspapers should always be seen as secondary to published research literature in books and journals. On the other hand, it should be remembered that it takes some time for academic articles to be published, so for recent events newspapers may be the only source of information.

Another valuable resource to supplement your literature searching is provided by the non-academic institutions that publish policy-oriented research on issues related to business and management, such as the Equal Opportunities Commission, the Work Foundation, the World Bank, the Institute for Public Policy Research, the Chartered Institute of Personnel and Development, and Demos. Reports are often published online and they can usually be downloaded free. They provide a faster route to publication than peer-reviewed journals. This is particularly useful when researching a currently emerging topic in management and business, or a government-led initiative such as Public–Private Partnerships.

However, we have an important word of warning about using Google and other search engines to locate research. Internet search engines are very useful for finding all sorts of things. However, they merely find things,

Using newspapers and other media to get information about a current management topic

In addition to using academic books and journal sources, Chris found that newspaper databases provided a valuable source of information on the subject of diversity, the debate about women in management, and the 'glass ceiling' effect. The British Equal Opportunities Commission website was also a useful source. Chris observed:

> I picked a relatively hot topic in the management field. It was interesting to learn that it isn't just the most obvious places that you do research. It's typing something into Google and looking in the newspaper daily. The *Independent* regularly had articles on this subject and so did the *Guardian*, so it wasn't just, you know, academic views that I was using.

However, it is important not to regard these sources of information as a substitute for academic research, which should provide the basis of your literature review. It is also important to remember that fashionable topics in management research will almost certainly have connections with former managerial practices. Therefore, an established theory can provide an invaluable means of understanding what is currently happening in the managerial context.

they do not evaluate them, so be prepared to look critically at what you've found. Remember that anyone can put information online, so you need to evaluate carefully whether what you have found is useful and legitimate. The following points are worth considering.

- Who is the author of the research, and what is their motive for publishing?

- What is the institutional location of the website? The URL can help you here. Is it an academic site (often .ac or .edu) or a government site (.gov), a non-commercial organization (.org) or a commercial one (.com or .co)?

- What is the motivation of the body that commissioned the research? Many think tanks, for example, promote a specific economic or political perspective, and commission research to support it.

There is a lot of very good research and analysis published outside peer-reviewed academic journals, and by non-academic publishers. However, it is more difficult to judge its status, so starting with databases such as those mentioned in this chapter is always the best approach to reviewing literature.

As part of your literature review, you may need to find out background information about markets or companies. There are numerous database sources that can provide you with this kind of company and market research data, including the Global Market Information Database (known as Passport GMID), which contains marketing profiles, consumer market sizing for 52 countries,

consumer lifestyle reports, data for over 200 countries, market forecasts, and information about 100,000 brands and 12,000 companies. A company called Mintel provides comprehensive market research reports on the UK retail and leisure sectors and conducts its own market research, while Reuters Business Insight provides access to hundreds of market research reports focused on energy, consumer goods, finance, health care, and technology. Depending on the library you belong to, you may also be able to access Datastream, Amadeus, or Investext, all of which contain company-specific information. Others are more subject-specific: for example, Creative Club provides an archive of advertisements in all UK media from 1997 onwards.

Finally, government statistics often offer good insights into a research topic. The UK National Statistics website, for example, offers a wide range of statistics about the UK, including social trends, regional trends, consumer trends, and the results of the General Household Survey: http://www.statistics.gov.uk/hub/index.html. European statistics relating to specific countries, industries, and sectors can be found on Europa, the portal to the European Union website: europa.eu.

Keywords and defining search parameters

For all databases, you need to decide on keywords to enter into the search engines that will result in suitable

TIPS AND SKILLS
Online searching

The strength of the internet in providing access to huge amounts of information is also its weakness. It can be very difficult to differentiate what is useful and reliable from that which is simplistic or plain wrong, commercially oriented, highly opinionated, or not sufficiently academic. Some online sources are misleading and incorrect. Therefore, it is important to be selective in your use of information on the internet and to build up a list of trusted sources such as Google Scholar.

references. Business and management dictionaries and subject handbooks can help you to define your area of research and to identify changes in the language used to describe the subject. For example, the term 'personnel management' has now been largely superseded by 'human resource management' (HRM), and 'payment systems' are now more widely referred to under the umbrella of 'reward management'. You will also need to think of synonyms and try to match your language to that of the source you are searching. For example, performance management may be more usually referred to in practitioner publications as 'employee evaluation' or 'appraisal'. Sometimes opposites are useful—for example, employment/unemployment. You also need to think about alternative spellings based on the forms used in different English-speaking countries—for example, organization/organisation, labor/labour. Be prepared to **experiment** and to amend your keywords as your research progresses—you may find that, as you search the literature, you come across alternative terms or other ways of describing your subject.

In most databases, typing in the title of your project, or a sentence or long phrase, as your search term is not advisable: unless someone has written something with the same title, you are unlikely to find very much, or you'll generate a very wide set of results that will take a long time to dig through. You need to think in terms of keywords to construct a focused literature set in a specific area. For example, if you are interested in 'the role of women in the management of banks' your keywords would be WOMEN and MANAG* and BANK*. This would mean that you captured articles containing the words manag*er*, manag*ers*, manag*ing*, and man*agement*, as well as bank*ing*, bank*s*, and bank*ers*, because the asterisk acts as a wild card that searches for all words that begin in this way. Consult the HELP function in the databases themselves, as well as supervisors and librarians, to find out how to use your keywords to best effect.

In some areas of research, there is an enormous amount of published material. In such a case, try to identify the most important research publications, for example through citation counts (the number of times a publication has been cited by other researchers), and work outwards from there.

STUDENT EXPERIENCE
The importance of identifying suitable keywords

Karen's experience of searching the literature highlights the importance of identifying the most accurate terms to describe the subject in which you are interested.

I went to Leeds University Library then and asked them, but it was just such a small area that not many people knew anything about it and so it was just a case really of going onto databases and searching on different words and seeing if that brought anything up. I was searching on 'cultural fit' and that didn't work. There was nothing. Nobody had written anything on the term 'cultural fit,' but then I tried 'organisational fit' and that was when it opened up and there were lots of things; and then once I had one, I had lots of other references and that was how it sort of snowballed.

Karen's metaphor of the snowball is striking here. Literature reviews frequently begin in this way—namely, by starting with a small number of references, following up citations within those, and continuing the process until a sizeable number of items has been accumulated.

Making progress

Be sure to move on to the next stage of your research at the point that you identified in your timetable (see Chapter 4), so that you can dig yourself out of the library. This is not to say that your search for the literature will cease, but that you need to force yourself to move on—all research projects are constrained by time. This is the second point of the literature review process when you really need your supervisor's advice; ask them for their thoughts on whether or not you need to search the literature much more. Figure 5.1 outlines

FIGURE 5.1
One way of searching the literature

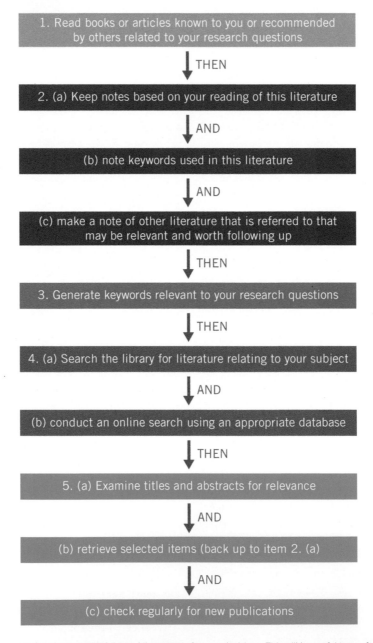

1. Read books or articles known to you or recommended by others related to your research questions

↓ THEN

2. (a) Keep notes based on your reading of this literature

↓ AND

(b) note keywords used in this literature

↓ AND

(c) make a note of other literature that is referred to that may be relevant and worth following up

↓ THEN

3. Generate keywords relevant to your research questions

↓ THEN

4. (a) Search the library for literature relating to your subject

↓ AND

(b) conduct an online search using an appropriate database

↓ THEN

5. (a) Examine titles and abstracts for relevance

↓ AND

(b) retrieve selected items (back up to item 2. (a)

↓ AND

(c) check regularly for new publications

Note: At each stage, keep a record of what you have done and the reasons for your decisions. This will be useful to you for remembering how you proceeded and for writing up a description and justification of your literature search strategy, which can form part of your 'Methods' section (see Chapter 7, 'Writing up business research'). When making notes on literature that you read, make notes on content and method, as well as relevance, and keep thinking about how each item will contribute to your critical review of the literature.

one way of searching the literature. The most important thing to do, as the note in the caption says, is to keep a record of the process so that you can keep track of what you have done.

Referencing

Referencing—providing publication details of the research you have consulted and built on—is a key part of all literature reviewing, especially if your dissertation is a systematic or narrative review in its entirety. Referencing the work of others is an important academic convention because it shows that you are aware of the historical development of your subject, and shows that you recognize how your own research builds on the work of others. Referencing in your literature review is thus a way of emphasizing your understanding and knowledge of the subject, and it is a key skill that all dissertations will be judged on. A reference is sometimes described as a 'citation' and the act of referencing as 'citing'.

As we mentioned earlier on in this chapter, keeping a record of what you have read is a key skill in constructing a literature review. For larger research projects it can be useful to use note cards or software packages that are designed specifically for this purpose, such as ProCite or EndNote. Some prefer to keep a record of all the research read in a Word document. It doesn't really matter how you do it. The main thing to make sure of is that you keep your bibliographic records up to date and do not leave this until the very end of the writing-up process, when you will probably be under significant time pressure.

Your university will probably have its own guidelines as to which style of referencing you should use in your dissertation, and if it does you should definitely follow them. However, the two main methods used are:

- **Harvard**. This system works as follows: whenever you paraphrase the argument or ideas of an author or authors in your writing, you add the surname of the author(s) and the year of publication in brackets at the end of the sentence. If you are quoting the author(s) directly, you put quotation marks around the text you take from them, then after the name and year of publication you add the page number where the quote is taken from. All books, articles, and other sources that you have cited in the text are then provided in full in a reference list at the end of the dissertation in alphabetical order by author surname. This is by far the most common referencing system in business and management research and the one that we follow in this book. It is, therefore, the style that we would encourage you to use if your university does not require you to follow its own guidelines.

- **Note or numeric**. This system works as follows: superscript numbers like this [5] are added to the text at the end of sentences. They refer to a note at the foot of the page (a footnote) or at the end of the text (an endnote), where the reference is given in full, together with the page number if it is a direct quotation. If a source is cited more than once, an abbreviated version of the reference is given in any subsequent citation (which is why this is often called the short-title system). Sometimes superscript numbers are used to provide additional detail, such as comments from the writer about the source being cited. This way of referencing is a particular feature of historical writing. One of the advantages of the note or numeric method is that it can be less distracting to the reader in terms of the flow of the text than the Harvard method, where long strings of references can make a sentence or a paragraph difficult to follow. Furthermore, software packages such as Word make the insertion of notes relatively simple, and many students find that this is a convenient way of referencing. However, when students use this method, they often use it incorrectly—it is difficult to use it well—and are sometimes unsure whether or not also to include a separate bibliography. For books and dissertations, a bibliography is sometimes recommended, and indeed this can be important in the assessment of students' work (see the section on avoiding plagiarism at the end of this chapter).

The role of the bibliography

What makes a good bibliography? You might think that length is a good measure, since a longer bibliography containing more references implies that the author has been comprehensive in their search of the existing literature. This is undoubtedly true, but only up to a point, since it is also important for the bibliography to be focused—that is, not to try to include everything that has ever been written about a subject but instead to reflect the author's informed judgement of the importance and suitability of sources. This incorporates some of the judgements about quality that were discussed earlier in this chapter. One common proxy for quality is the reputation of the journal in which an article is published. However, although this is a useful indicator, we recommend that it is not one you should rely on exclusively; there might be articles in lesser-status journals, for instance those targeted at practitioners, that have relevance to your subject. It is important to be aware of these judgements of quality and to

seek the advice of your supervisor when making them.

Another important feature of a good bibliography relates to secondary referencing. This is when you refer to an article or book that has been cited in another source such as a textbook and you do not, or cannot, access the original article or book from which it was taken. However, relying heavily on secondary references can be problematic because you are dependent upon the interpretation of the original text that is offered by the authors of the secondary text. This may be adequate for some parts of your literature review, but there is always the potential for different interpretations of the original text; this increases the further removed you are from the original source. So it is a good idea to be cautious in the use of secondary references and to go back to the original source if you can, particularly if the reference is an important one for your subject.

A further feature of a good reference list stems from the relationship between entries and the way they are used in the main body of the text. Obviously it is not helpful to include references in the bibliography that are not mentioned in the text. If references are integrated into the text in a way that shows that you have read them in detail and understood the theoretical perspective from which they are written, this is much more impressive than if a reference is inserted into the text in a way that does not clearly relate to what is being said in the text. Finally, Barnett (1994) argues that a good bibliography gives no indication of the quality of a piece of work, pointing out that some of the most influential academic books ever written do not even include one. Drawing on the ideas of Bourdieu (1984), he suggests that the main purpose of the bibliography is to enable the reader to understand the habitus that the author wants to be in, this being about understanding the beliefs and dispositions of the author combined with the constraints associated with their situation.

Avoiding plagiarism

An issue to bear in mind when writing up your literature review is the need to avoid plagiarizing the work that you are reading. Plagiarism is a notoriously slippery concept. It is defined in *Oxford Dictionary of English* (2nd edn, 2003: 1344) as 'the practice of taking someone else's work or ideas and passing them off as one's own'. As Callahan (2017) notes, plagiarism is usually seen as a form of theft, as the plagiarizer steals sentences, paragraphs or ideas from another author or researcher. In the Wikipedia entry on 'Academic dishonesty', plagiarism is defined as 'The adoption or reproduction of original creations of another author (person, collective, organization, community or other type of author, including anonymous authors) without due acknowledgment'. Plagiarism does not just relate to the literature you read in the course of preparing an essay or report. Taking material in a wholesale and unattributed way from sources such as essays written by others or from websites is also plagiarism. Further, it is possible to self-plagiarize (something that is not apparent in the Wikipedia definition above), as when a person lifts material that he or she has previously written and passes it off as new and original work (see Callahan 2017). Plagiarism is commonly regarded as a form of academic cheating, because the norms of the community have been broken, and as such is similar to other academic misdemeanours such as fabricating research findings.

There is a widespread view that plagiarism among students is increasingly common, though whether this is in fact the case is difficult to establish unambiguously. In a study of two assignments for a business course at a New Zealand university, Walker (2010) found that just over one-quarter of the two assignments together exhibited some level of plagiarism. However, he also found that the level of plagiarism declined between the two assignments, suggesting that students were less inclined to plagiarize for the second assignment when they had received the marker's comments on the first assignment. Many believe that the internet is a prominent—if not the main—driver behind the perceived increase in the prevalence of plagiarism. The ease with which text can be copied from websites, e-journal articles, e-books, or online essays sold commercially, and then pasted into essays is often said to be one of the main factors behind the alleged rise in plagiarism cases among students.

There are several difficulties with plagiarism as an issue in higher education. One is that universities vary in their definitions of what plagiarism is (Stefani and Carroll 2001)—community norms can be different depending on which community you belong to (Callahan 2017). Further, universities vary in their response to plagiarism when it is uncovered, especially in the type and severity of punishment. Moreover, within any university, academic and other staff may differ in their views of the sinfulness of plagiarism and how it should be handled (Flint et al. 2006). There is also evidence that students are less convinced than academic staff that plagiarism is wrong and that it should be punished.

In view of all these uncertainties of both the definition of plagiarism and the appropriate response to it, you may wonder whether you should take issues of plagiarism seriously. Our answer is that you most definitely should. All academic research communities place a high value on the originality of work that is presented in any form. To represent someone else's ideas or writings as your own is always seen as morally dubious, at best. Although there are grey areas with regard to plagiarism, it is important not to overstate their significance. The boundary between original and plagiarized work is usually clear. In addition, there *is* widespread condemnation of plagiarism in academic communities and it *is* nearly always punished when found in the work of students. You should, therefore, try to avoid plagiarizing the work of others at all costs. So concerned are universities about the growth in the number of plagiarism cases that come before examination boards, and the likely role of the internet in facilitating plagiarism, that they are making more and more use of plagiarism detection software, which compares work submitted to everything published on the internet and often across student submissions as well. As several writers (for example, McKeever 2006) have observed, the very technological development that is widely perceived as promoting the incidence of plagiarism—the internet—is also increasingly the springboard for its detection.

The most important point for students is that they should always try to avoid plagiarism, as the penalties may be severe. There are several basic practices that will help you avoid accusations of plagiarism. First, most obviously, do not include large sections of another author's text in your writing without making it very clear that they are in fact quotations. This shows that you know the text quoted is not your own work but that you are making a point by quoting someone else's work. It is easy to get this wrong. In June 2006, it was reported that a plagiarism expert at the London School of Economics had been accused of plagiarism in a paper he published on plagiarism! A paragraph was found that copied verbatim a published source by someone else and that had not been acknowledged properly as that person's work. The accused person defended himself by saying that this was due to a simple formatting error. It is common practice in academic publications to indent a large section of material that is being quoted, thus:

> The most important point for students is that they should always try to avoid plagiarism, as the penalties may be severe, regardless of the student's own views on the matter. There are several basic practices that will help you avoid accusations of plagiarism. First, most obviously, do not include large sections of another author's text in your writing without making it clear that they are in fact quotations. This shows that you know the text quoted is not your own work but that you are making a point by quoting someone. It is easy to get this wrong. In June 2006, it was reported that a plagiarism expert at the London School of Economics had been accused of plagiarism in a paper he published on plagiarism! A paragraph was found that copied verbatim a published source by someone else and that had not been acknowledged properly as that person's work. The accused person defended himself by saying that this was due to a formatting error. It is common practice in academic publications to indent a large section of material that is being quoted.

> (Bryman and Bell 2018: 105–106)

The lack of indentation meant that the paragraph in question looked as though it was being presented as the author's original work. While it may be that this is a case of 'unintentional plagiarism' (Park 2003), distinguishing the intentional from the unintentional is by no means easy. Either way, the credibility and possibly the integrity of the author may be undermined. It is also important to realize that, in most universities, copying large portions of text and changing a few words will also be regarded as plagiarism, and is relatively easy to identify.

Secondly, do not represent other people's ideas or arguments as your own. This means that you should acknowledge the source of any ideas or arguments that you use that are not your own.

Academics are on their guard against plagiarism by their peers too. Colquitt (2012) notes that when authors submit articles for consideration for publication via the Academy of Management's online journal portal, they encounter an automatic message that warns the author that all articles are screened for plagiarism. A number of other management journals routinely scan submitted manuscripts to check for plagiarism. Honig and Bedi

(2012) examined 279 papers that were presented at a conference associated with one of the divisions of the Academy of Management in 2009. They found evidence of some plagiarism in 25 per cent of the papers and, even more alarming, 'significant plagiarism' (where 5 per cent or more of the paper is found to be plagiarized) in 13 per cent of the papers. As Honig and Bedi note, the fact that papers undergo peer review when they are submitted clearly does not act as a deterrent and does not serve to identify cases of plagiarism.

Ultimately, the most important message of this section is that you should guard against plagiarism at all costs in your academic practice. It should be clear by now that you must inform yourself as to what your university and departmental guidelines are. Quite aside from the moral rights and wrongs of plagiarism (remember, it is theft), it is not likely to impress your tutor if it is clear from reading the text that large chunks of your essay or report have been lifted from another source with a few of your own words interspersing the plagiarized text. That is often in our experience a clear giveaway—the contrast in styles is very apparent and prompts the reader to explore the possibility that some or much of the assignment you submit has in fact been plagiarized. Nor is it likely to impress most tutors if much of the text has been lifted but a few words changed here and there, along with a few sprinkled words written by you. However, equally it has to be said that frequent quoting with linking sentences by you is not likely to impress either, even if the sources of the quotes are acknowledged. When presented with essays of that kind, we usually say to the student concerned that it is difficult to establish what his or her own thoughts on the issue are.

The solution is straightforward. Try to express ideas in your own words, and make clear acknowledgement to the authors who have introduced you to ideas that are not your own. Plagiarism is something you may get away with once or twice, but it is so imprinted on the consciousness of the academic communities working in universities nowadays that you are unlikely to get away with it regularly. Finally, put yourself in the position of the person being stolen from. It is extremely irritating to find that your own work has been plagiarized. One of this book's authors, Alan Bryman, was asked to act as an external examiner of a doctoral thesis and found that large sections of one of his books had been taken and presented as the student's own work. Bryman mentioned the incident to a colleague, who remarked that the only thing worse than plagiarism is incompetent plagiarism—incompetent because the student had plagiarized the work of someone he or she knew would be the external examiner.

One final point to note is that plagiarism is like a moving target. What it is, how it is defined, how it is detected, how it is penalized: all of these issues and others are in a state of flux as we write this chapter. It is very much a shifting situation precisely because of the perception that it is increasing in frequency. But whatever the changes in definition and detection, the penalties are always severe, and, as we have witnessed when students have been presented with evidence of their plagiarism, it can be profoundly embarrassing and distressing. The message is always simple at its centre: do not do it, and make sure that you know exactly what it is and how it is defined at your university so that you do not inadvertently commit plagiarism.

CHECKLIST
Questions to ask yourself when reviewing the literature

○ Is your list of references up to date? Does it include the most recently published research?

○ What literature searching have you done recently?

○ What have you read recently? Have you found time to read?

○ What have you learned from the research literature you have engaged with? Has this changed your understanding of the subject in any way?

○ Is your search for the literature and the review you are writing being guided by research questions or puzzles? Has your reading of the literature made you think about revising your research questions or made you think differently about a puzzle?

○ Have you addressed key controversies and debates in the literature, and different ways of conceptualizing your subject?

○ Have you been writing notes on what you have read?

○ Have you adopted a critical approach to presenting your literature review?

○ What story are you going to tell about the literature? In other words, have you worked out what the message is that you present about the literature?

○ Has someone read a draft of your review to check on your writing style and the strength of your arguments?

Adapted from Bruce (1994); Holbrook et al. (2007); Reuber (2010).

KEY POINTS

- Writing a literature review is a means of reviewing the main ideas and research relating to your chosen area of interest.

- A competent literature review confirms you as someone who is competent and knowledgeable in the subject area.

- A great deal of the work of writing a literature review consists of reading the work of other researchers in your subject area.

- Systematic review is a method that is gaining in popularity in business research; it is designed as a more reliable method of presenting literature searching and review.

- Narrative review is an alternative approach that has the advantage of flexibility, which can make it more appropriate for inductive research and qualitative research designs.

QUESTIONS FOR REVIEW

Reviewing the existing literature

- What are the main reasons for writing a literature review?
- How can you ensure that you get the most from your reading?
- What are the main advantages and disadvantages associated with systematic review?
- What type of research question or puzzle is systematic review most suited to addressing?
- What are the main reasons for conducting a narrative literature review?
- What type of research does narrative review work best for?

Searching the existing literature

- What are the main ways of finding existing literature on your subject?
- What is a keyword and how is it useful in searching the literature?

Referencing your work

- Why is it important to reference your work?
- What are the two main referencing styles used in academic work and which of these is preferred by your university?
- What is the role of the bibliography and what makes a good one?

Avoiding plagiarism

- What is plagiarism?
- Why is it taken so seriously by researchers?

ONLINE RESOURCES

www.oup.com/uk/brm5e/

Visit the Interactive Research Guide that accompanies this book to complete an exercise in reviewing the literature.

ETHICS IN BUSINESS RESEARCH

CHAPTER OUTLINE

This chapter is concerned with issues about ethics that might arise in the course of conducting research. It is important to remember that ethical issues can arise at various points in the research process. Business researchers therefore need to be aware of, and prepared to address, these issues in order to ensure the integrity of their study and the reputation of business research more generally. The professional bodies that represent business and social science researchers provide valuable guidance on ethical issues that can arise in research, and their statements will be reviewed in this chapter. The chapter explores:

- some famous, or infamous, cases where ethical principles have been transgressed, although it is important not to take the view that ethical concerns arise only in such extreme cases;

- the different stances that can be taken on ethics in business research;

- four ethical principles to which researchers are expected to adhere: avoidance of harm; informed consent; protection of privacy through confidentiality; and preventing deception;

- ethical considerations that relate specifically to online research;

- difficulties associated with ethical decision-making;

- the political context of business research and the ethical concerns that are raised by this.

Introduction

In this chapter, we will introduce the main issues and debates about research ethics. We are not going to try to resolve these debates, because they are not readily capable of resolution. What *is* crucial is to be aware of the ethical principles involved in business research and how to engage with them. It is only by being aware of these issues that you can make informed decisions about the ethics of your research. Discussions about the ethics of business research revolve around such concerns as the following.

- How should we treat the people on whom we conduct research?
- Are there unethical activities which we should not engage in?

Our chief concern in this chapter lies with the ethical issues that arise between researchers and research participants in the course of an investigation, as these are the most relevant considerations in a student research project. Writers on research ethics adopt different stances concerning research ethics. Key concept 6.1 outlines these stances. Towards the end of the chapter we broaden the discussion to look at the wider political context of business research, by considering issues related to university careers and research funding which have an effect on the type of research produced.

Questions about the ethics of business research also bring in the role of professional associations that have codes of ethics for their members, such as the Chartered Association of Business Schools (CABS) in the UK and the Academy of Management (AOM) in the USA. The statements of professional principles used by these organizations are readily accessed online and are useful examples of ethics codes for business researchers.

> Chartered Association of Business Schools (CABS), *Ethics Guide* (2015):
> https://charteredabs.org/publications/ethics-guide-2015-advice-guidance/
>
> Academy of Management (AOM), *AOM Code of Ethics* (2006):
> http://aom.org/About-AOM/AOM-Code-of-Ethics.aspx

It is also useful to look at how researchers in the social sciences more generally deal with ethical issues. In this chapter, the codes of ethics of the following professional associations will also be referred to.

> Australian Research Council/National Health and Medical Research Council/Universities Australia, *Australian Code for the Responsible Conduct of Research* (2007):
> https://www.nhmrc.gov.au/guidelines-publications/

> British Sociological Association (BSA), *Statement of Ethical Practice* (2017):
> https://www.britsoc.co.uk/media/24310/bsa_statement_of_ethical_practice.pdf
>
> Economic and Social Research Council (ESRC) [UK], *Framework for Research Ethics* (2015):
> http://www.esrc.ac.uk/funding/guidance-for-applicants/research-ethics/
>
> International Sociological Association (ISA), *Code of Ethics* (2001):
> https://www.isa-sociology.org/en/about-isa/code-of-ethics/
>
> Social Research Association (SRA) [UK], *Ethical Guidelines* (2003):
> http://the-sra.org.uk/research-ethics/ethics-guidelines/

Discussion about ethics in business and other social science research can be frustrating for four reasons.

1. Writers often differ quite widely from each other over ethical issues and questions. In other words, they differ over what is and is not ethically acceptable.

2. The main elements in the debates do not seem to move forward a great deal. The same kinds of points that were made in the 1960s were being rehashed in the late 1990s and in the present century.

3. Debates about ethics are often associated with well-known cases of alleged ethical transgression. Some of them, such as Dalton's (1959) covert ethnography of unofficial managerial activity, will also be encountered later in this book (see Chapter 19). A central issue that Dalton addresses in his study concerns the unofficial use of company resources, including pilfering or corporate theft (see Research in focus 6.2). There is considerable debate as to whether it was ethical to obtain such data through the method of covert observation (see Key concept 6.1). There are also several well-known psychological studies (e.g. Milgram 1963; Haney et al. 1973) that continue to be widely cited in the field of organizational behaviour, despite the fact that they were based on research designs that would now be widely considered extremely unethical (see Research in focus 6.3). However, the problem with this emphasis on notoriety is that it can be taken to imply that ethical concerns reside only in such extreme cases, when in fact the need to consider ethical issues applies to all types of business research.

4. Related to this last point, extreme and notorious cases of ethical violation tend to be associated with particular research methods, notably disguised (covert) observation and the use of deception in experiments. This can give the—incorrect—impression that other methods, such as questionnaires or semi-structured interviews, are immune from ethical issues. Again, the problem with this is that it implies that ethical concerns reside only or primarily in some methods but not others.

6.1 KEY CONCEPT
Stances on ethics

Authors on research ethics can be characterized according to the stance they take on the issue. The following positions can be distinguished:

- *Universalism.* A universalist stance takes the view that ethical precepts should never be broken. Infractions of ethical principles are wrong in a moral sense and are damaging to research. This kind of stance can be seen in the writings of Erikson (1967), Dingwall (1980), and Bulmer (1982). Bulmer does, however, point to some forms of disguised observation that may be acceptable. One is retrospective covert observation, which occurs when a researcher writes up his or her experiences in social settings in which he or she participated, but not as a researcher. An example would be Van Maanen (1991*b*), who wrote up his experiences as a ride operator in Disneyland many years after he had been employed there in vacation jobs. Even a universalist such as Erikson (1967: 372) recognizes that it 'would be absurd … to insist as a point of ethics that sociologists should always introduce themselves as investigators everywhere they go and should inform every person who figures in their thinking exactly what their research is all about'.

- *Situation ethics.* Goode (1996) has argued for deception to be considered on a case-by-case basis. In other words, he argues for what J. Fletcher (1966: 31) has called a 'situation ethics', or more specifically 'principled relativism', which can be contrasted with the universalist stance adopted by other writers. This argument has two ways of being represented:

  1. *The end justifies the means.* Some writers argue that, unless ethical rules are broken, we would never know about certain social phenomena. Dalton (1959) argues for this position in relation to his study of managers and the differences between official and unofficial action. Without some kind of disguised observation, this important aspect of organizational life would not have been studied. This is usually linked to the second form of a situationist argument.

  2. *No choice.* It is sometimes suggested that we have no choice but to conceal the purpose of a research investigation on occasions if we want to investigate the issues in which we are interested. This argument is related to the reactive effect that research can have on participants, who may be induced to change their behaviour as a consequence of being studied (see Research in focus 3.7). In such cases, some researchers argue that a degree of concealment, at least in advance of the study, is justifiable.

- *Ethical transgression is pervasive.* It is often observed that virtually all research involves ethically problematic elements. This occurs when participants are not given absolutely all the information about a study, or when there is variation between participants in the amount of knowledge they have about the research. Punch (1994: 91), for example, observes that 'some dissimulation is intrinsic to social life and, therefore, to fieldwork'. He quotes Gans (1962: 44) in support of this point: 'If the researcher is completely honest with people about his activities, they will try to hide actions and attitudes they consider undesirable, and so will be dishonest. Consequently, the researcher must be dishonest to get honest data.'

- *Anything goes (more or less).* Writers who advocate a situational stance towards research ethics are not arguing for an 'anything-goes' mentality, but for a certain amount of flexibility in ethical decision-making. However, Douglas (1976) has argued that the kinds of deception in which social researchers engage are trivial compared to those perpetrated by powerful institutions in modern society (such as the mass media, the police, and industry). His book is an inventory of tactics for deceiving people so that their trust is gained and they reveal themselves to the researcher. Very few researchers subscribe to this stance. Denzin (1968) comes close to an anything-goes stance when he suggests that social researchers are entitled to study anyone in any setting provided the work has a 'scientific' purpose, does not harm participants, and does not deliberately damage the discipline. The harm-to-participants criterion can also be seen in the cases reported in Research in focus 6.3.

6.2 RESEARCH IN FOCUS
A covert study of unofficial rewards

One of Dalton's (1959) central themes in his study of American managers and unofficial action revolves around the use of company materials and services as rewards for the **variable** contributions of individuals. He presents several cases, including that of a carpenter, Ted Berger, who was rewarded for his loyalty by not being required to operate machines, instead making such things as baby beds, tables, and rocking horses—custom-built objects for various managers—in exchange for which he was given 'gifts'. Another case concerns staff who routinely filled their car fuel tanks from the company garage and with this obtained free washing and waxing. Similarly, there is the case of Jim Speier, a factory foreman, who made use of machinery and materials to have constructed a rose arch, storm windows, and a set of wooden lawn sprinklers cut in the form of dancing girls and brightly painted!

Dalton's main strategy for preventing harm to his participants was to protect their anonymity, but the reader is left in no doubt as to the seriousness of consequences for the individuals concerned if their identities were to have been discovered. As Dalton explains, these individuals 'gave information and aid that, if generally known, would have jeopardized their careers' (1959: 275). One of the key ethical issues in this study concerns the lack of informed consent: participants were in no position to be able to judge whether or not to become involved in the research, as they were only vaguely aware that Dalton was doing some kind of research. They were almost certainly unaware of the risk of harm to their employment prospects that could result from their participation in the study. In his defence, Dalton adopts a situational ethical stance (see Key concept 6.1), arguing that it is impossible to study unofficial action other than by using covert methods which enable the researcher to get sufficiently close to the subject. As there has been very little study of this subject, it is difficult to see how we could compare Dalton's findings with those produced using overt methods, and therefore we have little choice but to take his word for this.

The importance of research ethics

Examples such as those summarized in Research in focus 6.2 and Research in focus 6.3 highlight the challenges of arriving at ethically informed decisions in business research. This might lead researchers to regard ethical issues as a series of obstacles that need to be overcome so that they can get on with their study. There is no doubt that the level of ethical scrutiny that researchers face has increased in recent years, and the burden of responsibility for demonstrating that ethical issues have been satisfactorily addressed, has been placed firmly on the researcher. The ethical principles that are covered by research ethics codes help researchers to ensure that ethical risks are minimized. However, these requirements can encourage a bureaucratic compliance-based, or 'tick-box' approach, where the researcher assumes that ethical considerations can be set to one side as dealt with once ethical approval has been obtained. Nothing could be farther from the truth; it is vital for business researchers to regard ethical considerations as an integral part of the research process and to continually revisit them throughout their study. For students undertaking a research project, it is likely that ethical decision-making will be undertaken in consultation with supervisors and other qualified researchers who have experience of how to deal with these complexities.

6.3 RESEARCH IN FOCUS
Two infamous studies of obedience to authority

Milgram's (1963) electric-shock experiments and Haney et al.'s (1973) prison studies have come to be seen as infamous because of the ethical issues they raise. Both studies aimed to measure the effects of group norms on the behaviour of the individual, and they have been widely applied in the field of organizational behaviour.

Milgram was concerned with the processes whereby a person can be induced to cause extreme harm to another by virtue of being ordered to do so. To investigate this issue further, he devised a laboratory experiment. Volunteers were recruited to act out the role of teachers and to punish learners (who were accomplices of the experimenter) by submitting them to electric shocks when the learners gave incorrect answers to questions.

The shocks were not, of course, real, but the teachers/volunteers were not aware of this. The level of electric shock was gradually increased with successive incorrect answers until the teacher/volunteer refused to administer more shocks. Learners had been trained to respond to the rising level of electric shock with simulated but appropriate howls of pain. In the room was a further accomplice of Milgram's, who cajoled the teacher/volunteer to continue to administer shocks, suggesting that it was part of the study's requirements to continue and that they were not causing permanent harm, in spite of the increasingly shrill cries of pain. However, in a later adaptation of the experiment, the teacher/volunteer was accompanied by a colleague who acted out the part of someone who refused to administer the shocks beyond a certain level. In this situation, the real subject continued to administer the shocks for a shorter period and then declined as the first teacher/volunteer had done. Milgram's study demonstrates the extent to which individuals display obedience to authority even if this involves causing considerable pain to others. It also shows how peer rebellion can be a powerful means of resisting the experimenter's authority.

Experiments conducted by Zimbardo and his graduate students from the department of psychology at Stanford University, California, involved creating a mock prison, in order to examine the roles played by prisoners and guards. Twenty-one male participants were selected from a group of seventy-five who responded to an advertisement in a local newspaper. Individuals were selected on the basis that they were mature, emotionally stable, middle-class, and well educated, and had no criminal record. Each was paid $15 per day to participate in the study. A coin was flipped in order to decide if the participant was to play the role of prisoner or guard. There were ten prisoners and eleven guards. However, only a few days into the planned fourteen-day study, the experiment took an unexpected turn. The relationship between prisoners and guards deteriorated to such an extent that guards began to subject prisoners to psychological cruelty. Within the first few days several of the prisoners had been released, suffering from severe depression and mental breakdown. Only six days into the study the experiment was abandoned owing to the extreme symptoms experienced by the prisoners. Haney et al.'s study shows that individual behaviour is determined by social and environmental conditions to a far greater extent than is commonly assumed.

Both studies raise complex and controversial ethical issues, particularly concerning the potential harm to participants as a result of the experiments. It is important to note that both studies were conducted in the middle of the last century, and it is extremely unlikely that either would be considered acceptable to a university ethics committee or indeed to most social researchers today. However, in 2006 Burger (2009) conducted what he refers to as a 'partial replication' of the Milgram experiment. Burger hypothesized that there would be little or no difference between Milgram's findings and his own some 45 years later. The **replication** is 'partial' for several reasons. Participants did not proceed beyond the lowest simulated voltage level that Milgram used (150 volts; 79 per cent of Milgram's teachers went beyond this point); participants were intensively screened for emotional and psychological problems and excluded if there was evidence of such problems; people who had studied some psychology were excluded (because the Milgram studies are so well known); and participants of all adult ages were included, rather than up to the age of 50, as in the original studies. Burger also reckons that his **sample** was more ethnically diverse than Milgram's would have been. The replication had to be partial because, as Burger puts it, 'current standards for the ethical treatment of participants clearly place Milgram's studies out of bounds' (Burger 2009: 2). Burger found that the propensity for obedience was only slightly lower than 45 years previously, though, as Miller (2009) observes, the adjustments Burger had to make probably render comparisons with Milgram's findings questionable.

Ethical principles

Discussions about ethical principles in business research, and perhaps more specifically transgressions of them, tend to revolve around certain recurrent issues. These are usefully broken down by Diener and Crandall (1978) into four main areas:

- whether there is *harm to participants*;
- whether there is a *lack of informed consent*;
- whether there is an *invasion of privacy*;
- whether *deception* is involved.

We will look at each of these ethical principles in turn, but it should be appreciated that they overlap somewhat. For example, it is difficult to imagine how the principle of informed consent could be built into an investigation in which research participants were deceived. However, these four ethical principles form a useful starting point for thinking about ethics in business research.

Avoidance of harm

Research that is likely to harm participants is regarded by most people as unacceptable. But what is harm? Harm can entail a number of facets: physical harm; harm to participants' development or self-esteem; stress; harm to career prospects or future employment; and 'inducing subjects to perform reprehensible acts', as Diener and Crandall (1978: 19) put it. In several studies that we have encountered in this book, there has been actual or potential harm to participants.

- In Dalton's (1959) study, his 'counselling' relationship with the female secretary in exchange for access to valuable personnel files (see Research in focus 19.3) was potentially harmful to her, both in terms of the personal relationship and in jeopardizing the security of her employment.
- In Haney et al.'s (1973) prison experiments (see Research in focus 6.3), several participants experienced severe emotional reactions, including mental breakdown.
- Many of the participants in the Milgram experiment (1963) on obedience to authority (see Research in focus 6.3) experienced high levels of stress and anxiety as a consequence of being incited to administer what they thought were electric shocks. It could also be argued that Milgram's observers were 'inducing subjects to perform reprehensible acts'. Another series of studies in which Milgram was involved placed participants in positions where they were being influenced to steal (Milgram and Shotland 1973).

The *AOM Code of Ethics* states that it is the responsibility of the researcher to assess carefully the possibility of harm to research participants, and that the possibility of harm should be minimized to the extent that it can be. Similar views are expressed by the Market Research Society (MRS), whose *Code of Conduct* (2014) advocates that 'the researcher must take all reasonable precautions to ensure that respondents are in no way directly harmed or adversely affected as a result of their participation in a marketing research project'. Some commentators cast the scope of ethical consideration wider than this, suggesting that it is also necessary to consider non-participants in evaluating the risk of harm (see Thinking deeply 6.4). This is consistent with recent changes in social research guidelines that extend the definition of what constitutes an ethical issue (see the section later in this chapter on 'Other ethical and legal considerations' for further discussion of these changes).

6.4 THINKING DEEPLY
Harm to non-participants?

Gorard (2002) argues that, although ethical guidance focuses on the responsibilities of the researcher in relation to research participants, there is also a need to consider the interests of non-participants in the research, especially when research has practical implications in determining social policies such as those relating to health, housing, transport, and education. He argues that 'most discussions of ethical considerations in research focus on possible harm to the research participants, to the exclusion of the possible harm done to future users of the evidence which research generates. They almost never consider the wasted resources, and worse, used in implementing treatments and policies that do not work' (2002: 3).

The need to ensure that respondents are in no way harmed as a result of their participation in research is of particular concern in situations involving vulnerable persons who may not be in a position to give their fully informed consent. An example of this might be marketing research that explores the effect of advertising on children. For example, Lawlor and Prothero (2007) conducted focus groups and individual interviews involving 52 children aged between 7 and 9 to explore their understanding of television advertisements. They carried out their data collection in two Irish primary schools during school hours. Consent to participate in the study was requested from the parents of the children, who expressed a preference that the interviews be conducted in the neutral setting of the school, rather than in the children's homes. Permission was also requested for the interviews to be tape-recorded. In cases such as this one, extreme diligence must be exercised over the gaining of informed consent because of the greater vulnerability of children as research participants and the difficulties in ensuring that they fully understand the implications of their agreement to participate in research.

A further ethical consideration relates to the possibility of harm to the researcher, an issue introduced in Tips and skills 'Safety in research'. In addition to the possibility of physical or emotional harm through exposure to a fieldwork setting, certain research methods, such as auto-ethnography (see Key concept 19.18), may carry a greater risk of emotional or professional harm to the researcher because the researcher's own personal self-disclosures constitute the basis for the analysis (Doloriert and Sambrook 2009). If this analysis is made public, sensitive or personal information pertaining to the researcher is placed in the public domain and the anonymity of the researcher cannot be maintained. Doloriert and Sambrook (2009) argue that this is a particular concern for student researchers, whose work will be examined by more experienced and more powerful senior researchers.

The issue of harm to participants is further addressed in ethical codes by advocating care over maintaining the confidentiality of records and the anonymity of accounts. This means the identities and records of individuals and organizations should be maintained as confidential. For example, the *AOM Code of Ethics* recommends that issues relating to confidentiality and anonymity should be negotiated and agreed with potential research participants, and, 'if confidentiality or anonymity is requested, this must be honored'. Similarly, the ISA code says that 'security, anonymity and privacy of research subjects and informants should be respected rigorously, in both quantitative and qualitative research'. This injunction means that care needs to be taken when findings are being published to ensure that individuals and organizations are not identified or identifiable, unless permission has been given for data to be passed on in a form that allows for this. The MRS *Code of Conduct* states that researchers 'should be particularly careful if sample sizes are very small (such as in business and employee research) that they do not inadvertently identify organisations or departments and therefore individuals'.

In quantitative research, it is often easier to anonymize records and to report findings in a way that does not

TIPS AND SKILLS
Safety in research

Although most business research carries a low risk of personal harm to the researcher, there are occasions when doing research could put you in a potentially dangerous situation. Just as you should ensure that no harm comes to research participants, you should at all costs avoid taking personal risks, including by putting yourself in situations where personal harm is a possibility. Individuals involved in supervising research also have a responsibility to ensure that researchers are not placed in situations that might pose a danger of harm to them. This is particularly the case for lone researchers. In some cases, there may be no obvious reason to think that a situation may be dangerous, but the researcher may be faced with a sudden outburst of abuse or threatening behaviour. This can arise when people react relatively unpredictably to an interview question or to being observed. If there are signs that such behaviour is imminent (for example, through body language), you should begin to withdraw from the research situation. R. M. Lee (2004) draws an important distinction between two kinds of danger in fieldwork: ambient and situational. The former refers to situations that are avoidable and where danger is a feature of the context. Situational danger occurs 'when the researcher's presence or activities evoke aggression, hostility or violence from those in the setting' (R. M. Lee 2004: 1285). While problems surrounding safety may be easier to anticipate in the case of ambient danger, they are less easy to foresee in connection with situational danger.

allow individuals to be identified. However, even here there are some instances where it is virtually impossible to make a company anonymous. The use of pseudonyms is a common recourse, but this may not eliminate entirely the possibility of identification. For example, in the case of Hofstede's (1984) research (discussed in Chapter 2), although a pseudonym—HERMES—was used for the company that was the focus of study, it was impossible to conceal its identity without completely distorting the original data because IBM is such a large, distinctive, and well-known organization. In Bell and Leonard's (2018) study of 'digital organizational storytelling' in an online branding company, it was impossible to analyse the organization's storytelling videos without disclosing its identity (see Chapter 20). Consequently the researchers decided not to use a pseudonym for the organization

in their published article. Issues of anonymity are particularly complex in relation to visual data (images and video). Sometimes researchers who use visual data have to go to quite extreme lengths to protect the anonymity of research participants (see Research in focus 6.9).

The issues of confidentiality and anonymity raise particular difficulties for many forms of qualitative research, where great care has to be taken with regard to the possible identification of persons, organizations, and places. The consequences of failing to protect individual anonymity are illustrated by M. Parker (2000: 238; see Chapter 19), who describes how a quotation in his report about the managing director was traced to an 'insufficiently anonymized source' whose reputation was damaged as a result of the incident. On the other hand, as Thinking deeply 6.5 illustrates, in some qualitative

STUDENT EXPERIENCE
Ethical considerations in a student research project

Tom was encouraged by his university to consider the ethical implications of his study of wellbeing among call-centre workers. His main focus was on protecting the anonymity of interviewees so that managers could not trace back comments to specific individuals.

> Birkbeck [College] are very concerned with encouraging an ethical approach to research and considering the implications of it. Given what I was doing, I didn't think there were huge ethical implications. I suppose my main concern was to make sure that I wasn't in any way harming the wellbeing of the people I was talking to and I suppose there was a vague possibility that, you know, we might have talked about very traumatic stuff in the interview, which might make them very stressed and so on, but I didn't think that was very likely. What was more likely was that they'd somehow feel that I'd kind of betrayed their confidentiality by feeding back to management what they were saying, even if it was in some sort of anonymized format. Because I only had a small sample size, you know, the boss could have said 'Right, who said this? I want to see all of you in my office.' So I wanted to set out as clearly as I could how I was going to use their data. What I did was when I transcribed my tapes I called them Interviewee A, Interviewee B, or whatever, and then I destroyed the tapes, so all I had was an anonymized interview. I did use quotes from interviews in my dissertation, but these were attributed to Interviewee A or Call handler B or whatever, but that report was confidential to Birkbeck. It didn't go to the organization that I did my research in.

In the report that went back to the organization Tom 'made sure that there was nothing in there that could be linked back to any individual. So it didn't say "A middle aged, Asian call handler said" because that could have been attributable back to individuals.'

However, Tom also became aware that employees could be pursuing their own political agendas through the research process.

> Although I made it clear that I wasn't there to check up on call handlers on behalf of the management and that it was all confidential and I wasn't going to make recommendations which would be traceable back to any individual, there'd still be a question about to what extent people thought that it was safe to talk to me or that all sorts of stuff was going on. People were asking themselves: 'Was it safe to talk to me?' Actually, I was possibly a mouthpiece for them to make comments back to management and they could say things that hopefully might get relayed on to management about working conditions or whatever.

research projects research participants may not wish to remain anonymous.

The issues of confidentiality and anonymity involve legal as well as ethical considerations. For example, in Cavendish's (1982) study of women factory workers on an assembly line, great care was taken by the researcher to invent names for all the women so that they could not be identified, in order to protect them from possible victimization by the company. Cavendish deliberately left the name of the firm unchanged to preserve the realism of the study and to provide 'concrete facts about the factory' (1982: vi). However, as she explains, the publisher's lawyers were resistant to this: 'if the firm was named, there was a risk both to me and to the publisher that the firm might bring a libel action against us' (1982: vi). For this reason, she decided to rewrite the account prior to publication so that the firm was unidentifiable. This involved changing not only the name of the firm, but also its location, details of the components manufactured, and the name of the trade union representing the women. In contrast, there are other instances where organizations do consent to be named in publications, for example in Pettigrew's (1985) study of changing culture at Imperial Chemical Industries (see Research in focus 3.16).

Issues of confidentiality and anonymity also raise particular problems with regard to the secondary analysis of

TIPS AND SKILLS
Confidentiality agreements

As part of the process of negotiating access, it is increasingly common for companies where research is to be carried out to ask their legal departments to prepare a confidentiality agreement, which you may be asked to sign, or someone from your university may be asked to sign on behalf of the institution. The main purpose of these agreements is to define and restrict the type of information that you are permitted to access and to establish what kind of information you are allowed to disclose about the company. This usually involves agreeing not to pass on information to a third party, particularly if it concerns commercially sensitive data, such as about new product development. There may be a clause that specifies that a representative from the company must have sight of the research once it has been written up, so that they can comment on the findings, particularly if they are going to be published. This kind of legally binding agreement grants a considerable amount of power to the company, and has the potential to cause considerable difficulties if your research throws up issues that the company would rather were kept out of the public domain. If you are asked to sign a confidentiality agreement, before signing it take it to your supervisor to ask for advice, and get it checked by someone who deals with legal issues on behalf of the university. It may be that there is some room for negotiation in relation to the exact wording of the agreement, and the company may be reassured if there is an undertaking that the research will guarantee anonymity.

6.5 THINKING DEEPLY
The assumption of anonymity

Grinyer (2002) argues that, although it is widely assumed that protecting the anonymity of research participants is ethical best practice, there are some circumstances where research participants do not wish to remain anonymous because making their identity explicit is an important way of retaining ownership of their stories. In the UK, there is a legal requirement to maintain anonymization wherever possible to increase the security of data processing. These guidelines are based on the assumption that research participants 'not only deserve the protection of anonymity, but that they actively desire it' (Grinyer 2002: 2). Grinyer argues that the allocation of pseudonyms to protect anonymity can cause unanticipated stress, since research participants sometimes feel that keeping their real names is an important recognition of their involvement in the research project. This, according to Grinyer, makes clear 'how problematic it is to make judgments on behalf of others, however well intentioned' (2002: 3). Grinyer recommends that this issue is dealt with on a case-by-case basis, through consultation with research participants throughout the research and publication process, so that individuals have the freedom to make a more informed choice and are less likely to feel that they have lost ownership of their stories.

STUDENT EXPERIENCE
Maintaining anonymity in a student research project

Karen devised an innovative way of keeping her research participants anonymous that still enabled her to reveal important details about a participant's position within the organization:

> I didn't put any names in the dissertation. It was very difficult to actually work out what I was going to do. With the questionnaire it was just a tick-box so it was a lot easier, but with the actual interviews I wanted to use quotes and that type of thing. So it was a lot more difficult so in the appendix I had a table which was a profile of all the people that I questioned, but with no names on it. So it just had the department that they were from and their level in the organization—not the job title—and then some other information like the length of the time they'd been there in the organization because I used that in the analysis. I could cross-reference that with the quotes that I used and say 'This person from the HR department or from another department said this.' So it maintained their anonymity.

Chris agreed to protect the anonymity of the bank where he did his research, and he sought informed consent from each of the interviewees who agreed to take part in the study. He gave the company and each of the people interviewed a pseudonym.

> The individuals knew from the beginning what I was doing and why I was doing it. I asked them would they want me to keep their names anonymous or not. One person said she did want to be kept anonymous, two said they weren't really bothered. So I thought if I'm going to do it with one, I'd best do it with the other two as well, which I did. I also had to get permission from the organization because I had information about the percentage of women at different levels of management within the organization, which I was freely given, but obviously I sought permission about actually putting that in my dissertation. They said they were fine about it as long as it's sort of not going to be published.

After having completed his degree, Chris was offered a job with the bank as a graduate management trainee. Since then he has become involved in diversity management within the company. Chris's experience shows how the need to act ethically in a research project cannot be separated from one's other roles, as his colleagues' impressions of him now will have undoubtedly been influenced by the way in which he conducted the research project. More generally, the importance of ethics in building trust through the research is something that Chris feels strongly about, as he explains: 'It's who you know and not what you know—and if you can get organizations to trust you and let you in, then you never know what that might lead to in the end.'

---

qualitative data (see Chapter 24), since it can be difficult to present field notes and interview transcripts in a way that will prevent people and places from being identified. As Alderson (1998) has suggested, the difficulty is in ensuring that the same safeguards concerning confidentiality can be guaranteed when secondary analysts examine such records as the safeguards provided by the original primary researcher.

One of the problems with the harm-to-participants issue is that it is not possible to identify in all circumstances whether or not harm is likely, though that fact should not be taken to mean that there is no point in seeking to protect participants. For example, in the prison experiments conducted by Haney et al. (see Research in focus 6.3) the extreme reactions of participants surprised the researchers. Arguably they did not

anticipate this level of harm to be incurred when they planned the study.

Informed consent

The principle of voluntary informed consent seeks to ensure that prospective research participants are given as much information as possible about a study in order to be able to make an informed decision about whether or not they wish to participate in it. This principle is set out in the *ESRC Framework for Research Ethics* (Section 2.2) as follows:

> Informed consent entails giving sufficient information about the research and ensuring that there is no explicit or implicit coercion ... so that prospective participants can make an informed and free decision on their

possible involvement. Information should be provided in a form that is comprehensible and accessible to participants, typically in written form (or in a form that participants can access after the end of the research interaction), and time should be allowed for the participants to consider their choices and to discuss their decision with others if appropriate.

The principle of informed consent means that participants should also be informed if observation techniques or recording equipment are to be used. However, some research, such as disguised or covert observation (as in Research in focus 6.2), or simple or contrived observation (see Key concept 14.11), involves a lack of informed consent. Lack of informed consent is also a feature of Research in focus 6.3. In Dalton's research, he went to great lengths in order to keep the purpose of his research from participants, presumably to maximize his chances

of obtaining specific information about such things as unofficial use of resources or pilfering. Even those who became key informants, or 'intimates', knew only of Dalton's general interest in 'personnel problems', and he took great care not to arouse suspicion. Dalton describes his undercover role as similar in indirect actions to that of an espionage agent or spy, although he stresses that his interest was in scientific rather than criminal evidence. Similarly, while Milgram's and Haney et al.'s experimental subjects (see Research in focus 6.3) were volunteers and therefore knew they were going to participate in research, there was a lack of informed consent because they were not given full information about the nature of the research and its possible implications for them.

While these examples are in the relatively distant past, a more recent experiment on Facebook users by Kramer et al. (2014) suggests that the principle

TIPS AND SKILLS
Getting to know what is expected from your university ethics committee

As well as making yourself familiar with the codes of ethics produced by professional associations such as the Academy of Management, you should be acquainted with the ethical guidelines of your university. Most universities have ethics committees that issue ethical guidelines to researchers employed by the university and to registered students. Ethical guidelines and ethics committees are there to protect research participants, but they are also involved in protecting researchers and institutions from the possibility of adverse publicity or legal action being taken against them.

In order to comply with these ethical requirements, you may need to submit an application form (see Tips and skills 'A sample university ethics form') to your university's ethics committee detailing how you have taken into account potential ethical issues that might arise from your study, particularly if the research involves collecting personal data (see the section later in this chapter on 'Data management'). If data are collected using audio or video recording equipment, informed consent can also be formally recorded in this way, by asking the participant for their informed consent at the start of the process, rather than by asking them to complete a form.

You may also be advised to submit a study information sheet for distribution to research participants (see Tips and skills 'A sample study information sheet'). The information sheet should cover the purpose of the research, what is involved in participating, and any benefits and risks associated with taking part. It may also include an explanation of how to withdraw from the study and what will happen to the data if this occurs. The information sheet also explains how the data will be collected, e.g. any audio or video recordings that will be made, and the ethical precautions that will be taken to protect participants from potential harm, e.g. the preserving of confidentiality and/or anonymity. The form will also provide contact information in case a participant has a question or complaint.

Participants may also be asked to complete a consent form to confirm that they have received and understood this information and agreed to participate (see Tips and skills 'A sample study consent form'). The consent form is usually signed by both parties to indicate consent.

If your university requires you to apply for ethical approval as part of your research project, this process can be time-consuming, so it is important to plan for this. It is also essential that you do not start the research until ethical approval has been granted.

TIPS AND SKILLS

A sample university ethics form

This form is intended to help researchers consider the ethical implications of research activity. Researchers are responsible for deciding, guided by university guidelines and professional disciplinary standards, whether a more extensive review is necessary.

Title of study:

Names of investigators:

	Yes	No
	(please tick)	
1. Is the study funded? (If yes, name the source)	☐	☐
2. Is the research compromised by the source of funding?	☐	☐
3. Are there potential conflicts of interest in the financial or organizational arrangements?	☐	☐
4. Will confidentiality be maintained appropriately at all stages of enquiry: at data collection, storage, analysis, and reporting?	☐	☐
5. Will human rights and dignities be actively respected?	☐	☐
6. Will highly personal, intimate, or other private or confidential information be sought?	☐	☐
7. Will there be any harm, discomfort, physical risks, or psychological risks?	☐	☐
8. Will participants be involved whose ability to give informed voluntary consent may be limited?	☐	☐
9. Will the study involve obtaining or processing personal data relating to living individuals (e.g. recording interviews with subjects even if the findings will subsequently be made anonymous)? (*Note: if the answer to this question is 'yes' you will need to ensure that relevant regulations and legal frameworks are complied with. In particular you will need to ensure that subjects provide sufficient consent and that personal data will be properly stored for an appropriate period of time.*)	☐	☐

10. Please provide a paragraph explaining any additional ethical issues that are relevant to the study. If none, explain why.

I confirm that the ethical issues pertaining to this study have been fully considered.

Signed (lead investigator): _____Date:_____

On behalf of the University Research Ethics Committee: _____Date:_____

---

of informed consent is occasionally violated today. A massive sample of 689,003 Facebook users was randomly selected in order to investigate whether exposure to positive or negative emotional expressions caused a change in users' own affective expressions as expressed in their own posts. Two experiments were created: one in which an experimental group was exposed for a one-week period to a reduction in positive emotions in friends' news feeds compared to a control group, and one in which the experimental group was exposed to a reduction in negative emotions. Participants were not offered the opportunity to give explicit informed consent to the study. Instead, the researchers claim that their investigation 'was consistent

with Facebook's Data Use Policy, to which all users agree prior to creating an account on Facebook, constituting informed consent for this research' (Kramer et al. 2014: 8789). The research prompted a storm of protest in the mass media in the UK and the USA because participants in the study were not given the opportunity to express, or withhold, explicit informed consent.

However, as Homan (1991: 73) has observed, implementing the principle of informed consent 'is easier said than done'. At least two major points stand out here.

• It is extremely difficult to present prospective participants with absolutely all the information that might be required to make an informed decision about their involvement. Relatively minor ethical transgressions probably pervade most business research, such as deliberately underestimating the amount of time that an interview is likely to take so that people are not put off being interviewed, and not giving absolutely all the details about one's research for fear of contaminating people's answers to questions.

- In ethnographic research, the researcher is likely to come into contact with a wide range of people, and ensuring that absolutely everyone has the opportunity for informed consent is not practicable because it would be extremely disruptive in everyday contexts. Also, even when all research participants in a certain setting are aware that the ethnographer is a researcher, it is doubtful whether they are all similarly (let alone identically) informed about the nature of the research. For example, in C. K. Lee's (1998) study of women factory workers in Hong Kong and China, she found it difficult to convey her 'version' of what she was doing to her co-workers. This was partly because the academic term 'thesis' did not make sense to them, so the women developed an alternative explanation, which involved the idea that Lee was writing a novel based on her experiences as a worker 'toiling side by side with "real" workers'. Lee explains: 'I had to settle for that definition too' (1998: 173). This example illustrates how difficult it can be for the researcher to fully explain the purpose and nature of the research, and so sometimes a compromise understanding is reached.

- The difficulties of obtaining informed consent are further complicated when data is collected in a public place, or using publicly available information about people or organizations. In such cases, it may not be practical to seek informed consent from all those present.

The passage acknowledges that covert research jeopardizes informed consent, along with the privacy principle (see below), but the BSA *Statement of Ethical Practice* says that covert research can be used 'only where it is impossible to use other methods to obtain essential data'. The difficulty here, clearly, is how a researcher is to decide whether or not it is impossible to obtain data other than by covert methods.

TIPS AND SKILLS
A sample study information sheet

Study Information

[Study Title]

You are being invited to consider taking part in the research study [insert title]. This study is being undertaken by [researcher name]. Before you decide whether or not you wish to take part, it is important for you to understand why this research is being done and what it will involve. Please take time to read this information carefully. Please ask if there is anything that is unclear or if you would like more information.

You have been invited to participate because [reason for participant selection]. The study will involve [brief details of methods, in language the reader will be able to understand]. You are free to decide whether you wish to take part or not. If you do decide to take part you will be asked to sign two consent forms; one is for you to keep and the other is for my records. You are free to withdraw from this study at any time and without giving reasons. Should you decide to withdraw from the study, your data will not be used and will be destroyed. The study is [details of how the research is being funded or, if it is part of a student project, explain: e.g. 'The study forms part of my MSc qualification at {name of university}'].

If you agree to take part, [explain what will happen from participant's perspective, e.g. you will be interviewed by the researcher involved in the study; the interview will last approximately one hour and will be audio-recorded for research purposes. The data will be anonymized and will not be used in a way which would enable identification of your individual responses. Data will be stored securely on a password-protected computer, and in hard copy in a locked filing cabinet, by the research investigators for a period not exceeding five years, after which point it will be disposed of securely. The data will not be shared with any third parties.].

If you have any questions about the study, please feel free to contact me at [researcher details: use university contact information rather than private phone number or personal email address]. Alternatively, if you are concerned about any aspect of this study you may contact [name and job title of contact within the university to whom issues should be addressed].

TIPS AND SKILLS
A sample study consent form

Consent Form

[Title of Research Project]

[Contact details of researcher: include university postal address, university telephone number, and university email address]

Request for informed consent:

- I have read the Study Information sheet provided and been given adequate time to consider it.
- I have been given the opportunity to ask questions about the Study and any questions have been answered to my satisfaction.
- I understand that my participation in the Study is voluntary.
- I understand that taking part in the Study will involve me being interviewed and I agree to this interview being audio-recorded.
- I understand that my personal details such as name and employer address will not be revealed to people outside the project.
- I understand that my words may be quoted in publications, reports, web pages, and other research outputs, but data collected about me during the Study will be anonymized before it is submitted for publication.
- I understand that I can withdraw from the Study at any time and I will not be asked any questions about why I no longer want to take part.
- I understand that if I withdraw from the Study my data will not be used.

Name of Participant: _____ Signature: _____ Date: _____

Name of Researcher: _____ Signature: _____ Date: _____

[Based on examples from the UK Data Archive and UK universities]

However, some researchers have expressed concerns about what they see as a 'tick-box approach' to informed consent, saying that it encourages ethical issues to be seen as a one-time consideration, rather than as something that needs to be considered throughout the research process (Sin 2005). The form-filling method of gaining informed consent is particularly problematic in certain qualitative research designs, where data collection can extend over a period of time and involve methods such as participant observation (see Chapter 19) for which it would be inappropriate to ask research participants to sign a form. Also, the direction of qualitative studies can be somewhat less predictable than with quantitative ones, so it is difficult to be specific within forms about some issues. The requirements of university ethics committees have led to concerns about 'ethics creep' (Haggerty 2004), a situation where bureaucratic structures of ethical regulation increase to such an extent that they become overly restrictive and dysfunctional, preventing certain types of research from being conducted, or leading researchers to avoid studying particular contexts where the requirements for ethical approval are particularly time consuming and difficult, such as in hospitals. A number of criticisms have been made of university systems and processes that are used to ensure the ethical conduct of researchers. These centre on several issues:

- ethical review committee members' lack of research experience and the secrecy that surrounds committee composition and practices (den Hoonaard 2011);
- inappropriate imposition of a biomedical model of research that follows the sovereignty of the positivist natural science paradigm and promotes a distanced, objectivist research stance that is insensitive to qualitative-interpretive study (Dingwall 2006);
- notions of potential harm applied in a social science context where risks of harm are much less than in the biomedical sciences (Thorne, 1980);

- the time-consuming and dysfunctional nature of bureaucratic review processes which encourage detachment from humanitarian values (Bell and Wray Bliss 2009);

- the unintended consequences of ethical regimes which encourage researchers to see ethics as a paper-based, tick-box exercise and a hurdle to be overcome, rather than an ongoing and essential feature of the research process (Sin 2005);

- the export of a research ethics model from scholars in the global north to those on the periphery without substantive dialogue and suitable modification (Riessman 2005).

[adapted from Bell and Kothiyal 2018, p.548]

Privacy

This third ethical principle relates to the need to protect the privacy of research participants. The right to privacy is a tenet that many of us hold dear, and transgressions of that right in the name of research are not regarded as acceptable. Under the heading 'Avoiding undue intrusion', the SRA guidance on this issue cites Cassell (1982) and states:

> People can feel wronged without being harmed by research: they may feel they have been treated as objects of measurement without respect for their individual values and sense of privacy. In many of the social enquiries that have caused controversy, the issue has had more to do with intrusion into subjects' private and personal domains, or by overburdening subjects by collecting 'too much' information, rather than with whether or not subjects have been harmed. In some cases a researcher's attitudes, demeanour or even their latent theoretical or methodological perspective can be interpreted as doing an injustice to subjects. Examples include an offhand manner on the part of a survey interviewer or studies which depend upon some form of social disruption. By exposing subjects to a sense of being wronged, perhaps by such attitudes, by such approaches, by the methods of selection or by causing them to acquire self knowledge that they did not seek or want, social researchers are vulnerable to criticism. Participants' resistance to future social enquiries in general may also increase as a consequence of such 'inconsiderateness'.
>
> (SRA, *Ethical Guidelines* 2003: 27)

Privacy is very much linked to the notion of informed consent, because, to the degree that informed consent is given on the basis of a detailed understanding of what the research participant's involvement is likely to entail, he or she in a sense acknowledges that the right to privacy has been surrendered for that limited domain. Of course, the research participant does not entirely abrogate the right to privacy by providing informed consent. When people agree to be interviewed, they may refuse to answer certain questions on whatever grounds they feel are justified. Often, these refusals will be based on a feeling that certain questions delve into private realms or cover topic areas that they find sensitive and they do not wish to make these known, regardless of the fact that the interview is conducted in private. The SRA statement highlights the potentially very broad and varied nature of the issues that can be interpreted as intrusive. Although there are some topics that can be judged sensitive to everyone, because of the nature of the subject, it is impossible for the researcher to know beforehand which topics may be sensitive to a particular individual. It therefore recommends that the researcher 'treat each case sensitively and individually, giving respondents a genuine opportunity to withdraw'.

Preventing deception

Deception occurs when researchers represent their research as something other than what it is. The obedience-to-authority study by Milgram referred to in Research in focus 6.3 involved deception, because participants were led to believe they were administering real electric shocks. A less extreme example is provided by Holliday (1995) in her ethnographic study of small firms (see Research in focus 6.6). In pretending to be a student interested in small firms in order to get information about a competitor's product, Holliday was clearly engaged in an element of deception.

The ethical objection to deception seems to turn on two points. First, it is not a nice thing to do. While the SRA *Guidelines* recognizes that deception is widespread in social interaction, it is hardly desirable. Secondly, there is the question of professional self-interest. If business researchers became known as snoopers who deceived people as a matter of course, the image of our work would be adversely affected and we might experience difficulty in gaining financial support and the cooperation of future prospective research participants. As the SRA *Guidelines* puts it:

> It remains the duty of social researchers and their collaborators, however, not to pursue methods of inquiry that are likely to infringe human values and sensibilities. To do so, whatever the methodological advantages, would be to endanger the reputation of social research and the mutual trust between social researchers and society which is a prerequisite for much research.

6.6 RESEARCH IN FOCUS
An example of an ethical dilemma in fieldwork

Holliday (1995: 17–18) describes an ethical dilemma that she faced during her fieldwork.

I arranged to visit a small electronics company owned by a friend of a colleague. The night before I was due to visit the company my temperature soared to 103 degrees and I went down with 'flu. However, I felt that I could not break the arrangement at such short notice, so I decided to go to the factory anyway ... I got to the factory at 10 am. Eventually Raj, the owner-manager, arrived. We had spent 10 minutes touring the factory when he asked me if I could drive. I said that I could, so he asked me if I would drive him to another factory about fifteen miles south ... Business and lunch over we walked back to the car (to my great relief—at last I could go home) ... As we pulled out of the car park, Raj turned to me and said, 'I'd just like to pop down to an exhibition in Birmingham—is that okay?' My heart sank, but I didn't have the strength to protest, so off to Birmingham we went.

During the journey down, Raj told me about a crisis which had occurred very recently within his company. Another small firm had ordered a very substantial piece of equipment from him, which had required a huge amount of development work. Once the item was supplied the company which placed the order promptly declared itself bankrupt and refused to pay ... By the time we reached Birmingham my sense of injustice was well and truly inflamed ... 'So', Raj continued, 'this company has a display of *our product* here today and I want to get their brochure on it. The trouble is they'll know me, so you'll have to get it. We'll split up at the door and I'll meet you in an hour. Tell them you're a customer or something ...' I couldn't believe it. I was being asked to commit industrial espionage in my first few hours of fieldwork.

I got the brochure pretending to be a student—from Southampton, interested in researching small firms. I even got an invitation to the factory to come and research them. Then I passed the intelligence to Raj and began the long drive back. I arrived home at 8.30 pm exhausted and feverish, and with a very guilty conscience.

One of the problems with the discussion of this aspect of ethics is that deception is, as some writers observe, widespread in business research (see the stance 'Ethical transgression is pervasive' in Key concept 6.1). As the example from C. K. Lee's (1998) research illustrates (discussed under 'Informed consent' earlier in the chapter), it is rarely feasible or desirable to provide participants with a totally complete account of what your research is about. Bulmer (1982), whose stance is predominantly that of a universalist in ethics terms (see Key concept 6.1), nonetheless recognizes that there are bound to be instances such as this and deems them justifiable. However, it is very difficult to know where the line should be drawn here.

Other ethical and legal considerations

In addition to the four main ethical issues identified by Diener and Crandall (1978), there are other ethical considerations that need to be taken into account in planning a research project. These relate to

- the impact of data protection legislation;
- copyright and the sharing of data;
- the role of reciprocity in determining the relationship between the researcher and research participants;

- the need to declare sources of funding and support that may cause a conflict of interest for the researcher.

Data management

The routine collection and storing of digital data and the practices of data sharing raise new concerns about confidentiality and other ethical issues. They raise questions about the extent to which information can legitimately be used for research purposes that may be different from the original reason for collecting the data. This issue focuses on who owns the data and under what circumstances people are entitled to use it. In obtaining informed consent from research participants, any long-term preservation and sharing plans should be made explicit, so these decisions need to be made at the outset of a project. A good source of advice on the management and sharing of data is the UK Data Archive (2009), which states:

> The ease with which digital data can be stored, disseminated and made accessible to secondary users via the internet means that many institutions embrace the sharing of research data to increase the impact and visibility of their research.
>
> (UK Data Archive 2011: 3, http://www.data-archive.ac.uk/media/2894/managingsharing.pdf)

As this statement highlights, it is increasingly common for researchers to be encouraged to make their data available to the wider scientific community so that maximum potential benefit may be gained from it. This raises issues relating to data security: the extent to which data need to be protected from unauthorized access or usage, particularly if they contain personal information relating to individuals, such as their names, addresses, occupations, or photographs.

In many countries, there is specific legislation governing data protection. Because legislation surrounding data protection varies from country to country, the Respect project set out to identify some common principles for European researchers to bear in mind when dealing with data-protection issues. This involved a group of legal specialists who reviewed the existing EU legislation and came up with a common set of guidelines for researchers to follow in dealing with this issue. These guidelines can be viewed in full at http://www.respectproject.org/data/415data.pdf. In 2018 the European Union's General Data Protection Regulations (GDPR) were made enforceable, meaning that organizations, including universities, that don't comply with the regulations will now face heavy fines. This is likely to have implications for how business researchers protect personal data. Further changes to legislation are likely following the UK's departure from the EU.

The length and detail of this report highlights the complexity of this issue, for which researchers may be advised to take legal advice. However, it is worth highlighting three of the recommendations that the authors of the report make. These are:

- Researchers should draft an outline of the processing operations (this is not limited to electronic processing) involved in their use of the data *before* they start to process it, so they can assess the legality of their usage in advance, rather than perform the operations and then find out afterwards whether or not they are permitted to use the data in this way. This point highlights the potential seriousness of using data unlawfully, for which criminal or administrative sanctions may be applied.

- Researchers should decide who is the controller of the data and thus responsible for its usage, and on the basis of this determine which national legislation applies to their study. This is a particular issue in situations involving a group of researchers working together on a research project but based in different countries. This decision also depends on where the data processing will be carried out.

- Prior to the data processing, the researcher should define who will be the data subjects and take precautions to respect their rights in relation to the data.

Copyright

A further issue affected by legal considerations is copyright. Copyright is an intellectual property right that protects the owner of copyright from unauthorized copying. Most research publications, reports, and books, as well as raw data such as spreadsheets and interview transcripts, are protected by copyright. For employed researchers, the first owner of copyright is usually the employer. However, many universities waive this right in relation to research data and publications and give it to the researcher. Some researchers use Creative Commons licences, which allow the creators of works to waive some of their rights in order to allow their work to be used more freely. The UK Data Archive provides an explanation of the situation regarding copyright:

> Researchers creating data typically hold copyright in their data … If researchers collect data using interviews, and make recordings or transcriptions of the interviewee's words, then the researcher holds the copyright of these recordings.
>
> (UK Data Archive 2011: 29)

The important thing to remember is that, if you want to share your data with other researchers, you will need to get copyright clearance from the interviewee for this at the time of the interview. There are also particular copyright issues pertaining to the use of visual data. For example, in order to reproduce a photograph in publication, consent may be required from the subject in the photograph as well as from the person who took it, who is usually the first owner of copyright; in such cases copyright is jointly shared.

Reciprocity and trust

Two of the authors of this book have argued elsewhere (Bell and Bryman 2007, Bell and Wray Bliss 2009) that ethics codes increasingly emphasize the importance of openness and honesty in communicating information about the research to all interested parties. Although this issue is related to the ethical principles of informed consent and avoiding deception discussed above, it goes further than these principles in placing the responsibility on researchers for taking action that helps to overcome the power inequalities between themselves and research participants, and for ensuring that the research

has benefits for them both. For example, the ESRC *Framework for Research Ethics* makes frequent mention of the need to communicate benefits to research participants. At its most advanced, this incorporates the concept of reciprocity, the idea that the research should be of mutual benefit to researcher and participants and that some form of collaboration or active participation should be built into the research project from the outset. This encourages a view of the research relationship as a mutually beneficial exchange between researcher and participants who see each other as moral beings and enforce on each other adherence to a set of agreed-upon moral norms (Wax 1982). It also resonates with developments in qualitative research that encourage the idea of 'researcher' and 'research subject(s)' to be rethought (see Chapter 17). Issues of trust may also arise in cases where the researcher is gathering data from people they know personally (see Research in focus 6.7).

STUDENT EXPERIENCE
Seeking to establish reciprocity by sharing research findings

One of the ways in which students can establish a degree of reciprocity within a student research project is through agreeing to share their findings with research participants by sending them a report based on the dissertation project or a copy of the dissertation. As Karen explained:

> There were a lot of people while I was doing the research who said, 'Oh, I'd love to see what your findings are and what your conclusions are' and that sort of thing. 'Cos it brings up a lot of issues sort of even more broadly than just recruitment as to, you know, 'Well, is it a good idea that we're doing this sort of thing?' and 'What is it doing to the whole organizational culture?' So there were lots of people who were very interested in it. So I sent them a copy [of the dissertation once I had] finished it. I don't know what they'll do with it! [*chuckles*] Whether anybody'll actually sit down and read all fifty pages of it I don't know.

The decision to share findings with research participants also raises particular ethical issues relating to the protection of anonymity, since it is especially important that individuals cannot be identified if decisions might be made by the organization based on the information collected through your research. If you have agreed to provide feedback findings from your research to people in the organization that you are studying, you need to be very clear about this when seeking informed consent from individuals involved in your research.

Sharing your findings with research participants can help to make the research process a more open exchange because it can take account of the power relations between the researcher and the people being studied (see the section on researcher–subject relationships in Chapter 17 for further discussion of this). This is particularly so if you share your findings during the research rather than at the end of it, so that research participants have the opportunity to question and add to your interpretations of the data. The views of research participants in response to your initial findings can then be written into the dissertation project. This helps to overcome the tendency towards interpretative omnipotence—a common feature of academic writing (see Chapter 19). However, these practices are more common in qualitative than quantitative research, because the former is less concerned with the possibility that this might introduce bias into the study.

6.7 RESEARCH IN FOCUS
Ethical issues in a study involving friends as respondents

Brewis (2014) discusses the ethical issues that arose in a research projects which involved gathering data about motherhood and life–work balance from six long-standing friends. She reflects on ethical issues that arose from the study, including whether or not her friend-respondents would have been as open with a researcher who was a stranger, and the need to be cautious in using prior knowledge about friend-respondents in the research. One of the things that is striking about Brewis's account of how she gained agreement from her research participants to participate in the study is the informality of the email exchanges in which she explained the study to the women and that led them to give their consent. As Brewis explains, although she had to go through a formal process of seeking ethical approval from her university, the informal process through which she negotiated research access with her friends ran parallel to and separate from this. It was not until much later that she began to question the ethics of her research relationships, upon realizing that the 'frankness and the depth of the narratives' she collected were 'in large part a product of our friendships' (2014: 854).

This example highlights the complexities involved in negotiating informed consent when research participants place a high degree of trust in the researcher to 'do the right thing'. Bhattacharya (2007) also writes about the difficulties that are raised with respect to formal processes of informed consent when research relationships are combined with friendship. When faced with a situation where she was collecting qualitative data from a friend, she describes how the friend refused to take seriously the formal processes of signing a form to indicate informed consent, insisting that she trusted Bhattacharya to do whatever she felt was right with the data. To insist on formalizing the consent process at this stage, Bhattacharya argues, would risk breaking this trust and dishonoring the friendship, although failure to meet formal ethical requirements also places the researcher in a vulnerable situation with their study and the university that supports it.

While these examples relate to research that involves friends as participants, Brewis argues that these ethical considerations also apply to other types of qualitative researcher project where the researcher uses existing contacts as participants, such as managers and other employees in an organization where the researcher works.

Affiliation and conflicts of interest

In all areas of scientific study, it is recognized that affiliations, particularly those related to funding, have the potential to influence the way that research issues are defined and findings presented. Owing in part to a number of high-profile ethical controversies (see Thinking deeply 6.8), it is increasingly expected that researchers will declare any sources of sponsorship and funding so that this can be taken into account in assessing research quality, particularly if the study is financially underwritten by an organization that has a vested interest in the results. This does not mean that the study is automatically biased but rather that it may be perceived to be biased, for example by the media, and therefore able to be discredited. Moreover, no research is truly independent. Even if it is not in receipt of funding from commercial sources, it is clear that the money must come from somewhere, such as a government source, which will also have interests in funding certain kinds of research and coming up with particular findings. In many MBA student research projects, the dissertation forms part of a degree that is supported or funded by their employer. Therefore, the main thing for researchers to be conscious of is the need to be explicit and open about sources of funding and support in order to ensure this does not adversely affect the credibility of the research.

6.8 THINKING DEEPLY
A funding controversy in a university business school

In December 2000, Nottingham University accepted £3.8 million from British American Tobacco to set up the International Centre for Corporate Social Responsibility within Nottingham University Business School. This prompted the professor leading one of Nottingham's top research teams working in the field of cancer research to leave, taking 15 of his staff with him. Cancer Research UK, which was funding medical research at the university, subsequently withdrew its £1.5 million grant and launched a new code of conduct that recommended research support not be provided to any university faculty that is in receipt of tobacco industry funding. However, Nottingham University insisted that it had been following these guidelines, because the money that funded the International Centre for Corporate Social Responsibility was kept completely separate from any area of research funded by Cancer Research UK. The case prompted a heated exchange among academics, one letter angrily commenting that it must only be a matter of time before someone founded a Pinochet Centre for the study of human rights. Because the tobacco industry has a history of subverting scientific research that does not support its commercial interests, as portrayed in the feature film *The Insider*, it was seen as unacceptable by some that Nottingham University should accept financial support from this source.

(Clark 2000; Tysome 2001)

TIPS AND SKILLS
ESRC recommendations for ethical review of student research projects

In line with Kent et al.'s (2002) prediction that developments within the social sciences would mean that ethical oversight regimes would become less 'light touch' in orientation than previous structures, the ESRC *Framework for Research Ethics* has a section entitled 'Student research and ethics approval', which deals specifically with undergraduate and postgraduate students. It states that research organizations

> should establish procedures specifically for reviewing research projects undertaken by undergraduate students and students on taught postgraduate courses. Student research poses particular challenges in relation to ethical review because of the large numbers, short timescales and limited scope of the projects involved. Supervisors should work closely with their students in considering ethical aspects of proposed research in keeping with this Framework.
>
> The same high ethical standards should be expected in student research. It cannot be assumed that all students' projects involve minimal risk. Student projects involving research potentially requiring a full ethics review may need careful consideration. However, in many cases student research may be managed at school/ department level and overseen by a light touch departmental ethics committee using an initial checklist . . . It should be made clear to potential research participants that the study is a student project. [Research organizations] also need to ensure that students are not exposed to undue risk in conducting their research.

(ESRC, *Framework for Research Ethics* 2015: Section 1.8)

A case could be made for considering student research through a particular form of expedited review. Undergraduate and taught postgraduate research might be reviewed by multidisciplinary committees with a proportion of the members from outside the school or faculty but within the university. As student projects are not externally funded individually, there is less risk of a conflict of interests within the university.

Visual methods and research ethics

In addition to the ethical considerations already highlighted, research that uses photographs, film, or video images raises particular issues for business researchers, particularly if individuals can be identified and hence their anonymity is not maintained. Prompted by the rapid growth in the use of these methods, the UK National Centre for Research Methods (2008) has published a useful review of guidelines for researchers on the ethical use of visual methods:

> http://eprints.ncrm.ac.uk/421/1/MethodsReview-PaperNCRM-011.pdf

This includes the following recommendations about filming or photography that takes place in public spaces:

> UK law enables individuals to film or take photos of places or individuals from or in a public place, including taking photos of private property.

However, the guidance goes on to note that

what is legal and what is sanctioned in practice do not always coincide … The situation is complicated by the difficulties in defining what constitutes a public space. Managers of shopping malls and public service organisations (such as hospitals, Local Authority leisure centres or libraries) may not view their organisations as public spaces for the purposes of researchers wishing to take images.

As this extract highlights, visual researchers need to be particularly cautious in their interpretation of what is acceptable and, wherever possible, need to seek fully informed consent from participants before collecting any data. Invasion of privacy can also be a particular issue when dealing with photographs (see Research in focus 6.9).

This discussion has drawn attention to the complexities associated with visual research and the need to ensure that individuals are protected from potential harm, such as by digitally manipulating the image so that individuals cannot be identified, even if this may be perceived by some as disconcerting.

6.9 RESEARCH IN FOCUS
Invasion of privacy in visual research

As S. Warren (2002: 240) notes, 'the very act of holding a camera up to one's eye and pointing it at someone is an obvious and potentially intrusive activity which cannot be "disguised" in the same way as making field-notes in a journal or even tape-recording an interview'. Ethical issues of anonymity and confidentiality are potentially more problematic because of the instant recognizability of photographic images. Legal issues can also be more complex, especially those pertaining to copyright ownership (Pink 2001). As a precaution, in her study of organizational aesthetics (see Research in focus 17.7), Warren did not use any photographs that revealed distinguishing organizational features, such as logos. She also used digital image manipulation software to obscure the faces of the few people in the photographs in order to protect their anonymity.

Another example of the consequences of the ethical sensitivity of using photographs in research is found in Bolton et al.'s (2001) research into child employment, where the researchers gave disposable cameras to the young people involved in the study so that they could take photographs of their place of work. Several of the young people chose to opt out of the photographic part of the study because they were worried that taking photographs might jeopardize their employment, while others, who had wanted to participate in the photographic study, found that when they took the cameras into work they were able to take only one or two shots before being asked by their employer not to take photographs. The researchers conclude: 'in these situations it is the absence of photographs that begins to tell us something about the work experiences of the children by providing an insight into the power relations that govern their employment' (2001: 512).

Ethical considerations in online research

The use of the internet as a method of data collection has introduced new ethical challenges for business researchers. These challenges arise in part from the vast array of online environments, including blogs, listservs, discussion groups, email, chatrooms, instant messaging, and newsgroups. The behaviour of internet users is to some extent governed by 'netiquette', the conventions of politeness or definitions of acceptable behaviour that are recognized by online communities, as well as by service providers' acceptable use policies and by data protection legislation. One problem faced by social researchers wanting to use the internet for data collection is that there is huge growth in the amount of research being conducted in this way (M. Williams 2007). Not only is this trend creating the problem of over-researched popu-lations who suffer from respondent fatigue; some of those involved in doing research with this new technology are not adhering to the ethical principles outlined earlier in this chapter. As a result, suspicion is beginning to set in among prospective research participants, creating a less than ideal environment for future online researchers.

The Association of Internet Researchers (AoIR) (2012, https://aoir.org/ethics/) recommends that research-ers start by considering the contextual norms established within the particular online venue (see Table 6.1) that they are studying, including terms of service or other

regulations. This is likely to give an indication of whether the site is public, or if users consider their exchanges to be private. The more the venue is acknowledged to be pub-lic, the less obligation there is on the researcher to protect the confidentiality and anonymity of individuals using the venue, or to seek their informed consent. However, distinctions between public and private space online are blurred and contested. Hewson et al. (2003) suggest that data that have been deliberately and voluntarily made available in public internet domains, such as newsgroups, can be used by researchers without the need for informed consent, provided the anonymity of individuals is pro-tected. However, other researchers (Hudson and Bruck-man 2004) found that, although certain online venues might be considered by some to be public spaces, entering chatrooms and recording the conversation for research purposes provoked an extremely hostile response from chatroom users (see Research in focus 6.10).

Barnes (2004) identifies five types of online message, each presenting slightly different ethical concerns for anonymity, confidentiality, and informed consent.

- *Messages exchanged in online public discussion lists.* A typical venue for this type of message is discussion groups or newsgroups. Although most group members see their messages as public, Barnes (2004) found that

TABLE 6.1
Internet venues and ethical questions

Type of internet venue	Example of ethical question raised*
Direct communication—including structured or semi-structured interviews, e.g. via Skype	How can the researcher ensure that the user understands and agrees that content and interaction will be used for research purposes?
Threaded discussion forums or chatrooms, e.g. newsgroups	How do Terms of Service articulate privacy of content and how is content shared with third parties?
Social networking—LinkedIn, Facebook	Does the user consider the content to be sensitive information?
Personal spaces—blogs, YouTube	If the content of a user's communication were to become known beyond the confines of the venue being studied, would harm be likely to result?
Avatar based social spaces, virtual worlds and online gaming spaces—e.g. Second Life	Should these virtual worlds be considered 'public'? What constitutes 'privacy' in such contexts?
Commercial web services—Google, Yahoo	What measures are in place to safeguard data at the site of data collection?
Data banks, repositories	In the case of shared data, what restrictions, if any, were placed on data use by the creator?

Source: adapted from Appendix 1, *Association of Internet Researchers (AoIR) Guidelines: Ethical Decision Making and Internet Research Ethics*, by Annette Markham (2016).

*Questions may apply to more than one type of venue.

6.10 RESEARCH IN FOCUS
Chatroom users' responses to being studied

Hudson and Bruckman (2004) designed an experiment to understand how potential participants react to being invited to participate in an online study. This involved entering a number of online moderated chatrooms and informing the participants that they were recording them, and then recording how they responded. They downloaded a list of available chatrooms on 'ICQ Chat' each evening at 9.50 p.m. Dividing the chatrooms by size from very small (2–4 participants) to large (30 or more participants), they then randomly selected sixteen chatrooms from each set, then subdivided these into groups of four. Each group of four chatrooms was sent a different message as follows:

- *no message*: the researchers entered the chatroom using the nickname 'chat study' and said nothing;
- *recording message*: the researchers entered the chatroom as 'chat study' and announced that they were recording the chatroom for a study;
- *opt-out message*: the researchers entered the chatroom in the same way as above but posted a message giving the participants the option not to be recorded;
- *opt-in message*: the researchers entered the chatroom in the same way as before but gave participants the option to volunteer to be recorded.

Based on a sample of 525 chatrooms studied over a two-week period, Hudson and Bruckman found that posting a message about the study resulted in significant hostility, greatly increasing the likelihood of researchers being kicked out of the chatroom by the **moderator**. Moreover, the likelihood of being kicked out of a chatroom decreased as the number of participants in the chatroom increased. The comments that accompanied the researchers being kicked out included referring to the study as 'spamming' (unwanted electronic communication often involving some form of commercial advertising), objection to being studied, general requests to leave, and insults. When given a chance to opt in, only 4 of the 766 potential respondents did so. Hence, even when the option of fully informed consent was given, chatroom participants still objected to being studied. The researchers conclude that 'these results suggest that obtaining consent for studying online chatrooms is impracticable' (Hudson and Bruckman 2004: 135). This example highlights the potential ethical difficulties in intruding on a pre-existing online communication venue for research purposes, even if it is considered a public space.

some consider them as private, despite having been sent statements upon joining the group indicating the public nature of the space. Barnes (2004) recommends as a general principle that the ideas of individuals who share their ideas on public lists should be attributed to authors in the same way as you would attribute something they had written in a printed text under traditional copyright law. However, it is a good idea to check the welcoming messages of public discussion lists for guidance on how to cite email messages. Some discussion groups state that researchers must notify the group in advance of any research being undertaken. Barnes advises that, when researching any online group, it is a good idea to contact it in advance and to ask for permission to observe the members.

- *Messages exchanged in private discussions between individuals and on private lists*. Barnes (2004) suggests that in this situation the names of the lists and participants should never be revealed. To protect individual identities further, she recommends that messages are combined, all headers and signatures are removed, references to the exact type of venue being studied are not made, and behaviour is described in general terms in a composite personality type rather than by referring to specific messages that could be traced to particular individuals.

- *Personal messages sent to the researcher*. In Barnes's (2004) research, these were sent on to her by a contact who had already deleted the names and email addresses of the original sender, but in any case, she suggests that headers and signatures are removed to protect the authors' anonymity.

- *Messages re-posted and passed around the internet*. This includes messages that people forward on to other people and discussion lists because they think they are interesting. They can contain the name of the original author or can be distributed as anonymous messages. If they are distributed anonymously, Barnes (2004) believes it is worth trying to find the original author, so he or she can be properly credited in the research publication. She advises emailing the author and asking for permission to use the message.

- *Messages generated by computer programs*. This refers to messages generated by natural language computer programs that form the basis for interaction with people.

There may also be specific ethical considerations associated with certain types of research, such as virtual ethnography (see Research in focus 19.13).

A further ethical issue relates to the principle of protecting research participants from harm, discussed previously, and the related issues of individual anonymity and confidentiality. Stewart and Williams (2005) suggest that complete protection of anonymity is almost impossible in online research, since, in computer-mediated communication, information about the origin of a computer-generated message, revealed for instance in the header, is very difficult to remove. It is also more difficult to guarantee confidentiality, because the data are often accessible to other participants. In a similar vein, DeLorme et al. (2001) suggest that the internet raises particular ethical concerns for qualitative researchers that arise from the difficulty of knowing who has access to information. For example, a message posted on an online discussion group can be accessed by anyone who has a computer and an internet connection. In addition, some online environments enable 'lurkers', people who listen to what is going on without making themselves identifiable. This makes it difficult for researchers to protect the confidentiality of data that they collect. A further concern arises from the potential for individuals to present a 'fake' identity during online interaction. If a research participant does this, it has implications for the validity of the data (see Chapter 17), but there is also potential for the researcher to deceive participants in the expectation that this will encourage them to respond more openly—for example, by pretending to be a man when conducting a focus group with all-male participants. This is thus a form of covert research which raises particular ethical issues because of the lack of informed consent.

The political context of business research

In addition to the ethical issues so far considered, it is important to be aware of the wider political context of business research. In recent years there has been increasing pressure on business researchers to publish in a small number of high-profile academic journals. The reasons for this are related to business-school globalization which has increased competition between business schools worldwide in recruiting students and staff. This in turn has increased the importance of business-school rankings, such those produced by the *Financial Times*, and accreditation systems such as the Association to Advance Collegiate Schools of Business (AACSB), which have become popular measures of business school education and research quality. A key indicator of business-school performance that informs such lists is the number of staff who publish in particular journals. Many of the highest-ranking business journals are North American and are dominated by the positivist tradition (Singh et al. 2007). This positions North American authors and journals as being at the centre of knowledge production, and European authors and journals (Grey 2010) and researchers from the global South (Kothiyal, Bell, and Clarke 2018) as peripheral.

This global political context has implications for the type of business research that is done and how it is carried out, including research strategy, design, and methods. Macdonald and Kam (2007) suggest that the 'publish or perish' culture that prevails in business schools encourages researchers to write articles that reviewers are likely to see as uncontroversial and to use methods that are broadly accepted within the field, rather than experimenting with new research approaches or challenging existing theory (Corbett et al. 2014). It has been argued that qualitative business researchers face increasing difficulty in convincing

key gatekeepers, including journal editors, reviewers, and funding bodies, of the credibility and quality of their research (Easterby-Smith et al. 2008; Symon et al. 2008; Harley 2015). Qualitative researchers can also be disadvantaged by contribution-to-length ratios, as quantitative findings can often be presented more concisely and authors who use these methods encounter less pressure to justify and explain in detail their choice of methods (Pratt 2008). This is confirmed by Bell and Clarke's (2014) study of student perceptions of management researchers in UK business schools (see Plates 6.1 and 6.2). Using free drawing and focus group methods, undergraduate students of business were asked: 'if a management researcher were an animal, what kind of animal would they be?' The dominant image was characterized by aggression, competitiveness and isolation. The images produced by the students suggested that they saw management researchers as a community 'engaged in instrumental, game-playing and primarily self-serving activities' and based on 'personal possession of intellectual knowledge and the domination of other researchers and research participants' (Bell and Clarke 2014: 14).

A further issue that arises from the political context of business research concerns the ethics of publishing. A key concern here is the issue of 'honorary authorship' (Greenland and Fontanarosa 2012), where someone is listed as

PLATE 6.1
The 'great wild beast' metaphor of a management researcher

Source: Bell and Clarke (2014).

PLATE 6.2
The 'exotic creature' metaphor of a management researcher

Source: Bell and Clarke (2014).

an author even though they have not made a substantive intellectual contribution to the work. As Greenland and Fontanarosa state, there can be several reasons for this, including 'coercive authorship', which is where 'a senior person informs a junior colleague that the senior person must be listed as an author even though she/he did not contribute substantially—or at all—to the work'. In other cases, the principal investigator may add the name of a prominent scientist in the field as a guest author in an attempt to boost the paper's chance of publication. To guard against this, the AOM code states that its members should take 'authorship credit, only for work they have actually performed or to which they have contributed'. The code further states that its members should 'usually list a student as principal author on multiple-authored publications that substantially derive from the student's dissertation or thesis'. The ISA code states that 'The contribution of scholars, sponsors, technicians or other collaborators who have made a substantial contribution in carrying out a research project should be acknowledged explicitly in any subsequent publication.'

Other ethical concerns relate to plagiarism, discussed in Chapter 5, and self-plagiarism, where researchers re-use material they have already published elsewhere. The AOM code states that members should 'explicitly cite others' work and ideas, including their own, even if the work or ideas are not quoted verbatim or paraphrased.

This standard applies whether the previous work is published, unpublished, or electronically available'. In relation to self-plagiarism, when researchers 'publish data or findings that overlap with work they have previously published elsewhere', the AOM code states that researchers should 'cite these publications' in their work to ensure that appropriate checks can be made. In some cases, it also appears that the pressure to publish may lead scholars to engage in unethical conduct in the form of fabrication or manipulation of results (Harley et al. 2014).

A final issue that can arise involves 'coercive citation', when journal editors, in an attempt to enhance the impact factor of their journal, put pressure on authors to add citations to their journal when no intellectual rationale for doing so exists (Wilhite and Fong 2012). Analysing 6672 responses to a survey sent to researchers across the social science disciplines, and data from 832 journals in those disciplines, they conclude that 'coercion is uncomfortably uncommon and appears to be practiced opportunistically', particularly in the business disciplines (Wilhite and Fong 2012: 542). They also found that senior researchers were more likely than junior researchers to resist coercive demands put upon them by journal editors. With the growth in prevalence of metric-based systems for literature searching and measuring the academic impact of researchers, such as Google Scholar, the potential for this kind of ethical issue to arise is likely to increase.

CHECKLIST
Ethical issues to consider

○ Have you read and incorporated into your research the ethical principles and recommendations of at least one of the professional research associations mentioned in this book?

○ Have you read and acted in accordance with your university's requirements for doing ethical research?

○ Have you found out whether or not there is a process of ethical approval required for your research project?

○ Have you checked to ensure that there is no prospect of any harm coming to participants?

○ Does your research conform to the principle of informed consent, so that research participants understand:

   ○ what the research is about?

   ○ the purposes of the research?

   ○ who is sponsoring it?

   ○ the nature of their involvement in the research?

   ○ how long their participation is going to take?

   ○ that their participation is voluntary?

   ○ that they can withdraw from participation in the research at any time?

   ○ what is going to happen to the data (i.e. where and for how long the data are going to be kept and who will have access to them)?

○ Are you confident that the privacy of the people involved in your research will not be violated?

○ Do you appreciate that you should not divulge information or views to your research participants that other research participants have given you?

○ Have you taken steps to ensure that your research participants will not be deceived about the research and its purposes?

○ Have you taken steps to ensure that the confidentiality of data relating to your research participants will be maintained?

○ Once the data have been collected, have you taken steps to ensure that the names of your research participants and the location of your research (such as the name of the organization(s) in which it took place) are not identifiable?

○ Does your strategy for keeping your data in electronic form comply with current data protection legislation?

○ Once your research has been completed, have you met obligations that were a requirement of doing the research (for example, submitting a report to an organization that allowed you access)?

KEY POINTS

● Concern about research ethics has been informed by a small number of cases where ethical principles have been transgressed, although it is important to be aware that ethical concerns arise in less extreme cases.

- Boundaries between ethical and unethical practices are not clear-cut; writers on social research ethics have adopted several different stances in relation to the issue.

- The four main ethical principles to which business researchers are expected to adhere relate to avoidance of harm; obtaining informed consent; protection of privacy through confidentiality; and preventing deception.

- The ethics codes and guidelines of professional research associations provide useful guidance while leaving the door open for some autonomy with regard to ethical issues.

- The primary concern of this chapter has been on maintaining ethical relations between researchers and research participants. However, in the conduct of business research ethical issues also arise that are not directly related to research participants, for example in relation to authorship and citation. These issue arise from the global political context in which business research is conducted.

QUESTIONS FOR REVIEW

- Why are ethical issues important in the conduct of business research?

- Outline the different stances on ethics in social research.

- How helpful are studies such as those conducted by Milgram, Haney et al., and Dalton in understanding the operation of ethical principles in business research?

Ethical principles

- Does 'harm to participants' refer to physical harm alone?

- What are some difficulties with following the ethical principle of avoiding harm to research participants?

- Why is it important to gain the informed consent of research participants?

- What are some of the challenges in following the ethical principle of informed consent?

- Why is the principle of privacy important?

- What principles concerning use of personal data are expressed in the 1998 Data Protection Act?

- Why should deception be avoided?

- Were the actions taken by Holliday (1995; Research in focus 6.6) ethical? Explain your viewpoint using the framework provided in this chapter. Would you have behaved differently in these circumstances? If so, how?

Ethical considerations in online research

- What ethical issues are raised by using the internet as a method of data collection?

The political context of business research

- Should we be concerned about the ethics of publishing in business research?

ONLINE RESOURCES
www.oup.com/uk/brm5e/

Visit the Interactive Research Guide that accompanies this book to complete an exercise on ethical issues in business research.

WRITING UP BUSINESS RESEARCH

CHAPTER OUTLINE

It is easy to forget that one of the main stages in any research project, regardless of its size, is that it has to be written up. This is, of course, how you will convey your findings, but being aware of the significance of writing is crucial because your audience must be persuaded about the credibility and importance of your research. This chapter presents some of the characteristics of the writing-up of business research, including writing up a student research project. The chapter explores:

- the nature of academic writing and why writing, and especially good writing, is important in business research;

- how to write up your research for a dissertation;

- how quantitative and qualitative research are written, using two of the examples introduced in Chapter 1.

Introduction

The aim of this chapter is to examine some of the strategies that are used in writing up business research. We will explore the features of academic writing. We will also consider the extent to which quantitative and qualitative research writing are different. However, the main point of this chapter is to provide students with practical advice on writing up a student research project. This is important, because no matter how well research is conducted, others (that is, your readers) have to be convinced about the credibility of the knowledge claims that you are making. Good writing is, therefore, very much to do with developing your style so that it is *persuasive* and *convincing*. Flat, lifeless, uncertain writing does not have the power to persuade and convince. Unclear, poorly expressed, and unstructured prose will not allow readers to understand your research fully, regardless of how good the research might be. This chapter will provide some ideas about structuring your own written work that will be extremely useful if you have to write a dissertation.

In exploring these issues, we will touch on rhetorical strategies in the writing of business research (see Key concept 7.1). Writers in the area of theory and research known as the social studies of science have been concerned with the limitations of accepted distinctions between rhetoric and logic and between the observer and the observed (e.g. Gilbert and Mulkay 1984). The problematizing of these distinctions, along with doubts about the possibility of a neutral language through which the natural and social worlds can be revealed, opened the door for an evaluation of scientific and social scientific writing.

Writing academically

In writing up business research it is important to write in a way that follows the conventions of logic, argumentation, and style that are associated with academic writing. Thinking deeply 7.2 provides some additional advice on how to write academically. One thing that can be noticed about Daft's (1995) list of reasons for rejecting academic manuscripts is that he makes little distinction between papers based on quantitative or qualitative methods, suggesting that they are evaluated according to similar conventions. These conventions, according to Czarniawska (1999), form part of the logico-scientific genre, which is the dominant form of writing in business and management research. They can be recognized as scientific because of the devices they use to indicate logical reasoning based on logical propositions. Genre boundaries define how texts should be constructed and impose constraints on the writing style that is adopted. In this chapter we will draw on the examples of quantitative (Elsesser and Lever 2011) and qualitative (Clarke et al. 2012) research which were referred to in Chapter 1, both of which are illustrative of the logico-scientific genre to which Czarniawska refers.

However, logico-scientific writing also uses aspects of storytelling—for example, literary devices such as metaphor—as well as rhetoric to engage the reader and convince them of the importance of the research subject

7.1 KEY CONCEPT
What is rhetoric?

The study of rhetoric is fundamentally concerned with the ways in which attempts to convince or persuade an audience are formulated. We often encounter the term in a negative context, such as 'mere rhetoric' or the opposition of 'rhetoric and reality'. However, rhetoric is an essential ingredient of writing, because when we write our aim is to convince others about the credibility of our knowledge claims. To suggest that rhetoric should somehow be suppressed makes little sense, since it is in fact a basic feature of writing. The examination of rhetorical strategies in written texts based on business research is concerned with the identification of the techniques in those texts that are designed to convince and persuade.

7.2 THINKING DEEPLY
How to write academically

In an attempt to make the tacit rules of journal publishing explicit, Daft (1995) draws on his own experiences of writing articles for journals. He lists 11 common problems based on analysis of 111 of his own peer reviews of work submitted to North American journals that took a **deductive** approach to theory. Common problems are:

- No theory: this involves a lack of explanation of the relationships among **variables**—'without a theory, there is nothing to pull the study together, nothing to justify why the variables should be studied' (1995: 167).

- **Concepts** and operationalization not in alignment: this problem occurs when the **research design** does not reflect the variables under study, sometimes because of differences in level of analysis. An example of this might involve using fluctuations in the number of employees in an organization as a measure of organizational change.

- Insufficient definition—theory: this occurs when authors do not explain what their concepts mean, since enacting a definition is often a part of theory development.

- Insufficient rationale—design: this problem arises when manuscripts fail to explain the procedures or methods used in the study, such as **sample** size or response rates, in sufficient detail.

- Macrostructure—organization and flow: this refers to whether or not the various parts of the paper, such as theory section, methods, and conclusions, fit together into a coherent whole. Problems arise when manuscripts contain measures in the results section that are not referred to in the theory section or when conclusions are reached that are not related to the paper's **research questions**.

- Amateur style and tone: indications of amateurism, according to Daft (1995: 170), include 'frequent use of underlining or exclamation marks'; exaggerating the importance of the research topic in order to make the case for publication; or tearing down the work of others to justify the author's own study rather than showing how the author's study builds on previous work.

- Inadequate research design: this involves the inappropriate use of methods that cannot address the research question posed by the study, such as the use of an undergraduate student sample to analyse the selection of business strategies by corporate executives, as undergraduate students have little or no experience of strategy selection. These issues often constitute a fatal problem which cannot be put right after the study has been conducted.

- Overengineering: sometimes authors concentrate so much on the methodology that it becomes an end in itself, at the expense of making a theoretical contribution.

- Conclusions not in alignment: this problem involves manuscripts where conclusions are too short or lack sufficient interpretation of the findings, as well as manuscripts which generalize far beyond the data; 'the important thing is to use the conclusion section to fully develop the theoretical contribution and to point out the new understanding from the study' (1995: 173).

Daft suggests that papers based on qualitative research studies are prone to similar shortcomings as those seen in quantitative papers, especially in relation to lack of theory and misalignment of concepts and operationalization. Qualitative papers were often rejected 'not because referees did not like qualitative research, but because the investigators had not used the manuscript to build theory' (1995: 174).

Daft then goes on to suggest ways of overcoming these common problems, or what you can do to lessen the likelihood of having your manuscript rejected. His suggestions include:

- Tell a story. Think of each variable in the research as a character and explain how the characters interact with each other. This will give meaning to the observed relationships between variables.

- Discuss fully your procedures and thought processes. Be open about weaknesses and limitations, because it gives reviewers confidence that you are not hiding anything.

- Concentrate on the macrostructure. Make sure that all sections of the paper are coordinated and flow logically from one to another.

- Find the operational base of your research and stick to it. Think of the research design as the core of an empirical paper, to which the theory, results, and discussion correspond.

- Don't exaggerate. It is better to be cautious in your argument than to overstate your claims. Avoid statements like 'these findings prove' and instead say 'these findings suggest'.

While these comments and suggestions relate to writing papers for academic journals, much of this advice is relevant to anyone writing for an academic audience, including students.

and the rightness of the argument. Czarniawska (1999) suggests this makes a written account of research similar to a detective story, because it is presented in the form of a problem or puzzle that needs to be solved. The central character, the detective or the researcher, is often an invisible narrator of the story who is called upon to investigate a situation and find a solution. As with any form of storytelling, it is important to write in a way which is engaging and interesting in order to grab the reader's attention, but at the same time to retain the specificity and precision that is the hallmark of good academic writing. This task is made easier if you are researching something which interests you. The vast range of business-related research topics that can be studied, and their importance in our lives today, means you should have much to choose from.

Writing up your research

It is easy to neglect the writing stage of your work because of the difficulties that you often encounter in getting your research underway. But—obvious though this point is—your dissertation has to be written. Your findings must be conveyed to an audience, something that all of us who carry out research have to face. The first piece of advice is ...

STUDENT EXPERIENCE
Using direct quotations to enhance confidence and demonstrate reflexivity

When students reach the stage of writing up qualitative research, they can find the previous work that they have done in recording the comments of research participants in their own words extremely valuable when presenting their findings. Karen found that, when she was writing up her research project, the ability to include direct quotations based on the detailed notes she had taken during interviews was invaluable and that this enhanced her dissertation. A direct quotation from a research participant can help to convey the views of people being studied in a way that is engaging and interesting. Direct quotations can also enhance the perceived **trustworthiness** of the research project by enabling the researcher to provide an example from the data that illustrates the theoretical point that he or she is trying to make. They can also help convince the reader that a methodical and thorough approach to data collection and analysis has been adopted. Direct quotations can also help the researcher to demonstrate **reflexivity** and awareness of researcher–subject relationships, by showing that he or she has been aware of the power relations between the researcher and the people being studied, and has sought to deal with this by 'giving voice' to participants in a way that is not mediated by his or her own interpretations. Of course, the process of selecting a direct quotation and any subsequent process of analysis does involve the researcher in imposing meaning, but this does not mean that the use of direct quotations has no value.

Start early

It is easy to take the view that the writing-up of your research findings is something that you can think about after you have collected and analysed your data. There is, of course, a grain of truth in this view, in that you could hardly write up your findings until you know what they are, which is something that you can know only once you have gathered and analysed your data. However, there are good reasons for beginning writing early on, since you might want to start thinking about such issues as how best to present and justify the research questions that are driving your research, or how to structure your account of the theoretical and research literature that you used to frame your research questions. Students often tend to underestimate the time that it will take to write up their research, so it is a good idea to allow plenty of time for this, especially if you are expecting your supervisor to read and comment on an early draft, since you will also need to allow him or her a reasonable amount of time for this. A further reason why it is advisable to begin writing earlier rather than later is an entirely practical one: many people find it difficult to get started and employ (probably unwittingly) procrastination strategies to put off the inevitable. This tendency can result in the writing being left until the last minute and consequently being rushed. Writing under this kind of pressure is not

ideal. Presenting your findings and conclusions is a crucial stage in the research process. If you do not provide a convincing account of your research, you will not do justice to it. It is also important to recognize that, while you should never start writing without having a plan of what you will be writing, in many cases it is difficult to get your ideas clear in your mind until you start writing them down. In that sense, writing can be seen not just as taking already-formulated ideas and writing them down, but as an integral part of the process of thinking about and clarifying ideas. The sooner you start writing, the sooner you will begin to clarify your ideas.

Be persuasive

This point is crucial. Writing up your research is not simply a matter of reporting your findings and drawing some conclusions. Writing up your research will contain many other features, such as referring to the literature on which you drew, explaining how you did your research, and outlining how you conducted your analysis. But, above all, you must be *persuasive*. This means that you must convince your readers of the credibility of your conclusions. Simply saying 'This is what I found; isn't it interesting?' is not enough. You must persuade your readers that your findings and conclusions are significant and that they are plausible.

STUDENT EXPERIENCE
The benefits of writing up early ... versus leaving it until later

Tom found that there were advantages to writing up his dissertation early. As he explained:

The deadline was to hand it in by the end of August, but I had a holiday at the beginning of August and I was going to move house, so I knew I had to finish by the end of July because otherwise it was going to be a nightmare. And that was quite good, because it meant I finished, went off on holiday, then I just let it sort of settle for a couple of weeks and when I came back I was able to look at it with a fresh eye and give it a final kind of tidy up and tweak.

Karen also found that writing up her dissertation early helped her to see her argument more clearly. 'I wanted to give it a lot of time to think about all the different issues'. She was also able to come back to the draft after a break before the deadline and make further changes, 'I think that's definitely the best way to do it, because I had so many friends who rushed it in the last two weeks, and I think then you lose all of the conceptual thinking and the ability to think more broadly about the topic and you just get a bit bogged down in all the detail.' Alex emphasized the importance of organizational skills in successful completion of a dissertation. This was a particular issue for him because he was in paid employment throughout the period when he was doing his research project and writing up.

The rewards of being a supervisor

The experience of supporting a student research project can be a rewarding experience for supervisors. Some of the rewards that supervisors mentioned included:

- reading a well-written dissertation;
- finding out interesting things they did not already know;
- discussing interesting topics with students;
- obtaining additional references for their own research and writing;
- helping students to discover they have become an expert in their sub-field;
- hearing of someone doing well in his or her career after leaving university.

Get feedback

Try to get as much feedback on your writing as possible and respond positively to the points anyone makes about what they read. Your supervisor is likely to be the main source of feedback, but universities vary in what supervisors are allowed to comment on. Provide your supervisor with drafts of your work to the fullest extent that regulations will allow. Give him or her plenty of time to provide feedback. There will be others like you who will want your supervisor to comment on their work, and, if he or she feels rushed, the comments may be less helpful. Also, you could ask others on the same degree programme to read your drafts and comment on them. They may ask you to do the same. Their comments may be very

useful, but, by and large, your supervisor's comments are the main ones you should seek out. Any output from a research project, whether it be a dissertation, a journal article, or a whole book, should emerge through a series of drafts. By getting feedback, particularly on early drafts, you will be able to develop and refine your argument as you work through a number of drafts to finalization of your work.

Avoid discriminatory language

Remember that your writing should be free of discriminatory language, which includes anything that could be interpreted as sexist. The British Sociological Association (BSA) publication *Language and the BSA: Sex and Gender*

The importance of an argument

One of the things that students can find difficult about writing up their research is the formulation of an argument. The writing-up of research should be organized around an argument that links all aspects of the research process from problem formulation, through literature review and the presentation of research methods, to the discussion and conclusion. The argument is a thread that runs through your dissertation (see Figure 7.1 for some examples of key phrases that can be used to construct and maintain an argument throughout the dissertation). Too often, students make a series of points without asking what the contribution of those points is to the overall argument that they are trying to present. Consider what your claim to knowledge is and try to organize your writing to support and enhance it. That will be your argument. Sometimes it is useful to think in terms of telling a story about your research and your findings. Try to avoid tangents and irrelevant material that may mean your readers will lose the thread of your argument. If you are not able to supply a clear argument, you are vulnerable to the 'so what?' question. Ask yourself: 'What is the key point or message that I want my readers to take away with them when they have finished reading my work?' If you cannot answer that question satisfactorily (and it may be worth trying it out on others), almost certainly you do not have an argument.

FIGURE 7.1
Typical ways of constructing an argument

Dissertation chapter		Commonly used phrases to make an argument
Introduction	**A**	In this dissertation I will argue that … This dissertation argues that … It is often argued that … It is argued here that … It could be argued that …
Literature review	**R** **G** **U** **M**	In the introduction I argued that … This argument is illustrated by exploring the concept of … The argument in this dissertation draws on … My arguments build on the work of Mintzberg (1973) … Some would argue that … Others have argued … As Bryman (1998) argued …/he suggests … Bell (1999) argues that …/she claims that … In this chapter I will situate my argument in the literature on …
Research methods	**E**	Following the arguments put forward by Willmott (1990) …
Results/findings/cases	**N**	This shows … This demonstrates that … This implies that … From this I suggest …
Discussion/analysis	**T**	Based on these findings I would argue that … In an earlier chapter I argued that …
Conclusion		In this dissertation I have argued for … I conclude that … In this dissertation I have argued for a more …

provides good guidelines on this issue. Specifically, they state:

> When reference to both sexes is intended, a large number of phrases use the word man or other masculine equivalents (e.g., 'father') and a large number of nouns use the suffix 'man', thereby excluding women from the picture we present of the world. These should be replaced by more precise non-sexist alternatives.

A number of the examples that the BSA give of how sexist language can be made non-sexist are highly relevant to business researchers. For example: 'chairman' should be changed to 'chair'; 'foreman' to 'supervisor'; 'manpower' to 'workforce staff, labour force, employees'; 'craftsman/men' to 'craftsperson/people'; 'manning' to 'staffing, working, running', 'manhours' to 'workhours' and 'policeman/fireman' to 'police officer/fire-fighter'.

Structure your writing

The length of your dissertation is likely to vary depending on the requirements of your university, but the structure of your dissertation is likely to be relatively consistent with standard structures. The following is a typical dissertation structure although, as the discussion that follows on quantitative and qualitative research writing, there is considerable variation, and so what follows should not be taken as prescriptive but rather as broad guidance.

Title page

Your university may require this to have a specific layout, likely to include details of your degree programme and year as well as your name and the dissertation title. You should examine your university's rules about what should be included here.

Acknowledgements

You might want to acknowledge the help of various people, such as gatekeepers who gave you access to an organization, people who have read your drafts and provided you with feedback, or your supervisor for their advice.

List of contents

Your university may have recommendations about the form this should take.

Abstract

This is a brief summary of your dissertation, usually around 200 to 300 words in length. Journal articles usually have abstracts, so you can draw on these for guidance on how to approach this task. As a guide, an abstract should include:

- Why is this topic interesting?
- What do we already know about it?
- What does this study focus on?
- How did I study it (research strategy/design/methods)?
- How does this study further our understanding of the topic?

Introduction

- You should explain what you are writing about and why it is important. Saying simply that it interests you because of a long-standing personal interest is not enough.
- You might indicate in general terms the theoretical approach or perspective you will be using and why.
- You should also at this point outline your research questions. In the case of dissertations based on qualitative research, it is likely that your research questions will be more open-ended than is the case with quantitative research. But do try to identify some research questions.
- The opening sentence or sentences are often the most difficult of all. Becker (1986) advises strongly against opening sentences that he describes as 'vacuous' and 'evasive'. He gives the example of 'This study deals with the problem of careers', and adds that this kind of sentence employs 'a typically evasive manœuvre, pointing to something without saying anything, or anything much, about it. *What* about careers?' (Becker 1986: 51). He suggests that such evasiveness often occurs because of concerns about giving away the plot. In fact, he argues, it is much better to give readers a

quick and clear indication of what is going to be meted out to them and where it is going. At the end of the introduction, it is useful to provide a brief overview of the structure of the dissertation, which you can think of as a 'map' for readers. This makes it easier for readers to follow your argument, because they have a general sense of how the argument will unfold.

Literature review

Detailed advice on how to go about writing this chapter of your dissertation is given in Chapter 5.

Research methods

The term 'research methods' is meant here as a kind of catch-all for several issues: your research design; your sampling approach; how access was achieved, if relevant; the procedures you used (e.g. if you collected data using a questionnaire, if you followed up non-respondents); the nature of your questionnaire, interview schedule, participant observation role, observation schedule, coding frame, or whatever (these will usually appear in full in an appendix, but you should comment on such things as your style of questioning or observation and why you asked the things you did); problems of non-response; note-taking; issues of ongoing access and cooperation; coding matters; and how you proceeded with your analysis. When discussing each of these issues, you should describe and defend the choices that you made, such as why you used a questionnaire rather than a structured interview approach, or why you focused upon a particular population for sampling purposes. However, you should not try to cover all possible alternative ontological and epistemological choices and all possible alternative methods in your dissertation: either your treatment of them would have to be relatively superficial, or your research methods chapter would have to become extremely long. As a rule of thumb, you should provide sufficient detail that readers can understand what you have done and why you have done it.

Results

In this chapter, you present the bulk of your findings. If you intend to have a separate 'Discussion' chapter, you may present your results with little commentary in terms of the literature or the implications of your findings. If there will be no 'Discussion' chapter, you will need to provide some reflections in the 'Results' chapter on the significance of your findings for your research questions and for the literature.

- Whichever approach you take, remember not to include *all* your results. You should present and discuss only those findings that relate to your research questions. This requirement may mean a rather painful process of leaving out many findings, but it is necessary so that the thread of your argument is not lost.

- Your writing should point to particularly salient aspects of the tables, graphs, or other forms of analysis you present. Do not just summarize what a table shows; you should direct the reader to the component or components of it that are especially striking from the point of view of your research questions. Try to ask yourself what story you want the table to convey and try to relay that story to your readers.

- Another mistake to be avoided is simply presenting a graph or table, or a section of the transcript of a semi-structured interview or focus group session, without any comment whatsoever, because the reader is left wondering how you think the findings should be interpreted and why you think they are important.

- When reporting quantitative findings, it is quite a good idea to vary wherever possible the method of presenting results—for example, provide a mixture of diagrams and tables. However, the methods of analysis you present must be appropriate to the types of variable involved: this will be covered in Chapter 15.

- A particular problem that can arise with qualitative research is that students find it difficult to leave out large parts of their data. As one experienced qualitative researcher has put it: 'The major problem we face in qualitative inquiry is not to get data, but to get rid of it!' (Wolcott 1990: 18). He goes on to say that the 'critical task in qualitative research is not to accumulate all the data you can, but to "can" (i.e., get rid of) most of the data you accumulate' (Wolcott 1990: 35). You simply have to recognize that much of the rich data you accumulate will have to be jettisoned. If you do not do this, any sense of an argument in your work is likely to be lost. There is also the risk that your account of your findings will appear too descriptive and lack an analytical edge. This is why it is important to use research questions as a focus and to orient the presentation of your findings to them. It is also important to keep in mind the theoretical ideas and the literature that have framed your work. The theory and literature that have influenced your thinking will also have shaped your research questions.

- Depending on length constraints, you may have more than one chapter in which you present your results. If so, Cryer (1996) recommends showing at the beginning of each chapter the particular issues that are being examined. You should indicate which research question or questions are being addressed and provide some signposts about what will be included in the chapter. In the conclusion of the chapter, you should make clear what your results have shown and draw out any links that might be made with the next results chapter or with the 'Discussion' chapter.

Discussion

In the discussion, you reflect on the implications of your findings for the research questions that have driven your research. In other words, how do your results illuminate your research questions? If you have specified hypotheses, the discussion will revolve around whether the hypotheses have been confirmed or not, and, if not, you might speculate about some possible reasons for their refutation and the implications of it. In this chapter, you need to address the fundamental question of 'So what?'—what do the findings mean, why is this important and why should readers care? This point should be amplified in the conclusion.

Conclusion

The main points here are as follows:

- A conclusion is not the same as a summary. However, it is frequently useful to bring out your argument thus far in the opening paragraph of the conclusion. This will mean relating your findings and your discussion of them to your research questions. Thus, your brief summary should be a means of hammering home to your readers the significance of what you have done. However, the conclusion should do more than merely summarize.

- You should make clear the implications of your findings for your research questions.

- You might suggest some ways in which your findings have implications for theories relating to your area of interest.

- You might also suggest some ways in which your findings have implications for practice in the field of business and management.

- You might draw attention to any limitations of your research with the benefit of hindsight, but it is probably best not to overdo this element, which would provide examiners with ammunition that might be used against you!

- It is often valuable to propose areas of further research that are suggested by your findings.

- Two things to avoid are engaging in speculations that take you too far away from your data or that cannot be substantiated by the data, and introducing issues or ideas that have not previously been brought up.

STUDENT EXPERIENCE
The challenges and constraints of length

For many students, their dissertation or research report will be by far the longest thing that they have so far written. The prospect of writing up a single piece of work of the length of a dissertation may at first seem a daunting prospect. However, the experiences of students interviewed for this book suggest that when it comes down to it the challenge is more often about how to keep within these limits. Chris's comments are typical: 'I'd never done a piece of work like this. You know, 3000 or 4000 words was probably as much as I'd written before and, although it was only meant to be 7000 words, it turned out to be 13,000.' Some students found the need to keep to a word limit a real struggle, particularly when presenting qualitative data. Karen found that her work exceeded the length guidelines provided by her university, so she tried to cut it down by putting graphs and tables into the appendices, but this had drawbacks because the reader had constantly to keep checking the appendices. Some supervisors may suspect that the student has done this just to get around the word limit. It is therefore important to plan your work carefully and to edit your work if necessary during the revision process. Editing to meet a word limit can also help you to focus on what you really want to say. For example, Tom realized that his first draft was quite descriptive and therefore he could cut out some of this detail, and this left him more space for the analysis.

Note that universities vary in both the length required for dissertations and the extent that they rigorously enforce a word limit, so check requirements carefully. But remember, while word limits may be viewed as a nuisance, especially when you feel that you have a lot to say or some really interesting data, they help ensure a level playing field for students, so that everyone has roughly the same amount of space in which to present their ideas and arguments. It is also worth noting that constraints of length apply to all academics, since the norm of writing in scholarly journals requires you to produce papers that are between 7000 and 12,000 words in length, so you are being required to conform to similar norms as other business researchers.

Appendices

In your appendices you might want to include such things as your questionnaire, coding frame, or observation schedule, letters sent to sample members, and letters sent to and received from gatekeepers where the cooperation of an organization was required.

References

Include here all references cited in the text. For the format of the references section you should follow whichever approach is prescribed by your department or school. Nowadays, the format is usually a variation of the Harvard method, such as the one employed for this book (discussed in Chapter 5).

TIPS AND SKILLS
Proofreading your dissertation

Before submitting your dissertation, make sure that it is spellchecked and check it for grammatical and punctuation errors. Although spellcheckers will pick up many errors, they are likely to be inadequate for fully correcting your work, which means that even when you have spellchecked your document you will need to read it carefully yourself and correct it. There are many useful guides and handbooks that can be used for this purpose. It may also be useful to ask someone else, such as a friend or family member, to proofread your work in case there are errors that you have missed. As well as being an important presentational issue, this will affect the ease with which your written work can be read and understood. Moreover, markers are likely to be less well-disposed to written work which is littered with mistakes. Proofreading therefore has the potential to affect significantly the quality of your dissertation.

Finally

Remember to fulfil any obligations you entered into, such as supplying a copy of your dissertation if, for example, your access to an organization was predicated on providing one; maintaining the confidentiality of information supplied and the anonymity of your informants and other research participants; and storing or disposing of your data properly (as discussed in Chapter 6).

Writing up quantitative and qualitative research

In the next two sections, research-based articles that have been published in journals are examined to discern some characteristic features. One article is based on quantitative research and another on qualitative research. The presentation of the quantitative and the qualitative research articles raises the question of whether or not practitioners of the two research strategies employ different writing approaches. It is sometimes suggested that they do, although when Bryman compared two articles based on research in the sociology of work, he found that the differences were less pronounced than he had anticipated on the basis of reading the literature on the topic (Bryman 1998). One difference we have noticed is that, in journals, quantitative researchers often give more detailed accounts of their research design, research methods, and approaches to analysis than qualitative researchers. This is surprising because in books reporting their research, qualitative researchers provide detailed accounts of these areas. Indeed, the chapters in Part Three of this book rely heavily on these accounts. Wolcott (1990: 27) has also noticed this tendency: 'Our [qualitative researchers'] failure to render full and complete disclosure about our data-gathering procedures give our methodologically orientated colleagues fits. And rightly so, especially for those among them willing to accept our contributions if we would only provide more careful data about our data.' Being informed that a study was based on a year's participant observation or a number of semi-structured interviews is not enough to gain an acceptance of the claims to credibility that a writer might be wishing to convey.

However, this point aside, although one article based on quantitative research and one based on qualitative research will be examined in the discussion that follows, we should not be too surprised if they turn out to be more similar than might have been expected. In other words, although we might have expected clear differences between the two in terms of their approaches to writing, the similarities are more noticeable than the differences.

In addition to looking at examples of writing in quantitative and qualitative research, in Chapter 27 we will examine how mixed methods research can be written up and explore some guidelines that are offered by practitioners.

An example of quantitative research

To illustrate some of the characteristics of the way quantitative research is written up for academic journals, we will return to the article about gender bias in attitudes towards leaders by Elsesser and Lever (2011) introduced in Chapter 1 (Research in focus 1.3). We are not suggesting that this article is somehow exemplary or representative, but rather that it exhibits some typical features in terms of presentation and structure, as well as a few less typical ones. The article is based on analysis of data from a US-based national survey conducted using the popular news website msnbc.com, and was published in the journal *Human Relations*. The article has the following components, aside from the abstract:

1. Introduction
2. Role congruity theory
3. Goals of the present study
4. Method
5. Results
6. Discussion (including subsections on 'limitations and strengths' and 'implications')

Introduction

Right at the beginning of the introduction, the opening sentence attempts to grab our attention, to give a clear indication of where the article's focus lies, and to provide an indication of the importance of the subject of study for practitioners, policy-makers, and academics. This is what the authors write:

> Although acceptance of female managers has increased in the last half-century, negative attitudes toward female leaders still persist (Carlson et al., 2006; Heilman, 2001; Heilman et al.,1995).
>
> (Elsesser and Lever 2011: 1556)

This is an impressive start, because, in just eighteen words (plus citations), the authors set out what the article is about and persuade us of its significance. They achieve this by first stating what progress has been achieved in increasing equality between men and women in business over the last 50 years, and then declaring the continued existence of negative attitudes towards female leaders. The inclusion of three citations to previous research at the end of this sentence provides support for their assertions and immediately situates the statement in relation to these earlier studies and existing literatures. Hence is it made clear which research audiences and debates the current study is addressing.

Next, Elsesser and Lever identify what they see as a limitation of existing research, which they suggest cannot be generalized to real world situations. 'While a few studies are based on actual bosses in work settings, many works base conclusions on student samples surveyed on vignettes of hypothetical leaders, attitudes about ideal leaders, or ratings of task leaders in laboratory settings' (2011: 1556). They provide five citations at the end of this sentence in order to support this claim. The criticism that the authors make thus focuses on the ecological validity of prior studies (see Chapter 3), which they claim calls into question the quality of existing research on this topic.

The authors go on to set out in much more precise terms how the research on which this article is based differs from this preceding research, and the research questions that it addresses.

> In the present study, subordinates rated their own female and male bosses, allowing us to examine whether biases exist against actual female leaders and, if so, under what conditions and management styles these biases are likely to emerge.
>
> (2011: 1556)

In so doing, the authors draw attention to a methodological deficiency in existing knowledge and tell us that they are going to correct this situation. The authors then go on to review the literature on role congruity theory.

Role congruity theory

In this literature review section of the article, the authors present existing research that addresses the topic of role congruity theory, which is the body of literature on which their study builds. Notice that it is not titled 'literature review'—instead the title reflects the specific theoretical focus of the article. The first paragraph explains the notion of role incongruity, where individuals act in ways that are incongruent with their sex roles as defined by society. They go on to suggest that role congruity theory predicts that female leaders suffer two kinds of prejudice: descriptive bias, 'where they are stereotyped as having less leadership potential than men'; and prescriptive bias, 'when female leaders are evaluated less favorably because leadership is seen as more desirable for men than for women' (2011: 1556–7). The rest of this section of the article is devoted to describing the existing literature in more detail and further elaborating on its methodological and empirical limitations.

Goals of the present study

In the second sentence of this section the authors clearly state their intentions:

> The goal of this paper is to examine respondents' ratings of their own current boss's competence and of their relationship with their boss, as well as their attitudes toward male and female managers more generally.
>
> (Elsesser and Lever 2011: 1558)

Their intention in doing so is to test whether stereotyping occurs in real-world settings, where people are rating their own supervisors. The researchers propose three sets of hypotheses.

- *Hypothesis 1a.* 'When rating one's own boss, respondents' ratings of male and female managers will not differ with regard to competence.'
- *Hypothesis 1b.* 'Competence ratings for male and female managers will not differ regardless of whether they work in male- or female-dominated environments.'
- *Hypothesis 1c.* 'Competence ratings for male and female managers will not differ regardless of the manager's style (sensitive or direct).'
- *Hypothesis 2a.* 'When rating one's own boss, respondents will not differ on reports of the quality of their relationships with male and female bosses.'

- *Hypothesis 2b.* 'Relationship ratings will not differ for male and female managers regardless of whether they work in male- or female-dominated environments.'

- *Hypothesis 2c.* 'Relationship ratings will not differ for male and female managers regardless of the manager's style (sensitive or direct).'

- *Hypothesis 2d.* 'Relationship ratings will not differ for extremely competent male managers and extremely competent female managers.'

- *Hypothesis 3a.* 'When stating their preference for managers in general, respondents will show a preference for male over female managers.'

- *Hypothesis 3b.* 'The general preference for male management will be strongest for those in male-dominated environments, by those with no previous experience with a female boss, and by those who currently report to a male boss.' (Elsesser and Lever 2011: 1558–9)

These hypotheses are intended to test whether gender bias is less in studies 'using actual bosses in actual organizations' (2011: 1558) than in experimental studies based on 'hypothetical managers or laboratory created leaders' (2011: 1557). They suggest a connection between bias against female leaders—the dependent variable—and relationships between employee and their bosses, whether they work in a male- or female-dominated environments, the manager's style (sensitive or direct), and the manager's competence, which constitute the independent variables in this study. We thus end up with a very clear research agenda, which has been arrived at by reflecting on existing theory and research in this area.

Methods

In this section, the authors outline the methods that were used in conducting the research and provide details about the data that they draw on. They begin by explaining that the data on which the paper is based came from a US-based national survey that was distributed online using a popular American news site, msnbc.com. The remainder of this section is then divided into three separate sub-sections titled: 'Participants', 'Measures', and 'Analyses'. The first of these subsections provides information about the participants, including a table detailing the industries they worked in. The second explains the measures used. For example:

> Relationship quality with the current boss was assessed with the item 'How would you rate your relationship with your current boss?' Responses were on a scale from 1 (Poor) to 7 (Excellent).

(Elsesser and Lever 2011: 1561)

The third subsection of the methods sets out the analyses used in the study, including the statistical tests that were used (t-tests, chi-square, factorial ANOVA—see Chapter 15 on tests of statistical significance). The paper also includes some analyses of what the authors describe as 'qualitative data', in the form of responses to open questions included in the survey (see Chapter 12). While we do not focus on this aspect here, it does illustrate the relative difficulty in clearly separating quantitative and qualitative methods in practice (see Chapter 26).

Results

In this section, the authors provide a description of their findings, setting out results in tables, and then consider what the results mean for the three sets of hypotheses. They move through the hypotheses in turn, discussing whether the hypotheses were supported or not. In this kind of research, the basis for theoretical conclusions is hypothesis testing, so careful consideration of whether each individual hypothesis is disproven or supported is essential to drawing conclusions.

Discussion

In this final section, Elsesser and Lever return to the issues that were presented in the introduction and theory sections. They begin with a short, clear summary of their findings in response to the question that has been driving their investigation:

> The answer to our title question (Does gender bias against female leaders persist?) is both 'yes' and 'no'.
> (2011: 1571)

The remainder of the paragraph is devoted to explaining in more detail how gender biases persist when participants are asked to imagine their ideal manager, although gender bias is less likely when evaluating their own boss. The authors go on to explain that their results are consistent with previous research 'that shows much larger gender bias in studies of hypothetical or abstract leaders, and little or no bias in studies of actual bosses, and should serve as a reminder that caution must be taken in extending laboratory results based on hypothetical bosses to actual organizational scenarios' (2011: 1571).

In the last few paragraphs of the paper, Elsesser and Lever discuss a surprising aspect of their findings which relates to the identification of a bias favouring 'cross-sex management'—male participants favouring female bosses and female participants favouring male bosses. At this point Elsesser and Lever begin to speculate about

about the reasons for this finding. The explanation that Elsesser and Lever offer for this surprising finding concerns 'intra-gender competition between women' and citing studies that suggest 'female employees devalue the competency of others of their own gender to enhance their own comparative worth' (2011: 1572). Overall, the findings as summarized in the first two subsections of the results suggest that (a) a slight majority of participants do not have a preference for the gender of their boss; and (b) of those participants who do have a preference for the gender of their boss, there is a general preference for male bosses.

The penultimate subsection of the 'Discussion' is titled 'Limitations and strengths'. Here, in addition to highlighting the strengths of the study, the authors discuss aspects of their research design that limit the findings and the conclusions that can be drawn, e.g. selection biases that arise because participants had to have access to the internet, leading to under-representation of certain groups. In the final subsection, 'Implications', the authors claim that their study offers 'encouraging evidence of changing attitudes towards female leaders … indicating a feminizing of the management role, with our participants favoring sensitive over direct managers, regardless of the manager's gender' (2011: 1574–5).

Elsesser and Lever do not have a separate 'Conclusion' section. Instead, the main conclusions are presented as part of the overall discussion. The article ends with acknowledgements to *Elle* magazine and msnbc.com for access to the 'Work and Power Survey' as well as to other individuals, including peer reviewers, who helped the authors to develop their work. This is followed by a list of references to literature cited in the article.

Lessons

It is worth spelling out the lessons that can be learned from Elsesser and Lever's article.

- There is a clear attempt to grab the reader's attention with strong opening statements, which also act as signposts to what the article is about.
- The authors spell out clearly the rationale of their research. This entails pointing to the significance of role congruity theory and the persistence of negative attitudes towards female leaders and managers, highlighting methodological limitations associated with existing literature and consequent gaps in our understanding.
- The research questions are spelled out in a very specific way. In fact, the authors present hypotheses that

are a highly specific form of research question (although hypotheses are framed as statements, to allow testing, they can nonetheless be thought of as a form of research question). As will be noted in Chapter 8, by no means all quantitative research is driven by hypotheses, even though outlines of the nature of quantitative research often imply that it is. Nonetheless, Elsesser and Lever chose to frame their research questions in this form.

- The research methods employed, the nature of the data, the measurement of concepts, the sampling, and the approaches to the analysis of the data are clearly and explicitly summarized.
- The presentation of the findings is orientated very specifically to the hypotheses.
- The discussion returns to the hypotheses and spells out the implications of the findings for them and for role congruity theory examined earlier in the paper. It is easy to forget that you should think of the research process as closing a circle in which you must return unambiguously to your research questions. There is no point inserting extraneous findings if they do not illuminate your research questions. At the same time, the discussion provides an opportunity for a degree of speculation in response to surprising or unanticipated findings arising from the study, using existing literature to substantiate these claims.
- While there is an element of rhetoric in the writing that seeks to convince and persuade, statements are made in a non-judgemental way in accordance with the conventions of the logico-scientific genre of writing.
- Finally, there is an attempt to consider the limitations of the study, in addition to its strengths. It is also common at this point to consider the implications of the study, e.g. for business or managers.

There is a clear sequential process moving from the formulation of the research questions (in the form of hypotheses) through the exposition of the nature of the data and the presentation of the findings to the discussion. Each stage is linked to and follows on from its predecessor (but see Thinking deeply 7.3). The structure used by Elsesser and Lever is based on a common one employed in the writing-up of quantitative research in business journals. It involved just one final section entitled 'Discussion', in which the authors drew their conclusions, but in other articles the discussion and conclusion may be separate sections.

7.3 THINKING DEEPLY
An empiricist repertoire?

Gilbert and Mulkay's (1984) research on scientists draws a distinction between an empiricist repertoire and a contingent repertoire. The former derived from 'the observation that the texts of experimental papers display certain recurrent stylistic, grammatical and lexical features which appear to be coherently related' (1984: 55–6). We should bear in mind that the same is true of papers written for social science journals. These too display certain features that suggest a degree of inevitability to the outcome of the research. In other words, the reader is given a sense that, in following the rigorous procedures outlined in the article, the researchers logically arrived at their conclusions. The contingent repertoire, with its recognition of the role of the researcher in the production of findings, is far less apparent in scientists' published work. Thus, we have to recognize the possibility that the impression of a series of linked stages leading to an inescapable culmination is to a large extent a reconstruction of events designed to persuade referees (who, of course, use the same tactics themselves) of the credibility and importance of one's findings. This means that the conventions for writing up a quantitative research project, some of which are outlined in this chapter, are in many ways an invitation to reconstruct an investigation in a particular way. The whole issue of the ways in which the writing-up of research represents a means of persuading others of the credibility of one's knowledge claims has been a particular preoccupation among qualitative researchers and has been greatly influenced by the surge of interest in postmodernism (Key concept 2.8). In Key concept 7.4, some of the rhetorical strategies involved in writing up quantitative research are outlined. Three points are worth making about these strategies in the present context. First, they are characteristic of the empiricist repertoire. Secondly, while the writing of qualitative research has been a particular focus since the 1980s (see below), some attention has also been paid to quantitative research. Thirdly, when Bryman (1998) compared the writing of quantitative and qualitative research articles, he found they were not as dissimilar in terms of rhetorical strategies as is sometimes proposed. However, he did find greater evidence of a management metaphor in writings on quantitative research (see Key concept 7.4).

7.4 KEY CONCEPT
What is a rhetorical strategy in quantitative research?

The rhetorical strategies used by quantitative researchers include the following:

- There is a tendency to remove the researcher from the text as an active ingredient of the research process in order to convey an impression of the objective nature of the findings—that is, as part of an external reality that is independent of the researcher (Gusfield 1976). Woolgar (1988a) refers to this as an externalizing device.

- The researcher surfaces in the text only to demonstrate his or her ingenuity in overcoming obstacles (Bazerman 1987; Bryman 1998).

- Key figures in the field are routinely cited to bestow credibility on the research (McCloskey 1985).

- The research process is presented as a linear one, to convey an air of inevitability about the findings that are reached (Gusfield 1976).

- Relatively strict rules are followed about what should be reported in published research and how it should be reported (Bazerman 1987).

- The use of a management metaphor is common in the presentation of findings, in which the researcher is depicted as ingeniously '"designing" research, "controlling" variables, "managing" data, and "generating" tables' (Bryman 1998: 146). See Shapiro (1985–6) and Richardson (1990) on this point.

Note that the first two points are somewhat inconsistent. There is some evidence that disciplines within the social sciences differ in respect of their use of an impersonal style of writing. But it may well also be that it sometimes depends on what the writer is trying to do; for example, sometimes getting across a sense of one's cunning in overcoming practical difficulties can be just as useful as giving a sense of the external nature of the findings. Therefore, the style of presentation may vary somewhat.

An example of qualitative research

Now we will look at an example of a journal article based on qualitative research. Again, we are not suggesting that the article is exemplary or representative, but that it exhibits some features that are often regarded as desirable qualities in terms of presentation and structure. The article is one that has been referred to in Chapter 1: a study of academic identity work by Clarke et al. (2012). The article is based on a semi-structured interview study and was published in the *Scandinavian Journal of Management*. The structure of the article runs as follows:

1. Introduction
2. Loving to labour: identity in business schools
3. Methodology
4. Research findings
5. Discussion
6. Summary and conclusion

What is immediately striking about the structure is that it is not dissimilar to that of Elsesser and Lever's (2011) article. Nor should this be all that surprising. After all, a structure that runs

Introduction → Literature review → Research design/ methods → Results → Discussion → Conclusions

is not obviously associated with one research strategy rather than the other. One difference from quantitative research articles is that the presentation of the results and the discussion of them are frequently rather more interwoven in qualitative research articles. We will see this in the case of Clarke et al.'s article. As with Elsesser and Lever's article, we will examine the writing in terms of the article's structure.

Introduction

The first paragraph gives an indication of the existing literature on which this article is based—related to the effects of new public management on academic work. However, before the start of the introduction, the authors present a direct quote from a play by Alan Bennett, *The History Boys* (2004). The words are those of a school headmaster who begins with the question, 'Shall I tell you what's wrong with Hector as a teacher?' and goes on to complain that his work is 'unpredictable, unquantifiable', which is problematic from a managerial perspective. This is an interesting and relatively unusual way to introduce an academic article; it illustrates the possibilities for being slightly creative in your writing—an issue we shall return to at the end of this chapter. The quote is not explained, or even directly referred to in the article; instead the reader is left to interpret it. It thus makes for an evocative and intriguing start to the article.

This first paragraph of the introduction is short, comprising just two sentences, and each is followed by a series of citations to existing literature. This enables the authors to immediately say what the article is about and where its focus lies. The authors then go on, in the second paragraph, to introduce the empirical research on which the article is based (a study of academic staff in UK business schools); the identity literature which provides the theory that is used in the study; and the objective of the article, which is to understand how 'academic subjectivities are sustained or transformed' as a consequence of the conditions in UK business schools. Three further paragraphs of the introduction are devoted to providing more detail on the authors' position before, in the final paragraph of this section, setting out the structure for what is to follow:

> We begin by providing a summary of what we understand by the concept of identity or identities … A section on the methods adopted and how the data was collected and analysed precedes our presentation of the main data from the research interviews … In the discussion section we reflect on how academics are increasingly confronted with managerialist intensifications of audit, accountability and performance demands … Finally in a summary and conclusion we examine the development of identities that are potentially resistant to these changing conditions, as well as on their implications for future academic work.
>
> (2012: 6)

Although for the purpose of this analysis we have been selective in our direct quotation from the introduction to this article, it is useful to look again at what each of these elements achieves.

- The direct quotation from a play right at the start catches the interest of the reader and hints at what is to follow.
- The first paragraph situates the study and provides a specific research focus—the effects of new public management on academic work.
- In the second paragraph the authors introduce their empirical study, the theoretical perspective that informs it, and the research objective (question).

- In the final paragraph of the introduction, Clarke et al. provide detailed signposting to indicate how the remainder of the article is structured. Phrases like 'We begin by ...' and 'Finally ...' let the reader know that this is what they are doing. The reader thus knows what to anticipate and this makes the argument easier to follow.

Loving to labour: identity in business schools

As with Elsesser and Lever's article, the title of the literature review reflects the topic of study. Here the authors set out their perspective on identity in organizations and provide some details about the organizational context of UK higher education, including changes in the way that performance is measured. Statements such as 'Identity is central to life in organizations ...' are followed by citations, which provide a clear, evidential warrant for the claims that are made. This section is relatively short but it is crucial in providing the foundations upon which the rest of the article builds.

Methodology

This section comprises three subsections that reflect the sequence of research steps involved: 'Research design', 'Data collection', and 'Data analysis'. In these sections the authors explain several elements of the methods they used.

- They set out the epistemological position taken (interpretive) and their rationale for focusing on their own organizational context, as business school academics themselves. This provides a degree of reflexivity (see later in this chapter), through which greater confidence in the findings can be claimed.
- They state how participants were selected (purposeful and self-selecting), the gender composition of the sample, and the number of UK business schools represented.
- They specify the nature of the data collected (including number of semi-structured interviews, when conducted, duration).
- They describe their approach to analysing the data (thematic analysis using NVivo—see Chapters 24 and 25).

Research findings

The research findings section is subtitled 'Love and labour' and the findings are presented in three separate sub-sections: 'Eros—romantic love', 'Agape—unconditional love', and 'Pragma—pragmatic love', using this typology to categorize and analyse the data. In each case, direct or verbatim quotations from the interview transcripts are used to illustrate and reinforce the theme presented. For example, the following sentence indicates the type of identity work that is observed in the data.

> Practices reflecting high commitment were pervasive in the data, with some participants narrating more extreme stories denoting an intense dependency on their work for meaning (Terkel, 1972).
>
> (Clarke et al. 2012: 9)

This is immediately followed by a data quote from one of the research participants to illustrate the point previously made. Italics are used to indicate that this is a direct quote:

> I work incredibly long hours ... I would prefer a more balanced life. You know, if I had an opportunity I would love to have children. I would like to be in a relationship but this [my job] has sort-of taken over in a way.
>
> (Lecturer, 2012: 9)

This is a common way of presenting qualitative data. However, as illustrated in Thinking deeply 7.5, the presentation of verbatim quotes can take other formats. Through the presentation of themes illustrated by verbatim quotes, the 'Research findings' section points forward to some of the arguments that are taken up in the 'Discussion' and the 'Summary and conclusion' sections. The 'Research findings' section also refers back to the previously discussed identity literature. This section includes more citations to the literature than the equivalent section in the quantitative article by Elsesser and Lever.

Discussion

This section of Clarke et al.'s article discusses the findings in the light of the study's research objective, which was to understand how academic identities are being sustained or transformed as a consequence of new public management in UK business schools. The key themes that have been developed through the data analysis—romantic, unconditional, or pragmatic love of academic work—are reiterated and reinforced. The second paragraph begins as follows:

> In exploring the identities of academics in UK business schools what is beyond question is the deep affection and love that most participants expressed for their working lives. Throughout the interviews, our respondents drew on different notions of love in describing their academic selves, three of which we selected out for analytical attention.
>
> (Clarke et al. 2012: 12)

This section is heavily referenced and slightly longer than the initial literature review section. This is an indication of the importance of the discussion in emphasizing the

7.5 THINKING DEEPLY
Using verbatim quotations from interviews

In presenting their findings, Clarke et al (2012) use verbatim interview quotations to illustrate the themes identified in the data. This is a common approach. However, many articles published in North American journals tend to take a slightly different approach. Here, the tone and mode of presenting the findings is very formal and conforms to traditional, mainstream expectations of what a research article should comprise. In particular, there is a 'definite harkening to a more positivistic style' in the presentation of findings, which is associated with a 'generic and impersonal' use of quotations (Adler and Adler 2008: 13, 14). One way in which this is revealed is through presentation of verbatim quotations in a formal manner in tables rather than *en passant*. An example can be found in Table 7.1, which is taken from Maitlis and Lawrence's (2007) multiple **case study ethnography** of three British orchestras. The article was published in a highly regarded journal and adopts what Adler and Adler (2008) refer to as the 'mainstream ethnography' frame. This can be discerned in the more formalistic tone than is usually encountered in the other writing frames. The article is about how 'sensegiving' takes place in organizations—that is, how leaders and others frame perceptions for others. One of the key themes identified was the competence of the leader, and this theme had three components (referred to as 'first-order concepts': see Key concept 24.6). Maitlis and Lawrence provided 'representative quotations' for each of the three components in a table (see Table 7.1). This style of presenting quotations has become noticeably popular in some leading journals. It is likely that there are several reasons for this: the provision of a table provides a sense of something equivalent to the more commonly encountered table summarizing the results of a statistical procedure; it provides a more formal style in keeping with the prevalent tone of such journals; and possibly it gives less of a sense that the quotations are anecdotal or 'cherry-picked'.

Corden and Sainsbury (2006) conducted research into qualitative researchers' use of such quotations. They found that researchers employ verbatim quotations for interview transcripts for a variety of reasons, such as to illustrate a point; to give voice to participants; to provide evidence; or to deepen readers' understanding. When Corden and Sainsbury examined a wide range of publications in the social policy field, they found a wide variety of approaches to the use of quotations. There was a great deal of variety in how those quoted are referred to and in editing conventions, such as the removal of 'er' and 'erm' and of false starts, as well as whether pauses or laughter are indicated. Thus, there is a wide variety of practice in the use of verbatim quotations. Corden and Sainsbury recommend that researchers should decide which approach they want to use and why, and be able to justify the choice made if necessary.

overall argument of the article and demonstrating how it contributes to our understanding of this subject, i.e. how it contributes to knowledge.

Summary and conclusion

In this section, the authors summarize their findings and draw out the implications that arise from them. They also reflexively analyse their own situated position as 'insider' researchers (see Chapter 19), noting the inherent tensions in seeking to commentate on the audit and performative culture in UK business schools by writing and publishing an academic article which 'serves to reproduce the very practices we criticize' (Clarke et al. 2012: 13). They also speculate on the broader significance of their findings as a potential form of organizational resistance. They end with a restatement of their main conclusion:

the institutionalization of the evaluation of academic output means that academics' identities are continually on the line, and individuals are often only perceived to be as 'good' as their last publication —despite academics possibly being successful in teaching or administration.

Clarke et al. (2012: 13)

This is followed by a warning about the potential negative implications of new public management in UK business schools:

as a consequence of this preoccupation, if notions of the aspirational academic recede or are reshaped too dramatically, then it is possible that passion and love for the job, with many of the meanings surrounding what it means to be an academic, are also at risk of further erosion.

The article ends with an acknowledgement to the editor and peer reviewers and a list of references to literature cited in the article.

TABLE 7.1
The use of verbatim interview quotations in a table

Data supporting the theme 'perceptions of a lack of leader competence'

Associated first-order concepts	Representative quotations
Poor organizational decision process	2.1 '[The associate leader] expressed concern over the lack of information from the office and wondered whether enough was being done to seek out potential leaders to work with the orchestra.' (minutes, BSO orchestra committee meeting) (BSO5)
	2.2 Commenting on the appointment decision process for an orchestra leader: 'It's one incredible grey area. Nobody seems to kn-ow what's happening with that and no one seems to know whose responsibility it is …. Eventually, the principals just made it so clear that basically they weren't happy [that the appointment was not made] …. But we have a theory that he may have promised the guy the job first, and got himself into a pickle.' (interview, BSO orchestra committee member) (BSO5)
	2.3 Commenting on a decision not to terminate a player, a LSO player board member commented: 'There was a decision over this player. The vote was taken and it went against the wishes of the chairman, and he said, 'Well okay, we'll call a council of principals meeting' …. Most of the principals are more than happy to sit on the fence. They've got a hard enough job. They don't want to put their oar in and stir things up, so of course the vote went the other way. Now I think that's a misuse of power, if you like. You're widening the goal posts and moving them at the same time. I was more than a little pissed off about that because it didn't seem to be fair. What was the point of having a [board]?' (interview, LSO player board member) (LSO5)
Poor outcomes of leader decision making	2.4 'Programming is [the senior producer]—you couldn't ask for better repertoire. [The senior producer] is very successful. He has organized some very good programmes and concerts.' (interview, BSO player) (BSO1)
	2.5 'Looking back on all this. I would say that those judgments [of the chief executive] were fatally flawed for our organization on two counts: [the principal conductor's] availability and commitment, and his financial cost.' (interview, PSO player director) (PSO2)
	2.6 'It was like lambs to the slaughter. The contract [the principal conductor] was offered should never have been accepted.' (interview, PSO deputy CEO) (PSO2)
	2.7 'If you look at the main [home city] concerts, something has happened there, and we've lost our thread, because we had three distinct series …. So I think the [PSO], represented by the board and the senior management, has a duty to make sure that the repertoire actually fulfils the artistic strategy.' (interview, PSO player chairman-elect) (PSO1)
Lack of leader expertise	2.8 '[We need] someone who knows what they're doing, who has sufficient commercial grasp to know the effect of what they're doing, and appreciates the need to create a programme for [the PSO home city] that will also apply in [other regional towns]. It's that thorough vision that is lacking at the moment, causing all sorts of orchestral problems.' (interview, PSO finance director) (PSO1)
	2.9 'You have someone here [the chief executive] who has no understanding of orchestras at all.' (observation, musicians' union representative, PSO players meeting with musicians' union) (PSO6)

Source: Maitlis and Lawrence (2007: 67); reproduced with permission.

Lessons

As with Elsesser and Lever's article, it is useful to review some of the lessons learned from the article by Clarke et al.

- As in the illustration of quantitative research writing, there are strong opening sentences, which attract our attention and give a clear indication of the nature and content of the article. There is some scope for creativity in order to grab the reader's attention, but this must be balanced against the need to conform to academic writing conventions.

- The rationale of the research is based on the idea of new public management, and the need to understand the effects of this new form of management on academic identity.

- The research question objective is specified, but this is more open-ended than in Elsesser and Lever's article, which is in keeping with the general orientation of qualitative researchers.

- The research methods are outlined, and an indication is given of the approach to analysis.

- The presentation of main themes corresponds to the overall research objective, but the typology that is developed is an opportunity to build theory inductively through data analysis. This is quite different from the article by Elsesser and Lever, which sought to test theory deductively using a series of hypotheses.

- The discussion section allows concepts and theories to be developed into a more general argument about the nature of academic work and the effects of audit and performative cultures.

- The summary and conclusion section gives the authors a final opportunity to recap the arguments made in the article, in a way which convinces and persuades, i.e. it is highly rhetorical (Key concept 7.1).

Reflexivity and its implications for writing

It is an increasing expectation (especially, but by no means exclusively, among qualitative researchers) that researchers display a degree of reflexivity in their research writing (Alvesson et al. 2008). In a general sense, reflexivity is about thinking deeply about the process of knowledge generation in research and questioning taken-for-granted assumptions about research. Reflexivity has several more specific meanings in the social sciences. The term is employed by ethnomethodologists to refer to the way in which speech and action are constitutive of the social world in which they are located; in other words, they do more than merely act as indicators of deeper phenomena (see Chapter 22). The other meaning of the term carries the connotation that business researchers should reflect on the implications of their methods, values, biases, and decisions for the knowledge that they generate about the social world, and that they should try to be aware of how personal idiosyncrasies and implicit assumptions affect their approach to study. Reflexivity also entails sensitivity to the researcher's cultural, political, and social context. As such, knowledge from a reflective position is always based on the researcher's location in time and social space. Also, unlike reflection, which takes place after the interaction or activity has passed, reflexivity is exercised in the moment as well as afterwards. Most importantly, according to Riach (2009: 359), reflexivity 'requires a fundamental requestioning of what is knowable in a given context'. This notion is especially explicit in Pink's (2001) formulation of a reflexive approach to analysing visual images (see Chapter 19) and in Plummer's (2001) definition of a reflexive approach to life histories (see Chapter 20).

Reflexivity is related to the concept of postmodernism (Key concept 2.8), which in one sense can be seen as a form of sensitivity—a way of seeing and understanding that results in a questioning of the taken-for-granted. Postmodernism questions the very notion of the dispassionate social scientist seeking to uncover a pre-given external reality. As a result, 'knowledge' of the social world is relative; any account is just one of many possible ways of rendering social reality.

There has been growing evidence of reflexivity in organizational research in the form of books that collect inside stories of the research process, detailing the nuts and bolts of research as distinct from the often-sanitized portrayal in research articles. Reflexivity encourages greater awareness and acknowledgement of the role of the researcher as part of the construction of knowledge. In other words, the reflexive attitude is highly critical of the notion that the researcher extracts knowledge from observations and conversations with others and then transmits knowledge to an audience. Instead, the researcher is viewed as implicated in the construction of knowledge through the stance that he or she assumes in relation to the observed and through the ways in which an account is transmitted in the form of a text. This entails an acknowledgement of the implications and significance of the researcher's choices as both observer and writer.

Writing differently

We have argued above that in practice the conventions of writing up qualitative and quantitative research are not so different as one might assume. Moreover, we have presented some general guidance on how you might present your research. It is important, however, to note that we are not proposing that there is a single 'formula' or 'recipe' for how you should write. Indeed, some scholars argue that the conventions of academic writing have become too restrictive, leading to a homogeneous and formulaic approach to writing, sometimes referred to as a 'boilerplate' which stifles creativity (Alvesson and Gabriel 2013; Corbett et al. 2014). It seems clear that papers which are presented in a 'scientific' format are more likely to be regarded as credible than those which are not (Harley and Hardy 2004). However, it is also possible that these conventions result in forms of writing that are difficult to read and understand. Billig (2013) argues that across the social sciences, the use of technical jargon and convoluted sentences has proliferated under conditions of higher education expansion and the requirement upon academics to continuously publish research. The use of such language means that new researchers often struggle to become proficient in the academic language that they are required to use. Related concerns have been raised in business research, where

Dane (2011) argues that much academic writing is stilted, distant, and difficult for practitioners to read. He recommends that authors use fictional writing as a source of inspiration and learn to think more creatively about their written work to enable a shift away from monotone stylistic conventions of article-writing towards creative innovation. For those early in their research careers, it may make sense to 'play it safe' by not straying too far from conventional approaches to writing up your research. As you develop your skills, however, you should not be afraid to think about presenting your ideas in creative ways which challenge these conventions to a certain degree, in order to better engage with your audience. Whatever writing style you eventually adopt, we cannot emphasize enough the value of practice in learning the craft of academic writing, for as Billig observes, 'William James once said that if there was anything good in his own style of writing, then was "the result of ceaseless toil in rewriting"' (Billig 2013: 6).

CHECKLIST
Issues to consider for writing up a piece of research

○ Have you clearly specified your research questions?

○ Have you clearly indicated how the literature you have read relates to your research questions?

○ Is your discussion of the literature critical and organized, so that it is not just a summary of what you have read?

○ Have you clearly outlined your research design and your research methods? This includes:

  ○ why you chose a particular research design;

  ○ why you chose a particular research method;

  ○ how you selected your research participants;

  ○ if there were any issues to do with cooperation (e.g. response rates);

  ○ why you implemented your research in a particular way (e.g. how the interview questions relate to your research questions, why you observed participants in particular situations, why your focus group guide asked the questions in a particular way and order);

  ○ if your research required access to an organization, how and on what basis was agreement for access forthcoming;

  ○ steps you took to ensure that your research was ethically responsible;

  ○ how you analysed your data;

  ○ any difficulties you encountered in the implementation of your research approach.

○ Have you presented your data in a manner that relates to your research questions?

○ Does your discussion of your findings show how they relate to your research questions?

○ Does your discussion of your findings show how they shed light on the literature that you presented?

○ Are the interpretations of your data that you offer fully supported with tables, figures, or segments from transcripts?

○ If you have presented tables and/or figures, are they properly labelled with a title and number?

○ If you have presented tables and/or figures, are they commented upon in your discussion?

○ Do your conclusions clearly allow the reader to establish what your research contributes to the literature?

○ Have you explained the limitations of your study?

○ Do your conclusions consist solely of a summary of your findings? If they do, rewrite them!

○ Do your conclusions make clear the answers to your research questions?

○ Does your presentation of the findings and the discussion allow a clear argument and narrative to be presented to the reader?

○ Have you broken up the text in each chapter with appropriate subheadings?

○ Does your writing avoid sexist, racist, and disablist language?

○ Have you included all appendices that you might need to provide (e.g. interview schedule, letters requesting access, communications with research participants)?

○ Have you checked that your list of references includes *all* the items referred to in your text?

○ Have you checked that your list of references follows precisely the style that your university requires?

○ Have you followed your supervisor's suggestions when he or she has commented on your draft chapters?

○ Have you got people other than your supervisor to read your draft chapters for you?

○ Have you checked to ensure that there is not excessive use of jargon?

○ Do you provide clear signposts in the course of writing, so that readers are clear about what to expect next and why it is there?

○ Have you ensured that your university's requirements for submitting projects are fully met in terms of such issues as word count (so that it is neither too long nor too short) and whether or not an abstract and table of contents are required?

○ Have you ensured that you do not quote excessively when presenting the literature?

○ Have you fully acknowledged the work of others so that you cannot be accused of plagiarism?

○ Is there a good correspondence between the title of your project and its contents?

○ Have you acknowledged the help of others where this is appropriate (e.g. your supervisor, people who may have helped with interviews, people who read your drafts)?

 # KEY POINTS

....

- Good writing is probably just as important as good research practice. Indeed, it is probably better thought of as a part of good research practice.

- Clear structure and a clear statement of your research questions are important components of writing up research.

- Be sensitive to the ways in which writers seek to persuade us of their points of view.

- The study of rhetoric and writing strategies generally teaches us that the writings of scientists and social scientists do more than simply report findings. They are designed to convince and to persuade.

- The emphasis on rhetoric is not meant to imply that there is no external social reality; it merely suggests that our understanding of that reality is profoundly influenced by the ways it is represented by writers.

- The basic structure of and the rhetorical strategies employed in most quantitative and qualitative research articles are broadly similar.

- We need to get away from the idea that rhetoric and the desire to persuade others of the validity of our work are somehow bad things. They are not. We all want to get our points across and to persuade our readers that we have got things right. The questions to ask are, do we do it well and do we make the best possible case? We all have to persuade others that we have got the right angle on things; the trick is to do it well. So when you write an essay or dissertation, do bear in mind the significance of your writing strategy.

QUESTIONS FOR REVIEW

- Why is it important to consider the ways in which business research is written?

Writing up quantitative research: an example

- Read an article based on quantitative research published in a business and management journal. How far does it exhibit the same characteristics as Elsesser and Lever's article?

- What is meant by 'rhetorical strategy'? Why might rhetorical strategies be important in writing up business research?

- Do Elsesser and Lever employ an empiricist repertoire?

Writing up qualitative research: an example

- Read an article based on quantitative research published in a business and management journal. How far does it exhibit the same characteristics as Clarke et al.'s article?

- How far is the structure of Clarke et al.'s article different from Elsesser and Lever's?

Reflexivity and its implications for writing

- How has postmodernism called into question established ways of writing business research?

- What is reflexivity?

Writing differently

- How might you cultivate creative innovation in your academic writing?

ONLINE RESOURCES
www.oup.com/uk/brm5e/

Visit the Interactive Research Guide that accompanies this book to complete an exercise in writing up business research.

PART TWO

QUANTITATIVE RESEARCH

THE NATURE OF QUANTITATIVE RESEARCH

CHAPTER OUTLINE

This chapter is concerned with the logic and key features of quantitative research. Broadly, quantitative research covers approaches which attempt to measure and/or count social phenomena and the relationships between them. This approach has long been the dominant one for conducting business research and remains so, in spite of qualitative research becoming more influential since the 1980s. The emphasis in this chapter is very much on what quantitative research *typically* entails, although at a later point in the chapter some of the ways in which there are often departures from this ideal type are outlined. This chapter explores the following areas:

- the main steps of quantitative research, which are presented as a linear succession of stages;

- the importance of concepts in quantitative research and the ways in which measures may be devised for concepts; this includes a discussion of the important idea of an indicator, which is devised as a way of measuring a concept for which there is no direct measure;
- the procedures for checking the reliability and validity of the measurement process;

- the main preoccupations of quantitative research, which are described in terms of four features—measurement, causality, generalization, and replication;
- some criticisms that are levelled at quantitative research.

Introduction

In Chapter 2, quantitative research was outlined as a distinctive research strategy. In very broad terms, it was described as involving the collection of numerical data and as exhibiting a view of the relationship between theory and research as deductive, a predilection for a natural science approach (and for positivism in particular), and an objectivist conception of social reality. A number of other features of quantitative research were outlined, but in this chapter we will examine the strategy in much more detail.

It should be made clear that the description of this research strategy as 'quantitative research' should not be taken to mean that quantification of aspects of social life is *all* that distinguishes it from a qualitative research strategy. The very fact that it has a distinctive epistemological and ontological position suggests that there is a good deal more to it than the mere presence of numbers. In this chapter, as well as outlining the main steps in quantitative research, we also examine some of the principal preoccupations of the strategy and how certain issues of concern among practitioners are addressed, such as questions about measurement validity.

The main steps in quantitative research

Figure 8.1 outlines the main steps in quantitative research. These steps reflect the underlying logic of quantitative research, which is deductive. This is very much an ideal-typical account of the process: it is probably never or rarely found in this pure form, but this outline represents a useful starting point for getting to grips with the main ingredients of the approach and the links between them. Research is rarely as linear and as straightforward as the figure implies, but its aim is to do no more than capture the main steps and provide a rough indication of their interconnections.

Some of the chief steps have been covered in the first two chapters of this book. The fact that we start off with theory signifies a deductive logic. It is common for outlines of the main steps of quantitative research to suggest that a hypothesis (or hypotheses) is (are) deduced from the theory and then tested. This notion has been incorporated into Figure 8.1. Hypothesis testing is characteristic of experimental research, and the popularity of this approach in quantitative social science reflects the

influence of the natural sciences on the development of the social sciences. It is important to note, however, that a good deal of quantitative research does not require the specification of a hypothesis, and instead theory acts loosely as a set of concerns in relation to which the business researcher collects data. The next step entails the selection of a research design, a topic that was explored in Chapter 3. As we have seen, the selection of research design has implications for a variety of issues, such as the external validity of findings and researchers' ability to impute causality to their findings. Step 4 involves devising quantitative measures of the concepts in which the researcher is interested. This process is often referred to as *operationalization*, a term that originally derives from physics to refer to the operations by which a concept (such as temperature or velocity) is measured (Bridgman 1927). Aspects of this issue will be explored later in this chapter.

The next two steps call for the selection of a research site or sites and then the selection of subjects/respondents.

FIGURE 8.1
The process of quantitative research

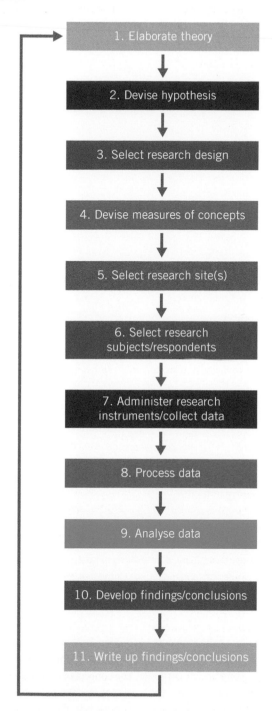

(Experimental researchers tend to call the people on whom they conduct research 'subjects', whereas social survey researchers typically call them 'respondents'.) Thus, in social survey research an investigator must first be concerned to establish an appropriate setting for his or her research. Research in focus 8.1 illustrates the process by which researchers might go about selecting research sites and sampling respondents. In experimental research, these two steps are likely to include the assignment of subjects into control and treatment groups.

Step 7 involves the administration of the research instrument(s). In experimental research, this is likely

8.1 RESEARCH IN FOCUS

Selecting research sites and sampling respondents: the Quality of Work and Life in Changing Europe project

The 'Quality of Work and Life in Changing Europe' is a research project funded by the European Commission (Abendroth and Den Dulk 2011; Lippe et al. 2009) that analyses international comparative data on the social wellbeing of citizens and social quality in European workplaces in eight partner countries: UK, Finland, Sweden, Germany, the Netherlands, Portugal, Hungary, and Bulgaria. The focus of the study was to understand the quality of working life among European workers, including how public and organizational policies in different countries affect these issues. The overall survey sample of 7867 service sector workers varied in size by country, ranging from 676 respondents in Sweden to 1373 respondents in Portugal. Service sector workers were chosen as the focus of the study because this is a growing sector of the economy that comprises both professional and lower-skilled workers. In each of the eight countries, a national team of researchers surveyed employees from the following types of workplace:

1. A bank/insurance company: included because these organizations are often at the forefront of supportive work–life policies and are highly visible, therefore susceptible to institutional pressures to provide work–life balance support (total of 1918 respondents).

2. A retail company: chains of shops were included because of the higher proportion of lower-skilled jobs and female workers employed there (total of 1670 respondents).

3. An information technology (IT)/telecom company: included because of the high proportion of professional workers and the highly competitive nature of careers in these organizations (total of 2628 respondents).

4. A public hospital: large hospitals in major cities were included as representative of public sector organizations (total of 1651 respondents).

Because this was a non-random quota sample selected to represent various categories of organization (sampling will be discussed in detail in Chapter 9), attempts were made in each country to select similar service sector organizations in order to increase comparability. These sector comparisons acted as a control variable on the sample. A questionnaire survey was developed by the researchers and translated into the language of each country, before being back-translated for comparability. Employees in the selected organizations received a letter in which they were asked to fill in the questionnaire, either on paper or online (see Chapter 11 for more about questionnaires and online surveys). The response rates in different countries were variable, ranging from 17 per cent (Hungary and the UK both being low) to 89 per cent (Bulgaria, Finland, and Sweden being relatively high). These findings enabled the researchers to trace differences between countries in terms of the level of support available (from the state, the workplace, and the family) for the development of work–life balance.

to mean pre-testing subjects, manipulating the independent variable for the experimental group, and post-testing subjects. In cross-sectional research using social survey research instruments, it will involve interviewing the sample members using a structured interview schedule (discussed in Chapter 10) or distributing a self-completion questionnaire (Chapter 11). In research using structured observation (Chapter 13), this step will mean an observer (or possibly more than one) watching the setting and the behaviour of people and then assigning categories to each element of behaviour.

Step 8 simply refers to the fact that, once information has been collected, it must be transformed into 'data'. In the context of quantitative research, this is likely to mean that it must be prepared so that it can be quantified. With some kinds of information this can be done in a relatively straightforward way—for example, for information relating to such things as people's ages, incomes, number of years spent at school, and so on. For other variables that are not readily measured in numbers, e.g. job satisfaction, quantification will entail coding the information—that is, transforming it into numbers to facilitate the quantitative analysis of the data, particularly if the analysis is going to be carried out by computer. 'Codes' act as tags that are placed on data about people to allow the information to be processed by the computer. This consideration leads into Step 9—the analysis of the data. In this step, the researcher uses techniques of quantitative data analysis to reduce the amount of data collected, to test for relationships between variables, to develop ways of presenting the results of the analysis to others, and so on.

The researcher must then interpret the results of the data analysis. It is at this stage that the 'findings' will emerge (Step 10). The researcher will consider the connections between the findings and the theorizing that acted as the impetus of the research. If there is a hypothesis, is it supported or disproven? What are the implications of the findings for the theoretical ideas that formed the background to the research?

Then the research must be written up (Step 11—covered in Chapter 7 of this book). The research cannot take on significance beyond satisfying the researcher's personal curiosity until it enters the public domain in some way, by being written up as a paper to be presented at a conference, or as a report to the agency that funded the research, or as a book or journal article for academic business researchers. In writing up the findings and conclusions, the researcher is doing more than simply relaying to others what has been found: readers must be convinced that the research conclusions are important and that the findings are robust. Thus, a significant part of the research process involves convincing others of the significance and validity of one's findings.

Once the findings have been published, they become part of the stock of knowledge (or 'theory' in the loose sense of the word) in their domain. Thus, there is a feedback loop from Step 11 back up to Step 1. The presence of both an element of deductivism (Step 2) and inductivism (the feedback loop) is indicative of the positivist foundations of quantitative research (see Key concept 2.10). Similarly, the emphasis on the translation of concepts into measures (Step 4) is symptomatic of the principle of phenomenalism, which is also a feature of positivism. It is to this important phase of translating concepts into measures that we now turn. As we will see, certain considerations follow on from the stress placed on measurement in quantitative research. By and large, these considerations are to do with the validity and reliability of the measures devised by social scientists. These considerations will figure prominently in the following discussion.

As we noted before presenting the model in Figure 8.1, this sequence of stages is a kind of ideal-typical account, and in practice not all quantitative research will adhere to these steps. At the end of this chapter, the section 'Is it always like this?' deals with some ways in which practice may diverge from this model.

Concepts and their measurement

What is a concept?

Concepts are the building blocks of theory and represent the points around which business research is conducted. Think of the numerous concepts that are mentioned in relation to just some of the research examples cited in this book:

> structure, agency, deskilling, organizational size, technology, charismatic leadership, followership, TQM, functional subcultures, knowledge, managerial identity, motivation to work, moral awareness, productivity, stress management, employment relations, organizational development, competitive success.

Each concept represents a label that we give to elements of the social world that seem to have common features and that strike us as significant. As Bulmer succinctly puts it, concepts 'are categories for the organization of ideas and observations' (1984: 43). One item mentioned in Chapter 3 but omitted from the list of concepts above is IQ. It has been omitted because it is not a concept! It is a *measure* of a concept—namely, intelligence. This is a rare case of a social scientific measure that has become so well known that the measure and the concept are almost as synonymous as temperature and the centigrade or Fahrenheit scales, or as length and the metric scale. The concept of intelligence has arisen as a result of noticing that some people appear to be very clever, some quite clever, and still others not at all clever. These variations in what we have come to call the concept of 'intelligence' seem important, because we might try to construct theories to explain these variations. We may try to incorporate the concept of intelligence into theories to explain variations in such things as job competence or entrepreneurial success. Similarly, with indicators of organizational *performance* such as 'productivity' or 'return on invest-ment', we notice that some organizations improve their relative performance, others remain static, and others decline in economic value. Out of such considerations, the concept of organizational performance is reached.

If a concept is to be employed in quantitative research, then logically it will have to be measured. Once they are measured, concepts are typically classified as independent or dependent variables. In other words, concepts may provide an explanation of a certain aspect of the social world (independent variables), or they may stand for things we want to explain (dependent variables). (There are other categories of variables, but for the sake of simplicity we will not deal with them here.) A concept such as organizational performance may be used in either capacity: for example, as a possible explanation of culture (are there differences between highly successful organizations and others, in terms of the cultural values, norms, and beliefs held by organizational members?) or as something to be explained (what are the causes of variation in organizational performance?). Equally, we might be interested in evidence of changes in organizational performance over time or in variations between comparable nations in levels of organizational performance. As we start to investigate such issues, we are likely to formulate theories to help us understand why, for example, rates of organizational performance vary between countries or over time. This will, in turn, generate new concepts, as we try to tackle the explanation of variation in rates.

Why measure?

The focus on measurement in quantitative research reflects the underlying ontological assumption that there is an objective external reality, and the epistemological assumption that to develop knowledge about reality we must be able to engage objectively with the phenomena we are researching. There are three more specific reasons for the preoccupation with measurement in quantitative research.

- Measurement allows us to delineate *fine differences* between people, organizations, or other entities in terms of the characteristic in question. This is very useful, since, although we can often distinguish between entities in terms of extreme categories, finer distinctions are much more difficult to recognize. For example, we can detect clear variation in levels of job satisfaction—people who love their jobs and people who hate their jobs—but small differences are much more difficult to detect without measurement of it.

- Measurement gives us a *consistent device* or yardstick for making such distinctions. A measurement device provides a consistent instrument for gauging differences. This consistency relates to two things: our ability to be consistent over time, and our ability to be consistent with other researchers. In other words, a measure should be something that is influenced neither by the timing of its administration nor by the person who administers it. The measure should generate consistent results, other than those that occur as a result of changes in the phenomenon being measured. Whether a measure actually possesses this quality has to do with the issue of *reliability*, which was introduced in Chapter 3 and which will be examined again below.

- Measurement provides the basis for *more precise estimates of the degree of relationship between concepts* (for example, through correlation analysis, which will be examined in Chapter 15). Thus, if we measure both job satisfaction and the things with which it might be related, such as stress-related illness, we will be able to produce more precise estimates of how closely they are associated than if we had not proceeded in this way.

Indicators

Some social phenomena can be measured more or less directly. For example, we can directly measure such things as age, annual income, or organizational size. Many phenomena, however, cannot be measured directly. In such cases, in order to provide a measure of a concept (often referred to as an operational definition, a term deriving from the idea of operationalization), it is necessary to have an indicator or indicators that will stand for the concept (see Key concept 8.2). There are various ways in which indicators can be devised:

- through a question (or series of questions) that is part of a structured interview schedule or self-completion questionnaire—the question(s) could be concerned with the respondents' report of an attitude (for example, job satisfaction) or their employment status (for example, job title) or a report of their behaviour (for example, job tasks and responsibilities);

- through the recording of individuals' behaviour using a structured observation schedule (for example, managerial activity);

- through the use of existing surveys, such as the Study of Australian Leadership (see Research in focus 3.13), which was used to measure aspects of Australian management practices;

- through an examination of mass media content by way of content analysis—for example, to determine changes in the salience of an issue, such as courage in managerial decision-making (Harris 2001).

Indicators, then, can be derived from a wide variety of sources and methods. Concepts can be operationalized using either single or multi-item indicators (see Research in focus 8.3 and 8.4).

Dimensions of concepts

The use of multiple-indicator measures reflects the fact that some phenomena are multi-dimensional. This view is associated particularly with Lazarsfeld (1958). The idea behind this approach is that, when the researcher is seeking to develop a measure of a concept, the different aspects or components of that concept should be considered. This specification of the dimensions of a concept would be undertaken with reference to theory and research associated with that concept. For his research on corporate social responsibility among Indian IT companies, Dhanesh (2014) needed to distinguish between the different dimensions of corporate social responsibility (CSR) because one of his research questions was: 'What dimensions of CSR are most significantly related to the employees' relationships with their employing organizations?' Following a review of theory and research on the subject, he proposed four dimensions of CSR, each of which was measured through a multiple-item scale comprising several statements requiring respondents to reply in terms of level of agreement or disagreement. The four dimensions are presented here, each with a representative item.

- *Discretionary CSR*: for example, 'This organization has a program in place to reduce the amount of energy and materials wasted in its business.'

8.2 KEY CONCEPT
What is an indicator?

It is worth making two distinctions here. First, there is a distinction between an *indicator* and a *measure*. The latter can be taken to refer to things that can be relatively unambiguously counted. At an individual level, measures might include personal salary, age, or years of service, whereas at an organizational level they might include annual turnover or number of employees. Measures, in other words, are quantities. If we are interested, for example, in some of the correlates of variation in the age of employees in part-time employment, age can be quantified in a reasonably direct way.

We use indicators to tap concepts that are less directly quantifiable. If we are interested in the causes of variation in job satisfaction, we will need indicators that will stand for the concept of job satisfaction. These indicators will allow job satisfaction to be measured and we can treat the resulting quantitative information as if it were a measure. An indicator, then, is something that is devised or already exists and that is employed *as though it were a measure of a concept*. It is viewed as an indirect measure of a concept such as job satisfaction. An IQ test is a further example, in that it is a battery of indicators of the concept of intelligence.

We see here a second distinction: between *direct* and *indirect* indicators of concepts. Indicators may be direct or indirect in their relationship to the concepts for which they stand. Thus, an indicator of marital status ('married' / 'single') has a much more direct relationship to its concept than an indicator (or set of indicators) relating to job satisfaction. Sets of attitudes always need to be measured by batteries of indirect indicators. So too do many forms of behaviour. When indicators are used that are not true quantities, they will need to be coded to be turned into quantities. Directness and indirectness are not qualities inherent to indicators: a particular indicator may be direct or indirect, depending on how it is applied. Data from a survey question on amount earned per month may be a direct measure of personal income, but if we treat amount earned per month as an indicator of social class, it becomes an indirect measure. The issue of indirectness raises the question of where an indirect measure comes from—that is, how does a researcher devise an indicator of something like job satisfaction? Usually, it is based on common-sense understandings of the forms the concept takes or on anecdotal or qualitative evidence relating to that concept. Many phenomena will already have been measured in prior research; in such cases, quantitative researchers often choose to use indicators which have been developed and validated in prior published work, rather than attempting to develop new ones.

8.3 RESEARCH IN FOCUS
A multiple-indicator measure of a concept

The research on cultural values and management ethics by Terence Jackson (2001) involved a questionnaire survey of part-time MBA and post-experience students in Australia, China, Britain, France, Germany, Hong Kong, Spain, India, Switzerland, and the USA. This contained 12 phrases, each describing a specific action, and respondents were asked to judge the extent to which they *personally* believed the action was ethical on a five-point scale: 1 = unethical, 5 = ethical. The middle point on the scale allowed for a neutral response. This approach to investigating a cluster of attitudes is known as a **Likert scale**. In some cases researchers use a seven-point scale rather than a five-point scale for responses.

The 12 phrases used in Jackson's research were as follows:

- accepting gifts/favours in exchange for preferential treatment;
- passing blame for errors to an innocent co-worker;
- divulging confidential information;
- calling in sick to take a day off;
- pilfering organization's materials and supplies;
- giving gifts/favours in exchange for preferential treatment;
- claiming credit for someone else's work;
- doing personal business on organization's time;
- concealing one's errors;
- taking extra personal time (breaks, etc.);
- using organizational services for personal use;
- not reporting others' violations of organizational policies.

Respondents were also asked to judge the extent to which they thought their peers believed the action was ethical, using the same scale. Finally, using the same type of Likert scale, they were asked to evaluate the frequency with which they and their peers act in the way implied by the statement: 1 = infrequently, 5 = frequently. 'Hence, respondents make a judgement as to the extent to which they believe (or they think their colleagues believe) an action is ethical: the higher the score, the higher the belief that the action is ethical' (2001: 1283). The study found that, across all national groups, managers saw their colleagues as less ethical than themselves. The findings also supported the view that ethical attitudes vary according to cultural context.

- *Ethical CSR*: for example, 'In this organization, fairness toward co-workers and/or business partners is an integral part of the employee evaluation process.'
- *Legal CSR*: for example, 'The managers of this organization try to comply with the law.'
- *Economic CSR*: for example, 'This organization has been successful at maximizing its profits.' (Dhanesh 2014: 144–5)

Dhanesh found that CSR was indeed associated with better relationships between employees and their organizations but that legal CSR was particularly important in this regard. He attributes this to India's recent economic past, in which it has emerged from a period of 'crippling crony capitalism', as he calls it (Dhanesh 2014: 141).

As well as capturing multiple dimensions of a concept and thus providing a more comprehensive measure, multiple-indicator measures offer another potential advantage. It is possible that a single indicator will incorrectly classify many individuals or organizations. This may be due to the wording of the question or it may be a product of misunderstanding. If there are a number of indicators, however, then even if people are misclassified through a particular question it will be possible to offset its effects.

8.4 RESEARCH IN FOCUS
Specifying dimensions of a concept: the case of job characteristics

A key question posed by Hackman and Oldham (1980) was: 'How can work be structured so that employees are internally motivated?' Their answer to this question relied on development of a model identifying five job dimensions that influence employee motivation. At the heart of the model is the suggestion that particular job characteristics ('core job dimensions') affect employees' experiences of work ('critical psychological states'), which in turn have a number of outcomes for both the individual and the organization. The three critical psychological states are:

- **experienced meaningfulness**: individual perceives work to be worthwhile in terms of a broader system of values;

- **experienced responsibility**: individual believes him or herself to be personally accountable for the outcome of his or her efforts;

- **knowledge of results**: individual is able to determine on a regular basis whether or not the outcomes of his or her work are satisfactory.

In addition, a particular employee's response to favourable job characteristics is affected by his or her 'growth need strength'—that is, his or her need for personal growth and development. It is expected that favourable work outcomes will occur when workers experience jobs with positive core characteristics; this in turn will stimulate critical psychological states.

In order to measure these factors, Hackman and Oldham devised the Job Diagnostic Survey (JDS), a lengthy questionnaire that can be used to determine the Motivating Potential Score (MPS) of a particular job—that is, the extent to which it possesses characteristics that are necessary to influence motivation. Below are the five dimensions; in each case an example is given of an item that can be used to measure it:

1. *Skill variety*: 'The job requires me to use a number of complex or high-level skills.'
2. *Task identity*: 'The job provides me with the chance completely to finish the pieces of work I begin.'
3. *Task significance*: 'This job is one where a lot of other people can be affected by how well the work gets done.'
4. *Autonomy*: 'The job gives me considerable opportunity for independence and freedom in how I do the work.'
5. *Feedback*: 'The job itself provides plenty of clues about whether or not I am performing well.'

Respondents are asked to indicate how far they think each statement is accurate, from 1 = very inaccurate to 7 = very accurate. In Hackman and Oldham's initial study, the JDS was administered to 658 individuals working in 62 different jobs across 7 organizations. Interpreting an individual's MPS score involves comparison with norms for specific job 'families', which were generated on the basis of this original sample. For example, professional/technical jobs have an average MPS of 154, whereas clerical jobs normally have a score of 106. Understanding the motivational potential of job content thus relies on interpretation of the MPS relative to that of other jobs and in the context of specific job families. Workers who exhibit adequate knowledge, high growth need strength, and skill, and who are satisfied with their job context, are expected to respond best to jobs with a high MPS.

Nonetheless, the use of single indicators of concepts is widespread. Boyd et al. (2012) have expressed concern about the fact that comparing articles published in *Strategic Management Journal* in 1998–2000 with those published in 2010, there has been an increase in the proportion of articles using single indicators. Moreover, this increase was from an already high level. The increase in the use of single indicators was particularly prominent for measures of dependent variables, with an increase from 57.7 per cent of articles in the earlier period to 76.5 per cent in 2010. It would be a mistake, however, to believe that investigations that use a single indicator of core concepts are somehow deficient. In any case, some studies employ both single- and multiple-indicator measures of concepts. What *is* crucial is whether or not measures are reliable and whether or not they are valid representations of the concepts they are supposed to be tapping. It is to this issue that we now turn.

Reliability of measures

Although the terms 'reliability' and 'validity' seem to be almost synonyms, they have quite different meanings in relation to the evaluation of measures of concepts, as was seen in Chapter 3. We deal with reliability in this section of the chapter and with validity in the next. As Key concept 8.5 suggests, reliability is fundamentally concerned with issues of consistency of measures. There are at least three different meanings of the term 'reliability': stability, internal reliability, and inter-rater reliability. These are outlined in Key concept 8.5 and elaborated upon in the next three subsections of this chapter.

Stability

The most obvious way of testing for the stability of a measure is the *test–retest* method. This involves administering a test or measure on one occasion and then readministering it to the same sample on another occasion, i.e.

T_1 T_2

Obs_1 Obs_2

If the measure is stable, we should expect to find a high correlation between Obs_1 and Obs_2. Correlation is a measure of the strength of the relationship between two variables. This topic will be covered in Chapter 15 in the context of a discussion about quantitative data analysis. Let us imagine that we develop a multiple-indicator measure that is supposed to tap a concept that we might call 'designerism' (a preference for buying goods, and especially clothing, with 'designer' labels). We would administer the measure to a sample of respondents and readminister it some time later. If the correlation is low, the measure would appear to be unstable, implying that respondents' answers cannot be relied upon as an indication of 'designerism'.

However, there are a number of problems with this approach to evaluating reliability. First, respondents' answers at T_1 may influence how they reply at T_2. This may result in greater consistency between Obs_1 and Obs_2 than is in fact the case. Secondly, events may intervene between T_1 and T_2 that influence the degree

---

8.5 KEY CONCEPT
What is reliability?

Reliability refers to the consistency of a measure of a concept. The following are three prominent factors involved when considering whether a measure is reliable:

- *Stability*. This consideration entails asking whether or not a measure is stable over time, so that we can be confident that the results relating to that measure for a sample of respondents do not fluctuate. This means that, if we administer a measure to a group and then readminister it, there will be little variation over time in the results obtained.

- *Internal reliability*. The key issue here is whether or not the indicators that make up the scale or index for a concept are consistent among themselves—in other words, whether or not respondents' scores on any one indicator tend to be related to their scores on the other indicators associated with that concept.

- *Inter-rater reliability*. When a great deal of subjective judgement is involved in the recording of observations or the translation of data into categories and where more than one rater is involved in such activities, there is the possibility that there is a lack of consistency in their decisions. This can arise in a number of contexts: for example, when answers to open-ended questions have to be categorized; where decisions have to be made about how to categorize media items, as in content analysis (discussed in Chapter 13); or when observers have to decide how to classify subjects' behaviour, as in structured observation (Chapter 13).

of consistency. For example, if a long span of time is involved, changes in the economy or in respondents' personal financial circumstances could influence their views about and predilection for designer goods. Of course, if we were measuring something which is relatively stable over time, for example aspects of personality, then we would not expect this problem to manifest itself. There are no obvious solutions to these problems, other than by introducing a complex research design and so turning the investigation of reliability into a major project in its own right. Perhaps for these reasons, many if not most reports of research findings do not appear to carry out tests of stability.

Internal reliability

This meaning of reliability applies to multiple-indicator measures such as those examined in Research in focus 8.3 and 8.4. When you have a multiple-item measure in which each respondent's answers to each question are aggregated to form an overall score, the possibility is raised that the indicators do not relate to the same concept; in other words, they lack coherence. We need to be sure that all our designerism indicators are related to each other. If they are not, some of the items may actually be unrelated to designerism and therefore indicative of something else. An example of a study that assessed internal reliability is given in Research in focus 8.8.

One way of testing internal reliability is the *split-half* method. We can take the management ethics measure developed by Terence Jackson (2001) as an example (see Research in focus 8.3). The twelve indicators would be divided into two halves, with six in each group. The indicators would be allocated on a random or an odd–even basis. The degree of correlation between scores on the two halves would then be calculated. In other words, the aim would be to establish whether respondents scoring high on one of the two groups also scored high on the other group of indicators. The calculation of the correlation will yield a figure, known as a coefficient, that varies between 0 (no correlation and therefore no internal consistency) and 1 (perfect correlation and therefore complete internal consistency). It is usually accepted that a result of 0.8 and above implies an acceptable level of internal reliability, although for many purposes 0.7 and above is accepted. Do not worry if these figures appear somewhat opaque. The meaning of correlation will be explored in much greater detail later on. The chief point to carry away with you at this stage is that the correlation establishes how closely respondents' scores on the two groups of indicators are related.

Nowadays, most researchers use a test of internal reliability known as *Cronbach's alpha* (see Key concept 8.6). Its use has grown as a result of its incorporation into computer software for quantitative data analysis.

Inter-rater reliability

The idea of inter-rater reliability is briefly outlined in Key concept 8.5. The issues involved are rather too advanced to be dealt with at this stage and will be briefly touched on in later chapters. Cramer (1998: Chapter 14) provides a very detailed treatment of the issues around inter-rater reliability and appropriate techniques.

8.6 KEY CONCEPT
What is Cronbach's alpha?

We may appear to be leaping ahead too much here, but it is important to appreciate the basic features of what this widely used test means. Cronbach's alpha is a commonly used test of internal reliability. It essentially calculates the average of all possible split-half reliability coefficients. A computed alpha coefficient will vary between 1 (denoting perfect internal reliability) and 0 (denoting no internal reliability). The figure 0.8 is typically employed as a rule of thumb to denote an acceptable level of internal reliability, though many writers accept a slightly lower figure. For example, in the case of the burnout scale replicated by Schutte et al. (2000; see Research in focus 8.9), alpha was 0.7, which they suggest 'as a rule of thumb' is 'considered to be efficient' (2000: 56).

Validity of measures

As noted in Chapter 3, the issue of measurement validity has to do with whether or not a measure of a concept really measures that concept (see Key concept 8.7). When people argue about whether or not a person's IQ score really measures or reflects that person's level of intelligence, they are raising questions about the measurement validity of the IQ test in relation to the concept of intelligence. Similarly, one often hears people say that they do not believe that the UK's Retail Price Index really reflects inflation and the rise in the cost of living. Again, in such comments a query is being raised about measurement validity. And whenever students or lecturers debate whether or not formal examinations provide an accurate measure of academic ability, they too are raising questions about measurement validity.

Writers distinguish between a number of ways of testing measurement validity, which really reflect different ways of gauging the validity of a measure of a concept. These different ways of testing validity will now be outlined.

Face validity

At the very minimum, a researcher who develops a new measure should establish that it has face validity—that is, that the measure apparently reflects the content of the concept in question. Face validity might be established by asking other people whether or not the measure seems to be getting at the concept that is the focus of attention. In other words, people, possibly those with experience or expertise in a field, might be asked to act as judges to determine whether or not, on the face of it, the measure seems to reflect the concept concerned. Face validity is, therefore, an essentially intuitive process. See Research in focus 14.7 for a discussion that uses the face validity

test in order to establish the quality of some measures in the field of strategic management.

Concurrent validity

The researcher might seek also to gauge the concurrent validity of the measure. Here the researcher employs a *criterion* on which cases (for example, people) are known to differ and that is relevant to the concept in question. A new measure of job satisfaction can serve as an example. A criterion might be absenteeism, because some people are more often absent from work (other than through illness) than others. In order to establish the concurrent validity of a measure of job satisfaction, we might see if people who are satisfied with their jobs are less likely than those who are not satisfied to be absent from work. If a lack of correspondence was found, such as frequent absentees not having lower levels of job satisfaction than other employees, doubt might be cast on whether or not our measure is really addressing job satisfaction. An example of a study that measured concurrent validity is given in Research in focus 8.8.

Predictive validity

Another possible test for the validity of a new measure is predictive validity, whereby the researcher uses a *future* criterion measure, rather than a contemporary one as in the case of concurrent validity. With predictive validity, the researcher would take future levels of absenteeism as the criterion against which the validity of a new measure of job satisfaction would be examined. The difference from concurrent validity is that a future rather than a simultaneous criterion measure is employed. Research in focus 8.8 provides an example of research

8.7 KEY CONCEPT
What is validity?

Validity, when used to describe indicators, refers to the issue of whether or not an indicator (or set of indicators) that is devised to gauge a concept really measures that concept. Several ways of establishing validity are explored in this section: face validity; concurrent validity; predictive validity; convergent validity; and discriminant validity. Here the term 'validity' is being used as a shorthand for what was referred to as measurement validity in Chapter 3. Measurement validity should therefore be distinguished from the other terms introduced in Chapter 3: internal validity; external validity; and ecological validity.

that administered the criterion measure at a point in the future. Sometimes, predictive validity is assessed by asking respondents whether they are likely to engage in a certain activity in the future. For example, Sonenshein et al. (2014) were interested in how people's self-evaluations influence their support for environmental issues. They developed a scale of 'self-assets' which asked respondents their level of agreement or disagreement with statements such as 'I stay up to date on environmental issues' and 'I am well practiced at making positive environmental change'. As a test of the predictive validity of the scale, the authors also asked respondents about such issues as the likelihood of them engaging in environmental issue-supportive behaviour in future and found a clear relationship between the two.

Convergent validity

In the view of some methodologists, the validity of a measure ought to be gauged by comparing it to measures of the same concept developed through other methods. For example, if we develop a questionnaire measure of how much time managers spend on various activities (such as attending meetings, touring their organization, informal discussions, and so on), we might examine its validity by tracking a number of managers and using a structured observation schedule to record how much time is spent in various activities and their frequency.

Discriminant validity

Discriminant validity entails ensuring that when a measure is used for one construct (Construct A) it is different in terms of its content from a measure used to measure another construct (Construct B). For example, Little et al. (2012) developed a scale comprising 20 items in order to measure 'interpersonal emotion management'. They sought to ensure that the scale did not overlap substantially with (i.e. had discriminant validity from) measures of related constructs such as self-reported emotional intelligence. As the authors put it, the tests of the scale's discriminant validity 'provided support for its distinctiveness' (Little et al. 2012: 417). Testing for discriminant validity is important in ensuring that there is not excessive overlap between measures of constructs that are related.

The connection between reliability and validity

The preceding discussion has explained a number of ways of assessing the merit of measures which are used to capture concepts. In quantitative research, it is important that measures are valid and reliable; when new measures are developed they should always be examined for validity and reliability. In practice, as noted earlier, researchers commonly employ measures which have previously been validated and published when they are gathering data on concepts which have featured in earlier research.

It should be borne in mind that, although reliability and validity are analytically distinguishable, they are related because validity presumes reliability. This means that if your measure is not reliable, it cannot be valid. This point can be made with respect to each of the three criteria of reliability that have been discussed. If the measure is not stable over time, it simply cannot be providing a valid measure. The measure could not be tapping the concept it is supposed to be related to if the measure fluctuated. If the measure fluctuates, it may be measuring different things on different occasions. If a measure lacks internal reliability, it means that a multiple-indicator measure is actually measuring two or more different things; therefore, the measure cannot be valid. Finally, if there is a lack of inter-observer consistency, it means that observers cannot agree on the meaning of what they are observing, which in turn means that a valid measure cannot be in operation.

The main preoccupations of quantitative researchers

Both quantitative and qualitative research can be viewed as exhibiting a set of distinctive and contrasting preoccupations. These preoccupations reflect epistemologically grounded beliefs about what constitutes acceptable knowledge, which are informed by ontological assumptions. In this section, four distinctive preoccupations that

8.8 RESEARCH IN FOCUS

Assessing the internal reliability and the concurrent and predictive validity of a measure of organizational climate

Patterson et al. (2005) describe the way they went about validating a measure of organizational climate that they developed. This is a rather loose concept that was first developed in the 1960s and 1970s to refer to the perceptions of an organization by its members. Four main dimensions of climate were developed, based around the following notions:

1. *Human relations model*: the extent of feelings of belonging and trust in the organization and the degree to which there is training, good communication, and supervisory support.

2. *Internal process model*: the degree of emphasis on formal rules and on traditional ways of doing things.

3. *Open systems model*: the extent to which flexibility and innovativeness are valued.

4. *Rational goal model*: the degree to which clearly defined objectives and the norms and values associated with efficiency, quality, and high performance are emphasized.

An Organizational Climate Measure, comprising 95 items in a 4-point Likert format (definitely false, mostly false, mostly true, definitely true) was developed and administered to employees in 55 organizations, with 6869 completing a questionnaire—a response rate of 57 per cent. A **factor analysis** (see Key concept 8.10) was conducted to explore the extent to which there were distinct groupings of items that tended to go together. This procedure yielded 17 scales, such as autonomy, involvement, innovation and flexibility, and clarity of organizational goals.

The *internal reliability* of the scales was assessed using Cronbach's alpha, showing that all scales were at a level of 0.73 or above. This suggests that the measure's constituent scales were internally reliable.

Concurrent validity was assessed following **semi-structured interviews** with each company's managers in connection with their organization's practices. The interview data were coded to provide criteria against which the validity of the scales could be gauged. In most cases, the scales were found to be concurrently valid. For example, the researchers examined the correlation between a scale designed to measure the emphasis on tradition and the degree to which practices associated with the 'new manufacturing paradigm' (Patterson et al. 2005: 397) were adopted, as revealed by the interview data. The correlation was −0.42, implying that those firms that were perceived as rooted in tradition tended to be less likely to adopt new manufacturing practices. Here the adoption of new manufacturing practices was treated as a criterion to assess the extent to which the scale measuring perceptions of tradition really was addressing tradition. If the correlation had been small or positive, the concurrent validity of the scale would have been in doubt.

To assess *predictive validity*, the researchers asked a senior **key informant** at each company to complete a questionnaire one year after the main survey had been conducted. The questionnaire was meant to address two of the measure's constituent scales, one of which was the innovation and flexibility scale. It asked the informants to assess their companies in terms of their innovativeness in a number of areas. For example, the correlation between the innovation and flexibility scale and informants' assessment of their companies in terms of innovativeness with respect to actual products achieved a correlation of 0.53. This implies that there was indeed a correlation between perceptions of innovativeness and flexibility and a subsequent indicator of innovativeness.

can be discerned in quantitative research will be outlined and examined: measurement, causality, generalization, and replication.

Measurement

The most obvious preoccupation is with measurement, a feature that is scarcely surprising in the light of much of the discussion in the present chapter so far. From the position of quantitative research, measurement carries a number of advantages that have been outlined in this chapter. It is not surprising, therefore, that issues of reliability and validity are a concern for quantitative researchers.

Causality

There is a very strong concern with causal explanation in most quantitative research. Quantitative researchers are rarely content merely to describe *how* things are, but are keen to say *why* things are the way they are. This emphasis is also often taken to be a feature of the ways in which the natural sciences proceed. Thus, researchers are often not only interested in *describing* a phenomenon, such as motivation to work—for example, describing how motivated a certain group of employees are, or what proportion of employees in a sample are highly motivated and what proportion are largely lacking in motivation. Rather, researchers are likely to want to *explain* the phenomenon, which means examining its causes. The researcher may seek to explain motivation to work in terms of personal characteristics (such as 'growth need strength', which refers to an individual's need for personal growth and development—see Research in focus 8.4) or in terms of the characteristics of a particular job (such as 'task interest' or 'degree of supervision'). In reports of research you will often come across the idea of *independent* and *dependent* variables, terms that reflect the tendency to think in terms of causes and effects. Motivation to work might be regarded as the dependent variable, which is to be explained, and 'growth need strength' as an independent variable, which therefore has a causal influence upon motivation.

When an experimental design is being employed, the independent variable is the variable that is manipulated by the researcher. There is little ambiguity about the direction of causal influence. However, with cross-sectional designs of the kind used in most social survey research, there is ambiguity about the direction of causal influence because data concerning variables are simultaneously collected. Therefore, we cannot say that an independent variable causes the dependent one. To refer to independent and dependent variables in the context of cross-sectional designs, we must *infer* that one causes the other, as in the example concerning 'growth need strength' and motivation to work in the previous paragraph. We must draw on common sense or theoretical ideas to infer the likely temporal precedence of variables. However, there is always the risk that the inference will be wrong.

The concern about causality is reflected in the preoccupation with internal validity that was referred to in Chapter 3. There, it was noted that a criterion of good quantitative research is frequently the extent to which there is confidence in the researcher's causal inferences. Research that exhibits the characteristics of an experimental design is often more highly valued than cross-sectional research, because of the greater confidence that can be enjoyed in the causal inferences associated with the former. For their part, quantitative researchers who employ cross-sectional designs continue to attempt to develop techniques that will allow causal inferences to be made with greater confidence.

Generalization

In quantitative research the researcher usually hopes to be able to say that his or her findings can be generalized beyond the confines of the particular context in which the research was conducted. This can be understood as another legacy of quantitative research attempting to mimic the natural sciences and to develop law-like generalizations about the social world. Thus, if a study of motivation to work is carried out using a questionnaire with a number of people answering the questions, we often want to say that the results can apply to individuals other than those who responded in the study. In survey research, this concern reveals itself in the attention given to the question of how one can create a representative sample. Given that it is rarely feasible to send questionnaires to, or interview, whole populations (such as all members of a town, or the whole population of a country, or all members of an organization)—i.e. to conduct a census—we have to sample. However, we will want the sample to be as representative as possible in order to be able to say that the results are not unique to the particular group upon whom the research was conducted; in other words, we want to be able to generalize the findings beyond the cases (for example, the people) that make up the sample.

Probability sampling, which will be explored in Chapter 9, is the main way in which researchers seek to generate a representative sample. This procedure largely eliminates bias from the selection of a sample by using a process of random selection. The use of a random selection process does not guarantee a representative sample, because, as will be seen in Chapter 9, there are factors that operate over and above the selection system used that can jeopardize the representativeness of a sample. A related consideration here is this: even if we did have a representative sample, what would it be representative *of*? The simple answer is that it will be representative of the population from which it was selected. This is certainly the answer that sampling theory gives us. Strictly speaking, we cannot generalize beyond that population. This means that, if the members of the population from which a sample is taken are all inhabitants of a town, city, or region, or are all members of an organization, we can generalize only to the inhabitants or members of that town, city, region, or organization. But it is very tempting to see the findings as having a more pervasive applicability, so that, even if the sample was selected from a single large organization such as IBM, the findings are relevant to all similar organizations. We should not make inferences beyond the population from which the sample was selected, but researchers frequently do so. The wish to be able to generalize is often so deeply ingrained that the limits to the generalizability of findings are frequently forgotten or sidestepped.

The concern with generalizability or external validity is particularly strong among quantitative researchers using cross-sectional and longitudinal designs. There is also concern about generalizability in experimental research, as the discussion of external validity in Chapter 3 suggests, but users of this research design usually give greater attention to internal validity issues.

Replication

Natural scientists are often depicted as wishing to reduce to a bare minimum the contaminating influence of the scientist's biases and values (Chalmers 2013). The results of a piece of research should be unaffected by the researcher's special characteristics or expectations. If biases and lack of objectivity were pervasive, the claims of the natural sciences to provide a definitive picture of the world would be seriously undermined. As a check upon the influence of these potentially damaging problems, scientists may seek to replicate—that is, to reproduce—each other's experiments. If replication failed, so that a scientist's findings repeatedly could not be reproduced, serious questions would be raised about the validity of his or her findings. Further, if a study can be replicated with consistent results in a number of different contexts, this strengthens the case for generalization from it (Bettis et al. 2016). Consequently, scientists often attempt to be highly explicit about their procedures so that an experiment is capable of replication. Likewise, quantitative researchers in the social sciences often regard replication, or more precisely the ability to replicate, as an important ingredient of their activity. It is easy to see why: the possibility of a lack of objectivity and of

the intrusion of the researcher's values would appear to be much greater when examining the social world than when the natural scientist investigates the natural order. Consequently, it is often regarded as important that the researcher spells out clearly his or her procedures so that they can be replicated by others, even if the research does not end up being replicated. The study by Schutte et al. (2000) described in Research in focus 8.9 relies on replication of the Maslach Burnout Inventory—General Survey, a psychological measure that has been used by the authors to test for emotional exhaustion, depersonalization, and reduced personal accomplishment across a range of occupational groups and nations.

It has been relatively straightforward and therefore quite common for researchers to replicate the Job Characteristics Model, developed by Hackman and Oldham (1980, see Research in focus 8.4), in order to enhance confidence in the theory and its findings. Several of these have attempted to improve the generalizability of the model through its replication in different occupational settings—for example, with teachers, university staff, nursery school teachers, and physical education and sport administrators. However, some criticism has been levelled at the original research for failing to make explicit how the respondent sample was selected, beyond the fact that it involved a diverse variety of manual and non-manual occupations in both manufacturing and service sectors; this lack of explicitness is seen to undermine the potential generalizability of the investigation (Bryman 1989a). A further criticism relates to the emphasis that the model places on particular characteristics of a job, such as feedback from supervisors, which may be less of a feature in today's working context than in the late 1970s. A final criticism made of subsequent replications of the initial study is that they fail to test the total model, focusing on the core job characteristics rather than incorporating the effects of the mediating psychological states, which Hackman and Oldham suggest are the 'causal core of the model' (1976: 255).

A study by Johns et al. (1992) attempts to address this last criticism by specifically focusing on the mediating and moderating effects of psychological states on the relationship between job characteristics and outcomes. Basing their research on a random sample of 605 first- and second-level managers in a large utility company (response rate approximately 50 percent), the authors used a slightly modified version of the JDS questionnaire to determine the relationship between job characteristics, psychological states, and outcome variables. Their results provide some support for the mediating role of psychological states in determining outcomes

8.9 RESEARCH IN FOCUS
Testing validity through replication: the case of burnout

The Maslach Burnout Inventory relies on the use of a questionnaire to measure burnout, which is characterized by emotional exhaustion, depersonalization, and reduced personal accomplishment. This syndrome is particularly associated with individuals who do 'people work of some kind'. Findings from the original North American study (Maslach and Jackson 1981) led the authors to conclude that burnout has certain debilitating effects, resulting ultimately in a loss of professional efficacy.

A study by Schutte et al. (2000) attempted to replicate these findings across a number of occupational groups (managers, clerks, foremen, technicians, blue-collar workers) in three different nations—Finland, Sweden, and the Netherlands. However, subsequent tests of the Maslach Burnout Inventory scale suggested a need for revisions that would enable its use as a measure of burnout in occupational groups other than the human services, such as nurses, teachers, and social workers, for whom the original scale was intended. Using this revised, General Survey version, the researchers sought to investigate its *factorial validity*, or the extent to which the dimensions of burnout could be measured using the same questionnaire items in relation to different occupational and cultural groupings than the original study (see Key concept 8.10 for an explanation of *factor analysis*).

Following Hofstede (1984; see Chapter 2), employees were drawn from the same multinational corporation in different countries, in order to minimize the possibility that findings would reflect 'idiosyncracies' associated with one company or another. The final sample size of 9055 reflected a response rate to the questionnaire of 63 percent.

The inventory comprises three subscales, each measured in terms of a series of items. An example of each is given below:

- *Exhaustion* (*Ex*): 'I feel used up at the end of the workday.'
- *Cynicism* (*Cy*): 'I have become less enthusiastic about my work.'
- *Professional Efficacy* (*PE*): 'In my opinion I am good at my job.'

The individual responds according to a seven-point scale, from 0 = never, to 6 = daily. High scores on Ex and Cy and low scores on PE are indicative of burnout. A number of statistical analyses were carried out; for example, the reliability of the subscales was assessed using Cronbach's alpha as an indicator of internal consistency, meeting the criterion of 0.70 in virtually all the (sub)samples.

Schutte et al. conclude that their study

- confirms that burnout is a three-dimensional concept;
- clearly demonstrates the factorial validity of the scale across occupational groups;
- reveals that the three subscales are sufficiently internally consistent.

Furthermore, significant differences were found in the pattern of burnout among white- and blue-collar workers, the former scoring higher on PE and lower on Cy. In interpreting these findings they argue that the higher white-collar PE scores may have arisen because 'working conditions are more favourable for managers than for workers, offering more autonomy, higher job complexity, meaningful work, and more respect for co-workers' (2000: 64).

Conversely: 'The relatively high scores on Cy for blue-collar workers reflect indifference and a more distant attitude towards their jobs. This might be explained by the culture on the shopfloor where distrust, resentment, and scepticism towards management and the organization traditionally prevail' (2000: 64).

Finally, Schutte et al. note that there were significant differences across national samples, the Dutch employees having scores that were consistently lower than those of their Swedish or Finnish colleagues. The authors conclude that the Maslach Burnout Inventory—General Survey is a suitable instrument for measuring burnout in occupational groups other than human services and in nations other than those in North America. Although alternative measurement scales exist, the majority of quantitative studies of burnout continue to rely on the Maslach Burnout Inventory—General Survey and the number of studies carried out is expanding rapidly. A recent **meta-analysis** (Key concept 14.8) of quantitative research on burnout identified 86 primary studies conducted since 2000, 48 of which had been published since 2006. This demonstrates the ongoing popularity of the measurement tool, especially in European and English-speaking countries (Reichl et al. 2014).

based on core job characteristics—however, not always in the way that is specified by the model. In particular, some personal characteristics, such as educational level, were found to affect psychological states in a reverse manner to that which was expected—those with less education responded more favourably to elevated psychological states.

Another significant interest in replication stems from the original Aston studies (see Research in focus 3.5), which stimulated a plethora of replications over a period of more than 30 years following publication of the first generation of research in the early 1960s. Most clearly associated with replication were the 'fourth-generation' Aston researchers, who undertook studies that:

- used a more homogenous sample drawn from a single industry, such as electrical engineering companies, 'to further substantiate the predictive power of the Aston findings' (Grinyer and Yasai-Ardekani 1980: 405); or

- extended the original findings to other forms of organization, such as churches (e.g. Hinings et al. 1976) or educational colleges (Holdaway et al. 1975).

Later proponents of the 'Aston approach' made international comparisons of firms in different countries in order to test the hypothesis that the relationship between the context and the structure of an organization was dependent on the culture of the country in which it operates. Studies conducted in China, Egypt, France, Germany, India, and Japan (e.g. Shenoy 1981) sought to test the proposition that some of the characteristic differences in organizational structure originally identified by the Aston researchers remained constant across these diverse national contexts.

However, replication is not a common strategy in research in the social sciences (Lucas et al. 2013). Standard replications do not form the basis for attractive articles, so far as many academic journal editors are concerned. Consequently, replications of research appear in print far less frequently than might be supposed. A further reason for the low incidence of published replications is that it is difficult to ensure in business research that the conditions in a replication are precisely the same as those that pertained in an original study. So long as there is some ambiguity about the degree to which the conditions relating to a replication are the same as those in the initial study, any differences in findings may be attributable to the design of the replication rather than to some deficiency in the original study.

Nonetheless, it is often regarded as crucial that the methods taken in generating a set of findings are made explicit, so that it is *possible* to replicate a piece of research. Thus, it is replicability that is often regarded as an important quality of quantitative research.

The critique of quantitative research

Over the years, quantitative research, along with its epistemological and ontological foundations, has been the focus of a great deal of criticism, particularly from exponents of qualitative research. To a very large extent, it is difficult to distinguish between different kinds of criticism when reflecting on the different critical points that have been proffered. These include: criticisms of quantitative research in general as a research strategy; criticisms of the epistemological and ontological foundations of quantitative research; and criticisms of specific methods and research designs with which quantitative research is associated.

Criticisms of quantitative research

To give a flavour of the critique of quantitative research, four criticisms will be covered briefly:

- *Quantitative researchers fail to distinguish people and social institutions from 'the world of nature'.* The phrase 'the world of nature' is from the writings of Schutz (1962; the passage from which it has been taken is quoted in full in Chapter 2 of this book). Schutz and other phenomenologists charge social scientists who employ a natural science model with treating the social world as if it were no different from the natural order. In so doing, they draw attention to one of positivism's central tenets—namely, that the principles of the scientific method can and should be applied to all phenomena that are the focus of investigation. As Schutz argues, this tactic essentially means turning a blind eye to the differences between the social and natural world. More particularly, as was observed in Chapter 2, it therefore means ignoring and riding roughshod over the fact that people interpret the world around them, whereas this capacity for self-reflection cannot be found among the objects of the natural sciences ('molecules, atoms, and electrons', as Schutz put it).

- *The measurement process possesses an artificial and spurious sense of precision and accuracy.* There are a number of aspects to this criticism, but the overarching criticism is that in social science quantitative data are often qualitative data which have been 'forced' into numerical form. More specifically, it has been argued that the connection between the measures developed by social scientists and the concepts they are supposed to be revealing is assumed rather than real; hence, Cicourel's (1964) notion of 'measurement by fiat'. Testing for validity in the manner described in the previous section cannot really address this problem, because the very tests themselves entail measurement by decree. A further way in which the measurement process is regarded by writers like Cicourel as flawed is that it presumes that when, for example, members of a sample respond to a question on a questionnaire (which is itself taken to be an indicator of a concept), they interpret the key terms in the question similarly. For many writers, respondents simply do not interpret such terms similarly. An often-used reaction to this problem is to use questions with fixed-choice answers, but this approach merely provides 'a solution to the problem of meaning by simply ignoring it' (Cicourel 1964: 108).

- *The reliance on instruments and procedures hinders the connection between research and everyday life.* This issue relates to the question of ecological validity that was raised in Chapter 3. Many methods of quantitative research rely heavily on administering research instruments to subjects (such as structured interviews and self-completion questionnaires) or on controlling situations to determine their effects (such as in experiments). However, as Cicourel (1982) asks, how do we know if survey respondents have the requisite knowledge to answer a question or if they are similar in their sense of the topic being important to them in their everyday lives? Thus, if respondents answer a set of questions designed to measure motivation to work, can we be sure that they are equally aware of what it is and its manifestations, and can we be sure that it is of equal concern to them in the ways in which it connects with their everyday working life? One can go even further and ask how well their answers relate to their everyday lives. People may answer a question designed to measure their motivation to work, but respondents' actual behaviour may be at variance with their answers (LaPiere 1934).

- *The analysis of relationships between variables creates a static view of social life that is independent of people's lives.* Blumer argued that studies that aim to bring out the relationships between variables omit 'the process of interpretation or definition that goes on in human groups' (1956: 685). This means that we do not know how what appears to be a relationship between two or more variables has been produced by the people to whom it applies. This criticism incorporates the first and third criticisms here—that the meaning of events to individuals is ignored and that we do not know how such findings connect to everyday contexts—but adds a further element: namely, that it creates a sense of a static social world that is separate from the individuals who make up that world. In other words, quantitative research is seen as embodying an objectivist ontology that reifies the social world.

We can see in these criticisms the application of a set of concerns associated with a qualitative research strategy. These criticisms combine an interpretivist epistemological orientation (an emphasis on meaning from the individual's point of view) and a constructionist ontology (an emphasis on viewing the social world as the product of individuals rather than as something beyond them). The criticisms may appear very damning, but, as we will see in Chapter 17, quantitative researchers have a powerful battery of criticisms of qualitative research in their arsenal as well!

Is it always like this?

One of the problems with characterizing any research strategy, research design, or research method is that to a certain extent one is always outlining an ideal-typical approach. In other words, we tend to create something that represents that strategy, design, or method by highlighting significant aspects of it, but that may not be reflected in its entirety in research practice. This gap between the ideal type and actual practice can arise as a result of at least two major considerations. First, it happens because those of us who write about and teach research methods cannot cover every eventuality that can arise in the process of business research, so we tend to provide accounts of the research process that draw upon common features. Thus a model of the process of quantitative research, such as that provided in Figure 8.1, should be thought of as a general *tendency* rather than as a definitive description of all quantitative research. A second reason why the gap can emerge is that, to a very large extent, when writing about and teaching research methods we are essentially providing an account of *good practice*. The fact of the matter is that these practices are often not followed in the published research that students are likely to encounter in the substantive courses that they will be taking. This failure to follow the procedures associated with good practice is not necessarily due to incompetence on the part of business researchers (though in some cases it can be!), but is much more likely to be associated with matters of time, cost, and feasibility—in other words, the pragmatic concerns that cannot be avoided when one does business research.

Reverse operationism

As an example of the first source of the gap between the ideal type and actual research practice we can take the case of something that Bryman has referred to as 'reverse operationism' (1988*a*: 28). The model of the process of quantitative research in Figure 8.1 implies that concepts are specified and measures are then provided for them. As we have noted, this means that indicators must be devised. This is the basis of the idea of 'operationism' or 'operationalism', a term that derives from physics (Bridgman 1927) and that implies a deductive view of how research should proceed. However, this view of research neglects the fact that measurement can entail much more of an inductive element than Figure 8.1 implies. Sometimes, measures are developed that in turn lead

to conceptualization. One way in which this can occur is when a statistical technique known as *factor analysis* is employed (see Key concept 8.10). In order to measure the concept of 'charismatic leadership', a term that owes a great deal to Weber's (1947) notion of charismatic authority, Conger and Kanungo (1998) generated 25 items to provide a multiple-item measure of the concept. These items derived from their reading of existing theory and research on the subject, particularly in connection with charismatic leadership in organizations. When the items were administered to a sample of respondents and the results were factor analysed, it was found that the items bunched around six factors, each of which to all intents and purposes represents a dimension of the concept of charismatic leadership:

- strategic vision and articulation behaviour;
- sensitivity to the environment;
- unconventional behaviour;
- personal risk;
- sensitivity to organizational members' needs;
- action orientation away from the maintenance of the status quo.

The point to note is that these six dimensions were not specified at the outset: the link between conceptualization and measurement was an inductive one. This is not an unusual situation so far as research is concerned (Bryman 1988*a*: 26–8).

Reliability and validity testing

The second reason why the gap between the ideal type and actual research practice can arise is because researchers do not always follow recommended practices. A classic case of this tendency is that while much time and effort are expended on the articulation of the ways in which the reliability and validity of measures should be determined, these procedures are not always followed. Boyd et al. (2012) found that for articles published in *Strategic Management Journal* between 1998 and 2000, 49.8 per cent of all possible reliability estimates were reported for measures of independent variables and 41 per cent for dependent variables; in 2010, these percentages had increased considerably to 87.5 and 64.7 per cent respectively. This is not to say that research that fails to report reliability

8.10 KEY CONCEPT
What is factor analysis?

Factor analysis is employed in relation to multiple-indicator measures to determine whether groups of indicators tend to bunch together to form distinct clusters, referred to as factors. Its main goal is to reduce the number of variables with which the researcher needs to deal. It is used in relation to multiple-item measures, such as Likert scales, to see how far there is an inherent structure to the large number of items that often make up such measures. Researchers sometimes use factor analysis to establish whether the dimensions of a measure that they expect to exist can be confirmed. The clusters of items that are revealed by a factor analysis need to be given names (for example, 'innovation and flexibility' or 'autonomy' in the example in Research in focus 8.8). It is a complex technique that is beyond the level at which this book is pitched (see Bryman and Cramer 2008: Chapter 13), but it has considerable significance for the development of measures in many social scientific fields.

estimates is necessarily *un*stable and *in*valid, but that we simply do not know.

The reasons why the procedures for determining stability and validity are not as commonly used as might be supposed are almost certainly the cost and time that are likely to be involved. Researchers tend to be concerned with substantive issues and are less than enthusiastic about engaging in the kind of development work that would be required for a thoroughgoing determination of measurement quality. These remarks on the lack of assessment of the quality of measurement should not be taken as a justification for readers to neglect this phase in their work. Our aim is merely to draw attention to some of the ways in which practices described in this book are not always followed and to suggest some reasons why they are not followed.

Sampling

A similar point can be made in relation to sampling, covered in Chapter 9. As we will see, good practice is strongly associated with the use of random samples or probability samples. However, quite a lot of research is based on non-probability samples—that is, samples that have not been selected in terms of the principles of probability sampling to be discussed in Chapter 9. Sometimes the use of non-probability samples will be due to the impossibility or extreme difficulty of obtaining probability samples. Yet another reason is that the time and cost involved in securing a probability sample are too great relative to the level of resources available. And a third reason is that sometimes the opportunity to study a certain group presents itself and represents too good an opportunity to miss. Again, such considerations should not be viewed as a justification and hence a set of reasons for ignoring the principles of sampling examined in the next chapter, because not following the principles of probability sampling carries implications for the kind of statistical analysis that can be employed (see Chapter 15). Instead, our purpose, as before, is to draw attention to the ways in which gaps between recommendations about good practice and actual research practice can arise.

KEY POINTS

....

- Quantitative research can be characterized as a linear series of steps moving from theory to conclusions, but the process described in Figure 8.1 is an ideal type from which there may be many departures.

- The measurement process in quantitative research entails the search for indicators.

- Establishing the reliability and validity of measures is important for assessing their quality.

- Quantitative research can be characterized as exhibiting certain preoccupations, the most central of which are: measurement; causality; generalization; and replication.

- Quantitative research has been subjected to many criticisms by qualitative researchers. These criticisms tend to revolve around the view that a natural science model is inappropriate for studying the social world.

QUESTIONS FOR REVIEW

The main steps in quantitative research

- What are the main steps in quantitative research?

- To what extent do the main steps follow a strict sequence?

- Do the steps suggest a deductive or inductive approach to the relationship between theory and research?

Concepts and their measurement

- Why is measurement important for the quantitative researcher?

- What is the difference between a measure and an indicator?

- Why might multiple-indicator approaches to the measurement of concepts be preferable to those that rely on a single indicator?

Reliability and validity

- What are the main ways of thinking about the reliability of the measurement process? Is one form of reliability the most important?

- 'Whereas validity presupposes reliability, reliability does not presuppose validity.' Discuss.

- What are the main criteria for evaluating measurement validity?

The main preoccupations of quantitative researchers

- Outline the main preoccupations of quantitative researchers. What reasons can you give for their prominence?

- Why might replication be an important preoccupation among quantitative researchers, in spite of replications in business research being fairly rare?

The critique of quantitative research

- 'The crucial problem with quantitative research is the failure of its practitioners to address adequately the issue of meaning.' Discuss.

- In the critique by qualitative researchers of quantitative research, how central is the adoption by quantitative researchers of a natural science model of conducting research?

ONLINE RESOURCES
www.oup.com/uk/brm5e/

Visit the Interactive Research Guide that accompanies this book to complete an exercise focused on the nature of quantitative research.

SAMPLING IN QUANTITATIVE RESEARCH

CHAPTER OUTLINE

This chapter and the three that follow it are very much concerned with principles and practices associated with social survey research. Sampling principles are not exclusively a concern for survey research; for example, they are relevant to the selection of documents for content analysis (see Chapter 13). However, in this chapter the emphasis will be on sampling in connection with the selection of people who would be asked questions by interview or questionnaire. The chapter explores:

- the related ideas of generalization (also known as external validity) and of a representative sample (the latter allows the researcher to generalize findings from a sample to a population);

- the idea of a probability sample—that is, one in which a random selection process has been employed;

- the main types of probability sample: the simple random sample; the systematic sample; the stratified random sample; and the multi-stage cluster sample;

- the main issues involved in deciding on sample size;

- different types of non-probability sample, including quota sampling, which is widely used in market research and opinion polls;

- potential sources of error in survey research;

- some sampling issues in online surveys.

Introduction

This chapter is concerned with some important aspects of conducting a survey, but it presents only a partial picture, because there are many other steps. In this chapter we are concerned with the issues involved in selecting respondents for survey research, although the principles involved apply equally to other approaches to quantitative research, such as content analysis. Chapters 9, 10, and 11 deal with the data collection aspects of conducting a survey, while Chapters 15 and 16 deal with the analysis of data.

Figure 9.1 is intended to outline the main steps involved in planning and conducting survey research. The planning will begin with an examination of general research issues that are to be investigated. These are gradually narrowed down so that they become research questions, which may take the form of hypotheses, though this is not necessarily the case. The movement from research issues to research questions is likely to be the result of reading the literature relating to the issues.

Once the research questions have been formulated, the planning of the fieldwork can begin. In practice, decisions relating to sampling and to the research instrument will overlap, but they are presented in Figure 9.1 as part of a sequence. The survey researcher needs to decide what kind of population is suited to the investigation of the topic and also needs to formulate a research instrument and decide how it should be administered. The 'research instrument' may be a structured interview schedule (discussed in Chapter 10) or a self-completion questionnaire (Chapter 11). There are several different ways of administering such instruments. Figure 9.2 outlines the main types that are likely to be encountered.

Quantitative research almost invariably involves sampling. In this chapter, we will be mostly concerned with sampling for social survey research involving data collection by structured interview or questionnaire. In social survey research, sampling constitutes a key step in the research process, as illustrated in Figure 9.1. However, other methods of quantitative research also involve sampling considerations, as will be seen in Chapter 13, where we will examine structured observation and content analysis. The principles of sampling involved are more or less identical in connection with these other methods, though frequently other considerations come to the fore as well.

FIGURE 9.1
Steps in planning a social survey

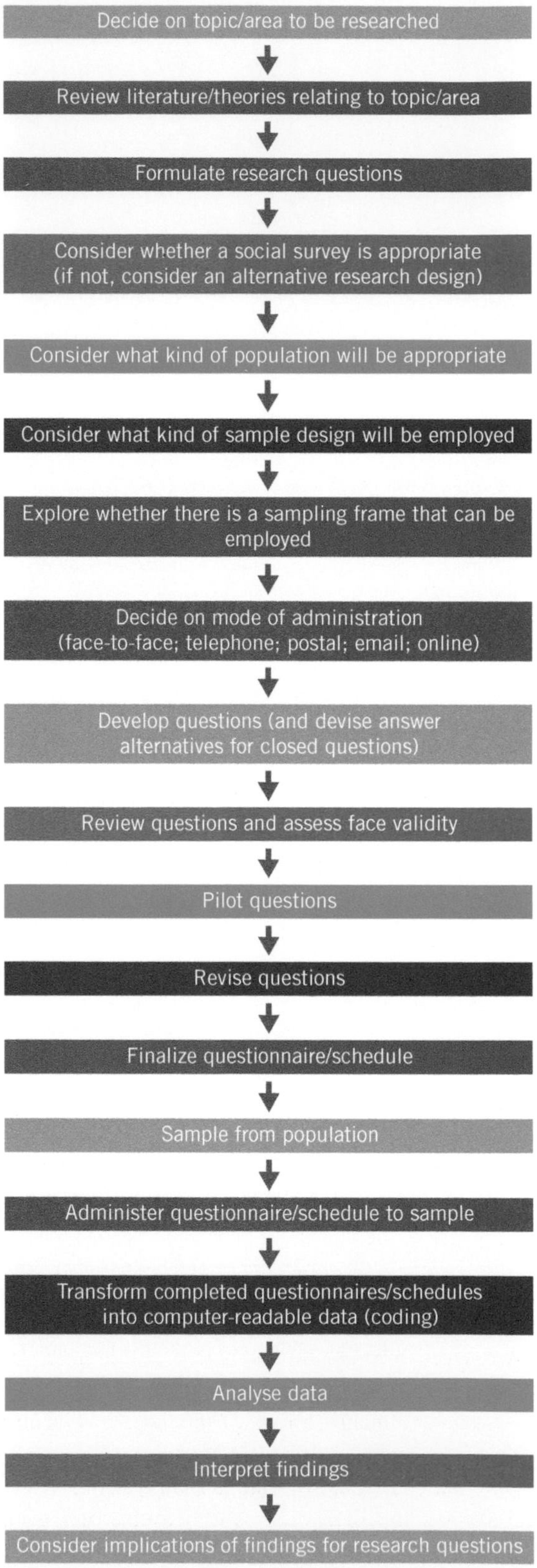

Decide on topic/area to be researched

↓

Review literature/theories relating to topic/area

↓

Formulate research questions

↓

Consider whether a social survey is appropriate (if not, consider an alternative research design)

↓

Consider what kind of population will be appropriate

↓

Consider what kind of sample design will be employed

↓

Explore whether there is a sampling frame that can be employed

↓

Decide on mode of administration (face-to-face; telephone; postal; email; online)

↓

Develop questions (and devise answer alternatives for closed questions)

↓

Review questions and assess face validity

↓

Pilot questions

↓

Revise questions

↓

Finalize questionnaire/schedule

↓

Sample from population

↓

Administer questionnaire/schedule to sample

↓

Transform completed questionnaires/schedules into computer-readable data (coding)

↓

Analyse data

↓

Interpret findings

↓

Consider implications of findings for research questions

FIGURE 9.2
Main modes of administration of a survey

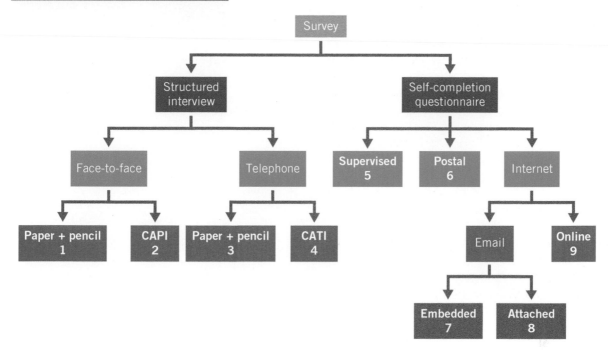

Introduction to sampling

Many of the readers of this book will be university or college students. At some point in your stay at your university (we will use this term from now on to include colleges) you may have wondered about the attitudes of your fellow students to various matters, or about their behaviour in certain contexts, or something about their backgrounds. If you were to decide to examine any or all of these three areas, you might consider conducting structured interviews or sending out questionnaires in order to find out about their behaviour, attitudes, and backgrounds. You would, of course, have to consider how best to design your interviews or questionnaires, and the issues that are involved in the decisions that need to be made about designing these research instruments and administering them will be the focus of Chapters 9–11. However, before getting to that point, you are likely to be confronted with a problem. Let us say that your university has around 10,000 students. It is extremely unlikely that you will have the time and resources to collect data from all these students. It is unlikely that you would be able to send questionnaires to all 10,000 and then process the results, and even more unlikely that you would be able to interview all of

them, since conducting survey research by interview is considerably more expensive and time-consuming, all things being equal, than by questionnaire (see Chapter 10). It is almost certain that you will need to *sample* students from the total population of students in your university to collect data from a manageable number of respondents.

But will any old sample suffice? Would it be sufficient to locate yourself in a central position on your campus (if your university has one) and then interview the students who come past you and whom you are in a position to interview? Alternatively, would it be sufficient to go around your student union asking people to be interviewed? Or to send questionnaires to everyone on your course?

The answer depends on whether or not you want to be able to *generalize* your findings to the entire student body in your university. If you do—and as discussed in Chapter 7, one of the preoccupations of quantitative researchers is generalization—it is unlikely that any of the three sampling strategies proposed in the previous paragraph would provide you with a *representative sample* of all students in your university. To be able to generalize your

9.1 KEY CONCEPT
Basic terms and concepts in sampling

- **Population**: basically, the universe of units from which the sample is to be selected. The term 'units' is employed because it is not necessarily people who are being sampled—the researcher may want to sample from a universe of nations, cities, regions, firms, etc. Thus, 'population' has a much broader meaning in sampling than it does in the everyday use of the term (meaning the total number of people in a nation or town).

- **Sample**: the segment of the population that is selected for investigation. It is a subset of the population. The method of selection may be based on a probability or a non-probability approach (see below).

- **Sampling frame**: the listing of all units in the population from which the sample will be selected.

- **Representative sample**: a sample that reflects the population accurately so that it is a microcosm of the population.

- **Sampling bias**: a distortion in the representativeness of the sample that arises when members of the population (or more precisely the sampling frame) vary in terms of how likely they are to be included in the sample, such that some groups are over-represented and others under-represented by comparison to their proportions in the population.

- **Probability sample**: a sample that has been selected using random selection so that each unit in the population has a known chance of being selected. It is generally assumed that a *representative sample* is more likely to be the outcome when this method of selection from the population is employed. The aim of probability sampling is to keep sampling error (see below) to a minimum.

- **Non-probability sample**: a sample that has not been selected using a random selection method. Essentially, this implies that some units in the population are more likely to be selected than others.

- **Sampling error**: the difference between a sample and the population from which it is selected, even though a probability sample has been selected.

- **Non-sampling error**: differences between the population and the sample that arise either from deficiencies in the sampling approach, such as an inadequate sampling frame or non-response (see below), or from such problems as poor question wording, poor interviewing, or flawed processing of data.

- **Non-response**: a source of non-sampling error that is particularly likely to happen when individuals are being sampled. It occurs whenever some members of the sample refuse to cooperate, cannot be contacted, or for some reason cannot supply the required data (for example, because they are no longer working in the organziation).

- **Census**: the collection of data from an entire population. Thus, if data are collected in relation to all units in a population, rather than in relation to a sample of units of that population, the data are treated as census data. The phrase '*the* census' typically refers to collection of data from all members of the population of a nation state—that is, a national census. Many countries around the world undertake a census every few years as a way of generating a snapshot of a range of social and economic features of their populations. However, in a statistical context, like the term *population*, the idea of a census has a broader meaning than this.

findings from your sample to the population from which it was selected, the sample must be representative. This is a fundamentally important point, because the aim of analyzing data from a sample is to make inferences about the larger population from which the sample was drawn, without having to try to collect data from the whole population. See Key concept 9.1 for an explanation of terms concerning sampling.

Why might the strategies for sampling students previously outlined be unlikely to produce a representative

sample? There are various reasons, of which the following stand out.

- The first two approaches depend heavily upon the availability of students during the time or times that you search them out. Not all students are likely to be equally available at that time, so the sample will not reflect those students who are not available.

- The first two approaches also depend on the students going to the locations. Not all students will necessarily pass the point where you locate yourself or go to the student union, or they may vary significantly in the frequency with which they do so. Their movements are likely to reflect such things as where their halls of residence or accommodation are situated, or where their departments are located, or their social habits. Again, to rely on these locations would mean missing out on students who do not frequent them.

- It is possible, not to say likely, that your decisions about which people to approach will be influenced by your judgements about how friendly or cooperative the people concerned are likely to be or by how comfortable you feel about interviewing students of the same (or opposite) gender to yourself, as well as by many other factors.

- The problem with the third strategy is that students on your course by definition take the same subject as each other and therefore will not be representative of all students in the university.

In other words, in the case of all three sampling approaches, your decisions about whom to sample are influenced too much by personal judgements, by prospective respondents' availability, or by your implicit criteria for inclusion. Such limitations mean that, in the language of survey sampling, your sample will be *biased*. A biased sample is one that does not represent the population from which the sample was selected. As far as possible, bias should be removed from the selection of your sample. In fact, it is incredibly difficult to remove bias altogether and to derive a truly representative sample. What needs to be done is to ensure that steps are taken to keep bias to an absolute minimum.

Three sources of bias can be identified (see Key concept 9.1 for an explanation of terms):

- *If a non-probability or non-random sampling method is used.* If the method used to select the sample is not random, there is a possibility that human judgement will affect the selection process, making some members of the population more likely to be selected than others. This source of bias can be eliminated through the use of probability or random sampling, the procedure for which is described later in this chapter.

- *If the sampling frame is inadequate.* If the sampling frame is not comprehensive or is inaccurate, or suffers from some other kind of similar deficiency, the sample that is derived cannot represent the population, even if a random or probability sampling method is employed.

- *If some sample members refuse to participate or cannot be contacted—in other words, if there is non-response.* The problem with non-response is that those who agree to participate may differ in various ways from those who do not agree to participate. Some of the differences may be significant to the research question or questions. If the data are available, it may be possible to check how far, when there is non-response, the resulting sample differs from the population. It is often possible to do this in terms of characteristics such as gender or age, or, in the case of something like a sample of university students, whether the sample's characteristics reflect the entire population in terms of the students' areas of study. However, after non-response it is usually extremely difficult to determine whether differences exist between the population and the sample in terms of 'deeper' factors, such as attitudes or patterns of behaviour.

Sampling error

In order to appreciate the significance of sampling error for achieving a representative sample, consider Figures 9.3–9.7. Imagine we have a population of 200 employees and we want a sample of 50. Imagine as well that one of the variables of concern to us is whether or not employees receive regular performance appraisals from their immediate supervisor, and that the population is equally divided between those who do and those who do not. This split is represented by the vertical line that divides the population into two halves (see Figure 9.3). If the sample is representative,

we would expect our sample of 50 to be equally split in terms of this variable, as in Figure 9.4. If there is a small amount of sampling error, so that we have one employee too many who is not appraised and one too few who is, it will look like Figure 9.5. In Figure 9.6 we see a rather more serious degree of over-representation of employees who do not receive appraisals. This time there are three too many who are not appraised and three too few who are. In Figure 9.7 we have a very serious over-representation of employees who do not receive performance appraisals, because there are

FIGURE 9.3
Having performance appraisals in a population of 200

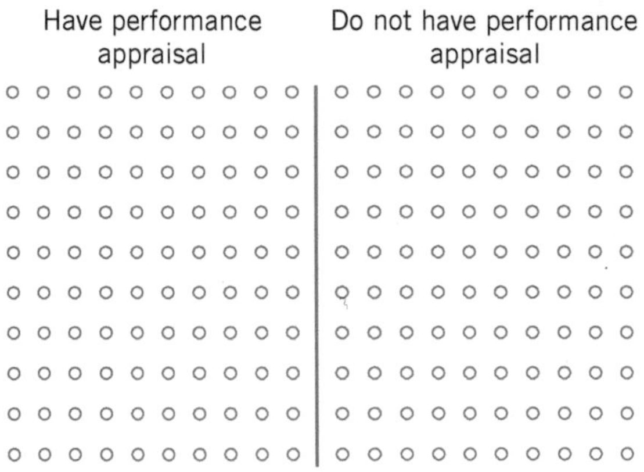

| Have performance appraisal | Do not have performance appraisal |

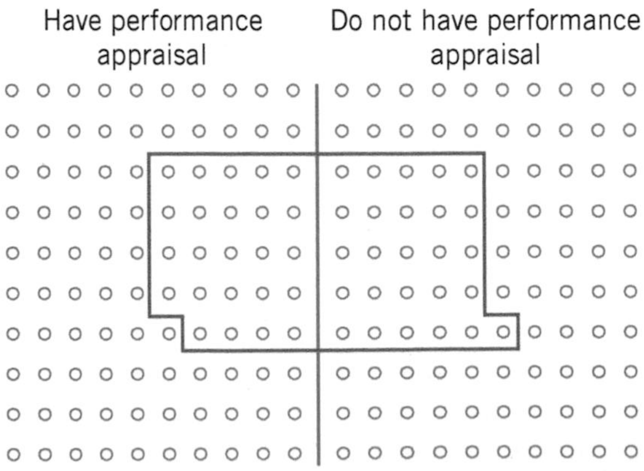

FIGURE 9.6
A sample with some sampling error

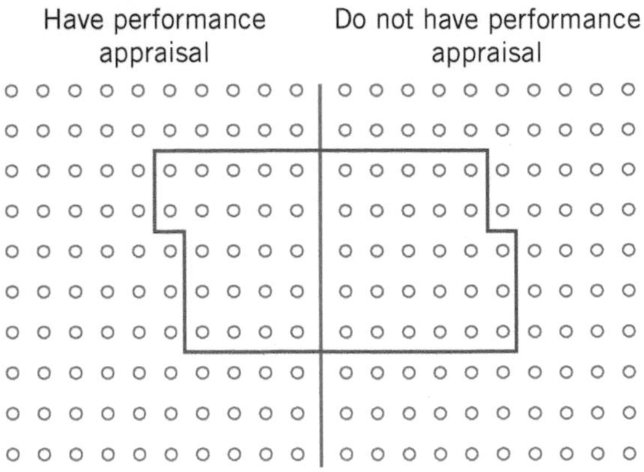

| Have performance appraisal | Do not have performance appraisal |

FIGURE 9.4
A sample with no sampling error

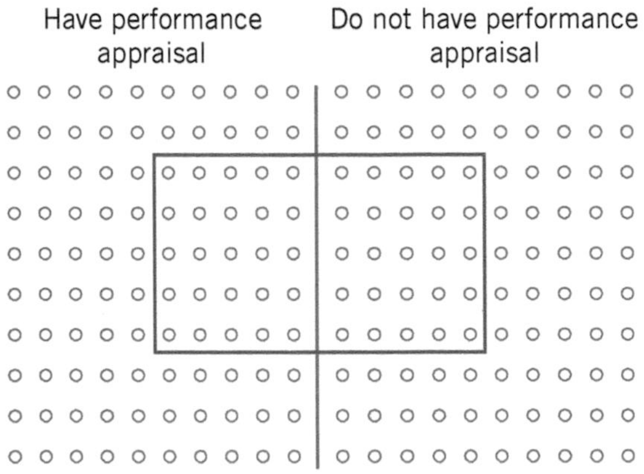

| Have performance appraisal | Do not have performance appraisal |

FIGURE 9.7
A sample with a lot of sampling error

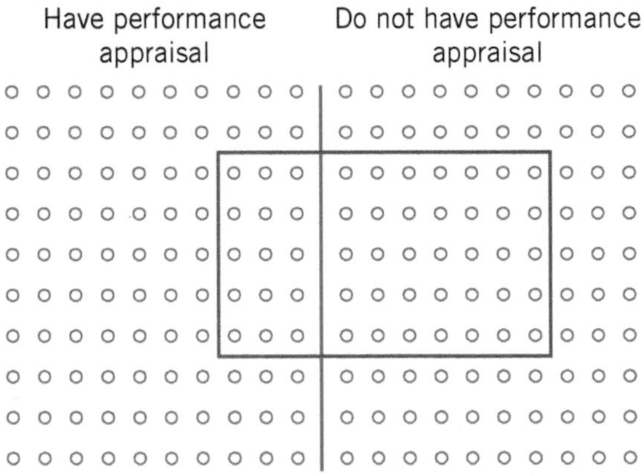

| Have performance appraisal | Do not have performance appraisal |

FIGURE 9.5
A sample with very little sampling error

| Have performance appraisal | Do not have performance appraisal |

35 employees in the sample who are not appraised, which is much larger than the 25 who should be in the sample.

It is important to appreciate that, as suggested above, probability sampling does not and cannot eliminate sampling error. Even with a well-crafted probability sample, a degree of sampling error is likely to creep in. However, probability sampling stands a better chance than non-probability sampling of keeping sampling error in check so that it does not end up looking like the outcome featured in Figure 9.7. Moreover, probability sampling allows the researcher to employ tests of statistical significance that permit inferences to be made about the population from which the sample was selected. These will be addressed in Chapter 15.

Types of probability sample

Imagine that we are interested in levels of training, skill development, and learning among employees, and that we want to examine the variables that relate to variation in levels of training they have undertaken. We might decide to conduct our research in a single nearby company. This means that our population will all be employees in that company, which in turn will mean that we will be able to generalize our findings only to employees of that company. We simply cannot assume that levels of training and their correlates will be the same in other companies. We might decide that we want our research to be conducted only on full-time employees, so that part-time and subcontracted workers are omitted. Imagine too that there are 9000 full-time employees in the company.

Simple random sample

The simple random sample is the most basic form of probability sample. With random sampling, each unit of the population has an equal probability of inclusion in the sample. Imagine that we decide that we have enough money to interview 450 employees at the company. This means that the probability of inclusion in the sample is

$$\frac{450}{9000} \text{ i.e. 1 in 20}$$

This is known as the *sampling fraction* and is expressed as

$$\frac{n}{N}$$

where n is the sample size and N is the population size.

The key steps in devising our simple random sample can be represented as follows:

1. Define the population. We have decided that this will be all full-time employees at the company. This is our N and in this case is 9000.

2. Select or devise a comprehensive sampling frame. It is likely that the company's HR department will keep records of all employees. This will enable us to exclude those who do not meet our criteria for inclusion—i.e. part-time employees and those who work on the premises but are not employees of the company.

3. Decide your sample size (n). We have decided that this will be 450.

4. List all the employees in the population and assign them consecutive numbers from 1 to N. In our case, this will be 1 to 9000.

5. Using a table of random numbers, or a computer program that can generate random numbers, select n (450) different random numbers that lie between 1 and N (9000). Select the 450 employees whose number corresponds to each of the random numbers.

6. The employees to which the n (450) random numbers refer constitute the sample.

Two points are striking about this process. First, there is almost no opportunity for human bias to manifest itself. Employees would not be selected on such subjective criteria as whether they looked friendly and approachable. The selection of whom to interview is entirely mechanical. Secondly, the process is not dependent on the employees' availability. They do not have to be working in the interviewer's proximity to be included in the sample. The process of selection is done without their knowledge. It is not until they are contacted by an interviewer that they know that they are part of a social survey.

It used to be common for researchers to use a table of random numbers to select a sample, and some textbooks still include such tables as an appendix. The easiest way to generate a table, however, is to use one of the many random number generators which can be found online. Alternatively, it is possible to generate a list of random numbers using Microsoft Excel, SPSS, or other statistical packages.

Systematic sample

A variation on the simple random sample is the systematic sample. With this kind of sample, you select units directly from the sampling frame—that is, without resorting to random numbers.

We know that we are to select 1 employee in 20. With a systematic sample, we would make a random start between 1 and 20 inclusive, possibly by using a table of random numbers. Let's assume that we start with the number 16. Thereafter, we would take every twentieth employee on the list. So the sequence will go:

16, 36, 56, 76, 96, 116, etc.

This approach obviates the need to assign numbers to employees' names and then to look up names of the employees whose numbers have been drawn by the random selection process. It is important to ensure, however, that there is no inherent ordering of the sampling frame, since this may bias the resulting sample. If there is some ordering to the list, the best solution is to rearrange it.

Stratified random sampling

In our imaginary study of company employees, one of the features that we might want our sample to exhibit is a proportional representation of the different departments in which employees work. It might be that the kind of department an employee works in is viewed as relevant to a wide range of attitudinal features that are in turn relevant to the study of skill development and training. Generating a simple random sample or a systematic sample *might* yield such a representation, so that the proportion of employees from the sales and marketing department in the sample would be the same as that in the employee population and so on. Thus, if there are 1800 employees in the sales and marketing department, using our sampling fraction of 1 in 20, we would expect to have 90 employees in our sample from this department of the company. However, because of sampling error, it is unlikely that this will occur and more likely that there will be a difference, so that there may be, say, 85 or 93 from this department.

Because it is very likely that the company will include in its records the department in which employees are based, or indeed may have separate lists of employees for each department, it will be possible to ensure that employees are accurately represented in terms of their departmental membership. In the language of sampling, this means stratifying the population by a criterion (in this case, departmental membership) and selecting either a simple random sample or a systematic sample from each of the resulting strata. In the present example, if there are five departments we would have five strata, with the numbers in each stratum being one-twentieth of the total for each department.

The advantage of stratified sampling in a case like this is clear: it ensures that the resulting sample will be distributed in the same way as the population in terms of the stratifying criterion. If you use a simple random or systematic sampling approach, you *may* end up with a distribution like that of the stratified sample, but it is unlikely. Two points are relevant here. First, you can conduct stratified sampling sensibly only when it is relatively easy to identify and allocate units to strata. If it is not possible or it would be very difficult to do so, stratified sampling will not be feasible. Secondly, you can use more than one stratifying criterion. Thus, it may be that you would want to stratify by department, by gender, and by whether or not employees are above or below a certain salary level or occupational grade. If it is feasible to identify employees in terms of these stratifying criteria, it is possible to use pairs of criteria or several criteria (such as departmental membership plus gender plus occupational grade).

Stratified sampling is really feasible only when the relevant information is available. In other words, when data are available that allow the ready identification of members of the population in terms of the stratifying criterion (or criteria), it is sensible to employ this sampling method. But it is unlikely to be practical or economical if the identification of population members for stratification purposes entails a great deal of work because there is no available listing in terms of strata.

Multi-stage cluster sampling

In the example we have been dealing with, employees to be interviewed are located in a single company. Interviewers will have to arrange their interviews with the sampled employees, but, because they are all working on the same premises (for the purposes of this hypothetical example we are assuming that the company has only one location), they will not be involved in a lot of travel. However, imagine that we wanted a *national* sample of employees. It is likely that interviewers would have to travel the length and breadth of the country to interview the sampled individuals. This would add a great deal to the time and cost of doing the research. This kind of problem occurs whenever the aim is to interview a sample that is to be drawn from a widely dispersed population, such as a national population, or a large region, or even a large city.

One way in which it is possible to deal with this potential problem is to employ *cluster sampling*. With cluster sampling, the primary sampling unit (the first stage of the sampling procedure) is not the units of the population to be sampled but groupings of those units. It is the latter groupings or aggregations of population units that are known as *clusters*. Imagine that we want a nationally representative sample of 5000 employees who are working for the 100 largest companies in the UK (this information is publicly available and generated through the FTSE—Financial Times Stock Exchange—index; company size is measured in terms of market capitalization). Using simple random or systematic sampling would yield a widely dispersed sample, which would result in a great deal of travel for interviewers. One solution might be

9.2 RESEARCH IN FOCUS
A cluster sample survey of Australian workplaces and employees

The 2015 Study of Australian Leadership (SAL) (see Research in focus 3.13) utilized a cluster-sampling approach. The aim of the study was to collect data from workplaces and their employees. Because no population frame of Australian workplaces exists, a sample of organizations was drawn from a commercial list of businesses. The sample of organizations was stratified by industry and size. Workplaces were then selected from within organizations, except in the case of single-site organizations, where the organization and the workplace were one and the same. In multi-site organizations, different numbers of workplaces were selected, depending on the total number of sites: one workplace was selected if the organization had 5 or fewer workplaces; two were selected if the organization had 6 to 20 workplaces; and three were selected if the organization had 21 or more workplaces. Employees were then sampled from within the sample of workplaces. In workplaces with fewer than 200 employees, all employees were surveyed. In larger workplaces a random sample of employees was surveyed. This design produced a representative sample of Australian workplaces and employees within them, which allowed workplace and employee data to be linked for the purposes of analysis.

to sample companies and then employees from each of the sampled companies. A probability sampling method would need to be employed at each stage. Thus, we might randomly sample ten companies from the entire population of the 100 largest companies in the UK, thus yielding ten clusters, and we would then interview 500 randomly selected employees at each of the ten companies. Research in focus 9.2 gives an example of a study that used cluster sampling.

A potential problem, however, is that there is no guarantee that these ten companies reflect the diverse range of industrial activities that are engaged in by the population as a whole. One solution to this problem would be to group the 100 largest UK companies by industry. This could be done using the codes from the Standard Industrial Classification system or SIC, which is used widely to classify companies for the purposes of collecting data. The next step would be to randomly sample companies from each of the major groups. One company might then

be sampled from each of the industries, and then approximately 400 employees from each of the companies would be interviewed. Thus, there are three separate stages:

- group 100 largest UK companies by market capitalization;
- sample one company from each of the major industries;
- sample 400 employees from each of the companies.

In a sense, cluster sampling is always a multi-stage approach, because clusters are always sampled first and then something else—either further clusters or population units—is sampled.

Many examples of multi-stage cluster sampling entail stratification. We might, for example, want further to stratify the companies according to whether their headquarters are located in the UK or abroad. To do this we would group companies according to whether their headquarters were based in the UK or elsewhere and then select one or two companies per industry from each of the two strata.

The qualities of a probability sample

The reason why probability sampling is such an important procedure in social survey research is that based on information about a random sample, it is possible to make inferences about the entire population from which it was selected. In other words, we can generalize findings derived from a sample to the population. This is not

to say that we treat the population data and the sample data as the same. Let us say we wish to examine the level of skill development in our sample of 450 employees. We will treat skill development as the number of training days completed in the previous 12 months. We can use the mean number of training days undertaken by the sample (X) to estimate the population mean (m). The mean, or more properly the **arithmetic mean**, is the simple average. This generalization from the sample mean to the population mean will have known margins of error. For more detail on this, see Tips and skills 'Generalizing from a random sample to the population'.

TIPS AND SKILLS
Generalizing from a random sample to the population

Using our imaginary study of training and skill development in a single nearby company, let us say that the sample mean is 6.7 days of training per employee (the average amount of training received in the previous 12 months in the sample). A crucial consideration here is: even if we used probability sampling, how confident can we be that the mean number of 6.7 training days is likely to be found in the population? If we take an infinite number of samples from a population, the sample estimates of the mean of the variable under consideration will vary in relation to the population mean. This variation will take the form of a bell-shaped curve known as a *normal distribution* (see Figure 9.8). The shape of the distribution implies that there is a clustering of sample means at or around the population mean. Half the sample means will be at or below the population mean; the other half will be at or above the population mean. As we move to the left (at or below the population mean) or the right (at or above the population mean), the curve tails off, implying that there would be fewer and fewer samples generating means that depart considerably from the population mean. The variation of sample means around the population mean is the *sampling error* and is measured using a statistic known as the **standard error of the mean**. This is an estimate of the amount that a sample mean is likely to differ from the population mean.

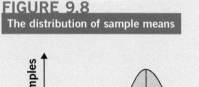

FIGURE 9.8
The distribution of sample means

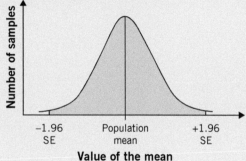

Note: 95 per cent of sample means will lie within the shaded area. SE = standard error of the mean.

This consideration is important, because sampling theory tells us that 68 per cent of all sample means will lie between plus or minus 1.00 standard error from the population mean and that 95 per cent of all sample means will lie between plus or minus 1.96 standard errors from the population mean. It is this second calculation that is crucial, because it is at least implicitly employed by survey researchers when they report their statistical findings. They typically employ 1.96 standard errors as the crucial criterion in how confident they can be in their findings. Essentially, the criterion implies that you can be 95 per cent certain that the population mean lies within plus or minus 1.96 sampling errors from the sample mean.

If a sample has been selected according to probability sampling principles, we know that we can be 95 per cent certain that the population mean will lie between the sample mean plus or minus 1.96 multiplied by the standard error of the mean. This is known as the *confidence interval*. If the mean number of training days in the previous twelve months in our sample of 450 employees is 6.7 and the standard error of the mean is 1.3, we can be 95 per cent certain that the population mean will lie between

$$6.7 + (1.96 \times 1.3)$$

and

$$6.7 - (1.96 \times 1.3)$$

i.e. between 9.248 and 4.152.

If the standard error was smaller, the range of possible values of the population mean would be narrower; if the standard error was larger, the range of possible values of the population mean would be wider.

If a stratified sample is selected, the standard error of the mean will be smaller; this is because the variation between strata is essentially eliminated, because the population will be accurately represented in the sample in terms of the stratification criterion or criteria employed. This consideration demonstrates the way in which stratification injects an extra increment of precision into the probability sampling process, since a possible source of sampling error is eliminated.

By contrast, a cluster sample without stratification exhibits a larger standard error of the mean than a comparable simple random sample. This occurs because a possible source of variability between employees (that is, membership of one department rather than another, which may affect levels of training undertaken) is disregarded. If, for example, some departments have a culture of learning in which a large number of employees were involved, and if these departments were not selected because of the procedure for selecting clusters, an important source of variability would have been omitted. It also implies that the sample mean would be on the low side, but that is another matter.

Sample size

One question about research methods that we are asked by students almost more than any other relates to the size of the sample: 'How large should my sample be?' or 'Is my sample large enough?' The decision about sample size is not a straightforward one: it depends on a number of considerations, and there is no one definitive answer. This is frequently a source of great disappointment to those who pose such questions. Moreover, most of the time decisions about sample size are affected by considerations of time and cost (see Tips and skills 'Sample size and probability sampling'). Therefore, invariably decisions about sample size represent a compromise between the constraints of time and cost, the need for precision, and a variety of further considerations that will now be addressed.

Absolute and relative sample size

One of the most basic considerations, and one that is possibly the most surprising, is that, contrary to what you might have expected, it is the *absolute* size of a sample that is important, not its *relative* size. This means that a

national probability sample of 1000 individuals in the UK is as likely to be representative as a national probability sample of 1000 individuals in the USA, even though the latter has a much larger population. It also means that increasing the size of a sample increases the precision of a sample. This means that the 95 per cent confidence interval referred to in Tips and skills 'Generalizing from a random sample to the population' narrows. However, a large sample cannot *guarantee* precision, so that it is probably better to say that increasing the size of a sample increases the *likely* precision of a sample. This means that as sample size increases, sampling error decreases. Therefore, an important component of any decision about sample size could be how much sampling error one is prepared to tolerate. The less sampling error one is prepared to tolerate, the larger a sample will need to be. Fowler (1993) however warns against a simple acceptance of this criterion. He argues that in practice researchers do not base their decisions about sample size on a single estimate of a variable. Most survey research is intended to generate a host of estimates—that is, of the variables that

Sample size and probability sampling

As we have said, the issue of sample size is the matter that most often concerns students and researchers. Basically, the bigger the sample, the more representative it is likely to be (provided the sample is randomly selected), regardless of the size of the population from which it is drawn. However, when doing research projects, students typically need to do their research with very limited resources. You should try to find out from your department or school if there are any guidelines about whether or not samples of a minimum size are expected. If there are no such guidelines, you will need to conduct your mini-survey in such a way as to maximize the number of interviews you can manage or the number of questionnaires you can send out and process, given the amount of time and resources available to you. Also, in many if not most cases, a truly random approach to sample selection may not be open to you. The crucial point is to be clear about and to justify what you have done, as well as to demonstrate the limitations of your sample. Explain the difficulties that you would have encountered in generating a random sample. Explain why you could not include any more in your sample of respondents. But, above all, do not make claims about your sample that are not sustainable. Do not claim that it is representative or that you have a random sample when it is clearly not the case that either of these is true. In other words, be frank about what you have done. People will be much more inclined to accept an awareness of the limits of your sample design than claims about a sample that are patently false. Also, it may be that there are lots of good features about your sample—the range of people included, the good response rate, the high level of cooperation you received from the firm. Make sure you play up these positive features at the same time as being honest about your sample's limitations.

make up the research instrument that is administered. He also observes that it is not normal for survey researchers to be in a position to specify in advance 'a desired level of precision' (1993: 34). Moreover, since sampling error will be only one component of any error entailed in an estimate, the notion of using a desired level of precision as a factor in a decision about sample size is not realistic. Instead, to the extent that this notion does enter into decisions about sample size, it often does so in a general rather than a calculated way.

Time and cost

Time and cost considerations become very relevant in this context. In the previous paragraph it is clearly being suggested that the larger the sample size, the greater the precision (because the amount of sampling error will be less). By and large, up to a sample size of around 1000, the gains in precision are noticeable as the sample size climbs from low figures of 50, 100, 150, and so on upwards. After a certain point, however, often in the region of 1000, the sharp increases in precision become less pronounced, and, although it does not plateau, there is a slow down in the extent to which precision increases (and hence the extent to which the sample error of the mean declines). Considerations of sampling size are likely to be profoundly affected by matters of time and

cost at such a juncture, since striving for smaller and smaller increments of precision becomes an increasingly uneconomic proposition.

Non-response

Considerations about sampling error do not end here. The problem of *non-response* should also be borne in mind. Most sample surveys include a certain amount of non-response. Thus, it is likely that only some of our sample will agree to participate in the research. If it is our aim to ensure as far as possible that 450 employees are interviewed and if we think that there may be a 20 per cent rate of non-response, it may be advisable to sample 540–550 individuals, on the grounds that approximately 90 will be non-respondents. For example, of the 143 survey questionnaires sent to companies in T. C. Powell's (1995) study of total quality management, only 40 were returned and of these only 36 were usable, making a response rate of 25 per cent. This raises the question of whether or not this sample is big enough to represent companies in the geographical area of the north-eastern USA that the study claims to represent (see Chapter 11 for a further discussion of acceptable response rates). The issue of non-response, and in particular of refusal to participate, is of particular significance, because it has been suggested by some researchers that response rates (see Key concept 9.3) to surveys are declining in many countries. This implies that there is a growing tendency towards people refusing to participate in survey research. As long ago as 1973, an article in the American magazine *Business Week* carried an article ominously entitled 'The Public Clams up on Survey Takers'. The magazine asked survey companies about their experiences and found considerable concern about declining response rates (*Business Week* 1973). Similarly, in Britain, a report from a working party on the Market Research Society's Research and Development Committee in 1975 pointed to concerns among market research companies. However, analyses of this issue by by Baruch and Holtom (2008) and Anseel et al. (2010) suggested that there is little evidence of a generalized decline in response rates in surveys in organizational research. Strategies that can improve responses to survey instruments such as structured interviews and questionnaires will be examined in Chapters 10 and 11.

Heterogeneity of the population

Yet another consideration is the homogeneity and heterogeneity of the population from which the sample is to be taken. When a sample is very heterogeneous, such as a sample of a whole country or city, the population which it represents is likely to be highly varied. When it is relatively homogeneous, such as members of a company or of an occupation, the amount of variation is less. The implication of this is that, the greater the heterogeneity of a population, the larger a sample will need to be.

Types of non-probability sampling

The term *non-probability sampling* is essentially an umbrella term to capture all forms of sampling that are not conducted according to the norms of probability sampling outlined above. It is not surprising, therefore, that the term covers a wide range of types of sampling strategy, at least one of which—the quota sample—is claimed by some practitioners to be almost as good as a probability sample. In this section we will cover two main types of non-probability sample: the convenience sample and the quota sample.

Convenience sampling

A convenience sample is one that is simply available to the researcher by virtue of its accessibility. Imagine that a researcher who teaches at a university business school is interested in the way that managers deal with ethical issues when making business decisions. The researcher might administer a questionnaire to several classes of students, all of whom are managers taking a part-time MBA degree. The chances are that the researcher will receive all or almost all the questionnaires back, so that there will be a good response rate. The findings may prove quite interesting, but the problem with such a sampling strategy is that it is impossible to generalize the findings, because we do not know of what population this sample is representative. They are simply a group of managers who are available to the researcher. They are almost certainly not representative of managers as a whole—the very fact they are taking this degree programme marks them out as different from managers in general.

This is not to suggest that convenience samples should never be used. Let us say that our lecturer/researcher is developing a battery of questions that are designed to measure the ethical decision-making processes used by managers. It is highly desirable to pilot such a research instrument before using it in an investigation, and administering it to a group who are not a part of the main study may be a legitimate way of carrying out some preliminary analysis of such issues as whether or not respondents tend to answer a particular question in identical ways, or whether or not one question is often omitted when managers respond to it. In other words, for this kind of purpose, a convenience sample may be acceptable, though not ideal. A second kind of context in which it may be at least fairly acceptable to use a convenience sample is when the chance presents itself to gather data from a convenience sample and it represents too good an opportunity to miss. The data will not allow definitive findings to be generated, because of the problem of generalization, but they could provide a springboard for further research or allow links to be forged with existing findings in an area.

It also perhaps ought to be recognized that convenience sampling probably plays a more prominent role than is sometimes supposed. In the field of business and management, convenience samples are certainly very common and in some areas, such as consumer behaviour research, they have become the norm. Nonetheless, there is evidence that we should be cautious in generalizing from convenience samples, particularly when they are samples of undergraduate students (Peterson and Merunka 2014).

It is common in some kinds of business research to use university undergraduate students as a convenience sample, particularly in experimental research. This has been criticized by Hooghe et al. (2010), who argue that it can endanger the validity and generalizability of findings because undergraduate students are likely to think and act differently from the general population. For instance, people from lower socio-economic groups are under-represented in undergraduate student populations; students are likely to have more socio-economic resources than is typical of the general population; and students may be inclined to exert more-than-typical cognitive effort in order to give the 'right' answer. Moreover, it is highly problematic to make claims about managerial or workplace phenomena based on such samples, as many undergraduates have little or no full-time workplace or managerial experience. This has led some management journals to refuse to publish papers based on student samples, unless the sample is merely a convenient way to sample managers, as in the case of part-time MBAs discussed above. The study described in Research in focus 9.4 used a convenience sample taken from the 'real world' rather than from among students.

Quota sampling

Quota sampling is used intensively in commercial research, such as market research and political opinion

STUDENT EXPERIENCE
Using convenience sampling in a dissertation

Jordan conducted research on self-expression in the workplace. Her approach required a fairly large sample of employees. The one-year duration of her honours program, and the need to fit her research around a demanding coursework load, meant that she had to find an efficient way to generate a sample which would allow her to conduct her analysis. She chose to survey graduate employees in a private-sector organization, who were undergoing a training program run by an NGO she had previously worked for. All 515 graduate employees who underwent the training program were given a paper survey to complete during their training program. She explained: '[the NGO] provides training to this particular organisation and to all of the graduate employees … 515 of them. They … provide this training in two places in Melbourne and Sydney … the reason why I got 515 surveys was because time was set aside during the workshop.' Jordan's use of convenience sampling provided her with an effective means to collect data which allowed her to conduct her analysis in a situation in which she did not have the time or resources to generate a random sample of employees.

9.4 RESEARCH IN FOCUS
Convenience sampling in a study of discrimination in hiring

Derous et al. (2017) conducted a study as a means of studying how ethnic cues influenced the outcomes of curriculum vitae (CV) screening during recruitment processes. Most studies of CV screening have used samples of university students (Derous et al. 2017: 862), but this study utilized a sample of human resource (HR) professionals as a means to increase the likelihood that the conclusions drawn were representative of processes and outcomes involving respondents who undertake recruitment in their daily working lives.

The study was conducted in Belgium. The authors needed a large sample for their study, but there was no sampling frame available from which to draw a random sample of respondents, so the sample was drawn from membership lists of HR professional associations, business publications, and the researchers' own networks. This generated a sample of 1463 respondents, of whom 424 agreed to participate. Participants were all Caucasian. Clearly this strategy did not generate a random sample and the sample cannot be regarded as representative in a statistical sense. Nonetheless, the sampling strategy represented a viable way to draw a large sample of actual HR professionals which could not otherwise have been generated.

The researchers provided each respondent with job advertisements for two different jobs in two different kinds of businesses. They were each also provided with four fictional CVs, each including a photo of a fictional applicant. The CVs showed a variety of combinations of skin tone (light versus dark) and name (Flemish versus Arab/Maghreb). Respondents were asked to rate each applicant using a three-item measure with **Likert scale** responses. For example, 'Given all the information you read about this applicant, how likely is it that you would invite this applicant for a job interview?' (1 = not likely at all; 7 = very likely). The findings showed the equally-qualified candidates with a dark skin tone were systematically rated less suitable for jobs than those with light skin tone, with the effect varying depending on the nature of the job. Name did not appear to matter. The findings suggested that there was systematic ethnically-based discrimination in CV screening and that there were subtle effects which arose from the kinds of jobs involved.

polling. The aim of quota sampling is to produce a sample that reflects a population in terms of the relative proportions of people in different categories, such as gender, ethnicity, age groups, socio-economic groups, and region of residence, and in combinations of these categories. However, unlike a stratified sample, the sampling of individuals is not carried out randomly, since the final selection of people is left up to the interviewer.

Once the categories and the number of people to be interviewed within each category (known as *quotas*) have been decided upon, it is then the job of interviewers to select people who fit these categories. The quotas will typically be interrelated. In a manner similar to stratified sampling, the population may be divided into strata in terms of, for example, gender, social class, age, and ethnicity. Census data might be used to identify the number of people who should be in each subgroup. The numbers to be interviewed in each subgroup will reflect the population. Each interviewer will probably seek out individuals who fit several subgroup quotas.

Accordingly, an interviewer may know that among the various subgroups of people, he or she must find and interview five Asian, 25-to-34-year-old, lower-middle-class females in the area in which the interviewer has been asked to work. The interviewer usually asks people who are available to him or her about their characteristics in order to determine their suitability for a particular subgroup. Once a subgroup quota (or a combination of subgroup quotas) has been achieved, the interviewer will no longer be concerned to locate individuals for that subgroup.

The choice of respondents is left to the interviewer, subject to the requirement of all quotas being filled, usually within a certain time period. Those of you who have ever been approached on the street by a person toting a clipboard and interview schedule and have been asked about your age, occupation, and so on, before being asked a series of questions about a product or whatever, have almost certainly encountered an interviewer with a quota sample to fill. Sometimes, he or she will decide not to interview you because you do not meet the criteria required to fill a quota. This may be due to a quota already having been filled or to the criteria for exclusion meaning that a person with a certain characteristic that you possess is not required.

A number of criticisms are frequently levelled at quota samples.

- Because the choice of respondent is left to the interviewer, the proponents of probability sampling argue that a quota sample cannot be representative. It may accurately reflect the population in terms of superficial characteristics, as defined by the quotas. However, in their choice of people to approach, interviewers may be unduly influenced by their perceptions of how friendly people are or by whether the people make eye contact with the interviewer (unlike most of us, who look at the ground and shuffle past as quickly as possible because we do not want to be bothered in our leisure time).

- People who are in an interviewer's vicinity at the times he or she conducts interviews, and are therefore available to be approached, may not be typical; in that case, those who are included in the sample will not be typical. There is a risk, for example, that people in full-time paid work may be under-represented.

- The interviewer is likely to make judgements about certain characteristics in deciding whether or not to approach a person: in particular, judgements about age. Those judgements will sometimes be incorrect—for example, when someone who is eligible to be interviewed, because a quota that he or she fits is unfilled, is not approached because the interviewer makes an incorrect judgement (perhaps that the person is older than he or she looks). In such a case, a possible element of bias is being introduced.

- It has also been argued that the widespread use of social class as a quota control can introduce difficulties, because of the problem of ensuring that interviewees are properly assigned to class groupings (Moser and Kalton 1971).

- It is not permissible to calculate a standard error of the mean from a quota sample, because the non-random method of selection makes it impossible to calculate the range of possible values of a population.

All of this makes the quota sample look a poor bet, and there is no doubt that it is not favoured by academic researchers. It does have some arguments in its favour, however.

- It is undoubtedly cheaper and quicker than an interview survey on a comparable probability sample. For example, interviewers do not have to spend a lot of time travelling between interviews.

- Interviewers do not have to keep calling back on people who were not available at the time they were first approached.

- Because calling back is not required, a quota sample is easier to manage. It is not necessary to keep track of people who need to be recontacted or to keep track of refusals. Refusals occur, of course, but it is not necessary (and indeed it is not possible) to keep a record of which respondents declined to participate.

- When speed is of the essence, a quota sample is invaluable when compared to the more cumbersome probability sample. Newspapers frequently need to know, quickly, how a national sample of voters feel about a certain topic or how they intend to vote at that time. Similarly, if there is a sudden major news event, such as a major terrorist attack or a natural disaster, the news media may seek a more or less instant picture of the nation's views or responses. Again, a quota sample will be much faster.

- As with convenience sampling, quota sampling is useful for conducting development work on new measures or on research instruments. It can also be usefully employed in relation to exploratory work from which new theoretical ideas might be generated.

- Although the standard error of the mean should not be computed for a quota sample, it frequently is. As Moser and Kalton (1971) observe, some writers argue that the use of a non-random method in quota sampling should not act as a barrier to such a computation because its significance as a source of error is small when compared to other errors that may arise in surveys (see Figure 9.9). However, they go on to argue that at least with random sampling the researcher can calculate the amount of sampling error and does not have to be concerned about its potential impact.

There is some evidence to suggest that, when compared to random samples, quota samples often result in biases (Yang and Banamah 2014). They under-represent people in lower social strata, people who work in the private sector and manufacturing, and people at the extremes of income, and they over-represent women in households with children and people from larger households (Marsh and Scarbrough 1990; Butcher 1994).

FIGURE 9.9
Four sources of error in social survey research

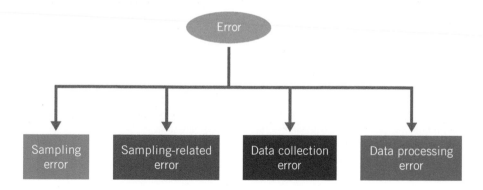

Limits to generalization

One point that is often not fully appreciated is that even when a sample has been selected using probability sampling, any findings can be generalized only to the population from which that sample was taken. This is an obvious point, but it is easy to think that findings from a study have some kind of broader applicability. If we take our imaginary study of training and skill development among employees of a company, any findings could be generalized only to that company. In other words, you should be very cautious about generalizing to employees at other companies. There are many factors that may imply that the level of training and skill development is higher (or lower) in that company than among company employees as a whole. There may be a higher (or lower) level of skill required in order to do the jobs that the company requires its employees to do; there may be more (or less) money in the company's training budget; there may be more (or less) of a culture of learning at this company; or the company may recruit a higher (or lower) proportion of employees who are already skilled. There may be many other factors too.

Similarly, we should be cautious of overgeneralizing in terms of locality. A frequent criticism made of research on employee motivation relates to the limited extent to which it can be assumed to be generalizable beyond the confines of the national or regional culture on which the study is based. For example, Herzberg et al. (1959) conducted semi-structured interviews with 203 accountants and engineers in the Pittsburgh area in the USA. Most of the companies that constituted sites for the study were involved in heavy industry, such as steel-making or shipbuilding. The population from which the sample was selected consisted of all accountants and engineers who worked for these companies. Respondents were chosen randomly according to certain criteria for stratification, including age, job title, level in the company, and length of service. It is interesting that there is no mention of gender in the study, although we can fairly safely assume that, given that this was a study of accountants and engineers in the late 1950s, there is likely to be a male bias to the study. The maximum number of individuals selected for interview in each company was approximately 50. As the authors acknowledge, 'the fact that this work was done within a thirty-mile radius around Pittsburgh will inevitably raise questions about the degree to which the findings are applicable in other areas of the country' (1959: 31). The findings may also reflect the values of high individualism, self-interest, and high masculinity that have been identified as characteristic of American culture (Hofstede 1984). This is part of the reason that there have been so many attempts to replicate the study on other occupational groups and in other localities, including different cultures and nationalities.

However, there could even be a further limit to generalization that is implied by the Herzberg et al. sample. The main study was conducted in the late 1950s. One issue that is rarely discussed in this context, and that is almost impossible to assess, is whether or not there is a time limit on the findings that are generated. Quite aside from the fact that we need to appreciate that the findings cannot (or at least should not) be generalized beyond the Pittsburgh area, is there a point at which we have to say, 'Well, those findings applied to the Pittsburgh area then, but things have changed and we can no longer assume that they apply to that or any other locality'? We are, after all, used to assuming that changed circumstances will prompt changed behaviour and attitudes. To take a simple example: no one would be prepared to assume that the findings of a study in 1980 of UK university students' budgeting and personal finance habits would apply to students in the early twenty-first century. Quite aside from changes that might have occurred naturally, the erosion and virtual dismantling of the student grant system in the UK and the introduction of tuition fees have changed the ways students finance their education, including perhaps a greater reliance on part-time work (Lucas 1997), a greater reliance on parents, and use of loans. But, even when there is no definable or recognizable source of relevant change of this kind, there is nonetheless the possibility (or even likelihood) that findings are temporally specific.

Error in survey research

We can think of 'error', a term that has been employed on a number of occasions, as being made up of four main factors (see Figure 9.9):

- *Sampling error*: see Key concept 9.1 for a definition. This kind of error arises because it is extremely unlikely that one will end up with a perfectly representative sample, even when probability sampling is employed.
- We can distinguish what might be thought of as *sampling-related error*. This is error that is subsumed under the category *non-sampling error* (see Key concept 9.1) but that arises from activities or events that are related to the sampling process and are connected with the issue of generalizability or external validity of findings. Examples are an inaccurate sampling frame and non-response.
- There is also error that is connected with the implementation of the research process. We might call this *data collection error*. This source of error includes such factors as poor question wording in self-completion questionnaires or structured interviews; poor interviewing techniques; and flaws in the administration of research instruments.
- Finally, there is *data processing error*. This arises from faulty management of data, in particular errors in the *coding* of answers.

The third and fourth sources of error relate to factors that are not associated with sampling and instead relate much more closely to concerns about the validity of measurement, which was addressed in Chapter 8. The kinds of steps that need to be taken to keep these sources of error to a minimum in the context of social survey research will be addressed in the next three chapters.

Sampling issues for online surveys

Online surveys have become increasingly popular in recent decades (Chapter 11 discusses them further). An obvious question to ask is how the material on sampling presented above might apply to them. Certainly, sampling in online surveys poses some specific challenges. A major issue and limitation is that not everyone in any nation is online, and of those who are, some may not have the technical ability to handle online questionnaires. Certain other features of online communications make the issue more problematic:

- Many people have more than one email address.
- Email addresses tend to be much more fleeting than postal addresses.
- Many people use more than one internet service provider (ISP).
- A household may have one computer but several users.
- Internet users are a biased sample of the population, in that they tend to be better educated, wealthier,

younger, and more often male than female (Blasius and Brandt 2010).

- Few sampling frames exist of the general online population, and most of these are likely to be expensive to acquire, since they are controlled by ISPs or may be confidential.

Such issues make the possibilities of conducting online surveys using probability sampling principles difficult to envisage. This is not to say that online surveys should not be considered. Indeed, for researchers in the field of business, there may be more opportunities than for researchers in other areas. For example, in many organizations, most if not all non-manual workers are likely to be online and familiar with the details of using email and the internet, so that a suitable sampling frame of email addressees is available or can relatively easily be compiled. In such circumstances, surveys can be conducted using essentially the same probability sampling procedures as those outlined above. For certain kinds of business research, such as investigations involving surveys of organizational members, email-based surveys may present sampling problems that differ little from offline modes of administration, other than the possibility of higher levels of non-response. Similarly, surveys of members of commercially relevant online groups can be conducted using probability sampling principles. If we are interested in collecting data from members of online communities, for example those using social networking technology for business purposes, then virtually by definition they would need to be contacted online to generate a sample. C. B. Smith (1997) conducted a survey of Web presence providers (people or organizations that are involved in creating and maintaining Web content). She acquired her sample from a directory of providers, which acted as her sampling frame.

As Couper (2000) notes of surveys of populations using probability sampling procedures:

> Intra-organizational surveys and those directed at users of the Internet were among the first to adopt this new survey technology. These restricted populations typically have no coverage problems . . . or very high rates of coverage. Student surveys are a particular example of this approach that are growing in popularity.
>
> (2000: 485)

Hewson and Laurent (2008) suggest that when there is no sampling frame, which is normally the case with samples to be drawn from the general population, the main approach taken to generating an appropriate sample is to post an invitation to answer a questionnaire on relevant newsgroup message boards, to suitable mailing lists, or on web pages and social media. The result will be a sample of entirely unknown representativeness, and it is impossible to know what the response rate to the questionnaire is, since the size of the population is also unknown. On the other hand, given that we have so little knowledge and understanding of online behaviour and attitudes relating to online issues, it could reasonably be argued that some information about these areas is a lot better than none at all, provided that the limitations of the findings in terms of their generalizability are appreciated.

More recently, there has been increasing interest in the use of online mechanisms for recruiting participants. These include systems for recruiting paid participants, for example Amazon Mechanical Turk and Google AdWords, as well as for seeking volunteers, for example on Facebook. It is important to note that such mechanisms generate convenience samples, rather than random samples. There is little research on their effectiveness in generating representative samples, but one recent study reports that volunteer-seeking methods appear to deliver more heterogeneous and thus perhaps more representative samples than systems which recruit paid participants (Antoun et al. 2016).

A further issue in relation to online sampling and sampling-related error is the matter of *non-response* (see Key concept 9.3). There is growing evidence that online surveys typically generate lower response rates than postal questionnaire surveys (Tse 1998; Sheehan 2001; Pedersen and Nielsen 2016). In the early years, in the late 1980s, response rates for email surveys were quite encouraging (Sheehan and Hoy 1999), but since the mid-1990s they have been declining to lower levels than those for most postal questionnaires (Sheehan 2001). Two factors may account for this decline: the novelty of email surveys in the early years and a growing antipathy towards unsolicited emails among online communities. A meta-analysis that compared Web surveys with other modes of survey administration found that on average, Web surveys produce a response rate that is 11 per cent lower (Lozar Manfreda et al. 2008). However, response rates can be boosted by following two simple strategies:

1. Contact prospective respondents before sending them a questionnaire. This is regarded as basic 'netiquette'. Bosnjak et al. (2008) found that response rates to a web-based panel survey could be enhanced by pre-notifying prospective participants. They found that pre-notifications sent by text (SMS) message were more effective than when sent by email but that

a combination of both was more effective than text messages alone.

2. As with postal questionnaire surveys, follow up non-respondents at least once.

3. There is evidence that incentives can increase response rates in online surveys (Pedersen and Nielsen 2016).

The case for the first of these two strategies in boosting response rates is not entirely clear (Sheehan 2001), but seems to be generally advisable. However, as previously noted, with many online surveys it is impossible to calculate a response rate, since, when participants are recruited through invitations and postings on discussion boards, etc., the size of the population of which they are a sample is almost impossible to determine.

Crawford et al. (2001) report the results of a survey of students at the University of Michigan that experimented with a number of possible influences on the response rate. Students in the sample were initially sent an email inviting them to visit the website, which allowed access, via a password, to the questionnaire. Some of those emailed were led to expect that the questionnaire would take 8–10 minutes to complete (in fact, it would take considerably longer); others were led to expect that it would take 20 minutes. As might be expected, those led to believe it would take longer were less likely to accept the invitation, resulting in a lower response rate for this group. However, Crawford et al. also found that those respondents who were led to believe that the questionnaire would take only 8–10 minutes were *more* likely to give up on the questionnaire part

of the way through, resulting in unusable partially completed questionnaires in most cases. Interestingly, they also found that respondents were most likely to abandon their questionnaires part of the way through when in the middle of completing a series of open questions. The implications of this finding reflect the advice you will encounter in Chapter 11: that it is probably best to ask as few open questions in self-completion questionnaires as possible.

Further evidence suggests that having a progress indicator in an online survey can reduce the number of people who abandon the questionnaire part of the way through completion (Couper et al. 2001). A progress indicator is usually a diagrammatic representation of how far the respondent has progressed through the questionnaire at any particular point. Couper et al. also found that it took less time for respondents to complete related items (for example, a series of Likert items) when they appeared on a screen together than when they appeared singly. Respondents also seemed less inclined to omit related questions when they appeared together on a screen rather than singly.

However, it is important not be too sanguine about some of these findings. One difficulty with them is that the samples derive from populations whose members are not as different from one another as would almost certainly be found in samples deriving from general populations. Another is that it must not be forgotten that, as previously noted, access to the internet is still not universal, and there is evidence that those with internet access differ from those without, both in terms of personal characteristics and attitudinally.

 KEY POINTS

....

- Probability sampling is a mechanism for reducing bias in the selection of samples.
- Ensure you become familiar with key technical terms in the literature on sampling, including representative sample; random sample; non-response; population; sampling error; etc.
- Randomly selected samples are important because they permit generalizations to the population and because they have certain known qualities.
- Sampling error decreases as sample size increases.
- Quota samples can provide reasonable alternatives to random samples, but they suffer from some deficiencies.
- Convenience samples may provide interesting data, but it is crucial to be aware of their limitations in terms of generalizability.
- Sampling and sampling-related error are just two sources of error in social survey research.
- Online surveys pose specific challenges in terms of sampling.

QUESTIONS FOR REVIEW

- What does each of the following terms mean: population; probability sampling; non-probability sampling; sampling frame; representative sample; and sampling and non-sampling error?

- What are the goals of sampling?

- What are the main areas of potential bias in sampling?

Sampling error

- What is the significance of sampling error for achieving a representative sample?

Types of probability sample

- What is probability sampling and why is it important?

- What are the main types of probability sample?

- How far does a stratified random sample offer greater precision than a simple random or systematic sample?

- If you were conducting an interview survey of around 500 people in a large city, what type of probability sample would you choose and why?

- A researcher positions herself on a street corner and asks one person in five who walks by to be interviewed: she continues doing this until she has a sample of 250. How likely is she to achieve a representative sample?

The qualities of a probability sample

- A researcher is interested in levels of job satisfaction among manual workers in a firm that is undergoing change. The firm has 1200 manual workers. The researcher selects a simple random sample of 10 per cent of the population. He measures job satisfaction on a Likert scale comprising ten items. A high level of satisfaction is scored 5 and a low level is scored 1. The mean job satisfaction score is 34.3. The standard error of the mean is 8.57. What is the 95 per cent confidence interval?

Sample size

- What factors would you consider in deciding how large your sample should be when devising a probability sample?

- What is non-response and why is it important to the question of whether or not you will end up with a representative sample?

Types of non-probability sampling

- Are non-probability samples useless?

- 'Quota samples are not true random samples, but in terms of generating a representative sample there is little difference between them, and this accounts for their widespread use in market research and opinion polling.' Discuss.

Limits to generalization

- 'The problem of generalization to a population is not just to do with the matter of getting a representative sample.' Discuss.

Error in survey research

- 'Non-sampling error, as its name implies, is concerned with sources of error that are not part of the sampling process.' Discuss.

Sampling for online surveys

- What are the main challenges in selecting a sample for an online survey?

....

ONLINE RESOURCES
www.oup.com/uk/brm5e/

Visit the Interactive Research Guide that accompanies this book to complete an exercise related to sampling.

....

STRUCTURED INTERVIEWING

CHAPTER OUTLINE

Once sampling issues have been taken into consideration, the next stage of the survey research process (see Figure 9.1) involves considering whether to administer the questionnaire face-to-face or to rely on self-completion. This chapter deals with the first option, the structured interview, while Chapter 11 addresses issues relating to self-completion. A further option to consider is whether to administer the questionnaire by email or online; this will also be covered in Chapter 11.

The structured interview is one of a variety of forms of research interview, but it is the one that is most commonly employed in survey research. The goal of the structured interview is for the interviewing of respondents to be standardized so that differences between interviews in any research project are minimized. As a result, there are many guidelines about how structured interviewing should be carried out so that variation in the conduct of interviews is small. This chapter explores a number of aspects of this:

- the reasons why the structured interview is a prominent research method in survey research, with consideration of the importance of standardization to the process of measurement;

- the different contexts of interviewing, such as the use of more than one interviewer and whether the administration of the interview is in person or by telephone;

- various requirements of structured interviewing, including establishing rapport with the interviewee, asking questions as they appear on the **interview schedule**, recording exactly what is said by interviewees, ensuring there are clear instructions on the interview schedule concerning question sequencing and the recording of answers, and keeping to the question order as it appears on the schedule;

- problems with structured interviewing, including the influence of the interviewer on respondents and the possibility of systematic bias in answers (known as **response sets**).

Introduction

The interview is a common occurrence in social life, because there are many different forms of interview. There are job interviews, media interviews, social work interviews, police interviews, appraisal interviews, to name a few. And then there are research interviews, which represent the kind of interview that will be covered in this and other chapters. These different kinds of interviews share some common features, such as the eliciting of information by the interviewer from the interviewee and the operation of rules of varying degrees of formality or explicitness concerning the conduct of the interview.

In the business research interview, the aim is for the interviewer to elicit from the interviewee or *respondent*, as he or she is frequently called in survey research, all manner of information: the interviewee's own behaviour or that of others; attitudes; norms; beliefs; and values. There are many different types or styles of research interview, but the kind that is primarily employed in survey research is the structured interview, which is the focus of this chapter. Other kinds of interview will be briefly mentioned in this chapter but will be discussed in greater detail in later chapters.

The structured interview

The research interview is a prominent data collection strategy in both **quantitative** and **qualitative research**. The **social survey** is probably the chief context within which business researchers employ the structured interview (see Key concept 10.1) in connection with quantitative research, and it is this form of the interview that will be emphasized in this chapter. The reason why survey researchers typically prefer this kind of interview is that it promotes standardization of *both* the asking of questions *and* the recording of answers. This feature has two closely related virtues from the perspective of quantitative research: the minimizing of error that could result from interviewer variability; and the ease of data processing provided by the standardized recording of answers.

Reducing error due to interviewer variability

The standardization of both the asking of questions and the recording of answers means that, if the interview is properly executed, variation in people's replies will be due to 'true' or 'real' variation and not due to the interview context. To take a simple illustration, when we ask a question that is supposed to be an **indicator** of a **concept**, we want to keep error to a minimum, an issue that was touched on at the end of Chapter 9. We can think of the answers to a question as constituting the values that a **variable** takes. These values, of course, exhibit variation. This could be the question on skill development and training among employees that was a focus of Chapter

10.1 KEY CONCEPT
What is a structured interview?

A structured interview, sometimes called a *standardized interview*, involves the administration of an interview schedule: a set of questions designed to be asked by an interviewer. The aim is for all interviewees to be given exactly the same context of questioning. This means that each respondent receives exactly the same interview stimulus as any other. The goal of this style of interviewing is to ensure that interviewees' replies can be aggregated, and this can be achieved reliably only if those replies are in response to identical cues. Interviewers are supposed to read out questions exactly as they are printed on the schedule, and in the same order. Questions are usually very specific and often offer the interviewee a fixed range of answers (this type of question is often called *closed, closed ended, pre-coded,* or *fixed choice*). The structured interview is the typical form of interview in social survey research.

9 at certain points. However, some respondents may be inaccurately classified in terms of the variable. There are several possible reasons for this.

Most variables will contain an element of error, so that it is helpful to think of variation as made up of two components: true variation and error. In other words:

variation = true variation + variation due to error

The aim is to keep the error component to a minimum, since error has an adverse effect on the validity of a measure. If the error component is quite high, validity will be jeopardized. In the structured interview, two sources of variation due to error—numbers 2 and 5 in Tips and skills 'Common sources of error in survey research'—are likely to be less pronounced, since the opportunity for variation in interviewer behaviour in these two areas (asking questions and recording answers) is reduced.

The significance of standardization and of thereby reducing interviewer variability is this: assuming that there is no problem with an interview question owing to such things as confusing terms or ambiguity (an issue that will be examined in Chapter 12, 'Asking questions'), we want to be able to say as far as possible that the variation that we find is connected with true variation between interviewees and not to variation in the way a question was asked or the way the answers were recorded. Interviewer variability can occur in either of two ways: first, *intra-interviewer variability,* whereby an interviewer is not consistent in the way he or she asks questions and/or records answers; second, when there is more than one interviewer, there may be *inter-interviewer variability,* whereby interviewers are not consistent with each other in the ways they ask questions and/or record answers. Needless to say, these two sources of variability are not mutually exclusive; they can coexist, compounding the problem even further. In view of the significance of standardization, it is hardly surprising that some writers prefer to call the structured interview a *standardized interview* (e.g. Oppenheim 1992) or *standardized survey interview* (e.g. Fowler and Mangione 1990).

TIPS AND SKILLS
Common sources of error in survey research

There are many sources of error in survey research, in addition to those associated with sampling. This is a list of the principal sources of error:

1. a poorly worded question;
2. the way the question is asked by the interviewer;
3. misunderstanding on the part of the interviewee;
4. memory problems on the part of the interviewee;
5. the way the information is recorded by the interviewer;
6. the way the information is processed, either when answers are coded or when data are entered into the computer.

Accuracy and ease of data processing

Like self-completion questionnaires (discussed in Chapter 11), most structured interviews contain mainly questions that are variously referred to as *closed, closed ended, precoded,* or *fixed choice.* This issue will be covered in detail in Chapter 11. However, this type of question has considerable relevance to the current discussion. With the closed question, the respondent is given a limited choice of possible answers. In other words, the interviewer provides respondents with two or more possible answers and asks them to select which one or ones apply. Ideally, this procedure will simply entail the interviewer placing a tick in a box by the answer(s) selected by a respondent, or circling the selected answer, or a similar procedure. The advantage of this practice is that the potential for interviewer variability is reduced: there is no problem of whether the interviewer writes down everything that the respondent says or of misinterpretation of the reply given. If an *open* or *open-ended* question is asked, the interviewer may not write down everything said, may embellish what is said, or may misinterpret what is said.

However, the advantages of the closed question in the context of survey research go further than this, as we will see in Chapter 11. One advantage that is particularly significant in the context of the present discussion is that closed questions greatly facilitate the processing of data. When an open question is asked, the answers need to be sifted and *coded* in order for the data to be analysed quantitatively. Not only is this a laborious procedure, particularly if there is a large number of open questions and/or of respondents; it also introduces the potential for another source of error, number 6 in Tips and skills 'Common sources of error in survey research': it is quite likely that error will be introduced as a result of variability in the coding of answers. When open questions are asked, the interviewer is supposed to write down as much of what is said as possible. Answers can, therefore, be in the form of several sentences. These answers have to be examined and then categorized, so that each person's answer can be aggregated with other respondents'

answers to a certain question. A number will then be allocated to each category of answer so that the answers can be entered into a computer database and analysed quantitatively. This general process is known as coding, and will be examined further in Chapter 11.

Coding introduces yet another source of error. First, if the rules for assigning answers to categories, collectively known as the coding frame, are flawed, the variation that is observed will not reflect the true variation in interviewees' replies. Secondly, there may be variability in the ways in which answers are categorized by the rater (the person doing the coding). As with interviewing, there can be two sources: *intra-rater variability,* whereby the rater varies over time in the way he or she applies the rules for assigning answers to categories; and *inter-rater variability,* whereby raters differ from each other in the way they apply the rules for assigning answers to categories. If either (or both) source(s) of variability occur, at least part of the variation in interviewees' replies will not reflect true variation and instead will be caused by error.

The closed question sidesteps this problem neatly, because respondents allocate *themselves* to categories. The coding process is then a simple matter of attaching a different number to each category of answer and of entering the numbers into a computer database. It is not surprising, therefore, that this type of question is often referred to as pre-coded, because decisions about the coding of answers are typically undertaken as part of the design of the schedule—that is, before any respondents have actually been asked questions. There is very little opportunity for interviewers or raters to vary in the recording or the coding of answers. Of course, if some respondents misunderstand any terms in the alternative answers with which they are presented, or if the answers do not adequately cover the appropriate range of possibilities, the question will not provide a valid measure. However, that is a separate issue. The chief points to register about closed questions for the moment is that, when compared to open questions, they reduce one potential source of error *and* are much easier to process for quantitative data analysis.

Other types of interview

The structured interview is by no means the only type of interview, but it is certainly the main type that is likely to be encountered in survey research and in quantitative research generally. Unfortunately, a host of different

terms have been employed by writers on research methods to distinguish the diverse forms of research interview. Key concept 9.1 represents an attempt to capture some of the major terms and types.

10.2 KEY CONCEPT
Major types of interview

- *Structured interview*: see Key concept 10.1.

- *Standardized interview*: see Key concept 10.1.

- *Semi-structured interview*. This is a term that covers a wide range of instances. It typically refers to a context in which the interviewer has a series of questions that are in the general form of an interview schedule but is able to vary the sequence of questions. The questions are frequently somewhat more general in their frame of reference than that typically found in a structured interview schedule. Also, the interviewer usually has some latitude to ask further questions in response to what are seen as significant replies. Sometimes such interview schedules will include closed questions, typically to gather data on variables such as gender, age, income, and job status, which may be needed as background or for analysis of responses to more open questions.

- *Unstructured interview*. The interviewer typically has only a list of topics or issues, often called an **interview guide** or *aide-mémoire*, that are covered. The style of questioning is usually informal. The phrasing and sequencing of questions will vary from interview to interview.

- *Intensive interview*. This term is employed by Lofland and Lofland (1995) as an alternative term to the *unstructured interview*. Spradley (1979) uses the term *ethnographic interview* to describe a form of interview that is also more or less synonymous with the *unstructured interview*.

- *Qualitative interview*. For some writers (e.g. Mason 1996), this term seems to denote an *unstructured interview*, but more frequently it is a general term that embraces interviews of both the semi-structured and unstructured kind (e.g. Rubin and Rubin 1995).

- *In-depth interview*. Like the term *qualitative interview*, this one sometimes refers to an *unstructured interview* but more often refers to both semi-structured and unstructured interviewing.

- *Focused interview*. This is a term devised by Merton et al. (1956) to refer to an interview using predominantly open questions to ask interviewees about a specific situation or event that is relevant to them and of interest to the researcher.

- *Focus group*. This is the same as the *focused interview*, but interviewees discuss the specific issue in groups. See Key concept 21.1 for a more detailed definition.

- *Group interview*. Some writers see this term as synonymous with the *focus group*, but a distinction may be made between the latter and a situation in which members of a group discuss a variety of matters that may be only partially related.

- *Oral history interview*. This is an *unstructured* or *semi-structured interview* in which the respondent is asked to recall events from his or her past and to reflect on them (discussed in Chapter 20). There is usually a cluster of fairly specific research concerns to do with a particular epoch or event, so there is some resemblance to a focused interview.

- *Life history interview*. This is similar to the *oral history interview*, but the aim of this type of *unstructured interview* is to glean information on the entire biography of each respondent (see Chapter 20).

All of the forms of interview outlined in Key concept 10.2, with the exception of the *structured interview* and the *standardized interview*, are primarily used in connection with qualitative research, and it is in that context that they will be encountered again in Part Three of this book. They are rarely used in connection with quantitative research, and survey research in particular, because the absence of standardization in the asking of questions and recording of answers makes respondents' replies difficult to aggregate and to process. This is not to say that they have no role at all. For example, the unstructured interview can have a useful role in helping the researcher to develop the fixed-choice alternatives with which respondents are provided in the kind of closed question that is typical of the structured interview.

Interview contexts

In an archetypal interview, an interviewer stands or sits in front of the respondent, asking the latter a series of questions and writing down the answers. Although this archetype is the most usual context for an interview, there are several possible departures from it.

More than one interviewee

In the case of group interviews or focus groups, there is more than one, and usually quite a few more than one, respondent or interviewee. Nor is this the only context in which more than one person is interviewed. Bell et al. (2001) carried out interviews with two managers in the same company, both of whom had been involved in the implementation of the people-management initiative Investors in People. The managers, who had often had different roles in relation to the initiative or been involved with it at different stages of its development, were together able to build a chronological understanding of its implementation. Similarly, in Bryman's research on visitors to Disney theme parks, not just couples but often their children took part in the interviews as well (Bryman 1999). However, it is very unusual for structured interviews to be used in connection with this kind of questioning. In survey research, it is almost always a single individual who is the object of questioning. Indeed, in survey interviews it is advisable to discourage as far as possible the presence and intrusion of others during the course of the interview. Investigations in which more than one person is being interviewed tend to be exercises in qualitative research, though this is not always the case.

More than one interviewer

This is a relatively unusual situation in business research, because of the considerable cost that is involved in dispatching two (or indeed more than two) people to interview someone. Bechhofer et al. (1984) describe research in which two people interviewed individuals, with one interviewer doing most of the talking and the other taking more extensive notes. However, while their approach achieved a number of benefits for them, their interviewing style was of the unstructured kind that is typically employed in qualitative research, and they argue that the presence of a second interviewer is unlikely to achieve any added value in the context of structured interviewing.

In person or by telephone?

A third departure from the archetype is that interviews may be conducted by telephone rather than face-to-face. While telephone interviewing is quite common in such fields as market research, it is less common in business research. Telephone interviewing can be carried out using landline, mobile or, increasingly, web-based applications such as Skype. See Research in focus 10.3 for an example of the use of telephone interviewing and Chapter 20 for a more detailed discussion of the use of Skype in interviews.

There are several advantages of telephone over personal interviews:

- On a like-for-like basis, they are far cheaper and quicker to administer. This arises because, for personal interviews, interviewers may have to spend a great deal of time and money travelling between respondents. This factor will be even more pronounced when a sample is geographically dispersed, a problem that is only partially mitigated in personal interview surveys by strategies such as cluster sampling. Of course, telephone interviews take time, and hired interviewers have to be paid, but the cost of conducting a telephone interview will still be lower than that of conducting a comparable personal one.

- The telephone interview is easier to supervise than the personal interview. This is a particular advantage when there are several interviewers, since it becomes easier to check on interviewers' transgressions in the asking of questions, such as rephrasing questions or the inappropriate use of probes by the interviewer (see the section on 'Probing' later in the chapter). Probes are stimuli introduced by the interviewer to elicit further information from the interviewee when the latter's response is inadequate, either because it fails to answer the question or because it answers the question but there is insufficient detail.

- Telephone interviewing has a further advantage: some evidence (which is not as clear-cut as one might want) suggests that, in personal interviews, respondents' replies are sometimes affected by characteristics of the interviewer (for example, class or ethnicity) and indeed by his or her mere presence (implying that the interviewees may reply in ways they feel will be deemed desirable by interviewers). The remoteness of the interviewer in telephone interviewing removes

10.3 RESEARCH IN FOCUS
A telephone survey of dignity at work

Berg and Frost (2005) used results from a telephone survey of over 500 low-skill, low-wage workers in hospitals in the USA in order to explore the factors that affect workers' perceptions of dignity at work. They also wanted to find out if union representation and/or changes in worker representation influenced workers' perceptions of dignity at work. The researchers identified three main dimensions to the concept of dignity at work: fair treatment, intrinsically satisfying work, and economic security. The kinds of jobs that their sample were engaged in included food service workers, housekeepers, and nursing assistants doing tasks that the authors describe as 'dead end jobs with little or no chance of upward mobility' (2005: 663). They observe that workers who do these jobs typically earn only the minimum wage and there tends to be a high level of annual turnover, between 50 and 100 per cent.

The data came from a sample of 15 community hospitals across the USA, focusing on the most representative group, hospitals with between 200 and 400 beds. The researchers chose telephone interviewing because of the 'inherent instability in the lives of this sector of the workforce' (2005: 669). This method was seen as being one way of reliably reaching the workers. The researchers carried out telephone interviews with 589 workers, asking them about all aspects of their jobs and careers. Telephone numbers were obtained from employers. However, there were a number of difficulties associated with the telephone interview method that stemmed from the nature of the **population** in which the research was interested. 'Many of the phone numbers we secured from employers were simply no good: the phone service had been disconnected; the person no longer lived at that phone number; or the respondent would not answer the telephone' (2005: 669). One of the reasons a phone call was not answered was because respondents had call display. If they did not recognize the number, they would not pick up the phone because they were trying to avoid debt collection agents. These difficulties adversely affected the response rate, which ended up at 45 per cent. The researchers conclude that the people they were able to survey probably represent the most stable part of this population, so the results are likely to overstate the positive aspects associated with these jobs: 'those whose work lives keep them living in a precarious fashion are likely those not responding to our telephone survey' (2005: 669).

this potential source of bias to a significant extent. The interviewer's personal characteristics cannot be seen, and the fact that he or she is not physically present may offset the likelihood of respondents' answers being affected by the interviewer. In the case of web-based applications such as Skype, interviewers may choose not to use the video capability precisely because it introduces the possibility of this kind of effect.

Telephone interviewing suffers from certain limitations when compared to the personal interview.

- The length of a telephone interview is unlikely to be sustainable beyond 20–25 minutes, whereas personal interviews can be much longer than this (Frey 2004).
- The question of whether response rates (see Key concept 9.3) are lower with surveys by telephone interview than with surveys by personal interview is unclear, in that there is little consistent evidence on this question. However, there is a general belief that telephone interviews achieve slightly lower rates than

personal interviews (Frey and Oishi 1995; Shuy 2002; Frey 2004).

- There is some evidence to suggest that telephone interviews are less effective for the asking of questions about sensitive issues, such as workplace bullying or drug and alcohol use. However, the evidence is not entirely consistent on this point, though it is probably sufficient to suggest that, when many questions of this kind are to be used, a personal interview may be superior (Shuy 2002).
- Developments in telephone communications, such as answerphones, other forms of call screening, and mobile phones, have almost certainly had an adverse effect on telephone surveys in terms of response rates and the general difficulty of getting access to respondents through conventional landlines. Households that rely exclusively on mobile phones represent a particular difficulty. On the other hand, the increased spread of internet access and the availability of web-based communication may limit this problem.

- Telephone interviewers have less opportunity to engage in observation. This means that they are not able to respond to signs of puzzlement or unease on the faces of respondents when they are asked a question. In a personal interview, the interviewer may respond to such signs by restating the question or attempting to clarify the meaning of the question, though this must be handled in a standardized way as far as possible. A further issue relating to the inability of the interviewer to observe is that, sometimes, interviewers may be asked to collect subsidiary information about their visits (for example, whether health and safety procedures are made evident at a business premises). Such information cannot be directly collected when telephone interviews are employed.

- It is frequently the case that specific individuals in households or firms are the targets of an interview. In other words, simply anybody will not do. This requirement is likely to arise from the specifications of the population to be sampled, which means that people in a certain role or position or with particular characteristics are to be interviewed. It is probably more difficult to ascertain by telephone interview whether or not the correct person is replying.

- There is some evidence to suggest that the quality of data derived from telephone interviews is inferior to that of comparable face-to-face interviews. A series of experiments reported by Holbrook et al. (2003) on the mode of survey administration in the USA using long questionnaires found that respondents interviewed by telephone were more likely to express no opinion or 'don't know' (see Chapter 12 for more on this issue); to answer in the same way to a series of linked questions; to provide socially desirable answers; to be apprehensive about the interview; and to be more likely to be dissatisfied with the time taken by the interview (even though interviews were typically shorter than in the face-to-face mode). Also, telephone interviewees tended to be less engaged with the interview process. While these results should be viewed with caution, since studies like these are bound to be affected by such factors as the use of a large questionnaire on a national sample, they do provide interesting food for thought.

Computer-assisted interviewing

In recent years, increasing use has been made of computers in the interviewing process, especially in commercial survey research of the kind conducted by market research and opinion polling organizations. There are two main formats for computer-assisted interviewing: computer-assisted personal interviewing (CAPI) and computer-assisted telephone interviewing (CATI). A very large percentage of telephone interviews are conducted with the aid of computers. Among commercial survey organizations, almost all telephone interviewing is of the CATI kind, and this kind of interview has become one of the most popular formats for such firms. The main reasons for the growing use of CAPI have been the increased portability and affordability of laptop computers and tablets, and the growth in the number and quality of software packages that provide a platform for devising interview schedules. If the interviewer is out in an organization all day, he or she may take a removable storage device with the saved data to the research office or upload the data.

With computer-assisted interviewing, the questions that comprise an interview schedule appear on the screen. As interviewers ask each question and the respondent replies, the interviewer inputs the appropriate reply and proceed to the next question. This process has the great advantage that, when *filter questions* are asked, so that certain answers may be skipped as a result of a person's reply, the computer 'jumps' to the next relevant question. This removes the possibility of interviewers inadvertently asking inappropriate questions or failing to ask ones that should be asked. In these ways, computer-assisted interviewing enhances the degree of control over the interview process and can therefore improve standardization of the asking and recording of questions. However, there is very little evidence to suggest that the quality of data deriving from computer-assisted interviews is demonstrably superior to that provided by comparable paper-and-pencil interviews (Couper and Hansen 2002).

It is possible that technophobic respondents may be a bit alarmed by the use of a laptop or tablet during an interview. One of us has had personal experience of this technique as a respondent in a market research survey: in this instance the laptop started to beep part of the way through the interview because the battery was about to expire and needed to be replaced with a back-up. An incident such as this could be disruptive to the flow of an interview and be alarming for technophobic respondents.

CAPI and CATI have not influenced academic survey research to anything like the same degree that they have in commercial survey research, although that picture is likely to change considerably because of the many advantages they possess. In any case, many of the large datasets that are used for secondary analysis (see Chapter 14 for examples) derive from computer-assisted interviewing studies undertaken by commercial or large social research organizations. One further point to register in connection with computer-assisted interviewing is that so far we have avoided discussion of online surveys. The reason for this is that such surveys are self-completion questionnaires rather than interviews. We cover them in Chapter 11.

Conducting interviews

Issues concerning the conduct of interviews are examined here in a very general way. In addition to the matters considered here, there is clearly the important issue of how to word the interview questions themselves. This area will be explored in Chapter 12; many of the rules of question-asking relate to self-completion questionnaire techniques such as postal or online questionnaires as well as to structured interviews. One further general point to make here is that the advice concerning the conduct of interviews provided in this chapter relates to structured interviews. The framework for conducting the kinds of interviewing used in qualitative research (such as unstructured and semi-structured interviewing and focus groups) will be handled in Part Three of the book.

Know the schedule

Before interviewing anybody, an interviewer should be fully conversant with the schedule. Even if you are the only person conducting interviews, make sure you know it inside out. Interviewing can be stressful for interviewers; in such cases, standard interview procedures such as filter questions (described under 'Clear instructions' below) can cause interviewers to get flustered and miss questions out or ask the wrong questions. If two or more interviewers are involved, they need to be fully trained to know what is required of them and to know their way around the schedule. Training is especially important to reduce the likelihood of interviewer variability in the asking of questions, which is a source of error.

Introducing the research

The researcher should give prospective respondents a credible rationale for the research in which they are being asked to participate and for giving up their valuable time. This aspect of conducting interview research is of particular significance at a time when response rates to social survey research appear to be declining (though, as noted in Chapter 9, the evidence on this issue is the focus of some disagreement). The introductory rationale may be either spoken by the interviewer or written down. It comes in

spoken form in such situations as when interviewers make contact with respondents on the street or when they 'cold call' respondents in their homes or at their place of work, whether in person or by telephone. A written rationale will be required to alert respondents that someone will be contacting them in person or on the telephone to request an interview. Respondents will frequently encounter both forms—for example, when they are sent a letter and then ask the interviewer who turns up to interview them what the research is all about. It is important for the rationale given by telephone to be consistent with the one given by letter, as if respondents pick up inconsistencies they may well be less likely to participate in the survey.

Introductions to research should typically contain the bits of information outlined in Tips and skills 'Topics and issues to include in an introductory statement'. Since interviewers represent the interface between the research and the respondent, they have an important role in maximizing the response rate for the survey. In addition, the following points should be borne in mind:

- Interviewers seeking respondents by phone should be prepared to keep calling back if interviewees are out or unavailable. This will require taking into account people's likely work and leisure habits—for example, there is no point in calling at home on people who work during the day. In addition, first thing in the morning may not be the best time to contact a busy manager who is likely to be briefing colleagues and responding to queries.

- Be self-assured; you may get a better response if you presume that people will agree to be interviewed rather than that they will refuse.

- Reassure people that you are not a salesperson. Because of the tactics of certain organizations whose representatives say they are doing market or business research, many people have become very suspicious of people saying they would just like to ask you a few questions.

- If you will be seen by respondents, dress in a way that will be acceptable to a wide spectrum of people.

- Make it clear that you will be happy to find a time to suit the respondent.

TIPS AND SKILLS
Topics and issues to include in an introductory statement

There are several issues to include in an introductory statement to a prospective interviewee. The following list comprises the principal considerations.

- Make clear the identity of the person who is contacting the respondent.

- Identify the auspices under which the research is being conducted—for example, a university, a market research agency.

- Mention any research funder, or, if you are a student doing an undergraduate or postgraduate dissertation, make this clear.

- Indicate what the research is about in broad terms and why it is important, and give an indication of the kind of information to be collected.

- Indicate why the respondent has been selected—for example, selected by a random process.

- Provide reassurance about the confidentiality of any information provided.

- Make it clear that participation is voluntary.

- Reassure the respondent that he or she will not be identified or be identifiable in any way. This can usually be achieved by pointing out that data are anonymized when they are entered into the computer and that analysis will be conducted at an aggregate level.

- Provide the respondent with the opportunity to ask any questions—for example, provide a contact telephone number if the introduction is in the form of a written statement, or, if in person, simply ask if the respondent has any questions.

These suggestions are also relevant to the covering letter that accompanies questionnaires (except that researchers wishing to receive responses on paper through the post need to remember to include a stamped addressed envelope!).

Rapport

It is frequently suggested that it is important for the interviewer to achieve *rapport* with the respondent. This means that very quickly a relationship must be established that encourages the respondent to want (or at least be prepared) to participate in and persist with the interview. Unless an element of rapport can be established, some respondents may initially agree to be interviewed but then decide to terminate their participation because of the length of time the interview is taking or perhaps because of the nature of the questions being asked. While this injunction essentially invites the interviewer to be friendly with respondents and to put them at ease, it is important that this quality is not stretched too far. Too much rapport may result in the interview going on too long and the respondent suddenly deciding that too much time is being spent on the activity. Also, the mood of friendliness may result in the respondent answering

questions in a way that is designed to please the interviewer. The achievement of rapport between interviewer and respondent is therefore a delicate balancing act. Moreover, it is probably somewhat easier to achieve in the context of the face-to-face interview rather than the telephone interview, since in the latter the interviewer is unable to offer obvious visual cues of friendliness like smiling or maintaining good eye contact, which are frequently regarded as conducive to gaining and maintaining rapport.

Asking questions

It was suggested earlier in the chapter that one of the aims of the structured interview is to ensure that each respondent is asked exactly the same questions. It was also pointed out that variation in the ways a question is asked is a potential source of error in survey research. The structured interview is meant to reduce the likelihood of this occurring, but it cannot guarantee that this will not occur, because there is always the possibility that interviewers will embellish or otherwise change a question when it is asked. There is considerable evidence that this occurs, even among centres of social research that have a solid reputation for being rigorous in following established methodological protocol (Bradburn and Sudman 1979). The problem with such variation in the asking of questions was outlined above: it is likely to engender variation in replies that does not reflect 'true' variation—in other words, error. Consequently, it is important for interviewers to appreciate the importance of keeping exactly to the wording of the questions they are charged with asking.

You might say: 'Does it really matter?' In other words, surely small variations to wording cannot make a significant difference to people's replies? While the impact of variation in wording obviously differs from context to context and is in any case difficult to quantify exactly, experiments in question wording suggest that even small variations in wording can exert an impact on replies (Schuman and Presser 1981). Three experiments in England conducted by Social and Community Planning Research concluded that a considerable number of interview questions are affected by interviewer variability. The researchers estimated that, for about two-thirds of the questions that were considered, interviewers contributed to less than 2 per cent of the total variation in each question (M. Collins 1997). On the face of it, this is a small amount of error, but the researchers regarded it as a cause for concern.

The key point to emerge, then, is the importance of getting across to interviewers the importance of asking questions as they are written. There are many reasons why interviewers may vary question wording, such as reluctance to ask certain questions, perhaps because of embarrassment (M. Collins 1997), but the general admonition to keep to the wording of the question needs to be constantly reinforced when interviewers are being trained. It also needs to be borne in mind for your own research.

Recording answers

An identical warning for identical reasons can be registered in connection with the recording of answers by interviewers, who should write down respondents' replies as exactly as possible. Not to do so can result in interviewers distorting respondents' answers and hence introducing error. Such errors are less likely to occur when the interviewer has merely to allocate respondents'

replies to a category, as in a closed question. This process can require a certain amount of interpretation on the part of the interviewer, but the error that is introduced is far less than when answers to open questions are being written down (Fowler and Mangione 1990).

Clear instructions

In addition to instructions about the asking of questions and the recording of answers, interviewers need instructions about their progress through an interview schedule. An example of the kind of context in which this is likely to occur is in relation to *filter questions*. Filter questions require the interviewer to ask questions of some respondents but not others. For example, the question

> How many days of on-the-job training have you received in the past 12 months?

presumes that the respondent is in employment. This option can be reflected in the fixed-choice answers that are provided, so that one of these is a 'not-in-employment' alternative. However, a better solution is not to presume anything about respondents' work behaviour but to ask them if they are currently in employment and then to filter out those respondents who are not. Tips and skills 'Instructions for interviewers in the use of a filter question' provides a simple example in connection with an imaginary study of feedback and job performance. The chief point to register about this example is that it requires clear instructions for the interviewer. If such instructions are not provided, there is the risk either that respondents will be asked inappropriate questions (which can be irritating for them) or that the interviewer will inadvertently fail to ask a question (which results in missing information).

Question order

In addition to warning interviewers about the importance of not varying the asking of questions and the recording of answers, they should be alerted to the importance of keeping to the order of asking questions. For one thing, varying the question order can result in certain questions being accidentally omitted, because the interviewer may forget to ask those that have been leapfrogged during the interview. Also, variation in question order may have an impact on replies: if some respondents have been previously asked a question that they should have been asked whereas others have not, a source of variability in the asking of questions will have been introduced and therefore a potential source of error.

TIPS AND SKILLS

Instructions for interviewers in the use of a filter question

1. Have you received any feedback concerning your job performance during the last twelve months?

   Yes ____

   No ____

   (if No proceed to question 4)

2. (*To be asked if respondent replied* Yes *to question 1*)

   Who provided you with this feedback?

   (*Ask respondent to choose the category that represents the person who most often gives them feedback and to choose one category only.*)

   Line manager ____

   HR manager ____

   Other _____ (specify)

3. How frequently do you receive feedback concerning your job performance?

   (*Ask respondent to choose the category that comes closest to his or her current experience.*)

   Once or twice a week ____

   Once or twice a month ____

   A few times a year ____

   Once or twice a year ____

4. (*To be asked if respondent replied* No *to question 1*)

   Have you received feedback concerning your job performance at any time during your employment by this organization?

   Yes ____

   No ____

Quite a lot of research has been carried out on the general issue of question order, but this has shown few, if any, consistent effects on people's responses as a result of asking questions at different points in a questionnaire or interview schedule. Different effects have been demonstrated on various occasions. There are two general lessons.

- Within a survey, question order should not be varied (unless, of course, question order is the subject of the study!).

- Researchers should be sensitive to the possible implications of the effect of early questions on answers to subsequent questions.

The following rules about question order are sometimes proposed:

- Early questions should be directly related to the topic of the research, about which the respondent has been informed. This removes the possibility that the respondent will be wondering at an early stage in the interview why he or she is being asked apparently irrelevant questions. This injunction means that personal questions about age, social background, and so on should *not* be asked at the beginning of an interview.

- As far as possible, questions that are more likely to be salient to respondents should be asked early in the interview schedule, so that their interest and attention are more likely to be secured. This suggestion may conflict with the previous one, in that questions specifically on the research topic may not be obviously salient to respondents, but it implies that as far as possible questions relating to the research topic that are more likely to grab their attention should be asked at, or close to, the start of the interview.

- Potentially embarrassing questions or ones that may be a source of anxiety should be left till later. In fact, research should be designed to ensure that as far as possible respondents are not discomfited, but it has to be acknowledged that with certain topics this effect may be unavoidable.

- With a long schedule or questionnaire, questions should be grouped into sections, since this allows a better flow than skipping from one topic to another.

- Within each group of questions, general questions should precede specific ones. Research in focus 10.4 provides an illustration of such a sequence.

- A further aspect of the rule that general questions should precede specific ones is that it has been argued that, when a specific question comes before a general one, the aspect of the general question that is covered by the specific one is discounted in the minds of respondents because they feel they have already covered it. Thus, if a question about how people feel about the amount they are paid precedes a general question about job satisfaction, there are grounds for thinking that respondents will discount the issue of pay when responding about job satisfaction.

- It is sometimes recommended that questions dealing with opinions and attitudes should precede questions to do with behaviour and knowledge. This is because it is felt that behaviour and knowledge questions are less affected by question order than questions that tap opinions and attitudes.

- During the course of an interview, it sometimes happens that a respondent provides an answer to a question that is to be asked later in the interview. Because of the possibility of a question order effect, when the interviewer arrives at the question that appears already to have been answered, it should be repeated.

However, question order effects remain one of the more frustrating areas of structured interview and questionnaire design, because of the inconsistent evidence that has beeen found and because it is difficult to formulate generalizations or rules from the evidence that does point to the existence of question order effects.

Probing

Probing is a highly problematic area for researchers employing a structured interview method. It frequently happens in interviews that respondents need help with their answers. One obvious case is where it is evident that

10.4 RESEARCH IN FOCUS
A question sequence

Here is hypothetical set of questions for an interview on the privatization of public authorities, the process by which government agencies are sold to commercial interests. It follows the recommendations of Foddy (1993: 61–2) about question order. The question order sequence is designed with a number of features in mind. It is designed to establish people's levels of knowledge of privatization before asking questions about it and to distinguish those who feel strongly about it from those who do not. The second question is open-ended, so respondents' frames of reference can be established with respect to the topic at hand. Subsequent questions are aimed at gathering data on people's views, and the strengths of those views.

1. Have you heard about the possible sale of public authorities to commercial interests?

   Yes _____ No _____

2. What do you think about the sale of public authorities?

3. Do you favour or not favour the sale of public authorities?

   Favour _____ Not favour _____

4. Why do you favour (not favour) the sale of public authorities?

5. How strongly do you feel about this?

   Very strongly _____

   Fairly strongly _____

   Not at all strongly _____

they do not understand the question—they may ask for further information, or it may be clear from what they say that they are struggling to understand the question or to provide an adequate answer. The second kind of situation the interviewer faces is when the respondent does not provide a sufficiently complete answer and must be probed for more information. The problem in either situation is obvious: the interviewer's intervention may influence the respondent and the nature of interviewers' interventions may differ. A potential source of variability in respondents' replies that does not reflect 'true' variation is introduced—that is, error.

Some general tactics regarding probes are as follows:

- If further information is required, usually in the context of an open-ended question, standardized probes can be employed, such as 'Could you say a little more about that?' or 'Are there any other reasons why you think that?' or simply 'Mmmm … ?' Probes have to be handled carefully. If they are not introduced in a consistent way or if they suggest a particular kind of answer to the interviewee, error will increase.

- If the problem is that when presented with a closed question the respondent replies in a way that does not allow the interviewee to select one of the pre-designed answers, the interviewer should repeat the fixed-choice alternatives and make it apparent that the answer needs to be chosen from the ones that have been provided.

- If the interviewer needs to know about something that requires quantification, such as the number of visits to banks in the last four weeks or the number of banks with which the respondent has accounts, but the respondent resists this by answering in general terms ('quite often' or 'I usually go to the bank every week'), the interviewer needs to persist with securing a number from the respondent. This will usually entail repeating the question. The interviewer should not try to second guess a figure on the basis of the respondent's reply and then suggest that figure to him or her, since the latter may be unwilling to demur from the interviewer's suggested figure.

Prompting

Prompting occurs when the interviewer suggests a possible answer to a question to the respondent. The key prerequisite here is that all respondents receive the same prompts. All closed questions entail standardized prompting, because the respondent is provided with a list of possible answers from which to choose. An unacceptable approach to prompting would be to ask an open question and to suggest possible answers only to some respondents, such as those who appear to be struggling to think of an appropriate reply.

During the course of a face-to-face interview, there are several circumstances in which it will be better for the interviewer to use 'show cards' rather than rely on reading out a series of fixed-choice alternatives. Show cards (sometimes called 'flash cards') display all the answers from which the respondent is to choose and are handed to the respondent at different points of the interview. Three kinds of context in which it might be preferable to employ show cards, rather than to read out the entire set of possible answers are as follows:

- There may be a very long list of possible answers. For example, respondents may be asked which daily newspaper they each read most frequently. To read out a list of newspapers would be tedious and it is probably better to hand the respondent a list of newspapers from which to choose.

- Sometimes, during the course of interviews, respondents are presented with a group of questions to which the same possible answers are attached. An example of this approach is Likert scaling, which is commonly used to measure attitudes. A typical strategy entails providing respondents with a series of statements and asking them how far they agree or disagree with the statements (see Chapter 8). These are often referred to as *items* rather than as *questions*, since, strictly speaking, the respondent is not being asked a question. An example was provided in Research in focus 8.3. It would be excruciatingly dull to read out all five possible answers 12 times. Also, it may be expecting too much of respondents if the interviewer reads out the answers once and then requires respondents to keep the possible answers in their heads for the entire batch of questions to which they apply. A show card that can be used for the entire batch and to which respondents can constantly refer is an obvious solution. As was mentioned in Research in focus 8.3, most Likert scales of this kind comprise five levels of agreement/disagreement and it is this conventional approach that is illustrated in Tips and skills 'A show card'.

- Some people are not keen to divulge personal details such as their age or their income. One way of neutralizing the impact of such questioning is to present respondents with age or income bands with a letter or number attached to each band. They can then be asked to say which letter applies to them (see Tips and skills 'Another show card'). This procedure will obviously not be appropriate if the research requires *exact* ages or incomes.

TIPS AND SKILLS
A show card

Card 6

Strongly agree

Agree

Undecided

Disagree

Strongly disagree

TIPS AND SKILLS
Another show card

Card 11

(a) Below 20

(b) 20–29

(c) 30–39

(d) 40–49

(e) 50–59

(f) 60–69

(g) 70 and over

Leaving the interview

Do not forget common courtesies such as thanking respondents for giving up their time. However, the period immediately after the interview is one in which some care is necessary, in that sometimes respondents try to engage the interviewer in a discussion about the purpose of the interview. Interviewers should resist elaboration beyond their standard statement, because respondents may communicate what they are told to others, which may bias the findings.

Training and supervision

On several occasions, reference has been made to the need for interviewers to be trained. The standard texts on survey research and on interviewing practice tend to be replete with advice on how best to train interviewers. Such advice is typically directed at contexts in which a

researcher hires an interviewer to conduct many or even all the interviews. It also has considerable importance in research in which several interviewers (who may be either collaborators or hired interviewers) are involved in a study, since the risk of interviewer variability in the asking of questions needs to be avoided.

For many readers of this book who are planning to do research, such situations are unlikely to be relevant, because they will be 'lone' researchers. You may be doing an undergraduate dissertation, or an exercise for a research methods course, or you may be a postgraduate conducting research for a Master's dissertation or for a PhD thesis. Most people in such a situation will not have the luxury of being able to hire a researcher to do any interviewing (though you may be able to find someone to help you a little). When interviewing on your own, you must train yourself to follow the procedures and advice provided above. This is a very different situation from a large research institute or market research agency, which relies on an army of hired interviewers who carry out the interviews. Whenever people other than the lead researcher are involved in interviewing, they will need training and supervision in the following areas:

- contacting prospective respondents and providing an introduction to the study;
- reading out questions as written and following instructions in the interview schedule (for example, in connection with filter questions);
- using appropriate styles of probing;
- recording exactly what is said;
- maintaining an interview style that does not bias respondents' answers.

Fowler (1993) cites evidence that suggests that training of less than one full day rarely creates good interviewers.

Supervision of interviewers in relation to these issues can be achieved in the following ways:

- checking individual interviewers' response rates;
- making audio recordings of at least a sample of interviews;
- examining completed schedules to determine whether any questions are being left out or if they are not being completed properly;
- call-backs on a sample of respondents (usually around 10 per cent) to determine whether or not they were interviewed and to ask about the interviewers' conduct.

Other approaches to structured interviewing

A number of other methods or techniques are used in business research as part of either the structured or the semi-structured interview. Three main types will be discussed in this section:

- the critical incident method;
- projective methods, pictorial methods, and photo-elicitation;
- the verbal protocol approach.

We have grouped these three methods together here because they can form part of a structured interview. However, they can also form part of a semi-structured interview (see Chapter 20) in a qualitative investigation, and so to an extent they cut across the quantitative/ qualitative divide (see Chapter 26). They are sometimes used as one part of an interview, in combination with other questions that form part of a more conventional interview schedule; in other research designs they form the basis for the entire interview. A further use of these methods is to check findings from more conventional quantitative approaches such as structured interviews or questionnaire surveys.

The critical incident method

The critical incident method involves asking respondents to describe *critical incidents*, which are defined very broadly by Flanagan (1954) as any observable human activity where the consequences are sufficiently clear as to leave the observer with a definite idea as to their likely effects. The term is derived from the analysis of near-disaster situations, where a version of the technique can be used to build up a picture of the events that contribute to a potential disaster and to develop a plan of action for dealing with them. The most common use of the critical incident method involves interviewing respondents about particular types of event or behaviour in order to develop an understanding of their sequence and their significance to the individual.

One of the earliest and most well-known illustrations of this method in business research is the study by Herzberg et al. (1959), which was mentioned in Chapter 9. The authors explain: 'We decided to ask people to tell us stories about times when they felt exceptionally good or bad about their jobs. We decided that from these stories we could discover the kinds of situations leading to negative or positive attitudes toward the job and the effects of these attitudes' (1959: 17). Their initial interview strategy was followed up by a series of probe questions that filled in missing information in the spontaneously told accounts. Content analysis (see Chapter 13) was then used to focus on exploring the essential features of the critical incident in order to reveal the values that they reflected. A more recent example of the use of the critical incident method is found in the study of managerial effectiveness described in Research in focus 10.5.

An example of the critical incident method

Chai et al. (2016) used the critical incident technique in interviews with Korean managerial and non-managerial employees. They interviewed 45 respondents across a number of large Korean organizations. Their aim was to develop an understanding of what was regarded as effective, and ineffective, management and leadership in the Korean context. Respondents were asked to identify four or more critical incidents which involved effective management and leadership and four or more which involved ineffective management and leadership. The time period was limited to six months before the interview. Respondents were asked three questions about each incident:

1. What was the background situation, circumstance, or context that led up to the critical incident you have in mind?

2. What exactly did the manager you observed do/say or not do/say, and/or in what way did s/he do/not do it or say/not say it that was either effective or ineffective?

3. What was the specific outcome of the critical incident that you have described, and on reflection why do you perceive this to be an example of effective or ineffective managerial behavior?

(Chai et al. 2016: 796)

The kinds of incidents which were recalled as indicating effective management included managers publicly praising staff and seeking to resolve problems for staff, while ineffective management was illustrated by examples including trying to force employees to do as they were told and setting overly ambitious targets for teams.

Finally, although we have introduced the critical incident method here in Part Two of the book, which deals with quantitative research, we should point out that this method is often used as part of a qualitative research investigation. An example of this is the study of small business owner-managers by Blackburn and Stokes (2000) (see Research in focus 21.3). In this instance, respondents were asked to recall a situation that had arisen in the previous two years in which they had lost a major customer and to explain what had happened and how they had coped with it. Blackburn and Stokes's analysis of the data was primarily qualitative, relying on the use of themes illustrated by the inclusion of direct quotes from respondents.

Projective methods, pictorial methods, and photo-elicitation

Projective methods classically involve the presentation of ambiguous stimuli to individuals, and responses

Using the critical incident method in a student research project

Tom followed the advice of his supervisor and used the critical incident technique when he was interviewing call centre workers about wellbeing and the experience of working in a call centre. He explained:

I did use critical incident technique in the interview to try and get people to give an example of a time when things have gone particularly well at work or particularly badly. It was quite a useful tool to get people to talk in an interesting way really about their work experience. And sometimes it wasn't really necessary because they would give lots of examples anyway, but it was quite a useful prompt to get people to be more specific and give examples of the sort of stuff that their work life was like.

are interpreted by the researcher to reveal underlying characteristics of the individual concerned. A common example is the Rorschach inkblot test, where respondents are asked to describe random inkblots. Analysis relies on expert psychological interpretation of the way that respondents have described the inkblots, and this is suggested to be indicative of their dominant channels of thinking. Another form of projective analysis involves the 'sentence completion test', where the individual is asked to complete a number of unfinished sentences; this technique has been used in the context of recruitment and selection, often as an assessment centre exercise.

One of the best-known examples of the use of projective techniques in management research involves the study by McClelland (1961) of leadership and the need for individual achievement. Informed by experimental psychology and the psychoanalytic insights of Freud, McClelland's study first involved stimulating the achievement motive in a group of subjects. He then sought to elicit their 'spontaneous thoughts' and fantasies in order to determine the effect of achievement motivation. The subjects were male college students who were told that they were going to be tested to determine their intelligence and leadership ability; it was assumed that this would arouse a desire in the subjects to do well. After the 'tests' had been completed, subjects were asked to write short five-minute stories suggested by pictures that flashed onto a screen for a few seconds. 'The pictures represented a variety of life situations centering particularly around work' (1961:

40). The stories were compared with those that had been written by a control group under normal conditions. The experimental group was found to refer more often in their stories to ideas related to achievement. From this, McClelland concluded that, if someone 'in writing his stories consistently uses achievement-related ideas of the same kind as those elicited in everyone under achievement "pressure," then he would appear to be someone with a "bias," a "concern," or a "need" for achievement' (1961: 43). This led him to develop a score for the need for achievement, defined as the number of achievement-related ideas in stories written by an individual under normal conditions.

A more recent example of projective methods can also be found in marketing research (see Research in focus 10.6). The authors of this study sought to investigate the influence of companies' corporate social responsibility on consumers' views of those companies and purchasing intentions. However, the use of projective methods is relatively uncommon in business research. They have largely been superseded by the use of visual techniques to stimulate creative thinking and problem solving, and to explore feelings, emotions, and values. For example, Stiles (2004) asked members of UK and North American business schools to express how they saw their organization's identity by drawing pictures (see Research in focus 10.7). The use of photo-elicitation can also be seen as an adaptation of projective methods (see Key concept 10.8 for an explanation and Research in focus 10.9 for an example).

10.6 RESEARCH IN FOCUS
Using projective methods in consumer research

McEachern (2015) was interested in the extent to which corporate citizenship behaviour by private companies (for example, voluntary philanthropic activity) influenced consumer views of those companies. More specifically, he was interested in levels of awareness by consumers and the nature and extent of their reactions to corporate citizenship behaviour. His study focused on the chocolate manufacturing industry and the production of 'Fairtrade' chocolate (using cocoa and other products which have been grown, processed, and transported ethically) and involved data collection from UK consumers. The study collected data using a number of techniques; the projective techniques were used as part of focus group interviews. Members of the groups were presented with magazines and chocolate wrappers and asked to construct collages in response to one of two questions: 'What does Fairtrade mean to you?' and 'Illustrate how you feel about leading, conventional chocolate brands becoming Fairtrade'. The intention was to provide participants with the opportunity to express their feelings on these issues without being influenced by the researcher. After the collages were constructed, interviews were conducted about them. McEachern's findings indicated that while consumers were aware of Fairtrade initiatives in the chocolate industry and while they approved of them, such initiatives had limited impact on decisions about which products to purchase.

10.7 RESEARCH IN FOCUS
Using pictorial exercises in a study of business school identity

Stiles (2004) used pictorial methods in a study of strategy in UK and North American business schools. The first stage of the research involved asking individual interviewees to imagine their organization as having a personality and then asking them to draw a picture of what that personality looks like. The second stage of the research involved showing these drawings to members of a focus group (see Chapter 21), who were invited to reach a consensus in choosing five pictures, ranging from an unfavourable depiction of the organization, to neutral, through to a favourable one. 'The group then produces a composite *free-drawn personality image* of its own' (2004: 130). The focus group discussion was video-recorded and transcribed. The importance of the pictures stems from the discussion that respondents had around their selection decisions, which revealed insights into the way academics perceived the management styles associated with their organizations and leaders. Stiles notes that, although this study was conducted in a business school setting, it could equally be applied in relation to a variety of other organizational settings. Stiles concludes that the pictorial exercises revealed constructs that were not identified using verbal research instruments, thus introducing the possibility that images are useful in revealing more latent perceptions.

10.8 KEY CONCEPT
What is photo-elicitation?

This method involves integrating photographs into the interview by asking the respondent questions about photographs that the researcher or the respondent has taken of the research setting. Respondents are asked to reflect, explain, and comment on the meaning of the objects in the photograph, the events that are taking place, or the emotions they associate with them. Photographs can provide a point of reference for the discussion and can help to move the interview from 'the concrete (a cataloguing of the objects in the photograph) to the socially abstract (what the objects in the photograph mean to the individual being interviewed)' (Harper 1986: 25). Harper suggests that the most useful photographs tend to be those that are visually arresting, because they are more likely to get the respondent's attention and provoke a response.

10.9 RESEARCH IN FOCUS
Using photo-elicitation to study tourist behaviour

Tonge et al. (2013) used photo-elicitation to study the reasons that tourists become attached to particular locations and visit them repeatedly, even when they are often distant and difficult to reach. Their study focused on visitors to Ningaloo Reef, in remote north-western Australia, and involved providing respondents (all of whom were repeat visitors to the reef) with digital cameras and asking them to take photographs which they felt summed up what the location meant to them and why they returned to it. The researchers uploaded the photographs to laptops and then conducted interviews with the participants while they looked at the photos they had taken. This method was chosen not just because it is an effective way of eliciting useful responses during interviews, but also because it involved respondents producing data while engaging in a familiar holiday activity—taking photographs.

The verbal protocol approach

The verbal protocol approach builds on the work of Newell and Simon (1972) in the area of human problem solving and has since been used in relation to a number of topics that are relevant to business researchers. The approach involves asking respondents to 'think aloud' while they are performing a task. The idea is to elicit the respondent's thought processes while he or she is making a decision or judgement or solving a problem. The subject's account of what he or she is doing and why is usually audio-recorded and transcribed and then content analysed (a process discussed in Chapter 13 of this book) using a coding scheme to discern different categories of thinking. An interesting example of the use of verbal protocol analysis can be found in a study by Ramiah and Banks (2015), who wanted to explore how decisions were made in the resolution of labour disputes (see Research in focus 10.10).

10.10 RESEARCH IN FOCUS
A study using the verbal protocol method

In their study of decision-making in labour disputes, Ramiah and Banks (2015) wished to understand processes of decision-making by actors involved in dispute resolution. In particular, they sought to make sense of the analytic processes involved in making decisions in real time while working to resolve disputes. For the study, 50 civil servants who worked in the Department of Labour in Malaysia were presented with realistic scenarios presenting labour disputes (all were based on actual disputes) which were characterized by complexity and uncertainty. These civil servants were responsible in their jobs for resolving disputes in ways which were intended to balance the rights and responsibilities of workers and employers. For the purposes of the study, they were divided into expert and novice groups based on their length of service and the extent of experience which they had in dealing with disputes. Participants had to analyse the scenarios and decide how to deal with them, while thinking aloud. The study found that experienced participants tended to construct arguments as they worked through the decision, rather than framing their decision as a narrative. The more experienced participants also tended to construct clear links between the evidence presented in the case and specific decisions at each stage of the process, which appeared to lead to better decisions. The use of the verbal protocol method allowed Ramiah and Banks to develop an understanding of the processes of decision-making which was more naturalistic than if they had simply asked respondents a series of questions about how they performed their roles at work.

Problems with structured interviewing

While the structured interview is a commonly used method of business research, certain problems associated with it have been identified over the years. These problems are not necessarily unique to the structured interview, in that they can sometimes be attributed to kindred methods, such as the self-completion questionnaire in survey research or even semi-structured interviewing in qualitative research. However, it is common for the structured interview to be a focus for the identification of certain limitations that are briefly examined below.

Characteristics of interviewers

There is evidence that interviewers' attributes can have an impact on respondents' replies, but, unfortunately, the literature on this issue does not lend itself to definitive generalizations. In large part, this ambiguity in the broader implications of experiments relating to the effects of interviewer characteristics is due to several problems, such as: the problem of disentangling the effects of interviewers' different attributes from each other (ethnicity, gender, socio-economic status); the interaction between the characteristics of interviewers and the characteristics of respondents; and the interaction between any effects observed and the topic of the interview. Nonetheless, there is undoubtedly some evidence that effects due to characteristics of interviewers can be discerned.

The ethnicity of interviewers is one area that has attracted some attention. Schuman and Presser (1981) cite a study that asked respondents to nominate two or three of their favourite actors or entertainers. Respondents were much more likely to mention African-American actors or entertainers when interviewed by African-American interviewers. Schuman and Converse (1971) interviewed 619 African-American Detroiters shortly after Martin Luther King's assassination in 1968. The researchers found significant response differences depending on whether the interviewers were also African-American in around one-quarter of the questions asked.

Although this proportion is quite striking, the fact that the majority of questions appear to have been largely unaffected does not give rise to a great deal of confidence that a consistent biasing factor is being uncovered. Similarly inconclusive findings tend to occur in relation to experiments with other sets of characteristics of interviewers. These remarks are not meant to play down the potential significance of interviewers' characteristics for measurement error, but to draw attention to the limitations of drawing conclusive inferences about the evidence. All that needs to be registered at this juncture is that almost certainly the characteristics of interviewers do have an impact on respondents' replies, but that the extent and nature of the impact are not clear and are likely to vary from context to context.

Response sets

Some writers have suggested that the structured interview is particularly prone to the operation among respondents of what Webb et al. (1966) call 'response sets', which they define as 'irrelevant but lawful sources of variance' (1966: 19). This form of response bias is especially relevant to multiple-indicator measure (see Chapter 8), where respondents reply to a battery of related questions or items, of the kind found in a Likert scale (see Research in focus 8.3). The idea of a response set implies that people respond to the series of questions in a consistent way but one that is irrelevant to the concept being measured. Two of the most prominent types of response set are known as the 'acquiescence' (also known as the 'yeasaying' and 'naysaying') effect, and the 'social desirability' effect.

Acquiescence

Acquiescence refers to a tendency for some people consistently to agree or disagree with a set of questions or items. Imagine respondents who replied to all the items in Research in focus 8.3 stating that they believed they were all unethical (scale = 5) and judging that they and their peers infrequently acted in the way implied by the statement (scale = 1). The problem with this multiple-item measure is that none of the item measure statements is written in a way that implies an opposite stance. In other words, there are no items that are ethical or likely to be engaged in frequently by many ethically responsible people. This could be seen as a potential source of bias in this multiple-item measure. A wording that would imply an opposite stance might be 'being prepared to take responsibility for errors' or 'refusing to accept gifts/favours in exchange for preferential treatment'. The inclusion of some items in this form would help to weed out those respondents who were replying within the framework of an acquiescence response set.

Social desirability bias

The social desirability effect refers to evidence that some respondents' answers to questions are related to their perception of the social desirability of those answers. An answer that is perceived to be socially desirable is more likely to be endorsed than one that is not. This phenomenon has been demonstrated in studies of ethical behaviour, managerial decision-making, and attitudes towards entrepreneurs (see Research in focus 10.11). In order to try to prevent social desirability bias, Terence Jackson (2001) framed questions in a way that was intended to enable the respondents to distance themselves from their responses, by imagining what a peer might do rather than having to state what they would do. It was expected that this would reduce the likelihood that individuals would respond in a way that they anticipated would be more acceptable. However, Steenkamp et al. (2010) have proposed that it is crucial to distinguish between social desirability bias that is conscious and that which is unconscious. The underlying motives and psychological processes associated with each are likely to differ, so that it is not obvious whether a procedure like that employed in Research in focus 10.11 applies to both or just one of the two forms.

In so far as these forms of response error go undetected, they represent sources of error in the measurement of concepts. However, while some writers have proposed outright condemnation of social research on the basis of evidence of response sets (e.g. Phillips 1973), it is

10.11 RESEARCH IN FOCUS
A study of the effects of social desirability bias

Ogbulu and Singh (2013) conducted a study on entrepreneurship by African Americans. As part of the study, they sought to measure social desirability bias and its impact on results from interviews on consumer perceptions of 'black' and 'white' (we note that this terminology is potentially problematic, but we are using the terms which the authors of the article use) entrepreneurs in the USA. The authors summarize their agenda as follows:

> The overarching hypothesis that guided the present research was that respondent data would differ based on both the race of the respondent and the race of the data collector when asked about racially different entrepreneurs and their firms. We focused on three areas of inquiry: attitudes toward entrepreneurs, perceptions of legitimacy and patronage intentions.

> (Ogbulu and Singh 2013: 4)

The study involved the administration of a structured questionnaire to a sample of 843 respondents, both black and white. The questionnaires were administered by both black and white data collectors.

The questionnaire included a series of questions about a fictional venture (a restaurant) which was being established in the city where data were collected. All the details in the questionnaires were the same except that one set of questionnaires included a photograph of a black male as the fictional entrepreneur while the other included a photograph of a white male. The biographical details of the fictional entrepreneur were identical and no mention of ethnic background was provided. Likert scale items were used to capture respondent attitudes to the entrepreneur, their opinion of the legitimacy of the venture, and their likelihood of patronizing the restaurant.

The results showed that black respondents did not rate the black entrepreneur more favourably or as more legitimate, but reported a greater likelihood of patronizing his restaurant. White respondents reported more favourable perceptions, higher legitimacy, and more likelihood of patronizing the restaurant if it were being established by a black entrepreneur. Significantly for our understanding of social desirability bias, white respondents responded more favourably to the black entrepreneur and indicated higher likelihood to patronize the restaurant when the questionnaire was administered by a black data collector than if it was administered by a white data collector. The researchers conclude that this provides evidence that social desirability bias is likely to influence how people respond to questions about issues of race and ethnicity and that this may generate misleading results in research on African-American entrepreneurs. This highlights the need to design studies and analyse data in ways which take account of this possible effect.

important not to get carried away with such findings. We cannot be sure how prevalent these effects are, and to some extent awareness of them has led to measures to limit their impact on data (for example, by weeding out cases obviously affected by them) or by instructing interviewers to limit the possible impact of the social desirability effect by not becoming overly friendly with respondents and by not being judgemental about their replies.

The problem of meaning

A critique of survey interview data and findings gleaned from similar techniques was developed by social scientists influenced by phenomenological and other interpretivist ideas of the kinds touched on in Chapter 2 (Cicourel 1964, 1982; Filmer et al. 1972; Briggs 1986; Mishler 1986). This critique revolves around what is often referred to in a shorthand way as the 'problem of meaning'. The kernel of the argument is that when humans communicate they do so in a way that not only draws on commonly held meanings but also simultaneously creates meanings. 'Meaning' in this sense is something that is worked at and achieved—it is not simply pre-given. Allusions to the problem of meaning in structured interviewing draw attention to the notion that survey researchers presume that interviewer and respondent share the same meanings of terms employed in the interview questions and answers. In fact, the problem of meaning implies that the possibility that interviewer and respondent may not be sharing the same meaning systems, and may hence imply different things in their use of words, is simply sidestepped in structured interview research. The problem of meaning is resolved by ignoring it.

KEY POINTS

- The structured interview is a research instrument that is used to standardize the asking of questions and often the recording of answers in order to keep interviewer-related error to a minimum.

- The structured interview can be administered in person, over the telephone, or via computer software such as Skype.

- It is important to keep to the wording and order of questions when conducting social survey research by structured interview.

- While there is some evidence that interviewers' characteristics can influence respondents' replies, the findings of experiments on this issue are somewhat equivocal.

- Response sets can be damaging to data derived from structured interviews, and steps need to be taken to identify respondents exhibiting them.

QUESTIONS FOR REVIEW

The structured interview

- Why is it important in interviewing for survey research to keep interviewer variability to a minimum?

- How successful is the structured interview in reducing interviewer variability?

- Why might a survey researcher prefer to use a structured rather than an unstructured interview approach for gathering data?

- Why do structured interview schedules typically include mainly closed questions?

Interview contexts

- Are there any circumstances in which it might be preferable to conduct structured interviews with more than one interviewer?

- 'Given the lower cost of telephone interviews as against personal interviews, the former are generally preferable.' Discuss.

Conducting interviews

- Prepare an opening statement for interviews to be conducted for a study of manual workers in a firm, in which access has already been achieved.

- To what extent is rapport an important ingredient of structured interviewing?

- How strong is the evidence that question order can significantly affect answers?

- How strong is the evidence that interviewers' characteristics can significantly affect answers?

- What is the difference between probing and prompting? How important are they and what dangers come with their use?

Other approaches to structured interviewing

- What is the critical incident method and how has it been applied in business research?

- Make a list of the projective methods that could be used in a study of organizational culture and consider how they might be applied.

Problems with structured interviewing

- What are response sets and why are they potentially important?

ONLINE RESOURCES
www.oup.com/uk/brm5e/

Visit the Interactive Research Guide that accompanies this book to complete an exercise in structured interviewing.

SELF-COMPLETION QUESTIONNAIRES

CHAPTER OUTLINE

Questionnaires that are completed by respondents themselves are one of the main instruments for gathering data using a social survey design, along with the structured interview that was covered in Chapter 10. The most common form was for a long time the mail or postal questionnaire, but in recent years this form of delivery has increasingly been displaced by email and online surveys. This chapter explores:

* the advantages and disadvantages of the questionnaire in comparison to the structured interview;

* how to address the potential problem of poor response rates, which is often a feature of postal, email, and online surveys;

* how questionnaires should be designed in order to make answering easier for respondents and less prone to error;

* some specific features of email and web-based surveys and their relative advantages and disadvantages;

* the use of diaries as a form of self-completion questionnaire.

Introduction

In a very real sense, the bulk of the previous chapter was about questionnaires. The structured interview is in many, if not most, respects a questionnaire that is administered by an interviewer. However, there is a tendency, which borders on a convention, to reserve the term 'questionnaire' for contexts in which a battery of usually closed questions is completed by respondents themselves.

Different kinds of self-completion questionnaires

The *self-completion questionnaire* is sometimes referred to as a self-administered questionnaire. The former term will be followed in this book. With a self-completion questionnaire, respondents answer questions by completing the questionnaire themselves. As a method, the self-completion questionnaire can come in several forms. Historically, the most prominent of these forms has been the mail or postal questionnaire, whereby, as its name implies, a questionnaire is sent through the post to the respondent. The latter, following completion of the questionnaire, is usually asked to return it by post; an alternative form of return is when respondents are requested to deposit their completed questionnaires in a certain location, such as a box in a supervisor's office in a firm, or on the top of a cashier's desk in a restaurant or shop. More recently, email or online delivery and completion of questionnaires has become much more common (these modes of delivery and completion are discussed in detail later in this chapter). The self-completion questionnaire may also have other forms of administration, such as when a researcher hands out questionnaires to all students in a class and collects them back after they have been completed. A variant of this is the 'drop-off and collect' approach that was used in a study of cardholders' satisfaction with loyalty programmes in Malaysia. Omar et al. (2011) delivered questionnaires to employees in several organizations. Each respondent was requested to select a loyalty programme of which he or she was a member and to answer questions about that programme. The questionnaires were then collected from the respondents. A high response rate of 87 per cent was achieved. 'Self-completion questionnaire' therefore covers more than postal or digital surveys, though it is probably true to say that the latter are the most prominent forms of the self-completion questionnaire.

In the discussion that follows, when points apply to all forms of self-completion questionnaire, this term will be employed. When points apply specifically or exclusively to postal, email, or online questionnaires, this will be specified. Because there are some quite specific issues concerning email and online surveys, we consider them separately and in more depth later in the chapter. We also consider a variant of the self-completion questionnaire when we discuss diaries at the end of the chapter.

Evaluating the self-completion questionnaire in relation to the structured interview

In many ways, the self-completion questionnaire and the structured interview are very similar methods of business research, and some studies use both (see Research in focus 11.1). The obvious difference between the two methods is that, with the self-completion questionnaire, there is no interviewer to ask the questions; instead, respondents must read each question themselves and answer the questions themselves. Beyond this obvious, but central, difference, they are remarkably similar. However, because there is no interviewer in the administration of the self-completion questionnaire, the research instrument must be especially easy to follow and its questions must be particularly easy to answer. After all, respondents cannot be trained in the way interviewers can be; nor do they know their way around a research instrument in the way a 'lone researcher' might.

11.1 RESEARCH IN FOCUS
Combining the use of structured interviews with self-completion questionnaires

Structured interviews can be used in conjunction with self-completion questionnaires to gain understanding of the perspectives of different groups of participants. The 2015 Study of Australian Leadership (SAL) (see Research in focus 3.13) is an example of a project that used different research methods to reach different categories of respondent. Structured interviews with senior managers were conducted by telephone, by a team of interviewers employing CATI technology. Surveys of frontline managers and non-managerial employees were administered by sending emails containing a link to an online self-completion survey (with the option of a paper survey if employees preferred that).

The SAL was designed to combine the views of different groups of participants in order to overcome the limitations and partiality of any one group of respondents. The combined use of structured interviews and self-completion questionnaires together enabled this aim to be achieved, despite the vast scale of the project.

Thus, self-completion questionnaires, as compared to structured interviews, tend to:

- have fewer open questions, since closed ones tend to be easier to answer;
- have easy-to-follow designs to minimize the risk that the respondent will fail to follow filter questions or will inadvertently omit a question;
- be shorter, to reduce the risk of 'respondent fatigue', since it is manifestly easier for a respondent who becomes tired of answering questions in a long questionnaire to consign it to a waste paper bin, or click away from it, than it is for a subject being interviewed to terminate the interview.

Advantages of the self-completion questionnaire over the structured interview

Cheaper to administer

Interviewing can be expensive. The cheapness of the self-completion questionnaire is especially advantageous if you have a sample that is geographically widely dispersed. When this is the case, a postal or online questionnaire will be much cheaper, because of the time and cost of travel for interviewers. This advantage is obviously less pronounced with telephone interviews, because of the lower costs of telephone charges relative to travel and time spent travelling. But, even in comparison to telephone interviewing, postal and online questionnaires enjoy cost advantages because they do not involve interviewers.

Quicker to administer

Self-completion questionnaires can be distributed in very large quantities at the same time. For example, a thousand questionnaires can be sent out by post in one batch (and virtually an unlimited number via email), but, even with a team of interviewers, it would take a long time to conduct personal interviews with a sample of one thousand respondents. However, it is important to bear in mind that the questionnaires do not all come back immediately and that they may take several weeks to be completed. Also, there is invariably a need to send out follow-up letters or emails and/or questionnaires to those who fail to complete them initially, an issue that will be returned to below.

Absence of interviewer effects

It was noted in Chapter 10 that various studies have demonstrated that characteristics of interviewers (and respondents) may affect the answers that people give. While the findings from this research are somewhat equivocal in their implications, it has been suggested that such characteristics as ethnicity, gender, and the social background of interviewers may combine to bias the answers that respondents provide. Obviously, since there is no interviewer present when a self-completion questionnaire is being completed, interviewer effects are eliminated. However, this advantage probably should be regarded fairly cautiously, since few consistent patterns have emerged over the years from research to suggest what kinds of interviewer characteristics produce a bias in answers. Probably of greater importance is the tendency for respondents to be more likely to exhibit social desirability bias when an interviewer is present.

No interviewer variability

Self-completion questionnaires do not suffer from the problem of interviewers asking questions in a different order or in different ways.

Convenience for respondents

Self-completion questionnaires are more convenient for respondents, because they can complete a questionnaire when they want and at the speed that they want to go.

Disadvantages of the self-completion questionnaire in comparison to the structured interview

Cannot prompt

There is no one present to help respondents if they are having difficulty answering a question. It is always important to ensure that the questions that are asked are clear and unambiguous, but this is especially so with the self-completion questionnaire, since there is no interviewer to help respondents with questions they find difficult to understand and hence to answer. Also, great attention must be paid to ensure that the questionnaire is easy to complete; otherwise questions will be inadvertently omitted if instructions are unclear.

Cannot probe

There is no opportunity to probe respondents to elaborate an answer. Probing can be very important when open-ended questions are being asked. Interviewers are often trained to get more from respondents. However, this problem largely applies to open questions, which are not used a great deal in self-completion questionnaire research.

Cannot ask many questions that are not salient to respondents

Respondents are more likely than in interviews to become tired of answering questions that are not very salient to them, and that they are likely to perceive as boring. Because of the risk of a questionnaire being abandoned by a respondent for this reason, it is important to avoid including many non-salient questions in a self-completion questionnaire. However, this point suggests that, when a research issue *is* salient to the respondent, a high response rate is feasible (Altschuld and Lower 1984). This means that, when questions are likely to be salient to the respondents, the self-completion questionnaire may be a good choice for researchers, especially when the much lower cost is borne in mind.

Difficulty of asking other kinds of question

In addition to the problem of asking many questions that are not salient to respondents, as previously suggested, it is also important to avoid asking more than a very small number of open questions (because respondents frequently do not want to write a lot). Questions with complex structures, such as filters, should be avoided as far as possible (because respondents often find them difficult to follow), although this problem can be largely eliminated in online surveys.

Questionnaire can be read as a whole

Respondents can read the whole questionnaire before answering the first question. When this occurs, none of the questions asked is truly independent of the others. It also means that you cannot be sure that questions have been answered in the correct order. It also means that the problems of question order effects, of the kind discussed in Chapter 10, may occur.

Do not know who answers

With postal and online questionnaires, you can never be sure that the right person has answered the questionnaire. If a questionnaire is sent to a certain person in a household, it may be that someone else in that household completes the questionnaire. It is also impossible to have any control over the intrusion of non-respondents (such as other members of a household) in the answering of questions. Similarly, if a questionnaire is sent to a manager in a firm, the task may simply be delegated to someone else. This advantage of the structured interview over the postal questionnaire does not apply when the former is administered by telephone, since the same problem is present.

Cannot collect additional data

With an interview, interviewers might be asked to collect snippets of information about the workplace, firm, manager, or whatever. This is not going to be possible with a postal or online questionnaire, but if self-completion questionnaires are handed out in an organization, it is more feasible to collect such additional data.

Difficult to ask a lot of questions

As signalled above, because of the possibility of 'respondent fatigue', long questionnaires are rarely feasible. Excessive length may even result in a greater tendency for questionnaires not to be answered in the first place, since they can be daunting.

Not appropriate for some kinds of respondent

Respondents whose literacy is limited are likely to experience difficulties in completing a questionnaire, as are those who do not speak the language in which the study is being conducted. In the case of the former problem, if a face-to-face interview is being conducted the literacy of the respondents is less important as communication is verbal and questions can be explained. In the case of the latter problem, researchers who need to collect data from speakers of other languages routinely deal with this issue by having questionnaires translated into the relevant language(s) and then responses translated back to the language of the study for checking (as in Research in focus 11.2). Although this practice is common, some scholars have argued that the process is problematic and can lead to questionable results because equivalent terms may have different meanings in different contexts and it may not be possible to translate questionnaires meaningfully (Chidlow et al. 2014).

Greater risk of missing data

Partially answered questionnaires are more likely, because of a lack of prompting or supervision, than partially completed interviews. It is also easier for respondents actively to decide not to answer a question when on their own than when being asked by an interviewer. Questions that appear boring or irrelevant to the respondent may be especially likely to be skipped. If questions are not answered, this creates a problem of missing data for the variables that are created.

Lower response rates

One of the most damaging limitations is that surveys by postal, email, and online questionnaire typically result in lower response rates (see Key concept 9.3) than comparable interview-based studies. The significance of a response rate is that, unless it can be proven that those who do not participate do not differ from those who do, there is likely to be the risk of bias. In other words, if, as is likely, there are differences between participants and refusals, it is probable that the findings relating to the sample will be affected. If a response rate is low, it seems likely that the risk of bias in the findings will be greater.

Steps to improve response rates to postal and online questionnaires

Because postal and online questionnaire surveys tend to generate lower response rates than comparable structured interview surveys, with implications for the validity of findings, a great deal of thought and research has gone into ways of improving survey response. The methods for improving responses to online surveys are much the same as those for postal surveys, although the method of application is likely to vary, eg. a follow-up letter versus a follow-up email. The following steps are frequently suggested.

- Write a good covering letter or email explaining the reasons for the research, why it is important, and why the recipient has been selected; mention sponsorship if any, and provide guarantees of confidentiality. The advice provided in Tips and skills 'Topics and issues to include in an introductory statement' (Chapter 10), on composing a letter or email to send out in advance of a respondent being asked to be interviewed, can also be followed to good effect when asking people to complete a questionnaire.

- Postal questionnaires should always be accompanied by a stamped addressed envelope or, at the very least, return postage.

11.2 RESEARCH IN FOCUS
Administering a survey in China

Mayes et al. (2017) conducted a survey of managers and employees in a large hotel in south-eastern China to explore associations between human resource management practices, perceived organisational support, and job satisfaction. They used multi-item scales previously published in English-language journals to capture most of their variables. This necessitated taking an English-language questionnaire and translating it into Chinese. This translation was undertaken by a Chinese national, who was fluent in Chinese and English, and familiar with business practices in China and the West. One of the authors, who was also Chinese-born, then translated the items back into English, to ensure that the initial translation was consistent with the original English-language questionnaire. The survey was then administered in Chinese in paper form and collected from respondents by the authors. This process of translation and back-translation gave the research team confidence that the Chinese-language version of the questionnaire was collecting data which accurately captured the variables which had previously been operationalized by English-speaking researchers collecting data from English-speaking respondents.

- Follow up individuals who do not reply at first, possibly with two or three further mailings or emails. The importance of reminders cannot be overstated—they do work. Our preferred and recommended approach is to send out a reminder letter or email to non-respondents two weeks after the initial mailing, reasserting the nature and aims of the survey and suggesting that the person should contact either the researcher or someone else in the research team to obtain a replacement copy of the questionnaire if the initial mailing has been mislaid or lost. Then, two weeks after that, all further non-respondents should be sent another letter along with a further copy of the questionnaire. These reminders have a demonstrable effect on the response rate. Some writers argue for further mailings of reminder letters to non-respondents. If a response rate is worryingly low, such further mailings would certainly be desirable. In the case of online surveys, it is generally recommended that follow-ups be sent earlier and more frequently, based on evidence suggesting that in the online environment, response and non-response times are shorter (Dillman et al. 2014).

- Unsurprisingly, shorter questionnaires tend to achieve better response rates than longer ones. However, this is not a clear-cut principle, because it is difficult to specify when a questionnaire becomes 'too long'. Also, the evidence suggests that the effect of the length of questionnaires on response rates cannot be separated very easily from the salience of the topic(s) of the research for respondents and from the nature of the sample. Respondents may be highly tolerant of longer questionnaires that contain many questions on topics that interest them.

- Clear instructions and an attractive layout improve response rates. Dillman et al. (2014), as part of what they call the total design method (TDM) for postal questionnaire research, recommend lower case for questions and upper case for closed-ended answers. However, with the growing use of electronic communication and the associated rise of 'netiquette', upper case is increasingly associated with 'shouting', so that this recommendation may become less desirable.

- Do not allow the questionnaire to appear unnecessarily bulky or long.

- As with structured interviewing (see Chapter 10), begin with questions that are more likely to be of interest to the respondent. This advice is linked to the issue of salience (see above) but has particular significance in the context of research that may have limited salience for the respondent.

- We are inclined to the view that, in general, postal and online questionnaires should comprise as few open questions as possible, since people are often deterred by the prospect of having to write or type a lot. In fact, many writers on the subject recommend that open questions are used as little as possible in self-completion questionnaires.

- Providing monetary incentives can be an effective way of increasing the response rate, although most students undertaking project work or research for their dissertation may not be able to do so due to limited resources. The evidence also suggests that quite small amounts of money have a positive impact on the response rate, but that larger amounts do not necessarily improve the response rate any further. In the case of online surveys, it is obviously not possible to include money. One solution is to automatically enter respondents in a lottery to win a gift voucher or similar reward when they complete their questionnaire (see Student experience 'Using a lottery').

STUDENT EXPERIENCE
Using a lottery as an incentive in a survey

Jordan conducted a survey of participants in a training program to collect data for her dissertation. The survey collected data at three points in time. She had a limited budget so chose to offer participants the chance to go into a lottery draw for an iPad as an incentive for participation. She explained: 'they went into a lottery draw if they did all the three time points. So there's an incentive ... as part of the program you get a five hundred dollar budget ... It's entirely your responsibility to manage that. And so my budget went into the lottery draw.' Jordan was able to use her resources very effectively to incentivize participation, by choosing a prize which appealed to the participants. This almost certainly played a central role in delivering the very high response rate which she achieved in her survey.

Response rates

As we have explained, response rates are important because, the lower a response rate, the more questions are likely to be raised about the representativeness of the achieved sample. This is likely, however, to be more of an issue with randomly selected samples. With samples that are not selected based on a probability sampling method, it could be argued that the response rate is less of an issue, because the sample would not be representative of a **population**, even if everyone participated! As discussed above, postal and online surveys commonly receive lower response rates than other surveys, which may lead you to wonder whether, if you use either approach, you are likely to end up with a response rate that is too low. Interestingly, while there is much discussion of response rates in the literature, when it comes to the question of what is acceptable in published research, there is considerable variation. Mellahi and Harris (2016) conducted a meta-analysis of over 1000 articles published in leading management journals between 2009 and 2013. They found that while much of the literature argues for a response rate of at least 50%, there was a great deal of variation in response rates for the papers in their sample. In fact, response rates ranged from 1 per cent to 100 per cent, with a **median** of 40 per cent and a mean of just under 45 per cent (Mellahi and Harris 2016: 430).

Our point here is not that response rate doesn't matter, but rather that you should recognize that much credible research is published with response rates lower than is commonly advocated. The important thing is that you recognize and acknowledge the implications of the possible limitations of a low response rate. On the other hand, if your research is based on a **convenience sample**, ironically it could be argued that a low response rate is less significant. Many students find self-completion questionnaires attractive because of their low cost and quick administration. The point of this discussion is that you should not be put off using such techniques because of the prospect of a low response rate.

Designing the self-completion questionnaire

In general, the principles set out in this section apply to email and online surveys as much as to postal surveys. There are, however, some issues concerning presentation which are specific to email and online surveys and which are discussed in the section after this one.

Do not cramp the presentation

Because of the well-known problem of low response rates, it is sometimes considered preferable to make the instrument appear as short as possible in order for it to be less likely to deter prospective respondents from answering. However, this is almost always a mistake. As Dillman (1983) observes, an attractive layout is likely to enhance response rates, whereas the kinds of tactics that are sometimes employed to make a questionnaire appear shorter than it really is—such as reducing margins and the space between questions—make it look cramped and thereby unattractive. Also, if questions are too close together, there is a risk that they will be inadvertently omitted.

This is not to say that you should be ridiculously liberal in your use of space, as this does not necessarily provide for an attractive format either and may run the risk of making the questionnaire look excessively long. As with so many other issues in business research, a steady course needs to be steered between possible extremes.

Clear presentation

Far more important than making a self-completion questionnaire appear shorter than is the case is to make sure that it has a layout that is easy on the eye and that it facilitates the answering of all questions that are relevant to the respondent. A variety of styles (for example, different fonts, font sizes, bold, italics, and capitals) can enhance the appearance *but must be used in a consistent manner*. This last point means that you should ensure that you use one style for general instructions, one for headings, perhaps one for specific instructions (e.g. 'Go to question 7'), one for questions, and one for closed-ended answers. Mixing styles, so that one style is sometimes used for both general instructions and questions, can be very confusing for respondents.

Vertical or horizontal closed answers?

Bearing in mind that most questions in a self-completion questionnaire are likely to be of the closed kind, one consideration is whether to arrange the fixed answers vertically or horizontally. Very often, the nature of the answers will dictate a vertical arrangement because of their sheer length. Many researchers prefer a vertical format whenever possible, because, in some cases where either arrangement is feasible, confusion can arise when a horizontal one is employed (Sudman and Bradburn 1982). Consider the following:

> What do you think of the CEO's performance in her job since she took over the running of this company? (*Please tick the appropriate response*)
>
> Very ____ Good ____ Fair ____ Poor ____ Very ____
> good   poor

There is a risk that, if the questionnaire is being answered in haste, the required tick will be placed in the wrong space—for example, indicating Good when Fair was the intended response. Also, a vertical format more clearly distinguishes questions from answers. To some extent, these potential problems can be obviated through the judicious use of spacing and print variation, but they represent significant considerations.

A further reason that vertical alignments can be superior is that they are probably easier to code, especially when pre-codes appear on the questionnaire. Very often, self-completion questionnaires are arranged so that to the right of each question are two columns: one for the column in which data relating to the question will appear in a data matrix; the other for all the pre-codes. The latter allows the appropriate code to be assigned to a respondent's answer by circling it for later entry into the computer. Thus, the choice would be between the formats presented in Tips and skills 'Closed question with a horizontal format' and Tips and skills 'Closed question with a vertical format'. In the second case, not only is there less ambiguity about where a tick is to be placed; the task of coding is easier. However, when there is to be a battery of questions with identical answer formats, as in a Likert scale, a vertical format will take up too much space. One way of dealing with this kind of questioning is to use abbreviations with an accompanying explanation. An example can be found in Tips and skills 'Formatting a Likert scale'. The four items presented there are taken from an 18-item Likert scale designed to measure job satisfaction (Brayfield and Rothe 1951).

TIPS AND SKILLS
Closed question with a horizontal format

What do you think of the CEO's performance in her job since she took over the running of this company? (*Please tick the appropriate response*)

Very good ____ Good ____ Fair ____ Poor ____ Very poor ____   5 4 3 2 1

TIPS AND SKILLS
Closed question with a vertical format

What do you think of the CEO's performance in her job since she took over the running of this company? (*Please tick the appropriate response*)

Very good   ____   5
Good   ____   4
Fair   ____   3
Poor   ____   2
Very poor   ____   1

TIPS AND SKILLS
Formatting a Likert scale

In the next set of questions, you are presented with a statement. You are being asked to indicate your level of agreement or disagreement with each statement by indicating whether you: Strongly agree (SA), Agree (A), are Undecided (U), Disagree (D), or Strongly disagree (SD).

Please indicate your level of agreement by circling the appropriate response.

23. My job is like a hobby to me.

    SA   A   U   D   SD

24. My job is usually interesting enough to keep me from getting bored.

    SA   A   U   D   SD

25. It seems that my friends are more interested in their jobs.

    SA   A   U   D   SD

26. I enjoy my work more than my leisure time.

    SA   A   U   D   SD

Identifying response sets in a Likert scale

One of the advantages of using closed questions is that they can be pre-coded, thus turning the processing of data for computer analysis into a fairly simple task (see Chapter 12 for more on this). However, some thought must go into the scoring of the items of the kind presented in Tips and skills 'Formatting a Likert scale'. We might for example score question 23 as follows:

Strongly agree = 5

Agree = 4

Undecided = 3

Disagree = 2

Strongly disagree = 1

Accordingly, a high score for the item (5 or 4) indicates satisfaction with the job and a low score (1 or 2) indicates low job satisfaction. The same applies to question 24. However, when we come to question 25, the picture is different. Here, agreement indicates a *lack* of job satisfaction. It is disagreement that is indicative of job satisfaction. We would have to reverse the coding of this item, so that

Strongly agree = 1

Agree = 2

Undecided = 3

Disagree = 4

Strongly disagree = 5

The point of including such items is to identify people who exhibit response sets, such as acquiescence (see Chapter 10). If someone were to agree with all 18 items, when some of them indicated *lack* of job satisfaction, it is likely that the respondent was affected by a response set and the answers are unlikely to provide a valid assessment of job satisfaction for that person.

Clear instructions about how to respond

Always be clear about how you want respondents to indicate their replies when answering closed questions. Are they supposed to place a tick by or circle or underline the appropriate answer, or are they supposed to delete inappropriate answers? Also, in many cases it is feasible for the respondent to choose more than one answer—is this acceptable to you? If it is not, you should indicate this in your instructions, for example:

(Please choose the one answer that best represents your views by placing a tick in the appropriate box.)

If you do not make this clear and if some respondents choose more than one answer, you will have to treat their replies as if they had not answered. This possibility increases the risk of missing data from some respondents.

If it is acceptable to you for more than one category to be chosen, you need to make this clear, for example:

(You may choose more than one answer. Please choose all answers that represent your views by placing ticks in the appropriate boxes.)

It is a common error for such instructions to be omitted and for respondents either to be unsure about how to reply or to make inappropriate selections.

Keep question and answers together

This is a simple and obvious, though often transgressed, requirement—namely, that you should never split up a question so that it appears on two separate pages. A common error is to have some space left at the bottom of a page into which the question can be slotted but for the closed answers to appear on the next page. Doing so carries the risk of the respondent forgetting to answer the question or providing an answer in the wrong group of closed answers (a problem that is especially likely when a series of questions with a common answer format is being used, as with a Likert scale).

Email and online surveys

Until fairly recently, the dominant approach to administration of surveys was the use of postal questionnaires, but the administration of surveys online is increasingly the norm. Most of the issues discussed above, particularly those concerning questionnaire design, apply to both online and on-paper surveys. The key difference between online and other forms of self-completion questionnaires is chiefly mode of delivery. Nonetheless, we consider there to be enough issues specific to online surveys that we have devoted part of this chapter specifically to this approach. So far as online surveys are concerned, there is a crucial distinction between surveys administered by email (email surveys) and surveys administered on a website (web-based surveys). In the case of the former, the questionnaire is sent via email to a respondent, whereas, with a web-based survey, the respondent is directed to a website to answer a questionnaire.

Email surveys

With email surveys it is important to distinguish between **embedded** and **attached email surveys**. In the case of the embedded questionnaire, the questions are to be found in the body of the email. There may be an introduction to the questionnaire followed by some marking that partitions the introduction from the questionnaire itself. Respondents have to reply to the email, indicating their replies using simple notations, such as an 'x', or they may be asked to delete alternatives that do not apply. If questions are open, they are asked to type in their answers. They then simply need to send the reply to return their completed questionnaires to the researcher. With an attached questionnaire, the questionnaire arrives as an attachment to an email that introduces it. As with the embedded questionnaire, respondents must select and/or type their answers. To return the questionnaire, it must be attached to a reply email, although respondents may also be given the opportunity to print out and send the completed questionnaire by postal mail to the researcher (Sheehan and Hoy 1999).

The chief advantage of the embedded questionnaire is that it is easier for the respondent to return to the researcher and it requires less computer expertise. Knowing how to read, fill in, and then return an attachment requires a certain facility with handling online communication that is still not universally applicable. Also, the recipients' operating systems or software may present problems with reading attachments, while many respondents may refuse to open the attachment because of concerns about viruses. On the other hand, the limited formatting that is possible with most email software, such as using bold, variations in font size, indenting, and other features, makes the appearance of embedded questionnaires rather dull and featureless, although this limitation is rapidly changing. Furthermore, it is slightly easier for the respondent to type material into an attachment that uses well-known software such as Microsoft Word, since, if the questionnaire is embedded in an email, the alignment of questions and answers may be lost.

Web-based surveys

Web-based surveys operate by inviting prospective respondents to visit a website at which the questionnaire can be found and completed online. The web-based survey has an important advantage over the email survey in that it can use a much wider variety of embellishments in terms of appearance. Plate 11.1 presents part of the questionnaire from the gym survey from Chapter 15 in a website survey format and answered in the same way as in Tips and skills 'A completed and processed questionnaire' (Chapter 15). There are also greater possibilities than with paper-based questionnaires in terms of the use of colour and variety in the format of closed questions. With open questions, the respondent is invited to type directly into a boxed area (for example, question 2 in Plate 11.1).

However, the advantages of the web-based survey are not just to do with appearance. The questionnaire can be designed so that, when there is a filter question (for example, 'if *yes* go to question 12, if *no* go to question 14'), it skips automatically to the next appropriate question. The questionnaire can also be programmed so that only one question ever appears on the screen

or so that the respondent can scroll down and look at all questions in advance. Finally, respondents' answers can be automatically programmed to download into a database, thus eliminating the daunting coding of a large number of questionnaires. In the early days of web-based surveys one of the chief problems was that in order to produce the attractive text and all the other features, the researcher had to be highly sophisticated in the use of HTML. There are now, however, numerous software packages for web-based surveys which are designed to produce questionnaires with all the features that have been described. For example, Plate 11.1 was created using Survey Monkey: www.survey-monkey.com.

With commercial applications such as these, you can design your questionnaire online and then create a URL to which respondents can be directed in order to complete it. Each respondent's replies are logged, and the entire dataset can be retrieved once you have decided that the data collection phase is complete. This means that there is no manual coding of replies (other than with open questions) or data entry. Not only does this save time; it also reduces the likelihood of errors in the processing of data.

PLATE 11.1
Gym survey in online survey format

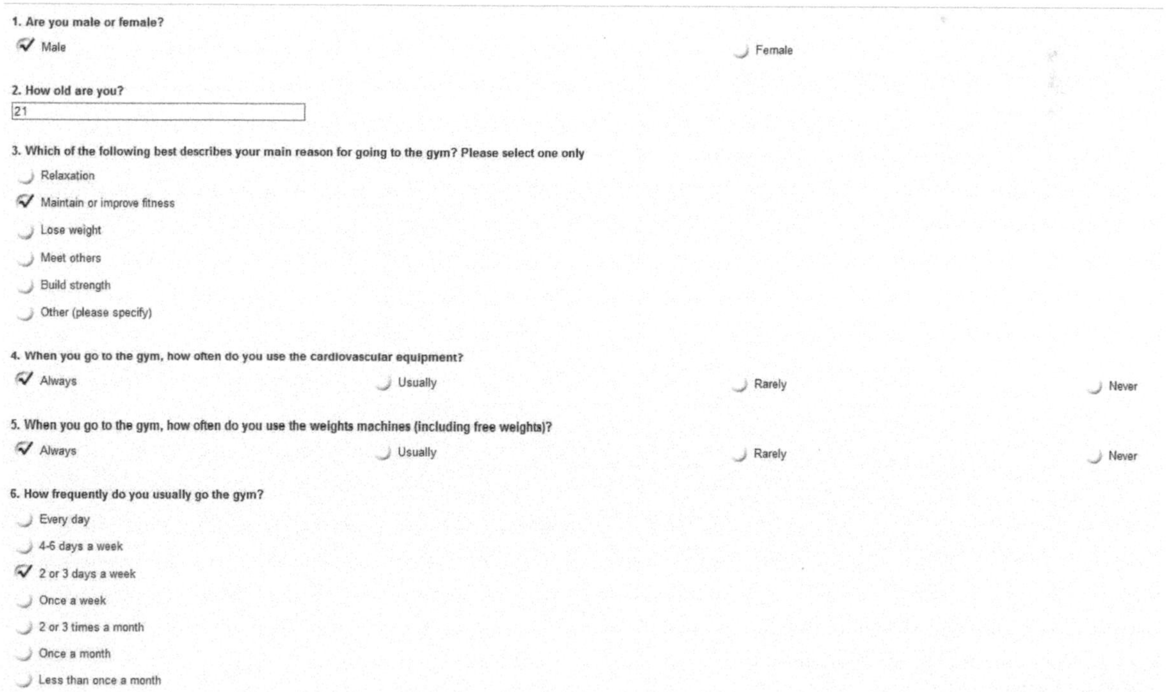

1. Are you male or female?
   - ☑ Male
   - ○ Female

2. How old are you?
   > 21

3. Which of the following best describes your main reason for going to the gym? Please select one only
   - ○ Relaxation
   - ☑ Maintain or improve fitness
   - ○ Lose weight
   - ○ Meet others
   - ○ Build strength
   - ○ Other (please specify)

4. When you go to the gym, how often do you use the cardiovascular equipment?
   - ☑ Always ○ Usually ○ Rarely ○ Never

5. When you go to the gym, how often do you use the weights machines (including free weights)?
   - ☑ Always ○ Usually ○ Rarely ○ Never

6. How frequently do you usually go the gym?
   - ○ Every day
   - ○ 4-6 days a week
   - ☑ 2 or 3 days a week
   - ○ Once a week
   - ○ 2 or 3 times a month
   - ○ Once a month
   - ○ Less than once a month

Potential respondents need to be directed to the website containing the questionnaire. Where there are possible problems to do with restricting who may answer the questionnaire, it may be necessary to set up a password system to filter out people for whom the questionnaire is not appropriate.

Comparing modes of survey administration

Experiments with different modes of administration are quite reassuring in terms of differences in how people's responses vary depending on mode, with differences often not large. For example, in a study of American students' attitudes to various aspects of college experience, respondents were found to reply more positively when answering questions online than when using paper questionnaires. However, with the exception of one of the scales, the differences were not large (Carini et al. 2003). Fleming and Bowden (2009) conducted a travel cost questionnaire survey, by mail and online, of visitors to Fraser Island, Australia. They found the results from the two modes of administration to be similar and that, in particular, the estimates of the 'consumer surplus' (the amount the tourist would be willing to spend on the visit less the amount actually spent) were similar across the two. Although there is some evidence of differences in response between modes of survey administration, mixing postal and online questionnaires is often recommended as a survey approach (Van Selm and Jankowski 2006). Trau et al. (2013) were interested in how far online questionnaires could be used as a means of achieving greater inclusion of stigmatized groups into organizational research. They compared questionnaires distributed online and by post and found that although data quality (amount of missing data) was worse for the online survey, the findings from various scales that were administered (e.g. an organizational commitment scale) were roughly equivalent. In other words, the mode of administration was unrelated to the responses derived. Further, Wolfe et al. (2008) conducted an experiment on teachers in Ohio and South Carolina comparing mail questionnaire and online surveys in terms of non-response at the level of the individual item or question in order to determine whether one mode of administration results in a higher level of failure to answer individual questions than the other. The authors found any differences to be very small.

Given that there do not appear to be great differences in findings resulting from different modes of administration in surveys that combine a web-based mode with a paper-based mode, there is often a good case to be made for offering respondents both options. A covering letter might draw prospective respondents' attention to a web-based option along with the necessary instructions for accessing it, so that those who prefer to work online are not put off responding to the questionnaire. However, there are grounds for caution when the survey is a mail questionnaire survey that offers respondents the option of responding through a web-based questionnaire. Medway and Fulton (2012) conducted a meta-analysis of studies that examined the impact of offering a web-based option and found a clear tendency for such surveys to produce *lower* response rates than those that do not provide such an option. The authors explain this possibly surprising finding in terms of such factors as the provision of an online option: increasing the overall complexity in responding; introducing a break in the process of responding; and sometimes causing technical difficulties that result in respondents giving up.

These findings suggest that it is difficult and probably impossible, given their relative newness, to provide a definitive verdict on online surveys compared to traditional forms of survey administration. For one thing, it is difficult to separate out the particular formats that researchers use when experimenting with modes of administration from the modes themselves. It may be that, if they had displayed online questions in a different manner, their findings would have been different—with obvious implications for how the online survey fares when compared with any of the traditional forms. Further, online surveys seem to work better than traditional survey forms in some respects more than others.

Tips and skills 'Advantages and disadvantages of online surveys compared to postal questionnaire surveys' summarizes the main factors to take into account when comparing online surveys with postal questionnaire surveys, and Table 11.1 compares the different methods of administering a survey.

TABLE 11.1

The strengths of email and web-based surveys in relation to face-to-face interview, telephone interview, and postal questionnaire surveys

Issues to consider	Mode of survey administration				
	Face-to-face interview	Telephone interview	Postal questionnaire	Email	Website
Resource issues					
Is the cost of the mode of administration relatively low?	★	★★	★★★	★★★	★ (unless researcher has access to low-cost software)
Is the speed of the mode of administration relatively fast?	★	★★★	★★★	★★★	★★★
Is the cost of handling a dispersed sample relatively low?	★ (★★ if clustered)	★★★	★★★	★★★	★★★
Does the researcher require little technical expertise for designing a questionnaire?	★★★	★★★	★★★	★★	★
Sampling-related issues					
Does the mode of administration tend to produce a good response rate?	★★★	★★	★	★	★
Is the researcher able to control who responds (i.e. to ensure that the target person is the person who answers)?	★★★	★★★	★★	★★	★★
Is the mode of administration accessible to all sample members?	★★★	★★	★★★	★(because of need for respondents to have online access)	★(because of need for respondents to have online access)
Questionnaire issues					
Is the mode of administration suitable for long questionnaires?	★★★	★★	★★	★★	★★
Is the mode of administration suitable for complex questions?	★★★	★	★★	★★	★★
Is the mode of administration suitable for open questions?	★★★	★★	★	★★	★★
Is the mode of administration suitable for filter questions?	★★★ (especially if CAPI used)	★★★ (especially if CATI used)	★	★	★★★ (if allows jumping)
Does the mode of administration allow control over the order in which questions are answered?	★★★	★★★	★	★	★★
Is the mode of administration suitable for sensitive questions?	★	★★	★★★	★★★	★★★
Is the mode of administration less likely to result in non-response to some questions?	★★★	★★★	★★	★★	★★
Does the mode of administration allow the use of visual aids?	★★★	★	★★★	★★	★★★
Answering context issues					
Does the mode of administration give respondents the opportunity to consult others for information?	★★	★	★★★	★★★	★★★
Does the mode of administration minimize the impact of interviewers' characteristics (gender, class, ethnicity)?	★	★★	★★★	★★★	★★★

Continued

Issues to consider	Mode of survey administration				
	Face-to-face interview	Telephone interview	Postal questionnaire	Email	Website
Does the mode of administration minimize the impact of the social desirability effect?	★	★★	★★★	★★★	★★★
Does the mode of administration allow control over the intrusion of others in answering questions?	★★★	★★	★	★	★
Does the mode of administration minimize the need for the respondent to have certain skills to answer questions?	★★★	★★★	★★	★(because of need to have online skills)	★ (because of need to have online skills)
Does the mode of administration enable respondents to be probed?	★★★	★★★	★	★★	★
Does the mode of administration reduce the likelihood of data entry errors by the researcher?	★	★	★★	★	★★★

Notes: Number of stars indicates the strength of the mode of administration of a questionnaire in relation to each issue. A single star implies that the mode of administering a questionnaire does not fare well in terms of the issue in question. Three stars imply that it does very well, and two stars imply that it is acceptable.

CAPI is computer-assisted personal interviewing; CATI is computer-assisted telephone interviewing.

Sources: This table is based on the authors' own experience and the following sources: Dillman (1978); Czaja and Blair (1996); **www.restore.ac.uk/orm/**.

TIPS AND SKILLS
Advantages and disadvantages of email and online surveys compared to postal questionnaire surveys

This box summarizes the main advantages and disadvantages of online surveys compared to postal questionnaire surveys. The tally of advantages and disadvantages in connection with online surveys relates to both email and web-based surveys. It should also be made clear that, by and large, online surveys and postal questionnaires suffer from one disadvantage relative to personal and telephone interviews—namely, that the researcher can never be certain that the person answering questions is who the researcher believes him or her to be. However, it has also been suggested that the impersonal feel of the internet means that the problem of social desirability effects is less likely to be pronounced than with surveys conducted by structured interview.

Advantages

1. Low cost. Even though postal questionnaire surveys are cheap to administer, there is evidence that email surveys in particular are cheaper. This is in part due to the cost of postage, paper, envelopes, and the time taken to stuff covering letters and questionnaires into envelopes with postal questionnaire surveys. However, with website-based surveys there may be start-up costs associated with the software needed to produce the questionnaire.

2. Faster response. Online surveys tend to be returned considerably more quickly than postal questionnaires.

3. Attractive formats. With web-based surveys, there is the opportunity to use a wide variety of stylistic formats for presenting questionnaires and closed-question answers. Also, automatic skipping when using filter questions and the possibility of immediate downloading of questionnaire replies into a database make this kind of survey quite attractive for researchers.

4. Mixed administration. Online surveys can be combined with postal questionnaire surveys, so that respondents have the option of replying by post or online. Moreover, the mode of reply does not seem to make a significant difference to the kinds of replies generated.

5. Unrestricted compass. There are no constraints in terms of geographical coverage with online surveys. The same might be said of postal questionnaire surveys, but these carry the complication of sending overseas respondents stamped and addressed envelopes that can be used in their own countries.

6. Fewer unanswered questions. There is evidence that online questionnaires are completed with fewer unanswered questions than postal questionnaires, resulting in less missing data. However, there is also evidence of little difference between the two modes of administering surveys.

7. Better response to open questions. To the extent that open questions are used, they tend to be more likely to be answered online and to result in more detailed replies.

8. Better data accuracy, especially in web-based surveys. Data entry is automated with online surveys, so that the researcher does not have to enter data into a spreadsheet, and therefore errors in data entry are largely avoided.

Disadvantages

1. Low response rate. Typically, response rates to online surveys are lower than those for comparable postal questionnaire surveys. However, the difficulty that is often encountered with online surveys of finding suitable **sampling frames** means that for many such surveys it is more or less impossible to calculate a response rate.

2. Restricted to online populations. Only people who are available online can reasonably be expected to participate in an online survey. This restriction may gradually ease over time, but, since the online population differs in significant ways from the non-online population, it is likely to remain a difficulty. On the other hand, if online populations are the focus of interest, this disadvantage is not an obstacle.

3. Requires motivation. Online survey respondents must be online to answer the questionnaire, so, if they are having to pay to use data or have poor connectivity, they may need a higher level of motivation to proceed than postal questionnaire respondents. This suggests that the solicitation to participate must be especially persuasive.

4. Confidentiality and anonymity issues. It is normal for **survey researchers** to indicate that respondents' replies will be confidential and that they will be anonymous. The same suggestions can and should be made with respect to online surveys. However, with email surveys, since the recipient must return the questionnaire either embedded within the message or as an attachment, respondents may find it difficult to believe that their replies really are confidential and will be treated anonymously. In this respect, website surveys may have an advantage over email surveys.

5. Multiple replies. With web-based surveys, there is a risk that some people may mischievously complete the questionnaire more than once. There is much less risk of this with email surveys.

Sources: Based on Schaeffer and Dillman (1998); Tse (1998); Kent and Lee (1999); Sheehan and Hoy (1999); Cobanoglu et al. (2001); Fricker and Schonlau (2002); Denscombe (2006).

Diaries as a form of self-completion questionnaire

An interesting and useful variant on traditional self-completion questionnaires is the **diary**. When the researcher is specifically interested in precise estimates of different kinds of behaviour, the diary warrants serious consideration, though it is still a relatively underused method. The term 'diary' has three different meanings in business research (see Key concept 11.3). It is the first of the three meanings—what Elliott (1997) calls the *researcher-driven diary*—that is the focus of attention here, especially in the context of its use in relation to **quantitative research**. When employed in this way, the researcher-driven diary functions in a similar way to the self-completion questionnaire. Equally, it could be said that the researcher-driven diary is an alternative method of data collection to observation in the sense that the research participants observe and record their

11.3 KEY CONCEPT
What is a research diary?

There are three major ways in which the term 'diary' has been employed in the context of business research.

The diary as a method of data collection. Here the researcher devises a structure for the diary and then asks a sample of diarists to complete the diaries so that they record what they do more or less contemporaneously with their activities. Elliott (1997) refers to this kind of use of the diary as *researcher-driven diaries*. Such diaries can be employed for the collection of data within the context of both quantitative and qualitative research. Sometimes, the collection of data in this manner is supplemented by a personal interview in which the diarist is asked questions about such things as what he or she meant by certain remarks. This *diary-interview*, as it is often referred to (Zimmerman and Wieder 1977), is usually employed when diarists record their behaviour in prose form rather than simply indicating the amount of time spent on different kinds of activity.

The diary as a document. The diary in this context is written spontaneously by the diarist and not at the behest of a researcher. Diaries in this sense are often used by historians but have some potential for business researchers working on issues that are of social scientific significance. As John Scott (1990) observes, the diary in this sense often shades into autobiography. Diaries as documents will be further addressed in Chapter 23.

The diary as a log of the researcher's activities. Researchers sometimes keep a record of what they do at different stages as an *aide-mémoire*. For example, the famous social anthropologist Malinowski (1967) kept an infamous log of his activities ('infamous' because it revealed his distaste for the people he studied and his inappropriate involvement with females). This kind of diary often shades into the writing of field notes by ethnographers, about which more is written in Chapter 19.

own behaviour. As such it can be thought of as the equivalent of structured observation (see Chapter 13) in the context of research questions that are framed in terms of quantitative research, or of ethnography (see Chapter 19) in the context of research questions framed in terms of qualitative research.

Corti (1993) distinguishes between 'structured diaries' and 'free text diaries'. Either may be employed by quantitative researchers. The research on managers and their jobs by Rosemary Stewart (1967) is an illustration of the structured kind of diary (see Research in focus 11.4). The diary has the general appearance of a questionnaire with largely closed questions. The kind of diary employed in this research is often referred to as a 'time-use' diary, in that it is designed so that diarists can record more or less contemporaneously the amount of time engaged in certain activities, such as time spent travelling, doing paperwork, in committee meetings, and so on. Ongoing estimates of the amount of time spent in different activities are often regarded as more accurate, because the events are less subject to memory problems or to the tendency to round up or down. Structured diaries are also regarded as more accurate in tracking events as they occur, as the example in Research in focus 11.4 illustrates.

An example of a free-text diary is provided by Huxley et al.'s (2005) study of stress and pressures among mental health social workers. In this study, a diary relating to the previous working week was sent to each of the 237 respondents, along with a postal questionnaire. The issues that diarists were invited to cover were based on findings from two focus groups with mental health social workers that the researchers had run prior to the diary study. The diary invited open-ended responses, which were entered into the qualitative software analysis package NVivo (discussed in Chapter 25) and were analysed thematically. One of the advantages of the diary in conjunction with a self-completion questionnaire in this study was that it provided contextual information about factors that had an impact on employee stress, such as the burden of paperwork and bureaucratic procedures, staff shortages and excessive workloads, and constant change and restructuring. This kind of information would probably have been much more difficult to glean from the questionnaires alone.

Using free-text recording of behaviour carries the same kinds of problems as those associated with coding answers to structured interview open questions—namely, the time-consuming nature of the exercise and the increased risks of inconsistency associated with the

11.4 RESEARCH IN FOCUS
A diary study of managers and their jobs

Rosemary Stewart's (1967) classic study of managerial time use focused on:

- the amount of time managers spent on particular activities;
- the frequency with which they undertook particular tasks.

'The diary method was chosen instead of observation because the research aimed to study more than 100 managers in a large number of companies. This aim could not be achieved by observation without a large team of observers' (1967: 7). In addition to recording the nature of the task that was being undertaken (such as paperwork, telephone calls, discussions, and so on), managers were asked to record in their diary:

1. the duration of the incident (hours and minutes);
2. where the work was done (own office, travelling, etc.);
3. who else was involved (boss, secretary, colleagues, etc.).

The diary entry took the form of a grid, which was filled in by ticking the appropriate boxes, which were subsequently coded. A distinction was made between episodes of work lasting 5 minutes or more, and 'fleeting contacts' of less than 5 minutes. The latter were recorded separately from the main section of the diary so managers could record as many of these short incidents as possible. Each day, the managers completed in addition to the main diary entry a form asking them to describe the three activities that had taken up the most work time. Each week, the managers filled in a form designed to check how well they had kept the diary, asking for example, 'How often did you fill in the diary?' A total of 160 managers kept diaries for a period of four weeks, a time period that Stewart considered was long enough to gain an impression of variations in the job but not so long that managers would lose interest in the exercise.

coding of answers. However, the free-text approach is less likely to be problematic when, as in Huxley et al. (2005), diarists can be instructed on what kind of information to write about, such as that relating to pressures of work, their affective commitment, and job satisfaction. It would be much more difficult to code free-text entries relating to more general questions such as in Stewart's (1967) study of how managers use their time.

Corti (1993) recommends that the person preparing the diary should follow these principles:

- provide explicit instructions for diarists;
- be clear about the time periods within which behaviour is to be recorded—for example, one working day, 24 hours, one week;
- provide a model of a completed section of a diary;
- provide checklists of 'items, events, or behaviour' that can jog people's memory—but the list should not become too daunting in length or complexity;
- include fixed blocks of time or columns showing when the designated activities start and finish: for example, diaries of the kind used by Stewart (1967), which showed how managers spend their time.

Advantages and disadvantages of the diary as a method of data collection

The two studies included here to illustrate the use of diaries (Research in focus 11.5 and 11.6) also suggest its potential advantages:

- When fairly precise estimates of the frequency and/or amount of time spent in different forms of behaviour are required, the diary may provide more valid and reliable data than questionnaire data (see Research in focus 11.5).
- When information about the sequencing of different types of behaviour and attitudes is required, the diary is likely to perform better than questionnaires or interviews (see Research in focus 11.6).
- The first two advantages could be used to suggest that structured observation would be just as feasible, but structured observation is probably less appropriate for producing data on behaviour that is personally sensitive, such as work-related gossip (see Research in focus 11.7). Moreover, although data on such behaviour can be collected by structured interview, it is likely that respondents will be less willing to divulge personal details in an interview situation. If such information were collected

by questionnaire, there is a greater risk of recall and rounding problems (see the first point in this list).

On the other hand, diaries may suffer from the following problems:

- They tend to be more expensive than personal interviews (because of the costs associated with recruiting diarists and of checking that diaries are being properly completed).

- Diaries can suffer from a process of attrition, as people decide they have had enough of the task of completing a diary.

- The previous point raises the possibility that diarists become less diligent over time about their record keeping.

- There is sometimes failure to record details sufficiently quickly, so that memory recall problems set in.

However, diary researchers argue that the resulting data are still more accurate than the equivalent data based on interviews or questionnaires.

Experience and event sampling

Scherbaum and Meade (2013) have called for greater use in business research of various methods that would reduce the reliance on questionnaires and other traditional techniques. Among these is **experience sampling** or *event sampling*, which capture participants' 'transient affective states'. With this method, participants are prompted to reply to questions about their behaviour and/or their affective states at particular points in time (or within a narrow timeframe). The method, which can be thought of as a variant of diary studies, allows something approximating to real-time data about the

11.5 RESEARCH IN FOCUS
A diary study of text messaging

Faulkner and Culwin (2005) used a questionnaire and a diary study to explore the uses of text messaging among UK university students. The diary study involved 24 mobile phone users who used text messaging. The researchers used a convenience sample made up of students in their mid-20s on a computer science course at a UK university, and the study formed part of their course work. The group was asked to keep diaries of sent and received text messages for a two-week period. Helpfully, 'The study started at midnight on February 15th to avoid the sample being affected by Valentine's Day greetings' (2005: 176). The following information was recorded in a structured format:

Book number

Message number

Date

Time

Send or receive

The original message

A translation if it was not in English

Sender's details

Relationship of sender to receiver

Although structured observation could have been used in this study, it would have entailed researchers following users around and waiting for participants to text someone, so a diary study is in this case a more directed method of focusing on one particular type of activity. This study focused on text messages that were predominantly of a personal nature, but text messaging is also a method of communication within business, where similar research methods could be applied.

11.6 RESEARCH IN FOCUS
A diary study of emotional labour in a call centre

Uy et al. (2017) conducted research in a call centre in Singapore to explore the effects of 'surface acting'—a type of emotional labour in which workers display positive emotions regardless of whether they feel them—in terms of emotional exhaustion and work engagement. They argued that a limitation of prior studies was that while they had shown associations between surface acting and emotional exhaustion, they had not looked at the pervasiveness of such effects nor at the factors which might mitigate them.

To explore these effects, the authors recruited a sample of just over 100 customer-service representatives in a Singaporean call centre and had them complete diaries over a five-day period. At the end of each day, respondents completed a short series of items, scored on 5-point Likert scales ('Never' to 'Always'), which measured surface acting. An example of the items is 'Today I faked a good mood'. Also at the end of the day, work engagement was measured using 5-point Likert scales ('Strongly Agree' to 'Strongly Disagree') with items such as 'At my work today, I really felt like I was bursting with energy'. Emotional exhaustion was measured by the respondents completing items before they went to bed, again scored on a 5-point scale ('Very slightly or not at all' to 'Extremely') and items such as 'I am feeling burned out now'. The authors were interested in whether helping behaviour involving co-workers—giving and receiving help—moderated the associations between surface acting and emotional exhaustion. Accordingly, data were also collected on giving and receiving help, also using a series of items with Likert scale responses.

The results showed that surface acting during the day was positively associated with emotional exhaustion, which spilled over into reduced engagement on the following day. This effect was apparently mitigated by giving help to co-workers, but not by receiving help. By using a diary, the authors were able to explore these effects over time, using data which were collected over time.

11.7 RESEARCH IN FOCUS
Using diaries to study a sensitive topic: work-related gossip

Kathryn Waddington (2005) argues that diary methods offer a solution to the problems of researching the often private, unheard, and unseen world of gossip in organizations. However, she also argues that diary methods alone are insufficient. Her mixed-method **research design** of nursing and health care organizations thus involved three phases. The first was aimed at exploring the characteristics of gossip and individual differences in relation to gender and organizational position, by developing an understanding of how respondents themselves understood the phenomena. Phase two of the research addressed the role of gossip in sensemaking and socialization and as an aspect of the expression and management of emotion in relation to workplace stress; in-depth interviews with nurses were used as the main method of data collection. The third phase of the study was where diary methods were used, along with a **critical incident method** (see Chapter 10) and telephone interviewing. The aim of this stage of the study was to add to the findings of the first two phases. Twenty health care workers were asked to keep an event-contingent structured diary record. When an incidence of gossip occurred, they were asked to record it on the incident sheet (see Figure 11.1) as soon as possible after it had occurred and at least once a day. The respondents were also asked to reflect upon an episode of work-related gossip in the form of a critical incident account detailing: (1) reasons for choosing the incident; (2) how they felt at the time it took place; (3) where and when it occurred and who was involved; (4) the content of the gossip; and (5) organizational factors contributing to the occurrence of the incident. Within four weeks of completion and return of the diaries and critical incident accounts, follow-up telephone interviews were carried out to clarify details relating to the critical incident accounts and to discuss the perceived accuracy and practicality of the diary records.

FIGURE 11.1

A sample diary record sheet

Record Sheet

Date......... Time.........am/pm   Length of time incident approx............... minutes

Number of people involved........ Females/.........Males

Where the incident took place:

Nature of *your* interpersonal relationship with the person(s) involved (please circle):
Work relationship only/friends at work/friends outside of work/partner/family member/other—please specify

I disclosed	Very little	1 2 3 4 5 6 7	A great deal
Others disclosed	Very little	1 2 3 4 5 6 7	A great deal
Social integration	I didn't feel part of the group	1 2 3 4 5 6 7	I felt part of the group
Quality	Unpleasant	1 2 3 4 5 6 7	Very pleasant
Initiation	I initiated	1 2 3 4 5 6 7	Others initiated

What did you gossip about?
How did you feel at the time the above took place?

Source: Waddington (2005).

occurrence and possibly intensity of the issue being asked about. The authors write:

> Individuals are typically prompted at specific points in time (e.g. every hour, once a day, during work breaks) or after specific events (e.g. after an interaction with a customer) to respond about their current states.
>
> (Scherbaum and Meade 2013: 140)

In addition, the participant might be prompted to complete the research instrument when a device that he or she carries around emits a sound. Experience/event sampling operates in a similar way to a diary in that participants record their feelings or impressions in terms of a predetermined format at the appropriate juncture.

The chief advantages of the method over the traditional way of administering a self-completion questionnaire is that the ensuing data tend to be more immediate (since participants reply *in situ*), less general (replies are not about feelings over a period of time), and less prone to memory distortions, though they share most of the limitations associated with the diary method (see above). Experience sampling may become more popular as smartphones have become so widely used, since they provide a very useful platform for prompting research participants to complete a research instrument and for completing and submitting answers. Hofmans et al. (2013) used smartphones to gather experience sampling data from 50 employees in a study of task characteristics and work effort. The employees were prompted with a beep five times a day for five working days to complete questions about their task at that time and their feelings about it. Beeps were not always responded to, so that there is an element of non-response, but the immediacy of the data that were received provides a significant alternative to conventional questionnaire answers. Uy et al. (2010) distinguish between three types of experience sampling approach:

a) *interval contingent*—where responses are provided at predetermined intervals, e.g. every hour, or at the same time each day, such as in Wagner et al.'s (2013) study of emotional labour and bus drivers;

b) *event contingent*—participants respond when the event takes place, such as when they experience certain moods;

c) *signal contingent*—participants are prompted to respond by a signalling device, such as an alarm, at randomly selected points in the day, as in Hofmans et al.'s (2013) study mentioned above.

Uy et al. (2010) suggest that experience sampling may offer benefits in terms of being able to capture dynamic processes as they unfold over time and offer greater **ecological validity** through the fact that reactions to events are recorded in naturalistic contexts where they occur. Chapter 13 returns to the issue of **time sampling** in relation to structured observation, where the observer records the observed behaviour of respondents at regularly timed intervals.

KEY POINTS

- Many of the recommendations relating to the self-completion questionnaire apply equally or almost equally to the structured interview, as has been mentioned on several occasions.

- Closed questions tend to be used in survey research rather than open ones. Coding is a particular problem when dealing with answers to open questions.

- Structured interviews and self-completion questionnaires both have their respective advantages and disadvantages, but a particular problem with questionnaires sent by post or email or presented online is that they frequently produce a low response rate. However, steps can be taken to boost response rates.

- Presentation of closed questions and the general layout constitute important considerations in the design of the self-completion questionnaire.

- Both email and web-based surveys are increasingly common. They have advantages and disadvantages when compared to other forms of questionnaire delivery, but overall represent a very effective delivery mode.

- The researcher-driven diary was also introduced as a possible alternative to using questionnaires and interviews when the research questions are very specifically concerned with aspects of people's behaviour.

QUESTIONS FOR REVIEW

Evaluating the self-completion questionnaire in relation to the structured interview

- 'The low response rates frequently achieved in research with postal, email, and online questionnaires mean that the structured interview is invariably a more suitable choice.' Discuss.

- What steps can be taken to boost postal and online questionnaire response rates?

Designing the self-completion questionnaire

- Why are self-completion questionnaires usually made up mainly of closed questions?

- Why might a vertical format for presenting closed questions be preferable to a horizontal format?

Internet-based surveys

- What is the difference between email and web-based surveys?

- What are the main advantages and disadvantages of email and web-based surveys?

Diaries as a form of self-completion questionnaire

- What are the main kinds of diary used in the collection of business research data?

- Are there any circumstances when the diary approach might be preferable to the use of a self-completion questionnaire?

ONLINE RESOURCES
www.oup.com/uk/brm5e/

Visit the Interactive Research Guide that accompanies this book to complete an exercise in self-completion questionnaires.

ASKING QUESTIONS

CHAPTER OUTLINE

This chapter is concerned with the considerations that are involved in asking questions that are used in **structured interviews** and **questionnaires** of the kinds discussed in Chapters 10 and 11. As such, it continues the focus upon **survey research** that began in Chapter 8 and moves on to the next stage in the process that we outlined in Figure 9.1. This chapter explores the following:

- the issues involved in deciding whether or when to use open or **closed questions**;
- the different kinds of question that can be asked in structured interviews and questionnaires;
- rules to bear in mind when designing questions;
- vignette questions in which respondents are presented with a scenario and are asked to reflect on the scenario;
- the importance of piloting questions;
- the possibility of using questions that have been used in previous survey research.

Introduction

How we ask questions largely determines what we find out when we do survey research. Thus, in using survey instruments such as structured interviews or self-completion questionnaires, how we ask questions is fundamental in determining the quality and usefulness of the data we collect. Of course, as the previous two chapters have sought to suggest, there is much more to the design and administration of such research instruments than how best to phrase questions. There is no doubt, however, that the issue of how questions should be asked is a crucial concern for the survey researcher and it is not surprising that this aspect of designing survey instruments has been a major focus of attention over the years and preoccupies many practising researchers.

Open or closed questions?

One of the most significant considerations for many researchers is whether to ask a question in an open or closed format. This distinction was first introduced in Chapter 9. The issue of whether to ask a question in an open or closed format is relevant to the design of both structured interview and self-administered questionnaire research.

With an open or open-ended question, respondents are asked a question and can reply however they wish. With a closed question, they are presented with a set of fixed alternatives from which they must choose an appropriate answer. All the questions in Tips and skills 'Instructions for interviewers in the use of a filter question' (Chapter 10) are of the closed kind. So too are the Likert-scale items in Research in focus 8.3 and Research in focus 8.4, as well as Tips and skills 'Closed question with a horizontal format' and Tips and skills 'Closed question with a vertical format' (Chapter 11); these form a particular kind of closed question. What, then, are some of the advantages and limitations of these two types of question format?

Open questions

Open questions present both advantages and disadvantages to the survey researcher, though, as the following discussion suggests, the problems associated with the processing of answers to open questions tend to mean that closed questions are more likely to be used in most structured interviews and surveys.

Advantages

Although survey researchers typically prefer to use closed questions, open questions do have certain advantages over closed ones, as outlined in the list below:

- Respondents can answer in their own terms. They are not forced to answer in the same terms as those foisted on them by the closed answers.

- They allow unusual responses to be derived. Replies that the survey researcher may not have contemplated (and that would therefore not form the basis for fixed-choice alternatives) are possible.

- The questions do not suggest certain kinds of answer to respondents. Therefore, respondents' levels of knowledge and understanding of issues can be uncovered. The salience of issues for respondents can also be explored.

- They are useful for exploring new areas or ones in which the researcher has limited knowledge.

- They are useful for generating possible answers to closed or fixed-choice questions for future use. This is a point that will be returned to in the section on 'Piloting and pre-testing questions' later in this chapter.

Disadvantages

However, open questions present problems for the survey researcher, as the following list reveals:

- In interviewing, they are time-consuming for interviewers to administer. Interviewees are likely to talk for longer than is usually the case with a comparable closed question.

- Answers must be 'coded'. This is very time-consuming. For each open question, it entails reading through answers, deriving themes that can be employed to form the basis for codes, and then going through the answers again so that the answers can be coded for entry into a computer spreadsheet. The process is essentially identical to that involved in content analysis (discussed in

Chapter 13) and is sometimes called *post-coding* to distinguish it from *pre-coding*, whereby the researcher designs a coding frame in advance of administering a survey instrument and often includes the pre-codes in the questionnaire (as in Tips and skills 'Processing a closed question'). However, in addition to being time-consuming, post-coding can be an unreliable process, because it can introduce the possibility of variability in the coding of answers and therefore of measurement error (and hence lack of validity). This is a form of data processing error (see Figure 9.9). Research in focus 12.1 deals with aspects of the coding of open questions.

- They require greater effort from respondents. As mentioned above, respondents being interviewed are likely to talk for longer than would be the case for a comparable closed question, or, in the case of a self-completion questionnaire, would need to write for much longer. Therefore, it is often suggested that open questions have limited utility in the context of self-completion questionnaires. Because of the greater effort involved, many prospective respondents are likely to be put off by the prospect of having to write extensively, which may exacerbate the problem of low response rates with postal and online questionnaires in particular (see Chapter 11).

- In research based on open question structured interviews, there is the possibility of variability between interviewers in the recording of answers. This possibil-

ity is likely to arise because of the difficulty of writing down verbatim what respondents say to interviewers. The obvious solution is to use an audio recorder; however, this may not be practicable, for example, in a noisy environment. Also, the transcription of answers to audio-recorded open questions is immensely time-consuming and adds additional costs to a survey. The problem of transcription is one continually faced by qualitative researchers using semi-structured and unstructured interviews (see Chapter 20).

Closed questions

The advantages and disadvantages of closed questions are in many respects implied in some of the considerations relating to open questions.

Advantages

Closed questions offer the following advantages to researchers:

- It is easy to process answers. For example, the respondent in a self-completion questionnaire, or the interviewer using a structured interview schedule, will place a tick or circle an answer for the appropriate response. The appropriate code can then be almost mechanically derived from the selected answer, since the pre-codes are placed to the side of the fixed-choice answers. See Tips and skills 'Processing a closed question' for an

---

12.1 RESEARCH IN FOCUS
Coding a very open question

Coding an open question usually involves reading and rereading transcripts of respondents' replies and formulating distinct themes in their replies. A coding frame then needs to be designed that identifies the types of answer associated with each question and their respective codes (i.e. numbers). A coding schedule may also be necessary to keep a record of rules to be followed in the identification of certain kinds of answer in terms of a theme. The numbers allocated to each answer can then be used in the computer processing of the data.

Foddy (1993) reports the results of an exercise in which he asked a small sample of his students, 'Your father's occupation is (was) …?' and requested three details: nature of business; size of business; and whether owner or employee. In giving the size of the business, the replies were particularly variable in kind, including 'big', 'small', 'very large', '3000 acres', 'family', 'multinational', '200 people', and 'Philips'. The problem here is obvious: you simply cannot compare and therefore aggregate people's replies. In a sense, the problem is only partly to do with the difficulty of coding an open question. It is also due to a lack of specificity in the question. If, instead, Foddy had asked, 'How many employees are (were) there in your father's organization?', a more comparable set of answers should have been forthcoming. Whether his students would have known this information is, of course, yet another issue. However, the exercise does illustrate the potential problems of asking an open question, particularly one such as this that lacks a clear reference point for gauging size.

TIPS AND SKILLS
Processing a closed question

What do you think of the CEO's performance in her job since she took over the running of this company?

(Please tick the appropriate response)

Very good	____	5
Good	✓	④
Fair	____	3
Poor	____	2
Very poor	____	1

example based on Tips and skills 'Closed question with a vertical format' (Chapter 11). In the case of online surveys, it is generally possible to set up surveys so that data are coded as they are entered.

- Closed questions enhance the comparability of answers, making it easier to show the relationship between variables and to make comparisons between respondents or types of respondents. Although contingency tables (discussed in Chapter 15) can also be generated by post-coding respondents' answers to open questions, with post-coding there is always a problem of knowing how far respondents' answers that receive a certain code are genuinely comparable. As previously noted, the assignment of codes to people's answers may be unreliable (see the sixth point in Tips and skills 'Common sources of error in survey research' in Chapter 10). Checks are necessary to ensure that there is a good deal of agreement between coders and that coders do not change their coding conventions over time. Closed questions essentially circumvent this problem.

- Closed questions may clarify the meaning of a question for respondents. Sometimes respondents may not be clear about what a question is getting at, and the availability of answers may help to clarify the situation for them.

- Closed questions are easy for interviewers and/or respondents to complete. Precisely because interviewers and respondents are not expected to write extensively and instead must place ticks or circle answers, closed questions are easier and quicker to complete.

- In interviews, closed questions reduce the possibility of variability in the recording of answers in structured interviewing. As noted in Chapter 10, if interviewers do not write down exactly what respondents say to them when answering questions, a source of bias and

hence of invalidity is in prospect. Closed questions reduce this possibility, though there is still the potential problem that interviewers may have to *interpret* what is said to them to assign answers to a category.

Disadvantages

However, closed questions exhibit certain disadvantages:

- There is a loss of spontaneity in respondents' answers. There is always the possibility that people might come up with interesting replies that are not covered by the fixed answers that are provided. One solution to this possible problem is to ensure that, before the survey is designed, an open question is used to generate the categories of answers to closed questions. Also, there may be a good case for including a possible response category of 'Other' and allowing respondents to indicate what they mean by this category.

- It is difficult to make fixed-choice answers exhaustive. All possible answers should be catered for, although in practice this may be difficult to achieve, since this rule may result in excessively long lists of possible answers. Again, a category of 'Other' may be desirable to allow for a wide range of answers.

- There may be variation among respondents in the interpretation of fixed-choice answers. There is always a problem when asking a question that certain terms may be interpreted differently by respondents. If this is the case, then validity will be jeopardized. The presence of fixed-choice answers can exacerbate this possible problem, because there may be variation in the understanding of key terms in the answers.

- Closed questions may be irritating to respondents when they are not able to find a category that they feel applies to them.

- In interviews, a large number of closed questions may make it difficult to establish rapport, because the respondent and interviewer are less likely to engage with each other in a conversation. The interview is more likely to have an impersonal feel to it. However, because it is difficult to determine the extent to which rapport is a desirable attribute of structured interviewing (see Chapter 10), this is not necessarily too much of a problem.

Types of question

It is worth bearing in mind that, when you are using a structured interview or self-completion questionnaire, you will probably be asking several different types of question. There are various ways of classifying these, but here are some prominent types of question:

- *Personal factual questions*. These are questions that ask the respondent to provide *personal information*, by which is meant information about themselves such as age, gender, education, employment status, income, and so on. This kind of question also includes questions about *behaviour*. Such factual questions may have to rely on the respondents' memories, as when they are asked about such things as frequency of individual performance appraisal meetings, how often they visit certain shops, or when they last had any time off work.

- *Factual questions about others*. Like the previous type of question, this one asks for information about others, sometimes in combination with the respondent. An example of such a question would be one about team performance, which would require respondents to consider their own productivity (measured in terms of such things as daily work rate, frequency of lateness for work, and so on) in conjunction with the productivity of fellow team members. However, a criticism of such research is precisely that it relies on the possibly distorted views of respondents concerning their own and others' behaviour. Like personal factual questions, an element of reliance on memory recall is also likely to be present and potentially problematic.

- *Informant factual questions*. Sometimes, we place people who are interviewed or who complete a questionnaire in the position of informants rather than as respondents answering questions about themselves. This kind of question can also be found when people are asked about such things as the size of the firm for which they work, who owns it, whether it employs certain technologies, and whether it has certain specialist functions. Such questions are essentially about characteristics of an entity of which they have knowledge, in this case, a firm.

- *Questions about attitudes*. Questions about attitudes are very common in both structured interview and self-completion questionnaire research. This type of question would seek to collect data about such things as job satisfaction, work engagement, or organizational commitment. The Likert scale is one of the most frequently encountered formats for measuring attitudes. Tips and skills 'Response formats for scales' provides a number of ways of presenting response formats.

- *Questions about beliefs*. Respondents are frequently asked about their beliefs. One form of asking questions about beliefs is when respondents are asked whether they believe that certain matters are true or false—for example, a question asking whether the respondent believes current equal employment opportunity policies in their organization are effective. Or a survey about workplace stress might ask respondents to indicate whether they believe that the incidence of stress-related absence from work is increasing.

- *Questions about normative standards and values*. Respondents may be asked to indicate what principles of behaviour influence them or they hold dear. The elicitation of such norms of behaviour is likely to have considerable overlap with questions about attitudes and beliefs, since norms and values can be construed as having elements of both.

- *Questions about knowledge*. Questions can sometimes be employed to 'test' respondents' knowledge in an area. For example, a study of health and safety in the workplace might ask questions about the legal requirements that companies must comply with, to test respondents' awareness of these issues.

Most structured interview schedules and self-completion questionnaires will comprise more than one, and often several, of these types of question. It is important to bear in mind the distinction between different types of question. There are several reasons for this.

- It is useful to keep the distinctions in mind because they force you to clarify in your own mind what you are asking about, albeit in rather general terms.

Response formats for scales

There are several ways of presenting the response formats for the individual items that make up a scale such as a Likert scale. The kind used in Tips and skills 'Formatting a Likert scale' (Chapter 11) is an example of a verbal format (see below).

Binary response format
My job is usually interesting enough to keep me from getting bored.

Agree _____   Disagree _____

(This format is sometimes elaborated to include a 'don't know' response.)

Numerical response format
My job is usually interesting enough to keep me from getting bored.

5   4   3   2   1

(where 5 means Strongly agree and 1 means Strongly disagree)

Verbal format
My job is usually interesting enough to keep me from getting bored.

Strongly agree _____   Agree _____   Undecided _____   Disagree _____   Strongly disagree _____

Bipolar numerical response format
I love my job   7   6   5   4   3   2   1   I hate my job

Frequency format
My job is usually interesting enough to keep me from getting bored

All of the time _____   Often _____   Fairly often _____   Occasionally _____   None of the time _____

The bipolar numerical response format is used in connection with *semantic differential* scales. With such scales, the respondent is given lists of pairs of adjectives. Each pair represents adjectival opposites (for example, masculine/feminine). A well-known example is the Fiedler (1967) least-preferred co-worker (LPC) scale. With this scale, each leader in a sample of leaders is given a set of between 16 and 25 pairs of adjectives and is asked to describe the person with whom he or she has least preferred co-working. Examples of the pairs are:

Pleasant	8	7	6	5	4	3	2	1	Unpleasant
Friendly	8	7	6	5	4	3	2	1	Unfriendly
Rejecting	1	2	3	4	5	6	7	8	Accepting
Distant	1	2	3	4	5	6	7	8	Close

Each leader's score on each pair is aggregated to give a total score for that leader. Fiedler argued that leaders who describe their least-preferred co-workers in largely positive terms (pleasant, friendly, accepting, close) were predominantly relationship-oriented; those who described their least-preferred co-workers in largely negative terms (unpleasant, unfriendly, rejecting, distant) were predominantly task-oriented.

- It will help to guard against asking questions in an inappropriate format. For example, a Likert scale is problematic when asking factual questions about behaviour.

- When building scales such as a Likert scale, it is best not to mix different types of question. For example,

attitudes and beliefs sound similar and you may be tempted to use the same format for mixing questions about them. However, it is best not to do this and instead to have separate scales for attitudes and beliefs. If you mix them, the questions cannot really be measuring the same thing, so that measurement validity is threatened.

Rules for designing questions

Over the years, numerous rules (and rules of thumb) have been devised about the dos and don'ts of asking questions. Despite this, it is one of the easiest areas for making mistakes. There are three simple rules of thumb as a starting point; beyond that, the rules specified below act as a means of avoiding further pitfalls.

General rules of thumb

Always bear in mind your research questions

The questions that you will ask in your self-completion questionnaire or structured interview should always be geared to answering your research questions. This first rule of thumb has at least two implications. First, it means that you should make sure that you ask questions that relate to your research questions. Ensure, in other words, that the questionnaire questions you ask will allow your research questions to be addressed. You will not want to find out at a late stage that you forgot to include some crucial questions. Secondly, it means that there is little point in asking questions that do not relate to your research questions. It is also not fair to waste your respondents' time answering questions that are of little value to you.

What do you want to know?

Rule of thumb number two is to decide exactly what it is you want to know. Consider the seemingly harmless question:

Do you have a car?

What is it that the question is seeking to tap? Is it car ownership? If it is car ownership, the question is inadequate, largely because of the ambiguity of the word 'have'. The question can be interpreted as personally owning a car; having access to a car in a household; and 'having' a company car or a car for business use. Thus, an answer of 'yes' may or may not be indicative of car ownership. If you want to know whether your respondent owns a car, ask her/him directly about this matter. Similarly, there is nothing wrong with the question:

How many people does your organization employ?

However, this question does not clarify whether you are interested in the workplace, the company, or the business as a whole—which may include a number of subsidiary companies. In addition, it does not distinguish between full- and part-time workers, or temporary and permanent employees. Hence, if you are interested in knowing how many full-time or full-time equivalent employees there are, then you need to specify this. Similarly, if you are interested only in people who are employed directly by the firm (rather than temporary or contract staff who work on the premises), you need to make this clear in your question.

How would *you* answer it?

Rule of thumb number three is to put yourself in the position of the respondent. Ask yourself the question and try to work out how you would reply. If you do this, there is at least the possibility that the ambiguity that is inherent in the 'Do you have a car?' question will manifest itself and its inability to tap car ownership would become apparent. Let us say as well that there is a follow-up question to the previous one:

Have you driven the car this week?

Again, this looks harmless, but, if you put yourself in the role of a respondent, it will be apparent that the phrase 'this week' is vague. Does it mean the last seven days or does it mean the week in which the questioning takes place, which will, of course, be affected by such things as whether the question is being asked on a Monday or a Friday? In part, this issue arises because the question designer has not decided what the question is about. Equally, however, a moment's reflection in which you put yourself in the position of the respondent might reveal the difficulty of answering this question.

Taking account of these rules of thumb and the following rules about asking questions may help you to avoid the more obvious pitfalls.

Specific rules when designing questions

Avoid ambiguous terms in questions

Avoid terms such as 'often' and 'regularly' as measures of frequency. They are very ambiguous, because respondents will operate with different frames of reference when employing them. Sometimes their use is unavoidable, but, when there is an alternative that allows actual frequency to be measured, this will nearly always be preferable. So, a question such as

How often do you usually visit the cinema?

Very often   ‒‒‒‒

Quite often   ‒‒‒‒

Not very often   ‒‒‒‒

Not at all   ‒‒‒‒

suffers from the problem that, apart from 'not at all', the terms in the response categories are ambiguous. Instead, try to ask about actual frequency, for example:

How frequently do you usually visit the cinema? (*Please tick whichever category comes closest to the number of times you visit the cinema.*)

More than once a week   ‒‒‒‒

Once a week   ‒‒‒‒

Two or three times a month   ‒‒‒‒

Once a month   ‒‒‒‒

A few times a year   ‒‒‒‒

Once a year   ‒‒‒‒

Less than once a year   ‒‒‒‒

Alternatively, you might simply ask respondents about the number of times they have visited the cinema in the previous four weeks.

Words like 'colleagues' or 'management' are also ambiguous, because people will have different notions of who their colleagues are or who makes up the management. As previously noted, words like 'have' can also be sources of ambiguity.

It is also important to bear in mind that certain common words, such as 'quality' and 'customer', mean different things to different people. For some, quality is dependent on the purpose of the product, whereas for others it is an absolute measure of the standard of the product. Similarly, some people refer to colleagues from different departments as customers, whereas others take the word to mean those external to the organization who consume the products or services that the firm provides. In such cases, it will be necessary to define what you mean by such terms.

Avoid long questions

It is commonly believed that long questions are undesirable. In a structured interview the interviewee can lose the thread of the question, and in a self-completion questionnaire the respondent may be tempted to omit such questions or to skim them and therefore not give them sufficient attention. However, Sudman and Bradburn (1982) have suggested that this advice applies better to attitude questions than to ones that ask about behaviour. They argue that, when the focus is on behaviour, longer questions have certain positive features in interviews— for example, they are more likely to provide memory cues and they facilitate recall because of the time taken to complete the question. However, the general advice to keep questions short is the main piece of advice to be followed.

Avoid double-barrelled questions

Double-barrelled questions are ones that in fact ask about two things. The problem with this kind of question is that it leaves respondents unsure about how best to respond. Take the question:

How satisfied are you with pay and conditions in your job?

The problem here is obvious: the respondent may be satisfied with one but not the other. Not only will the respondent be unclear about how to reply, but any answer that is given is unlikely to be a good reflection of the level of satisfaction with pay *and* conditions. Similarly:

How frequently does your boss give you information concerning your daily work schedule and new developments within the company?

suffers from the same problem. A boss may provide extensive information about the daily work schedule but be totally uninformative about what is going on in the company more generally, so any stipulation of frequency of information is going to be ambiguous and will create uncertainty for respondents.

The same rule applies to fixed-choice answers. Further instances of double-barrelled questions are provided in Tips and skills 'Matching question and answers in closed questions'.

Avoid very general questions

It is easy to ask a very general question when in fact what is wanted is a response to a specific issue. The problem with questions that are very general is that they lack a frame of reference. Thus:

How satisfied are you with your job?

seems harmless, but it lacks specificity. Does it refer to pay, conditions, the nature of the work, or all of these? If there is the possibility of such diverse interpretations, respondents are likely to vary in their interpretations too, and this will be a source of error. One of our favourite

Matching question and answers in closed questions

You can sometimes find examples of badly designed questions in situations that you encounter in your everyday life. A recent example we have come across is a feedback questionnaire produced by a publisher and inserted into the pages of a novel that one of us was reading. At one point in the questionnaire there was a series of Likert-style items regarding the book's quality. In each case, the respondent is asked to indicate whether the attribute being asked about is poor; acceptable; average; good; or excellent. However, in each case, the items are presented as questions, for example:

Was the writing elegant, seamless, imaginative?

The problem here is that an answer to this question is 'yes' or 'no'. At most, we might have gradations of yes and no, such as: definitely; to a large extent; to some extent; not at all. However, 'poor' or 'excellent' cannot be answers to this question. The problem is that the questions should have been presented as statements, such as:

Please indicate the quality of the book in terms of each of the following criteria.

The elegance of the writing:

Poor _____ Acceptable _____ Average _____ Good _____ Excellent _____

Of course, we have changed the sense slightly here, because a further problem with the question as it was stated is that it is a double-barrelled question. In fact, it is 'treble-barrelled', because it asks about three attributes of the writing in one question. The reader's views about the three qualities may vary. A similar question asked:

Did the plot offer conflict, twists, and a resolution?

Again, not only does the question imply a 'yes' or 'no', it asks about three attributes. How would you answer if you had different views about each of the three criteria?

It might be argued that the issue is a nit-picking one: someone reading the question obviously knows that he or she is being asked to rate the quality of the book in terms of each attribute. The problem is that we simply do not know what the impact might be of a disjunction between question and answer, so you may as well get the connection between question and answers right (and do not ask double- or treble-barrelled questions either!).

examples of an overly general question comes from Karl Marx's *Enquête Ouvrière*, a questionnaire that was sent to 25,000 French socialists and others (though there is apparently no record of any being returned). The final (one-hundredth) question reads:

What is the general, physical, intellectual, and moral condition of men and women employed in your trade?

(Bottomore and Rubel 1963: 218)

Avoid leading questions

Leading or loaded questions are ones that appear to lead the respondent in a particular direction. Questions of the kind 'Do you agree with the view that … ?' fall into this class of question. The obvious problem with such a question is that it is suggesting a particular reply to respondents, although of course they do have the ability to rebut any implied answer. However, it is the fact that they might feel pushed in a certain direction that they do not naturally incline towards that is the problem. Such a question as:

Do you think that UK corporate directors receive excessive financial compensation?

is likely to make it difficult for some people to answer in a way that indicates they do not believe that UK corporate directors are overpaid for what they do. Once again, Marx is the source of a favourite example of a leading question:

If you are paid piece rates, is the quality of the article made a pretext for fraudulent deductions from wages?

(Bottomore and Rubel 1963: 215)

Avoid questions that are actually asking two questions

The double-barrelled question is a clear instance of the transgression of this rule, but in addition there is the case of a question like:

When did you last discuss your training needs with your supervisor/line manager?

What if the respondent has never discussed his or her training needs with the line manager? It is better to ask two separate questions:

Have you ever discussed your training needs with your supervisor/line manager?

Yes   ____

No   ____

If yes, when did your most recent discussion take place?

Another way in which more than one question can be asked is with a question like this:

How effective have your different job search strategies been?

Very effective   ____

Fairly effective   ____

Not very effective   ____

Not at all effective   ____

The obvious difficulty is that, if the respondent has used more than one job search strategy, his or her estimation of effectiveness will vary for each strategy. A mechanism is needed for assessing the success of each strategy, rather than forcing respondents to average out their sense of how successful the various strategies were.

Avoid questions that include negatives

The problem with questions with 'not' or similar formulations in them is that it is easy for the respondent to miss the word out when completing a self-completion questionnaire or to miss it when being interviewed. If this occurs, a respondent is likely to answer in the opposite way from the one intended. There are occasions when it is impossible to avoid negatives, but a question like the following should be avoided as far as possible:

Do you agree with the view that students should not have to take out loans to finance higher education?

Instead, the question should be asked in a positive format. Questions with double negatives should be totally avoided, because it is difficult to know how to respond to them. A hypothetical example of such a question is:

Would you rather not buy products from a confectionary company which did not produce Fairtrade chocolate?

It is quite difficult to establish what an answer of 'yes' or 'no' would actually mean in response to this question.

One context in which it is difficult to avoid using questions with negatives is when designing Likert scale items. Since you are likely to want to identify respondents who exhibit response sets and will therefore want to reverse the direction of your question asking (see Chapter 10), the use of negatives will be difficult to avoid.

Avoid technical and obscure terms

Use simple, plain language and avoid jargon. Do not ask a question such as:

Do you sometimes feel alienated from work?

The problem here is that many respondents will not know what is meant by 'alienated', and furthermore they are likely to have different views of what it means, even if it is a remotely meaningful term to them.

Consider the following question:

The influence of the TUC on management–worker relations has declined in recent years.

Strongly agree __ Agree __ Undecided __ Disagree __ Strongly disagree __

The use of acronyms such as 'TUC' (the Trades Union Congress in the UK) can be a problem, because some people may be unfamiliar with what they stand for.

TIPS AND SKILLS
Common mistakes when asking questions

Over the years, we have read many projects and dissertations based on structured interviews and self-completion questionnaires. We have noticed that a small number of mistakes recur. Here is a list of some of them:

1. An excessive use of open questions. Students sometimes include too many open questions. While a resistance to closed questions may be understandable, open questions are likely to reduce your response rate and will cause you analysis problems. Keep the number to an absolute minimum.

2. An excessive use of yes/no questions. Sometimes students include lots of questions that provide just a yes/no form of response. This is usually the result of lazy thinking and preparation. The world rarely fits into this kind of response. Take a question like:

Are you satisfied with opportunities for promotion in the firm?

Yes _____   No _____

This does not provide for the possibility that respondents will vary in their satisfaction. So why not rephrase it as:

How satisfied are you with opportunities for promotion in the firm?

Very satisfied   _____

Satisfied   _____

Neither satisfied nor dissatisfied   _____

Dissatisfied   _____

Very dissatisfied   _____

3. Students often fail to give clear instructions on self-completion questionnaires about how the questions should be answered. Make clear whether you want a tick, something to be circled or deleted, or whatever. If only one response is required, make sure you say so—for example, 'Tick the answer that comes closest to your view'.

4. Be careful about letting respondents choose more than one answer. Sometimes it is unavoidable, but questions that allow more than one reply are often difficult to analyse.

5. In spite of the fact that we always warn about the problems of overlapping categories, students still formulate closed answers that are not mutually exclusive. In addition, some categories may be omitted. For example:

How many times per week do you consult with your line manager?

1–3 times _____   3–6 times _____   6–9 times _____   More than 10 times _____

Not only does the respondent not know where to answer if his or her answer might be 3 or 6, there is no answer for someone who would want to answer 10.

6. Students sometimes do not ensure the answers correspond to the question. For example:

Do you regularly meet with your appraiser for an appraisal interview?

Never   _____

Once a year   _____

Twice a year   _____

More than twice a year   _____

The problem here is that the answer to the question is logically either 'yes' or 'no'. However, the student quite sensibly wants to gain some idea of frequency (something that we would agree with in the light of our second point in this list!). The problem is that the question and the response categories do not match up. The question should be:

How frequently do you meet with your appraiser in any year (January to December)?

Never   _____

Once a year   _____

Twice a year   _____

More than twice a year   _____

If you never committed any of these 'sins', you would be well on the way to producing a questionnaire that would stand out from the rest, provided you considered the other advice we give in this chapter as well!

Does the respondent have the requisite knowledge?

There is little point in asking respondents lots of questions about matters of which they have no knowledge. It is very doubtful whether meaningful data about computer use could be extracted from respondents who have never used or come into direct contact with a computer.

Make sure that there is a symmetry between a closed question and its answers

A common mistake is for a question and its answers to be out of phase with each other. Tips and skills 'Matching question and answers in closed questions' describes such an instance.

Make sure that the answers provided for a closed question are balanced

A common error when asking closed questions is for the answers that are provided to be unbalanced. For example, imagine that a respondent is given a series of options such as:

Excellent   _____

Good   _____

Acceptable   _____

Poor   _____

In this case, the response choices are balanced towards a favourable response. Excellent and Good are both positive; Acceptable is a neutral or middle position; and Poor is a negative response. In other words, the answers are loaded in favour of a positive rather than a negative reply, so that a further negative response choice (perhaps Very Poor) is required.

Memory problems

Do not rely too much on stretching people's memories to the extent that the answers for many of them are likely to be inaccurate. It would be nice to have accurate replies to a question about the number of times respondents have visited the cinema in the previous 12 months, but it is highly unlikely that most will in fact recall events accurately over such a long space of time (other perhaps than those who have not gone at all or only once or twice in the preceding 12 months). It was for this reason that, in the question on cinema visiting above, the time frame was predominantly just one month.

Don't know

One area of controversy when asking closed questions is whether to offer a 'don't know' or 'no opinion' option. The issue chiefly relates to questions concerning attitudes. The chief argument for including the 'don't know' option is that *not* to include one risks forcing people to express views that they do not really hold. Converse and Presser (1986: 35–6) strongly advocate that survey respondents should be offered a 'don't know' option but argue that it should be implemented by a filter question to filter out those who do not hold an opinion on a topic. This means that the interviewer needs to ask two questions, with the second question just relating to those respondents who do not hold an opinion.

The alternative argument about 'don't know' is that presenting it as an option allows respondents to select it when they cannot be bothered to think about the issue. In other words, presenting the option may prevent some respondents from thinking about the issue. A series of experiments conducted in the USA suggests that many respondents who express a lack of opinion on a topic do in fact hold an opinion (Krosnick et al. 2002). It was found that respondents with lower levels of education were especially prone to selecting the 'don't know' option and that questions that are later in a questionnaire are more likely to suffer from a tendency for 'don't know' to be selected. The latter finding implies a kind of question order effect. It implies that respondents become increasingly tired or bored as the questioning proceeds and therefore become prone to laziness in their answers. The researchers conclude that data quality is not enhanced by the inclusion of a 'don't know' option and that it may even be the case that some respondents become inhibited from expressing an opinion that they probably hold. Consequently, these researchers err on the side of *not* offering a 'don't know' option unless it is felt to be absolutely necessary.

Vignette questions

A form of asking mainly closed questions that has been used in connection with the examination of people's normative standards is the vignette technique. The technique essentially comprises presenting respondents with one or more scenarios and then asking them how they would respond when confronted with the circumstances of that scenario. Research in focus 12.2 describes a vignette that was employed in the context of a longitudinal study of the ethical behaviour of managers.

Sixteen different vignettes were used in this study to tease out respondents' responses to questionable ethical practices of different kinds. The scenarios presented in Research in focus 12.2 were concerned with a wide variety of business situations and were designed to address different functional areas of business. Each one dealt with a different questionable ethical practice, including some that were illegal. For example, scenario A concerns the issue of corporate theft; scenario B, law-breaking; and scenario C, professional malpractice. Many aspects of the issues being tapped by the vignette questions could be accessed through attitude items, such as:

> If a senior marketing professional has private business interests that are also related to the business of the firm, he has a duty to declare these interests to other senior executives immediately they arise.

Strongly agree__ Agree __ Undecided __ Disagree __ Strongly disagree__

The advantage of the vignette over such an attitude question is that it anchors the choice in a situation and as such reduces the possibility of an unreflective reply. In addition, when the subject matter is a sensitive area (in this case, dealing with ethical behaviour), there is the possibility that the questions may be seen as threatening by respondents. Respondents may feel that they are being judged by their replies. If the questions are about other people (and imaginary ones at that), this permits a certain amount of distance between the questioning and the respondent and results in a less threatening context. However, it is hard to believe that respondents will not feel that their replies will at least in part be seen as reflecting on them, even if the questions are not about them as such.

One obvious requirement of the vignette technique is that the scenarios must be believable, so that considerable effort needs to go into the construction of credible situations. Finch (1987) points out two further considerations in relation to this style of questioning. First, it is more or less impossible to establish how far assumptions are being made about the characters in the scenario (such as their ethnicity) and what the significance of those assumptions might be for the validity and comparability

12.2 RESEARCH IN FOCUS
Using vignette questions in a tracking study of ethical behaviour

The following vignettes were used by Longenecker et al. (2006: 177) in a study of ethical perceptions of managers of large corporations and owner/managers of smaller companies over 17 years. Using a **postal questionnaire** which contained 16 vignettes of business decisions with ethical overtones, a random sample of 10,000 respondents was surveyed at three points in time, in 1985, 1993, and 2001. The nationwide sample of US business professionals was generated from a mailing list used by publishers of major business periodicals. Some of the situations described in the vignettes were illegal; others were not, but involved debatably ethical actions. Respondents were asked to what extent they found each action compatible with their own ethical views, using a seven-point scale ranging from (1) never acceptable to (7) always acceptable. Three of the 16 vignettes are presented below.

A) An executive earning $50,000 a year padded his expense account by about $1500 a year.

B) In order to increase profits, a general manager used a production process which exceeded legal limits for environmental pollution.

C) Because of pressure from his brokerage firm, a stockbroker recommended a type of bond which he did not consider a good investment.

This longitudinal study enabled the researchers to track whether the ethical decision-making of managers was changing over time. However, unlike in a panel or a cohort study (see Chapter 3), the samples surveyed in each case were not the same, which limits the comparability of the data over time. Also, the nature of these questions makes it clear that they all involve ethical transgression of some sort, so respondents may be tempted to indicate the unacceptability of the actions because of **social desirability bias** (see Chapter 10), even if they might take a different view in practice.

of people's replies. Secondly, it is also difficult to establish how far people's answers reflect their own normative views or indeed how they themselves would act when confronted with the kinds of choices revealed in the scenarios. However, in spite of these reservations, the vignette technique warrants serious consideration when the research focus is concerned with an area that lends itself to this style of questioning.

Piloting and pre-testing questions

It is always desirable, if possible, to conduct a pilot study before administering a self-completion questionnaire or structured interview schedule to your sample. A pilot study involves administering your questionnaire or schedule to a small number of people who are in important ways like the respondents you intend to collect data from, but are not likely to be part of your sample. If, for example, you were planning a survey of call centre workers, ideally you would pilot your study using call centre workers (but not call centre workers who would be likely to be part of your sample). By doing this, you can assess whether someone doing the kind of work that you are interested in can make sense of, and answer, the questions you are planning to use.

In fact, the desirability of piloting such instruments is not solely to do with trying to ensure that survey questions operate well; piloting also has a role in ensuring that the research instrument as a whole functions well. Pilot studies may be particularly crucial in relation to research based on the self-completion questionnaire, since there will not be an interviewer present to clear up any confusion. Also, with interviews, persistent problems may emerge after a few interviews have been carried out, and these can then be addressed. However, with self-completion questionnaires, since they are sent or handed out in large numbers, considerable wastage may occur prior to any problems becoming apparent.

Here are some uses of pilot studies in survey research.

- If the main study is going to employ mainly closed questions, open questions can be asked in the pilot to generate the fixed-choice answers. Glock (1988), for example, extols the virtues of conducting qualitative

interviews in preparation for a survey, for precisely this kind of reason.

- Piloting an interview schedule can provide interviewers with some experience of using it and can infuse them with a greater sense of confidence.

- If everyone (or virtually everyone) who answers a question replies in the same way, the resulting data are unlikely to be of interest because they do not form a variable. A pilot study allows such a question to be identified.

- In interview surveys, it may be possible to identify questions that make respondents feel uncomfortable and to detect any tendency for respondents' interest to be lost at certain junctures.

- Questions that seem not to be understood (more likely to be realized in an interview than in a self-completion questionnaire context) or questions that are often not answered should become apparent. The latter problem of questions being skipped may be due to confusing or threatening phrasing, poorly worded instructions, or confusing positioning in the interview schedule or questionnaire. Whatever the cause might be, such missing data are undesirable, and a pilot study may be instrumental in identifying the problem.

- Pilot studies allow the researcher to determine the adequacy of instructions to interviewers, or to respondents completing a self-completion questionnaire.

- It may be possible to consider how well the questions flow and whether it is necessary to move some of them around to improve this feature.

Using existing questions

One final observation regarding the asking of questions is that you should also consider using questions that have been employed by other researchers for at least part of your questionnaire or interview schedule. This may seem like stealing, but if the questions have been published in prior research you should be able to use them as long as you cite the relevant publication and seek permission as required. Employing existing questions allows you to use questions that have been 'pre-tested'. If reliability and validity testing has taken place, which it typically will have if the relevant paper is published in a good journal, you will know about the measurement qualities of the existing questions you use. A further advantage of using existing questions is that they allow you to draw comparisons with other research. This might allow you to indicate whether change has occurred or whether place makes a difference to findings. For example, if you are researching job satisfaction, using one of the standard job satisfaction scales would allow you to compare your new findings with another researcher's previous findings. Alternatively, using the same questions as another researcher may allow you to explore whether the location of your sample appears to make a difference to the findings. While you need to be cautious about inferring too much from such comparisons between your own and other researchers' data, the findings can none the less be illuminating. At the very least, examining questions used by others might give you some ideas about how best to approach your own questions, even if you decide not to make use of any existing questions as they stand. An example of how questions developed by other researchers were used in a study of high performance work systems is given in Research in focus 12.3.

12.3 RESEARCH IN FOCUS
Using scales developed by other researchers in a study of high performance work systems

Van de Voorde and Beijer (2015) conducted a study of high performance work systems (HPWS)—systems of mutually-reinforcing human resource management (HRM) practices—and their associations with employees' experiences of job strain (a negative outcome) or commitment (a positive outcome). The authors argued that while there were many studies which examined such associations, little was known about the 'HR attributions' of employees—their understanding of the aims of management in implementing HPWS—and how these influenced the associations between HPWS and employee outcomes. Put simply, the authors argued that it is important to understand not just what HRM practices are in place, but also the meanings which employees attach to them, if we are to understand how HPWS influence employees' experiences of work.

The authors surveyed over 1000 Dutch employees across 105 work units in a variety of industries, in for-profit and not-for-profit organizations. The study also collected data from the line manager in each work unit. In conducting this study, the authors used a series of questionnaire items which had previously been used and had been published:

- The prevalence of HPWS was measured using 23 pre-existing items drawn from Kroon et al. (2009) and 3 from Boselie (2002), which asked each manager to rate the extent to which employees in that work unit were subject to specific HRM practices. Examples of items:

    Does your company offer formal internal training?

    Does your company pay higher than average salaries?

    Are employees involved in strategic decisions in your organization?

- Answers were provided using the following four responses:

    Yes, for all employees in this unit

    Yes for a majority of employees in this unit (> 50 per cent)

    Yes for a minority of employees in this unit (< 50 per cent)

    No, for none of the employees in this unit

    The 26 items were used to construct a single composite measure of the experience of HPWS at work unit level.

- Employees' organizational commitment—the extent to which employees feel they share the values of the organization—was measured using a scale developed by Moideenkutty et al. (2001). A sample item is: 'I really feel as if this organization's problems are my own'. The responses were captured using a seven-point Likert scale (1 = Strongly disagree to 7 = Strongly agree).

- Employees' job strain—a form of stress—was measured using a scale developed by Van Veldhoven and Meijman (1994). An example item is 'I find it difficult to relax at the end of a working day'. Participants responded on a four-point scale (never, sometimes, often, always).

- HR attributions were measured by asking each employee to rate each HR practice in terms of whether it was aimed at promoting employee wellbeing and, in a separate set of questions, whether it was aimed at getting the most work out of employees. This approach was based on items developed by Nishii et al. (2008). Employees provided answers on a five-point Likert scale (1 = Strongly disagree to 5 = Strongly agree).

By drawing on a number of prior studies, the authors were able to utilize pre-tested measures, which captured all the variables which they needed for their study. Based on their analysis of the data, the authors found that the more prevalent were HPWS practices, the higher were attributions of both wellbeing and performance, which they argue suggests that HPWS practices signal managerial intentions to employees and that employees can attribute both employee- and managerially-focused intentions in using such systems. Significantly, however, the study suggests that the more that employees attribute HPWS to the desire by management to improve wellbeing, the higher are their levels of commitment and the lower their levels of job strain. Where employees attribute HPWS to a desire for higher performance, job strain is higher. These findings, the authors argue, show that the meanings that employees attach to HPWS influence the outcomes of HPWS.

The process of finding questions has been made a great deal easier by the creation of 'question banks', which act as repositories of questions employed in surveys and elsewhere. The UK Data Archive (UKDA), which aims to improve standards in UK survey research, has a very good question bank providing access to questionnaires from major surveys (including the **Census**) and associated commentary to assist survey design. It is freely available and can be found at https://discover.ukdataservice.ac.uk/variables. The Australian Data Archive also holds numerous questionnaires which have been used in prior studies and which can be accessed at http://www.ada.edu.au. It is essential, whenever you use questions from prior studies, that you seek permission as necessary and attribute the questions to their sources. You will find that data archives almost always specify what attribution is required, so make sure that you understand what is required and comply with requirements.

STUDENT EXPERIENCE
Using a questionnaire designed by another researcher

Karen used a questionnaire designed by an author that she had identified during her **literature review** to measure the cultural profile of the company where she was doing her research. For each of the 54 characteristics of the culture, each respondent had to 'identify whether it was highly characteristic, moderately characteristic, or not characteristic at all of the culture'. This quantitative element of her research project was combined with qualitative **semi-structured interviews** involving a sample of 15 managers within the business from different departments and different levels of the organization. Each research participant completed the questionnaire and was also interviewed. In explaining her **research design**, Karen said:

> I chose [a sample of] fifteen because I only had a limited amount of time and I thought, 'If I go for more than that, then I'm going to end up with like an overwhelming amount of data and information to sift through.' I thought, 'I'd rather get more valuable information and sort of have longer interviews and get more sort of time to explore things, than to just cut them short and only have a few.'

For a detailed discussion of the issues involved in combining **quantitative** and **qualitative research**, see Chapter 27.

TIPS AND SKILLS
Getting help in designing questions

When designing questions, as we suggested earlier, try to put yourself in the position of someone who has been asked to answer the questions. This can be difficult, because some (if not all) of the questions may not apply to you—for example, if you are a student doing a survey of managers. However, try to think about how you would reply. This means concentrating not just on the questions themselves but also on the links between the questions. For example, do filter questions work in the way you expect them to? Then try the questions out on some people you know, as a form of a pilot study. Ask them to be critical and to consider how well the questions connect to each other. Also, do look at the questionnaires and structured interview schedules that experienced researchers have devised. They may not have asked questions on your topic, but the way they have asked the questions and the flow of the questions should give you an idea of what to do and what to avoid when designing such instruments.

CHECKLIST
Issues to consider for your structured interview schedule or self-completion questionnaire

○ Have you devised a clear and comprehensive way of introducing the research to interviewees or questionnaire respondents?

○ Have you considered whether there are any existing questions used by other researchers to investigate this topic that could meet your needs?

○ Do the questions allow you to answer all your research questions?

○ Could any questions that are not strictly relevant to your research questions be dropped?

○ Have you tried to put yourself in the position of answering as many of the questions as possible?

○ Have you piloted the questionnaire with some appropriate respondents?

○ If it is a structured interview schedule, have you made sure that the instructions to yourself and to anyone else involved in interviewing are clear (for example, with filter questions, which questions should be answered next)?

○ If it is a self-completion questionnaire, have you made sure that the instructions to the respondent are clear (for example, with filter questions, which questions should be answered next)?

○ Are instructions about how to record responses clear (for example, whether to tick or circle; whether more than one response is allowable)?

○ Have you included as few open questions as possible?

○ Have you allowed respondents to indicate levels of intensity in their replies, so that they are not forced into 'yes' or 'no' answers where intensity of feeling or frequency of a behaviour may be more appropriate?

○ Have you ensured that questions and their answers do not span more than one page?

○ Have socio-demographic questions been left until the end of the questionnaire?

○ Have you put questions that are central to the research topic at, or very close to, the beginning?

○ Have you taken steps to ensure that the questions you are asking really do supply you with the information you need?

○ Have you taken steps to ensure that there are no:

  ○ ambiguous terms in questions or closed answers?

  ○ long questions?

  ○ double-barrelled questions?

  ○ very general questions?

  ○ leading questions?

  ○ questions that are asking about two or more things?

  ○ questions that include negatives?

  ○ questions using technical terms?

○ Have you made sure that your respondents will have the requisite knowledge to answer your questions?

○ Is there an appropriate match between your questions and your closed answers?

○ Do any of your questions rely too much on your respondents' memory?

○ If you are using a Likert scale approach:

  ○ Have you included some items that can be reverse scored to minimize response sets?

  ○ Have you made sure that the items really do relate to the same underlying cluster of attitudes so that they can be aggregated?

○ Have you ensured that your closed answers are exhaustive?

○ Have you ensured that your closed answers do not overlap?

○ Where appropriate, have you ensured that there is a category of 'other' (or similar category such as 'unsure' or 'neither agree nor disagree') so that respondents are not forced to answer in a way that is not indicative of what they think or do?

KEY POINTS

- While open questions undoubtedly have certain advantages, closed questions are typically preferable for a survey, because of the ease of asking questions and recording and processing answers.

- This applies particularly to the self-completion questionnaire.

- Open questions of the kind used in qualitative interviewing have a useful role in relation to the formulation of fixed-choice answers and in piloting.
- It is crucial to learn the rules of question-asking to avoid some of the more obvious pitfalls.
- Remember always to put yourself in the position of the respondent when asking questions and to make sure you will generate data appropriate to your research questions.
- Vignette questions can be used to investigate people's normative standards.
- Piloting or pre-testing may clear up problems in question formulation.

QUESTIONS FOR REVIEW

Open or closed questions?

- What difficulties do open questions present in survey research?
- Why are closed questions frequently preferred to open questions in survey research?
- What are the limitations of closed questions?
- How can closed questions be improved?

Types of question

- What are the main types of question that are likely to be used in a structured interview or self-administered questionnaire?

Rules for designing questions

- What is wrong with each of the following questions?

  What is your annual salary?

  > Below £10,000
  >
  > £10,000–15,000
  >
  > £15,000–20,000
  >
  > £20,000–25,000
  >
  > £25,000–30,000
  >
  > £30,000–35,000
  >
  > £35,000 and over

  Do you ever feel alienated from your work?

  > All the time
  >
  > Often
  >
  > Occasionally
  >
  > Never

  How satisfied are you with the customer services and products provided by this company?

  > Very satisfied
  >
  > Fairly satisfied
  >
  > Neither satisfied nor dissatisfied
  >
  > Fairly dissatisfied
  >
  > Very dissatisfied

Vignette questions

- In what circumstances are vignette questions appropriate?

Piloting and pre-testing questions

- Why is it important to pilot questions?

Using existing questions

- Why might it be useful to use questions devised by others?

....

 ONLINE RESOURCES

www.oup.com/uk/brm5e/

Visit the Interactive Research Guide that accompanies this book to complete an exercise in asking questions.

....

CHAPTER 13

QUANTITATIVE RESEARCH USING NATURALLY OCCURRING DATA

CHAPTER OUTLINE

Structured observation involves the direct observation of behaviour and the recording of that behaviour in terms of categories that have been devised prior to the start of data collection. Content analysis is an approach to the analysis of documents and texts (which may be printed or online text and/or visual images) that seeks to quantify content in terms of predetermined categories and in a systematic and replicable manner. Neither method is as widely used in business research as other methods outlined in this book, but nonetheless they are important approaches.

This chapter explores:

- the potential of structured observation for the study of behaviour;
- how to devise an observation schedule;
- different strategies for observing behaviour in structured observation;
- sampling issues in structured observation research—with this method, the issue of sampling is to do not just with people but also with the sampling of time and contexts;
- issues of reliability and validity in structured observation;
- some criticisms of structured observation;
- the kinds of research question to which content analysis is suited;
- how to approach the sampling of documents to be analysed;
- what kinds of features of documents or texts are counted;
- how to go about coding, which is probably the central and most distinctive stage of doing a content analysis;
- the advantages and disadvantages of content analysis.

Introduction

In the previous three chapters, we have discussed ways of collecting quantitative data which involve asking people questions, either individually or in groups, and either face-to-face, on the phone, or via a questionnaire. These approaches are popular, primarily because they are effective means of gathering data. The earlier chapters have touched on a number of criticisms of the various approaches discussed. One common criticism of interviews and surveys is that the researcher does not collect data in naturally occurring situations and environments.

That is, interviews and surveys are 'artificial' settings, which strictly speaking only tell us about how people answer interview or survey questions, not about how they actually behave or think. By contrast, the principle of naturalism informs several qualitative methods such as ethnography and participant observation (see Chapter 19). There are, however, quantitative methods which can also be used to gather and analyse naturally occurring data. Two of these, structured observation and content analysis, will be discussed in this chapter.

Structured observation

As noted above, surveys and interviews have been criticized for being artificial situations. This general problem is manifested in a variety of ways. Some of these are listed below:

- *Problem of meaning*. People may vary in their interpretations of key terms in a question.
- *Problem of omission*. When answering the question, respondents may inadvertently omit key terms in the question.
- *Problem of memory*. People may misremember aspects of the occurrence of certain forms of behaviour.

- *Social desirability effect*. People may exhibit a tendency towards replying in ways that are meant to be consistent with their perceptions of the desirability of certain kinds of answer.
- *Question threat*. Some questions may appear threatening and result in a failure to provide an honest reply.
- *Interviewer characteristics*. Aspects of the interviewer may influence the answers provided.
- *Gap between stated and actual behaviour*. How people say they are likely to behave and how they actually behave may be inconsistent.

13.1 KEY CONCEPT
What is structured observation?

Structured observation, often also called systematic observation, is a technique in which the researcher employs explicitly formulated rules for the observation and recording of behaviour. The rules inform observers about what they should look for and how they should record behaviour. Each person who is part of the research (we will call these people 'participants') is observed for a predetermined period using the same rules. These rules are articulated in what is usually referred to as an *observation schedule*, which bears many similarities to a structured interview schedule with closed questions. The aim of the observation schedule is to ensure that each participant's behaviour is systematically recorded so that it is possible to aggregate the behaviour of all those in the sample in respect of each type of behaviour being recorded. The rules that constitute the observation schedule are as specific as possible in order to direct observers to exactly what aspects of behaviour they are supposed to be looking for. The resulting data resemble questionnaire data considerably, in that the procedure generates information on different aspects of behaviour that can be treated as variables. Moreover, structured observation research is typically underpinned by a cross-sectional research design.

An obvious solution to problems of these kinds is to observe people's behaviour directly rather than to rely on research instruments such as questionnaires to elicit such information. A useful way of doing this is structured observation (see Key concept 13.1), also often called systematic observation.

It has been implied that structured observation can be viewed as an alternative to survey methods of research. After all, in view of the various problems identified above, it would seem an obvious solution to observe people instead. Central to any structured observation study will be the *observation schedule* or *coding scheme*.

This specifies the categories of behaviour that are to be observed and how behaviour should be allocated to those categories. It is best to illustrate what this involves by giving an example. One of the best-known studies to have used structured observation is Mintzberg's (1973) ground-breaking study of managerial work. Mintzberg studied five chief executives, for one week each, as they went about their normal business days. The detailed nature of his investigation restricted the amount of quantitative data that could be generated, but it also enabled very detailed analysis of the kind of work that managers do (see Research in focus 13.2).

13.2 RESEARCH IN FOCUS
Mintzberg's categories of basic activities involved in managerial work

Mintzberg (1973) identified five categories into which the activities of managerial work could be placed. They are listed below:

- *Scheduled meeting*. A prearranged face-to-face meeting involving the manager and one or more other participants is defined as scheduled.

- *Unscheduled meeting*. A meeting is defined as unscheduled if it is arranged hastily, as when someone just 'drops in'.

- *Desk work*. This refers to the time the manager spends at his or her desk, processing mail, scheduling activities, writing letters, or communicating with the secretary.

- *Call*. This category refers to telephone calls.

- *Tour*. This refers to a chance meeting in the hall, or to the 'promenades' taken by the manager to observe activity and to deliver information.

Structured data were collected using three records:

- *chronology record*: described activity patterns, noting the time, nature, and duration of the activity;
- *mail record*: described each piece of incoming/outgoing mail and the action that was taken to respond to it;
- *contact record*: described each verbal contact, noting the participants and where it took place.

In Mintzberg's coding scheme, time and activities were coded separately, so that the distribution of clock time might overlap an activity or vice versa. For example, 'tours' of the work site and 'desk work' included time spent talking (i.e. verbal contact). Almost 40 per cent of activities were meetings; this accounted for 70 per cent of the managers' work time. From such data, a number of features could be derived. Mintzberg's main conclusions were that managerial work is highly fragmented, varied, and characterized by brief spells of any one activity, and that managers have a need for instant communication on which to base further verbal contact and action. These findings ran contrary to the traditional view that was dominant at the time, which suggested that managerial activity was planned and rational.

The observation schedule

Devising a schedule for the recording of observations is clearly a crucial step in the structured observation project. The considerations that go into this phase are very like those involved in producing a structured interview schedule:

- A clear focus is necessary. There are two aspects to this point. First, it should be clear to the observer exactly who or what (and possibly both) is to be observed. For example, if people are the focus of attention, the observer needs to know precisely who is to be observed. The second sense in which a clear focus is necessary is that the research problem needs to be clearly stated so that the observer knows which of the many things going on in any setting are to be recorded.
- As with the production of a closed question for a structured interview schedule or self-completion questionnaire, the forms taken by any category of behaviour must be both mutually exclusive (that is, not overlap) and inclusive (that is, cover all relevant forms of behaviour). It is often desirable for a certain amount of unstructured observation to take place prior to the construction of the observation schedule and for there to be some piloting of it, so that possible problems associated with a lack of inclusiveness can be anticipated.

- The recording system must be easy to operate. Complex systems with large numbers of types of behaviour will be undesirable. In a similar way to interviewers using a structured interview schedule, observers need to be trained, but even after training it is easy for an observer to become flustered or confused if faced with too many options.

- One possible problem with some observation schedules is that they require a certain amount of interpretation on the part of the observer. For example, it might be difficult to distinguish in any meaningful sense between an unscheduled meeting and a discussion with two or three colleagues that takes place in a corridor. To the extent that it may be difficult to distinguish between the two, some interpretation on the part of the observer may be needed.

Strategies for observing behaviour

There are different ways of conceptualizing how behaviour should be recorded:

- We can record in terms of *incidents*. This means waiting for something to happen and then recording what follows from it. Essentially, this is what Mintzberg (1973) did, as the following account of his method illustrates: 'The researcher observes the manager as he performs his work. Each observed event (a verbal contact or a piece of incoming or outgoing mail) is categorized by the researcher in several ways (for example, duration, participants, purpose)' (1973: 231). In this study, the categories, or activity codes, are developed either during the observation or shortly after it takes place, rather than beforehand. Only after the observation had taken place did Mintzberg begin to draw connections between the activities to develop his final activity codes.

- We can observe and record in terms of *short periods* of time, observing one individual for a couple of minutes but returning at structured intervals to conduct further observations. This can help to ensure the generalizability of what goes on in the setting. For example, if a manager holds regular meetings each day at 4 p.m., three observations, each lasting 20 minutes, con-

ducted in the morning, at lunchtime, and in the afternoon, will ensure a more representative sample of activities than would an observation lasting an hour from 4 to 5 p.m.

- We can observe and record observations for quite *long periods* of time. The observer watches and records more or less continuously, doing what Martin and Bateson (1986) refer to as continuous recording, whereby the observer observes for extended periods, thus allowing the frequency and duration of forms of behaviour to be measured.

Sampling for structured observation

Just like survey research, structured observation necessitates decisions about sampling. Mintzberg's study was somewhat unusual in that it relied on a very small sample of only five individuals—a decision that he explains was forced partly by practical constraints, as the research was done for his doctoral dissertation. This meant that 'the time of only one researcher was available, and that for only 12 months or so' (Mintzberg 1973: 237). Research in focus 13.3 describes a study done with a sample of just one individual. However, with structured observation it is more usual to sample a larger number of people, and also to incorporate several other sampling issues.

Sampling people

When people are being sampled, considerations very similar to those encountered in Chapter 9 in respect of probability sampling come to the fore. This means that the observer will ideally want to sample on a random basis.

Sampling in terms of time

It is often necessary to ensure that, if certain individuals are sampled on more than one occasion, they are not always observed at the same time of the day. This means that, if particular individuals are selected randomly for observation on several different occasions for short periods, it is desirable for the observation periods to be randomly selected. For example, it would not be desirable for a certain manager working in her office always to be observed at the end of the day. She might be tired

and this would give a false impression of that manager's behaviour.

Further sampling considerations

The sampling procedures mentioned so far conform to probability sampling principles, because it is feasible to construct a sampling frame for individuals. However, this is not always possible for different kinds of reasons. Studies in public areas, for example, do not permit random sampling, because we cannot very easily construct a sampling frame of people walking along a street. Similarly, it is not feasible to construct a sampling frame of interactions—for example, of meetings between managers and their subordinates. The problem with doing structured observation research on such a topic is that it does not lend itself to the specification of a sampling frame, and therefore the researcher's ability to generate a probability sample is curtailed.

As suggested in Chapter 8, considerations relating to probability sampling derive largely from concerns surrounding the external validity of findings. Such concerns are not necessarily totally addressed by resorting to probability sampling, however. For example, if a structured observation study is conducted over a relatively short span of time, issues of the representativeness of findings are likely to arise. Consequently, consideration must be given to the question of the timing of observation. Furthermore, how are the sites in which structured observation is to take place selected? Can we presume that they are themselves representative? Clearly, a random sampling procedure for the selection of organizations may assuage concerns in this connection. However, in view of the difficulty of securing access to settings such as business organizations, it is likely

13.3 RESEARCH IN FOCUS
Structured observation with a sample of one

Louhiala-Salminen (2002) observed a Finnish business manager who worked in a multinational corporation for one day to identify the features that characterize the discourse in a multinational corporation. The aim of the study 'was to describe the discourse activities of a professional who is a non-native speaker of English and uses English "as a business lingua franca"' (2002: 215). Most of the day was recorded using audio tapes, and an observation protocol was used to make notes about the nature of the activity, including type of communication and language used. Louhiala-Salminen undertook the observation between 09.00 and 16.00 and followed the manager all day except for one 20-minute meeting that entailed confidential information. The manager stayed at work for a further 90 minutes after the observation ended, 'catching up with some planning and writing which he was not able to do in the day' (2002: 217). On the day following the observation, the manager, his superior, and his subordinates were interviewed to seek clarification of events the previous day and to gain background information about the manager's education, experience, and attitudes towards language, communication, and culture.

One of the issues this study had to deal with is the impact of technology on managerial time use, specifically the use of email as a communication medium as opposed to writing letters or making telephone calls. The researcher explains: 'The written documents that the manager read or wrote during the day were e-mail messages. Because of the large number of the messages (about 150 altogether) it would have been impossible to have copies of all without seriously disturbing the normal flow of work. Therefore about one third of the email messages were printed as examples' (2002: 214). Louhiala-Salminen notes the crucial role of email in structuring the events of the working day. The manager spent the first two hours of his day working through the 95 emails that had arrived for him during the previous two days when he had been out of the office, and the majority of subsequent interactions were initiated by email messages. The study also highlights the blurred boundaries between different kinds of activity: 'throughout the day spoken and written communication were totally intertwined, there was hardly any activity in either mode where the other would not be present as well; many of the phone calls were to confirm an issue in an e-mail message, e-mail messages referred to phone calls, and they were constantly discussed in face-to-face communication with colleagues' (2002: 217).

This study is also interesting in terms of **reactive effects**. When discussing the nature of the observation and in particular the low number of direct spoken encounters, which Louhiala-Salminen found puzzling given the open-plan nature of the office, the manager suggested that more people would have stopped to talk to him had the researcher not been sitting near his desk. Finally, although this study involved the structured observation of just one manager for one day, it was intended to form part of a bigger international comparative study across four different countries once the research design and data collection methods had been tested. One of the things that Louhiala-Salminen discovered from the study was that, because of the hectic pace of work involving different communication media, the observation protocol was too detailed to be completed during the observation. She suggests that a video recording would make analysis of simultaneous and interconnected activities easier.

---

that the organizations to which access is secured will not be representative of the population of appropriate ones.

A further set of distinctions between types of sampling in structured observation have been drawn by Martin and Bateson (1986):

- **ad libitum sampling**, whereby the observer records whatever is happening at the time;

- **focal sampling**, in which a specific individual is observed for a set period of time—the observer records all examples of whatever forms of behaviour are of interest in terms of a schedule;

- **scan sampling**, whereby an entire group of individuals is scanned at regular intervals and the behaviour of all of them is recorded at that time—this sampling strategy allows only one or two types of behaviour to be observed and recorded; and

- **behaviour sampling**, whereby an entire group is watched and the observer records who was involved in a particular kind of behaviour.

Most structured observation research seems to employ focal sampling, as in Mintzberg's (1973) study.

Issues of reliability and validity

One researcher has concluded that, when compared to interviews and questionnaires, structured observation 'provides (*a*) more reliable information about events; (*b*) greater precision regarding their timing, duration, and frequency; (*c*) greater accuracy in the time ordering of variables; and (*d*) more accurate and economical reconstructions of large-scale social episodes' (McCall 1984: 277). This is a very strong endorsement for structured observation, but, as McCall notes, there are several issues of reliability and validity that confront practitioners of the method. Some of these issues are like those faced by researchers when seeking to develop measures in business research in general (see Chapter 8) and by those using survey research in particular. However, certain concerns are specific to structured observation.

Reliability

Practitioners of structured observation have been concerned with the degree to which two or more observers of the same behaviour agree in terms of their coding of that behaviour on the observation schedule—that is, *inter-observer consistency*. The chief mechanism for assessing this component of reliability is a statistic called *kappa* (see Key concept 13.4; *this can be ignored if you feel unsure about addressing more complex statistical issues at this stage*).

A second consideration in relation to reliability is the degree of consistency of an observer's application of the observation schedule over time—that is, *intra-observer consistency*. This is clearly a difficult notion, because of the capacity for and often necessity for people to behave in different ways on different occasions and in different contexts. Assessing the consistency of observation ratings across all possibilities is clearly a difficult undertaking. The procedures for assessing this aspect of reliability are broadly similar to those applied to the issue of inter-observer consistency.

It is clearly not an easy matter to achieve reliability in structured observation. This is a point of some significance, given that validity presupposes reliability (see Chapter 8). Reliability may be difficult to achieve on occasions, because of the effects of such factors as observer fatigue and lapses in attention. However, this point should not be exaggerated, because some studies have been able to achieve high levels of reliability for many of their measures, and indeed two critics of structured observation have written that 'there is no doubt that observers can be trained to use complex coding schedules with considerable reliability' (Delamont and Hamilton 1984: 32).

Validity

Measurement validity relates to the question of whether a measure is measuring what it is supposed to measure. The validity of any measure will be affected by:

- whether or not the measure reflects the concept it has been designed to measure (see Chapter 8); and
- error that arises from the implementation of the measure in the research process (see Chapter 10).

13.4 KEY CONCEPT
What is Cohen's kappa?

Cohen's kappa is a measure of the degree of agreement over the coding of items by two people. As such, it could be applied to the coding of any textual information, as in the content analysis of newspaper articles or of answers to open interview questions, as well as to the coding of observation. Much like Cronbach's alpha (see Key concept 8.6), you will end up with a coefficient that will vary between 0 and 1. The closer the coefficient is to 1, the higher the agreement and the better the inter-observer consistency. A coefficient of 0.75 or above is considered very good; between 0.6 and 0.75, it is considered good; and between 0.4 and 0.6, it is regarded as fair. The meaning of kappa is that it measures the degree of agreement between observers beyond that which would occur by chance. Croll (1986) refers to a very similar statistic, the Scott coefficient of agreement, which can be interpreted in an identical way.

The first of these issues simply means that in structured observation it is necessary to attend to the same kinds of issues concerning the checking of validity (assessing face validity, concurrent validity, and so on) that are encountered in research-based interviews and questionnaires. The second aspect of validity—error in implementation—relates to two matters in particular:

- Is the observation instrument administered as it is supposed to be? This is the equivalent of ensuring that interviewers using a structured interview schedule follow the research instrument and its instructions exactly as they are supposed to. If there is variability between observers or over time, the measure will be unreliable and therefore cannot be valid. It is therefore crucial to ensure that observers have as complete an understanding as possible of how the observation schedule should be implemented.

- Do people change their behaviour because they know they are being observed? This is an instance of what is known as the 'reactive effect'—after all, if people adjust the way they behave because they know they are being observed (perhaps because they want to be viewed in a favourable way by the observer), their behaviour would have to be considered atypical. As a result, we could hardly regard the results of structured observation research as indicative of what happens in reality. As McCall (1984) notes, there is evidence that a reactive effect occurs in structured observation, but that by and large research participants become accustomed to being observed, so that the researcher essentially becomes less intrusive the longer he or she is present.

Criticisms of structured observation

Structured observation has, in the past, been quite controversial. Certain criticisms have been implied in some of the previous discussion of reliability and validity issues, as well as in connection with the issue of generalizability. However, other areas of criticism warrant further discussion.

- There is a risk of imposing a potentially inappropriate or irrelevant framework on the setting being observed. This point is similar to the problem of the closed question in questionnaires. This risk is especially great if the setting is one about which little is known. One solution is for the structured observation to be preceded by a period of unstructured observation, so that appropriate variables and categories can be specified.

- Because it concentrates upon directly observable behaviour, structured observation is rarely able to get at intentions behind behaviour. Sometimes, when intentions are of concern, they are imputed by observers. Thus, in Mintzberg's basic activity categories of managerial behaviour, it is not entirely clear what the difference is between an 'unscheduled meeting' and a 'tour' that involves a chance meeting. Essentially, the problem is that structured observation does not readily allow the observer to get a grasp of the meaning of behaviour.

- There is a tendency for structured observation to generate lots of bits of data. The problem here can be one of trying to piece them together to produce an overall picture, or one of trying to find general themes that link the fragments of data together. It becomes difficult, in other words, to see a bigger picture that lies behind the segments of behaviour that structured observation typically uncovers. It has been suggested, for example, that the tendency for structured observation studies of managers at work to find little evidence of planning in their everyday work (e.g. Mintzberg 1973) is due to the tendency for the method to fragment a manager's activities into discrete parts. As a result, something like planning, which may be an element in many managerial activities, becomes obscured from view (Snyder and Glueck 1980).

- It is often suggested that structured observation neglects the context within which behaviour takes place. For example, Martinko and Gardner (1990) found that some of Mintzberg's categories of basic activity were represented differently among school principals, rather than general managers, and, in particular, the amount of time spent on unscheduled meetings was much greater. Of course, if data were collected about the context in which behaviour takes place, this criticism would have little weight, but the tendency of structured observation researchers to concentrate on overt behaviour engenders this kind of criticism.

On the other hand …

It is clear from the previous section that there are undeniable limitations to structured observation. However, it also has to be remembered that, when overt behaviour is the focus of analysis and perhaps issues of meaning are less salient, structured observation is almost certainly more accurate and effective than getting people to report on their behaviour through questionnaires. It may also be that structured observation is a method that works best when accompanied by other methods. Since it can rarely provide reasons for observed patterns of behaviour, if it is accompanied by another method that can probe reasons, it is of greater utility.

Another form of quantitative analysis that uses naturally occurring data is content analysis, to which we will now turn.

Content analysis

Imagine that you are interested in the amount and nature of the interest shown by the mass media, such as newspapers, in a business news item such as the sexual harassment allegations made against Uber in 2017 and the impact this has had on corporate accountability and ethical behaviour. You might ask such questions as:

- When did news items on this topic first begin to appear?
- Which newspapers were fastest in generating an interest in the topic?
- Which newspapers have shown the greatest interest in the topic?
- At what point did media interest begin to wane?
- Have journalists' stances on the topic changed, for example, in terms of their support for self-regulation by business, or in calling for increased government regulation of corporate behaviour?

If you want to know the answers to research questions such as these, you are likely to need to use content analysis of the texts involved in order to answer them.

Content analysis emphasizes two qualities: objectivity and being systematic. The former quality means that rules are clearly specified in advance for the assignment of the raw material (such as newspaper stories) to categories. Objectivity in this sense resides in the fact that there is transparency in the procedures for assigning the raw material to categories so that the analyst's personal biases intrude as little as possible in the process. The content analyst is simply applying the rules in question. The quality of being systematic means that the application of the rules is done in a consistent manner so that bias is again suppressed. Because of these two qualities, anyone could employ the rules and (hopefully) come up with the same results. These qualities of the process of analysis mean that the results are not an extension of the analyst and his or her personal biases. The rules in question may, of course, reflect the researcher's interests and concerns and therefore these might be a product of subjective bias, but the key point is that, once formulated, the rules can be (or should be capable of being) applied without the intrusion of bias.

Content analysis is firmly rooted in the quantitative research strategy, in that the aim is to produce quantitative accounts of the raw material in terms of the categories specified by the rules. The feature of quantification adds to the general sense of the systematic and objective application of neutral rules, so that it becomes possible to say with some certainty and in a systematic way that, for example, management blogs carried far more coverage of an issue than online news sites.

Further, content analysis is concerned with uncovering the apparent content of the item in question: what it is clearly about. The latter essentially opens the door to conducting an analysis in terms of what we might term 'latent content'—that is, of meanings that lie beneath the superficial indicators of content. Uncovering such latent content means interpreting meanings that lie beneath the surface, such as whether the impression is given that the author construes the Uber allegations as being of interest only to the transport industry, or as having a broader set of implications for business practice and corporate accountability across the globe.

Content analysis becomes applicable to many different forms of unstructured information, such as transcripts of semi- and unstructured interviews (e.g. Bryman et al. 1996) and even qualitative case studies of organizations (e.g. Hodson 1996). Nor is it necessary for the medium being analysed to be in a written form. This type of research has been conducted on a range of topics and materials, for example:

13.5 KEY CONCEPT
What is content analysis?

Content analysis. An approach to the analysis of documents and texts that seeks to quantify content in terms of predetermined categories and in a systematic and replicable manner.

Content analysis can usefully be contrasted with two other approaches to the analysis of the content of communication:

- *Semiotics*, the study/science of signs: an approach to the analysis of documents and other phenomena that emphasizes the importance of seeking out the deeper meaning of those data. A semiotic approach is concerned to uncover the processes of meaning production and how signs are designed to have an effect upon actual and prospective consumers of those signs.

- *Ethnographic content analysis*, a term employed by Altheide (1996) to refer to an approach to documents that emphasizes the role of the investigator in the construction of the meaning of and in texts. It is sometimes also referred to as qualitative content analysis. As with most approaches that are described as ethnographic, there is an emphasis on allowing categories to emerge out of data and on recognizing the significance for understanding meaning of the context in which an item being analysed (and the categories derived from it) appeared. This approach will be explored in Chapter 24.

When the term 'content analysis' is employed in this chapter, it will be referring to quantitative content analysis—that is, the first of the three forms of analysis referred to in the passage above.

- the visual images (as well as the text) of company annual reports to explore how these reflect organizational beliefs about customers (Dougherty and Kunda 1990);

- motivational videos featuring management guru Frederick Herzberg giving a live lecture to managers (Jackson and Carter 1998);

- the pictures drawn by managers to express their views about organizational change (Broussine and Vince 1996).

However, the main use of content analysis has been to examine mass media items, as well as texts and documents that are either produced by an organization, such as annual reports, or written about it, such as articles in the business press. In this regard, content analysis is one of a number of approaches to the examination of texts that have been developed over the years (see Key concept 13.5).

What are the research questions?

As with most quantitative research, it is necessary to specify the research questions precisely, as these will guide both the selection of the media to be content analysed and the coding schedule. If the research questions are not clearly articulated, there is a risk that irrelevant media will be analysed or that the coding schedule will miss out key dimensions. Most content analysis is likely to entail several research questions. For example, the aim of Harris's (2001) study (discussed in Research in focus 13.6) was to investigate the way the word 'courage' was used in the business community. In itself this is not very specific and hardly directs you to a clear

specification of the media to be examined or the development of a coding schedule. However, to achieve this aim Harris sought to content analyse stories in newspapers that were about courage in order to compare a definition of courage derived from the literature with the way the word 'courage' is used in the community (especially in business, commerce, and government). This gave rise to other, more specific research questions, including:

- Is it possible to categorize the types of courage event described in the newspaper stories?

- What tools, if any, are said to have helped people show courage?

- Are obstacles identified in accounts of courage, and, if so, what are they?

- Are aspects of the accounts linked to specific professions or sectors of activity?

- Is courage used to describe dispositions, actions, or a virtue?

Such questions seem to revolve around the questions of: *who* (gets reported); *what* (gets reported); *where* (does the issue get reported); *location* (of coverage within the items analysed); *how much* (gets reported); and *why* (does the issue get reported).

As with much content analysis, the researcher was just as interested in omissions in coverage as in what *does* get reported. For example, details about the profession, qualifications, and beliefs of the courageous person were frequently omitted. Such omissions are in themselves potentially interesting, as they may reveal what is and is not important to reporters and their editors.

Selecting a sample for content analysis

There are several phases in the selection of a sample for content analysis. Because it is a method that can be applied to many kinds of documents, the case of applying it to the mass media will be explored here. However, the basic principles have a broader relevance to a wide range of applications of content analysis.

Sampling media

Many studies of the mass media entail the specification of a research problem in the form of 'the representation of *X* in the mass media'. The *X* may be trade unions, HRM, or women and leadership. But which mass media might one choose to focus upon? Will it be newspapers or television or radio or magazines or news websites or blogs? And, if newspapers, will it be all newspapers or only the business press? Will it be printed newspapers, online newspapers or both? Will it be a sample of newspapers? And will it include free newspapers? And if newspapers, will all news items be candidates for analysis—for example, would feature articles and letters to the editor be included? And will newspapers from more than one country be included?

Typically, researchers will opt for one or possibly two of the mass media and may sample within that type or types. In the research described in Research in focus 13.6; Harris (2001) chose to focus on just four newspapers over one year, 1996, which is just as well, since the author was able to locate a large number of appropriate items (news items containing one or more of the words 'courage', 'courageous', or 'courageously')—610 in total. However, the study also incorporated a cross-cultural element by sampling one newspaper each from Australia, the UK, the USA, and China. Other media that typically have a smaller, more carefully selected audience can also form the focus for content analysis. For example, Barley et al. (1988) conducted content analysis on items from business and management journals. Although these periodicals cannot be classified as mass media in the conventional sense, as the average peer-reviewed journal article is read by only a relatively small number of people compared to mass media, these journals do represent a highly influential medium for the subcultural groups that Barley and his colleagues were concerned to investigate.

Sampling dates

Sometimes, the decision about dates is more or less dictated by the occurrence of a phenomenon. With a research question that entails an ongoing general phenomenon, such as the representation of courage in managerial decision-making or the cultural values of companies, the matter of dates is more open. The principles of probability sampling outlined in Chapter 9 can readily be adapted for sampling dates—for example, generating a systematic sample of dates by randomly selecting one day of the week and then selecting every *n*th day thereafter.

One important factor is whether the focus will be on an issue that entails keeping track of representation as it happens, in which case the researcher may begin at any time and the key decision becomes when to stop, or whether or not it is necessary to go backwards in time to select media from one or more time periods in the past.

13.6 RESEARCH IN FOCUS
A content analysis of courage and managerial decision-making

The aim of Harris's (2001) study was to investigate the way the word 'courage' was used in the business community and to compare this with a theoretical definition of the construct defined prior to data collection—based on a selective review of the literature. The content analysis procedure that followed relied on searching through the 1996 editions of four daily newspapers—the *Australian Financial Review*, *The Guardian* (UK), the *Los Angeles Times*, and the *South China Morning Post*. These newspapers were selected because they all had substantial coverage of business and commerce, they covered a wide geographical spread, and they could provide information about the way that courage was perceived in the business community.

Using a searchable database, Harris included items where the word 'courage', or derivatives such as 'courageous', appeared in the text. This gave him a total population of 610 items. Each of the items was coded by the researcher using a specially designed form that allowed for inclusion of information about the nature of the article, the characteristics of the individual who was described as courageous, and the features of the courage that was being described. A coding 'dictionary' was devised that showed the coding rules, so that more than one coder could be involved in the classification and thereby increase validity. Findings showed that the newspaper stories about courage confirmed the theoretical definition of the construct that had been developed during the first stage of the study.

What is to be counted?

Obviously, decisions about what should be counted during a content analysis are bound to be profoundly affected by the nature of the research questions under consideration. Content analysis offers the prospect of different kinds of 'units of analysis' being considered. The following kinds of units of analysis are frequently encountered and can be used as guides to the kinds of objects that might be the focus of attention. However, what you would actually *want* or *need* to count will be dictated by your research question.

Significant actors

Particularly in the context of mass media news reporting, the main figures in any news item and their characteristics are often important items to code. These considerations are likely to result in the following questions being asked in the course of a content analysis:

- What kind of person has produced the item (for example, general or specialist news reporter)?
- Who is or are the main focus of the item (for example, senior executive of an organization, manager, politician, or employee representative)?

- Who provides alternative voices (for example, consumer representative, official from a professional association, or employee)?
- What was the context for the item (for example, publication of financial results, major organizational event, or disaster)?

The chief objective in recording such details is to map the main protagonists in news reporting in an area and to begin to reveal some of the mechanics involved in the production of information for public consumption.

Words

While it may seem a dull and time-consuming activity, counting the frequency with which certain words occur is sometimes undertaken in content analysis. Deciding what the unit of analysis will be, whether word, phrase, or sentence, is an important consideration in content analysis research. It would be difficult to contemplate using manual analysis for a very large sample, and so researchers tend to use computer-aided content analysis (see Research in focus 13.7).

13.7 RESEARCH IN FOCUS
A computer-aided content analysis of microlending to entrepreneurs

Allison et al. (2013) were interested in the factors that might be associated with the propensity of investors to lend through microlending to entrepreneurs in developing countries. They anticipated that one set of factors involved in the decision to invest was how entrepreneurs represent themselves in entrepreneurial investment profiles. These provide narratives about the entrepreneurs, their businesses, and rationales for investing in them. One of their **hypotheses** was: 'There is a negative correlation between use of accomplishment **rhetoric** and the speed with which individual investors fund microloans' (Allison et al. 2013: 695). Narratives were acquired through a microlending organization (Kiva.org). In order to examine the narratives, the researchers employed DICTION 6.0, a program that compares texts to dictionaries comprising groups of words that are thematically organized. Thus, the word 'accomplishment' is described as associated with a series of words associated with task-completion. For this dictionary, the authors supply the following example with the relevant words that trigger an attribution of accomplishment in bold:

> When she **started** her business she actually had no car but now due to her **success** and **increased** working capital she has bought a car to **expand** her territory.
>
> (Allison et al. 2013: 699)

The number of narratives analysed varied greatly across the 39 countries in the dataset, with a range of 4 in Haiti to 1804 in Philippines. The length of the narratives also varied greatly, with a range of 27 to 1379 words and a mean of 163 words. In line with the hypothesis quoted above, it was found that an accomplishment rhetoric reduced the speed with which investors were prepared to fund ventures. Information about DICTION can be found at http://www.dictionsoftware.com/.

Subjects and themes

Frequently in a content analysis the researcher will want to code text in terms of certain subjects and themes. Essentially, what is being sought is a categorization of the phenomenon or phenomena of interest. While categorizations of specific words are often relatively straightforward, when the process of coding is thematic a more interpretative approach needs to be taken. At this point, the analyst is searching not just for manifest content but for latent content as well. It becomes necessary to probe beneath the surface in order to ask deeper questions about what is happening.

Dispositions

A further level of interpretation is likely to be entailed when the researcher seeks to demonstrate a disposition in the texts being analysed. For example, it may be that the researcher wants to establish whether the journalists reporting an issue in the news media are favourably inclined or hostile towards an aspect of it, such as in their stances on the practice of paying chief executives large financial bonuses. Alternatively, the researcher may be interested in the views of a news article reader, rather than the writer. Such an analysis entails establishing whether a judgemental stance can be discerned in the items being coded and, if so, what the nature of the judgement is.

Images

A further alternative focus for content analysis involves counting the frequency and type of images contained within a text. For example, Hunter (2008), a researcher in the field of tourism studies, analysed photographic representations appearing in tourist brochures and guidebooks relating to 21 destinations. In fact such methods are relatively common in tourism research and have been applied in the analysis of a wide range of documents such as postcards. Hunter (2008) analysed a sample of 10 per cent or 375 of the photographic images contained in the selected brochures and guidebooks. Images were categorized in terms of space, defined as 'the kind of physical tourism environment that is represented by means of the photograph' (Hunter 2008: 359);

categories included 'natural landscapes', 'cultivated landscapes', 'heritage and material culture', and 'tourism products' such as cuisine. They were also categorized by 'subject', defined as the kinds of people found in the photograph; categories include 'no people', 'host only', 'guest only', and 'host and guest'. He could thereby analyse the frequency with which each category appeared, using this as the basis for critical analysis of the social effects of tourism on places and peoples. The content analysis of images has significant application in other areas of business research such as marketing, where the visual plays an influential role.

Coding in content analysis

As much of the foregoing discussion has implied, coding is a crucial stage in the process of doing a content analysis. There are two main elements to a content analysis coding scheme: designing a coding schedule and designing a coding manual. To illustrate their use, imagine a student who is interested in reports of employment tribunal hearings dealing with workplace discrimination on the basis of gender, ethnicity, or disability, reported on a news website over a three-month period. The student chooses to focus on the reporting of the employment tribunal hearing and of the outcomes of the hearing. To simplify the issue, the following variables might be among those considered:

1. nature of the claim (for example, denial of promotion);
2. gender of the complainant;
3. ethnicity of the complainant;
4. disability status of the complainant;
5. occupation of the complainant;
6. age of the complainant;
7. marital status of the complainant;
8. nature of the employer's business;
9. number of employees in the business;
10. outcome of tribunal (case sustained/not sustained; nature of award);
11. position of the news item on the website;
12. number of words in the item.

Analysis would enable the student to record information about the kinds of gender, ethnicity, or disability discrimination issues that employment tribunals deal with and also to look for patterns in the characteristics of complainants and employers. The content analysis could thereby provide valuable insight—for example, into the way that gendered managerial structures, cultures, and organizational practices are reproduced. Content analysts would normally be interested in a much larger number of variables than this, but a simple illustration like this can be helpful to show the kinds of variables that might be considered.

Coding schedule

The coding schedule is a form into which all the data relating to an item being coded will be entered. Figure 13.1 provides an example of a coding schedule based on the study of managerial courage and decision-making described in Research in focus 13.6. The schedule is very much a simplification in order to facilitate the discussion of the principles of coding in content analysis and of the construction of a coding schedule in particular.

Each of the roman numerals in Figure 13.1 relates to a specific dimension that is being coded—for example, 'iii' relates to the dimension 'qualifications' of the actor. The blank cells on the coding form are the places where codes are written. A new coding schedule form would be used for each media item coded. The codes can then be transferred to a computer data file for analysis with a software package such as IBM SPSS (see Chapter 16).

Coding manual

On the face of it, the coding schedule in Figure 13.1 seems very bare and does not appear to provide much information about what is to be done or where. This is where the coding manual comes in. The coding manual, sometimes referred to as the content analysis dictionary, is a statement of instructions to coders that specifies the categories that will be used to classify the text based on a set of written rules that define how the text will be classified. It provides: a list of all the dimensions; the different categories subsumed under each dimension; the letters or numbers (that is, *codes*) that correspond to each category; and guidance on what each dimension is concerned with, the definitions or rules to be used in assigning words to categories, and any factors that should be taken into account in deciding how to allocate any particular code to each dimension. The coding manual enables the message content to be coded in a consistent manner. The coding categories for each dimension need to be mutually exclusive and exhaustive so that there is no sense of overlap.

For example, in his study of managerial courage and managerial decision-making, Harris (2001) constructed a coding manual to define the features of courage that he was looking for in the newspaper stories. Figure 13.2

FIGURE 13.1
Coding schedule

No.	Information about the actor	Code	No.	Features of courage displayed, sought, or observed	Code
i	Gender of actor		viii	Word used to describe courage	
ii	Age of actor		ix	Tools mentioned	
iii	Qualifications		x	Obstacles mentioned	
iv	Profession		xi	Involves choice between personal values and corporate values	
v	Place		xii	Involves defence of corporate/ organizational values or vision	
vi	Rank		xiii	Involves choice between personal advantage and corporate/community good	
vii	Evidence of being a risk-taker		xiv	Courage refers to the action or to disposition of actor or to a virtue	

Source: adapted from Harris (2001).

FIGURE 13.2
Coding manual

Information about the actor	Features of courage displayed, sought, or observed
i. Gender of actor Male (1); Female (2); Unknown (3)	**viii. Word used to describe courage** Courage/ous/ly (1); Moral courage (2); Brave/ry (3); Dare/ing (4); Moral fibre (5); Strong will (6); Persevera/nce (7)
ii. Age of actor (at the time the event occurred) Record age in years (0 if unknown)	**ix. Tools mentioned (activities, circumstances, or events that facilitated the courage)** Bind (1) = made a public statement so as to make it harder to avoid the intended action Devil's advocate (2) = a person specifically designated to put contrary views Example (3) = e.g. 'seeing what A did gave me courage' Horror (4) = can't allow it to continue, sheer enormity (to the actor) of what is proposed/happening meant that major obstacles had to be overcome Others (5) = support expressed by others who may not necessarily be being courageous themselves Vision (6) = clear focus Faith (7) = inspiration or belief in a higher force
iii. Qualifications (only include if unambiguous) Degree/professional (1); Trade (2); Unknown (3)	**x. Obstacles mentioned (something faced or overcome, a difficulty, concern, temptation, or hurdle)** Easy path (1) = temptation to avoid the hard work Name calling (2) = personal abuse directed at the actor Physical threat (3) = violence or threat of violence to actor, family, etc. Commercial risk (4) = includes potential financial consequences Unpopular (5) = what is planned is unpleasant or trenchantly opposed
iv. Profession (only include if unambigious) Law (1); Medicine (2); Engineering (3); Accounting (4); Journalism (5); Other (6); Not clear or combined (7)	**xi. Involves choice between personal values and corporate values** Yes, personal values chosen (1); Yes, corporate and community values chosen (2); Unknown (3)
v. Place in which the event occurred Use 2-letter ISO country code; if many, code as World (−1)	**xii. Involves defence of corporate/organizational values or vision** Yes (1); No (2)
vi. Rank (only include if unambiguous) Minister and ranking opposition, US senator (1); Member of Parliament (2); Manager (3); Company owner (4); Board member (5); Self-employed (6); Corporate professional, e.g. engineer or lawyer (7); other (8)	**xiii. Involves choice between personal advantage and corporate/community good** Yes, personal advantage chosen (1); Yes, corporate and community good chosen (2); Unknown (3)
vii. Evidence of being a risk-taker (evidence in the item apart from courage event of the actor being a risk-taker) Yes (1); No (2)	**xiv. Courage refers to the action or to disposition of actor or to a virtue** The word 'courage' is used to describe an act or action, or some other outcome—*a courageous act, acted courageously, acted with courage* (1); Courage is attributed to the actor in relation to the act(s)—*to show courage, to be courageous* (2); Courage is mentioned without attribution to either act or person— e.g. *reference to a disembodied virtue* (3)

Source: adapted from Harris (2001).

provides a simplified version of the coding manual that corresponds to the coding schedule developed by Harris in this study (see Figure 13.1 and Research in focus 13.6). The coding manual includes all the dimensions that would be employed in the coding process, indications of guidance for coders, and the lists of categories that were created for each dimension. The coding manual includes instructions for classification of information about the actor in addition to categories for various features of the courage referred to in the newspaper article: how it was

FIGURE 13.3
Completed coding schedule

No.	Information about the actor	Code	No.	Features of courage displayed, sought, or observed	Code
i	Gender of actor	2	viii	Word used to describe courage	1
ii	Age of actor	35	ix	Tools mentioned	4
iii	Qualifications	1	x	Obstacles mentioned	4
iv	Profession	6	xi	Involves choice between personal values and corporate values	3
v	Place	14	xii	Involves defence of corporate/ organizational values or vision	1
vi	Rank	4	xiii	Involves choice between personal advantage and corporate/community good	2
vii	Evidence of being a risk-taker	2	xiv	Courage refers to the action or to disposition of actor or to a virtue	1

Source: adapted from Harris (2001).

displayed, sought, or observed. The coding schedule and manual permit only one obstacle or tool to be recorded in relation to a particular phrase or sentence in a newspaper article. However, if a phrase contains two or more obstacles or tools, the coder may break down the phrase and code a single word or a few words at a time.

The coding manual is crucial, because it provides coders with complete listings of all categories for each dimension they are coding and guidance about how to interpret the dimensions. At this stage, decisions must be made regarding the treatment of words that have more than one meaning. It is on the basis of these lists and guidance that a coding schedule of the kind presented in Figure 13.1 will be completed. Even if you are a lone researcher, such as a student conducting a content analysis for a dissertation, it is important to spend a lot of time providing yourself with instructions about how to code. While you may not face the problem of inter-rater reliability, the issue of intra-rater reliability is still significant for you and you will probably need to use the coding manual to keep reminding yourself of your rules for coding the data.

Figure 13.3 illustrates how a fictitious example of a news item that presents an act of courage might be coded according to Harris's coding manual. The news story, published in the UK newspaper *The Guardian*, focuses on a 35-year-old female entrepreneur, owner of a small business, who is described as having acted courageously in

taking the decision to turn down a contract with a major distributor and retailer because of concerns, which were subsequently proved correct, about the tactics being used to undermine the competition. The coding of the incident would then appear as in Figure 13.3 and the data would be entered into a computer program, such as SPSS, as follows:

2 35 1 6 14 4 2 1 4 4 3 1 2 1

Each newspaper item that mentions the word 'courage' would create a row of data with an identical structure.

Potential pitfalls in devising coding schemes

There are several potential dangers in devising a content analysis coding scheme, and they are very similar to the kinds of consideration that are involved in the design of structured interview and structured observation schedules:

* *Discrete dimensions*. Make sure that your dimensions are entirely separate; in other words, there should be no conceptual or empirical overlap between them. For example, coding manual rules may be needed to distinguish between 'management' positions (such as the administrators of a firm) and 'management' actions (like the management of innovation).

- *Mutually exclusive categories*. Make sure that there is no overlap in the categories supplied for each dimension. If the categories are not mutually exclusive, coders will be unsure about how to code each item.

- *Exhaustive*. For each dimension, all possible categories should be available to coders.

- *Clear instructions*. Coders should be clear about how to interpret what each dimension is about and what factors to take into account when assigning codes to each category. Sometimes, these will have to be very elaborate. Coders should have little or no discretion in how to allocate codes to units of analysis.

- *Be clear about the unit of analysis*. For example, in Harris's (2001) study of courage and managerial decision-making, more than one courage event per media item can be recorded. The coding schedule needs to be clear in distinguishing between the media item (for example, a newspaper article) and the event being coded. In practice, a researcher is interested in both but needs to keep the distinction in mind.

In order to be able to enhance the quality of a coding scheme, it is highly advisable to pilot early versions of the scheme. Piloting will help to identify difficulties in applying the coding scheme, such as uncertainty about which category to employ when considering a certain dimension or discovering that no code was available to cover a particular case. Piloting will also help to identify any evidence that one category of a dimension tends to subsume an extremely large percentage of items. If this occurs, it may be necessary to consider breaking that category down so that it allows greater discrimination between the items being analysed.

The reliability of coding is a further potential area of concern. Coding must be done in a consistent manner. As with structured observation, coding must be consistent between coders (inter-rater reliability) and each coder must be consistent over time (intra-rater reliability). An important part of piloting the coding scheme will be testing for consistency between coders and, if time permits, intra-coder reliability. However, coding may not be consistent, and the extent of inter-coder reliability may vary depending on the type of content that is being analysed (see Research in focus 13.8 for an example).

13.8 RESEARCH IN FOCUS
Issues of inter-coder reliability in a study of text messaging

The results of the **diary** study of patterns of text messaging carried out by Faulkner and Culwin (2005) described in Research in focus 11.5 were analysed according to the content of text messages sent by the participants in the study. The categories identified were:

1. advertisements;
2. questions;
3. rendezvous immediate and ongoing;
4. rendezvous near future;
5. events;
6. instructions;
7. reminders;
8. jokes;
9. signon;
10. signoff;
11. gossip;
12. dates;
13. information—personal;
14. information—commercial;
15. information—operational.

The results of the coding exercise were entered onto an online database. To check for inter-coder reliability, the participants were then shown a random selection of text messages from the entire pool and asked to code them; a consensus was drawn up based on the number of times a text message was assigned to a particular category. However, the degree of consensus between coders was not high. Total consensus was achieved for approximately 16 per cent of the items and 50 per cent consensus was achieved for 75 per cent of the items. Faulkner and Culwin explain this in terms of the specificity of text messaging, which is a method of communication between one sender and receiver, unlike newspapers, which are a medium of mass communication. They conclude: 'these classifications were applied by people who had not necessarily received nor sent the individual text message. To a large extent the interpretation of content depends on the receiver of that content' (2005: 180).

Advantages of content analysis

Content analysis has several significant advantages, which are outlined below:

- Content analysis is a very transparent research method. The coding scheme and the sampling procedures can be clearly set out so that replications and follow-up studies are feasible. It is this transparency that often causes content analysis to be referred to as an objective method of analysis.

- It can allow a certain amount of longitudinal analysis with relative ease. In the example of employment tribunal hearings concerning gender, ethnicity, or disability discrimination, a temporal analysis could be introduced through comparison of employment tribunal reporting in newspapers during two different time periods, such as the 1960s and the 1990s. Changes in emphasis could thus be examined.

- It is a highly flexible method. It can be applied to a wide variety of kinds of unstructured information.

- Content analysis can allow information to be generated about social groups that are difficult to gain access to directly.

Disadvantages of content analysis

Like all research techniques, content analysis suffers from certain limitations, which are described below:

- A content analysis can only be as good as the documents on which the practitioner works. John Scott (1990) recommends assessing documents in terms of such criteria as: authenticity (that the document is what it purports to be); credibility (whether there are grounds for thinking that the contents of the document have been or are distorted in some way); and representativeness (whether or not the documents examined are representative of all possible relevant documents, as, if certain kinds of document are unavailable or no longer exist, generalizability will be jeopardized). These kinds of consideration will be especially important to bear in mind when a content analysis is being conducted on documents such as company reports or internal memoranda.

- It is almost impossible to devise coding manuals that do not entail some interpretation on the part of coders.

Coders must draw upon their everyday knowledge as participants in a common culture in order to be able to code the material with which they are confronted (Cicourel 1964; Garfinkel 1967). To the extent that this occurs, it is questionable whether or not it is justifiable to assume a correspondence of interpretation between the persons responsible for producing the documents being analysed and the coders (Beardsworth 1980).

- Particular problems are likely to arise when the aim is to impute latent rather than manifest content.

- It is difficult to ascertain the answers to 'Why?' questions through content analysis. For example, although Rosén (2014) was able to trace the increasing level of professionalization in job advertisements for strategic communication experts in Sweden, she was unable to explain in any detail why this had occurred (see Research in focus 13.9).

13.9 RESEARCH IN FOCUS
A content analysis of Swedish job advertisements 1960–2010

Rosén (2014) used content analysis to evaluate changes in the description and requirements of professional communicators in Swedish job advertisements from 1960 to 2010. A total of 196 job advertisements were collected at ten-year intervals over the period from the largest morning newspapers in Sweden—*Dagens Nyheter*, *Svenska Dagbladet*, and *Sydsvenska Dagbladet*. In each case, the sample was taken from 31 days in August, which is a busy recruitment month in Sweden. Advertisements relating to information, marketing, communication, and consultancy were selected. A coding scheme covering 17 major recruitment aspects was developed, including job title, function/role, education, and qualifications. This enabled understanding of the process whereby strategic communication roles have become increasingly professionalized, requiring college-level qualifications and specialist expertise. As might be expected, the analysis also indicated a shift over time in job titles, away from those that used the term 'man', e.g. 'advertising man' in the 1960s, towards more gender-neutral labels by 2010.

KEY POINTS

- Structured observation and content analysis are methods for quantitatively analysing naturally occurring data.

- Structured observation is an approach to the study of behaviour that is an alternative to survey-based measures.

- It comprises explicit rules for the recording of behaviour.

- It shares with survey research many common problems concerning reliability, validity, and generalizability.

- Reactive effects have to be taken into account but should not be exaggerated.

- Problems with structured observation revolve around the difficulty of imputing meaning and ensuring that a relevant framework for recording behaviour is being employed.

- Content analysis is very much located within the quantitative research tradition of emphasizing measurement and the specification of clear rules that exhibit reliability.

- While traditionally associated with the analysis of mass-media content, content analysis is in fact a very flexible method that can be applied to a wide range of phenomena.

- It is crucial to be clear about your research questions in order to be certain about your units of analysis and what exactly is to be analysed.

- You also need to be clear about what is to be counted.

- The coding schedule and coding manual are crucial stages in the preparation for a content analysis.

- Content analysis becomes particularly controversial when it is used to seek out latent meaning and themes.

QUESTIONS FOR REVIEW

Problems with survey research on behaviour

- What are the chief limitations of survey research with regard to the study of behaviour?

So why not observe behaviour?

- What are the chief characteristics of structured observation?

- To what extent does it provide a superior approach to the study of behaviour than questionnaires or structured interviews?

The observation schedule

- What is an observation schedule?

- 'An observation schedule is much like a self-completion questionnaire or structured interview except that it does not involve asking questions.' Discuss.

- Devise an observation schedule of your own for observing an area of social interaction in which you are regularly involved. Ask people with whom you normally interact in those situations how well they think it fits what goes on. Have you missed anything out?

Strategies for observing behaviour

- What are the main ways in which behaviour can be recorded in structured observation?

Sampling for structured observation

- Identify some of the main sampling strategies in structured observation.

Issues of reliability and validity

- How far do considerations of reliability and validity in structured observation mirror those encountered in relation to the asking of questions in structured interviews and self-completion questionnaires?

- What is the reactive effect and why might it be important in relation to structured observation research?

Criticisms of structured observation

- 'The chief problem with structured observation is that it does not allow us access to the intentions that lie behind behaviour.' Discuss.

- How far do you agree with the view that structured observation works best when used in conjunction with other research methods?

Applying content analysis

- To what kinds of documents and media can content analysis be applied?

- What is the difference between manifest and latent content? What are the implications of this distinction for content analysis?

What are the research questions?

- Why are precise research questions especially crucial in content analysis?

- With what general kinds of research questions is content analysis concerned?

Selecting a sample for content analysis

- What special sampling issues does content analysis pose?

What is to be counted?

- What kinds of things might be counted in the course of doing a content analysis?
- To what extent do you need to infer latent content when you go beyond counting words?

Coding in content analysis

- Why is coding so crucial in content analysis?
- What is the difference between a coding schedule and a coding manual?
- What potential pitfalls need to be guarded against when devising coding schedules and manuals?

Advantages of content analysis

- 'One of the most significant virtues of content analysis is its immense flexibility, in that it can be applied to a wide variety of documents.' Discuss.

Disadvantages of content analysis

- To what extent is content analysis undermined by the need for coders to interpret meaning?
- To what extent are content analysis studies atheoretical?

....

ONLINE RESOURCES
www.oup.com/uk/brm5e/

Visit the Interactive Research Guide that accompanies this book to complete an exercise relating to quantitative research using naturally occurring data.

....

14

SECONDARY ANALYSIS AND OFFICIAL STATISTICS

CHAPTER OUTLINE

This chapter explores the possibilities associated with the analysis of data that have been collected by others. There are two main types discussed in this chapter:

- the secondary analysis of data collected, either for commercial or research purposes, by other people;

- the secondary analysis of official statistics—that is, statistics collected by government departments in the course of their work or specifically for statistical purposes.

This chapter explores:

- the advantages and disadvantages of carrying out secondary analysis of data collected by other researchers, particularly in view of many datasets being based on large, high-quality investigations that are invariably beyond the means of students;

- how to obtain such datasets;

- the potential of official statistics in terms of their reliability and validity;

- the notion that official statistics are a form of unobtrusive method—that is, a method that does not provoke a reaction on the part of those being studied to the fact that they are research participants.

Introduction

Many of the techniques we have covered so far—survey research by questionnaire or structured interview; structured observation; content analysis—can be extremely time-consuming and expensive. Students in particular may have neither the time nor the financial resources to conduct very extensive research. Further, in many institutions there are ethics approval processes, which can be onerous and time-consuming, that are required before it is possible to collect data. Yet we know that large amounts of quantitative data about business and management are collected by social scientists, market intelligence firms, professional associations, and others. Some of this information, such as that produced by market research organizations, can be expensive to access. However, many organizations, most notably government departments and their various representatives, collect data that are presented in statistical form and that may be usable without charge by students and university researchers. Would it not be a good idea to analyse such data rather than collect new data?

This is where *secondary analysis* comes in. Secondary analysis offers this kind of opportunity. Key concept 14.1 contains a brief definition of secondary analysis and

raises one or two basic points about what it involves. As the chapter outline suggests, in this chapter we will be concerned with two kinds of issue:

- the secondary analysis of data that have been collected by other researchers;
- the secondary analysis of data that have been collected by other organizations in the course of their business.

In business and management, secondary analysis is of increasing interest to researchers. Traditionally, it has been the province of economists to analyse secondary data and draw conclusions about how it relates to the world of business. However, since the 1960s, more researchers, particularly those from an industrial relations background, have begun to take greater interest in the analysis of large-scale workplace survey data. Part of the reason for this relates to the success of the UK's Workplace Employment Relations Survey (WERS), and similar surveys in other countries, e.g. the Australian Workplace Industrial Relations Survey (AWIRS). These have considerably opened up the potential for secondary analysis of work-related issues, largely because of their breadth and scope.

Other researchers' data

There are several reasons why secondary analysis should be seriously considered as an alternative to collecting new data. The main advantages of secondary

analysis have been covered by Dale et al. (1988), from whom we have borrowed most of the following observations. In considering the various advantages of

14.2 RESEARCH IN FOCUS
Exploring corporate reputation in three Scandinavian countries

Vidaver-Cohen and Brønn (2013) conducted an exploratory study of corporate responsibility, corporate reputation, and stakeholder support among firms in Norway, Sweden, and Denmark. In doing so, they used data from the Reputation Institute's RepTrak® survey, which collects data on corporate reputation among leading companies on an annual basis across the world. The Reputation Institute is a commercial enterprise which consults to corporations on measuring, managing, and communicating their reputations. By using this data, the authors were able to analyse data from over 170,000 individual evaluations of nearly 600 firms across the years 2010–12. The evaluations took the form of data collected from random **samples** of people in each country, using multiple questions with **Likert-scale** responses. By using the RepTrak® data, the authors were able to assess levels of perceived corporate responsibility across and within the three countries, as well as to measure associations between perceived corporate responsibility on one hand and reputation and support on the other, using a dataset much bigger than they could possibly have collected themselves.

secondary analysis, we have in mind the particular needs of the lone student conducting a small research project as an undergraduate or a more substantial piece of work as a postgraduate. However, this emphasis should definitely not be taken to imply that secondary analysis is really appropriate or relevant only to students. Quite the contrary: secondary analysis should be considered by all business researchers. However, secondary data need not necessarily have been collected by other researchers; instead, they may be collected by a company or another type of organization for its own purposes (see Research in focus 14.2). It is also possible for secondary analysis to be used in combination with the collection of primary data, as the example in Research in focus 14.3 illustrates. This can enable a comparative element to be incorporated into the **research design**. However, we have one other reason for emphasizing the prospects of secondary analysis for students: based on our personal experience, students tend to assume that any research they carry out has to entail the collection of primary data. Provided secondary analysis does not conflict with the guidelines students are given regarding projects they are asked to complete, we feel there is a strong case for students considering the use of secondary analysis, as it frees them up to spend more time on searching the literature, designing their **research questions**, and analysing and interpreting the data.

Advantages of secondary analysis

Secondary analysis offers numerous benefits to students carrying out a research project. These are outlined below:

- *Cost and time*. As noted at the start of the chapter, secondary analysis offers the prospect of having access to good-quality data, such as that available from the UK Data Archive (see section on 'Accessing the UK Data Archive' below) and other national data archives, for a tiny fraction of the resources involved in carrying out a data collection exercise yourself.

- *High-quality data*. Many of the datasets that are employed most frequently for secondary analysis are of extremely high quality. By this we mean several things. First, the sampling procedures have been rigorous, in most cases resulting in samples that are as close to being representative as one is likely to achieve. While the organizations responsible for these studies suffer the same problems of survey non-response as anybody else, well-established procedures are usually in place for following up non-respondents and thereby keeping this problem to a minimum. Second, the samples are often national samples or at least cover a wide variety of regions. In addition, some datasets enable cross-national comparison (see Research in focus 14.4). The degree of geographical spread and the sample size of such datasets are invariably attained only in research that attracts quite substantial resources. It is inconceivable that student projects could even get close to the coverage that such datasets attain. Third, many datasets have been generated by highly experienced researchers and, in the case of some of the large datasets, such as the WERS, the data have been gathered by research organizations that have developed structures and control procedures to check on the quality of the emerging data

14.3 RESEARCH IN FOCUS

Combining primary and secondary data in a single study of the implications of marriage structure for men's attitudes to women in the workplace

In order to understand the implications of marriage structure, Sreedhari et al. (2014) conducted a total of five studies combining the analyses of secondary data from US and UK survey sources with quasi-experiments on managers and undergraduate students. The secondary analyses were based on two sources of data:

1. Data from the 1996 General Social Survey (GSS), a US national probability survey of adults, focusing on the attitudes of 282 heterosexual married men and analysing items that asked them to indicate their level of agreement/disagreement to questions such as: 'wife should help husband's career first' using a four-point Likert scale, correlating these with the predictor **variable** 'marriage structure', classifying respondents according to 'traditional' (wife not employed), 'semi traditional' (wife works part-time), and 'dual earner' marriage structure.

2. Data from two 2002 surveys, the GSS and the National Organizations Survey (NOS). For the NOS, the employers of some GSS respondents were contacted and asked about employment practices in their firms. Using data from the two surveys enabled organization-level data and responses from individuals to be linked, resulting in a sample of 89 full-time male employees and focusing on the variable 'perceived smoothness of workplace operations' and its **correlation** with the same predictor variable of 'marriage structure'.

The results from both of these studies indicated that marriage structures predicted how egalitarian men are, those in traditional marriages being more likely to hold negative attitudes toward women in their workplace.

The researchers then conducted a controlled **quasi-experiment** based on a recruitment scenario on 89 male undergraduate students, which indicated that men from traditional marriage backgrounds were less attracted to organizations with female leaders. This was followed by another quasi-experiment, this time involving a **convenience sample** of 232 managers recruited from a US accounting organization, to examine whether men in traditional marriage structures were more likely to behave in ways that would prevent women in the organization advancing in their careers. This involved an online organizational simulation, in which the gender of the imaginary potential leader was manipulated. The fifth and final study sought to establish whether the attitudes of men who were single would change their attitudes to those of women in the workplace once they were married. The researchers also wanted to test whether these findings would generalize to a non-US sample. They therefore used data relating to a sample of 304 men from the 1991 and 1993 British Household Panel Survey (BHPS). The sample was comprised of men who were single in the first wave of data collection but had married by the time of the second data collection point. The findings from all five of the studies carried out by Sreedhari et al. (2014) showed that men in traditional marriages tend to hold negative views towards the presence of women in the workplace.

(see Research in focus 14.5 for an example of research that drew on the WERS). Some large datasets that are suitable for secondary analysis are described in Table 14.1. Due to space constraints, we have only listed UK and European datasets, but there are many similar sources of data available in most countries (see the discussion of national statistical agencies and data archives below for some guidance on locating data sources).

- *Opportunity for longitudinal analysis*. Partly linked to the last point is the fact that secondary analysis can offer the opportunity for longitudinal research. Sometimes, as with the WERS, a panel design has been employed and it is possible to chart trends and connections over time. Such data are sometimes analysed cross-sectionally, but there are obviously opportunities for longitudinal analysis as well. Also, with datasets such as the Labour Force Survey (LFS), where similar

TABLE 14.1
Large UK and European datasets suitable for secondary analysis

Title	Dataset details	Topics covered
Business Register and Employment Survey (BRES), UK	Produces UK annual employment statistics and collects data on local units and business structures to update the Inter-Departmental Business Register, which is used as a **sampling frame** in many surveys. Survey conducted annually, sample size approximately 82,000. Accessed via the Office for National Statistics and Nomis official labour market statistics website: **http://www.nomisweb.co.uk/**.	Data are collected on the number of jobs by geographical location, detailed industrial activity (SIC code), and whether full- or part-time.
Understanding Society, UK	Builds on 18 years of the British Household Panel Survey (BHPS), which it replaced in 2009/10. Like the BHPS, which started in 1991, the Understanding Society survey uses interviews and questionnaires and follows the same nationally **representative sample** of individuals within a household, but is based on a much larger panel of 40,000 households. See **http://www.understandingsociety.org.uk./**	Household organization, labour market behaviour, income and wealth, housing, health, and socio-economic values.
British Social Attitudes (BSA) survey	More or less annual survey since 1983 of a representative sample aged 18 and over by interview and questionnaire. Each survey comprises an hour-long interview and a self-completion questionnaire. Accessible through the National Centre for Social Research: **http://www.natcen.ac.uk/our-research/research/british-social-attitudes/**.	Covers wide range of areas of social attitudes and behaviour. The survey focuses mainly on people's attitudes, but also collects details of their behaviour patterns, household circumstances, and work.
European Community Studies and Eurobarometer	Since the early 1970s, public opinion surveys have been conducted on behalf of the European Commission at least twice a year in all member states of the European Union. The Eurobarometer series began in 1974. It comprises individual face-to-face interviews with national samples and is conducted biannually, in spring and autumn. Accessible through the European Commission: **http://ec.europa.eu/commmfrontoffice/publicopinion/index.cfm**.	Cross-national comparison of wide range of social and political issues, including European integration, life satisfaction, social goals, currency issues, working conditions, and travel.
European Working Conditions Survey (EWCS)	A cross-sectional survey conducted every five years since 1990 by the European Foundation for the Improvement of Living and Working Conditions (Eurofound). The fifth survey, of nearly 44,000 workers, was conducted in 2010 and covered 34 countries. Accessible via the European Working Conditions Observatory: **https://www.eurofound.europa.eu/data/european-working-conditions-survey**.	Areas covered include precarious employment, leadership styles, and worker participation, as well as the general job context, working time, work organization, pay, work-related health risks, cognitive and psychosocial factors, work–life balance and access to training. Questions were also asked about the effects of the economic downturn on working conditions.
International Social Survey Programme (ISSP)	Annual programme since 1983 based on cross-national collaboration covering survey topics important for social science research. Accessible through the GESIS Leibniz Institute for the Social Sciences: **http://www.issp.org/menu-top/home/**.	Attitudes towards legal systems and the economy. Covers special topics, including work orientations (see Research in focus 14.4), the environment, and national identity.
Labour Force Survey (LFS), UK	Largest regular household survey in the UK. Biennial interviews, 1973–83, and annual interviews, 1984–91, comprising a quarterly survey of around 15,000 addresses per quarter and an additional survey in March–May; since 1991, quarterly survey of around 60,000 addresses. Since 1998, core questions have also been administered in member states of the European Union. Accessible via UK Data Servicet: **ukdataservice.ac.uk/**.	Covers hours worked, job search methods, training, and personal details, such as nationality and gender.
Population Census, UK	A simple questionnaire survey of the **population** of England and Wales held every ten years since 1801. The most recent **Census** was held in 2011 and the one before that in 2001. Accessed via the Office for National Statistics and Nomis, official labour market statistics website: **http://www.nomisweb.co.uk/census/2011**.	Contains information about households and individuals covering topics as diverse as age, gender, occupation, qualifications, ethnicity, social class, employment, family structure, amenities, and tenure.
Annual Survey of Hours and Earnings (ASHE), UK	The most comprehensive source of earnings information in the UK, conducted annually since 1970 and surveying the earnings of employees. Reports are free to view or download from the UK National Statistics Publication Hub: **http://www.statistics.gov.uk/hub/index.html**.	Looks at levels, composition, and distribution of earnings and details of hours worked, broken down by industry, occupation, age group, and gender.

TABLE 14.1
(continued)

Title	Dataset details	Topics covered
Workplace Employment Relations Survey (WERS), UK	This survey was carried out in 1980, 1984, 1990, 1998, 2004, and 2011. The sample comprised workplaces where interviews were carried out with managers and worker representatives, and questionnaires administered to employees. Accessible through UK Data Service: **ukdataservice.ac.uk/**.	Wide range of areas covered, including: pay determination, recruitment and training, equal opportunities, workplace change, work attitudes, management organization, and employee representation.

14.4 RESEARCH IN FOCUS
Cross-national comparison of work orientations: an example of a secondary dataset

The International Social Survey Programme (ISSP) conducted four surveys focusing on the topic of work orientations, in 1989, 1997, 2005, and 2015. A total of 37 countries participated in the 2015 survey. The survey uses a standardized questionnaire and focuses on respondents' general attitudes towards work and leisure, work organization, and work content. Opinions were elicited on such issues as preferred time budget for selected activities such as work, leisure time, etc.; work orientation; importance of selected demands of a job (scale); preference for being self-employed or being an employee, working in a small or in a large firm, and working in private business or civil service; advantages of employee status (greater job security and lower impairment of family life); importance of unions for job security and working conditions of employee; preference for full-time employment or part-time employment; preference for more work (and money) or for reduction in working hours. Demographic variables include age, gender, education, marital status, personal and family income, employment status, household size and composition, occupation, religion and church attendance, social class, union membership, political party, voting history, size of community, region, and ethnicity. Full details and links to the datasets can be accessed via the International Social Survey Programme Data Archive: **http://www.issp.org/menu-top/home/**

14.5 RESEARCH IN FOCUS
Workplace gender diversity and union density: an example of secondary analysis using the WERS data

Haile (2017) used data from the 2004 Workplace Employment Relations Survey (WERS) to explore associations between gender diversity and workplace union density in Britain. Her motivation was the fact that union decline in Britain had coincided with growth of female employment. Using the WERS data, Haile was able to measure associations between the gender diversity of workplaces (an index based on the relative proportions of male and female employees in a workplace) on one hand and union density (the percentage of employees in a workplace who are union members) on the other. The WERS allowed the analysis to be done using a nationally representative sample of workplaces, which meant that the findings could be generalized with confidence. The dataset also included data on numerous workplace characteristics (e.g. size, industry) which meant that potentially confounding factors could be controlled for.

Haile's results showed a negative association between gender diversity and union density within the sample. Further analysis, however, showed that the negative association was stronger in workplaces with a majority of male employees, relative to those with a majority of female workers. On this basis, she speculates that as women increasingly enter workplaces, which are often characterized by gender discrimination, gender-based conflict may increase, thereby undermining the ability of unions to organize and recruit members. She argues that unions may have to reconsider their approach to workplace organization and recruitment, to take account of increased female participation in the workforce.

data are collected over time, usually because certain interview questions are recycled each year, trends (such as changes in working time or shifting patterns of employment) can be identified over time. With such datasets, respondents differ from year to year so that causal inferences over time cannot be readily established, but nonetheless it is still possible to gauge trends.

- *Subgroup or subset analysis.* When large samples are the source of data, there is the opportunity to study what can often be quite sizeable subgroups of individuals or subsets of questions. Very often, in order to study specialized categories of individuals, small, localized studies are the only feasible way forward because of costs. However, large datasets can frequently yield quite large nationally representative samples of specialized categories of individuals, such as workers in a particular industry or occupation or with a particular set of personal characteristics. These can form the basis for representative sampling of individuals. Similarly, when a large-scale survey covers several topic areas, analysis may involve focusing on a smaller subset of questions that are covered by the survey (see Research in focus 14.6).

- *Opportunity for cross-cultural analysis.* Cross-cultural research has considerable appeal at a time when social scientists are more attuned to the processes associated with globalization and to cultural differences, though it is easy to forget that many findings should not be taken to apply to countries other than the one in which the research was conducted. However, cross-cultural research presents barriers to the social scientist. There are obvious barriers to do with the cost and practical difficulties of doing research in a different country, especially when language and cultural differences are likely to be significant. The secondary analysis of comparable data from two or more countries provides one possible model for conducting cross-cultural research. The ISSP is explicitly concerned with bringing together findings from existing social science surveys from different countries and contexts. An example of the kind of cross-cultural analysis the programme has produced is given in Research in focus 14.4.

- *More time for data analysis.* Precisely because data collection is time-consuming, the analysis of data is often squeezed. It is easy to perceive the data collection as the difficult phase and to take the view that the analysis of data is relatively straightforward. This is not the case. Working out what to make of your data is no easy matter and requires considerable thought and often a preparedness to consider learning about unfamiliar techniques of data analysis. While secondary analysis invariably entails a lot of data management—partly so that you can get to know the data and partly so that you can get it into a form that you need (and this phase should not be underestimated)—the fact that you are freed from

14.6 RESEARCH IN FOCUS

Age and work-related health: methodological issues involved in secondary analysis using the Labour Force Survey

Davies et al. (2014) used data from the UK Labour Force Survey (LFS) to consider two methodological issues related to age and work-related health. Their first point is that the LFS is unusual in asking questions relating to health of people who are not in employment. This enables a more representative analysis than through focusing only on people currently in work. Data from the LFS also enable comparison between work-related health problems that arise from the person's current job with those arising from previous employment. The LFS data are also based on self-reporting, which relies on an individual's 'perception of the attribution of an illness being caused or made worse by their occupation, rather than verification of work attribution made by a medical practitioner' (Davies et al. 2014: 4). While the researchers acknowledge that this is a subjective measure which may result in reporting bias, the under-reporting of work-related health data by employers makes those supposedly more objective measures equally problematic. The LFS data thus enable better understanding of the health advantages and disadvantages associated with government policies to encourage people to work longer.

having to collect fresh data means that your approach to the analysis of data can be more considered than it might otherwise have been.

- *Reanalysis may offer new interpretations.* It is easy to take the view that, once a set of data has been analysed, the data have in some sense been drained of further insight. What, in other words, could possibly be gained by going over the same data that someone else has analysed? In fact, data can be analysed in so many different ways that it is very unusual for the range of possible analyses to be exhausted. Several possibilities can be envisaged. First, a secondary analyst may decide to consider the impact of a certain variable on the relationships between variables of interest. Such a possibility may not have been envisaged by the initial researchers. Secondly, the arrival of new theoretical ideas may suggest analyses that could not have been conceived of by the original researchers. In other words, the development of such new theoretical directions may prompt a reconsideration of the relevance of the data. Thirdly, an alternative method of quantitative data analysis may be employed which offers the prospect of a rather different interpretation of the data. Fourthly (and related to the last point), new techniques of quantitative data analysis are continuously emerging. As awareness of such techniques spreads, and their potential relevance is recognized, researchers become interested in applying them to other datasets.

- *The wider obligations of the business researcher.* For all types of business research, research participants give up some of their time, usually for no reward. It is not unreasonable that the participants should expect that the data that they participate in generating should be mined to their fullest extent. However, much business research is chronically under-analysed. Primary researchers may feel they want to analyse only data relating to central research questions, or lose interest as a new set of research questions interpose themselves into their imagination. Making data available for secondary analysis enhances the possibility that fuller use will be made of the data.

- *University ethical clearance procedures.* As discussed in Chapter 6, most universities require staff and students to apply for ethics clearance before they collect data. Procedures vary across institutions, but in some cases they are onerous and time consuming. Most secondary analysis does not require ethical clearance, as you will not be collecting data. This can save a good deal of time and effort, which can be devoted to data analysis. If you are in doubt about whether such clearance is required for a particular piece of secondary analysis, however, it is always best to check with your institution.

Limitations of secondary analysis

The foregoing list of benefits of secondary analysis sounds almost too good to be true. In fact, there are not very many limitations, but the following warrant some attention:

- *Lack of familiarity with data.* When you collect your own data, when the dataset is generated, you are very familiar with the structure and contours of your data. However, with data collected by others, a period of familiarization is necessary. You have to get to grips with the range of variables, the ways in which the variables have been coded, and various aspects of the organization of the data. The period of familiarization can be quite substantial with large complex datasets and should not be underestimated.

- *Complexity of the data.* Many datasets that are employed for secondary analysis are very large in the sense of having large numbers of both respondents and variables. Sometimes, the sheer volume of data can present problems with the management of the information at hand, and, again, a period of acclimatization may be required. Also, some of the most prominent datasets that have been employed for secondary analysis are known as *hierarchical* datasets, such as the WERS. The difficulty here is that the data are collected and presented at the level of both the organization and the individual, as well as other levels. The secondary analyst must decide which level of analysis is going to be employed. If the decision is to analyse individual-level data, the individual-level data must then be extracted from the dataset. Different data will apply to each level. Thus, at the organizational level, the WERS provides data on such variables as number of employees and level of ownership, while, at the individual level, data on age, qualifications, and salary level can be found.

- *No control over data quality.* The point has been made on several occasions that secondary analysis offers the opportunity for students and others to examine data of far higher quality than they could collect themselves. However, this point applies mainly to datasets commissioned by a government department and conducted by researchers who are regarded as independent or at least somewhat distanced from the issues that are being investigated, such as academics working for a university research unit. While the quality of data should never be taken for granted, in the case of such datasets it is reasonably assured. With other datasets, though, more caution may be necessary in connection with assessment of data quality. This may be of particular concern when using data that are the result of commercially commissioned research, for example market research or surveys that have been conducted in-house by a company that wants to measure the effectiveness of its HRM strategy.

- *Absence of key variables*. Because secondary analysis involves the analysis of data collected by others for their own purposes, it may be that one or more key variables are not present. You may, for example, want to examine whether or not a relationship between two variables holds when one or more *other* variables are taken into account. Such an analysis is known as multivariate analysis, an area that will be touched on in Chapter 15. The inability to examine the significance or otherwise of a theoretically important variable can be frustrating and can arise when, for example, a theoretical approach that has emerged since the collection of the data suggests its importance. In other cases, variables may be available which are close to what is required, but not exactly so. In such cases, it is necessary to make a decision about whether the variable in question is near enough to the required one to allow for meaningful analysis.

Accessing data archives

In many countries, there are data archives where data collected by government agencies, university researchers, and commercial organizations are stored and are available for researchers to use, often free of charge:

- The US government provides access to a vast range of government data in machine readable format via the http://Data.Gov website.

- The Social Science Japan Data Archive is a repository for Japanese datasets which are available for secondary analysis and can be found at http://csrda.iss.u-tokyo.ac.jp/en/.

- In Australia, the Australian Data Archive is a repository for numerous studies: https://www.ada.edu.au/.

- The Consortium for European Social Science Data Archives brings together data archives from a number of member countries; details can be found at https://www.cessda.eu/.

These are just a few examples of data archives which are available to researchers. A comprehensive listing of data archives can be found via re3data, a global registry of research data repositories: https://www.re3data.org/.

To illustrate briefly what is offered by data archives, we will use the example of the UK Data Archive. Containing over 4000 datasets, the Archive is the largest collection of accessible digital data on social and economic topics in the UK. Data are acquired from academic, commercial, and government sources and are preserved and made available for further analysis.

Access to the Archive's holdings is provided to all academic researchers unless restrictions have been placed on the dataset by the owners. In addition to UK cross-sectoral studies from academic, government, and commercial sources, the Archive holds time series data, major longitudinal studies, panel surveys, and major cross-sectional studies. Data holdings include UK Census data; Office for National Statistics (ONS) Omnibus Survey; LFS; and the survey of British Social Attitudes (BSA). Data are made available over the network, on CD-ROM, and on other media. The Archive can also be used to locate and acquire data from other archives within Europe and worldwide, using a series of reciprocal agreements with other institutions. By far the most straightforward route to find out whether or not the Archive contains data on the topic you are interested in is by going to the UK Data Service's online catalogue, 'Discover', which provides a single point of access to data for social and economic researchers. It can be accessed by going to the home page at http://ukdataservice.ac.uk/.

Enter your terms into the box and click 'Search' (see Plate 14.1). You can use Boolean logic search terms AND, NOT, OR to refine your search, and you can combine search terms with filters. For example, we asked for studies with the keywords 'consumers' and 'technolog*' (* is used as a 'wild card' in searches so that it covers 'technology', 'technological', 'technologies', etc.) found anywhere in the study description. We refined the search using the following filters: **Type** 'data collections', **Subject** 'employment and labour', and **Date** 2010–2014. This resulted in nine studies being found (see Plate 14.2). We selected Study Number SN 6676 which is described in the title as 'Understanding Society: Waves 1-3 2009-2011', and selected **Full record**,

PLATE 14.1
The UK Data Service 'Discover' Catalogue

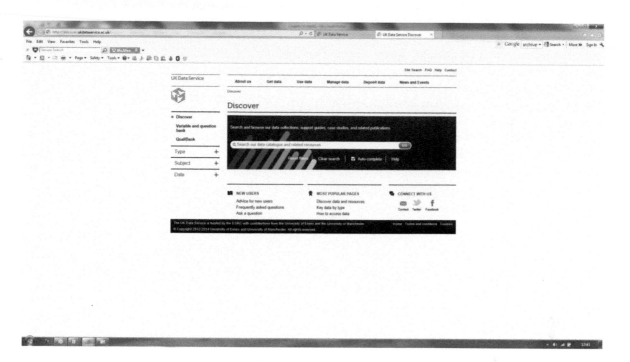

Webpage created for the UK Data Service, an ESRC-funded resource. Reproduced with permission from the University of Essex. The page is available at **http://discover.ukdataservice.ac.uk**.

PLATE 14.2
Results of a search

Webpage created for the UK Data Service, an ESRC-funded resource. Reproduced with permission from the University of Essex. The page is available at **http://discover.ukdataservice.ac.uk**.

which provided a two-page abstract of the study, including information about the sponsors; sampling details; method of data collection; main topics of the survey; and information about publications deriving from the study. At the bottom of this page is a further section on administrative and access information, which informs you of any special conditions relating to access. With the one we specified, we are told that because the data 'are more sensitive and/or pose a higher risk of disclosure' there are access restrictions which mean that data cannot be downloaded except by registration as a Secure User, which would normally be a professional researcher, rather than a student or member of the public. But for others, such as the LFS, access to data is via registration or by setting up an account that will allow you to download data. You will need to find out if there is an administrative charge for receiving the data, but it is likely that, if you are a student at (or a member of staff in) a UK institution of higher education, there will be no charge. A small number of quantitative and qualitative datasets, including World Bank macrodata, are also available without registration or authentication via the UK Data Service Data Open Access Policy, including some that can be used as a teaching resource. See the website for more details.

Information about searching for qualitative data for the purpose of conducting a secondary analysis can be found in Chapter 24.

Archival proxies and meta-analysis

It need not necessarily be the case that secondary analysis entails the analysis of primary data collected by other researchers, as illustrated by the discussion of the use of archival proxies in strategic management in Research in focus 14.7. Another context in which secondary analysis of other researchers' data may be carried out is through meta-analysis of existing research studies. With this method, the secondary researcher analyses data provided in articles that relate to the research question(s) of interest. See Key concept 14.8 and Research in focus 14.9.

14.7 RESEARCH IN FOCUS
The use of archival proxies in the field of strategic management

In the field of strategic management, considerable use is made of archival proxies, that is, quantitative data collected by organizations that can be used to represent an underlying theoretical construct. Such data are routinely collected by firms and are usually publicly accessible through such outlets as company reports. Ketchen et al. (2012) have considered how far such proxy measures (which are are a form of unobtrusive measure—see Key concept 14.11) can be used as valid indicators of underlying concepts. In the strategic management field, the issue is of considerable importance because their use has been increasing since the 1980s while the use of questionnaires and laboratory experiments has declined (Boyd et al. 2012). Ketchen et al. consider three archival proxy measures: research and development (R&D) intensity, patent counts, and patent citations. An examination of the use of these proxies in two prominent journals—*Academy of Management Journal* and *Strategic Management Journal*—shows that they have been used to represent a wide variety of theoretical constructs. For example, patent counts have been used to indicate constructs as diverse as the quantity of innovations carried out by a firm and a firm's technological capabilities. Ketchen et al. propose that the former use is reasonable and has face validity but the latter use is stretching its meaning, since, as the authors observe, applying for a patent does not necessarily mean that a firm has the capacity to develop the technology. Similarly, R&D intensity can usefully be regarded as a reasonable measure of some underlying constructs such as 'technological capabilities', but others have treated it as a measure of innovations and innovativeness, which seems less acceptable since whether a firm has the capacity to innovate is a different issue from the amount of money spent on research and development. While the discussion by Ketchen et al. does not depart from a consideration of the basic issue of the face validity of these measures, it provides an instructive warning about the need to ensure a reasonable correspondence between concepts and measures.

14.8 KEY CONCEPT
What is meta-analysis?

Meta-analysis involves summarizing the results of a large number of quantitative studies and conducting various analytical tests to show whether or not a particular variable has an effect. This provides a means whereby the results of large numbers of quantitative studies of a particular topic can be summarized and compared. The aim of this approach is to establish whether or not a particular variable has a certain effect by comparing the results of different studies. Meta-analysis thus involves pooling the results from various studies in order to estimate an overall effect by correcting the various sampling and non-sampling errors that may arise in relation to a particular study. In a sense, a meta-analysis lies between two kinds of activity covered in this book: doing a literature review of existing studies in an area in which you are interested (the focus of Chapter 5), and conducting a secondary analysis of other researchers' data, as has been discussed in this chapter. However, the technique relies on all the relevant information being available for each of the studies examined. Since not all the same information relating to methods of study and sample size is included in published papers, meta-analysis is not always feasible. One particular problem that meta-analysts face is known as the 'file drawer problem', whereby research that does not generate interesting publishable findings tends to be filed away and never sees the light of day. This tendency almost certainly creates a bias in meta-analytic reviews, since findings that fail to support a hypothesis or are equivocal in their implications may be less likely to be published.

14.9 RESEARCH IN FOCUS
A meta-analysis of research on corporate social responsibility and performance in East Asia

A question which is often asked in business research is whether theory and practice from Europe, the UK, and the USA can be applied in other contexts, especially Asian ones. Hou et al. (2015) were interested in whether corporate social responsibility (CSR), which has been shown to be associated with positive organizational outcomes in a number of settings, was also associated with them in East Asia. To explore this question, they conducted a meta-analysis of published articles based on East Asian data which investigated links between CSR and various measures of organizational performance.

Using a combination of database and journal searches, the authors identified 28 relevant papers based on empirical data, published over 15 years. Together, the papers covered over 30,000 firms. They included various different measures of two different kinds of CSR—social and environmental—and of financial and operational performance. By conducting meta-analysis, the authors found that overall CSR was positively associated with organizational performance, but that environmental CSR had a stronger association with performance than did social CSR. Overall, CSR had a stronger association with operational performance than with financial performance. The associations did not vary over the 15-year period during which the studies appeared. This meta-analysis allowed Hou and colleagues to evaluate the apparent outcomes of CSR in East Asia in way which could not have been done with a single study, thereby allowing them to draw theoretical and practical inferences about its importance in this context.

14.10 KEY CONCEPT
What is the ecological fallacy?

The ecological fallacy is the error of assuming that inferences about individuals or organizations can be made from findings relating to aggregate data. For example, official statistics might demonstrate a positive relationship between size of firm and the number of labour disputes involving strike action. Such a finding could be taken to imply that employees in larger firms are more likely than those in small firms to take strike action. However, it would be wrong to draw such an inference about individual firms or groups of employees from aggregate data. A particular large firm may show quite low levels of strike activity, while a particular small firm might show a high level. The fallacy can arise for several reasons—the reason highlighted in this case being that it may not be the size of the firm that is responsible for the level of strike activity.

Official statistics

The analysis of official statistics has been a feature of business research for many years. In most countries, agencies of the state, in the course of their business, are required to keep a record of their areas of activity. When these records are aggregated, they form the official statistics in an area of activity. Virtually every country in the world has an agency responsible for statistics. You can find a list of national statistics agencies at https://unstats.un.org/home/nso_sites/. Such statistics offer considerable potential benefits to business researchers:

- The data have already been collected. Therefore, as with other kinds of secondary analysis of data (see above), considerable time and expense may be saved. Also, some data are likely to be based on national censuses rather than samples, so that a complete picture can be obtained.

- Since the people who are the source of the data are not being asked questions that are part of a research project, the problem of reactivity will be much less pronounced than when data are collected by interview or questionnaire.

- There is the option of analysing the data both cross-sectionally and longitudinally. When analysing the data cross-sectionally, we could examine employment rates (in addition to unemployment rates) in terms of such standard variables as social class, income, ethnicity, age, gender, and region. Such analyses allow us to search for the factors that are associated with employment. Also, we can analyse the data over time. Precisely because the data are compiled over many years, it is possible to chart trends over time and perhaps to relate these to wider social changes.

- There is the prospect as well of cross-cultural analysis, since the official statistics from different nation-states can be compared for a specific area of activity.

However, readers who recall the discussion of convergent validity introduced in Chapter 8 will already be on their guard. The official statistics concerned with an area of social life such as employment can be very misleading, because they record only those individuals who are processed by the agencies that have the responsibility for compiling the statistics. In addition, the process whereby official statistics are generated involves an element of interpretation. In the case of labour disputes, this means that a substantial number of disputes are likely to go unrecorded as a result either of not being reported or of not being recognized as a labour dispute according to the criteria used by the agency. This level of unrecorded activity is sometimes referred to in relation to the field of crime (which has been one of the main areas for discussions about the uses and limitations of official statistics) as 'the dark figure' (Coleman and Moynihan 1996). Nor can the example of labour disputes be regarded as unique in this connection. To push the point even further, the deficiencies of official statistics also extend to the recording of levels of employment and unemployment. For example, the 'claimant count', which is used to gain a picture each month of the level of unemployment, may misrepresent the 'real' level of unemployment: people who are unemployed but who do not claim benefits or whose claim is disallowed will not be counted in the statistics, while those who form part of the claimant count but who work in part of what is known as the 'black' or 'informal' economy (and who therefore are not really unemployed) *will* be included in the unemployment statistics.

14.11 KEY CONCEPT
What are unobtrusive measures?

An unobtrusive measure is 'any method of observation that directly removes the observer from the set of interactions or events being studied' (Denzin 1970). Webb et al. (1966) distinguished four main types of such observation:

1. *Physical traces.* These are the 'signs left behind by a group' and include such things as graffiti and rubbish.

2. *Archive materials.* This category includes statistics collected by governmental and non-governmental organizations, such as diaries, the mass media, and historical records. See Research in focus 14.7 for a discussion of such data.

3. *Simple observation.* This refers to 'situations in which the observer has no control over the behaviour or sign in question, and plays an unobserved, passive, and non-intrusive role in the research situation' (Webb et al. 1966: 112).

4. *Contrived observation.* This is the same as simple observation, but the observer either actively varies the setting in some way (but without jeopardizing the unobtrusive quality of the observation) or employs hidden hardware to record observations, such as video cameras.

Official statistics would be subsumed under Category 2. It is important to realize that Webb et al. (1966) were not intending that unobtrusive methods should supplant conventional methods. Instead, they argued that the problem they were identifying was the almost exclusive reliance upon methods that were likely to be affected by reactivity. Webb et al. argued for greater 'triangulation' in social research, whereby conventional (reactive) and unobtrusive (non-reactive) methods would be employed in conjunction. For example, they wrote that they were providing an inventory of unobtrusive methods, 'because they demonstrate ways in which the investigator may shore up reactive infirmities of the interview and questionnaire' (1966: 174).

It is worth noting that unobtrusive methods or measures encapsulate at least two ways of thinking about the process of capturing data. First, many so-called unobtrusive measures are in fact *sources* of data, such as graffiti, diaries, media articles, and official statistics. Such sources require analysis in order to be rendered interesting to a business school audience. Secondly, such measures include *methods* of data collection, such as simple and contrived observation. While the data generated by such methods of data collection also require analysis, the data have to be produced by the methods. The data are not simply out there awaiting analysis in the way in which diaries or newspaper articles are (although, of course, a great deal of detective work is often necessary to unearth such sources). This means that neither of the terms 'unobtrusive methods' or 'unobtrusive measures' captures the variety of forms very well. A further disadvantage of the term 'unobtrusive measure' is that it seems to imply a connection to quantitative research alone, whereas certain approaches employed by qualitative researchers may qualify as unobtrusive methods.

An interesting use of unobtrusive methods can be found in Chatterjee and Hambrick's (2007) research on narcissistic CEOs. Rather than use one of the standard questionnaire inventories that have been devised to measure narcissism, the researchers used five unobtrusive indicators that they felt captured the sense of superiority and self-absorption that typifies this personality type:

(1) the prominence of the CEO's photograph in the company's annual report; (2) the CEO's prominence in the company's press releases; (3) the CEO's use of first-person singular pronouns in interviews; (4) the CEO's cash compensation divided by that of the second-highest-paid executive in the firm; and (5) the CEO's non-cash compensation divided by that of the second-highest-paid executive in the firm.

(Chatterjee and Hambrick 2007: 363)

All of these indicators are unobtrusive in that the data do not entail the involvement of the CEOs. From the point of view of the reader, the credibility of these indicators rests or falls on how far the researchers are convincing in the case that they make for their use as measures of narcissism.

Reliability and validity

Issues of reliability and validity seem to loom large in these considerations. Reliability seems to be jeopardized because definitions and policies regarding the phenomena to be counted vary over time. To the extent that such factors operate, the reliability of the data will be adversely affected and, as a result, validity will be similarly impaired.

Also, the problems with official statistics extend to the examination of the variables with which the rate of occurrence is associated. For example, it might be assumed that, if an examination of differences in labour disputes demonstrates that the rate varies by sector—say, with industries such as manufacturing and transport having consistently high strike rates and sectors such as agriculture having very low ones—this implies that the industrial sector is subject to labour militancy leading to strike action. There are two problems with drawing such an inference. First, there is an analytic difficulty known as the ecological fallacy (see Key concept 14.10). Secondly, even if we could ignore the problem of the ecological fallacy (which we cannot, of course), we would still be faced with an issue that is related to the matter of validity. Variations between industrial sectors may be a product of factors other than the difference in their propensity to take strike action. Instead, the variations may be due to such factors as variations in the average rates of pay and the terms and conditions of employment in different industrial sectors; likelihood of employers in different industrial sectors to report a dispute; differences in the number of employees working in these sectors; variation in the average number of people employed by organizations in different sectors; differences in the level of union membership and union activity; and variations in the effectiveness of formal communication systems.

Official statistics as a form of unobtrusive measure

One of the most compelling and frequently cited cases for the continued use of official statistics is that they can be considered a form of unobtrusive measure, although nowadays many writers prefer to use the term unobtrusive methods (R. M. Lee 2000). This term is derived from the notion of 'unobtrusive measure' coined by Webb et al. (1966). In a highly influential book, Webb et al. argued that social researchers are excessively reliant on measures of social phenomena deriving from methods of data collection that are prone to *reactivity* (see Research in focus 3.7, where this idea is introduced). This means that, whenever people know that they are participating in a study (which is invariably the case with methods of data collection such as structured interviewing, self-completion questionnaire, and structured observation), a component of their replies or behaviour is likely to be influenced by their knowledge that they are being investigated. In other words, their answers to questions or the behaviour they exhibit may be untypical.

Official statistics fit fairly squarely in the second of the four types of unobtrusive measures outlined in Key concept 14.11. As noted there, this second grouping covers a very wide range of sources of data, which includes statistics generated by organizations that are not agencies of the state. This is a useful reminder that potentially interesting statistical data are frequently compiled by a wide range of organizations, such as market research agencies. There may be greater potential for searching out and mining statistical data produced by organizations that are relatively independent of the state.

 # KEY POINTS

- Secondary analysis of existing data offers the prospect of being able to explore research questions of interest to you without having to go through the process of collecting the data yourself.

- Very often, secondary analysis offers the opportunity of being able to employ high-quality datasets that are based on large, reasonably representative samples.

- The analysis of official statistics may be thought of as a special form of secondary analysis but one that is more controversial because of the unease about the reliability and validity of certain types of official data, especially those relating to unemployment and labour disputes.

- Official statistics can be thought of as a form of unobtrusive measure.

QUESTIONS FOR REVIEW

- What is secondary analysis?

Other researchers' data

- Outline the main advantages and limitations of secondary analysis of other researchers' data.

- Does the possibility of conducting a secondary analysis apply only to quantitative data produced by other researchers?

Official statistics

- What reliability and validity issues do official statistics pose?

- What are unobtrusive methods or measures? What is the chief advantage of such methods?

ONLINE RESOURCES
www.oup.com/uk/brm5e/

Visit the Interactive Research Guide that accompanies this book to complete an exercise in secondary analysis and the use of official statistics.

CHAPTER

15

QUANTITATIVE DATA ANALYSIS

CHAPTER OUTLINE

In this chapter, some of the basic but nonetheless most frequently used methods for analysing quantitative data will be presented. To illustrate the use of the methods of data analysis, a small imaginary set of data based on attendance at a gym is used. It is the kind of small research project that would be feasible for most students doing undergraduate research projects for a dissertation or similar exercise. The chapter explores:

- the importance of *not* leaving considerations of how you will analyse your quantitative data until after you have collected all your data—you should be aware of the ways in which you would like to analyse your data from the earliest stage of your research;

- the distinctions between the different kinds of variables that can be generated in quantitative research. Knowing how to distinguish types of variables is crucial so that you appreciate which methods of analysis can be applied when you examine variables and relationships between them;

- methods for analysing a single variable at a time (univariate analysis);
- methods for analysing relationships between two variables (bivariate analysis);
- the analysis of relationships between three or more variables (multivariate analysis).

Introduction

In this chapter, some basic techniques for analysing quantitative data will be examined. In Chapter 16, the ways in which these techniques can be implemented using computer software will be introduced. The software is known as IBM SPSS and the version discussed in Chapter 16 is Release 24. The statistical formulae that underpin the techniques discussed in this chapter will not be presented here, since the necessary calculations can easily be carried out by using SPSS. Two chapters cannot do justice to the topics involved in statistical analysis, and readers are advised to move on as soon as possible to books that provide more detailed and advanced treatments (e.g. Bryman and Cramer 2011).

Before beginning this exposition of techniques, we would like to give you advance warning of one of the biggest mistakes that people make about quantitative data analysis:

I don't have to concern myself with how I'm going to analyse my survey data until after I've collected my data. I'll leave thinking about it till then, because it doesn't impinge on how I collect my data.

This is a common error that arises because quantitative data analysis looks like a distinct phase that occurs after the data have been collected (see, for example, Figure 8.1, in which the analysis of quantitative data is depicted

as a late step—number 9—in quantitative research). Quantitative data analysis is indeed something that occurs typically at a late stage in the overall process and is also a distinct stage.

However, that does not mean that you should not be considering how you will analyse your data until then. In fact, you should be fully aware of what techniques you will apply at a fairly early stage—for example, when you are designing your questionnaire, observation schedule, coding frame, or whatever. The two main reasons for this are as follows:

1. You cannot apply just any technique to any variable. Techniques must be appropriately matched to the types of variables that you have created through your research. This means that you must be fully conversant with the ways in which different types of variables are classified.

2. The size and nature of your sample are likely to impose limitations on the kinds of techniques you can use.

In other words, you need to be aware that decisions that you make at quite an early stage in the research process, such as the kinds of data you collect and the size of your sample, will have implications for the sorts of analysis that you will be able to conduct.

A small research project

This discussion of quantitative data analysis will be based upon an imaginary piece of research carried out by an undergraduate marketing student for a dissertation. The student in question is interested in the role of the sport and leisure industry and in particular, because of her own enthusiasm for leisure clubs and gyms, in the ways in which such venues are used and people's reasons for joining them. She has read an article that suggests that participant involvement in adult fitness programmes

is associated with their attitudinal loyalty, comprising investment of time and money, social pressure from significant others, and internalization of or commitment to the fitness regime (Park 1996). She intends to use this theory as a framework for her findings. The student is also interested in issues relating to gender and body image, as she suspects that men and women will differ in their reasons for going to a gym and the kinds of activities in which they engage in the gym. Her final issue of interest relates to the importance of age in determining gym involvement. In particular, she has discovered that previous research has shown that older people tend to show higher levels of attitudinal loyalty to recreational activities more generally and she wants to find out if this finding also applies to involvement in leisure clubs and gyms.

She secures the agreement of a gym close to her home to contact a sample of its members by post. The gym has 1200 members and she decides to take a simple random sample of 10 per cent of the membership (that is, 120 members). She sends out questionnaires to members of the sample with a covering letter testifying to the gym's support of her research. One thing she wants to know is how much time people spend on each of the three main classes of activity in the gym: cardiovascular equipment, weights equipment, and exercises. She defines each of these carefully in the covering letter and asks members of the sample to keep a note of how long they spend on each of the three activities on their next visit. They are then requested to complete the questionnaires. She ends up with a sample of 90 questionnaires—a response rate of 75 per cent.

Part of the questionnaire is presented in Tips and skills 'A completed and processed questionnaire' and has been completed by a respondent, then coded by the student. The entire questionnaire runs to four pages, but only 12 of the questions are provided here. Many of the questions (1, 3, 4, 5, 6, 7, 8, and 9) are pre-coded, and the student doing the coding simply has to circle the code to the far right of the question under the column 'code'. With the remainder of the questions, specific figures are requested, and the student doing the coding simply transfers the relevant figure to the code column.

TIPS AND SKILLS
A completed and processed questionnaire

Questionnaire		Code
1. Are you male or female (please tick)?		
Male ✓ Female ____		① 2
2. How old are you?		
_21_ years		*21*
3. Which of the following best describes your main reason for going to the gym? (please tick one only)		
Relaxation	____	1
Maintain or improve fitness	✓	②
Lose weight	____	3
Meet others	____	4
Build strength	____	5
Other (please specify)	____	6
4. When you go to the gym, how often do you use the cardiovascular equipment (treadmill, step machine, bike, rower)? (please tick)		
Always	✓	①
Usually	____	2
Rarely	____	3
Never	____	4
5. When you go to the gym, how often do you use the weights machines (including free weights)? (please tick)		
Always	✓	①
Usually	____	2
Rarely	____	3
Never	____	4

6. How frequently do you usually go to the gym? (please tick)

Every day	____	1
4–6 days a week	____	2
2 or 3 days a week	✓	③
Once a week	____	4
2 or 3 times a month	____	5
Once a month	____	6
Less than once a month	____	7

7. Are you usually accompanied when you go to the gym or do you usually go on your own? (please tick one only)

On my own	✓	①
With a friend	____	2
With a partner/spouse	____	3

8. Do you have sources of regular exercise other than the gym?

    Yes ____ No ✓   1 ②

    If you have answered No to this question, please proceed to question 10

9. If you have replied **Yes** to question **8**, please indicate the main source of regular exercise in the last six months from this list. (please tick one only)

Sport	____	1
Cycling on the road	____	2
Jogging	____	3
Long walks	____	4
Other (please specify)	____	5

10. During your last visit to the gym, how many minutes did you spend on the cardiovascular equipment (treadmill, step machine, bike, rower)?

    33 minutes   *33*

11. During your last visit to the gym, how many minutes did you spend on the weights machines (including free weights)?

    17 minutes   *17*

12. During your last visit to the gym, how many minutes did you spend on other activities (e.g. stretching exercises)?

    5 minutes   *5*

Missing data

The data for all 90 respondents are presented in Tips and skills 'Gym survey data'. Each of the 12 questions is known for the time being as a variable number (var00001, etc.). The variable number is a default number that is imposed by SPSS, the statistical package that is described in Chapter 16. Each variable number corresponds to the question number in Tips and skills 'A completed and processed questionnaire' (i.e. var00001 is question 1, var00002 is question 2, etc.). In the management of data, an important issue arises as to how to handle missing data. Missing data arise when respondents fail to reply to a question—either by accident or because they do not want to answer the question. Thus, respondent 24 has failed to answer question 2, which is concerned with age. This has been coded as a zero (0) and it will be important to ensure that the computer software is notified that zero will represent missing data for this question, since it needs to be taken into account during the analysis. Also, question 9 has a large number of zeros: many people did not answer it, because they have been filtered out by the previous question (that is, they do not have other sources of regular exercise). These have also been coded as zero

TIPS AND SKILLS
Gym survey data

var00001	var00002	var00003	var00004	var00005	var00006	var00007	var00008	var00009	var00010	var00011	var00012
1	21	2	1	1	3	1	2	0	33	17	5
2	44	1	3	1	4	3	1	2	10	23	10
2	19	3	1	2	2	1	1	1	27	18	12
2	27	3	2	1	2	1	2	0	30	17	3
1	57	2	1	3	2	3	1	4	22	0	15
2	27	3	1	1	3	1	1	3	34	17	0
1	39	5	2	1	5	1	1	5	17	48	10
2	36	3	1	2	2	2	1	1	25	18	7
1	37	2	1	1	3	1	2	0	34	15	0
2	51	2	2	2	4	3	2	0	16	18	11
1	24	5	2	1	3	1	1	1	0	42	16
2	29	2	1	2	3	1	2	0	34	22	12
1	20	5	1	1	2	1	2	0	22	31	7
2	22	2	1	3	4	2	1	3	37	14	12
2	46	3	1	1	5	2	2	0	26	9	4
2	41	3	1	2	2	3	1	4	22	7	10
1	25	5	1	1	3	1	1	1	21	29	4
2	46	3	1	2	4	2	1	4	18	8	11
1	30	3	1	1	5	1	2	0	23	9	6
1	25	5	2	1	3	1	1	1	23	19	0
2	24	2	1	1	3	2	1	2	20	7	6
2	39	1	2	3	5	1	2	0	17	0	9
1	44	3	1	1	3	2	1	2	22	8	5
1	0	1	2	2	4	2	1	4	15	10	4
2	18	3	1	2	3	1	2	1	18	7	10
1	41	3	1	1	3	1	2	0	34	10	4
2	38	2	1	2	5	3	1	2	24	14	10
1	25	2	1	1	2	1	2	0	48	22	7
1	41	5	2	1	3	1	1	2	17	27	0
2	30	3	1	1	2	2	2	0	32	13	10
2	29	3	1	3	2	1	2	0	31	0	7
2	42	1	2	2	4	2	1	4	17	14	6
1	31	2	1	1	2	1	2	0	49	21	2
2	25	3	1	1	2	3	2	0	30	17	15
1	46	3	1	1	3	1	1	3	32	10	5

var00001	var00002	var00003	var00004	var00005	var00006	var00007	var00008	var00009	var00010	var00011	var00012
1	24	5	2	1	4	1	1	2	0	36	11
2	34	3	1	1	3	2	1	4	27	14	12
2	50	2	1	2	2	3	2	0	28	8	6
1	28	5	1	1	3	2	1	1	26	22	8
2	30	3	1	1	2	1	1	4	21	9	12
1	27	2	1	1	2	1	1	3	64	15	8
2	27	2	1	2	4	2	1	4	22	10	7
1	36	5	1	1	3	2	2	0	21	24	0
2	43	3	1	1	4	1	2	0	25	13	8
1	34	2	1	1	3	2	1	1	45	15	6
2	27	3	1	1	2	1	1	4	33	10	9
2	38	2	1	3	4	2	2	0	23	0	16
1	28	2	1	1	3	3	1	2	38	13	5
1	44	5	1	1	2	1	2	0	27	19	7
2	31	3	1	2	3	2	2	0	32	11	5
2	23	2	1	1	4	2	1	1	33	18	8
1	45	3	1	1	3	1	1	2	26	10	7
2	34	3	1	2	2	3	2	0	36	8	12
1	27	3	1	1	2	3	1	3	42	13	6
2	40	3	1	1	2	2	1	4	26	9	10
2	24	2	1	1	2	1	1	2	22	10	9
1	37	2	1	1	5	2	2	0	21	11	0
1	22	5	1	1	4	1	1	1	23	17	6
2	31	3	1	2	3	1	1	4	40	16	12
1	37	2	1	1	2	3	2	0	54	12	3
2	33	1	2	2	4	2	2	0	17	10	5
1	23	5	1	1	3	1	1	1	41	27	8
1	28	3	1	1	3	3	2	0	27	11	8
2	29	2	1	2	5	2	1	2	24	9	9
2	43	3	1	1	2	1	2	0	36	17	12
1	28	5	1	1	3	1	1	1	22	15	4
1	48	2	1	1	5	1	1	4	25	11	7
2	32	2	2	2	4	2	2	0	27	13	11
1	28	5	1	1	2	2	2	0	15	23	7
2	23	2	1	1	5	1	1	4	14	11	5
2	43	2	1	2	5	1	2	0	18	7	3
1	28	2	1	1	4	3	1	2	34	18	8
2	23	3	1	1	2	1	2	0	37	17	17

var00001	var00002	var00003	var00004	var00005	var00006	var00007	var00008	var00009	var00010	var00011	var00012
2	36	1	2	2	4	2	1	4	18	12	4
1	50	2	1	1	3	1	1	2	28	14	3
1	37	3	1	1	2	2	2	0	26	14	9
2	41	3	1	1	2	1	1	4	24	11	4
1	26	5	2	1	5	1	1	1	23	19	8
2	28	3	1	1	4	1	2	0	27	12	4
2	35	2	1	1	3	1	1	1	28	14	0
1	28	5	1	1	2	1	1	2	20	24	12
2	36	2	1	1	3	2	2	0	26	9	14
2	29	3	1	1	4	1	1	4	23	13	4
1	34	1	2	2	4	2	1	0	24	12	3
1	53	2	1	1	3	3	1	1	32	17	6
2	30	3	1	1	4	1	2	0	24	10	9
1	43	2	1	1	2	1	1	2	24	14	10
2	26	5	2	1	4	1	1	1	16	23	7
2	44	1	1	1	4	2	2	0	27	18	6
1	45	1	2	2	3	3	2	0	20	14	5

to denote missing data, though strictly speaking their failure to reply is more indicative of the question not being applicable to them. Note also that there are zeros for var00010, var00011, and var00012. However, these do *not* denote missing data but indicate that the respondent spends 0 minutes on the activity in question. Everyone has answered questions 10, 11, and 12, so there are in fact no missing data for these variables. If there had been missing data, it would be necessary to code missing data with a number that could not also be a true figure. For example, nobody has spent 99 minutes on these activities, so this might be an appropriate number, as it is easy to remember and could not be read by the computer as anything other than missing data.

Types of variable

One of the things that might strike you when you look at the questions is that the kind of information that you receive varies by question. Some of the questions call for answers in terms of real numbers: questions 2, 10, 11, and 12. Questions 1 and 8 yield either/or answers and are therefore in the form of dichotomies. The rest of the questions take the form of lists of categories, but there are differences between these too. Some of the questions are in terms of answers that are rank ordered: questions 4, 5, and 6. Thus we can say in the case of question 6 that the category 'every day' implies greater frequency than '4–6 days a week', which in turn implies greater frequency than '2 or 3 days a week', and so on. However, in the case of questions 3, 7, and 9, the categories are *not* capable of being rank ordered. We cannot say in the case of question 3 that 'relaxation' is more of something than 'maintain or improve fitness' or 'lose weight'.

These considerations lead to a classification of the different types of variable that are generated in the course of research. There are four main types:

TABLE 15.1
Types of variable

Type	Description	Examples in gym study	Variable name in SPSS (see Chapter 16)
Interval/ratio	Variables where the distances between the categories are identical across the range	var00002	age
		var00010	cardmins
		var00011	weimins
		var00012	othmins
Ordinal	Variables whose categories can be rank ordered but where the distances between the categories are not equal across the range	var00004	carduse
		var00005	weiuse
		var00006	frequent
Nominal	Variables whose categories cannot be rank ordered; also known as *categorical*	var00003	reasons
		var00007	accomp
		var00009	exercise
Dichotomous	Variables containing data that have only two categories	var00001	gender
		var00008	othsourc

- **Interval variables/ratio variables** are variables where the distances between the categories are identical across the range of categories. In the case of variables var00010 and var00011, the distance between the categories is 1 minute. Thus, a person may spend 32 minutes on cardiovascular equipment, which is 1 minute more than someone who spends 31 minutes on this equipment. That difference is the same as the difference between someone who spends 8 minutes and another who spends 9 minutes on the equipment. This is the highest level of measurement, and a very wide range of techniques of analysis can be applied to interval/ratio variables. There is, in fact, a distinction between interval and ratio variables, in that the latter are interval variables with a fixed zero point. However, since most ratio variables exhibit this quality in business research (for example, income, age, number of employees, revenue), they are not being distinguished here.

- **Ordinal variables** are variables whose categories can be rank ordered (as in the case of interval/ratio variables) but the distances between the categories are not equal across the range. Thus, in the case of question 6, the difference between the category 'every day' and '4–6 days a week' is not the same as the difference between '4–6 days a week' and '2 or 3 days a week', and so on. Nonetheless, we can say that 'every day' is more frequent than '4–6 days a week', which is more frequent than '2 or 3 days a week', etc. You should also bear in mind that, if you subsequently group an interval/ratio variable such as var00002, which refers to people's ages, into categories (e.g. 20 and under; 21–30; 31–40; 41–50; 51 and over), you are transforming it into an ordinal variable.

- **Nominal variables**, also known as **categorical variables**, comprise categories that cannot be rank ordered. As noted previously, we cannot say in the case of question 3 that 'relaxation' is more of something than 'maintain or improve fitness' or 'lose weight'.

- **Dichotomous variables** contain data that have only two categories (for example, gender). Their position in relation to the other types is slightly ambiguous, as they have only one interval. They therefore can be considered as having attributes of the other three types of variable. They look as though they are nominal variables, but because they have only one interval they are sometimes treated as ordinal variables. However, it is probably safest to treat them for most purposes as if they were ordinary nominal variables.

The four main types of variable and illustrations of them from the gym survey are provided in Table 15.1.

Multiple-**indicator** (or multiple-item) measures of **concepts**, such as **Likert scales**, produce strictly speaking ordinal variables. However, many writers argue that they can be treated as though they produce interval/ratio variables, because of the relatively large number of categories they generate. For a brief discussion of this issue, see Bryman and Cramer (2011), who distinguish between 'true' interval/ratio variables and those produced by **multiple-indicator measure** (2011: 71–3).

Figure 15.1 provides guidance about how to identify variables of each type.

FIGURE 15.1
Deciding how to categorize a variable

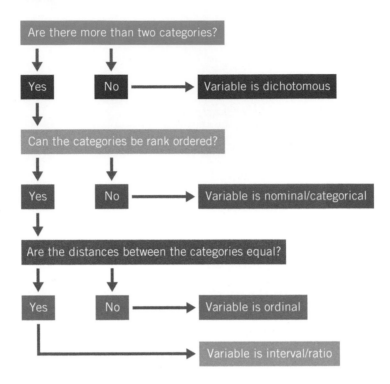

Univariate analysis

Univariate analysis refers to the analysis of one variable at a time. In this section, the commonest approaches will be outlined.

Frequency tables

A frequency table provides the number of people and the percentage belonging to each of the categories for the variable in question. It can be used in relation to all the different types of variable. An example of a frequency table is provided for var00003 in Table 15.2. Notice that nobody chose two of the possible choices of answer—'meet others' and 'other'—so these are not included in the table. The table shows, for example, that 33 members of the sample go the gym to lose weight and that they represent 37 per cent (percentages are often rounded up and down in frequency tables) of the entire sample. The procedure for generating a frequency table with SPSS is described in Chapter 16.

If an interval/ratio variable (such as people's ages) is to be presented in a frequency table format, it is almost invariably the case that the categories will need to be grouped. When grouping in this way, take care to ensure that the categories you create do not overlap (for example, like this: 20–30, 30–40, 40–50, etc.). An example of a frequency table for an interval/ratio variable is shown in Table 15.3: it provides a frequency table for var00002, which is concerned with the ages of those visiting the gym. If we did not group people in terms of age ranges, there would be 34 different categories, which is too many to take in. By creating five categories, we make the

TABLE 15.2
Frequency table showing reasons for visiting the gym

Reason	n	%
Relaxation	9	10
Maintain or improve fitness	31	34
Lose weight	33	37
Build strength	17	19
TOTAL	90	100

TABLE 15.3

Frequency table showing ages of gym members

Age	*n*	%
20 and under	3	3
21–30	39	44
31–40	23	26
41–50	21	24
51 and over	3	3
TOTAL	89	100

distribution of ages easier to comprehend. Notice that the sample totals 89 and that the percentages are based on a total of 89 rather than 90. This is because this variable contains one missing value (respondent 24). The procedure for grouping respondents with SPSS is described in Chapter 16.

Diagrams

Diagrams are among the most frequently used methods of displaying quantitative data. Their chief advantage is that they are relatively easy to interpret and understand. If you are working with nominal or ordinal variables, the *bar chart* and the *pie chart* are two of the easiest methods to use. A bar chart of the data from Table 15.2 is shown in Figure 15.2. Each bar represents the number of people falling into each category. This figure was produced with SPSS. The procedure for generating a bar chart with

FIGURE 15.3

Pie chart showing the main reasons for visiting the gym (SPSS output)

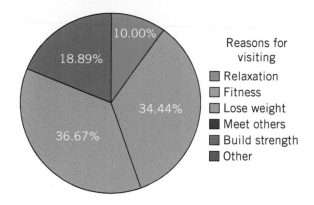

SPSS is described in Chapter 16.

Another way of displaying the same data is with a pie chart, like the one in Figure 15.3. This shows the relative size of the different categories but brings out as well the size of each slice relative to the total sample. The percentage that each slice represents of the whole sample is also given in this diagram, which was also produced with SPSS. The procedure for generating a pie chart with SPSS is described in Chapter 16.

If you are displaying an interval/ratio variable, like var00002, a *histogram* is likely to be employed. Figure 15.4, which was also generated by SPSS, uses the

FIGURE 15.2

Bar chart showing the main reasons for visiting the gym (SPSS output)

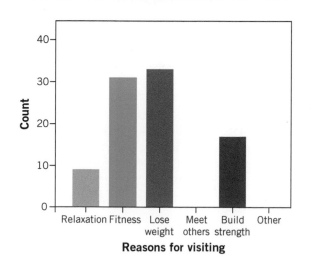

FIGURE 15.4

Histogram showing the ages of gym visitors (SPSS output)

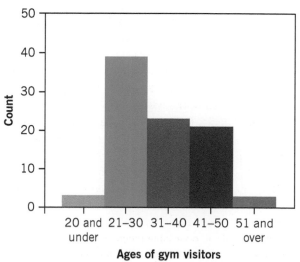

same data and categories as Table 15.3. As with the bar chart, the bars represent the relative size of each of the age bands. However, note that, with the histogram, there is no space between the bars, whereas there is a space between the bars of a bar chart. Histograms are produced for interval/ratio variables, whereas bar charts are produced for nominal and ordinal variables. The procedure for generating a histogram with SPSS is described in Chapter 16.

Measures of central tendency

Measures of central tendency encapsulate in one figure a value that is typical for a distribution of values. In effect, we are seeking out an average for a distribution, but, in quantitative data analysis, three different forms of average are recognized:

- *Arithmetic mean*. This is the 'average' as we understand it in everyday use—that is, we sum all the values in a distribution and then divide by the number of values. Thus, the arithmetic mean (or more simply the *mean*) for var00002 is 33.6, meaning that the average age of gym visitors is nearly 34 years of age. The mean should be employed only in relation to interval/ratio variables, though it is not uncommon to see it being used for ordinal variables as well.

- *Median*. The median is the mid-point in a distribution of values. Whereas the mean is vulnerable to outliers (extreme values at either end of the distribution), which will exert considerable upwards or downwards pressure on the mean, by taking the mid-point of a distribution the median is not affected in this way. The median is derived by arraying all the values in a distribution from the smallest to the largest and then finding the middle point. If there is an even number of values, the median is calculated by taking the mean of the two middle numbers of the distribution. In the case of var00002, the median is 31. This is slightly lower than the mean, in part because some considerably older members (especially respondents 5 and 10) inflate the mean slightly. The median can be employed in relation to both interval/ratio and ordinal variables.

- *Mode*. The mode is the value that occurs most frequently in a distribution. The mode for var00002 is 28. The mode can be employed in relation to all types of variable.

The procedure for generating the mean, median, and mode with SPSS is described in Chapter 16.

Measures of dispersion

The amount of variation in a sample can be just as interesting as providing estimates of the typical value of a distribution. For one thing, it becomes possible to draw contrasts between comparable distributions of values. For example, is there more or less variability in the amount of time spent on cardiovascular equipment as compared to weights machines?

The most obvious way of measuring dispersion is by the range. This is simply the difference between the maximum and the minimum value in a distribution of values associated with an interval/ratio variable. We find that the range for the two types of equipment is 64 minutes for the cardiovascular equipment and 48 minutes for the weights machines. This suggests that there is more variability in the amount of time spent on the former. However, like the mean, the range is influenced by outliers, such as respondent 60 in the case of var00010.

Another measure of dispersion is the standard deviation, which is essentially the average amount of variation around the mean. Although the calculation is somewhat more complicated than this, the standard deviation is calculated by taking the difference between each value in a distribution and the mean and then dividing the total of the differences by the number of values. The standard deviation for var00010 is 9.9 minutes and for var00011 it is 8 minutes. Thus, not only is the average amount of time spent on the cardiovascular equipment higher than for the weights equipment; the standard deviation is greater too. The standard deviation is also affected by outliers, but, unlike the range, their impact is offset by dividing by the number of values in the distribution. The procedure for generating the standard deviation with SPSS is described in Chapter 16.

A type of figure that has become popular for displaying interval/ratio variables is the *boxplot* (see Figure 15.5). This form of display provides an indication of both central tendency (the median) and dispersion (the range). It also indicates whether there are any outliers. Figure 15.5 displays a boxplot for the total number of minutes users spent during their last gym visit. There is an outlier—case number 41, who spent a total of 87 minutes in the gym. The box represents the middle 50 per cent of users. The upper line of the box indicates the greatest use of the gym within the 50 per cent and the lower line of the box represents the least use of the gym within the 50 per cent. The line going across the box indicates the median. The line going upwards from the box goes up to the person whose use of the gym was greater than any other user, other than case number 41. The line going downwards from

FIGURE 15.5

A boxplot for the number of minutes spent on the last visit to the gym

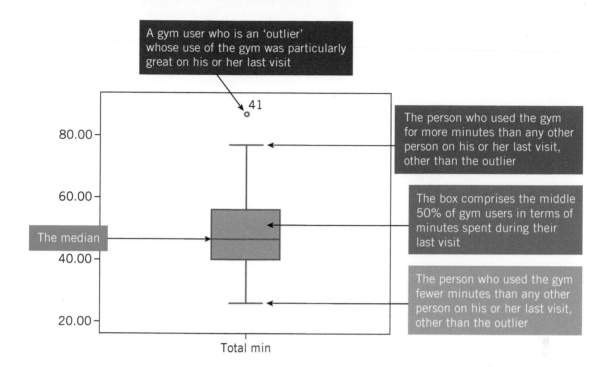

the box goes down to the person whose use of the gym was lower than that of any other user. Boxplots are useful because they display both central tendency and dispersion. They vary in their shape depending on whether cases tend to be high or low in relation to the median.

With Figure 15.5, the box and the median are closer to the bottom end of the distribution, suggesting less variation among gym users below the median. There is more variation above the median. The procedure for generating a boxplot with SPSS is described in Chapter 16.

Bivariate analysis

Bivariate analysis is concerned with the analysis of two variables at a time to uncover whether or not the two variables are related. Exploring relationships between variables means searching for evidence that the variation in one variable coincides with variation in another variable. A variety of techniques is available for examining relationships, but their use depends on the nature of the two variables being analysed. Figure 15.6 portrays the main types of bivariate analysis according to the types of variable involved.

Relationships, not causality

An important point to bear in mind about all of the methods for analysing relationships between variables is that

it is precisely relationships that they uncover. As was noted in Chapter 3 in relation to cross-sectional designs, this means that you cannot infer that one variable *causes* another. Indeed, there are cases when what appears to be a causal influence working in one direction actually works in the other way.

Sometimes, we may feel quite confident that we can infer a causal direction when a relationship between two variables is discerned—for example, if we find that age and voting behaviour are related. It is impossible for the way people vote to influence their age, so, if we do find the two variables to be related, we can rule out that causal relationship. We cannot infer with complete confidence that age is the independent variable, but we can entertain this as a highly plausible explanation. It

FIGURE 15.6

Methods of bivariate analysis

	Nominal	Ordinal	Interval/ratio	Dichotomous
Nominal	Contingency table + chi-square (χ^2) + Cramér's V	Contingency table + chi-square (χ^2) + Cramér's V	Contingency table + chi-square (χ^2) + Cramér's V If the interval/ratio variable can be identified as the dependent variable, compare means + eta	Contingency table + chi-square (χ^2) + Cramér's V
Ordinal	Contingency table + chi-square (χ^2) + Cramér's V	Spearman's rho (ρ)	Spearman's rho (ρ)	Spearman's rho (ρ)
Interval/ratio	Contingency table + chi-square (χ^2) + Cramér's V If the interval/ratio variable can be identified as the dependent variable, compare means + eta	Spearman's rho (ρ)	Pearson's r	Spearman's rho (ρ)
Dichotomous	Contingency table + chi-square (χ^2) + Cramér's V	Spearman's rho (ρ)	Spearman's rho (ρ)	phi (ϕ)

is not uncommon for researchers, when analysing their data, to draw inferences about causal direction based on their assumptions about the likely causal direction among related variables. Although such inferences may be based on sound reasoning, they can only be inferences, and there is the possibility that the real pattern of causal direction is the opposite of that which is anticipated.

Contingency tables

Contingency tables are probably the most flexible of all methods of analysing relationships in that they can be employed in relation to any pair of variables, though they are not the most efficient method for some pairs, which is the reason why the method is not recommended in all the cells in Figure 15.6. A contingency table is like a frequency table but it allows two variables to be simultaneously analysed so that relationships between the two variables can be examined. It is normal for contingency tables to include percentages, since these make the tables easier to interpret. Table 15.4 examines the relationship between two variables from the gym survey: gender and reasons for visiting the gym. The percentages are *column percentages*—that is, they calculate the number in each cell as a percentage of the total number in that column. Thus, to take the top left-hand cell, the three men who go to the gym for relaxation are 7 per cent of all 42 men in the sample. Users of contingency tables often present

the presumed independent variable (if one can in fact be presumed) as the column variable and the presumed dependent variable as the row variable. In this case, we are presuming that gender influences reasons for going to the gym. In fact, we know that going to the gym cannot influence gender. In such circumstances, it is column rather than row percentages that will be required. The procedure for generating a contingency table with SPSS is described in Chapter 16.

Contingency tables are generated so that patterns of association can be searched for. In this case, we can see clear gender differences in reasons for visiting the gym. As our student anticipated, females are much more likely

TABLE 15.4

Contingency table showing the relationship between gender and reasons for visiting the gym

Reasons	Gender			
	Male		Female	
	No.	%	No.	%
Relaxation	3	7	6	13
Fitness	15	36	16	33
Lose weight	8	19	25	52
Build strength	16	38	1	2
TOTAL	42	100	48	100

Note: $\chi^2 = 22.726$; $p < 0.0001$.

than men to go to the gym to lose weight. They are also somewhat more likely to go to the gym for relaxation. By contrast, men are much more likely to go to the gym to build strength. There is little difference between the two genders in terms of fitness as a reason.

Pearson's *r*

Pearson's *r* is a method for examining relationships between interval/ratio variables. The chief features of this method are as follows:

- the coefficient will almost certainly lie between 0 (zero, or no relationship between the two variables) and 1 or −1 (a perfect relationship)—this indicates the *strength* of a relationship;

- the closer the coefficient is to 1 or −1, the stronger the relationship; the closer it is to 0, the weaker the relationship;

- the coefficient will be either positive or negative—this indicates the *direction* of a relationship.

To illustrate these features, consider Tips and skills 'Imaginary data from five variables to show different types of relationship', which gives imaginary data for five variables, and the scatter diagrams in Figures 15.7–15.10, which look at the relationship between pairs of interval/ratio variables. The scatter diagram for variables 1 and 2 is presented in Figure 15.7 and shows a perfect positive relationship, which would have a Pearson's *r* correlation of 1. This means that, as one variable increases, the other variable increases by the same amount.

The scatter diagram for variables 2 and 3 (see Figure 15.8) shows a perfect negative relationship, which would have a Pearson's *r* correlation of −1. This means that, as one variable increases, the other variable decreases.

If there was no or virtually no correlation between the variables, there would be no apparent pattern to the markers in the scatter diagram. This is the case with the relationship between variables 2 and 5. The correlation is virtually zero at −0.041. This means that the variation in each variable is not associated with variation in the other variable. Figure 15.9 shows the appropriate scatter diagram.

If a relationship is strong, a clear patterning to the variables will be evident. This is the case with variables 2 and 4, whose scatter diagram appears in Figure 15.10. There is clearly a positive relationship, and in fact the Pearson's *r* value is +0.88 (usually, positive correlations are presented without the + sign). This means that the variation in the two variables is very closely connected.

Going back to the gym survey, we find that the correlation between age (var00002) and the amount of time spent on weights equipment (var00011) is −0.27, implying a weak negative relationship. This suggests that there is a tendency such that, the older a person is, the less likely he or she is to spend much time on such equipment.

TIPS AND SKILLS
Imaginary data from five variables to show different types of relationship

	Variables			
1	2	3	4	5
1	10	50	7	9
2	12	45	13	23
3	14	40	18	7
4	16	35	14	15
5	18	30	16	6
6	20	25	23	22
7	22	20	19	12
8	24	15	24	8
9	26	10	22	18
10	28	5	24	10

FIGURE 15.7
Scatter diagram showing a perfect positive relationship

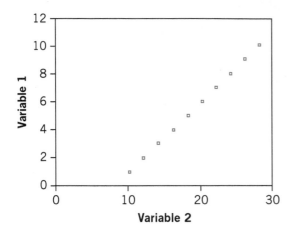

FIGURE 15.8
Scatter diagram showing a perfect negative relationship

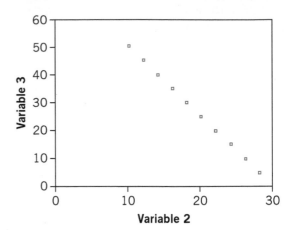

FIGURE 15.9
Scatter diagram showing two variables that are not related

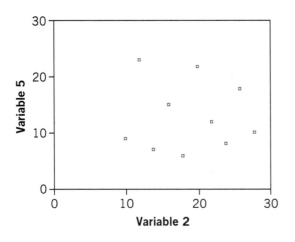

FIGURE 15.10
Scatter diagram showing a strong positive relationship

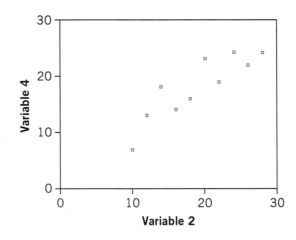

In order to be able to use Pearson's r, the relationship between the two variables must be broadly *linear*—that is, when plotted on a scatter diagram, the values of the two variables approximate to a straight line (even though they may be scattered, as in Figure 15.10) and do not curve. Therefore, plotting a scatter diagram before using Pearson's r is important, in order to determine that the nature of the relationship between a pair of variables does not violate the assumptions being made when this method of correlation is employed.

If you square a value of Pearson's r, you can derive a further useful statistic—namely the *coefficient of determination*, which expresses how much of the variation in one variable is accounted for by the other variable. Thus,

if r is -0.27, r^2 is 0.0729. We can then express this as a percentage by multiplying r^2 by 100. The product of this exercise is 7 per cent. This means that just 7 per cent of the variation in the use of cardiovascular equipment is accounted for by age. The coefficient of determination is a useful adjunct to the interpretation of correlation information.

The procedures for generating Pearson's r and scatter diagrams with SPSS are described in Chapter 16.

Spearman's rho

Spearman's rho, which is often represented with the Greek letter ρ, is designed for the use of pairs of ordinal variables, but is also used, as suggested by Figure 15.6, when one variable is ordinal and the other is interval/ratio. It is exactly the same as Pearson's r in terms of the outcome of calculating it, in that the computed value of rho will be either positive or negative and will vary between 0 and 1 or −1. If we look at the gym study, there are three ordinal variables: var00004, var00005, and var00006 (see Table 15.1). If we use Spearman's rho to calculate the correlation between the first two variables, we find that the correlation between var00004 and var00005—frequency of use of the cardiovascular and weights equipment—is low at 0.2. A slightly stronger relationship is found between var00006 (frequency of going to the gym) and var00010 (amount of time spent on the cardiovascular equipment), which is 0.4. Note that the latter variable is an interval/ratio variable. When confronted with a situation in which we want to calculate the correlation between an ordinal and an interval/ratio variable, we cannot use Pearson's r, because both variables must be at the interval/ratio level of measurement. Instead, we must use Spearman's rho (see Figure 15.6). The procedure for generating Spearman's rho with SPSS is described in Chapter 16.

Phi and Cramér's V

Phi (φ) and Cramér's *V* are two closely related statistics. The phi coefficient is used for the analysis of the relationship between two dichotomous variables. Like Pearson's r, it results in a computed statistic that varies between 0 and +1 or −1. The correlation between var00001 (gender) and var00008 (other sources of regular exercise) is 0.24, implying that males are somewhat more likely than females to have other sources of regular exercise, though the relationship is weak.

Cramér's *V* uses a similar formula to phi and can be employed with nominal variables (see Figure 15.6). However, this statistic can take on only a positive value, so that it can give an indication only of the strength of the relationship between two variables, not of the direction.

The value of Cramér's *V* associated with the analysis presented in Table 15.4 is 0.50. This suggests a moderate relationship between the two variables. Cramér's *V* is usually reported along with a contingency table and a chi-square test (see section on 'The chi-square test' below). It is not normally presented on its own. The procedure for generating phi and Cramér's *V* with SPSS is described in Chapter 16.

Comparing means and eta

If you need to examine the relationship between an interval/ratio variable and a nominal variable, and if the latter can be relatively unambiguously identified as the independent variable, a potentially fruitful approach is to compare the means of the interval/ratio variable for each subgroup of the nominal variable. As an example, consider Table 15.5, which presents the mean number of minutes spent on cardiovascular equipment (var00010) for each of the four categories of reasons for going to the gym (var00003). The means suggest that people who go to the gym for fitness or to lose weight spend considerably more time on this equipment than people who go to the gym to relax or to build strength.

This procedure is often accompanied by a test of association between variables called eta (η). This statistic expresses the level of association between the two variables and, like Cramér's *V*, will always be positive. The level of eta for the data in Table 15.5 is 0.48. This suggests a moderate relationship between the two variables. Eta-squared expresses the amount of variation in the interval/ratio variable that is accounted for by the nominal variable. In the case of this example, eta-squared is 22 per cent. Eta is a very flexible method for exploring the relationship between two variables, because it can be employed when one variable is nominal and the other interval/ratio. Also, it does not make the assumption that the relationship between variables is linear. The procedure for comparing means and for generating eta with SPSS is described in Chapter 16.

TABLE 15.5

Time	Reasons				
	Relaxation	Fitness	Lose weight	Build strength	Total
Mean number of minutes spent on cardiovascular equipment	18.33	30.55	28.36	19.65	26.47
n	9	31	33	17	90

Comparing subgroup means: time spent on cardiovascular equipment by reasons for going to the gym

Multivariate analysis

Multivariate analysis entails the simultaneous analysis of three or more variables. This is quite an advanced topic, and it is recommended that readers examine a textbook on quantitative data analysis for an exposition of techniques (e.g. Bryman and Cramer 2011). There are three main contexts within which multivariate analysis might be employed.

Could the relationship be spurious?

In order for a relationship between two variables to be established, not only must there be evidence that there is a relationship but the relationship must be shown to be *non-spurious*. A spurious relationship exists when there appears to be a relationship between two variables, but the relationship is not real: it is being produced because each variable is itself related to a third variable. For example, if we find a relationship in a firm between employees' levels of organizational commitment and job satisfaction, we might ask: could the relationship be an artefact of the leadership style of respondents' immediate managers (see Figure 15.11)? The more committed people are to their organization, the more job satisfaction they are likely to exhibit. However, whether leaders are considerate to their subordinates or not is likely to influence both organizational commitment *and* job satisfaction. If leadership style were found to be producing the apparent relationship between organizational commitment and job satisfaction, we would conclude that the relationship is spurious. In this case, the variable of leadership style would be known as a confounding variable.

Could there be an intervening variable?

Let us say that we do not find that the relationship is spurious; we might ask *why* there is a relationship between two variables. For example, there have been several studies that have explored the relationship between an organization's market orientation and its business performance. However, the mixed nature of the findings to have emerged from these studies led Piercy et al. (2002) suggest that there is a more complex relationship between these two variables than previous studies have assumed. In particular, they speculated that higher levels of market orientation are associated with higher levels of employee motivation, satisfaction, and commitment, which in turn leads to enhanced organizational performance. Employee attitudes are thus an intervening variable (also called a mediator):

| market orientation | → | employee attitudes | → | organizational performance |

An intervening variable allows us to answer questions about the bivariate relationship between variables. It suggests that the relationship between the two variables is not a direct one, since the impact of market orientation on organizational performance is viewed as occurring via employee attitudes.

Could a third variable moderate the relationship?

We might ask a question such as: does the relationship between two variables hold for men but not for women?

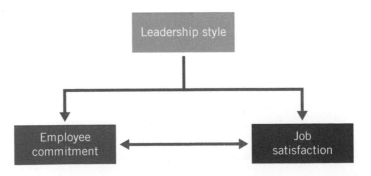

FIGURE 15.11
A spurious relationship

TABLE 15.6

Contingency table showing the relationship between age and whether or not gym visitors have other sources of regular exercise (%)

Other source of exercise	Age		
	30 and under	31–40	41 and over
Other source	64	43	58
No other source	36	57	42
n	42	23	24

If it does, the relationship is said to be moderated by gender. We might ask in the gym study, for example, if the relationship between age and whether visitors have other sources of regular exercise (var00008) is moderated by gender. This would imply that, if we find a pattern relating age to other sources of exercise, that pattern

will vary by gender. Table 15.6 shows the relationship between age and other sources of exercise. In this table, age has been broken down into just three age bands to make the table easier to read. The table suggests that the 31–40 age group is less likely to have other sources of regular exercise than the 30-and-under and 41-and-over age groups. However, Table 15.7, which breaks the relationship down by gender, suggests that the pattern for males and females is somewhat different. Among males, the pattern shown in Table 15.6 is very pronounced, but for females the likelihood of having other sources of exercise declines with gender. It would seem that the relationship between age and other sources of exercise is a moderated relationship because it is moderated by gender. This example illustrates the way in which contingency tables can be employed for multivariate analysis. However, there is a wide variety of other techniques (Bryman and Cramer 2011: Chapter 10). The procedure for conducting such an analysis with SPSS is described in Chapter 16.

TABLE 15.7

Contingency table showing the relationship between age and whether or not gym visitors have other sources of regular exercise for males and females (%)

Other source of exercise	Gender					
	Male			Female		
	30 and under	31–40	41 and over	30 and under	31–40	41 and over
Other source	70	33	75	59	50	42
No other source	30	67	25	41	50	58
n	20	9	12	22	14	12

Statistical significance

One difficulty with working on data deriving from a sample is that there is often the lingering worry that, even though you have employed a probability sampling procedure (as in the gym survey), your findings will not be generalizable to the population from which the sample was drawn. As we saw in Chapter 9, there is always the possibility that sampling error (difference between the population and the sample that you have selected) has occurred, even when probability sampling procedures have been followed. If this happens, the sample will be unrepresentative of the wider population and therefore any findings will be invalid. To make matters worse, there is no feasible way of finding out whether or not they do in fact apply to the population! What you can do is provide

an indication of how confident you can be in your findings. This is where statistical significance and the various tests of statistical significance come in.

We need to know how confident we can be that our findings can be generalized to the population from which that sample was selected. Since we cannot be absolutely certain that a finding based on a sample will also be found in the population, we need a technique that allows us to establish how confident we can be that the finding exists in the population and what risk we are taking in inferring that the finding exists in the population. These two elements—confidence and risk—lie at the heart of tests of statistical significance (see Key concept 15.1). However, it is important to appreciate that tests of statistical

15.1 KEY CONCEPT
What is a test of statistical significance?

A test of statistical significance allows the analyst to estimate how confident he or she can be that the results deriving from a study based on a randomly selected sample are generalizable to the population from which the sample was drawn. When examining statistical significance in relation to the relationship between two variables, it also tells us about the risk of concluding that there is in fact a relationship in the population when there is no such relationship in the population. If an analysis reveals a statistically significant finding, this does not mean that the finding is intrinsically significant or important. The word 'significant' seems to imply importance. However, statistical significance is solely concerned with the confidence researchers can have in their findings. It does not mean that a statistically significant finding is substantively significant.

significance can be employed only in relation to samples that have been drawn using probability sampling. The process of inferring findings from a probability sample to the population from which it was selected is known as statistical inference.

In Chapter 9 (see Tips and skills 'Generalizing from a random sample to the population'), in the context of the discussion of the standard error of the mean, we began to get an appreciation of the ideas behind statistical significance. For example, we know that the mean age of the gym sample is 33.6. Using the concept of the standard error of the mean, we can calculate that we can be 95 per cent confident that the population mean lies between 31.72 and 35.47. This suggests that we can determine in broad outline the degree of confidence that we can have in a sample mean.

In the rest of this section, we will look at the tests that are available for determining the degree of confidence we can have in our findings when we explore relationships between variables. All of the tests have a common structure:

- *Set up a null hypothesis.* A null hypothesis stipulates that two variables are not related in the population—for example, that there is *no* relationship between gender and visiting the gym in the population from which the sample was selected.
- *Establish the level of statistical significance that you find acceptable.* This is essentially a measure of the degree of risk that you might reject the null hypothesis (implying that there *is* a relationship in the population) when you should support it (implying that there is no relationship in the population). Levels of statistical significance are expressed as probability levels—that is, the probability (expressed as *p*) of rejecting the null hypothesis when you should be confirming it. See Key concept 15.2 on this issue. The convention among

most business researchers is that the maximum level of statistical significance that is acceptable is $p < 0.05$, which implies that there are fewer than 5 chances in 100 that you could have a sample that shows a relationship when there is not one in the population.

- *Determine the statistical significance of your findings.* That is, use a statistical test such as chi-square—see section on 'The chi-square test'. If your findings are statistically significant at the 0.05 level—so that the risk of getting a relationship as strong as the one you have found when there is *no* relationship in the population is no higher than 5 in 100—you would *reject* the null hypothesis. Therefore, you are implying that the results are unlikely to have occurred by *chance*.

There are in fact two types of error that can be made when inferring statistical significance. These errors are known as Type I and Type II errors (see Figure 15.12). A Type I error occurs when you reject the null hypothesis when it should in fact be confirmed. This means that your results have arisen by chance and you are falsely concluding that there is a relationship in the population when there is not one. Using a $p < 0.05$ level of significance means that we are more likely to make a Type I error than when using a $p < 0.01$ level of significance. This is because with 0.01 there is less chance of falsely rejecting the null hypothesis. However, in doing so, you increase the chance of making a Type II error (accepting the null hypothesis when you should reject it). This is because you are more likely to confirm the null hypothesis when the significance level is 0.01 (1 in 100) than when it is 0.05 (1 in 20).

The chi-square test

The chi-square (χ^2) test is applied to contingency tables such as Table 15.4. It allows us to establish how confident

15.2 KEY CONCEPT
What is the level of statistical significance?

The level of statistical significance is the level of risk that you are prepared to take that you are inferring that there is a relationship between two variables in the population from which the sample was taken when in fact no such relationship exists. The maximum level of risk that is conventionally taken in business research is to say that there are up to 5 chances in 100 that we might be falsely concluding that there is a relationship when there is not one in the population from which the sample was taken. This means that, if we drew 100 samples, we are recognizing that as many as 5 of them might exhibit a relationship when there is not one in the population. Our sample might be one of those 5, but the risk is fairly small. This significance level is denoted by $p < 0.05$ (p means probability). If we accepted a significance level of $p < 0.1$, we would be accepting the possibility that as many as 10 in 100 samples might show a relationship where none exists in the population. In this case, there is a greater risk than with $p < 0.05$ that we might have a sample that implies a relationship when there is not one in the population, since the probability of our having such a sample is greater when the risk is 1 in 10 (10 out of 100 when $p < 0.1$) than when the risk is 1 in 20 (5 out of 100 when $p < 0.05$). Therefore, we would have greater confidence when the risk of falsely inferring that there is a relationship between 2 variables is 1 in 20, as against 1 in 10. But, if you want a more stringent test, perhaps because you are worried about the use that might be made of your results, you might choose the $p < 0.01$ level. This means that you are prepared to accept as your level of risk a probability of only 1 in 100 that the results could have arisen by chance (that is, due to sampling error). Therefore, if the results, following administration of a test, show that a relationship is statistically significant at the $p < 0.05$ level, but not the $p < 0.01$ level, you would have to confirm the null hypothesis.

we can be that there is a relationship between the two variables in the population. The test works by calculating for each cell in the table an expected frequency or value—that is, one that would occur on the basis of chance alone. The chi-square value, which in Table 15.4 is 22.726, is produced by calculating the differences between the actual and expected values for each cell in the table and then summing those differences (it is slightly more complicated than this, but the details

need not concern us here). The chi-square value means nothing on its own and can be meaningfully interpreted only in relation to its associated level of statistical significance, which in this case is $p < 0.0001$. This means that there is only 1 chance in 10,000 of falsely rejecting the null hypothesis (that is, inferring that there is a relationship in the population when there is no such relationship in the population). You could be extremely confident that there is a relationship between gender and reasons

FIGURE 15.12
Type I and Type II errors

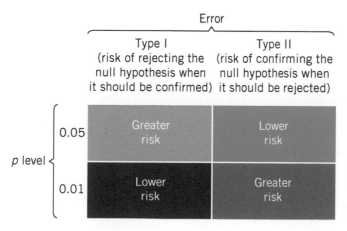

for visiting the gym among all gym members, since the chance that you have obtained a sample that shows a relationship when there is no relationship among all gym members is 1 in 10,000.

Whether or not a chi-square value achieves statistical significance depends not just on its magnitude but also on the number of categories of the two variables being analysed. This latter issue is governed by what is known as the 'degrees of freedom' associated with the table. The number of degrees of freedom is governed by the simple formula:

number of degrees of freedom
= (number of columns −1) × (number of rows −1).

In the case of Table 15.4, this will be (2 − 1) × (4 − 1) = 3. In other words, the chi-square value that is arrived at is affected by the size of the table, and this is taken into account when deciding whether the chi-square value is statistically significant or not. The procedure for generating chi-square in conjunction with a contingency table with SPSS is described in Chapter 16.

Correlation and statistical significance

Examining the statistical significance of a computed correlation coefficient, which is based on a randomly selected sample, provides information about the likelihood that the coefficient will be found in the population from which the sample was taken. Thus, if we find a correlation of −0.62, what is the likelihood that a relationship of at least that size exists in the population? This tells us if the relationship could have arisen by chance.

If the correlation coefficient r is −0.62 and the significance level is $p < 0.05$, we can reject the null hypothesis that there is no relationship in the population. We can infer that there are only 5 chances in 100 that a correlation of at least −0.62 could have arisen by chance alone. You *could* have 1 of the 5 samples in 100 that shows a relationship when there is not one in the population, but the degree of risk is reasonably small. If, say, it was found that $r = -0.62$ and $p < 0.1$, there could be as many as 10 chances in 100 that there is no correlation in the population. This would *not* be an acceptable level of risk for most purposes. It would mean that in as many as 1 sample in 10 we might find a correlation of −0.62 or above when there is not a correlation in the population. If $r = -0.62$ and $p < 0.001$, there is only 1 chance in 1000 that no correlation exists in the population. There would be a very low level of risk if you inferred that the correlation had not arisen by chance.

Whether a correlation coefficient is statistically significant or not will be affected by two factors:

1. the size of the computed coefficient; and
2. the size of the sample.

This second factor may appear surprising. Basically, the larger a sample, the more likely it is that a computed correlation coefficient will be found to be statistically significant. Thus, even though the correlation between age and the amount of time spent on weights machines in the gym survey was found to be just −0.27, which is a fairly weak relationship, it is statistically significant at the $p < 0.01$ level. This means that there is only 1 chance in 100 that there is no relationship in the population. Because the question of whether or not a correlation coefficient is statistically significant depends so much on the sample size, it is important to realize that you should always examine *both* the correlation coefficient *and* the significance level. You should not examine one at the expense of the other.

This treatment of correlation and statistical significance applies to both Pearson's r and Spearman's rho. A similar interpretation can also be applied to phi and Cramér's V. SPSS automatically produces information regarding statistical significance when Pearson's r, Spearman's rho, phi, and Cramér's V are generated.

Comparing means and statistical significance

A test of statistical significance can also be applied to the comparison of means that was carried out in Table 15.5. This procedure entails treating the total amount of variation in the dependent variable—amount of time spent on cardiovascular equipment—as made up of two types: variation *within* the four subgroups that make up the independent variable, and variation *between* them. The latter is often called the *explained variance* and the former the *error variance*. A test of statistical significance for the comparison of means entails relating the two types of variance to form what is known as the F statistic. This statistic expresses the amount of explained variance in relation to the amount of error variance. In the case of the data in Table 15.5, the resulting F statistic is statistically significant at the $p < 0.001$ level. This finding suggests that there is only 1 chance in 1000 that there is no relationship between the two variables among all gym members. SPSS produces information regarding the F statistic and its statistical significance if the procedures described in Chapter 16 are followed.

KEY POINTS

- You need to think about your data analysis before you begin designing your research instruments.

- Techniques of data analysis are applicable to some types of variable and not others. You need to know the difference between nominal, ordinal, interval/ratio, and dichotomous variables.

- You need to think about the kinds of data you are collecting and the implications your decisions will have for the sorts of techniques you will be able to employ.

- Become familiar with computer software such as SPSS before you begin designing your research instruments, because it is advisable to be aware at an early stage of difficulties you might have in presenting your data in SPSS.

- Make sure you are thoroughly familiar with the techniques introduced in this chapter and when you can and cannot use them.

- The basic message, then, is not to leave these considerations until your data have been collected, tempting though it may be.

- Do not confuse statistical significance with substantive significance.

QUESTIONS FOR REVIEW

- At what stage should you begin to think about the kinds of data analysis you need to conduct?

- What are missing data and why do they arise?

Types of variable

- What are the differences between the four types of variable outlined in this chapter: interval/ratio; ordinal; nominal; and dichotomous?

- Why is it important to be able to distinguish between the four types of variable?

- Imagine the kinds of answers you would receive if you administered the following four questions in an interview survey. What kind of variable would each question generate: dichotomous; nominal; ordinal; or interval/ratio?

  1. Do you enjoy going shopping?

     Yes   ____
     No   ____

  2. How many times have you shopped in the last month? Please write in the number of occasions below.

     ____

  3. For which kinds of items do you most enjoy shopping? Please tick one only.

     Clothes (including shoes)   ____
     Food   ____
     Things for the house   ____
     Presents   ____
     Entertainment (CDs, videos, etc.) ____

4. How important is it to you to buy clothes with designer labels?

Very important   ____

Fairly important   ____

Not very important   ____

Not at all important   ____

Univariate analysis

● What is an **outlier** and why might one have an adverse effect on the mean and the range?

● In conjunction with which **measure of central tendency** would you expect to report the standard deviation: the mean; the median; or the mode?

Bivariate analysis

● Can you infer causality from bivariate analysis?

● Why are percentages crucial when presenting contingency tables?

● In what circumstances would you use each of the following: Pearson's *r*; Spearman's rho; phi; Cramér's *V*; eta?

Multivariate analysis

● What is a spurious relationship?

● What is an intervening variable?

● What does it mean to say that a relationship is moderated?

Statistical significance

● What does statistical significance mean and how does it differ from substantive significance?

● What is a significance level?

● What does the chi-square test achieve?

● What does it mean to say that a correlation of 0.42 is statistically significant at $p < 0.05$?

ONLINE RESOURCES

www.oup.com/uk/brm5e/

Visit the Interactive Research Guide that accompanies this book to complete an exercise in quantitative data analysis.

USING IBM SPSS STATISTICS

CHAPTER OUTLINE

In order to implement the techniques that you learned in Chapter 15, you would need to do either of two things: learn the underlying formula for each technique and apply your data to it, or use computer software to analyse your data. The latter is the approach chosen in this book for two main reasons:

- it is closer to the way in which quantitative data analysis is carried out in real research nowadays;
- it helps to equip you with a useful transferable skill.

You will be learning IBM SPSS Statistics, which is the most widely used package of computer software for doing this kind of analysis. It is relatively straightforward to use. We will be continuing to refer to the techniques introduced in Chapter 15 and will continue to use the gym survey as an example.

This chapter largely operates in parallel to Chapter 15, so that you can see the links between the techniques learned there and the use of SPSS to implement them.

Introduction

This chapter aims to provide a familiarity with some basic aspects of SPSS for Windows, which is possibly the most widely used computer software for the analysis of quantitative data for social scientists. SPSS, which originally was short for Statistical Package for the Social Sciences, has been in existence since the mid-1960s and over the years has undergone many revisions, particularly since the arrival of personal computers. It is now known as IBM SPSS Statistics and the version that was used in preparing this chapter was Release 24. The gym survey used in Chapter 15 will be employed to illustrate SPSS operations and methods of analysis. The aim of this chapter is to introduce ways of using SPSS to implement the methods of analysis discussed in Chapter 15.

SPSS operations will be presented in **bold**, for example, **Variable Name:** and **Analyze**. Names given to variables in the course of using SPSS will be presented in ***bold italics***, e.g. ***gender*** and ***reasons***. Labels given to values or to variables are also in **bold**, e.g. **reasons for visiting** and **male**. Tips and skills 'Basic operations in SPSS' presents a list summarizing these. One further element in the presentation is that a right-pointing arrow (→) will be used to denote 'click once with the left-hand button of your mouse'. This action is employed to make selections and for similar activities.

TIPS AND SKILLS
Basic operations in SPSS

- The **SPSS Data Editor**. This is the sphere of SPSS into which data are entered and subsequently edited and defined. It is made up of two screens: the **Data Viewer** and the **Variable Viewer**. You move between these two viewers by selecting the appropriate tab at the bottom left of the screen.

- The **Data Viewer**. This is the spreadsheet into which your data are entered. When you start up SPSS, the **Data Viewer** will be facing you.

- The **Variable Viewer**. This is another spreadsheet, but this one displays information about each of the variables and allows you to change that information. It is the platform from which you provide, for each variable, such information as the variable name; a variable label; and value labels (see below).

- The **Output Viewer**. When you perform an analysis or produce a diagram (called a 'chart' in SPSS), your output will be deposited here. The **Output Viewer** superimposes itself over the **Data Editor** after an analysis has been performed or a chart generated.

- A **Variable Name**. This is the name that you give to a variable, e.g. ***gender***. The name must be no more than eight characters. Until you give a variable a name, it will be referred to as var00001, etc. When the variable has been given a name, it will appear in the column for that variable in the Data View window. It is generated from the **Variable Viewer**.

- A **Variable Label**. This is a label that you can give to a variable but which is not restricted to eight characters. Spaces can be used, e.g. **reasons for visiting**. The Label will appear in any output you generate. It is generated from the **Variable Viewer**.

- A **Value Label**. This is a label that you can attach to a code that has been used when entering data for all types of variables other than interval/ratio variables. Thus, for var00001, we would attach the label 'male' to 1 and 'female' to 2. When you generate output, such as a frequency table or chart, the labels for each value will be presented. This makes the interpretation of output easier. It is generated from the **Variable Viewer**.

- **Missing Values.** When you do not have data for a particular variable when entering data for a case, you must specify how you are denoting missing values for that variable. Missing values are generated from the **Variable Viewer**.

- **Recode**. A procedure that allows codes or numbers to be changed. It is especially helpful when you need to combine groups of people—for example, when producing age bands.

- **Compute**. A procedure that allows you to combine two or more variables to form a new variable.

- **Analyze**. This is the point on the menu bar above the **Data Editor** from which you choose (via a dropdown menu) which method of analysis you want to select. Note that, whenever an item on a menu appears with a right-pointing arrowhead (→) after it, this means that, if you select that option, a further menu will follow on.

- **Graphs**. This is the point on the menu bar above the **Data Editor** from which you choose (via a drop-down menu) which chart you want to select.

- **Chart Editor**. When you produce a graph, you can edit it with the **Chart Editor**. To activate this editor, double-click anywhere in the graph. A small chart editor window will appear and your main graph will appear opaque until you exit the Editor. From the Editor, you can make various changes and enhancements to your graph.

Getting started in SPSS

Beginning SPSS

To start SPSS, double-click on the **IBM SPSS Statistics** icon on your computer screen. If there is no icon, → the Start button in the bottom left-hand corner of your screen. From the menu of programs, → **IBM SPSS Statistics**. A follow-on menu will appear, from which you should select **IBM SPSS Statistics 24**. When SPSS loads, you *may* be faced with an opening dialog box with the title 'What do you want to do?' and a list of options. Many users prefer to disable this opening box. It is not important in relation to the following exposition, so → **Close**. You will then be faced with the **SPSS Data Editor**. This is made up of two components: **Data View** and **Variable View**. In the following discussion, these two screens are referred to as the **Data Viewer** and the **Variable Viewer**. You move between these two viewers by selecting the appropriate tab at the bottom of the screen. The **Data Viewer** is in the form of a spreadsheet grid into which you enter your data. The columns represent *variables*—in other words, information about characteristics of each person in the gym study sample. Until data are entered and names are given to variables, each column simply has **var** as its heading. The rows represent *cases*, which can be people (as in the example you will be working through) or any unit of analysis. Each block in the grid is referred to as a cell. Note also that when the data are in the SPSS spreadsheet, they will look different; for example, 1 will be 1.00.

Entering data in the Data Viewer

To input the data into the **Data Viewer**, make sure that the top left-hand cell in the grid is highlighted (see Plate 16.1). If it is not highlighted, simply click once in that cell. Then, type the appropriate figure for that cell—that is, 1. This number goes directly into that cell and into the box beneath the toolbar. As an alternative to using the mouse, many people find it easier to use the arrow keys on their keyboard to move from cell to cell. If you make a mistake at any point, simply click once in the cell in question, type in the correct value, and click once more in that cell. When you have finished, you should end up in the bottom right-hand cell of what will be a perfect rectangle of data. Plate 16.2 shows the **Data Viewer** with the data from the gym survey entered (though only part of the set of data is visible, in that only the first 37 respondents are visible). The top row of the Data Viewer contains the coded answers from the completed questionnaire in Chapter 15 (see Tips and skills 'A completed and processed questionnaire' in Chapter 15).

In order to proceed further, you will find that SPSS works in the following typical sequence for defining variables and analysing your data:

1. You make a selection from the menu bar at the top of the screen, e.g. → **Analyze**.

2. From the menu that will appear, make a selection, e.g. → **Descriptive Statistics** → **Descriptives**.

3. This will bring up a *dialog box* in which you will usually inform SPSS of what you are trying to do—e.g. which variables are to be analysed.

4. Very often, you then need to convey further information and to do this you have to → a button that will bring up what is called, following Bryman and Cramer (2011), a *sub-dialog box*.

PLATE 16.1
The SPSS Data Viewer

Each row represents a case

Each column represents a variable

PLATE 16.2
The Data Viewer with 'gym study' data entered

This row shows the data for the first person who answered the Gym Survey questionnaire

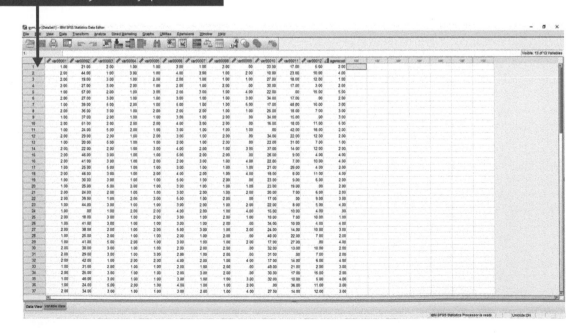

5. You then provide the information in the sub-dialog box and then go back to the dialog box. Sometimes, you will need to bring up a further sub-dialog box and then go back to the dialog box.

When you have finished going through the entire procedure, → **OK**. The toolbar beneath the menu bar allows shortcut access to certain SPSS operations.

Defining variables: variable names, missing values, variable labels, and value labels

Once you have finished entering your data, you need to define your variables. The following steps will allow you to do this:

1. → the **Variable View** tab at the bottom of the **Data Viewer** (opens the **Variable Viewer** shown in Plate 16.3).

2. To provide a variable name, click on the current variable name (e.g. *var00003*) and type the name you want to give it (e.g. *reasons*). Remember that this name must be no more than eight characters and you *cannot* use spaces.

3. You can then give your variable a more detailed name, known in SPSS as a variable label. To do this, → cell in the **Label** column relating to the variable for which you want to supply a variable label. Then, simply type in the variable label (i.e. **reasons for visiting**).

4. Then you will need to provide 'value labels' for variables that have been given codes. The procedure

generally applies to variables that are not interval/ratio variables. The latter, which are numeric variables, do not need to be coded (unless you are grouping them in some way). To assign value labels, → in the **Values** column relating to the variable you are working on. A small button with three dots on it will appear. → the button. The **Value Labels** dialog box will appear (see Plate 16.4). → the box to the right of **Value** and begin to define the value labels. To do this, enter the value (e.g. **1**) in the area to the right of **Value** and then the value label (e.g. **relaxation**) in the area to the right of **Label**. Then → **Add**. Do this for each value. When you have finished, → **OK**.

5. You will then need to inform SPSS of the value that you have nominated for each variable to indicate a missing value. In the case of *reasons*, the value is 0 (zero). To assign the missing value, → the cell for this variable in the **Missing** column. Again, → the button that will appear with three dots on it. This will generate the **Missing Values** dialog box (see Plate 16.5). In the **Missing Values** dialog box, enter the missing value (**0**) below **Discrete missing values**: and then → **OK**.

In order to simplify the following presentation, *reasons* will be the only variable for which a variable label will be defined. Following the procedure in step 2, the variables in the dataset are renamed for the remainder of the presentation: *var00001* is *gender*, *var00002* is *age*, *var00003* is *reasons*, *var00004* is *carduse* (uses cardio equipment), *var00005* is *weiuse* (uses weights), *var00006* is *frequent* (frequency of visits), *var00007*

PLATE 16.3
The Variable Viewer

To create **Missing Values** for **var0003**, click here. A little button with three dots will appear.

*gym.sav [DataSet1] - IBM SPSS Statistics Data Editor

File Edit View Data Transform Analyze Direct Marketing Graphs Utilities Extensions Window Help

	Name	Type	Width	Decimals	Label	Values	Missing	Columns	Align	Measure	Role
1	var00001	Numeric	8	2		None	None	8	Right	Scale	Input
2	var00002	Numeric	8	2		None	None	8	Right	Scale	Input
3	var00003	Numeric	8	2		None	None	8	Right	Scale	Input
4	var00004	Numeric	8	2		None	None	8	Right	Scale	Input
5	var00005	Numeric	8	2		None	None	8	Right	Scale	Input
6	var00006	Numeric	8	2		None	None	8	Right	Scale	Input
7	var00007	Numeric	8	2		None	None	8	Right	Scale	Input
8	var00008	Numeric	8	2		None	None	8	Right	Scale	Input
9	var00009	Numeric	8	2		None	None	8	Right	Scale	Input
10	var00010	Numeric	8	2		None	None	8	Right	Scale	Input
11	var00011	Numeric	8	2		None	None	8	Right	Scale	Input
12	var00012	Numeric	8	2		None	None	8	Right	Scale	Input

PLATE 16.4
The Value Labels dialog box

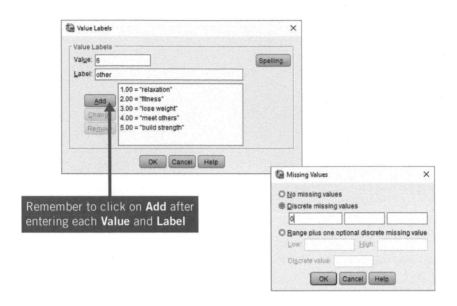

Remember to click on **Add** after entering each **Value** and **Label**

PLATE 16.5
The Missing Values dialog box

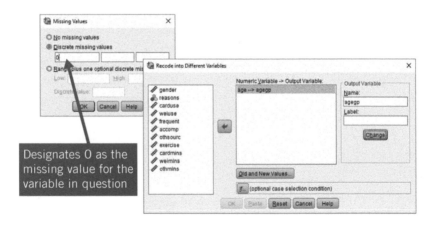

Designates 0 as the missing value for the variable in question

is *accomp* (has accomplished set goals), *var00008* is *othsourc* (uses other sources of exercise beyond visiting the gym), *var00009* is *exercise* (number of exercises), *var00010* is *cardmins* (minutes of cardio), *var00011* is *weimins* (minutes of weights), *var00012* is *othmins* (minutes of other sport).

Recoding variables

Sometimes you need to recode variables—for example, when you want to group people. You would need to do this in order to produce a table like Table 15.3 for an interval/ratio variable such as *var00002*, which we will give the variable name *age*. SPSS offers two choices: you can recode *age* so that it will be changed in the Data Viewer, or you can keep *age* as it is and create a new variable. This latter option is desirable whenever you want to preserve the variable in question as well as create a new one. Since we may want to carry out analyses involving *age* as an interval/ratio variable, we will recode it so that a new variable, which we will call *agegp*, for *age* groups, will be created. The aim of the following operations is to create a new variable—*agegp*—which will comprise five age bands, as in Table 15.3.

PLATE 16.6
The Recode into Different Variables dialog box

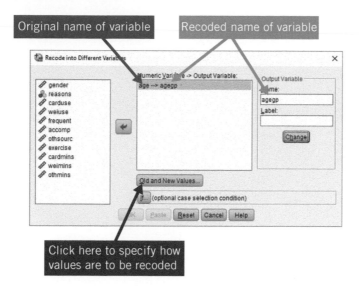

Original name of variable

Recoded name of variable

Click here to specify how values are to be recoded

1. →**Transform** → **Recode into Different Variables** … [opens **Recode into Different Variables** dialog box shown in Plate 16.6]

2. → *age* → [puts *age* in **Numeric Variable** – > **Output Variable:** box] → box beneath **Output Variable Name:** and type *agegp* → **Change** [puts *agegp* in the **Numeric Variable** – > **Output Variable:** box] → **Old and New Values** … [opens **Recode into Different Variables: Old and New Values** sub-dialog box shown in Plate 16.7]

3. → the circle by **System- or user-missing** and by **System-missing** under **New Value**, if you have missing values for a variable, which is the case for this variable

4. → circle by **Range, LOWEST through value:** and type **20** in the box → box by **Value** under **New Value** and type **1** → **Add** [the new value will appear in the **Old** – > **New:** box]

PLATE 16.7
The Recode into Different Variables: Old and New Values sub-dialog box

Recode into Different Variables: Old and New Values

Old Value
○ Value:
○ System-missing
● System- or user-missing
○ Range:

through

○ Range, LOWEST through value:
○ Range, value through HIGHEST:
○ All other values

New Value
○ Value:
● System-missing
○ Copy old value(s)

Old --> New:

MISSING --> SYSMIS
Lowest thru 20 --> 1
21 thru 30 --> 2
31 thru 40 --> 3
41 thru 50 --> 4
51 thru Highest --> 5

Add
Change
Remove

☐ Output variables are strings Width: 8
☐ Convert numeric strings to numbers ('5'->5)

Continue   Cancel   Help

PLATE 16.8
The Compute Variable dialog box

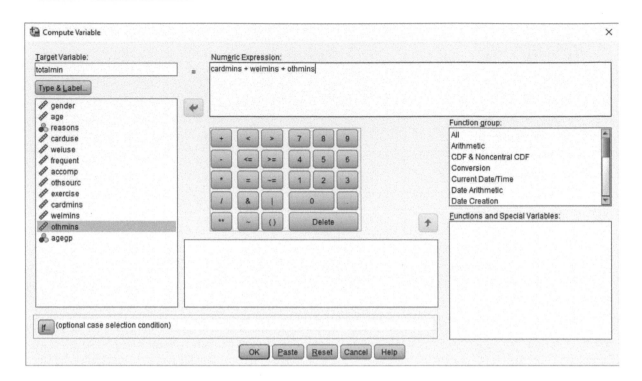

5. → first box by **Range:** and type **21** and in box after **through** type **30** → box by **Value** under **New Value** and type **2** → **Add**

6. → first box by **Range:** and type **31** and in box after **through** type **40** → box by **Value** under **New Value** and type **3** → **Add**

7. → first box by **Range:** and type **41** and in box after **through** type **50** → box by **Value** under **New Value** and type **4** → **Add**

8. → circle by **Range, value through HIGHEST** and type **51** in the box → box by **Value** in **New Value** and type **5** → **Add** → **Continue** [closes the **Recode into Different Variables: Old and New Values** sub-dialog box shown in Plate 16.7 and returns you to the **Recode into Different Variables** dialog box shown in Plate 16.6]

9. → **OK**

The new variable *agegp* will be created and will appear in the **Data Viewer**. You would then need to generate **value labels** for the five age bands and possibly a **variable label** using the approach described above.

Computing a new variable

A person's total amount of time spent in the gym is made up of three variables: *cardmins*, *weimins*, and *othmins*. If we add these up, we should arrive at the total number of minutes spent on activities in the gym. In so doing, we will create a new variable *totalmin*. To do this, this procedure should be followed:

1. → **Transform** → **Compute Variable** ... [opens the **Compute Variable** dialog box shown in Plate 16.8]

2. under **Target Variable:** type *totalmin*

3. from the list of variables at the left, → *cardmins* [puts *cardmins* in box beneath **Numeric Expression:**] → +button → *weimins* [puts *weimins* after + sign] → +button; → *othmins* [puts *othmins* after + sign]

4. → **OK**

The new variable *totalmin* will be created and will appear in the **Data Editor**.

Now at last, we can begin to analyse the data!

Data analysis with SPSS

Generating a frequency table

To produce a frequency table like the one in Table 15.2:

1. → **Analyze** → **Descriptive Statistics** → **Frequencies** … [opens the **Frequencies** dialog box shown in Plate 16.9]

2. → **reasons for visiting** → [image: arrow button] [puts **reasons for visiting** in **Variable[s]:** box]

3. → **OK**

The table will appear in the **Output Viewer** (see Plate 16.10).

PLATE 16.9
The Frequencies dialog box

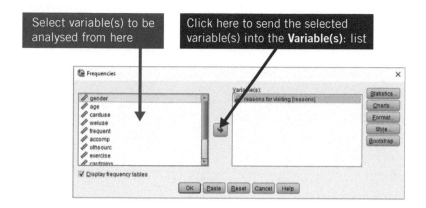

PLATE 16.10
The Output Viewer with Frequency table

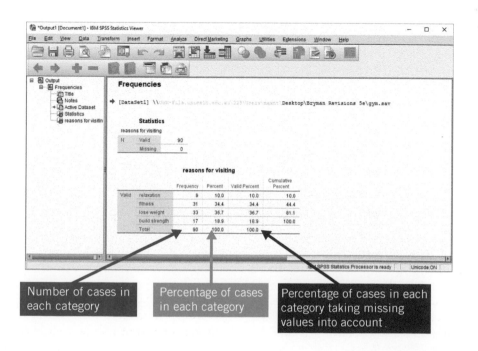

Note that in the Frequencies dialog box, variables that have been assigned labels will appear in terms of their variable labels, but those that have not been assigned labels will appear in terms of their variable names. This is a feature of all dialog boxes produced via **Analyze** and **Graphs** (see below).

Generating a bar chart

To produce a bar chart like the one in Figure 15.2:

1. → **Graphs** → **Chart Builder** … [opens **Chart Builder** dialog box shown in Plate 16.11]

2. → **Bar** below **Choose from:** and then → the simple bar format in the top left-hand corner of the **Gallery** and drag and drop it into the area above it. Then → *age* and drag and drop in the same way as for a bar chart.

3. → **reasons for visiting** from below **Variables:** and drag and drop into area marked in blue **X-Axis?**

4. → **OK**

Generating a pie chart

To produce a pie chart like the one in Figure 15.3:

1. → **Graphs** → **Chart Builder** … [opens the **Chart Builder** dialog box shown in Plate 16.12] → **Pie/Polar** below **Choose from:** and then → the pie chart format in the top left-hand corner of the **Gallery** and drag and drop it into the area above it.

2. → **reasons for visiting** from below **Variables:** and drag and drop into area marked in blue **Slice by?**]

3. → **OK**

In order to include percentages, as in Figure 15.3, *double-click* anywhere in the chart in order to bring up the **Chart Editor**. The chart will appear in the **Chart Editor** and the main figure will become opaque. Then → **Elements** and then → **Show Data Labels**. This will place percentages in each slice as a default. If you want the frequencies, → **Count** in the **Properties** sub-dialog box that appears simultaneously (see Plate 16.12).

PLATE 16.11
Creating a bar chart with the Chart Builder

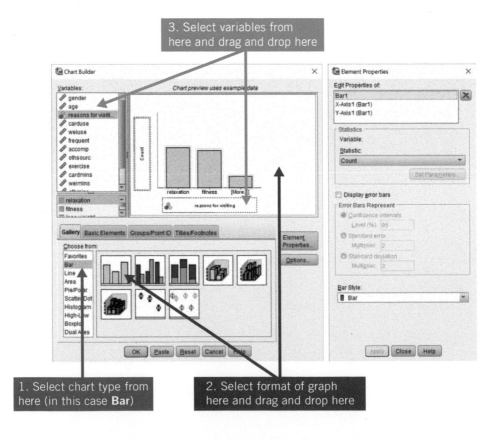

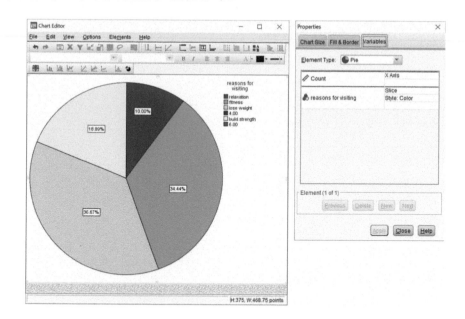

Your chart will be in colour, but, if you want to print it and have access only to a monochrome printer, you can change your pie chart into patterns, which allows the slices to be clearer. This can be done through the **Chart Editor**.

Generating a histogram

In order to generate a histogram for an interval/ratio variable such as *age*, → **Graphs** → **Chart Builder** … [opens the Chart Builder dialog box shown in Plate 16.12] → **Histogram** below **Choose from:** and then → the histogram format you prefer from the **Gallery** and drag and drop it into the area above it. Then → *age* and drag and drop it in the same way as for a bar chart. This procedure will generate a histogram whose age bands are defined by the software. By double-clicking on the diagram, the histogram can be edited using the **Chart Editor**.

Generating the arithmetic mean, median, standard deviation, range, and boxplots

To produce the mean, median, standard deviation, and the range for an interval/ratio variable such as *age*, the following steps should be followed:

1. → **Analyze** → **Descriptive Statistics** → **Explore** … [opens the **Explore** dialog box]

2. → *age* → ⟦⟧ to the left of **Dependent List:** [puts *age* in the **Dependent List:** box] → **Statistics** under **Display** → **OK**

The output will also include the 95 per cent confidence interval for the mean, which is based on the standard error of the mean. The output can be found in Table 16.1. If you select **Plots …**, the **Explore: Plots** sub-dialog box will come up and you can elect to generate a histogram. To do this, you will need to select either **Both** or **Plots** under **Display** on the **Explore** dialog box. In addition, selecting **Both** or **Plots** will produce two further types of figure, one of which is a boxplot, which was covered in Chapter 15.

Generating a contingency table, chi-square, and Cramér's *V*

In order to generate a contingency table, like that in Table 15.4, along with a chi-square test and Cramér's *V*, use the following procedure:

1. → **Analyze** → **Descriptive Statistics** → **Cross-tabs …** [opens the **Crosstabs** dialog box shown in Plate 16.13]

2. → **reasons for visiting** → ⟦⟧ by **Row[s]** [**reasons for visiting** will appear in the **Row[s]:** box] → *gender* → ⟦⟧ by **Column[s]:** [*gender* will appear in the **Column[s]:** box] → **Cells …** [opens **Cross-tabs: Cell Display** sub-dialog box shown in Plate 16.14]

TABLE 16.1
Explore output for *age* (SPSS output)

Explore

Case Processing Summary

	Cases					
	Valid		Missing		Total	
	N	Percent	N	Percent	N	Percent
age	89	98.9%	1	1.1%	90	100.0%

Descriptives

			Statistic	Std. Error
age	Mean		33.5955	.94197
	95% Confidence Interval for Mean	Lower Bound	31.7235	
		Upper Bound	35.4675	
	5% Trimmed Mean		33.3159	
	Median		31.0000	
	Variance		78.971	
	Std. Deviation		8.88656	
	Minimum		18.00	
	Maximum		57.00	
	Range		39.00	
	Interquartile Range		14.00	
	Skewness		.446	.255
	Kurtosis		−.645	.506

3. Make sure **Observed** in the **Counts** box has been selected. Make sure **Column** under **Percentages** has been selected. If either of these has not been selected, simply click at the relevant point. → **Continue** [closes **Crosstabs: Cell Display** sub-dialog box and returns you to the **Crosstabs** dialog box shown in Plate 16.13]

4. → **Statistics** ... [opens the **Crosstabs: Statistics** sub-dialog box shown in Plate 16.15]

5. → **Chi-square** → **Phi and Cramér's *V*** → **Continue** [closes **Crosstabs: Statistics** sub-dialog box and returns you to the **Crosstabs** dialog box shown in Plate 16.13]

6. → **OK**

The resulting output can be found in Table 16.2.

If you have a table with two dichotomous variables, you would use the same sequence of steps to produce phi.

Generating Pearson's *r* and Spearman's rho

To produce Pearson's *r* in order to find the correlations between *age*, *cardmins*, and *weimins*, follow these steps:

1. → **Analyze** → **Correlate** → **Bivariate** ... [opens **Bivariate Correlations** dialog box shown in Plate 16.16]

2. → *age* → [→] → *cardmins* → [→] → *weimins* → [→] [*age*, *cardmins*, and *weimins* should now be in the **Variables:** box] → **Pearson** [*if* not already selected] → **OK**

The resulting output is in Table 16.3.

To produce correlations with Spearman's rho (ρ), follow the same procedure, but, instead of selecting **Pearson**, you should → **Spearman** instead.

PLATE 16.13
The Crosstabs dialog box

Select and place here the variable that will make up the rows. This will be the dependent variable if it is possible and legitimate to make a claim about likely causality

Select and place here the variable that will make up the columns. This will be the independent variable if it is possible and legitimate to make a claim about likely causality

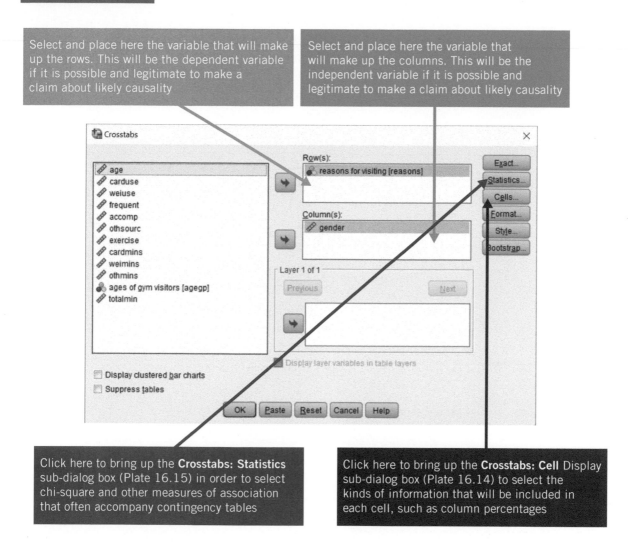

Click here to bring up the **Crosstabs: Statistics** sub-dialog box (Plate 16.15) in order to select chi-square and other measures of association that often accompany contingency tables

Click here to bring up the **Crosstabs: Cell** Display sub-dialog box (Plate 16.14) to select the kinds of information that will be included in each cell, such as column percentages

Generating scatter diagrams

Scatter diagrams, known as *scatterplots* in SPSS, are produced in the following way. Let us say that we want to plot the relationship between *age* and *cardmins*. There is a convention that, if one variable can be identified as likely to be the independent variable, it should be placed on the *x* axis—that is, the horizontal axis. Since *age* is bound to be the independent variable, we would follow these steps:

1. → **Graphs** → **Chart Builder** [opens the **Chart Builder** dialog box shown in Plate 16.17]

2. → **Scatter/Dot** from below **Choose from:**. Then select from the scatter diagram formats, the basic

format which is in the top left-hand corner and drag and drop into the area above the scatter diagram formats

3. → *cardmins* and drag and drop into area designated **Y-Axis?** and → *age* and drag and drop into area designated **X-Axis?** (see Plate 16.17)

A scatter diagram in the default format is shown in Figure 16.1. The scatter diagram can then be edited by bringing up the **Chart Editor** by double-clicking anywhere in the diagram. For example, the type and size of the markers can be changed by clicking anywhere in the chart in the **Chart Editor**. This brings up a **Properties** sub-dialog box, which allows a variety of changes to the appearance

PLATE 16.14
The Crosstabs: Cell Display sub-dialog box

Select **Observed** to show the number of cases in each cell in the table

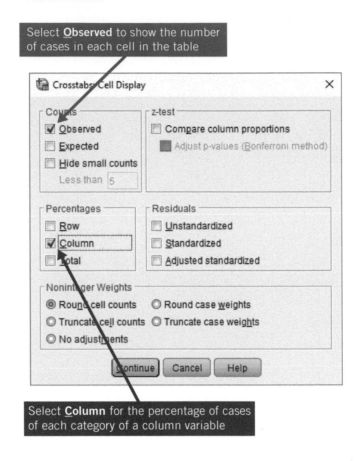

Select **Column** for the percentage of cases of each category of a column variable

of the diagram, such as colour and appearance of the points on the plot.

Comparing means and eta

To produce a table like Table 15.5, these steps should be followed:

1. → **Analyze** → **Compare Means** → **Means** ... [opens the **Means** dialog box shown in Plate 16.18]

2. → *cardmins* → 🔽 to the left of **Dependent List:** [puts *cardmins* in the **Dependent List: box**] → **reasons for visiting** → 🔽 to the left of **Independent List:** [puts **reasons for visiting** in the **Independent List:box**] → **Options** ... [opens the **Means: Options** sub-dialog box]

3. → **Anova table and eta** underneath **Statistics for First Layer** → **Continue** [closes the **Means: Options** sub-dialog box and returns you to the **Means** dialog box shown in Plate 16.18] → **OK**

Generating a contingency table with three variables

To create a table like that in Table 15.7, you would need to follow these steps:

1. → **Analyze** → **Descriptive Statistics** → **Crosstabs** ... [opens the **Crosstabs** dialog box shown in Plate 16.13]

2. → *othsourc* → **Independent List:** by **Row[s]** [*othsourc* will appear in the **Row[s]:** box]

3. → *age3* [this is the name we gave when we created a new variable with *age* recoded into three categories] → **Independent List:** by **Column[s]:** [*age3* will appear in the **Column[s]:** box] → *gender* → **Independent List:** beneath **Previous** [*gender* will appear in the box underneath **Layer 1 of 1**] → **Cells** [opens **Crosstabs: Cell Display** sub-dialog box shown in Plate 16.14]

4. Make sure **Observed** in the **Counts** box has been selected. Make sure **Column** under **Percentages** has been selected. If either of these has not been selected,

PLATE 16.15
The Crosstabs: Statistics sub-dialog box

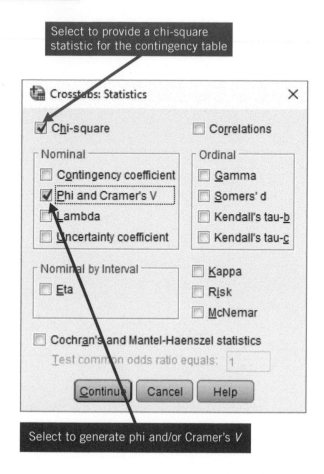

Select to provide a chi-square statistic for the contingency table

Select to generate phi and/or Cramer's *V*

---

simply click at the relevant point. → **Continue** [closes **Crosstabs: Cell Display** sub-dialog box and returns you to the **Crosstabs** dialog box shown in Plate 16.13]

5. → **OK**

The resulting table will look somewhat different from Table 15.7 in that gender will appear as a row rather than as a column variable.

Further operations in SPSS

Saving your data

You will need to save your data for future use. To do this, make sure that the **Data Editor** is the active window. Then:

→ **File** → **Save As …**

The **Save Data As** dialog box will then appear. You will need to provide a name for your data, which will be placed after **File name:** We called the file 'gym study'. You also need to decide where you are going to save the data—for example, onto a memory stick. To select the destination drive, → the downward pointing arrow to the left of **Look in** and then select the drive and folder into which you want to place your data. Then → **Save**.

Remember that this procedure saves your data *and* any other work you have done on your data—for example, value labels and recoded variables. If you subsequently use the data again and do more work on your data, such as creating a new variable, you will need to save the data again or the new work will be lost. SPSS will give you a choice of renaming your data, in which case you will have two files of data (one with the original data and one with any changes), or keeping the same name, in which case the file will be changed and the existing name retained.

TABLE 16.2

Contingency table for *reasons for visiting* by *gender* (SPSS output

Crosstabs

Case Processing Summary

	Cases					
	Valid		Missing		Total	
	N	Percent	N	Percent	N	Percent
reasons for visiting * gender	90	100.0%	0	0.0%	90	100.0%

reasons for visiting * gender Crosstabulation

				gender		
				Male	Female	Total
reasons for visiting	relaxation	Count		3	6	9
		% within gender		7.1%	12.5%	10.0%
	fitness	Count		15	16	31
		% within gender		35.7%	33.3%	34.4%
	lose weight	Count		8	25	33
		% within gender		19.0%	52.1%	36.7%
	build strength	Count		16	1	17
		% within gender		38.1%	2.1%	18.9%
Total		Count		42	48	90
		% within gender		100.0%	100.0%	100.0%

Chi-Square Tests

	Value	df	Asymp. Sig. (2-sided)
Pearson Chi-Square	22.726[a]	3	.000
Likelihood Ratio	25.805	3	.000
Linear-by-Linear Association	9.716	1	.002
N of Valid Cases	90		

[a]2 cells (25.0%) have expected count less than 5. The minimum expected count is 4.20.

Symmetric Measures

		Value	Approx. Sig.
Nominal by Nominal	Phi	.503	.000
	Cramer's *V*	.503	.000
N of Valid Cases		90	

PLATE 16.16
The Bivariate Correlations dialog box

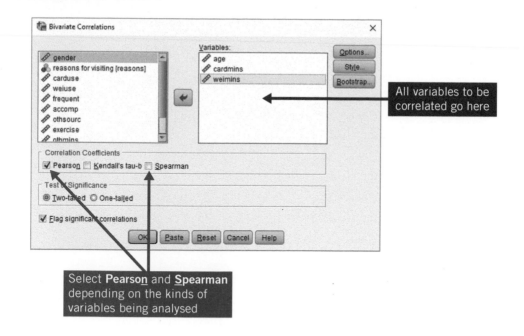

All variables to be correlated go here

Select **Pearson** and **Spearman** depending on the kinds of variables being analysed

TABLE 16.3
Correlations output for *age*, *weimins*, and *cardmins* (SPSS output)

Correlations

Correlations

		age	cardmins	weimins
age	Pearson Correlation	1	−.109	−.273**
	Sig. (2-tailed)		.311	.010
	N	89	89	89
cardmins	Pearson Correlation	−.109	1	−.161
	Sig. (2-tailed)	.311		.130
	N	89	90	90
weimins	Pearson Correlation	−.273**	−.161	1
	Sig. (2-tailed)	.010	.130	
	N	89	90	90

**.Correlation is significant at the 0.01 level (2-tailed).

PLATE 16.17

Creating a scatter diagram with the Chart Builder

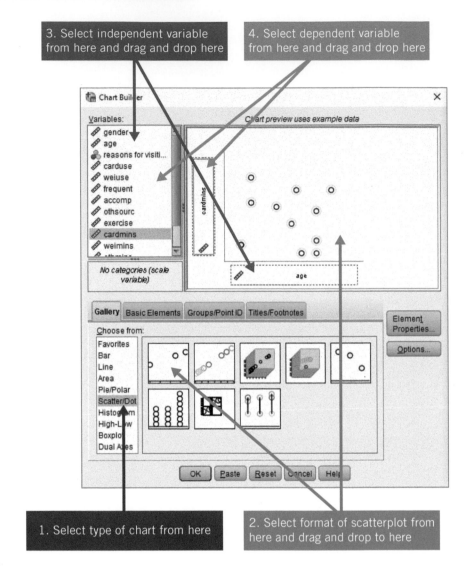

FIGURE 16.1

Scatter diagram showing the relationship between *age* and *cardmins* (SPSS output)

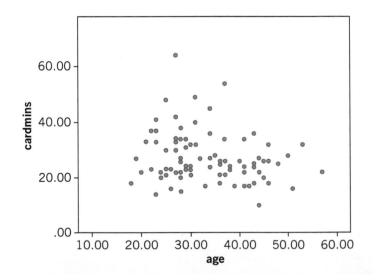

PLATE 16.18
The Means dialog box

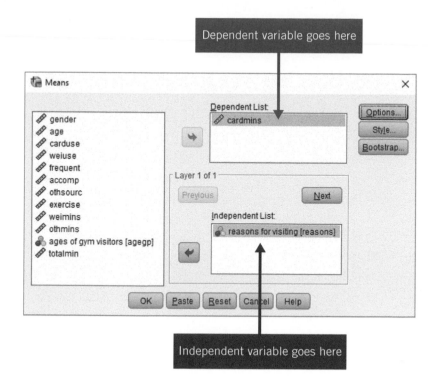

Dependent variable goes here

Independent variable goes here

Retrieving your data

When you want to retrieve the data file you have created, → **File** → **Open** → **Data** ... The **Open File** dialog box will appear. You then need to go to the location in which you have deposited your data to retrieve the file containing your data and then → **Open**. A shortcut alternative to this procedure is to → the first button on the toolbar (it looks like an open file), which brings up the **Open File** dialog box.

Printing output

To print all the output in the **SPSS Output Viewer**, make sure that the **Output 1—SPSS Viewer** is the active window and then → **File** → **Print** ... The **Print** dialog box will appear and then → **OK**. To print just some of your output, hold down the Ctrl button on your keyboard and click once on the parts you want to print. The easiest way to do this is to select all the elements you want in the output summary in the left-hand segment of the **Output Viewer** shown in Plate 16.10. Then bring up the **Print** dialog box. When the **Print** dialog box appears, make sure **Selection** under **Print range** has been selected. The third button on the toolbar (which appears as a printer) provides a shortcut to the **Print** dialog box.

KEY POINTS

- SPSS can be used to implement the techniques learned in Chapter 15, but learning new software requires perseverance and at times the results obtained may not seem to be worth the learning process.

- But it is worth it—it would take you far longer to perform calculations on a sample of around 100 than to learn the software.

- If you find yourself moving into much more advanced techniques, the time saved is even more substantial, particularly with large samples.
- It is better to become familiar with SPSS before you begin designing your research instruments, so you are aware of difficulties you might have in presenting your data in SPSS at an early stage.

QUESTIONS FOR REVIEW

Getting started in SPSS

- Outline the differences between variable names, variable labels, and value labels.
- In what circumstances might you want to recode a variable?
- In what circumstances might you want to create a new variable?

Data analysis with SPSS

- Using the gym survey data, create:
    - a frequency table for *exercise*;
    - a bar chart and pie chart for *exercise* and compare their usefulness;
    - a histogram for *cardmins*;
    - measures of central tendency and dispersion for *cardmins*;
    - a contingency table and chi-square test for *exercise* and *gender*;
    - Pearson's r for *age* and *cardmins*;
    - Spearman's rho for *carduse* and *weiuse*;
    - a scatter diagram for *age* and *cardmins*;
    - a comparing means analysis for *totalmin* and **reasons for visiting**.

ONLINE RESOURCES
www.oup.com/uk/brm5e/

Visit the Interactive Research Guide that accompanies this book to complete an exercise in using IBM SPSS.

PART THREE
QUALITATIVE RESEARCH

THE NATURE OF QUALITATIVE RESEARCH

CHAPTER OUTLINE

Qualitative research is a research strategy that usually emphasizes words rather than numbers in the collection and analysis of data. As a research strategy it is in general inductive, constructionist, and interpretive, though qualitative researchers do not always subscribe to all of these intellectual positions. This chapter is concerned with outlining the main features of qualitative business research. The chapter explores:

- the main steps in qualitative research—which are more complex than in quantitative research;

- the relationship between theory and research;

- the nature of concepts in qualitative research and their differences from concepts in quantitative research;

- how far reliability and validity are appropriate criteria for qualitative researchers and whether alternative criteria that are more tailored to the research strategy are needed;
- the main preoccupations of qualitative researchers—five areas are identified:
  - seeing through the eyes of research participants
  - description and context
  - process
  - flexibility and lack of structure
  - concepts and theory as outcomes of the research process;
- some common criticisms of qualitative research;
- the main contrasts between qualitative and quantitative research;
- the stance of feminist researchers on qualitative research.

Introduction

We began Chapter 8 by noting that *quantitative* research had been outlined in Chapter 2 as a distinctive research strategy. Much the same kind of general point can be made in relation to *qualitative* research. In Chapter 2 it was suggested that qualitative research differs from quantitative research in several ways. Most obviously, qualitative research tends to be concerned with words rather than numbers, but four further features are particularly noteworthy:

- an inductive view of the relationship between theory and research, whereby the former is generated out of the latter;
- an epistemological position described as interpretivist, meaning that, in contrast to the adoption of a natural scientific model in quantitative research, the stress is on the understanding of the social world through an examination of the interpretation of that world by its participants (see Chapter 2);
- an ontological position described as constructionist, which implies that social properties are outcomes of the interactions between individuals, rather than phenomena 'out there' and separate from those involved in their construction (see Chapter 2);
- an emphasis on naturalism, as the practice of seeking to understand social reality in its own terms by providing rich descriptions of people and interactions in settings that arise without the researcher attempting to influence them for the purposes of data collection. Naturalism is taken to imply that people attribute meaning to behaviour and are active creators of their social world, rather than passive subjects.

As Bryman and Burgess (1999) observe, although there has been a proliferation of writings on qualitative research since the 1970s, stipulating what it is and is not as a distinct research strategy is by no means straightforward. They propose that one of the reasons for this uncertainty is because as a term, 'qualitative research' is sometimes taken to imply an approach to study in which quantitative data are not collected or generated. Consequently, qualitative research ends up being addressed in terms of what quantitative research is *not*. Many writers on qualitative research are critical of such a view, because the distinctiveness of qualitative research does not reside solely in the absence of numbers. It is also important to note that when we describe qualitative research in this chapter, we are making generalizations just as we did when describing quantative research. There are, of course, always divergences from such generalizations, a point which we return to later in this chapter.

Silverman (1993) is critical of accounts of qualitative research that do not acknowledge the variety of forms that the research strategy can take. Other writers, such as Denzin and Lincoln (2005), have argued that qualitative research has evolved over time into a series of distinct phases or 'moments'. In other words, these writers are critical of attempts to specify the nature of qualitative research as a general approach. In writing about the characteristics of qualitative research we therefore need to be sensitive to the different orientations of qualitative researchers. Yet it is also clear that the label 'qualitative research' is commonly used in business and management studies. This can be seen from the popularity of specialist journals, such as *Qualitative Research in Organizations and Management*, and the number of texts and handbooks, such as the *SAGE Handbook of Qualitative Business and Management Research Methods* (Cassell et al. 2018).

Several reasons might be proposed for the unease among some writers about specifying the nature of qualitative research. First, qualitative research subsumes several diverse research methods that differ from each other considerably. The following are the main research methods associated with qualitative research.

- *Ethnography/participant observation*. While some caution is advisable in treating ethnography and participant observation as synonyms, they refer to similar approaches to data collection in which the researcher is immersed in a social setting for some time in order to observe and listen with a view to gaining an appreciation of the culture of a social group. These methods, discussed in Chapter 19, were used in Dalton's (1959) study of managerial work in the USA and by Alcadipani and Tonelli in their exploration of life on the shopfloor of a newspaper printing factory in the north of England (Alcadipani and Tonelli 2014) (see Chapter 19).

- *Qualitative interviewing*, covered in Chapter 20. This broad term encompasses a wide range of interviewing styles (see Key concept 10.2 for an introduction).

- *Focus groups*, discussed in Chapter 21 (see Key concept 10.2 for an introduction).

- *Language-based approaches to the collection of qualitative data*, such as discourse and conversation analysis (covered in Chapter 22).

- *The collection and qualitative analysis of texts and documents* (covered in Chapter 23).

Each of these approaches to data collection will be examined in Part Three. As will be seen, there are overlaps between these approaches. Researchers employing ethnography or participant observation frequently conduct qualitative interviews; they also often collect and analyse texts and documents as well. Thus, there is considerable variability in the collection of data among studies that are deemed to be qualitative. Of course, quantitative research also subsumes several different methods of data collection (these were covered in Part Two), but the methods associated with qualitative research imply somewhat greater variability.

A second reason why there is resistance to specifying the nature of qualitative research is that the connection between theory and research is more ambiguous than in quantitative research. With the latter research strategy, theoretical issues typically drive the formulation of a research question, which in turn drives the collection and analysis of data. Findings then feed back into the relevant theory. In qualitative research, theory is supposed to be an outcome of an investigation rather than something that precedes it. However, some writers, including Silverman (1993: 24), argue that such a depiction of qualitative research is 'out of tune with the greater sophistication of contemporary field research design, born out of accumulated knowledge of interaction and greater concern with issues of reliability and validity'. Nonetheless, qualitative research is more usually regarded as denoting an approach in which theory and categorization emerge out of the collection and analysis of data. The more general point being made is that such a difference within qualitative research may account for the unease about depicting research strategy in terms of a set of stages.

The main steps in qualitative research

The sequence outlined in Figure 17.1 illustrates the process of qualitative research. In order to illustrate these steps, a study by Ladge et al. (2012) of identity transitions among women professionals in early pregnancy will be used.

- *Step 1. General research questions* (see Thinking deeply 17.1). Ladge et al.'s (2012) study focused on how professional women in pregnancy experience identity changes. Their theoretical interest, as they explain, 'is in understanding how a life-altering change in an individual's nonwork self often instigates a need to reorient his/her work identity' (Ladge et al. 2012: 1450).

They therefore chose to focus on professional women in the early stages of their first pregnancy, asserting that these women start to explore and enact the identity of motherhood long before the child is born. Through this, Ladge et al. (2012) make a theoretical contribution to understanding how work and nonwork identities coevolve in 'liminal periods', when identity is in flux. Drawing on the identity literature, they assume that this liminal period will be characterised by 'feelings of ambiguity, openness, disorientation, self-questioning and indeterminacy' (Ladge et al. 2012: 1451), as women are no longer fully connected to their old professional identity and are anticipating a new iden-

FIGURE 17.1
An outline of the main steps of qualitative research

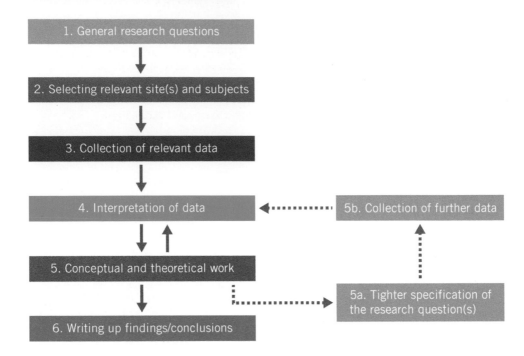

1. General research questions

2. Selecting relevant site(s) and subjects

3. Collection of relevant data

4. Interpretation of data ← 5b. Collection of further data

5. Conceptual and theoretical work

5a. Tighter specification of the research question(s)

6. Writing up findings/conclusions

tity where they will be mothers and professionals. This led the researchers towards the development of their research goal which was to 'study women's experiences of the liminal period of pregnancy as they develop their new maternal identity and begin reconstructing their professional identity in light of impending motherhood' (Ladge et al. 2012: 1453). A set of general questions including 'How do women manage their work identity while pregnant?' guided the research, 'but as we moved through the data, we were open to making adjustments to these questions ... based on our own interpretations of the data and the interpretations of respondents' (Ladge et al. 2012: 1455).

- *Step 2. Selecting relevant site(s) and subjects.* The first stage of the project involved a pilot study of ten interviews with women who were either pregnant with their first child or within six months of having given birth to their first child. Interviewees had a minimum of three years' professional experience and were planning on returning to work after their maternity leave.

- *Step 3. Collection of relevant data.* The researchers justify their choice of qualitative research methods as a response to calls from work–life scholars for more research that explores the lived experience of partici-

pants, their choice of semi-structured interview methods enabling the exploration of women's work experience while pregnant. Interviews were between 60 and 90 minutes' duration and were taped and transcribed verbatim.

- *Step 4. Interpretation of data.* Ladge et al. describe their study as based on a grounded theory approach. The process of analysis began by developing a set of codes that emerged inductively from the interviews. The three researchers worked together to develop shared agreement on these codes, each coding a subset of the transcripts independently and then meeting up to compare and consolidate, returning to the literature and then recoding. Following techniques developed by Strauss and Corbin (1990), they went through several cycles of this process. Eventually, 'after coding 29 interviews, we felt we had reached the point of theoretical saturation because no new codes were being generated' (Ladge et al. 2012: 1456).

- *Step 5. Conceptual and theoretical work.* Consistent with their grounded theory approach, Ladge et al. describe their goal as to expand knowledge about liminal periods and to build new theory about identity transitions. The researchers therefore develop a theoretical model (in the form of a detailed flow diagram) to illustrate the experiences of identity transitions in

17.1 THINKING DEEPLY
Research questions in qualitative research

The research questions posed in qualitative research are stated with varying degrees of explicitness. Sometimes, the question is embedded within a general statement about the orientation of an article. Other studies are more explicit in stating research questions. Ashforth et al. (2007) were interested in the phenomenon of 'dirty work', a term that refers to work that is tainted 'physically, socially or morally' (E. C. Hughes 1958: 122, quoted in Ashforth et al. 2007: 149). They conducted semi-structured interviews with managers in 18 such occupations in order to explore how this work is 'normalized'—that is, how managers develop ways of dealing with or reducing the significance of the taint of dirty work. After a discussion of the literature and their view of its implications for their own work, they write:

> In summary, our research questions were:
>
> *Research Question 1. What normalization challenges do managers in dirty work occupations face?*
>
> *Research Question 2. What tactics do managers report using to normalize dirty work?*
>
> (Ashforth et al. 2007: 151; emphasis in original)

One factor that may affect the degree of explicitness with which research questions are stated is the outlet in which the research is published. Ashforth et al. (2007) published this article in the *Academy of Management Journal*, which publishes mainly empirical articles deriving from quantitative research. It may be that Ashforth et al. chose this format for presenting their research questions so that it would exhibit some of the characteristics of research questions or hypotheses in quantitative research that tend to be stated explicitly. Another article in the same issue of that journal also states its research questions very explicitly, though not in the same way.

> Thus two research questions guided this article: (1) What conditions trigger organizational stakeholders and leaders to engage in sensemaking activities? and (2) What conditions enable sensegiving on the part of stakeholders and leaders motivated to engage in sensemaking activities?
>
> (Maitlis and Lawrence 2007: 59)

The researchers investigated these two research questions by collecting qualitative data from semi-structured interviews, observation, and examination of documents related to three British symphony orchestras. Since the early 2010s there has been increasing expectation upon qualitative business researchers to articulate a research question in this way when presenting their findings.

liminal periods. In this model, pregnancy is labelled as a 'triggering event' that evokes identity uncertainty. The emphasis in this model is on explaining the process of identity transition as it unfolds in the liminal period.

- *Step 5a. Tighter specification of the research question(s).* Having done the pilot study, Ladge et al. refined their definition of the population being studied, their theoretical frame, and the questions that comprised the interview protocol. The extent of these changes illustrates the extent to which qualitative researchers are flexible in their approach to study, changing direction in the course of the investigation, a point which we will return to later in this chapter. They explain: 'we learned from the pilot study that we needed to focus on a precise segment of working women … Thus, we decided to focus our attention on women who had at least three years' professional experience'. The women in this second sample held a variety of professional occupations, including manager, lawyer, and college professor. Through analysis of the interview transcripts from the pilot study, the researchers returned to the literature on identity transitions 'and recognized that pregnancy represents a liminal space. Thus, we modified our full study to focus exclusively on pregnant women, excluding those who had given birth' (Ladge et al. 2012: 1453–4). They then interviewed a further 25 women (Step 5b) based on these refined sampling criteria. Such a research strategy is frequently referred to as iterative: the stages of data collection and analysis take place in parallel, as initial stages of data collection and analysis are used to refine subsequent phases of data collection and analysis.

- *Step 5b. Collection of further data.* A snowball sampling technique (discussed in Chapter 18) was used to identify participants for the main study. Initially this involved publicizing the study via university alumni and professional networks. Although the authors do not make this explicit, all of the interviews appear to have been conducted in the USA, where the three researchers are based. Ladge et al. give much more detail about the interview questions they asked in the main study than they do for the pilot. Questions covered three main themes. The first set asked participants to share thoughts and ideals related to work and pregnancy in light of their backgrounds—an example would be 'What aspects of your youth and history have formulated your views of motherhood?' A second set probed women's experiences of pregnancy and work, e.g. 'Tell the story about when you first found out that you were pregnant.' A third group of questions explored women's specific experiences in the workplace related to their pregnancy and the ways they managed pregnancy in the workplace.

- *Step 6. Writing up findings/conclusions.* There is no real difference between the significance of writing up in quantitative research and qualitative research, so that the same points made in relation to Step 11 in Figure 8.1 apply here. An audience must be convinced about the credibility and significance of the interpretations offered. The salience of what researchers have seen and heard has to be impressed on the audience. Ladge et al. do this by making clear the theoretical and practical implications of their study. They suggest that the findings from this study may be generalizable to other situations where a future nonwork role has an impact on one's work role, such as when a manager finds himself with responsibilities to care for an aging parent. Practical implications arising from the study relate to the role of organizations in more proactively supporting women during pregnancy, 'as they wrestle with conceptualizing possible selves' (Ladge et al. 2012: 1467), but do not relate to providing work–life support for working mothers when they return to work after the baby is born.

Two distinctive aspects of the sequence of steps in qualitative research are the related issues of theory and concepts, issues to which we now turn.

Theory and research

Most qualitative researchers when writing about their craft emphasize a preference for treating theory as something that emerges inductively (see Chapter 2) out of the collection and analysis of data. For example, Marshall (1984) describes her approach to the analysis of research data on women managers' career histories as 'immersion'. This involves trying to appreciate inherent patterns rather than to impose preconceived ideas on the data. As she explains, in the early stages of data analysis impressions seem to dominate; although there is a sense that something is coming out of the data, it is not clear what. At the same time, she articulates a common fear among qualitative researchers that '*nothing* is going to come out of the research and that I'm going to be left with a pile of tapes and nothing to say at the end' (1981: 396). Structuring the data involves Marshall picking certain things out and putting them under some headings, but again she states: 'I'm a bit unsure about this, because this seems to *rob* the individual case of its wholeness. So I have to compensate for parcelling out little bits of

a person and putting them under different categories and headings, and try to appreciate the wholeness of each person as well' (1981: 396). Marshall's final stage involves attention and 'mental space in order to allow insights to emerge from an unconscious level so that connections can be made at lots of different levels'. Only towards the end does it 'become more solid and understandable. That feeling gives me confidence that I can put it together' (1981: 398). As will be seen in Chapter 24, practitioners of grounded theory stress the importance of allowing theoretical ideas to emerge out of one's data.

One key point implied by Figure 17.1 is that the typical sequence of steps in qualitative research entails generating theories inductively rather than testing theories that are specified at the outset. But some qualitative researchers argue that qualitative data can be used to *test* theories as well. Silverman (1993) argues that qualitative researchers have become increasingly interested in the testing of theories and that this is a reflection of the growing maturity of the strategy. Certainly, there is no reason why qualitative research cannot be used to test theories that are specified in advance of data collection. In any case, much qualitative research involves testing theories in the course of the research process. So, in Figure 17.1, the loop back from Step 5a 'Tighter specification of the research question(s)' to Step 5b 'Collection of further data' implies that a theoretical position may emerge in the course of research and may spur the collection of further data to test that theory.

This oscillation between testing emerging theories and collecting data is a common feature of qualitative research. However, it is presented as a dashed line in Figure 17.1, because it is not as necessary a feature of the process of qualitative research as the other steps. Silverman (1993) is undoubtedly correct that pre-specified theories *can be* and sometimes *are* tested with qualitative data, but the generation of theory tends to be the preferred approach.

Concepts in qualitative research

A central feature of Chapter 8 was the discussion of concepts and their measurement. For most qualitative researchers, developing measures of concepts will not be a significant consideration, but concepts are very much part of the landscape in qualitative research. However, the way in which concepts are developed and used is often rather different from in quantitative research. Blumer's (1954) distinction between 'definitive' and 'sensitizing' concepts helps to explain some of these differences.

Blumer (1954) argued against the use of definitive concepts in social research. The idea of definitive concepts is typified by the way in which, in quantitative research, a concept, once developed, becomes fixed through the elaboration of indicators. For Blumer, such an approach is overly restrictive, because the concept in question comes to be seen exclusively in terms of the indicators that have

been developed for it. Fine nuances in the form that the concept can assume, or alternative ways of viewing the concept and its manifestations, are sidelined. In other words, definitive concepts are excessively concerned with what is common to the phenomena that the concept is supposed to subsume rather than with variety. Instead, Blumer recommended that social researchers should use sensitizing concepts to provide 'a general sense of reference and guidance in approaching empirical instances' (1954: 7).

As the example in Research in focus 17.2 suggests, the researcher frequently starts out with a broad outline of a concept, which is revised and narrowed during the course of data collection. Subsequent researchers may take up and revise the concept and use it in different organizational contexts or in relation to different research questions.

17.2 RESEARCH IN FOCUS
The emergence of a concept in qualitative research: 'emotional labour'

Hochschild's (1983) idea of emotional labour—labour that 'requires one to induce or suppress feelings in order to sustain the outward countenance that produces the proper state of mind in others' (1983: 7)—has become an influential concept in the sociology of work and emotions. Somewhat surprisingly for a qualitative study, Hochschild's initial conceptualization appears to have emerged from a questionnaire she distributed to 261 university students. The questionnaire posed two open-ended questions: 'Describe a real situation that was important to you in which you experienced a deep emotion' and 'Describe as fully and concretely as possible a real situation that was important to you in which you either changed the situation to fit your feelings or changed your feelings to fit the situation' (1983: 13). Thus, although a self-completion questionnaire was employed, the resulting data were qualitative. Hochschild's data analysis drew on the idea of 'emotion work', which is the same as emotional labour but occurs in a private context. Emotional labour is essentially emotion work performed as part of one's paid employment.

In order to develop the idea of emotional labour, Hochschild looked to the world of work. She chose to focus on flight attendants, as an occupational group that was likely to engage in emotional labour. Several sources of data on emotional labour among flight attendants were used. She gained access to Delta Airlines, a large American airline. Data collection involved

- observing training sessions for attendants and having many conversations with trainees and experienced attendants;
- interviewing other personnel, such as section managers and advertising agents;
- examining Delta advertisements spanning 30 years;
- observing the flight attendant recruitment process at Pan American Airways, since she had not been allowed to do this at Delta;
- conducting 'open-ended interviews lasting three to five hours each with thirty flight attendants in the San Francisco Bay Area' (1983: 15).

As a contrasting occupational group that is also involved in emotional labour, she also interviewed five debt-collectors.

From this it can be seen that Hochschild's concept of emotional labour began as a somewhat imprecise idea which emerged out of a concern with emotion work and gradually developed. The concept has been picked up by numerous other business and management researchers. For example, Leidner (1993) has explored, through ethnographic studies of a McDonald's restaurant and an insurance company, the ways in which organizations seek to 'routinize' the display of emotional labour.

Reliability and validity in qualitative research

In Chapters 3 and 8 it was noted that reliability and validity are important criteria in establishing and assessing the quality of business research. However, there has been discussion among qualitative researchers concerning the relevance of reliability and validity. Even writers who take the view that these criteria are relevant suggest that the meanings of these terms need to be altered. For example, the criterion of validity carries connotations of measurement. Since measurement is not a major preoccupation among qualitative researchers, the criterion of validity would seem to have limited application in such studies.

Adapting reliability and validity for qualitative research

One approach is to assimilate reliability and validity into qualitative research with little change of meaning other than playing down the salience of measurement. Mason (1996), for example, argues that reliability, validity, and generalizability (which is the main component of external validity; see Chapter 3) 'are different kinds of measures of the quality, rigour and wider potential of research, which are achieved according to certain methodological and disciplinary conventions and principles'

(1996: 21). She sticks closely to the meaning that these criteria have in quantitative research, where they have been largely developed. Thus, validity refers to whether 'you are observing, identifying, or "measuring" what you say you are' (1996: 24). LeCompte and Goetz (1982) and Kirk and Miller (1986) also write about reliability and validity in relation to qualitative research but invest the terms with a somewhat different meaning from Mason. LeCompte and Goetz discuss the following aspects.

- *External reliability*: the degree to which a study can be replicated. This is a difficult criterion to meet in qualitative research, since, as LeCompte and Goetz recognize, it is impossible to 'freeze' a social setting and the circumstances of an initial study to make it replicable in the sense in which the term is usually used (see Chapter 8). However, they suggest several strategies that enable the requirements of external reliability to be approached. For example, they suggest that a qualitative researcher replicating ethnographic research needs to adopt a similar social role to that adopted by the original researcher. Otherwise, what a researcher sees and hears when attempting to conduct a replication will not be comparable to the original research.
- *Internal reliability*: when there is more than one observer, do members of the research team agree

about what they see and hear? This is a similar notion to *inter-observer consistency* (see Key concept 13.4).

- *Internal validity*: is there a good match between researchers' observations and the theoretical ideas they develop? LeCompte and Goetz argue that internal validity tends to be a strength of qualitative research, particularly ethnographic research, because prolonged participation in the social life of a group over a long period of time allows the researcher to ensure a high level of congruence between concepts and observations.

- *External validity*, which refers to the degree to which findings can be generalized across social settings. LeCompte and Goetz argue that, unlike internal validity, external validity represents a problem for qualitative researchers because of their tendency to use case studies and small samples.

As this suggests, some qualitative researchers tend to use the terms reliability and validity in similar ways to quantitative researchers when seeking to develop criteria for assessing research.

Alternative criteria for evaluating qualitative research

However, some writers have suggested that qualitative studies should be evaluated according to quite different criteria from those used by quantitative researchers. Lincoln and Guba (1985) and Guba and Lincoln (1994) propose that it is necessary to specify ways of establishing and assessing the quality of qualitative research that provide an alternative to reliability and validity. They propose two primary criteria for assessing a qualitative study: trustworthiness and *authenticity*.

Trustworthiness is made up of four criteria, each of which has an equivalent criterion in quantitative research:

- *credibility*, which parallels internal validity;
- *transferability*, which parallels external validity;
- *dependability*, which parallels reliability;
- *confirmability*, which parallels objectivity.

A major reason for Guba and Lincoln's unease about the simple application of reliability and validity standards to qualitative research is that the criteria presuppose that a single absolute account of social reality is feasible. In other words, they are critical of the view (described in Chapter 2 as realist) that there are absolute truths about the social world that it is the job of the social scientist to reveal. Instead, they argue that there can be more than one and possibly several accounts.

Credibility

The significance of this stress on multiple accounts of social reality is especially evident in the trustworthiness criterion of *credibility*. After all, if there can be several possible accounts of an aspect of social reality, the plausibility or credibility of the account that a researcher arrives at is going to determine its acceptability to others. The establishment of the credibility of findings entails both ensuring that research is carried out according to the canons of good practice *and* submitting research findings to the members of the social world who were studied, for confirmation that the investigator has correctly understood that social world. This latter technique is often referred to as respondent validation or member validation (see Key concept 17.3). Another technique Guba and Lincoln recommend is triangulation (see Key concept 17.4).

17.3 KEY CONCEPT
What is respondent validation?

Respondent validation, which is also sometimes called *member validation*, is a process whereby a researcher provides research participants with an account of his or her findings. The purpose of this is to seek corroboration of the account that the researcher has arrived at. Respondent validation is particularly popular among qualitative researchers, because they frequently want to ensure that there is a good correspondence between their findings and the perspectives and experiences of their research participants. There are several forms of respondent validation.

- The researcher provides each research participant with an account of what they have said to the researcher in an interview and conversations, or of what the researcher observed by watching that person in an observational study. For example, Marshall (1995) wanted to tell the stories of a small group of women managers who had left or were leaving senior organization positions, from these women's points of view. To achieve this, she met with each manager for one-and-a-half to two hours and asked the woman to tell her story. Marshall stated that she would be happy to discuss her own views and experiences if relevant. Once the story had been transcribed, she wrote an initial draft of the story and invited the manager to read it.

- The researcher feeds back to a group of people or an organization his or her impressions and findings in relation to that group or organization. In Marshall's (1995) research, after reading the story, each of the managers met Marshall again, or exchanged letters and phone calls, in order to develop the story to their mutual satisfaction. Most of the women were generally happy with the drafts but wanted minor amendments. Marshall revised the stories, taking their comments into account. She states that, ultimately, the woman manager had the right of veto over what appeared in 'her' chapter of the book that Marshall wrote.

Later, all participants were invited to a one-day collaborative enquiry workshop, in which they jointly reviewed their experiences of employment and discussed issues of mutual interest.

In each case, the goal is to seek confirmation that the researcher's findings and impressions are congruent with the views of those on whom the research was conducted and to seek out areas where there is a lack of correspondence and the reasons for it. However, the idea is not without practical difficulties.

- Respondent validation may provoke defensive reactions and even censorship on the part of research participants. Marshall was prepared to accept this as a consequence of her collaborative approach. Hence one participant decided that her story made her too identifiable and vulnerable. Her reasons for this centred on the difficulties of establishing a positive, accepted identity as a manager because she self-identified as gay. Marshall therefore agreed to write a brief account of 'Ruth's' experience.

- Research participants cannot validate the scientific legitimacy of a researcher's analysis. Even if participants are prepared to corroborate the researcher's account, the researcher still has to develop concepts and theories that make a contribution to knowledge. Marshall was therefore careful to differentiate between data—over which participants had a right of veto (i.e. the women's stories)—and other material over which she wished to retain control, to put her own views and pursue her 'more academic concerns' (1995: 336).

Respondent validation can provide a means of confirming the validity of individual accounts. It can also help to redress power imbalances between researcher and researched by providing participants with a degree of involvement in and authority over the research findings. However, it is important to distinguish between seeking validation from individuals and seeking validation from organizations, or—as is more likely—powerful individuals within organizations, such as senior managers. The latter option, by giving powerful groups within the organization control over the research, can introduce problems of censorship.

17.4 KEY CONCEPT
What is triangulation?

Triangulation involves using more than one method or source of data in the study of social phenomena. The triangulation metaphor is taken from navigation and military strategy, where it refers to the process whereby multiple reference points are used to locate an object's exact position. The term has been used more broadly by Denzin (1970: 310) to refer to an approach that uses 'multiple observers, theoretical perspectives, sources of data, and methodologies', but the emphasis has tended to be on methods of investigation and sources of data. One of the reasons Webb et al. (1966) advocate greater use of unobtrusive methods is because of their potential as a strategy of triangulation. Triangulation was originally conceptualized by Webb et al. (1966) as an approach to the development of measures of concepts, whereby more than one method would be employed in the development of measures, resulting in greater confidence in findings. As such, triangulation was strongly associated with a quantitative research strategy. However, triangulation can also take place within a qualitative research strategy. In fact, ethnographers often check out their observations with interview questions to determine whether they might have misunderstood what they had seen. Increasingly, triangulation is used to refer to a process of cross-checking findings deriving from both quantitative and qualitative research (Deacon et al. 1998). For example, Kanter (1977) draws attention to the triangulation of methods that characterized her approach, stating, 'I used each source of data, and each informant, as a check against the others' (1977: 337). She suggests that 'a combination of methods . . . emerges as the most valid and reliable way to develop understanding of such a complex social reality as the corporation' (1977: 337).

In addition to allowing the cross-checking of qualitative data, the combined use of quantitative and qualitative methods may allow access to different levels of reality. However, triangulation is just one way of thinking about the integration of these two research strategies, as will be discussed in depth in Chapter 27.

Transferability

As qualitative research typically entails the intensive study of a small group, or of individuals sharing certain characteristics (that is, depth rather than the breadth that is a preoccupation in quantitative research), qualitative findings tend to be orientated to the contextual uniqueness and significance of the aspect of the social world being studied. As Guba and Lincoln put it, whether or not findings 'hold in some other context, or even in the same context at some other time, is an empirical issue' (Lincoln and Guba 1985: 316). Instead, qualitative researchers are encouraged to produce what Geertz (1973) calls thick description—that is, rich accounts of the details of a culture. Guba and Lincoln argue that a thick description provides others with what they refer to as a database for making judgements about the possible transferability of findings to other milieux.

Dependability

As a parallel to reliability in quantitative research, and in order to demonstrate that qualitative research is trustworthy, Guba and Lincoln propose the idea of *dependability*. This involves adoption of an 'auditing' approach which ensures that complete records are kept of all phases of the research process—problem formulation, selection of research participants, fieldwork notes, interview transcripts, data analysis decisions—in an accessible manner. Peers then act as auditors, possibly during the course of the research and certainly at the end, to establish how far proper procedures are being and have been followed. This would include assessing the degree to which theoretical inferences can be justified. Auditing has not become a popular approach to enhancing the dependability of qualitative business research, partly because of problems associated with it. One is that it is very demanding for the auditors, bearing in mind that qualitative research frequently generates extremely large datasets: this may be a major reason why it has not become a pervasive approach to validation.

Confirmability

Confirmability is concerned with ensuring that, while recognizing that complete objectivity is impossible in business research, the researcher can be shown to have acted in good faith; in other words, it should be apparent that he or she has not overtly or manifestly allowed personal values or theoretical inclinations to sway the conduct of the research and findings deriving from it. Guba and Lincoln propose that establishing confirmability should be one of the objectives of auditors.

Overview of the issue of criteria

Qualitative researchers who apply the criteria of reliability and validity with little or no adaptation broadly position themselves as realists—that is, as saying that social reality exists independently of those who are engaged with it. Johnson et al. (2006) refer to this kind of business research as 'positivist-qualitative', because it involves the use of non-quantitative methods but is informed by largely positivistic assumptions, including the idea that 'there is a world out there to be discovered and explored in an objective manner' (Johnson et al., 2006: 138). Lincoln and Guba reject this view, arguing instead that qualitative researchers' concepts and theories are representations and that there may, therefore, be other equally credible representations of the same phenomena. In addition to the four criteria discussed above, Lincoln and Guba propose a fifth criterion of *authenticity*, which raises issues concerning the wider social and political impact of research. Authenticity places responsibility on the researcher to fairly represent different viewpoints within a social setting, so as to enable research participants to arrive at a better understanding of their situations and empower them to engage in action to change their circumstances. According to Johnson et al. (2006), this criteriology is consistent with critical theory and is aligned with participatory action research, which aims to engender emancipatory change.

Although qualitative researchers have sought to formulate quality criteria appropriate to their approach, this has not had as much impact in business research as might be expected. Pratt (2008) has shown that qualitative business researchers believe their work continues to be judged by criteria of validity and reliability that are more suited to quantitative research. Cornelissen et al. (2012) argue that the dominance of criteria informed by a positivist epistemology, such as validity and reliability, puts pressure on business researchers to try to conform to them, even if this is inconsistent with the principles of qualitative research, introduced at the start of this chapter, that may guide their study. According to Johnson et al. (2006), the most important thing for qualitative researchers is to make sure that the quality criteria they use are logically consistent with their philosophical assumptions.

The main preoccupations of qualitative researchers

The preoccupations of qualitative researchers reflect epistemologically grounded beliefs about what constitutes acceptable knowledge. Whereas quantitative research is profoundly influenced by a natural science approach to producing knowledge, qualitative researchers are more influenced by *interpretivism* (see Key concept 2.12). This position is the product of the confluence of three related stances: Weber's notion of *Verstehen*; symbolic interactionism; and phenomenology. In this section, six distinctive preoccupations of qualitative researchers will be examined.

Seeing through the eyes of people being studied

An underlying premise of many qualitative researchers is that the subject matter of business (that is, people and their social world) differs from the subject matter of the natural sciences. A key difference is that the objects of analysis of the natural sciences (atoms, molecules, gases, chemicals, metals, and so on) cannot attribute meaning to events and to their environment. However, people *do*. This argument is especially evident in the work of Schutz (1962) and can particularly be seen in the passage quoted in Chapter 2, where Schutz draws attention to the fact that, unlike the objects of the natural sciences, the objects of the social sciences—people—are capable of attributing meaning to their environment. Consequently, many qualitative researchers suggest that a methodology is required for studying people that reflects these differences between people and the objects of the natural sciences. As a result, many qualitative researchers express a commitment to viewing events and the social world through the eyes of the people that they study, rather than as though those people were incapable of their own interpretations and reflections. The epistemology underlying qualitative research has been expressed by the authors of one widely read text as involving two central tenets: '(1) … face-to-face interaction is the fullest condition of participating in the mind of another human being, and (2) … you must participate in the mind of another human being (in sociological terms, "take the role of the other") to acquire social knowledge' (Lofland and Lofland 1995: 16). An example of this approach is given in Research in focus 17.5.

It is not surprising, therefore, that many researchers make claims in their reports of their investigations about having sought to take the views of the people they studied as the point of departure (see Research in focus 17.5). This tendency reveals itself in frequent references to getting close to research participants and seeing from the perspective of those who are studied. Here are some other examples.

- Jackall (1988), in his ethnographic study of bureaucracy and morality in large corporations, seeks to understand 'how men and women in business actually experience their work' (1988: 5) in order to ascertain its moral salience for them.

- Marshall (1984) describes herself as an 'interpreter' rather than a manipulator of data, 'concerned with capturing other people's meanings rather than testing hypotheses' (1984: 116).

The preference for seeing from the perspective of the people studied in qualitative research is often accompanied by the closely related goal of seeking to probe beneath surface appearances. After all, if you take the position of the people you are studying, the prospect is raised that they might view things differently from the way an outsider with little direct contact might have expected. This stance reveals itself in various studies.

17.5 RESEARCH IN FOCUS
Seeing practice-based learning from the perspective of train dispatchers

Willems' (2018) study of Dutch train dispatchers in a railway control room illustrates the commitment that qualitative researchers have to trying to appreciate events and the social world from the perspective of the people who are being studied. In explaining his approach, he states: 'I encouraged dispatchers to explain work from their own understandings … rather than probing them to fit experience into pre-determined or theoretical categories' (Willems 2018: 29). Willems was interested in understanding the role of embodied, sensory practices in practice-based learning. His research focus was informed by a phenomenological approach which suggests that the body is a primary means through which human beings experience and engage with the world. Willems' analysis shows the importance of sensory knowledge in the work of train dispatchers—such as by touching the tracks, seeing the switches, and recalling the experience of feeling a train enter a tunnel—that enable train dispatchers to safely coordinate the movement of trains. The study thereby challenges the emphasis within mainstream management learning scholarship on cognition, showing instead how the dispatchers learn by experiencing the railways in bodily, material, and emotional ways.

- Dalton's (1959) research study of the informal organization found that the boundaries between unofficial reward obtained through expense accounting, and organizational theft or pilfering, were defined quite differently by individual managers, depending on their position within the hierarchy.

- Collinson (1992a) found that shopfloor workers at 'Slavs' dealt with their occupational status partly by channelling their personal ambitions and energies outside the workplace into the alternative domains of family and home, investing in 'the self-sacrificing role of parental breadwinner' (1992a: 185).

- Marshall's (1984) study of women in management showed that this issue could not be understood without taking into account the wider social context, including society's values about work, and the way of life in large organizations, in order to make sense of the kinds of job roles that women in employment adopt.

- Ram's (1994) study of management in small firms showed that workers were not just controlled through direct supervision and intensive working methods, as previous studies had suggested. Using ethnographic methods, Ram was able to pick up on a variety of largely informal negotiating processes, whereby employees negotiated a 'fair' rate for the job, taking into account considerations such as the time of the year, the type of work, caste, and culture.

The empathetic stance of seeking to see things from the perspective of one's research participants is very much in tune with interpretivism and demonstrates well the epistemological links with phenomenology, symbolic interactionism, and *Verstehen*. However, it is not without practical problems. For example: the risk of 'going native' and losing sight of what you are studying (see Key concept 19.6); the problem of how far the researcher should go, such as the potential question of participating in illegal or dangerous activities; and the possibility that the researcher will be able to see the social world from the perspective of only some of the people who form part of a social scene but not others, such as only people of the same gender.

Description and emphasis on context

Qualitative researchers are more inclined than quantitative researchers to provide a great deal of descriptive detail when reporting their research. This is not to say that they are exclusively concerned with description. They *are* concerned with explanation, and indeed the extent to which qualitative researchers ask 'Why?' questions is frequently understated. In addition, more critical or radical qualitative researchers are often concerned with understanding the political and economic interests that inform organizational actions, in order to enhance the possibilities for changing them. For example, in her ethnography of a multinational corporation, Casey (1995) describes herself as concerned with understanding dominant social constructions about work, the self, and society, in the hope that this might increase the likelihood of societal transformation.

Many qualitative studies provide a detailed account of what goes on in the setting being investigated. Very often qualitative studies seem to be full of apparently trivial details. However, these details are frequently important for the qualitative researcher because of their significance for research participants and because they provide an account of the context where the behaviour takes place. It is with this point in mind that Geertz (1973) recommends the thick description of social settings, events, and often individuals. On the surface, some of this detail may appear irrelevant, and, indeed, there is a risk of the researcher becoming too embroiled in descriptive detail. Lofland and Lofland (1995: 164–5), for example, warn against what they call 'descriptive excess' in qualitative research, whereby the amount of detail inhibits the analysis of data.

One of the main reasons why qualitative researchers are keen to provide considerable descriptive detail is that they typically emphasize the importance of the contextual understanding of social behaviour. This means that behaviour and values must be understood in the situations where they arise. This recommendation implies that we cannot understand the behaviour of members of a social group other than in terms of the specific environment in which they operate. In this way, behaviour that may appear odd or irrational can make perfect sense when we understand the context within which that behaviour takes place. The emphasis on context in qualitative research goes back to many of the classic studies in social anthropology, which demonstrated how a particular practice, such as the magical ritual that may accompany the sowing of seeds, made little sense unless we understand the belief systems of that society. It is often precisely this detail that provides the mapping of context in terms of which behaviour is understood. The propensity for description can also be interpreted as a manifestation of the naturalism that pervades much qualitative research.

Emphasis on process

Qualitative research tends to view social life in terms of processes. This tendency reveals itself in a number of ways. One of the main ways is that there is often a concern to show how events and patterns unfold over time. As a result, qualitative evidence often conveys a strong sense of change and flux. As Pettigrew (1997: 338) explains, process is 'a sequence of individual and collective events, actions, and activities unfolding over time in context'. This includes understanding how the history of an organization shapes the present reality and how the 'interchange between agents and contexts occurs over time and is cumulative' (Pettigrew 1997: 339).

Qualitative research based on ethnographic methods is particularly associated with this emphasis on process. It is the element of participant observation, a key feature of ethnography, that is especially instrumental in generating this feature. Ethnographers are typically immersed in a social setting for a long time—sometimes years, as in Michel's (2011) study of Wall Street bankers (Research in focus 19.2). Consequently, ethnographers are able to observe the ways in which events develop over time or the ways in which the different elements of a social system (values, beliefs, behaviour, and so on) interconnect. Such findings can inject a sense of process by seeing social life in terms of streams of interdependent events and elements (see Research in focus 17.6 for an example).

This is not to say, however, that ethnographers are the only qualitative researchers who inject a sense of process into our understanding of social life. This can also be achieved through semi-structured and unstructured interviewing, by asking participants to reflect on the

17.6 RESEARCH IN FOCUS
Studying process and change in the Carlsberg group

Hatch et al.'s (2015) study of organizational identity and culture was conducted in the Carlsberg group—the global beer brand headquartered in Denmark—at a time when the organization was going through a period of transformational change. The longitudinal study was carried out between 2009 and 2012 and combined ethnographic methods of data collection, using semi-structured interviews, participant observation, and documentary data including annual reports and press coverage relating to the company. Data analysis involved the use of grounded theory methods to identify themes 'as they emerged during data collection' (2015: 63). The researchers describe their study as 'engaged scholarship' because it involved studying a problem 'up close' (Van de Ven, 2007), in a way which was relevant to organizational members, including senior managers who were closely involved in the study (see also Chapter 19).

processes leading up to or following on from an event, or through the life history method of qualitative interviewing (see Chapter 20).

Flexibility and limited structure

Many qualitative researchers are disdainful of approaches to research that entail the imposition of predetermined formats on the social world. This position is largely to do with the preference for seeing things from the perspective of people being studied. After all, if a structured method of data collection is used, certain decisions must have been made about what the researcher expects to find. Therefore, the researcher is limited in the degree to which they can genuinely adopt the world view of people being studied. Consequently, most qualitative researchers prefer a research orientation that entails as little prior contamination of the social world as possible. To do otherwise risks imposing an inappropriate frame of reference on people. Keeping structure to a minimum is intended to enhance the opportunity of genuinely revealing the perspectives of the people you are studying. Also, in the process, aspects of people's social world that are particularly important to them, but that might not even have crossed the mind of a researcher unfamiliar with it, are more likely to be forthcoming. Because of this, qualitative research tends to be a strategy that tries not to delimit areas of enquiry too much, asking general rather than specific research questions (see Figure 17.1).

Owing to the preference for a loosely structured approach to the collection of data, qualitative researchers adopt methods that do not require the investigator to develop highly specific research questions in advance. Ethnography, with its emphasis on participant observation, is particularly well suited to this orientation. It allows researchers to submerge themselves in a social setting with a general research interest in mind and gradually to narrow their focus by making as many observations of that setting as possible. They can then formulate more specific research questions out of their collected data. Similarly, interviewing is an extremely prominent method in the qualitative researcher's repertoire, but, as we will see in Chapter 20, it is less structured than the kind of interviewing encountered in Chapter 10. Blumer's (1954) argument for sensitizing rather than definitive concepts (definitive being the kind employed by quantitative researchers) is symptomatic of the preference for a more open-ended, and hence less structured, approach.

An advantage of the unstructured nature of most qualitative research (that is, in addition to gaining access to people's world views) is that it offers the prospect of flexibility. The researcher can change direction during their investigation much more easily than in quantitative research, which tends to have a built-in momentum once the data collection is under way.

Concepts and theory grounded in data

For qualitative researchers, concepts and theories are usually inductively arrived at from the data that are collected through a process of development (see Research in focus 17.2). In recent years, attempts have been made to enhance the transparency surrounding this process and to introduce greater rigour into this aspect of qualitative research (see Chapter 24).

Not just words

Qualitative business researchers, like other researchers across the social sciences (Banks 2001; Pink 2001; Rose 2001), have become increasingly interested in the analysis of visual data. Writers such as Meyer (1991) and Holliday (2001) have argued that there has been an undue emphasis on the importance of language in constituting meaning and this has led to a tendency to overlook the importance of the visual (Bell and Davison 2013, Meyer et al. 2013). They highlight the unique aspects of the visual, including aesthetic attributes and mimetic potential to induce immediate, memorable effects on audiences. Photographs may be used in qualitative organizational research in a number of ways.

- Photographs may be as an *aide-mémoire* in fieldwork— the images essentially become components of the ethnographer's field notes.

- Photographs may be a source of data in their own right and not simply adjuncts to the ethnographer's field notes, as in Bell's research focusing on visual messages of death and loss following the closure of a car factory (Research in focus 17.7).

- Photographs may serve prompts for discussion by research participants. This includes the use of photographs taken by the ethnographer or by research participants, such as in the study of aesthetics by S. Warren (2002, 2005; Research in focus 17.7). In the case of photographs taken by research participants, Pink (2004: 399) writes: 'By working with informants to produce images that are meaningful for them we can gain insights into their visual cultures and into what is important for them as individuals living in particular localities.'

17.7 RESEARCH IN FOCUS
An example of dialogical visual research

Dialogical visual research (Meyer et al. 2013) involves using visual artefacts as a means of communication between the researcher and research participants. S. Warren (2002) used photographs in her study of aesthetics and organization in the website design department of a global IT company. She was prompted to use visual methods 'to explore the relationship between the feel, sights, smells, and even the tastes of the organizational setting' (2002: 230) which could not be spoken about or written down. Warren gave a camera to employees and asked them to take photographs that would 'show' how it 'felt' to work there. She claims that 'the photographs make an interesting data set in their own right regarding the ways in which the respondents chose to define their work environments, what they felt to be worthy (and not worthy) of photographing, and the individual and sometimes innovative ways they framed their subjects' (2002: 232).

Plates 17.1–17.3 show three photographs taken by respondents. Plate 17.1 is a photograph of a cup of tea from a vending machine. When the respondent was asked why he had taken this particular picture, he raised issues concerning his dissatisfaction with the amount of money that had been spent on the office at the expense of other things that were more important to employees. Plate 17.2 shows a meeting room that was photographed by a respondent who found it to be an escape and a contrast from the normal work environment. However, Warren argues that in her study the use of photographs did not primarily entail analysis of their content. Instead the photographs formed part of a data-generating triangle involving the image, respondent, and researcher, focusing on the reasons why they were taken. Plate 17.3 provides a good illustration of this, since the blurred nature of this photograph of the office space means it would be difficult to distinguish the content at all without the account provided by the respondent, who explains that they were trying to capture the 'busyness' and 'colour' that defined the atmosphere of the workplace. Warren also notes that photographs such as this one show how intangible emotional concepts that are hard to communicate through language can be conveyed through images.

PLATE 17.1
'Cup of tea from vending machine'

Copyright Samantha Warren. Reproduced with thanks.

The photographs were then discussed in the context of an interview conversation with the respondent in a form of qualitative photo-elicitation. Warren suggests the photographs added to the richness of data collected and were used by respondents to give an emotional sense of the work environment.

PLATE 17.2
'Thinktank: aestheticized meeting room'

Copyright Samantha Warren. Reproduced with thanks.

PLATE 17.3
'Blurred view of office space'

Copyright Samantha Warren. Reproduced with thanks.

Pink (2001) draws attention to two different ways in which visual images have been conceptualized in social research. She calls these *realist* and *reflexive* approaches. The latter approach to the visual is frequently collaborative, in the sense that research participants may be involved in decisions about what photographs should be taken and then how they should be interpreted. Further, there is recognition of the fluidity of the meaning of images, implying that they can never be fixed and will always be viewed by different people in different ways. For example, in Bell's (2012) study of the closure of a Jaguar car manufacturing plant (Research in focus 17.8), she analysed the positionality of the person who took the photograph or produced the image, as well as the content of the photograph itself.

Meyer et al. (2013) provide an overview of how visuals have been integrated into qualitative organizational research and identify five ideal-typical approaches:

- *Archaeological:* based on analysis of visual artefacts in which socially constructed meaning is embodied; Davison's (2009) study of iconography in a UK bank (Research in focus 23.6) provides an example.

- *Practice:* involving the study of visual artefacts *in situ*, including how they are used by social actors in various processes of organizing; an example is Bell's (2012) study of visual expression of change and loss surrounding the closure of a car manufacturing plant (Research in focus 17.8).

- *Strategic:* this builds on psychological, linguistic, or semiotic theory and involves the use of visual methods to elicit desired responses from audiences; an example is Bell and Clarke's (2014) study of undergraduate student perceptions of management researchers (see Chapter 6).

- *Dialogical:* this type of research uses visuals as a form of communication between the researcher and the field, such as through the use of **projective techniques**, pictorial, and photo-elicitation (Key concept 10.8).

- *Documenting:* this involves the use of visual artifacts as a form of field notes to document the research process; examples include Buchanan's (1998) study of the hospital patient trail discussed below.

17.8 RESEARCH IN FOCUS
An example of practice visual research

Practice-oriented visual research involves studying how visual artefacts are used by social actors in processes of organizing. Bell (2012) was interested in processes of loss and mourning in response to organizational change involving the closure of a Jaguar car manufacturing plant in the UK city of Coventry (Bell 2012). She became aware of the role of visual images in communicating messages about the closure when an image was published in the local newspaper featuring a Jaguar E-Type vehicle with the letters 'RIP JAG' written across the front of the vehicle, accompanied by a story about the decision of the Ford Motor Company to close the factory. In addition to studying historical photographs and artefacts held in the Jaguar company archives, she analysed images produced by employees and managers in response to the intended closure. She also analysed more than 600 photographs of the manufacturing plant that were taken by the organization's picture archivist in the last days before car production ceased (Plates 17.4 and 17.5). Through this she developed an analysis of the significance of the visual in constructing organizational memory and narrating stories about the organization's history and identity. The findings from the case led her to conclude that the visual are an important resource in enabling managerial narratives to be contested and alternatives to be constructed.

However, Meyer et al. (2013) suggest there is still some way to go before the inclusion of visual data in empirical analyses becomes the norm rather than the exception. The Researcher Development pages on the website of the International Network for Visual Studies in Organizations, *in Visio* (http://moodle.in-visio.org/) contain information about visual methods and the theory that informs them.

Photographs produced as part of fieldwork may be analysed by the researcher alongside other types of documents containing written words, such as interview transcripts, as in the study of business process re-engineering in a UK hospital by Buchanan (2001). Buchanan used photographs taken by himself as a way of gaining insight into the 'patient trail', the temporal and spatial process experienced by patients. Buchanan (2001: 151)

argues that using photographs in conjunction with other methods of data collection helps the organizational researcher to:

- develop a richer understanding of organizational processes;

- capture data not disclosed in interview;

- reveal to staff aspects of work in other sections of the organization with which they have little or no regular contact;

- offer a novel channel for respondent validation of data;

- involve staff in debate concerning the implications of research findings for organization process redesign and improvement.

PLATE 17.4
'An empty staff break area on the last day of production'

Copyright Karam Ram and Jaguar Heritage. Reproduced with thanks.

PLATE 17.5
'After the last car has left the track'

Copyright Karam Ram and Jaguar Heritage. Reproduced with thanks.

Visual organizational research has great potential. However, Pink (2004) reminds us that visual research methods are never purely visual. There are two aspects to this point. First, visual research methods are usually accompanied by other (often traditional) research methods such as interviewing and observation. Second, the visual is almost always accompanied by the non-visual—words—which is the medium of expression for both the research participants and the researchers themselves. Further consideration of the use of visual methods in ethnographic research and in the qualitative analysis of documents will be provided in Chapters 19 and 23.

The critique of qualitative research

In a similar way to the criticisms that have been levelled at quantitative research, mainly by qualitative researchers, a parallel critique has been built up of qualitative research. These are some of the more common issues raised.

Qualitative research is too subjective

Quantitative researchers sometimes criticize qualitative research as being too impressionistic and subjective. By these criticisms they usually mean that qualitative findings rely too much on the researcher's often unsystematic views about what is significant and important, and also upon the close personal relationships that the researcher frequently strikes up with the people studied. Precisely because qualitative research often begins in a relatively open-ended way and entails a gradual narrowing-down of research questions or problems, the consumer of the writings deriving from the research may be given few clues as to why one area was the chosen area upon which attention was focused rather than another. By contrast, quantitative researchers point to the tendency for the problem formulation stage in their work to be more explicitly stated in terms of such matters as the existing literature on that topic and key theoretical ideas.

Qualitative research is difficult to replicate

Quantitative researchers also often argue that these tendencies are made more problematic because of the difficulty of replicating a qualitative study, although replication is by no means a straightforward matter regardless of this particular issue (see Chapter 8). Precisely because qualitative research is relatively unstructured and reliant upon the qualitative researcher's ingenuity, it is almost impossible to conduct a true replication, since there are hardly any standard procedures to be followed. In qualitative research, the investigator him or herself is the main instrument of data collection, so that what is observed and heard and also what the researcher decides to concentrate upon is very much a product of his or her preferences. There are several possible components of this criticism: what qualitative researchers (especially perhaps in ethnography) choose to focus upon while in the field is a product of what strikes them as significant, whereas other researchers are likely to empathize with other issues; the responses of participants (people being observed or interviewed) to qualitative researchers are likely to be affected by the characteristics of the researcher (personality, age, gender, and so on); and, because of the unstructured nature of qualitative data, interpretation will be profoundly influenced by the subjective leanings of a researcher. Because of such factors it is difficult to replicate qualitative findings. The difficulties ethnographers experience when they revisit grounds previously trodden by another researcher (often referred to as a 'restudy') do not inspire confidence in the replicability of qualitative research (Bryman 1994).

Problems of generalization

It is often suggested that the scope of the findings of qualitative investigations is restricted. When participant observation is used or when unstructured interviews are conducted with a small number of individuals in a certain organization or locality, they argue that it is impossible to know how the findings can be generalized to other settings. How can just one or two cases be representative of all cases? In other words, can we really treat Perlow's (1997) research, discussed in Chapter 27, on the time and the work–life balance of software engineers in a high-tech corporation in the USA as representative of all software engineers? Can we treat Ladge et al.'s (2012) research on pregnant women professionals as representative of the identity transition experiences of women working in non-professional occupations? In the case of research based on interviews rather than participation, can we treat interviewees who have not been selected through a probability procedure or even quota sampling as representative? Are Watson's (1994*a*) managers typical of all managers working within the telecommunications industry, or are Ram's (1994; see Research in focus 19.4) small-firm case studies in the West Midlands typical of small firms elsewhere?

The answer in all these cases is that, although we cannot make empirical generalizations about entire populations from a single case study, this is not the purpose of qualitative case study research (Flyvbjerg 2006). Similarly, the people who are interviewed in qualitative research are not meant to be representative of a population in any precise manner. Instead, the findings of qualitative research are used to make theoretical generalizations. It is 'the cogency of the theoretical reasoning' (J. C. Mitchell 1983: 207), rather than statistical criteria, that is decisive in considering the generalizability of the findings of qualitative research. In other words, it is the quality of the theoretical inferences that are derived from qualitative data that is crucial to the assessment of generalization.

These three criticisms reflect many of the preoccupations of quantitative research that were discussed in Chapter 8. A further criticism that is often made of qualitative research, but that is perhaps less influenced by quantitative research criteria, is the suggestion that

reports of qualitative research frequently lack transparency in terms of how the research was conducted.

Lack of transparency

It is sometimes difficult to establish from qualitative research what the researcher actually *did* and how they arrived at the study's conclusions. For example, qualitative research reports are sometimes unclear about such matters as how people were chosen for observation or interview. This deficiency contrasts sharply with the—sometimes laborious—accounts of sampling procedures in reports of quantitative research. However, it does not seem plausible to suggest that outlining in some detail the ways in which research participants are selected constitutes the application of quantitative research criteria. Readers have a right to know to what extent research participants were selected to correspond to a wide range of people. Also, the process of qualitative data analysis is frequently unclear (see Bryman and Burgess 1994*a*). It is often not obvious how the analysis was conducted—in other words, what the researcher was actually doing when the data were analysed and therefore how the study's conclusions were arrived at. These issues of lack of transparency are being addressed (see Thinking deeply 17.9), but not always in ways that are consistent with the principles of qualitative research.

17.9 THINKING DEEPLY
A quantitative review of qualitative research in management and business

Bluhm et al. (2011) conducted a quantitative review of 198 articles based on qualitative research published in leading US and European management journals over a ten-year period (1998–2008). They assert that support for qualitative research grew in this period and that overall quality standards rose, a trend they attribute to greater standardization and increased scientific and methodological rigour and validity. The authors identify the most common theoretical purpose of these articles as theory elaboration and theory generation. In terms of research design, most (59 per cent) used more than one method of data collection, with interviewing being by far the most popular method used. One interesting finding to emerge from the review was that studies using novel or innovative qualitative methods, such as focus groups or diaries, tend to be cited more often than those that use conventional research designs. The authors therefore recommend greater use of innovative qualitative techniques by drawing on methods used in other disciplines, such as sociology or linguistics. The authors used a combination of quantitative **content analysis** (see Chapter 13) and citation analysis in their review, which, they argue, enabled them to 'draw precise conclusions and make more accurate comparisons' (Bluhm et al. 2011: 1872). However, their application of positivist quality criteria, such as removal of researcher bias and replicability, could be seen as a somewhat contradictory and inappropriate imposition of quantitative standards of evaluation on qualitative research.

Is it always like this?

This heading was used in Chapter 8 in relation to quantitative research, but the question is less easy to answer in relation to qualitative research. To a large extent, this is because qualitative research is less codified than quantitative research—that is, it is less influenced by strict guidelines and directions about how to go about data collection and analysis. For example, Dalton (1959, 1964) (see Chapter 19) explains that no explicit hypotheses formed the basis for his participant-observational study of managerial work, for three reasons. First, he was not able to be sure what was relevant until he had gained 'some intimacy with the situation'; secondly, once uttered, a hypothesis becomes somewhat 'obligatory'; and, thirdly, there is a danger that the hypothesis carries a quasi-scientific status. Instead he worked on the basis of 'hunches', which guided him through the research.

As a result, accounts of qualitative research are often less prescriptive than those encountered in relation to quantitative research. Instead, they tend to have a more descriptive tenor, outlining the different ways qualitative researchers have gone about research or suggesting possible ways of doing research based on the writer's own experiences or those of others. To a large extent, this picture is changing, in that there is a growing number of books and articles that seek to make clear-cut recommendations about how qualitative research should be carried out (see Thinking deeply 17.9 for an illustration of this type of standardizing approach).

However, if we look at some of the preoccupations of qualitative research that were described above, we can see certain ways in which there are departures from the practices that are implied by these preoccupations. One of the main departures is that qualitative research is sometimes a lot more focused than is implied by the suggestion that the researcher begins with general research questions and narrows it down so that theory and concepts are arrived at during and after the data collection. There is no *necessary* reason why qualitative research cannot be employed to investigate a specific research problem. A related way in which qualitative research differs from the standard model is in connection with the notion of a lack of structure in approaches to collecting and analysing data. As will be seen in Chapter 22, such techniques as conversation analysis entail the application of a highly codified method for analysing talk. Moreover, the use of computer-assisted qualitative data analysis software (CAQDAS), which will be the subject of Chapter 25, has led to greater transparency in the procedures used for analysing qualitative data. This may lead to more codification in qualitative data analysis than has previously been the case.

Contrasts between quantitative and qualitative research

Several writers have explored the contrasts between quantitative and qualitative research (e.g. Halfpenny 1979; Bryman 1988a; Hammersley 1992b). Table 17.1 draws out the main contrasting features.

- *Numbers versus Words*. Quantitative researchers are often portrayed as preoccupied with applying measurement procedures to social life, while qualitative researchers are seen as using words in the presentation of analyses of society, although, as we have emphasized, qualitative researchers are also concerned with the analysis of visual data.
- *Point of view of researcher versus points of view of participants*. In quantitative research, the investigator is in the driving seat. The set of concerns that he or she brings to an investigation structures the investigation. In qualitative research, the perspective of those being studied—what they see as important and significant—provides the point of orientation.

- *Researcher is distant versus researcher is close*. In quantitative research, researchers are uninvolved with their subjects and in some cases, as in research based on postal questionnaires or on interviews conducted by hired assistants, may have no contact with them at all. Sometimes, this lack of a relationship with the subjects of an investigation is regarded as desirable by quantitative researchers, because they feel that their objectivity might be compromised if they become too

TABLE 17.1
Contrasting features of quantitative and qualitative research

Quantitative	Qualitative
Numbers	Words
Point of view of researcher	Points of view of participants
Researcher is distant	Researcher is close
Theory testing	Theory emergent
Static	Process
Structured	Unstructured
Generalization	Contextual understanding
Hard, reliable data	Rich, deep data
Macro	Micro
Behaviour	Meaning
Artificial settings	Natural settings

involved with the people they study. The qualitative researcher seeks close involvement with the people being investigated, so that he or she can approach genuine understanding of the world from their perspective.

- *Theory and concepts tested in research versus theory and concepts emergent from data.* Quantitative researchers typically bring a set of concepts to bear on the research instruments being employed, so that theoretical work precedes the collection of data, whereas in qualitative research concepts and theoretical elaboration tend to emerge out of data collection.

- *Static versus process.* Quantitative research is frequently depicted as presenting a static image of social reality with its emphasis on relationships between variables. Change and connections between events over time tend not to surface, other than in a mechanistic fashion. Qualitative research is often depicted as attuned to the unfolding of events over time and to the interconnections between the actions of participants of social settings.

- *Structured versus unstructured.* Quantitative research is typically highly structured, so that the investigator is able to examine the precise concepts and issues that are the focus of the study; in qualitative research the approach is invariably unstructured, so that the possibility of getting at actors' meanings and of concepts emerging out of data collection is enhanced.

- *Generalization versus contextual understanding.* Whereas quantitative researchers want their findings

to be generalizable to the relevant population, the qualitative researcher seeks an understanding of behaviour, values, beliefs, and so on in terms of the context in which the research is conducted.

- *Hard, reliable data versus rich, deep data.* Quantitative data are often depicted as 'hard' in the sense of being robust and unambiguous, owing to the precision offered by measurement. Qualitative researchers claim, by contrast, that their contextual approach and their—often prolonged—involvement in a setting engender rich data.

- *Macro versus micro.* Quantitative researchers are often depicted as involved in uncovering large-scale social trends and connections between variables, whereas qualitative researchers are seen as concerned with small-scale aspects of social reality, such as interaction.

- *Behaviour versus meaning.* It is sometimes suggested that the quantitative researcher is concerned with people's behaviour and the qualitative researcher with the meaning of action.

- *Artificial settings versus natural settings.* Whereas quantitative researchers conduct research in a contrived context, qualitative researchers investigate people in natural environments.

However, as we will see in Chapter 26, while these contrasts depict reasonably well the differences between quantitative and qualitative research, they should not be viewed as constituting hard and fast distinctions.

Similarities between quantitative and qualitative research

It is also worth bearing in mind the ways in which quantitative and qualitative research are *similar* rather than different, as Hardy and Bryman (2004) have pointed out. They draw attention to the following points.

- *Both are concerned with data reduction*. Both quantitative and qualitative researchers collect large amounts of data. These large amounts of data represent a problem for researchers, because they then have to distil the data. By reducing the amount of data, they can then begin to make sense of it. In quantitative research, the process of data reduction takes the form of statistical analysis—something like a mean or frequency table is a way of reducing the amount of data on large numbers of people. In qualitative data analysis, as will be seen in Chapter 24, qualitative researchers develop concepts out of their often rich data.

- *Both are concerned with answering research questions*. Although the kinds of research questions asked in quantitative and qualitative research are typically different (more specific in quantitative research, more open-ended in qualitative research), both approaches are fundamentally concerned with answering questions about the nature of social reality.

- *Both are concerned with relating data analysis to the research literature*. Both quantitative and qualitative researchers are typically concerned to relate their findings to points thrown up by the literature relating to the topics on which they work. In other words, the researcher's findings take on significance in large part when they are related to the literature.

- *Both are concerned with variation*. In different ways, both quantitative and qualitative researchers seek to uncover variation and then to represent the variation that they uncover. This means that both groups of researchers are keen to explore how organizations (or whatever the unit of analysis is) differ and to explore some of the factors connected to that variation, although, once again, the *form* that variation takes differs.

- *Both treat frequency as a springboard for analysis*. In quantitative research, frequency is a core outcome of collecting data, as the investigator typically wants to reveal the relative frequency with which certain types of behaviour occur or how many newspaper articles emphasize a certain issue. In qualitative research, issues of frequency arise in the fact that, in reports of findings in publications, such terms as 'often' or 'most' are commonly employed. Also, when analysing qualitative data, the frequency with which certain themes occur commonly informs which ones tend to be emphasized when writing up findings.

- *Both seek to ensure that deliberate distortion does not occur*. Few business researchers nowadays subscribe to the view that it is possible to be an entirely objective and dispassionate student of organizational life. As discussed in Chapter 2, personal values often play a significant role in the selection of research topics and the approach to study taken by business researchers. However, that does not imply that 'anything goes'. In particular, researchers seek to ensure that 'wilful bias' (Hammersley and Gomm 2000) or what Hardy and Bryman (2004: 7) call 'consciously motivated misrepresentation' does not occur.

- *Both argue for the importance of transparency*. Both quantitative and qualitative researchers seek to be clear about their research procedures and how their findings were arrived at. This allows others to judge the quality and importance of their work. In the past, it has been suggested that some qualitative researchers were opaque about how they went about their investigations, but increasingly transparency is an expectation.

- *Both must address the question of error*. In Chapter 9, we introduced the significance of error for quantitative research (or, more specifically, survey research) and the steps that can be taken to reduce its likelihood. For the quantitative researcher, error must be reduced as far as possible so that the investigator can be confident that any variation uncovered is real, and not the product of problems with how questions are asked or how research instruments are administered. In qualitative research, the investigator seeks to reduce error by ensuring that, for example, there is a good fit between his or her concepts and the evidence that has been amassed.

- *Research methods should be appropriate to the research questions*. This is not addressed by Hardy and Bryman (2004), but a further issue is that both groups of researchers seek to ensure that, when they specify research questions, they select research methods and approaches to the analysis of data that are appropriate to those questions.

These tend to be rather general points of similarity, but they are an important corrective to any view that portrays the two approaches as completely different. There *are* differences between quantitative and qualitative research, but that is not to say that there are no points of similarity.

Researcher–participant relationships

A further difference between quantitative and qualitative research arises from the way that qualitative researchers relate to research participants. Qualitative researchers tend to take greater account of the power relations that exist between the researcher himself or herself and the people who are the subject of study. This has led to the development of several qualitative approaches that enable research participants to play a more active part in designing the research and to influence the outcomes of the process. Action research, feminist, collaborative, and participative forms of enquiry all fall into this category. We will consider the main features of each of these approaches and explore the implications that they have for researcher–participant relationships.

Action research

There is no single type of action research, but business researchers generally characterize it as an approach to study in which there is an explicit commitment 'towards achieving social or organizational change at various levels through intense contact between researcher and community members researched' (Burns et al. 2014: 133). A common theme concerns the need for research to be useful to research participants. Action research is therefore based on close 'involvement with members of an organization' over a matter that is of 'genuine concern to them' (Eden and Huxham 1996: 75). The action researcher works closely with the research community to co-produce knowledge that is of mutual benefit. Action research is defined by Argyris et al. (1985) as follows:

- Experiments are on real problems within an organization and are designed to assist in their solution.
- This involves an iterative process of problem identification, planning, action, and evaluation.
- Action research leads eventually to re-education, changing patterns of thinking, and action. This depends on working closely with research participants (sometimes referred to in action research as 'clients') in identifying new courses of action.

- It is intended to contribute both to academic theory and practical action.

Eden and Huxham (1996) define the characteristics of action research in terms of outcomes and processes. Good and effective action research should have the following outcomes.

- It should have implications that relate to situations other than the one that is studied.
- As well as being usable in everyday life, action research should also be concerned with theory.
- It should lead to the generation of emergent or grounded theory, which emanates from the data in gradual incremental steps.
- Action researchers must recognize that their findings will have practical implications and they should be clear about what they expect participants to take away from the project.
- The collection of data is likely to be involved in the formulation of the diagnosis of a problem and in the evaluation of a problem. Data collection methods can include keeping a diary of subjective impressions, a collection of documents relating to a situation, observation notes of meetings, questionnaire surveys, interviews, audio or video recordings of meetings, and written descriptions of meetings or interviews (which may be given to participants for them to validate or amend). In action research, the investigator becomes part of the field of study, and, as with participant observation, this has its own attendant problems. In their action research study of an outpatient health centre, Ramirez and Bartunek (1989) found themselves caught up in a conflict about organizational roles and loyalties. Some members of the organization began to spread rumours intended to discredit the action researcher (who was an internal consultant), suggesting that she was using the project to further her career within the organization.

17.10 RESEARCH IN FOCUS
Using visual methods in participatory action research study of a Ghanaian cocoa value chain

McCarthy and Muthury (2016) suggest that business and society researchers have tended to overlook those with less power, including women, non-literate people, and indigenous peoples, referring to them as 'fringe stakeholders'. They attribute this oversight in part to the dominance of quantitative methods within this field, which are insensitive to issues of power in research relationships. Instead, business and society research has tended to prioritize the collection of data from leaders of workers' groups, including trades unions, NGOs, and managers. McCarthy and Muthury argue that visual participatory methods provide a means of addressing this gap, by enabling groups with less power to participate more effectively in research.

Their study was a case study of Ghanaian cocoa farmers, focusing on gender equality issues. The researchers ran participant workshops with a translator, a cooperative supplier, and 48 cocoa farmers in four villages in Ghana. The researchers used participant-produced drawings and group discussion as the main sources of data. One of the benefits of this method was that it helped to overcome difficulties associated with studying groups that have low levels of literacy. The image data and focus group discussions were analysed thematically in **NVivo** (the use of NVivo will be covered in Chapter 25).

One of the drawing exercises involved asking participants to draw a 'gender tree' in the form of a simple image of a tree with roots and branches (see Plate 17.6 for an example). On one side of the tree participants were asked to represent women's work/expenditure or ownership, using a series of pictorial symbols to indicate the type of activity (Plate 17.7), and on the other men's work/expenditure or ownership. In the middle they were asked to indicate shared work/expenditure or ownership. In facilitated, same-sex focus groups (focus groups are covered in Chapter 21), participants were subsequently asked questions about whether the tree was 'balanced'. Crucially, the participant-produced drawings provided a basis for discussion through which the farmers and suppliers were able to explore the reasons for women's marginalization from cocoa farming, as a consequence of unequal distribution of domestic work, and to think about how these inequalities could be addressed in future.

Burns et al. (2014) use the term 'participatory organizational research' to refer to a specific type of action-oriented research that is concerned with enabling 'less powerful members of organizations, those who may normally go unheard, to gain a voice' (2014: 134). P. Park (1999) describes participatory research as focused on disempowered groups who can be helped through research that addresses problems related to their welfare in an organized way. The researcher should ideally be someone who is familiar with the community and committed to working towards improving their conditions. This, he argues, is what differentiates participatory research from other types of action research which is concerned only with solving problems of an organizational, job-related nature. Burns et al. (2014) suggest that participatory organizational research is especially important in studies that involve vulnerable groups who might otherwise be at a power disadvantage in their

interactions with researchers. Their particular study focused on the treatment of older people living in care homes. Key to their use of this method was the organization of panel group meetings where residents met with other stakeholders to engage in open discussion. The creation of spaces for people to engage openly with one another enabled issues to be raised that might otherwise have gone unexplored. For an example of participatory action research using visual methods, see Research in focus 17.10.

Action research is criticized, in a similar way to other qualitative methods, for its lack of repeatability and consequent lack of rigour and for concentrating too much on organizational action at the expense of research findings. In their defence, action researchers claim that involvement with practitioners concerning issues that are important to them provides a richness of insight that cannot be gained in other ways. It is also

PLATE 17.6

Gender tree and summary explanations, drawn by female participant in Western Region, Ghana

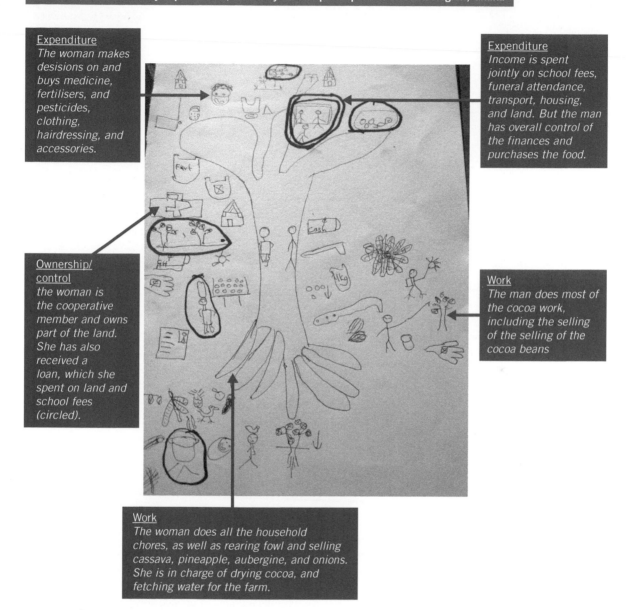

Expenditure
The woman makes desisions on and buys medicine, fertilisers, and pesticides, clothing, hairdressing, and accessories.

Expenditure
Income is spent jointly on school fees, funeral attendance, transport, housing, and land. But the man has overall control of the finances and purchases the food.

Ownership/control
the woman is the cooperative member and owns part of the land. She has also received a loan, which she spent on land and school fees (circled).

Work
The man does most of the cocoa work, including the selling of the selling of the cocoa beans

Work
The woman does all the household chores, as well as rearing fowl and selling cassava, pineapple, aubergine, and onions. She is in charge of drying cocoa, and fetching water for the farm.

Source: Copyright McCarthy and Muthury (2016). Reproduced with thanks.

---

claimed that theory generated from action research is 'grounded in action' (Eden and Huxham 1996), thereby overcoming some of the difficulties of relying on talk as a source of data, instead of action or overt behaviour.

Action research should not be confused with **evaluation research** (see Key concept 3.9), which usually denotes the study of the impact of an intervention, such as a new social policy or a new innovation in organizations.

Feminism and qualitative research

A further dimension to this discussion is that, in the view of some writers, qualitative research is aligned with feminist philosophical principles, whereas quantitative research is not. **Feminist research** has an important role to play in business research, which is often designed and conducted from implicitly male or masculine perspectives (see Thinking deeply 17.11).

PLATE 17.7
Example of symbols co-created between researchers and local staff

Source: Copyright McCarthy and Muthury (2016). Reproduced with thanks.

Note: from top left, symbols represent work including—

Cocoa work: planting cocoa seeds, weeding, clearing land, fermenting, drying, bagging, fertilising/spraying pesticides, cutting open pods, carrying cocoa, selling, harvesting.

Other paid work: growing cassava, bananas/plantain, tomatoes, aubergine; palm oil processing; tailoring; trading small goods; growing maize, onions; batik making; soap making; gari proceessing; mechanic; taxi driving; carpentry.

Unpaid work: cooking; childcare; sweeping; cooperative membership; carrying water; carrying firewood; washing and drying clothes; cooperative committee membership.

17.11 THINKING DEEPLY
Feminist research in business

Organizational research has typically been pursued from a male-orientated perspective, which, according to Wilson (1995), regards men and women as alike and fails to consider gender as a significant variable within organizational processes. To illustrate this, Wilson cites the example of the Hawthorne studies (see Research in focus 3.7), which involved the observational study of a group of female employees in the 'test room' and a group of male employees in the 'bank wiring room'. 'The men were observed under normal working conditions while the female group was pressured, by male supervisors, into an experimental situation. Despite the fact that output was increased by the women and restricted by the men, the overall findings were presented as an explanation of the behaviour of employees *per se*' (1995: 1–2). Other studies have tended to treat women as entirely peripheral to organizational life. This bias is particularly evident in the study of management. As the majority of managers are men, studies of management have mainly focused on observation of male managers. Therefore, recommendations about what makes effective management often erroneously assume that better managers are more masculine, reinforcing this masculine gender stereotype. Despite the growth of feminist research in various disciplines, much of this has occurred outside the boundaries of business research. If, as Wilson suggests, we need to 'see reality differently' and reformulate the way in which work organizations are understood, feminist methods provide a means whereby male-orientated values can be exposed and challenged.

Quantitative research is frequently viewed as incompatible with feminism for the following reasons:

- Mies (1993) argues that quantitative research suppresses the voices of women either by ignoring them or by researching women in a value-neutral way, when in fact the goal of feminist research should be to conduct research specifically *for* women.

- The criterion of validity, which is commonly associated with quantitative research, turns women, when they are the focus of research, into objects. This means that women are subjected to exploitation, in that knowledge and experience are extracted from them with nothing in return, even when the research is conducted by women (Mies 1993).

- The emphasis on controlling variables adds to this, if the idea of control is viewed as a masculine approach to study.

- The use of predetermined categories in quantitative research emphasizes what is already known and consequently perpetuates 'the silencing of women's own voices' (Maynard 1998: 128).

- The quest for universal laws may be inconsistent with feminism's emphasis on the situated nature of social reality, which is seen as embedded in social identities (based on gender, ethnicity, sexual orientation, class, etc.) that are unique to individuals (Miner-Rubino et al. 2007).

By contrast, qualitative research is viewed by many feminists as either more compatible with feminism's central ideas or as more capable of being adapted to its purpose because it allows:

- women's voices to be heard;

- exploitation to be reduced by giving as well as by receiving in the course of fieldwork (for an example of personal connections made during the course of fieldwork, see Research in focus 17.12);

- women to be researched without attempts being made to control them through the researcher's application of technical procedures; and consequently,

- the emancipatory goals of feminism to be furthered.

How qualitative research contributes towards these goals will be addressed in Chapters 19, 20, and 21, by looking at feminist approaches to ethnography, qualitative interviewing, and focus groups. However, business research has a tendency to ignore or marginalize gender in terms of the way that research topics are defined. Mirchandani (1999) observes that research on women's experiences of entrepreneurship focuses on identifying similarities and differences between female and male business-owners, and on providing explanations of these differences. She argues that, although this is useful in compensating for the exclusion of women in earlier studies, it does not explain why entrepreneurship is defined and understood only in terms of the behaviour of men. Mirchandani argues that the construction of the category

17.12 RESEARCH IN FOCUS
A feminist analysis of embodied identity at work

The subject of embodied identities at work has attracted interest from feminist researchers, who see feminist theories as key to understanding how women's bodies are treated in the workplace. Trethewey (1999), a Foucauldian feminist, interviewed 19 professional women about their definitions and experiences of their professional bodies using the friendship model of interviewing (Oakley 1981), explained in Chapter 20. Trethewey explains: 'I felt more comfortable approaching the participants as friends rather than as subjects or data. I have since formed friendships with several of the participants, have joined the reading group of another participant, and was invited to participate in a local women's mentoring committee by yet another participant' (1999: 427). This shows how feminist researchers seek to break down the boundaries between the researcher and (female) research participants as a means of trying to make the research relationship more equal.

of 'the female entrepreneur' prioritizes gender over other important aspects of identity, such as social stratification, business ownership, organizational structure, and industry, that need to be explored in relation to female *and* male business-owners.

However, some feminist researchers are positive towards quantitative research. Some of their arguments follow:

- The worst discrimination against women might not have been recognized so clearly if not for the collection and analysis of statistics revealing exclusion (Maynard 1994; Oakley 1998). Factual evidence of this kind allows the case for equal opportunities legislation to be made much more clearly, for example.

- Miner-Rubino et al. (2007) suggest that knowledge about the distribution of attitudes and behaviours in a sample can be used to establish the most appropriate course of action for social change.

- As Jayaratne and Stewart (1991) and Maynard (1994, 1998) note, research that combines quantitative and qualitative methods is not incompatible with the feminist cause.

- There has also been a recognition of the fact that qualitative research is not *ipso facto* feminist in orientation. If, for example, ethnography (see Chapter 19) *required* a feminist sensitivity, we would expect subjects such as social anthropology, which have been virtually founded on the approach, to be almost inherently feminist, which is definitely not the case (Reinharz 1992: 47–8). The answer to the question 'What are the best approaches to feminist research?' seems to lie in the *application* of methods rather than in something that is inherent in them. Consequently, some writers have preferred to write about *feminist*

research practice rather than about *feminist methods* (Maynard 1998: 128).

Postcolonial and indigenous research

A further way in which researcher–participant relationships have been challenged in recent years is through postcolonialist critique of practices of social scientific knowledge production, which are based on a conception of research which developed in the countries of Europe and North America that was subsequently exported to the global South. This relies on the assertion that 'social science can have only one, universal, body of concepts and methods, the one created in the global North' (Connell 2007: ix). Writers such as Connell challenge this by exposing the hidden biases contained within theories produced from within the global North which claim universal relevance based on the assumption that 'all societies are knowable, and they are knowable in the same way and from the same point of view' (Connell 2007: 44). Such an approach is suggested to be inherently colonizing, involving the abandonment of local cultural knowledge and the imposition of discourses of scientific research that are claimed to be neutral but that involve the assertion of imperialist neocolonial power relations of oppression and domination. This can be seen from the ways in which scientific research has been used as a tool of colonialist exploitation: for example, Prasad (2003) points out that ethnography (see Chapter 19) was used in the nineteenth century and the early twentieth by imperialist European powers of Britain, France, and the Netherlands, to gather data about Asian and African cultures which enabled their subjugation and explanation, 'by carving out identities of the Western self and

17.13 RESEARCH IN FOCUS
Indigenous ways of understanding leadership

Warner and Grint (2006) explore Native American traditions of leadership which they assert can displace the imperialist foundations of the American approach to studying this subject and open up alternatives. One of the challenges they faced in this project related to the dominance of the English language, and the difficulty of translating meanings from indigenous cultural contexts: 'when discussing leadership with American Indians whose second language is English, the first author sought to have them give their own tribal word for "leader"' (Warner and Grint 2006: 231). This prompted discussion of numerous terms related to leadership, which the authors found very difficult to translate in a way which preserved their cultural meaning. A key characteristic of their research involved an obligation actively to work with research participants to question the methods and processes of research, including the reliance on observation and the privileging of the written word, and to question what is actually meant by 'leadership'. They conclude 'that we need more studies of [Native American] leadership by insiders not simply of insiders if we are ever to get beyond a superficial comprehension of the "other"' (Warner and Grint 2006: 240).

the non-Western Other, and by delineating relationships between them through a series of hierarchical oppositional categories' (Prasad 2003: 155). She argues that the concept of the ethnographic imagination, based on discourses of primitivism, orientalism, and tropicalization, which the colonial project entailed, can still be seen in many recent ethnographic accounts of fieldwork which celebrate risky adventures in 'foreign' lands.

These critiques have opened up spaces for the construction of alternative approaches to knowledge production, in the form of indigenous research methodologies, a term which invites exploration of methods that enable the voices of colonized peoples to be heard, in addition to non-human interests related to ecosystems (Tuhiwai Smith 1999). Informed by feminist approaches to research, indigenous methodologies seek to disrupt established relationships between (mostly non-indigenous) researchers and indigenous peoples and enable

them to find their own academic voice and identity; the focus is thus on the ethics of research and the implications for communities of research. These ideas are potentially highly significant in understanding globalization and its effects in fields such as international and comparative management and business. For example, Jack and Westwood (2006) use ideas from postcolonialism to argue that researchers in these fields, even those committed to qualitative methods, have been slow to acknowledge the political nature of research in reflecting the interests and values of the researcher. They propose an alternative, in the form of a postcolonial epistemology which enables the universalizing tendencies of Western knowledge systems, which construct and legitimate the dominance of the West as a source of knowledge about international business, to be resisted. Research in focus 17.13 provides an example of how these ideas have also been applied in the field of leadership.

KEY POINTS

....

- There is disagreement over what precisely qualitative research is.
- Qualitative research does not lend itself to the delineation of a clear set of linear steps.
- It tends to be a more open-ended research strategy than is typically the case with quantitative research.
- Theories and concepts are viewed as outcomes of the research process.
- Visual materials, such as photographs and video, have attracted considerable interest among qualitative business researchers in recent years, not just as adjuncts to data collection but as objects of interest in their own right.

- There is considerable unease about the simple application of the reliability and validity criteria associated with quantitative research to qualitative research. Indeed, some writers prefer to use alternative criteria that have parallels with reliability and validity.

- Most qualitative researchers reveal a preference for seeing the social world from the perspective of research participants.

- Several writers have depicted qualitative research as having a far greater affinity with a feminist standpoint than quantitative research.

- Action research, feminism, and indigenous methods of enquiry have changed the relationship between researchers and research participants.

QUESTIONS FOR REVIEW

- What are some of the difficulties with providing a general account of the nature of qualitative research?

- Outline some of the traditions of qualitative research.

- What are some of the main research methods associated with qualitative research?

The main steps in qualitative research

- Does a research question in qualitative research have the same significance and characteristics as in quantitative research?

Theory and research

- Is the approach to theory in qualitative research inductive or deductive?

Concepts in qualitative research

- What is the difference between definitive and sensitizing concepts?

Reliability and validity in qualitative research

- How have some writers adapted the notions of reliability and validity to qualitative research?

- Why have some writers sought alternative criteria for the evaluation of qualitative research?

- Evaluate Lincoln and Guba's criteria.

- What is respondent validation?

- What is triangulation?

The main preoccupations of qualitative researchers

- Outline the main preoccupations of qualitative researchers.

- How do these preoccupations differ from those of quantitative researchers, which were considered in Chapter 8?

The critique of qualitative research

- What are some of the main criticisms that are frequently levelled at qualitative research?

- To what extent do these criticisms reflect the preoccupations of quantitative research?

Is it always like this?

- Can qualitative research be employed in relation to hypothesis testing?

Some contrasts and similarities between quantitative and qualitative research

- 'The difference between quantitative and qualitative research revolves entirely around the concern with numbers in the former and with words in the latter.' How far do you agree with this statement?

Researcher–participant relationships

- What is action research?
- What is participatory organizational research and how has it been used by business researchers?
- What is the relationship between feminism and qualitative research and how might this be important in the study of business and management?
- What are the distinguishing features of indigenous and postcolonial methodologies and how can they be applied in business research?

....

ONLINE RESOURCES
www.oup.com/uk/brm5e/

Visit the Interactive Research Guide that accompanies this book to complete an exercise relating to the nature of qualitative research.

....

SAMPLING IN QUALITATIVE RESEARCH

CHAPTER OUTLINE

This chapter describes some of the main ways of thinking about conducting sampling in qualitative research. Whereas, in survey research, there is an emphasis on probability sampling, qualitative researchers tend to emphasize the importance of purposive sampling for their work. Purposive sampling places the investigator's research questions at the heart of the sampling considerations. This chapter explores:

- the significance of levels of sampling;
- the nature of purposive sampling and the reasons for the emphasis on it among many qualitative researchers;
- theoretical sampling, which is a key ingredient of the grounded theory approach, and the nature of theoretical saturation, which is one of the main elements of this sampling strategy;
- the importance of not assuming that theoretical and purposive sampling are the same thing;
- the generic purposive sampling approach as a means of distinguishing theoretical sampling from purposive sampling in general;
- the use of more than one sampling approach in qualitative research.

Introduction

In much the same way that, in quantitative research, the discussion of sampling revolves around probability sampling, discussions of sampling in qualitative research tend to revolve around the notion of purposive sampling (see Key concept 18.1). This type of sampling is essentially to do with the selection of units (which may be people, organizations, documents, departments, and so on), with direct reference to the research questions being asked. The idea is that the research questions should give an indication of what units need to be sampled. Research questions are likely to provide guidelines as to what categories of people (or whatever the unit of analysis is) need to be the focus of attention and therefore sampled. In this chapter, purposive sampling will act as the master concept around which different sampling approaches in qualitative research can be distinguished.

Probability sampling may be used in qualitative research, though it is more likely to occur in interview-based rather than in ethnographic qualitative studies. There is no obvious rule of thumb to help the qualitative researcher in deciding when it might be appropriate to employ probability sampling, but two criteria may be applied. First, if it is highly significant or important for the qualitative researcher to be able to generalize to a wider population, probability sampling is likely to be a more compelling sampling approach. This might occur when the audience for one's work is one for whom generalizability in the traditional sense of the word is important. Second, if the research questions do not suggest that particular categories of people (or whatever the unit of analysis is) should be sampled, there may be a case for sampling randomly.

However, in many cases, probability sampling is not feasible, because of the constraints of ongoing fieldwork and also because it can be difficult and often impossible to map 'the population' from which a random sample might be taken—that is, to create a sampling frame. However, the reason why qualitative researchers rarely seek to generate random samples is not due to these technical constraints but because, like researchers basing their investigations on qualitative interviewing, they typically want to ensure that they gain access to as wide a range of individuals relevant to their research questions as possible, so that many different perspectives and ranges of activity are the focus of attention.

18.1 KEY CONCEPT
What is purposive sampling?

Purposive sampling is a non-probability form of sampling. The researcher does not seek to sample research participants on a random basis. The goal of purposive sampling is to sample cases/participants in a strategic way, so that those sampled are relevant to the research questions that are being posed. Very often, the researcher will want to sample in order to ensure that there is a good deal of variety in the resulting sample, so that sample members differ from each other in terms of key characteristics relevant to the research question. Because it is a non-probability sampling approach, purposive sampling does not allow the researcher to generalize to a population. Although a purposive sample is not a random sample, it is not a convenience sample either (see Chapter 9 for a description of convenience sampling). A convenience sample is simply available by chance to the researcher, whereas in purposive sampling the researcher samples with his or her research goals in mind. In purposive sampling, sites, such as organizations, and people (or whatever the unit of analysis is) within sites, are selected because of their relevance to the research questions. The researcher needs to be clear in his or her mind what the criteria are that will be relevant to the inclusion or exclusion of units of analysis (whether the 'units' are sites, people, or something else). Examples of purposive sampling in qualitative research are theoretical sampling (see Key concept 18.3 and, for an example, Research in focus 18.5) and snowball sampling (see Research in focus 18.6 for an example). In quantitative research, quota sampling is a form of purposive sampling.

Levels of sampling

Writers on sampling in qualitative research sometimes provide lists of the different sampling approaches that may be found (see Key concept 18.2 for some of the main types that are frequently identified). While these are useful, they sometimes intermingle two different levels of sampling, an issue that is particularly relevant to the consideration of sampling in qualitative research based on single case study or multiple case study designs. With such research designs, the researcher must first select the case or cases; subsequently, the researcher must sample units within the case. When sampling contexts or cases, qualitative researchers have a number of principles of purposive sampling on which to draw. To a significant extent, the ideas and principles behind these were introduced in Chapter 3 in connection with the different types of case, particularly following Yin's (2009) classification.

An example is a study by Pringle (1988) of power relations and secretarial work. This study involved interviews with secretarial students and with a range of workers, both secretarial and non-secretarial, in a variety of Australian workplaces. The first stage of this process involved groups of three secretarial students who were interviewed for 20–30 minutes about their course. A smaller sample (*n* = 30) were interviewed again near the end of their course and then followed up as they entered the workforce. Fifteen were interviewed a third time individually at home and asked to reflect on the value of their course. The second stage of interviews was carried out in a representative range of workplaces. 'Of 244 interviews 72 were with employees in the public sector, 32 with unions, 92 with large corporations and 44 with small companies, agencies and partnerships' (Pringle 1988: 268). A breakdown of interviewees by occupation is given in Table 18.1.

18.2 KEY CONCEPT
Some purposive sampling approaches

The following is a list of some prominent types of purposive sample that have been identified by writers such as Patton (1990) and Palys (2008).

1. *Extreme or deviant case sampling*: sampling cases that are unusual or that are unusually at the far end(s) of a particular dimension of interest.

2. *Typical case sampling*: sampling a case because it exemplifies a dimension of interest.

3. *Critical case sampling*: sampling a crucial case that permits a logical inference about the phenomenon of interest—for example, a case might be chosen precisely because it is anticipated that it might allow a theory to be tested.

4. *Maximum variation sampling*: sampling to ensure as wide a variation as possible in terms of the dimension of interest.

5. *Criterion sampling*: sampling all units (cases or individuals) that meet a particular criterion.

6. *Theoretical sampling*: see Key concept 18.3.

7. *Snowball sampling*: see Research in focus 18.6.

8. *Opportunistic sampling*: capitalizing on opportunities to collect data from certain individuals, contact with whom is largely unforeseen but who may provide data relevant to the research question.

9. *Stratified purposive sampling*: sampling of usually typical cases or individuals within subgroups of interest.

The first three purposive sampling approaches are ones that are particularly likely to be employed in connection with the selection of cases or contexts. The others are likely to be used in connection with the sampling of individuals as well as cases or contexts.

TABLE 18.1
A stratified interview sample

Interviewees by occupation	Number	%
Top and middle management	54	22
Lower management	22	9
Administrative	18	7.5
Supervisory	9	3.5
Personal assistant	3	1.5
Secretary (1 boss)	67	27.5
Secretary (2+ bosses)	29	12
Word processor/typist	22	9
Clerical assistant	20	8
Total	244	100

Source: adapted from Pringle (1988).

Purposive sampling

Most sampling in qualitative research entails purposive sampling of some kind. What links the various kinds of purposive sampling approaches is that the sampling is conducted with reference to the goals of the research, so that units of analysis are selected in terms of criteria that will allow the research questions to be answered. This term is explained in Key concept 18.1.

In order to contextualize the discussion, we will draw on two useful distinctions that have been employed in relation to purposive sampling. First, Teddlie and Yu (2007) distinguish a sampling approach that they refer to as sequential sampling, which implies a distinction between sequential and non-sequential approaches. Non-sequential approaches to sampling might be termed 'fixed sampling strategies'. With a sequential approach, sampling is an evolving process in that the researcher usually begins with an initial sample and gradually adds to the sample as befits the research questions. Units are selected by virtue of their relevance to the research questions, and the sample is gradually added to as the investigation evolves. With a fixed purposive sampling strategy, the sample is more or less established at the outset of the research, and there is little or no adding to the sample as the research proceeds. The research questions guide the sampling approach, but the sample is more or less fixed early on in the research process. Second, Hood (2007) distinguishes between *a priori* and contingent sampling approaches. A purposive sampling approach is contingent when the criteria for sampling units of analysis evolve over the course of the research. The research questions again guide the sampling of participants, but the relevant sampling criteria shift over the course of the research as the research questions change or multiply. With an *a priori* purposive sample, the criteria for selecting participants are established at the outset of the research. The criteria will again be ones that are designed to answer the research questions, but the criteria do not evolve as the research progresses.

Theoretical sampling

One form of purposive sampling is theoretical sampling (see Key concept 18.3), advocated by Glaser and Strauss (1967) and Strauss and Corbin (1998) in the context of an approach to qualitative data analysis they developed known as grounded theory, which will be touched on here and discussed in greated depth in Chapter 24. In Glaser and Strauss's view, because of its reliance on statistical rather than theoretical criteria, probability sampling is not appropriate to qualitative research. Theoretical sampling is meant to be an alternative strategy. As they put it: 'Theoretical sampling is done in order to discover categories and their properties and to suggest the interrelationships into a theory. Statistical sampling is done to obtain accurate evidence on distributions of people among categories to be used in descriptions and

STUDENT EXPERIENCE
Purposive sampling in a student's research project

Anna's experience of **semi-structured interview** shows how interviewees may be selected purposively on the basis of their likely ability to contribute to theoretical understanding of a subject. Her qualitative study in the area of marketing ethics focused on the lived experience of women who become commercial egg donors and her chosen method was semi-structured interviewing. However, finding women who had experience of being a commercial egg donor who fitted the criteria for the study, and were willing to be interviewed, was challenging in a number of respects. As Anna explained: 'I had to find women who had donated in a commercial environment.' Although Anna was based in Australia, this led her to focus on finding women in the USA, where the commercial activity of egg donorship is legal. Further criteria for sampling were that the women had to have received compensation, to have donated to a complete stranger, and to have donated at least 12 months, and up to 20 years, ago. Anna then put out a call for participants:

> So the first thing I did was create a Facebook page for the study. Then I created an 'Expression of Interest Form' on Google forms. I used that link to put on the Facebook page and created some flyers. Then I created a Facebook advertisement which targeted potential women within Facebook. I was targeting people who had gone to university because we know that the women who go to prestigious universities are targeted through advertising for a donation.

Having communicated the information about her research project to prospective participants, she waited to see if they would respond, by completing an 'Expression of Interest Form' and emailing this to her. Over 20 women responded to her in this way. Eventually, and based on further filtering according to her sampling criteria, her purposive strategy resulted in a sample of 10 US-based women whom she interviewed via Skype.

18.3 KEY CONCEPT
What is theoretical sampling?

According to Glaser and Strauss (1967: 45), theoretical sampling 'is the process of data collection for generating theory whereby the analyst jointly collects, **codes**, and analyzes his data and decides what data to collect next and where to find them, in order to develop his theory as it emerges. The process of data collection is *controlled* by the emerging theory, whether substantive or formal.' This definition conveys a crucial characteristic of theoretical sampling—namely, that it is an ongoing process rather than a distinct and single stage, as it is, for example, in probability sampling. Moreover, it is important to realize that it is not just people who are the 'objects' of sampling, as can be seen in a more recent definition: 'Data gathering driven by concepts derived from the evolving theory and based on the concept of "making comparisons," whose purpose is to go to places, people, or events that will maximize opportunities to discover variations among concepts and to densify categories in terms of their properties and dimensions' (Strauss and Corbin 1998: 201). For Charmaz (2000: 519), theoretical sampling is a 'defining property of grounded theory' and is concerned with the refinement of the theoretical categories that emerge in the course of analysing data that have been collected, rather than boosting sample size. Theoretical sampling differs from generic purposive sampling, which is outlined below, in that its practitioners emphasize using it to provide a springboard for the generation of theory and the refinement of theoretical categories. It is **iterative** in the sense that it is not a one-off but an ongoing process that entails several stages. It emphasizes theoretical saturation (see Key concept 18.4) as a criterion for deciding when to cease collecting new data on a particular theoretical idea and to move on to the investigation of some ramifications of the emerging theory.

verifications' (Glaser and Strauss 1967: 62). What distinguishes theoretical sampling from other sampling approaches is the emphasis on the selection of cases and units with reference to the quest for the generation of a theoretical understanding. Figure 18.1 outlines the main steps in theoretical sampling.

In grounded theory, you carry on collecting data (observing, interviewing, collecting documents) through theoretical sampling until theoretical saturation (see Key concept 18.4) has been achieved. This means that successive interviews/observations have both formed the basis for the creation of a category and confirmed its importance, and there is no need to continue with data collection in relation to that category or cluster of categories; instead, the researcher should move on and generate hypotheses out of the categories that are building up and then move on to collecting data in relation to these hypotheses. As Charmaz (2006) puts it, when new data no longer stimulate new theoretical understandings or new dimensions of the principal theoretical categories, the relevant categories are saturated. Proponents of grounded theory argue that there is a great deal of redundancy in statistical sampling. For example, committing yourself to interviewing x per cent of an organization's members may mean that you end up wasting time and

resources because you could have confirmed the significance of a concept and/or its connections with other concepts by using a much smaller sample. Instead, grounded theory advocates that you sample in terms of what is relevant to and meaningful for your theory. The key is to ensure you sample so as to test your emerging theoretical ideas. The approach is supposed to be an iterative one—that is, one in which there is a movement backwards and forwards between sampling and theoretical reflection—but it may be that the researcher feels that his or her categories achieve theoretical saturation (see Key concept 18.4) at a relatively early stage. For example, for their research on organization dress, referred to in Research in focus 20.5, Rafaeli et al. (1997: 14) initially 'identified a stratified random sample of 20 people from the population of full-time, permanent administrative employees in the organization' (1997: 13–14). They then evaluated their data 'after completing interviews with the 20 individuals selected and concluded that, because we had reached theoretical saturation (Glaser and Strauss 1967), no additional interviews were necessary'. The use of theoretical saturation as a criterion for deciding when to cease further sampling does not necessarily imply that a theoretical sampling approach has been employed. This is suggested by the quotation from Rafaeli et al., where there is no suggestion of an iterative movement between sampling and theory development. What we see here is an approach that is more redolent of what we call below a generic purposive sampling approach than of theoretical sampling.

A sampling approach that is more in tune with Glaser and Strauss's (1967) idea of theoretical sampling is provided by Treviño et al. (2014) in their study of ethics and compliance officers (see Research in focus 18.5). The chief virtue of theoretical sampling is that the emphasis is upon using theoretical reflection on data as the guide to whether more data are needed. It therefore places a premium on theorizing rather than the statistical adequacy of a sample, which may be a limited guide to sample selection in many instances. However, O'Reilly and Parker (2013) argue that the notion of theoretical saturation has become overused in qualitative research in generic ways that do not respect the true meaning of the term or the diversity of qualitative research methods. Crucially, they distinguish between data saturation, which is when sampling continues until no new findings are generated, and theoretical saturation, which involves continuing to sample until conceptual categories are fully developed and relationships between them are accounted for. This latter usage is integral to the approach of grounded theory, which will be examined in

FIGURE 18.1

The process of theoretical sampling

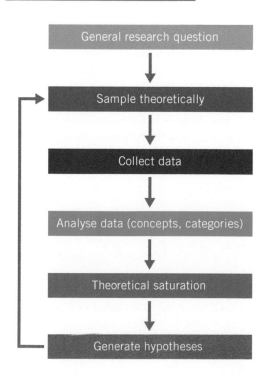

General research question

↓

Sample theoretically

↓

Collect data

↓

Analyse data (concepts, categories)

↓

Theoretical saturation

↓

Generate hypotheses

18.4 KEY CONCEPT
What is theoretical saturation?

The key idea is that you carry on sampling theoretically until a category has been saturated with data. 'This means, until (*a*) no new or relevant data seem to be emerging regarding a category, (*b*) the category is well developed in terms of its properties and dimensions demonstrating variation, and (*c*) the relationships among categories are well established and validated' (Strauss and Corbin 1998: 212). In the language of grounded theory, a category operates at a somewhat higher level of abstraction than a concept in that it may group together several concepts that have common features denoted by the category. Saturation does not mean, as is sometimes suggested, that the researcher develops a sense of déjà vu when listening to what people say in interviews but that new data no longer suggest new insights into an emergent theory or new dimensions of theoretical categories.

18.5 RESEARCH IN FOCUS
An example of theoretical sampling

Treviño et al. (2014) conducted an interview study of 40 ethics and compliance officers in order to address research questions relating to the origins of the role in the officers' respective organizations and the nature of their work. Initially, they sampled a varied group of officers, so that their first sampling approach was influenced by purposive sampling. Then they used the insights gleaned from their early examination of their data to establish who to interview next. Thus, their initial analysis of their data from the first sampling phase influenced which officers should be interviewed next in order to flesh out and elaborate their emerging theoretical understanding of the data.

greater detail in the context of qualitative data analysis in Chapter 24. O'Reilly and Parker are also critical of the lack of transparency that surrounds the notion of saturation, as researchers rarely explain in a transparent way how this was achieved. Further, in the context of inductive research, they suggest that data saturation may be an unrealistic target, as the number of themes emerging from a dataset is potentially limitless.

Generic purposive sampling

Hood (2007: 152) has usefully pointed out that there is a tendency among many writers and researchers to 'identify all things qualitative with "grounded theory"'. This is particularly the case with the notion of theoretical sampling, which is often treated as synonymous with purposive sampling when in fact it is one form of purposive sampling (see Key concept 18.3). Hood usefully contrasts grounded theory with what she calls a 'generic inductive qualitative model', which is relatively open-ended and emphasizes the generation of concepts and

theories but does not entail (among other things) the iterative sampling style of grounded theory. Sampling considerations are particularly prominent in this contrast between grounded theory and the generic inductive qualitative model. Whereas, as we have seen, theoretical sampling is a sequential sampling process whereby sampling is conducted in order to develop theoretical categories and inferences, in the generic inductive qualitative model, sampling is conducted purposively but not necessarily with regard to the generation of theory and theoretical categories. We are going to call this sampling approach *generic purposive sampling*, a category that subsumes several of the sampling strategies identified in Key concept 18.2, though not theoretical sampling. Generic purposive sampling may be employed in a sequential or in a fixed manner and the criteria for selecting cases or individuals may be formed *a priori* (for example, socio-demographic criteria) or be contingent or a mixture of both. In most of the examples discussed in this book, generic purposive sampling is fixed and *a priori*. However, the criteria employed are ones that are informed by the research questions. When using a generic purposive sampling approach with respect to the selection of cases or contexts, the researcher establishes criteria concerning the kinds of cases needed to address the research questions, identifies appropriate cases, and then samples from those cases that have been identified. When contexts are being sampled, it is common for some form of generic purposive sampling to be employed.

In business research, generic purposive sampling is often used to gain an insight into a wide range of roles within an organization. For example, Casey (1995) describes how she interviewed 60 people during her research at the Hephaestus Corporation, in an effort to gain a wide sample of occupation, rank, tenure, and demographic features such as gender, race, ethnicity, and regional origin. She goes on to describe how interviewees came from a variety of occupational groupings, including engineers, computer professionals, scientists, technical analysts, financial analysts, administrators, managers, and manufacturing workers. Finally, some individuals were chosen on the basis of their strategic importance within the team or division, including the vice-president, a union representative, a new entry employee, and a returned retiree. The primary stratifying criteria, then, were at occupational and strategic levels.

Generic purposive sampling (or variations of it) is often employed in relation to the selection of participants. For their study of the meaning of work–life balance issues for trade union representatives in two sectors (retailing and media), Rigby and O'Brien-Smith (2010) selected a purposive sample based on three criteria: making sure that representatives were at each of three levels (national officials, full-time officials, and lay representatives); union respondents were at 'better organised workplaces' (2010: 206); and there was variety in

the geographical location of the representatives who were interviewed. Finally, for the research referred to in Research in focus 20.6, the authors purposively sampled employees from each of six quite different organizations. They write: 'We aimed for diversity in terms of age, organization and occupation, and approximately equal numbers of men and women. Our assumption was that this would maximize the likelihood of accessing variation and highlight any common core of experience more than a homogeneous sample would' (Bosley et al. 2009: 1499). What we see in all these examples is a quest for appropriate samples in terms of the research questions in which the researcher is interested.

Snowball sampling

In certain respects, snowball sampling is a form of convenience sample, but it is worth distinguishing because it has attracted quite a lot of attention over the years. With this approach to sampling, the researcher makes initial contact with a small group of people who are relevant to the research topic and then uses these to establish contacts with others. Bryman used an approach like this to create a sample of British visitors to Disney theme parks (Bryman 1999). Another example of snowball sampling is given in the study by Venter et al. (2005) (see Research in focus 18.6), where this technique was used to identify owner-managers and successors of small and medium-sized family businesses in South Africa. A snowball sample is in no sense random, because there is no way of knowing the precise extent of the population from which it would have to be drawn. In other words, there is no accessible sampling frame for the population from which the sample is to be taken, and the difficulty of creating such a sampling frame means that such an

---

STUDENT EXPERIENCE
Stratified sampling in a student's research project

Lucie's interview sampling strategy within the organization she was studying was based on stratified sampling in order to understand how the concept of enterprise was understood at different levels of the organization.

There aren't that many staff in the institute and the main people basically oversee everything. So I interviewed the Director and the Administrator, because they were the people that I was dealing with, so they were the easiest to access for an interview I suppose. And then I interviewed a few people who worked as temps just to get their perspective, because obviously the Director and the Administrator, they'd be very positive about their institute. So I wanted to get a smaller person's—if that's the right word—perspective on the institute as well, to see whether that was how it was really run.

approach is the only feasible one. Moreover, even if one could create a sampling frame of 'strategic decision-makers' or of 'British visitors to Disney theme parks', it would almost certainly be inaccurate straight away, because this is a shifting population. People will constantly be becoming and ceasing to be associated with the decision-making network, while new theme park visitors are arriving all the time. The problem with snowball sampling is that it is very unlikely that the sample will be representative of the population, though, as we have just suggested, the very notion of a population may be problematic in some circumstances. However, by and large, snowball sampling is used not within a quantitative research strategy, but within a qualitative one: both Franwick's and Bryman's studies were carried out within a predominantly qualitative research framework. Concerns about external validity and the ability to generalize do not loom as large within a qualitative research strategy as they do in a quantitative research one (see Chapters 8 and 17). In qualitative research, the orientation to sampling is more likely to be guided by a preference for *theoretical sampling* than with the kind of statistical sampling that has been the focus of this chapter. There is a much better 'fit' between snowball sampling and the theoretical sampling strategy of qualitative research than with the statistical sampling approach of quantitative research. This is not to suggest that snowball sampling is entirely irrelevant to quantitative research: when the researcher needs to focus upon or to reflect relationships between people, tracing connections through snowball sampling may be a better approach than conventional probability sampling (J. S. Coleman 1958).

Snowball sampling is a sampling technique in which the researcher samples initially a small group of people relevant to the research questions, and these sampled participants propose other participants who have had the experience or characteristics relevant to the research. These participants will then suggest others and so on. As noted in Chapter 9, it is sometimes (though rarely) used in survey research when probability sampling is more or less impossible. It is also sometimes recommended when networks of individuals are the focus of attention (Coleman 1958). In fact, Noy (2008) points out that snowball sampling is frequently presented as a strategy to be employed when probability sampling is impossible or not feasible—for example, when trying to sample hard-to-reach populations because of the absence of a sampling frame. This is often how it is represented in discussions of its use in survey research and sometimes in qualitative research too (see Research in focus 18.6). However, Noy observes that one advantage the technique offers is that it is able simultaneously to capitalize on and to reveal the connectedness of individuals in networks.

The sampling of informants in ethnographic research is sometimes a combination of opportunistic sampling and snowball sampling. Much of the time ethnographers are forced to gather information from whatever sources are available to them. Very often they face opposition or at least indifference to their research and are relieved to glean information or views from whoever is prepared to divulge such details. An example of opportunistic sampling is provided by Jackall (1988), who went into several large organizations in order to study how bureaucracy shapes moral consciousness. Analysis of the occupational

18.6 RESEARCH IN FOCUS
A snowball sample

Venter et al. (2005) were interested in factors that influence the succession process in small and medium-sized family businesses. Their initial intention was to obtain access to a mailing list of small and medium-sized family businesses in South Africa from banks and other large organizations that had family businesses as clients. This would then have formed the basis of their sample. However, these large organizations declined to share their client information with the research team, which instead used snowball sampling. This involved research associates, who were employed in different regions of the country, contacting small and medium-sized businesses with the aim of identifying those that were family businesses. Potential respondents were then asked to refer the researchers on to other family businesses that they knew about. As the researchers explain, 'following up on referrals proved to be the most effective approach and eventually yielded the majority of the potential respondents listed on the sampling frame' (2005: 291). A questionnaire survey was then mailed to 2458 respondents, comprising current owner-managers, potential successors, successors, and retiring owner-managers in 1038 family businesses, and a total of 332 usable questionnaires were returned.

ethics of corporate managers was based on core data of 143 intensive, semi-structured interviews with managers at every level of the organization. This formed the basis for selection of a smaller stratified group of 12 managers, who were reinterviewed several times and asked to interpret materials that Jackall was collecting. However, as the study progressed Jackall realized that an investigation of organizational morality should also explore managerial dissenters, or 'whistleblowers'—individuals who had taken stands against their organizations on grounds that they defined as moral. Between 1982 and 1988, Jackall conducted case studies of these dissenters, interviewing 18 'whistleblowers' and reviewing large amounts of documentary evidence. In order to explore managerial morality further, he then presented these cases to the stratified group of 12 managers and asked them 'to assess the dissenters' actions and motives by their own standards' (1988: 206).

Sample size

One of the problems that the qualitative researcher faces is that it can be difficult to establish at the outset how many people will be interviewed if theoretical considerations guide selection. It is impossible to know, for example, how many people should be interviewed before theoretical saturation has been achieved. To a certain extent, this is not helped by the fact that the criteria for recognizing or establishing when or whether saturation has been achieved are rarely articulated in detail (Guest et al. 2006). Also, as an investigation proceeds, it may become apparent that groups will need to be interviewed who were not anticipated at the outset. This necessity arose because parents' accounts flagged the importance of there being uncertainty about which groups of professionals had primary responsibility in such circumstances. With probability sampling, such considerations can be specified, taking into account the size of the population and time and cost constraints.

As a rule of thumb, however, the broader the scope of a qualitative study and the more comparisons between groups in the sample that are required, the more interviews will need to be carried out (Warren 2002; Morse 2004). Taking the second of these two criteria, if several comparisons are likely to be wanted—between males and females, different age groups, different types of research participants in terms of locally relevant factors—a larger sample is likely to be necessary. Also, in a study of the experience of relationship breakdown, fewer respondents are likely to be necessary if the emphasis is on those who have been formally married as opposed to the more general category of being in a relationship. Nonetheless, Warren (2002: 99) makes the interesting remark that, for a qualitative interview study to be published, the minimum number of interviews required seems to be between 20 and 30. This suggests that, although there is an emphasis on the importance of sampling purposively in qualitative research, minimum levels of acceptability operate, although there are almost certainly exceptions to Warren's rule (for example, very intensive interviews of the kind conducted in life story interviews, where there may be just one or two interviewees). Moreover, by no means all practitioners would agree with Warren's figure. Gerson and Horowitz (2002: 223) write that 'fewer than 60 interviews cannot support convincing conclusions and more than 150 produce too much material to analyse effectively and expeditiously'. The differences between these authors' views suggest how difficult it can be to try to specify minimum sample sizes (see also Guest et al. (2006) and Mason (2010) for other summaries of some researchers' suggestions on this issue). The size of sample that is considered able to support convincing conclusions is likely to vary somewhat from situation to situation in purposive sampling terms, and qualitative researchers have to recognize that they are engaged in a delicate balancing act:

> In general, sample sizes in qualitative research should not be so small as to make it difficult to achieve data saturation, theoretical saturation, or informational redundancy. At the same time, the sample should not be so large that it is difficult to undertake a deep, case-oriented analysis.

> (Onwuegbuzie and Collins 2007: 289)

Given the ranges of opinion about appropriate sample sizes, it is not surprising that, when Mason (2010) examined the abstracts of doctoral theses derived from interview-based qualitative research in Great Britain and Ireland, he found that the 560 theses varied in sample size from 1 to 95, with a mean of 31 and a median of 28. The difference between the mean and median suggests that the mean is being inflated by some rather large samples. Mason refers to a study that reviewed 50 grounded theory-based research articles, which found sample sizes to vary between 5 and 350.

It is also likely that the orientation of the researchers and the purposes of their research will be significant. What is probably crucial is to justify rigorously any sample size. In other words, rather than rely on others' impressions of suitable sample sizes in qualitative research, it is almost certainly better to be clear about the sampling method you employed, why you used it, and why the sample size you achieved is appropriate. It may be that the reason why you feel that a sample of a certain size is adequate is because you feel you have achieved theoretical saturation, a term that, while strongly linked to grounded theory, is often used by researchers operating within a variety of approaches. If saturation is the criterion for sample size, specifying minimum or maximum sample sizes is pointless. Essentially, the criterion for sample size is whatever it takes to achieve saturation. The problem is that, as several writers observe (e.g. Guest et al. 2006; Mason 2010), saturation is often *claimed* but not justified or explained (Bowen 2008). See Thinking deeply 18.7 for more on this question.

Related to this issue is that you need to be sure that you do not generalize inappropriately from your data. Onwuegbuzie and Leech (2010) observe that for the most part there are two kinds of generalization that may be inferred from a qualitative study. One is analytic generalization, which is much the same as theoretical generalization (J. C. Mitchell 1983) and refers to the credibility of the theoretical inferences that the researcher draws from his or her findings. The other they call 'case-to-case transfer', which refers to making generalizations from one case to another case that is broadly similar. This is more or less the same as the notion of *moderatum* generalization suggested by M. Williams (2000: 215) who has argued that, in many cases, qualitative researchers are in a position to produce what he calls *moderatum* generalizations—that

is, ones in which aspects of the focus of enquiry (e.g. a small network of female entrepreneurs, a big data processing firm) 'can be seen to be instances of a broader set of recognizable features'. In addition, Williams argues that not only is it the case that qualitative researchers *can* make such generalizations but that in fact they often *do* make them. Thus, when generating findings relating to a firm that processes big data, a researcher is likely to draw comparisons with findings by other researchers relating to comparable organizations (e.g. information technology firms). When forging such comparisons and linkages, the researcher is engaging in *moderatum* generalization. *Moderatum* generalizations will always be limited and somewhat more tentative than those associated with statistical generalizations of the kind associated with probability sampling (see Chapter 9). On the other hand, they do permit an element of generalization and help to counter the view that generalization beyond the immediate evidence and the case is impossible in qualitative research.

Generalization to a population may be legitimate when a probability sampling procedure has been employed. Onwuegbuzie and Leech analysed all 125 empirical articles that had been published in the *Qualitative Report*, an academic journal that has been in publication since 1990. They found that 29.6 per cent of the articles contained generalizations that illegitimately went beyond the sample participants. In other words, just under one-third of articles made inferences to a population beyond the study's participants. As the authors note, when this occurs, there is an inconsistency between the design of the research and the interpretations that are made about the resulting data. There is clearly a lesson here about the need to be clear about what you can and cannot infer from a sample of any kind, something that applies to sampling in quantitative research too.

STUDENT EXPERIENCE
How many interviews in a student research project?

One of the questions that we are often asked by students is: How many interviews should they do for their research project? As Tom explained:

I think this is one of the key questions that people ask. You say 'What's the minimum number of interviews I have to do to make this project viable?' [*chuckles*] and my tutor did say that because I'd decided to cut myself free from the bounds of positivism I could just do one interview if I wanted to and that would be quite legitimate. I didn't quite feel up to doing that.

This is also an area where advice can vary from one university to another, depending on the degree level (undergraduate or postgraduate), the word limit and credit weighting of the dissertation, and the time allocated to its completion, so you should definitely refer to the advice given by your university and your supervisor. However, it is useful to compare the experiences of some of the students we interviewed.

- Tom interviewed eight of the approximately 40 staff at the call centre he was studying.

- Anna did 10 interviews via Skype, rather than face-to-face, with commercial egg donors. She did not use video, in order to protect the respondents' anonymity, given the sensitivity of the topic she was studying.

- Chris conducted four interviews with three female managers and the head of diversity in the organization he was studying.

- Karen carried out 15 interviews with managers in one organization, each lasting one hour, taking notes throughout.

As the above summaries illustrate, there is quite a difference in the number of interviews carried out by students doing a dissertation project. However, it is important not to place too much emphasis on the number of interviews conducted in qualitative research because the emphasis should be on quality, detail, and depth of the interview data collected, rather than on achieving an acceptable number of interviewees. This point was made by Alex, who struggled to persuade entrepreneurs to be interviewed:

> Because I was targeting such a small group, the single biggest challenge was finding people and then getting them to commit. So I had quite a few people pull out because they were too busy at work or someone was unavailable. Things like that. In the end I only got six interviews including in the company I worked for. Once I knew I wasn't going to get massive sample size, that's where I said 'okay these interviews need to be really comprehensive, I need to compensate for this best I can.'

18.7 THINKING DEEPLY
Saturation and sample size

As noted in the text, it is very difficult to know in advance how many interviews you need to conduct if theoretical saturation (see Key concept 18.4) is the principle used to assess the adequacy of a sample. Further, the criteria for deciding when theoretical saturation has been achieved are more or less absent. In their study of ethics and compliance officers which was referred to in Research in focus 18.5, Treviño et al. (2014) found that after their thirtieth interview only one new code was generated and after the thirty-fifth interview no new codes were arrived at. Therefore, in this case, the last ten interviews (there were 40 in total) hardly generated any new theoretical insights at all. This finding should not be taken as a rule of thumb, as it may not apply in other instances, but it does suggest that saturation may be achieved earlier than might be anticipated.

Not just people

Sampling is not just about people but also about sampling other things. For one thing, principles of purposive sampling can be applied to such things as documents, in much the same way that probability sampling can be applied to different kinds of phenomena to generate a representative sample. However, there is another dimension to sampling in qualitative research that is worth bearing in mind. This is to do with needing to sample the different contexts within which interviewing or observation take place. Writing about ethnographic research, Hammersley and Atkinson (1995) mention time and context as units that need to be considered in the context of sampling. Attending to *time* means that the ethnographer must make sure that people or events are observed at different times of the day and different days of the week. To do otherwise risks drawing inferences about certain people's behaviour or about events that are valid only for mornings or for weekdays rather than weekends. It is impossible to be an ethnographer all the time for several reasons: need to take time out to write up notes; other commitments (work or domestic); and body imperatives (eating, sleeping, and so on). When the group in question operates a different cycle from the ethnographer's normal regime (such as night shifts in a factory or hospital), the requirement to time sample may necessitate a considerable change of habit. Delbridge (1998), for example, describes how tired he felt after a day making windscreen wipers or circuit boards for televisions. In addition, he explains that 'there was real pressure and intensity during the fieldwork, particularly during the early stages when I was negotiating my informal access and acceptance into the group. I developed a nervous tic in my cheek during the first two weeks, something I have never experienced before or since' (1998: 19).

It can also be important to sample in terms of *context*. People's behaviour is influenced by contextual factors, so that it is important to ensure that such behaviour is observed in a variety of locations. For example, in his study of masculinity and workplace culture in a lorry-making factory in the north-west of England, Collinson (1992a) draws attention to the ways in which shopfloor workers resist managerial control by spending time chatting and joking. As Collinson spent time with workers during lunch and unofficial breaks, in the toilet, the canteen, the car park, on the works' bus, in the pub, and occasionally in people's homes, he was able to explore these cultural practices in far more detail than if he had confined his study and himself to observing practices within formal workplace settings.

Using more than one sampling approach

Purposive sampling often involves more than one of the approaches outlined above. For example, it is quite common for snowball sampling to be preceded by another form of purposive sampling. This process can entail sampling initial participants without using a snowball approach and then using these initial contacts to broaden out through a snowballing method. Thus, in their study of the role of power in the branding of a tourist destination—the Gold Coast in Australia—Marzano and Scott (2009) initially purposively sampled key stakeholders in the branding process. These were individuals who had key roles in the agencies responsible for and with an interest in the branding of this tourist destination. As a result of the snowballing process, people such as senior managers in hotels and theme parks were also identified and became candidates for inclusion in the research, which was conducted by semi-structured interview.

A further sense in which more than one sampling approach may be employed is when researchers try to introduce an element of purposiveness into a snowball sample. For example, Marshall (1984) describes how, in order to identify her sample of 30 women managers, she would first make a contact within a particular company (sometimes a woman manager and sometimes a helpful member of the personnel department) and then ask him or her to suggest other potential interviewees. However,

Marshall also made a number of decisions in advance of her study about the type of participants she was interested in. First, she decided to interview only in and around London, to reduce the significance of whether or not managers were geographically mobile; second, to impose an upper age limit of 45 years, to reduce the potential differences between generations; third, to contact several people in each company to provide a guide to the influence of the company; and, fourth, to restrict the number of personnel managers in the sample, to avoid weighting her sample towards this 'traditional stronghold of female employment' (1984: 115). Her approach thus also involved an element of *a priori* purposive sampling.

There is evidence of a quest for both purposiveness and representativeness in these studies. With the work of Marshall the purposiveness reveals itself mainly in the search for women managers with appropriate characterics; in the case of Marzano and Scott's research, the purposive sample was boosted through subsequent snowball sampling. At the same time, there is a strong sense of wanting to generate a sample with at least a semblance of representativeness. This is quite an interesting development, since sampling in qualitative research, as we have seen, is primarily associated with purposive sampling. At the same time, it raises an interesting question that may at least in part lie behind the use of representativeness in these studies. Given that, when you sample purposively, in many cases several individuals (or whatever the unit of analysis is) will be eligible for inclusion, how do you decide which one or ones to include? In other words, if your research questions direct you to select a subsample that has criteria *a* and *b* and another subsample that has criteria *a* and *c*, so that you can compare them, how do you choose between the individuals who meet each of the two pairs of criteria? Sampling for at least a modicum of representativeness, as these researchers appear to have done, may be one way of making such a decision.

KEY POINTS

- Purposive sampling is the fundamental principle for selecting cases and individuals in qualitative research.

- Purposive sampling places the investigation's research questions at the forefront of sampling considerations.

- It is important to bear in mind that purposive sampling will entail considerations of the levels at which sampling needs to take place.

- It is important to distinguish between theoretical sampling and the generic purposive sampling approach, as they are sometimes treated synonymously.

- Theoretical saturation is a useful principle for making decisions about sample size, but there is evidence that it is often claimed rather than demonstrated.

QUESTIONS FOR REVIEW

- How does purposive sampling differ from probability sampling, and why do many qualitative researchers prefer to use the former?

- In what circumstances might you employ snowball sampling?

Levels of sampling

- Why might it be significant to distinguish between the different levels at which sampling can take place in a qualitative research project?

Purposive sampling

- Why is theoretical sampling such an important facet of grounded theory?

- How does theoretical sampling differ from the generic purposive sampling approach?

- Why is theoretical saturation such an important ingredient of theoretical sampling?

- What are the main reasons for considering the use of snowball sampling?

Sample size

- Why do writers seem to disagree so much on what is a minimum acceptable sample size in qualitative research?

- To what extent does theoretical sampling assist the qualitative researcher in making decisions about sample size?

Not just people

● Why might it be important to remember in purposive sampling that it is not just people who are candidates for consideration in sampling issues?

Using more than one sampling approach

● How might it be useful to select people purposively following a survey?

ONLINE RESOURCES
www.oup.com/uk/brm5e/

Visit the Interactive Research Guide that accompanies this book to complete an exercise in sampling for qualitative research.

ETHNOGRAPHY AND PARTICIPANT OBSERVATION

CHAPTER OUTLINE

Ethnography and participant observation entail the extended involvement of the researcher in the social life of those he or she studies (see Key concept 19.1). The former term is also frequently taken to refer to the written output of that research. This chapter explores:

- the problems of gaining access to different settings and some suggestions about how they might be overcome;

- the issue of whether or not a covert role is practicable and acceptable;

- the role of key informants and gatekeepers for the ethnographer;

- the different kinds of roles that ethnographers can assume in the course of their fieldwork;

- the role of field notes in ethnography and the variety of forms they can assume;

- bringing an ethnography study to an end;

- a focus on four particular types of ethnography: feminist, global and multi-site, virtual, and visual;

- a discussion of the writing of ethnography.

Introduction

Prior to the 1970s, ethnography was primarily associated with social anthropological research, where the investigator visits a (usually) foreign land, gains access to a group (for example, a tribe or village), and spends a considerable amount of time (often many years) with that group with the aim of uncovering its culture. This form of ethnography involves the ethnographer watching and listening to what people say and do, engaging people in conversations to probe specific issues of interest, taking copious field notes, and returning home to write an account of their fieldwork experiences. This might lead you to think that ethnography is a relatively simple process, but doing an ethnography is nowhere nearly as straightforward as this implies.

This chapter will outline some of the main decisions that confront ethnographers, along with some of the many contingencies they face. However, it is not easy to generalize about the ethnographic research process in such a way as to provide definitive recommendations about research practice because the diversity of experiences that confront ethnographers, and the variety of ways in which they deal with them, does not readily permit clear-cut generalizations. The following comment in a book on ethnography makes this point well.

> Every field situation *is* different and initial luck in meeting good informants, being in the right place at the right time and striking the right note in relationships may be just as important as skill in technique. Indeed, many successful episodes in the field do come about through good luck as much as through sophisticated planning, and many unsuccessful episodes are due as much to bad luck as to bad judgement.
>
> (Sarsby 1984: 96)

However, this statement should not be taken to imply that forethought and an awareness of alternative ways of doing things are irrelevant. It is with this kind of issue that the rest of this chapter will be concerned. The chapter will also be concerned with identifying similarities and differences between 'ethnography' and 'participant observation' (see Key concept 19.1 for an explanation of the relationship between these terms).

19.1 KEY CONCEPT
Differences and similarities between ethnography and participant observation

Definitions of ethnography and participant observation are difficult to distinguish. Both draw attention to the fact that the participant observer/ethnographer immerses him or herself in a group for an extended period of time, observing behaviour, listening to what is said in conversations both between others and with the fieldworker, and asking questions. A typical account of the ethnographic research process, and the importance of participant observation within this, is provided by Lok and de Rond's (2013) ethnographic study of the Cambridge University Boat Race. The researchers wanted to understand the institutional practices of the club which determine how crew are selected to participate in the race. As Lok and de Rond explain: 'true to the ethnographic tradition one of us spent an entire Boat Race season (September 9, 2006, to April 7, 2007) with the squad full-time. The researcher joined the squad for their daily training sessions, sat in on all coaches' meetings, and socialized with the squad and coaches outside of training hours.' When the squad trained off-site 'he traveled with them, slept in their rooms, worked along side them in rigging boats, loading equipment, driving club vans, mopping floors, cooking breakfast and studying video footage of water outings and past boat races' (Lok and de Rond 2013: 192).

The term 'ethnography' is often preferred, because 'participant observation' seems to imply just observation, though in practice participant observers do more than simply observe. Typically, participant observers and ethnographers will both gather further data through interviews and the collection of documents. However, as we will discuss at the end of this chapter, the term 'ethnography' has an additional meaning, in that it also refers to the account of the culture that the researcher writes at the end of their study.

Organizational ethnography

Business researchers have imported the methods and many of the conventions of ethnography into the study of organizational settings. Rosen (1991) understands organizational ethnography to be distinctive because it is concerned with social relations that are connected to certain goal-directed activities. He suggests that the rules, strategies, and meanings within a structured work situation are different from those that affect other areas of social life. An ethnographic approach implies intense researcher involvement in the day-to-day running of an organization, so that the researcher can understand it from an insider's point of view. In order to become immersed in other people's realities, organizational ethnographers, like their anthropological predecessors, engage in fieldwork that tends to commit them to a period of time spent in the organization, or a long stay 'in the field'. One reason for this is because many ethnographers report that after a period of time they become less obtrusive to participants in social settings, who become familiar with their presence (e.g. Atkinson 1981: 128). Here are some examples of classic and more recent organizational ethnographies.

- D. Roy (1958) spent two months working as a machine operator in the 'clicking room' of a factory in Chicago. The same factory was later used as a research setting by Burawoy (1979), who worked as a machine operator for ten months in the same plant.

- Beynon (1975) studied the Ford Motor Company's Halewood assembly plant in Liverpool over a period of five years to produce an account of factory life that described the process whereby people became shop stewards, the way they understood the job, and the kinds of pressures they experienced. This study also involved understanding the experience of people who worked on the assembly lines and the way they made sense of industrial politics.

- Willems (2018) made a two-year study of embodied, sensory learning through participant observation of train dispatchers in the Dutch railways (Research in focus 17.5). In addition to participant observation involving 30 shifts, each observational episode lasting 2–8 hours, Willems took detailed field notes, consulted internal documents, and carried out semi-structured interviews.

- Alcadipani became a participant observer in a newspaper printing factory in the North of England in order to explore how the predominantly white, male workforce was responding to the threat of shutdown in a declining industry. His study involved spending nearly nine months observing 'daily activities at the plant, typically for 8–12 hours a day, five days a week … on both day and night shifts' (Alcadipani and Tonelli 2014: 326).

Ethnography, which denotes the practice of writing (*graphy*) about people and cultures (*ethno*), provides business researchers with an obvious method for understanding work organizations as cultural entities. Many organizational ethnographies focus on the construction of cultural norms, expressions of organizational values, and patterns of workplace behaviour; for example:

- Hatch et al.'s (2015) study of organizational identity and culture over a five-year period of transformational change in the Danish-headquartered Carlsberg group (Research in focus 17.6);

- Michel's (2011) nine-year study of Wall Street investment bankers' practices of habitual overwork and the effects this has on their bodies (Research in focus 19.2);

- Kunda's (1992) study of cultural norms and practices in a high-technology company, 'Lyndsville Tech', in Silicon Valley, USA.

19.2 RESEARCH IN FOCUS
An example of an organizational ethnography lasting nine years

Michel's (2011) ethnography of investment banks focuses on Wall Street investment bankers' bodies, including how they are adversely affected by their intense working conditions and why the bankers engage in habitual overwork which causes such strain on their bodies, even though they have a high degree of autonomy and ability to control their workload. Her nine-year study of two investment banking departments involved tracking four cohorts of employees, two in each bank, from the point of joining, for as long as they stayed with the bank. Michel is very detailed in her description of the data collection process that formed the basis for her study.

Participant and non-participant observation: over two years, about 7000 hours in years 1–2 of the study;

Semi-structured formal interviews: 136 (30–45 minutes in length) in year 2 of the study, followed by almost 500 1–3 hour follow-up interviews in years 3–9 of the study;

Informal interviews: 200, based on themes evolving from the study.

The banks were highly restrictive in terms of how they allowed Michel to use the data. For instance, they did not allow her to reveal the size of the cohorts or the dates of the study, nor did they allow her to audio-record the interviews. Although nine years is an unusually long time for an ethnographic study to continue, this longitudinal aspect of the study enabled Michel to track long-term physical and mental health problems experienced by the bankers and to trace how this affected their relationships to their bodies and their careers.

TIPS AND SKILLS
Micro-ethnography

If you are doing research for a dissertation project, it is unlikely that you will be able to conduct a full-scale ethnography, because this would almost certainly involve you spending a considerable period of time in an organizational setting. Nevertheless, it may be possible for you to carry out a form of *micro-ethnography* (Wolcott 1995). This involves focusing on a particular aspect of an organizational culture, such as the way the organization has implemented TQM, and showing how the culture is reflected through this managerial initiative. A shorter time period (ranging from a couple of weeks to a few months) could be spent in the organization—on either a full-time or a part-time basis—to achieve this more closely defined cultural understanding.

STUDENT EXPERIENCE
Participant observation in a student research project

Lucie felt that participant observation would enable her to gain an insider perspective on the process of constructing entrepreneurial identity among university students. As a university student herself, she was in a good position to be accepted into the research setting and to try to view these events through the eyes of the people she was studying. She arranged to attend events and workshops designed to help university students to develop entrepreneurial behaviour. As Lucie explained, this meant 'I could get the feel of how the organizers were trying to present enterprise to me as a student. I could get first-hand experience of it and embrace what they were trying to say.'

Lucie found the pressures associated with ethnographic participant observation significant.

Because I was trying to research this, I don't know if I was looking at things a bit too deeply and not just kind of taking it for what it was. I found myself looking around and trying to kind of gauge other people's reactions as well, so I don't know if I sat there and did it as much as kind of just sitting there and taking everything in really. It was quite difficult. I was trying to write everything down because they didn't want me to tape record anything so I had to take notes and I didn't want to miss anything. So it was quite difficult really to decide 'Is that important or is that irrelevant?' and it got a bit kind of confusing at times. It was quite a lot of information to take in I suppose.

Access

One of the key and yet most difficult steps in ethnography is gaining access to a social setting that is relevant to the research problem in which you are interested. The way that access is approached differs according to whether the setting is a relatively open one or a relatively closed one (Bell 1969). The majority of organizational ethnography is done in predominantly closed or non-public settings of various kinds, such as factories or offices. The negotiation of access involves gaining permission to enter these privately managed spaces or situations. Gaining access to organizations can initially be a very formal process involving a lengthy sequence of letter-writing and meetings, in order to deal with managerial concerns about your goals. However, the distinction between open and closed settings is not a hard-and-fast one. Many organizations also have a highly public character, made visible through marketing and public relations activities.

Buchanan et al. (1988) suggest that researchers should adopt an opportunistic approach towards fieldwork in organizations, balancing what is desirable against what is possible. 'The research timetable must therefore take into account the possibility that access will not be automatic and instant, but may take weeks and months of meetings and correspondence to achieve' (1988: 56). Gaining access is the result of 'strategic planning, hard work and dumb luck' (Van Maanen and Kolb 1985: 11). Sometimes, sheer perseverance pays off. Leidner (1993) was determined that one of the organizations in which she conducted ethnographic research on the routinization of service work should be McDonald's. She writes:

> I knew from the beginning that I wanted one of the case studies to be of McDonald's. The company was a pioneer and exemplar of routinized interaction, and since it was locally based, it seemed like the perfect place to start. McDonald's had other ideas, however, and only after tenacious pestering and persuasion did I overcome corporate employees' polite demurrals, couched in terms of protecting proprietary information and the company's image.
>
> (Leidner 1993: 234–5)

This kind of determination was necessary because Leidner was committed to studying a specific organization—rejection would have required a complete rethink of the research project. However, with many research questions, several potential cases are likely to meet your criteria. During his year of participant observation at ZTC Ryland, Watson (1994a) joked with managers that he had chosen the company for the study because of its convenient location, just a 20-minute walk from his house. Another, more serious, reason given for choosing the company as a research site was because management had been involved in a succession of change initiatives associated with the development of a 'strong' corporate culture.

Organizational researchers use a range of tactics, many of which may seem rather unsystematic, but they are worth drawing attention to.

- Use friends, contacts, colleagues, academics to help you gain access; provided the organization is relevant to your research question, the route should not matter. Sometimes, access negotiated through contacts from the researcher's previous employment. For example, Michel's (2011) access to investment banks was enabled by the fact that she had been an associate at a Wall Street bank before entering academic life. This enabled her to cultivate relationships that were the basis for her nine-year ethnographic study. Similarly, Zhang and Spicer's (2014: 744) ten-month ethnographic study of the production of hierarchical space was enabled by the first author's former employment in a 'large tax authority in a coastal metropolis in eastern China … By courtesy of his former colleagues, he was granted otherwise rare research access to the organization'.

- Try to get the support of someone within the organization who will act as your champion. This person may be prepared to vouch for you and the value of your research. Such people are placed in the role of 'sponsors' and 'gatekeepers'. Sometimes, an ethnographer's path will be smoothed by an individual who acts as both sponsor and gatekeeper.

- Usually you will need to get access through top management/senior executives. Even though you may secure a certain level of agreement lower down the hierarchy, you will usually need clearance from them. In Hatch et al.'s (2015) case, the researchers gained access to the Carlsberg Group through a senior manager, Anne Marie Skov, who was Carlsberg's senior vice-president of group communication and corporate social responsibility. In addition to enabling access to the organization, Skov became a co-author of a published journal article written about the study. In explaining these relationships, the authors state:

We are well aware that procuring entry through Skov, a senior executive, influenced how the researchers (Hatch and Schutz) were treated and affected the information with which they were entrusted. However, informants showed great willingness to be frank and open about their issues and concerns with the company. Many saw their interview as an avenue to communicate with top managers and all were assured that we would not publish anything without corporate approval (by written agreement with Carlsberg).

(2015: 62)

- Offer something in return (for example, a report). Gaining access is often based on an exchange whereby the organizational ethnographer cannot gain access to collect data without giving something in return, e.g. in the form of their physical, mental, or emotional labour, which involves finding a role within the organization (see Research in focus 19.3). However, this strategy also carries risks, in that it may turn you into a cheap consultant and may invite restrictions on your activities, such as insistence on seeing what you write or limitations on who is willing to talk to you. For example, Milkman (1997) in her study of General Motors found that, although her research approach gained her legitimacy in the eyes of management, it stimulated scepticism and lack of trust among the workers.

- Provide a clear explanation of your aims and methods and be prepared to deal with concerns. Suggest a meeting at which you can deal with worries, and provide an explanation of what you intend to do in terms that can readily be understood by others.

- Be prepared to negotiate—you will want complete access, but it is unlikely you will be given *carte blanche*. Milkman (1997) describes how, in negotiating access to the General Motors automobile assembly plant, the promise to produce 'hard', quantitative data to management, through survey research, was what eventually secured the researcher's access to the plant—even though she had no previous experience in designing or conducting surveys!

- Be reasonably honest about the amount of people's time you are likely to take up. This is a question you will almost certainly be asked if you are seeking access to commercial organizations and probably many not-for-profit ones too.

'Hanging around' is another common access strategy. This typically entails either loitering in an area until you are noticed or gradually becoming incorporated into or asking to join a group. For example, as well as interviewing shop stewards who represented assembly-line workers and a selection of workers from each of the four main

19.3 RESEARCH IN FOCUS
Finding a working role in the organization

Organizational ethnography involves seeking to manage the impressions that others have of you in a way which helps you to be accepted into the organizational setting. One way of acheiving this is by developing a working role (see Table 19.1 later in the chapter for descriptions of different types of role a researcher might take). One type of working role involves casting yourself in the role of a management consultant who is seen as a credible, trusted outsider who can work closely with management. Watson (1994a) illustrates how he used this working role to gain access to the organization he was studying. It was agreed that his year-long access to the company would result in the development of a competency identification scheme that the company could use to select and develop future managers. However, there may be dangers in becoming too closely identified with managerial groups, as this can cut off access to potentially valuable informants within the organization. Milkman (1997) describes how the very fact that she had legitimacy with both management and the union at General Motors rendered her untrustworthy in the eyes of workers whom she was most interested in studying. This was because, 'in the intensely political world of the factory, academic researchers were an entirely unknown quantity and could only be understood as servicing someone else's immediate interests' (1997: 192).

A second type of role involves the researcher being seen as an apprentice who contributes to the practical running of the organization. For example, Sharpe (1997) describes how she gained insider status by taking up employment as a shopfloor worker in a Japanese car manufacturing company on a six-month student job placement contract. She explains: 'by immersing myself in the shopfloor life, I believed I would be able to offer a richer, reflexive understanding of social processes and dynamics than if I took a more conventional approach of research as an outsider or distant observer' (1997: 230). Holliday (1995), who also took on the role of the apprentice, calculated the financial value of the work that she did for the company in exchange for access, estimating that it cost her approximately £2500.

A third type of working role adopted by organizational ethnographers involves becoming a confidant. For example, Dalton (1959) describes how a female secretary helped him to obtain confidential data about managerial salaries. In exchange, she asked Dalton, given his sociological training, to provide her with some relationship counselling to help her to work out the feelings she held towards a man she was seriously dating. Dalton obliged, in exchange for the data, and the secretary married the man within a year. Similarly, M. Parker (2000) suggests that the role of the confidant is the most productive for revealing insights into the politics of the organization. D. Fletcher (2002) describes how she adopted a role as 'emotional-nurturer' in her study of a small engineering company. She explains that she subconsciously chose this role in a masculine organizational setting as a way of responding to her feelings of 'femaleness' and difference. To try to gain acceptance among members of the organization, she 'provided positive stroking concerning job/marital problems' (2002: 411) and 'tried to create a non-threatening comfort zone in which people could have a break from work and talk about their work' (2002: 412). However, Fletcher also explains that she felt that something of herself was 'lost' through this process, making her sometimes tired, depressed, and frustrated, as 'constantly providing emotional nurture is exhausting and neverending' (2002: 414).

The working roles adopted by organizational ethnographers often overlap; more than one may be adopted in a particular setting. They are also likely to change over time as the fieldwork progresses. Even if it were possible to adopt a single ethnographic role over the entire course of a project, this could be undesirable, because the researcher would not have as much flexibility in handling situations and people, and there could be a greater risk of excessive involvement ('going native'—Key concept 19.6) or detachment.

production departments, Beynon (1975) spent a day each week at the Ford plant observing and listening to the shop stewards 'as they negotiated, argued and discussed issues amongst themselves and with their members' (1975: 13). He describes how he 'sat at tables in the canteens and at benches around the coffee-vending machines at break times' and 'talked with workers as they queued up for their dinner, for buses or to clock their cards at the beginning and the end of every day' (1975: 13). Similarly, Casey, in her study of a group of professional workers at the multinational 'Hephaestus' Corporation, tells how she 'spent a great deal of time lingering around individual people' (1995: 201). M. Parker (2000: 236) describes how he spent time waiting 'outside managers' offices, often for long periods of time, and wandering around the factory or offices' just to collect small details or fragments of data.

As these anecdotes suggest, gaining access to social settings is a crucial first step in ethnographic research, in that, without access, your research plans will be halted in their tracks. As Ram (1994) illustrates in his study of employment relations in small firms (see Research in focus 19.4), attention to cultural context and local norms and values can be important considerations

when seeking access to closed settings. Gender can also be an important consideration when negotiating access to organizational settings that are dominated by one or another gender (as in the study described in Research in focus 19.9 later in the chapter).

When studying contexts where the researcher is already involved as a complete participant, for example as an organizational employee, other problems can arise. Brannick and Coghlan (2007) refer to this type of study as 'insider research' while Alvesson (2003) uses the term 'self-ethnography'. In such situations the researcher is likely to be extremely familiar with the organizational culture and will already have relationships with organizational members, making access easier. However, it can be more difficult to recognize the distinctive features of a culture in which you are completely immersed, and conflicts of interest can arise in studying people with whom you have ongoing working relationships, particularly if a report of findings will be presented to them or to others in the organization.

In summary, gaining access is often fraught with difficulties. Therefore, this discussion of access strategies can be only a starting point in deciding what approach to take.

19.4 RESEARCH IN FOCUS
A complete participant?

One of the aims of Ram's (1994) ethnographic study of employment relations in small firms was to consider how employees and employers negotiated the labour process.

However, just getting into clothing companies in the West Midlands, which formed the focus of his study, was 'notoriously difficult' (1994: 26). In order to gain access to the three clothing firms that formed the basis for his study, Ram relied on his family and community connections to establish the trust necessary for him to 'tap into the workplace culture' (1994: 23). Being able to speak fluent Punjabi was essential to understanding people in the workplace, but equally important for Ram in becoming an 'insider' was being able to understand how the shopfloor manufacturing industry culture worked. Crucial to this was his own first-hand experience of the clothing industry. Ram describes himself as having been involved in the clothing trade for most of his life.

> My two elder sisters and one younger sister are married into clothing families, where they work as sewing machinists and assist in the management of the in-laws' firms. My elder brother runs a clothing manufacturing business with a cousin … My younger brother is in charge of the family-owned warehouse.
>
> (1994: 24)

Ram adopted an 'opportunistic' approach to the fieldwork, relying on his friends and relatives and on his personal background as a member of a 'respected' family in the local Asian community. Ram's own father was in charge of 'Company A', which formed one of Ram's case studies. In addition, Ram himself had worked for this company either full- or part-time 'since it came into being' (1994: 30). He had the power to 'sign cheques, purchase stock, make use of the firm's equipment and give instructions to the company's workers' (1994: 30), and during one period of the fieldwork his father went on holiday, leaving Ram and his younger brother to run the firm. However, despite his apparent role as a total participant, it was hard for Ram to talk to the shopfloor machinists, who were mostly women, because of the customary regulation of gender relationships within Asian society. He therefore used a chaperone, a senior female machinist, who accompanied him when he questioned individual female operatives.

Overt versus covert?

One way to ease the access problem is to assume a *covert* role—in other words, not to disclose the fact that you are a researcher. This strategy obviates the need to negotiate access to organizations or to explain why you want to intrude into people's lives and make them objects of study. Using a covert role also reduces **reactivity**, because participants do not know the person conducting the study is a researcher. Therefore, they are less likely to adjust their behaviour because of the researcher's presence.

There are some historical examples of covert ethnography in business. Dalton's (1959) study of managers, *Men Who Manage*, focused on the gap between official and unofficial action. Dalton describes how, in setting up access, he made no formal approach to the top management of any of the four firms he studied in the heavily industrialized area of 'Mobile Acres' in the USA. Instead he became an employee in two of the firms he studied and engaged in covert participant observation. Describing some of the difficulties associated with his **covert**

research role, Dalton describes how his situation became more sensitive as he acquired more unofficial information about practices such as 'pilfering' (employee theft of materials). However, his work role gave him 'great freedom of movement and wide contacts' (1959: 278) within the firm. In another classic study, Donald Roy (1958) was similarly oblique with his co-workers about why he was working at the factory. Working under the pseudonym 'Danelly', he describes how workers knew that he had been attending 'college' but 'the specific course of study remained somewhat obscure' (1958: 164) to them. In answer to the question 'Why are you working here?', Roy stressed the importance of working 'lots of overtime' and this, according to Roy, seemed to 'suffice' for the workers. Covert study also makes it difficult for the ethnographer to record their observations, such as by writing field notes (Research in focus 19.5).

Ethnographers are far more likely to be in an overt role than a covert one. The reasons for this are predominantly related to ethical considerations (see Chapter 6). Covert study transgresses two important ethical tenets:

19.5 RESEARCH IN FOCUS
An example of the difficulties of covert observation: the case of field notes in the lavatory

Ditton's (1977) research on 'fiddling' in a bakery provides an interesting case of the practical difficulties of taking notes during covert observation, as well as an illustration of an ethnographer who shifted his position from covert to overt observation at least in part because of those difficulties.

> Nevertheless, I *was* able to develop personal covert participant–observation skills. Right from the start, I found it impossible to keep everything that I wanted to remember in my head until the end of the working day … and so had to take rough notes as I was going along. But I was stuck 'on the line', and had nowhere to retire to privately to jot things down. Eventually, the wheeze of using innocently provided lavatory cubicles occurred to me. Looking back, all my notes for that third summer were on Bronco toilet paper! Apart from the awkward tendency for pencilled notes to be self-erasing from hard toilet paper … my frequent requests for 'time out' after interesting happenings or conversations in the bakehouse and the amount of time I was spending in the lavatory began to get noticed. I had to pacify some genuinely concerned work-mates, give up totally undercover operations, and 'come out' as an observer—albeit in a limited way. I eventually began to scribble notes more openly, but still not in front of people when they were talking. When questioned about this, as I was occasionally, I coyly said that I was writing things down that occurred to me about 'my studies'.
>
> (1977: 5)

it does not provide participants with the opportunity for informed consent (whereby they can agree or disagree to participate on the basis of information supplied to them) and it entails deception. It can also be taken to be a violation of the principle of privacy. Indeed, ethics politics and approval procedures in many universities make it very difficult to gain approval for covert ethnography. Also, many writers take the view that, in addition to being potentially damaging to research participants, it can also harm the practice of research: there are fears about social researchers being identified by the public as snoopers or voyeurs if they are found out. The discussion of access that follows will therefore focus upon ethnographers seeking to take an overt role.

Ongoing access

Negotiation of access does not finish when you have made contact and gained an entrée to the organization. You still need access to *people*. Securing access is in many ways an ongoing activity, which takes considerable effort and time.

There are various concerns that organization members may have about being studied, and these will affect the level of ongoing access that you are able to achieve.

- People may have suspicions about you, perhaps seeing you as an instrument of top management. It is common for members of organizations to believe that researchers are placed there to check up on them or even for the researcher to be mistaken for someone playing a different role. For example, Roethlisberger and Dickson (1939) describe how one of the interviewers in the Hawthorne studies was mistaken for a rate setter.

> There was a buzz of conversation and the men seemed to be working at great speed. Suddenly there was a sharp hissing sound. The conversation died away, and there was a noticeable slowing up in the work pace. The interviewer later discovered from an acquaintance in the department that he had been mistaken for a rate setter. One of the workmen, who acted as a lookout, had stepped on a valve releasing compressed air, a prearranged signal for slowing down.
>
> (Roethlisberger and Dickson 1939: 386)

- People may worry that what they say or do may get back to bosses or to colleagues. Van Maanen (1991a) notes from his research on the police that, when conducting ethnographic research among officers, you are likely to observe activities that may be deeply discrediting and even illegal. Your credibility among police officers will be determined by your reactions to situations and events that are known to be difficult for individuals.

- If organization members have these worries, they may give the appearance of going along with your research while in fact sabotaging it, engaging in deceptions, misinformation, and not allowing access to 'back regions' (Goffman 1959).

There are four things you can do to smooth the path of ongoing access.

- Play up your credentials—your past work and experience; your knowledge of the organization and/or its sector; your understanding of organization members' problems—and be prepared for tests of either competence or credibility. For example, Perlow (1997) observes that a critical factor in gaining the support of engineers at the Ditto corporation was that she came from the Massachusetts Institute of Technology (MIT), as 'there is no institution that the engineers we studied hold in higher regard' (1997: 142).

- Pass tests—be non-judgemental when things are said to you about informal activities or about the organization; make sure information given to you does not get back to others, whether bosses or peers. M. Parker (2000) describes how, when at the end of his fieldwork he submitted his report to management, an uncomplimentary comment about the managing director was traced back to an insufficiently anonymized source. Parker subsequently came in for a humiliating grilling from three of the company directors. He claims that this event probably damaged the manager's reputation in the organization and the manager's trust in him.

- You may need a role—if your research involves quite a lot of participant observation, the role will be related to your position within the organization (see Research in focus 19.3). Otherwise, you will need to construct a 'front', as Ditton (1977; see Research in focus 19.5) did when referring to 'his studies'. This will involve thinking about your appearance and your explanations about what you are doing there, and possibly helping out occasionally with work or offering advice. Make sure you have thought about ways in which people's suspicions can be allayed and do not behave ambiguously or inconsistently.

- Be prepared for changes in circumstances that may affect your access, such as changes of senior management.

Cunliffe and Alcadipani (2016) draw on examples from the second author's ethnographic study of a police force in Latin America to propose that access can be understood in the following ways.

- *Instrumental*—within this approach the researcher concentrates on 'maximizing information gained from respondents' (2016: 541) in order to achieve research goals. Research relationships are usually short-term, formal, and disengaged. Access is obtained through deliberate, instrumental use of techniques to win people's trust.

- *Transactional*—access is understood as a reciprocal relationship where an informal or formal agreement is made between the researcher and the organization in exchange for data. This is similar to finding a working role (Research in focus 19.3) and can involve the researcher using 'reputational capital', such as the status of the university which is sponsoring them, to gain access.

- *Relational*—access is characterized as a fluid relationship based on integrity, trust, and mutuality. This requires longer-term relationships to be built.

Cunliffe and Alcadipani (2016: 536–7) frame access as 'an emergent, political process of immersion, backstage dramas and deception'. In relation to deception, they argue that research practice inevitably involves presenting certain impressions of oneself which are misleading, perpetrating certain betrayals, and failing to be transparent about one's motives. As this analysis highlights, the distinctions we made earlier between covert and overt study are not as clear as might be imagined.

A further point arising from Cunliffe and Alcadipani's typology is that the type of access an ethnographer has is likely to have implications for their capacity to penetrate the surface layers of an organization. One strength of organizational ethnography is that it offers the prospect of being able to find out what an organization is 'really' like, as opposed to how it formally depicts itself. For example, Michael Humphreys conducted ethnographic research in the UK headquarters of a US bank referred to pseudonymously as Credit Line (Humphreys and Watson 2009). He was aware of the firm's commitment to corporate social responsibility but became increasingly aware that, although people working in the organization were publicly enthusiastic about its ethical stance, many were privately sceptical about the firm's actual commitment. For example, he quotes one employee (Charity) as saying: 'My problem is that, in this organization, corporate social responsibility is a sham—it's just rhetoric—I mean how can we call ourselves responsible when we give credit cards to poor people and charge them 30 per cent APR [annual percentage rate] just because they are high risk?' (Humphreys and Watson 2009: 50). For employees to divulge such private views, which cast doubt on the integrity of their organization, the ethnographer will probably need to be closer to the confidant role referred to in Table 19.1, since it requires the organizational participants to be comfortable about sharing their private views, which could lead to them being censured by senior managers.

Key informants

One aspect of having sponsors or gatekeepers who smooth access for the ethnographer is that they may become *key informants* in the fieldwork. Ethnographers tend to rely on several informants, but certain informants may become particularly important to the research. They often develop an appreciation of the research and direct the ethnographer to situations, events, or people likely to be helpful to the progress of the investigation.

An example is provided by Kanter (1977), who describes the relationships she developed with a small group of people at Indsco Corporation. 'These people were largely in functions where they were well placed to see a large number of people in a large number of levels ... They could tell me about the history of the company and a variety of experiences in the organization as well as provide information about the issues in their own careers. I could also use them to check out stories I gathered elsewhere' (1977: 336). Collinson (1992*b*) describes how being a man researching equal opportunities sometimes resulted in research respondents withholding cooperation. He describes how the identification of key women informants, who were prepared to assist the 'young lad from the university', was crucial in providing him with 'insider' information. One woman trade unionist in particular provided extensive help with the project. Collinson and the woman trade unionist developed 'a much closer and mutually supportive working relationship than would usually be the case between researcher and respondents' (1992*b*: 115). This provided him with 'deeper insight into the difficulties faced by women in employment and within the trade union movement' (1992*b*: 115) and greater understanding of the problems of managing work and home.

In summary, key informants can clearly be of great help to the ethnographer and frequently provide a support that helps with the stress of fieldwork. However, this carries risks in that the ethnographer may develop an undue reliance on the key informant, and, rather than seeing social reality through the eyes of a range of members of the social setting, the researcher is seeing social reality primarily through the eyes of the key informant.

Roles for ethnographers

Related to the issue of ongoing access is the question of the type of role the ethnographer adopts. One of the most widely cited schemes to describe the roles that ethnographers adopt is Gold's (1958) classification of participant observer roles, which can be arrayed on a continuum of degrees of involvement with and detachment from members of the social setting (see Figure 19.1). There are four roles.

- *Complete participant.* According to Gold, the complete participant is a fully functioning member of the social setting and his or her true identity is not known to members. As such, the complete participant is a covert observer, like D. Roy (1958) and Dalton (1959).

- *Participant-as-observer.* This role is the same as the complete participant one, but members of the social setting are aware of the researcher's status as a

FIGURE 19.1

Gold's classification of participant observer roles

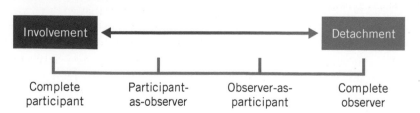

researcher. The ethnographer is engaged in regular interaction with people, participates in their daily lives, and is open about their research. In organizational ethnography this frequently involves taking up either paid or unpaid employment in the research setting, as did Delbridge (1998) in his study of contemporary manufacturing under TQM and Alcadipani in his study of factory shopfloor workers in a printing factory in the North of England (Alcadipani and Tonelli, 2014).

- *Observer-as-participant*. In this role, the researcher is mainly an interviewer. There is some observation, but very little of it involves any participation. Many of the studies covered in Chapter 20 are of this type.
- *Complete observer*. The researcher does not interact with people. According to Gold, people do not have to take the researcher into account. This kind of role relies on forms of observation that are unobtrusive in character. For example, in studies at the Western Electric Company's Hawthorne plant, investigators spent a total of six months observing the informal social relationships between operators in the Bank Wiring Observation Room. Investigations involved an observer, who maintained a role as 'disinterested spectator' with the aim of observing and describing what was going on. Observation involved certain general rules: the investigator should not give orders or answer any questions that necessitated the assumption of authority; he should not enter voluntarily into any argument and generally should remain as non-committal as possible; he should not force himself into any conversation or appear anxious to overhear; he should never violate confidences or give information to supervisors; and he should not by his manner of speech or behaviour 'set himself off from the group' (Roethlisberger and Dickson 1939: 388–9).

Each role carries its own advantages and risks. The issues concerning being a complete participant were touched on in Research in focus 19.4. According to Gold, the participant-as-observer role carries the risk of over-identification and hence of 'going native' (see Key concept 19.6) through getting too close to people. Gold argues that the observer-as-participant role carries the risk of not understanding the social setting and people in it sufficiently and therefore of making incorrect inferences. The complete observer role shares with complete participation the removal of the possible problem of reactivity, but it carries even further risks than the observer-as-participant role of failing to understand situations.

However, most writers would take the view that, since ethnography entails immersion in a social setting and fairly prolonged involvement, the complete observer role should not be considered as participant observation or ethnography at all, since participation is likely to be missing.

Table 19.1 outlines the working roles that organizational ethnographers may adopt in order to gain access to closed settings (Research in focus 19.4). The point here is that such roles, whether paid or unpaid, are likely to require a significant investment of time and effort on the part of the researcher, in addition to that required for the study.

Active or passive?

A further issue that is raised about any situation in which the ethnographer participates is the degree to which he or she should be or can be an active or a passive participant (Van Maanen 1978). Even when the ethnographer is in an observer-as-participant role, there may be contexts in which either participation is unavoidable or a compulsion to join in a limited way may be felt. For example, Fine's (1996) research on the work of chefs in restaurants was carried out largely by semi-structured interview. In spite of his limited participation, he found himself involved in washing up in the kitchens to help out during busy periods. Sometimes ethnographers may *feel* they have no choice but to get involved, because a failure to participate

19.6 KEY CONCEPT
What is 'going native'?

'Going native' refers to a situation that ethnographers can find themselves in when they lose their sense of being a researcher and become wrapped up in the world view of the people they are studying. The prolonged immersion of ethnographers in the lives of the people they study, coupled with the commitment to seeing the social world through their eyes, lie behind the risk and actuality of going native. Going native is a potential problem for several reasons but especially because the ethnographer can lose sight of his or her position as a researcher and therefore find it difficult to develop a social-scientific angle on the collection and analysis of data.

TABLE 19.1
Working roles in organizational ethnography

	Role		
	Consultant	Apprentice	Confidant
Characteristics	Competent, knowledgeable, professional	Naive, unthreatening, personable	Mature, attentive, trustworthy
	A credible outsider who secures the trust of management	A younger person who can make him- or herself useful within the organization	An impartial outsider who is able to listen to people's problems
	Exchange of access for knowledge or information, often in the form of a written report or verbal presentation	Exchange of access for productive labour	Exchange of access for psycho-social support or therapy

actively might indicate to members of the social setting a lack of commitment and lead to a loss of credibility. Another example is provided by Holliday (1995), who describes how in smaller organizations active work-role participation is more likely to be expected of the ethnographer than in larger companies where there is more space to 'hang around'. She describes how at FranTech she was given 'a variety of jobs, from typing and answering the telephone to "managerial" tasks such as auditing the production schedule and writing procedures for the BS5750' (Holliday 1995: 27). Ram (1994; see Research in focus 19.4), in his study of family-owned and managed firms in the West Midlands clothing industry, talks about helping with social security queries, housing issues, and passport problems, advising on higher education, and even tying turbans while in the field.

Ethnography also includes the use of non-observational methods and sources such as interviewing and documents. For example, Lok and de Ronde's (2013) ethnography of the Cambridge University Boat Club involved the ethnographer being copied in on all email correspondence between the squad and coaches, generating a total of around 150 emails. This, in addition to archival data including media post-race reports and a log book kept by former club captains, formed the basis for their analysis of 'practice breakdowns', where things did not go as anticipated for crew members. Similarly, Zhang and Spicer (2014), in their study of a Chinese bureaucracy, used visual methods, taking photographs and asking participants to take photographs of the building, in addition to traditional ethnographic methods such as field notes and interviews.

Shadowing

A form of observation that has affinities with the notion of passive participant observation and which may be feasible for some students when doing research for their dissertations is the notion of *shadowing*, which McDonald (2005) used in her study of team leaders in a high-tech organization. She defines shadowing as 'a research technique which involves a researcher closely following a member of an organization over an extended period of time' (2005: 456). This includes shadowing him or her at meetings as well as time spent writing at his or her desk. Although shadowing need not necessarily form part of an ethnographic study—it could also be used as a stand-alone method—it does bear some similarity to the kinds of participant observation that ethnographers typically engage in. In addition to following the member of the organization throughout his or her working day, the researcher also asks him or her questions about what he or she is doing: 'some of the questions will be for clarification, such as what was being said on the other end of a phone call, or what a departmental joke means. Other questions will be intended to reveal purpose, such as why a particular line of argument was pursued in a meeting, or what the current operational priorities are' (2005: 456). During this process, the researcher may write field notes recording the times and subject of conversation and the body language and moods of the person being shadowed. McDonald claims that one of the advantages of shadowing is that, rather than relying on an individual's account of his or her role in an organization, it enables the researcher to view the behaviour directly. Also, as Czarniawska (2007) notes, shadowing is likely to involve mobility, so that the researcher is able to view the work of the person being shadowed in a variety of contexts.

Gill et al. (2014) suggest that shadowing comprises three phases. First, there is the 'arriving phase' during which the shadower should attend to a range of initial pre-fieldwork issues such as negotiating with the shadowee what areas of organizational activity can be subjected to the shadowing method. Second, there is the shadowing phase itself, during which the shadower should consider such issues as different note-taking strategies and learning the behavioural rules suggested by the organizational culture so that these are not transgressed. Third, there is the 'leaving' phase during which the shadower has to consider how best to make an acceptable exit and to do so in a way that will allow some ongoing contact: for example, so that the shadowee might appraise items written by the shadower. Urban and Quinlan's (2014: 47) experiences of shadowing in Canadian health care organizations suggests that the method, as they put it, is 'not for the faint of heart'. The sometimes frantic world of nurses and the ethical dilemmas that are regularly faced (since informed consent cannot be continually negotiated with those with whom shadowees come into contact) suggest that the method can be challenging to implement.

Field notes

Because of the importance of descriptive detail in qualitative research, ethnographers often take notes based on their observations. These include summaries of events, accounts of behaviour, and the researcher's initial reflections on them. The main equipment that you are likely to need for this is a digital recorder, notepad, and pen. Here are some general principles for writing fieldnotes.

- Write down notes, however brief, as quickly as possible after seeing or hearing something interesting.

- Write up full field notes at the very latest at the end of the day and include such details as location, who was involved, what prompted the exchange, date and time of the day, etc.

- You may prefer to use a digital recorder to record initial notes, but this may create a problem of needing to transcribe a lot of speech.

- Notes must be vivid and clear—you should not have to ask at a later date, 'What did I mean by that?'

- You need to take copious notes, so, if in doubt, write it down. The notes may be of different types (see the section on 'Types of field notes' below).

Obviously, it can be very useful to take your notes down straight away—that is, as soon as something interesting happens. However, wandering around with a notebook and pencil in hand and scribbling notes down on a continuous basis runs the risk of making people self-conscious. It may be necessary, therefore, to develop strategies of taking small amounts of time out, though hopefully without generating the anxieties Ditton (1977) appears to have caused (see Research in focus 19.5). Keeping field notes on top of the demands of being an observer in organizations requires energy and dedication. For example, in their participant observation study of the Cambridge University Boat Race, Lok and de Rond (2013: 192) describe how at the end of each day the ethnographer 'transcribed each day's extensive fieldnotes'.

To some extent, strategies for taking field notes will be affected by the degree to which the ethnographer enters the field with clear research questions. As noted in Chapter 17, most qualitative research adopts a general approach of beginning with general research questions (as shown in Figure 17.1), but there is considerable variation in this. Ditton (see Research in focus 19.5) provides an illustration of a very open-ended approach when he writes that his research 'was not set up to answer any empirical questions' (1977: 11).

However, starting an ethnographic study without having a specific research question can lead to difficulties later on. Kunda (1992) describes how he was swamped with information, partly because he did not seek to define his focus of study. His interest in any event that was occurring in the organization led to the generation of a vast quantity of data. During his year in the field he 'generated thousands of pages of fieldnotes and interview transcripts (produced each day from the fragmented notes hastily scribbled during and between events and interviews), collections of archival material, computer output, newsletters, papers, memos, brochures, posters, textbooks, and assorted leftovers' (1992: 237). Usually the ethnographer will begin to narrow down the focus of his or her research and to match observations to the emerging research focus. M. Parker (2000: 239) describes how, as each case study progressed, he began to focus down on certain key issues and ideas that began to guide his interviews and observation. This was partly a result of feeling the need to develop a framework that could enable him to cope with the 'huge quantity of ideas' and 'incoherent impressions' that he had generated. This approach is implied by the sequence shown in Figure 17.1.

Speaking into a digital recorder may rekindle an awareness of the ethnographer's presence. Also, in shops, offices, and factories it may be difficult to use a recorder without the availability of an interview room, because of the impact of extraneous noise.

Types of field notes

Some writers classify the types of field notes that are generated in the process of conducting an ethnography. The following classification is based on categories suggested by Lofland and Lofland (1995) and Sanjek (1990).

- *Mental notes*: particularly useful when it is inappropriate to be seen taking notes.
- *Jotted notes* (also called *scratch notes*): very brief notes written down on pieces of paper or in small notebooks to jog one's memory about events that should be written up later. Lofland and Lofland (1995: 90) refer to these as being made up of 'little phrases, quotes, key words, and the like'. They need to be jotted down inconspicuously, preferably out of sight, since detailed note-taking in front of people may make them self-conscious. Willems (2018: 29) describes how he 'jotted down significant observations' while observing train dispatchers in the railway control room which he then wrote down in a more detailed ethnographic style in the field notes' (see Research in focus 17.5 and 19.7).

- *Full field notes*: as soon as possible, make detailed notes, which will be your main data source. They should be written at the end of the day or sooner if possible. Write as promptly and as fully as possible. Write down information about events, people, conversations, etc. Write down initial ideas about interpretation. Record impressions and feelings.

As Research in focus 19.7 illustrates, the content of field notes includes descriptive observations of behaviour and settings, as well as the ethnographer's emotional reflections on their experiences. For example, in describing her fieldwork experience, Holliday (1995) draws attention to her prevailing fear of incompetence, her concern about being liked, and her anxiety about whether or not to disagree with or challenge people. Field notes are used by ethnographers as a basis for personal reflection (Coffey 1999), and as a source of data that is used in writing up an account of the social setting and the culture in question (see Research in focus 19.7).

19.7 RESEARCH IN FOCUS
Using field note extracts in data analysis and writing

Willems' (2018) two-year ethnographic study of train dispatchers in the Dutch railway system relied heavily on observing the dispatchers as they went about their daily work in the control room. Through observing, talking to, and interviewing the train dispatchers, Willems began to develop his theoretical focus and research question, which was concerned with understanding the role of the body and the senses in practice-based learning. In presenting his analysis, Willems makes significant use of his fieldnotes and observations, giving examples of them to illustrate particular themes. As the following extract shows, there can be significant literary and creative skill that goes into writing field notes in a way which conveys the experience of being in a situation.

> There is something about the sound here, but I don't know what it is. Sometimes the sound of phones and voices swells into a roar after which it tones down near to a silence, only to be followed by a new eruption of noise (Field notes 5 December 2013).

(2018: 32)

However, on other occasions Willem's writing from his field notes is more factually descriptive, as in this extract:

> The phone of Mandy rings. She does not pick up her phone but gazes at it and then at her screens, after which she turns to me and starts counting, '4, 3, 2, 1,' and then the phone 'magically' stops ringing. She smiles: 'I just knew he'd hang up.' (Observation 15 July 2014).

(2018: 30)

In both cases, the extracts evoke an atmosphere, including of sounds and physical actions, which convey the embodied, sensory experience of being in the control room in a way which would be difficult to achieve using other methods such as qualitative interviewing.

Bringing ethnographic fieldwork to an end

Knowing when to stop is not an easy or straightforward matter in ethnography. Because of its unstructured nature and the absence of specific hypotheses to be tested (other than those that might emerge during data collection and analysis), there is a tendency for ethnographic research to lack an obvious end point. Traditions within anthropology have dictated that long-term continuous fieldwork should usually consist of a period of 12 months, to enable the study of a culture through a full seasonal cycle of activity (C. A. Davies 1999). These conventions also apply, though perhaps to a lesser extent, within organizational ethnography, where a 'long stay' in the field is still seen as crucial to securing 'insider' status. At some point, however, ethnographic research does come to an end! Career, personal, and family reasons will necessitate leaving the field; dissertation deadlines or research funding commitments will bring fieldwork to a close. A deadline for concluding an ethnographic study may have been negotiated with the organization as a condition of access.

Ethnographic research is likely to be demanding for many reasons: the nature of the topic, which may place the fieldworker in stressful situations; the marginality of the researcher in the social setting and the need constantly to manage a front; and the prolonged absence from one's normal life that is often necessary. The ethnographer may feel that he or she has simply had enough. A further possibility that may start to bring about moves to bring fieldwork to a close is that the ethnographer may begin to feel that the research questions on which he or she has decided to concentrate are answered, so that there are no new data worth generating. The ethnographer may even feel a strong sense of déjà vu towards the end of data collection. Altheide (1980: 310) has written that his decision to leave the various news organizations in which he conducted ethnographic research was often motivated by 'the recurrence of familiar situations and the feeling that little worthwhile was being revealed'. In the language of grounded theory, all the researcher's categories are thoroughly *saturated*, although Glaser and Strauss's (1967) approach would invite you to be certain that there are no new questions to be asked of the area you are investigating, or no new comparisons to be made.

The reasons for bringing ethnographic research to a close can involve a wide range of factors, from the personal to matters of research design. Whatever the reason, disengagement has to be *managed*. For one thing, this means that promises must be kept, so that, if you promised a report to an organization as a condition of entry, that promise should not be forgotten. It also means that ethnographers must provide good explanations for their departure. If members of a social setting are aware of a researcher's presence they will know that he or she is a temporary fixture, but over a long period of time, and especially if there was genuine participation in activities within that setting, people may forget that the ethnographer's presence is finite. The farewells have to be managed and in an orderly fashion. Buchanan et al. (1988) recommend that leaving the research site is handled in such a way as to leave the door open to the possibility of future research or fieldwork visits. At this stage it is useful to confirm the conclusion of the research in writing, thanking staff for their cooperation.

Also, the ethnographer's *ethical* commitments must not be forgotten, such as the need to ensure that persons and settings are anonymized. It is common practice within organizational ethnography to change the name of a company in order to protect the anonymity of the organization, as well as the names of individuals who participated in the study—even place names and locations may be changed. For example, Dalton (1959) protected the anonymity of his 'intimates' or informants by changing the place names and locations associated with the study. He also did not disclose his job role in the companies he worked in because he felt this would endanger the exposure of 'intimates' to their superiors. Whatever happens, it is wise to reach an agreement with senior members of the organization before disclosing the identity of an organization, and it may be less threatening for senior managers and employers if the researcher offers anonymity as an explicit aspect of the access agreement. Humphreys, in his research on Credit Line referred to earlier, went even further in his efforts to ensure that organizational participants remained anonymous (Humphreys and Watson 2009). He was concerned that the gulf between the company's public position on corporate social responsibility, and the private views of many staff about that position, presented him with an ethical dilemma in that he needed to protect their anonymity so that they would not get into trouble with the firm. His use of direct quotes from a respondent named 'Charity' are quoted, but Charity is not a pseudonym, the usual tactic used by researchers to preserve the identity of their informants. Instead 'Charity' is a composite, rather than a real person; her words are an aggregation of the remarks of several employees who expressed similar positions.

Feminist ethnography

In this section we will review some of the debates within feminist research and relate them to the ethnographic tradition. There are several examples of ethnographies done by women and of women's work (e.g. Cavendish 1982; Westwood 1984; see also Research in focus 19.8 and 19.9), but few ethnographic studies are informed by feminist tenets of the kind outlined in Chapter 17.

Reinharz (1992) sees feminist ethnography as significant because it

- documents women's lives and activities, which were previously largely seen as marginal and subsidiary to men's;

- understands women from their perspective, so that the tendency that 'trivializes females' activities and thoughts, or interprets them from the standpoint of men in the society or of the male researcher' (1992: 52) is mitigated; and

- understands women in context.

Such commitments and practices go only part of the way towards understanding feminist ethnography. Feminist researchers are concerned with the question of whether research allows for a non-exploitative relationship between researcher and researched. One of the main elements of such a strategy is that the ethnographer does not treat the relationship as a one-way process of extracting information from others, but actually provides something in return. Yet Stacey (1988) argues, based on her fieldwork experience, that the situations she encountered as a feminist ethnographer placed her

> in situations of inauthenticity, dissimilitude, and potential, perhaps inevitable, betrayal situations that I now believe are inherent in fieldwork method. For no matter how welcome, even enjoyable the fieldworker's presence may appear to 'natives', fieldwork represents an intrusion and intervention into a system of relationships, a system of relationships that the researcher is far freer to leave.
>
> (1988: 23)

19.8 RESEARCH IN FOCUS
An ethnography of work from a woman's perspective

In her study of women employed in unskilled manual jobs in Britain, Pollert (1981) set out to understand the lived experience of working under modern capitalism from a woman's perspective. The study is based on informal interviews and observation on the shopfloor of a Bristol tobacco factory in 1972. 'It is a glimpse into the everyday working lives of the young girls and older women who worked there: about how they got on with their jobs, their bosses and each other—and in a background sense, their boyfriends, their husbands and their families—and how all these strands wove together into their experience and consciousness' (1981: 6).

Pollert was not employed in the factory and was open about her status as a researcher. Her role was one of observer-as-participant, according to Gold's classification scheme. Being a female researcher was, according to Pollert, vitally important to the study and an important factor in breaking down barriers with women workers. However, while she was a woman among women, she was also middle-class, had a middle-class accent, and was not there to earn money—factors that clearly set her apart from the women. To begin with she was 'naturally scrutinized with a mixture of hostility, suspicion and curiosity' (1981: 7) and was called upon to answer more questions than she asked. In managing to break down some of these barriers, Pollert explains that she tried to be open with her opinions, in wanting to argue with and challenge attitudes as well as to learn, and not to set herself up as a 'reporter' who was interested in 'how the masses think'. Interestingly, unlike many male organizational ethnographers, Pollert kept a degree of social distance from her research subjects, having very little direct involvement with home, community, and social life. 'It was simply not on to suggest we meet for a drink in a pub, the normal "neutral" meeting-place for men.' Instead, what she learned about home and social life was filtered through factory experience.

Pollert's research goes some way towards being what could be described as a feminist ethnography (she focuses on the working lives of women and seeks to understand the women from their own perspective and in their own context). However, as Pollert managed the power relations between herself and the women mainly as a one-way process, the study does not conform to the ideals of feminist ethnography in this respect.

19.9 RESEARCH IN FOCUS
'Not one of the guys': ethnography in a male-dominated setting

The male-dominated cultures that are associated with some organizational settings, such as factory shopfloors and management boardrooms, means that gender and sexuality is often an important consideration in fieldwork encounters. For example, Collinson (1992*a*) describes the collectivist, masculine practices of 'piss taking' and swearing on the shopfloor, while Watson (1994*a, b*) draws attention to the jokes and 'dirty talking' that reinforced his inclusion among managers at ZTC Ryland.

The emphasis that some male ethnographers place on jokes, humour, swearing, and 'becoming one of the lads' could be interpreted as an attempt to demonstrate their 'insider' status. However, an ethnographer's ability to participate in masculine practices does not necessarily confirm their status as an insider (Bell 1999). Although female organizational ethnographers sometimes experience masculine organizational settings in a way that confirms their 'difference' and can make them feel uncomfortable, for example, through constant exposure to pornographic images on the wall (D. Fletcher 2002) or not having access to women-only toilets (Bell 1999), this does not necessarily preclude them from collecting ethnographic data. Instead, gender roles can be understood as a dynamic feature of the researcher's identity in fieldwork settings (C. Warren 1988) that changes over time.

Stacey also argues that, when the research is written up, it is the feminist ethnographer's interpretations and judgements that come through and have authority.

Reinharz (1992: 74–5) argues that, although ethnographic fieldwork relationships may sometimes *seem* manipulative, a clear undercurrent of reciprocity often lies beneath them. The researcher may offer help or advice to research participants, or she may exhibit reciprocity by giving a public airing to normally marginalized voices (although the ethnographer is always the mouthpiece for such voices and may be imposing a particular 'spin' on them). However, it would be wrong to abandon feminist ethnography on the grounds that the ethnographer cannot fulfil all possible obligations simultaneously or is not entirely at ease in the research situation (see Research in focus 19.9). Indeed, this would be a recipe for the abandonment of all research, feminist or otherwise. What is crucial is transparency—both in the feminist ethnographer's dealings with the women she studies and in the account of the research process.

Global and multi-site ethnography

Traditionally, the boundaries of an ethnographic study were determined by place—the ethnographer travelled to the location where the community was located and studied what he or she found there. However, in organizational ethnography it can be difficult to set spatial or geographic boundaries around the community being studied, especially in cases where the organization is part of a multinational corporation. A further feature of organizational ethnography that distinguishes it from traditional ethnography is the need to understand the wider societal and economic context within which a given organization is situated. This has given rise to new forms of ethnographic research that are not so dependent on place, in the form of multi-site and global ethnography.

Global ethnography focuses on understanding how cultures are affected by globalization in ways that have contributed to the dissolution of traditional ways of working (Burawoy et al. 2000). In so doing it extends the tradition of ethnographic studies of industrial and large bureaucratic organizations, as studied by Casey (1995), with relatively fixed boundaries. Some global ethnographers seek to gain insight into the lived experience of globalization by studying mobile occupational groups, such as job-hopping Irish software engineers or Indian

19.10 RESEARCH IN FOCUS
A multi-site ethnography of diversity management

Prasad et al. (2011) conducted a four-year long multi-sited ethnography of six organizations from the Canadian petroleum and insurance industries. Their focus was on the workplace diversity management programmes that had been implemented in these organizations, and on the discourse of fashion that had shaped the implementation process. In each of the six organizations, three components of data collection were involved.

1. Ethnographic observations: primarily this involved observing diversity training sessions, internal meetings, a diversity conference, and diversity training for HR professionals delivered by external consultants.

2. In-depth ethnographic interviews: these were conducted with diversity consultants and trainers, personnel and HR directors, diversity managers, and participants in diversity workshops.

3. Examination of documents: these were related to the diversity management process, including brochures, videos, training exercises, and cases.

What is interesting about this study is that the focus on fashion relies on understanding the relationships between fashion setters and followers, which a multi-site ethnographic approach enables more effectively than a single-site approach.

nurses working in the USA. This shift opens up opportunities to study phenomena such as the effects of advances in telecommunications and information technologies on working practices.

Related to global ethnography is the concept of multi-site ethnography (Prasad and Prasad 2009). In such studies 'the researcher does not confine his/her observations and analysis to a single organization or location but follows specific social phenomena as they travel between different actors and networks in multiple institutional domains' (Prasad et al. 2011: 707). As with global ethnography, there is a recognition that organizations have permeable boundaries and are influenced

by other organizations and institutions. Hence there is a need to move beyond single sites and locations and to reconnect local meaning-making practices with 'wider social events and mindsets' (Prasad et al. 2011: 707). These writers are influenced by Marcus (1999) in suggesting the strategy of 'following', as a distinguishing feature of such research, tracking 'people (e.g. expatriate managers, minority executives, female bond traders, etc.), products (e.g. coffee, sushi, T-shirts, etc.), conflicts (over resources or social issues), life-histories, laws, policies, and an array of discourses as they wind in and out of multiple organizational locations' (Prasad et al. 2011: 708; see Research in focus 19.10).

Virtual ethnography

Ethnography may not seem to be an obvious arena for collecting data via the internet. The image of the ethnographer is that of someone who visits places or locations, and, particularly in the context of business research, organizations. The internet seems to go against that because it is a decidedly placeless space. As V. Hine (2000) has observed, conceiving of the internet as a place—a cyberspace—has been one strategy for an ethnographic study of the internet, and from this it is just a short journey to the examination of online communities

or virtual communities. In this way, our concepts of place and space that are constitutive of the way in which we operate in the real world are grafted onto the internet and its use. A further issue is that, as already noted, ethnography entails participant observation, but in cyberspace what is the ethnographer observing and in what is he or she participating? In particular, a virtual ethnography requires getting away from the idea that an ethnography is of or in a 'place' in any traditional sense. It is also an ethnography of a domain that infiltrates other spaces and times in the lives of its participants, so that the boundaries of the 'virtual' in a virtual ethnography are problematic to participants and analysts alike.

Early ethnographic research in connection with the internet often entailed the use of semi-structured interviews which were administered online (e.g. Markham 1998). As the use of the internet has changed, there has been a burgeoning of online discussion groups and these have increasingly become a focus of attention for researchers wanting to conduct online ethnographic research. One of the most significant approaches to doing such research is *netnography* (see Research in focus 19.11), which has been developed by Kozinets (2010, 2012). For Kozinets, netnography is a form of ethnography because it entails the researcher's immersion in the online worlds under investigation; because it is an essentially naturalistic method; and because it relies considerably on observation, though often supported by forms of online interview. Netnography is tailored to the examination of communities that have an exclusively online existence, although it can play a role in relation to communities that have both an online and an offline existence. With cases where a community has both an online and an offline presence, the offline element needs to be examined through a conventional ethnographic approach.

The growing focus on online communities suggests a number of different formats through which they can be studied using various combinations of netnography, traditional ethnography, and some interviewing. Three types of study are described here. The three types entail a considerable degree of immersion in the postings, but Type 1 is the least likely of the three to be viewed as a form of online ethnography, as the researcher largely occupies a position as external observer.

Type 1. Study of online interaction only with no participation. These are studies that typically entail solely the examination of blogs, discussion groups, listservs, etc., without any participation or intervention on the part of the researcher(s). This can take the form of 'lurking' and conducting an analysis without the authors of the materials being aware of the researcher's(s') presence. However, a more ethical approach that is consistent with netnography is for the researcher to announce his/her presence, as Kozinets (2002; see Research in focus 19.11) did in his study of an online group of coffee enthusiasts and Chan and Li (2010; see Research in focus 27.7) did in their mixed methods study of a virtual community of consumers. The goal of such research is to uncover themes that derive from the threads in the online discussions.

Type 2. Study of online interaction with some participation plus online or offline interviews. These are studies that typically entail the examination of blogs, discussion groups, listservs, etc., but with some participation or intervention on the part of researcher(s). The researcher

19.11 RESEARCH IN FOCUS
Netnography

Kozinets (2002, 2010) has coined the term 'netnography' to refer to a marketing research method that investigates computer-mediated communications in connection with market-related topics. The author defines online communities in a particular way for the purposes of his research: 'Online communities are contexts in which consumers often partake in discussions whose goals include attempts to inform and influence fellow consumers about products and brands' (2002: 61). Kozinets illustrates his approach with reference to a study of the meanings surrounding coffee and its consumption. As with most specialized online discussion forums, groups that engage in computer-mediated communications about a certain topic are likely to be knowledgeable enthusiasts. Therefore, they are well placed to provide interesting market-related information about trends and meanings in relation to a consumer topic such as coffee. Kozinets began with a search for newsgroups that contained the word 'coffee' and homed in on one—<alt.coffee>—that contained a large amount of traffic. He read hundreds of posted messages but narrowed these down to 179. He followed through particular threads (for example, those to do with Starbucks) in terms of their connection with his research questions. For example, the netnography suggests that, among many of these enthusiasts, Starbucks is seen as having commodified coffee, and, as a result, its 'baristas' lack passion in their craft. There is a sense that the discussion participants felt that this lack of passion was transmitted to the quality of the coffee. Kozinets suggests that his analysis shows that 'coffee marketers have barely begun to plumb the depths of taste, status, and snob appeal that are waiting to be explored by discriminating coffee consumers' (2002: 70).

is not passive and instead intervenes (overtly or covertly) in the ongoing postings and discussions. In addition, the researcher interviews some of the people involved in the online interaction. The interviews may be online or offline. Research in focus 19.12 illustrates this kind of study. So too does Kozinets's (2001) study of *Star Trek* fandom and the construction of consumption, in particular in relation to memorabilia and merchandise. Kozinets, himself a *Star Trek* fan, collected data from three websites devoted to *Star Trek* which exhibited a substantial amount of interaction between fans. In addition, he was a participant observer at meetings and conventions for fans and conducted face-to-face and email interviews with fans. Kozinets also contributed to some of the online interactions between fans on the websites.

Type 3. Study of online interaction plus offline research methods (in addition to online or offline interviews). Same as Type 2, but in addition there is active participation of the researcher(s) in the offline worlds of those being studied, such as attending gatherings, as well as interviews (which may be online or offline). An example is Chen's (2012) study of group buying online, whereby groups of consumers approach businesses concerning their intention to purchase goods and services with a view to negotiating better terms by virtue of their greater leverage as a result of being part of a group. Chen focused on Ihergo.com, which is the largest Taiwanese online

community dedicated to group buying. Chen's methods are described as follows: 'This study used Netnography to gather data, including online participant-observation (e.g., observing participants' online discussion and buying behaviour in Ihergo), online interviews (e.g., e-mail exchanges and online immediate interviews), offline participant observation (e.g., joining private parties/meetings), and offline (face-to-face in-depth) interviews' (Chen 2012: 258). Through the resulting data, Chen was able to identify four motivations for online group purchasing.

A further example of the use of ethnography in relation to the study of online worlds can be found in Research in focus 19.11, which shows how the study of online discussion groups can be revealing about enthusiasms in our era of consumerism and brands.

Studies such as these are clearly inviting us to consider the nature of the internet as a domain for investigation, but they also invite us to consider the nature and the adaptiveness of our research methods. In the examples discussed in this section, the question of what is and is not ethnography is given a layer of complexity that adds to the considerations referred to earlier in this chapter. But these studies are also invariably cases of using internet-based research methods to investigate internet use. Future online ethnographic investigations of issues unrelated to the internet will give a clearer indication

19.12 RESEARCH IN FOCUS
Using blogs in a study of word-of-mouth marketing

Kozinets et al. (2010) carried out a netnographic (see Research in focus 19.11) study of word-of-mouth marketing (WOMM), a technique increasingly used by firms who intentionally influence individuals who they believe are likely to communicate positive impressions of a product to others. Word of mouth has been known to be an important factor in influencing whether new products or changes to existing ones will take root. As a marketing device, WOMM is used to influence a formerly spontaneous process. A North American specialist WOMM firm (Buzzablog) 'seeded' a new camera-equipped mobile phone with 90 influential bloggers whom the firm had previously screened and who were known to write about relevant issues and also to attract 400 or more readers per day. The authors did not participate in the study in the sense of contributing to any of the discussion surrounding the blogs, though they did have some discussions with Buzzablog, some of whose managers were interviewed. They focused upon the 83 bloggers whose blogs were maintained for the duration of the study. Their dataset comprised 220 postings by the bloggers and around 700 comments from readers. These were divided into postings that were sent before, during, or after the WOMM campaign. Through a **qualitative content analysis** of the blogs and associated discussions, four communication strategies were identified and were taken to suggest that WOMM does not simply amplify marketing messages. The content and meaning of marketing messages were transformed at the same time that they were being implanted. The authors conclude: 'Word-of-mouth marketing operates through a complex process that transforms commercial information into cultural stories relevant to the members of particular communities' (Kozinets et al. 2010: 86).

of the possibilities that the method offers. At the same time, both C. Hine (2008) and Garcia et al. (2009) have observed that there is a growing tendency and need for online ethnographers to take into account offline worlds, because even the most committed internet user has a life beyond the computer. This means taking into account that the members of the online communities that tend to be the focus of ethnographic studies have lives offline and that the two will have implications for the other. There is a corollary to this observation: as the internet becomes increasingly embedded in people's lives, practitioners of what might be thought of as conventional ethnography (in the sense of the ethnographic study of non-virtual lives and communities) will increasingly have to take into account individuals' commitments to life online. Earlier online/virtual ethnographies tended to emphasize people's involvement and participation in online worlds, perhaps because the relative newness of the internet and its lack of reach into everyday life during those days meant that the virtual could be treated as a relatively autonomous domain.

One area of debate in recent years regarding online ethnography has been over the status of 'lurking'. This practice is disliked by members of online communities and can result in censure from participants, who are often able to detect the practice. Online ethnographers sometimes lurk as a prelude to their fieldwork in order to gain an understanding of the setting prior to their overt participation. Even when websites are used in this way, ethical issues arise (see Research in focus 19.13), and it has been suggested that 'ethnographers will get a more authentic experience of an online setting if they jump straight into participation' (Garcia et al. 2009: 60).

19.13 RESEARCH IN FOCUS
Ethical issues in a virtual ethnography of change in the NHS

There have been some attempts to highlight the ethical considerations associated with virtual ethnography. Clegg Smith (2004) was interested in organizational change and the role played by professionals in the NHS. While she was doing her research, she came across a listserv that was being used by British general practitioners (GPs) as a forum to discuss their feelings about the proposed reforms to the British health care system and their likely effects. She explains, 'essentially, I had stumbled on a "setting" in which GPs were "talking" among themselves about the significance of the proposed health care reforms for them as individuals, for the wider profession and generally about the future of general practice in Britain' (2004: 225). The geographically dispersed nature of GPs' work meant that the list provided a unique opportunity for them to interact with each other. Clegg Smith argues that one of the advantages of such virtual methods is that they provide the opportunity to conduct research with virtually no observer effects (see Research in focus 3.7). Therefore, her strategy was covert because, she explains, 'I anticipated difficulties in informing participants about my research without intruding in the ongoing interaction to an unacceptable extent' (2004: 232), and she feared that this might also arouse hostility because she observed that 'spam' messages were received unfavourably. For 15 months she 'participated' in the list by receiving and reading messages daily without explicitly stating or explaining her presence to the majority of the listserv's members. A further difficulty in seeking informed consent arose from the nature of the list as an unmoderated forum; therefore there was no gatekeeper to whom she could address her request. Added to this, the membership of the list of around 500 members was in constant flux, so any single request for consent would have been impossible. Hence 'the only appropriate way to gain informed consent would be to repeatedly post requests to the entire list. Through my previous exposure to the list, however, I knew that such behaviour was clearly out of line with accepted practice in this domain' (2004: 233).

However, as Clegg Smith explains, 'I am aware that in making the decision not to expound my presence on the list, I may face considerable ethical critique. My research appears analogous with the notion of "covert" research so demonized in the usual discussions of research ethics' (2004: 225). One of the ways in which she justifies this is through discussion of the features of her study that distinguish it from other studies of virtual interaction. She notes how her study examined interaction between participants who were not engaged in the kind of 'fantasy interaction' associated with sexual or social virtual interaction. Therefore, Clegg Smith argues, her participants were not taking the opportunity to 'engage in behaviour with which they would not be comfortable engaging as part of their "real" lives' (2004: 228). A further ethical justification of her research arises from the extent to which participants saw the list as a public rather than a private space. The warning posted to each member on subscription and at monthly intervals stated 'MEMBERS ARE ADVISED TO CONSIDER COMMENTS POSTED TO LISTX TO BE IN THE PUBLIC DOMAIN' (2004: 229; capitalization in original). In addition, list members received guidelines on the copyright implications of email messages, which stated that comments posted to public lists are comparable to sending letters to a newspaper editor. Clegg Smith suggests that this provided justification for her 'electronic eavesdropping', since the ethical guidelines she was working to suggested that it was 'not necessary to explicitly seek permission for recording and analyzing publicly posted messages' because this is 'akin to conducting research in a marketplace, library or other public area, where observers are not necessarily expected to obtain informed consent from all present' (2004: 230).

A final ethical issue arising from the study concerns the principle of anonymity. Initially, Clegg Smith assumed she should protect the identity of participants when reporting her research findings, but through her involvement in the list she became aware that 'participants might wish to be "credited" for their postings' (2004: 234) because of the reaction when journalists used list messages without crediting the authors. However, despite this, she felt that, because she had not sought informed consent from all list members, it would be wrong to do this.

Visual ethnography

The term 'visual ethnography' (see Key concept 19.14) refers to ethnographic research where visual materials feature prominently in the setting and the researchers' analysis (Peñaloza 1999; Pink 2001). However, as with virtual ethnography, the term is sometimes used in a way that does not imply the kind of sustained immersion in a social setting that is a feature of traditional ethnography. Photographs are the visual medium that has received the greatest attention. An example of visual ethnography is provided by Peñaloza (2000), a marketing researcher, who was interested in how the cultural meaning of the American West is produced through activities at cattle trade shows. The rich imagery of the American West,

reflected by such examples as Marlboro cigarettes, Wrangler jeans, and Jeep Cherokees, is represented through the trade show where animals are bought and sold, but also where the culture of the American West is enacted and celebrated. In addition to participant observation and in-depth interviewing, her ethnographic study incorporated 550 photographs taken at the shows over a six-year period. These were mainly photographs of the events—including cattle sales, breed shows, and rodeos. As a visible record of people and activities, the photographs helped Peñaloza to build up a profile of the ethnicity and gender of event attendees and the types of activities at the show.

19.14 KEY CONCEPT
What is visual ethnography?

Pink (2001) distinguishes between scientific–**realist** approaches to the use of visual methods in ethnographic research, which suggest that visual images are a way of observing and recording reality, and reflexive approaches, which involve exploring how informants and ethnographers experience their social setting. She also argues that, while visual images should be accorded higher status in the generation of ethnographic knowledge, they should not be seen as a replacement for data that rely on the written or spoken word. 'Thus visual images, objects, descriptions should be incorporated when it is appropriate, opportune or enlightening to do so' (2001: 5). Visual ethnography often involves the ethnographer taking photographs or making video recordings of research participants in their social setting. Pink suggests that this has the advantage of being an activity that is more visible and comprehensible to participants, in contrast to the writing of field notes, which is a relatively solitary activity.

Analysis focuses on interpreting the meaning of these visual images within their cultural context. Photographs and video footage can also provide a basis for interviewing members of a social group about their social setting and culture in a similar way to photo-elicitation, described in Chapter 10. Finally, visual ethnography can also include the analysis of visual images in the form of documents containing photographs or artwork that are collected by the ethnographer during his or her involvement in the research setting.

Writing ethnography

In addition to denoting a way of doing research, as mentioned earlier, the label 'ethnography' is also used describe the end result or written product of such studies. Since the 1980s, there has been an interest not just in how ethnography is carried out in the field but also in the rhetorical conventions used to produce ethnographic texts.

Realist tales

Ethnographic texts are designed to convince readers of the *reality* of the events and situations described and the plausibility of the analyst's explanations. The ethnographic text must not simply present a set of findings: it must provide an 'authoritative' account of the group or culture in question. In other words, the ethnographer must convince us that he or she has arrived at an account of social reality that has strong claims to truth.

The ethnographic text is permeated by stylistic and rhetorical devices whereby the reader is persuaded to enter into a shared framework of facts and interpretations, observations and reflections. As with the scientific paper and the kind of approach to writing found in reporting quantitative business research, the ethnographer typically works within a writing strategy that is imbued with *realism*. This simply means that the researcher presents an authoritative, dispassionate account that represents an external, objective reality. In this respect, there is little difference between the writing styles of quantitative and qualitative researchers. Van Maanen (1988) calls ethnography texts that conform to these characteristics *realist tales*. These are the most common type of ethnographic writing, though he distinguishes two other types (see Key concept 19.15 and Research in focus 19.6). However, the *form* that this realism takes differs. Van Maanen also distinguishes four characteristics of realist tales: experiential authority; typical forms; the native's point of view; and interpretative omnipotence. These traits will be discussed in the sections that follow.

Experiential authority

Just as in much quantitative research writing, the author in a realist tale disappears from view. We are told what members of a group say and do, and they are the only people directly visible in the text. The author provides a narrative in which he or she is not seen. As

19.15 KEY CONCEPT
Three forms of ethnographic writing

Van Maanen (1988) has distinguished three major types of ethnographic writing.

- *Realist tales*: apparently definitive, confident, and dispassionate third-person accounts of a culture and of the behaviour of members of that culture. This is the most prevalent form of ethnographic writing.

- *Confessional tales*: personalized accounts in which the ethnographer is fully implicated in the data-gathering and writing-up processes. These are warts-and-all accounts of the trials and tribulations of doing ethnography. They have become more prominent since the 1970s and reflect a growing emphasis on reflexivity in qualitative research in particular. In the edited volume *Doing Research in Organizations* (Bryman 1988b), several of the contributors provide inside accounts of doing qualitative research in industrial enterprises. Beynon (1988), for example, describes how his account, published in *Working for Ford* (1975), of how a dead man was left lying on the factory floor for ten minutes while the line continued to run provoked a response from the Ford Motor Company, which sought to discredit his research. As this example illustrates, confessional tales are more concerned with detailing how research was carried out than with presenting findings. Very often the confessional tale is told in a particular context (such as an invited chapter in a book of similar tales), but the main findings are written up in realist tale form.

- *Impressionist tales*: accounts that place a heavy emphasis on 'words, metaphors, phrasings, and … the expansive recall of fieldwork experience' (Van Maanen 1988: 102). There is a heavy emphasis on stories of dramatic events that provide 'a representational means of cracking open the culture and the fieldworker's way of knowing it' (1988: 102). However, as Van Maanen notes, impressionist tales 'are typically enclosed within realist, or perhaps more frequently, confessional tales' (1988: 106).

a result, an impression is conveyed that the findings presented are what any reasonable, similarly placed researcher would have found. As readers, we have to accept that this is what the ethnographer saw and heard while working as a participant observer or whatever. The personal subjectivity of the author/ethnographer is essentially played down by this strategy. The possibility that the fieldworker may have his or her own biases or may have become too involved with the people being studied is suppressed. To this end, when writing up the results of their ethnographic work, authors play up their academic credentials and qualifications, their previous experience, and so on. All this enhances the degree to which it appears the author's account can be relied upon. The author/ethnographer can then appear as a reliable witness.

19.16 RESEARCH IN FOCUS
Realism in organizational ethnography

Many organizational ethnographies tend to be written as realist tales (see Key concept 19.15), narrated dispassionately to reinforce the authenticity of the account. Typically, the author is absent from the text, or is a minor character in the story, and methods are revealed only at the end, in the form of a 'confessional' chapter or appendix, where the ethnographer 'reveals his hand' (Watson 1994a) by disclosing personal details about the fieldwork experience. However, this is not to say that organizational ethnographers are unaware of the representational difficulties caused by such an approach to writing. Consider, for example, the first few sentences of the methodological appendix that is provided by Kunda (1992) in the book *Engineering Culture: Control and Commitment in a High-Tech Corporation*.

> This study belongs to the genre known as 'ethnographic realism'. This identification says much about presentational style, little about the actual research process. The descriptive style of this genre presents an author functioning more or less as a fly on the wall in the course of his sojourn in the field—an objective, unseen observer following well-defined procedures for data collection and verification. It requires no great insight, however, to recognize that ethnographic realism is a distortion of convenience. Fieldwork, as all who have engaged in it will testify, is an intensely personal and subjective process, and there are probably at least as many 'methods' as there are fieldworkers.
>
> (Kunda 1992: 229).

Kunda questions the extent to which the ethnographer is an objective observer, suggesting instead that he or she experiences organizational life from a situated position as an insider. He implies that it is, therefore, impossible for ethnographers to distance themselves from the fieldwork experience. However, despite this recognition of the need for greater 'reflexivity' within organizational ethnography, only a few organizational ethnographies are actually written in the first person, with the researcher as a main character who is telling the story. Even in cases when this does occur, the main-character narrative tends to be located peripherally, in the appendices or footnotes of an article or book (Hatch 1996), as Kunda himself has done.

A further element of experiential authority is that, when describing their methods, ethnographers invariably make a great deal of the intensiveness of the research that they carried out—they spent so many months in the field, had conversations and interviews with countless individuals, worked hard to establish rapport, and so on. These features are also added to by drawing the reader's attention to such hardships as the inconvenience of the fieldwork—the danger, the poor food, the disruptive effect on normal life, the feelings of isolation and loneliness, and so on.

Typical forms

The author often writes about typical forms of institutions or of patterns of behaviour. What is happening here is that the author is generalizing about a number of recurring features of the group in question to create a typical form that that feature takes. He or she may use examples based on particular incidents or people, but basically the emphasis is on the general.

The native's point of view

One of the distinguishing features of much qualitative research is the commitment to seeing through the eyes of the people being studied. This is an important feature for ethnographic researchers, because it is part of a strategy of getting at the meaning of social reality from the perspective of those studied. However, it also represents an important element in creating a sense of authoritativeness on the part of the ethnographer. After all, claiming to see social reality from the perspective of the group being studied means that the ethnographer is in an excellent position to speak authoritatively and write definitively about them. Realist tales frequently include numerous references to the steps taken by the ethnographer to get close to the people studied and his or her success in this regard. In her study of Afro-Caribbean women working in high-tech informatics, Freeman (2000) writes about the small group of six women at Multitext who became the focus of more intense, long-term data collection:

> After many Sunday lunches, picnics, church services, birthday celebrations, and family outings, I got to know these few women better, seeing them not only as workers but also as members of families, as partners in complex relationships, as mothers, as daughters, as co-workers, and as friends. We spent time together in my rented flat, and in their wood and 'wall house' homes, cooking and eating meals together, sometimes watching videos as we talked. I persuaded them, on rare occasions, to picnic at the beach, and they took me to their churches and fetes and on special outings—to the circus, to the

calypso contests, and to national sites enjoyed by tourists and locals alike. Sometimes we went shopping, and sometimes we bought ice cream after work.

> (2000: 17)

Interpretive omnipotence

When writing up an ethnography in the realist style, the author rarely presents possible alternative interpretations of an event or pattern of behaviour. Instead, the phenomenon in question is presented as having a single meaning or significance, which the fieldworker alone has cracked. Indeed, the evidence provided is carefully marshalled to support the singular interpretation that is placed on the event or pattern of behaviour. We are presented with an inevitability. It seems obvious or inevitable that someone would draw the inferences that the author has drawn when faced with such clear-cut evidence.

Other approaches

Consideration of the four characteristics of realist tales discussed in the previous sections leads to the observation that what the researcher did *qua* researcher is only one part of creating a sense of having worked out the nature of a culture. It is also very much to do with how the researcher represents what he or she did through writing about ethnography.

Van Maanen (1996) has suggested that 'in these textually sophisticated times, few argue that a research report is anything more (or, certainly, anything less) than a framework- or paradigm-dependent document, crafted and shaped within the rules and conventions of a particular research community, some articulated (and written in the back of research journals) and some tacitly understood' (1996: 376). This statement is linked to the influence of postmodernism (Key concept 2.8) and the linguistic turn in qualitative research (Key concept 19.17). Postmodernism has led to a questioning of ethnographic accounts and the authority that is inscribed into them (Clifford 1983). The ethnographic text 'presumes a world out there (the real) that can be captured by a "knowing" author through the careful transcription and analysis of field materials (interviews, notes, etc.)' (Denzin 1994: 296) This thinking can be discerned in Van Maanen's (1988) critique of 'realist tales' (see Key concept 19.15). Postmodernism problematizes such accounts and their authority to represent a reality because there 'can never be a final, accurate representation of what was meant or said, only different textual representations of different experiences' (Denzin 1994:

19.17 KEY CONCEPT
What is the linguistic turn?

Postmodernism can also be seen as the stimulus for the linguistic turn in the social sciences. The linguistic turn is based on the idea that language shapes our understanding of the world. Moreover, because knowledge is constructed through language, and language can never create an objective representation of external reality, meaning is uncontrollable and undiscoverable. This leads to a rejection of positivist scientists' claims to be able to produce reliable knowledge through a neutral process of exploration. Postmodernists argue that knowledge is never neutral and is constantly open to revision. They reject what they see as scientific 'grand' or 'meta' narratives that seek to explain the world from an objective viewpoint. Scientific investigation is thus suggested by postmodernists to be nothing more than a type of 'language game' (Rorty 1979) used by this particular community to produce localized understandings.

Postmodernists have also suggested that certain methods can be more easily adapted to the linguistic turn, in particular ethnography, because it can be used to deconstruct claims to represent reality and can provide alternative versions of reality that attempt to blur the boundary between 'fact' and 'fiction' (Linstead 1993). Auto-ethnography (see Key concept 19.18) can be seen as an attempt to modify the way we use language in research that reflects the linguistic turn. These new forms of writing are sometimes described as being part of the *narrative* turn that seeks to expose the 'fiction' of ethnographic writing by deconstructing its conventions. The narrative turn involves the use of different writing styles that do not involve the creation of ethnographic authority (Woolgar 1988b) and instead encourage a number of perspectives to be represented.

296). This has led to interest in the privilege conveyed in ethnographic texts and how voices, particularly of marginal groups, are often suppressed. These concerns have led to the development of new forms of writing such as auto-ethnography (see Key concept 19.18).

The concerns within these and other traditions (including postmodernism) have led to experiments in writing ethnography (Richardson 1994) that involve the identity of the ethnographer being written into the text (see Research in focus 19.19). An example is the use of a 'dialogic' form of writing that seeks to raise the profile of the multiplicity of voices that can be heard in the course of fieldwork. As Lincoln and Denzin (1994: 584) put it: 'Slowly it dawns on us that there may … be … not one "voice," but polyvocality; not one story, but many tales, dramas, pieces of fiction, fables, memories, histories, autobiographies, poems, and other texts to inform our sense of lifeways, to extend our understandings of the Other.' This postmodern preference for seeking out multiple voices and for turning the ethnographer into a 'bit player' reflects the mistrust among postmodernists of 'meta-narratives'—that is, positions or grand accounts that implicitly make claims about absolute truths and that therefore rule out the possibility of alternative versions of reality. On the other hand, 'mini-narratives, micronarratives, local narratives are just stories that make no truth claims and are therefore more acceptable to postmodernists' (Rosenau 1992: p. xiii).

19.18 KEY CONCEPT
What is auto-ethnography?

One of the ways in which more reflexive, narrative forms of ethnographic writing have been cultivated is through the emerging cross-disciplinary genre of auto-ethnography. This relates to the interest of anthropologists in auto-anthropology (Strathern 1987), which is an autobiographical form of research that is concerned with researching settings where the cultural backgrounds of the observer and observed are shared. Auto-ethnography involves the writing of a highly personalized text in which the personal is related to the cultural and the political in a way that claims the conventions associated with literary writing. However, it is difficult to summarize what auto-ethnography is about, precisely because its purpose is to challenge the conventions of social scientific writing by blurring the boundaries of genre that separate art and science, a practice referred to as 'genre bending'. An example of this is a book by Ellis (2004) entitled *The Ethnographic I: A Methodological Novel about Teaching and Doing Autoethnography*, which uses a fictitious account of her teaching a graduate course on auto-ethnography as the basis for discussion of doing and writing auto-ethnography. This involves blending the highly personalized accounts of her own and her students' lives with methodological discussions in a way that has come to be labelled as 'creative non-fiction'. Crucial to the auto-ethnographic style of writing is the focus on 'creating a palpable emotional experience' (Holman Jones 2005: 767) for readers so that they experience the narrative 'as if it were happening to them' (Ellis 2004: 116). Although there are few signs so far of auto-ethnography having been imported into the study of management and business, one example is found in a book by Goodall (1994) entitled *Casing a Promised Land: The Autobiography of an Organizational Detective as Cultural Ethnographer*, which describes the adventures of an organization communication specialist who enters a variety of organizational settings and, like a detective, looks for clues in order to understand them. Watson (2000) has argued that ethnographic research accounts can be written in a way that bridges the genres of creative writing and social science, calling this 'ethnographic fiction science'. One of the challenges for many social science researchers is that this entails having the skills of a fiction writer as well as the abilities of a researcher, which is a demanding combination that their experience may not have prepared them for.

19.19 RESEARCH IN FOCUS
Identity and ethnographic writing

In her study of everyday life on the shopfloor of a Japanese factory, Kondo (1990) provides an example of ethnographic writing in which the self is central to the account. Kondo describes how, as a Japanese–American academic studying Japanese factory life, she had to learn how to act and behave as a Japanese woman: 'My first nine months of fieldwork were characterised by an attempt to reduce the distance between expectation and inadequate reality, as my informants and I conspired to rewrite my identity as Japanese' (1990: 25). Her sense of self and identity was thereby mediated 'by the experiences, relations and interactions of her fieldwork' (Coffey 1999: 24).

Writing partly in the first person, Kondo seeks to reveal her identity through the text in order to emphasize the point that the ethnographic text is constructed through the stance assumed in relation to the observed. For example, she states: 'what I write is no mere academic exercise; for me it matters, and matters deeply' (Kondo 1990: 302).

Kondo is also critical of conventional ethnographic writing, which 'sandwiches the "data" into the body of the book, leaving "theory" for the beginning and the end' (1990: 304). Instead she 'scatters' theoretical discussion 'in different parts of the text, and the "ethnographic" vignettes and anecdotes are marshaled analytically' (1990: 304).

Kondo's work thus provides an example of a contemporary organizational ethnography that seeks to achieve a postmodern reflexivity, partly through exploration of experimental writing strategies.

KEY POINTS

- 'Ethnography' is a term that refers to both a method and the written product of research based on that method.

- The ethnographer is typically a participant observer who also uses non-observational methods and sources such as interviewing and documents.

- The ethnographer may adopt an overt or a covert role, but the latter carries ethical difficulties.

- The negotiation of access to a social setting can be a lengthy process. It may depend on establishing an exchange relationship.

- Key informants frequently play an important role for the ethnographer, but care is needed to ensure that their impact on the direction of research is not excessive.

- There are several different ways of classifying the kinds of role that the ethnographer may assume. These are not necessarily mutually exclusive.

- Field notes are important for prompting the ethnographer's memory.

- Feminist approaches to ethnography have led to examination and questioning of traditional ethnographic methods.

- Global and multi-site ethnography illustrate the ways in which ethnographic methods have been adapted in order to study mobile social groups, effects of globalization, and spatially distributed contexts.

- Virtual and visual ethnographies of organization are becoming increasingly common, but they sometimes differs from how ethnography is traditionally understood.

- The writing of ethnography is increasingly seen not as a detached account of 'reality' but rather as a narrative produced by, and involving, the researcher.

QUESTIONS FOR REVIEW

- Is it possible to distinguish ethnography and participant observation?

- How does participant observation differ from structured observation?

Organizational ethnography

- To what extent do participant observation and ethnography rely solely on observation?

- What distinguishes organizational ethnography from other forms of ethnography?

Access

- 'Covert ethnography obviates the need to gain access to inaccessible settings and therefore has much to recommend it.' Discuss.

- Examine some articles in business and management journals in which ethnography and participant observation figure strongly. Was the researcher in an overt or a covert role? How was access achieved?

- Does the problem of access finish once access to a chosen setting has been achieved?

- What might be the role of key informants in ethnographic research? Is there anything to be concerned about when using them?

Roles for ethnographers

- How does Gold's scheme classify participant observer roles?
- Should ethnographers be active or passive in the settings in which they conduct research?
- How does shadowing differ from participant observation?

Field notes

- Why are field notes important for ethnographers?
- Why is it useful to distinguish between different types of field notes?

Bringing ethnographic fieldwork to an end

- How do you decide when to cease data collection in ethnographic research?

Feminist ethnography

- What are the main features of feminist ethnography?

Global and multi-site ethnography

- What are the main features of global ethnography?

Virtual ethnography

- How has ethnography been adapted to collect data via the internet?

Visual ethnography

- What role can visual materials play in ethnography?
- What distinguishes visual ethnography from other research methods that focus on visual data?

Writing ethnography

- Why are some ethnographic styles of writing imbued with realism?
- What are the main characteristics of realist tales?
- What forms of ethnographic writing other than realist tales can be found?
- What are the implications of the linguistic turn for ethnographic writing?

....

ONLINE RESOURCES

www.oup.com/uk/brm5e/

Visit the Interactive Research Guide that accompanies this book to complete an exercise relating to ethnography and participant observation.

....

INTERVIEWING IN QUALITATIVE RESEARCH

CHAPTER OUTLINE

This chapter is concerned with the interview in qualitative research. The term *qualitative interview* is often used to capture the different types of interview that are used in qualitative research. Such interviews tend to be far less structured than the kind of interview associated with survey research, which was discussed in Chapter 10. This chapter is concerned with individual interviews in qualitative research; the focus group method, which is a form of interview but with several people, is discussed in Chapter 21. The t wo forms of qualitative interviewing discussed in this chapter are unstructured and semi-structured interviewing. The chapter explores:

- the differences between structured interviewing and qualitative interviewing;

- the main characteristics of and differences between unstructured and semi-structured interviewing—this entails a recognition that the two terms refer to extremes and that in practice a wide range of interviews with differing degrees of structure lie between the extremes;

- how to devise and use an interview guide for semi-structured interviewing;

- the kinds of question that can be asked in an interview guide;

- the importance of audio-recording and transcribing qualitative interviews;

- the advantages and disadvantages of non-face-to-face interviewing via telephone, online, or using Skype;
- the significance of qualitative interviewing in feminist research;
- the advantages and disadvantages of qualitative interviewing relative to participant observation.

Introduction

The interview is probably the most widely used method in qualitative research. Of course, as we have seen in Chapter 19, ethnography often involves a substantial amount of interviewing, and this undoubtedly contributes to the widespread use of the interview by qualitative researchers. However, it is the flexibility of the interview that makes it so attractive. Since ethnography involves an extended period of participant observation, which is very disruptive for researchers because of the sustained absence(s) required from work and/or family life, research based mainly on interviews is an attractive alternative for the collection of qualitative data. Interviewing, the transcription of interviews, and the analysis of transcripts are all very time-consuming, but they can be more readily accommodated into researchers' personal lives than ethnographic work.

In Key concept 10.2 several types of interview were briefly outlined. Two of the types outlined there—the

structured interview and the standardized interview—are associated with quantitative research. However, the predominant use of interviewing is as part of a qualitative research strategy. Focus group interviewing will be examined in Chapter 21. Other forms of interview associated with qualitative research will be explored in this chapter, including the life history interview and oral history interview. However, the two main types are the unstructured interview and the *semi-structured interview*. Researchers sometimes use the term *qualitative interview* to encapsulate these two types of interview. There is clearly the potential for confusion here, but the types and definitions offered in Key concept 10.2 are intended to provide consistency of terminology. One final point to note at the outset is that, in qualitative research, no single interview stands alone. 'It has meaning to the researcher only in terms of other interviews and observations' (Whyte 1953: 22).

STUDENT EXPERIENCE
Intensive interviewing

Sometimes the conditions of research access combined with other work and personal commitments mean that students have to interview a number of participants in a short period of time. For Chris, this meant he carried out all of his interviews in just one day. Although these practical constraints sometimes just have to be worked with, it is important to recognize that interviewing can be quite a stressful and tiring activity and doing a large number of interviews in one day particularly so. This makes it even more important to have considered the issues covered in this chapter before doing your interviews.

In Chris's case, practical constraints also affected the time in which he conducted the interviews.

I did all the interviews on the same day, which was a matter of convenience because I was coming from Birmingham to London so I didn't really have the budget to make several journeys but looking back on it, it might have been a good idea to say, 'Right. Well, I did the first one. These are the questions I asked. These are the responses. That's an interesting response,' or, 'I didn't get quite what I'd expect there. Let me tailor the question or maybe the questions. Go and change it slightly.'

Chris acknowledges that, if he had piloted and pre-tested his questions (see Chapter 12), this might have enhanced the overall quality of his data. However, although he carried out the interviews in a short time period, Chris had already built up relationships with his interviewees beforehand as a result of his internship. As he explained:

> I'd known all of them for at least eight weeks so I suppose that would have obviously had an effect on the style of conversation that I had with them in the interviews as opposed to somebody I'd interviewed without knowing them beforehand. I'm sure that did have an effect and it meant that some of the questions I asked were more personal because I had background about what they'd done, families, that kind of thing. And they brought that kind of thing into the interviews. Whether somebody who didn't know me would have been so happy to do that, I don't know.

Differences between the structured interview and the qualitative interview

Qualitative interviewing is different from interviewing in quantitative research in a number of ways.

- The approach tends to be much less structured in qualitative research. In quantitative research, the interview is structured to maximize the reliability and validity of measurement of key concepts. It is also more structured because the researcher has a clearly specified set of research questions that are to be investigated. The structured interview is designed to answer these questions. Instead, in qualitative research, there is an emphasis on greater generality in the formulation of initial research ideas and on interviewees' own perspectives.

- In qualitative interviewing, there is much greater interest in the interviewee's point of view; in quantitative research, the interview reflects the researcher's concerns. This contrast is a direct outcome of the previously mentioned one. For example, Ram (1994) describes his qualitative interviewing style as owing little to the 'textbook' approach, which 'exhorts the interviewer to remain aloof while seeking to extract information from the respondent' (1994: 32), as it would have been 'absurd and counter-productive' to assume this degree of social distance from family and friends whom he had known for years.

- In qualitative interviewing, 'rambling' or going off at tangents is often encouraged—it gives insight into what the interviewee sees as relevant and important;

in quantitative research, it is usually regarded as a nuisance and discouraged.

- In qualitative interviewing, interviewers can depart significantly from any schedule or guide that is being used. They can ask new questions that follow up interviewees' replies and can vary the order of questions and even the wording of questions. In quantitative research, none of these things should be done, because they will compromise the standardization of the interview process and hence the reliability and validity of measurement.

- As a result, qualitative interviewing tends to be flexible (see Research in focus 20.2 for an example), responding to the direction in which interviewees take the interview and perhaps adjusting the emphases in the research as a result of significant issues that emerge in the course of interviews. By contrast, structured interviews are typically inflexible, because of the need to standardize the way in which each interviewee is dealt with.

- In qualitative interviewing, the researcher wants rich, detailed answers; in quantitative research, the interview is supposed to generate answers that can be coded and processed quickly.

- In qualitative interviewing, the interviewee may be interviewed on more than one and sometimes even several occasions. In quantitative research, unless the research is longitudinal in character, the person will be interviewed on one occasion only.

Asking questions in the qualitative interview

Qualitative interviewing varies a great deal in the approach taken by the interviewer. The two major types were mentioned at the beginning of the chapter.

- The almost totally *unstructured interview*. Here the researcher uses at most an *aide-mémoire* as a brief set of self-prompts to deal with a certain range of topics. There may be just a single question that the interviewer asks, and the interviewee is then allowed to respond freely, with the interviewer simply responding in turn to points that seem worth following up. Unstructured interviewing tends to be very similar in character to a conversation (Burgess 1984). Dalton (1959) refers to the importance of 'conversational interviewing' as the basis for his data collection strategy. These are not interviews in the usual sense, but a series of broken and incomplete conversations that, when written up, may, according to Dalton, be 'tied together as one statement' (1959: 280). Conversational interviews are characterized by being precipitated by events. In some instances, these were prompted by Dalton, who asked managers at the end of an important meeting an open-ended question such as 'How did things go?', but in others they were simply the result of overheard exchanges in shops or offices. See Research in focus 20.1 for an example of an unstructured interview.

- A *semi-structured interview*. The researcher has a list of questions on fairly specific topics to be covered, often referred to as an *interview guide*, but the interviewee has a great deal of leeway in how to reply. Questions may not follow on exactly in the way outlined on the guide. Questions that are not included in the guide may be asked as the interviewer picks up on things said by interviewees. But, by and large, all the questions will be asked and a similar wording will be used from interviewee to interviewee. For example, Willman et al. (2002) carried out semi-structured interviews with traders in financial markets in London. The interviews covered a range of issues, including motivations, emotions, trading strategies, and questions about organizational culture. They also included questions about control incentives and management style. In this analysis, the researchers focused on sections of the interview that dealt with the aversion to and seeking of risk; this formed the basis for their conclusion that traders focus on avoiding losses rather than making gains. Research in focus 20.2 provides a further example of this type of interview.

In both cases, the interview process is *flexible*. Also, the emphasis is on how the interviewee frames and understands issues and events—that is, what the interviewee views as important in explaining and understanding events, patterns, and forms of behaviour. Thus, Leidner (1993) describes the interviewing she carried out in a McDonald's restaurant as involving a degree of structure, but adds that the interviews also 'allowed room to pursue topics of particular interest to the workers' (1993: 238). Milkman (1997), in her study of auto workers at General Motors, describes how in the second stage of her research she interviewed a total of 30 buyout takers and workers, using a 'very general interview guide', trying to be as casual as she could, and never discouraging anyone from going off on tangents. Most interviews were with individuals. However, in a few cases workers invited their friends from the plant as well. Milkman claims that 'these turned out to be among the best interviews, since they developed a group dynamic in which my presence often became marginal' (1997: 198). In an interview study of secretarial work involving almost 500 office workers, Pringle (1988) followed an oral history format. She explains:

> We did not restrict the subject matter to work. Initially people were asked to start by talking about a typical day ... Over time, our interests shifted or became more focused on the relation between different parts of their lives, on home and family, and their views on a range of political and social issues, and on their notions of a 'good boss' and 'good secretary'.

> (1988: 270)

Once again, we must remember that qualitative research is *not* quantitative research with the numbers missing. The two different types of interview in qualitative research are extremes, and there is quite a lot of variability between them, but most qualitative interviews are close to one type or the other. In neither case does the interviewer slavishly follow a schedule, as is done in quantitative research interviewing but in semi-structured interviews the interviewer does follow a script to a certain extent. The choice of whether to veer towards one type rather than the other is likely to be affected by a variety of factors.

- If it is important to the researcher to gain a genuine understanding of the world views of members of a social setting or of people sharing common attributes, an unstructured interviewing approach may be prefer-

20.1 RESEARCH IN FOCUS
An example of unstructured interviewing

Whyte (1953) presents an example of a 'non-directive', or unstructured, interview conducted in 1952 during a one-day visit to the Chicago plant of the Inland Steel Container Company. The aim of this interview was to catch up with developments in union–management relations that had taken place since his previous visit to the plant and since Whyte's publication of a book on this subject. Whyte suggests that the book had been received favourably at the plant, as it showed management and union officials in a positive light. Publication was marked by a public meeting, and every worker in the plant had been presented with a copy. This helped to ensure positive rapport with the respondent, the vice-president of the union and chairman of its grievance committee, on the day in question. Whyte provides a commentary on his interview with the vice-president that involves analysing his own interviewing technique, including such 'mistakes' as presenting a leading question.

Although Whyte suggests that he was following the 'rules' of non-directive interviewing—by concentrating on listening, not interrupting or arguing with the informant, and periodically restating what had been said—in certain important respects he was not. In particular, Whyte attempted to direct Gary towards an account of the social process. Specifically, how the problem came to the attention of the person concerned, and what steps were involved in the action taken?

> Right at the outset I sought to move him from a statement of sentiments to an account of interpersonal events. I was interested not only in what happened at a particular time, but in how that event related to others that took place before or afterwards. For all these events I wanted answers to the question: Who did what, with whom, and where?

(1953: 21–2)

Therefore, although Whyte describes his approach to organizational interviewing as non-directive, it is not as unstructured as it at first seems.

20.2 RESEARCH IN FOCUS
Flexibility in semi-structured interviewing

Between February and April 1990, Prasad (1993) interviewed 34 employees as part of her study of computerization at the Paragon Corporation. Interviews focused on understanding employees' experiences of computerized work. Each one lasted between 45 minutes and one-and-a-half hours and was 'semi-structured'. Prasad explains that in some cases the interviews corroborated her own assessment of the situation, while in others they offered a different interpretation that helped her to rethink her analysis. This meant that 'there was no one set of questions administered to all interviewees and no specific sequencing of the issues raised' (1993: 1408). She writes that the interviews were informed by the idea of 'grand tour' and 'mini tour' questions (Spradley and McCurdy 1972).

> The broad and exploratory grand tour questions gave the interviews focus and were developed keeping my research interests in mind. For the most part, grand tour questions got interviewees talking about aspects of computerization and related organizational issues. If the interviewee touched on something that was closely connected with the symbolism of computers or seemed particularly concerned about certain aspects of computerization, I pursued those areas through the use of more specific and detailed mini tour questions.

(Prasad 1993: 1409)

able. With a more unstructured approach, the researcher is less likely to come at participants' world views with presuppositions or expectations and is more likely to see things as the participants see them.

- If the researcher is beginning the investigation with a fairly clear focus, rather than a very general notion of wanting to do research on a topic, it is likely that the interviews will be semi-structured ones, so that the more specific issues can be addressed. More structure is also likely to be imposed when the researcher has a clear idea of how the data will be analysed. In the case of using interviews to generate data about critical incidents, a set of subject themes can be used to guide respondents to recall examples of specific events that illustrate each theme.

- If more than one person is to carry out the fieldwork, then to ensure a degree of comparability in interviewing style it is likely that semi-structured interviewing will be preferred.

- If you are doing multiple **case study** research, you are likely to find that you will need some structure to ensure cross-case comparability. All Bryman's qualitative research on different kinds of organization entailed semi-structured interviewing, and most of it was multiple case study research (e.g. Bryman et al. 1994; Bryman et al. 1996).

In business research there are some additional considerations that relate to qualitative interviewing.

Interviewing managers often raises specific issues: the status and power held, particularly at a senior level, mean that gaining access to this group of people can be extremely difficult, and arranging a mutually convenient time in which to conduct an interview, which may last several hours, even more so. Given the number of outside requests for information and assistance that most managers receive, it is particularly important to express a request for interview in a way that is most likely to lead to a favourable response. A request for interview may be made by email, letter, or telephone. Healey and Rawlinson (1993) recommend a dual approach: first make a telephone call, 'fishing' for a named person who is most likely to be appropriate for the interview; then follow this up with an introductory letter, delivered via email or post. In the letter, it may be appropriate to enclose a short outline of the nature and purpose of the project and an indication of how the findings might be useful to the respondent. If the research is supported by a high-profile sponsor (for example, a company or university), it may be worth enclosing a letter from a senior person in the sponsor organization endorsing the aims of the research. Finally, a telephone call made a few days after receipt of the letter can provide an opportunity for the researcher to deal with any queries the manager may have. The most important thing to remember, however, is that 'polite persistence' is often crucial (Healey and Rawlinson 1993).

TIPS AND SKILLS
Learning how to interview by watching movies

If you have never done any qualitative interviewing before, a useful way of familiarizing yourself with the method and the techniques involved is by watching movies that sensitize you to some of the issues involved in **naturalistic** inquiry. Saldaña (2009) recommends several popular movies to simulate the kinds of real-world dilemmas and human interaction that researchers commonly face in their practice. For qualitiative interviewing, his recommendations include *Kinsey* (2004), a movie about the controversial biologist Dr Alfred Kinsey, who studied sexual behaviour in the USA in the 1940s and 50s. Kinsey used a combination of structured and semi-structured interviews, observation, and participational methods. The film provides insight into the issues involved in researching a highly sensitive topic and the influence of the researcher's personal values (see Chapter 2) on his choice of research subject. Saldaña also recommends *The Matrix* (1999) to gain insight into the **concepts** of **epistemology** and **ontology** and *The Truman Show* (1998) to illustrate the principles of participant observation (see Chapter 19) and the ethical issues (see Chapter 6) raised by acting without having obtained someone's **informed consent**. Another way to familiarize yourself with the techniques involved in qualitative interviewing is to watch a recording of a news reporter or documentary moviemaker interviewing someone—take notes on their body language, their listening skills, and how they interact with the person whom they are interviewing.

Interviewing in organizations also involves encroaching on an individual's work time, and in some cases, it may not be possible to take people away from their work during their hours of employment. Managers may be unwilling to grant employees time away from work to conduct an interview, or there may simply be no one available to cover their duties. When employees are paid on an hourly basis, this becomes a particularly important issue. For example, in her research into work roles in restaurants, Hall (1993) wanted to interview a sample of the servers (waiters and waitresses) who worked in the five selected restaurants. To do this, she had to approach servers on duty to schedule individual interviews for off-duty times, usually before or after their work shift. This relied on servers' willingness to devote an hour of their unpaid time to this task.

However, sometimes managers demonstrate a willingness to enable the interview process despite the time and cost implications. Bell et al. (2001) were able to conduct a group interview with employees in one plant because the section manager and his team agreed to cease production for a period of time to allow the interview to take place. However, it is not only the interviewer who benefits from the interview process. Sometimes interviewees welcome the opportunity to offload issues and concerns or think through a problem in a structured way, particularly if they are able to see a copy of the transcript afterwards. In these instances, the interview is very much a two-way process, with both parties gaining something beneficial from it.

Preparing an interview guide

The idea of an interview guide is much less specific than the notion of a structured interview schedule. Such a guide may comprise no more than a brief list of memory prompts of areas to be covered in the interview. Moreover, an interview guide does not necessarily have to comprise written words; instead it can take the form of a series of visual prompts related to a subject (see Research in focus 20.3). Researchers often offer to provide a copy of the interview guide or schedule to participants in the study. This can help to strengthen the dependability of the research (see Chapter 17). What is essential is that the questioning allows interviewers to understand how research participants view their social world and that there is flexibility in the conduct of the interviews.

In preparing for qualitative interviews, Lofland and Lofland (1995: 78) suggest asking yourself the question 'Just what about this thing is puzzling me?' This can be applied to each of the research questions you have already generated, or it may be a mechanism for generating some research questions. They suggest that your puzzlement can be stimulated by various activities: random thoughts

20.3 RESEARCH IN FOCUS
Using photographs as prompts in a study of consumer behaviour

Hurworth (2003) suggests some ways that photographs can be integrated into the interviewing process (see also the discussion of photo-elicitation in Chapter 10). Showing an interviewee a photo can help him or her recall events from the past, articulate abstract concepts, or express complex emotions. Photographs also have advantages in overcoming interviewees' discomfort in being interviewed and can encourage them to discuss issues in more detail.

Heisley and Levy (1991) used photo-interviewing in a study of consumer behaviour related to family meals. They met each family and took photographs of them preparing and consuming dinner as a family. The researchers edited the photographs into a chronological set that represented the main events of the evening and the family members involved. Next, the informants were interviewed and asked to 'tell me whatever you think about when you look at [these photographs]' (Heisley and Levy 1991: 263). Finally, informants were shown the photographs again, accompanied by an audio recording of the first interview, and asked to comment on the data generated. One of the findings from the study related to how interviewees commented on the consumer products in the photograph, such as furnishings and table utensils, their responses highlighting how these objects are embedded in social relationships—for example, fondue sets as wedding gifts. They conclude: 'A photograph motivates people to provide a perspective of action, to explain what lies behind the pictures, and to relate how the frozen moment relates to the reality as they see it' (Heisley and Levy 1991: 269).

in different contexts, which are then written down as quickly as possible; discussions with colleagues, friends, and relatives; and, of course, the existing literature on the topic. The formulation of the research question(s) should not be so specific that alternative avenues of enquiry that might arise during the collection of field-work data are closed off. Such premature closure of your research focus would be inconsistent with the process of qualitative research (see Figure 17.1), with the emphasis on the world view of the people you will be interviewing, and with the approaches to qualitative data analysis such as grounded theory that emphasize the importance of not starting out with too many preconceptions (qualitative data analysis will be discussed in Chapter 24). Gradually, an order and structure will begin to emerge in your meanderings around your research question(s) and will form the basis for your interview guide.

You should also consider 'What do I need to know in order to answer each of the research questions I am interested in?' This means trying to get an appreciation of what the interviewee sees as significant and important in relation to each of your topic areas. Thus, your questioning will need to cover the areas that you think you need to know about, but from the perspective of your interviewees. Some basic elements in the preparation of your interview guide will be the following:

- create a certain amount of order on the topic areas, so that your questions about them flow reasonably well, but be prepared to alter the order of questions during the actual interview;

- formulate interview questions or topics in a way that will help you to answer your research questions (but try not to make them too specific);

- try to use a language that is comprehensible and relevant to the people you are interviewing;

- just as in interviewing in quantitative research, do not ask leading questions;

- remember to ensure that you ask or record 'facesheet' information of a general kind (name, age, gender, etc.) and a specific kind (position in company, number of years employed, number of years involved in a group, etc.), because such information is useful for contextualizing people's answers.

There are some practical details to attend to before the interview:

- Make sure you are familiar with the setting in which the interviewee works, lives, or engages in the behaviour of interest to you. This will help you to understand what he or she is saying in the interviewee's own terms.

- Use a good digital audio recorder or ensure that your phone has the capacity to serve as a reliable recorder (see Tips and skills 'Digital audio recording' later in the chapter). Qualitative researchers nearly always audio-record and then transcribe their interviews. This procedure is important for the detailed analysis required in qualitative research and to ensure that the interviewees' answers are captured in their own terms. If you are taking notes, it is easy to lose the phrases and language used. Also, because the interviewer is supposed not to be following a strictly formulated schedule of questions of the kind used in structured interviewing, he or she will need to be responsive to the interviewee's answers so that it is

TIPS AND SKILLS
Where to conduct an interview?

Finding a quiet, private space to conduct an interview uninterrupted can be one of the most difficult tasks for the qualitative researcher. Many organizations will struggle to find you a spare room that is not being used and is suitable. Think carefully before agreeing to interview someone in their office; are there likely to be frequent telephone calls or interruptions that make the interview difficult? Also, traffic, aircraft, or machinery can contribute to background noise that can make the audio-recorded speech inaudible. It is a good idea to spend some time in the room prior to the interview; do a speech recording to test the acoustics of the room and position the furniture; if there is noise from outside the room, think about closing doors or windows. Similarly, you may wish to turn off a noisy heater. Position the microphone as near to your interviewees as possible and make sure that they are unlikely to knock it. You will, of course, need to balance these issues against the comfort and convenience of your interviewee (it would not be sensible to insist on having all the windows closed in the middle of summer!). But do not be afraid to explain what you need in order to conduct the interview, even though you may have to be prepared to compromise when it comes to actually getting it.

Criteria of a successful interviewer

Kvale (1996) has proposed a list of ten criteria of a successful interviewer.

1. *Knowledgeable*: is thoroughly familiar with the focus of the interview; pilot interviews of the kind used in survey interviewing can be useful as a preparation for the main interviewing process.

2. *Structuring*: gives purpose for interview; rounds it off; asks whether interviewee has questions.

3. *Clear*: asks simple, easy, short questions; no jargon.

4. *Gentle*: lets people finish; gives them time to think; tolerates pauses.

5. *Sensitive*: listens attentively to what is said and how it is said; is empathetic in dealing with the interviewee.

6. *Open*: responds to what is important to interviewee; flexible.

7. *Steering*: knows what he or she wants to find out.

8. *Critical*: is prepared to challenge what is said—for example, dealing with inconsistencies in interviewees' replies.

9. *Remembering*: relates what is said to what has previously been said.

10. *Interpreting*: clarifies and extends meanings of interviewees' statements, but without imposing meaning on them.

To Kvale's list we would add the following.

- *Balanced*: does not talk too much, which may make the interviewee passive, and does not talk too little, which may result in the interviewee feeling he or she is not talking along the right lines.

- *Ethically sensitive*: is sensitive to the ethical dimension of interviewing, ensuring the interviewee appreciates what the research is about, its purposes, and that his or her answers will be treated confidentially.

---

possible to follow them up. A good microphone is highly desirable, because many interviews are let down by poor recording.

- Make sure as far as possible that the interview takes place in a setting that is quiet and private (so the interviewee does not have to worry about being overheard).

- Prepare yourself for the interview by cultivating as many as possible of the traits of a quality interviewer suggested by Kvale (see Tips and skills, 'Where to conduct an interview?').

After the interview, make notes about:

- how the interview went (was interviewee talkative, cooperative, nervous, well dressed/scruffy, etc.?);

- where the interview took place;

- any other feelings about the interview (did it open up new avenues of interest?);

- the setting (busy/quiet, many/few other people in the vicinity, new/old building, use of computers).

Kinds of questions

The kinds of question asked in qualitative interviews are highly variable. Kvale (1996) has suggested nine different kinds of question. Most interviews will contain virtually all of these types, although interviews that rely on lists of topics are likely to follow a somewhat looser format. Kvale's nine types of question are as follows.

1. *Introducing questions*: 'Please tell me about when your interest in X first began'; 'Have you ever … ?'; 'Why did you go to … ?'

2. *Follow-up questions*: getting the interviewee to elaborate his or her answer, such as 'Could you say some more about that?'; 'What do you mean by … ?'; 'Can you give me an example … ?'; even 'Yeeees?'

3. *Probing questions*: following up what has been said through direct questioning.

4. *Specifying questions*: 'What did you do then?'; 'How did X react to what you said?'

5. *Direct questions*: 'Do you find it easy to keep smiling when serving customers?'; 'Are you happy with the

amount of on-the-job training you have received?' Such questions are perhaps best left until towards the end of the interview, in order not to influence the direction of the interview too much.

6. *Indirect questions*: 'What do most people round here think of the ways that management treats its staff?', perhaps followed up by 'Is that the way you feel too?', in order to get at the individual's own view.

7. *Structuring questions*: 'I would now like to move on to a different topic.'

8. *Silence*: allow pauses to signal that you want to give the interviewee the opportunity to reflect and amplify an answer.

9. *Interpreting questions*: 'Do you mean that your leadership role has had to change from one of encouraging others to a more directive one?'; 'Is it fair to say that you don't mind being friendly towards customers most of the time, but when they are unpleasant or demanding you find it more difficult?'

In their study of ethics and compliance officers, Treviño et al. (2014) used a final question that does not fit easily in any of these categories. This is a 'what do you think I should have asked you about that I haven't?' question. They asked: 'If I really want to understand your role what should I have asked that I didn't?' (Treviño et al. 2014: 204). This kind of question is worth considering as a means of catching perspectives that your other question failed to reveal but which may be very significant to the interviewee.

As this list of question types suggests, one of the main ingredients of the interview is listening—being very attentive to what the interviewee is saying or even not

TIPS AND SKILLS
Interviewing for the first time

The prospect of doing your first interview can be daunting. Also, it is easy to make some fundamental mistakes when you begin interviewing. An American study of postgraduates' experiences of a lengthy interview training course showed that novice interviewers were easily thrown off by a number of events or experiences in the course of the interview process (Roulston et al. 2003). The researchers' findings suggest five challenges that are worth bearing in mind when approaching your first interview(s).

1. *Unexpected interviewee behaviour or environmental problems*. These inexperienced interviewers were easily discomfited by unexpected responses or behaviour on the part of the interviewees or by problems such as noise in the vicinity of the interview. When you go into the interview, bear in mind that things may not go according to plan. Interviewees may say things that you find surprising or shocking. Equally, there can be many distractions close to where the interview takes place. You clearly cannot plan for or control these things, but you can bear in mind that they might happen and try to limit their impact on you and on the course of the interview.

2. *Intrusion of own biases and expectations*. Roulston et al. report that some of the trainees were surprised when they read their own transcripts at how their own biases and expectations were evident in the ways they asked questions and followed up on replies.

3. *Maintaining focus in asking questions*. Students reported that they sometimes had difficulty probing answers, asking follow-up questions, and clarifying questions in a way that did not lose sight of the research topic and what the questions were getting at.

4. *Dealing with sensitive issues*. Some students asked questions that caused interviewees to become upset, and this response could have an adverse effect on the conduct of the interview. However, most students felt that they coped reasonably well with such emotionally charged situations.

5. *Transcription*. Many reported finding transcription difficult and time-consuming—more so than they had imagined.

There are, of course, many other possible issues that impinge on first-time interviewees. Many do not go away, either, no matter how experienced you are. It is very difficult to know how to deal with some of these contingencies. However, it is worth bearing in mind that they do arise and that their impact may be greatest when you have less interviewing experience.

saying. It means that the interviewer is active without being too intrusive—a difficult balance. But it also means that, just because the interview is being audio-recorded (the generally recommended practice whenever it is feasible), the interviewer cannot take things easy. In fact, an interviewer must be very attuned and responsive to what the interviewee is saying and doing. This is also important because something like body language may indicate that the interviewee is becoming uneasy or anxious about a line of questioning. An ethically sensitive interviewer will not want to place undue pressure on the person he or she is talking to and will need to be prepared to cut short that line of questioning if it is clearly a source of concern.

Remember as well that in interviews you are going to ask about different kinds of things, such as:

- values: of interviewee, of group, of organization;
- beliefs: of the interviewee or others;
- behaviour: of the interviewee or others;
- formal and informal roles: of the interviewee or others;
- relationships: of the interviewee or others;
- places and locales;
- emotions: particularly of the interviewee, but also possibly of others;
- encounters;
- stories.

Try to vary the questioning in terms of types of question (as suggested by Kvale's nine types outlined above) *and* the types of phenomena you ask about.

Finally, you must think about how to end interviews satisfactorily, making sure that your interviewees have had a chance to comment fully on the topic concerned and giving them the opportunity to raise any issues that they think you have overlooked in your questions. The closing moments of an interview also provide an opportunity to include a final 'catch-all' question. Journalists sometimes refer to this as the 'doorknob question', since it is asked at the end, when rapport has been established and the interviewee has relaxed into the situation. This type of closing question tends to seek a directive response—for example, 'If you were advising the organization on this subject, what are the main changes or improvements that you would recommend?' or 'From your experience in this area, what advice would you offer to other managers facing similar problems?' This encourages the interviewee to comment on specific issues and to put forward a personal opinion.

Using an interview guide: an example

Research in focus 20.4 is taken from an interview from Bell and Leonard's (2018) study of online responses to concerns about business ethics and corporate social responsibility. Bell and Leonard's research design involved a single case study of a US-based branding and design company, founded in 2003, that specializes in 'digital organizational storytelling' by producing online animated videos on behalf of non-profit third sector organizations and small to medium-sized businesses. The researchers were interested in understanding the process of organizational storytelling online and the

STUDENT EXPERIENCE
Learning how to interview

Karen found that through the experience of doing a research project involving qualitative interviewing she had acquired a new and potentially transferable skill.

I learned a lot through the interviews that I did about how to probe and to get what you want out of it. You can so easily just go into an interview and just sit there and listen to what they're saying and then you go out and think, 'Actually they didn't give me anything that I wanted. They just talked at me.' But you need to balance that with not actually telling them what you want to know, but just sort of guiding them towards it so that you can achieve the objectives that you've got. That's another skill that I wouldn't say I've managed to learn completely, but I think it's something that you pick up and you can get better at through doing this sort of research. Since then I've done quite a lot of sort of client-based consultancy projects and I think this is definitely one of the main skills I applied there. Having it clear in your own mind what you want to get and asking the questions in a way that can get what you want without leading people to tell you what you want to hear.

20.4 RESEARCH IN FOCUS
Part of the transcript of a semi-structured interview

1. Interviewer	Okay, thank you ever so much for agreeing to have a talk to me today … I've got a few questions that I just wanted to go through with you in a fairly sort of informal way … I wonder if I could talk with you a little bit first of all about your own process of joining Free Range Studios?
2. Participant	Sure … [*participant talks in detail about educational and employment background*] … while I was in DC I was working for a big environmental group and [they] hired Free Range when it was just the two founders … and literally as I walked through the door and looked around I thought 'I totally miss this world.' And so literally on the spot I said 'oh, I miss this world!' and Steve said 'looking for a job?' [*chuckling*]. We kind of went back and forth and I was interviewing them to hire them while they were interviewing me to hire me.
3. Interviewer	Oh, okay.
4. Participant	And so then I came in and it was my job to grow Free Range … it was my job to get things kind of sorted out and [people] hired and start to grow it out.
5. Interviewer	Right. When you say studio experience are you talking there about a creative design background or a film background specifically?
6. Participant	Creative design, uh-huh.
7. Interviewer	And when was that? How long have you been with Free Range now?
8. Participant	Oh, 10½, almost 11 years.
9. Interviewee	Okay, so pretty much from the beginning.

relationship between online storytellers and audiences. They interviewed five senior members of the 24-member company and two key informants from a client organization via Skype (see section later in this chapter on Skype interviewing). They also analyzed publicly available documents, including online videos produced by the company and comments posted online by audiences. The semi-structured interview guide focused on questions related to the backgrounds of employees, how they experienced the organizational culture, relationships to client organizations, and accounts of the company's history and growth.

This sequence of exchanges begins at the start of the interview with the interviewer (1) asking what would be considered an 'introducing question' in terms of the list of nine question types suggested by Kvale (1996), outlined above. The participant responds in some detail (this extract has been edited so does not include her response in its entirety). The participant's response concludes with an account of an interaction which took place between organizational members. You will notice

that this is worded as though it is being acted out, rather like a play. Such recounted, scripted narratives are not unusual in qualitative interviewing. This response is very helpful in providing insight into how the participant experiences and characterizes the organization's culture. The researcher then briefly interjects to confirm that they are listening (3) and the participant continues to explain the role she has played within the company. While it is important not to interrupt the participants' flow of speech too frequently, such gestures are helpful in ensuring that a dialogue is maintained, rather than leaving the participant to lapse into monologue. The interviewer (5) then asks an 'interpreting question' in order to seek clarification about the participant's career background. Next, the interviewer (7) asks a 'direct question' about the length of time the participant has worked for the organization. The participant responds (8) and the interviewer confirms (9), based on their prior understanding gleaned from other data sources, that the participant has been with the organization almost from the beginning.

As can be seen from this short extract, qualitative interview exchanges are not dissimilar to normal conversation. The main difference between them is that the interviewer is working with the aid of an interview guide and is continually reviewing and seeking to actively guide the conversation so that all the relevant themes are covered.

Recording and transcription

We have already made the point on several occasions that, in qualitative research, the interview is usually audio-recorded and transcribed whenever possible (see Tips and skills 'Why you should record and transcribe interviews'). Qualitative researchers are frequently interested not just in *what* people say but also in the *way* that they say it. If this aspect is to be fully woven into an analysis, it is necessary for a complete account of the

series of exchanges in an interview to be available. Also, because the interviewer is supposed to be highly alert to what is being said—following up interesting points made, prompting and probing where necessary, drawing attention to any inconsistencies in the interviewee's answers—it is best if he or she is not distracted by having to concentrate on getting down notes on what is said.

As with just about everything in conducting business research, there is a cost, in that the use of a digital audio recorder may disconcert respondents, who become self-conscious or alarmed at the prospect of their words being preserved. Most people accede to the request for the interview to be audio-recorded, though it is not uncommon for a small number to refuse (see Research in focus 20.5). When faced with refusal, you should still go ahead with the interview, as it is highly likely that useful information will still be forthcoming. For example, Prasad (1993; Research in focus 20.2) recounts that, in

TIPS AND SKILLS
Why you should record and transcribe interviews

With approaches that entail detailed attention to language, such as **conversation analysis** and **discourse analysis** (see Chapter 22), the recording of conversations and interviews is to all intents and purposes mandatory. However, researchers who use qualitative interviews and focus groups (see Chapter 21) also tend to record and then transcribe interviews. Heritage (1984: 238) suggests that the procedure of recording and transcribing interviews has the following advantages.

* It helps to correct the natural limitations of our memories and of the intuitive glosses that we might place on what people say in interviews.

* It allows more thorough examination of what people say.

* It permits repeated examinations of the interviewees' answers.

* It opens up the data to public scrutiny by other researchers, who can evaluate the analysis that is carried out by the original researchers of the data (that is, a **secondary analysis**).

* It therefore helps to counter accusations that an analysis might have been influenced by a researcher's values or biases.

* It allows the data to be reused in other ways from those intended by the original researcher—for example, in the light of new theoretical ideas or analytic strategies.

However, it has to be recognized that the procedure is very time-consuming. It also requires good equipment, usually in the form of a digital audio recorder and microphone. Transcription also very quickly results in a daunting pile of paper. Also, recording equipment may be daunting for interviewees.

It is also worth bearing in mind that, in our experience, focus group research, which is the subject of Chapter 21, can be difficult to transcribe. This is because people in the discussions often talk over each other, in spite of warnings by the **moderator** not to do so. Even a high-quality microphone will not readily deal with this issue. One possibility is to video-record, as well as audio-record. However, this is likely to be beyond the means of most students and also requires a particular environment suitable for video recording the focus group. The possible problems of transcription should be borne in mind if you are considering using a focus group.

the few instances where employees at Paragon indicated discomfort with being recorded, she took notes during the interview and wrote these up after the session. The summary notes were then shown to the interviewee, who evaluated their accuracy. This advice also applies in cases of recorder malfunction (Research in focus 20.5). Among those who do agree to be audio-recorded, there will be some who nonetheless feel alarm at being confronted with a microphone. As a result, some interviews may not be as interesting as you might have hoped.

In qualitative research, there is often quite a large amount of variation in the amount of time that interviews take. For example, in Milkman's (1997) study of technological change at General Motors, the length of the interviews ranged between 45 minutes and four hours. Similarly, Marshall's (1995) (Key concept 17.3) research involved interviews with women managers that lasted between one-and-a-half and two hours. It should not be assumed that shorter interviews are necessarily inferior to longer ones, but very short ones that are a product of interviewee non-cooperation or anxiety about being audio-recorded are likely to be less useful. In the extreme, when an interview has produced very little of significance, it may not be worth the time and cost of transcription. Thankfully, such occasions are relatively unusual. If people do agree to be interviewed, they usually do so in a cooperative way and loosen up after initial anxiety about the microphone. As a result, even short interviews are often quite revealing.

The problem with transcribing interviews is that it is very time-consuming. In their study of traders and managers in four investment banks, Willman et al. (2002) interviewed 118 traders and trader-managers and 10 senior managers. Interviews averaged one hour in duration. They were all recorded and transcribed. It is best to allow around five to six hours for transcription for every hour of speech. Also, transcription yields vast numbers of pages of text, which you will need to wade through when analysing the data. Prasad (1993) reports that her 34 interviews on computerization (see Research in focus 20.2) generated nearly 800 pages of interview transcripts that needed to be analysed, in addition to over 1800 pages of field notes from observations. It is clear, therefore, that while transcription has the advantage of keeping intact the interviewee's (and interviewer's) words, it does so by piling up the amount of text to be analysed. It is no wonder that writers such as Lofland and Lofland (1995) advise that the analysis of qualitative data is not left until all the interviews have been completed and transcribed. To procrastinate may give the researcher the impression that he or she faces a monumental task. Also, there are good grounds for making analysis an ongoing activity, because it allows the researcher to be more aware of emerging themes that he or she may want to ask about in a more direct way in later interviews. Ongoing analysis is also very much recommended by proponents of approaches to qualitative data analysis such as grounded theory (see Chapter 24).

20.5 RESEARCH IN FOCUS
Getting it recorded and transcribed: an illustration of two problems

Rafaeli et al. (1997) conducted semi-structured interviews with 20 female administrators in a university business school in order to study the significance of dress at the workplace. They write:

> Everyone we contacted agreed to participate. Interviews took place in participants' offices or in a school lounge and lasted between 45 minutes and three hours. We recorded and transcribed all but two interviews: 1 participant refused to be taped, and the tape recorder malfunctioned during another interview. For interviews not taped, we recorded detailed notes. We assured all participants that their responses would remain confidential and anonymous and hired an outside contractor to transcribe the interviews.
>
> (1997: 14)

Even though overall this interview study was highly successful, generating 18 interviews that were recorded and transcribed, it does show two kinds of problems qualitative interviewers can face—namely, hardware malfunctions and refusals to be recorded.

TIPS AND SKILLS
Transcribing interviews

If you are doing research for a project or dissertation, you may not have the resources to pay for professional transcription, and, unless you are an accurate touch typist, it may take you longer than the suggested five to six hours per hour of speech. The important thing to bear in mind is that you must allow sufficient time for transcription and be realistic about how many interviews you are going to be able to transcribe in the time available.

TIPS AND SKILLS
Transcription conventions and using direct quotes in a dissertation

When you are transcribing an interview, it is important that the written text reproduces exactly what the interviewee said, word for word. Do not paraphrase the words of the speaker because this is not consistent with the commitment of qualitative researchers to see through the eyes of the people studied. Transcribing an interview verbatim helps to give the reader confidence in your data collection process and makes them less likely to question the validity of your study.

The use of certain conventions when transcribing interviews helps to ensure this:

- If there are parts of the interview that are unclear on the recording, do not be tempted to guess or make them up. Instead indicate in your transcript that there is a missing word or phrase, for example by using the convention [???]. People rarely speak in fully formed sentences. They often repeat themselves and they may have verbal 'tics' in the form of a common word or phrase that is repeated through habit or because they like it! When you write up your research, and quote directly from your transcripts, it is likely that you will edit out some of these digressions for the sake of length and ease of understanding.

- If you wish to quote the first sentence from a section of speech and then a sentence or two further on from the transcript, use the convention of three consecutive dots (...) to indicate the break point.

- If an interviewee omits a word from a sentence that is a grammatical omission or if the interviewee refers to a subject in a way that does not make its meaning clear and you need to provide readers with more contextual information so that they can understand the quote, use the convention of square brackets [ ] in which you insert the words you have added.

When quoting from an interview in your dissertation, you should use the following conventions:

- Use quotation marks to indicate a direct quote from an interview, or, for longer extracts, set them apart from the main text—for example, by indenting them or using a different font. This makes it immediately apparent to the reader that this is a direct quotation, and it enables you to differentiate between presentation of the data and your analysis of it.

- Indicate who is speaking in the quotation, either introducing the speaker before the quotation by saying something like 'As John put it,' or 'Anne explained her reasons for this', or attribute the quotation to the interviewee immediately afterwards, for example by writing his or her pseudonym or [Interviewee 1] in square brackets. This may be accompanied by relevant biographical information, such as their job role in the organization.

Given the emphasis that is placed on transcription in qualitative interview research, it is important to think about how you will go about this if you are planning on using interviews as a method. The first question to consider is whether to do the transcription yourself or use a professional transcription service. Transcribers need to be trained in much the same way that interviewers do. Moreover, even among experienced transcribers, errors can creep in. For example, Spender (1989) describes how, of the 34 interviews in his sample, 25 were transcribed. During the exploratory stages of the research this was done by assistants. However, this proved unsatisfactory, as 'there are important data in the respondent's intonations, hesitations, etc. which need to be available'. He concluded that 'the recording can help to recapture the actual data, which is neither the recording, nor the transcript, but the researcher's experience of the interview in its own context' (1989: 82). Poland (1995) has provided some fascinating examples of mistakes in transcription that can be the result of many different factors (mishearing, fatigue, carelessness). For example, one transcript contained the following passage:

> I think unless we want to become like other countries, where people have, you know, democratic freedoms . . .

But the actual words on the audio recording were:

> I think unless we want to become like other countries, where people have no democratic freedoms . . .

(Poland 1995: 294)

Steps clearly need to be taken to check the quality of transcription.

Flexibility in the interview

One further point to bear in mind is that you need to be generally flexible in your approach to interviewing in qualitative research. This advice is not just to do with needing to be responsive to what interviewees say to you and following up interesting points that they make. Such flexibility *is* important and will help to prevent the qualitative interview from turning into a kind of structured interview but with open questions. Flexibility is also important in such areas as varying the order of questions, following up leads, and clearing up inconsistencies in answers. Flexibility is important in other respects, such as coping with audio recording equipment breakdown and refusals by interviewees to allow a recording to take place (see Research in focus 20.5). A further element is that interviewers often find that, as soon as they switch off their audio recorders, the interviewee continues to talk on the topic of interest and frequently will say more interesting things than in the recorded interview. It is usually not feasible to switch the machine back on again, so try to take some notes, either while the person is talking or as soon as possible after the interview. Such 'unsolicited accounts' can often be the source of revealing information or views (Hammersley and Atkinson 1995). This is certainly what M. Parker (2000) found in connection with his research on three British organizations—a National Health Service district health authority, a building society, and a manufacturing company—which was based primarily on semi-structured interviews:

> Indeed, some of the most valuable parts of the interview took place after the tape had been switched off, the closing intimacies of the conversation being prefixed with a silent or explicit 'Well, if you want to know what I really think …'. Needless to say, a visit to the toilet to write up as much as I could remember followed almost immediately.

(2000: 236)

TIPS AND SKILLS
Transcribing sections of an interview

Some interviews or at least large portions of them may not be very useful, perhaps because interviewees are reticent or because their answers are not as relevant to your research topic as you had hoped. There seems little point in transcribing material that you know is unlikely to be fruitful. It may be that, for many of your interviews, it would be better to listen to them closely first, at least once or more usually twice, and then transcribe only those portions that you think are useful or relevant. However, this may mean that you miss certain things or that you have to go back to the recordings at a later stage in your analysis to try to find something that emerges as significant only later on.

To transcribe or not to transcribe?

Lucie found the process of transcribing her interviews to be very time-consuming, but she did also see benefits in the process:

> It was quite tedious because you have to write down everything that they say, even the kind of things that you know you won't be using. And I'm not a touch-typist or anything, so I had to like go back and listen over again. It took a long time. It would take three times the amount of time of the interview to transcribe it. Even longer actually! But it was quite useful because listening over again you pick up on things that you didn't pick up initially, but I didn't know if it was me reading into it too much because I'd heard it so many times. I was like 'Oh, that's interesting!' and 'What did she mean by that?' So I thought it was useful in that sense, but it was quite a long process.

A further example is given by Tom, who transcribed only the sections of his interviews that he judged were likely to be useful:

> I didn't actually transcribe everything that was said to me because sometimes people would go off on a big explanation of technical procedures in the call centre, which I knew wasn't going to answer any of my research questions because I wasn't interested in making any technical recommendations about the organization of the work and so when people started going on into kind of procedures and how they prioritized calls I thought 'There's no point in me transcribing this because it's not going to help me in any way.' So I was a bit selective although I still had to transcribe most of it.

Digital audio recording and speech-recognition software

Digital voice recording provides you with a permanent record of the interview that can be listened to repeatedly (for example, to try to catch a word that is difficult to hear). Digital voice recorders are often installed as apps on smartphones, which makes them very unobtrusive in a research interview and easy to carry.

Digital recording also enables the use of digital editing programs to adjust recording levels, adjust volume between different speakers, reduce background noise, extract information to protect anonymity, or cut out unwanted sections of recording (Stockdale 2002). Transcription software can be used to insert tags that show up in the transcribed text. When reading the transcript, you can click the tag and listen to the appropriate section of the audio recording. There are various speech-recognition or speech-to-text software programmes available, which can assist in the process of transcription. Given the time-consuming nature of manual transcription, this might seem an attractive option. However, these programmes are limited in their accuracy and often require time to set up so that they can recognize the speaker's voice, which research participants are likely to be unwilling to do. For some time now, technology writers have been saying that the software is improving rapidly, and while this is true, at the time of writing, we are not aware of any software that approaches the accuracy of a person.

TIPS AND SKILLS
Translating interview data

With business research becoming increasingly international, this introduces considerations related to translation when the researcher is collecting data in a language other than English and translating it into English for the purposes of reporting findings. These issues were also discussed in Chapter 11 in the context of survey research. Xian (2008) argues that much of the discussion about this issue to date has been positivistic in orientation, seeing translation purely as a technical exercise rather than an interpretative process. She argues that interview translation is based on the negotiation of cultural differences between the interviewer and the interviewee. Drawing on her study of Chinese women's narratives, she suggests that 'the translation process constitutes a (re)construction of the social reality of a culture in a different language, in which the translator interacts with the data, actively interpreting social concepts and meanings' (2008: 233). Xian identifies three types of problem associated with translating interview data.

1. *Linguistic.* This includes situations where interviewees use words for which there is no equivalent in English, or grammatical structures that cannot be translated easily.

2. *Socio-cultural.* This includes difficulties associated with translating idioms or proverbs from one language to another that rely on socio-historical knowledge for their meaning. Xian recommends the use of footnotes to provide the contextual understanding through which the translation can be made meaningful. However, Xian is cautious about back-translating the transcript into the primary language and asking interviewees to verify the back-translation because of concern that they would just not be able to recognize their own accounts.

3. *Methodological.* Taking a postmodern perspective (see Key concept 2.8), Xian argues that translation is a process that involves the translator imposing his or her authority on the foreign culture. Instead she recommends a more reflexive approach that involves acknowledging and working with the difficulties associated with translation and not allowing silences to be overlooked.

Translation, she concludes, is therefore a sensemaking process that involves the translator's knowledge, social background, and personal experience.

TIPS AND SKILLS
Keeping the recorder going

Since interviewees sometimes 'open up' at the end of the interview, perhaps just when the audio recorder has been switched off, there are good grounds for suggesting that you should keep it switched on for as long as possible. So, when you are winding the interview down, don't switch off the recorder immediately.

Non-face-to-face interviews

So far, this chapter has been concerned with interviews that are conducted face-to-face. This involves the researcher arranging to meet up with the interviewee at a set time, and in a particular place, for the purpose of conducting the interview. However, there are several ways of conducting qualitative interviews that do not rely on meeting face-to-face. In this section we discuss three types of non-face-to-face interviewing—using telephone, online, and Skype technologies. Some qualitative researchers suggest that non-face-to-face interviewing lessens the rapport that can be established and maintained between the interviewer and the researcher.

Overall, it is our view that the pervasive use of these technologies in everyday life means that they have become entirely normal as a way of interacting for many people. Hence concerns about non-face-to-face interviewing being inherently less naturalistic are becoming less important.

Telephone interviewing

Telephone interviewing is common in survey research, as noted in Chapter 10. However, it has not been widely used in qualitative research even though it has certain benefits when compared to face-to-face interviewing. One of these is cost, since it will be much cheaper to conduct qualitative interviews by telephone, just as it is with survey interviewing. It is likely to be especially useful for hard-to-reach groups and when interviewer safety is a consideration. Further, it may be that asking sensitive questions by telephone will be more effective, since interviewees may be less distressed about answering when the interviewer is not physically present. It may also be that for interviewing in organizations where the telephone is a core means of service delivery, such as call centres, or in organizations located overseas, the use of telephone interviewing as a research method may be more appropriate and more practical. For example, Patwardhan et al. (2009) were interested in the use of strategic deception by call centre operators to develop relationships with consumers, through such tactics as giving a Western 'pseudo name' (2009: 321) or pretending that the call centre was in a location in the USA or UK rather than in India. They carried out twelve face-to-face and nine telephone interviews with call centre operators who worked for a health care financial service company in India in order qualitatively to explore the types of deception used with Western consumers. The authors state that the decision to carry out face-to-face versus telephone interviews was made purely for practical reasons; international telephone interviews made from the USA where the researchers worked were the second choice in cases where it was not possible to meet the interviewee face-to-face. However, it may be argued that, because call centre workers use the telephone as their main medium of communication with consumers, they might be more comfortable participating in a telephone interview study than other groups of employees. Furthermore, since this study focused on ethically sensitive practices—that is, call centre workers lying to consumers, and the training given by the company to support these deceptive practices—it could be that the lack of physical proximity between the researcher and the participants enabled by telephone interviewing increased the employees' sense of anonymity and encouraged them to participate in the study.

Certain issues about the use of telephone interviewing in qualitative research need to be borne in mind. Most obviously, it will not be appropriate to some groups of interviewees, such as those with no or limited access to telephones. Secondly, it is unlikely to work well with very long interviews. It is much easier for the interviewee to terminate a telephone interview than one conducted in person. This is especially significant for qualitative interviews, which are often time-consuming for interviewees. Thirdly, it is not possible to observe body language to see how interviewees respond in a physical sense to questions. Body language may be important, because through it the interviewer may be able to discern such things as discomfort, puzzlement, or confusion. It should also be borne in mind that there can be technical difficulties with recording telephone interviews. Special equipment may be needed, and there is always the possibility that the line will be poor.

Online interviews

The issues involved in conducting online interviews raises additional issues related to whether the interactions are synchronous or asynchronous. In synchronous online interviews, communication takes place in real time so that the questions posed by the researcher are answered more or less immediately by the participant. An example of this would be interviews based on an instant messaging application such as WhatsApp or WeChat. In asynchronous online interviewing, exchanges are not in real time: instead, the researcher sends the participant a question or set of questions via email and they respond to them over a period of a few days. Hewson and Laurent (2008) point out that methods writers imply that asynchronous online interviews tend to generate richer, more thorough, and more thoughtful data than synchronous ones, which often produce data they describe as 'playful' and less detailed. O'Connor et al. (2008) maintain that the adoption of synchronous interviews has been low, perhaps because of greater understanding of what can be gleaned from asynchronous interviews.

Although online interviews run the risk relative to face-to-face interviews that the respondent is somewhat more likely to drop out of the exchange (especially in asynchronous mode, since the interviews can sometimes be very protracted), Mann and Stewart (2000: 138–9) suggest that a relationship of mutual trust can be built up. This kind of relationship can make it easier for a longer-term commitment to the interview to be maintained, but also makes it easier for the researcher to go back to his or her interviewees for further information or reflections, something that is more difficult to do with the face-to-face personal interview. The authors also suggest it is important for interviewers to keep sending messages to respondents to reassure them that their written utterances are helpful and significant, especially since there is a lack of visual cues, such as nodding.

A further issue for the online personal interviewer to consider is whether to send all the questions at once or to interview by sending one question at a time followed by a reply. The problem with the former is that respondents may read all the questions and then reply only to those that they feel interested in or to which they feel they can make a genuine contribution, so that asking one question at a time is likely to be more reliable.

There is evidence to suggest that prospective interviewees are more likely to agree to participate if agreement is solicited prior to sending them questions and if the researcher uses some form of self-disclosure, such as directing the person being contacted to the researcher's website, which contains personal information, particularly information that might be relevant to the research issue (Curasi 2001; O'Connor and Madge 2001). The argument for obtaining prior agreement from interviewees before sending them questions to be answered is that unsolicited emails (spam) are regarded as a nuisance among online users. Receiving what is thought to be spam could result in an immediate refusal to take the message seriously.

Curasi (2001) conducted a comparison in which 24 online interviews carried out through email correspondence (and therefore asynchronous) were contrasted with 24 parallel face-to-face interviews. The interviews were concerned with online shopping. She found the following:

- Face-to-face interviewers are better able than online interviewers to maintain rapport with respondents.

- Greater commitment and motivation are required for completing an online interview, but, because of this, replies are often more detailed and considered than with face-to-face interviews.

- Online interviewers are less able to have an impact on whether the interview is successful or not because they are more remote.

- Online interviewees' answers tend to be more considered and grammatically correct, because they have more time to ponder their answers and because they

can tidy them up before sending them. Whether this is a positive feature is debatable: there is the obvious advantage of a 'clean' transcript, but there may be some loss of spontaneity, which Gibson (2010) found in connection with her research when she compared email and face-to-face interviews.

- Follow-up probes can be carried out in online interviews, as well as in face-to-face ones.

On the other hand, Curasi also found that the worst interviews, in terms of the amount of detail forthcoming, were online interviews. It may be that these differences are to do with the fact that, whereas a qualitative face-to-face interview is *spoken*, the online interview is usually *typed*.

It is clear from many of the discussions about online interviews by email that a significant problem for interviewers is that of keeping respondents involved when questions are being sent one or two at a time. Respondents tend to lose momentum or interest. However, Kivits (2005) has shown that recontacting interviewees on regular occasions and adopting an accessible and understanding style can not only help to maintain momentum for many interviewees but also bring some who have lost interest, or forgotten to reply, back into the research.

An interesting issue with asynchronous personal interviews is whether it is appropriate to describe them as qualitative interviews at all and indeed whether they are experienced by participants as interviews. Given that the process of answering questions in an asynchronous online interview entails writing, particularly if there is minimal interaction with the researcher, it may be experienced by the participant as more akin to answering open questions in a self-administered questionnaire.

Interviews using Skype

The previous discussion of online personal interviewing assumes that the exchange is conducted entirely by text. However, software applications such as Skype offer further possibilities for synchronous online interviewing. Skype, or the various alternatives technologies for making online audio and video calls, makes online interviewing similar to a telephone interview, but with the added possibility of face-to-face interaction via webcam. Some researchers have reported and reflected on their experiences of using Skype in qualitative interviewing and they are broadly positive (Deakin and Wakefield 2014; Hanna 2012; Weinmann et al. 2012). In addition to enabling a visual element that is akin to a face-to-face interview, they suggest several other advantages:

- Skype interviewing is more flexible than face-to-face interviewing, in that last-minute adjustments to the scheduling of the interview can be easily accommodated.

- There are obvious time and cost savings as the need to travel to the interview is removed, which is a particular advantage with geographically dispersed samples.

- The convenience of being interviewed by Skype may encourage some people to agree to be interviewed when they might otherwise have declined.

- There are fewer concerns about the safety of both parties in an interview situation, particularly when the interview is being conducted at night.

- There is little evidence that the interviewer's capacity to secure rapport is significantly reduced in comparison with face-to-face interviews.

There are some limitations that warrant mention too:

- There are potential technological problems with the use of Skype. Not everyone has the necessary wifi connection and familiarity with Skype is not universal.

- Skype can be prone to fluctuations in the quality of the connection (and sometimes outages) which can make the flow of the interview less than smooth. Breaking up of speech can result in poor recordings of the interview, which makes transcription difficult or at times impossible.

- One of the principal advantages of the online text-based interview is lost, in that the respondent's answers need to be transcribed as in face-to-face qualitative interviewing.

- Although it is clearly advantageous for interviewers and interviewees to see each other so that visual cues can be picked up, responses may be affected by visible characteristics of the interviewer, such as gender, age, and ethnicity.

- There is some evidence that prospective Skype interviewees are more likely than face-to-face interviewees to fail to be present for an interview.

Clearly, interviewing via Skype clearly has great potential and it may be that some of the difficulties reported above will gradually become less pronounced.

STUDENT EXPERIENCE

Using Skype interviews in a study of women egg donors

For her dissertation research project, Anna carried out interviews with 10 women who had been commercial egg donors (Anna's research is also discussed in Chapter 18 in the context of sampling). Because the women were based in the USA, and Anna was in Australia, Skype or an equivalent technology provided the only means through which she was able to interview this group of research participants. Below she describes how she went about setting this up:

> So we would set a time to chat and, of course, the people who were going to be interviewed need to have the technology to be able to talk from one continent to another. But most people have smartphones these days. I helped them with some directions if they hadn't used either Skype or FaceTime or Google Chat—I used all of those with different people. We would book a time to talk. I made sure that our time zones were correct. And then I would ring them and they would pick up. With some women I spoke to it was just like a phone call, just voice-to-voice. I would offer that we don't have to see each other—whatever we feel comfortable with—just to make it so that there was no added pressure on having to look a certain way. People become self-conscious when there's a video camera on them.

> I used my computer at home and I used QuickTime to record the conversation on the computer. But I also had my phone recording, and I had a voice recorder recording, just in case anything got lost—which it did once.

What is striking about Anna's study is the extent to which Skype interviewing enabled her to access a difficult-to-reach group, both in terms of the sensitivity of the topic and their geographical location. Skype interviewing was also helpful in protecting participants' anonymity and confidentiality, including by enabling them to leave off the webcam so that their faces were not visible to the researcher.

Life history and oral history interviews

Two special forms of the kind of interview associated with qualitative research are *life history* and *oral history* interviews.

The life history interview is associated with the life history method, where it is often combined with various kinds of personal documents such as diaries, photographs, and letters. This method is also referred to as the biographical method. A life history interview is a kind of unstructured interview covering the totality of an individual's life. It documents 'the inner experience of individuals, how they interpret, understand, and define the world around them' (Faraday and Plummer 1979: 776).

Life history methodology is useful in situations when the researcher is attempting to understand the complex processes whereby people make sense of their organizational reality. Musson (1998) suggests that it can provide answers to such research questions as: How does socialization take place in organizations? How are organizational careers created and maintained? How do certain managerial styles come to be accepted as inevitable? What influence do leaders and founders have on organizational culture?

Despite the suggested relevance of life history interviews to organizational research, there has been only a trickle of empirical studies that have used this approach over the years. Bowen and Hisrich (1986) suggest that a very 'uneven picture' emerges of the female entrepreneur owing to a lack of published research. The few studies that exist tend to employ 'very small samples' and 'seldom attempt to be representative' (1986: 404). They suggest that longitudinal studies following the careers of entrepreneurs over time would enable development of a life cycle conception of the careers of female entrepreneurs and they recommend the use of a life history approach.

The life history method has tended to suffer because the life in question is erroneously seen as a sample of one and hence of limited generalizability. However, it has clear strengths from the point of view of the qualitative researcher: its unambiguous emphasis on the point of view of the life in question and a clear commitment to the processual aspects of social life, showing how events unfold and interrelate in people's lives. The terms *life history* and *life story* are sometimes employed interchangeably, but R. L. Miller (2000: 19) suggests that the latter is an account someone gives about his or her life and that a life history dovetails a life story with other sources, such as diaries and letters (of the kind discussed in Chapter 23).

An example of the life history interview approach in organizational research is provided by Musson in the context of her research on how general medical practitioners (GPs) in the UK experienced and understood the 1990 health care reforms. As the research progressed, it became apparent to Musson that life histories of key actors were significant in the way that changes were understood and experienced.

> I directed the storytelling process to a large extent by asking individuals to tell me about when and how their understanding of the purpose of the organization shifted ... These stories differed from focusing on the history of an individual's marital difficulties, to telling me a story about an individual patient and the way she was treated by the GPs in the practice ... Likewise, I asked people to tell me about their lives in previous organizations and how they had experienced these; what they had found rewarding, constraining or difficult to make sense of, and how this differed in their current organization. Again, the open ended structure of the narratives allowed people to introduce subjects of major importance to them.
>
> (Musson 1998: 16)

Miller suggests there has been a resurgence of interest in life history methods in recent years, and Chamberlayne et al. (2000) argue that there has been a recent 'turn to biographical methods'. To a large extent, the revival of this approach derives from a growth of interest in the role and significance of agency in social life. The revival is largely associated with the growing use of life story interviews and especially in association with narrative analysis (see Chapter 22). The growing use of such interviews has come to be associated less and less with the study of a single life (or indeed just one or two lives) and increasingly with the study of several lives (see Research in focus 20.6 for an example).

Plummer (2001) draws a useful distinction among three types of life story:

1. *Naturalistic life stories*. These are life stories that occur whenever people reminisce or write autobiographies, or when job applicants write out letters of application and are interviewed.

2. *Researched life stories*. These are life stories that are solicited by researchers with a social scientific purpose in mind. Most research based on life history/ story interviews are of this kind.

20.6 RESEARCH IN FOCUS
Constructionism in a life history study of occupational careers

In an article on the concept of occupational career by Bosley et al. (2009), an explicitly constructionist stance was taken. Rather than viewing careers as a relatively fixed series of stages through which people progress, Bosley et al. researched careers as social constructions that are highly contingent on experiences and on other individuals who influence the occupational directions that people take. As the authors put it: 'career is seen as social practice, constituted by actors themselves in and through their relationships with others, and as they move through time and space. It is an **iterative** and on-going process' (2009: 1498). The authors employed a life story method in which 28 employees were interviewed. The interviews 'elicited participants' accounts of their careers from school-leaving to present day. Describing encounters with helpers in the context of preceding and subsequent events enabled participants to recall and identify significant career helpers and the role played by helpers in shaping their careers' (2009: 1499). For each interviewee, a narrative account was generated that portrayed each interviewee's career in terms of contacts, relationships, and encounters that shaped his or her career direction. Out of these narratives, the authors forged a typology of career-shaping roles: adviser, informant, witness, gatekeeper, and intermediary. Each role is associated with a different kind of impact on employees' career trajectories and decision-making. The authors write: 'shaping encounters served as a vehicle through which participants negotiated with and navigated through the structural environments in which they were situated' (2009: 1515). The constructionism associated with this research lies in its emphasis on interviewees, and the events and people that were significant in the course and direction of their careers.

3. *Reflexive and recursive life stories.* This recognizes that the life story is always a construction in which the interviewer is implicated. An *oral history* interview is usually somewhat more specific in tone in that the subject is asked to reflect upon specific events or periods in the past. It too is sometimes combined with other sources, such as documents. The chief problem with the oral history interview (which it shares with the life history interview) is the possibility of bias introduced by memory lapses and distortions (Grele 1998). On the other hand, oral history testimonies have allowed the voices to come through of groups that are typically marginalized in historical research (a point that also applies to life history interviews), either because of their lack of power or because they are typically regarded as unexceptional (Samuel 1976).

Feminist interviewing

Unstructured and semi-structured interviewing have become prominent methods of data gathering within a feminist research framework. In part, this is a reflection of the preference for qualitative research among feminist researchers, but it also reflects a view that the kind of interview with which qualitative research is associated allows many of the goals of feminist research to be realized. Indeed, the view has been expressed that 'Whilst several brave women in the 1980s defended quantitative methods, it is nonetheless still the case that not just qualitative methods, but the in-depth face-to-face interview has become the paradigmatic "feminist method"' (Kelly et al. 1994: 34). This comment is enlightening because it implies that it is not simply that qualitative research is seen by many writers and researchers as more consistent with a feminist position than quantitative research, but that specifically qualitative interviewing is seen as especially appropriate. The point that is being made here is not necessarily that such interviewing is somehow more in tune with feminist values than, say, ethnography (especially since it is often an ingredient of ethnographic research). Instead, it could be that the intensive and time-consuming nature of ethnography means that, although it has great potential as an approach to feminist research (see Chapter 19), qualitative interviewing is often preferred because it is usually less invasive in these respects.

However, it is specifically interviewing of the kind conducted in qualitative research that is seen as having potential for a feminist approach, not the structured interview with which survey research is associated. Why might one type of interview be consistent with a sensitivity to feminism and the other not? In a frequently cited article, Oakley outlines the following points about the standard survey interview.

- It is a one-way process—the interviewer extracts information or views from the interviewee.

- The interviewer offers nothing in return for the extraction of information. For example, interviewers using a structured interview do not offer information or their own views if asked. Indeed, they are typically advised not to do such things because of worries about contaminating their respondents' answers.

- The interviewer–interviewee relationship is a form of hierarchical or power relationship. Interviewers arrogate to themselves the right to ask questions, implicitly placing their interviewees in a position of subservience or inferiority.

- The element of power is also revealed by the fact that the structured interview seeks out information from the perspective of the researcher.

- Because of these points, the standard survey interview is inconsistent with feminism when women interview other women. This view arises because it is seen as indefensible for women to 'use' other women in these ways.

Instead of this framework for conducting interviews, feminist researchers advocate one that establishes:

- a high level of rapport between interviewer and interviewee;

- a high degree of reciprocity on the part of the interviewer;

- the perspective of the women being interviewed;

- a non-hierarchical relationship.

In connection with the reciprocity that she advocates, Oakley noted, for example, that in her research on the transition to motherhood, she was frequently asked questions by her respondents. She argues that it was ethically indefensible for a feminist not to answer when confronted with questions of a certain kind. For Oakley, therefore, the qualitative interview was a means of resolving the dilemmas that she encountered as a feminist interviewing other women. An interesting dilemma is the question of what feminist researchers should do when their interpretation of women's accounts differs from how research participants see their own situation (Kelly et al. 1994). This raises the tricky question of how far the commitment to seeing through the eyes of the people you study can and/or should extend. Two examples are relevant here. Reinharz (1992: 28–9) cites the case of an American study by M. Andersen (1981), who interviewed 20 'corporate wives' who came across as happy with their lot and were supportive of feminism only in relation to employment discrimination. Andersen interpreted their responses to her questions as indicative of 'false consciousness'—in other words, she did not really believe her interviewees. When Andersen wrote an article on her findings, the women wrote a letter rejecting her account, affirming that women can be fulfilled as wives and mothers. A similar situation confronted Millen (1997) when she interviewed 32 British female scientists using 'semi-structured, in-depth individual interviewing' (1997: 4.6). As Millen puts it:

> There was a tension between my interpretation of their reported experience as sex-based, and the meaning the participants themselves tended to attribute to their experience, since the majority of respondents did not analyse these experiences in terms of patriarchy or sex–gender systems, but considered them to be individualised, or as 'just something that had to be coped with' … From my external, academically privileged vantage point, it is clear that sexism pervades these professions, and that men are assumed from the start by other scientists to be competent scientists of status whilst women have to prove themselves, overcome the barrier of their difference before they are accepted. These women, on the other hand, did not generally view their interactions in terms of gendered social systems. There is therefore a tension between their characterisation of their experience and my interpretation of it.

(1997: 5.6, 5.9)

Three interesting issues are thrown up by these two accounts. First, how can such a situation arise? Qualitative research makes claims to reveal social reality as viewed by members of the setting in question. If researchers are genuinely seeing through others' eyes, the 'tension' to which Millen refers should not arise. However, it clearly can and does, and this suggests that qualitative researchers are more affected by their own perspectives and research questions when collecting and analysing data than might be expected from textbook accounts of the research process. Second, there is the question of how to handle such a 'tension'—that is, how do you reconcile the two accounts? M. Andersen's (1981) solution to the tension she encountered was to reinterpret her findings in terms of the conditions that engender the contentment she uncovered. Third, given that feminist research is often concerned with wider political goals of emancipation, a tension between participants' world views and the researcher's position raises moral questions about the appropriateness of imposing an interpretation that is not shared by research participants themselves.

A further dilemma relates to the responsibilities of the researcher when interviewing male participants whose views directly challenge feminist commitments. Such as situation was experienced by Arendell (1997) in her study of divorced fathers. Arendell argues that, while feminist research has focused on women interviewing other women and men interviewing women, insufficient attention has been devoted to understanding the gender and power dynamics involved when women interview men. Her study involved face-to-face interviews with divorced fathers who had children. Many of the men in the study were critical and denigrating of women, some expressing considerable hostility towards their ex-wives. Yet Arendell found herself in the paradoxical position of being treated as a confidant to whom the men disclosed their feelings and experiences in great detail precisely *because* she was a woman—the men perceiving it to be more appropriate to share their emotions with a woman rather than a man. Arendell did not voluntarily tell the fathers that she was a feminist and many of them assumed she was not, instead presuming she was committed to understanding their situation and exposing the wrongs perpetrated upon them as divorced fathers. One of the questions that Arendell poses concerns whether or not she was inadvertently endorsing, or even contributing to, sexist, misogynist behaviours by not objecting to the views expressed by the men during the interviews. In answering this question, she argues that had she declared her objections, the men would probably not have spoken openly to her and she therefore 'needed to allow them to tell their stories in their own fashion, whatever the content, style, or tone' (1997: 363).

As these examples highlight, while interviewing is a popular research method for feminist researchers, the ways in which feminists write about interviews as a research method is also of general significance in the conduct of qualitative business research because it raises important questions about the power relationships between, and ethical responsibilities of, researchers and participants.

Merits and limitations of qualitative interviewing

The aim of this section is to consider the merits and limitations of interviewing in qualitative research in comparion to other qualitative methods such as participant observation (discussed in Chapter 19). We summarize here first the advantages and then the disadvantages.

Advantages of qualitative interviews

1. *Qualitative interviews can be used to investigate issues that are resistant to observation.* There is a wide range of issues that are simply not amenable to observation, so asking people about what has happened is the only viable means of finding out about such issues within a qualitative research strategy. This is particularly so when dealing with perceptions, attitudes, and motives, which may be held privately by individuals, rather than expressed openly in organizational contexts. An example of where this can arise is in the study of organizational spirituality and religion. It is not always possible within a qualitative study to find out how employees' spiritual and religious values influence their working practices without asking them about this privately in an interview. Given the sensitivity of such issues, it is particularly important to provide participants with assurances of confidentiality and anonymity (see the discussion of research ethics in Chapter 6).

2. *Qualitative interviewing enables the reconstruction of events.* This is done by asking interviewees to think back over how a certain series of events unfolded in relation to a current situation. An example is Pettigrew's (1985) research on ICI, which involved 'retrospective interviewing' (see Research in focus 3.16). This reconstruction of events is something that cannot be accomplished using methods such as participant observation.

3. *Qualitative interviewing makes obtaining informed consent from participants more straightforward.* Gaining informed consent by using a signed consent form is an increasingly common ethical requirement in business research (see Chapter 6). It is relatively easy to have a discussion with participants about the nature of a study prior to commencing an interview and to ask them for their signature to indicate their consent to participate. This is much more difficult in participant observation or ethnography, where the precise moment at which to request consent is unclear and may involve discussions with several people who are present, each of whom may feel differently.

4. *Qualitative interviews may be less prone to reactive effects.* Methods such as participant observation are prone to reactive effects. People's knowledge of the fact that they are being observed may make them behave less naturally. Interviewers clearly do not suffer from the same kind of problem, but it could be argued that the unnatural character of the interview encounter can also be regarded as a context within which reactive effects may emerge. It seems likely that both participant observation and qualitative interviewing set in motion reactive effects, but of different kinds.

5. *Qualitative interviews are less intrusive in people's lives.* In comparison to methods like participant observation, interviews are time-bounded and take up a lot less time. The impact on people's lives is therefore likely to be less than having to have a researcher hanging around for a period of weeks, months, or even years.

6. *Qualitative interviews can make longitudinal research easier.* Within a qualitative interview study, the researcher may negotiate to re-interview individuals at a later date, thereby enabling a longitudinal element to be built into the study. Michel's (2011) nine-year study of Wall Street investment bankers (Research in focus 19.2) provides an example of this. While other qualitative methods such as participant observation are inherently longitudinal in character, because the observer is present in a social setting for a period of time, there are often limits to the amount of time that researchers can spend doing fieldwork away from their normal routines. Following up interviewees on several occasions is likely to be easier than returning to research sites on a regular basis.

7. *Qualitative interviewing can give greater breadth of coverage.* In qualitative interviewing, the researcher is less constrained in their selection of individuals and is better able to construct a stratified sample, for example of individuals at different hierarchical levels within a large organization. This enables greater breadth of coverage than in participant observation, where interactions and observations are likely to be fairly restricted to a specific group of people.

8. *Qualitative interviews enable the researcher to maintain a specific focus.* As noted in Chapter 17, qualitative research sometimes begins with a specific focus. Qualitative interviewing is well suited to such forms of qualitative study, since the interview can be directed towards addressing specific research questions. For example, the research by Bryman and his colleagues on the police had a very specific research focus in line with its Home Office funding—namely, conceptions of leadership among police officers (Bryman et al. 1996). The bulk of the data gathering was in two police forces and entailed the interviewing of police officers at all levels using a semi-structured interview guide.

Disadvantages of qualitative interviews

1. *Qualitative interviewing is less naturalistic.* As noted in Chapter 17, naturalism is one of the main tenets of qualitative research. Interviewing, even when it is at its most informal, disrupts the normal flow of events, and consequently is less naturalistic than methods such as participant observation. Research that relies on interviewing alone is likely to entail much more fleeting, structured contacts.

2. *Qualitative interviews provide limited insight into how language naturally occurs.* Related to the previous point, and as will be discussed in Chapter 22, qualitative researchers are concerned with how language is used in situations of everyday usage. The deliberately constructed nature of the qualitative interview means that the language participants use is likely to be influenced by their awareness of being studied—this is a form of reactive effect. This may cause them to self-censor their language use and produce accounts that they think are likely to be more acceptable to outsiders, including the researcher. This is potentially more likely if the participant is highly accustomed to giving other types of interviews, e.g. to the media.

3. *Qualitative interviewing tends to produce over-rationalistic accounts of the self.* Atkinson and Silverman (1997) argue that interviews invite participants to narrate their past behaviour in ways which elevate individual perceptions and accounts of experience and position them as 'authentic'. They argue that this

encourages an overly rationalistic view of human behaviour. They argue that 'the interview becomes a personal confessional' that conceals the deliberate identity work that is entailed in the production of such (auto)biographical accounts (1997: 305). Twenty years on, Silverman (2017: 145) argues that little has changed, and that the interview remains unquestioned as the 'Gold Standard' of qualitative methods. He argues that there is a need for greater transparency in qualitative interviewing, including by researchers making explicit the exchanges between researchers and participants (as shown in Research in focus 20.4), rather than presenting participants' words in isolation.

4. *Qualitative interviews provide limited insight into social interactions and behaviours.* The interview relies primarily on verbal accounts of behaviour, so implicit features in social life are less likely to be revealed and matters that interviewees take for granted are less likely to surface than from observing behaviour. For example, few interviewees will be able to accurately recollect exactly who said what in a meeting involving several people, so for this, researchers must continue to rely on observation.

5. *Qualitative interviewing is not conducive to exposing deviant or hidden activities.* Much of what we know about patterns of resistance at work, industrial sabotage, and other criminal or deviant activity within organizations has been gleaned from participant observation. For example, Linstead's (1985) study of the practical jokes, general kidding, and games played by bakery workers was based on participant observation. Similarly, Collinson's (1988) analysis of humour in the context of a male-dominated workplace (see Chapter 19) relied partly on non-participant observation to obtain data about the daily jibes, socialization rituals, and initiation ceremonies that characterized daily life on the factory shopfloor. These are aspects of behaviour that insiders are likely to be reluctant to talk about in an interview. Understanding is likely to come through prolonged interaction.

6. *Qualitative interviews are less flexible in dealing with unexpected topics or issues.* Except with the most unstructured forms of interview, the interview process is likely to entail some degree of structure through the interview guide. There is also a tendency for interviewers to try to maintain a degree of comparability in their questioning of different people, and hence to impose a structure on the interview. This may discourage them from exploring issues that arise unexpectedly, even if they may turn out to be important to the study. Ditton's (1977) decision at a very late stage in the data collection process to focus on pilferage in the bakery in which he was a participant observer is an example that illustrates the importance of flexibility in qualitative research.

CHECKLIST
Issues to consider for your qualitative interview

○ Have you devised a clear and comprehensive/informative way of introducing the research to interviewees?

○ Does your interview guide clearly relate to your research questions?

○ Have you piloted the guide with some appropriate respondents?

○ Have you thought about what you will do if your interviewee does not turn up for the interview?

○ Does the guide contain a good mixture of different kinds of questions, such as probing, specifying, and direct questions?

○ Have you ensured that interviews will allow novel or unexpected themes and issues to arise?

○ Is your language in the questions clear, comprehensible, and free of unnecessary jargon?

○ Are your questions relevant to the people you are proposing to interview?

○ Does your interview guide include requests for information about the interviewee, such as his or her age, work experience, position in the firm?

○ Have your questions been designed to elicit reflective discussions, so that interviewees are not tempted to answer only in 'yes' or 'no' terms?

○ Do your questions offer a real prospect of seeing the world from your interviewees' point of view rather than imposing your own frame of reference on them?

○ Are you familiar with the setting(s) in which the interviews will take place?

○ Are you thoroughly familiar with and have you tested your recording equipment?

○ Have you thought about how you will present yourself in the interview, such as how you will be dressed?

○ Have you thought about how you will go about putting into operation the skills that make a good interviewer (see Tips and skills 'Criteria of a successful interviewer')?

KEY POINTS

- Interviewing in qualitative research is typically of the unstructured or semi-structured kind.

- In qualitative research, interviewing may be the sole method in an investigation or may be used as part of an ethnographic study, or indeed in tandem with another qualitative method.

- Qualitative interviewing is meant to be flexible and to seek out the world views of research participants.

- If an interview guide is employed, it should not be too structured in its application and should allow some flexibility in the asking of questions.

- The qualitative interview should be audio-recorded and then transcribed.

- As with ethnographic research, investigations using qualitative interviews tend not to employ random sampling to select participants.

- The qualitative interview has become a popular method of data collection in feminist studies.

- Whether to use qualitative interviews sometimes depends on the relative suitability of the method to the research questions being addressed.

QUESTIONS FOR REVIEW

Differences between the structured interview and the qualitative interview

- How does qualitative interviewing differ from structured interviewing?

Asking questions in the qualitative interview

- What kinds of skill does the interviewer need to develop in qualitative interviewing?

- What kinds of consideration need to be borne in mind when preparing an interview guide?
- What are the differences between unstructured and semi-structured interviewing?
- Could semi-structured interviewing stand in the way of flexibility in qualitative research?
- What kinds of question might be asked in an interview guide?
- Why is it important to record and transcribe qualitative interviews?

Life history and oral history interviews

- What are the differences between life history and oral history interviews?

Feminist research and interviewing in qualitative research

- Why has the qualitative interview become such a prominent research method for feminist researchers?
- What dilemmas might be posed for feminist researchers using qualitative interviewing?

Merits and limitations of qualitative interviewing

- Outline the relative advantages and disadvantages of qualitative interviewing.

ONLINE RESOURCES
www.oup.com/uk/brm5e/

Visit the Interactive Research Guide that accompanies this book to complete an exercise in interviewing for qualitative research.

FOCUS GROUPS

CHAPTER OUTLINE

The focus group method is an interview with several people on a specific topic or issue. This chapter explores:

- the possible reasons for preferring focus group interviews to individual interviews of the kind discussed in Chapter 20;
- the role of focus groups in market research, to determine how to sell products and services to consumers;
- how focus groups should be conducted in terms of such features as the need for recording, the number and size of groups, how participants can be selected, and how direct the questioning should be;
- the significance of interaction between participants in focus group discussions;
- the use of online focus groups;
- the use of the focus group method as an emancipatory research approach;
- some practical difficulties with focus group sessions, such as the possible loss of control and the potential for unwanted group effects.

Introduction

We are used to thinking of the interview as something that involves an interviewer and one interviewee. Most textbooks reinforce this perception by concentrating on individual interviews. The focus group technique is a method of interviewing that involves more than one, usually at least four, interviewees. Essentially it is a group interview. Some authors draw a distinction between focus group and group interview techniques. Three reasons are sometimes put forward to suggest a distinction.

- Focus groups typically emphasize a specific theme or topic that is explored in depth, whereas group interviews often span very widely.

- Sometimes group interviews are carried out so that the researcher is able to save time and money by carrying out interviews with a number of individuals simultaneously. However, focus groups are not carried out for this reason.

- The focus group practitioner is invariably interested in the ways in which individuals discuss a certain issue *as members of a group*, rather than simply as individuals. In other words, with a focus group the researcher will be interested in such things as how people respond to each other's views and build up a view out of the interaction that takes place within the group.

However, the distinction between the focus group method and the group interview is by no means clear-cut, and the two terms are often used interchangeably. Boddy (2005) suggests that the confusion is even broader than this, and also includes terms such as the 'nominal group interview', making it difficult for researchers to talk to each other in a common language. Nonetheless, the definition proposed in Key concept 21.1 provides a starting point.

Most focus group researchers undertake their work within the traditions of qualitative research. This means that they are explicitly concerned to reveal how the group participants view the issues they encounter. Therefore, the researcher will aim to provide a fairly unstructured setting for the extraction of their views and perspectives. The person who runs the focus group session is usually called the moderator or facilitator, and he or she will be expected to guide the session but not to be too intrusive.

Another general point about the focus group method is that it is one of the most widely used qualitative research methods outside of academic contexts. Focus groups have been used commercially for many years in market and consumer research to test reactions to products and advertising initiatives. They are also used by politicians, not only quantitatively to predict the outcome of an election, but also qualitatively to shape their policies and images. Focus groups are used by movie-makers to determine when a major film run should end, by art entrepreneurs to determine what paintings will sell, and by CEOs to test corporate communications. The popularization of the focus group method may make it more difficult to convince research audiences of the significance of focus group research, because they are used for so many other purposes. Cowley (2000) suggests that, in order to distinguish research based on 'strategic qualitative market research focus groups' from research that is done by those who simply decide 'they can run' focus groups, despite their lack of experience, a professional code of conduct is

21.1 KEY CONCEPT
What is the focus group method?

The focus group method is a form of group interview in which there are several participants (in addition to the moderator/facilitator); there is an emphasis in the questioning on a particular fairly tightly defined topic; and the accent is upon interaction within the group and the joint construction of meaning. As such, the focus group contains elements of two methods: the group interview, in which several people discuss a number of topics; and what has been called a focused interview, in which interviewees are selected because they 'are known to have been involved in a particular situation' (Merton et al. 1956: 3) and are asked about that involvement. The focused interview may be administered to individuals or to groups. Thus, the focus group method appends to the focused interview the element of interaction within groups as an area of interest and is more focused than the group interview.

needed. However, it must be remembered that, while the use of focus groups is becoming more widespread, it is by no means a new technique, as it has a long-established use in various forms of research. Based on his experience of academic and market research in an international context, Boddy (2005) distinguishes between the 'focus group interview' and the 'focus group discussion'. The focus group discussion is loosely directed by a facilitator and involves a group of people who are brought together to discuss a subject of interest with the other members of the group; this can include argument and disagreement but is generally conducted in an open, friendly manner. The focus group interview is more closely controlled by the facilitator and discussion is mainly between the facilitator and the group, rather than between participants.

Group members may use hand-held electronic devices to select their preferences, and 'mini-questionnaires' may also be used. The focus group interview is more associated with market research, rather than with qualitative research of the kind we are discussing here.

One final point to make is that there is growing interest in the use of online focus groups, discussed later in this chapter. There is evidence that, although they tend to be shorter than comparable face-to-face focus groups, they can generate a considerable amount of relevant data for the researcher (Reid and Reid 2005). When this is viewed in relation to the saving in travel time and cost for both researchers and participants, it is clear why this is becoming an increasingly commonly used variation on the method.

Uses of focus groups

What are the uses of the focus group method? In many ways its uses are bound up with the uses of qualitative research in general, but, over and above these, the following points can be registered.

- The original idea for the focus group—the focused interview—was that people who were known to have had a certain experience could be interviewed in a relatively unstructured way about that experience. The bulk of the discussion by Merton et al. (1956) of the notion of the focused interview was in terms of individual interviews, but their book also considered the extension of the method into group interview contexts. Subsequently, the focus group has become a popular method for researchers examining the ways in which people, in conjunction with one another, construe the general topics in which the researcher is interested. In management research, early use of the focus group technique was also seen as a way of helping individuals to define problems and work together to identify potential solutions (Hutt 1979). The dynamics of group discussion could lead individuals to define business problems in new and innovative ways and to formulate creative ideas for their solution.

- The technique allows the researcher to develop an understanding about *why* people feel the way they do. In an individual interview the interviewee is often asked about his or her reasons for holding a particular view, but the focus group approach offers the opportunity of allowing people to probe each other's reasons for holding a certain view. This can be more interesting than the question-followed-by-answer approach of individual interviews. For one thing, an individual may answer in a certain way during a focus group, but, as he or she listens to others' answers, he or she may want to qualify or modify a view; or alternatively may want to voice agreement to something that he or she probably would not have thought of without the opportunity of hearing the views of others. These possibilities mean that focus groups may also be very helpful in the elicitation of a wide variety of views about a particular issue.

- In focus groups, participants are able to bring to the fore issues that they deem to be important and significant in relation to the given topic. This is clearly an aim of individual interviews too, but, because the moderator has to relinquish a certain amount of control to the participants, the issues that concern them can surface. This is clearly an important consideration in the context of qualitative research, since the viewpoints of the people being studied are an important point of departure.

- In conventional one-to-one interviewing, interviewees are rarely challenged; they might say things that are inconsistent with earlier replies or that patently could not be true, but we are often reluctant to point out such deficiencies. In the context of a focus group, individuals will often argue with each other and challenge each other's views. This process of arguing means that the researcher may stand a chance of ending up with more realistic accounts of what people think, because they are forced to consider and possibly revise their views.

- The focus group offers the researcher the opportunity to study the ways in which individuals collectively make sense of a phenomenon and construct meanings around it. It is a central tenet of such theoretical positions as symbolic interactionism (discussed in Chapter 2) that the process of coming to terms with (that is, understanding) social phenomena is not undertaken by individuals in isolation from each other. Instead, it is something that occurs in interaction and discussion with others. In this sense, therefore, focus groups reflect the processes through which meaning is constructed in everyday life and to that extent can be regarded as more naturalistic than individual interviews (Wilkinson 1998).

As we mentioned in the introduction to this chapter, focus groups have been used extensively in market research for many years, where the method is employed for such purposes as testing responses to new products and advertising initiatives. According to the UK Association of Qualitative Market Research Practitioners, focus groups represent the most commonly used research method in market research; see the Association for Qualitative Research website for more on this: https://www.aqr.org.uk/. Such focus groups typically involve groups of six to twelve consumers, who are brought together to discuss their reactions to new products, packaging, advertisements, or promotions. There is a large literature in market research on focus group research and its implementation (e.g. Calder 1977).

However, the use of focus group methods in market research has attracted its fair share of controversy. Some researchers have suggested that it is a weaker method than, say, experiments or surveys (to name two research approaches that are common in market research). The most frequently mentioned problem is the perceived lack of generalizability—results are not always a reliable indicator of the reactions of the wider population. Criticism is also made of the unsystematic nature of the sample, which is not as rigorous as probability sampling (see Chapter 9). For example, Sudman and Blair (1999: 272) have suggested that, although the focus group method is an excellent tool for gaining insight about markets, 'it should be evident that a group of 10 or so people chosen haphazardly at a single location cannot be expected to reflect the total population of consumers'. A further difficulty stems from the lack of realism associated with focus groups. Participants may be given written or verbal descriptions of a product, or an artist's sketch, but this bears little relation to the real-life experience of choosing a product in a competitive context. Criticisms also stem from problems of reliability. This relates to the role of the moderator and the suggestion that there can be variation in the interpretation of transcripts. Fern (2001) has provided a rebuttal of these criticisms by arguing that the generalizability of focus group findings, as with other research methods, depends on the scale of the sample—a two-group study may have limited generalizability but a 32-group study is another matter. He also defends the reliability of focus groups, suggesting that representativeness can be achieved by stratifying the population and drawing random samples from each stratum. Fern suggests that greater reliability can be gained by using different moderators with different backgrounds or from different groups (for example, male and female) to conduct group discussions on a relevant topic (for example, gender). The results from each group can then be compared for consistency of interpretation. What seems slightly puzzling is that market researchers attempt to defend their use of focus group methods in terms of quantitative rather than qualitative criteria. This is likely to be because quality criteria associated with quantitative study are applied, even though the focus group interview is a qualitative method.

Conducting focus groups

There are a number of practical issues in conducting focus group research that warrant discussion.

Recording and transcription

As with interviewing for qualitative research, the focus group interview will work best if it is recorded and subsequently transcribed. The following reasons are often used to explain this preference.

- One reason is the simple difficulty of writing down not only exactly what people say but also who says it. The researcher will be interested in who expresses views within the group, such as whether certain individuals seem to act as opinion leaders or dominate the discussion. This also means that there is an interest in ranges of opinions within groups; for example, in a session, does most of the range of opinion derive from just one or two people or from most of the people in the group? In an individual interview you might be able to ask the respondent to hold on while you write something down, but to do this in the context of a discussion involving several people would be extremely disruptive.

- A major reason for conducting focus group research is the fact that it is possible to study the processes whereby meaning is collectively constructed within each session, as discussed earlier in the chapter. It would be very difficult to do this by taking notes, because of the need to keep track of *who says what* (see also previous point). If this element is lost, the dynamics of the focus group session would also be lost, and a major rationale for doing focus group interviews rather than individual ones would be undermined.

- Like all qualitative researchers, the focus group practitioner will be interested in not just what people say but *how* they say it—for example, the particular language that they use. There is every chance that the nuances of language will be lost if the researcher has to rely on notes.

It should be borne in mind that transcribing focus group sessions is more complicated and hence more time-consuming than transcribing traditional interview recordings. This is because you need to take account of *who* is talking in the session, as well as what is said. This is sometimes difficult, since people's voices are not always easy to distinguish. Also, people sometimes talk over each other, which can make transcription even more difficult. In addition, it is extremely important to ensure that you equip yourself with a very high-quality microphone, which is capable of picking up voices, some of which may be quite faint, from many directions. Focus group transcripts always seem to have more missing bits

owing to lack of audibility than transcripts from conventional interviews.

A recent development in market research has involved the introduction of online focus groups. This overcomes some of the problems associated with recording what goes on in focus groups, but it also raises difficulties. Online focus groups are discussed later in this chapter.

How many groups?

How many groups do you need? There is a good deal of variation in the number of focus groups used in any particular study, with the norm being somewhere between 12 and 15. However, much lower numbers are not uncommon. Chan et al. (2012) conducted focus group research into the management of stress among Hong Kong construction professionals in mainland China and held just six groups. Four were from different parts of mainland China, one was a group of Hong Kong professionals who had repatriated from China, and one was group of Hong Kong professionals without expatriate experience.

Clearly, it is unlikely that just one group will suffice the needs of the researcher, since there is always the possibility that the responses are particular to that one group. Obviously, time and resources will be a factor, but there are strong arguments for saying that too many groups will be a waste of time. Calder (1977) proposes that, when the moderator reaches the point that he or she is able to anticipate fairly accurately what the next group is going to say, then there are probably enough groups already. This notion is very similar to the theoretical saturation criterion that was briefly introduced in Key concept 18.4. In other words, once your major analytic categories have been saturated, there seems little point in continuing, and so it would be appropriate to bring data collection to a halt. For their study of audience discussion programmes, Livingstone and Lunt (1994: 181) used this criterion: 'The number of focus groups was determined by continuing until comments and patterns began to repeat and little new material was generated.'

TIPS AND SKILLS
Transcribing focus group interviews

In Chapter 20, we suggested that it may not always be desirable or feasible to transcribe the whole of an interview. The same applies to focus group research, which is often more difficult and time-consuming to transcribe than individual interview recordings because of the number of speakers involved. The suggestions made in Chapter 20 in relation to transcribing sections of an interview therefore apply equally well to focus group recordings.

When this point of theoretical saturation is reached, as an alternative to terminating data collection, there may be a case for moving on to an extension of the issues that have been raised in the focus group sessions that have been carried out.

One factor that may affect the number of groups is whether the researcher feels that the kinds and range of views are likely to be affected by socio-demographic factors such as age, gender, class, and so on. Many focus group researchers like to use stratifying criteria such as these to ensure that groups with a wide range of features will be included. If so, a larger number of groups may be required to reflect the criteria. In the research described in Research in focus 21.2, Richards and Sang (2016) used a self-selected sample of trade union members who responded to their email request for study participants. Although this was a self-selected sample, and therefore no stratifying criteria were used to determine it, the researchers were able to put together a relatively diverse group of managers, employees and trade union representatives, in terms of their experience of neurological conditions. Thus, out of 44 participants overall, 27 per cent had a neurological impairment, 30 per cent worked with someone with neurological impairment, 32 per cent had a family member or friend with neurological impairment, 11 per cent represented neurologically impaired employees at work, and 16 per cent had no experience of neurological impairments in any situation. This provided the basis for a focus group discussion between participants with diverse experience relevant to the study, even if participants were not stratified based on socio-demographic factors.

One further point to bear in mind when considering the number of groups is that more groups will increase the complexity of your analysis. For example, Schlesinger et al. (1992: 29) report that the 14 audio-recorded sessions they organized produced over 1400 pages of transcription. This large quantity was accumulated from

21.2 RESEARCH IN FOCUS
Using focus groups to study trade union representation of disabled employees

Richards and Sang (2016) were interested in the extent to which trade unions represent disabled employees. Their research project focused on studying an initiative set up by a union that represents rail/transport industry workers in the UK, to address the needs of neurologically impaired employees. The purpose of the 'Neurodiversity' project is to raise awareness and provide education related to five neurological impairments (dyslexia, dyspraxia, dyscalculia, ADHD, and Asperger's syndrome) and enable specialist knowledge to be applied by Neurodiversity Champions in the workplace. A key aspect of Richards and Sang's research project involved evaluating the success of this initiative (see Key concept 3.9, 'What is evaluation research?').

The researchers adopted a qualitative research strategy as the most efficient way of understanding the attitudes of a range of trade union stakeholders towards the initiative. They decided to use focus groups as their main method of data collection because 'it is possible to tap into group dynamics and "safety in numbers" raises the willingness of participants to talk about sensitive topics'; this was also 'a quick and easy way to speak to many people at once' (Richards and Sang 2016: 1648). Focus group participants were recruited by email, using the trade union's membership database. Individuals were encouraged to participate if they had any experience of dyslexia, dyspraxia, dyscalculia, ADHD, or Asperger's syndrome; the sample was self-selecting. The researchers also conducted semi-structured telephone and face-to-face interviews with neurologically impaired employees, Neurodiversity Champions, and trade union organizers.

Six one-hour focus groups were held in two locations. The discussion focused on exploring participants' knowledge of neurological impairments and workplace experiences of those who self-identified as having a neurological impairment. The focus group discussion was recorded and transcribed verbatim. What is striking about Richards and Sang's analysis are the discrepancies between the focus group and interview responses. Specifically, the focus group discussion unearthed more sceptical, critical views concerning the behaviours of management, including employer human resource departments, to support employees with neurological impairment. This example shows how two different methods of qualitative data collection can be used in tandem to expose tensions between different stakeholders.

discussions in each group of an average of one hour for each of four screenings that session participants were shown. Although this means that the sessions were longer than is normally the case, it does demonstrate that the amount of data to analyse can be very large, even though a total of 14 sessions may not sound like a lot to someone unfamiliar with the workings of the method.

Size of groups

How large should groups be? Morgan (1998a) suggests that the typical group size is six to ten members. In Richards and Sang's (2016: 1649) study of neurologically impaired employees in the rail/transport industry, the size of focus group ranged from three to nine members, 'with an average of just over six members per focus group'. With such a variation in the size of groups, it is likely that different interactional dynamics will arise.

One problem faced by focus group researchers is people who agree to participate but who do not turn up on the day. It is almost impossible to control for 'no-shows' other than by deliberately over-recruiting, a strategy that is sometimes recommended (e.g. Wilkinson 1999a: 188). Almost the opposite problem was faced by Milkman (1997) in her study of auto factory workers at the General Motors plant in New Jersey. Milkman and a colleague conducted three focus group discussions at the plant—two with production workers and one with skilled trades workers. Each discussion was held in a conference room inside the plant during regular working hours, lasted around two hours, and was audio-recorded and transcribed. Workers were selected randomly from the plant roster and they were paid their normal wage for the time spent in discussion. This, according to Milkman, 'ensured perfect attendance', but it also 'underscored the project's official status' (1997: 195). She suspects that this made some participants suspicious and less inclined to speak freely.

Morgan (1998a) recommends smaller groups when participants are likely to have a lot to say on the research topic. This is likely to occur when participants are very involved in or emotionally preoccupied with the topic. He also suggests smaller groups when topics are controversial or complex and when gleaning participants' personal accounts is a major goal. Morgan recommends larger groups when involvement with a topic is likely to be low or when the researcher wants 'to hear numerous brief suggestions' (1998a: 75). However, larger groups are not necessarily better for addressing topics that participants have little involvement with, since it may be more difficult to stimulate discussion in such a context.

Level of moderator involvement

How involved should the moderator/facilitator be? In qualitative research, the aim is to get at the perspectives of those being studied. Consequently, the approach should not be intrusive and structured. Researchers tend to use a small number of general questions to guide the focus group session, and moderators tend to allow quite a lot of latitude to participants, so that the discussion can range fairly widely. Obviously, if the discussion goes off at a total tangent, it may be necessary to refocus the participants' attention, but even then it may be necessary to be careful, because what may appear to be digressions may in fact reveal something of interest to the group participants. The advantage of allowing a fairly free rein to the discussion is that the researcher stands a better chance of getting access to what individuals see as important or interesting. On the other hand, too much totally irrelevant discussion may prove unproductive, especially in the commercial environment of market research. It is not surprising, therefore, that, as Wilkinson (1999a) observes, some writers on focus groups warn against the possibility that participants come to take over the running of a session from the moderator, and offer advice on how to reassert control (e.g. Krueger 1988). Research in focus 21.3 demonstrates how the level of moderator involvement can vary.

21.3 RESEARCH IN FOCUS
Moderator involvement in a focus group discussion

The following extracts are taken from a study of small businesses owner-managers by Blackburn and Stokes (2000: 59–60). The first instance involves an exchange between participants where three quite different opinions emerge in relation to the issue of succession planning without any moderator involvement.

Michael	… talking about your family taking over the business—that's something I wouldn't do with my family because I don't think they've got the fire. I just don't think my daughters have got the same fire as I've got.
Mike	You're forcing them down a particular channel—there are so many things they can do … I think that they may or may not have the right qualities to do that—they may wish to go out and do other things … plus you might think that in giving them a thriving business you're spoiling them so I just think this whole family business thing is an absolute can of worms.
Gary	If they're in it already though it's a different situation.
Mike	… Well I accept that … my exit strategy is that at some point I've got to sell the business and I think the management team realise that. So they know when we're discussing share options there's only one point—you know we were discussing what's the point in owning shares in a private business—there is only one point when it is worth it and that's when the business is sold. So what it is, is when the business is sold they get a share of the benefit—so that's the sort of logic there.

In this first part of the discussion there is broad agreement between Michael and Mike about the issues involved in handing over the business to a family member, with Mike building on the preceding remarks made by Michael. This *complementary* interaction is then interrupted by Gary, who suggests that this depends on whether or not the family member is actively involved in the day-to-day running of the business. This more *argumentative* interaction leads Mike to revert to an alternative exit strategy which involves selling the business.

In the second extract, the moderator provides a prompt to guide the discussion of planned business succession to find out if any of the participants have taken advice on this issue. This encourages the group to share their experiences.

Moderator	Has anyone other than Gary taken advice on exit routes?
Lilian	We took advice when we made our plan in the first place about moving ourselves away from the front end of the business. How we geared our pension schemes …
Mike	I've taken advice and their advice was you need to be bigger … to make the amount of money you need to actually walk away from it … I'm in the process of doing that …
Marina	We started this actually about two years ago and we have taken advice and put plans into place. I do believe it is very important to have those plans and the correct ones. They always advise you to get bigger and you have to be a certain size …

One way in which the moderator may need to be involved is in responding to specific points that are of potential interest to the research questions but that are not picked up by other participants. The moderator has to straddle two positions: allowing the discussion to flow freely and intervening to bring out especially salient issues, particularly when group participants do not do so. This is not easy, and each tactic—intervention and non-intervention—carries risks. The best advice is to err on the side of minimal intervention—other than to start the group on a fresh set of issues—but to intervene when the group is struggling in its discussions or when it has not picked up on something that has been said in the course of the session that appears significant for the research topic. Kandola (2012) recommends tactics to keep the discussion flowing, such as acknowledging what has been said, summarizing and stimulating reflection on what has been said, and allowing adequate time for participants to speak. Equally, she recommends that the moderator should avoid certain forms of intervention, notably agreeing or disagreeing, expressing personal opinions, and interrupting. She also cautions against the use of bodily responses like frowning, looking distracted, fidgeting, and shaking one's head (nodding is recommended, though we would recommend caution here as nodding can be interpreted by participants as agreement).

One of the challenges for focus group moderators is ensuring that there is a good level of participation among members. Getting equal participation is unrealistic, but it is clearly preferable for all group members to participate to a reasonable degree. One technique that Kandola (2012) suggests as a means of stimulating participation is writing comments that arise in the course of a discussion onto a flipchart. Chan et al. (2012) wrote comments onto a board when they conducted focus group research into the management of stress among expatriate Hong Kong construction professionals in mainland China. The moderator noted points made by participants, which allowed them to reflect on what had been said and acted as a stimulus to further discussion. As Chan et al. observe, doing this also proffered the opportunity for participants to check on the researchers' emerging understanding. However, Kandola cautions that as far as possible, participants' own language should be used when making such notes so that the researchers' own understandings are not imposed.

Selecting participants

Who should participate in a focus group? This depends on who will find the topic relevant and who can represent specific occupational or organizational groupings that have an interest in the topic concerned. Usually, a wide range of organizational members or stakeholders from different organizations is required, but they are organized into separate groups in terms of stratifying criteria, such as age, gender, occupation, profession, hierarchical position within the organization, or length of service. Participants for each group can then be selected randomly or through some kind of snowball sampling method. The aim is to establish whether or not there is any systematic variation in the ways in which different groups discuss a matter.

A further issue in relation to the selection of group participants is whether to select people who are unknown to each other (for example, members of the same professional association or employees from different divisions within the same organization) or to use natural groupings (for example, co-workers or students on the same course). Some researchers prefer to exclude people who know each other, on the grounds that pre-existing styles of interaction or status differences may contaminate the session. Not all writers accept this rule of thumb. Some prefer to select natural groups whenever possible. For example, in marketing research, companies such as Procter & Gamble tend to go back repeatedly to the same pool from which they draw focus groups (Kiely 1998).

However, opting for a strategy of recruiting people entirely from natural groups is not always feasible, because of difficulties of securing participation. For example, it is not always feasible to remove a number of employees from work activity at the same time; in such cases other strategies of selection may have to be used. Morgan (1998a) suggests that one problem with using natural groups is that people who know each other well are likely to operate with taken-for-granted assumptions that they feel do not need to be brought to the fore. He suggests that, if it is important for the researcher to bring out such assumptions, groups of strangers are likely to work better. On the other hand, if the focus group is intended to explore collective understandings or shared meanings held within a work group, this can be achieved more readily by using participants who are all members of the same work group.

Asking questions

An issue that is close to the question of the degree of involvement on the part of the moderator is the matter of how far there should be a set of questions that must be addressed. This issue is very similar to the considerations about how unstructured an interview should be in qualitative interviewing (see Chapter 20). Some researchers prefer to use just one or two very general questions to stimulate discussion, with the moderator intervening as necessary along the lines outlined above. However, other researchers prefer to inject somewhat more structure into the organization of the focus group sessions. A clear example of this is given in Figure 21.1: in research on small business owner-managers, which moderators worked with a topic agenda with times allocated to the discussion of each topic. Opening questions were designed to generate initial reactions in a relatively open-ended way, to put the owner-managers at ease, and to get them talking as soon as possible in an informal manner. Then the moderator moved the discussion on to the substantive issues of trading climate, challenges in the business environment, government policies, and business succession and exit strategies. Such a general approach

FIGURE 21.1

An example of a topic agenda for a small business owner-manager focus group

	Topic Agenda
1.	**Introduction (15 mins.)** Introduce the research team and roles Aim and format of the focus group **Conventions** (confidentiality, speak one at a time, recordings, everybody's views, open debate, report of proceedings) Personal introduction of participants and their businesses

2.	**Discussion Topics**
	(i) *Current trading climate* (15 mins.)
	    (e.g. comparative order levels)
	(ii) *Main challenges in the business environment* (20 mins.)
	    (e.g. exchange rates, recruitment, raising money)
	(iii) *Government policies and small firms* (20 mins.)
	    (e.g. the minimum wage, entry into the Euro)
	(iv) *Topical issues* (20 mins.)
	    (e.g. business succession and exit strategies)

3.	**Summing Up** Thanks for participation and report back Invite back to next event in six months Reimburse expenses
4.	**Lunch** Sandwiches and drinks Close

Source: Blackburn and Stokes (2000).

to questioning, which is fairly common in focus group research, allows the researcher to navigate the channel between, on the one side, addressing the research questions and ensuring comparability between sessions, and, on the other side, allowing participants to raise issues they see as significant and in their own terms.

Clearly, there are different questioning strategies and approaches to moderating focus group sessions. Most lie somewhere in between the rather open-ended approach employed by Tyler and Cohen (2010) (see Research in focus 21.3) and the more structured one used by Richards and Sang (2016) (see Research in focus 21.2). There is no one best way, and the style of questioning and moderating is likely to be affected by various factors, such as the nature of the research topic (for example, is it one that the researcher already knows a lot about, in which case a degree of structure is feasible?) and levels of interest and/or knowledge among participants in the research (for example, a low level of participant interest may require a somewhat more structured approach).

Kandola (2012) recommends asking for examples and further elaboration as a means of stimulating further discussion that may allow amplification of key points. Whichever strategy of questioning is employed, the focus group researcher should generally be prepared to allow at least some discussion that departs from the interview guide, since such debate may provide new and unexpected insights. A more structured approach to questioning might inhibit such spontaneity, but it is unlikely to remove it altogether.

Beginning and finishing

It is recommended that focus group sessions begin with an introduction, whereby the moderators thank people for coming and introduce themselves, the goals of the research are briefly outlined, the reasons for recording the session are given, and the format of the focus group session is sketched out. It is also important to present some of the conventions of focus group participation, such as that only one person should speak at a time (perhaps explaining the problems that occur with recordings when people speak over each other); that all data will be treated confidentially and anonymized; that the session is open and everyone's views are important; and the amount of time that will be taken up. During the introduction phase, focus group researchers also often ask participants to fill in forms providing basic socio-demographic information about themselves, such as age, gender, and occupation. Participants should then be encouraged to introduce themselves and to write out their first names on a badge or a card placed in front of them, so that everyone's name is known.

At the end the moderators should thank the group members for their participation and explain briefly what will happen to the data they have supplied. If a further session is to be arranged, steps should be taken to coordinate this.

Group interaction in focus group sessions

Kitzinger (1994) has observed that reports of focus group research frequently do not take into account interaction within the group. This is surprising because it is precisely the operation of social interaction and its forms and impact that would seem to distinguish the focus group session from the individual interview. Yet, as Kitzinger observes, few publications based on focus group research cite or draw inferences from patterns of interaction within the group (see Research in focus 21.4 for an exception). Wilkinson (1998) reviewed over 200 studies based on focus groups published between 1946 and 1996. She concluded: 'Focus group data is most commonly presented as if it were one-to-one interview data, with interactions between group participants rarely reported, let alone analysed' (1998: 112).

Interactions between focus group participants may be either complementary or argumentative (Kitzinger 1994). The extract from a focus group discussion with some moderator involvement in Research in focus 21.3 illustrates these two types of interaction. The former brings out the elements of the social world that provide participants' own frameworks of understanding, so that agreement emerges in people's minds. However, as Kitzinger suggests, arguments in focus groups can be equally revealing. She suggests that moderators can play an important role in identifying differences of opinion and exploring with participants the factors that may lie behind them. Disagreement can provide participants with the opportunity to revise their opinions or to think more about the reasons why they hold the view that they do. Drawing attention to patterns of interaction within focus groups allows the researcher to determine how group participants view the issues with which they are confronted in their own terms. The posing of questions by, and agreement and disagreement among, participants helps to bring out their own stances on these issues. The resolution of disagreements also helps to force participants to express the grounds on which they hold particular views. The important point to note here is that the ability to capture *group* opinion, including

21.4 RESEARCH IN FOCUS
Using focus groups in a study of female entrepreneurs

In a qualitative analysis of female entrepreneurs' accounts of their role, Buttner (2001) used the focus group method to explore the leadership and management style of women entrepreneurs in their own organizations. Although the study was exploratory, 'designed to capture the women's "voice" as they spoke about their role in their businesses' (2001: 258), a **structured interview** protocol was used. A total of 129 women entrepreneurs from 12 research sites across the USA participated in the focus groups, and the results were video-recorded and transcribed. In addition to recording the content of comments made by participants, the study also analysed the frequency with which they spoke about particular issues. This is an example of how qualitative researchers sometimes undertake a limited amount of quantification of their data (see Chapter 26).

what Tadejewski (2016: 332) refers to as 'the boundaries of social convention and discourse', rather than the viewpoints of individuals, is a particular feature of focus groups that distinguishes this method from others. It is therefore likely that analyzing the patterns of interaction between members of the group will enable insight into the process whereby these social perspectives are formed.

Online focus groups

Online focus groups use the internet as a means of communication between focus group participants and moderators in a way which removes the need for face-to-face interaction. The discussion is either typed or spoken. There is a crucial difference between synchronous and asynchronous online focus groups. With synchronous focus groups participants are online simultaneously, so the discussion takes place in real time. Comments are made more or less immediately in response to previous comments and questions (whether from the moderator or from other participants). As Mann and Stewart (2000) observe, because several participants can type in a response to a contribution at the same time, the conventions of normal turn-taking in conversations are largely sidelined.

With asynchronous groups, focus group exchanges are not in real time. Email is sometimes used for this purpose (see Research in focus 21.5 for an example). For example, the moderator may send a question by email to focus group participants. Participants will be able to reply to the moderator and to other group members at some point in the future. Such groups get around the time zone problem and are probably easier than synchronous groups for participants who are less skilled at using a keyboard. However, the risk of dropouts is greater. Huang and Hsu (2009) were interested in the experiences among cruise passengers of interaction with fellow North American passengers. They undertook both individual interviews and virtual focus groups. The researchers were participants in online cruise forums and used these as a springboard for securing participation in the online focus groups. Two of the groups were able to proceed despite some dropouts and took 25 and 28 days to complete. Four out of an initial seven completed the first group and six out of an initial seven completed the second group. The third group began with five participants and ended up with one person so that it became in effect an online individual interview.

One of the advantages of both types of online focus groups stems from the possibility of using a 'captive

21.5 RESEARCH IN FOCUS
An asynchronous focus group study

Adriaenssens and Cadman (1999) report their experiences of conducting a market research exercise to explore the launch of an online share-trading platform in the UK. Participants were in two groups: one group of active shareholders (20 participants) and a second group of passive shareholders (10 participants). They were identified through the MORI (Market & Opinion Research International) Financial Services database as 'upmarket shareholders who were also Internet users' (1999: 418–19). The participants who were identified were very geographically spread, so online focus groups were ideal. Questions were emailed to participants in five phases, with a deadline for returning replies, which were then copied anonymously to the rest of the participants. The questions were sent in the body of the email, rather than as attachments, to solve problems of software incompatibility. After each phase, a summary document was produced and circulated to participants for comment, thus injecting a form of respondent validation into the project. The researchers found it difficult to ensure that participants kept to the deadlines, which in fact were rather tight, although it was felt that having a schedule of deadlines that was kept to as far as possible was helpful in preventing dropouts. The researchers felt that the group of active shareholders was too large to manage and suggest groups of no more than ten participants.

population' of people who are already communicating with each other, unlike face-to-face focus groups that are brought together for the purpose of the focus group meeting. This means researchers are often able to take advantage of pre-existing social groups of people who are already communicating with one another online (Stewart and Williams 2005). Online focus groups also enable geographical distances to be overcome. International focus groups can enable cross-cultural discussions at a relatively low cost. However, setting up a time and place for synchronous online focus group discussions between international participants may be problematic because of time zone differences, making it hard to find a time that is convenient to everyone (Stewart and Williams 2005).

Conferencing software is used for synchronous groups and is often used for asynchronous groups as well. This may mean that focus group participants will require access to the software. One possibility for selecting participants for online focus groups is to use questionnaires as a springboard for identifying potential participants. Another possibility is to contact them by email or social media, this being a relatively quick and economical way of contacting a large number of possible participants. For their study of virtual communities concerned with consumption issues, Evans et al. (2001) used a combination of questionnaires (both paper and online) and focus groups made up of respondents to the questionnaires who had indicated a willingness to take further part in the research. The British focus groups were of the face-to-face kind, but, in addition, international respondents to the questionnaire who were prepared to be further involved in the research participated in an online focus group. Other sources of participants for online focus groups might involve postings on appropriate special interest websites or on such outlets as special interest bulletin boards or chatrooms.

The requisite number of participants is affected by the question of whether the online focus group is being conducted synchronously or asynchronously. Mann and Stewart (2000) advocate that, with the former type, the group should not be too large, because it can make it difficult for some people to participate, possibly because of limited keyboard skills, and they recommend groups of between six and eight participants. Also, moderating the session can be more difficult with a large number. In asynchronous mode, such problems do not exist, and very large groups can be accommodated—certainly much larger ones than could be envisaged in a face-to-face context, although Adriaenssens and Cadman

(1999) suggest that large groups can present moderation problems.

Before starting the focus group, moderators are advised to send out a welcome message introducing the research and laying out some of the ground rules for the ongoing discussion. There is evidence that participants respond more positively if the researchers reveal something about themselves (Curasi 2001). This can be done in the opening message or by creating links to personal websites.

One problem with the asynchronous focus group is that moderators cannot be available online 24 hours a day, although it is not inconceivable that moderators could have a shift system to deal with this limitation. This lack of continuous availability means that emails or postings may be sent and responded to without any ability of the moderator to intervene or participate. This is not inherently a problem but could become so if offensive messages were being sent or if the discussion were to go off at a complete tangent, from which it became difficult to redeem the situation. Further, because focus group sessions in asynchronous mode may go on for a long time, perhaps several days or even weeks, there is a greater likelihood of participants dropping out of the study. A further problem arises from response rates, which may be lower than for face-to-face focus groups (Stewart and Williams 2005). Even though it is relatively easy for the researcher to contact a large number of possible respondents using email, the response rates of those wishing to participate in an online focus group has been found to be quite low (between 5 and 20 per cent). Further reservations have been expressed about the lack of non-verbal data obtained from online focus groups, such as facial expression.

Online focus groups are unlikely to replace their face-to-face counterparts. Instead, they are likely to be used in connection with certain kinds of research topic and/or sample. As regards the latter, dispersed or inaccessible people are especially relevant to online focus group research. As Sweet (2001) points out, relevant topics are likely to be ones involving sensitive issues and ones concerned with internet use—for example, the study discussed in Research in focus 21.5 and studies such as O'Connor and Madge (2001).

The discussion in Tips and skills 'Advantages and disadvantages of online compared to face-to-face focus groups' enables the features of online focus groups to be compared. This tally of advantages and disadvantages applies more or less equally well in comparing virtual with face-to-face interviewing (see Chapter 20).

Advantages and disadvantages of online compared to face-to-face focus groups

Here is a summary of the main advantages and disadvantages of online focus groups compared to their face-to-face counterparts.

Advantages of online focus groups

- More cost- and time-efficient than face-to-face equivalents, eliminating the time and cost of travel to participate.

- Participants who would otherwise be inaccessible (for example, because they are in another country) or hard to involve in research (for example, because they work from home) can more easily be involved.

- Large numbers of potential participants can be contacted by email or via social media.

- Participants are able to reread what they, and others, have previously written in their replies.

- The discussion does not have to be audio-recorded, thus eliminating interviewee apprehension about speaking and being recorded.

- There is no need for transcription. This represents a significant advantage because of the time and cost involved in transcribing focus group sessions.

- Discussion is more accurately recorded, avoiding the problems of face-to-face focus groups that may arise from mishearing or being able to identify who is speaking.

- Participants can use pseudonyms so that their identity can be more easily concealed from others in the group. This can make it easier for participants to disclose difficult information about themselves, discuss potentially sensitive issues, or divulge potentially unpopular views, especially in asynchronous mode.

- Shy or quiet participants may find it easier to come to the fore; equally, overbearing participants are less likely to predominate.

- Participants are less likely to be influenced by characteristics such as the age, ethnicity, or appearance (and possibly even gender if pseudonyms are used) of other participants.

- Participants are less likely to be affected by characteristics of moderators respectively, so interviewer bias is less likely.

- When interviewees and participants are online at home, they are essentially being provided with an 'anonymous, safe and non-threatening environment' (O' Connor and Madge 2001: 11.2), which may be especially helpful to vulnerable groups.

- Similarly, researchers do not need to gain physical access to organizations and other workplaces, which can be unsafe environments.

Disadvantages of online focus groups

- Only people with internet access, other requisite technological resources, and the competencies required to operate them are likely to be able to participate.

- The tendency for individuals to decline to participate can be higher.

- Responses are likely to be less spontaneous. However, this can be construed as an advantage in some respects, since participants can reflect on their answers to a much greater extent than is possible in a face-to-face situation and thus may give more considered replies (Adriaenssens and Cadman 1999).

- The researcher cannot be certain that the people who are interviewed are who they say they are (though this issue may apply to face-to-face interviews as well).

- Online connections may be lost, perhaps because of a server crashing or a respondent's broadband going down.

- Moderators cannot observe body language or other forms of non-verbal data that might suggest puzzlement, or a thwarted desire to contribute to the discussion.

- It can be more difficult for the moderator to establish rapport and engage with participants. However, when the topic is of interest to participants, this may not be a major problem.

- Online focus groups require considerable commitment from participants, for example if they need to install software onto their computers and remain online for extended periods of time.

- The moderator may not be aware if the participant is distracted by something and, in such circumstances, may continue to ask questions as if he or she had the person's full attention.

- Asynchronous interviews can take a long time, depending on the availability and enthusiasm of participants.

- Probing is more difficult in asynchronous interviews. Curasi (2001) reports some success in eliciting further information from respondents, but it is easier for interviewees to ignore or forget about requests for further information or expansion on answers given.

- With asynchronous focus groups, there may be a greater tendency for participants to discontinue their involvement before the end of the process.

- In synchronous focus groups, variations in keyboard skills may make equal levels of participation difficult.

Sources: Clapper and Massey (1996); Adriaenssens and Cadman (1999); Tse (1999); Mann and Stewart (2000); Curasi (2001); O'Connor and Madge (2001); Sweet (2001); Hewson and Laurent (2008).

The focus group as an emancipatory method

The use of focus groups as a method that seeks to give voice to groups of participants who are systematically marginalized or oppressed in organizations and society stems from the work of feminist researchers (Wilkinson 1998, 1999b). Three aspects of the method make it suited to being used in this way.

- Focus group research is more naturalistic than many other methods, because, in emphasizing group interaction, which is a normal part of social life, it does not suffer from the problem of gleaning information in an unnatural situation. Moreover, the tendency of many focus group researchers to recruit participants from naturally occurring groups underpins the higher degree of naturalism associated with the method, since people are able to discuss issues in situations that are quite normal for them. As a result, there is greater opportunity to derive understandings that chime with the 'lived experience' of participants. However, not all writers accept the contention that focus groups are more naturalistic than individual interviews. Even when natural groups are used, gathering people to discuss a certain topic (such as a television advertisement) is not inherently naturalistic, because the social setting is to a significant extent contrived (Morrison 1998: 154–5). Indeed, completing questionnaires or

being interviewed may appear more natural, because such instruments are fairly commonplace, whereas being asked to discuss in a group an issue not necessarily of one's choosing is less so.

- Because the individual is very much part of a group in the focus group method, it enables analysis of 'the self as relational or as socially constructed' (Wilkinson 1999b: 229–30), which is a key tenet of feminist research. By studying the individual within a social context, focus group methods endeavour to avoid *decontextualization*—which feminists argue is a tendency in most research methods to treat the individual as a separate entity devoid of a social context.

- As we have seen in previous chapters, feminist researchers are critical of research methods that are exploitative and that create a power relationship between the researcher and participants. Wilkinson observes that the risk of this occurring is greatly reduced with focus groups, because participants are able to take over much of the direction of the session from the moderator. Indeed, they may even subvert the goals of the session in ways that could be of considerable interest to the moderator. As a result, participants' points of view are much more likely to be revealed than in a traditional interview. Using research methods such as the focus group to subvert established power relations, in ways which seek to emancipate oppressed and marginalized groups, is of potential interest to a wide range of business researchers who are interested in understanding and challenging inequalities, including those that are based on colonialism as well as gender. Tyler and Cohen's (2010) study of women's embodied experiences of the workplace (Research in focus 21.6) provides an example that illustrates the emancipatory potential of focus groups. Tadajewski (2015) suggests that the potential of focus groups as a method in marketing and consumer behaviour research is significantly underutilized. He argues that greater use of focus groups could enable a shift away from focusing predominantly on the thoughts and perceptions of individuals, and towards more contextualized understandings of consumer behaviour as situated and social. He also highlights the critical emancipatory potential of this type of research, 'by providing voice to those who are denied it' and helping people to understand 'the structural barriers that constrain their lived reality' (Tadajewski 2015: 336–7). This approach to focus groups highlights its use as a method of 'consciousness raising' (Wilkinson, 1998, 1999*a*, 1999*b*).

21.6 RESEARCH IN FOCUS
An example of the focus group as an emancipatory method

Tyler and Cohen (2010) used a combination of focus groups and interviews with women working in diverse roles in a university setting, to explore how gender is materialized through workspace. Their research was inspired by the work of a contemporary video artist, Sofia Hulten, called *Grey Area*, which features the artist in a grey suit hiding in various places in an office and eventually getting inside a bin-liner, in a gesture of throwing herself away. Tyler and Cohen's interest in this topic was also prompted by personal experiences at work, where they were criticized by a female colleague for displaying pictures of their family and children's drawings in their office because it portrayed them in stereotypically gendered ways. They therefore used still images from *Grey Area* as the basis for focus groups and individual interviews with women, to discuss their lived, embodied experiences of the workplace. Their convenience sample relied on posting an invitation on the website of the university where they both worked, inviting participation in the study. They ran three focus groups, each held a week apart: 9 participants, duration 80 minutes, 22 pages of transcript; 11 participants, duration 70 minutes, 20 pages of transcript; and 10 participants, duration 90 minutes, 24 pages of transcript.

They describe the method used in focus groups as follows:

> We used printed colour sheets of stills from Grey Area as a starting point for the focus groups … laying the room out so that participants sat around a large table facing each other, with an A3 sheet of the stills in front of them. We were loosely guided by an interview schedule, in which we asked the women taking part to reflect on the images and on how they might relate (if at all) to their own experiences of the workplace, and of their own workspace. We asked participants about their first impressions, if there were any images in the sequence that struck them as particularly interesting or important, and why. We then talked about how the images made them feel, and about how they thought the woman in the video might be feeling. At various points, we focused on the theme of hiding, and particularly on the woman throwing herself away at the end of the sequence. We also had lengthy discussions in each group about why the video is called Grey Area, and about what greyness connotes in relation to gender, identity and workspace. In each of the sessions, participants asked questions of themselves, of us and of each other.
>
> (Tyler and Cohen 2010: 183)

The focus groups were facilitated by the two researchers together with a part-time researcher and a research student. This enabled them to delegate responsibility for the recording equipment and taking notes, leaving them free to concentrate on the discussion. Following iterative analysis of the focus group transcripts, they developed an interview schedule which formed the basis for individual follow-up interviews with 23 of the women who had participated in the focus groups, in addition to a further 24 women who volunteered to participate. The researchers' choice of artwork as a prompt for these discussions sought to 'move' participants and to encourage them to reflect on their experiences in ways which they might otherwise struggle to articulate.

Limitations of focus groups

Focus groups clearly have considerable potential for research questions in which the processes through which meaning is jointly constructed are likely to be of particular interest. Indeed, it may be that even when this is not a prominent emphasis, the use of the focus group method may be appropriate and even advantageous, since it allows participants' perspectives—an important feature of much qualitative research (see Chapter 17)—to be revealed in ways that are different from individual interviews (for example, through discussion, participants' questions, arguments, and so on). It also offers considerable potential for feminist researchers. What, then, might be its chief limitations?

- The researcher probably has less control over proceedings than with the individual interview. As we have seen, by no means all writers on focus groups perceive this as a disadvantage. However, the question of control raises issues for researchers of how far they can allow a focus group to 'take over' the running of proceedings. There is clearly a delicate balance to be taken into account over how involved moderators should be and how far a set of prompts or questions should influence the conduct of a focus group, as some of the earlier discussions have suggested. What is not clear is the degree to which it is appropriate to surrender control of a focus group to its participants, especially when there is a reasonably explicit set of research questions to be answered.

- The data are difficult to analyse. A huge amount of data can be very quickly produced. Developing a strategy of analysis that incorporates both themes in what people say and patterns of interaction is not easy. Also, as previously pointed out, focus group recordings are particularly prone to inaudible elements, which affects transcription.

- They are difficult to organize. Not only do you have to secure the agreement of people to participate in your study; you also need to persuade them to turn up at a particular time. Small inducements, such as payment of expenses or provision of lunch, are sometimes made to induce participation, but nonetheless it is common for people not to turn up.

- The recordings are probably more time-consuming to transcribe than equivalent recordings of individual interviews, because of variations in voice pitch and the need to take account of who says what.

- There are possible problems of group effects. This includes the obvious problem of dealing with reticent speakers and with those who hog the stage! Krueger (1998) suggests in relation to the problem of overly prominent participants that the moderator should make clear to the speaker and other group participants that other people's views are definitely required; for example, he suggests saying something like: 'That's one point of view. Does anyone have another point of view?' (1998: 59). As for those who do not speak very much, it is recommended that they are actively encouraged to say something. Also, as the well-known Asch experiments showed (see Research in focus 21.7), an emerging group view may mean that a perfectly legitimate perspective held by just one individual may be suppressed. There is also evidence that, as a group comes to share a certain point of view, group members come to think uncritically about it and to develop almost irrational attachments to it (Janis 1982). It is not known how far such group effects have an adverse impact on focus group findings, but it is clear that they cannot be entirely ignored. In this context, it would be interesting to know how far agreement among focus group participants is more frequently encountered than disagreement: we have a hunch that it is, since the effects to which both Asch and Janis referred would lead us to expect more agreement than disagreement in focus group discussions. Related to this, in group contexts participants may be more prone to expressing culturally expected views than in individual interviews.

- Madriz (2000) proposes that there are circumstances when focus groups may not be appropriate because of their potential for causing discomfort among participants. When such discomfort might arise, individual interviews are likely to be preferable. Situations in which unease might be occasioned are when intimate details of private lives need to be revealed; when participants may not be comfortable in each other's presence (for example, bringing together people in a hierarchical relationship to each other); and when participants are likely to disagree profoundly with each other.

Tadejewski (2015) suggests that market research is sometimes used to support commercial interests in ways that are unethical and thus at odds with the emancipatory aims of critical researchers. Using the example of market

21.7 RESEARCH IN FOCUS
Group conformity and the focus group method

Asch's (1951) laboratory studies into individual conformity to group norms provide us with an indication of the risks that are associated with focus groups. One experiment involved seven men who were brought together as a group and seated at a table. The men were told that they were participating in a study on visual perception. However, only one of the men was a real participant; the rest were 'actors' paid by Asch to participate. The group was shown a series of lines and asked to judge which were equal in length.

However, the actor-participants had been instructed to lie about which of the lines was equal. Despite the obviousness of the task, in most of the trials that Asch conducted the individual subject conceded to the group judgement, rather than giving the response he or she judged to be correct. The research showed that it was difficult for individuals to express their opinions when they contradict the views of other group members. These findings have obvious implications for the conduct of focus groups, particularly since Asch also found that conformity increased when group members had to continue working together in the future—a distinct possibility within organizational research. However, Asch also found that conformity decreased when subjects were not face-to-face.

research conducted by the tobacco industry in the 1950s and 1960s, he notes that tobacco industry insiders knew of the negative health effects of smoking. This meant that their use of focus groups, to better understand the symbolic appeal of particular cigarette brands, was unethical because it was directed towards maintaining the status quo and preventing it from being questioned in ways which would undermine the industry.

CHECKLIST
Issues to consider for your focus group

○ Have you devised a clear and comprehensive way of introducing the research to participants?

○ Do the questions or topics you have devised allow you to answer all your research questions?

○ Have you piloted the questions in your interview guide with some appropriate respondents?

○ Have you devised a strategy for encouraging respondents to turn up for the focus group meeting?

○ Have you thought about what you will do if some participants do not turn up for the session?

○ Have you ensured that interviews will allow novel or unexpected themes and issues to arise?

○ Is your language in the questions clear and comprehensible?

○ Are your questions relevant to the people participating in the focus groups?

○ Have your questions been designed to elicit reflective discussions so that participants are not tempted to answer in 'yes' or 'no' terms?

○ Are your questions designed to encourage group interaction and discussion?

○ Do your questions offer a real prospect of seeing the world from your interviewees' point of view rather than imposing your own frame of reference on them?

○ Are you familiar with the setting(s) in which the interview will take place?

○ Are you thoroughly familiar with and have you tested your recording or audio-visual equipment?

○ Have you thought about how you will present yourself in the session, such as how you will be dressed?

○ Have you devised a strategy for dealing with silences?

○ Have you devised a strategy for dealing with participants who are reluctant to speak?

○ Have you devised a strategy for dealing with participants who speak too much and hog the discussion?

○ Do you have a strategy for how far you are going to intervene in the focus group discussion?

○ Do you have a strategy for dealing with the focus group if the discussion goes off at a tangent?

○ Have you tested out any aids that you are going to present to focus group participants (e.g. visual aids, segments of film, case studies)?

KEY POINTS

....

- The focus group is a group interview that is concerned with exploring a certain topic.
- The moderator generally tries to provide a relatively free rein to the discussion. However, there may be contexts in which it is necessary to ask fairly specific questions, especially when cross-group comparability is an issue.
- There is concern with the collective production of meaning.
- Focus group discussions need to be recorded and transcribed.
- There are several issues concerning the recruitment of focus group participants—in particular, whether to use natural groupings or to employ stratifying criteria.
- Group interaction is an important component of discussions.
- Some writers view focus groups as well suited to emancipatory standpoints.

QUESTIONS FOR REVIEW

....

- Why might it be useful to distinguish between a focus group and a group interview?

Uses of focus groups
- What advantages might the focus group method offer in contrast to an individual qualitative interview?

Conducting focus groups
- How involved should the moderator be?
- Why is it necessary to record and transcribe focus group sessions?

- Are there any circumstances in which it might be a good idea to select participants who know each other?

- What might be the advantages and disadvantages of using an interview guide in focus group sessions?

Group interaction in focus group sessions

- Why might it be important to treat group interaction as an important issue when analysing focus group data?

The focus group as an emancipatory method

- Evaluate the argument that the focus group can be supportive of oppressed and marginalized groups in organizations and society.

- To what extent are focus groups a naturalistic approach to data collection?

Limitations of focus groups

- Does the potential for the loss of control over proceedings and group effects damage the potential utility of the focus group as a method?

- How far do the greater problems of transcription and difficulty of analysis undermine the potential of focus groups?

....

ONLINE RESOURCES
www.oup.com/uk/brm5e/

Visit the Interactive Research Guide that accompanies this book to complete an exercise relating to focus groups.

....

LANGUAGE IN QUALITATIVE RESEARCH

CHAPTER OUTLINE

This chapter is concerned with approaches to the analysis of language, including discourse analysis. The chapter explores

- discourse analysis, which examines how language is used and the effects on understanding reality that are accomplished through this—such approaches include critical discourse analysis, where there is an emphasis on understanding the effects of historical and social context on the type of language that is produced;

- two further approaches that focus on specific forms of language and their effects in creating meaning—narrative analysis (also sometimes referred to as storytelling research), and rhetorical analysis, which concentrates on the use of specific forms of language to convince or persuade;

- and finally, conversation analysis, which is a fine-grained approach to analysing the detail of how language is used, especially in naturally occurring conversations.

Introduction

Language is bound to be of importance for organizational researchers. It is, after all, through language that we ask people questions in interviews and through which the questions are answered. Language is also central to the structuring of organizations, if only because people in work organizations rely so heavily on talk—in meetings, on the telephone, in the cafeteria—to accomplish their everyday business. It is through language that people in organizations exchange information, skills, services, and resources and make sense of their situation through interaction with each other. In managerial work a great deal of emphasis is placed on verbal interaction or talk, as numerous research studies highlight. For example, Mintzberg's (1973) study reports that verbal contacts, face-to-face and on the telephone, accounted for 75 per cent of senior managers' time and 67 per cent of their activities (see Chapter 13 for an explanation of Mintzberg's study). Other studies have shown that between 57 and 89 per cent of managerial time is spent in verbal interactions of one kind or another (Boden 1994). The role of the business researcher who focuses on language is to explore the nature of the relationship between language and action in these instances.

What is crucial about the approaches discussed in this chapter is that, unlike other methods that use language in business research, they treat language as a topic rather than as a resource. This means that language is treated as

significantly more than a medium through which business research is conducted (such as by asking questions in interviews). Instead language is treated as a focus of attention in its own right. This type of research is broadly constructionist in orientation, hence language is not just seen as reflective of what goes on in an organization; instead, it is a way of constructing particular understandings of phenomena. This means, for example, that as soon as managers in a public-sector organization start to talk of their clients as 'customers', a whole new way of defining the organization's purpose and activities is introduced.

The first part of the chapter is concerned with what may be characterized as meso-level (Alvesson and Kärreman 2000) or 'context-sensitive approaches' (Grant et al. 2004) to the study of language which take account of factors beyond the text itself. In addition to being sensitive to the context in which language is produced, these approaches are concerned with finding generalizable patterns and going beyond the detail of the text. They therefore explore social and historical context, and other factors that influence how language is produced, disseminated, and consumed. Discourse, including critical discourse analysis, and to a lesser extent narrative and rhetorical analysis, can be considered context-sensitive approaches. The final part of the chapter deals with a more fine-grained approach to analyzing language use, in the form of conversation analysis.

Discourse analysis

While discourse analysis is not the only way of analyzing language qualitatively, it represents a widely used method in business research. There is an international conference dedicated to discursive approaches to organizational analysis as well as a handbook (Grant et al. 2004) and a journal, *Discourse and Society*. As researchers who study discourse note, the focus on language in business research is not surprising because language plays such a significant role in 'constructing, situating, facilitating and communicating the diverse cultural, institutional, political and socio-economic parameters of "organizational being"' (Grant, et al. 1998: 12). A key strength of discourse analysis concerns its ability to be applied to naturally occurring conversation and documents as well as other forms of written and spoken language.

The first part of this chapter will outline the main features associated with a particular type of discourse analysis which has evolved its own technical vocabulary and set of techniques. This approach is associated with such writers as Potter (1997), Potter and Wetherell (1987, 1994), Billig (1992), and Gilbert and Mulkay (1984); it is suggested to be characterized by two distinctive features at the level of epistemology and ontology (Potter 1997) (see also Key concept 22.4).

- It is anti-realist: in other words, it denies that there is an external reality awaiting a definitive portrayal by the researcher and it therefore rejects the notion that any researcher can arrive at a privileged account of the aspect of the social world being investigated.

22.1 KEY CONCEPT
What is discourse analysis?

According to Potter (1997), discourse analysis 'emphasizes the way versions of the world, of society, events and inner psychological worlds are produced in discourse' (1997: 146). This definition of discourse analysis means that discourse is not just a mirror on the social world around us but in many ways plays a key role in producing that world. *How* we say things—our phrases, our emphases, the things we leave out—is meant to accomplish certain effects in others. In so doing, we have an impact on others' perceptions and understandings and as such on their and our reality.

Some discourse analysts, however, adopt a stance that is closer to a realist position, but most seem to be anti-realist in orientation.

- It is *constructionist*: in other words, the emphasis is placed on the versions of reality propounded by members of the social setting being investigated and on the fashioning of that reality through their renditions of it (see Key concepts 2.7 and 22.1). More specifically, the constructionist emphasis requires a recognition that discourse entails a selection from many viable renditions and that in the process a particular depiction of reality is built up.

Thus, discourse is not simply a neutral device for imparting meaning. People seek to accomplish things when they talk or when they write; discourse analysis is concerned with the strategies they employ in trying to create different kinds of effect. This version of discourse analysis is, therefore, action orientated—that is, it is a way of getting things done. This is revealed in three basic discourse-analytic questions:

1. What is this discourse doing?
2. How is this discourse constructed to make this happen?

3. What resources are available to perform this activity?

(Potter 2004: 609)

The consideration of discourse analysis that follows draws on two studies:

- research into the discourses applied to unemployed older workers in Australia (Ainsworth and Hardy 2009);
- a study of MBA students' use of role models in professional identity formation (Kelan and Mah 2014).

The first study, by Ainsworth and Hardy (2009; see Research in focus 22.2), shows how discourses of the mind and body are used to discipline unemployed older workers in a way that is disempowering; the second study, by Kelan and Mah (2014; see Research in focus 22.3), provides an illustration of how the notion of interpretative repertoire can be used to understand gendered processes of identity formation among MBA students.

Main features of discourse analysis

1. *Not just speech*. Discourse analysis is an approach that can be applied to forms of communication and not

22.2 RESEARCH IN FOCUS
The application of mind and body discourses to older workers

Ainsworth and Hardy (2009) studied the discourses pertaining to the employment of older workers through a discursive analysis of a parliamentary inquiry in Australia, which was set up to examine the barriers that older unemployed workers face in regaining employment. The inquiry lasted just over a year (1998–9) and comprised a series of written submissions and public hearings held throughout Australia, where employee and lobby groups, unions, government representatives, and private individuals were invited to appear. A final report was then published in 2000 on the findings of the inquiry. One of the reasons for selecting the inquiry as a research site was because of the accessibility, volume, and range of available texts relating to it, which included media releases, written submissions, and more than 1000 pages of oral evidence and testimony relating to the public hearings, which had been transcribed verbatim. There was the further advantage that many of these documents could be obtained from the government website. Ainsworth and Hardy (2009) claim that, because these 'naturally occurring' texts were generated independently of the researcher, they have the advantage of not being subject to reactive effect and provided very useful materials for systematic analysis.

The authors identify two discourses in the texts:

1. *physical discourses relating to the body*, which portray ageing as a process of inevitable decline;
2. *discourses of the mind*, which psychologize and individualize the problem of unemployment.

They argue that, while these discourses have separate effects, their consequences for identity formation are even greater when brought together through a normative 'mechanism of grief', which encourages older unemployed workers to make use of labour market interventions that help them to accept their loss of employment rather than locate permanent job opportunities. Unemployed older workers were thus advised to 'manage the grief' associated with their loss of employment and to 'resolve the anger' that they felt in relation to job loss because this was deemed 'unhealthy' and claimed to be harming their chances of re-employment. The personal stories told by unemployed older workers were thereby discursively regulated through retelling and reframing by others in a way that deflected responsibility away from government agencies or employers. The authors conclude that, 'rather than provide space for resistance, the intersection of these discourses disempowers an already disadvantaged group' (Ainsworth and Hardy 2009: 1200).

22.3 RESEARCH IN FOCUS
Interpretative repertoires in the identification of role models by MBA students

Kelan and Mah (2014) were interested in how MBA students construct a professional self-identity through identification of gendered role models. Their interest in this topic arose from previous research findings which suggested that women managers struggle to find examples of women leaders with whom they can identify. They conducted 20 in-depth interviews with full-time MBA students at an elite British business school, ten of whom were men and ten women, each interview lasting between 45 and 110 minutes. The researchers also used visual methods to encourage interviewees' engagement with this topic; their questions related to a person the interviewee admired, as follows:

> We asked you to bring along a picture of a person in business you admire. Who have you chosen? What do you admire in this person?

(Kelan and Mah, 2014: 94)

Although only half of the interviewees brought a photo of a person they admired, by asking interviewees to bring along a picture to the interview, the researchers were able to encourage interviewees to think about this in advance. All the male interviewees selected men as the people they admired, whereas the female interviewees selected men and women. Through their analysis, Kelan and Mah identified two interpretative repertoires, comprised of common tropes which interviewees used to talk about the person they admired. They refer to these as the 'idealization' repertoire and the 'admiration' repertoire. They found significant differences between men and women MBA students in their study in terms of the way students used these two interpretative repertoires to construct a professional self-identity. The idealization repertoire was used by all the male students, whereas the repertoire of admiration was used almost exclusively by women students when talking about individuals they admired.

only to spoken language or talk. This involves treating texts (see Chapter 23) as interrelated to each other and dependent on context. The types of texts that may be analysed using a discourse analytic approach are wide ranging, and include corporate annual reports, government inquiries into organizational disasters, and the content on organizational websites. Moreover, in discourse analysis there is much less of an emphasis on naturally occurring talk, so that talk in research interviews can be a legitimate target for analysis.

2. *Contextual understanding*. Discourse analysts have a preference towards locating the situational specifics of talk in the context of their occurrence. As Potter (1997: 158) puts it, discourse analysts prefer to avoid making reference in their analyses to what he refers to as 'ethnographic particulars' and argues that instead they prefer 'to see things as things that are worked up, attended to and made relevant in interaction rather than being external determinants'. However, discourse analysis practitioners are less committed to this principle than conversation analysts, in that the former sometimes show a greater preparedness to make reference to 'ethnographic particulars'.

3. *Resists codification*. Discourse analysts are opposed to the idea that their analytical practices can be codified and argue that such a codification is probably impossible. One useful point of departure for discourse analysis research that has been suggested by Gill (1996), following Widdicombe (1993), is to treat the way that something is said as being 'a solution to a problem' (Widdicombe 1993: 97, quoted in Gill 1996: 146). Gill (2000) also suggests adopting a posture of 'sceptical reading'. This means searching for a purpose lurking behind the ways that something is said or presented.

4. *Sensitivity to what is unsaid*. A further feature to be aware of is that what is said is always a way of *not* saying something else. In other words, either total silence on a topic, or formulating an argument in a conversation or article in one way rather than in another way, is a crucial component of seeing discourse as a solution to a problem. For example, Ainsworth and Hardy (2009; see Research in focus 22.2) argue that discourse shapes the rules that determine how we speak and act in relation to a given topic, in a way that gives certain actors more legitimacy and rights to commentate than others. They found that discourses that represent the physical process of human ageing as a process of inevitable decline and discourses of the mind that focus on psychologizing feelings of loss and anger associated with job losses were used to marginalize older workers and to exclude them from the labour market. Formulating understandings of unemployment in this way thus discourages collective acknowledgement of responsibility for the problem of older worker unemployment and invites older unemployed people to accept their disempowered situation. This example illustrates the potential for discourses to affect power relations between social actors, a point to which we will return to in the section on critical discourse analysis that follows.

Interpretive repertoires and detailed procedures

Potter and Wetherell (1994) highlight two tendencies within discourse analysis, although they acknowledge that the distinction is somewhat artificial. One is the identification of 'the general resources that are used to construct discourse and enable the performance of particular actions' (1994: 48–9), and is concerned with identifying *interpretative repertoires*. The other is concerned to identify 'the detailed procedures through which versions are constructed and made to look factual' (1994: 49). We will now explore these two strands of discourse analysis.

To illustrate the idea of an interpretative repertoire, we will refer to the study of professional role models adopted by MBA students described in Research in focus 22.3.

TIPS AND SKILLS
Using existing material

As some of these examples of discourse analysis illustrate, you may be able to use the technique to study an issue of interest to you based on materials that are publicly available, such as speeches. This means that you do not have to collect new data and you can devote more attention analysing the materials. Research in focus 22.2 provides an example of a study that relied exclusively on publicly available written texts.

Kelan and Mah (2014: 93) define the interpretative repertoire as 'a repeatedly encountered construction employed in sensemaking. It is a repertoire because only a limited number of terms are used'. They go on to say that these common-sense units of understanding have 'an "off-the-shelf" character and can be used flexibly to make a point in any given situation'. They identify two interpretative repertoires that reflect the ways that individuals talked about people in business whom they admire.

- *The idealization repertoire.* This is comprised of respondents' talk about people who are business founders or very senior in organizations, such as CEOs. Themes include 'being self-made', having achieved success through hard work and perseverance, and 'being authentic'. This is illustrated by one of their respondents, Luke, who talks about the person he admires in these terms, stating:

He got a football scholarship to school (…) and started up a load of car dealerships. And made kind of five or six hundred million dollars by the time he was fifty (…) it's that sort of completely self-made, incredibly sharp (…) he's got very high levels of integrity, you know, what you see is what you get.

(Kelan and Mah 2014: 96)

While the themes of being self-made and being authentic might seem contradictory, Kelan and Mah suggest that they justify and balance the two ideals of 'wealth, status and power' and 'integrity, passion and being true to the self'. They then go on to contrast this with a second repertoire.

- *The admiration repertoire.* This is characterized by ambivalence and caveats in talking about the admired person, such as the 'Superwoman' who appears to do it all. This includes talk about their not-admired characteristics (neutral or negative), as well as the positive traits of the individual. It thereby involves more critical evaluation of the person with whom one identifies. For example:

Frances: 'I like her' cause she's a woman who's basically lived her life according to her own values (…) I was always a bit suspicious that she'd be a bit of a fraud. Until I actually saw her speak (…) And then I realized that she's just very, very open, you know, and what you see is what there is.

(Kelan and Mah 2014: 98)

A key difference, then, between the second and the first interpretative repertoire is that the admiration repertoire contains much greater ambivalence, reflecting tensions and suspicions about whether a person such as this could really exist. The notion of the interpretative repertoire is interesting because it brings out the idea that belief and action take place within templates that guide and influence the writer or speaker. However, the interpretative repertoires identified by Kelan and Mah (2014) by no means exhaust the range of possibilities for analysis, as the advantages of the notion of interpretative repertoires stem primarily from its flexibility in accounting for a diverse range of social practices. Hence, Potter and Wetherell (1987) suggest that repertoires are available to people with many different social group memberships. They also point out that there is no need to attempt to find consensus with regard to repertoires—because they are used to perform different sorts of accounting tasks, individuals are able to draw upon a variety of repertoires in different situations. Finally, they emphasize that 'the concept of repertoire is but one component in a systematic approach to the study of discourse' (Potter and Wetherell 1987: 157), one that in a few years' time may be developed further or even discarded.

In discourse analysis there is also an emphasis on the resources that are employed in conveying allegedly factual knowledge—or what Potter and Wetherell (1994) might describe as *quantification rhetoric*, by which is meant the ways in which numerical and non-numerical statements are made to support or refute arguments. Instead, the texts largely consist of general statements, claims, and conclusions. This is interesting, given the importance of quantification in everyday life and the tendency for many social scientists to make use of this strategy themselves (John 1992).

A number of further characteristics apply to discourse analysis, the most important of which are presented below.

- *Reading the detail*: discourse analysts incorporate the conversation analysis preference for attention to the details of discourse.

- *Looking for rhetorical detail*: attention to rhetorical detail entails a sensitivity to the ways in which arguments are constructed.

- *Looking for accountability*: discourse analysts draw on conversation analysis practitioners' interest in and approach to accounts. From the point of view of both conversation analysis and discourse analysis, discourse can and should be regarded as accounts. For discourse analysis practitioners, the search for accountability entails attending to the details through which these accounts are constructed.

- *Cross-referencing discourse studies*: Potter and Wetherell suggest that reading other discourse studies is itself an important activity. First, it helps to sharpen the analytic mentality at the heart of discourse analysis. Secondly, other studies often provide insights that are suggestive for one's own data.

This approach to discourse analysis has been criticized for being too narrow in focus or not sufficiently sensitive to context. The anti-realist inclination of some discourse analysis practitioners has been a source of controversy. It has been claimed that the emphasis on representational practices through discourses sidelines any notion of a pre-existing material reality that can constrain individual agency (Thompson and Harley 2012). Reality becomes little more than that which is constituted in and through discourse. This lack of attention to a material reality that lies behind and underpins discourse has proved too abstracted for some social researchers and theorists. This is an issue that we will deal with next, when we examine critical discourse analysis. The main point to note at this stage is that, while many discourse analysis practitioners are anti-realist, an alternative realist or critical realist position in relation to discourse is also feasible (Fairclough 2005).

Critical discourse analysis

Critical discourse analysis is principally concerned with capturing and analysing how language is used in specific socio-historical contexts in order to generate particular effects. It also emphasizes the role of language as a power resource. This approach is associated with writers such as Fairclough (1992, 1995, 2003), Hardy (2001), and Phillips and Hardy (2002). Critical discourse analysis additionally draws on the writings of the social theorist Michel Foucault (1974, 1979, 1980), whose work uncovers the representational properties of discourse as a vehicle for the exercise of power. Foucault draws attention to the disciplinary practices that enable particular versions of subjectivity to be constructed in different socio-cultural moments, and the role of language within this. Consequently, the notion of discourse is broader than in other forms of discourse analysis, as this summary by Phillips and Hardy (2002) highlights.

> We define a discourse as an interrelated set of texts, and the practices of their production, dissemination, and reception, that brings an object into being (I. Parker 1992) … In other words, social reality is produced and made real through discourses, and social interactions cannot be fully understood without reference to the discourses that give them meaning. As discourse analysts, then, our task is to explore the relationship between discourse and reality.
>
> (Phillips and Hardy 2002: 3)

In an organizational context, one of the things that critical discourse analysis practitioners seek to trace is how discourses are constructed and maintained in relation to certain phenomena, such as globalization or strategic management. Analysis seeks to reveal the meaning of a phenomenon by exploring how

- the discourse has come to have a particular meaning today, when 40 or 50 years ago it might have had none or a quite different meaning;

- the discourse draws on and influences other discourses;

- the discourse is constructed through texts (such as academic articles or journalistic writing);

- the discourse gives meaning to social life and makes certain activities possible, desirable, or inevitable;

- particular actors draw on the discourse to legitimate their positions and actions (Phillips and Hardy 2002: 8).

As the second point in the above list indicates, discourses are conceived of as drawing on and influencing other discourses. So, for example, the discourse of globalization might affect discourses on new technology, free trade and liberalism, or corporate social responsibility. However, this is not always a complementary process, as in some cases discourses compete with each other for dominance in what is termed *dialogical struggle* (Keenoy et al. 1997). An example of this can be seen in the analysis by Legge (1995) that traces the changing rhetorics of personnel management and HRM in the UK. Legge argues that 'the importance of HRM, and its apparent overshadowing of personnel management, lies just as much and (possibly more so) in its function as rhetoric about how employees should be managed to achieve competitive advantage than as a coherent new practice' (1995: xvi). This has the potential to give rise to a rhetoric–reality gap, in which discourses coexist and are translated into social practice in a variety of ways (Watson 1994a). Critical discourse analysis thus involves exploring why some meanings become privileged or taken for granted and others become marginalized. In other words, discourse does not just provide an account of what goes on in organizations; it is also a process whereby meaning is created. This involves asking 'who uses language, how, why and when' (Van Dijk 1997: 2).

Analysis of a *discursive event* is usually carried out according to a 'three-dimensional' framework, which proceeds as follows:

- examination of the actual content, structure, and meaning of the text under scrutiny (*the text dimension*);

- examination of the form of discursive interaction used to communicate meaning and beliefs (*the discursive practice dimension*);

- consideration of the social context in which the discursive event is taking place (*the social practice dimension*) (Grant et al. 2004: 11).

A further key concept within critical discourse analysis is the notion of *intertextuality*, which draws attention to the notion of discourse as existing beyond the level of any particular discursive event on which analysis is focused. The notion of intertextuality thus enables a focus on the social and historical context in which discourse is embedded.

As noted earlier, there has been some criticism of discourse analysis for apparently ignoring material reality which exists separately from the discursive realm (Reed 2000; Thompson and Harley 2012). A strong critic of discourse analysis on this basis has been Fairclough, who has argued that it should be developed in a direction which adopts the tenets of critical realism. Fairclough is sceptical of the anti-realist assumptions of some discourse analysts who reject objectivist conceptions of organization as social structure in favour of seeing it as 'an interactive accomplishment' (2005: 917), according to a constructionist perspective (see Chapter 2). He quotes Mumby and Clair (1997) as typical of the latter position in saying 'we suggest that organizations exist only in so far as their members create them through discourse' (1997: 181).

Instead, Fairclough recommends an approach that centres on the tension between organizational discourse and organizational structure. Therefore, a critical realist approach to discourse analysis involves analysing not just the discourse *per se* but also its relationship to non-discursive elements. This is particularly important in relation to the study of organizational change because, 'while change in discourse is a part of organizational change, and organizational change can often be understood partly in terms of the constructive effects of discourse on organizations, organizational change is not simply

change in discourse' (2005: 931). Fairclough identifies four sets of organizational research issues that a critical realist approach to discourse analysis can address:

- *emergence*: founded on the notion that 'new' organizational discourses emerge 'through "reweaving" relations between existing discourses' (2005: 932);

- *hegemony*: focusing on how particular discourses become hegemonic in particular organizations and on 'how discourse figures within the strategies pursued by groups of social agents to change organizations in particular directions' (2005: 933);

- *recontextualization*: involving identification of the principles through which 'external' discourses are internalized within particular organizations;

- *operationalization*: focusing on how discourses are operationalized, transformed into new ways of acting and interacting, inculcated into new ways of being, or materialized, within organizations.

Discourse analysis has also been criticized because what different researchers understand the term 'discourse' to mean varies considerably, and so does their approach to analysis. There is thus a danger, noted by Alvesson and Kärreman (2000), that the term 'discourse analysis' is too broad to be meaningful, authors treating the term as though it has a clear, broadly agreed-upon meaning, which, just from reading this chapter, you will be able to see it does not. Consequently, 'discourse sometimes comes close to standing for everything, and thus nothing' (Alvesson and Kärreman 2000: 1128). Building on their earlier article, Alvesson and Kärreman (2011) also warn that the privileging of discourse, and primarily of talk and language as the central force in organizational meaning-making, contributes towards a marginalization of the non-discursive, which includes the material, embodied, and unarticulated. This criticism does not mean that discourse analysis should not be employed, of course, but rather that when working in this tradition it is important to recognize some of the pitfalls and omissions which critics have identified.

Narrative analysis

Narrative analysis is an approach to the elicitation and analysis of language that is sensitive to the sense of temporal sequence that people, as tellers of stories about their lives or events around them, detect in their lives and surrounding episodes and inject into their accounts. Proponents of narrative analysis argue that most approaches

to the collection and analysis of data neglect the fact that people perceive their lives in terms of continuity and process; attempts to understand social life that are not attuned to this feature neglect the perspective of those being studied. Life history research (see Chapter 20) is an obvious location for the application of a narrative analysis, but its use can be much broader than this. Mishler (1986: 77), for example, has argued for greater interest in 'elicited personal narratives'. In his view, and that of many others, the answers that people provide in qualitative interviews can be viewed as stories that are potential fodder for a narrative analysis. In other words, narrative analysis relates not just to the life span but also to accounts relating to events and the interconnections between them. Some researchers apply narrative analysis to interview accounts (e.g. Riessman 1993), while others deliberately ask people to recount stories (e.g. R. L. Miller 2000). Coffey and Atkinson (1996) argue that a narrative should be viewed in terms of the functions that the narrative serves for the teller. The aim of narrative interviews is to elicit interviewees' reconstructed accounts of connections among events and between events and contexts.

In business research, the study of narratives in organizations is well established (see Key concept 22.4 for a definition). Such analyses generally entail exploration of 'spoken or written accounts of connected events' (Boje et al. 2016: 392), which are used to generate insight into organizational sensemaking processes (Weick 1995). In a now classic study, Boje (1991) analyses the types and uses of stories in an office supply firm to develop a theory of organizations as a collective storytelling system. He gives an example of a strategic planning session where the CEO of the company uses stories to explain how the printing industry has changed and to convey a sense of things being better now than they used to be. Boje argues that through this the CEO gains political advantage by portraying the current context as more favourable than the past one. However, not all organizational stories are as coherent as this example implies. The concept of 'microstoria', or 'little stories', is used to refer to the telling of fragmented, terse stories. Boje et al. (2016) conducted an historical archive analysis (see Chapter 23) into the Burger King Corporation (1978–2015) to explore the role of alternative and competing 'antenarratives' in stakeholders' retrospective and prospective sensemaking about strategic change. Basing their study on analysis of documents such as corporate annual reports, the authors argue that this narrative method draws attention to stories that sometimes 'speak against organizational power in situated context' (2016: 401). This more complex approach acknowledges that while narrative analysis often focuses on 'relatively coherent narratives that have a clear beginning and an end' (Vaara et al. 2016: 496), this is not a necessary requirement for narrative analysis (see Key concept 22.4).

22.4 KEY CONCEPT
What are organizational narratives?

Vaara et al. (2016) suggest that organizational narratives have at least six key features.

1) Organizational narratives are 'temporal, discursive constructions that provide a means for individual, social and organizational sensemaking and sensegiving' (2016: 498). They are associated with other language-based approaches to analysis, including discourse and rhetorical analysis. However, Vaara et al. argue that it is the *temporal* aspect of narratives which makes them distinct from these other approaches. This makes them particularly suited to use in the study of change.

2) Organizational narratives are 'not often fully fledged stories or accounts' (2016: 498), in the way that classical literary theory suggests. Instead their plotlines remain implicit and they are often fragmented rather than fully formed or consensually agreed upon.

3) Analysis of organizational narratives requires a focus on how they are produced and consumed. The authors use the term 'story' to refer to 'existing narratives that can be told and retold in various forms' (2016: 498).

4) Organizational narratives are part of multifaceted structures. At the macro level they are linked to societal narratives (in a similar way to discourse analysis), while at the micro level they are comprised of discursive and rhetorical elements which ensure their spread or appeal.

5) While organizational narratives are usually associated with written or spoken language, they also relate to other modes of communication such as visual or audio.

6) Organizational narratives fulfil a key function in processes of organizational stability and change. Specifically, they argue that narratives have both *performative power*, through providing accounts of events that frame them as either change or stability, and *agency*, the potential to influence how events unfold or reproducing the status quo.

22.5 RESEARCH IN FOCUS
An example of narratives in a hospital

Brown (1998) has examined the competing narratives involved in the aftermath of the introduction of a hospital information support system (HISS) at a British hospital trust referred to as 'the City'. The IT implementation was largely seen as unsuccessful because of cost overruns and the absence of clear clinical benefits. Drawing on his interviews with key actors regarding the IT implementation and its aftermath, Brown presents three contrasting narratives—the ward narrative; the laboratory narrative; and the implementation team's narrative—thereby presenting the perspectives of the main groups of participants in the implementation.

The three contrasting narratives provide a very clear sense of the organization as a political arena in which groups and individuals contest the legitimacy of others' interpretations of events. Thus, 'the representations of each group's narrative are described as vehicles for establishing its altruistic motives for embarking on the project, and for attributing responsibility for what had come to be defined as a failing project to others' (Brown 1998: 49).

Thus, while the three groups had similar motivations for participating in the initiative, largely in terms of the espousal of an ethic of patient care, they had rather different latent motivations and interpretations of what went wrong. In terms of motivations, whereas the ward narrative implied a latent motivation to save doctors' and nurses' time, the laboratory team emphasized the importance of retaining the existing IT systems, and the implementation team placed the accent on the possible advantages for their own careers, in large part by the increased level of dependence on their skills. In terms of the contrasting narratives of what went wrong, the ward narrative was to do with the failure of the implementation team to coordinate the initiative and meet deadlines, and the laboratory team emphasized the tendency for the implementation team not to listen or communicate. As for the implementation team, their diagnosis was to do with the ward staff failing to communicate their needs, lack of cooperation from the laboratory staff, and poorly written software.

Narrative analysis is suggested to be particularly suited to the study of organizational culture and change. This approach is also useful in studying issues of power and politics in organizations, as indicated by the study in Research in focus 22.5. As Brown (1998) notes, one of the advantages of using narrative analysis in this study was that it enabled exploration of the organization as an arena where a variety of perspectives and viewpoints coexist, rather than a monolithic entity with a single voice. This is an example of a 'composite narrative' that captures the collective meanings held by a group of organizational members (Vaara et al., 2016).

Rhetorical analysis

Related to narrative analysis is an approach that focuses on the importance of rhetorical devices as a means of communication and persuasion within management and organization. This includes analysis of classic rhetorical devices, such as argumentation, as well as various literary devices, including tropes such as metaphor, synecdoche, metonymy, and irony. Rhetoric and tropes are argued to be an unavoidable feature of organizational life (Oswick et al. 2004). Analyses often focus on their role in communicating with large audiences. For example, rhetorical analysis has been used to critique management fashions and management gurus by exploring how language is used to communicate ideas to global audiences (B. Jackson 2001). It is also applied in the study of leadership, as another organizational context in which language is targeted at large audiences. For example, the study by Heracleous and Klaering (2014) described in Research in focus 22.6 analysed the rhetorical dynamics and metaphors used by the charismatic former CEO of Apple

22.6 RESEARCH IN FOCUS
The rhetorical construction of charismatic leadership

Heracleous and Klaering (2014) were interested in exploring the effect of rhetorical competence on charismatic leadership and whether leaders changed their rhetorical discourse in different contexts. Their empirical study of this question relied on an in-depth **case study** of Apple Inc. former CEO, the late Steve Jobs. A key aspect of charismatic leadership is suggested to involve the use of metaphors to communicate with followers. Their approach involved the analysis of three texts which were selected to represent temporal and contextual diversity and to reflect diversity in the leader's perceived 'ethos', or credibility in the situation:

1. a Securities and Exchange Commission (SEC) deposition by Steve Jobs given in 2008 concerning stock option backdating (119-page document comprising over 18,000 words), a situation of low ethos because Apple was being investigated for potential illegal practices;

2. a CNCB interview with Steve jobs regarding Apple's supplier shift from IBM to Intel conducted in 2005 (521 words), a situation of medium ethos where the leader was not particularly admired;

3. a discussion with Steve Jobs about media and technology in the *Wall Street Journal*, 2010 (transcript length: 12,006 words), a situation of high ethos where the leader was being 'worshipped'.

One 500-word portion was selected for detailed analysis from each of the three texts, looking for central themes and the root metaphors employed. In addition to ethos, or speaker credibility, the researcher focused on two other aspects of rhetoric: 'logos', use of logic in arguments, and 'pathos', ability to ignite audience emotions.

Inc., the late Steve Jobs, in his communications with diverse audiences.

This study highlights the importance of rhetorical devices in provoking identification and commitment among listeners. It suggests that how a leader's message is framed, through the use of metaphors, rhythm, contrasts, and lists, is as important as what the speech is about in gaining commitment from followers. These 'tools for framing' define the form and construction of the message by providing vivid images for the audience. According to Heracleous and Klaering (2014), they include pathos and metaphor.

- *Pathos*. Here the speaker, Steve Jobs, attempts to evoke sympathy from the audience by presenting himself as a human being rather than as the CEO of a successful multi-million dollar company, as the following extract from the SEC deposition illustrates:

Steve Jobs: Well it was a tough situation, you know. It wasn't so much about the money ... And as we've seen in the discussions of the past hour, I spent a lot of time trying to take care of people at Apple and to, you know, surprise and delight them with what a career at Apple

could be ... And I felt that the Board wasn't really doing the same with me ... So I was hurt, I suppose would be the most accurate word ... I had been working, you know, 4 years, 5 years of my life and not seeing my family very much and stuff and I just felt like there is nobody looking out for me here ...

(Heracleous and Klaering 2014: 141)

By describing the Board of Director's lack of care for him, Steve Jobs invokes the rhetorical dynamic of pathos to evoke audience sympathy by portraying himself as 'a self-sacrificing businessman who places the company above his own interests' (Heracleous and Klaering 2014: 142). However, in the interview with the *Wall Street Journal*, where Steve Jobs is being interviewed as a respected expert and invited to share his wisdom, he draws on a much wider range of rhetorical techniques, including metaphor.

- *Metaphor*. Steve Jobs also uses root metaphors, such as the 'circle of life', as illustrated by the following extract:

Steve Jobs: The way we've succeeded is by choosing what horses to ride really carefully, technically. We try to look for these technical vectors, that have a future and that are headed up and you know. Technology, different pieces of technology, kinda go in cycles, they have their springs and summers and autumns, and then they, you know, go to the graveyard of technology. So we try to pick things that are in their springs.

Here, Steve Jobs is speaking in a context of high ethos, i.e. he has strong credibility and therefore he adopts a more entertaining and expansive rhetorical style, using the four seasons to describe products, with 'spring' referring to their birth, and 'graveyard' to describe their death. This 'circle of life' metaphor is also repeated in relation to the Apple company, which Jobs describes as 'on its way to oblivion', and then struggling for survival, before experiencing a rebirth.

Rhetorical analysis thereby enables a focus on the persuasive acts that help to engender identification and foster co-operation within a group.

Conversation analysis

Conversation analysis is a fine-grained approach to the analysis of language in use, whether in conversation or in dialogue, that seeks to understand its organizing properties—in other words, the rules and structures that determine what people say in a given interaction. The roots of conversation analysis lie in ethnomethodology, a sociological position developed by Harold Garfinkel and Harvey Sacks, though it is the latter with whom conversation analysis is most associated. Ethnomethodology is concerned with the 'methods or procedures that competent members of that social group use to go about "organizing" themselves' (Whittle 2018: 217). Ethnomethodologists are fundamentally concerned with the notion of organization as something that is worked at and accomplished through social processes of interaction, rather than pre-given. Contrary to what its name implies, ethnomethodology is *not* a research methodology; it is the study of the methods employed in everyday life though which social order is accomplished.

The research that ethnomethodologists do involves 'studying actual scenes as they unfold in real time in order to identify the kinds of knowledge and reasoning—the "ethno-methods"—that enable people to organize themselves to accomplish some kind of joint activity' (Whittle 2018: 219). These ideas mean that ethnomethodology satisfies two of the preoccupations of qualitative researchers—the preference for a contextual understanding of action (see Chapter 17) and an ontological position associated with constructionism (discussed in Chapter 2). The preference for analysing talk in naturally occurring situations suggests that conversation analysis chimes with another preoccupation among qualitative researchers—namely, a commitment to naturalism.

Two ideas are central to ethnomethodology and find clear expression in conversation analysis: indexicality and reflexivity. Indexicality means that the meaning of an act, which in conversation analysis essentially means spoken words or utterances including pauses and sounds, depends upon the context in which it is used. Reflexivity means that spoken words are constitutive of the social world in which they are located; in other words, the principle of reflexivity in ethnomethodology means that talk is not a 'mere' representation of the social world—it does much more than just stand for something else. While ethnomethodological research is not a unified field, the approach on which we focus here is associated with the work of Sacks (e.g. Sacks et al. 1974). It involves conducting fine-grained analyses of talk in naturally occurring situations and is referred to as conversation analysis (Key concept 22.7).

22.7 KEY CONCEPT
What is conversation analysis?

Conversation analysis is the fine-grained analysis of talk in naturally occurring situations. To conduct such investigations, a premium is placed on the recording and transcription of naturally occurring conversations for the purposes of intensive analysis. These analyses are concerned with uncovering the underlying structures of talk and understanding how order is achieved through interaction.

Heritage (1984, 1987) has proposed that conversation analysis is governed by three basic assumptions.

- *Talk is structured*. Talk comprises invariant patterns—that is, it is structured. Participants are implicitly aware of the rules that underpin these patterns. As a result, conversation analysts eschew attempts to infer the motivations of speakers from what they say or to ascribe their talk to personal characteristics. Such information is unnecessary, since the conversation analyst is orientated to the underlying structures of action, as revealed in talk.

- *Talk is forged contextually*. Action is revealed in talk, and as such talk must be analysed in terms of its context. This means that we must seek to understand what someone says in terms of the talk that has preceded it and that therefore talk is viewed as exhibiting patterned sequences.

- *Analysis is grounded in data*. Conversation analysts shun prior theoretical schemes and instead argue that characteristics of talk and of the constitutive nature of social order in each empirical instance must be induced out of data. Heritage (1987: 258) has written: 'It is assumed that social actions work in *detail* and hence that the specific details of interaction cannot simply be ignored as insignificant without damaging the prospects for coherent and effective analyses.' This assumption represents a manifesto for the emphasis on fine-grained details (including length of pauses, prolongation of sounds, and so on) that is the hallmark of conversation analysis.

As the third of the three assumptions indicates, conversation analysis requires the analyst to produce detailed transcripts of natural conversation that includes all the pauses, interruptions, and intonations used by speakers. Some of the basic notational symbols employed in conversation analysis are listed below.

- A figure in parentheses is used to indicate the length of a period of silence, usually measured in tenths of one second. Thus, (0.3) signals three-tenths of a second of silence.

- Punctuation marks, such as an exclamation mark, are used to capture characteristics of speech delivery rather than as grammatical notation.

- Italics are indicative of an emphasis in the speaker's delivery of a word.

- A hyphen represents a cut-off of a prior word or syllable, which may arise because a speaker is interrupted by someone else.

- Brackets indicate the point at which simultaneous speech overlaps—for example when more than one speaker talks at the same time.

- A colon in the middle of a word indicates that the sound that occurs directly before the colon is prolonged (e.g. we:ll). More than one colon means further prolongation (e.g. ::::).

- The notation .hhh preceded by a dot indicate an intake of breath. If no dot is present, it means breathing out.

- A bracketed full stop (.) indicates a very slight pause.

The attention to detail in conversation analysis is very striking and represents a clear difference from the way in which talk is normally treated by qualitative researchers such as when transcribing and analysing interviews. Attention to fine details is an essential ingredient of conversation analysis work. Pauses and emphases are not to be regarded as incidental or of little significance in terms of what the speaker is trying to achieve; instead, they are part of 'the specific details of interaction [that] cannot simply be ignored as insignificant', as Heritage (1987: 248) puts it. The gradual accumulation of detailed analyses of talk in interaction has resulted in recognition of recurring features in the way that talk is organized. These features can be regarded as tools that can be applied to sequences of conversation.

One of the most basic ideas in conversation analysis is the notion that one of the ways in which order is achieved in everyday conversation is through turn-taking. This is a particularly important tool of conversation analysis, because it illustrates that talk depends on shared codes. If such codes did not exist, there would not be smooth transitions in conversation. In other words, there must be codes to indicate the ends of utterances. One of the ways in which turn-taking is revealed is through the examination of adjacency pairs. The idea of the adjacency pair draws attention to the well-attested tendency for some kinds of activity as revealed in talk to involve two linked phases: a question followed by an answer; an invitation followed by a response (accept/decline); or a greeting followed by a returned greeting. The first phase invariably implies that the other part of the adjacency pair will be forthcoming—for example, that an invitation will be responded to. The second phase is of interest to the conversation analyst not just because it becomes a springboard for a response but because compliance with the normative structure of the pairing indicates an appreciation of how one is supposed to respond to the initial phase. In this way, 'intersubjective understandings' are continuously reinforced (Heritage 1987: 259–60). This is not to imply that the second phase will *always* follow the first; indeed, the response to a failure to comply with the expected response is itself the focus of attention by conversation analysts.

Conversation analysts study talk in a range of organizational settings, such as television news interviews, courtroom trials, and medical settings. For example, Boden (1994) uses conversation analysis to explore how talk is organized in formal and informal meetings. She shows how interactional order is constructed through sequences of talk that enable people to transmit information, make decisions, and sort out misunderstandings. It has sometimes been suggested that conversation analysis fails to capture body movements. However, the growth of video-based methods has enabled this limitation to be addressed, as the analysis of teamwork in hospital anaesthesia teams by Hindmarsh and Pilnick illustrates (Research in focus 22.8).

The insistence of conversation analysts that understanding must be based on sequences of talk, and must avoid extraneous inferences about the meanings of that talk, marks it as a somewhat different approach from much qualitative research. As we have seen in previous chapters, qualitative researchers often seek to achieve understanding from the perspective of those being studied. Conversation analysts claim to do this only in so far as that understanding can be revealed in the specific contexts of talk. To import elements that are not specifically grounded in the here-and-now of what has just been said during a conversation risks implanting understanding that is not grounded in participants' own terms (Schegloff 1997). In so doing, conversation analysis reduces the risk of making unwarranted speculations about what is happening in social interactions and has contributed much to our understanding of the accomplishment of social order.

22.8 RESEARCH IN FOCUS
A study of hospital teamwork using ethnomethodology and conversation analysis

Hindmarsh and Pilnick's (2007) research focused on understanding embodiment in the workplace. The organizational setting that they selected for study was a hospital pre-operative anaesthetic team, where embodied conduct and coordination is critical in ensuring successful outcomes. They describe their approach as involving consideration of 'the fine-grained, closely organized practices of teamwork among personnel involved in administering and managing anaesthetic procedures' (2007: 1396). In addition to interviewing members of the team and conducting observational fieldwork, a key method of data collection involved 'naturalistic audio-visual recordings of everyday anaesthetic work' (2007: 1398). These recordings were made on 14 days over a period of several months. Crucially, this method enabled the study of non-vocal, i.e. embodied interactions, in addition to talk.

A key analytical focus was on the 'sequential' organization of activity in 'real-time' as a means of understanding how each 'participant's conduct emerges in relation to the actions of others' (2007: 1401). They present their data using a series of 'fragments', very short (around 15 seconds) extracts from the video recording. These are presented in conjunction with a sequence of still images showing how the bodies of organizational members move as they work. Plate 22.1 shows an extract from an image sequence involving two members of the anaesthetic team conducting a procedure on a patient. What is striking about this example is relative absence of talk, for as the researchers' note 'aside from a quiet "okay" by the anaesthetist at one point, this is all completed without talk' (2007: 1404). By presenting and analysing these short sequences of everyday anaesthetic work, the researchers demonstrate the competence of team members as evidenced by their ability to sensitively and seamlessly coordinate their bodily movements, a practice which they refer to as 'intercorporeal knowing'. As this example demonstrates, conversation analysis has moved beyond analysis of talk in isolation towards incorporation of the non-verbal aspects through which interactional orders are produced.

PLATE 22.1
Images for fragment 1 (Hindmarsh and Pilnick 2007)

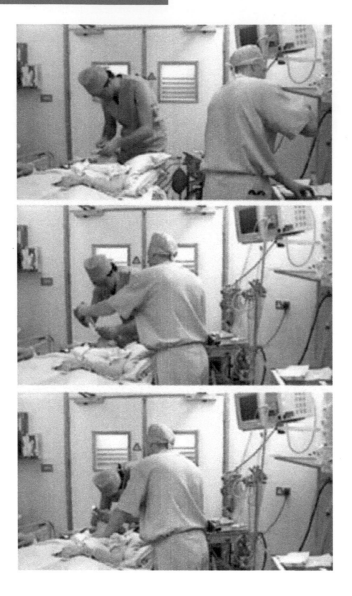

Overview

As the discussion in this chapter has emphasized, different approaches to analysing language tend to draw on
each other to a greater or lesser extent. Discourse analysis, including critical discourse analysis, narrative analysis, and rhetorical analysis, can be understood as more
flexible approaches to the study of language in business
research than conversation analysis, because they are not
solely concerned with the analysis of naturally occurring
talk and enable broader acknowledgement of the socio-
historical context within which language use is situated.
Discourse and narrative analysis also enable the use of a
wider range of data sources, including interviews.

KEY POINTS

- The approaches examined in this chapter take the position that language is itself a focus of interest, and not just a medium through which research participants communicate with each other or with researchers.

- Discourse analysis is an anti-realist, constructionist approach for the analysis of language that conceives of discourse as a means of conveying meaning.

- Critical discourse analysis conceives of a discourse as an interrelated set of texts and sees discourses as drawing on and influencing other discourses. It emphasizes the role of language as a power resource that is related to ideology and socio-cultural change.

- Narrative analysis is an approach to the elicitation and analysis of language that is sensitive to the stories that people tell about their lives or events around them.

- Rhetorical analysis examines the use of persuasive forms of language that help to engender identification and foster cooperation within a group, focusing on the importance of rhetorical devices in this process.

- Fine-grained approaches such as conversation analysis focus in detail on the organizing properties of language and the rules and structures that determine what people say in a given interaction. Conversation analysis is a highly detailed approach to the analysis of naturally occurring conversation and dialogue that uses systematic rules to reveal the underlying structures of language.

QUESTIONS FOR REVIEW

Discourse analysis

- What is the significance of saying that discourse analysis is anti-realist and constructionist?

- What is an interpretative repertoire?

- What questions might a critical discourse analyst ask in seeking to reveal the meaning of current discourses about mindfulness in the workplace?

- Why is the notion of intertextuality important to critical discourse analysts?

Narrative analysis

- What is the main purpose of seeking to uncover organizational stories?

- How is it that the writing-up of research is in itself a process of narrative construction?

Rhetorical analysis

- List some of the main areas of business and management where rhetorical analysis has been applied and explain why rhetorical analysis is useful in understanding them.

Conversation analysis

- What three basic assumptions underpin the conversation analyst's approach?

- List three of the notational symbols used in conversation analysis.

- What are the main criticisms of fine-grained approaches?

ONLINE RESOURCES

www.oup.com/uk/brm5e/

Visit the Interactive Research Guide that accompanies this book to complete an exercise relating to language in qualitative research.

DOCUMENTS AS SOURCES OF DATA

CHAPTER OUTLINE

The term 'documents' covers a wide range of different sources. This chapter aims to reflect that variability by examining a range of documentary sources that can be used in qualitative business research. In addition, the chapter touches on approaches to the analysis of such sources. The chapter explores:

- four criteria for evaluating documents;
- diaries as a type of personal document;
- public documents deriving, for example, from an official inquiry or legal investigation;
- organizational documents such as websites and company annual reports;
- media outputs such as newspaper articles;
- visual documents including photographs and other images;
- the idea that documents are 'texts' that must be read for meaning;
- three approaches to the analysis of documents: qualitative content analysis, semiotics, and historical analysis.

Introduction

This chapter will be concerned with a heterogeneous set of documentary data sources including diaries, autobiographies, organizational websites and reports, newspaper articles, and photographs. Many of these documents have not been produced at the request of a business researcher—instead, this data is simply 'out there' waiting to be collected and analysed. Despite the accessibility of documentary data, considerable research skill is involved in deciding what data to collect and how to go about analysing it.

An idea that will be developed later in this chapter is the notion that documents are 'texts' which can be 'read', although this term is understood in a somewhat looser fashion than is normally the case when we think of written words. This enables a distancing from realist ontological assumptions which assume there is a reality that can be discovered by analysing documents, towards an interpretive epistemology where documents are treated as privileging particular viewpoints or perspectives (see also the discussion of discourse analysis in Chapter 22).

Documents have already been encountered in this book. For example, photographs can be the focus of content analysis (discussed briefly in Chapter 13) or may be used as prompts in connection with structured interviewing (see Key concept 10.8 and Research in focus 10.9) or experiments. A further way in which documents have been considered previously is in the discussion in Key concept 14.11, which noted that studying archive materials is an unobtrusive method of conducting research.

Indeed, this points to an often-noted advantage of using documents—namely, they are non-reactive. This means that, because they have not been created specifically for the purposes of business research, the possibility of a reactive effect (see Research in focus 3.7 on the Hawthorne effect) can be largely discounted as a limitation on the validity of data. However, the emphasis in this chapter is on the use of documents in qualitative organizational research.

In discussing the different kinds of documents used in social science research, John Scott (1990) distinguishes between personal documents and official documents, and further classifies the latter in terms of private as opposed to state documents. These distinctions will be used in the discussion that follows. In addition, Scott proposes the following criteria for assessing the quality of documents (1990: 6):

- *Authenticity*: is the evidence genuine and of unquestionable origin?
- *Credibility*: is the evidence free from error and distortion?
- *Representativeness*: is the evidence typical of its kind, and, if not, is the extent of its untypicality known?
- *Meaning*: is the evidence clear and comprehensible?

This is a useful set of criteria in assessing documents, and reference to them will be made in the following discussion.

Personal documents

Personal documents produced by individuals such as diaries, including video diaries and blogs (see Research in focus 23.1), and autobiographies may be used as the primary source of data in a qualitative study or to complement other methods, such as interviews or participant observation. They may be produced at the request of the researcher, or they may exist independently of the researcher's interest in a topic or setting. An example of the latter is the study by Schoneboom (2011), in which she analysed online diaries or 'workblogs', where individuals or loosely connected groups of workers wrote about their jobs in an online diary a satirical way (Research in focus 23.1).

Diaries may also be produced specifically for the purposes of research, in which case the diarist is normally given some sort of topic guide to help them. This is different from quantitative diary studies (see Chapter 11), because a lesser degree of structure is imposed on the diarist. Increasingly, there is a move away from traditional diaries towards video diaries in business research. The ubiquity of video cameras in smartphones and computers presents opportunities for greater use of video diary methods in business research (Zundel et al. 2016). Zundel et al. focus on self-directed video diaries, which they compare to other forms of diaries (written and audio). They argue that this method has the potential to

23.1 RESEARCH IN FOCUS
A study of online diaries written by white-collar workers

Schoneboom (2011) suggests that 'workblogs', serving as employee diaries, provide a unique insight into the labour process from a worker's perspective. Focusing on workblogs produced by white-collar workers in Greater Manchester and Lancashire in the north of England, she suggests these online documents illustrate the countercultural values and creative aspirations of the bloggers, challenging the view of knowledge workers as atomized and apathetic, and instead showing them to be part of an organized and vocal movement. The anonymous bloggers were identified through a combination of snowball sampling and internet searching. Using these methods, Schoneboom identified 'bloggers who worked in white-collar office environments and wrote critically about their work either as the primary topic of their blog or as an occasional theme' (2011: 407). Concentrating on bloggers in a specific geographical region enabled Schoneboom to study face-to-face interaction and local networking at 'blogmeets'. She complemented this with email and telephone interviews with the bloggers, in addition to analysis of archived material on the blogs, which she also contributed to in order to avoid being seen as 'lurking' (see Chapter 19). She also sought to build trust with the bloggers by referring them to her own online identity, in the form of a long-established personal website.

Schoneboom suggests that although these accounts are written 'pseudonymously, and are often fictionalised, they reveal employees' critical responses to the corporate cultures in which they are immersed' (Schoneboom 2011: 133). However, because of the potential negative repercussions of workblogging, several bloggers have faced disciplinary action from their employers. Workbloggers have therefore become increasingly subtle in their approaches, for example by hiding work-related content within blogs that do not have an explicitly work-related theme. Consequently, bloggers are increasingly reluctant to enagage with researchers, and Schoneboom advises that posted content is 'harvested' quickly and regularly, as it can be taken down suddenly and often without warning. She adds that the emergence of Twitter and Facebook provides new opportunities for employees to talk about work. However, employer surveillance of these activities means that these opportunities do not necessarily enable employees to speak openly.

produce more and richer data, especially in relation to bodily expressions and identity (by enabling social actors to reflect on the roles they inhabit and how they change over time), and by generating practice-related insights into the work worlds of participants. An example of the potential of diaries in generating insight into embodied, sensory experiences can be seen from Riach and Warren's (2015) study of employee's experiences of smell in the workplace. By asking participants to keep 'smell diaries', in the form of an audio-recorded account of odours experienced such as perfume and coffee, and their reactions to them at various points in the day, the researchers were able to gain an insight into bodily experiences that would have been very difficult using any other method.

Tips and skills 'Using self-directed video diaries' provides advice on how to use the self-directed video diary method. These advantages must be offset, however, against the relative lack of control that the researcher has over the content of the diary entries and also against

potential ethical issues (see Chapter 6). These insights are based on Zundel et al.'s (2016) study of strategic decision-making in an engineering service firm. The study involved asking managers 'to upload a video diary at least weekly using a private YouTube channel where the researchers could see entries from all of the diarists but each participant could only access their own recordings' (2016: 2). Such methods are suggested to enable more participatory, dialogical relationships to be developed between researchers and research participants (see the section in Chapter 17 on 'Researcher-participant relationships').

Other kinds of personal documents are sometimes used to trace the history of an organization or an approach to management thought, such as by analysing letters and other archival documents. Many of these documents are held in private collections, which can make research access potentially difficult. They are particularly important in historical analysis, which will be discussed at the end of this chapter. Research in focus 23.9 includes

TIPS AND SKILLS
Using self-directed video diaries in business research

Zundel et al. (2016) suggest that video diaries that are directed by participants offer an efficient method for collecting data from multiple respondents over time. They provide five recommendations for researchers thinking of using this method in their research.

1. While video diaries can be very useful in collecting data about embodied practices and identities as they evolve over time and *in situ*, this method is probably best used 'in combination with other research methods that better capture the sequential structure of events and that offer the researcher opportunities to clarify issues or redirect attention in the data gathering process' (2016: 20).

2. The utility of video diaries may be enhanced by providing research participants with focused instructions, such as to describe their work surroundings or organizational practices. The research participant is thereby cast in the role of a documentary filmmaker of their own situation.

3. Effective use of the method relies on building a relationship of trust between the researcher and research participants. These relationships take time and effort to build.

4. Sometimes the level of disclosure of personal information by participants can far exceed what was anticipated by the researcher. This raises ethical concerns about the responsibilities of the researcher to protect participants from potential harm if this information were made public (see Chapter 6). This recommendation also relates to a point made in Chapter 6 about the potential difficulties in anonymizing visual data.

5. Pay attention to the practicalities of video diaries. The researchers encountered technical difficulties related to participants' use of their own devices and uploading recordings to a private YouTube channel. This carries the risk of lost video recordings and can cause participants to become frustrated with and disengaged from the research process.

an example of a study by Cooke (2006) that involves the use of a further type of personal document, in the form of a series of letters exchanged between two men, Ronald Lippit (1914–86) and John Collier (1884–1968), who contributed to the development of action research.

When they are written for wider consumption, diaries are difficult to distinguish from another kind of personal document—the autobiography. Like diaries, autobiographies can be written at the request of the researcher, particularly in connection with life history studies (see Chapter 20 for a full explanation of the life history method). However, commercially published autobiographical sources can also be used for research purposes. While these are in a sense 'public' documents, on the basis of their ready accessibility, we deal with them here as personal documents because they are produced by individuals. For example, in the research by Kapasi et al. (2016) on the construction of gendered leadership identities, the authors analysed the autobiographies of four women leaders in business and politics—Sheryl Sandberg, Karren Brady, Hillary Clinton, and Julia Gillard (Research in focus 23.2).

When we evaluate personal documents, the *authenticity* criterion is clearly of considerable importance. Is the purported author of the diary or autobiography the real author or has the document been written by someone else? Turning to the issue of *credibility*, John Scott (1990) observes that there are at least two major concerns with respect to personal documents: the factual accuracy of reports, and whether or not they report the true feelings of the writer. Scott recommends that the researcher maintains a healthy scepticism when analyzing personal documents. Famous business people, such as Elon Musk or Sheryl Sandberg, know that their letters, diaries, autobiographies or biographies are likely to be of considerable interest to others and it is likely that they will have a public image that they want to project (see Research in focus 23.2).

Representativeness is an additional concern for personal documents. Personal documents are often only preserved, such as in archives, when they relate to influential business leaders and companies, such as Cadbury, Unilever, or the Ford Foundation. Therefore, such historical documents are likely to be biased in terms of the organizations and individuals they represent.

23.2 RESEARCH IN FOCUS
Using autobiographical sources to study high-profile women leaders

Kapasi et al (2016) were interested in understanding how high-profile women leaders construct gendered leadership identities that are perceived to be 'authentic'. They focused on autobiographies, rather than biographies, because the latter tend to be written from an 'outsider, objective perspective', whereas the former provide insight into 'how organisational actors construct and present a self to other parties' (2016: 343). Their analysis is based on four published autobiographies authored by two business leaders—Sheryl Sandberg, COO of Facebook, and Karren Brady, a senior football club manager—and two political leaders—the American politician Hillary Clinton, and former Australian prime minister, Julia Gillard.

The analysis focuses on the specific stories that these leaders 'choose to tell' (2016: 342) in their autobiographies in order to construct an (authentic) leader identity. They analysed the documents thematically (see Chapter 24), looking for underlying themes that inform the leadership **narrative**, such as 'personal journeys', 'authenticity', and 'family'. A key finding to emerge from the study concerns the 'consciously gendered' nature of the narratives in conforming to gender stereotypes which locate the women in domestic contexts and emphasize 'feminine' leadership traits. This study is interesting because it acknowledges the challenge of *credibility* in assessing autobiographies and deals with this by actively focusing on the constructed nature of these documentary sources. The authors conclude by suggesting that autobiographies are an important data source in understanding the identity work involved in contemporary leadership.

Public documents

Public documents are a source of a great deal of information for business researchers. This includes statistical information generated by official bodies, discussed in Chapter 14. In addition to such quantitative data, there is a lot of publicly available textual material that is of relevance to business researchers, such as legislative documents and official reports. For example, in Ainsworth and Hardy's (2009) study of unemployed older workers, all the documents analysed by the researchers were obtained via an Australian government website, including media releases, transcripts of public hearings, and reports (see Research in focus 22.2).

An example of a study that relied more or less exclusively on public documents is B. A. Turner's (1994) study of large-scale disasters. Turner's analysis was based entirely on the detailed accounts of decisions and actions provided by public inquiry reports into three disasters, one of which was a fire at a leisure centre in 1973 that resulted in 50 deaths.

Turner was primarily interested in the preconditions of the fire—the factors that were deemed by the inquiry to have led to the fire itself and the way in which the handling

of the incident produced such disastrous consequences. In his initial analysis, which was based on a grounded theory approach, Turner aimed to produce a theoretical account of the fire's preconditions. Turner describes the process for this and the other two public inquiry reports he examined as one of slowly going through the details of the report. He describes the process as follows:

> I asked, for each paragraph, what names or 'labels for ideas' I needed in order to identify those elements, events or notions which were of interest to me in my broad and initially very unfocused concern to develop a theory of disaster preconditions.

> (1994: 198)

Turner recorded these 'labels for ideas', which provided the raw materials for building his theoretical model. This type of analysis, which uses publicly available data to analyse critical events or disasters, has been referred to as 'organizational post mortem' research (Orton 1997). A further example of organizational post mortem research is provided in Research in focus 23.3, involving two separate studies of a police shooting of an innocent man in the

23.3 RESEARCH IN FOCUS
Two studies using public documents to analyse a policing disaster

Colville et al.'s (2013) analysis focuses on the 2005 Stockwell shooting, when specialist firearms officers from the London Metropolitan Police Service shot dead Jean Charles de Menezes in a tube train at Stockwell Underground station because they wrongly suspected him of being a terrorist and carrying a bomb. Adopting a sensemaking perspective, Colville et al.'s primary data source is the report which followed the official inquiry into the shooting conducted by the Independent Police Complaints Commission, the *IPCC Stockwell One Report* (2007). This, in combination with witness statements, voice recordings, and CCTV footage, provided the basis for the 194-page report. The authors suggest that their ability to interpret the data was enhanced by the insider status of the third author, who had been a police officer and had counter-terrorism experience. In contrast to other research on organizational disaster sensemaking, such as Gephart's (1993) and Turner's (1994), these researchers chose to examine only this single report, rather than multiple documents and media sources, as their analysis focused on the organizational/operational details of the incident and because this 'legally upheld document ... in terms of its timelines and recorded explanations ... [remains] uncontested' (Colville et al. 2013: 1206).

A separate analysis by Cornelissen et al. (2014) also takes a sensemaking approach to analysing the same incident. Cornelissen et al. used different documentary data sources from those used by Colville et al., including transcripts of the official inquest into the death of de Menezes. They assert that the data give insight into 'real-time sensemaking in the context of an unprecedented, complex and dynamic situation' (Cornelissen et al. 2014: 8).

Although these researchers may not have been aware of the others' interest in this subject (the authors do not cite each other's articles), the studies take a very similar approach to analysis. Both focus on the written logs of decisions taken by senior police officers on the day the incident happened, which give insight into events as they unfolded minute by minute. They also use similar theoretical **concepts** and focus on the framing of decisions that defined the situation.

London Underground. Familiarizing oneself with these kinds of research materials can be very time-consuming, mainly because of the vastness and detail of documents associated with official events and inquiries. This needs to be taken into account when planning to use such materials as a potential source of data. In terms of John Scott's (1990) four criteria, such materials can certainly be seen as authentic and having meaning (in the sense of being clear and comprehensible to the researcher), but the two other standards require greater consideration. The question of credibility raises the issue of whether or not the documentary source is biased. In other words, such documents can be interesting precisely because of the biases they reveal. Equally, this point suggests that caution is necessary in attempting to treat them as depictions of reality. The issue of representativeness is complicated in that materials like these are in a sense unique, and it is precisely their official or quasi-official character that makes them interesting in their own right. There is also, of course, the question of whether or not the case itself is representative, but in the context of qualitative research this is not a meaningful question, because no case can be representative in a statistical sense. The issue is one of establishing a cogent theoretical account and possibly examining that account in other contexts. B. A. Turner's (1994) examination of three separate disasters led him to conclude that there were many common factors associated with behaviour in organizational crisis situations.

Organizational documents

This heterogeneous group of sources is of particular importance to business researchers, not least because of the vast quantity of documentary information that organizations generate. Many of these documents are in the public domain and can readily be accessed online, including minutes of meetings, annual reports, mission statements, reports to shareholders, transcripts of business leaders' speeches, press releases, advertisements, and websites. An example of a study that used websites as a source of documentary data is Coupland's (2005) analysis of CSR reporting in four multinational organizations in the petrochemical industry. The purpose of this study was to identify the discourses used by the organizations to describe their socially responsible activities. Other documents are not (or may not be) in the public domain, such as company newsletters, organizational charts, external consultancy reports, minutes of meetings, emails, policy statements, company regulations, and so on. Given the proliferation of email as a form of organizational communication, and its demonstrated negative effects on miscommunication through intentional and unintentional communication of emotion (Byron 2008), it is perhaps surprising that there is not more analysis of emails as documents in qualitative business research.

In case study and ethnographic research, documents can provide the researcher with valuable background information about the company and its history. Because documents can offer insights into past managerial decisions and actions, they can also be useful in building up a 'timeline', particularly in processual studies of organizational change (see Chapter 17). For his study of ICI, Pettigrew (1985; see Research in focus 3.16) was given access to company archives, so that, in addition to interviewing, he was allowed to examine 'materials on company strategy and personnel policy, documents relating to the birth and development of various company OD (organizational development) groups, files documenting the natural history of key organizational changes, and information on the recruitment and training of internal OD consultants, and the use made of external OD consultants' (1985: 41). Such information can be very important for researchers conducting case studies of organizations using such methods as participant observation or (as in Pettigrew's case) qualitative interviews.

Such documents need to be evaluated using Scott's four criteria. As with the materials considered in the previous section, documents deriving from private sources such as companies are likely to be authentic and meaningful, in the sense of being clear and comprehensible to the researcher, but issues of credibility and representativeness are likely to be more complex. For instance, organizational documents that are in the public domain, such as company annual reports, are intended to represent the official view of senior management and promote a favorable view of the organization to outsiders, including shareholders. Hence, they are likely to contain limited information about the company's problems or failings. To overcome these issues of credibility and representativeness, it may be necessary to consult alternative documentary sources that are likely to have greater credibility, such as reputable newspaper reports.

Issues of authenticity and representativeness are particularly important when using documents accessed online. The first and perhaps biggest challenge concerns authenticity. Current concerns about 'fake news'—stories that are demonstrably false but nevertheless circulate widely online—are indicative of the difficulties experienced by many people in ascertaining what is true and what is not when information is accessed online. Authenticity is also related to the difficulties that are sometimes encountered in ascertaining who produced the document. An example given by Bell and Leonard (2018) in their study of 'digital organizational storytelling' concerns a satirical animated film on YouTube entitled 'Al Gore's Penguin Army', which called into question the existence of climate change. Originally thought to have been produced by an amateur, the film was later discovered to have been produced by a public relations and lobbying firm whose clients include ExxonMobil and General Motors. Representativeness is also important when assessing documents accessed online because of the speed with which information circulates and changes. An important consideration related to this issue stems from the dynamic nature of the content of websites, which may be updated on a weekly or even daily basis. It is important, therefore, to record the date on which a website was consulted and to 'cut and paste' relevant content into a saved document in case the content changes. Indeed, these changes may be important to the analysis: for example, Coupland's (2005) study of CSR in multinational oil companies involved monitoring the organizations' website coverage of corporate social responsibility issues over time. She therefore conducted regular website keyword searches relating to 'social responsibility' over a six-month period and noted any major changes in the reporting during this time.

People who write organizational documents, such as managers, are likely to have a particular point of view that they want to get across. An illustration of this simple observation is Forster's (1994) study of career development in a large retail organization. Forster carried out extensive analysis of company documents relating primarily to HRM issues, as well as interviews and a questionnaire survey. Because he was able to interview many of the authors of the documents about what they had written, 'both the accuracy of the documents and their authorship could be validated by the individuals who had produced them' (1994: 155). This allowed the authenticity and credibility of the documents to be confirmed.

However, the documents also showed up divergent interpretations of the same events and processes 'among the three subgroups within the company—senior executives, HQ personnel staff and regional personnel managers' (1994: 160). This enabled Forster to show how the different groups expressed their views through the documents. As this example illustrates, documents are not necessarily 'free from error and distortion', as John Scott puts it.

Therefore, they have to be interrogated and examined in the context of other sources of data.

A final consideration with organizational documents is that gaining access to confidential or potentially sensitive sources such as personnel files, as Dalton (1959) did (see Chapter 19), raises particular ethical issues (discusssed in Chapter 6).

Media outputs

Newspapers, magazines, television programmes, films, and other mass media are potential sources for business research. An example is given in Research in focus 23.4 of a study that relied exclusively on articles about a well-known business leader published in the popular press. In addition to exploring mass-media outputs using a quantitative form of data analysis such as content analysis, such sources can also be examined in terms of their qualitative nature. Typically, such analysis entails searching for themes in the sources examined (see Chapter 24 for more on thematic analysis).

Authenticity issues are sometimes difficult to assess in the case of mass-media outputs. While the outputs can usually be deemed to be genuine, the authorship of articles is often unclear (for example, editorials, some magazine articles), so that it is difficult to know if they can be relied upon as being written by someone in a position to provide an accurate account. Representativeness is rarely an issue for analyses of newspaper or magazine articles, since the population from which a sample has been drawn is usually ascertainable, especially when a wide range of newspapers is employed. Finally, the evidence is usually clear and comprehensible but may require considerable awareness of contextual factors relating to the organization or company, such as information about share prices, movements of key personnel, and merger speculation.

23.4 RESEARCH IN FOCUS
An analysis of public documents in leadership research

Chen and Meindl (1991) analysed articles in the popular press about Donald Burr, an entrepreneur who in 1980 started the low-cost US airline, People Express. Burr was widely revered as a charismatic leader because of the early success of his business and the high level of commitment exhibited by his staff. However, in 1984 the company began to founder, and it was taken over by a rival in 1987.

The researchers carried out two analyses of magazine and newspaper articles about Burr. The first followed traditional content analysis methods (of the kind described in Chapter 13); it involved identifying themes and then recording the frequency of their occurrence in the text. However, the second analysis was more interpretative; it involved identification of the metaphors used to describe Burr over the course of the airline's history. The first analysis sought to analyse Burr's image from the perspective of the *reader* of the news article, whereas the second analysis concentrated on gaining an impression from the point of view of the *writer*.

Articles were presented to a sample of 75 undergraduate business students, who were asked to write a description of Burr based on the materials they had just read. Fourteen different themes were extracted from the image descriptions and these were subjected to traditional content analysis to establish a pattern of frequency. The analysis revealed that the themes used to describe Burr varied according to the time period in the company's history that the articles covered. For example, when the company was doing well, Burr was seen as ambitious, fair, and caring, but when it was doing badly he was seen as determined and instrumental.

In the qualitative content analysis, Chen and Meindl (1991) focused on the journalists' descriptions of Burr (that is, the writers rather than the readers of the text):

> We screened, sentence by sentence, the same sampled journal articles that were presented to the respondents. Those words, phrases, or clauses that metaphorically described Burr's personality, his behaviours, or his impact were identified as metaphorical expressions. Altogether, 46 such expressions were identified.
>
> (1991: 539)

One of the most common metaphors uncovered was that of Burr as an unorthodox preacher who was visionary, charismatic, and dedicated to his mission, as these journalistic quotes illustrate:

> Within the new structure … Burr will go on preaching his unorthodox management approach.
>
> (1991: 550)

> Burr works hard when he talks. He paces, he sits; he stands; he throws out his arms; he condemns and praises, implores and jokes.
>
> (1991: 550)

The study found a high degree of correspondence between images constructed through metaphors and images constructed by the readers. This finding demonstrates the influence of the business press in constructing particular images of organizational leaders.

Visual documents

As we highlighted in Chapter 19, visual research is an expanding area in business research. Organizations produce a wide array of documents that contain images, for example in reports, in branding, and on websites. There are also various types of publicly available visual documents that are of relevance to business researchers. For example, Bell and Leonard's (2018) study of digital organizational storytelling (discussed in Chapter 20) explored the production and circulation of online animated videos which are critical of business practices such as factory farming. Visual documents that can be considered as main or supplementary sources of data in qualitative analysis include photographs, graphic and artistic images, sketches and drawings, and moving images in the form of video, feature film, and television. Davison's (2009) study of the Bradford & Bingley bank illustrates the potential for analysis of corporate brand images (see Research in focus 23.6).

In Chapter 19, we made a distinction between visual materials produced by the researcher or by participants at the researcher's request and those that form part of the research setting and are *extant* to the research process (see Thinking deeply 23.5). An example of a study using the latter type of visual document can be seen in Research in focus 23.6, which analyses images found in company annual reports.

However, photographs must not be taken at face value when used as a research source; it is also necessary to have considerable additional knowledge of the social context to probe beneath the surface. Glossy photographs of happy, smiling employees in corporate brochures or newsletters, for example, might suggest that there is a gap between the photographic image of the company and the underlying reality as experienced at a day-to-day level. Scott sees the issue of *representativeness* as a particular problem for the analyst of photographs. As he suggests, the photographs that survive the passage of time—for example, in archives—are unlikely to be representative. It is therefore important for the researcher to remain sensitive to what is not photographed.

23.5 THINKING DEEPLY
Three ways of using photographs as documents

Qualitative researchers distinguish between the use of *extant* photographs that have not been produced for the research and *research-generated* photographs that have been produced by the researcher or at the researcher's request. Three common uses of photographs are the following.

1. *Illustrative*. Photographs may be used to do little more than illustrate points and thereby enliven what might otherwise be a rather dry discussion of findings.

2. *As data*. Photographs may be viewed as data in their own right. See, for example, the study of organizational aesthetics by Warren (2002; Research in focus 17.7). Extant photographs can be understood as a main source of data about the field in which the researcher is interested. The examples given in Research in focus 17.16 are in this category.

3. *As prompts*. Photographs may be used as prompts to entice people to talk about what is represented in them. Both research-driven photographs, such as in the example of S. Warren's (2002, 2005) study of organizational aesthetics discussed in Chapter 17, and extant photographs may be used in this way.

23.6 RESEARCH IN FOCUS
Analysing photographs in a study of brand identity in a UK bank

Davison's (2009) study of Bradford & Bingley shows how changes in lending and funding practices since its formation in the 1960s, which were indicative of shifts in the UK bank's ethos, were mirrored by changes in the visual iconography that the company used in its marketing campaigns and annual reporting documents. Davison traces the way that the iconography of the bowler hat, which formed an enduring part of the bank's brand identity, changed over time. Davison locates the icon of the bowler hat in popular culture, citing a diverse range of sources from film and television that have shaped its changing meaning. She thus argues that the bowler hat has been used as a symbol of class, as epitomized by the character John Steed in the 1960s UK TV series *The Avengers*; as a way of representing professionalism, as in the film *Men in Black* (1997); and to denote eroticism and entertainment, as when worn by Liza Minelli in the film *Cabaret* (1972). Two of the images from Davison's analysis are presented here. Plate 23.1 shows a relatively recent image from the company's website. Davison argues that, through the wearing of this item of traditionally male attire by a woman, the company seeks to shift the brand from its former values of masculine, anonymous, traditional, and reserved, to an identity that is more feminine, proactive, and seductive. Plate 23.2 shows a further use of the icon that is based on abstract representation in a manner that echoes the style of the artist Andy Warhol. Davison states that 'here the icon of the bowler hat has been separated from its wearer to acquire a life and importance of its own in these repetitive stylised motifs' (Davison 2009: 897) in a way that provides memorability through repetition. Through this detailed reading of the visual meaning of the brand, Davison highlights its role and importance even in documents as apparently objective and numerically focused as the annual financial reports produced by banks.

PLATE 23.1

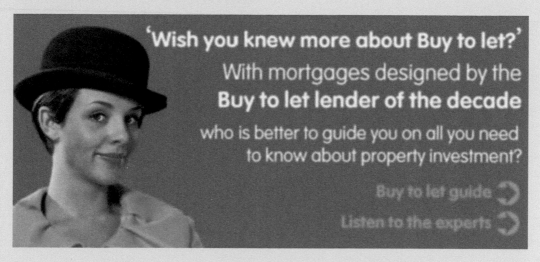

Source: Davison (2009: 896) Copyright Bradford and Bingley. Reproduced with thanks.

PLATE 23.2

Bradford & Bingley logo from the 1990s, '20 coloured bowler hats'

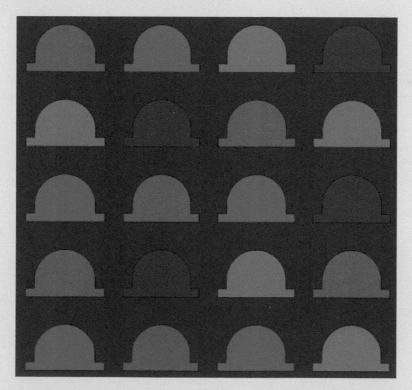

Source: Davison (2009: 897) Copyright Bradford and Bingley. Reproduced with thanks.

Documents as 'texts'

The word 'text' is sometimes used as a synonym for 'document'. However, the word 'text' can be applied to a wide range of phenomena, so that theme parks, landscapes, heritage attractions, technologies, and a wide range of other objects are treated as texts out of which a 'reading' can be fashioned (e.g. Grint and Woolgar 1997). In Barthes's (1972) influential collection of essays, objects as varied as wrestling matches, Citroën cars, and strip-tease acts are submitted to readings. In a sense, therefore, just about everything can be treated as a text which can be read.

As mentioned in the introduction to this chapter, this has implications for the interpretation of documents (the focus of the next section) in terms of the different ontological assumptions that the researcher makes. It is clearly tempting to assume that documents reveal something about an underlying social reality, so that the documents created within an organization (minutes of meetings, newsletters, mission statements, job specifications, etc.) are viewed as representations of the reality of that organization. In other words, we might take the view that such documents tell us something about what goes on in that organization and will help us to uncover such things as its culture. According to such a view, documents are windows onto social and organizational realities. This type of approach to analyzing documents is thus guided by realist ontological assumptions (see Chapter 2).

However, treating documents as texts implies a more constructionist ontological approach. Rather than view documents as ways of gaining access to an underlying reality, Atkinson and Coffey (2004) suggest that documents should be viewed as a distinct level of 'reality' in their own right. Atkinson and Coffey argue that documents should be examined in terms of, on the one hand, the context in which they were produced and, on the other hand, their implied readership. When viewed in this way, documents are significant for what they are supposed to accomplish and who they are written for. They are written in order to convey an impression, one that will be favourable to the author and those whom they represent. Moreover, any document should be viewed as linked to other documents, because invariably it refers to and/or is a response to other documents. Other documents form part of the context or background to the writing of a document. Atkinson and Coffey refer to the interconnectedness of documents as *inter-textuality*.

The minutes of a meeting in an organization might be the kind of document that would interest a business researcher. On the face of it, this document provides a record of issues raised at the meeting; the discussion of those issues; views of the participants; and actions to be taken. As such, they might be deemed interesting for a business researcher for their ability to reveal such things as the culture of the organization or department responsible for the minutes, its preoccupations, and possible disputes among the meeting participants. However, precisely because the minutes are a document that is to be read not only by participants but also by others (members of other departments or other organizations; in the case of a UK public-sector organization, the minutes may be accessed by the public under the Freedom of Information Act), they are likely to be written with a view to prospective scrutiny by others. Disagreements may be suppressed and actions to be taken may reflect a desire to demonstrate that important issues are to be addressed rather than because of a genuine desire to act on them. Also, the minutes are likely to be connected either explicitly or implicitly to other documents of that organization, such as previous minutes, mission statements, organizational regulations, and external documents (such as legislation). Further, following Atkinson and Coffey's suggestions, the minutes should be examined for the ways in which language is used to convey certain messages.

Atkinson and Coffey's central message is that documents have a distinctive ontological status, in that they form a separate reality, which the authors refer to as a 'documentary reality', and they should not be taken to be 'transparent representations' of an underlying organizational or social reality. They go on to write: 'We cannot ... learn through written records alone how an organization actually operates day by day. Equally, we cannot treat records—however "official"—as firm evidence of what they report' (Atkinson and Coffey 2004: 58). Hence documents need to be recognized for what they are—namely, texts written with distinctive purposes in mind, and not as simply reflecting reality. This means that if the researcher wishes to employ documents as a means of understanding aspects of an organization and its operations, it is likely that he or she will need to buttress an analysis of documents with other sources of data. An example of this relates to Vaughan's (1990) analysis of the Space Shuttle *Challenger* accident. As Vaughan (2006) points out, examining documents such as presidential commission reports can be extremely illuminating about the kinds of issues that they emphasize and the kinds of ways in which the issues are framed. This is precisely the point that Atkinson and Coffey (2004) are making. Vaughan (2006) examined three commission reports: the *Challenger* Report; the *Columbia* Accident Investigation Board Report, which dealt with another space shuttle disaster that took place in February 2003; and the 9/11 Commission Report. She shows that each report was shaped by a dominant frame: respectively an 'accident investigation frame'; a 'sociological frame'; and a 'historical/war frame' (2006: 304). Further, she notes that the 9/11 report locates causation in what she calls 'regulatory failure' (2006: 300), which is to do with problems with the activities of the agencies charged with upholding national security. An effect of that attribution of causation is to absolve the president and to some extent US foreign policy of responsibility. This examination of documents implies that they can tell us about such things as how those responsible for reporting officially on major incidents construct the background and the causes of those incidents. These documents are rhetorically designed to 'do something': they are designed to assign moral and practical responsibility and to identify possible recommendations.

This orientation to documents represents a shift in how they are conceived for research purposes because it implies that there is no single truth awaiting discovery in a text. Rather, there are different readings and intentions involved in the production of texts that privilege particular versions of reality.

Interpreting documents

Although it means straying into areas that are relevant to Chapter 24, this section will briefly consider the question of how to interpret documents qualitatively. Three approaches are outlined: qualitative content analysis; semiotics; and historical analysis. In addition to these, discourse analysis, which was covered in Chapter 22, has been used as an approach for the analysis of documents.

Qualitative content analysis

This is probably the most prevalent approach to the qualitative analysis of documents, although in business research it remains less frequently used than quantitative content analysis (Insch et al. 1997). It comprises a searching-out of underlying themes in the materials being analysed and can be discerned in several of the studies referred to earlier, such as Colville et al. (2013) and Cornelissen et al. (2014). A further example is provided in Chen and Meindl's (1991) study of the metaphors used to describe the entrepreneur and business leader Donald Burr (see Research in focus 23.4). Unlike quantitative content analysis, the processes through which the themes are extracted are usually left implicit. The extracted themes are usually illustrated—for example, with brief quotations from a newspaper article or magazine. The procedures adopted by B. A. Turner (1994) in his research on organizational disasters is an example of the search for themes in texts.

Altheide (1996) has outlined an approach that he calls ethnographic content analysis (referred to by him as ECA; also called qualitative content analysis), which he contrasts with quantitative content analysis of the kind outlined in Chapter 13. Altheide's approach represents a codification of certain procedures that might be viewed as typical of the kind of qualitative content analysis on which many of the studies referred to so far are based. He describes his approach as differing from traditional quantitative content analysis, in that the researcher is constantly revising the themes or categories that are distilled from the examination of documents. As he puts it:

> ECA follows a recursive and reflexive movement between concept development, sampling-data, collection-data, coding-data, and analysis-interpretation. The aim is to be systematic and analytic but not rigid. Categories and variables initially guide the study, but others are allowed and expected to emerge during the study, including an orientation to *constant discovery* and *constant comparison* of relevant situations, settings, styles, images, meanings, and nuances.
>
> (Altheide 1996: 16; emphases in original)

Thus, with ECA there is much more movement back and forth between conceptualization, data collection, analysis, and interpretation than is the case with the kind of content analysis described in Chapter 13. Quantitative content analysis typically entails applying predefined categories to the sources; ECA employs some initial categorization, but there is greater potential for refinement of those categories and the generation of new ones.

Qualitative content analysis as a strategy for searching for themes in data lies at the heart of the coding approaches that are often employed in the analysis of qualitative data, such as grounded theory. This was the approach used by Colville et al. (2013) in their analysis of the Stockwell shooting of Jean Charles de Menezes in 2005 (Research in focus 23.3).

Semiotics

Semiotics is invariably referred to as the 'science of signs'. It is an approach to the analysis of symbols in everyday life and as such can be employed in relation not only to documentary sources but also to all kinds of other data because of its commitment to treating phenomena as texts. The main terms employed in semiotics are:

- the sign—that is, something that stands for something else;

- the things the sign is made up of—a *signifier* and the *signified*;

- the *signifier*, which is the thing that points to an underlying meaning (the term *sign vehicle* is sometimes used instead of *signifier*);

- the *signified*, which is the meaning to which the signifier points;

- a *denotative meaning*, which is the manifest or more obvious meaning of a signifier and as such indicates its function;

- a *sign-function*, which is an object that denotes a certain function;

- a *connotative meaning*, which is a meaning associated with a certain social context that is in addition to its denotative meaning;

- *polysemy*, which refers to a quality of signs—namely, that they are always capable of being interpreted in many ways;

- the *code*, which is the generalized meaning that interested parties may seek to instil in a sign; a code is sometimes also called a *sign system*.

Semiotic analysis focuses on the way that messages are communicated as systems of cultural meaning. It is based on semiotic theory, which suggests that the symbolic order of a culture is constructed and interpreted through a system of signs. A *sign* constitutes the relationship between the *signifier* (the recognizable word, sound, or picture that attracts our attention and communicates a particular message) and the *signified* (the message or concept itself). The link between the signifier and the signified is arbitrary; its meaning depends on the conventions held by groups of sign users about the mental concept (signified) that the material object (signifier) is intended to represent. Barley (1983) provides the following example:

> As you drive toward me in your speeding car, I hold up my hand, palm out, intending an expression signifying the content, 'Stop while I cross the street.' From your vantage point behind the wheel, you wonder why I am so brash as to say hello from the middle of the crosswalk and you step on the gas. Obviously our conventions differ.
>
> (1983: 395–6)

This example places greater emphasis on the recipient of the message, who must actively interpret the signifier in order to establish its meaning by drawing on his or her cultural knowledge. The task of the researcher in semiotic analysis is to discover the rules that bind users of a sign together and enable them to make sense of their cultural world.

Signs contribute to systems of signification or *codes*, which provide a model for social action; these are composed of *denotative* and *connotative* elements. The denotative code represents meaning that is associated directly with the sign-vehicle itself, whereas the connotative code represents meaning that links the sign with its cultural context.

Despite the potential for applying semiotic analysis in the study of organizational cultures, its use has instead been mainly confined to studies of marketing and advertising. In advertising, semiotic analysis encourages recognition of the way that individuals interpret the same advertising message in slightly different ways. Combe and Crowther (2000) suggest, for example, that signs and symbols influence the positioning and repositioning of brands, such as Murphy's Irish Stout, in recipients' minds. A further application of semiotic analysis in an organizational context is provided by Barley (1983) in his study of funeral work (see Research in focus 23.7).

Historical analysis

Historical analysis is in this chapter because the kind of research that we are referring to in this section often involves documents and other artefacts that can be used to trace the history of an organization or an industry. As mentioned earlier in this chapter, this can include letters and diaries of company founders and other members of the organization, financial reports, and records of meetings, which are often held in private or public archives for

23.7 RESEARCH IN FOCUS
A semiotic analysis of a funeral business

Over a three-month period, Barley (1983) engaged in observation and conducted interviews in a US funeral home, with the intention of uncovering the signs used by funeral directors to make sense of their work. After interviewing funeral directors about various aspects of their work, including the history of the business, the layout and decor of the home, and the tasks involved in preparing a body or making a removal, Barley began to develop maps of connotative codes through which he saw funeral directors as striving to achieve the quality of 'naturalness' in the funeral scene by making arrangements in a way that they believe is least likely to disturb mourners. This might involve arranging the corpse in such a way as to convey the image of a restfully sleeping person or furnishing the funeral home in a way that simulates a comfortable living room, with coffee tables and comfortable chairs. Barley concludes that the funeral director's role relies on a system of signs or codes that create a subtle illusion of everyday life, in order to obscure the strangeness of death and thereby to reassure mourners.

the purposes of historical study by researchers. However, historical analysis relates not just to the study of documents from the past but also to the methods that are used to interpret them. In recent years there has been growing interest in historical analysis in business research. Some writers have been critical of the approach traditionally taken by business historians, suggesting it is overly real-ist (see Chapter 2), or possibly empiricist (see Key concept 2.1), and suffers from a tendency towards 'myopic fact-collect[ing] without a method' (Kieser 1994: 612). Decker (2016) argues that business historians need to

do more to explain their methods in a way that is comprehensible to other social scientists. She suggests that this involves explaining the role of archives, historical materials preserved in a specific location, as the basis for 'reconstruction'. Importantly, this involves acknowledging the colonizing tendencies of many archives, and the silences that are perpetuated through this (see the section in Chapter 17 on 'Postcolonial and indigenous research'). This has led to the emergence of more diverse approaches to historical research (see Thinking deeply 23.8 and Research in focus 23.9).

23.8 THINKING DEEPLY
Three arguments for historical analysis in studying organizations

Rowlinson (2004a: 8) outlines three arguments for a historical perspective in organization studies.

1. The *factual approach* argues that 'if organization studies were to take account of the facts revealed by history then a number of erroneous assumptions would be undermined' (2004a: 8). It can thus be seen as is aligned with positivism because history is viewed as 'a repository of facts which, so long as historians properly interpret them, can conveniently confirm or refute preferred or non-preferred theoretical positions' (2004a: 10).

2. The *narrative approach* suggests that history is not a skillfully crafted recounting of factual events from the past, but a well-crafted story about the past constructed by the historian through the careful use of narrative. This takes inspiration from the work of White (1987), who argues that historical analysis relies on narrative construction, through the choices made by the researcher about which historical elements to focus on and how they are ordered. History can therefore be understood as a discourse (see Chapter 22) that is actively constructed, including by organizational leaders and managers who have a vested interest in promoting a particular view of the past in order to shape the present. This 'has shifted the emphasis away from seeing archival research as the historian's craft towards a view that it is the conventions and customs of writing that constitute the craft of history' (Rowlinson 2004b: 11).

3. The *archaeo-genealogical approach* is derived from the work of Foucault and his attempts to deconstruct the present through analyses of the past. In his archaeological phase, Foucault explored 'in language the sedimented evidence of the assumptions; the values; the common sense through which, for instance, a phenomenon such as madness could have one set of meanings in one era and a contradictory set of meanings in another' (Jacques 2010: 310). Foucault used this genealogical approach to examine 'the conditions under which the different ways of interpreting and evaluating ourselves have come to exist. The purpose of the genealogical method is to analyse and excavate the taken-for-granted' assumptions that define the present ... and to understand how it has transpired that the present has come to be accepted as inevitable or natural' (Poutanen and Kovalainen 2010: 263, 418). An example of the genealogical approach is provided in Research in focus 23.9.

23.9 RESEARCH IN FOCUS
A genealogical historical analysis of management thought

Genealogical historical analysis of documentary sources (see Thinking deeply 23.8) can be a powerful way of challenging taken-for-granted assumptions. For example, Cooke (2003) argues that American slavery has been wrongly excluded from the history of management. His analysis shows that nineteenth-century US slave plantations were a key site in the emergence of industrial discipline. This argument is based on an historical study of documents that include contemporaneous accounts written by people living and working on the plantations in addition to academic analyses. Using these sources, Cooke argues that management theorists have actively written out the shameful roots of many practices that we accept now as normal or rational, terming this a 'denial'.

In another study by Cooke (2006), his analysis of the history of management thought focuses on an historical dataset comprised of a series of letters written between 1949–50. The letters were exchanged between two American men—Ronald Lippit, an academic psychologist, and John Collier, a public administrator and campaigner—who contributed to the development of action research (see Chapter 17). By quoting directly from the letters, Cooke shows how at the time of the cold war between the USA, the Soviet Union, and their various allies, there was disagreement about the purposes that action research should serve. While Collier was instrumental in promoting a broadly social perspective, Lippit prioritized a narrower, more instrumental and managerial version of action research, and it was the more conservative version that won out. The overall aim of both studies is similar, as the social, political, and ethical contexts of what we now take to be rationally-based, neutral managerial ideas are picked apart. In common with many business researchers involved in the 'historical turn', Cooke uses historical methods to put a more critical slant on the history of management thought.

CHECKLIST
Evaluating documents

Can you answer the following questions?

○ Who produced the document?

○ Why was the document produced?

○ Was the person or group that produced the document in a position to write authoritatively about the subject or issue?

○ Is the material genuine?

○ Did the person or group have a particular agenda, and if so can you identify a particular slant?

○ Is the document typical of its kind, and if not, is it possible to establish how untypical it is and in what ways?

○ Is the meaning of the document clear?

○ Can you corroborate the events or accounts presented in the document?

○ Are there different possible interpretations of the document from the one you offer, and if so, what are they and why have you discounted them?

KEY POINTS

- Documents constitute a very heterogeneous set of sources of data, which include personal documents, official documents from both the state and private sources, and the mass media.

- Such materials can be the focus of both quantitative and qualitative enquiry, but the emphasis in this chapter has been upon the latter.

- Documents of the kinds considered may be in printed, visual, digital, or indeed any other retrievable format.

- For many writers, just about anything can be 'read' as a text.

- Criteria for evaluating the quality of documents are authenticity; credibility; representativeness; and meaning. The relevance of these criteria varies somewhat according to the kind of document being assessed.

- There are several ways of analysing documents within qualitative research. In this chapter we have covered qualitative content analysis, semiotics, and historical analysis.

QUESTIONS FOR REVIEW

- What is meant by a document?
- What are John Scott's four criteria for assessing documents?

Personal documents

- How can diaries be used in business research?
- How do they fare in terms of John Scott's criteria?

Public documents

- What do the studies by Turner, Colville et al., and Cornelissen et al. suggest in terms of the potential for business researchers to use official documents?

- How do such documents fare in terms of John Scott's criteria?

Organizational documents

- What kinds of documents might be obtained from organizational sources?
- How do such documents fare in terms of John Scott's criteria?

Media outputs

- What kinds of documents are media outputs?
- How do such documents fare in terms of John Scott's criteria?

Visual documents

- Name three ways that photographs can be used as a source of data in business research and explain the differences between them.

Documents as 'texts'

- What is a text?
- What ontological assumptions about the nature of reality are implied by the use of this term?

Interpreting documents

- How does qualitative content analysis differ from the kind of content analysis discussed in Chapter 13?
- What is a sign? How central is it to semiotics?
- What is the difference between denotative meaning and connotative meaning?
- What is historical analysis and how can it be applied in business research?

....

 ONLINE RESOURCES

www.oup.com/uk/brm5e/

Visit the Interactive Research Guide that accompanies this book to complete an exercise relating to documents as sources of data.

....

QUALITATIVE DATA ANALYSIS

CHAPTER OUTLINE

Because qualitative data deriving from interviews, participant observation, or documents typically comprise a large corpus of unstructured textual material, they are not straightforward to analyse. Moreover, unlike quantitative data analysis, there are no clear-cut rules about how qualitative data analysis should be carried out. In this chapter, some general approaches to qualitative data analysis will be examined. The chapter explores:

- two of the most widely used strategies of qualitative data analysis—thematic analysis and grounded theory—in each case, we examine the main features, processes, and outcomes, along with some of the criticisms;

- coding as a basic operation in qualitative data analysis and grounded theory specifically;

- the main criticism that is made of coding in relation to qualitative data—namely, that it tends to fragment data;

- secondary analysis of qualitative data collected by other researchers.

Introduction

One of the main difficulties with qualitative research is that it rapidly generates a large, complex dataset because of its reliance on unstructured language in the form of field notes, interview transcripts, or documents as well as visual images. Miles (1979) describes qualitative data as an 'attractive nuisance', because, while the richness associated with qualitative data is valued by qualitative researchers, it can be very difficult to find analytic pathways through this richness. Because of this, the researcher must try to avoid being overly captivated by the richness of the data collected such that they are unable to interpret the data's broader significance.

Finding a path through qualitative data is not easy, and it can be difficult to know where to start when confronting such data for the first time. In large part, this is because, unlike the analysis of quantitative data, there are few well-established and widely accepted rules for the analysis of qualitative data. In dealing with quantitative data you still have to interpret your analyses, but at least there are relatively clear rules for getting to that point. Qualitative data analysis is not characterized by this degree of codification of analytic procedures, and many writers would argue that such codification is not desirable (Bryman and Burgess 1994*b*; Bell et al. 2017).

What *can* be provided are broad guidelines (Okely 1994), and it is in the spirit of this suggestion that this chapter is written.

The chapter considers two strategies for the analysis of qualitative data—thematic analysis and grounded theory. These are probably the most frequently used approaches, though others do exist. As we will see, one of the differences between qualitative and quantitative data analysis is that, with the latter, analysis invariably occurs after your data have been collected. In contrast, qualitative analytical approaches such as grounded theory are often described as iterative—that is, there is a repetitive interplay between the collection and analysis of data. This means that analysis starts after some of the data have been collected and the ideas that emerge from this analysis then shape the next steps in data collection. Consequently, while grounded theory and thematic analysis are described as strategies of analysis, they can also be viewed as strategies for the *collection* of data as well. The outcome of quantitative data analysis is also associated with an inductive approach to research, where theory is the outcome of the analytical process rather than a precursor to it (see Tips and skills 'Analysing data inductively').

TIPS AND SKILLS
Analysing data inductively

When analysing qualitative data it can be difficult for students to know how to deal with the emergence of themes in the data that do not relate to theories identified in the literature review. Should they be included in the analysis, in which case you will probably need to read additional literature in order to support your analysis, or should you stick to the subject of your literature review, leaving themes that do not closely relate to it out of the analysis?

This dilemma is associated with inductive research (see Chapter 2), where data are collected to build theory rather than test it. This process of theory building is usually iterative, involving tracking back and forth between theory and data. While it may be desirable to pursue an inductive logic by following emergent themes back to the literature, so that theory can be built from the data, conceptual constraints, such as linking to your research questions, and practical constraints, such as submission deadlines and constraints on dissertation length, can make this difficult (see Chapter 7). If you explore every theme that emerges through your data analysis there also is a danger that you will try to cover too many literature items in your project, and consequently your treatment of them will become superficial.

The main point to bear in mind is that it is important to try to achieve a balance between exploring new themes that emerge through your data analysis and sticking to the subject area that provided the basis for your review of the literature. As experienced qualitative researchers will tell you, there are multiple themes that can be generated out of a rich qualitative dataset, and it is impossible to pursue them all.

Thematic analysis

One of the most common approaches to qualitative data analysis entails what is often referred to as thematic analysis. The study by Clarke et al. (2012) discussed in Chapter 1 provides an example of a study that uses thematic analysis. However, unlike several other strategies of qualitative data analysis, this is not an approach to analysis that has an identifiable heritage or a distinctive cluster of techniques. Indeed, the search for themes is an activity that can be discerned in most approaches to qualitative data analysis, such as grounded theory, critical discourse analysis (see Chapter 22), qualitative content analysis (Chapter 23), and narrative analysis (Chapter 22). Also, for some writers a theme is more or less the same as a code, whereas for others it transcends any one code and is built up out of groups of codes. Key concept 24.1 provides some criteria for identifying what a theme is.

When searching for themes, Ryan and Bernard (2003) recommend looking for:

- *repetitions*—topics that recur again and again;
- *indigenous typologies or categories*—local expressions that are either unfamiliar or used in an unfamiliar way;
- *metaphors and analogies*—the ways in which participants represent their thoughts in terms of metaphors or analogies;
- *transitions*—the ways in which topics shift in transcripts and other materials;
- *similarities and differences*—exploring how interviewees might discuss a topic in different ways or differ from each other in certain ways, or exploring whole texts such as transcripts and asking how they differ;
- *linguistic connectors*—examining the use of words like 'because' or 'since', because such terms point to causal connections in the minds of participants;
- *missing data*—reflecting on what is *not* in the data by asking questions about what interviewees, for example, omit in their answers to questions;
- *theory-related material*—using social scientific concepts as a springboard for themes.

An emphasis on repetition is probably one of the most common criteria for establishing that a pattern within the data warrants being considered a theme. Repetition may refer to recurrence within a data source (for example, an interview transcript or document) or, as is more often the case, across data sources (for example, a corpus of interview transcripts or documents). However, repetition *per se* is an insufficient criterion for something to warrant being labelled a theme. Most importantly, it must be relevant to the investigation's research questions or research focus. In other words, simply because a large number of people who have been interviewed say much the same thing, this does not mean it warrants being considered a theme. The identification of a theme is a stage or two further on from coding data in terms of initial or open codes (Braun and Clarke 2006). In the research by Corley and Gioia (2004) discussed later in the chapter (Research in focus 24.5), themes were derived from 'first-order concepts'. Figure 24.3 shows how the theme 'Change in social referents' was derived from three

24.1 KEY CONCEPT
What is a theme?

In spite of its apparent frequency of use in the analysis of qualitative data (see main text), there are relatively few specifications of the processes involved in thematic analysis. This is changing (e.g. Ryan and Bernard 2003; Braun and Clarke 2006), but, even so, understandings of what constitutes a theme vary. By and large, we can say that a theme:

- is a category identified by the analyst through his/her data;
- relates to the analyst's research focus (and quite possibly the research questions);
- builds on codes identified in transcripts and/or field notes;
- provides the researcher with the basis for a theoretical understanding of his or her data that can make a theoretical contribution to the literature relating to the research focus.

first-order concepts. This process requires the researcher to reflect on the initial codes that have been generated and to gain a sense of the continuities and linkages between them (see Key concept 24.6).

While thematic analysis lacks clearly specified procedures, it is the flexibility of this analytical strategy—the fact that it can be used to analyse a wide variety of types of qualitative data and as part of a narrative, grounded theory, or critical discourse analytic approach—that accounts for its popularity.

STUDENT EXPERIENCE
Dealing with large amounts of unstructured data

Tom found that in one key respect his experience of doing a research project confirmed what he had been led to expect—the tendency for qualitative research to generate large amounts of textual data that are difficult to analyse systematically. 'All textbooks say, don't they, that inexperienced researchers are likely to collect too much data and then not be able to process it all or analyse it all properly and it's true! [*laughs*] It's true! I certainly found it hard to process the amount of stuff that I'd collected.'

Lucie had a similar experience.

It was really hard. It was probably the biggest part of my project. It just took me so long—the whole summer—because there was so much. I had to go through it all and try and look for the themes. I knew while I was doing it kind of what type of themes were emerging, so I went through the data looking for things to support that, but I had such a lot of data it was really difficult not to miss out anything and to try and get through all the data. It was really hard to pick out emerging themes—just going through the data was so difficult. At first I was a bit overwhelmed. I didn't really know how to do it. I hadn't carried out qualitative research before, so I didn't really know how to approach it that well. Eventually I broke it down into the different themes and talked about those and used the data as evidence that supported what I was trying to say. The interview data was really useful because I could quote from it and what people said was really useful. They said it better than I could have said it.

STUDENT EXPERIENCE
The experience of analysing qualitative data

The supervisors we spoke to said that sometimes students can end up describing the data rather than analysing it. However, students who have put more time and effort into studying research methods are better able to analyse qualitative data and explain how they have done this. This was also confirmed by several of the students we interviewed. When Anna got to the stage of analysing her qualitative interview data she used Dedoose, **http://www.dedoose.com/**, a software application that supports the analysis of qualitative text, photos, videos, and audio (see Chapter 25 on using computers in qualitative analysis).

The transcriptions were in a word document and I would upload them and just go through them line-by-line listening for different themes and highlighting anything that was possibly interesting or unusual. I did that a couple times for all the interviews using the themes to figure out what kind of stories are being told here. There was a lot in there, and when discussing the various aspects with my supervisor, I found I had to just put some aside.

She went on to explain: 'I was definitely finding things every time I went back that I didn't see maybe the first time. It took a long time to distil what was I actually seeing.' Anna's experience highlights the importance of investing time and effort in the analysis process. It is often at this point that the whole purpose of studying research methods suddenly starts to make sense.

Grounded theory

Grounded theory (see Key concept 24.2) is by far the most widely used framework for analysing qualitative data. The book that is the chief wellspring of the approach, *The Discovery of Grounded Theory: Strategies for Qualitative Research* by Barney G. Glaser and Anselm L. Strauss (published in 1967), must be one of the most widely cited books in the social sciences. However, providing a definitive account of this approach is by no means a straightforward matter, for the following reasons:

- Glaser and Strauss developed grounded theory along different paths after the publication of the above book. Glaser felt that the approach to grounded theory that Strauss was promoting (most notably in Strauss 1987 and Strauss and Corbin 1990) was too prescriptive and emphasized too much the development of concepts rather than of theories (Glaser 1992). However, because of the greater prominence of Strauss's writings, his version is largely the one followed in the exposition below. There is, however, considerable controversy about what grounded theory is and entails (Charmaz 2000).

- Straussian grounded theory has changed a great deal over the years. This is revealed in a constant addition to the tool chest of analytic devices that is revealed in his writings.

- Some writers have suggested that grounded theory is honoured more in the breach than in the observance, implying that claims are often made that grounded theory has been used but that evidence of this being the case is at best uncertain (Bryman 1988a: 85, 91; Locke 1996; Charmaz 2000). Sometimes the term is used simply to imply that the analyst has grounded his or her theory in data. Grounded theory is more than this and refers to a set of procedures that are described in this section. Referencing academic publications is

often part of a tactic of persuading readers of the legitimacy of one's work (Gilbert 1977), and this process can be discerned in researchers' claims to have used grounded theory. Alternatively, researchers sometimes appear to have used just one or two features of grounded theory but refer without qualification to their having used the approach (Locke 1996).

Against such a background, writing about the essential elements of grounded theory is not an easy matter. It is not going to be possible to describe here grounded theory in all its facets; instead, its main features will be outlined. In organizing this discussion, we find it helpful to distinguish between *tools* and *outcomes* in grounded theory.

Tools of grounded theory

Some of the tools of grounded theory have been referred to in previous chapters. The locations of relevant discussions in this book are indicated in the list that follows.

- *Theoretical sampling*: see Key concept 18.3.

- *Coding*: the key process in grounded theory, whereby data are broken down into component parts, which are given names. It begins soon after the collection of initial data. As Charmaz (2000: 515) puts it: 'We grounded theorists code our emerging data as we collect it … Unlike quantitative research that requires data to fit into *preconceived* standardized codes, the researcher's interpretations of data shape his or her emergent codes in grounded theory' (emphasis in original). In grounded theory, different types or levels of coding are recognized (see Key concept 24.3).

- *Theoretical saturation*: see Key concept 18.4. Theoretical saturation is a process that relates to two phases in grounded theory: the coding of data (implying that

24.2 KEY CONCEPT
What is grounded theory?

In its most recent incarnation, grounded theory has been defined as 'theory that was derived from data, systematically gathered and analysed through the research process. In this method, data collection, analysis, and eventual theory stand in close relationship to one another' (Strauss and Corbin 1998: 12). Thus, two central features of grounded theory are that it is concerned with the development of theory out of data *and* that the approach is *iterative*, or *recursive*, as it is sometimes called, meaning that data collection and analysis proceed in tandem, repeatedly referring back to each other.

you reach a point where there is no further point in reviewing your data to see how well they fit with your concepts or categories) and the collection of data (implying that, once a concept or category has been developed, you may wish to continue collecting data to determine its nature and operation but then reach a point where new data are no longer illuminating the concept).

- *Constant comparison*: an aspect of grounded theory that was prominent in Glaser and Strauss (1967) and that is often referred to as a significant phase by practitioners, but that seems to be an implicit, rather than an explicit, element in more recent writings. Constant comparison refers to a process of maintaining a close connection between data and conceptualization, so that the correspondence between concepts and categories with their indicators is not lost. More specifically, attention to the procedure of constant comparison enjoins the researcher constantly to compare phenomena being coded under a certain category so that a theoretical elaboration of that category can begin to emerge. Glaser and Strauss advised writing a memo (see below) on the category after a few phenomena had been coded. It also entails being sensitive to contrasts between the categories that are emerging.

Outcomes of grounded theory

The following are the products of different phases of grounded theory.

- *Concept(s)*—refers to labels given to discrete phenomena; concepts are referred to as the 'building blocks of theory' (Strauss and Corbin 1998: 101). The value of concepts is determined by their usefulness or utility. One criterion for deciding whether a concept is useful is that a useful concept will typically be found frequently, and members of the organization under study will be able to recognize it and relate it to their experiences. Concepts are produced through *open coding* (see Key concept 24.3). Concepts can be recorded using incidents in the data as examples to illustrate and remind the researcher of the type of data to be coded under them (see Research in focus 24.4 and Figure 24.3).

- *Category, categories*—a concept that has been elaborated so that it is regarded as representing real-world phenomena. A category may subsume two or more concepts. As such, categories are at a higher level of abstraction than concepts. A category may become a

core category around which the other categories pivot (see Key concept 24.3). The number of core categories may, in fact, be relatively few. For example, Martin and Turner (1986) give an example of one study in which from a large dataset and an initial 100 concepts, fewer than 40 of these proved to be very useful and only 10 provided the basis for the final analysis.

- *Properties*: attributes or aspects of a category.

- *Hypotheses*: initial hunches about relationships between concepts.

- *Theory*: according to Strauss and Corbin (1998: 22), 'a set of well-developed categories … that are systematically related through statements of relationship to form a theoretical framework that explains some relevant social … or other phenomenon'. Since the inception of grounded theory, writings have pointed to two types or levels of theory: *substantive theory* and *formal theory*. The former relates to theory in a certain empirical instance or substantive area, such as occupational socialization. A formal theory is at a higher level of abstraction and has a wider range of applicability to several substantive areas, such as socialization in a number of spheres, suggesting that higher-level processes are at work. The generation of formal theory requires data collection in contrasting settings.

The different elements of the grounded theory process are portrayed in Figure 24.2. As with all diagrams, this is a representation, and it is particularly so in the case of grounded theory, because the existence of different versions of the approach does not readily permit a definitive rendition. Also, it is difficult to get across diagrammatically the iterative nature of grounded theory—in particular, its commitment to the idea that data collection and analysis occur in parallel. This is partly achieved in the diagram through the presence of arrows pointing in both directions in relation to certain steps. The figure suggests the following process.

- The researcher begins with a general research question (step 1).

- Relevant people and/or incidents are theoretically sampled (step 2).

- Relevant data are collected (step 3).

- Data are coded (step 4), which at the level of open coding may generate concepts (step 4a).

- There is a constant movement backwards and forwards between the first four steps, so that early coding suggests the need for new data, which results in the need to sample theoretically, and so on.

24.3 KEY CONCEPT
Coding in grounded theory

Coding is one of the most central processes in grounded theory. It entails reviewing transcripts and/or field notes and giving labels (names) to component parts that seem to be of potential theoretical significance and/or that appear to be particularly salient within the social worlds of those being studied. As Charmaz (1983: 186) puts it: 'Codes … serve as shorthand devices to *label*, *separate*, *compile*, and *organize* data' (emphases in original). Coding is a somewhat different process from coding in relation to quantitative data, such as survey data. With the latter, coding is more or less solely a way of managing data, whereas in grounded theory, and indeed in approaches to qualitative data analysis that do not subscribe to the grounded theory approach, it is an important first step in the generation of theory. Coding in grounded theory is also somewhat more tentative than in relation to the generation of quantitative data, where there is a tendency to think of data and codes as very fixed. Coding in qualitative data analysis tends to be in a constant state of potential revision and fluidity. The data are treated as potential indicators of concepts and the indicators are *constantly compared* (see under 'Tools of grounded theory') for concepts they best fit with. As Strauss (1987: 25) put it: 'Many indicators (behavioral actions/events) are examined comparatively by the analyst who then "codes" them, naming them as indicators of a class of events/behavioral actions.'

Strauss and Corbin (1990), drawing on their grounded theory approach, distinguish between three types of coding practice:

- **Open coding**: 'the process of breaking down, examining, comparing, conceptualizing and categorizing data' (1990: 61); this process of coding yields concepts, which are later to be grouped and turned into categories.

- **Axial coding**: 'a set of procedures whereby data are put back together in new ways after open coding, by making connections between categories' (1990: 96). This is done by linking codes to contexts, to consequences, to patterns of interaction, and to causes.

- **Selective coding**: 'the procedure of selecting the core category, systematically relating it to other categories, validating those relationships, and filling in categories that need further refinement and development' (1990: 116). A core category is the central issue or focus around which all other categories are integrated. It is what Strauss and Corbin call the storyline that frames your account.

The three types of coding are really different *levels* of coding, and each relates to a different point in the elaboration of categories in grounded theory.

24.4 RESEARCH IN FOCUS
Categories in grounded theory

Prasad (1993) used techniques of grounded theory to analyse the vast quantity of field notes and interview transcripts that were generated by her study (see Chapter 20). She identified important *concepts* in the data, and accumulated incidents, events, or pieces of conversation—*elements*—that related to a particular concept. She then grouped the elements together (see Figure 24.1) under a meaningful *label*. The initial aim of labels was to find a level of abstraction that was high enough to avoid creating too many new concepts but low enough to ensure that each concept accurately represented a phenomenon.

Maintaining these concepts was an iterative process that began early in the research process. New concepts were generated, and further elements were added to them as more data were collected. Prasad then scanned the concepts for relationships between them. She states that this led to the development of new second-order concepts that helped her to further develop her analysis.

FIGURE 24.1

Elements used by Prasad (1993) to identify the label 'organizational turmoil' related to work computerization

Data source	Organization member	Incident, quotation, opinion, event
Field notes No. 7, p. 3	Project manager	Discussing possible resistance to computers: 'Yes . . . we have got to pull out all our weapons to fight this thing out. But until we win . . . It's going to mean confusion.'
Interview No. 8, p. 23	Receptionist	Describing the first two weeks of computerization: 'What I hated was the anger and, well, the confusion. It was almost like my divorce all over again . . . blaming each other and mistakes every minute.'
Field notes No. 33, p. 24	Nurse supervisor	Official memo to trainers: 'We need to be well prepared for the next few weeks of chaos. Even the people you work with will not seem the same any more.'
Interview No. 24, pp. 8–9	Senior manager	'I finally know what army generals feel like . . . that's exactly what it was like. Fighting people all the time . . . the girls, the nurses, Joe, and the big brass at Paragon . . . and not knowing where the next attack would come from.'

Source: adapted from Prasad (1993).

- Through a constant comparison of indicators and concepts (step 5), categories are generated (step 5*b*). The crucial issue is to ensure that there is a fit between indicators and concepts.

- Categories are saturated during the coding process (step 6).

- Relationships between categories are explored (step 7) in such a way that hypotheses about connections between categories emerge (step 7*a*).

- Further data are collected via theoretical sampling (steps 8 and 9).

- The collection of data is likely to be governed by the theoretical saturation principle (step 10) and by the testing of the emerging hypotheses (step 11), which leads to the specification of substantive theory (step 11*a*).

- The substantive theory is explored using grounded theory processes in relation to different settings from that in which it was generated (step 12), so that formal theory may be generated (step 12*a*). A formal theory will relate to more abstract categories, which are not specifically related to the research area in question.

Step 12 is relatively unusual in grounded theory, because researchers typically concentrate on a certain setting,

although the study described in Research in focus 24.5 did examine other settings to explore the emerging concepts. A further way in which formal theory can be generated is by using existing theory and research in comparable settings.

Concepts and categories are perhaps the key elements in grounded theory. Indeed, it is sometimes suggested that, as a qualitative data analysis strategy, it works better for generating categories than for generating theory (see Key concept 24.6 for an illustration of how this happens through first- and second-order analysis). In part, this may be because studies purporting to use the approach often generate grounded *concepts* rather than grounded theory as such. Concepts and categories are nonetheless at the heart of the approach, and key processes such as coding, theoretical sampling, and theoretical saturation are designed to guide their generation.

Memos

One aid to the generation of concepts and categories is the *memo*. Memos in grounded theory are notes that researchers might write for themselves and for those with whom they work concerning such elements of grounded theory as coding or concepts. They serve as reminders about what is meant by the terms being used and provide

FIGURE 24.2
Processes and outcomes in grounded theory

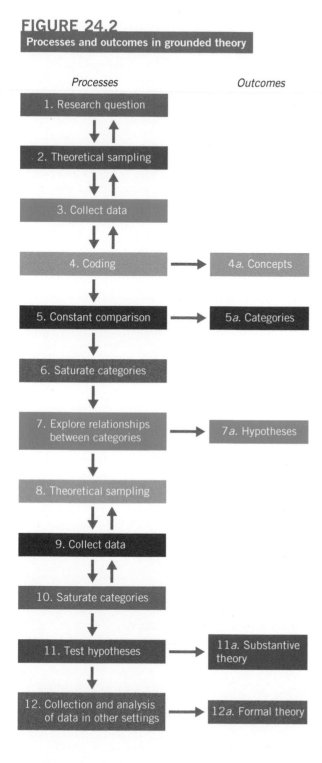

Processes   Outcomes

1. Research question
2. Theoretical sampling
3. Collect data
4. Coding → 4a. Concepts
5. Constant comparison → 5a. Categories
6. Saturate categories
7. Explore relationships between categories → 7a. Hypotheses
8. Theoretical sampling
9. Collect data
10. Saturate categories
11. Test hypotheses → 11a. Substantive theory
12. Collection and analysis of data in other settings → 12a. Formal theory

the building blocks for a certain amount of reflection. Memos are potentially very helpful to researchers in helping them to crystallize ideas and not to lose track of their thinking on various topics. An illustration of a memo from research in which Bryman was involved is provided in Research in focus 24.7.

Finding examples of grounded theory that reveal all its facets and stages is very difficult, and it is unsurprising that many expositions of grounded theory fall back on the original illustrations provided in Glaser and Strauss (1967). Many studies show some of its elements but not others. For example, Prasad's (1993) study of technological change (see Chapter 20, Research in focus 24.4, and Figure 24.1) incorporates some of the features of a grounded theory approach, such by keeping a record of coded concepts and using this to develop 'second-order' or core categories. However, other tools of grounded theory, such as memos, were not used in this study. Similarly, although Gersick (1994) used a grounded theory approach in her study of the effects of time on organizational adaptation, her coding was based partly on themes that she had been interested in prior to data collection, in addition to those that emerged during the interviews.

It is clear that grounded theory provides qualitative researchers with tools and potential resources that can be employed in the analysis of qualitative data as well as in the research process as a whole. Terms such as constant comparison, theoretical sampling, coding, theoretical saturation, memos, and so on have crept into the discourse of research method without carrying with them the implication that a full-blooded grounded theory study has been conducted. O'Reilly et al. (2012) have been critical of what they call the à la carte approach in which particular components of grounded theory are selected while others are ignored. They argue that this results in a number of problems: for example, a tendency for theoretical sampling not to be followed through properly, a tendency for the link between coding and data collection to become disrupted, and a tendency for coding not to be extended into the production of theory. However, it is also the case that grounded theory writers and researchers have produced a valuable set of techniques. It may be that picking just one or two of these does not make a genuine grounded theory study, but at the same time those techniques may be valuable to those researchers who do not see themselves as committed to a fully-fledged grounded theory. Also, following through on all the steps in a grounded theory study can be very demanding in terms of the time required, so even when the aim is to conduct a grounded theory study, certain compromises have to be made in some instances.

Criticisms of grounded theory

In spite of the frequency with which it is cited, and the frequent lip service paid to it, grounded theory is not without its limitations, which include the following:

24.5 RESEARCH IN FOCUS
A grounded theory approach in a study of a corporate spin-off

The research discussed here derives from a case study investigation of a corporate spin-off (referred to as 'Bozkinetic') from a large US company (referred to as 'Bozco') and the issue of how the organizational identity of the new organization changed in the course of the process of spinning it off. The findings are reported in Corley and Gioia (2004), and various aspects of the research methods used are discussed in Gioia et al. (2013). Data collection and analysis took place in three distinct stages—before, during, and following the spin-off—and entailed semi-structured interviewing, examination of written and electronic documents, and non-participant observation of employees as they went about their work and during key meetings. The qualitative data analysis followed a classic grounded theory sequence.

1. Open coding: preliminary concepts were identified (often based on *in vivo* language, i.e. language used in the data) from the data and grouped.

2. Axial coding: connections between the emergent themes were detected and grouped into higher-order conceptual categories.

3. Themes deriving from the axial coding were themselves grouped into theoretically fertile dimensions.

At the final stage, three 'aggregate' dimensions were proposed: triggers of identity ambiguity; change context; and leaders' responses to sense-giving imperative. We can take the first of these as an illustration.

Triggers of identity ambiguity were built up from three emergent themes derived at the axial coding stage referred to as 'change in social referents'; 'temporal identity discrepancies'; and 'construed external image discrepancies'. Each of these had been derived from an open coding process in which initial first-order concepts were identified. These were relatively low-level in terms of theoretical elaboration but nonetheless pulled together key motifs in the data. 'Change in social referents', for example, was derived from three first-order concepts that the researchers described as

- loss of parent company as direct (internal) comparison;

- shift in focus to comparisons with competitors;

- media attention shifts away from Bozco to industry (Gioia et al. 2013: 21).

For each of the three emergent themes that were derived from the axial coding process, Corley and Gioia (2004) provided representative quotations. For example, a quotation from an executive vice-president that was indicative of 'Change in social referents' was:

> I think that instead of getting hung up on the fact that you want to be different than (Bozko) you are supposed to be differentiating yourself from your competition. Who cares if you are different from (Bozco)?

> (Corley and Gioia 2004: 188)

This quotation relates particularly well to the first-order concept of 'loss of parent company as direct (internal) comparison'. Thus, we see a process in which the aggregate dimension 'triggers of identity ambiguity' is derived as outlined in Figure 24.3. This sequence shows a gradual building up of theoretical level from relatively simple concepts that are closely tied to the interviewees' words (first-order concepts), to a bringing together of elements that are common to the underlying first-order concepts into a higher level of theoretical abstraction (second-order theme), which is combined with the two other second-order themes to produce a theoretical concept that operates at a high level of abstraction. By combining the theoretical concepts that were developed ('change in social referents'; 'temporal identity discrepancies'; and 'construed external image discrepancies') and specifying the temporal connections between them, it was possible to build up a grounded theory of the process of organizational identity change (Corley and Gioia 2004: 185; Gioia et al. 2012: 23).

This analytical approach provides the basis for what has come to be referred to as the Gioia methodology (Gioia et al. 2013), in which second-order data analysis forms the basis for generation of theoretical models and concepts that are propositional and transferable, lending them to deductive testing through quantitative research (Key concept 24.6).

FIGURE 24.3
Producing a theoretical construct

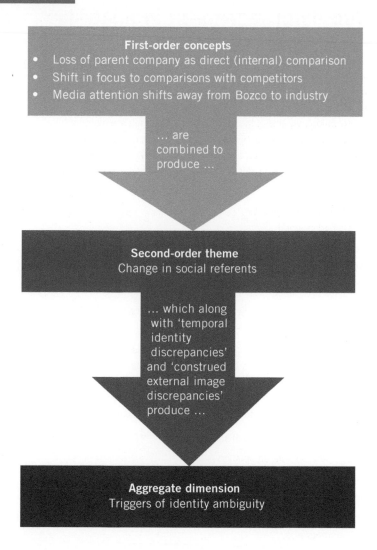

First-order concepts
- Loss of parent company as direct (internal) comparison
- Shift in focus to comparisons with competitors
- Media attention shifts away from Bozco to industry

... are combined to produce ...

Second-order theme
Change in social referents

... which along with 'temporal identity discrepancies' and 'construed external image discrepancies' produce ...

Aggregate dimension
Triggers of identity ambiguity

Source: based on Corley and Gioia (2004).

- Bulmer (1979) has questioned whether or not, as prescribed by the advocates of grounded theory, researchers can suspend their awareness of relevant theories or concepts until quite a late stage in the process of analysis. Business researchers are typically sensitive to the conceptual armoury of their disciplines, and it seems unlikely that this awareness can be put aside. Indeed, nowadays it is rarely accepted that theory-neutral observation is feasible. In other words, it is generally agreed that what we 'see' when we conduct research is conditioned by many factors, one of which is what we already know about the social world being studied (in terms both of social scientific conceptualizations and

as members of society). Also, many writers might take the view that it is desirable that researchers are sensitive to existing conceptualizations, so that their investigations are focused and can build upon the work of others.

- Related to this first point is the fact that, in many circumstances, researchers are required to spell out the possible implications of their planned investigation. For example, a lecturer making a bid for research funding or a student applying for funding for postgraduate research is usually required to demonstrate how his or her research will build upon what is already known or to demonstrate that he or she has a reasonably tightly

24.6 KEY CONCEPT
What is first- and second-order analysis?

Gioia et al. (2013) describe their approach to developing concepts and building theory through data which they have developed through their research practice over more than 20 years. This systematic process involves two levels or orders:

First-order analysis, using informant-centric terms and codes;

Second-order analysis, which develops researcher-centric concepts, themes and dimensions.

While this distinction bears close relation to grounded theory—first-order analysis sharing many characteristics with open coding, and second-order analysis being closely related to the development of categories—the next stage involves developing the data into a 'data structure', a visual map illustrating the progression from raw data to terms and themes, which forces researchers to think about their data theoretically. This systematic approach enabled Gioia et al. to demonstrate the rigorous nature of their conceptual and theory development in a way which was convincing to reviewers less familiar with a qualitative approach. However, the first-/second-order distinction has now become so prevalent in business research that Gioia et al. suggest it may be being overused and treated as a template, as data structure formats from previously published work are simply reproduced. They caution against this 'cookbook' approach because it goes against the use of this methodology, which must be open to innovation in order to remain effective.

24.7 RESEARCH IN FOCUS
A memo

In a study of the bus industry that Bryman carried out with colleagues in the early 1990s (Bryman et al. 1996), they noticed that the managers they interviewed frequently referred to the notion that their companies had *inherited* features that derived from the running of those companies before deregulation. They often referred to the idea of inheriting characteristics that held them back in trying to meet the competitive environment they faced in the 1990s. As such, 'inheritance' is what Strauss (1987) calls an *in vivo code* (one that derives from the language of people in the social context being studied), rather than what he calls *sociologically constructed codes*, which are labels employing the analyst's own terminology. The following memo outlines the concept of inheritance, provides some illustrative quotations, and suggests some properties of the concept.

Memo for Inheritance

Inheritance: many of our interviewees suggest that they have inherited certain company traits and traditions from the period prior to deregulation (i.e. pre-1985). It is a term that many of them themselves employed to denote company attributes that are not of their choosing but have survived from the pre-deregulation period. The key point about inheritance is that the inherited elements are seen by our interviewees as hindering their ability to respond to the changing environment of the post-deregulation era.

Inherited features include:

- expensive and often inappropriate fleets of vehicles and depots;
- the survival of attitudes and behaviour patterns, particularly among bus drivers, which are seen as inappropriate to the new environment (for example, lack of concern for customer service) and which hinder service innovation;
- high wage rates associated with the pre-deregulation era; means that new competitors can enter the market while paying drivers lower wages.

Sample comments:

> We *inherited* a very high cost structure because of deregulation. 75% of our staff were paid in terms of conditions affected by [rates prior to deregulation].
>
> (Commercial Director, Company B)
>
> I suppose another major weakness is that we are very tied by conditions and practices we've *inherited*.
>
> (Commercial Director, Company G)
>
> We have what we've *inherited* and we now have a massive surplus of double decks … We have to go on operating those.
>
> (Managing Director, Company B).

Managing Director of Company E said the company had inherited staff who were steeped in pre-deregulation attitudes, which meant that 'we don't have a staff where the message is "the customer is number one". We don't have a staff where that is emblazoned on the hearts and minds of everyone, far from it.'

Pre/post-deregulation: interviewees make a contrast between the periods before and after deregulation to show how they have changed. This shows in a sense the *absence* of inherited features and their possible impact; it can also refer to how the impact of possibly inherited features was negated or offset. For example, X referring to the recent end of the three-week strike: 'there was no way we were going to give in to this sort of thing, this sort of blackmail. We just refused to move and the trade unions had never experienced that. It was all part of the change in culture following deregulation.'

Inheriting constraints: such as staff on high wage rates and with inappropriate attitudes.

Inheriting surplus capacity: such as too many buses or buses of the wrong size.

defined research question, something that is also frequently disdained in grounded theory.

- There are practical difficulties with grounded theory. The time taken to transcribe audio recordings of interviews, for example, can make it difficult for researchers, especially when they have tight deadlines, to carry out a genuine grounded theory analysis with its constant interplay of data collection and conceptualization.

- It is somewhat doubtful whether grounded theory in many instances really results in *theory*. As previously suggested, it provides a rigorous approach to the generation of concepts, but it is often difficult to see what theory, in the sense of an explanation of something, is being put forward. Moreover, in spite of the frequent lip service paid to the generation of formal theory, most grounded theories are substantive in character; in other words, they pertain to the specific social phenomenon being researched and not to a broader range of phenomena (though, of course, they *may* have such broader applicability).

- In spite of the large amount written on grounded theory, but perhaps because of the many subtle changes in its presentation, it is still vague on certain points, such as the difference between concepts and catego-

ries. For example, while Strauss and Corbin (1998: 73) refer to theoretical sampling as 'sampling on the basis of emerging *concepts*' (emphasis added), Charmaz (2000: 519) writes that it is used to 'develop our emerging *categories*' (emphasis added). The term 'categories' is increasingly being employed rather than 'concepts', but such inconsistent use of key terms is not helpful to people trying to understand the overall process.

- Grounded theory is very much associated with an approach to data analysis that invites researchers to fragment their data by coding the data into discrete chunks. However, in the eyes of some writers, this kind of activity results in a loss of a sense of context and of narrative flow (Coffey and Atkinson 1996), a point to which we will return below.

- The presence of competing accounts of the elements of grounded theory does not make it easy to characterize it or to establish how to use it. This situation has been made even more problematic by Charmaz's (2000) suggestion that most grounded theory is objectivist and that an alternative, constructionist (she calls it *constructivist*) approach is preferable. She argues that the grounded theory associated with Glaser, Strauss, and Corbin is objectivist in that it aims to uncover a reality that is external to social actors. She offers an alternative, constructionist version that 'assumes that people create and maintain meaningful worlds through dialectical processes of conferring meaning on their realities and acting within them … Thus, social reality does not exist independent of human action' (Charmaz 2000: 521). Such a position stands in contrast to earlier grounded theory texts that 'imply that categories and concepts inhere within the data, awaiting the researcher's discovery … Instead, a constructivist approach recognizes that the categories, concepts, and theoretical level of an analysis emerge from the researcher's interaction within the field and questions about the data' (Charmaz 2000: 522). One difficulty here is that the two meanings of constructionism referred to in Key concept 2.7 seem to be conflated. The first quotation refers to constructionism as an ontological position in relating to social objects and categories; the second is a reference to constructionism in relation to the nature of know-ledge of the social world. It is certainly fair to suggest that Glaser, Strauss, and Corbin in their various writings neglect the role of the researcher in the generation of knowledge, but it is not clear that they are indifferent to the notion that social reality exists independently of social actors. Strauss was, after all, the lead of the study referred to in Chapter 2 concerning the hospital as a negotiated order, which was used as an illustration of constructionism (Strauss et al. 1973). However, there is little doubt that there is considerable confusion currently about the nature of grounded theory. According to Partington (2000), there is little evidence of the successful application of Strauss and Corbin's (1990) grounded theory within management and business research. This is partly because of the greater difficulty in following this more prescriptive, proceduralized approach, which contrasts sharply with Glaser and Strauss's (1967) earlier emphasis on the development of insight based on open-minded sensitivity.

Nonetheless, grounded theory probably represents the most influential general strategy for conducting qualitative data analysis, though how far the approach is followed varies from study to study. Locke (2001) argues that grounded theory is particularly well suited to organizational research. She suggests that it is particularly good at the following.

- *Capturing complexity*: grounded theory is good at capturing the complexity of contexts as action unfolds.

- *Linking with practice*: grounded theory frequently facilitates an appreciation among organizational members of their situations. Such understanding can provide a helpful springboard for organizational action.

- *Facilitating theoretical work in substantive areas that have not been well researched by others*: as new forms of organizational or technological change emerge and become prominent in the business world, grounded theory is ideal for an open-ended research strategy that can then be employed for the generation of theory out of the resulting data.

- *Putting new life into well-established fields*: grounded theory can provide the basis for an alternative view of well-established fields, such as group effectiveness and leadership, through its open-ended approach to data collection followed by a rigorous approach to theoretical work.

In addition, many of grounded theory's core processes, such as coding, memos, and the very idea of allowing theoretical ideas to emerge out of one's data, have been hugely influential. Indeed, it is striking that one of the main developments in qualitative data analysis in recent years—computer-assisted qualitative data analysis—has implicitly promoted many of these processes, because the software programs have often been written with grounded theory in mind (Richards and Richards 1994; Lonkila 1995).

More on coding

Coding is the starting point for most forms of qualitative data analysis, including ethnography. The principles involved have been well developed by writers on grounded theory and others. The main considerations in developing codes, some of which are derived from Lofland and Lofland (1995), are as follows.

- Of what general category is this item of data an instance?
- What does this item of data represent?
- What is this item of data about?
- Of what topic is this item of data an instance?

- What question about a topic does this item of data suggest?
- What sort of answer to a question about a topic does this item of data imply?
- What is happening here?
- What are people doing?
- What do people say they are doing?
- What kind of event is going on?

Steps and considerations in coding

The following steps and considerations need to be borne in mind in preparation for and during coding.

- *Code as soon as possible*. It is well worth coding as you go along, as grounded theory suggests. This may sharpen your understanding of your data and help with theoretical sampling. Also, it may help to alleviate the feeling of being swamped by your data, which may happen if you defer analysis entirely until the end of the data collection period. At the very least, you should ensure that, if your data collection involves recording interviews, you begin transcription at a relatively early stage.
- *Read through your initial set of transcripts, field notes, documents, etc.*, without taking any notes or considering an interpretation; perhaps at the end jot down a few general notes about what struck you as especially interesting, important, or significant.
- *Do it again*. Read through your data again, but this time begin to make marginal notes about significant remarks or observations. Make as many as possible. Initially, they will be very basic—perhaps keywords used by your respondents, names that you give to themes in the data. When you do this you are *coding*—generating an index of terms that will help you to interpret and theorize in relation to your data.
- *Review your codes*. Begin to review your codes, possibly in relation to your transcripts. Are you using two or more words or phrases to describe the same phenomenon? If so, remove one of them. Do some of your codes relate to concepts and categories in the existing literature? If so, might it be sensible to use these instead? Can you see any connections between the codes? Is there some evidence that respondents believe that one thing tends to be associated with or caused by something else? If so, how do you characterize and therefore code these connections?
- *Consider more general theoretical ideas in relation to codes and data*. At this point, you should be beginning to generate some general theoretical ideas about your data. Try to outline connections between concepts and categories you are developing. Consider in more detail how they relate to the existing literature. Develop hypotheses about the linkages you are making and go back to your data to see if they can be confirmed.
- Remember that any one item or slice of data can and often should be coded in more than one way.
- *Do not worry about generating what seem to be too many codes*, at least in the early stages of your analysis; some will be fruitful and others will not—the important thing is to be as inventive and imaginative as possible; you can worry about tidying things up later.
- *Keep coding in perspective*. Do not equate coding with analysis. It is part of your analysis, albeit an important one. It is a mechanism for thinking about the meaning of your data *and* for reducing the vast amount of data that you are facing (Huberman and Miles 1994). Miles and Huberman (1984) have developed several techniques for the display of data that have been coded through content analysis as a way of overcoming the difficulty of representing the complexity of qualitative analysis. One of the most important of these is the matrix format, which identifies constructs along one axis and occurrences along the other. This technique introduces an element of quantification into the qualitative analysis by drawing attention to the frequency of occurrences in the data. Another data display mechanism described by Gersick (1994) in her study of a new business venture is the timeline; this is used to represent the company's history, including major events and decisions, the time period over which they were implemented, and the eventual outcome of the actions. Whatever data display techniques you use, you must still interpret your findings. This means attending to issues such as the significance of your coded material for the lives of the people you are studying, forging interconnections between codes, and reflecting on the overall importance of your findings for the research questions and the research literature that have driven your data collection.

Turning data into fragments

The coding of such materials as interview transcripts has typically entailed writing marginal notes on them and gradually refining those notes into codes. In this way, portions of transcripts become seen as belonging to certain names or labels. In the past, this process was accompanied by cutting and pasting in the literal sense of using

Coded data from the 'Collaborative Organisations' project

Below is an extract from a coded interview undertaken as part of the project that features in Chapter 25.

Organizer:	Oldbrook desperately needs it, but there isn't anywhere—no one picked up that. What the ladies who'd come from outside to Share Fair felt was that they hadn't been able to engage with the local community sufficiently to be able to hand it over. So they brought all their energy, there were inordinate amount of—they were very gratified that so many of their people had come over to support this thing, but that's not really the way it's supposed to work. So it was a bit of—and the reason for that was because I was running a BLE gathering at the same time and that was as a consequence of somebody not, kind of like, breaking their ankle and then deciding that wasn't the job for them and then … So there was a whole series of completely unrelated incidents, as life culminates in, right, well I'll just do a Share Fair and I'll do a gathering at the same time, right, so we're … So I was meeting two agendas and two sets of needs really which, in retrospect, was why I was so exhausted at the end of it! I was pushing against the tide, whereas I believe that what's going to happen in Essex is we're actually doing it because it's a Share Fair. If other BLEs want to come and join in that's great and they'll be encouraged, but it's not going to be run with that in mind. You've got natural leaders already in place and I'd say that Share Fair is not something that you can do, it isn't a big lunch. It isn't something that anyone can do. It's, you have to have access to some sort of venue, space, you have to have some sort of infrastructure, you have to have communication and network with a number of different community organizations, you need to have some kind of muscle just for the day and you need some experience of how you do this kind of stuff. You need PLI.	**Typical issues faced** **Lack of engagement** **Support from non-local organizations** **Changed plans** **Organization requirements** **Leader role** **Uniqueness of share fairs** **Organizing essentials**	**Decision-making factors** **Uncertainty** **Event identity** **Funds required** **Social capital**
Researcher:	What is that?		
Organizer:	Public Liability Insurance. So you need a certain set of resources before you start. I believe that once you've got that, once these good things become regular and once they become more well known then it will become easier for other people to adopt them, but at this instance I think you need … I need to push at open doors and I need the people who are doing that to also push at open doors. So that's why we're kind of develop—I'm going to be developing a pack with the people who are actually doing it. So they are keeping a **diary**, both H_* in St Lawrence and M_ and R_ in Stanford Le Hope. So they're going to be writing down what it is that they're doing and what it is that they're needing and then it's kind of like answering those questions we will hopefully put together a handbook.	**Organizing essentials** **Leader role** **Systematic reflections**	**Health and safety** **Enabling social capital** **Knowledge creation**

*Individuals referred to by single letter to ensure anonymity scissors and paste. It entailed cutting up one's transcripts into files of chunks of data, with each file representing a code. The process of cutting and pasting is useful for data retrieval, though it is always important to make sure that you have ways of identifying the origins of the chunk of text (for example, name, position, date). Word-processing programs allow this to be done in a way that does not rely on your cutting-and-pasting skills so much through the use of the 'find' function. Nowadays, computer-assisted qualitative data analysis software (CAQDAS) is increasingly used to perform these tasks (see Chapter 25).

As has been emphasized throughout this chapter, there is no one correct approach to coding your data. However, it is common to conceive of different types and levels of code (see Key concept 24.3). Tips and skills 'Coded data from the "Collaborative Organisations" project' shows an extract from an interview from the research conducted by Akash Puranik, a doctoral student at the Open University in the UK. Further details about this project are discussed in Chapter 25. The extract presented here illustrates the different levels of coding.

- The first level is basic or first-order coding. This involves identifying basic aspects of *how* the organizing happened. Examples include codes such as 'changed plans', 'typical issues faced', 'support from non-local organizations'. Such coding primarily extracts and summarizes what the interviewee has said. It is therefore unlikely to get us very far analytically.

- A second level of coding comprises a deeper awareness of the content. This is achieved by recoding, comparing, consolidating, and re-grouping the codes to generate concepts. In the example above, basic codes such as 'changed plans' and 'typical issues faced' were grouped together under 'decision-making factors'. Conversely, a single code, 'organizing essentials', was later split into two codes—'funds required' and 'social capital'. Figure 25.1 shows the different codes generated through this process of regrouping and consolidation.

- A final level of coding moves even further away from close association with what the interviewee says, towards a concern with broad analytic themes. This involves asking questions about the properties and interconnections between codes. Through this it becomes possible to see codes and concepts as dimensions of a broader phenomenon. This level of coding enables second-order analysis, as the basis for generating theory inductively from the data (see Key concept 24.6 and Research in focus 24.5).

As Coffey and Atkinson (1996) observe, codes should not be thought of purely as mechanisms for the fragmentation

and retrieval of text. In other words, they do more than simply manage the data you have gathered. For example, as will be shown in Chapter 25, in the 'Collaborative Organisations' project the code 'decision-making factors' came to be seen as a dimension of 'formalized aspects', which was contrasted with 'informal aspects', both of which were identified as dimensions of 'organizing process' (referred to Figure 25.1). In this way, we can begin to map more general or formal properties of concepts that are being developed. Finally, it is important to mention that narrative analysis (Chapter 22) was also used in this project to map timelines as well as organizational and individual narratives. In addition, the analytical themes were generated only after being contrasted with and validated through analysis of visual data collected. As this example highlights, qualitative analysis often involves the flexible use of some of the techniques associated with grounded theory in combination with aspects of other analytical approaches.

The critique of coding

One of the most common criticisms of the coding approach to qualitative data analysis is the possibility of losing the context of what is said. By picking chunks of text out of the context within which they appeared, such as a particular interview transcript, the social setting can be lost.

A second criticism of coding is that it results in a fragmentation of data, so that the narrative flow of what people say is lost (Coffey and Atkinson 1996). Marshall (1981) became concerned about the fragmentation of data that occurs as a result of coding themes when she came to analyse the data she had collected based on qualitative interviews with women managers. She writes:

> The next stage involves picking certain things out and putting them under some headings. I'm a bit unsure about this, because this seems to rob the individual case of its wholeness. So I have to compensate for parceling out little bits of a person and putting them under different categories and headings, and try to appreciate the wholeness of each person as well. (1981: 396).

Marshall's account is interesting because it suggests that the coding method of qualitative data analysis fragments data and that some forms of data or theoretical perspectives may be unsuitable for the coding method.

A third critique that has emerged in recent years in business research is associated with the application of a quantitative logic in qualitative research, by adding accuracy checks, reliability assessments, triangulation, and measures to enhance transparency (Cornelissen 2017). Some writers are concerned that qualitative business research is becoming increasingly similar to quantitative studies. The craft of analysis is an important aspect of what makes qualitative research distinctive. But, as Cornelissen notes, in the past decade there has been a shift towards 'factor-analytic' approaches. These approaches follow the principles of grounded theory but use them in a way which reduces large amounts of qualitative data to meaningful 'factors' which are suggested to be transferrable to other contexts. He suggests that this has led to a worrying decline in theorizing based on thick description and pattern description, which are central to qualitative research (see Chapter 17). Cornelissen is also critical of the 'Gioia methodology' (Key concept 24.6) because he suggests this analytical approach entails 'methodological slippage' in moving 'beyond the idiosyncrasies of a particular case' to 'produce transferable constructs and propositions' (Cornelissen 2017: 378).

The approaches to analyzing qualitative data discussed in this chapter must therefore be considered in conjunction with alternatives such as narrative analysis (see Chapter 22), discourse analysis (Chapter 23), and the life history approach (Chapter 20). Nonetheless, the coding method is likely to remain prominent, because of several factors: its widespread acceptance in business research; the influence of grounded theory and its associated techniques; and the growing use of computer software for qualitative data analysis, which encourages a coding approach (see Chapter 25).

Regardless of which analytical strategy you use, you cannot simply say: 'this is what my participants said and did—isn't that incredibly interesting?' While it may be interesting, your work can acquire significance only when you theorize in relation to it. Many qualitative researchers are wary of this—they worry that, in the process of interpretation and theorizing, they may fail to do justice to what they have seen and heard: that they may contaminate their participants' words and behaviour. This is a risk, but it has to be balanced against the fact that your findings acquire significance only when you have reflected on, interpreted, and theorized your data.

Secondary analysis of qualitative data

So far, this discussion of qualitative data analysis has been solely concerned with the analysis of data that the analyst has played a part in collecting. While the secondary analysis of quantitative data has been on the research agenda for many years (see Chapter 14), similar use of qualitative data has only more recently come to the fore. The general idea of secondary analysis was addressed in Key concept 14.1.

There is no obvious reason why qualitative data cannot be the focus of secondary analysis, though such data do present certain problems that are not fully shared by quantitative data. The possible grounds for conducting a secondary analysis are more or less the same as those associated with quantitative data (see Chapter 14). Some data archives include qualitative datasets (see Chapter 14 for a discussion of data archives). For example, Qualidata, an archival resource centre, was created in the UK in 1994. The centre is concerned with 'locating, assessing and documenting qualitative data and arranging their deposit in suitable public archive repositories' (Corti et al. 1995). Qualidata can be accessed via the UK Data Service's online catalogue, 'Discover', which provides a single point of access to data for social and economic researchers. It can be accessed via the home page: https://www. ukdataservice.ac.uk.

An example involving secondary analysis of qualitative data is provided by Savage (2005), who analysed field notes that had been collected by Goldthorpe et al. in the Affluent Worker studies in the early 1960s, which he accessed through the Qualidata archive. Savage argues that, although a huge amount of qualitative data was generated through the Affluent Worker studies, very little of this part of the research made its way into publication. Instead, the researchers focused on aspects of their data that could be quantified and consistently coded and 'a huge amount of evocative material was "left on the cutting room floor"' (Savage 2005: 932). Savage (2005) uses the field notes, which contain many verbatim quotes from respondent interviews, to argue that rereading the field notes with a contemporary understanding of issues of money, power, and status indicates that the respondents had different understandings of class from those of Goldthorpe et al. that the researchers did not pick up on, and this difference of understanding affected how the data were interpreted.

Qualidata's focus is on acquiring datasets created from research projects funded by the Economic and Social Research Council. This includes mixed methods (see Chapter 27) and purely qualitative studies. Qualidata acknowledges certain difficulties with the reuse of qualitative data, such as the difficulty of making settings and people anonymous and the ethical problems involved in such reuse associated with promises of confidentiality. Hammersley (1997) has suggested that reuse of qualitative data may be hindered by the secondary analyst's lack of an insider's understanding of the social context within which the data were produced. This possible difficulty may hinder the interpretation of data but would seem to be more of a problem with ethnographic field notes than with interview transcripts. Such problems even seem to affect researchers revisiting their own data many years after the original research had been carried out (Mauthner et al. 1998: 742). There are also distinctive ethical issues deriving from the fact that the original researcher(s) may not have obtained the consent of research participants for the analysis of data by others. This is a particular problem with qualitative data which invariably contains detailed accounts of contexts and people that can make it difficult to conceal their identities in the presentation of raw data (as opposed to publications, where such concealment is usually feasible). Nonetheless, in spite of certain practical difficulties, secondary analysis offers rich opportunities not least because of the tendency for qualitative research to generate large and rich datasets, which means much of the material remains under-explored.

Key concept 24.8 and Research in focus 24.9 illustrate meta-ethnography, which is an approach to secondary analysis. Rather than analysing data collected by others, this approach involves synthesizing the interpretations and explanations offered in other studies. This approach should not be confused with the approach used by Hodson (1996) (see Chapter 26) which involved the application of *quantitative* techniques to the analysis of a large number of ethnographic studies.

24.8 KEY CONCEPT
What is meta-ethnography?

Meta-ethnography is a method that is used to achieve interpretative synthesis of qualitative research and other secondary sources. It can be used to synthesize and analyse information about a phenomenon that has been extensively studied. However, in contrast to meta-analysis in quantitative research (Key concept 14.8 and Research in focus 14.9), meta-ethnography 'refers not to developing overarching generalizations but, rather, translations of qualitative studies into one another' (Noblit and Hare 1988: 25). Meta-ethnography involves a series of seven phases that overlap and repeat as the synthesis progresses.

1. *Getting started.* This involves the researcher in identifying an intellectual interest that the qualitative research might inform through the reading of interpretative accounts.

2. *Deciding what is relevant to the initial interest.* Unlike positivists, interpretative researchers are not concerned with developing an exhaustive list of studies that might be included in the review. Instead the primary intent is to determine what accounts are likely to be credible and interesting to the intended audience for the synthesis.

3. *Reading the studies.* This involves the detailed, repeated reading of the studies, rather than moving to analysis of their characteristics.

4. *Determining how the studies are related.* This stage entails 'putting together' the various studies by determining the relationships between them and the metaphors used within them.

5. *Translating the studies into one another.* This phase is concerned with interpreting the meaning of studies in relation to each other: are they directly comparable or 'reciprocal' translations; do they stand in opposition to each other as 'refutational' translations; or do they, taken together, represent a line of argument that is neither 'reciprocal' nor 'refutational'?

6. *Synthesizing translations.* The researcher compares the different translations and shows how they relate to each other. This may involve grouping them into different types.

7. *Expressing the synthesis.* This involves translating the synthesis into a form that can be comprehended by the audience for which it is intended.

Crucial to this is that the synthesis focuses on the interpretations and explanations offered by studies that are included, rather than on the data that these studies are based on.

24.9 RESEARCH IN FOCUS

A meta-ethnography of research on the experiences of people with common mental disorders when they return to work

Andersen et al. (2012) used meta-ethnography as a method for synthesizing qualitative research concerned with the experiences of employees with common mental disorders (CMD) when they return to work (RTW). The synthesis was guided by three research questions:

1. What kinds of opportunities and obstacles do employees with CMD experience in relation to RTW?

2. What is the nature of the RTW process that they experience?

3. What is an optimal RTW intervention from their perspective?

Using keywords associated with each of the three main concepts—mental health (e.g. mental illness, depression, stress), work status (e.g. employability, sick leave, returning to work), and method (e.g. semi-structured interview, qualitative method, **focus group**)—six different online databases were searched for the period 1995–2011. This stage led to the identification of 4072 articles. Articles were included if they met the following conditions: a qualitative research method was used; research questions addressed both RTW and CMD; and the research was undertaken from the perspective of people with CMD. The initial stage of identifying relevance produced 64 articles and these were then examined in greater detail, resulting in just eight relevant studies. These studies were appraised for quality using 17 of the 18 quality criteria employed by the UK National Centre for Social Research. The authors elected to include in their synthesis studies that were of least 'medium' quality, resulting in eight studies being included in the final dataset of articles. These eight studies then became the focus of *data extraction*, that is, the process of identifying and summarizing key elements in each investigation. This number may seem like a rather small sample to end up with given that the initial trawl produced over 4000 articles, but this is a common outcome. The initial trawl is based entirely on the identification of articles through keywords and combinations of keywords. When the abstracts of these articles are examined it becomes clear that a great many are not relevant to the research questions and have to be excluded. When the remaining articles are examined in even greater detail (i.e. the entire article is read), there is a further loss of articles due to lack of relevance. There is then often a further reduction if articles are appraised for quality and some are found to be of insufficient quality. In the case of the synthesis by Andersen et al., no articles fell below the criterion of medium quality that they established. If they had relied on only articles that were of at least high quality, only three studies would have been the focus of the meta-ethnography.

For the actual synthesis method, the authors write that they mainly employed 'reciprocal translation analysis' (step 5 in Key concept 24.8). This process entailed examining all the articles in detail and inductively identifying what Andersen et al. call 'first-order concepts' and then developing higher-level 'second-order key concepts' out of these. For example, one of the five second-order key concepts associated with the RTW was called 'accommodations and social support', which was made up of three first-order concepts: gradual RTW, accommodations, and social support. The authors show that three articles provided evidence of the first of these three first-order concepts, five articles provided evidence of the second, and four of the third. The articles were summarized in terms of the second-order key concepts. For example:

> The reviewed studies showed that reduced work hours alone were insufficient to secure RTW. Responsibilities and workload also needed to be increased gradually through relevant work accommodations (32, 36, 38, 39).
>
> (Andersen et al. 2012: 97–8)

The four numbers at the end of this quotation refer to the four studies that specifically identified that responsibilities and workload need to be increased gradually. The authors then describe their third-order interpretations of the findings from the second-order analysis. Andersen et al. arrive at two third-order interpretations of their examination of the key concepts: 'pre-illness conditions influence the RTW process' and an 'unfortunate lack of coordination between the different systems with which the employee is in contact during the RTW process' (Andersen et al. 2012: 100).

KEY POINTS

- Qualitative research frequently results in the accumulation of a large volume of rich, unstructured data.

- The analysis of qualitative data is not determined by codified rules in the same way as quantitative data analysis.

- There are different approaches to qualitative data analysis, of which thematic analysis and grounded theory are two of the most commonly used.

- Coding is a key process in most qualitative data analysis strategies, but it is sometimes criticized for fragmenting and decontextualizing data.

- Secondary analysis of qualitative data is becoming more prominent than in the past.

QUESTIONS FOR REVIEW

- What is meant by suggesting that qualitative data are an 'attractive nuisance'?

Strategies of qualitative data analysis

- What criteria can be used to identify themes, and how should you search for them in your data?

- What are the main tools and outcomes of grounded theory?

- What is the role of coding in grounded theory and what are the different types of coding?

- What is *in vivo* coding?

- What is the role of memos in grounded theory?

- Charmaz has written that theoretical sampling 'represents a defining property of grounded theory' (2000: 519). Why do you think she feels this is the case?

- What are the main criticisms of grounded theory?

More on coding

- Is coding associated solely with grounded theory?

- What are the main steps in coding?

- To what extent does coding result in excessive fragmentation of data?

- To what extent does narrative analysis provide an alternative to data fragmentation?

Secondary analysis of qualitative data

- How feasible is it for researchers to analyse qualitative data collected by another researcher?

ONLINE RESOURCES
www.oup.com/uk/brm5e/

Visit the Interactive Research Guide that accompanies this book to complete an exercise in qualitative data analysis.

COMPUTER-ASSISTED QUALITATIVE DATA ANALYSIS: USING NVIVO

CHAPTER OUTLINE

One of the most significant developments in qualitative research since the mid 1980s is the emergence of software designed to assist in the analysis of qualitative data. This software is often referred to as computer-assisted (or computer-aided) qualitative data analysis software (CAQDAS). CAQDAS removes the clerical tasks associated with the manual coding and retrieving of data. While there is no industry leader among the different programs, this chapter introduces NVivo, a widely-used CAQDAS package. This chapter explores:

- some of the debates about the desirability of CAQDAS;
- how to set up your research materials for analysis with NVivo;
- how to code using NVivo;
- how to retrieve coded data;
- how to create memos;
- basic operations in NVivo.

Introduction

One of the most notable developments in qualitative research has been the arrival of computer software that facilitates the analysis of qualitative data. Computer-assisted qualitative data analysis software, or CAQDAS as it is conventionally abbreviated, has been a growth area in terms of both the proliferation of programs that perform such analysis and the numbers of people using them. The term and its abbreviation were coined by Lee and Fielding (1991).

Most of the best-known programs are variations on the code-and-retrieve theme. This means that they allow the analyst to code text while working at the computer and to retrieve the coded text. Thus, if we code a large number of interviews, we can retrieve all those sequences of text to which a code (or combination of codes) was attached. This means that the computer takes over manual tasks associated with the coding process referred to in Chapter 24. Typically, the analyst would:

- go through a set of data marking sequences of text in terms of codes (coding);
- for each code, collect together all sequences of text coded in a particular way (retrieving).

The computer takes over the physical task of writing marginal codes, making photocopies of transcripts or field notes, cutting out all chunks of text relating to a code, and pasting them together. CAQDAS does not automatically do these things: the researcher must still interpret the data, code it, and then retrieve the data, but the computer takes over the manual processes involved (wielding scissors and pasting small pieces of paper together, for example).

Is CAQDAS like quantitative data analysis software?

One of the comments often made about CAQDAS is that it does not and cannot help with decisions about the coding of textual materials or about the interpretation of findings (Sprokkereef et al. 1995; Weitzman and Miles 1995). However, this situation is no different from quantitative data analysis software. In quantitative research, the investigator sets out the crucial concepts and ideas in advance rather than generating them out of his or her data. Also, it would be wrong to represent the use of quantitative data analysis software such as SPSS as purely mechanical: once the analyses have been conducted, it is still necessary to interpret them. Indeed, the choice of variables and the techniques of analysis are areas in which a considerable amount of interpretative expertise is required. Creativity is required in using both types of software.

No industry leader

With quantitative data analysis, SPSS is both widely known and widely used. It is not the only statistical software used by business researchers, but it is certainly dominant. It has competitors, but SPSS is the industry leader. The same is not true in the field of qualitative data analysis, in which there is no industry leader. Advice on alternative qualitative data analysis software can be found at onlineqda.hud.ac.uk/Which_software/what_packages_are_available/index.php.

Limited acceptance of CAQDAS

Unlike quantitative data analysis, in which the use of computer software is both widely accepted and to all intents and purposes a necessity, the use of CAQDAS is by no means universally embraced. There are several reasons for this.

- Some researchers are concerned that the ease with which coded text can be quantified, either within qualitative data analysis packages or by importing coded information into quantitative data analysis packages such as SPSS, will increase the likelihood of quantifying findings. They are concerned that this will lead to qualitative research becoming colonized by reliability and validity criteria applied in quantitative research (Hesse-Biber 1995).

- Weaver and Atkinson (1994) suggest that CAQDAS reinforces the tendency for the code-and-retrieve process that underpins most approaches to qualitative data analysis and that this leads to fragmentation of the textual materials on which researchers work. As a result, the narrative flow of interview transcripts and events recorded in field notes may be lost.

- The fragmentation process of coding text into chunks that are then retrieved and put together into groups of related fragments risks decontextualizing data (Buston 1997; Fielding and Lee 1998: 74). Having an awareness of context is crucial to many qualitative researchers, and the prospect of this element being marginalized is of concern to them.

- Catterall and Maclaran (1997) argue that CAQDAS is not very suitable for focus group data because the code-and-retrieve function tends to result in a failure to capture the communication between participants. Many writers view the interaction that occurs in focus groups as an important feature of the method (Kitzinger 1994).

- Stanley and Temple (1995) suggest that most of the necessary coding and retrieval features are achievable through word-processing software. They show how this can be accomplished using Microsoft Word. The advantage of using such software is that it does not require a lengthy period of getting acquainted with it.

- Researchers working in teams may experience difficulties in coordinating the coding of text when different people are involved in this activity (Sprokkereef et al. 1995).

- Coffey et al. (1996) have argued that the style of qualitative data analysis enshrined in most CAQDAS software (including NVivo) is resulting in the emergence of a new orthodoxy. This arises because these programs presume a certain style of analysis—one based on coding and retrieving text—that owes a great deal to grounded theory. Coffey et al. argue that the emergence of a new orthodoxy is inconsistent with the growing experimentation with a variety of representational modes in qualitative research.

On the other hand, several writers are enthusiastic about CAQDAS software on a variety of grounds.

- Most obviously, CAQDAS can make the coding and retrieval process faster and more efficient.

- CAQDAS offers new analytical opportunities. For example, Mangabeira (1995) has argued that the ability to relate coded text to what are often referred to as 'facesheet variables' (sociodemographic and personal information such as age, title of job, number of years in school education) offers new opportunities in the process of analysing data.

- CAQDAS can potentially enhance the transparency of the process of qualitative data analysis. It is often noted that the ways in which qualitative data are analysed are unclear in reports of findings (Bryman and Burgess 1994b). CAQDAS requires researchers to be more explicit about the process of analysis and provides an audit trail that can be easily referred to at a later stage.

- CAQDAS invites the analyst to think about codes that are developed in terms of 'trees' of interrelated ideas. This can be a useful, in that it urges the analyst to consider possible connections between codes.

- Writers including Silverman (1985) have commented on the tendency towards anecdotalism in qualitative research—that is, the tendency to use quotations from interview transcripts or field notes but with little sense of the prevalence of the phenomenon they are supposed to exemplify. CAQDAS offers the opportunity to count such things as the frequency with which a form of behaviour occurred or a viewpoint was expressed in interviews, although as noted previously, some qualitative researchers perceive risks in this.

- Sinkovics and Penz (2011) argue that CAQDAS supports greater structuring and systematization of the research process. Using an example of a study involving multilingual interviews, they suggest that CAQDAS helps in the management of multidimensional research teams, cultural context and language. They also suggest that CAQDAS encourages early, concrete decision-making around nodes (see Key concept 25.1) which aids synchronization and overall equivalence when dealing with varied and complex datasets.

- Paulus, Lester, and Britt (2013) suggest there are generational differences in researchers' attitudes to CAQDAS, particularly among senior researchers who lack exposure to CAQDAS. They show that introductory methods textbooks on qualitative research tend to frame the use of technology using a 'discourse of caution' rather than a 'discourse of possibility' (Paulus, Lester, and Britt 2013: 642) and focus more on limitations than potential advantages. They claim that this cautionary approach is based on an outdated understanding of what the software can and cannot do and they urge researchers to embrace new technological affordances.

So, should you use CAQDAS? If you have a very small dataset it may not be worth the time and effort to learn how to use new software. Another reason not to use CAQDAS is related to access; if you cannot access the software via a university licensing agreement, it may be too expensive for personal purchase. On the other hand, if you think you may use this or similar software in future, it may be worthwhile learning how to use it. You should bear in mind however, that while there is high awareness of CAQDAS among academic researchers, its use in commercial contexts may be quite low. For example, Rettie et al. (2008) conducted a questionnaire survey of UK market research companies and found that, while the majority of commercial market researchers were aware of the potential applications of CAQDAS, only 13 out of 153 respondents used it as a data analysis tool. There is further discussion of the pros and cons of CAQDAS at onlineqda.hud.ac.uk/Intro_CAQDAS/software_debates.php.

The rest of this chapter provides an introduction to NVivo using an example dataset. The dataset used is based on a qualitative study of 'organizational collaboration' carried out by Akash Puranik, a PhD student at the Open University. Akash's research explores how non-contractual, informal collaborations, set up with the intention of benefiting communities, are organized. One such collaboration, Share Fair, is the focus of the data analysis presented here. Share Fairs are an initiative developed by the UK educational charity and social enterprise The Eden Project in Cornwall. Participating organizations and individuals come together and set up a day-market where no money changes hands and people are encouraged to collaborate informally by sharing skills, stories, things, and community spirit.

Learning NVivo

This explanation of NVivo 11 and its functions addresses just its most basic features. There may be features not covered here that you would find useful in your own work, so it is worth taking some time to familiarise yourself with the program's capabilities. There is a good 'Help' facility and online tutorials are available.

As in Chapter 16, → signifies 'click once with the left-hand button of your mouse'—that is, select.

On opening NVivo, you will be presented with a welcome screen (see Plate 25.1). This screen shows

any existing NVivo projects on the left-hand side and is the springboard for either opening one of the existing projects or starting a new one. If you are starting a new project, as in the example that follows, → **File** → **New**. The **New Project** dialog box appears, and you are asked to provide a **Title** for your project. For this exercise, the title 'Collaborative Organisations' was chosen. You are also asked to give a **Description** of the project, but this is optional. When you have done this, → **OK**.

PLATE 25.1
The opening screen

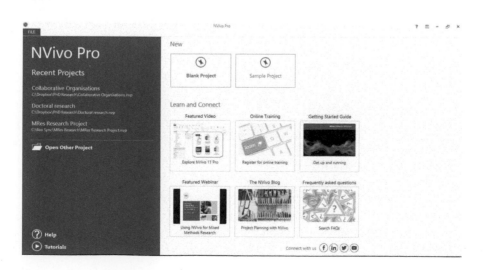

You then need to import the documents you want to code. In this case, the documents are various data collected from the Share Fair events. Within this project numerous kinds of documents such as field notes, unstructured and semi-structured interviews, participant reflections, brochures and pamphlets, emails, social media posts, photos, videos etc. were used. In addition to supporting data analysis, NVivo was helpful in organizing these diverse data sources. NVivo 11 can accept documents in a range of formats:

- rich text (.rtf, .txt)
- Word (.doc, .docx)
- portable document (.pdf)
- datasets (.xls, .xlsx)
- image (.bmp, .gif, .jpeg, .jpg, .png, .tif, .tiff)
- audio (.mp3, .m4a, .wma, .wav)
- video (.mpg, .mpeg, .mpe, .mp4, .avi, .wmv, .mov, .qt, .3gp, .mts, .mt2s)

Some of the audio and video formats might require codecs, computer programs that are used to encode or decode digital data, to run the files. Further information on this can be found at http://help-nv11.qsrinternational.com/desktop/deep_concepts/media_file_formats_supported_by_nvivo.htm.

To import the documents, → **Internals** (below **Sources** at the top of the **Navigation view**) → **DATA** tab on the **Ribbon** → **Documents** button on the **Find bar** [opens the **Import Internals** dialog box] → the documents to be imported (you can hold down the **Ctrl** key to select several documents, or if you want to select all of them hold down the **Ctrl** key and tap the **A** key) → **Open**. (See Plate 25.2 for the series of steps.) The documents will then be visible in the Document Viewer. Once the documents have been imported, they can be read and edited. All you need to do is double-click on the ▤ icon to the left of each interview in Viewer.

Coding

Coding your data is one of the key phases in the whole process of qualitative data analysis. For NVivo, coding is accomplished through *nodes* (see Key concept 25.1).

PLATE 25.2
Stages in importing documents into NVivo

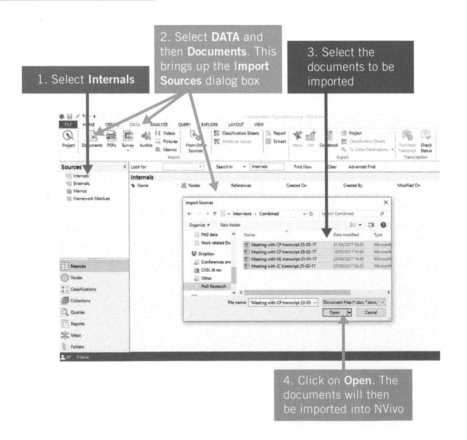

25.1 KEY CONCEPT
What is a node?

NVivo's Help system defines coding as 'a way of gathering all the references to a specific topic, theme, person or other entity'. This is accomplished by marking passages of text in a project's documents with nodes. Nodes are, therefore, the route by which coding is undertaken. A node is defined as 'a collection of references about a specific theme, place, person or other area of interest'. When a document has been coded, the node will incorporate references to those portions of documents in which the code appears. Once established, nodes can be changed or deleted.

There are several ways of going about the coding process in NVivo. The approach Akash took in relation to the coding of the Collaborative Organisations project was to follow these steps:

1. He read through the interviews in the Document Viewer several times (see Plate 25.3).

2. Through this initial reading, he highlighted parts of text that seemed interesting, worked out some codes that seemed relevant to the project, while taking notes using memos (see below)

3. He went back into the documents and coded them using NVivo.

An alternative strategy is to code while browsing the documents.

Creating nodes

Some of the nodes that Akash used are presented in Figure 25.1. In prior versions of NVivo, when creating a node, the researcher chose between creating a 'free node' or a 'tree node'. The latter is a node that is organized in a hierarchy of connected nodes, whereas free nodes were not organized in this way. This distinction was dropped in later editions, and the software now assumes that a hierarchically organized node is being created. (It is possible, though, for a node to be non-hierarchical or 'free': that is, neither a 'child' nor a 'parent' of another node.) Notice that there are two main groups of *hierarchically organized nodes* in the example 'tree' of nodes shown in Figure 25.1.

Nodes can be created in the following way.

FIGURE 25.1
Nodes used in the Collaborative Organisations project

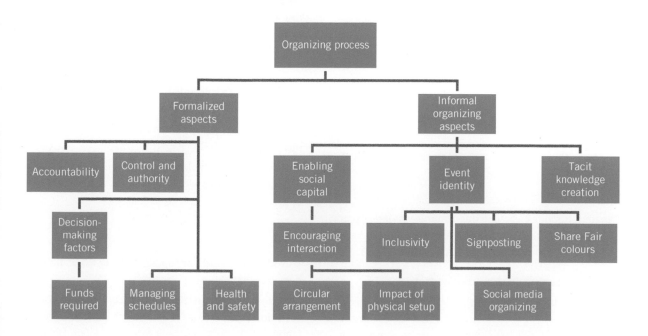

PLATE 25.3
The NVivo workspace

Ribbon contains the main Nvivo commands. The find bar changes when you select a different command

The Document Viewer and its components

Find bar – to search for items in your Nvivo project

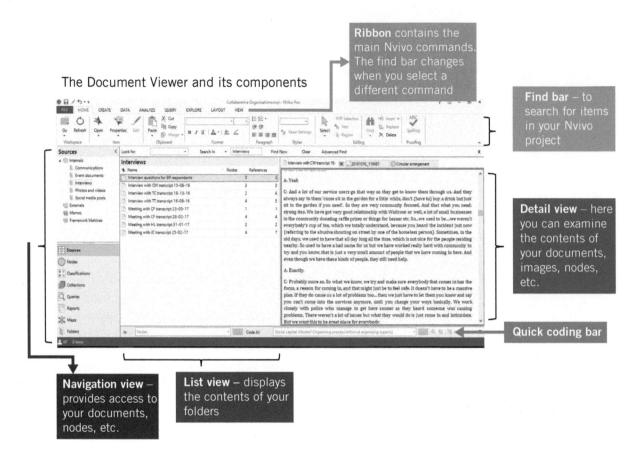

Detail view – here you can examine the contents of your documents, images, nodes, etc.

Quick coding bar

Navigation view – provides access to your documents, nodes, etc.

List view – displays the contents of your folders

Creating a non-hierarchically organized node

This sequence of steps demonstrates how to create a 'free' or non-hierarchically organized node for the concept of *'Accountability'*.

1. While in the **Document Viewer** [the term used to describe the general screen shown in Plate 25.3] → **CREATE** in the Ribbon

2. → **Node** in the **Find bar** [opens the **New Node** dialog box—see Plate 25.4]

3. Enter the node **Name** [*Accountability*] and a **Description** (this is optional)

4. → **OK**

Note that the node created in this example was later organized hierarchically. This particular project did not have any non-hierarchically organized nodes (free nodes).

Creating hierarchically organized nodes

To create a hierarchically organized node, the initial process is exactly the same as with a non-hierarchically organized node. We will explain how to create the hierarchically organized node *Funds required*, which is a child of the hierarchically organized node *Decision making factors*, which is itself a child of the hierarchically organized node *Formalised aspects* that is organized under the core node *Organising process* (see Figure 25.1). The following steps will generate this node.

1. While in the **Document Viewer** → **CREATE** in the Ribbon

2. → **Node** in the Find bar [opens the New Node dialog box—see Plate 25.5]

3. Enter the node Name [Organising process] and a Description (the latter is optional)

4. → OK

5. → Organising process in the list of nodes in the List viewer

6. → **Node** in the **Find bar** [opens the **New Node** dialog box—see Plate 25.5]

7. Enter the node **Name** [*Formalised aspects*] and a **Description** (the latter is optional). This node will form a child of the hierarchically organized node [make

PLATE 25.4
Stages in creating a non-hierarchically organized node

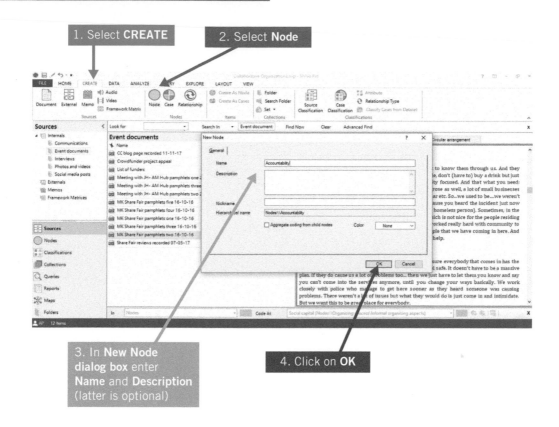

1. Select **CREATE**

2. Select **Node**

3. In **New Node** dialog box enter **Name** and **Description** (latter is optional)

4. Click on **OK**

sure that in Hierarchical name it reads *Nodes\\Organising process*, as this will mean it is a child of *Organising process*]. See Plate 25.5.

8. These steps should be repeated to create further child nodes as required for your project. Ensure that you select the parent node in each step before clicking on Node in Find bar to create the new node as a child of previous node. In this example, the hierarchically organized nodes 'Organising process—Formalised aspects—Decision making factors—Funds required' were created. See Plate 25.5.

Applying nodes in coding text

Coding is carried out by applying nodes to segments of text. Once you have set up some nodes (and do remember you can add and alter them at any time), assuming that you are looking at a document in the viewer, you can highlight the area of the document that you want to code and then right-click on the mouse while holding the cursor over the highlighted text. Then, → **Code** This opens the **Select Code Items** dialog box. This dialog box can be

used to select the node at which you want to the text to be coded, as well as for creating a new node.

If the code you want to use has been created, one of the easiest ways of coding in NVivo is to drag and drop text into an existing code (see Plate 25.6). To do this, highlight the text to be coded and then, holding down the left-hand button, drag the text over to the appropriate node in the **List view**.

Another way is to right click over the highlighted text and then → **Code** which opens the **Select Code Items** dialog box. You can then select the appropriate nodes and → **OK**. If you want to use a hierarchically organized code you would need to find the appropriate parent in the list and click the small arrow to the left of it. Multiple nodes can be selected by using **Ctrl** key.

One more way is to highlight the text you want to code is by using the **Quick coding bar** (see Plate 25.3). To do this, highlight the text to be coded and then click the **Quick coding button** (see Plate 25.7). Tick the node(s) you want to use and → **OK**. It is important to finalize this coding by → the button with blue tick ⟐. Thus, in the example in Plate 25.7, the tick by *Social media*

PLATE 25.5
Stages in creating a hierarchically organized node

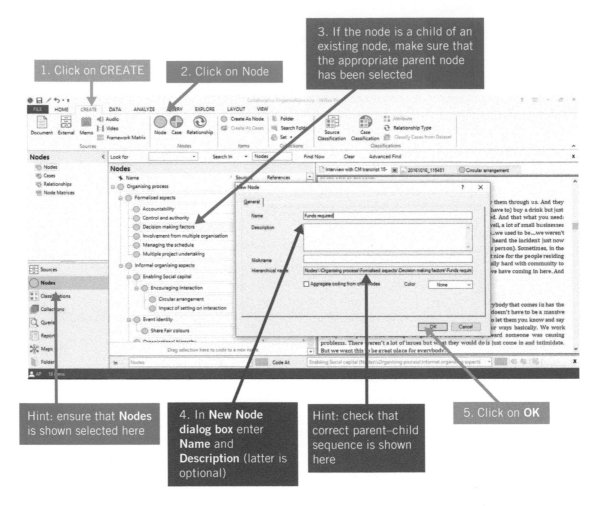

1. Click on CREATE

2. Click on Node

3. If the node is a child of an existing node, make sure that the appropriate parent node has been selected

Hint: ensure that **Nodes** is shown selected here

4. In New Node dialog box enter **Name** and **Description** (latter is optional)

Hint: check that correct parent–child sequence is shown here

5. Click on OK

organising and Enabling social capital will select these nodes for coding the highlighted text at them. If you want to use a hierarchically organized node, you would need to find the appropriate parent in the list of nodes within the List view and then click on the plus to the left of it. To *uncode* at any point, simply highlight the passage to be uncoded, and → the button with a red cross in it in the **Quick coding bar** (see Plate 25.3). Alternatively, right-click on the highlighted text and → **Uncode**.

Applying nodes in coding data in other formats

In the Collaborative Organisations project, besides the interview and reflection notes, which were transcribed in Word document format, various other forms of data were analysed. As discussed before, NVivo can be a useful tool to organize these data. Now we will look at how coding can be applied to some other forms of data such as images and PDF documents.

Images can be coded in NVivo using the region selection function in the coding process. To use this, double-click the image to be coded; this will open the image in the **Detail View** in **Document Viewer** (see Plate 25.3). Hover the mouse over to the area to be coded, keep the mouse button clicked and drag across to make the selection (see Plate 25.8). The selected area can be coded using the buttons in the **Quick coding area** or by right clicking on the area and → **Code**. The instructions in the previous section for coding text are equally applicable to the images after the area selection is made.

PDF files are rather unusual as NVivo allows for both text and region selection for coding, depending upon the permissions and the type of file. For example, in the Collaborative Organisations project, brochures and pamphlets used to promote events were *scanned* and stored as PDF files. These were treated in the same way as images because the underlying document text could

PLATE 25.6

Using drag and drop to code

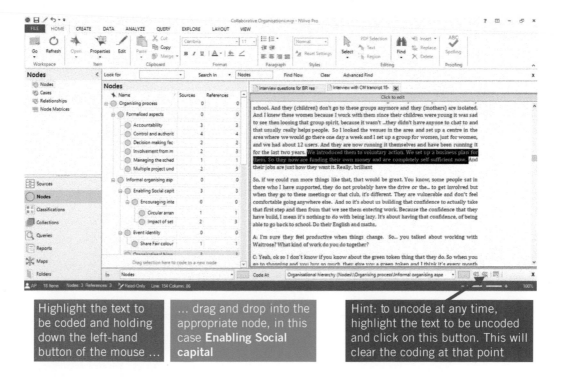

Highlight the text to be coded and holding down the left-hand button of the mouse …

… drag and drop into the appropriate node, in this case **Enabling Social capital**

Hint: to uncode at any time, highlight the text to be uncoded and click on this button. This will clear the coding at that point

PLATE 25.7

Using the Quick coding bar to code

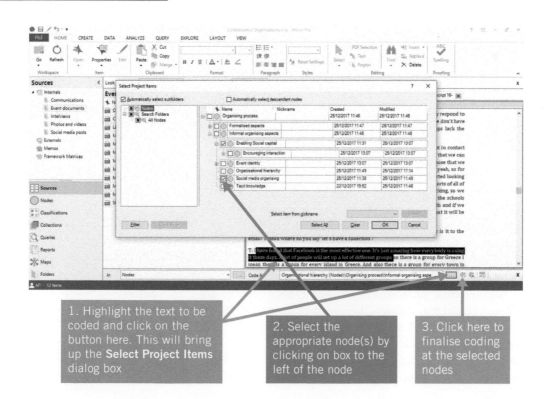

1. Highlight the text to be coded and click on the button here. This will bring up the **Select Project Items** dialog box

2. Select the appropriate node(s) by clicking on box to the left of the node

3. Click here to finalise coding at the selected nodes

PLATE 25.8
Coding images in NVivo

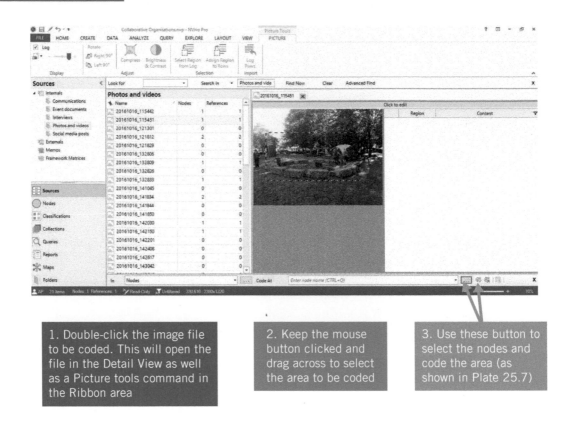

1. Double-click the image file to be coded. This will open the file in the Detail View as well as a Picture tools command in the Ribbon area

2. Keep the mouse button clicked and drag across to select the area to be coded

3. Use these button to select the nodes and code the area (as shown in Plate 25.7)

PLATE 25.9
Text and region selection for a PDF file

Both the Text and Region selection functions are available for some PDF files

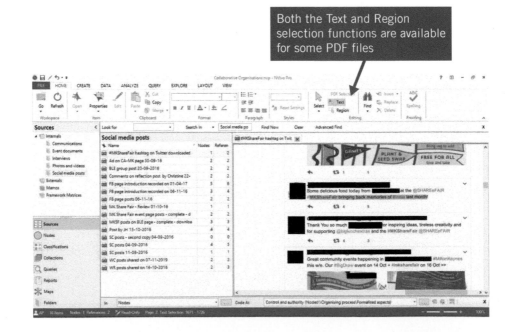

PLATE 25.10
Coding stripes

not be accessed. Social media posts related to the events were also *saved* as PDF files (if using Chrome as web browser this can be done by using the print command—**Ctrl** key pressed together with **P** key—when browsing social media pages; in the resulting page you can click on **Change** under the printer name and the dialog box gives you the option to **Save as PDF**). Saving them as PDF files allows for text selection as well as region selection (see

Plate 25.9). As social media posts consisted of textual as well as pictorial data, this enables flexibility in coding.

Coding stripes

It is helpful to be able to see the data that have been coded and the nodes applied to them. NVivo has a useful aid to this called *coding stripes*. Selecting this facility allows you to see multicoloured stripes that represent

PLATE 25.11
Searching for text that has been coded under a particular node

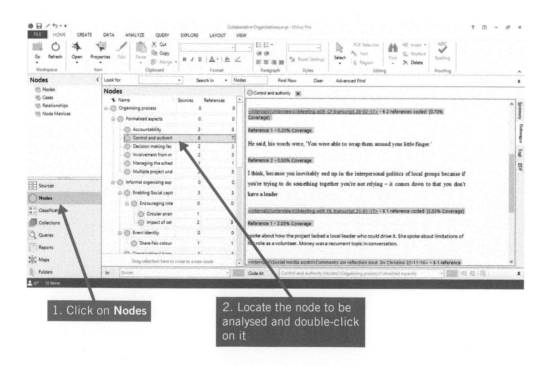

1. Click on **Nodes**

2. Locate the node to be analysed and double-click on it

PLATE 25.12

Searching for the intersection of two nodes using the Coding Query dialog box

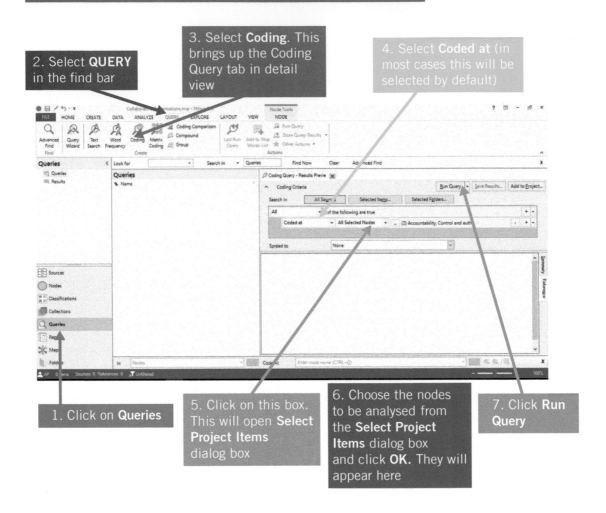

2. Select **QUERY** in the find bar

3. Select **Coding**. This brings up the Coding Query tab in detail view

4. Select **Coded at** (in most cases this will be selected by default)

1. Click on **Queries**

5. Click on this box. This will open **Select Project Items** dialog box

6. Choose the nodes to be analysed from the **Select Project Items** dialog box and click **OK.** They will appear here

7. Click **Run Query**

portions of coded data and the nodes used. Overlapping codes do not represent a problem.

To activate coding stripes → **VIEW** in the **Ribbon** and then → **Coding Stripes** in the **Find** bar → **Nodes Recently Coding**. Plate 25.10 shows these stripes. We can see that some segments have been coded at two or more nodes—such as *Tacit knowledge*, *accountability*, and *Enabling social capital*. All the nodes that have been used are clearly displayed.

Searching data

Once you have done some coding, however preliminary, you will want to conduct searches of your data. For example, you may want to retrieve all occurrences of a particular node. NVivo allows you to trawl through all your documents so you end up with all the data that

was coded at a particular node. This is very easy to do in NVivo.

To search for occurrences of a single node

These steps describe how to conduct a search for sequences of text that have been coded using the node *Control and authority*. The stages are outlined in Plate 25.11.

1. In the **Document Viewer** → **Nodes** in the **Navigation view**. This will bring up your list of nodes in the **List view**.

2. If you cannot find the parents of *Control and authority* → on the little box with a + sign ⊞ to the left of *Organising process* [this brings up a list of all branches of the node *Organising process*].

PLATE 25.13
Searching for specific text using the Find Content dialog box

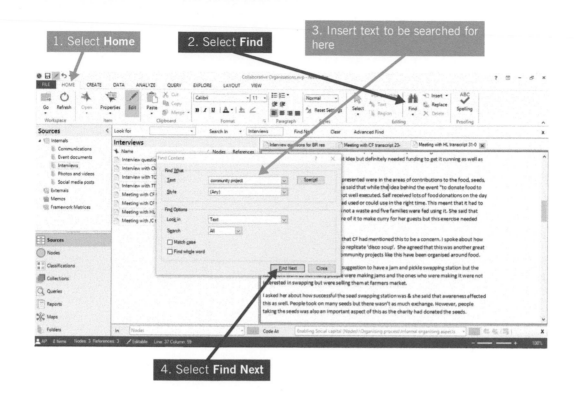

1. Select **Home**

2. Select **Find**

3. Insert text to be searched for here

4. Select **Find Next**

3. → on the + sign ⊞ to the left of *Formalised aspects* [this brings up a list of all branches of the node *Formalised aspects*].

4. Double-click on *Control and authority*.

5. All instances of coded text at the node *Control and authority* will appear at the bottom of the screen, as in Plate 25.11.

To search for text coded in terms of a free node, the process is simpler, in that you simply double-click on the relevant **Free Node** to generate all the text coded at that node. The regions coded for images and PDF files will also show in the detail view but in the form of coordinates of the region. However, in this case a separate tab is added to the right-hand edge of the detail view. By clicking on the appropriate tab (*Images* or *PDF*) you will be able to see the specific regions that are coded.

To search for the intersection of two nodes

This section is concerned with searching for sequences of text that have been coded at two nodes: *Accountability* and *Control and authority*. This type of search is known

as a 'Boolean search'. It will locate text coded in terms of the two nodes together (that is, where they intersect), *not* text coded in terms of each of the two nodes. The following steps need to be followed:

1. In the **Document Viewer** → **Queries** in the **Navigation view**

2. → **Query** on the **Find** bar

3. → 🔍 [opens the **Coding Query** tab in Detail View as in Plate 25.12]

4. Ensure **Coded at** is selected in search options; in most cases, this will be the default option

5. → ⋯ and then select the two nodes to be analysed from the **Select Project Items** dialog box

6. Once the nodes have been selected, → **OK**

7. → **Run Query**

To search for specific text

NVivo can also perform searches for specific words or phrases, often referred to as 'strings'. For example, to

PLATE 25.14
Stages in creating a memo

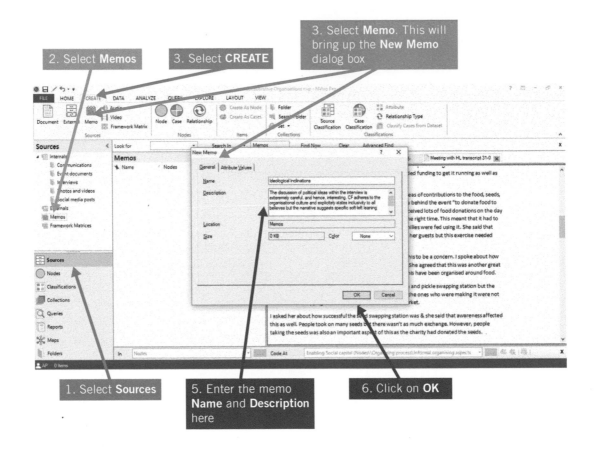

2. Select **Memos**

3. Select **CREATE**

3. Select **Memo**. This will bring up the **New Memo** dialog box

1. Select **Sources**

5. Enter the memo **Name** and **Description** here

6. Click on **OK**

search for the phrase '*community project*', the following steps need to be taken:

1. → **Home** on the **Ribbon**

2. → [image: Find] [opens the Find Content dialog box in Plate 25.13]

3. Insert *community project* to the right of **Text**

4. To the right of **Look in**, make sure **Text** has been selected

5. → **Find Next**

Text searching can be useful for the identification of possible *in vivo* codes (see Chapter 24). You would then need to go back to the documents to create nodes to allow you to code using *in vivo* language.

Output

To find the results of coding at a particular node, → use the **Nodes** button in the bottom left. This will bring up your node structure. Find the node that you are interested in and simply double-click on that node. This will bring up all text coded at that node along with information about which interview(s) the text comes from.

Memos

In Chapter 24, it was noted that one feature of the grounded theory approach to qualitative data analysis is the use of memos in which ideas and illustrations might be stored. Memos can be easily created in NVivo using the following steps, which are outlined in Plate 25.14:

1. In the **Navigation View** → **Sources**

2. Under **Sources** → **Memos**

3. → **Create** tab on the **Find bar** and then

4. → **Memo** [opens the **New Memo** dialog box shown in Plate 25.14]

5. To the right of **Name**, type in a name for the memo (e.g. *Ideological inclinations*)—you can also provide

a brief description of the document in the window to the right of Description, as in Plate 25.14

6. → **OK**

Saving an NVivo project

When you have finished working on your data, you will need to save it for future use. To do this, on the menu bar at the top, → **File** → **Save**. This will save all the work you

have done. You will then be given the opportunity to exit NVivo or to create or open a project without worrying about losing all your hard work.

Opening an existing NVivo project

To retrieve a project you have created, at the Welcome screen, → **File** → **Open**. This opens the **Open Project** dialog box. Search for and then select the project you want to work on. Then → **Open**.

Final thoughts

As with the chapter on SPSS (Chapter 16), a short chapter such as this can provide help only with the most basic features of the software. In so doing, we hope that it will have given students who may be uncertain about whether CAQDAS is for them an impression of what the software is like and a sense of its capabilities. Some readers may decide it is not for them and that the tried-and-tested cut-and-paste (for example in Microsoft Word)

will do the trick, but the NVivo software warrants serious consideration because of its power and flexibility.

Some useful online help in the use of NVivo can be found at the Online QDA website, http://onlineqda. hud.ac.uk/, and the CAQDAS Networking Project website, https://www.surrey.ac.uk/computer-assisted-qualitative-data-analysis.

KEY POINTS

....

- CAQDAS programs such as NVivo can be a useful tool in coding and analysing qualitative data that makes many of the tasks associated with handling large amounts of unstructured data faster and easier.

- Using CAQDAS does not remove the need for interpretation of findings, which remains the responsibility of the researcher.

- If you have a very small dataset, you should think carefully about whether it is worth the time investment in learning a new software program versus analysing the data manually or using word-processing software.

- If you have a larger dataset, or are intending to use the software skills that you acquire on other research projects in the future, CAQDAS can be an invaluable tool.

QUESTIONS FOR REVIEW

....

Is CAQDAS like quantitative data analysis software?

- What are the main points of difference between CAQDAS and quantitative data analysis software such as SPSS?

- Why is the use of CAQDAS controversial?
- To what extent does CAQDAS help with qualitative data analysis?

Learning NVivo

- What is a node?
- What is the difference between a non-hierarchically organized node and a hierarchically organized node?
- Do nodes have to be set up in advance? How does your analysis change if you create nodes while coding?
- In NVivo, what is the difference between a document and a memo?
- How do you go about searching for a single node and the intersection of two nodes?
- Why might it be useful to display coding stripes?
- How do you search for specific data?

ONLINE RESOURCES

www.oup.com/uk/brm5e/

Visit the Interactive Research Guide that accompanies this book to complete an exercise in computer-assisted qualitative data analysis using NVivo.

PART FOUR
MIXED METHODS RESEARCH

BREAKING DOWN THE QUANTITATIVE/ QUALITATIVE DIVIDE

CHAPTER OUTLINE

This chapter is concerned with the degree to which the quantitative/qualitative divide should be regarded as a hard-and-fast one. It shows that, while there are many differences between the two research strategies, there are also many examples of research that transcend the distinction. One way in which this occurs is through research that combines quantitative and qualitative research, which is the focus of Chapter 27. The present chapter is concerned with points of overlap between them. This chapter explores:

- aspects of qualitative research that can contain elements of the natural science model;

- aspects of quantitative research that can contain elements of interpretivism;

- the idea that research methods are less rigidly determined by epistemological and ontological assumptions than is sometimes supposed;

- ways in which aspects of the quantitative/qualitative contrast sometimes break down;

- studies in which quantitative and qualitative research are employed in relation to each other, so that qualitative research is used to analyse quantitative research and vice versa;

- the use of quantification in qualitative research.

Introduction

With this book structured so far around the distinction between quantitative and qualitative research, it may appear perverse to raise the prospect that the distinction might be overblown at this stage. The distinction has been employed so far for two main reasons:

- There *are* differences between quantitative and qualitative research in terms of research strategy, and many researchers and writers on research methodology perceive this to be the case.

- It is a useful means of organizing research methods and approaches to data analysis.

However, while epistemological and ontological commitments may be associated with certain research methods—such as the often-cited links between a natural science epistemology (in particular, positivism) and survey research, or between an interpretivist epistemology (for example, phenomenology) and qualitative interviewing—the connections are not deterministic. In other words, while qualitative interviews may often reveal a predisposition towards or a reflection of an interpretivist and constructionist position, this is not always the case, as in an example we cited early in this book: see the discussion of the study by Hochschild (1983) in Chapter 2) This means that the connections that were posited in Chapter 2 between epistemology and ontology, on the one hand, and research method, on the other, are best thought of as tendencies rather than as definitive connections. Such connections were implied by the suggestion that within each of the two research strategies—quantitative and qualitative—there is a distinctive mix of epistemology, ontology, and research methods. This is not to say that one's method should not follow from one's ontological and epistemological assumptions, but rather that there is not a simple mechanistic link, whereby the use of a structured interview or self-completion questionnaire *necessarily* implies a commitment to a natural scientific model or that ethnographic research *must* mean an interpretivist epistemology. Research methods are much more free-floating than is sometimes supposed. A method of data collection such as participant observation can be employed in such a way that it is in tune with the tenets of constructionism, but equally it can be used in a manner that reveals an objectivist orientation. Also, it is easy to underemphasize the significance of practical considerations in the way in which business research is conducted (though look again at Figure 2.2). Conducting a study of humour and resistance on the shopfloor by postal questionnaire may not be totally impossible, but it is unlikely to succeed in terms of yielding valid answers to questions.

In the rest of this chapter, we will examine a variety of ways in which the contrast between quantitative and qualitative research should not be overdrawn.

The natural science model and qualitative research

One of the chief difficulties with the links that are frequently forged between issues of epistemology and matters of research method or technique is that they often entail a characterization of the natural sciences as necessarily or inherently positivist in orientation. There are three notable difficulties here.

- There is no agreement on the epistemological basis of the natural sciences. As noted in Chapter 2, such writers as Harré (1972) and Keat and Urry (1975) have argued that positivism is but one version of the nature of the natural sciences, realism being one alternative account (Bhaskar 1975).

- If we assume that the practices of natural scientists, and of social scientists who seek to emulate their approach, are those that are revealed in their written accounts of what they do, we run into a problem because studies by social researchers of scientists' practices suggest that there is often a disparity between their work behaviour and their writings. It could be argued that to an extent 'science' is just one way of presenting results, which may or may not correspond to how research is actually conducted (Harley and Hardy 2004; Corbett et al. 2014).

- As Platt (1981) has argued, a term such as 'positivist' has to be treated in a circumspect way, because, while it does refer to a distinctive characterization of scientific enquiry (see Key concept 2.10), it is also frequently employed in a polemical way. When employed in this manner, it is rarely helpful, because the term is usually a characterization (a negative one) of the work of others rather than of one's own work.

Quite aside from the difficulty of addressing the natural science model and positivism, there are problems with associating them solely with quantitative research. Further, qualitative research frequently exhibits features that one would associate with a natural science model. This tendency is revealed in several ways.

- *Empiricist overtones.* Although empiricism (see Key concept 2.1) is typically associated with quantitative research, many writers on qualitative research display an equal emphasis on the importance of direct contact with social reality as the springboard for any investigation. Thus, writers on qualitative research frequently stress the importance of direct experience of social settings and fashioning an understanding of social worlds via that contact. The very idea that theory is to be grounded in data (see Chapter 24) seems to constitute a manifesto for empiricism, and it is unsurprising, therefore, that some writers claim to detect 'covert positivism' in qualitative research. Another way in which empiricist overtones are revealed is in the suggestion that social reality must be studied from the vantage point of research participants but that the only way to gain access to their interpretations is through extended contact with them, implying that meaning is accessible to the senses of researchers. The empiricism of qualitative research is perhaps most notable in conversation analysis, which was examined in Chapter 22. This is an approach that takes precise transcriptions of talk as its starting point and applies rules of analysis to such data. The analyst is actively discouraged from engaging in speculations about intention or context that might derive from an appreciation of the ethnographic particulars of the social setting.
- *A specific problem focus.* As noted in Chapter 17, qualitative research can be employed to investigate quite specific, tightly defined research questions of the kind normally associated with a natural science model of the research process.
- *Hypothesis- and theory-testing.* Following on from the previous point, qualitative researchers typically discuss hypothesis- and theory-testing in connection with hypotheses or theories generated in the course of conducting research, as in analytic induction or grounded theory. However, there is no obvious reason why this cannot occur in relation to previously specified hypotheses or theories.

- *Realism.* Realism (see Key concept 2.11) is one way in which the epistemological basis of the natural sciences has been construed. It has entered into the social sciences in a number of ways, but one of the most significant of these is Bhaskar's (1989) notion of critical realism. This approach accepts neither a constructionist nor an objectivist ontology and instead takes the view that the 'social world is reproduced and transformed in daily life' (1989: 4). Social phenomena are produced by mechanisms that are real, but that are not directly accessible to observation and are discernible only through their effects. For critical realism the task of business research is to seek to uncover causal mechanisms and thus to explain how social phenomena come into being. Within business research there is increasing interest in this ontological approach, which has undergone something of an intellectual revitalization in recent years (Thompson and Harley 2012; Edwards et al. 2014). Critical realism has also been popular in marketing research because it offers an alternative to the predominantly positivist paradigm in marketing (Easton 2002). Fleetwood (2005) suggests that critical realism offers a more fruitful alternative to postmodernism (see Key concept 2.8) for organization and management studies because it overcomes the ambiguity associated with postmodernism, which stems from 'ontological exaggeration' of the role of language in determining reality. Critical realists occupy a middle position between positivism and postmodernism by claiming that an entity can exist independently of our knowledge of it, while also asserting that access to the social world is always mediated and thus subjective. Critical realists also believe in the notion of material and non-material entities that are said to be real if they have an effect on behaviour. In addition to the empirical domain of observable events, there is a real domain 'in which generative mechanisms capable of producing patterns of events reside' (Tsang and Kwan 1999: 762). The critical realist approach was applied in the study discussed in Research in focus 26.1.

In addition, writers on qualitative research sometimes distinguish stances on qualitative research that contain elements of both quantitative and qualitative research. R. L. Miller (2000), in connection with an examination of Life history interviews (see Chapter 20), distinguishes three approaches to such research. One of these, which he calls 'neo-positivist', uses 'pre-existing networks of concepts ... to make theoretically based predictions concerning people's experienced lives' (2000: 12).

A critical realist study of innovation in Australia

Jackson et al. (2016) carried out a study of innovation in Australia, informed by a critical realist approach. Their study began with an analysis of statistics on national levels of innovation from the Organisation for Economic Cooperation and Development (OECD) and other sources, which was aimed at assessing Australia's innovation performance in comparison to other developed economies (this is an example of the use of secondary data, as discussed in Chapter 14). The analysis showed that Australia was a relatively poor performer. The rest of the study was aimed at seeking to discover the underlying causal mechanisms, through a process of 'retroduction'. Retroduction involves starting from an observed social or economic phenomenon, and then 'working backwards' from it to discover what caused it. Through a mixture of theoretical conjecture, further analysis of the statistical data, and examination of various other data sources, the authors put forward preliminary explanations of Australia's poor innovation performance, which they suggest may help inform policy.

Therefore, one approach to the life history method, which is associated with qualitative rather than quantitative research, would seem to entail a theory-testing approach to the collection and analysis of qualitative data. A further illustration is Charmaz's (2000) suggestion that two approaches to grounded theory can be distinguished: objectivist and constructionist (she uses the term 'constructivist'). She argues that, in spite of the differences that developed between Glaser (1992) and Strauss (e.g. Strauss and Corbin 1998), both held to the view of an objective, external reality. In other words, in the eyes of both the major writers on grounded theory, there is a social world beyond the researcher, whose job it is to reveal its nature and functioning.

Quantitative research and interpretivism

Qualitative research would seem to have a monopoly of the ability to study meaning. Its proponents essentially claim that it is only through qualitative research that the world can be studied through the eyes of the people who are studied. This claim can be challenged by the observation that attitude surveys are widely used to measure how people feel about a wide range of phenomena. In fact, it would seem that quantitative researchers frequently address meanings. An example is the concept of 'orientation to work', associated with the Affluent Worker research in the 1960s, which sought to uncover the nature and significance of the meanings that industrial workers bring with them to the workplace (Goldthorpe et al. 1968).

The widespread inclusion of questions about attitudes in surveys suggests that quantitative researchers are interested in matters of meaning. It might be objected that survey questions do not really tap issues of meaning because they are based on categories devised by the designers of the interview schedule or questionnaire. Two points are relevant here. First, in the absence of respondent validation exercises, the notion that qualitative research is more adept at gaining access to the point of view of those being studied than quantitative research is invariably assumed rather than demonstrated. Qualitative researchers frequently claim to have tapped into participants' world views because of, for example, their extensive participation in the everyday lives of those they study, the length of time they spent in the setting being studied, or the lengthy and intensive interviews conducted. However, the explicit demonstration that interpretative understanding has been accomplished—for example, through respondent validation (see Key concept 17.3)—is rarely undertaken. Secondly, if the design of attitude questions is based on prior questioning that seeks to bring out the range of possible attitudinal positions on an issue, attitudinal questions may be better able to gain access to meaning.

Quantitative research and constructionism

It was noted in Chapter 2 that one keynote of constructionism is a concern with issues of representation, as these play an important role in the construction of the social world. Qualitative content analysis has played an important role in developing such an understanding, just as discourse analysis has in relation to the social construction of events and meanings in business leaders' speeches and mission statements. However, it is easy to forget that conventional quantitative content analysis can also be useful in this way.

Chen and Meindl's (1991) research into the entrepreneurial leadership of the founder of the low-cost US airline People Express, Donald Burr, referred to in Research in focus 23.4, provides an example of the combined use of quantitative and qualitative content analysis. Much of their understanding of Burr's leadership style was derived from qualitative content analysis, but they also employed a quantitative content analysis, 'identifying leader-charismatic themes, recording frequency, and analyzing trends' (1991: 530) using data from magazine and newspaper articles that focused on the company. Rather than simply content-analysing the articles themselves, the researchers involved 72 undergraduate business students, who were asked to read the new articles and write a description of Burr, as a person and as a CEO, based on the materials they had read. Content analysis was then conducted on the students' descriptions. This showed that the language used by the students to describe Burr changed as the performance of the company varied. Chen and Meindl conclude that images portrayed of Burr in the past interacted with indications of current performance to determine the reconstruction of the leader's image. In other words, instead of being rejected, old themes were modified and injected with new meaning. The second stage of the content analysis was more qualitative in nature. It involved qualitative content analysis of the actual newspaper articles in order to identify the metaphors used to describe Burr. The results of this analysis were broadly consistent with the first, thereby reinforcing the validity of the overall findings. More generally, this example shows how quantitative research can play a significant role in relation to a constructionist stance.

Epistemological and ontological considerations

If we review the argument so far, it is being suggested that:

- there are differences between quantitative and qualitative research in terms of their epistemological and ontological commitments; *but*
- the connection between research strategy, on the one hand, and epistemological and ontological commitments, on the other, is not deterministic. In other words, there is a tendency for quantitative and qualitative research to be associated with the epistemological and ontological positions outlined in Chapter 2, but there are important exceptions to this general trend.

However, some writers have suggested that research methods carry with them a cluster of epistemological and ontological commitments such that to elect to use a self-completion questionnaire is more or less simultaneously and inevitably to select a natural science model and an objectivist world view. Similarly, the use of participant observation is often taken to imply a commitment to interpretivism and constructionism. The difficulty with such a view is that, if we accept that there is no perfect correspondence between research strategy and matters of epistemology and ontology, the notion that a method is inherently or necessarily indicative of certain wider assumptions about knowledge and the nature of social reality begins to founder.

In business research, if Burrell and Morgan's (1979) influential 'four-paradigm' framework were consistently applied, one would expect to see a clear correspondence between the paradigm adopted (see Chapter 2) and the research methods used: the functionalist paradigm community using, for example, questionnaire surveys, and the interpretative paradigm community using, for example, ethnographic methods. In fact, research methods are much more 'free-floating' in terms of epistemology and ontology than this proposition suggests, and it is often not possible to uncover an unambiguous pattern linking the grounding of an article in one of the four paradigms with the research methods used.

Furthermore, because of the dominance of mixed methods case study research in the business and management field, it is common for several methods to be used in the same research study. In summary, although there is undoubtedly a general tendency for specific paradigm communities to favour certain research methods, the reality is more complex than this picture at first suggests.

Problems with the quantitative/qualitative contrast

The contrasts between quantitative and qualitative research that were drawn in Chapter 17 suggest a somewhat hard-and-fast set of distinctions and differences (see Table 17.1). However, there is a risk that this kind of representation tends to exaggerate the differences between them. A few of the distinctions will be examined to demonstrate this point.

Behaviour versus meaning

The distinction is sometimes drawn between a focus on behaviour and a focus on meanings. However, as already noted, quantitative research frequently involves the study of meanings in the form of attitude scales (such as the Likert scaling technique) and other techniques. Qualitative researchers may feel that the tendency for attitude scales to be preformulated and imposed on research participants means that they do not really gain access to meanings. The key point being made here is that at the very least quantitative researchers frequently *try* to address meanings. Also, somewhat ironically, many of the techniques with which quantitative research is associated, most notably survey research based on questionnaires and interviews, have been shown to relate poorly to people's actual behaviour. Moreover, looking at the other side of the divide, qualitative research frequently, if not invariably, entails the examination of behaviour in context. Qualitative researchers often want to interpret people's behaviour in terms of the norms, values, and culture of the group or organization in question. In other words, quantitative and qualitative researchers are typically interested in both what people do and what they think, but they go about the investigation of these areas in different ways. Therefore, the degree to which the behaviour-versus-meaning contrast coincides with quantitative and qualitative research should not be overstated.

Theory tested in research versus theory emergent from data

A further related point is that the suggestion that theory and concepts are developed prior to undertaking a study in quantitative research is something of a caricature that is true only up to a point. It reflects a tendency to characterize quantitative research as driven by a theory-testing approach. However, while experimental investigations probably fit this model well, survey-based studies are often more exploratory than this view implies. Although concepts have to be measured, the nature of their interconnections is frequently not specified in advance. Quantitative research is far less driven by a hypothesis-testing strategy than is frequently supposed. As a result, the analysis of quantitative data from social surveys is often more exploratory than is generally appreciated and consequently offers opportunities for the generation of theories and concepts (see Research in focus 26.2). As one American survey researcher has commented in relation to a large-scale survey he conducted in the 1950s, but that has much relevance today: 'There are so many questions which might be asked, so many correlations which can be run, so many ways in which the findings can be organized, and so few rules or precedents for making these choices that a thousand different studies could come out of the same data' (Davis 1964: 232).

The common depiction of quantitative research as solely an exercise in testing preformulated ideas fails to appreciate the degree to which findings frequently suggest new departures and theoretical contributions. Therefore, the suggestion that, unlike an interpretivist stance, quantitative research is concerned solely with the testing of ideas that have previously been formulated (such as hypotheses) fails to recognize the creative work that goes into the analysis of quantitative data and into the interpretation of findings (see Research in focus 26.2 for an example). Equally, as noted above, qualitative research can be used in relation to the testing of theories (again, Research in focus 26.2 provides an example).

Numbers versus words

Even perhaps this most basic element in the distinction between quantitative and qualitative research is not without problems. Much, if not most, quantitative analysis in social science involves taking qualitative data (eg. attitudes) and fitting them into numerical categories (eg.

Likert scales). Qualitative researchers often undertake a limited amount of quantification of their data. Silverman (1984, 1985) has argued that some quantification of findings from qualitative research can often help to uncover the generality of the phenomena being described. However, he warns that such quantification should reflect research participants' own ways of understanding their social world. Similarly, Miles and Huberman (1994), whose approach is commonly used in business research, recommend the use of a contact summary sheet as a means of recording themes that arise during a qualitative interview. Using the interview transcript, the researcher categorizes interview responses by theme, eventually generating a single-page summary of the interview. Not only does the contact summary sheet highlight the main concepts, themes, and issues, it also provides a record of their frequency of occurrence. This technique illustrates how qualitative interview data can be analysed in a way that involves a degree of quantification. In any case, it has often been noted that qualitative researchers engage in 'quasi-quantification' through the use of such terms as 'many', 'often', and 'some' (see below). All that is happening is that the researcher is injecting greater precision into such estimates of frequency.

Artificial versus natural

The artificial/natural contrast referred to in Table 17.1 can similarly be criticized. It is often assumed that because much quantitative research employs research instruments that are applied to the people being studied (questionnaires, structured interview schedules, structured observation schedules, and so on), it provides an artificial account of how the social world operates. Qualitative research is often viewed as more naturalistic (see Chapters 3 and 17). Ethnographic research in particular would seem to exhibit this quality, because the participant observer studies people in their normal social worlds and contexts—in other words, as they go about normal activities. However, when qualitative research is based on interviews (such as semi- and unstructured interviewing and focus groups), the depiction 'natural' is possibly less applicable. Interviews still have to be arranged and interviewees have to be taken away from activities that they would otherwise be engaged in, even when the interviewing style is of the more conversational kind. We know very little about interviewees' reactions to and feelings about being interviewed. M. Parker (2000), in describing his ethnographic role as a confidant, recounts a comment made by one of his interviewees: 'it's nice to have somebody to talk to and moan to you know. I try

to talk to my wife like this but she doesn't listen' (2000: 237). While this interviewee clearly enjoyed being interviewed, it is likely that he was very conscious of the fact that he had been engaged in an interview rather than a conversation. The interview was clearly valuable in allowing this individual to express his concerns, but the point being made here is that the view that the methods associated with qualitative research are naturalistic is to exaggerate the contrast with the supposed artificiality of the research methods associated with quantitative research. Atkinson and Silverman (1997) have further suggested that qualitative researchers' obsession with the semi-structured interview as a naturalistic form of enquiry reflects a media-led societal trend towards confessional interviewing as a source of truth and meaning. They suggest that descriptive research of this nature is little different from chat shows or human interest journalism.

As noted in Chapter 21, focus group research is often described as more natural than qualitative interviewing because it emulates the way people discuss issues in real life. Natural groupings are often used to emphasize this element. However, whether or not this is how group participants view the nature of their participation is unclear. In particular, when it is borne in mind that people are sometimes strangers, have to travel to a site where the session takes place, are paid for their trouble, and frequently discuss topics they rarely if ever talk about, it is not hard to take the view that the naturalism of focus groups is assumed rather than demonstrated.

In participant observation, the researcher can be a source of interference that renders the research situation less natural than it might superficially appear to be. Whenever the ethnographer is in an overt role, a certain amount of reactivity is possible—even inevitable. It is difficult to estimate the degree to which the ethnographer represents an intrusive element that has an impact on what is found, but once again the naturalism of such research is often assumed rather than demonstrated, although it is admittedly likely that it will be less artificial than the methods associated with quantitative research. However, when the ethnographer also engages in interviewing (as opposed to casual conversations), the naturalistic quality is likely to be less pronounced.

These observations suggest that there are areas and examples of studies that lead us to question the degree to which the quantitative/qualitative contrast is a rigid one. Once again, this is not to suggest that the contrast is unhelpful, but that we should be wary of assuming that in writing and talking about quantitative and qualitative research we are referring to two absolutely divergent and inconsistent research strategies.

Reciprocal analysis

There is one further thing which highlights the lack of a clear boundary between quantitative and qualitative research. This is the fact that each can be used to analyse the other.

Qualitative analysis of quantitative data

There has been a growing interest in the examination of the writings of quantitative researchers using some of the methods associated with qualitative research. In part, this trend can be seen as an extension of the growth of interest among qualitative researchers in the writing of ethnography, which can be seen in such work as Van Maanen (1988) and Atkinson (1990). The attention to quantitative research is very much part of this trend because it reveals a concern in both cases with the notion the written account of research constitutes not only the presentation of findings but also an attempt to persuade the reader of the credibility of those findings.

One way in which a qualitative research approach to quantitative research is manifested is through what Gephart (1988, 2014) has called *ethnostatistics*, by which is meant 'the study of the construction, interpretation, and display of statistics in quantitative social research'. Gephart shows that there are a number of ways in which the idea of ethnostatistics can be realized, but it is with just one of these—approaching statistics as rhetoric—that we will be concerned here. Research in focus 26.2 provides an example of ethnostatistics in use in research. Directing attention to the idea of statistics as rhetoric means becoming sensitive to the ways in which statistical arguments are deployed to bestow credibility on research for target audiences. More specifically, this means examining the language used in persuading audiences about the validity of research. Indeed, the very use of statistics themselves can be regarded as a rhetorical device because the use of quantification means that business research can bestow upon itself the appearance of

26.2 RESEARCH IN FOCUS
The construction of meaning from numerical data

Gephart undertook an ethnostatistical study of the way statistics were used to justify budget cuts in the province of Alberta, Canada (Gephart 2014). The provincial government in Alberta, which had previously told its constituents that the economy was growing strongly, suddenly announced cuts to public spending. Gephart wanted to understand the rhetorical processes by which a political speech created a perceived economic crisis which could be used to justify budget cuts.

The primary data used in the study were a speech given by the premier of Alberta in 2013 and two statistical charts related to the speech, which were published on the Government of Alberta website. The premier's speech announced that due to a 'bitumen bubble' (bitumen is a substance which is mined and forms the basis for a form of crude oil), the price of the oil produced by Alberta was much lower than expected and thus provincial revenue would be much lower, creating an economic crisis for the state. Gephart's analysis focuses on the rhetorical devices used by the premier in presenting the statistical evidence to persuade listeners of the reality of the crisis and thus the legitimacy of spending cuts. Gephart explains his analytical approach:

> To undertake rhetorical analysis, I read the key documents and uncovered key themes related to the bitumen bubble based crisis. I coded all statements in the key documents in terms of these following key themes that emerged from reading the documents: 1) features of the bitumen bubble, 2) key features of Alberta budgets in 2012–13 and 2013–14, 3) economic prosperity in Alberta, 4) forecasts and forecasting practices, 5) the causes of the bubble, 6) implications of the bubble for Alberta, and 7) how to resolve or remove the bubble. Next, I examined the core data passages for evidence of: 1) tropes, in particular metaphors, 2) textual practices, and 3) exclusions, and identified all examples of each of these phenomena.

> (2014: 45–6).

By conducting this detailed analysis, Gephart was able to show how rhetorical devices were used to construct particular meanings from numerical data, to create particular accounts of prosperity and the threat to it from the 'bitumen bubble' and to justify a particular response from the government.

a natural science and thereby achieve greater legitimacy and credibility by virtue of that association (McCartney 1970; John 1992).

Quantitative analysis of qualitative data

We can also find examples of situations where quantitative methods are applied to qualitative data. For example, Hodson (1996) applied a quantitative research approach to qualitative research on workplaces, conducting content analysis of 'book-length ethnographic studies based on sustained periods of direct observation' (1996: 724). Hodson's approach is a form of research that may have potential in other areas of business research in which ethnography has been a popular method and a good deal of ethnographic evidence has been built up. Hodson (1999) suggests that the study of social movements may be one such field; managerial fads and fashions may be yet another. Hodson's research presents one solution to the problem of making comparisons between ethnographic studies in a given area.

Certain key issues need to be resolved when conducting analyses of the kind carried out by Hodson. One relates to the issue of conducting an exhaustive literature search for suitable studies for possible inclusion. Hodson chose to analyse just books, rather than articles, because of the limited amount of information that can usually be included in the latter. Even then, criteria for the inclusion of a book needed to be stipulated. Hodson employed three: 'The criteria for inclusion were (a) the book had to be based on ethnographic methods of observation over a period of at least 6 months, (b) the observations had to be in a single organization, and (c) the book had to

focus on at least one clearly identified group of workers' (1999: 22). The application of these criteria resulted in the exclusion of 279 out of 365 books uncovered. A second crucial area relates to the coding of the studies. Hodson stresses the importance of having considerable knowledge of the subject area, adopting clear coding rules, and pilot testing the coding schedule. In addition, he recommends checking the reliability of coding by having 10 per cent of the documents coded by two people. The process of coding was time-consuming, in that Hodson calculates that each book-length ethnography took forty or more hours to code. (A detailed description of Hodson's project can be seen at https://www.icpsr. umich.edu/icpsrweb/ICPSR/studies/3979.)

Hodson's approach has many attractions, not the least of which is the impossibility of a quantitative researcher being able to conduct investigations in such a varied set of organizations. Also, it means that more data of much greater depth can be used than can typically be gathered by quantitative researchers. It also allows hypotheses deriving from established theories to be tested, such as the 'technological implications' approach, which sees technologies as having impacts on the experience of work (Hodson 1996). However, the loss of a sense of social context is likely to be unattractive to many qualitative researchers.

Of particular significance for this discussion is the remark that 'the fundamental contribution of the systematic analysis of documentary accounts is that it creates an analytic link between the in-depth accounts of professional observers and the statistical methods of quantitative researchers' (Hodson 1999: 68). In other words, the application of quantitative methods to qualitative research may provide a meeting ground for the two research strategies.

Quantification in qualitative research

As noted in Chapter 17, the numbers-versus-words contrast is perhaps the most basic in many people's minds when they think about the differences between quantitative and qualitative research. After all, it seems to relate in a most fundamental way to the very terms used to denote the two approaches that seem to imply the presence and absence of numbers. However, it is simply not the case that there is a complete absence of quantification in qualitative research.

Thematic analysis

In Chapter 24, it was observed that one of the most common approaches to qualitative data analysis is

undertaking a search for themes in transcripts or field notes. However, as Bryman and Burgess (1994b: 224) point out, the criteria employed in the identification of themes are often unclear. One possible factor that these authors suggest may be in operation is the frequency of the occurrence of certain incidents, words, phrases, and so on that denote a theme. In other words, a theme is more likely to be identified the more times the phenomenon it denotes occurs in the course of coding. This process may also account for the prominence given to some themes over others when writing up qualitative data analysis. In other words, a kind of implicit quantification may be in operation that influences the identification of themes and the elevation of some themes over others.

Quasi-quantification in qualitative research

It has often been noted that qualitative researchers engage in 'quasi-quantification' through the use of terms such as 'many', 'frequently', 'rarely', 'often', and 'some'. In order to be able to make such allusions to quantity, the qualitative researcher should have some idea of the relative frequency of the phenomena being referred to. However, as expressions of quantities, they are imprecise, and it is often difficult to discern why they are being used at all. The alternative would seem to be to engage in a limited amount of quantification when it is appropriate, such as when an expression of quantity can bolster an argument. This point leads directly on to the next section.

Combating anecdotalism through limited quantification

One of the criticisms that is often levelled against qualitative research is that the publications on which it is based are often anecdotal, giving the reader little guidance as to the prevalence of the issue to which the anecdote refers. The widespread use of brief sequences of conversation, snippets from interview transcripts, and accounts of encounters between people provides little sense of the prevalence of whatever such items of evidence are supposed to indicate. There is the related risk that a particularly striking statement by someone or an unexpected activity may have more significance attached to it than might be warranted in terms of its frequency.

Perhaps at least partly in response to these problems, qualitative researchers sometimes undertake a limited amount of quantification of their data. Numbers can be used to give a fairly straightforward indication of the scale of the research project. Casey (1995), for example, explains that she interviewed 60 people during the course of her ethnographic study. However, numbers can also be used to interpret the significance of qualitative data. For example, in their research on concepts of leadership employed by British police officers, Bryman et al. (1996) counted the frequency with which certain leadership styles were cited in interview transcripts. This exercise allowed them to demonstrate that the kind of leadership preferred by police officers was different from what was in vogue among theorists of leadership at the time. Similarly, Gabriel (1998) describes how he studied organizational culture in a variety of organizations by collecting, during interviews, stories about the organizations in question. Computers and information technology were a particular focus of the stories elicited. Altogether 377 stories were collected in the course of 126 interviews in five organizations. Gabriel shows that the stories were of different types: comic stories (which were usually a mechanism for disparagement of others); epic stories (survival against the odds); tragic stories (undeserved misfortune); gripes (personal injustices); and so on. He counted the number of each type: comic stories were the most numerous at 108; then epic stories (82); tragic stories (53); gripe stories (40); and so on. Themes in the stories were also counted, such as when they involved a leader, a personal trauma, an accident, and so forth. In all these cases, the types of stories and the themes could have been treated in an anecdotal way, but the use of such simple counting conveys a clear sense of their relative prevalence. Exercises like these can be used to counter the suggestion that is sometimes made that the approach to presenting qualitative data can be too anecdotal, so that readers are not given enough of a sense of the *extent* to which certain beliefs are held or a certain behaviour occurs.

 KEY POINTS

....

- There are differences between quantitative and qualitative research, but it is important not to exaggerate them.

- The connections between epistemology and ontology, on the one hand, and research methods, on the other, are not deterministic.

- Qualitative research sometimes exhibits features normally associated with a natural science model.

- Quantitative research aims on occasions to engage with an interpretivist stance.

- Research methods are more autonomous in relation to epistemological commitments than is often appreciated.

- The artificial/natural contrast that is often an element in drawing a distinction between quantitative and qualitative research is frequently exaggerated.

- A quantitative research approach can be employed for the analysis of qualitative studies, and a qualitative research approach can be employed to examine the rhetoric of quantitative researchers.

- Some qualitative researchers employ quantification in their work.

QUESTIONS FOR REVIEW

The natural science model and qualitative research

- Are the natural sciences positivistic?

- To what extent can some qualitative research be deemed to exhibit the characteristics of a natural science model?

Quantitative research and interpretivism

- To what extent can some quantitative research be deemed to exhibit the characteristics of interpretivism?

Quantitative research and constructionism

- To what extent can some quantitative research be deemed to exhibit the characteristics of constructionism?

Epistemological and ontological considerations

- How far do research methods necessarily carry epistemological and ontological implications?

Problems with the quantitative/qualitative contrast

- Outline some of the ways in which the quantitative/qualitative contrast may not be as hard and fast as is often supposed.

Reciprocal analysis

- How have statistics been used to bestow credibility upon management and business research?

- How might Hodson's approach to the analysis of qualitative data be applied in business and management research?

Quantification in qualitative research

- How far is quantification a feature of qualitative research?

ONLINE RESOURCES
www.oup.com/uk/brm5e/

Visit the Interactive Research Guide that accompanies this book to complete an exercise related to breaking down the quantitative/qualitative divide.

MIXED METHODS RESEARCH: COMBINING QUANTITATIVE AND QUALITATIVE RESEARCH

CHAPTER OUTLINE

This chapter is concerned with mixed methods research—that is, research that combines quantitative and qualitative research. While this may seem a straightforward way of resolving and breaking down the divide between the two research strategies, it is controversial. Moreover, there may be practical difficulties associated with mixed methods research. This chapter explores:

- arguments against the combination of quantitative and qualitative research—two kinds of argument are distinguished and are referred to as the embedded methods argument and the paradigm argument;

- the suggestion that there are two versions of the debate about the possibility of combining quantitative and qualitative research, one that concentrates on methods of research and another that is concerned with epistemological issues;

- the different ways in which mixed methods research has been carried out;

- the need to recognize that mixed methods research is not inherently superior to research that employs a single research strategy.

Introduction

So far throughout the book an emphasis has been placed on the strengths and weaknesses of the research methods associated with quantitative and qualitative research. One possible response to this kind of recognition is to propose combining them. After all, such a strategy would seem to allow the various strengths to be capitalized upon and the weaknesses offset somewhat. However, not all writers on research methods agree that such integration is either desirable or feasible. On the other hand, in business research combined research appears to be particularly popular. In discussing the combination of quantitative and qualitative research, this chapter will be concerned with three main issues:

1. an examination of the arguments against integrating quantitative and qualitative research;

2. the different ways in which quantitative and qualitative research have been combined;

3. an assessment of combined research, which asks if it is necessarily superior to investigations relying on just one research strategy and if there are any additional problems deriving from it.

Key concept 27.1 explains what defines mixed methods research and what differentiates it from other apparently similar approaches.

The arguments against mixed methods research

The argument against mixed methods research tends to be based on either, and sometimes both, of two kinds of argument:

- the idea that research methods carry epistemological commitments; and

- the idea that quantitative and qualitative research are separate *paradigms*.

These two arguments will now be briefly reviewed.

The embedded methods argument

This first position, which was outlined in Chapter 26, implies that research methods are ineluctably rooted in epistemological and ontological commitments. Such a view of research methods can be discerned in statements like the following:

> every research tool or procedure is inextricably embedded in commitments to particular versions of the world and to knowing that world. To use a questionnaire, to use an attitude scale, to take the role of participant observer, to select a random sample, to measure rates of population growth, and so on, is to be involved in conceptions of the world which allow these instruments to be used for the purposes conceived.
>
> (Hughes 1990: 11)

According to such a position, the decision to employ, for example, participant observation is not simply about

27.1 KEY CONCEPT
What is mixed method research?

There is sometimes confusion about distinctions between mixed methods research and other approaches which use more than one method. The term *mixed methods research* is used as a simple shorthand to stand for research that integrates quantitative and qualitative research within a single project. Of course, there is research that, for example, combines structured interviewing with structured observation or ethnography with semi-structured interviewing. There is also research which combines surveys and experiments. However, these instances of the combination of research methods are associated with just one research strategy—qualitative and quantitative research respectively—and might better be thought of as *multi-method research*. By mixed methods research we are referring to research that combines research methods that cross the *two research strategies*. The term multi-strategy research can also be used to describe this approach, but 'mixed method' is the more commonly used term.

how to go about data collection but also a commitment to an epistemological position that is inimical to positivism and that is consistent with interpretivism.

This kind of view of research methods has led some writers to argue that mixed methods research is not feasible or even desirable. An ethnographer may collect questionnaire data to gain information about a slice of social life that is not amenable to participant observation, but this does not represent an integration of quantitative and qualitative research, because the epistemological positions in which the two methods are grounded constitute irreconcilable views about how social reality should be studied. Bazeley (2015: 27) observes that 'differences in ontology, epistemology, and in disciplinary traditions have hindered the willingness of some to engage with what appears to be a compromise (and paradigmatically compromised) position'.

The chief difficulty with the argument against mixed methods on the basis of ontological and epistemological 'purity' is that, as was noted in Chapter 26, the idea that research methods automatically carry with them fixed epistemological and ontological implications is very difficult to sustain. The research methods we have discussed are capable of being put to a wide variety of tasks.

The paradigm argument

The paradigm argument was introduced in Chapter 2 in order to categorize some of the ontological and epistemological assumptions that are made in business research. It conceives of quantitative and qualitative research as *paradigms* (see Key concept 2.14) in which epistemological assumptions, values, and methods are inextricably intertwined and are incompatible between paradigms (e.g. Guba 1985; D. L. Morgan 1998*b*). Therefore, when researchers combine participant observation with a questionnaire, they are not really combining quantitative and qualitative research, since paradigms are incommensurable—that is, they are incompatible: the integration is at only a superficial level and within a single paradigm.

The problem with the paradigm argument is that it rests, as with the embedded methods argument, on contentions about the interconnectedness of method, and epistemology in particular, connections that cannot—in the case of business research—be demonstrated. Moreover, while Kuhn (1970) certainly argued that paradigms are incommensurable, it is by no means clear that quantitative and qualitative research are in fact paradigms. As suggested in Chapters 2 and 26, there are areas of overlap and commonality between them.

Two versions of the debate about quantitative and qualitative research

There would seem to be two different versions of the debate about the nature of quantitative and qualitative research, and these two different versions have implications in researchers' minds about whether or not the two can be combined:

- A *philosophical version*, as in the embedded methods argument and the paradigm argument, sees quantitative and qualitative research as grounded in incompatible epistemological principles (and ontological ones too, but these tend not to be given as much attention). According to this version of their nature, mixed methods research is not possible.

- A *technical or practical version*, which is the position taken by most researchers whose work is mentioned in the next section, gives greater prominence to the strengths of the data collection and data analysis techniques with which quantitative and qualitative research are each associated and sees these as capable of being fused. There is a recog-

nition that quantitative and qualitative research are each connected with distinctive epistemological and ontological assumptions, but the connections are not viewed as fixed and ineluctable. Research methods are perceived, unlike in the epistemological version of the debate, as autonomous. A research method from one research strategy is viewed as capable of being pressed into the service of another. Indeed, in some instances, as will be seen in the next section, the notion that there is a 'leading' research strategy in a mixed methods investigation may not even apply in some cases.

The technical version of the debate about the nature of quantitative and qualitative research essentially views the two research strategies as compatible. As a result, mixed methods research becomes both feasible and desirable. It is in that spirit that we now turn to a discussion of the ways in which quantitative and qualitative research can be combined.

The rise of mixed methods research

Mixed methods research has become an increasingly used and accepted approach to conducting business research and in the social sciences more generally. Bryman (2009) examined published articles based on mixed methods research in the period 1994–2003 and found a threefold increase over that period. Mixed methods have been the focus of a specialist handbook, which has gone into a second edition (Tashakkori and Teddlie 2003, 2010), and specialist journals, such as the *Journal of Mixed Methods Research*. In the field of marketing, Hanson and Grimmer (2005) found that nearly 9 per cent of all articles in three major marketing journals in the period 1993–2002 derived from mixed methods research, representing around 14 per cent of all empirical articles. An examination of the research methods used in the *Leadership Quarterly*, a US-based journal that specializes in academic articles concerned with leadership, found that over the first two decades of its existence (1990–2009), the proportion of empirical articles combining quantitative and qualitative research was around 12–13 per cent (Lowe and Gardner 2000; Gardner et al. 2010). Hummerinta-Peltomäki and Nummela (2006) examined four journals in the international business field. They found that 17 per cent of all empirical articles derived from mixed methods research. Molina-Azorín (2009, 2012) found that 17 per cent of all empirical articles published in *Strategic Management Journal* between 1997 and 2006 were based on mixed methods research. In 2011, Bluhm et al. published a review of qualitative research (which encompassed both purely qualitative and mixed-method research) published in leading US and European management journals between 1999 and 2008. Of the 198 papers included in the sample, around a third employed mixed methods.

Bryman's (2009) research shows that there has been an increase in articles based on mixed methods research, and the various studies discussed above show rates between 9 and 31 percent. This is somewhat higher than was found in an examination by Alise and Teddlie (2010) of articles published in journals in the fields of psychology, sociology, nursing, and education. Alise and Teddlie found that 11 per cent of all empirical articles were based on mixed methods research, with education having a much larger proportion than the three other fields (24 per cent of all empirical articles, against 7, 5, and 9 per cent, respectively). These findings strongly suggest that mixed methods research has acquired credibility in the field of business studies and that it is being employed on a fairly regular basis as a distinctive research strategy.

In the three sections that follow, we examine some discussions about the nature of mixed methods research that have been a focus for writers concerned with these issues. The three foci are:

1. the priority and order through which quantitative research and qualitative research were carried out;

2. the different types of mixed methods design;

3. the purpose(s) of doing mixed methods research.

This section will be structured in terms of a classification Bryman developed many years ago of the different ways in which mixed methods research has been undertaken (Bryman 1988*a*, 1992). The classification has been changed slightly from the one presented in his earlier publications.

Classifying mixed methods research in terms of priority and sequence

Several writers (e.g. D. L. Morgan 1998*b*, 2014) have distinguished various forms of mixed methods research in terms of two issues:

- *The priority decision*. To what extent is a qualitative or a quantitative method the principal data-gathering tool, or do they have equal weight?

- *The sequence decision*. Which method precedes which? In other words, does the qualitative method precede the quantitative one or vice versa, or is the data collection associated with each method concurrent?

These criteria yield nine possible types (see Figure 27.1). In this illustration, capital letters indicate priority—for example, QUAL indicates that the qualitative component was the main data collection approach; lower case indicates a more subsidiary role—for example, qual. Arrows refer to the sequence—for example, QUAN→qual means

FIGURE 27.1
Classifying mixed methods research in terms of priority and sequence

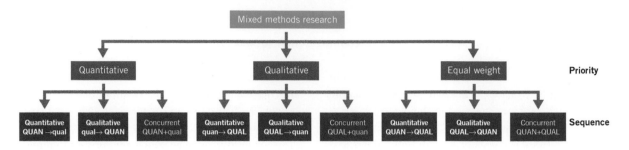

Capitals and lower case indicate priority
Arrows indicate sequence; + indicates concurrent

that the collection of quantitative data was the main data collection approach and that the collection of these quantitative data was undertaken before the collection of qualitative data, which occupies a subsidiary role. The + simply means that the collection of the quantitative and the qualitative data was conducted more or less concurrently. One difficulty with this and related classifications is that when reading the report of a study it is not always easy to establish the priority and sequence used. However, it is useful as a way of thinking about fundamental aspects of the design of mixed methods studies.

Table 27.1 summarizes the percentages of mixed methods articles in four business research fields (marketing, leadership, strategic management, and organizational behaviour) in terms of sequence and priority. The findings show that a clear tendency for mixed methods research in these fields to be sequential and for quantitative research to be the dominant partner in the conduct of the research. The latter finding almost certainly reflects a continued tendency for quantitative research to be the dominant research approach in fields such as these. Molina-Azorín and Cameron (2010) found that the typical article in *Strategic Management Journal* is qual→QUAN, which implies that qualitative research typically acts as preparation for the main phase of mixed methods research which is quantitative in nature. Similarly, in connection with 45 mixed methods articles published in the field of international business studies, Hummerinta-Peltomäki

TABLE 27.1
Sequence and priority in mixed methods research articles in four business research fields

	Nine marketing journals 2003–9 (43 mixed methods articles); based on Harrison and Reilly (2011)	Articles in *Leadership Quarterly* 2004–June 2012 (15 mixed methods articles); based on Stentz et al. (2012)	Articles in *Strategic Management Journal* 2003–9 (64 mixed methods articles); based on Molina-Azorín and Cameron (2010)	Articles in *Journal of Organizational Behavior* 2003–9 (20 mixed methods articles); based on Molina-Azorín and Cameron (2010)
Sequence				
Sequential	79%	60%	95%	75%
Concurrent	19%[1]	33%[1]	5%	25%
Priority				
Quantitative	63%	47%	83%[2]	60%[2]
Qualitative	7%	20%	17%	40%
Equal weight	30%	33%		

[1]These figures do not add up to 100 because one study had both sequential and concurrent elements.

[2]The authors do not provide figures to distinguish between studies in which the quantitative or the qualitative research was dominant but do say that the quantitative component was the dominant one.

and Nummela (2006) report that 27 of them were quite similar in that data were collected sequentially with the qualitative research preceding the quantitative phase. We suspect that this applies to the other fields referred to in Table 27.1 in view of the fact that they were all sequential and the quantitative component was dominant.

Different types of mixed methods design

Writers on mixed methods research have drawn on several of the distinctions outlined in the previous section to distinguish between different types of mixed methods design. Different ways of distinguishing them have been put forward by various writers, but the ones provided by Creswell and Plano Clark (2011) is probably the most commonly employed. They distinguish six designs, of which the four presented in Figure 27.2 are the most commonly referred to.

The convergent parallel design entails the simultaneous collection of quantitative and qualitative data which have equal priority. The resulting analyses are then

FIGURE 27.2
Four basic mixed methods designs

(a) *Convergent parallel design*

(b) *Exploratory sequential design*

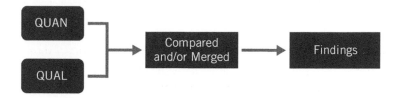

(c) *Explanatory sequential design*

(d) *Embedded design*

Source: Based on Creswell and Plano Clark (2011).

compared and/or merged to form an integrated whole. This kind of design tends to be associated with triangulation exercises, whereby the researcher aims to compare the two sets of findings, and also situations in which the researcher aims to offset the weaknesses of both quantitative and qualitative research by capitalizing on the strengths of both.

The exploratory sequential design entails the collection of qualitative data prior to the collection of quantitative data. It is associated with investigations in which the researcher wants to generate hypotheses or hunches, which can then be tested using quantitative research, and with investigations in which the aim is to develop research instruments such as questionnaire questions which can then be employed in a quantitative investigation. Another purpose is to follow up qualitative findings with quantitative research which allows the scope and generalizability of the qualitative findings to be assessed. Although Creswell and Plano Clark depict the quantitative element as typically having priority within this design, this is not always the case: it may have a largely subsidiary role in relation to the quantitative research.

The explanatory sequential design involves the collection and analysis of quantitative data followed by the collection and analysis of qualitative data in order to elaborate or explain the quantitative findings. The need for such an approach can arise when the researcher feels that the broad patterns of relationships uncovered through quantitative research require an explanation which the quantitative data on their own are unable to supply or when further insight into the quantitative findings is required. Again, although Creswell and Plano Clark show the quantitative element as having priority in this design, it may not always, such as when the explanation

or elaboration to be provided by the qualitative findings is especially significant for the study's research questions. The research by Holmberg et al. (2008) discussed in Research in focus 2.15 provides examples of the use of this design. Although Figure 27.2 (c) implies that qualitative research is the priority approach, there are likely to be occasions when there is a strong quantitative research orientation and the qualitative research acts largely as a follow-up, in which case it will be the quantitative research that is the priority.

The embedded design can have either quantitative or qualitative research as the priority approach but draws on the other approach as well within the context of a study. The need for an embedded design can arise when the researcher needs to enhance either quantitative or qualitative research with the other approach. The phasing of the data collection may be simultaneous or sequential. The need for the design arises when the researcher feels that quantitative (or qualitative) research alone will be insufficient for understanding the phenomenon of interest. For example, the researcher may be interested in examining a research question principally using quantitative research but may have a subsidiary research question that is best addressed through qualitative research. The research by Perlow (1997, 1999), discussed later in this chapter, provides an example of the use of this design.

One of the issues that should emerge from this brief exposition of the different types of mixed methods design is that the choice of design is closely bound up with the anticipated use(s) of a mixed methods approach in the eyes of the researcher. Thus the choice of mixed methods design should be based on the role that it is expected that mixed methods research will play. Possible roles are considered in the next section.

Approaches to mixed methods research

The logic of triangulation

The idea of triangulation has been previously encountered in Key concept 17.4. When applied to the present context, it implies that the results of an investigation employing a method associated with one research strategy are cross-checked against the results of using a method associated with the other research strategy. It is an adaptation of the argument by writers such as Webb et al. (1966) that confidence in the findings deriving

from a study using a quantitative research strategy can be enhanced by using more than one way of measuring a concept. For example, in their longitudinal study of culture in a governmental organization in the USA, Zamanou and Glaser (1994) collected different types of data in order to examine different aspects of organizational reality. By using survey, interview, and observational data, they were able to combine 'the specificity and accuracy of quantitative data with the ability to interpret idiosyncrasies and complex perceptions, provided by qualitative analysis' (1994: 478). Ratings on the 190 questionnaires were combined with data from the interviews, 76 of which were conducted before and 94 after the introduction of a communication intervention programme that was designed to change the organizational culture. One of the researchers also became a participant observer in the organization for a period of two months. Zamanou and Glaser suggest that this triangulated approach enabled the collection of different types of data that related to different cultural elements, from values to material artefacts—something that other cultural researchers have found difficult to achieve.

As mentioned in Key concept 17.4, triangulation can also be associated with a quantitative strategy, as an approach to the development of multiple measures in order to improve confidence in findings (Webb et al. 1966); some writers have suggested that this kind of triangulation is declining in use. This can be demonstrated by reference to an article that has reviewed the methods used within business research. Scandura and Williams (2000) analysed all articles published in three top-ranking American journals, *Academy of Management Journal*, *Administrative Science Quarterly*, and *Journal of Management*, over two time periods, 1985–7 and 1995–7. They were particularly interested in tracing changing practice in triangulation of methods and the use of different measures of validity. A total of 614 articles was coded for the primary research methodologies they employed. The research showed that 'to publish in these three top-tier general management journals, researchers are increasingly employing research strategies and methodological approaches that compromise triangulation' (2000: 1259). A further finding indicated that internal, external, and construct validity had also declined during the period. They conclude that 'management research may be moving even further away from rigour' (2000: 1259), limiting the applicability of findings by failing to triangulate: that is, by not using various designs in a programme of research in order to help counterbalance the strengths and weaknesses of each.

An illustration of a study that does use a triangulation approach is an investigation by P. Stiles (2001) into the impact of boards of directors on corporate strategy. Stiles used a multi-method research design, which involved the following methods:

- *In-depth semi-structured interviews with 51 main board directors of UK public companies*. This was Stiles's primary means of collecting data. In order to develop a grounded understanding of board activities, he sought to allow directors 'to reveal their perceptions' (2001:

632). Pilot interviews, using a schedule based on analysis of existing literature, were carried out with five directors, and these were used to develop the final set of topics. Stiles also carried out a number of supplementary interviews with other stakeholders, among them a journalist, a representative from the Consumers' Association, and a number of leading academics.

- *A questionnaire survey of 121 company secretaries*. The quantitative element in Stiles's research design relied on a questionnaire, which was sent to 900 members of the Institute of Company Secretaries and Administrators. This generated a response rate of 14 per cent. Had this been the main research method upon which the study relied, the low response rate would have called into question the external validity of the findings. However, Stiles points out that questionnaire results are used 'to support the main findings, which emerged from the qualitative data and … are meant to be illustrative rather than definitive' (2001: 633).

- *Four case studies of UK public limited companies, where several board members were interviewed and secondary archival data were collected*. Stiles chose four large UK businesses in which to test findings that emerged from data collected using his two preliminary research methods. The cases were chosen because they had strong reputations but had experienced periods of turbulence and change. Stiles claims that 'this buttressing of the original findings through testing in four different research sites affords a further element of triangulation into the study, with the new data from the case testing the validity and generality of the initial findings' (2001: 634). Validity was also improved through respondent validation (see Key concept 17.3), involving a draft of the findings being sent to the case companies on which individuals were invited to comment.

Stiles's main finding, that multiple perspectives are required in order to understand fully the nature of board activity, owes something to his research approach, which enabled exploration of the strategy-making role of the board and its multifunctional nature. In this research, the use of a triangulation strategy seems to have been planned by the researcher, and the two sets of results were broadly consistent. However, researchers may carry out mixed methods research for other purposes, but in the course of doing so discover that they have generated quantitative and qualitative findings on related issues, so that they can treat such overlapping findings as a triangulation exercise. Yauch and Steudel (2003: 467) provide an example of unplanned triangulation, in a study that was conducted 'to identify key cultural factors that aided or hindered a company's ability to successfully implement manufacturing cells'. They collected qualitative data in two case study firms that had recently introduced cellular manufacturing and also developed and administered in these firms a questionnaire instrument called the 'Organizational Culture Inventory'. The main goal of using both quantitative and qualitative research was to glean through the latter some of the factors that lay behind the patterns that were uncovered through the questionnaire. However, the researchers also found that, while the two sets of data were congruent for one company, for the other they were not, prompting the researchers to explore possible reasons for the two sets of data to be inconsistent between the companies.

Whether planned or unplanned, when a triangulation exercise is undertaken, the possibility of a failure to corroborate findings always exists. This raises the issue of what approach should be taken towards inconsistent results. One approach is to treat one set of results as definitive. However, simply and arbitrarily favouring one set of findings over another is not an ideal approach to reconciling conflicting findings deriving from a triangulation exercise.

Qualitative research facilitates quantitative research

There are several ways in which qualitative research can be used to guide quantitative research.

- *Providing hypotheses*. Because of its tendency towards an unstructured, open-ended approach to data collection, qualitative research is often very helpful as a source of hypotheses or hunches that can be subsequently tested using a quantitative research strategy. An example is a study by Tripp et al. (2002) of revenge in the workplace. Initially, 88 working MBA students in the USA were asked to give an account of two incidents in which the student or someone else had sought to gain revenge against another person. The revenge episodes were examined to establish the activities involved in taking revenge. The overriding finding was that the initial episode and the revenge should be in line with each other: there should be symmetry between them. This symmetry has two elements: symmetry of consequences—the revenge should do the same amount of harm as the original wrongdoing; and symmetry of method—the way in which revenge is exacted should resemble that involved in the initial harm that was done. Drawing on this distinction, the researchers conducted a second study, using an experimental design, to test their prediction, which emerged

out of the qualitative study, that 'the symmetry of consequences will influence individual judgments of revenge [and] symmetry of method should shape individual judgments about revenge' (Tripp et al. 2002: 972–3). In fact, the experiment did not entirely support these expectations. When revenge is symmetric in terms of consequences, the experiment showed that the vengeful act is viewed more positively. This was in line with the researchers' expectations. However, symmetry of method operated in a manner contrary to their expectations: vengeful acts were viewed *more* harshly when they were symmetric with the original harmful act.

- *Aiding measurement*. The in-depth knowledge of social contexts acquired through qualitative research can be used to inform the design of survey questions for structured interviewing and self-completion questionnaires. An example is given in Research in focus 27.2, where focus groups and qualitative interviews informed the design of a questionnaire to collect data on HR competencies.

Quantitative research facilitates qualitative research

One of the chief ways in which quantitative research can prepare the ground for qualitative research is through the selection of people to be interviewed, or companies to be selected as case studies. For example, Scase and Goffee (1989) used the results of their questionnaire survey of 374 UK managers (see Research in focus 3.14) to generate a smaller, representative sample of 80 managers for in-depth interviews. Similarly, in the research by Gardner on the effects of pressure on team performance (see Research in focus 27.3), a survey of teams was followed up with a small number of case studies which were used to explain the patterns which were observed in the survey data.

Filling in the gaps

This approach to mixed methods research occurs when the researcher cannot rely on either a quantitative or a qualitative method alone and must buttress his or her findings with a method drawn from the other research strategy. Its most typical form is when ethnographers employ structured interviewing or possibly a self-completion questionnaire, because not everything they need to know about is accessible through participant observation. This kind of need can arise for several reasons, such as the need for information that is not accessible to

27.2 RESEARCH IN FOCUS
Using qualitative data to inform quantitative measurement

Lo et al. (2015) conducted a mixed-method study to understand HR competencies—the personal characteristics and behaviour which HR practitioners bring to their jobs—and the role of different competencies in contributing to organizational performance. They wished to investigate HR practitioners' *own* assessments of which competencies were important in which contexts. To do this, they began with a focus group involving 10 experienced practitioners, to generate a list of statements about what competencies were required in their roles. They also conducted a **content analysis** of a sample of job descriptions to see what competencies were listed there. On the basis of these two sources of data, they derived a list of 44 competencies which appeared to be important for HR roles.

The list was used to develop an **online survey**, which was administered anonymously to 63 HR professionals. They were asked to rate their own job on a seven-point **Likert scale** from 'mostly function' to 'mostly strategic' and to sort the 44 labels into themes. They were then asked to rate each theme in terms of importance in their current job on seven-point Likert scale from 'not at all important' to 'highly important'. The authors then used specialized software to analyse the results and create a concept map, which facilitated the identification of seven clusters of HR competencies, which varied in terms of (a) the number of individual competencies in each and (b) their relative importance from the perspective of HR practitioners in terms of functional or strategic HR roles. This mixed-method approach allowed the initial list to be developed **inductively** using qualitative data, then used to conduct quantitative analysis to map patterns. On the basis of the results, the authors were able to demonstrate the importance of context in understanding which set of competencies was important, which went beyond prior research.

observation or to qualitative interviewing (e.g. systematic information about social backgrounds of people in a particular setting), or the difficulty of gaining access to certain groups of people. For example, in her study of working couples with children Hochschild (1989) used quantitative analysis of time use to assess levels of participation in everyday domestic work. This formed the basis for her qualitative exploration based on interviews

27.3 RESEARCH IN FOCUS
Using quantitative research to facilitate qualitative research

In a study which explored the outcomes of pressure on team performance, Gardner (2012) used two complementary methods: an online survey of members of teams in a large accounting firm, combined with a matched survey of clients of the teams (there were 72 teams in the final sample); and six in-depth case studies of teams across two large firms. The survey of team members collected data on perceived pressure to perform and a number of characteristics of team members and teams. The client survey collected data on team performance. The data were used to test a series of hypotheses about associations between pressure and performance. The results showed that pressure was a 'double-edged sword', in that it increased motivation to perform, but at the same time increased the use of general skills and decreased the use of specialist skills, thereby undermining performance. The six case studies were used to explore the mechanisms which appeared to lead to these apparent outcomes of pressure. The author concluded on the basis of the case studies that the outcomes arose due to four factors: a drive towards consensus; a focus on shared knowledge; a focus on project completion rather than learning; and increased conformity to status hierarchy. By using this approach, Gardner was able to test hypotheses and demonstrate statistical associations, but also to go beneath the surface of the statistics and explore causal processes.

27.4 RESEARCH IN FOCUS
Using quantitative data about time use to fill in the gaps in a qualitative study

Hochschild (1989) took a 'naturalistic approach' to understanding the way that working parents deal with the demands of work and home life. Together with her two research associates, she interviewed 50 couples where both parents were in paid work; two-thirds of them were interviewed several times. She also interviewed 45 other individuals, including babysitters, daycare workers, schoolteachers, couples with one working parent and small children, and divorcees who had formerly been part of two-job couples. The main part of her study was thus qualitative. However, she first carried out quantitative analysis of her respondents' time use, measuring how much time they spent working and on domestic tasks using a short questionnaire sent to every thirteenth name from the personnel list of a large corporation. This quantitative aspect of Hochschild's research design enabled her to gain information that was not accessible from interview data alone. Although it would have been possible to collect information about time use through observational methods, this would have been very time-consuming. At the end of the questionnaire, respondents were asked if they were willing to volunteer to be interviewed. This sample then formed the basis for the qualitative aspect of the study.

and observation of the gender strategies that working couples use (see Research in focus 27.4). Equally, qualitative methods may be used to provide important contextual information that supplements the findings from a larger quantitative study. For example, Zamanou and Glaser (1994) used semi-structured interviews and participant observation in order to help interpret and place in context the results of statistical analyses of the Organizational Culture Scale (OCS), which formed the basis for their questionnaire survey of culture change in a government organization. They state:

> the results of the OCS provided a quantitative description of the culture of the organization, but the study still lacked an exploration of the deeper, more subjective, and less observable layers of culture. Thus qualitative measures (i.e. interviews, observations) were combined with the questionnaire results to illustrate the quantitative findings and to provide an examination of the depth of the culture.

(1994: 479)

Static and processual features

One of the contrasts suggested by Table 17.1 is that, whereas quantitative research tends to bring out a static picture of social life, qualitative research is more processual. The term 'static' can easily be viewed in a rather negative light. In fact, it is very valuable on many occasions to uncover regularities, and it is often the identification of such regularities that allows a processual analysis to proceed. A mixed methods research approach offers the prospect of being able to combine both elements.

For example, Zamanou and Glaser (1994) wanted to explore the impact of a communication intervention programme designed to change the culture of a governmental organization from hierarchical and authoritarian to participative and involved. They argue that the study of organizational culture lends itself to a mixed methods research approach because different methods can be used to capture different cultural elements and processes. In addition, as we mentioned in Chapter 17, a longitudinal research design can enable understanding of events over time (see Research in focus 19.2). The questionnaire survey used by Zamanou and Glaser provided a static picture of the organizational culture prior to the intervention (Time 1) and again after it had ended (Time 2). It was hypothesized that ratings on scales such as teamwork, morale, and involvement would be significantly higher after the intervention than before it. Interviews were then used to explore employees' perceptions of culture in more detail, asking them to describe cultural incidents, events, and stories that had helped to form their perceptions. However, it is not only qualitative research that can incorporate processual analysis. Quantitative diary study research by Rosemary Stewart (1967) analysed the way in which 160 managers spent their time during a four-week period in order to discover similarities and differences in their use of time and the reasons for those differences (see Research in focus 11.4). In focusing on managerial activity over a period of time, this study provided a dynamic, rather than a static, analysis of what managers actually do.

Research issues and participants' perspectives

Sometimes, researchers want to gather two kinds of data: qualitative data that will allow them to gain access to the perspectives of the people they are studying; and quantitative data that will allow them to explore specific issues in which they are interested. They are seeking to explore an area in both ways, so that they can both adopt an unstructured approach to data collection in which participants' meanings are the focus of attention and investigate a specific set of issues through the more structured approach of quantitative research.

An example of this is Ruth Milkman's (1997) study of a General Motors car manufacturing plant in the USA, referred to in Chapter 20. Milkman was interested in the nature of the labour process in the late twentieth century and whether or not new factory conditions were markedly different for car workers from the negative portrayals of such work in the 1950s and early 1960s (e.g. Blauner 1964). As such, she was interested in the meaning of industrial work. She employed semi-structured interviews and focus groups with car production workers to elicit data relevant to this aspect of her work. However, in addition she had some specific interests in a 'buyout' plan that the company's management introduced in the mid-1980s after it had initiated a variety of changes to work practices. The plan gave workers the opportunity to give up their jobs for a substantial cash payment. In 1988, Milkman carried out a questionnaire survey of workers who had taken up the company's buyout offer. These workers were surveyed again the following year and in 1991. The reason for the surveys was that Milkman had some very specific interests in the buyout scheme, such as reasons for taking the buyout, how they had fared since leaving General Motors, how they felt about their current employment, and differences between social groups (in particular, different ethnic groups) in current earnings relative to those at General Motors.

The problem of generality

As noted in Chapter 26, a problem that is often made of qualitative research is that because findings are sometimes presented in an anecdotal fashion we are given little sense of the relative importance of the themes identified. Silverman (1984, 1985) has argued that some quantification of findings from qualitative research can often help to uncover the generality of the phenomena being described.

The combined use of qualitative and quantitative research methods represents a common pattern in case study research in business research, used by researchers in order to enhance the generality of their findings. An illustration of this tendency is given in Research in focus 27.5, where Kanter, in her classic book *Men and Women of the Corporation* (1977), describes the diverse range of methods that she used in her case study of a single organization, Indsco Supply Corporation. Even though the fieldwork was undertaken in just one company and the case constituted a focus of interest in its own right, Kanter claims that its findings are typical of other large corporations. However, it is not coincidental that she makes this claim only after having accounted in some detail for the complex set of methods that were involved in her mixed methods research approach.

Other studies have attempted to counter the criticism of anecdotalism that is levelled at qualitative research by introducing a quantitative aspect into their analysis. These include Bryman et al.'s (1996) study of leadership in the British police force and Gabriel's (1998) study of organizational culture (see Chapter 26), both of which calculate the frequency of themes in order to provide a sense of their relative importance. However, Silverman warns that such quantification should reflect research participants' own ways of understanding their social world. If this occurs, the quantification is more consistent with the goals of qualitative research.

Interpreting the relationship between variables

One problem frequently encountered by quantitative researchers is how to explain relationships between variables. One strategy is to look for what is called an intervening variable, which is influenced by the independent variable but which in turn has an effect on the dependent variable. Thus, if we find a relationship between gender and small business ownership, we might propose that entrepreneurial attitude is one factor behind the relationship:

gender → entrepreneurial attitude → small business ownership.

This sequence implies that the variable of gender has an impact on how an individual feels about taking on an entrepreneurial role and becoming committed to the ideals associated with it (for example, belief in economic self-advancement, individualism, self-reliance, and a strong work ethic), which in turn has implications for the kinds of choices they make within the labour market. However, an alternative approach might be to seek

27.5 RESEARCH IN FOCUS
A mixed methods case study

Kanter (1977) describes her research at Indsco as a 'case study of a single organization'. Kanter describes how, over a five-year period, she spent time as a consultant, participant-observer, and researcher at Indsco Supply Corporation. Her sources of data included:

- a **postal questionnaire** survey, taking 2–3 hours to complete, of 205 sales workers and managers out of a **population** of 350;
- semi-structured interviews with the first 20 women to enter the sales force;
- access to a survey of employees on attitudes towards promotion;
- content analysis of 100 performance appraisal forms;
- group discussions with employees—from managers to secretaries—recorded verbatim;
- participation in meetings;
- participant observation in training programmes;
- internal reports, memoranda, and public documents relating to personnel policies;
- conversations in offices, at social gatherings, or in people's homes.

Overall, Kanter suggests that she spent over 120 personal contact days on-site, and the number of people with whom she held conversations was well over 120. A further 500 people participated in written surveys—the primary source of quantitative data used in the study. Kanter draws attention to the potential for generalizability from a single case, by suggesting that 'the case provided material out of which to generate the concepts and flesh for giving meaning to the abstract propositions I was developing' (1977: 332).

Although Kanter does not claim statistical generalizability for her data, she does draw attention to the way that she used the data from the case to generate concepts that could be transferred to other organizational contexts. Hence she states that, after having formulated her initial impressions about Indsco, she had conversations with informants in three other large corporations 'in order to satisfy myself that Indsco … was not particularly unique in the relationships I observed. I learned that Indsco, indeed, was typical, and its story could be that of many large corporations' (1977: 332).

to explore the relationship between the variables further by conducting a qualitative investigation of the ways in which entrepreneurial work is situated within gendered processes that are embedded within society (Mirchandani 1999). This would involve challenging the sequence of these variables, drawing attention to the gendered nature of entrepreneurial values.

A good example of this is Katie Truss's (2001) argument that more qualitative research is needed in order to increase our understanding of the link between HRM and organizational performance. She suggests that many existing studies rely on a single informant in each organization and focus on financial performance, rather than on a broader range of outcome variables. In contrast, adopting a mixed methods longitudinal research design, Truss was able to explain how Hewlett-Packard's people management philosophy, known as 'The HP Way', was translated into policies by the HR function. The questionnaire

data enabled comparison with other companies, showing, for example, that employees were significantly more positive regarding the effectiveness of recruitment at Hewlett Packard (HP). Overall, employees received more training and development than in the other high-performance companies, and appraisals were regularly conducted. However, once the researchers attempted to probe beneath the surface, it emerged that 'The HP Way' was open to quite different interpretations. For example, during the first wave of data collection it was found that, prior to the redundancies in the 1980s, employees had believed that 'The HP Way' meant they would have 'jobs for life'. It was also found that the move towards flexible working was having an adverse effect on staff loyalty.

In terms of recruitment and selection, the strength of corporate values expressed in 'The HP Way' had given rise to a rather narrow view of the HP employee, and individuals who did not fit this profile were unlikely to survive within the company. These findings suggest that changes in the company's environment, which was becoming increasingly competitive and hostile, were having a negative effect on HRM. In conclusion, the research provides only limited support for the view that effective HRM is the key to achieving sustained competitive advantage, instead suggesting that environmental events and conditions play a significant part. Finally, Truss concludes that these findings are the direct result of the qualitative aspect of the study:

> Had we relied on questionnaire data obtained from a single informant (the HR director, as in other studies) and carried out a quantitative analysis linking performance with human resource processes, we would have concluded that this organization was an example of an organization employing 'High Performance Work Practices' to good effect. However, employing a contextualized, case-study method has enabled us to see below the surface and tap into the reality experienced by employees, which often contrasts sharply with the company rhetoric.
>
> (2001: 1145)

The quantitative research results could thus be seen as somewhat misleading, in that they reflect the organization's rhetorical position rather than the reality experienced by employees. Truss is suggesting that the latter would not have been exposed without the addition of qualitative methods of investigation.

Another mixed methods study in which qualitative findings allowed the authors to arrive at a more rounded picture than the quantitative data alone revealed can be found in Research in focus 2.15. The questionnaire data collected by Holmberg et al. (2008) revealed the general pattern whereby leadership was found to influence the success or failure of the implementation of evidence-based treatment practices for drug abuse and criminal behaviour in Sweden, but the qualitative data brought out the specific significance of leaders being actively interested in the programme and being available for support. A futher example of qualitative data shedding light on the connections between variables may be seen in Research in focus 27.6.

Studying different aspects of a phenomenon

This category of mixed methods research incorporates two forms that Bryman referred to as 'the relationship between "macro" and "micro" levels' and 'stages in the research process' (Bryman 1988a: 147–51). This draws attention to the tendency to think of quantitative research as most suited to the investigation of 'macro' phenomena (such as social mobility) and qualitative research as better suited to 'micro' ones (such as small-group interaction).

In the example shown in Research in focus 27.7, Chan and Li (2010) combined quantitative research and qualitative research in order to examine different facets of consumer interactions in a virtual community. The combination produced greater understanding than might have been possible using only one research strategy.

In Table 17.1, the category 'stages in the research process' draws attention to the possibility that quantitative and qualitative research may be suited to different phases in a study. However, it now seems to us that these are simply aspects of a more general tendency for quantitative and qualitative researchers to examine different aspects of their area of interest.

A further illustration of the use of mixed methods research to explore different aspects of a phenomenon can be found in a study conducted by Perlow (1997, 1999) of how people use their time at work. Although this study mainly comprised ethnographic methods, which included participant observation and semi-structured interviewing, Perlow also used a time-use diary (see Chapter 11), similar to the one used by R. Stewart (1967; see Research in focus 11.4), to record and measure quantitatively the time that software engineers spent on various activities each day. Perlow explains:

> On randomly chosen days, I asked three or four of the twelve software engineers to track their activities from when they woke up until they went to bed. I asked them to wear a digital watch that beeped on the hour and, at each beep, to write down everything that they had done during the previous hour. I encouraged them to write down interactions as they occurred and to use the beeps as an extra reminder to keep track of their activities.
>
> (Perlow 1999: 61)

The ethnographic methods were intended to capture the cultural norms and values held by the software engineers, while the time-use diary was specifically directed towards measurement of their time use. Using this combined approach, Perlow was able to build up a picture of *how* the engineers use their work time (using a quantitative strategy) and an understanding of *why* they use their work time in this way (using qualitative methods). In this study, mixed methods research was geared to addressing different kinds of research question. After each tracking log had been completed, Perlow conducted a debriefing interview with each engineer, who explained the

27.6 RESEARCH IN FOCUS
Expanding on quantitative findings with qualitative research in a study of leadership

Currie et al. (2009) drew on institutional theory to illuminate the connections between leadership and organizational change. They note that school leaders in the UK operate within a system in which a particular kind of leadership (results-oriented leadership) is increasingly valued over traditional leadership patterns within the sector (professional value-based leadership). They wanted to examine whether the former leadership approach was more effective than the latter and to examine how far institutional forces (especially values and norms about leadership) affect leadership as it is practised on the ground. In order to investigate the relationship between leadership and effectiveness, the researchers conducted a content analysis of 200 reports by the UK Office of Standards in Education (Ofsted) covering the period 2002–4. These are reports produced by inspectors acting for Ofsted after they inspect standards in a school. Inspections are carried out on a regular basis. Through the content analysis it was possible to identify the leadership pattern for 182 of the 200 reports. Of these, 49 were results-oriented and 133 were professional value-based. School performance was measured as the percentage of students at each school who achieved grade C or above in five or more General Certificate of Secondary Education subjects. Currie et al. found that whether the predominant leadership approach was results-oriented or professional value-based was unrelated to school performance. The researchers then conducted semi-structured interviews with heads or deputy heads at 30 schools. Some of the questions asked were informed by the findings deriving from the content analysis. The findings from this phase of the research strongly suggest that professional value-based leadership is still prevalent and that the old institutional environment is fairly resistant to policy-driven values that emphasize results. As one of the researchers' interviewees put it:

We educate children, not make widgets. Good lessons. Nothing else matters at all. All we need is high quality teachers that teach high quality lessons. My job is to provide a role model and give them a receptive context in which to do it. I don't care for anything else. Obviously this leads to better results.

(a school principal, quoted in Currie et al. 2009: 673)

The researchers show that heads and deputy heads sometimes grafted a results-based orientation onto a traditional professional value-based leadership, as can be seen in this quotation. Principals who express a commitment to professional value-based leadership are in effect moderating their approach by instilling a focus on results as well. Straddling both leadership approaches allowed the heads and deputy heads to enhance the legitimacy of their leadership in the eyes of the two different constituencies—peers and colleagues, and policy-makers and inspectors. Adopting a mixed methods approach allowed Currie et al. to establish the lack of a relationship between the predominant leadership approach and performance and to embellish that finding with qualitative findings that demonstrate the subtle interplay between the two leadership approaches and the institutional forces at play. As Stentz et al. (2012) observe, this is a good example of a sequential explanatory study in which the quantitative component has priority (i.e. QUAN→qual).

patterns of interaction recorded on the log sheets. From this Perlow was able to calculate the total time the engineer spent at work and the proportion of that time spent on interactive versus individual activities. Perlow found that, although 60 per cent of the engineers' time was spent on individual activities, and just over 30 per cent was spent on interactive activities, the time spent alone did not occur in one consecutive block:

Rather, examination of the sequences of individual and interactive activities revealed that a large proportion of

the time spent uninterrupted on individual activities was spent in very short blocks of time, sandwiched between interactive activities. Seventy-five percent of the blocks of time spent uninterrupted on individual activities were one hour or less in length, and, of those blocks of time, 60 percent were half an hour or less in length.

(Perlow 1999: 64)

This finding forms the basis for the theoretical conclusions that Perlow is able to draw in relation to the crisis mentality induced by the engineers, their work

27.7 RESEARCH IN FOCUS
Combining netnography and an online survey in a study of a virtual community of consumers

Chan and Li (2010) were interested in virtual communities: in particular the reasons why participants help each other and how such help relates to participants' commitment to the communities, as well as their behavioural intentions in the form of online shopping. The researchers set up several hypotheses. In order to address these hypotheses, the researchers combined netnography (see Research in focus 19.11) and an online survey. However, the survey was used for testing all of the hypotheses and the netnography's role was to explore and provide 'a preliminary understanding of the practice, potential drivers, and impacts of reciprocity' (Chan and Li 2010: 1037) among participants in an online community. The netnography comprised an examination of postings on a popular Chinese website designed for women (http://www.onlylady.com) and in particular on its cosmetic message board, which is a source of information and discussions concerning beauty products. The researchers read and interpreted postings covering the period September 2004 to January 2005. The researchers show through their netnography that conveying information and support through virtual interactions was itself a motivator of reciprocal help and support. In some cases, the discussion threads indicate that participants felt impelled to purchase products to get bigger discounts for others and for themselves in the future. For the survey, the researchers obtained permission to conduct a survey of participants. They initiated a thread and invited members of the online community to participate in the survey, resulting in a sample of 899. The resulting data allowed the researchers to test their hypotheses and as a result to find, for example, that stronger social ties among participants and greater enjoyment derived from interaction are associated with greater reciprocity. Reciprocity in turn was found to be associated with the propensity to co-shop.

This is an example of a study in which the combination of quantitative research and qualitative research allowed different facets of the phenomenon of interest—consumer interactions in a virtual community—to be examined. Greater understanding could be gleaned than from one research strategy alone. The research has the characteristics of an embedded mixed methods design with the quantitative research as the priority approach.

patterns, and the heroic acts that this culture encourages and rewards. In her analysis, she is able to illustrate these themes through presentation of the ethnographic research data. However, it is the *quantitative* analysis of time use that provides the initial impetus for the theoretical conclusions that Perlow is able to draw.

This form of mixed methods research entails making decisions about which kinds of research question are best answered using a quantitative research method and which by a qualitative research method, and about how best to interweave the different elements, especially since, as suggested in the context of the discussion about triangulation, the outcomes of mixtures of methods are not always predictable.

Solving a puzzle

The outcomes of research are, as suggested by the last sentence, not always easy to anticipate. Although people sometimes cynically suggest that social scientists

find what they want to find or that social scientists just convey the obvious, the capacity of the obvious to provide us with puzzling surprises should never be underestimated. When this occurs, employing a research method associated with a research strategy not initially used can be helpful. One context in which this might occur is when qualitative research is used as a salvage operation, when an anticipated set of results from a quantitative investigation fails to materialize (Weinholtz et al. 1995). Research in focus 27.8 provides an interesting illustration of this use of mixed methods research. Another situation arises when questionnaire response rates are too low to be used as the sole data source upon which to base findings. P. Stiles (2001), for example, generated only a 14 per cent response rate from the 900 questionnaires that were sent to members of the Institute of Company Secretaries and Administrators. Interview and case study data provided him with alternative data sources upon which to focus.

27.8 RESEARCH IN FOCUS

Using mixed methods research to solve a puzzle: the case of displayed emotions in convenience stores

An example of combining quantitative and qualitative research to solve a puzzle is Sutton and Rafaeli's (1988) study of the display of emotions in organizations. Following a traditional quantitative research strategy, based on their examination of such studies as Hochschild (1983), Sutton and Rafaeli formulated a **hypothesis** suggesting a **positive relationship** between the display of positive emotions to retail shoppers (smiling, friendly greeting, eye contact) and the level of retail sales. In other words, we would expect that, when retail staff are friendly and give time to shoppers, sales will be better than when they fail to do so. Sutton and Rafaeli had access to data that allowed this hypothesis to be tested. The data derived from a study of 576 convenience stores in a national retail chain in the USA.

Structured observation of retail workers provided the data on the display of positive emotions, and sales data provided information for the other variable. The hypothesis implied that there would be a positive relationship—that is, that stores in which there was a more pronounced display of positive emotions would report superior sales. When the data were analysed, a relationship was confirmed, but it was found to be negative; that is, stores in which retail workers were less inclined to smile, be friendly, and so on tended to have better sales than those in which such emotions were in evidence. This was the reverse of what the authors had anticipated they would uncover. Sutton and Rafaeli (1992: 124) considered restating their hypothesis to make it seem that they had found what they had expected, but fortunately resisted the temptation!

Instead, they conducted a qualitative investigation of four case study stores to help understand what was happening. This involved a number of methods: unstructured observation of interactions between staff and customers; semi-structured interviews with store managers; brief periods of participant observation; casual conversations with store managers, supervisors, executives, and others; and data gathered through posing as a customer in stores. The stores were chosen in terms of two criteria: high or low sales, and whether or not staff typically displayed positive emotions. The qualitative investigation suggested that the relationship between the display of positive emotions and sales was negative, but that sales were likely to be a cause rather than a consequence of the display of emotions. This pattern occurred because, in stores with high levels of sales, staff were under greater pressure and encountered longer queues at checkouts. Staff therefore had less time and inclination for the pleasantries associated with the display of positive emotions. The quantitative data were then re-analysed with this alternative interpretation in mind and it was supported.

Thus, instead of the causal sequence being

more displays of positive emotions → higher retail sales

it was

higher retail sales → fewer displays of positive emotions.

This exercise also highlights the main difficulty associated with inferring causal direction from a cross-sectional research design (see Key concept 3.11).

Like unplanned triangulation, this category of mixed methods research is more or less impossible to plan for. It essentially provides the quantitative researcher with an alternative either to reconstructing a hypothesis or to filing the results away (and probably never looking at them again) when findings are inconsistent with a hypothesis. It is probably not an option in all cases in which a hypothesis is not confirmed. There may also be instances in which a quantitative study could shed light on puzzling findings drawn from a qualitative investigation.

Quality issues in mixed methods research

There can be little doubt that mixed methods research is far more common than when one of us first started writing about it (Bryman 1988*a*). Two significant factors in prompting this development are:

1. a growing preparedness to think of research methods as techniques of data collection or analysis that are not rigidly determined by epistemological and ontological baggage; and

2. a softening in the attitude towards quantitative research among feminist researchers, who had previously been highly resistant to its use (see Chapter 17 for a discussion of this point).

Other factors are doubtless relevant, but these two developments do seem especially significant. However, it is important to realize that mixed methods research is not intrinsically superior to research which uses only one method or works within a single strategy. It is tempting to think that mixed methods research is more or less inevitably superior to research that relies on a single method on the grounds that more, and more varied, findings are inevitably 'a good thing'. Indeed, social scientists sometimes display such a view (Bryman 2007*b*).

However, several points must be borne in mind. These reflections are influenced by writings concerned with indicators of quality in mixed methods research (e.g. Bryman et al. 2008; O'Cathain et al. 2008). Rather than include all possible quality criteria that can or have been applied to mixed methods research (e.g. O'Cathain 2010), the approach taken here is to emphasize criteria that recur in discussions of quality in connection with mixed methods research (Bryman 2014):

1. Mixed methods research must be competently designed and conducted. Poorly conducted research will yield suspect findings, no matter how many methods are employed.

2. Mixed methods research must be appropriate to the research questions and the research area with which you are concerned. There is no point collecting more data simply on the basis that 'more is better'. Mixed methods research has to be dovetailed to research questions, just as all research methods must be. It is, after all, likely to consume considerably more time and financial resources than research relying on just one method.

3. It is best to be explicit about why you have conducted mixed methods research. Providing a rationale for its use gives the reader a better sense of the relationship between the research questions and the research methods and also what the use of two or more methods was meant to achieve in terms of the overall project.

4. Try not to think of mixed methods research as made up of separate components. It is best to consider how the quantitative and qualitative components are related to each other from the outset. There is a feeling among many writers with an interest in such research that many so-called mixed methods projects are not really mixed at all, because the researchers do not adequately integrate their quantitative and qualitative findings. This is particularly evident when researchers present and discuss their quantitative and qualitative findings separately rather than bringing the evidence together.

5. Make sure that you provide a sufficiently detailed account of all of the methodological details of the research for both the quantitative and the qualitative components. Sometimes researchers provide more detail concerning one element or give only a surface treatment of both. So, make sure that information about sampling, design, and administration of research instruments, analysis of the data, and the like are provided for both components.

6. As awareness of the different types of mixed methods design has spread, there is a growing expectation that the researcher stipulates the kind of design he or she is using and the reasons for that choice. The designs outlined in the section above on 'Different types of mixed methods design' provides an outline of the fundamental types of design.

In other words, mixed methods research should not be considered as an approach that is universally applicable or as a panacea. It may provide a better understanding of a phenomenon than if just one method had been used. It may also frequently enhance our confidence in our own or others' findings—for example, when a triangulation exercise has been conducted. It may even improve our chances of access to settings to which we might otherwise be excluded; Milkman (1997: 192), for example, has suggested in the context of her research on a General Motors factory that the promise that she 'would produce "hard," quantitative data through survey research was what secured [her] access', even though she had no experience in this method. But the general point remains: that mixed methods research, while offering great potential in many instances, is subject to similar constraints and considerations as research relying on a single method or research strategy.

On the other hand, Molina-Azorín (2012) compared the mixed methods articles published between 1980 and 2006 in *Strategic Management Journal* with an equivalent set of single-strategy articles from the same journal. He found that mixed methods articles were noticeably more likely to be cited in other publications. ('Citation', making reference to a particular article in other articles, is sometimes treated as an indicator of the impact of a piece of work within its field.) For example, eight years after publication the mean number of citations of a mixed methods article was around 6 but the equivalent number of citations of a single-strategy article was around 3.5. Molina-Azorín's findings suggest that mixed methods articles typically make a greater impact.

KEY POINTS

- While there has been a growth in the amount of mixed methods research, not all writers support its use.
- Objections to mixed methods research tend to be the result of a view that there are epistemological and ontological impediments to the combination of quantitative and qualitative research.
- There are several ways of combining quantitative and qualitative research and of representing mixed methods research.
- The outcomes of combining quantitative and qualitative research can be planned or unplanned.

QUESTIONS FOR REVIEW

- What is mixed methods research?

The arguments against mixed methods research

- What are the main elements of the embedded methods argument and the paradigm argument against mixed methods research?

Two versions of the debate about quantitative and qualitative research

- What are the main elements of the philosophical and the technical or practical versions of the debate about quantitative and qualitative research? What are the implications of these two versions of the debate for mixed methods research?

The rise of mixed methods research

- How does the field of business research compare with other areas of the social sciences in terms of the frequency with which mixed methods research is employed?

Approaches to mixed methods research

- Why might it be helpful to distinguish between different mixed methods research designs in terms of the priority and the sequence of the quantitative and the qualitative components?
- What are the chief ways in which quantitative and qualitative research have been combined?
- What is the logic of triangulation?

- Traditionally, qualitative research has been depicted as having a preparatory role in relation to quantitative research. To what extent do the different forms of mixed methods research reflect this view?

Quality issues in mixed methods research

- Why is it important to integrate the quantitative and the qualitative strands in mixed methods research as far as possible?

- Is mixed methods research necessarily superior to single strategy research?

ONLINE RESOURCES

www.oup.com/uk/brm5e/

Visit the Interactive Research Guide that accompanies this book to complete an exercise relating to mixed methods research.

GLOSSARY

Abductive A type of reasoning with strong ties to *inductive* reasoning. Abductive reasoning starts with observation of phenomena and then seeks to develop explanations for them, often by working iteratively between theory and data. This form of reasoning can be based on quantitative or qualitative data and informed by objectivist or constructionist *ontological* assumptions.

Action research An approach in which the action researcher and client collaborate in the diagnosis of an organizational or job-related problem and seek to develop a solution to the problem based on this diagnosis.

Adjacency pair A term used in *conversation analysis* referring to the tendency for certain kinds of activity in talk to be characterized by linked phases.

Ad libitum sampling A sampling approach in *structured observation* whereby, at previously determined time intervals, whatever is happening at the moment is recorded.

Arithmetic mean Also known simply as the mean, this is what we know in everyday usage as the average—namely, the total of a distribution of values divided by the number of values.

Asynchronous online interview or focus group Online interviews may be asynchronous or *synchronous*. In the case of the former, the transactions between participants are not in real time, so that there may be long spaces of time between interviewers' questions and participants' replies, and in the case of focus groups, between participants' contributions to the discussion.

Attached email survey A survey in which respondents are sent a questionnaire, which is received as an email attachment. Compare with *embedded email survey*.

Behaviour sampling A sampling approach in *structured observation* whereby an entire group is watched and the observer records who was involved in a particular kind of behaviour.

Biographical method See *life history method*.

Bivariate analysis The examination of the *relationship* between two *variables*, as in *contingency tables* or correlation.

CAQDAS An acronym of computer-*assisted* (or -aided) qualitative *data* analysis software.

Case study A *research design* that entails the detailed and intensive analysis of a single case. The term is sometimes extended to include the study of just two or three cases for comparative purposes.

Categorical variable See *nominal variable*.

Causality A causal connection between *variables*, rather than a mere *relationship* or association between them.

Cell The point in a table, such as a *contingency table*, where the rows and columns intersect.

Census The enumeration of an entire *population*. Unlike a *sample*, which comprises a count of *some* units in a population, a census relates to *all* units in a population. Thus, if a *questionnaire* is sent to every person in a town or to all members of a profession, the research should be characterized as a census.

Chi-square test Chi-square (χ^2) is a test of *statistical significance*, which is typically employed to establish how confident we can be that the findings displayed in a *contingency table* can be generalized from a *probability sample* to a *population*.

Closed question A question employed in an *interview schedule* or *self-completion questionnaire* that presents the respondent with a set of possible answers to choose from. Also called fixed-choice question and *pre-coded question*.

Cluster sample A sampling procedure in which at an initial stage the researcher samples areas (i.e. clusters) and then samples units from these clusters, usually using a *probability sampling* method.

Code, coding In *quantitative research*, codes are numbers that are assigned to data about people or other units of analysis when the data are not inherently numerical. In *questionnaire*-based research, the answer to a question (e.g. 'strongly agree') is assigned a number (e.g. 5) so that the information can be statistically processed. Thus, each person who answers 'strongly agree' will receive the same number (in this case 5). When answers are textual, respondents' answers must be grouped into categories and those categories are then coded. In *qualitative research*, coding is the process whereby data are broken down into component parts, which are given names.

Coding frame A listing of the codes used in relation to the analysis of data. In relation to answers to a *structured* *interview* schedule or *questionnaire*, the coding frame will delineate the categories used in connection with each question. It is particularly crucial in relation to the coding of *open questions*. With *closed questions*, the coding frame is essentially incorporated into the pre-given answers, hence the frequent use of the term *pre-coded question* to describe such questions.

Coding manual In *content analysis*, this is the statement of instructions to coders that outlines all the possible categories for each dimension being coded.

Coding schedule In *content analysis*, this is the form onto which all the data relating to an item being coded will be entered.

Comparative design A *research design* that entails the comparison of two or more cases in order to illuminate existing theory or generate theoretical insights as a result of contrasting findings uncovered through the comparison.

Concept A name given to a category that organizes observations and ideas by virtue of their possessing common features.

Concurrent validity One of the main approaches to establishing *measurement validity*. It entails relating a measure to a criterion on which cases (e.g. people) are known to differ and that is relevant to the *concept* in question.

Confounding variable A *variable* that is related to each of two variables the result of which is to produce the appearance of a *relationship* between the two variables. Such a relationship is a spurious relationship.

Constant An attribute in terms of which cases do not differ. Compare with *variable*.

Constant comparison A central tool of *grounded theory* that entails constantly comparing new data with existing data, concepts, and categories. It also entails comparing categories with each other and categories with concepts.

Construct The same as a *concept*, but in much *quantitative research* 'construct' is the preferred term.

Constructionism, constructionist An *ontological* position (often also referred to as 'constructivism') that asserts that social phenomena and their meanings are continually being accomplished by social actors. It is antithetical to *objectivism*.

Constructivism See *constructionism*.

Content analysis An approach to the analysis of documents and texts that seeks to quantify content in terms of predetermined categories and in a systematic and replicable manner. The term is sometimes used in connection with qualitative research as well—see *qualitative content analysis*.

Contingency table A table, comprising rows and columns, that shows the *relationship* between two *variables*. Usually, at least one of the variables is a *nominal variable*. Each cell in the table shows the frequency of occurrence of that intersection of categories of each of the two variables and usually a percentage.

Continuous recording A procedure in *structured observation* whereby observation occurs for extended periods, so that the frequency and duration of certain types of behaviour can be carefully recorded.

Convenience sample A sample that is selected because of its availability to the researcher. It is a form of *non-probability sample*.

Convergent validity An assessment of the *measurement validity* of a measure that compares it to another measure of the same concept that has been generated from a different method.

Conversation analysis The fine-grained analysis of talk as it occurs in interaction in naturally occurring situations. The talk is recorded and *transcribed* so that the detailed analyses can be carried out. The analysis is concerned with uncovering the underlying structures of talk in interaction and as such with the achievement of order through interaction. Conversation analysis is grounded in *ethnomethodology*.

Correlation An approach to the analysis of *relationships* between *interval/ratio variables* and/or *ordinal variables* that seeks to assess the strength and direction of the relationship between the variables concerned. *Pearson's r* and *Spearman's rho* are both methods for assessing the level of correlation between variables.

Covert observation, covert research Terms frequently used in connection with *ethnographic* research in which the researcher does not reveal his or her true identity. Such research violates the ethical principle of *informed consent*.

Cramér's *V* A method for assessing the strength of the *relationship* between two *variables*, at least one of which must have more than two categories.

Critical incident method A technique that usually relies on *structured interviewing* to elicit from respondents an account of key events or specific kinds of behaviour (critical incidents) and their consequences. Analysis involves interpretation of critical incidents so as to identify common patterns of behaviour.

Critical realism A *realist* methodology that asserts that the study of the social world should be concerned with the identification of the structures that generate that world. Critical realism is 'critical' because its practitioners aim to identify structures in order to change them, so that inequalities and injustices may be counteracted. Unlike *positivism*, critical realism accepts that the structures that are identified may not be perceptible by the senses. Thus, whereas *positivism* is *empiricist*, critical realism is not.

Cross-sectional design A *research design* that entails the collection of data on more than one case (usually quite a lot more than one) and at a single point in time in order to collect a body of quantitative or quantifiable data in connection with two or more *variables* (usually many more than two), which are then examined to detect patterns of association. The cross-sectional design is also often called 'social survey design'.

Deductive An approach to the relationship between theory and research in which the latter is conducted with reference to hypotheses and ideas inferred from the former. Compare with *inductive*.

Dependent variable A *variable* that is causally influenced by another variable (i.e. an *independent variable*).

Diary In the context of social research methods, a term that can mean different things. Three types of diary can be distinguished: diaries written or completed at the behest of a researcher; personal diaries that can be analysed as *personal documents*, but that were produced spontaneously; and diaries written by social researchers to log their activities and reflections.

Dichotomous variable A *variable* with just two categories.

Dimension Refers to an aspect of a *concept*.

Discourse analysis An approach to the analysis of talk and other forms of language that emphasizes the ways in which versions of reality are accomplished through language.

Discriminant validity The extent to which a *measure* used for a concept is different in content from another measure used for the same concept, so that there is not excessive overlap between related measures of that concept.

Distribution of values A term used to refer to the entire data relating to a *variable*. Thus, the ages of members of a *sample* represent the distribution of values for that variable for that sample.

Ecological fallacy The error of assuming that inferences about individuals can be made from findings relating to aggregate data.

Ecological validity A concern with the question of whether or not social scientific findings are relevant and applicable to people's everyday, natural social settings.

Embedded email survey A social survey in which respondents are sent an email that contains a *questionnaire* in the body of the email. Compare with *attached email survey*.

Empiricism An approach to the study of reality that suggests that only knowledge gained through experience and the senses is acceptable.

Epistemology, epistemological A theory of knowledge. It is particularly employed in this book to refer to a stance on what should pass as acceptable knowledge. See *positivism*, *realism*, and *interpretivism*.

Eta (η) A test of the strength of the *relationship* between two *variables*. The *independent variable* must be a *nominal*

variable and the *dependent variable* must be an *interval variable* or *ratio variable*. The resulting level of correlation will always be positive.

Ethnographic content analysis See *qualitative content analysis*.

Ethnography, ethnographer Like *participant observation*, a research method in which the researcher immerses him- or herself in a social setting for an extended period of time, observing behaviour, listening to what is said in conversations both between others and with the fieldworker, and asking questions. However, the term has a more inclusive sense than participant observation, which seems to emphasize the observational component. Also, the term 'an ethnography' is frequently used to refer to the written output of ethnographic research.

Ethnomethodology A sociological perspective concerned with the way in which social order is accomplished through talk and interaction. It provides the intellectual foundations of *conversation analysis*.

Evaluation research Research that is concerned with the evaluation of real-life interventions in the social world.

Experience sampling Also called 'event sampling', experience sampling refers to various methods that seek to capture affective states and/or behaviour at certain points in time. These 'points in time' are determined by the researcher and when they occur, research participants have to record such things as what they are doing or how they are feeling.

Experiment A *research design* that strives to rule out alternative explanations of findings deriving from it (i.e. possessing *internal validity*) by having at least (*a*) an experimental group, which is exposed to a treatment, and a control group, which is not; and (*b*) *random assignment* to the two groups.

External validity A concern with the question of whether or not the results of a study can be generalized beyond the specific research context in which it was conducted.

Face validity A concern with whether or not an *indicator* appears to reflect the content of the *concept* in question.

Facilitator See *moderator*.

Factor analysis A statistical technique used for large numbers of *variables* to establish whether there is a tendency for groups of them to be inter-related. It is often used with *multiple-indicator measures* to see if the *indicators* tend to bunch to form one or more groups of indicators. These groups of indicators are called factors and each must then be given a name.

Feminist research Research which is conducted with the purpose of furthering the interests of women by challenging gendered power relations and practices of exploitation and oppression, focusing on issues of concern to women and enabling their voices to be heard.

Field notes A detailed chronicle by an *ethnographer* of events, conversations, and behaviour, and the researcher's initial reflections on them.

Fixed-choice question See *closed question*.

Focal sampling A sampling approach in *structured observation* whereby a sampled individual is observed for a set period of time. The observer records all examples of whatever forms of behaviour are of interest.

Focus group A form of group interview in which there are several participants (in addition to the *moderator* or facilitator); there is an emphasis in the questioning on a fairly tightly defined topic; and the emphasis is upon interaction within the group and the joint construction of meaning.

Frequency table A table that displays the number and/or percentage of units (e.g. people) in different categories of a *variable*.

Generalization, generalizability A concern with the *external validity* of research findings.

Grounded theory An approach to the analysis of qualitative data that aims to generate theory out of research data by achieving a close fit between the two.

Hawthorne effect See *reactivity*.

Hermeneutics A term drawn from theology that, when imported into the social sciences, is concerned with the theory and method of the interpretation of human action. It emphasizes the need to understand from the perspective of the social actor.

Hypothesis An informed speculation, which is set up to be tested, about the possible *relationship* between two or more *variables*.

Independent variable A *variable* that has a causal impact on another variable (i.e. on a *dependent variable*).

Index See *scale*.

Indicator A *measure* that is employed to refer to a *concept* when no direct measure is available.

Indigenous research Research that seeks to overcome oppressive, colonizing biases within the social sciences and to enable the development of alternative *paradigms*, by giving voice to the interests of participants and researchers in the global South, in addition to considering non-human interests related to ecosystems.

Inductive An approach to the relationship between theory and research in which the former is generated out of the latter. Compare with *deductive*.

Informed consent A key principle in social research ethics. It implies that prospective research participants should be given as much information as might be needed to make an informed decision about whether or not they wish to participate in a study.

Inter-coder reliability See *inter-rater reliability*.

Internal reliability The degree to which the indicators that make up a *scale* are consistent.

Internal validity A concern with the question of whether or not a finding that suggests a causal *relationship* between two or more *variables* is sound.

Interpretative repertoire A collection of linguistic resources that are drawn upon in order to characterize and assess actions and events.

Interpretivism, interpretive An *epistemological* position that requires the social scientist to grasp the subjective meaning of social action.

Inter-rater reliability The degree to which two or more individuals agree about the *coding* of an item. Inter-rater reliability is likely to be an issue in *content analysis*, *structured observation*, and when *coding* answers to *open questions* in research based on *questionnaires* or *structured interviews*.

Interval variable A *variable* where the distances between the categories are identical across its range of categories.

Intervening variable A *variable* that is apparently affected by another variable and that in turn has an apparent causal impact on another variable. Taking an intervening variable into account often facilitates the understanding of the *relationship* between two variables.

Interview guide A rather vague term for the brief list of memory prompts of areas to be covered in *unstructured interviewing* or to the somewhat more structured list of issues to be addressed or questions to be asked in *semi-structured interviewing*.

Interview schedule A collection of questions designed to be asked by an interviewer. An interview schedule is always used in a *structured interview*.

Intra-coder reliability See *intra-rater reliability*.

Intra-rater reliability The degree to which an individual differs over time in the *coding* of an item. Intra-rater reliability is likely to be an issue in *content analysis*, *structured observation*, and when *coding* answers to *open questions* in research based on *questionnaires* or *structured interviews*.

Iterative Describes a process in which the stages of data collection and analysis take place in parallel: analysis starts after some of the data have been collected, and the ideas that emerge from this analysis then shape the next steps in data collection.

Key informant Someone who offers the researcher, usually in the context of conducting an *ethnography*, perceptive information about the social setting, important events, and individuals.

Life history interview Similar to the *oral history interview*, but the aim of this type of unstructured interview is to glean information on the entire biography of each respondent.

Life history method Also often referred to as the 'biographical method', this method emphasizes the inner experience of individuals and its connections with changing events and phases throughout the life course. The method usually entails *life history interviews* and the use of *personal documents* as data.

Likert scale A widely used format developed by Rensis Likert for asking attitude questions. Respondents are typically asked their degree of agreement (e.g from 1 'strongly disagree' to 5 'strongly agree') with a series of statements that together form a *multiple-indicator* (also called multiple-item) *measure*. The scale is deemed then to measure the intensity with which respondents feel about an issue.

Literature review The process of searching for, reading, and evaluating published materials that are relevant to research that you are planning, and documenting your evaluation. See *narrative review*, *rapid review* and *systematic review*.

Longitudinal research A *research design* in which data are collected on a *sample* (of people, documents, etc.) on at least two occasions.

Mail questionnaire Traditionally, this term has been synonymous with the *postal questionnaire*, but, with the arrival of email-based questionnaires (see *embedded email survey* and *attached email survey*), many writers prefer to refer to 'postal' rather than 'mail' questionnaires.

Mean See *arithmetic mean*.

Measure A device for making quantifiable distinctions that provides a consistent instrument for gauging differences and that ideally is influenced neither by the timing of its administration nor by the person who administers it. A measure should generate consistent results, other than those that occur as a result of changes in the phenomenon being measured. Compare with *indicator*.

Measurement validity The degree to which a measure of a concept truly reflects that concept. See also *face validity* and *concurrent validity*.

Measure of central tendency A statistic, such as the *arithmetic mean*, *median*, or *mode*, that summarizes a *distribution of values*.

Measure of dispersion A statistic, such as the *range* or *standard deviation*, that summarizes the amount of variation in a *distribution of values*.

Median The mid-point in a *distribution of values*.

Member validation See *respondent validation*.

Meta-analysis A form of *systematic review* that involves summarizing the results of a large number of quantitative studies and conducting various analytical tests to show whether or not a particular *variable* has an apparent effect across the studies.

Meta-ethnography A form of *systematic review* that is used to achieve interpretative synthesis of *qualitative research*

and other secondary sources, thus providing a counterpart to *meta-analysis* in *quantitative research*. It can be used to synthesize and analyse information about a phenomenon that has been extensively studied.

Missing data Data relating to a case that are not available, for example, when a respondent in *survey research* does not answer a question. These are referred to as 'missing values' in *SPSS*.

Mixed methods research A term that is increasingly employed to describe research that combines the use of both *quantitative research* and *qualitative research*.

Mode The value that occurs most frequently in a *distribution of values*.

Moderated relationship A *relationship* between two *variables* is said to be moderated when it varies systematically with the value of a third variable.

Moderator The person who guides the questioning of a *focus group*. Also called a 'facilitator'.

Multiple-indicator measure A measure that employs more than one *indicator* to measure a *concept*.

Multi-strategy research A term used to describe research that combines *quantitative* and *qualitative research*; see also *mixed methods research*.

Multivariate analysis The examination of *relationships* between three or more *variables*.

Narrative analysis An approach to the elicitation and analysis of data that is sensitive to the sense of temporal sequence that people, as tellers of stories about their lives or events around them, detect in their lives and surrounding episodes and inject into their accounts. However, the approach is not exclusive to a focus on life histories.

Narrative review A method of conducting a *literature review* that is often contrasted with a *systematic review*. It tends to be less focused than a systematic review and seeks to arrive at a critical interpretation of the literature that it covers.

Naturalism A philosophical position and a style of research that seeks to minimize the intrusion of artificial methods of data collection. It implies that the social world should be as undisturbed as possible by the processes of research, in order to remain true to the phenomenon that is being investigated.

Negative relationship A *relationship* between two *variables* whereby as one increases the other decreases.

Nominal variable Also known as a 'categorical variable', this is a *variable* that comprises categories that cannot be rank ordered.

Non-manipulable variable A *variable* that cannot readily be manipulated either for practical or for ethical reasons and that therefore cannot be employed as an *independent variable* in an *experiment*.

Non-probability sample A sample that has not been selected using a *random sampling* method. Essentially, this implies that some units in the population are more likely to be selected than others.

Non-response A source of *non-sampling error* that occurs whenever some members of a sample refuse to cooperate, cannot be contacted, or for some reason cannot supply the required data.

Non-sampling error Differences between the *population* and the *sample* that arise either from deficiencies in the sampling approach, such as an inadequate *sampling frame* or *non-response*, or from such problems as poor question wording, poor interviewing, or flawed processing of data.

Null hypothesis A *hypothesis* of no *relationship* between two *variables*.

NVivo A software package used for the analysis of qualitative data (*CAQDAS*).

Objectivism An *ontological* position that asserts that social phenomena and their meanings have an existence that is independent of social actors. Compare with *constructionism*.

Observation schedule A device used in *structured observation* that specifies the categories of behaviour that are to be observed and how behaviour should be allocated to those categories.

Official statistics Statistics compiled by or on behalf of government agencies in the course of conducting their business.

Online survey A very general term used to include any survey conducted online. As such, it includes the *website-based survey*, the *attached email survey*, and the *embedded email survey*.

Ontology, ontological A theory of the nature of reality. See *objectivism* and *inductivism*.

Open question A question employed in an *interview schedule* or *self-completion questionnaire* that does not present the respondent with a set of possible answers to choose from. Compare with *closed question*.

Operational definition The definition of a *concept* in terms of the operations to be carried out when measuring it.

Operationism, operationalism A doctrine, mainly associated with physics, that emphasizes the search for *operational definitions* of *concepts*.

Oral history interview A largely *unstructured interview* in which the respondent is asked to recall events from his or her past and to reflect on them.

Ordinal variable A *variable* whose categories can be rank ordered (as in the case of *interval* and *ratio variables*), but for which the distances between the categories are not equal across the range.

Outlier An extreme value in a distribution of values. If a *variable* has an extreme value—either very high or very low—the *arithmetic mean* or the *range* will be distorted by that value.

Paradigm(s) A term deriving from the history of science, where it was used to describe a cluster of beliefs and dictates that, for scientists in a particular discipline, influence what should be studied, how research should be done, and how results should be interpreted.

Participant observation Research in which the researcher immerses him- or herself in a social setting for an extended period of time, observing behaviour, listening to what is said in conversations both between others and with the fieldworker, and asking questions. Participant observation usually includes interviewing key informants and studying documents, and as such is difficult to distinguish from *ethnography*. In this book, 'participant observation' is employed to refer to the specifically observational aspect of ethnography.

Participatory research Research that focuses on working with and helping disempowered groups by addressing problems related to their welfare and wellbeing. Includes participatory *action research*.

Pearson's *r* A measure of the strength and direction of the *relationship* between two *interval* or *ratio variables*.

Personal documents Documents such as *diaries*, letters, and autobiographies that are not written for an official purpose. They provide first-person accounts of the writer's life and events within it.

Phenomenology A philosophy that is concerned with the question of how individuals make sense of the world around them and how in particular the philosopher should bracket out preconceptions concerning his or her grasp of that world.

Photo-elicitation A visual research method that typically entails getting interviewees to discuss one or more photographs in the course of an interview. The photograph(s) may be extant or may have been taken by the interviewee for the purpose of the research.

Phi (φ) A method for assessing the strength and direction of the *relationship* between two *dichotomous variables*.

Population The universe of units from which a *sample* is to be selected.

Positive relationship A *relationship* between two *variables* whereby as one increases the other increases as well.

Positivism, positivist An *epistemological* position that advocates the application of the methods of the natural sciences to the study of social reality and beyond.

Postal questionnaire A form of *self-completion questionnaire* that is sent to respondents, and usually returned by them, by non-electronic mail.

Postmodernism A philosophical position that displays a distaste for master-narratives and for a *realist* orientation. In the context of research methodology, postmodernists display a preference for qualitative methods and a concern with the modes of representation of research findings.

Pre-coded question Another name for a *closed question*. The term 'pre-coded' is often preferred, because it describes an approach that removes the need for the application of a *coding frame* to the question after it has been answered. This is because the range of answers has been predetermined and a numerical *code* will have been pre-assigned to each possible answer. The term is particularly appropriate when the codes appear on the *questionnaire* or *interview schedule*.

Predictive validity An assessment of the *measurement validity* of a measure of a concept that uses a future benchmark as a criterion.

Probability sample A sample that has been selected using *random sampling* and in which each unit in the population has a known probability of being selected.

Projective techniques A method involving the presentation of ambiguous stimuli, e.g. inkblots, to individuals; their responses are interpreted by the researcher with the aim of revealing the underlying characteristics of the individual.

Purposive sampling, sample A form of *non-probability sample* in which the researcher aims to sample cases/participants in a strategic way, so that those sampled are relevant to the research questions that are being posed.

Qualitative content analysis An approach to documents that emphasizes the role of the investigator in the construction of the meaning of and in texts. There is an emphasis on allowing categories to emerge out of data and on recognizing the significance for understanding the meaning of the context in which an item being analysed (and the categories derived from it) appeared.

Qualitative research Research that typically emphasizes words rather than quantification in the collection and analysis of data. As a *research strategy* it is *inductivist*, *constructionist*, and *interpretivist*, but qualitative researchers do not always subscribe to all three of these features. Compare with *quantitative research*.

Quantitative research Research that emphasizes quantification in the collection and analysis of data. As a *research strategy* it is typically *deductivist* and *objectivist* and incorporates a natural science model of the research process (in particular, one influenced by *positivism*), but quantitative researchers do not always subscribe to all of these features. Compare with *qualitative research*.

Quasi-experiment A *research design* that is close to being an experiment but that does not meet the requirements fully and therefore does not exhibit complete *internal validity*.

Questionnaire A collection of questions administered to respondents. When used on its own, the term usually denotes a *self-completion questionnaire*.

Quota sample A *sample* that non-randomly samples a *population* in terms of the relative proportions of people in different categories. It is a type of *non-probability sample*.

Random assignment A term used in connection with *experiments* to refer to the random allocation of research participants to the experimental group and the control group.

Random sampling Sampling whereby the inclusion of a unit of a *population* occurs entirely by chance.

Range The difference between the maximum and the minimum value in a *distribution of values* associated with an *interval* or *ratio variable*.

Rapid review A *literature review* that conforms to the main principles of a *systematic review* but is deliberately limited in scope so that the review can be completed in a relatively short time.

Ratio variable An *interval variable* with a true zero point.

Reactivity, reactive effect A term used to describe the response of research participants to the fact that they know they are being studied, also sometimes referred to as the Hawthorne effect. Reactivity is deemed to result in untypical behaviour.

Realism, realist An epistemological position that acknowledges a reality that is independent of the senses and that is accessible to the researcher's tools and theoretical speculations. It implies that the categories created by scientists refer to real objects in the natural or social worlds. See also *critical realism*.

Reflexivity This term is used in a variety of ways, but in research methods it typically refers to an awareness on the part of researchers of their *ontological* and epistemological assumptions and of the ways in which their actions in conducting research shape the knowledge they produce.

Relationship An association between two *variables* whereby the variation in one variable coincides with variation in another variable. See *negative relationship* and *positive relationship*.

Reliability The degree to which a measure of a concept is stable and consistent. See also *internal reliability*; *interrater reliability*; *stability*.

Replicability The degree to which the results of a study can be reproduced by another researcher following the same procedures. See also *internal reliability*.

Replication The carrying out of a study using the same procedures as a previous study, with the aim of seeing whether the results resemble those of the previous study (i.e. replicate it) or are different.

Representative sample A *sample* that reflects the population accurately, so that it is a microcosm of the *population*.

Research design This term is employed in this book to refer to a framework or structure within which the collection and analysis of data takes place. A choice of research design reflects decisions about the priority being given to a range of dimensions of the research process (such as *causality* and *generalization*) and is influenced by the kind of *research question* that is posed.

Research question An explicit statement in the form of a question of what it is that a researcher intends to find out about. A research question influences not only the scope of an investigation but also how the research will be conducted (the *research design*).

Research strategy A term used in this book to refer to a general orientation to the conduct of social research (see *quantitative research* and *qualitative research*).

Respondent validation Sometimes called 'member validation', this is a process whereby a researcher provides the people on whom he or she has conducted research with an account of his or her findings and requests feedback on that account.

Response set The tendency among some respondents to *multiple-indicator measures* to reply in the same way to each constituent item.

Rhetoric A concern with the ways in which appeals to convince or persuade are devised.

Rhetorical analysis An approach to analysing language that focuses on the importance of rhetorical devices as a means of communication and persuasion, including analysis of classic rhetorical devices such as argumentation, as well as literary devices such as metaphor, synecdoche, metonymy, and irony.

Sample The segment of the population that is selected for research. It is a subset of the *population*. The method of selection may be based on *probability sampling* or *non-probability sampling*.

Sampling error Differences between a *random sample* and the *population* from which it is selected.

Sampling frame The listing of all units in the *population* from which a *sample* is selected.

Scale A term that is usually used interchangeably with 'index' to refer to a *multiple-indicator measure* in which the score a person gives for each component *indicator* is used to provide a composite score for that person.

Scan sampling A sampling approach in *structured observation* whereby an entire group of individuals is scanned at regular intervals and the behaviour of all of them is recorded at each occasion.

Secondary analysis The analysis of data by researchers who will probably not have been involved in the collection of those data, for purposes that may not have been envisaged by those responsible for the data collection. Secondary analysis may be performed on either quantitative data or qualitative data.

Self-administered questionnaire See *self-completion questionnaire*.

Self-completion questionnaire A *questionnaire* that the respondent answers without the aid of an interviewer. Sometimes called a 'self-administered questionnaire'.

Semiotics The study/science of *signs*; an approach to the analysis of documents and other phenomena that emphasizes the importance of seeking out the deeper meaning of those phenomena. A semiotic approach is concerned to uncover the processes of meaning production and how signs are designed to have an effect upon actual and prospective consumers of those signs.

Semi-structured interview A term that covers a wide range of types. It typically refers to a context in which the interviewer has a series of questions that are in the general form of an *interview guide* but is able to vary the sequence of questions. The questions are frequently somewhat more general in their frame of reference from that typically found in a *structured interview* schedule. Also, the interviewer usually has some latitude to ask further questions in response to what are seen as significant replies.

Sensitizing concept A term devised by Blumer to refer to a preference for treating a *concept* as a guide in an investigation, so that it points in a general way to what is relevant or important. This position contrasts with the idea of an *operational definition*, in which the meaning of a concept is fixed in advance of carrying out an investigation.

Sign A term employed in *semiotics*. A sign is made up of a signifier (the manifestation of a sign) and the signified (that idea or deeper meaning to which the signifier refers).

Simple observation The passive and unobtrusive observation of behaviour.

Simple random sample A *sample* in which each unit has been selected entirely by chance. Each unit of the *population* has a known and equal probability of inclusion in the sample.

Snowball sampling A *non-probability sample* technique in which the researcher makes initial contact with a small group of people who are relevant to the research topic and then uses these to establish contacts with others.

Social desirability bias A distortion of response that is caused by respondents' attempts to construct an account that conforms to a socially acceptable model of belief or behaviour.

Social survey See *cross-sectional design*.

Spearman's rho (ρ) A measure of the strength and direction of the *relationship* between two *ordinal variables*.

SPSS Originally short for Statistical Package for the Social Sciences, SPSS is a widely used computer program that allows quantitative data to be managed and analysed.

Spurious relationship A *relationship* between two *variables* is said to be spurious if it is being produced by the impact of a third variable on each of the two variables that form the spurious relationship. When the third variable is controlled, the relationship disappears.

Stability The extent to which a *measure* is stable over time, so that a researcher can be confident that the results relating to that measure for a sample of respondents do not fluctuate if that measure is administered and later readministered.

Standard deviation A measure of dispersion around the mean.

Standard error of the mean An estimate of the amount that a *sample* mean is likely to differ from the *population* mean.

Statistical inference See *statistical significance (test of)*.

Statistical significance (test of) Allows the analyst to estimate how confident he or she can be that the results deriving from a study based on a randomly selected *sample* are generalizable to the *population* from which the sample was drawn. Such a test does not allow the researcher to infer that the findings are of substantive importance. The *chi-square test* is an example of this kind of test. The process of using a test of statistical significance to generalize from a sample to a population is known as 'statistical inference'.

Stratified random sample A *sample* in which units are *randomly sampled* from a *population* that has been divided into categories (strata).

Structured interview A research interview in which all respondents are asked exactly the same questions in the same order with the aid of a formal *interview schedule*.

Structured observation Often also called 'systematic observation', structured observation is a technique in which the researcher employs explicitly formulated rules for the observation and recording of behaviour. The rules inform observers about what they should look for and how they should record behaviour.

Survey research A *cross-sectional design* in relation to which data are collected predominantly by *self-completion questionnaire* or by *structured interview* on more than one case (usually quite a lot more than one) in order to collect a body of quantitative or quantifiable data in connection with two or more *variables* (usually many more than two) which are then examined to detect patterns of *relationship*.

Symbolic interactionism A theoretical perspective in sociology and social psychology that views social interaction as taking place in terms of the meanings actors attach to action and things.

Synchronous online interview or focus group Online interviews or focus groups may be *asynchronous* or synchronous. In the case of the latter, the transactions between participants are in real time, so that there will be only brief time lapses between interviewers' questions and participants' replies, and, in the case of focus groups, between participants' contributions to the discussion.

Systematic observation See *structured observation*.

Systematic review A method of conducting a *literature review* that uses explicit procedures and exhaustive searches; the aim is to conduct a comprehensive and unbiased literature review and to leave a transparent record of the process used.

Systematic sample A *probability sampling* method in which units are selected from a *sampling frame* according to fixed intervals, such as every fifth unit.

Text A term that is used either in the conventional sense of a written work or in more recent years to refer to a wide range of phenomena including e.g. images or speech. For example, in arriving at a *thick description*, Geertz refers to treating culture as a text.

Thematic analysis A term used in connection with the analysis of qualitative data to refer to the extraction of key themes in one's data. It is a rather diffuse approach and there are few generally agreed principles for defining core themes in data.

Theoretical sampling A term used mainly in relation to *grounded theory* to refer to sampling carried out so that emerging theoretical considerations guide the selection of cases and/or research participants. Theoretical sampling is supposed to continue until a point of *theoretical saturation* is reached.

Theoretical saturation In *grounded theory*, the point when emerging concepts have been fully explored and no new theoretical insights are being generated. See also *theoretical sampling*.

Thick description A term devised by Geertz to refer to detailed accounts of a social setting that can form the basis for the creation of general statements about a culture and its significance in people's social lives.

Time sampling A sampling method in *structured observation* that entails using a criterion for deciding when observation will occur.

Transcription, transcript, transcribe A transcript is the written translation of an audio-recorded interview or *focus group* session; transcribing is the act of making such a transcript.

Triangulation The use of more than one method or source of data in the study of a social phenomenon so that findings may be cross-checked.

Trustworthiness A set of criteria advocated by some writers for assessing the quality of *qualitative research*.

Turn-taking The notion from *conversation analysis* that order in everyday conversation is achieved through orderly taking of turns in conversations.

Univariate analysis The analysis of a single *variable* at a time.

Unobtrusive methods Research methods that do not entail the awareness among research participants that they are being studied and that are therefore not subject to *reactivity*.

Unstructured interview An interview in which the interviewer typically has only a list of topics or issues, often called an *interview guide*, that he or she expects to cover. The style of questioning is usually very informal. The phrasing and sequencing of questions will vary from interview to interview.

Validity A concern with the integrity of the conclusions that are generated from a piece of research. There are different aspects of validity. See, in particular, *measurement validity*, *internal validity*, *external validity*, and *ecological validity*. When used on its own, *validity* is usually taken to refer to *measurement validity*.

Variable An attribute in terms of which cases vary. See also *dependent variable* and *independent variable*. Compare with *constant*.

Verbal protocol approach A method that involves asking respondents to think aloud while they are performing a task in order to capture their thought processes while they are making a decision or judgement or solving a problem.

Web-based survey A *cross-sectional survey* conducted so that respondents complete a *questionnaire* via a website.

REFERENCES

Abendroth, A. K., and den Dulk, L. (2011). 'Support for the Work–life Balance in Europe: The Impact of State, Workplace and Family Support on Work–life Balance Satisfaction', *Work, Employment and Society*, 25(2): 234–56.

Academy of Management (2006). *AOM Code of Ethics*, http://aom.org/About-AOM/AOM-Code-of-Ethics.aspx.

Adler, N. (1983). 'A Typology of Management Studies Involving Culture', *Journal of International Business Studies*, 14(2): 29–47.

Adler, P. A., and Adler, P. (2008). 'Of Rhetoric and Representation: The Four Faces of Ethnography', *Sociological Quarterly*, 49: 1–30.

Adriaenssens, C., and Cadman, L. (1999). 'An Adaptation of Moderated E-mail Focus Groups to Assess the Potential of a New Online (Internet) Financial Services Offer in the UK', *Journal of the Market Research Society*, 41: 417–24.

Agerström, J. and Rooth, D. (2011). 'The Role of Automatic Obesity Stereotypes in Real Hiring Discrimination', *Journal of Applied Psychology*, 96(4): 790–805.

Ainsworth, S., and Hardy, C. (2009). 'Mind over Body: Physical and Psychotherapeutic Discourses and the Regulation of the Older Worker', *Human Relations*, 62(8): 1199–229.

Alcadipani, R., and Tonelli, M. J. (2014). 'Imagining Gender Research: Violence, Masculinity and the Shopfloor', *Gender, Work and Organization*, 21(4): 321–39.

Alderson, P. (1998). 'Confidentiality and Consent in Qualitative Research', *Network: Newsletter of the British Sociological Association*, 69: 6–7.

Aldrich, H. E. (1972). 'Technology and Organizational Structure: A Re-Examination of the Findings of the Aston Group', *Administrative Science Quarterly*, 17(1): 6–43.

Alise, M. A., and Teddlie, C. (2010). 'A Continuation of the Paradigm Wars? Prevalence Rates of Methodological Approaches across the Social/Behavioral Sciences', *Journal of Mixed Methods Research*, 4(2): 103–26.

Allison, T. H., McKenny, A. F., and Short, J. C. (2013). 'The Effect of Entrepreneurial Rhetoric on Microlending Investment: An Investigation of the Warm-Glow Effect', *Journal of Business Venturing*, 28(6): 690–707.

Altheide, D. L. (1980). 'Leaving the Newsroom', in W. Shaffir, R. A. Stebbins, and A. Turowetz (eds), *Fieldwork Experience: Qualitative Approaches to Social Research*. New York: St Martin's Press.

Altheide, D. L. (1996). *Qualitative Media Analysis*. Thousand Oaks, CA: Sage.

Altschuld, J. W., and Lower, M. A. (1984). 'Improving Mailed Questionnaires: Analysis of a 96 Percent Return Rate', in D. C. Lockhart (ed.), *Making Effective Use of Mailed Questionnaires*. San Francisco: Jossey-Bass.

Alvesson, M. (2002). *Postmodernism and Social Research*. Buckingham: Open University Press.

Alvesson, M. (2003). 'Methodology for Close Up Studies: Struggling with Closeness and Closure', *Higher Education*, 46: 167–93.

Alvesson, M., and Gabriel, Y. (2013). 'Beyond Formulaic Research: In Praise of Greater Diversity in Organizational Research and Publications', *Academy of Management Learning and Education*, 12: 245–63.

Alvesson, M., and Kärreman, D. (2000). 'Varieties of Discourse: On the Study of Organization through Discourse Analysis', *Human Relations*, 53(9): 1125–49.

Alvesson, M., and Kärreman, D. (2007). 'Constructing Mystery: Empirical Matters in Theory Development', *Academy of Management Review*, 32: 1265–81.

Alvesson, M., and Kärreman, D. (2011). 'Decolonializing Discourse: Critical Reflections on Organizational Discourse Analysis', *Human Relations*, 64(9): 1121–46.

Alvesson, M., and Sandberg, J. (2011). 'Generating Research Questions through Problematization', *Academy of Management Review*, 36(2): 247–71.

Alvesson, M., and Thompson, P. (2005). 'Post-Bureaucracy', in S. Ackroyd, R. Batt, P. Thompson, and P. Tolbert (eds), *The Oxford Handbook of Work and Organizations*. Oxford: Oxford University Press.

Alvesson, M., Hardy, C. and Harley, B. (2008). 'Reflecting on Reflexivity: Reflective Textual Practices in Organization and Management Theory', *Journal of Management Studies*, 45(3): 480–501.

Andersen, M. (1981). 'Corporate Wives: Longing for Liberation or Satisfied with the Status Quo?', *Urban Life*, 10: 311–27.

Andersen, M. F., Nielsen, K. M., and Brinkmann, S. (2012). 'Meta-Synthesis of Qualitative Research on Return to Work among Employees with Common Mental Disorders', *Scandinavian Journal of Work and Environmental Health*, 38(2): 93–104.

Anonymous (2014). 'The Case of the Hypothesis that Never Was: Uncovering the Deceptive Use of Post-hoc Hypotheses', *Journal of Management Inquiry*, 24(2): 214–16.

Anseel, F., Lievens, F., Schollaert, E., and Choragwicka, B. (2010). 'Response Rates in Organizational Science, 1995–2008: A Meta-Analytic Review and Guidelines for Survey Researchers', *Journal of Business and Psychology*, 25(3): 335–49.

Antoun, C., Zhang, C., Conrad, F., and Schober, M. (2016). 'Comparisons of Online Recruitment Strategies for Convenience Samples: Craigslist, Google AdWords, Facebook, and Amazon Mechanical Turk', *Field Methods*, 28(3): 231–46.

Arendell, T. (1997). 'Reflections on the Researcher-Researched Relationship: A Woman Interviewing Men', *Qualitative Sociology*, 20(3): 341–68.

Argyris, C., Putnam, R., and Smith, M. (1985). *Action Science: Concepts, Methods and Skills for Research and Intervention*. San Francisco: Jossey-Bass.

Aronson, E., and Carlsmith, J. M. (1968). 'Experimentation in Social Psychology', in G. Lindzey and E. Aronson (eds), *The Handbook of Social Psychology*. Reading, MA: Addison-Wesley.

Asch, S. E. (1951). 'Effect of Group Pressure upon the Modification and Distortion of Judgments', in H. Guetzkow (ed.), *Groups, Leadership and Men*. Pittsburgh: Carnegie Press.

Ashforth, B. E., Kreiner, G. E., Clark, M. A., and Fugate, M. (2007). 'Normalizing Dirty Work: Tactics for Countering Occupational Taint', *Academy of Management Journal*, 50: 149–74.

Association of Internet Researchers (AoIR) (2002). 'Ethical Decision Making and Internet Research: Recommendations from the AoIR Ethics Working Committee', aoir.org/reports/ethics.pdf.

Atkinson, P. (1981). *The Clinical Experience*. Farnborough: Gower.

Atkinson, P. (1990). *The Ethnographic Imagination: Textual Constructions of Society*. London: Routledge.

Atkinson, P., and Coffey, A. (2004). 'Analysing Documentary Realities', in D. Silverman (ed.), *Qualitative Research: Theory, Method and Practice*, 2nd edn. London: Sage.

Atkinson, P., and Silverman, D. (1997). 'Kundera's Immortality: The Interview Society and the Invention of Self', *Qualitative Inquiry*, 3(3): 324–45.

Atkinson, P., Coffey, A., and Delamont, S. (2003). *Key Themes in Qualitative Research: Continuities and Changes*. Oxford: AltaMira Press.

Australian Research Council, National Health and Medical Research Council, and Universities Australia (2007). *Australian Code for the Responsible Conduct of Research*, https://www.nhmrc.gov.au/guidelines-publications/.

Banks, M. (2001). *Visual Methods in Social Research*. London: Sage.

Barley, S. (1983). 'Semiotics and the Study of Occupational and Organizational Cultures', *Administrative Science Quarterly*, 28: 393–413.

Barley, S., Meyer, G., and Gash, D. (1988). 'Cultures of Culture: Academics, Practitioners and the Pragmatics of Normative Control', *Administrative Science Quarterly*, 33: 24–60.

Barnes, S. (2004). 'Issues of Attribution and Identification in Online Social Research', in M. D. Johns, S.-L. S. Chen, and G. J. Hall (eds), *Online Social Research*. New York: Peter Lang.

Barnett, R. (1994). 'Editorial', *Studies in Higher Education*, 19(2): 123–4.

Barthes, R. (1972). *Mythologies*. London: Jonathan Cape.

Bartunek, J. M., Bobko, P., and Venkatraman, N. (1993). 'Toward Innovation and Diversity in Management Research Methods', *Academy of Management Journal*, 36(6): 1362–73.

Baruch, Y., and Holtom, B. (2009). 'Survey Response Rate Levels and Trends in Organizational Research', *Human Relations*, 61(8): 1139–60.

Bauman, Z. (1978). *Hermeneutics and Social Science: Approaches to Understanding*. London: Hutchison.

Bazeley, P. (2015). 'Mixed Methods in Management Research: Implications for the Field', *Electronic Journal of Business Research Methods*, 13(1): 27–35.

Bazerman, C. (1987). 'Codifying the Social Scientific Style: The APA *Publication Manual* as a Behaviorist Rhetoric', in J. S. Nelson, A. Megill, and D. N. McClosky (eds), *The Rhetoric of the Human Sciences*. Madison: University of Wisconsin Press.

Beardsworth, A. (1980). 'Analysing Press Content: Some Technical and Methodological Issues', in H. Christian (ed.), *Sociology of Journalism and the Press*. Keele: Keele University Press.

Bechhofer, F., Elliott, B., and McCrone, D. (1984). 'Safety in Numbers: On the Use of Multiple Interviewers', *Sociology*, 18: 97–100.

Becker, H. S. (1982). 'Culture: A Sociological View', *Yale Review*, 71: 513–27.

Becker, H. S. (1986). *Writing for Social Scientists: How to Start and Finish your Thesis, Book, or Article*. Chicago: University of Chicago Press.

Bell, C. (1969). 'A Note on Participant Observation', *Sociology*, 3: 417–18.

Bell, C., and Newby, H. (1977). *Doing Sociological Research*. London: George Allen & Unwin.

Bell, E. (1999). 'The Negotiation of a Working Role in Organizational Ethnography', *International Journal of Social Research Methodology*, 2(1): 17–37.

Bell, E. (2012). 'Ways of Seeing Death: A Critical Semiotic Analysis of Organizational Memorialization', *Visual Studies*, 27(1): 4–17.

Bell, E., and Bryman, A. (2007). 'The Ethics of Management Research: An Exploratory Context Analysis', *British Journal of Management*, 18(1): 63–77.

Bell, E., and Clarke, D. (2014). 'Beasts, Burrowers and Birds: The Enactment of Researcher Identities in UK Business Schools', *Management Learning*, 45(3): 249–66.

Bell, E., and Davison, J. (2013). 'Visual Management Studies: Empirical and Theoretical Approaches', *International Journal of Management Reviews*, 15(2): 167–84.

Bell, E., and Kothiyal, N. (2018). 'Ethics Creep from the Core to the Periphery', in C. Cassell, A. Cunliffe, and G. Grandy (eds), *SAGE Handbook of Qualitative Business and Management Research Methods: History and Traditions*. London: Sage, 546–61.

Bell, E., and Leonard, P. (2018). 'Digital Organizational Storytelling on YouTube: Constructing Plausibility through Network Protocols of Amateurism, Affinity and Authenticity', *Journal of Management Inquiry*, 27(3): 339–51.

Bell, E., and Taylor, S. (2016), 'Vernacular Mourning and Corporate Memorialization in Framing the Death of Steve Jobs', *Organization*, 23(1): 114–32.

Bell, E., and Thorpe, R. (2013). *A Very Short, Fairly Interesting and Reasonably Cheap Book about Management Research*. London: Sage.

Bell, E., and Wray Bliss, E. (2009). 'Research Ethics: Regulations and Responsibilities', in D. Buchanan and A. Bryman (eds), *The Sage Handbook of Organizational Research Methods*. London: Sage, 78–92.

Bell, E., Kothiyal, N., and Willmott, H. (2017). 'Methodology-as-Technique and the Meaning of Rigor in Globalized Management Research', *British Journal of Management*, 28(3): 534–50.

Bell, E., Taylor, S., and Thorpe, R. (2001). 'Investors in People and the Standardization of Professional Knowledge in Personnel Management', *Management Learning*, 32(2): 201–19.

Bell, E., Taylor, S., and Thorpe, R. (2002). 'Organizational Differentiation through Badging: Investors in People and the Value of the Sign', *Journal of Management Studies*, 39(8): 1071–85.

Berg, P., and Frost, A. C. (2005). 'Dignity at Work for Low Wage, Low Skill Service Workers', *Industrial Relations*, 60(4): 657–82.

Bettis, R., Helfat, C., and Shaver, J. (2016). 'The Necessity, Logic, and Forms of Replication', *Strategic Management Journal*, 37(11): 2193–203.

Beynon, H. (1975). *Working for Ford*, 2nd edn. Harmondsworth: Penguin.

Beynon, H. (1988). 'Regulating Research: Politics and Decision Making in Industrial Organizations', in A. Bryman (ed.), *Doing Research in Organizations*. London: Routledge.

Bhaskar, R. (1975). *A Realist Theory of Science*. Leeds: Leeds Books.

Bhaskar, R. (1989). *Reclaiming Reality: A Critical Introduction to Contemporary Philosophy*. London: Verso.

Bhattacharya, K. (2007). 'Consenting to the Consent Form: What are the Fixed and Fluid Understandings between the Researcher and the Researched?', *Qualitative Inquiry*, 13(8): 1095–115.

Billig, M. (1992). *Talking of the Royal Family*. London: Routledge.

Billig, M. (2013). *Learn to Write Badly: How to Succeed in the Social Sciences*. Cambridge: Cambridge University Press.

Blackburn, R., and Stokes, D. (2000). 'Breaking down the Barriers: Using Focus Groups to Research Small and Medium-Sized Enterprises', *International Small Business Journal*, 19(1): 44–67.

Blasius, J., and Brandt, M. (2010). 'Representativeness in Online Surveys Through Stratified Sampling', *Bulletin de Methodologie Sociologique*, 107(1): 5–21.

Blauner, R. (1964). *Alienation and Freedom*. Chicago: University of Chicago Press.

Bluhm, D. J., Harman, W., Lee, T. W., and Mitchell, T. R. (2011). 'Qualitative Research in Management: A Decade of Progress', *Journal of Management Studies*, 48(8): 1866–91.

Blumer, H. (1954). 'What is Wrong with Social Theory?', *American Sociological Review*, 19: 3–10.

Blumer, H. (1956). 'Sociological Analysis and the "Variable"', *American Sociological Review*, 21: 683–90.

Blumer, H. (1962). 'Society as Symbolic Interaction', in A. M. Rose (ed.), *Human Behavior and Social Processes*. London: Routledge & Kegan Paul.

Boddy, C. (2005). 'A Rose by Any Other Name may Smell as Sweet but "Group Discussion" is Not Another Name for a "Focus Group" nor Should it Be', *Qualitative Market Research*, 8(3): 248–55.

Boden, D. (1994). *The Business of Talk: Organizations in Action*. Cambridge: Polity Press.

Bogdan, R., and Taylor, S. J. (1975). *Introduction to Qualitative Research Methods: A Phenomenological Approach to the Social Sciences*. New York: Wiley.

Boje, D. (1991). 'The Storytelling Organization: A Study of Performance in an Office Supply Firm', *Administrative Science Quarterly*, 36: 106–26.

Boje, D. M., Haley, U. C. V., and Saylors, R. (2016). 'Antenarratives of Organizational Change: The Microstoria of Burger King's Storytelling in Space, Time and Strategic Context', *Human Relations*, 69(2): 391–418.

Bolton, A., Pole, C., and Mizen, P. (2001). 'Picture This: Researching Child Workers', *Sociology*, 35(2): 501–18.

Born, G. (2004). *Uncertain Vision: Birt, Dyke and the Reinvention of the BBC*. London: Secker & Warburg.

Boselie, P. (2002). *Human Resource Management, Work Systems and Performance: A Theoretical-Empirical Approach*, Tinbergen Institute, Rotterdam.

Bosley, S. L. C., Arnold, J., and Cohen, L. (2009). 'How Other People Shape our Careers: A Typology Drawn from Career Narratives', *Human Relations*, 62: 1487–520.

Bosnjak, M., Neubarth, W., Couper, M. P., Bandilla, W., and Kaczmirek, L. (2008). 'Prenotification in Web-Based Access Panel Surveys: The Influence of Mobile Text Messaging Versus E-mail on Response Rates and Sample Composition', *Social Science Computer Review*, 26: 213–23.

Bottomore, T. B., and Rubel, M. (1963). *Karl Marx: Selected Writings in Sociology and Social Philosophy*. Harmondsworth: Penguin.

Bourdieu, P. (1984). *Distinction: A Social Critique of the Judgement of Taste*. Cambridge, MA: Harvard University Press.

Bowen, D. D., and Hisrich, R. D. (1986). 'The Female Entrepreneur: A Career Development Perspective', *Academy of Management Review*, 11: 393–407.

Bowen, G. A. (2008). 'Naturalistic Inquiry and the Saturation Concept: A Research Note', *Qualitative Research*, 8: 137–52.

Boyce, G., and Lepper, L. (2002). 'Assessing Information Quality Theories: The USSCo. Joint Venture with William Holyman and Sons and Huddart Parker Ltd, 1904–35', *Business History*, 44(4): 85–120.

Boyd, B. K., Haynes, K. T., Hitt, M. A., Bergh, D. D., and Ketchen, D. J. (2012). 'Contingency Hypotheses in Strategic Management: Use, Disuse, or Misuse', *Journal of Management*, 38(1): 278–313.

Bradburn, N. A., and Sudman, S. (1979). *Improving Interview Method and Questionnaire Design*. San Francisco: Jossey-Bass.

Brannick, T., and Coghlan, D. (2007). 'In Defense of Being "Native": The Case for Insider Academic Research', *Organizational Research Methods*, 10(1): 59–74.

Braun, V., and Clarke, V. (2006). 'Using Thematic Analysis in Psychology', *Qualitative Research in Psychology*, 3: 77–101.

Brayfield, A., and Rothe, H. (1951). 'An Index of Job Satisfaction', *Journal of Applied Psychology*, 35: 307–11.

Brengman, M., Geuens, M., Weijters, B., Smith, S. M., and Swinyard, W. R. (2005). 'Segmenting Internet Shoppers Based on their Web-Usage Related Lifestyle: A Cross-Cultural Validation', *Journal of Business Research*, 58: 79–88.

Brewis, J. (2005). 'Signing My Life Away? Researching Sex and Organization', *Organization*, 12(4): 439–510.

Brewis, J. (2014). The Ethics of Researching Friends: On Convenience Sampling in Qualitative Management and Organization Studies, *British Journal of Management*, 25: 849–62.

Bridgman, P. W. (1927). *The Logic of Modern Physics*. New York: Macmillan.

Briggs, C. L. (1986). *Learning How to Ask: A Sociolinguistic Appraisal of the Role of the Interview in Social Science Research*. Cambridge: Cambridge University Press.

Briner, R. B., Denyer, D., and Rousseau, D. (2009). 'Evidence-Based Management: Concept Cleanup Time?', *Academy of Management Perspectives*, 23(4): 5–18.

British Sociological Association (2017). *Statement of Ethical Practice*, https://www.britsoc.co.uk/media/24310/bsa_statement_of_ethical_practice.pdf

Broussine, M., and Vince, R. (1996). 'Working with Metaphor towards Organizational Change', in C. Oswick and D. Grant (eds), *Organization Development: Metaphorical Explanations*. London: Pitman Publishing.

Brown, A. D. (1998). 'Narrative, Politics and Legitimacy in an IT Implementation', *Journal of Management Studies*, 35: 35–58.

Bruce, C. S. (1994). 'Research Students' Early Experiences of the Dissertation Literature Review', *Studies in Higher Education*, 19(2): 217–29.

Bryman, A. (1988a). *Quantity and Quality in Social Research*. London: Routledge.

Bryman, A. (1988b). *Doing Research in Organizations*. London: Routledge.

Bryman, A. (1989a). *Research Methods and Organization Studies*. London: Routledge.

Bryman, A. (1992). 'Quantitative and Qualitative Research: Further Reflections on their Integration', in J. Brannen (ed.), *Mixing Methods: Qualitative and Quantitative Research*. Aldershot: Avebury.

Bryman, A. (1994). 'The Mead/Freeman Controversy: Some Implications for Qualitative Researchers', in R.G. Burgess (ed.), *Studies in Qualitative Methodology*, vol. 4. Greenwich, CT: JAI Press.

Bryman, A. (1995). *Disney and his Worlds*. London: Routledge.

Bryman, A. (1998). 'Quantitative and Qualitative Research Strategies in Knowing the Social World', in T. May and M. Williams (eds), *Knowing the Social World*. Buckingham: Open University Press.

Bryman, A. (1999). 'Global Disney', in P. Taylor and D. Slater (eds), *The American Century*. Oxford: Blackwell.

Bryman, A. (2004a). *Social Research Methods*, rev. edn. Oxford: Oxford University Press.

Bryman, A. (2004b). *The Disneyization of Society*. London: Sage.

Bryman, A. (2007a). 'Effective Leadership in Higher Education', *Studies in Higher Education*, 32: 693–710.

Bryman, A. (2007b). 'The Research Question in Social Research: What is its Role?', *International Journal of Social Research Methodology*, 9: 5–20.

Bryman, A. (2009). 'Mixed Methods in Organizational Research', in D. A. Buchanan and A. Bryman (eds), *The Sage Handbook of Organizational Research Methods*. London: Sage.

Bryman, A. (2014). 'June 1989 and Beyond: Julia Brannen's Contribution to Mixed Methods Research', *International Journal of Social Research Methodology*, 17: 121–31.

Bryman, A., and Burgess, R. G. (1994a). 'Developments in Qualitative Data Analysis: An Introduction', in A. Bryman and R. G. Burgess (eds), *Analyzing Qualitative Data*. London: Routledge.

Bryman, A., and Burgess, R. G. (1994b). 'Reflections on Qualitative Data Analysis', in A. Bryman and R. G. Burgess (eds), *Analyzing Qualitative Data*. London: Routledge.

Bryman, A., and Burgess, R. G. (1999). 'Introduction: Qualitative Research Methodology: A Review', in A. Bryman and R. G. Burgess (eds), *Qualitative Research*. London: Sage.

Bryman, A., and Cramer, D. (2008). *Quantitative Data Analysis with SPSS 14, 15 and 16: A Guide for Social Scientists*. London: Routledge.

Bryman, A., and Cramer, D. (2011). *Quantitative Data Analysis with IBM SPSS 17, 18 and 19: A Guide for Social Scientists*. London: Routledge.

Bryman, A., Becker, S., and Sempik, J. (2008). 'Quality Criteria for Quantitative, Qualitative and Mixed Methods Research: The View from Social Policy', *International Journal of Social Research Methodology*, 11: 261–76.

Bryman, A., Gillingwater, D., and McGuinness, I. (1996). 'Industry Culture and Strategic Response: The Case of the British Bus Industry', *Studies in Cultures, Organizations and Societies*, 2: 191–208.

Bryman, A., Haslam, C., and Webb, A. (1994). 'Performance Appraisal in UK Universities: A Case of Procedural Compliance?', *Assessment and Evaluation in Higher Education*, 19: 175–88.

Bryman, A., Stephens, M., and A Campo, C. (1996). 'The Importance of Context: Qualitative Research and the Study of Leadership', *Leadership Quarterly*, 7: 353–70.

Buchanan, D. A. (1998). 'Representing Process: The Contribution of a Re-engineering Frame', *International Journal of Operations and Production Management*, 18(12): 1163–88.

Buchanan, D. A. (2001). 'The Role of Photography in Organization Research: A Reengineering Case Illustration', *Journal of Management Inquiry*, 10: 151–64.

Buchanan, D. A. (2012). 'Case Studies in Organizational Research', in G. Symon and C. Cassell (eds), *Qualitative Organizational Research: Core Methods and Current Challenges*. Los Angeles: Sage.

Buchanan, D., and Bryman, A. (2007). 'Contextualizing Methods Choice in Organizational Research', *Organizational Research Methods*, 10(3): 483–501.

Buchanan, D. A., Boddy, D., and McCalman, J. (1988). 'Getting In, Getting Out and Getting Back', in A. Bryman (ed.), *Doing Research in Organizations*. London: Routledge.

Bulmer, M. (1979). 'Concepts in the Analysis of Qualitative Data', *Sociological Review*, 27: 651–77.

Bulmer, M. (1982). 'The Merits and Demerits of Covert Participant Observation', in M. Bulmer (ed.), *Social Research Ethics*. London: Macmillan.

Bulmer, M. (1984). 'Facts, Concepts, Theories and Problems', in M. Bulmer (ed.), *Social Research Methods*. London: Macmillan.

Burawoy, M. (1979). *Manufacturing Consent*. Chicago: University of Chicago Press.

Burawoy, M. (2003). 'Revisits: An Outline of a Theory of Reflexive Ethnography', *American Sociological Review*, 68: 645–79.

Burawoy, M., Blum, J. A., George, S., Gille, Z., Gowan, T., Haney, L., Klawiter, M., Lopez, S. H., Riain, S. O., and Thayer, M. (2000). *Global Ethnography: Forces, Connections and Imaginations in a Postmodern World*. Berkeley and Los Angeles: University of California Press.

Burger, J. M. (2009). 'Replicating Milgram: Would People Still Obey Today?', *American Psychologist*, 64(1): 1–11.

Burgess, R. G. (1984). *In the Field*. London: Allen & Unwin.

Burman, E. (1994). 'Interviewing', in P. Banister, E. Burman, I. Parker, M. Taylor, and C. Tindall (eds.), *Qualitative Methods in Psychology: A Research Guide*. Buckingham: Open University Press: 49–71.

Burns, D., Hyde, P., Killet, A., Poland, F., and Gray, R. (2014). 'Participatory Organizational Research: Examining Voice in the Co-production of Knowledge', *British Journal of Management*, 25: 133–44.

Burrell, G., and Morgan, G. (1979). *Sociological Paradigms and Organisational Analysis*. Aldershot: Gower.

Business Week (1973). 'The Public Clams up on Survey Takers', 15 September, 216–20.

Buston, K. (1997). 'NUD*IST in Action: Its Use and its Usefulness in a Study of Chronic Illness in Young People', *Sociological Research Online*, 2, http://www.socresonline.org.uk/socresonline/2/3/6.html.

Butcher, B. (1994). 'Sampling Methods: An Overview and Review', *Survey Methods Centre Newsletter*, 15: 4–8.

Buttner, E. H. (2001). 'Examining Female Entrepreneurs' Management Style: An Application of a Relational Frame', *Journal of Business Ethics*, 29: 253–69.

Byron, K. (2008). 'Carrying Too Heavy a Load? The Communication and Miscommunication of Emotion by Email', *Academy of Management Review*, 33(2): 309–27.

Calder, B. J. (1977). 'Focus Groups and the Nature of Qualitative Marketing Research', *Journal of Marketing Research*, 14: 353–64.

Callahan, J. (2017). 'The Retrospective (Im)Moralization of Self-Plagiarism: Power Interests in the Social Construction of New Norms for Publishing'. *Organization*, doi: 10.1177/1350508417734926.

Campbell, D. T. (1957). 'Factors Relevant to the Validity of Experiments in Social Settings', *Psychological Bulletin*, 54: 297–312.

Campbell, M. L. (1998). 'Institutional Ethnography and Experience as Data', *Qualitative Sociology*, 21(1): 55–73.

Carini, R. M., Hayek, J. C., Kuh, G. D., Kennedy, J. M., and Ouimet, J. D. (2003). 'College Student Responses to Web and Paper Surveys: Does Mode Matter?', *Research in Higher Education*, 44(1): 1–19.

Casey, C. (1995). *Work, Self and Society: After Industrialism*. London: Routledge.

Cassell, C., Cunliffe, A. L., and Grandy, G. (2018). *The SAGE Handbook of Qualitative Business and Management Research Methods: History and Traditions*. London: SAGE.

Cassell, J. (1982). 'Harms, Benefits, Wrongs and Rights in Fieldwork', in J. E. Sieber (ed.), *The Ethics of Social Research: Surveys and Experiments*. New York: Springer, 7–31.

Catterall, M., and Maclaran, P. (1997). 'Focus Group Data and Qualitative Analysis Programs: Coding the Moving Picture as well as Snapshots', *Sociological Research Online*, 2, http://www.socresonline.org.uk/socresonline/2/1/6.html.

Cavendish, R. (1982). *Women on the Line*. London: Routledge & Kegan Paul.

Chai, D., Jeong, S., Kim, J., Kim, S., and Hamlin, R. (2016). 'Perceived Managerial and Leadership Effectiveness in a Korean Context: An Indigenous Qualitative Study', *Asia Pacific Journal of Management*, 33(3): 789–820.

Chalmers, A. (2013). *What is This Thing Called Science?* St Lucia: UQ Press.

Chamberlayne, P., Bornat, J., and Wengraf, T. (2000). 'Introduction: The Biographical Turn', in P. Chamberlayne, J. Bornat, and T. Wengraf (eds), *The Turn to Biographical Methods in Social Science: Comparative Issues and Examples*. London: Routledge.

Chan, I. Y. S., Leung, M.-Y., and Yu, S. S. W. (2012). 'Managing the Stress of Hong Kong Expatriate Professionals in Mainland China: Focus Group Study Exploring Individual Coping Strategies and Organizational Support', *Journal of Construction Engineering and Management*, 138(10): 1150–60.

Chan, K. W., and Li, S. Y. (2010). 'Understanding Consumer-to-Consumer Interactions in Virtual Communities: The Salience of Reciprocity', *Journal of Business Research*, 63: 1033–40.

Charmaz, K. (1983). 'The Grounded Theory Method: An Explication and Interpretation', in R. M. Emerson (ed.), *Contemporary Field Research: A Collection of Readings*. Boston: Little, Brown.

Charmaz, K. (2000). 'Grounded Theory: Objectivist and Constructivist Methods', in N. K. Denzin and Y. S. Lincoln (eds), *Handbook of Qualitative Research*, 2nd edn. Thousand Oaks, CA: Sage.

Charmaz, K. (2006). *Constructing Grounded Theory: A Practical Guide through Qualitative Analysis*. London: Sage.

Chartered Association of Business Schools (2015). *Ethics Guide*, https://charteredabs.org/publications/ethics-guide-2015-advice-guidance/.

Chatterjee, A., and Hambrick, D. C. (2007). 'It's All About Me: Narcissistic Chief Executive Officers and their Effects on Company Strategy and Performance', *Administrative Science Quarterly*, 52: 351–86.

Chen, C. C., and Meindl, J. R. (1991). 'The Construction of Leadership Images in the Popular Press: The Case of Donald

Burr and People Express', *Administrative Science Quarterly*, 36: 521–51.

Chen, C.-P. (2012). 'Online Group Buying Behavior in CC2B e-Commerce: Understanding Consumer Motivations', *Journal of Internet Commerce*, 11: 254–70.

Chidlow, A., Ployiannaki, E., and Welch, C. (2014). 'Translation in Cross-Language International Business Research: Beyond Equivalence', *Journal of International Business Studies*, 45(5): 462–82.

Cicourel, A. V. (1964). *Method and Measurement in Sociology*. New York: Free Press.

Cicourel, A. V. (1982). 'Interviews, Surveys, and the Problem of Ecological Validity', *American Sociologist*, 17: 11–20.

Clapper, D. L., and Massey, A. P. (1996). 'Electronic Focus Groups: A Framework for Exploration', *Information and Management*, 30: 43–50.

Clark, C. (2000). 'Letter: Stub out BAT Cash', *Times Higher Education Supplement*, 8 December.

Clarke, C., and Knights, D. (2014). 'It's a Bittersweet Symphony, This Life: Fragile Academic Selves and Insecure Identities at Work', *Organization Studies*, 35(3): 335–7.

Clarke, C., Knights, D., and Jarvis, C. (2012). 'A Labour of Love? Academics in Business Schools', *Scandinavian Journal of Management*, 28: 5–15.

Clegg Smith, K. (2004). '"Electronic Eavesdropping": The Ethical Issues Involved in Conducting a Virtual Ethnography', in M. D. Johns, S.-L. S. Chen, and G. J. Hall (eds), *Online Social Research*. New York: Peter Lang.

Clifford, J. (1983). 'On Ethnographic Authority', *Representations*, 1: 118–46.

Cobanoglu, C., Ward, B., and Moreo, P. J. (2001). 'A Comparison of Mail, Fax and Web-Based Survey Methods', *International Journal of Market Research*, 43: 441–52.

Coffey, A. (1999). *The Ethnographic Self: Fieldwork and the Representation of Reality*. London: Sage.

Coffey, A., and Atkinson, P. (1996). *Making Sense of Qualitative Data: Complementary Research Strategies*. Thousand Oaks, CA: Sage.

Coffey, A., Holbrook, B., and Atkinson, P. (1996). 'Qualitative Data Analysis: Technologies and Representations', *Sociological Research Online*, 2, http://www.socresonline.org.uk/socresonline/1/1/4.html.

Coghlan, D. (2001). 'Insider Action Research Projects: Implications for Practising Managers', *Management Learning*, 32(1): 49–60.

Coleman, C., and Moynihan, J. (1996). *Understanding Crime Data: Haunted by the Dark*. Buckingham: Open University Press.

Coleman, J. S. (1958). 'Relational Analysis: The Study of Social Organization with Survey Methods', *Human Organization*, 16: 28–36.

Collins, G., and Wickham, J. (2004). 'Inclusion or Exploitation: Irish Women Enter the Labour Force', *Gender, Work and Organization*, 11(1): 26–46.

Collins, M. (1997). 'Interviewer Variability: A Review of the Problem', *Journal of the Market Research Society*, 39: 67–84.

Collins, R. (1994). *Four Sociological Traditions*, rev. edn. New York: Oxford University Press.

Collinson, D. L. (1988). 'Engineering Humour: Masculinity, Joking and Conflict in Shop Floor Relations', *Organisation Studies*, 9(2): 181–99.

Collinson, D. L. (1992a). *Managing the Shopfloor: Subjectivity, Masculinity and Workplace Culture*. Berlin: DeGruyter.

Collinson, D. L. (1992b). 'Researching Recruitment: Qualitative Methods and Sex Discrimination', in R. Burgess (ed.), *Studies in Qualitative Methodology*, vol. 3. London: JAI Press.

Colquitt, J. (2012). 'From the Editors: Plagiarism Policies and Screening at *AMJ*', *Academy of Management Journal*, 55(4): 749–51.

Colville, I., Pye, A., and Carter, M. (2013). 'Organizing to Counter Terrorism: Sensemaking amidst Dynamic Complexity', *Human Relations*, 66(9): 1201–23.

Combe, I. A., and Crowther, D. E. (2000). 'The Semiology of an Advertising Campaign: Brand Repositioning', University of North London, Social Marketing Working Paper Series, 1–32.

Conger, J. A., and Kanungo, R. N. (1998). *Charismatic Leadership in Organizations*. Thousand Oaks, CA: Sage.

Conklin, J. (ed.) (2006). *Dialogue Mapping: Building Shared Understanding of Wicked Problems*. Chichester: Wiley.

Connell, R. (2007). *Southern Theory*. Cambridge: Polity.

Converse, J. M., and Presser, S. (1986). *Survey Questions: Handcrafting the Standardized Questionnaire*. Beverly Hills, CA: Sage.

Cook, T. D., and Campbell, D. T. (1979). *Quasi-Experimentation: Design and Analysis for Field Settings*. Boston, MA: Houghton Mifflin.

Cooke, B. (2003). 'The Denial of Slavery in Management Studies', *Journal of Management Studies*, 40(8): 1895–918.

Cooke, B. (2006). 'The Cold War Origin of Action Research as Managerialist Cooptation', *Human Relations*, 59(5): 665–93.

Corbett, A., Cornellisen, J., Delios, A., and Harley, B. (2014). 'Variety, Novelty, and Perceptions of Scholarship in Research on Management and Organizations: An Appeal for Ambidextrous Scholarship', *Journal of Management Studies*, 51(1): 3–18.

Corden, A., and Sainsbury, R. (2006). *Using Verbatim Quotations in Reporting Qualitative Social Research: Researchers' Views*. Social Policy Research Unit Report, http://www.york.ac.uk/inst/spru/pubs/pdf/verbquotresearch.pdf.

Corley, K. G., and Gioia, D. A. (2004). 'Identity Ambiguity and Change in the Wake of a Corporate Spin-Off', *Administrative Science Quarterly*, 49: 173–208.

Cornelissen, J. P. (2017). 'Preserving Theoretical Divergence in Management Research: Why the Explanatory Potential of Qualitative Research should be Harnessed rather than Suppressed', *Journal of Management Studies*, 54(3): 368–83.

Cornelissen, J., Gajewska-De Mattos, H., Piekkari, R., and Welch, C. (2012). 'Writing Up as a Legitimacy Seeking Process: Alternative Publishing Recipes for Qualitative Research', in G. Symons and C. Cassell (eds), *Qualitative Organizational Research*. London: Sage, 184–203.

Cornelissen, J. P., Mantere, S., and Vaara, E. (2014). 'The Contradiction of Meaning: The Combined Effect of Communication, Emotions, and Materiality on Sensemaking in the

Stockwell Shooting', *Journal of Management Studies*, doi: 10.1111/joms.12073.

Corti, L. (1993). 'Using Diaries in Social Research', *Social Research Update*, no. 2.

Corti, L., Foster, J., and Thompson, P. (1995). 'Archiving Qualitative Research Data', *Social Research Update*, no. 10.

Couper, M. P. (2000). 'Web Surveys: A Review of Issues and Approaches', *Public Opinion Quarterly*, 64: 464–94.

Couper, M. P., and Hansen, S. E. (2002). 'Computer-Assisted Interviewing', in J. F. Gubrium and J. A. Holstein (eds), *Handbook of Interview Research: Context and Method*. Thousand Oaks, CA: Sage.

Couper, M. P., Traugott, M. W., and Lamias, M. J. (2001). 'Web Survey Design and Administration', *Public Opinion Quarterly*, 65: 230–53.

Coupland, C. (2005). 'Corporate Social Responsibility on the Web', *Journal of Business Ethics*, 62: 355–66.

Cowley, J. C. P. (2000). 'Strategic Qualitative Focus Group Research: Define and Articulate our Skills or We Will be Replaced by Others', *International Journal of Market Research*, 42(1): 17–38.

Cramer, D. (1998). *Fundamental Statistics for Social Research*. London: Routledge.

Crawford, S. D., Couper, M. P., and Lamias, M. J. (2001). 'Web Surveys: Perception of Burden', *Social Science Computer Review*, 19: 146–62.

Creswell, J., and Plano Clark, V. L. (2011). *Designing and Conducting Mixed Methods Research*, 2nd edn. Los Angeles: Sage.

Croll, P. (1986). *Systematic Classroom Observation*. London: Falmer Press.

Cryer, P. (1996). *The Research Student's Guide to Success*. Buckingham: Open University Press.

Cunliffe, A., and Alcadipani, R. (2016). 'The Politics of Access in Fieldwork: Immersion, Backstage Dramas and Deception', *Organizational Research Methods*, 19(4): 535–61.

Curasi, C. F. (2001). 'A Critical Exploration of Face-to-Face Interviewing vs Computer-Mediated Interviewing', *International Journal of Market Research*, 43: 361–75.

Currie, G., Lockett, A., and Suhomlinova, O. (2009). 'Leadership and Institutional Change in the Public Sector: The Case of Secondary Schools in England', *Leadership Quarterly*, 20: 664–79.

Czaja, R., and Blair, J. (1996). *Designing Surveys: A Guide to Decisions and Procedures*. Thousand Oaks, CA: Sage.

Czarniawska, B. (1998). *A Narrative Approach to Organization Studies*. Thousand Oaks, CA: Sage.

Czarniawska, B. (1999). *Writing Management: Organization Theory as a Literary Genre*. Oxford: Oxford University Press.

Czarniawska, B. (2007). *Shadowing and other Techniques for Doing Fieldwork in Modern Societies*. Malmö: Liber.

Czarniawska, B. (2014). 'Why I Think Shadowing is the Best Field Technique in Management and Organization Studies', *Qualitative Research in Organizations and Management*, 9(1): 90–93.

Daft, R. L. (1995). 'Why I Recommended that your Manuscript be Rejected and What You can Do About It', in L. L. Cummings and P. J. Frost (eds), *Publishing in the Organizational Sciences*. London: Sage.

Daigneault, P.-M., Jacob, S., and Ouimet, M. (2012). 'Using Systematic Review Methods within a Ph.D. Dissertation in Political Science: Challenges and Lessons Learned from Practice', *International Journal of Social Research Methodology*, doi: 10.1080/13645579.2012.730704.

Dale, A., Arber, S., and Proctor, M. (1988). *Doing Secondary Analysis*. London: Unwin Hyman.

Dalton, M. (1959). *Men who Manage: Fusion of Feeling and Theory in Administration*. New York: Wiley.

Dalton, M. (1964). 'Perceptions and Methods in Men who Manage', in P. Hammond (ed.), *Sociologists at Work*. New York: Basic Books.

Dane, E. (2011). 'Changing the Tune of Academic Writing: Muting Cognitive Entrenchment', *Journal of Management Inquiry*, 20(3): 332–6.

Davies, C. A. (1999). *Reflexive Ethnography: A Guide to Researching Selves and Others*. London: Routledge.

Davies, J. (2001). 'International Comparisons of Labour Disputes in 1999', *Labour Market Trends*, April: 195–201.

Davies, R., Jones, M., and Lloyd-Williams, H. (2014). 'Age and Work-Related Health: Insights from the UK Labour Force Survey', *British Journal of Industrial Relations*, doi: 10.1111/bjir.12059.

Davis, J. A. (1964). 'Great Books and Small Groups: An Informal History of a National Survey', in P. Hammond (ed.), *Sociologists at Work*. New York: Basic Books.

Davison, J. (2009). 'Icon, Iconography, Iconology: Visual Branding, Banking and the Case of the Bowler Hat', *Accounting, Auditing and Accountability Journal*, 22(6): 883–906.

Deacon, D., Bryman, A., and Fenton, N. (1998). 'Collision or Collusion? A Discussion of the Unplanned Triangulation of Quantitative and Qualitative Research Methods', *International Journal of Social Research Methodology*, 1: 47–63.

Deakin, H., and Wakefield, K. (2014). 'Skype Interviewing: Reflections of Two PhD researchers', *Qualitative Research*, doi: 10.1177/1468794113488126.

Decker, S. (2016). 'The Silence of the Archives: Business History, Post-colonialism and Archival Ethnography', *Management and Organizational History*, 8(2): 155–73.

Delamont, S., and Hamilton, D. (1984). 'Revisiting Classroom Research: A Continuing Cautionary Tale', in S. Delamont (ed.), *Readings on Interaction in the Classroom*. London: Methuen.

Delanty, G., and Strydom, P. (2003). *Philosophies of Social Science: The Classic and Contemporary Readings*. Maidenhead: Open University Press.

Delbridge, R. (1998). *Life on the Line: The Workplace Experience of Lean Production and the 'Japanese' Model*. Oxford: Oxford University Press.

DeLorme, D. E., Zinkhan, G. M., and French, W. (2001). 'Ethics and the Internet: Issues Associated with Qualitative Research', *Journal of Business Ethics*, 33: 271–86.

den Hoonaard, W. C. (2011). *The Seduction of Ethics: Transforming the Social Sciences*. Toronto: University of Toronto Press.

Denscombe, M. (2006). 'Web-Based Questionnaires and the Mode Effect: An Evaluation Based on Completion Rates and Data Contents of Near-Identical Questionnaires Delivered in Different Modes', *Social Science Computer Review*, 24: 246–54.

Denscombe, M. (2010). *Ground Rules for Good Research: Guidelines for Good Practice*, 2nd edn. Maidenhead: Open University Press.

Denyer, D., and Tranfield, D. (2009). 'Producing a Systematic Review', in D. Buchanan and A. Bryman (eds), *The Sage Handbook of Organizational Research Methods*. London: Sage.

Denzin, N. K. (1968). 'On the Ethics of Disguised Observation', *Social Problems*, 15: 502–4.

Denzin, N. K. (1970). *The Research Act in Sociology*. Chicago: Aldine.

Denzin, N. K. (1994). 'Evaluating Qualitative Research in the Poststructural Moment: The Lessons James Joyce Teaches us', *International Journal of Qualitative Studies in Education*, 7: 295–308.

Denzin, N. K., and Lincoln, Y. S. (2005). 'Introduction: The Discipline and Practice of Qualitative Research', in N. K. Denzin and Y. S. Lincoln (eds), *Handbook of Qualitative Research*, 3rd edn. Thousand Oaks, CA: Sage.

Derous, E., Pepermans, R., and Ryan, A. M. (2017). 'Ethnic Discrimination During Resume Screening: Interactive Effects of Applicants' Ethnic Salience with Job Contexts', *Human Relations*, 70(7): 860–82.

Dhanesh, G. S. (2014). 'CSR as Organization-Employee Relationship Management Strategy: A Case Study of Socially Responsible Information Technology Companies in India', *Management Communication Quarterly*, 28(1): 130–49.

Diener, E., and Crandall, R. (1978). *Ethics in Social and Behavioral Research*. Chicago: University of Chicago Press.

Dillman, D. A. (1978). *Mail and Telephone Surveys: The Total Design Method*. New York: Wiley.

Dillman, D. A. (1983). 'Mail and Other Self-Administered Questionnaires', in P. H. Rossi, J. D. Wright, and A. B. Anderson (eds), *Handbook of Survey Research*. Orlando, FL: Academic Press.

Dillman, D., Smyth, D., and Christian, L. (2014). *Internet, Phone, Mail and Mixed-Mode Surveys: The Tailored Design Method*, 4th edn. Hoboken: Wiley.

Dingwall, R. (1980). 'Ethics and Ethnography', *Sociological Review*, 28: 871–91.

Dingwall, R. (2006). 'Confronting the Anti-Democrats: The Unethical Nature of Ethical Regulation in Social Science', *Medical Sociology Online*, 1: 51–8.

Dingwall, R. (2008). 'The Ethical Case Against Ethical Regulation in Humanities and Social Science Research', *Twenty-First Century Society*, 3(1): 1–12.

Ditton, J. (1977). *Part-Time Crime: An Ethnography of Fiddling and Pilferage*. London: Macmillan.

Doloriert, C., and Sambrook, S. (2009). 'Ethical Confessions of the "I" of Autoethnography: The Student's Dilemma', *Qualitative Research in Organizations and Management*, 4(1): 27–45.

Dougherty, D., and Kunda, G. (1990). 'Photograph Analysis: A Method to Capture Organizational Belief Systems', in P.

Gagliardi (ed.), *Symbols and Artefacts: Views of the Corporate Landscape*. Berlin: DeGruyter.

Douglas, J. D. (1976). *Investigative Social Research: Individual and Team Field Research*. Beverly Hills, CA: Sage.

Dyer, W. G., and Wilkins, A. L. (1991). 'Better Stories, not Better Constructs, to Generate Better Theory: A Rejoinder to Eisenhardt', *Academy of Management Review*, 16: 613–19.

Easterby-Smith, M., Golden-Biddle, K., and Locke, K. (2008). 'Working with Pluralism: Determining Quality in Qualitative Research', *Organizational Research Methods*, 11(3): 419–29.

Easton, G. (2002). 'Marketing: A Critical Realist Approach', *Journal of Business Research*, 55(2): 103–9.

Economic and Social Research Council [UK] (2015). *Framework for Research Ethics*, http://www.esrc.ac.uk/funding/guidance-for-applicants/research-ethics/

Eden, C., and Huxham, C. (1996). 'Action Research for Management Research', *British Journal of Management*, 7(1): 75–86.

Edwards, P., Collinson, M., and Rees, C. (1998). 'The Determinants of Employee Responses to Total Quality Management: Six Case Studies', *Organization Studies*, 19(3): 449–75.

Edwards, P., O'Mahoney, J., and Vincent, S. (2014). *Studying Organisations Using Critical Realism: A Practical Guide*. Oxford: Oxford University Press.

Eisenhardt, K. M. (1989). 'Building Theories from Case Study Research', *Academy of Management Review*, 14: 532–50.

Eisenhardt, K. M., and Graebner, M. E. (2007). 'Theory Building from Cases: Opportunities and Challenges', *Academy of Management Journal*, 50(1): 25–32.

Elliott, H. (1997). 'The Use of Diaries in Sociological Research on Health Experience', *Sociological Research Online*, 2, http://www.socresonline.org.uk/socresonline/2/2/7.html.

Ellis, C. (2004). *The Ethnographic I: A Methodological Novel about Teaching and Doing Autoethnography*. Walnut Creek, CA: AltaMira.

Elsesser, K. M., and Lever, J. (2011). 'Does Gender Bias Against Female Leaders Persist? Quantitative and Qualitative Data from a Large-scale Survey', *Human Relations*, 64(12): 1555–78.

Erikson, K. T. (1967). 'A Comment on Disguised Observation in Sociology', *Social Problems*, 14: 366–73.

Evans, M., Wedande, G., Ralston, L., and van't Hul, S. (2001). 'Consumer Interaction in the Virtual Era: Some Qualitative Insights', *Qualitative Market Research*, 4: 150–9.

Fairclough, N. (1992). *Discourse and Social Change*. Cambridge: Polity Press.

Fairclough, N. (1995). *Critical Discourse Analysis: The Critical Study of Language*. London: Longman.

Fairclough, N. (2003). *Analysing Discourse: Textual Analysis for Social Research*. London: Routledge.

Fairclough, N. (2005). 'Discourse Analysis in Organization Studies: The Case for Critical Realism', *Organization Studies*, 26(6): 915–39.

Faraday, A., and Plummer, K. (1979). 'Doing Life Histories', *Sociological Review*, 27: 773–98.

Faulkner, X., and Culwin, F. (2005). 'When Fingers Do the Talking: A Study of Text Messaging', *Interacting with Computers*, 17: 167–85.

Fenton, N., Bryman, A., and Deacon, D. (1998). *Mediating Social Science*. London: Sage.

Fern, E. F. (2001). *Advanced Focus Group Research*. Thousand Oaks, CA: Sage.

Ferraro, F., Etzion, D., and Gehman, J. (2015). 'Tackling Grand Challenges Pragmatically: Robust Action Revisited', *Organization Studies*, 36: 363–90.

Fiedler, F. E. (1967). *A Theory of Leadership Effectiveness*. New York: McGraw Hill.

Fielding, N., and Lee, R. M. (1998). *Computer Analysis and Qualitative Research*. London: Sage.

Filmer, P., Phillipson, M., Silverman, D., and Walsh, D. (1972). *New Directions in Sociological Theory*. London: Collier-Macmillan.

Finch, J. (1987). 'The Vignette Technique in Survey Research', *Sociology*, 21: 105–14.

Fine, G. A. (1996). 'Justifying Work: Occupational Rhetorics as Resources in Kitchen Restaurants', *Administrative Science Quarterly*, 41: 90–115.

Flanagan, J. C. (1954). 'The Critical Incident Technique', *Psychological Bulletin*, 1: 327–58.

Fleetwood, S. (2005). 'Ontology in Organization and Management Studies: A Critical Realist Perspective', *Organization*, 12(2): 197–222.

Fleming, C., and Bowden, M. (2009). 'Web-Based Surveys as an Alternative to Traditional Mail Methods', *Journal of Environmental Management*, 90: 284–92.

Fletcher, D. (2002). '"In the Company of Men": A Reflexive Tale of Cultural Organizing in a Small Organization', *Gender, Work and Organization*, 9(4): 398–419.

Fletcher, J. (1966). *Situation Ethics*. London: SCM Press.

Flint, A., Clegg, S., and Macdonald, R. (2006). 'Exploring Staff Perceptions of Student Plagiarism', *Journal of Further and Higher Education*, 30: 145–56.

Flyvbjerg, B. (2006). 'Five Misunderstandings about Case Study Research', *Qualitative Inquiry*, 12: 219–45.

Foddy, W. (1993). *Constructing Questions for Interviews and Questionnaires: Theory and Practice in Social Research*. Cambridge: Cambridge University Press.

Forster, N. (1994). 'The Analysis of Company Documentation', in C. Cassell and G. Symon (eds), *Qualitative Methods in Organizational Research*. London: Sage.

Foucault, M. (1974). *The Order of Things: An Archaeology of the Human Sciences*. New York: Vintage.

Foucault, M. (1979). *Discipline and Punish: The Birth of the Prison*. New York: Random House.

Foucault, M. (1980). *The History of Sexuality, i. An Introduction*. New York: Random House.

Fowler, F. J. (1993). *Survey Research Methods*, 2nd edn. Newbury Park, CA: Sage.

Fowler, F. J., and Mangione, T. W. (1990). *Standardized Survey Interviewing: Minimizing Interviewer-Related Error*. Beverly Hills, CA: Sage.

Franzosi, R. (1995). 'Computer-Assisted Content-Analysis of Newspapers: Can We Make an Expensive Research Tool More Efficient?', *Quantity and Quality*, 29(2): 157–72.

Freeman, C. (2000). *High Tech and High Heels in the Global Economy: Women, Work and Pink-Collar Identities in the Caribbean*. Durham, NC: Duke University Press.

Frey, J. H. (2004). 'Telephone Surveys', in M. S. Lewis-Beck, A. Bryman, and T. F. Liao (eds), *The Sage Encyclopedia of Social Science Research Methods*. Thousand Oaks, CA: Sage.

Frey, J. H., and Oishi, S. M. (1995). *How to Conduct Interviews by Telephone and in Person*. Thousand Oaks, CA: Sage.

Fricker, S., and Schonlau, M. (2002). 'Advantages and Disadvantages of Internet Research Surveys: Evidence from the Literature', *Field Methods*, 14: 347–67.

Gabriel, Y. (1998). 'The Use of Stories', in G. Symon and C. Cassell (eds), *Qualitative Methods and Analysis in Organizational Research*. London: Sage.

Gallupe, R. B., Dennis, A. R., Cooper, W. H., Valacich, J. S., Bastianutti, L. M., and Nunamaker, J. F. (1992). 'Electronic Brainstorming and Group Size', *Academy of Management Journal*, 35: 350–69.

Gans, H. J. (1962). *The Urban Villagers*. New York: Free Press.

Garcia, A. C., Standlee, A. I., Bechkoff, J., and Cui, Y. (2009). 'Ethnographic Approaches to the Internet and Computer-Mediated Communication', *Journal of Contemporary Ethnography*, 38(1): 52–84.

Gardner, H. (2012). 'Performance Pressure as a Double-edged Sword: Enhancing Team Motivation but Undermining the Use of Team Knowledge', *Administrative Science Quarterly*, 57(1): 1–46.

Gardner, W. L., Lowe, K. B., Moss, T. W., Mahoney, K. T., and Cogliser, C. C. (2010). 'Scholarly Leadership of the Study of Leadership: A Review of *The Leadership Quarterly*'s Second Decade, 2000–2009', *Leadership Quarterly*, 21: 922–58.

Garfinkel, H. (1967). *Studies in Ethnomethodology*. Englewood Cliffs, NJ: Prentice-Hall.

Geertz, C. (1973). 'Thick Description: Toward an Interpretive Theory of Culture', in C. Geertz, *The Interpretation of Cultures*. New York: Basic Books.

Gephart, R. (2014). 'Using Prosperity to Construct an Economic Crisis: Alberta's "Bitumen" Bubble', *Recherches en Sciences de Gestion/Management Sciences/Ciencias de Gestión*, 105(6): 37–57.

Gephart, R. P. (1988). *Ethnostatistics: Qualitative Foundations for Quantitative Research*. Newbury Park, CA: Sage.

Gephart, R. P. (1993). 'The Textual Approach: Risk and Blame in Disaster Sensemaking', *Academy of Management Journal*, 36(6): 1465–514.

Gersick, C. J. G. (1994). 'Pacing Strategic Change: The Case of a New Venture', *Academy of Management Journal*, 37(1): 9–45.

Gerson, K., and Horowitz, R. (2002). 'Observation and Interviewing: Options and Choices', in T. May (ed.), *Qualitative Research in Action*. London: Sage.

Ghobadian, A., and Gallear, D. (1997). 'TQM and Organization Size', *International Journal of Operations and Production Management*, 17(2): 121–63.

Gibbons, M., Limoges, C., Nowotny, H., Schwartzman, S., Scott, P., and Trow, M. (1994). *The New Production of Knowledge*. London: Sage.

Gibson, L. (2010). 'Realities Toolkit #09: Using Email Interviews', *Realities* series, Morgan Centre for the Study of Relationships and Personal Life, University of Manchester.

Gilbert, G. N. (1977). 'Referencing as Persuasion', *Social Studies of Science*, 7: 113–22.

Gilbert, G. N., and Mulkay, M. (1984). *Opening Pandora's Box: A Sociological Analysis of Scientists' Discourse*. Cambridge: Cambridge University Press.

Gill, R. (1996). 'Discourse Analysis: Practical Implementation', in J. T. E. Richardson (ed.), *Handbook of Qualitative Research Methods for Psychology and the Social Sciences*. Leicester: BPS Books.

Gill, R. (2000). 'Discourse Analysis', in M. W. Bauer and G. Gaskell (eds), *Qualitative Researching with Text, Image and Sound*. London: Sage.

Gill, R., Barbour, J., and Dean, M. (2014). 'Shadowing in/as Work: Ten Recommendations for Shadowing Fieldwork Practice', *Qualitative Research in Organizations and Management*, 9(1): 69–89.

Gioia, D. A., Corley, K. G., and Hamilton, A. L. (2013). 'Seeking Qualitative Rigor in Inductive Research: Notes on the Gioia Methodology', *Organizational Research Methods*, 16(1): 15–31.

Glaser, B. G. (1992). *Basics of Grounded Theory Analysis*. Mill Valley, CA: Sociology Press.

Glaser, B. G., and Strauss, A. L. (1967). *The Discovery of Grounded Theory: Strategies for Qualitative Research*. Chicago: Aldine.

Glock, C. Y. (1988). 'Reflections on Doing Survey Research', in H. J. O'Gorman (ed.), *Surveying Social Life*. Middletown, CT: Wesleyan University Press.

Godard, J. (1994). 'Beyond Empiricism: Towards a Reconstruction of IR Theory and Research', *Advances in Industrial and Labour Relations*, 6: 1–35.

Goffman, E. (1959). *The Presentation of Self in Everyday Life*. New York: Anchor Books.

Gold, R. L. (1958). 'Roles in Sociological Fieldwork', *Social Forces*, 36: 217–23.

Golden-Biddle, K., and Locke, K. D. (1993). 'Appealing Work: An Investigation of how Ethnographic Texts Convince', *Organization Science*, 4: 595–616.

Golden-Biddle, K., and Locke, K. D. (1997). *Composing Qualitative Research*. Thousand Oaks, CA: Sage.

Goldthorpe, J. H., Lockwood, D., Bechhofer, F., and Platt, J. (1968). *The Affluent Worker: Industrial Attitudes and Behaviour*. Cambridge: Cambridge University Press.

Goodall, H. L., Jr (1994). *Casing a Promised Land: The Autobiography of an Organizational Detective as Cultural Ethnographer*. Carbondale: Southern Illinois University Press.

Goode, E. (1996). 'The Ethics of Deception in Social Research: A Case Study', *Qualitative Sociology*, 19: 11–33.

Gorard, S. (2002). 'Ethics and Equity: Pursuing the Perspective of Non-Participants', *Social Research Update*, no. 39.

Grant, A. M., and Wall, T. D. (2009). 'The Neglected Science and Art of Quasi-Experimentation: Why-to, When-to, and How-to Advice for Organizational Researchers', *Organizational Research Methods*, 12(4): 653–86.

Grant, D., Hardy, C., Oswick, C., and Putnam, L. L. (eds) (2004). *The Sage Handbook of Organizational Discourse*. London: Sage.

Grant, D., Keenoy, T., and Oswick, C. (1998). *Discourse and Organization*. London: Sage.

Greene, J. C. (1994). 'Qualitative Program Evaluation: Practice and Promise', in N. K. Denzin and Y. S. Lincoln (eds), *Handbook of Qualitative Research*. Thousand Oaks, CA: Sage.

Greene, J. C. (2000). 'Understanding Social Programs through Evaluation', in N. K. Denzin and Y. S. Lincoln (eds), *Handbook of Qualitative Research*, 2nd edn. Thousand Oaks, CA: Sage.

Greenland, P., and Fontanarosa, P. B. (2012). 'Ending Honorary Authorship', *Science Magazine*, 337: 1019.

Grele, R. J. (1998). 'Movement without Aim: Methodological and Theoretical Problems in Oral History', in R. Perks and A. Thomson (eds), *The History Reader*. London: Routledge.

Grey, C. (2010). 'Organizing Studies: Publications, Politics and Polemic', *Organization Studies*, 31(6): 677–94.

Grint, K., and Woolgar, S. (1997). *The Machine at Work: Technology, Work and Organization*. Cambridge: Polity Press.

Grinyer, A. (2002). 'The Anonymity of Research Participants: Assumptions, Ethics and Practicalities', *Social Research Update*, 36, sru.soc.surrey.ac.uk/SRU36.html.

Grinyer, P., and Yasai-Ardekani, M. (1980). 'Dimensions of Organizational Structure: A Critical Replication', *Academy of Management Journal*, 23: 405–21.

Gronn, P. (2011). 'Hybrid Configurations of Leadership', in A. Bryman, D. Collinson, K. Grint, B. Jackson, and M. Uhl-Bien (eds), *SAGE Handbook of Leadership*. London: Sage.

Guba, E. G. (1985). 'The Context of Emergent Paradigm Research', in Y. S. Lincoln (ed.), *Organization Theory and Inquiry: The Paradigm Revolution*. Beverly Hills, CA: Sage.

Guba, E. G., and Lincoln, Y. S. (1994). 'Competing Paradigms in Qualitative Research', in N. K. Denzin and Y. S. Lincoln (eds), *Handbook of Qualitative Research*. Thousand Oaks, CA: Sage.

Guest, G., Bunce, A., and Johnson, L. (2006). 'How Many Interviews are Enough? An Experiment with Data Saturation and Variability', *Field Methods*, 18: 59–82.

Gummesson, E. (2000). *Qualitative Methods in Management Research*, 2nd edn. London: Sage.

Gusfield, J. (1976). 'The Literary Rhetoric of Science: Comedy and Pathos in Drinking Driving Research', *American Sociological Review*, 41: 16–34.

Hackman, J., and Oldham, G. (1980). *Work Redesign*. Reading, MA: Addison-Wesley.

Haggerty, K. D. (2004). 'Ethics Creep: Governing Social Science Research in the Name of Ethics', *Qualitative Sociology*, 27: 391–414.

Haile, G. A. (2017). 'Union Decline in Britain: Does Gender have Anything to Do with It?', *Scottish Journal of Political Economy*, 64(1): 25–49.

Halfpenny, P. (1979). 'The Analysis of Qualitative Data', *Sociological Review*, 27: 799–825.

Hall, E. (1993). 'Smiling, Deferring and Flirting: Doing Gender by Giving "Good Service"', *Work and Occupations*, 20(4): 452–71.

Hammersley, M. (1989). *The Dilemma of Qualitative Method: Herbert Blumer and the Chicago Tradition*. London: Routledge.

Hammersley, M. (1992a). 'By what Criteria should Ethnographic Research be Judged?', in M. Hammersley, *What's Wrong with Ethnography?* London: Routledge.

Hammersley, M. (1992b). 'Deconstructing the Qualitative–Quantitative Divide', in M. Hammersley, *What's Wrong with Ethnography?* London: Routledge.

Hammersley, M. (1997). 'Qualitative Data Archiving: Some Reflections on its Prospects and Problems', *Sociology*, 31: 131–42.

Hammersley, M., and Atkinson, P. (1995). *Ethnography: Principles in Practice*, 2nd edn. London: Routledge.

Hammersley, M., and Gomm, R. (2000). 'Bias in Social Research', in M. Hammersley (ed.), *Taking Sides in Social Research: Essays in Partisanship and Bias*. London: Routledge.

Hammond, P. (1964). *Sociologists at Work*. New York: Basic Books.

Hand, M. (2014). 'From Cyberspace to the Dataverse: Trajectories in Digital Social Research', *Big Data*, 13: 1–27.

Haney, C., Banks, C., and Zimbardo, P. (1973). 'Interpersonal Dynamics in a Simulated Prison', *International Journal of Criminology and Penology*, 1: 69–97.

Hanna, P. (2012). 'Using Internet Technologies (such as Skype) as a Research Medium: A Research Note', *Qualitative Research*, 12(2): 239–42.

Hanson, D., and Grimmer, M. (2005). 'The Mix of Qualitative and Quantitative Research in Major Marketing Journals', *European Journal of Marketing*, 41(1/2): 58–70.

Hantrais, L. (1996). 'Comparative Research Methods', *Social Research Update*, no. 13.

Hardy, C. (2001). 'Researching Organizational Discourse', *International Studies of Management and Organization*, 31(3): 25–47.

Hardy, M., and Bryman, A. (2004). 'Introduction: Common Threads among Techniques of Data Analysis', in M. Hardy and A. Bryman (eds), *Handbook of Data Analysis*. London: Sage.

Harley, B. (2015). 'The One Best Way? "Scientific" Research on HRM and the Threat to Critical Scholarship', *Human Resource Management Journal*, 25(4): 399–407.

Harley, B., and Hardy, C. (2004). 'Firing Blanks? An Analysis of Discursive Struggle in HRM', *Journal of Management Studies*, 41(3): 377–400.

Harley, B., Faems, D., and Corbett, A. (2014). 'A Few Bad Apples or the Tip of an Iceberg? Academic Misconduct in Publishing', *Journal of Management Studies*, 51(8): 1361–3.

Harper, D. (1986). 'Meaning and Work: A Study in Photo Elicitation', *Current Sociology*, 34(3): 24–68.

Harré, R. (1972). *The Philosophies of Science*. Oxford: Oxford University Press.

Harris, H. (2001). 'Content Analysis of Secondary Data: A Study of Courage in Managerial Decision Making', *Journal of Business Ethics*, 34(3–4): 191–208.

Harrison, R. L., and Reilly, T. M. (2011). 'Mixed Methods Designs in Marketing Research', *Qualitative Market Research: An International Journal*, 14(1): 7–26.

Haslam, C., and Bryman, A. (1994). 'The Research Dissemination Minefield', in C. Haslam and A. Bryman (eds), *Social Scientists Meet the Media*. London: Routledge.

Hatch, M. J. (1996). 'The Role of the Researcher: An Analysis of Narrative Position in Organization Theory', *Journal of Management Inquiry*, 5(4): 359–74.

Hatch, M. J., Schultz, M., and Skov, A. (2015). 'Organizational Identity and Culture in the Context of Managed Change: Transformation in the Carlsberg Group', *Academy of Management Discoveries*, 1(1): 58–90.

Healey, M. J., and Rawlinson, M. B. (1993). 'Interviewing Business Owners and Managers: A Review of Methods and Techniques', *Geoforum*, 24(3): 339–55.

Heap, J. L., and Roth, P. A. (1973). 'On Phenomenological Sociology', *American Sociological Review*, 38: 354–67.

Heisley, D. D., and Levy, S. J. (1991). 'Autodriving: A Photoelicitation Technique', *Journal of Consumer Research*, 18(4): 257–72.

Heracleous, L., and Klaering, L. A. (2014). 'Charismatic and Rhetorical Competence: An Analysis of Steve Job's Rhetoric', *Group and Organization Management*, 39(2): 131–61.

Heritage, J. (1984). *Garfinkel and Ethnomethodology*. Cambridge: Polity Press.

Heritage, J. (1987). 'Ethnomethodology', in A. Giddens and J. H. Turner (eds), *Social Theory Today*. Cambridge: Polity Press.

Herzberg, F., Mausner, B., and Snyderman, B. B. (1959). *The Motivation to Work*, 2nd edn. New York: Wiley.

Hesse-Biber, S. (1995). 'Unleashing Frankenstein's Monster? The Use of Computers in Qualitative Research', *Studies in Qualitative Methodology*, 5: 25–41.

Hewson, C., and Laurent, D. (2008). 'Research Design and Tools for Internet Research', in N. Fielding, R. M. Lee, and G. Blank (eds), *The Sage Handbook of Online Research Methods*. London: Sage.

Hewson, C., Yule, P., Laurent, D., and Vogel, C. (2003). *Internet Research Methods: A Practical Guide for the Social and Behavioural Sciences*. London: Sage.

Hill, F., Leitch, C., and Harrison, R. (2006). 'Desperately Seeking Finance? The Demand for Finance by Women-Owned and -Led Businesses', *Venture Capital: An International Journal of Entrepreneurial Finance*, 8: 159–82.

Hilton, G. (1972). 'Causal Inference Analysis: A Seductive Process', *Administrative Science Quarterly*, 17(1): 44–54.

Hindmarsh, J., and Pilnick, A. (2007). 'Knowing Bodies at Work: Embodiment and Ephemeral Teamwork in Anaesthesia', *Organization Studies*, 28: 1395–416.

Hine, C. (2008). 'Virtual Ethnography: Models, Varieties, Affordances', in N. Fielding, R. M. Lee, and G. Blank (eds), *The Sage Handbook of Online Research Methods*. London: Sage.

Hinings, C. R., Ranson, S., and Bryman, A. (1976). 'Churches as Organizations', in D. S. Pugh and C. R. Hinings (eds), *Organizational Structure: Extensions and Replications, The Aston Programme II*. Farnborough: Saxon House.

Hochschild, A. R. (1983). *The Managed Heart*. Berkeley and Los Angeles: University of California Press.

Hochschild, A. R. (1989). *The Second Shift: Working Parents and the Revolution at Home*. New York: Viking.

Hodson, R. (1996). 'Dignity in the Workplace under Participative Management', *American Sociological Review*, 61: 719–38.

Hodson, R. (1999). *Analyzing Documentary Accounts*. Thousand Oaks, CA: Sage.

Hofmans, J., Gelens, J., and Theuns, P. (2013). 'Enjoyment as a Mediator in the Relationship Between Task Characteristics and Work Effort: An Experience Sampling Study', *European Journal of Work and Organizational Psychology*, 23(5): 693–705.

Hofstede, G. (1984). *Culture's Consequences: International Differences in Work Related Values*. Beverly Hills, CA: Sage.

Holbrook, A., Bourke, S., Fairburn, H., and Lovat, T. (2007). 'Examiner Comment on the Literature Review in Ph.D. Theses', *Studies in Higher Education*, 32: 337–56.

Holbrook, A., Green, M. C., and Krosnick, J. A. (2003). 'Telephone versus Face-to-Face Interviewing of National Probability Samples with Long Questionnaires: Comparisons of Respondent Satisficing and Social Desirability Response Bias', *Public Opinion Quarterly*, 67: 79–125.

Holdaway, E. A., Newberry, J. F., Hickson, D. J., and Heron, R. P. (1975). 'Dimensions of Structure in Complex Societies: The Educational Sector', *Administrative Science Quarterly*, 20: 37–58.

Holliday, R. (1995). *Investigating Small Firms: Nice Work?* London: Routledge.

Holliday, R. (2001). 'We've Been Framed: Visualising Methodology', *Sociological Review*, 48(4): 503–21.

Holman Jones, S. (2005). 'Autoethnography: Making the Personal Political', in N. K. Denzin and Y. S. Lincoln (eds), *Handbook of Qualitative Research*, 3rd edn. London: Sage.

Holmberg, R., Fridell, M., Arnesson, P., and Bäckvall, M. (2008). 'Leadership and Implementation of Evidence-Based Practices', *Leadership in Health Services*, 21(3): 168–84.

Homan, R. (1991). *The Ethics of Social Research*. London: Longman.

Honig, B., and Bedi, A. (2012). 'The Fox in the Hen House: A Critical Examination of Plagiarism among Members of the Academy of Management', *Academy of Management Learning and Education*, 11(1): 101–23.

Hood, J. C. (2007). 'Orthodoxy vs. Power: The Defining Traits of Grounded Theory', in A. Bryant and K. Charmaz (eds), *The SAGE Handbook of Grounded Theory*. Los Angeles: Sage.

Hooghe, M., Stolle, D., Mahéo, V., and Vissers, S. (2010). 'Why Can't a Student be more Like an Average Person? Sampling and Attrition Effects in Social Science Field and Laboratory Experiments', *Annals of the American Academy of Political and Social Science*, 628: 85–96.

Hou, M., Liu, M., Fan, P., and Wei, Z. (2015). 'Does CSR Pay Off in East Asian firms? A Meta-analytic Investigation', *Asia Pacific Journal of Management*, 33: 195–228.

Huang, J., and Hsu, C. H. C. (2009). 'Interaction Among Fellow Cruise Passengers: Diverse Experiences and Impacts', *Journal of Travel and Tourism Marketing*, 26: 547–67.

Huberman, A. M., and Miles, M. B. (1994). 'Data Management and Analysis Methods', in N. K. Denzin and Y. S. Lincoln (eds), *Handbook of Qualitative Research*. Thousand Oaks, CA: Sage.

Hudson, J. M., and Bruckman, A. S. (2004). '"Go Away": Participant Objections to Being Studied and the Ethics of Chatroom Research', *Information Society*, 20: 127–39.

Hughes, E. C. (1958). *Men and their Work*. Glencoe, IL: Free Press.

Hughes, J. A. (1990). *The Philosophy of Social Research*, 2nd edn. Harlow: Longman.

Hummerinta-Peltomäki, L., and Nummela, N. (2006). 'Mixed Methods in International Business Research', *Management International Review*, 46(4): 439–59.

Humphreys, M., and Watson, T. (2009). 'Ethnographic Practices: From "Writing-up Ethnographic Research" to "Writing Ethnography"', in S. Ybema, D. Yanow, H. Wels, and F. Kamsteeg (eds), *Organizational Ethnography: Studying the Complexities of Everyday Life*. London: Sage.

Hunter, W. C. (2008). 'A Typology of Photographic Representations for Tourism: Depictions of Groomed Spaces', *Tourism Management*, 29: 354–65.

Hurworth, R. (2003). 'Photo-Interviewing for Research', *Social Research Update*, 40, sru.soc.surrey.ac.uk/SRU40. html.

Hutt, R. W. (1979). 'The Focus Group Interview: A Technique for Counseling Small Business Clients', *Journal of Small Business Management*, 17(1): 15–20.

Huxley, P., Evans, S., Gately, C., Webber, M., Mears, A., Pajak, S., Kendall, T., Medina, J., and Catona, C. (2005). 'Stress and Pressures in Mental Health Social Work: The Worker Speaks', *British Journal of Social Work*, 35: 1063–79.

Hyde, P., McBride, A., Young, R., and Walshe, K. (2006). 'Role Redesign: New Ways of Working in the NHS', *Personnel Review*, 34(6): 697–712.

Insch, G., Moore, J., and Murphy, L. (1997). 'Content Analysis in Leadership Research: Examples, Procedures and Suggestions for Future Use', *Leadership Quarterly*, 8(1): 1–25.

International Sociological Association (2001). *Code of Ethics*, https://www.isa-sociology.org/en/about-isa/code-of-ethics/.

Jack, G., and Westwood, R. (2006). 'Postcolonialism and the Politics of Qualitative Research in International Business', *Management International Review*, 46(4): 481–500.

Jack, L., and Kholief, A. (2007). 'Introducing Strong Structuration Theory for Informing Qualitative Case Studies in Organization, Management and Accounting Research', *Qualitative Research in Organizations and Management: An International Journal*, 2(3): 208–25.

Jackall, R. (1988). *Moral Mazes: The World of the Corporate Manager*. Oxford: Oxford University Press.

Jackson, B. (2001). *Management Gurus and Management Fashions*. London: Routledge.

Jackson, N., and Carter, P. (1998). 'Management Gurus: What are we to Make of Them?', in J. Hassard and R. Holliday (eds), *Organization-Representation: Work and Organization in Popular Culture*. London: Sage.

Jackson, P., Runde, J., Dobson, P., and Richter, N. (2016). 'Identifying Mechanisms: Influencing the Emergence and Success of Innovation Within National Economies—A Realist Approach', *Policy Sciences*, 49(3): 233–56.

Jackson, T. (2001). 'Cultural Values and Management Ethics: A Ten Nation Study', *Human Relations*, 54(10): 1267–302.

Jacques, R. S. (2010). 'Discourse Analysis', in A. J. Mills, G. Durepos, and E. Wiebe (eds), *Sage Encyclopedia of Case Study Research*. Thousand Oaks, CA: Sage, i: 304–8.

Janis, I. L. (1982). *Groupthink: Psychological Studies of Policy Decisions and Fiascos*, 2nd edn. Boston: Houghton-Mifflin.

Jayaratne, T. E., and Stewart, A. J. (1991). 'Quantitative and Qualitative Methods in the Social Sciences: Current Feminist Issues and Practical Strategies', in M. M. Fonow and J. A. Cook (eds), *Beyond Methodology: Feminist Scholarship as Lived Research*. Bloomington: Indiana University Press.

John, I. D. (1992). 'Statistics as Rhetoric in Psychology', *Australian Psychologist*, 27: 144–9.

Johns, G., Xie, J., and Fang, Y. (1992). 'Mediating and Moderating Effects in Job Design', *Journal of Management*, 18(4): 657–76.

Johnson, P., Buehring, A., Cassell, C. M., and Symon, G. (2006). 'Evaluating Qualitative Management Research: Towards a Contingent Criteriology', *International Journal of Management Reviews*, 8: 131–56.

Jones, M. L. (2004). 'Application of Systematic Review Methods to Qualitative Research: Practical Issues', *Journal of Advanced Nursing*, 48(3): 271–8.

Kabanoff, B., Waldersee, R., and Cohen, M. (1995). 'Espoused Values and Organizational Change Themes', *Academy of Management Journal*, 38(4): 1075–104.

Kandola, B. (2012). 'Focus Groups', in G. Symon and C. Cassell (eds), *Qualitative Organizational Research: Core Methods and Current Challenges*. Los Angeles: Sage.

Kanter, R. M. (1977). *Men and Women of the Corporation*. New York: Basic Books.

Kapasi, I., Sang, K. J. C., and Sitko, R. (2016). 'Gender, Authentic Leadership and Identity: Analysis of Women Leaders' Autobiographies', *Gender in Management: An International Journal*, 31(5/6): 339–58.

Keat, R., and Urry, J. (1975). *Social Theory as Science*. London: Routledge & Kegan Paul.

Keenoy, T., Oswick, C., and Grant, D. (1997). 'Organizational Discourses: Text and Context', *Organization*, 2: 147–58.

Kelan, E. K., and Mah, A. (2014). 'Gendered Identification: Between Idealization and Admiration', *British Journal of Management*, 25: 91–101.

Kelly, L., Burton, S., and Regan, L. (1994). 'Researching Women's Lives or Studying Women's Oppression? Reflections on what Constitutes Feminist Research', in M. Maynard and J. Purvis (eds), *Researching Women's Lives from a Feminist Perspective*. London: Taylor & Francis.

Kent, J., Williamson, E., Goodenough, T., and Ashcroft, R. (2002). 'Social Science Gets the Ethics Treatment: Research Governance and Ethical Review', *Sociological Research Online*, 7(4), http://www.socresonline.org.uk/7/4/williamson.html.

Kent, R., and Lee, M. (1999). 'Using the Internet for Market Research: A Study of Private Trading on the Internet', *Journal of the Market Research Society*, 41: 377–85.

Ketchen, D. J., Ireland, R. D., and Baker, L. T. (2012). 'The Use of Archival Proxies in Strategic Management Studies', *Organizational Research Methods*, 16(1): 32–42.

Kiely, T. (1998). 'Wired Focus Groups', *Harvard Business Review*, 76(1): 12–16.

Kieser, A. (1994). 'Crossroads: Why Organization Theory Needs Historical Analyses—and How This Should Be Performed', *Organization Science*, 5(4): 608–20.

King, E. B., Hebl, M. R., Morgan, W. B., and Ahmad, A. S. (2012). 'Field Experiments on Sensitive Organizational Topics', *Organizational Research Methods*, 16(4): 501–21.

Kirk, J., and Miller, M. L. (1986). *Reliability and Validity in Qualitative Research*. Newbury Park, CA: Sage.

Kitzinger, J. (1994). 'The Methodology of Focus Groups: The Importance of Interaction between Research Participants', *Sociology of Health and Illness*, 16: 103–21.

Kivits, J. (2005). 'Online Interviewing and the Research Relationship', in C. Hine (ed.), *Virtual Methods: Issues in Social Research on the Internet*. Oxford: Berg.

Knights, D., and McCabe, D. (1997). '"How Would You Measure Something Like That?": Quality in a Retail Bank', *Journal of Management Studies*, 34(3): 371–88.

Kondo, D. K. (1990). *Crafting Selves: Power, Gender and Discourses of Identity in a Japanese Workplace*. Chicago: University of Chicago Press.

Kostova, T. (1999). 'Transnational Transfer of Strategic Organizational Practices: A Contextual Perspective', *Academy of Management Review*, 24(2): 308–24.

Kothiyal, N., Bell, E., and Clarke, C. (2018). 'Moving Beyond Mimicry: Creating Hybrid Spaces in Indian Business Schools', *Academy of Management Learning and Education*, 17(2): 137–54.

Kozinets, R. V. (2001). 'Utopian Enterprise: Articulating the Meanings of *Star Trek*'s Culture of Consumption', *Journal of Consumer Research*, 28(1): 67–88.

Kozinets, R. V. (2002). 'The Field behind the Screen: Using Netnography for Marketing Research in Online Communities', *Journal of Marketing Research*, 39: 61–72.

Kozinets, R. V. (2012). 'Marketing Netnography: Prom/ot(ulgat)ing a New Research Method', *Methodological Innovations Online*, 7(1): 37–45, http://www.methodologicalinnovations.org.uk/previous-issues/.

Kozinets, R. V. (2010). *Netnography: Doing Ethnographic Research Online*. London: Sage.

Kozinets, R. V., de Valck, K., Wojnicki, A. C., and Wilner, S. J. S. (2010). 'Networked Narratives: Understanding Word-of-Mouth Marketing in Online Communities', *Journal of Marketing*, 74: 71–89.

Kramer, A. D. I., Guillory, J. E., and Hancock, J. T. (2014). 'Experimental Evidence of Massive-Scale Emotional Contagion Through Social Networks', *Proceedings of the National Academy of Sciences*, 111(24): 8788–90, http://www.pnas.org/content/111/24/8788.

Krause, R., Whitler, K., and Semadeni, M. (2014). 'Power to the Principals! An Experimental Look at Shareholder Say-on-Pay Voting', *Academy of Management Journal*, 57: 94–115.

Kroon, B., van de Voorde, K., and van Veldhoven, M. (2009). 'Cross level Effects of High Performance Work Practices on Burnout: Two Counteracting Mediating Mechanisms Compared', *Personnel Review*, 38(5): 509–25.

Krosnick, J. A., Holbrook, A. L., Berent, M. K., Carson, R. T., Hanemann, W. M., Kopp, R. J., Mitchell, R. C., Presser, S., Ruud, P. A., Smith, V. K., Moody, W. R., Green, M. C., and

Conaway, M. (2002). 'The Impact of "No Opinion" Response Options on Data Quality: Non-Attitude Reduction or an Invitation to Satisfice?', *Public Opinion Quarterly*, 66: 371–403.

Krueger, R. A. (1988). *Focus Groups: A Practical Guide for Applied Research*. Newbury Park, CA: Sage.

Krueger, R. A. (1998). *Moderating Focus Groups*. Thousand Oaks, CA: Sage.

Kuhn, T. S. (1970). *The Structure of Scientific Revolutions*, 2nd edn. Chicago: University of Chicago Press.

Kunda, G. (1992). *Engineering Culture: Control and Commitment in a High-Tech Corporation*. Philadelphia: Temple University Press.

Kvale, S. (1996). *InterViews: An Introduction to Qualitative Research Interviewing*. Thousand Oaks, CA: Sage.

Ladge, J. J., Clair, J. A., and Greenberg, D. (2012). 'Cross-domain Identity Transition During Liminal Periods: Constructing Multiple Selves as Professional and Mother During Pregnancy', *Academy of Management Journal*, 55(6): 1449–71.

LaPiere, R. T. (1934). 'Attitudes vs Actions', *Social Forces*, 13: 230–37.

Lawlor, M. A., and Prothero, A. (2007). 'Exploring Children's Understanding of Television Advertising: Beyond the Advertiser's Perspective', *European Journal of Marketing*, 42(11/12): 1203–23.

Lawrence, P. R., and Lorsch, J. W. (1967). *Organization and Environment*. Boston: Addison Wesley.

Layder, D. (1993). *New Strategies in Social Research*. Cambridge: Polity Press.

Lazarsfeld, P. (1958). 'Evidence and Inference in Social Research', *Daedalus*, 87: 99–130.

Learmonth, M. (2009). 'Rhetoric and Evidence: The Case of Evidence-Based Management', in D. Buchanan and A. Bryman (eds), *The Sage Handbook of Organizational Research Methods*. London: Sage.

LeCompte, M. D., and Goetz, J. P. (1982). 'Problems of Reliability and Validity in Ethnographic Research', *Review of Educational Research*, 52: 31–60.

Lee, B., Collier, P. M., and Cullen, J. (2007). 'Reflections on the Use of Case Studies in the Accounting, Management and Organizational Disciplines', *Qualitative Research in Organizations and Management: An International Journal*, 2(3): 169–78.

Lee, C. K. (1998). *Gender and the South China Miracle: Two Worlds of Factory Women*. Berkeley and Los Angeles: University of California Press.

Lee, R. M. (2000). *Unobtrusive Methods in Social Research*. Buckingham: Open University Press.

Lee, R. M. (2004). 'Danger in Research', in M. S. Lewis-Beck, A. Bryman, and T. F. Liao (eds), *The Sage Encyclopedia of Social Science Research Methods*. Thousand Oaks, CA: Sage.

Lee, R. M., and Fielding, N. G. (1991). 'Computing for Qualitative Research: Options, Problems and Potential', in N. G. Fielding and R. M. Lee (eds), *Using Computers in Qualitative Research*. London: Sage.

Lee, T. W. (1999). *Using Qualitative Methods in Organizational Research*. London: Sage.

Legge, K. (1995). *Human Resource Management: Rhetorics and Realities*. Basingstoke: Macmillan.

Leidner, R. (1993). *Fast Food, Fast Talk: Service Work and the Routinization of Everyday Life*. Berkeley and Los Angeles: University of California Press.

Leitch, C. M., Hill, F. M., and Harrison, R. T. (2010). 'The Philosophy and Practice of Interpretivist Research in Entrepreneurship: Quality, Validation, and Trust', *Organizational Research Methods*, 13: 67–84.

Lilley, S., Harvie, D., Lightfoot, G., and Weir, K. (2012). 'What are We to Do with Feral Publishers?', *Organization*, 19(6): 905–14.

Lincoln, Y. S., and Denzin, N. K. (1994). 'The Fifth Moment', in N. K. Denzin and Y. S. Lincoln (eds), *Handbook of Qualitative Research*. Thousand Oaks, CA: Sage.

Lincoln, Y. S., and Guba, E. (1985). *Naturalistic Inquiry*. Beverly Hills, CA: Sage.

Linstead, S. (1985). 'Jokers Wild: The Importance of Humour and the Maintenance of Organizational Culture', *Sociological Review*, 33(4): 741–67.

Linstead, S. (1993). 'From Postmodern Anthropology to Deconstructive Ethnography', *Human Relations*, 46(1): 97–120.

Little, L. M., Kluenper, D., Nelson, D. L., and Gooty, J. (2012). 'Development and Validation of the Interpersonal Emotion Management Scale', *Journal of Occupational and Organizational Psychology*, 85(2): 407–20.

Livingstone, S., and Lunt, P. (1994). *Talk on Television: Audience Participation and Public Debate*. London: Routledge.

Lo, L., Macky, K., and Pio, E. (2015). 'The HR Competency Requirements for Strategic and Functional HR Practitioners', *International Journal of Human Resource Management*, 26(18): 2308–28.

Locke, K. (1996). 'Rewriting The Discovery of Grounded Theory after 25 Years?', *Journal of Management Inquiry*, 5: 239–45.

Locke, K. (2001). *Grounded Theory in Management Research*. London: Sage.

Locke, R. (1996). *The Collapse of the American Management Mystique*. Oxford: Oxford University Press.

Lofland, J., and Lofland, L. (1995). *Analyzing Social Settings: A Guide to Qualitative Observation and Analysis*, 3rd edn. Belmont, CA: Wadsworth.

Lok, J., and de Rond, M. (2013). 'On the Plasticity of Institutions: Containing and Restoring Practice Breakdowns at the Cambridge University Boat Club', *Academy of Management Journal*, 56(1): 185–207.

Longenecker, J., Moore, C. W., Petty, J. W., Palich, L. E., and McKinney, J. A. (2006). 'Ethical Attitudes in Small Business and Large Corporations: Theory and Empirical Findings from a Tracking Study Spanning Three Decades', *Journal of Small Business Management*, 44(2): 167–83.

Lonkila, M. (1995). 'Grounded Theory as an Emergent Paradigm for Computer-Assisted Qualitative Data Analysis', in U. Kelle (ed.), *Computer-Aided Qualitative Data Analysis*. London: Sage.

Louhiala-Salminen, L. (2002). 'The Fly's Perspective: Discourse in the Daily Routine of a Business Manager', *English for Specific Purposes*, 21: 211–31.

Lowe, K. B., and Gardner, W. L. (2000). 'Ten Years of *The Leadership Quarterly*: Contributions and Challenges for the Future', *Leadership Quarterly*, 11(4): 459–514.

Lozar Manfreda, K., Bosnjak, M., Berzelak, J., Haas, I., and Vehovar, V. (2008). 'Web Surveys versus Other Survey Modes', *International Journal of Market Research*, 50(1): 79–104.

Lucas, J., Morrell, K., and Posard, M. (2013). 'Considerations on the "Replication Problem" in Sociology', *American Sociologist*, 44(2): 217–32.

Lucas, R. (1997). 'Youth, Gender and Part-Time Work: Students in the Labour Process', *Work, Employment and Society*, 11: 595–614.

Macdonald, S., and Kam, J. (2007). 'Ring a Ring o' Roses: Quality Journals and Gamesmanship in Management Studies', *Journal of Management Studies*, 44(4): 640–55.

Madriz, M. (2000). 'Focus Groups in Feminist Research', in N. K. Denzin and Y. S. Lincoln (eds), *Handbook of Qualitative Research*, 2nd edn. Thousand Oaks, CA: Sage.

Maitlis, S., and Lawrence, T. B. (2007). 'Triggers and Enablers of Sensegiving in Organizations', *Academy of Management Journal*, 50: 57–84.

Malinowski, B. (1967). *A Diary in the Strict Sense of the Term*. London: Routledge & Kegan Paul.

Mangabeira, W. (1995). 'Qualitative Analysis and Microcomputer Software: Some Reflections on a New Trend in Sociological Research', *Studies in Qualitative Methodology*, 5: 43–61.

Mann, C., and Stewart, F. (2000). *Internet Communication and Qualitative Research: A Handbook for Researching Online*. London: Sage.

Mantere, S., and Ketokivi, M. (2013). 'Reasoning in Organizational Science', *Academy of Management Review*, 38(1): 70–89.

Marcus, C. (1999). *Ethnography Through Thick and Thin*. Princeton, NJ: Princeton University Press.

Market Research Society (2014). *Code of Conduct*, https://www.mrs.org.uk/standards/code_of_conduct.

Markham, A. (1998). *Life Online: Researching the Real Experience in Virtual Space*. London and Walnut Creek, CA: AltaMira Press.

Marsden, R. (1982). 'Industrial Relations: A Critique of Empiricism', *Sociology*, 16(2): 232–50.

Marsh, C. (1982). *The Survey Method: The Contribution of Surveys to Sociological Explanation*. London: Allen & Unwin.

Marsh, C., and Scarbrough, E. (1990). 'Testing Nine Hypotheses about Quota Sampling', *Journal of the Market Research Society*, 32: 485–506.

Marshall, J. (1981). 'Making Sense as a Personal Process', in P. Reason and J. Rowan (eds), *Human Inquiry*. Chichester: John Wiley.

Marshall, J. (1984). *Women Managers: Travellers in a Male World*. Chichester: Wiley.

Marshall, J. (1995). *Women Managers Moving On: Exploring Career and Life Choices*. London: Routledge.

Martin, J. (1992). *Cultures in Organizations: Three Perspectives*. Oxford: Oxford University Press.

Martin, P., and Bateson, P. (1986). *Measuring Behaviour: An Introductory Guide*. Cambridge: Cambridge University Press.

Martin, P. Y., and Turner, B. A. (1986). 'Grounded Theory and Organizational Research', *Journal of Applied Behavioral Science*, 22(2): 141–57.

Martinko, M. J., and Gardner, W. L. (1990). 'Structured Observation of Managerial Work: A Replication and Synthesis', *Journal of Management Studies*, 27(3): 329–57.

Marx, G. T. (1997). 'Of Methods and Manners for Aspiring Sociologists: 37 Moral Imperatives', *American Sociologist*, 28(1): 102–25.

Marzano, G., and Scott, N. (2009). 'Power in Destination Branding', *Annals of Tourism Research*, 36: 247–67.

Maslach, C., and Jackson, S. (1981). 'The Measurement of Experienced Burnout', *Journal of Occupational Behavior*, 2: 99–113.

Mason, J. (1996). *Qualitative Researching*. London: Sage.

Mason, M. (2010). 'Sample Size and Saturation in PhD Studies Using Qualitative Interviews' [63 paragraphs], *Forum Qualitative Sozialforschung/Forum: Qualitative Social Research*, 11/3, art. 8, http://www.qualitative-research.net/index.php/fqs/article/view/1428.

Masterman, M. (1970). 'The Nature of a Paradigm', in I. Lakatos and A. Musgrave (eds), *Criticism and the Growth of Knowledge*. Cambridge: Cambridge University Press.

Mauthner, N. S., Parry, O., and Backett-Milburn, K. (1998). 'The Data are Out There, or Are They? Implications for Archiving and Revisiting Qualitative Data', *Sociology*, 32: 733–45.

Mayes, B. T., Finney, T. G., Johnson, T. W., Shen, J., and Yi, L. (2017). 'The Effect of Human Resource Practices on Perceived Organizational Support in the People's Republic of China', *International Journal of Human Resource Management*, 28(9): 1261–90.

Maynard, M. (1994). 'Methods, Practice and Epistemology: The Debate about Feminism and Research', in M. Maynard and J. Purvis (eds), *Researching Women's Lives from a Feminist Perspective*. London: Taylor & Francis.

Maynard, M. (1998). 'Feminists' Knowledge and the Knowledge of Feminisms: Epistemology, Theory, Methodology and Method', in T. May and M. Williams (eds), *Knowing the Social World*. Buckingham: Open University Press.

Mays, N., Pope, C., and Popay, J. (2005). 'Sytematically Reviewing Qualitative and Quantitative Evidence to Inform Management and Policy-Making in the Health Field', *Journal of Health Services Research and Policy*, 10(Supplement 1): S6–S20.

McCall, M. J. (1984). 'Structured Field Observation', *Annual Review of Sociology*, 10: 263–82.

McCarthy, L., and Muthuri, J. N. (2016). 'Engaging Fringe Stakeholders in Business and Society Research: Applying Visual Participatory Research Methods', *Business and Society*, https://doi.org/10.1177/0007650316675610.

McCartney, J. L. (1970). 'On Being Scientific: Changing Styles of Presentation of Sociological Research', *American Sociologist*, 5: 30–5.

McClelland, D. C. (1961). *The Achieving Society*. Princeton: Van Nostrand.

McCloskey, D. N. (1985). *The Rhetoric of Economics*. Brighton: Wheatsheaf.

McDonald, G. (2000). 'Cross-Cultural Methodological Issues in Ethical Research', *Journal of Business Ethics*, 27: 89–104.

McDonald, S. (2005). 'Studying Actions in Context: A Qualitative Shadowing Method for Organizational Research', *Qualitative Research*, 5(4): 455–73.

McEachern, M. G. (2015). 'Corporate Citizenship and its Impact upon Consumer Moralisation, Decision-making and Choice', *Journal of Marketing Management*, 31(3–4): 430–52.

McKeever, L. (2006). 'Online Plagiarism Detection Services: Saviour or Scourge?', *Assessment and Evaluation in Higher Education*, 31: 155–65.

McPhail, C., and Rexroat, C. (1979). 'Mead vs Blumer: The Divergent Methodological Perspectives of Social Behaviorism and Symbolic Interactionism', *American Sociological Review*, 44: 449–67.

Medway, R. L., and Fulton, J. (2012). 'When More Gets You Less: A Meta-analysis of the Effect of Concurrent Web Options on Mail Survey Response Rates', *Public Opinion Quarterly*, 76(4): 733–46.

Mellahi, K., and Harris, L. (2016). 'Response Rates in Business and Management Research: An Overview of Current Practice and Suggestions for Future Direction', *British Journal of Management*, 27(2): 426–37.

Meltzer, B. N., Petras, J. W., and Reynolds, L. T. (1975). *Symbolic Interactionism: Genesis, Varieties and Criticism*. London: Routledge & Kegan Paul.

Merton, R. K. (1967). *On Theoretical Sociology*. New York: Free Press.

Merton, R. K., Fiske, M., and Kendall, P. L. (1956). *The Focused Interview: A Manual of Problems and Procedures*. New York: Free Press.

Meyer, A. D. (1991). 'Visual Data in Organizational Research', *Organization Science*, 2(2): 218–36.

Meyer, R. E., Höllerer, M. A., Jancsary, D., and Van Leeuwen, T. V. (2013). 'The Visual Dimension in Organizing, Organization and Organization Research', *Academy of Management Annals*, 7(1): 487–553.

Michel, A. (2011). 'Transcending Socialization: A Nine-year Ethnography of the Body's Role in Organizational Control and Knowledge Workers' Transformation', *Administrative Science Quarterly*, 56(3): 325–68.

Michels, R. (1962). *Political Parties: A Study of the Oligarchal Tendencies of Modern Democracy*. New York: Collier Books [first published 1915].

Mies, M. (1993). 'Towards a Methodology for Feminist Research', in M. Hammersley (ed.), *Social Research: Philosophy, Politics and Practice*. London: Sage.

Miles, M. B. (1979). 'Qualitative Data as an Attractive Nuisance', *Administrative Science Quarterly*, 24: 590–601.

Miles, M. B., and Huberman, A. M. (1984). *Qualitative Data Analysis: A Sourcebook of New Methods*. London: Sage.

Miles, M. B., and Huberman, A. M. (1994). *Qualitative Data Analysis: An Expanded Sourcebook*. London: Sage.

Milgram, S. (1963). 'A Behavioral Study of Obedience', *Journal of Abnormal and Social Psychology*, 67: 371–8.

Milgram, S., and Shotland, L. (1973). *Television and Antisocial Behavior: Field Experiments*. New York: Academic Press.

Milkman, R. (1997). *Farewell to the Factory: Auto Workers in the Late Twentieth Century*. Berkeley and Los Angeles: University of California Press.

Millen, D. (1997). 'Some Methodological and Epistemological Issues Raised by Doing Feminist Research on Non-Feminist Women', *Sociological Research Online*, 2, http://www.socresonline.org.uk/socresonline/2/3/3.html.

Miller, A. G. (2009). 'Reflections on "Replicating Milgram" (Burger, 2009)', *American Psychologist*, 64(1): 20–7.

Miller, R. L. (2000). *Researching Life Stories and Family Histories*. London: Sage.

Miner-Rubino, K., Jayaratne, T. E., and Konik, J. (2007). 'Using Survey Research as a Quantitative Method for Feminist Social Change', in S. N. Hesse-Biber (ed.), *Handbook of Feminist Research: Theory and Praxis*. Thousand Oaks, CA: Sage.

Mintzberg, H. (1973). *The Nature of Managerial Work*. New York: Harper & Row.

Mirchandani, K. (1999). 'Feminist Insight on Gendered Work: New Directions in Research on Women and Entrepreneurship', *Gender, Work and Organization*, 6(4): 224–35.

Mishler, E. G. (1986). *Research Interviewing: Context and Narrative*. Cambridge, MA: Harvard University Press.

Mitchell, J. C. (1983). 'Case and Situation Analysis', *Sociological Review*, 31: 186–211.

Moideenkutty, U., Blau, G., Kumar, R., and Nalakath, A. (2001). 'Perceived Organisational Support as a Mediator of the Relationship of Perceived Situational Factors to Affective Organisational Commitment'. *Applied Psychology*, 50(4): 615–34.

Molina-Azorín, J. F. (2009). 'Understanding how Mixed Methods Research is Undertaken within a Specific Research Community', *International Journal of Multiple Research Approaches*, 3: 47–57.

Molina-Azorín, J. F. (2012). 'Mixed Methods in Strategic Management: Impact and Applications', *Organizational Research Methods*, 15(1): 33–56.

Molina Azorín, J. F., and Cameron, R. (2010). 'The Application of Mixed Methods in Organisational Research: A Literature Review', *Electronic Journal of Business Research Methods*, 8(2): 95–105, http://www.ejbrm.com/volume8/issue2/p95.

Morgan, D. L. (1998a). *Planning Focus Groups*. Thousand Oaks, CA: Sage.

Morgan, D. L. (1998b). 'Practical Strategies for Combining Qualitative and Quantitative Methods: Applications for Health Research', *Qualitative Health Research*, 8: 362–76.

Morgan, D. L. (2014). *Integrating Qualitative and Quantitative Methods: A Pragmatic Approach*. Los Angeles: Sage.

Morgan, G. (1997). *Images of Organization*. Thousand Oaks: CA: Sage.

Morrell, K., and Learmonth, M. (2015). 'Against Evidence-Based Management, For Management Learning', *Academy of Management Learning and Education*, 14(4): 520–33.

Morrison, D. E. (1998). *The Search for a Method: Focus Groups and the Development of Mass Communication Research*. Luton: University of Luton Press.

Morse, J. M. (2004). 'Sampling in Qualitative Research', in M. S. Lewis-Beck, A. Bryman, and T. F. Liao (eds), *The Sage Encyclopedia of Social Science Research Methods*, 3 vols. Thousand Oaks, CA: Sage.

Moser, C. A., and Kalton, G. (1971). *Survey Methods in Social Investigation*. London: Heinemann.

Mumby, D., and Clair, R. (1997). 'Organizational Discourse', in T. A. Van Dijk (ed.), *Discourse as Social Interaction,* vol. 2 of *Discourse Studies: A Multidisciplinary Introduction*. Newbury Park, CA: Sage.

Musson, G. (1998). 'Life Histories', in G. Symon and C. Cassell (eds), *Qualitative Methods and Analysis in Organizational Research*. London: Sage.

Newell, A., and Simon, H. A. (1972). *Human Problem Solving*. Englewood Cliffs, NJ: Prentice Hall.

Nielsen, K., Randall, R., and Christensen, K. B. (2010). 'Does Training Managers Enhance the Effects of Implementing Team-Working? A Longitudinal Mixed Methods Field Study', *Human Relations,* 63: 1719–41.

Nishii, L.H., Lepak, D. P., and Schneider, B. (2008). 'Employee Attributions of the "Why" of HR Practices: Their Effects on Employee Attitudes and Behaviors, and Customer Satisfaction', *Personnel Psychology*, 61(3): 503–45.

Noblit, G. W., and Hare, R. D. (1988). *Meta-ethnography: Synthesizing Qualitative Studies*. Newbury Park, CA: Sage.

Noy, C. (2008). 'Sampling Knowledge: The Hermeneutics of Snowball Sampling in Qualitative Research', *International Journal of Social Research Methodology*, 11: 327–44.

Oakley, A. (1981). 'Interviewing Women: A Contradiction in Terms', in H. Roberts (ed.), *Doing Feminist Research*. London: Routledge & Kegan Paul.

Oakley, A. (1998). 'Gender, Methodology and People's Ways of Knowing: Some Problems with Feminism and the Paradigm Debate in Social Science', *Sociology*, 32: 707–31.

O'Cathain, A. (2010). 'Assessing the Quality of Mixed Methods Research: Toward a Comprehensive Framework', in A. Tashakkori and C. Teddlie (eds.), *The Sage Handbook of Mixed Methods in Social and Behavioral Research*, 2nd edn. Los Angeles: Sage, 531–55.

O'Cathain, A., Murphy, E., and Nicholl, J. (2008). 'The Quality of Mixed Methods Studies in Health Services Research', *Journal of Health Services Research and Policy*, 13: 92–8.

O'Connor, H., and Madge, C. (2001). 'Cyber-Mothers: Online Synchronous Interviewing using Conferencing Software', *Sociological Research Online*, 5, http://www.socresonline.org.uk/5/4/oconnor.html.

O'Connor, H., Madge, C., Shaw, R., and Wellens, J. (2008). 'Internet-Based Interviewing', in N. Fielding, R. M. Lee, and G. Blank (eds), *The Sage Handbook of Online Research Methods*. London: Sage.

Ogbolu, M. N., and Singh, R. P. (2013). 'Researching Black Entrepreneurship: Exploring the Challenge of Response Bias', *Journal of Developmental Entrepreneurship*, 18(4), https://doi.org/10.1142/S1084946713500234 (18 pages).

O'Gorman, C., Bourke, S., and Murray, J. A. (2005). 'The Nature of Managerial Work in Small Growth-Oriented Businesses', *Small Business Economics*, 25: 1–16.

Okely, J. (1994). 'Thinking Through Fieldwork', in A. Bryman and R. G. Burgess (eds), *Analyzing Qualitative Data*. London: Routledge.

Omar, N. A., Aziz, N. A., and Nazri, M. A. (2011). 'Understanding the Relationship of Program Satisfaction, Program Loyalty and Store Loyalty among Cardholders of Loyalty Programs', *Asian Academy of Management Journal*, 16(1): 21–41.

Onwuegbuzie, A. J., and Collins, K. M. T. (2007). 'A Typology of Mixed Methods Sampling Designs in Social Sciences Research', *Qualitative Report*, 12: 281–316, http://www.nova.edu/ssss/QR/QR12-2/onwuegbuzie2.pdf.

Onwuegbuzie, A. J., and Leech, N. L. (2010). 'Generalization Practices in Qualitative Research: A Mixed Methods Case Study', *Quality and Quantity*, 44: 881–92.

Oppenheim, A. N. (1992). *Questionnaire Design, Interviewing and Attitude Measurement*. London: Pinter.

O'Reilly, K., Paper, D., and Marx, S. (2012). 'Demystifying Grounded Theory for Business Research', *Organizational Research Methods*, 15(2): 247–62.

O'Reilly, M., and Parker, N. (2013). '"Unsatisfactory Saturation": A Critical Exploration of the Notion of Saturated Sample Sizes in Qualitative Research', *Qualitative Research*, 13(2): 190–97.

Orton, J. D. (1997). 'From Inductive to Iterative Grounded Theory: Zipping the Gap between Process Theory and Process Data', *Scandinavian Journal of Management*, 13(4): 419–38.

Oswick, C., Putnam, L., and Keenoy, T. (2004). 'Tropes, Discourse and Organizing', in D. Grant, C. Hardy, C. Oswick, and L. Putnam (eds), *Handbook of Organizational Discourse*. London: Sage.

Palys, T. (2008). 'Purposive Sampling', in L. M. Given (ed.), *The Sage Encyclopedia of Qualitative Research Methods*, vol. 2. Thousand Oaks, CA: Sage.

Parboteeah, K. P., Hoegl, M., and Cullen, J. (2009). 'Religious Dimensions and Work Obligation: A Country Institutional Profile Model', *Human Relations*, 62(1): 119–48.

Park, C. (2003). 'In Other (People's) Words: Plagiarism by University Students—Literature and Lessons', *Assessment and Evaluation in Higher Education*, 28: 471–88.

Park, P. (1999). 'People, Knowledge, and Change in Participatory Research', *Management Learning*, 30(2): 141–57.

Park, S. H. (1996). 'Relationships between Involvement and Attitudinal Loyalty Constructs in Adult Fitness Programmes', *Journal of Leisure Research*, 28(4): 233–50.

Parker, I. (1992). *Discourse Dynamics*. London: Routledge.

Parker, M. (2000). *Organizational Culture and Identity*. London: Sage.

Partington, D. (2000). 'Building Grounded Theories of Management Action', *British Journal of Management*, 11: 91–102.

Patterson, M. G., West, M. A., Shackleton, V. J., Dawson, J. F., Lawthom, R., Maitlis, S., Robinson, D. L., and Wallace, A. M. (2005). 'Validating the Organizational Climate Measure: Links to Managerial Practices, Productivity and Innovation', *Journal of Organizational Behavior*, 26: 379–408.

Patton, M. (1990). *Qualitative Evaluation and Research Methods*. Beverly Hills, CA: Sage.

Patwardhan, A., Noble, S. M., and Nishihara, C. M. (2009). 'The Use of Strategic Deception in Relationships', *Journal of Services Marketing*, 23(5): 318–25.

Paulus, T. M., Lester, J. N., and Britt, V. G. (2013). 'Constructing Hopes and Fears Around Technology: A Discourse Analysis of Introductory Research Methods Texts', *Qualitative Inquiry*, 19(3): 639–51.

Pedersen, M., and Nielsen, C. (2016). 'Improving Survey Response Rates in Online Panels: Effects of Low-Cost Incentives and Cost-Free Text Appeal Interventions', *Social Science Computer Review*, 34(2): 229–43.

Peñaloza, L. (1999). 'Just Doing It: A Visual Ethnographic Study of Spectacular Consumption Behavior at Nike Town', *Consumption, Markets and Culture*, 2: 337–400.

Peñaloza, L. (2000). 'The Commodification of the American West: Marketers' Production of Cultural Meanings at the Trade Show', *Journal of Marketing*, 64: 82–109.

Peräkylä, A. (1997). 'Reliability and Validity in Research Based on Transcripts', in D. Silverman (ed.), *Qualitative Research: Theory, Method and Practice*. London: Sage.

Perlow, L. A. (1997). *Finding Time: How Corporations, Individuals and Families can Benefit from New Work Practices*. Ithaca, NY: ILR Press.

Perlow, L. A. (1999). 'Time Famine: Toward a Sociology of Work Time', *Administrative Science Quarterly*, 44: 57–81.

Peterson, R., and Merunka, D. (2014). 'Convenience Samples of College Students and Research Reproducibility', *Journal of Business Research*, 67(5): 1035–41.

Petticrew, M., and Roberts, H. (2006). *Systematic Reviews in the Social Sciences: A Practical Guide*. Oxford: Blackwell.

Pettigrew, A. (1985). *The Awakening Giant: Continuity and Change in Imperial Chemical Industries*. Oxford: Blackwell.

Pettigrew, A. (1990). 'Longitudinal Field Research on Change: Theory and Practice', *Organization Science*, 1(3): 267–92.

Pettigrew, A. (1997). 'What is a Processual Analysis?', *Scandinavian Journal of Management*, 13: 337–48.

Phillips, D. L. (1973). *Abandoning Method*. San Francisco: Jossey-Bass.

Phillips, N., and Hardy, C. (2002). *Discourse Analysis: Investigating Processes of Social Construction*. London: Sage.

Piekkari, R., Welsh, C., and Paavilainen, E. (2009). 'Case Study as Disciplinary Convention: Evidence from International Business Journals', *Organizational Research Methods*, 12(3): 567–89.

Piercy, N. F., Harris, L. C., and Lane, N. (2002). 'Market Orientation and Retail Operatives' Expectations', *Journal of Business Research*, 55: 261–73.

Pink, S. (2001). *Doing Visual Ethnography*. London: Sage.

Pink, S. (2004). 'Visual Methods', in C. Seale, G. Gobo, J. F. Gubrium, and D. Silverman (eds), *Qualitative Research Practice*. London: Sage.

Plate, L. (1993). 'From Reading "Against" to Reading "With": Feminism and the Subject of Reading', *Reader*, 30(Fall): 27–47.

Platt, J. (1981). 'The Social Construction of "Positivism" and its Significance in British Sociology, 1950–80', in P. Abrams, R. Deem, J. Finch, and P. Rock (eds), *Practice and Progress: British Sociology 1950–1980*. London: George Allen & Unwin.

Plummer, K. (2001). 'The Call of Life Stories in Ethnographic Research', in P. Atkinson, A. Coffey, S. Delamont, J. Lofland, and L. Lofland (eds), *Handbook of Ethnography*. London: Sage.

Poland, B. D. (1995). 'Transcription Quality as an Aspect of Rigor in Qualitative Research', *Qualitative Inquiry*, 1: 290–310.

Pollert, A. (1981). *Girls, Wives, Factory Lives*. London: Macmillan.

Popper, K. (2003). 'The Problem of Induction', in G. Delanty and P. Strydom (eds), *Philosophies of Social Science: The Classic and Contemporary Readings*. Maidenhead: Open University Press.

Potter, J. (1996). *Representing Reality: Discourse, Rhetoric and Social Construction*. London: Sage.

Potter, J. (1997). 'Discourse Analysis as a Way of Analysing Naturally Occurring Talk', in D. Silverman (ed.), *Qualitative Research: Theory, Method and Practice*. London: Sage.

Potter, J. (2004). 'Discourse Analysis', in M. Hardy and A. Bryman (eds), *Handbook of Data Analysis*. London: Sage.

Potter, J., and Wetherell, M. (1987). *Discourse and Social Psychology: Beyond Attitudes and Behaviour*. London: Sage.

Potter, J., and Wetherell, M. (1994). 'Analyzing Discourse', in A. Bryman and R. G. Burgess (eds), *Analyzing Qualitative Data*. London: Routledge.

Poutanen, S., and Kovalainen, A. (2010). 'Critical Theory', in A. J. Mills, G. Durepos, and E. Wiebe (eds), *Sage Encyclopedia of Case Study Research*. Thousand Oaks, CA: Sage, i: 260–64.

Powell, T. C. (1995). 'Total Quality Management as Competitive Advantage: A Review and Empirical Study', *Strategic Management Journal*, 16: 15–37.

Prasad, A., Prasad, P., and Mir, R. (2011). 'One Mirror in Another: Managing Diversity and the Discourse of Fashion', *Human Relations*, 64(5): 703–24.

Prasad, P. (1993). 'Symbolic Processes in the Implementation of Technological Change: A Symbolic Interactionist Study of Work Computerization', *Academy of Management Journal*, 36(6): 1400–29.

Prasad, P. (2003). 'The Return of the Native: Organizational Discourses and the Legacy of the Ethnographic Imagination', in A. Prasad (ed.), *Postcolonial Theory and Organizational Analysis: A Critical Engagement*. New York: Palgrave, 149–70.

Prasad, P., and Prasad, A. (2009). 'Endless Crossroads: Debates, Deliberations and Disagreements on Studying Organizational Culture', in B. Buchanan and A. Bryman (eds.), *The Sage Handbook of Organizational Research Methods*. London: Sage.

Pratt, M. G. (2008). 'Fitting Oval Pegs into Round Holes: Tensions in Evaluating and Publishing Qualitative Research in Top-Tier North American Journals', *Organizational Research Methods*, 11: 481–509.

Pringle, R. (1988). *Secretaries Talk: Sexuality, Power and Work* (London: Verso).

Pugh, D. S. (1998). 'Introduction', in D. S. Pugh (ed.), *The Aston Study and its Developments, The Aston Programme I*. Dartmouth: Ashgate.

Pugh, D. S., Hickson, D. J., Hinings, C. R., and Turner, C. (1968). 'Dimensions of Organization Structure', *Administrative Science Quarterly*, 13: 65–105.

Punch, M. (1994). 'Politics and Ethics in Qualitative Research', in N. K. Denzin and Y. S. Lincoln (eds), *Handbook of Qualitative Research*. Thousand Oaks, CA: Sage.

Purkayastha, S., Manolova, T. S., and Edelman, L. F. (2012). 'Diversification and Performance in Developed and Emerging Market Contexts: A Review of the Literature', *International Journal of Management Reviews*, 13: 18–38.

Rafaeli, A., Dutton, J., Harquail, C. V., and Mackie-Lewis, S. (1997). 'Navigating by Attire: The Use of Dress by Female Administrative Employees', *Academy of Management Journal*, 40: 9–45.

Ram, M. (1994). *Managing to Survive: Working Lives in Small Firms*. Oxford: Blackwell.

Ramiah, S. P., and Banks, A. P. (2015), 'Naturalistic Decision Making through Argumentation: Resolving Labour Disputes', *Journal of Occupational and Organizational Psychology*, 88(2): 364–81.

Ramirez, I., and Bartunek, J. (1989). 'The Multiple Realities and Experiences of Internal Organization Development in Healthcare', *Journal of Organizational Change Management*, 2(1): 40–57.

Reay, T., Berta, W., and Kohn, M. K. (2009). 'What is the Evidence on Evidence-Based Management?', *Academy of Management Perspectives*, 23(4): 19–32.

Reed, M. I. (2000). 'The Limits of Discourse Analysis in Organizational Analysis', *Organization*, 7: 524–30.

Reichl, C., Leiter, M. P., and Spinath, F. M. (2014). 'Work–Nonwork Conflict and Burnout: A Meta-analysis', *Human Relations*, doi: 10.1177/0018726713509857.

Reid, D. J., and Reid, F. J. M. (2005). 'Online Focus Groups: An In-depth Comparison of Computer-Mediated and Conventional Focus Group Discussions', *International Journal of Market Research*, 47(2): 131–62.

Reinharz, S. (1992). *Feminist Methods in Social Research*. New York: Oxford University Press.

Rettie, R., Robinson, H., Radke, A., and Ye, X. (2008). 'CAQDAS: A Supplementary Tool for Qualitative Market Research', *Qualitative Market Research: An International Journal*, 11(1): 76–88.

Reuber, A. R. (2010). 'Strengthening your Literature Review', *Family Business Review*, 23: 105–8.

Rhodes, C., and Brown, A. D. (2005). 'Narrative, Organizations and Research', *International Journal of Management*, 7(3): 167–88.

Riach, K. (2009). 'Exploring Participant-Centred Reflexivity in the Research Interview', *Sociology*, 43(2): 356–70.

Riach, K., and Warren, S. (2015). 'Smell Organizations: Bodies and Corporeal Porosity in Office Work', *Human Relations*, 68(5): 789–809.

Richards, J., and Sang, K. (2016). 'Trade Unions as Employment Facilitators for Disabled Employees', *International Journal of Human Resource Management*, 27(14): 1642–61.

Richards, L., and Richards, T. (1994). 'From Filing Cabinet to Computer', in A. Bryman and R. G. Burgess (eds), *Analyzing Qualitative Data*. London: Routledge.

Richardson, L. (1990). 'Narrative and Sociology', *Journal of Contemporary Ethnography*, 19: 116–35.

Richardson, L. (1994). 'Writing: A Method of Inquiry', in N. K. Denzin and Y. S. Lincoln (eds), *Handbook of Qualitative Research*. Thousand Oaks, CA: Sage.

Riessman, C. K. (1993). *Narrative Analysis*. Newbury Park, CA: Sage.

Riessman, C. K. (2005). 'Exporting Ethics: A Narrative About Narrative Research in South India', *Health*, 9(4): 473–90.

Rigby, M., and O'Brien-Smith, F. (2010). 'Trade Union Interventions in Work–Life Balance', *Work, Employment and Society*, 24: 203–20.

Ritzer, G. (1975). 'Sociology: A Multiple Paradigm Science', *American Sociologist*, 10: 156–67.

Roethlisberger, F. J., and Dickson, W. J. (1939). *Management and the Worker: An Account of a Research Programme Conducted by the Western Electric Company, Hawthorne Works, Chicago*. Cambridge, MA: Harvard University Press.

Rorty, R. (1979). *Philosophy and the Mirror of Nature*. Princeton: Princeton University Press.

Rose, G. (2001). *Visual Methodologies*. London: Sage.

Rosen, M. (1991). 'Coming to Terms with the Field: Understanding and Doing Organizational Ethnography', *Journal of Management Studies*, 28(1): 1–24.

Rosén, M. E. (2014). 'From Ad-man to Digital Manager: Professionalization through Swedish Job Advertisements 1960–2010', *Journal of Communications Management*, 18(1): 16–39.

Rosenau, P. M. (1992). *Post-Modernism and the Social Sciences: Insights, Inroads, and Intrusions*. Princeton: Princeton University Press.

Rosnow, R. L., and Rosenthal, R. (1997). *People Studying People: Artifacts and Ethics in Behavioral Research*. New York: W. H. Freeman.

Roulston, K., DeMarrais, K., and Lewis, J. (2003). 'Learning to Interview in the Social Sciences', *Qualitative Inquiry*, 9: 643–68.

Rousseau, D. (1985). 'Issues of Level in Organizational Research: Multi-Level and Cross-Level Perspectives', in L. Cummings and B. Staw (eds), *Research in Organizational Behavior*, vol. 7. London: JAI Press.

Rousseau, D. M. (2006). 'Is There Such a Thing as Evidence-Based Management?' *Academy of Management Review*, 31(2): 256–69.

Rowlinson, M. (2004a). 'Historical Perspectives in Organization Studies: Factual, Narrative, and Archeo-Genealogical', in D. E. Hodgson and C. Carter (eds), *Management Knowledge and the New Employee*. Burlington, VT: Ashgate, 8–20.

Rowlinson, M. (2004b). 'Historical Analysis of Company Documents', in C. Cassell and G. Symon (eds), *Essential Guide to Qualitative Methods in Organizational Research*. London: Sage, 301–10.

Roy, A., Walters, P., and Luk, S. (2001). 'Chinese Puzzles and Paradoxes: Conducting Business Research in China', *Journal of Business Research*, 52: 203–10.

Roy, D. (1958). 'Banana Time: Job Satisfaction and Informal Interaction', *Human Organisation*, 18: 156–68.

Rubin, H. J., and Rubin, I. S. (1995). *Qualitative Interviewing: The Art of Hearing Data*. Thousand Oaks, CA: Sage.

Ruppert, E., Law, J., and Savage, M. (2013). 'Reassembling Social Science Methods: The Challenge of Digital devices', *Theory, Culture and Society*, 30(4): 22–46.

Ryan, G. W., and Bernard, H. R. (2003). 'Techniques to Identify Themes', *Field Methods*, 15: 85–109.

Rynes, S. L., Hillman, A., Ireland, R. D., Kirkman, B., Law, K., Miller, C. C., Rajagopalan, N., and Shapiro, D. (2005). 'Everything you've Always Wanted to Know about *AMJ* (but May have been Afraid to Ask)', *Academy of Management Journal*, 48(5): 732–7.

Sacks, H., Schegloff, E. A., and Jefferson, G. (1974). 'A Simplest Systematics for the Organization of Turn-Taking in Conversation', *Language*, 50: 696–735.

Saldaña, J. (2009). 'Popular Film as an Instructional Strategy in Qualitative Research Methods Courses', *Qualitative Inquiry*, 15(1): 247–61.

Samuel, R. (1976). 'Oral History and Local History', *History Workshop Journal*, 1: 191–208.

Sandberg, J., and Alvesson, M. (2011). 'Ways of Constructing Research Questions: Gap-Spotting or Problematization?', *Organization*, 18: 23–44.

Sanjek, R. (1990). 'A Vocabulary for Fieldnotes', in R. Sanjek (ed.), *Fieldnotes: The Making of Anthropology*. Ithaca, NY: Cornell University Press.

Sarsby, J. (1984). 'The Fieldwork Experience', in R. F. Ellen (ed.), *Ethnographic Research: A Guide to General Conduct*. London: Academic Press.

Savage, M. (2005). 'Working-Class Identities in the 1960s: Revisiting the Affluent Worker Study', *Sociology*, 39(5): 929–46.

Scandura, T. A., and Williams, E. A. (2000). 'Research Methodology in Management: Current Practices, Trends and Implications for Future Research', *Academy of Management Journal*, 43(6): 1248–64.

Scase, R., and Goffee, R. (1989). *Reluctant Managers: Their Work and Lifestyles*. London: Routledge.

Schaeffer, D. R., and Dillman, D. A. (1998). 'Development of a Standard E-mail Methodology', *Public Opinion Quarterly*, 62: 378–97.

Schegloff, E. A. (1997). 'Whose Text? Whose Context?', *Discourse and Society*, 8: 165–87.

Scherbaum, C. A., and Meade, A. W. (2013). 'New Directions for Measurement in Management Research', *International Journal of Management Reviews*, 15: 132–48.

Schlesinger, P., Dobash, R. E., Dobash, R. P., and Weaver, C. K. (1992). *Women Viewing Violence*. London: British Film Institute.

Schoneboom, A. (2011). 'Workblogging in a Facebook Age', *Work, Employment and Society*, 25(1): 132–40.

Schoonhoven, C. B. (1981). 'Problems with Contingency Theory: Testing Assumptions Hidden within the Language of Contingency Theory', *Administrative Science Quarterly*, 26: 349–77.

Schuman, H., and Converse, J. (1971). 'The Effects of Black and White Interviewers on Black Responses in 1968', *Public Opinion Quarterly*, 35: 44–68.

Schuman, H., and Presser, S. (1981). *Questions and Answers in Attitude Surveys: Experiments on Question Form, Wording, and Context*. San Diego, CA: Academic Press.

Schutte, N., Toppinnen, S., Kalimo, R., and Schaufeli, W. (2000). 'The Factorial Validity of the Maslach Burnout Inventory—General Survey (MBI—GS) across Occupational Groups and Nations', *Journal of Occupational and Organizational Psychology*, 73(1): 53–67.

Schutz, A. (1962). *Collected Papers, i: The Problem of Social Reality*. The Hague: Martinus Nijhof.

Schwartzman, H. B. (1993). *Ethnography in Organizations*, Qualitative Research Methods Series 27. Newbury Park, CA: Sage.

Schwartz-Shea, P., and Yanow, D. (2012). *Interpretive Research Design*. London: Routledge.

Scott, J. (1990). *A Matter of Record*. Cambridge: Polity Press.

Shapiro, M. (1985–6). 'Metaphor in the Philosophy of the Social Sciences', *Cultural Critique*, 2: 191–214.

Sharpe, D. (1997). 'Managerial Control Strategies and Subcultural Proccesses', in S. Sackmann (ed.), *Cultural Complexity in Organizations*. London: Sage.

Sheehan, K. (2001). 'E-Mail Survey Response Rates: A Review', *Journal of Computer-Mediated Communication*, 6(2), http://www.ascusc.org/jcmc/vol6/issue2/sheehan.html.

Sheehan, K., and Hoy, M. G. (1999). 'Using E-mail to Survey Internet Users in the United States: Methodology and Assessment', *Journal of Computer-Mediated Communication*, 4(3), http://www.ascusc.org/jcmc/vol4/issue3/sheehan.html.

Shenoy, S. (1981). 'Organization Structure and Context: A Replication of the Aston Study in India', in D. J. Hickson and J. McMillan (eds), *Organization and Nation, The Aston Programme IV*. Aldershot: Gower.

Shepherd, C., and Challenger, R. (2013). 'Revisiting Paradigm(s) in Management Research: A Rhetorical Analysis of the Paradigm Wars', *International Journal of Management Reviews*, 15(2): 225–44.

Shepherd, D. A., and Suddaby, R. (2017). 'Theory Building: A Review and Integration', *Journal of Management*, 43(1): 59–86.

Shrivasta, P., Mitroff, I. I., Miller, D., and Miglani, A. (1988). 'Understanding Industrial Crises', *Journal of Management Studies*, 25: 283–304.

Shuy, R. W. (2002). 'In-person versus Telephone Interviewing', in J. F. Gubrium and J. A. Holstein (eds), *Handbook of Interview Research: Context and Method*. Thousand Oaks, CA: Sage.

Silverman, D. (1984). 'Going Private: Ceremonial Forms in a Private Oncology Clinic', *Sociology*, 18: 191–204.

Silverman, D. (1985). *Qualitative Methodology and Sociology: Describing the Social World*. Aldershot: Gower.

Silverman, D. (1993). *Interpreting Qualitative Data: Methods for Analysing Qualitative Data*. London: Sage.

Silverman, D. (2017). 'How Was It for You? The Interview Society and the Irresistible Rise of the (Poorly Analysed) Interview', *Qualitative Inquiry*, 17(2): 144–58.

Sin, C. H. (2005). 'Seeking Informed Consent: Reflections on Research Practice', *Sociology*, 39(2): 277–94.

Singh, G., Haddad, K. M., and Chow, C. W. (2007). 'Are Articles in Top Management Journals Necessarily of Higher Quality?', *Journal of Management Inquiry*, 16(4): 319–31.

Sinkovics, R., and Penz, E. (2011). 'Multilingual Elite-Interviews and Software-Based Analysis: Problems and Solutions based on CAQDAS', *International Journal of Market Research*, 53(5): 705.

Smeaton, D., and White, M. (2017). 'Britain's Older Employees in Decline, 1990–2006: A Panel Analysis of Pay', *Work, Employment and Society*, 1–12.

Smith, C. B. (1997). 'Casting the Net: Surveying an Internet Population', *Journal of Computer-Mediated Communication*, 3(1), http://www.ascusc.org/jcmc/vol3/issue1/yun.html.

Snyder, N., and Glueck, W. F. (1980). 'How Managers Plan: The Analysis of Managers' Activities', *Long Range Planning*, 13: 70–6.

Social Research Association [UK] (2003). *Ethical Guidelines*, http://the-sra.org.uk/research-ethics/ethics-guidelines/.

Sonenshein, S., DeCelles, K. A., and Dutton, J. E. (2014). 'It's Not Easy Being Green: The Role of Self-Evaluations in Explaining Support of Environmental Issues', *Academy of Management Journal*, 57(1): 7–37.

Sørensen, J. B. (2004). 'The Organizational Demography of Racial Employment Segregation', *American Journal of Sociology*, 110(3): 626–71.

Spender, J. (1989). *Industry Recipes: An Enquiry into the Nature and Sources of Managerial Judgement*. Oxford: Blackwell.

Spradley, J. P. (1979). *The Ethnographic Interview*. New York: Holt, Rinehart & Winston.

Spradley, J. P., and McCurdy, D. (1972). *The Cultural Experience*. Chicago: Science Research Associates.

Sprokkereef, A., Larkin, E., Pole, C. J., and Burgess, R. G. (1995). 'The Data, the Team, and the Ethnograph', *Studies in Qualitative Methodology*, 5: 81–103.

Sprouse, M. (ed.) (1992). *Sabotage in the American Workplace*. San Francisco: Pressure Drop Press.

Sreedhari, D. D., Chugh, D., and Brief, A. P. (2014). 'The Implications of Marriage Structure for Men's Workplace Attitudes, Beliefs, and Behaviours Towards Women', *Administrative Science Quarterly*, 59(2): 330–65.

Stacey, J. (1988). 'Can there be a Feminist Ethnography?', *Women's International Studies Forum*, 11: 21–7.

Stake, R. E. (1995). *The Art of Case Study Research*. Thousand Oaks, CA: Sage.

Stake, R. E. (2005). 'Qualitative Case Studies', in N. K. Denzin and Y. S. Lincoln (eds), *The Sage Handbook of Qualitative Research*, 3rd edn. Thousand Oaks, CA: Sage.

Stanley, L., and Temple, B. (1995). 'Doing the Business? Evaluating Software Packages to Aid the Analysis of Qualitative Data Sets', *Studies in Qualitative Methodology*, 5: 169–97.

Steenkamp, J.-B. E. M., de Jong, M. G., and Baumgartner, H. (2010). 'Socially Desirable Response Tendencies in Survey Research', *Journal of Marketing Research*, 48: 199–214.

Stefani, L., and Carroll, J. (2001). 'A Briefing Note on Plagiarism', *Assessment Series 10*, http://www.sussex.ac.uk/tldu/documents/plag_ass0101.doc.

Stentz, J. E., Plano Clark, V. L., and Matkin, G. S. (2012). 'Applying Mixed Methods to Leadership Research: A Review of Current Practices', *Leadership Quarterly*, 23: 1173–83.

Stewart, K., and Williams, M. (2005). 'Researching Online Populations: The Use of Online Focus Groups for Social Research', *Qualitative Research*, 5(4): 395–416.

Stewart, R. (1967). *Managers and their Jobs*. London: Macmillan.

Stiles, D. R. (2004). 'Pictorial Representation', in C. Cassell and G. Symon (eds), *Essential Guide to Qualitative Methods in Organizational Research*. London: Sage.

Stiles, P. (2001). 'The Impact of the Board on Strategy: An Empirical Examination', *Journal of Management Studies*, 38(5): 627–50.

Stockdale, A. (2002). 'Tools for Digital Audio Recording in Qualitative Research', *Social Research Update*, 38.

Strathern, M. (1987). 'The Limits of Auto-Anthropology', in A. Jackson (ed.), *Anthropology at Home*. London: Tavistock.

Strauss, A. (1987). *Qualitative Analysis for Social Scientists*. New York: Cambridge University Press.

Strauss, A., and Corbin, J. M. (1990). *Basics of Qualitative Research: Grounded Theory Procedures and Techniques*. Newbury Park, CA: Sage.

Strauss, A., and Corbin, J. M. (1998). *Basics of Qualitative Research: Techniques and Procedures for Developing Grounded Theory*. Thousand Oaks, CA: Sage.

Strauss, A., Schatzman, L., Ehrich, D., Bucher, R., and Sabshin, M. (1973). 'The Hospital and its Negotiated Order', in G. Salaman and K. Thompson (eds), *People and Organizations*. London: Longman.

Streiner, D. L., and Sidani, S. (2010). *When Research Goes Off the Rails: Why it Happens and What You Can Do About It*. New York: Guilford.

Sudman, S., and Blair, E. (1999). 'Sampling in the Twenty-First Century', *Journal of the Academy of Marketing Science*, 27(2): 269–77.

Sudman, S., and Bradburn, N. M. (1982). *Asking Questions: A Practical Guide to Questionnaire Design*. San Francisco: Jossey-Bass.

Sutton, R. I., and Rafaeli, A. (1988). 'Untangling the Relationship between Displayed Emotions and Organizational Sales: The Case of Convenience Stores', *Academy of Management Journal*, 31: 461–87.

Sutton, R. I., and Rafaeli, A. (1992). 'How we Untangled the Relationship between Displayed Emotion and Organizational Sales: A Tale of Bickering and Optimism', in P. J. Frost and R. Stablein (eds), *Doing Exemplary Research*. Newbury Park, CA: Sage.

Sweet, C. (2001). 'Designing and Conducting Virtual Focus Groups', *Qualitative Market Research*, 4: 130–5.

Symon, G., Buehring, A., Johnson, P., and Cassell, C. (2008). 'Positioning Qualitative Research as Resistance to the Institutionalization of the Academic Labour Process', *Organization Studies*, 29(10): 1315–36.

Tadajewski, M. (2016). 'Focus Groups: History, Epistemology and Non-individualistic Consumer Research', *Consumption, Markets and Culture*, 19(4): 319–45.

Tashakkori, A., and Teddlie, C. (2003). *Handbook of Mixed Methods in Social and Behavioral Research*. Thousand Oaks, CA: Sage.

Tashakkori, A., and Teddlie, C. (2010). *Handbook of Mixed Methods in Social and Behavioral Research*, rev. edn. Thousand Oaks, CA: Sage.

Teddlie, C., and Yu, F. (2007). 'Mixed Methods Sampling: A Typology with Examples', *Journal of Mixed Methods Research*, 1: 77–100.

Thomas, R., and Linstead, A. (2002). 'Losing the Plot? Middle Managers and Identity', *Organization*, 9(1): 71–93.

Thompson, P., and Harley, B. (2012). 'Beneath the Radar? A Critical Realist Analysis of "The Knowledge Economy" and "Shareholder Value" as Competing Discourses', *Organization Studies*, 33(10): 1363–81.

Thorne, B. (1980). '"You Still Takin' Notes?": Fieldwork and Problems of Informed Consent', *Social Problems*, 27(3): 284–97.

Tight, M. (2010). 'The Curious Case of Case Study: A Viewpoint', *International Journal of Social Research Methodology*, 13(4): 329–39.

Tonge, J., Moore, S., Ryan, M., and Beckley, L. (2013). 'Using Photo-Elicitation to Explore Place Attachment in a Remote Setting', *Electronic Journal of Business Research Methods*, 11(1): 41–50.

Townsend, K., and Burgess, J. (2009). 'Serendipity and Flexibility in Social Science Research: Meeting the Unexpected', in K. Townsend and J. Burgess (eds), *Method in the Madness: Research Stories you Won't Read in Textbooks*. Oxford: Chandos.

Tracy, S. J., Lutgen-Sandvik, P., and Alberts, J. K. (2006). 'Nightmares, Demons and Slaves: Exploring the Painful Metaphors of Workplace Bullying', *Management Communication Quarterly*, 20(2): 148–85.

Tranfield, D., and Starkey, K. (1998). 'The Nature, Social Organisation and Promotion of Management Research: Towards Policy', *British Journal of Management*, 9: 341–53.

Tranfield, D., Denyer, D., and Smart, P. (2003). 'Towards a Methodology for Developing Evidence-Informed Management Knowledge by Means of Systematic Review', *British Journal of Management*, 14: 207–22.

Trau, R. N. C., Härtel, C. E. J., and Härtel, G. F. (2013). 'Reaching and Hearing the Invisible: Organizational Research on Invisible Stigmatized Groups via Web Surveys', *British Journal of Management*, 24: 532–41.

Trethewey, A. (1999). 'Disciplined Bodies: Women's Embodied Identities at Work', *Organization Studies*, 20(3): 423–50.

Treviño, L. K., den Nieuwenboer, N. A., Kreiner, G. E., and Bishop, D. G. (2014). 'Legitimating the Legitimate: A Grounded Theory Study of Legitimacy Work among Ethics and Compliance Officers', *Organizational Behavior and Human Decision Processes*, 123: 186–205.

Tripp, T. M., Bies, R. J., and Aquino, K. (2002). 'Poetic Justice or Petty Jealousy? The Aesthetics of Revenge', *Organizational Behavior and Human Decision Processes*, 89: 966–84.

Truss, C. (2001). 'Complexities and Controversies in Linking HRM with Organizational Outcomes', *Journal of Management Studies*, 38(8): 1121–49.

Tsang, E., and Kwan, K.-M. (1999). 'Replication and Theory Development in Organizational Science: A Critical Realist Perspective', *Academy of Management Review*, 24(4): 759–80.

Tse, A. C. B. (1998). 'Comparing the Response Rate, Response Speed and Response Quality of Two Methods of Sending Questionnaires: E-mail vs. Mail', *Journal of the Market Research Society*, 40: 353–61.

Tse, A. C. B. (1999). 'Conducting Electronic Focus Group Discussions among Chinese Respondents', *Journal of the Market Research Society*, 41: 407–15.

Tuhiwai Smith, L. (1999). *Decolonizing Methodologies: Research and Indigenous Peoples*. London: Zed Books.

Turner, B. A. (1994). 'Patterns of Crisis Behaviour: A Qualitative Inquiry', in A. Bryman and R. G. Burgess (eds), *Analyzing Qualitative Data*. London: Routledge.

Tyler, M., and Cohen, L. (2010). 'Spaces that Matter: Gender Performativity and Organizational Space', *Organization Studies*, 31(2): 175–98.

Tysome, T. (2001). 'Tobacco Link Causes Cancer Team to Leave', *Times Higher Education Supplement*, 23 March.

UK Data Archive (2009). *Managing and Sharing Data: A Best Practice Guide for Researchers*. Colchester, Essex: UK Data Archive.

UK Data Archive (2011). *Managing and Sharing Data: Best Practice for Researchers*, 3rd edn. Colchester, Essex: UK Data Archive.

Urban, A.-M., and Quinlan, E. (2014). 'Not for the Faint of Heart: Insider and Outsider Shadowing Experiences within Canadian Health Care Organizations', *Qualitative Research in Organizations and Management*, 9(1): 47–65.

Usunier, J. C. (1998). *International and Cross-Cultural Management Research*. London: Sage.

Uy, M. A., Foo, M., and Aguinis, H. (2010). 'Using Experience Sampling Methodology to Advance Entrepreneurship Theory and Research', *Organizational Research Methods*, 13(1): 31–54.

Uy, M. A., Lin, K. J., and Ilies, R. (2017). 'Is it Better to Give or Receive? The Role of Help in Buffering the Depleting Effects of Surface Acting', *Academy of Management Journal*, 60(4): 1442–61.

Vaara, E., Soneshein, S., and Boje, D. M. (2016). 'Narratives as Sources of Stability and Change in Organizations: Approaches and Directions for Future Research', *Academy of Management Annals*, 10(1): 495–560.

van der Lippe, T., den Dulk, L., van Doorne-Huiskes, A., Schippers, J., Lane, L., and Bäck-Wiklund, M. (2009). *Final Report: Quality of Life in a Changing Europe* [report of the European Commission's 'Quality' research project]. Utrecht: Utrecht University.

Van de Ven, A. H. (2007). *Engaged Scholarship: A Guide for Organizational and Social Research*. Oxford: Oxford University Press.

van de Voorde, K., and Beijer, S. (2015). 'The Role of Employee HR Attributions in the Relationship Between High-Performance Work Systems and Employee Outcomes'. *Human Resource Management Journal*, 25(1): 62–78.

Van Dijk, T. A. (1997). 'Discourse as Interaction in Society', in T. A. Van Dijk (ed.), *Discourse as Social Interaction*, vol. 2 of

Discourse Studies: A Multidisciplinary Introduction. Newbury Park, CA: Sage.

Van Maanen, J. (1978). 'On Watching the Watchers', in P. Manning and J. Van Maanen (eds), *Policing: The View from the Street*. Santa Monica, CA: Goodyear.

Van Maanen, J. (1988). *Tales of the Field: On Writing Ethnography*. Chicago: University of Chicago Press.

Van Maanen, J. (1991a). 'Playing Back the Tape: Early Days in the Field', in W. B. Shaffir and R. A. Stebbins (eds), *Experiencing Fieldwork: An Inside View of Qualitative Research*. Newbury Park, CA: Sage.

Van Maanen, J. (1991b). 'The Smile Factory: Work at Disneyland', in P. J. Frost, L. F. Moore, M. R. Louis, C. C. Lundberg, and J. Martin (eds), *Reframing Organizational Culture*. Newbury Park, CA: Sage.

Van Maanen, J. (1996). 'On the Matter of Voice', *Journal of Management Inquiry*, 5(4): 375–81.

Van Maanen, J., and Kolb, D. (1985). 'The Professional Apprentice: Observations on Fieldwork Roles in Two Organizational Settings', *Research in the Sociology of Organizations*, 4: 1–33.

Van Selm, M., and Jankowski, N. W. (2006). 'Conducting Online Surveys', *Quality and Quantity*, 40(3): 435–56.

van Veldhoven, M., and Meijman, T. F. (1994). *Het meten van psychosociale arbeidsbelasting met eenvragenlijst: De vragenlijst beleving en beoordeling van de arbeid (VBBA)*. Amsterdam: Nederlands Instituut voor Arbeidsomstandigheden.

Vaughan, D. (1990). 'Autonomy, Independence and Social Control: NASA and the Space Shuttle *Challenger*', *Administrative Science Quarterly*, 35: 225–57.

Vaughan, D. (2006). 'The Social Shaping of Commission Reports', *Sociological Forum*, 21: 291–306.

Venter, E., Boshoff, C., and Maas, G. (2005). 'The Influence of Successor Related Factors on the Succession Process in Small and Medium-Sized Family Businesses', *Family Business Review*, 18(4): 283–303.

Vidaver-Cohen, D., and Brønn, P. S. (2015). 'Reputation, Responsibility, and Stakeholder Support in Scandinavian Firms: A Comparative Analysis', *Journal of Business Ethics*, 127(1): 49–64.

Waddington, K. (2005). 'Using Diaries to Explore the Characteristics of Work-Related Gossip: Methodological Considerations from Exploratory Multimethod Research', *Journal of Occupational and Organizational Psychology*, 78: 221–36.

Wagner, D. T., Barnes, C. M., and Scott, B. A. (2013). 'Driving it Home: How Workplace Emotional Labor Harms Employee Home Life', *Personnel Psychology*, doi: 10.1111/peps.12044.

Walker, J. (2010). 'Measuring Plagiarism: Researching What Students Do, Not What They Say', *Studies in Higher Education*, 35(1): 41–59.

Walsh, D. (1972). 'Sociology and the Social World', in P. Filmer, M. Phillipson, D. Silverman, and D. Walsh (eds), *New Directions in Sociological Theory*. London: Collier-Macmillan.

Warner, L. S., and Grint, K. (2006). 'American Indian Ways of Leading and Knowing', *Leadership*, 2(2): 225–44.

Warren, C. (1988). *Gender Issues in Field Research*. London: Sage.

Warren, C. A. B. (2002). 'Qualitative Interviewing', in J. F. Gubrium and J. A. Holstein (eds), *Handbook of Interview Research: Context and Method*. Thousand Oaks, CA: Sage.

Warren, S. (2002). 'Show Me How it Feels to Work Here: Using Photography to Research Organizational Aesthetics', *Ephemera*, 2(3): 224–45.

Warren, S. (2005). 'Photography and Voice in Critical, Qualitative, Management Research', *Accounting, Auditing and Accountability Journal*, 18(6): 861–82.

Warren, S. (2009). 'Visual Methods in Organizational Research', in D. Buchanan and A. Bryman (eds), *The Sage Handbook of Organizational Research Methods*. London: Sage.

Wasko, J., Phillips, M., and Meehan, E. R. (eds) (2001). *Dazzled by Disney: The Global Disney Audiences Project*. London: Leicester University Press.

Watson, T. (1994a). *In Search of Management: Culture, Chaos and Control in Managerial Work*. London: Routledge.

Watson, T. (1994b). 'Managing, Crafting and Researching: Words, Skill and Imagination in Shaping Management Research', *British Journal of Management*, 5S: S77–87.

Watson, T. (2000). 'Ethnographic Fiction Science: Making Sense of Managerial Work and Organizational Research Processes with Caroline and Terry', *Organization*, 7(3): 489–510.

Wax, M. L. (1982). 'Research Reciprocity Rather than Informed Consent in Fieldwork', in J. E. Sieber (ed.), *The Ethics of Social Research: Fieldwork, Regulation and Publication*. New York: Springer-Verlag.

Weaver, A., and Atkinson, P. (1994). *Microcomputing and Qualitative Data Analysis*. Aldershot: Avebury.

Webb, E. J., Campbell, D. T., Schwartz, R. D., and Sechrest, L. (1966). *Unobtrusive Measures: Nonreactive Measures in the Social Sciences*. Chicago: Rand McNally.

Weber, M. (1930). *The Protestant Ethic and the Spirit of Capitalism*. London: George Allen & Unwin.

Weber, M. (1947). *The Theory of Social and Economic Organization*, translated by A. M. Henderson and T. Parsons. New York: Free Press.

Weick, K. E. (1995). *Sensemaking in Organizations*. Thousand Oaks, CA: Sage.

Weinholtz, D., Kacer, B., and Rocklin, T. (1995). 'Salvaging Quantitative Research with Qualitative Data', *Qualitative Health Research*, 5: 388–97.

Weinmann, T., Thomas, S., Brilmayer, S., Heinrich, S., and Radon, K. (2012). 'Testing Skype as an Interview Method in Epidemiologic Research: Response and Feasibility', *International Journal of Public Health*, 57: 959–61.

Weitzman, E. A., and Miles, M. B. (1995). *Computer Programs for Qualitative Data Analysis*. Thousand Oaks, CA: Sage.

Westwood, S. (1984). *All Day Every Day: Factory, Family, Women's Lives*. London: Pluto Press.

White, H. (1987). *The Content of the Form: Narrative Discourse and Historical Representation*. London: Johns Hopkins University Press.

White, P. (2009). *Developing Research Questions: A Guide for Social Scientists*. Basingstoke: Palgrave Macmillan.

Whittington, R. (1989). *Corporate Strategies in Recession and Recovery*. London: Unwin Hyman.

Whittle, A. (2018). 'Ethnomethodology', in C. Cassell, A. L. Cunliffe, and G. Grandy (eds), *The SAGE Handbook of Qualitative Business and Management Research Methods: History and Traditions*. London: Sage.

Whyte, W. F. (1953). 'Interviewing for Organizational Research', *Human Organization*, 12(2): 15–22.

Widdicombe, S. (1993). 'Autobiography and Change: Rhetoric and Authenticity of "Gothic" Style', in E. Burman and I. Parker (eds), *Discourse Analytic Research: Readings and Repertoires of Text*. London: Routledge.

Wilhite, A. W., and Fong, E. A. (2012). 'Coercive Citation in Academic Publishing', *Science Magazine*, 335: 542–3.

Wilkinson, S. (1998). 'Focus Groups in Feminist Research: Power, Interaction, and the Co-production of Meaning', *Women's Studies International Forum*, 21: 111–25.

Wilkinson, S. (1999a). 'Focus Group Methodology: A Review', *International Journal of Social Research Methodology*, 1: 181–203.

Wilkinson, S. (1999b). 'Focus Groups: A Feminist Method', *Psychology of Women Quarterly*, 23: 221–44.

Willems, T. (2018). 'Seeing and Sensing the Railways: A Phenomenological View on Practice-Based Learning', *Management Learning*, 49(1): 23–39.

Williams, M. (2000). 'Interpretivism and Generalization', *Sociology*, 34: 209–24.

Williams, M. (2007). 'Cybercrime and Online Methodologies', in R. King and E. Wincup (eds), *Doing Research on Crime and Justice*. Oxford: Oxford University Press.

Williams, R. (1976). 'Symbolic Interactionism: Fusion of Theory and Research', in D. C. Thorns (ed.), *New Directions in Sociology*. London: David & Charles.

Willman, P., Renton-O'Creevy, M., Nicholson, N., and Soane, E. (2002). 'Traders, Managers and Loss Aversion in Investment Banking: A Field Study', *Accounting, Organizations and Society*, 27: 85–98.

Wilson, F. (1995). *Organizational Behaviour and Gender*. London: McGraw Hill.

Winch, P. (1958). *The Idea of a Social Science and its Relation to Philosophy*. London: Routledge & Kegan Paul.

Wolcott, H. F. (1990). *Writing up Qualitative Research*. Newbury Park, CA: Sage.

Wolcott, H. F. (1995). 'Making a Study More Ethnographic', in J. Van Maanen (ed.), *Representation in Ethnography*. London: Sage.

Wolfe, E. W., Converse, P. D., and Oswald, F. L. (2008). 'Item-Level Nonresponse Rates in an Attitudinal Survey of Teachers Delivered by Mail and Web', *Journal of Computer-Mediated Consumption*, 14: 35–66.

Woodward, J. (1965). *Industrial Organization: Theory and Practice*. Oxford: Oxford University Press.

Woolgar, S. (1988a). *Science: The Very Idea*. Chichester: Ellis Horwood.

Woolgar, S. (1988b). *Knowledge and Reflexivity: New Frontiers in the Sociology of Knowledge*. London: Sage.

Wright, A. L., Zammuto, R. F., Liesch, P. W., Middleton, S., Hibbert, P., Burke, J., and Brazil, V. (2016). 'Evidence-Based Management in Practice: Opening up the Decision Process, Decision-Maker and Context', *British Journal of Management*, 27(1): 161–78.

Xian, H. (2008). 'Lost in Translation? Language Culture and the Roles of Translator in Cross-Cultural Management Research', *Qualitative Research in Organizations and Management*, 3(3): 231–45.

Yang, K., and Banamah, A. (2014). 'Quota Sampling as an Alternative to Probability to Sampling? An Experimental Study', *Sociological Research Online*, 19(1): 1–11.

Yauch, C. A., and Steudel, H. J. (2003). 'Complementary Use of Qualitative and Quantitative Cultural Assessment Methods', *Organizational Research Methods*, 6: 465–81.

Yin, R. K. (1984). *Case Study Research: Design and Methods*. Beverly Hills, CA: Sage.

Yin, R. K. (2003). *Case Study Research: Design and Methods*, 3rd edn. Thousand Oaks, CA: Sage Publications.

Yin, R. K. (2009). *Case Study Research: Design and Methods*, 4th edn. Los Angeles: Sage.

Zamanou, S., and Glaser, S. R. (1994). 'Moving toward Participation and Involvement', *Group and Organization Management*, 19(4): 475–502.

Zhang, Z., and Spicer, A. (2014). 'Leader, You First: The Everyday Production of Hierarchical Space in a Chinese Bureaucracy', *Human Relations*, 67(6): 739–62.

Zimmerman, D. H., and Wieder, D. L. (1977). 'The Diary: Diary–Interview Method', *Urban Life*, 5: 479–98.

Zundel, M., MacIntosh, R., and Mackay, D. (2018). 'The Utility of Video Diaries for Organizational Research', *Organizational Research Methods*, 21(2): 386–411.

NAME INDEX

Note: Tables and figures are indicated by an italic *t* and *f* following the page number.

SUBJECT INDEX

Note: Tables and figures are indicated by an italic *t* and *f* following the page number.